Holman
Concise
Topical
Concordance

Holman
Concise
Topical
Concordance

An easy to use alphabetical reference
covering hundreds of topics.

HOLMAN
REFERENCE

Nashville, Tennessee

Dewey Decimal Classification: 220.5
Subject Heading: Bible—Bible.Concordances
Library of Congress Catalog Number: 98–34784

Library of Congress Cataloging-in-Publication Data

Holman concise Bible concordance / Steve Bond, editor
   p.   cm.
   Includes index.
   ISBN 0-8054-9349-2 (hb)
    1. Bible—concordances, English.   I. Bond, Steve, 1944–   .
II. Holman Bible Publishers (Nashville, Tenn.)
BS425.H635   1998
220.5'20813—dc21   98–34784
CIP

CONTENTS

BIBLE BOOK ABBREVIATIONS
IN CANONICAL ORDER

OLD TESTAMENT

Gen.	Genesis
Exod.	Exodus
Lev.	Leviticus
Num.	Numbers
Deut.	Deuteronomy
Josh.	Joshua
Judg.	Judges
Ruth	Ruth
1 Sam.	1 Samuel
2 Sam.	2 Samuel
1 Kings	1 Kings
2 Kings	2 Kings
1 Chron.	1 Chronicles
2 Chron.	2 Chronicles
Ezra	Ezra
Neh.	Nehemiah
Esther	Esther
Job	Job
Ps. (pl. Pss.)	Psalms
Prov.	Proverbs
Eccles.	Ecclesiastes
Song of Sol.	Song of Solomon
Isa.	Isaiah
Jer.	Jeremiah
Lam.	Lamentations
Ezek.	Ezekiel
Dan.	Daniel
Hos.	Hosea
Joel	Joel
Amos	Amos
Obad.	Obadiah
Jon.	Jonah
Mic.	Micah
Nah.	Nahum
Hab.	Habakkuk
Zeph.	Zephaniah
Hag.	Haggai
Zech.	Zechariah
Mal.	Malachi

NEW TESTAMENT

Matt.	Matthew
Luke	Luke
Mark	Mark
John	John
Acts	Acts of the Apostles
Rom.	Romans
1 Cor.	1 Corinthians
2 Cor.	2 Corinthians
Gal.	Galatians
Eph.	Ephesians
Phil.	Philippians
Col.	Colossians
1 Thess.	1 Thessalonians
2 Thess.	2 Thessalonians
1 Tim.	1 Timothy
2 Tim.	2 Timothy
Titus	Titus
Philem.	Philemon
Heb.	Hebrews
James	James
1 Pet.	1 Peter
2 Pet.	2 Peter
1 John	1 John
2 John	2 John
3 John	3 John
Jude	Jude
Rev.	Revelation

BIBLE BOOK ABBREVIATIONS
IN ALPHABETICAL ORDER

1 Chron.	1 Chronicles	Hos.	Hosea
1 Cor.	1 Corinthians	Isa.	Isaiah
1 John	1 John	James	James
1 Kings	1 Kings	Jer.	Jeremiah
1 Pet.	1 Peter	Job	Job
1 Sam.	1 Samuel	Joel	Joel
1 Thess.	1 Thessalonians	John	John
1 Tim.	1 Timothy	Jon.	Jonah
2 Chron.	2 Chronicles	Josh.	Joshua
2 Cor.	2 Corinthians	Jude	Jude
2 John	2 John	Judg.	Judges
2 Kings	2 Kings	Lam.	Lamentations
2 Pet.	2 Peter	Lev.	Leviticus
2 Sam.	2 Samuel	Luke	Luke
2 Thess.	2 Thessalonians	Mal.	Malachi
2 Tim.	2 Timothy	Mark	Mark
3 John	3 John	Matt.	Matthew
Acts	Acts of the Apostles	Mic.	Micah
Amos	Amos	Nah.	Nahum
Col.	Colossians	Neh.	Nehemiah
Dan.	Daniel	Num.	Numbers
Deut.	Deuteronomy	Obad.	Obadiah
Eccles.	Ecclesiastes	Phil.	Philippians
Eph.	Ephesians	Philem.	Philemon
Esther	Esther	Prov.	Proverbs
Exod.	Exodus	Ps. (pl. Pss.)	Psalms
Ezek.	Ezekiel	Rev.	Revelation
Ezra	Ezra	Rom.	Romans
Gal.	Galatians	Ruth	Ruth
Gen.	Genesis	Song of Sol.	Song of Solomon
Hab.	Habakkuk	Titus	Titus
Hag.	Haggai	Zech.	Zechariah
Heb.	Hebrews	Zeph.	Zephaniah

HOW TO USE THIS
TOPICAL CONCORDANCE

T ake almost any topic of human concern. Almost always, the Bible speaks to that concern. *The Holman Concise Topical Concordance* is your link from a topic of interest to the Bible passages that speak to that topic.

Topics are arranged alphabetically. Simply turn to the topic of interest and note the Scripture references related to that topic. You will find here both traditional and contemporary topics such as Abortion, AIDS, Animal Rights, Assisted Suicide, and many more.

The *Holman Concise Topical Concordance* joins a growing family of Concise Bible Reference tools from Holman. These include *Holman Concise Bible Dictionary* and *Holman Concise Bible Commentary*.

ABILITY
From God. 1 Pet. 4:11.
Giving according to. Ezra 2:69;
　Acts 11:29.
Greater, promised. John 14:12.
Limited only by faith. Mark 9:23.
Measured by one's readiness.
　2 Cor. 8:12.
Of Jesus, through the Father.
　John 5:19.
Of Paul, through Christ. Phil. 4:13.
Of the woman who anointed Jesus.
　Mark 14:8.
Spiritual, assigned by God.
　Rom. 12:3–8.
Spiritual, inspired by the Spirit.
　1 Cor. 12:4–11.
Talents given according to.
　Matt. 25:15.
To build the tabernacle. Exod. 36:2.
To make the priests' garments.
　Exod. 28:3.

ABORTION
Killing of unborn children.
　Exod. 21:22–25; 2 Kings 8:12;
　Hos. 13:16; Amos 1:13.
Look to interests of others. Phil. 2:4.
Personhood of unborn children.
　Exod. 21:22–25; Pss. 51:5;
　139:13–15; Eccles. 11:5 (RSV).

*Principles relevant to development
　of unborn children*
　Consciousness of unborn child.
　　Luke 1:41, 44.
　Controlled by God. Job 31:15;
　　Pss. 119:73; 139:13–15;
　　Isa. 44:2; 46:3.

For a purpose. Isa. 49:5; Jer. 1:5;
　Rom. 9:11; Gal. 1:15.
Life begins at conception.
　Ruth 4:13; Hos. 9:11.
Mysterious. Eccles. 11:5.
With Holy Spirit. Luke 1:15.
Speak for those who cannot.
　Prov. 31:8.

Value of life
　Children a reward from God.
　　Ps. 127:3–5.
　God gives and takes life. Job 1:21.
　Infants blessed by Jesus.
　　Luke 18:15–16.
　In image of God.
　　Gen. 1:26–27; 9:6.
　Preference for life.
　　Deut. 30:15, 19;
　　1 Cor. 15:25–26.
　Sanctity of life.
　　Gen. 1:26–27; 2:7; Ps. 8:5.

ABSENCE
From the body means presence with
　the Lord. Phil. 1:20–23.
Of body, presence in spirit.
　1 Cor. 5:3.
Of Christ necessary. John 16:7.
Or presence under the Lord.
　2 Cor. 5:9.

ABUNDANCE
Of blessings promised the righteous.
　Prov. 28:20.
Of divine grace. Rom. 5:20;
　2 Cor. 8:7.
Of divine mercy. Ps. 86:5.

Of entrance into the kingdom.
2 Pet. 1:11.
Of harvest promised Israel.
Lev. 26:5; Deut. 30:9.
Of the heart, source of our words.
Matt. 12:34.
Of human life commanded.
Gen. 1:28.
Of joy with the Lord. Ps. 16:11.
Of life at the creation. Gen. 1:20.
Of life in Christ. John 10:10.
Of spiritual riches. Phil. 4:18–19.

ACCEPTANCE
By the grace of God. Rom. 5:17;
Eph. 1:6.
Of prayers. Gen. 19:21.
Of sacrifices. Ps. 119:108.
Of sinners. Ezek. 20:40–41;
36:23–29.

ACCESS TO GOD
See God, Access to

ACCOMPLISHMENT
Cost of. Luke 14:28.
Of all things. Rev. 16:17.
Of the Christian race.
1 Cor. 9:24–27.
Of collection for Paul. 2 Cor. 8:11.
Of creation Gen. 1:31.
Of entry into the promised land.
Josh. 3:1–17.
Of idol destruction. 2 Chron. 34:7.
Of Israel's warfare. Isa. 40:2.
Of Jesus, source of. John 5:19–20.

ACCUSATION
Against Jesus. Matt. 27:13;
Luke 23:2.
Against Stephen. Acts 6:11.
Against the woman taken in adultery.
John 8:4, 10.

Answered. Rom. 8:1; 1 John 3:21.
False, and restitution. Luke 19:8.
False, forbidden. Luke 3:14.
Of Adam and Eve. Gen. 3:12–13.
Of Satan against Job. Job 1:9–11;
2:4–5.

ACHIEVEMENT
See Accomplishment

ADOPTION
Being gathered together in one by
Christ. John 11:52.
Believers become brethren of Christ
by. John 20:17; Heb. 2:11–12.
Believers predestined to. Rom. 8:29;
Eph. 1:5, 11.
Believers receive the Spirit of.
Rom. 8:15; Gal. 4:6.
Believers wait for the final
consummation of. Rom. 8:19, 23;
1 John 3:2.
Confers a new name. Num. 6:27;
Isa. 62:2; Acts 15:17. (*See also*
Believers, Titles of.)
Entitles to an inheritance.
Matt. 13:43; Rom. 8:17;
Gal. 3:29; 4:7; Eph. 3:6.
Evidenced by being led by the Spirit.
Rom. 8:14.
Explained. 2 Cor. 6:18.
Of Gentiles, predicted. Hos. 2:23;
Rom. 9:24–26; Eph. 3:6.
God is long-suffering and merciful
toward the partakers of.
Jer. 31:1, 9, 20.
Holy Spirit a witness of. Rom. 8:16.
Illustrated by Esther. Esther 2:7.
Is a privilege of believers. John 1:12;
1 John 3:1.
Is according to promise. Rom. 9:8;
Gal. 3:29.
Is by faith. Gal. 3:7, 26.

Is of God's grace. Ezek. 16:3–6;
Rom. 4:16–17; Eph. 1:5–6, 11.
Is through Christ. John 1:12;
Gal. 4:4–5; Eph. 1:5;
Heb. 2:10, 13.
Joseph's sons. Gen. 48:5, 14,
16, 22.
Moses. Exod. 2:10.
New birth connected with.
John 1:12–13.
Safety of those who receive.
Prov. 14:26.
Should lead to holiness.
2 Cor. 6:17–18, with 2 Cor. 7:1;
Phil. 2:15; 1 John 3:2–3.

Should produce
An avoidance of being pretentious.
Matt. 6:1–4, 6, 18.
A desire for God's glory.
Matt. 5:16.
A forgiving spirit. Matt. 6:14
A love of peace. Matt. 5:9.
A merciful spirit. Luke 6:35–36.
A spirit of prayer. Matt. 7:7–11.
Childlike confidence in God.
Matt. 6:25–34.
Likeness to God. Matt. 5:44–45,
48; Eph. 5:1.
Subjects believers to the fatherly
discipline of God. Deut. 8:5;
2 Sam. 7:14; Prov. 3:11–12;
Heb. 12:5–11.
To be pleaded in prayer. Isa. 63:16;
Matt. 6:9.
Typified. Israel. Exod. 4:22;
Hos. 11:1; Rom. 9:4.

ADORATION
To God, ascribed. Jude 25; Rev. 4:8.
Of God, commanded.
1 Chron. 16:29; Pss. 95:6; 96:1;
99:9; 100:1–2; 107:1; 112:1;
113:1; 117.

Of Jesus.
Matt. 8:2; 9:18; 14:33; 18:26;
28:16–17; Mark 5:6;
John 20:28; Phil. 2:10; Heb. 1:6.
Observed by Isaiah. Isa. 6:1–3.
Of the wise men. Matt. 2:2.

ADVENT OF CHRIST
See Christ, Advent of

ADVERTISING, PRINCIPLES RELEVANT TO

Everything to be
Done with integrity. Prov 10:9;
11:3.
Done without deception and lies.
Prov. 30:8.
For the good of others.
1 Cor. 10:24, 33.
To the glory of God. 1 Cor. 10:31.
Truthful. Prov. 8:7; 12:17;
Eph. 4:25.

ADVOCATE
See also Comforter

The Holy Spirit
Another Helper. John 14:16.
Christ to send. John 16:7.
Will teach us all things.
John 14·26.
Will testify of Christ. John 15:26

Jesus
Our advocate with the Father.
1 John 2:1.

AFFAIRS
See also Premarital sex; Rape

Compared to behavior of horses.
Jer. 5:8.

Examples of
Amnon and Tamar.
2 Sam. 13:1–14.
David and Bathsheba.
2 Sam. 11:2–5.
Gomer. Hos. 3:1.
Judah and Tamar.
Gen. 38:12–26.
Levite and concubine.
Judg. 19:2 (KJV).
Samaritan woman.
John 4:17–18.
With prostitute. Prov. 7:6–23;
1 Cor. 6:13–20.
Forbidden. Exod. 20:14; Prov.
5:15–20; Matt. 5:27–28; 1 Cor.
6:9, 18; 7:1–3; Col. 3:5–6;
1 Thess. 4:3–5; Heb. 13:4.

Forgiven by
God. 2 Sam. 12:13; Ps. 51.
Jesus. John 8:10–11.
Spouse. Judg. 19:1–4.

*Have consequences that affect
   others*
Alienation. 1 Cor. 5:12.
Destroys oneself.
Prov. 6:27–32; 7:21–27; 9:13–
18; Rom. 1:26–27.
Family. Gen. 35:22; 2 Sam.
13:21–22.
Guilt. Ps. 51:1–14.
Hatred. Deut. 22:13–14;
2 Sam. 13:15, 22.
Illegitimate child. 2 Sam. 12:14.
Innocent people. 2 Sam.
12:10–11.
Innocent spouse. 2 Sam.
11:6–21; Job 31:9–10.
Lust equated with. Matt. 5:28.
Marriage partners one flesh.
Gen. 2:24; 1 Cor. 6:16–17.

Public embarrassment.
Gen. 38:23–26; 1 Sam.
2:22–24; 2 Sam. 12:11–12;
Matt. 1:19.
Refused by Joseph. Gen. 39:7–18.
Temptation to engage in. 1 Cor.
10:12–13.

AFFECTIONS
Of believers, supremely set on God.
Pss. 42:1; 73:25; 119:10.
Blessedness of making God the
object of. Ps. 91:14.
Christ claims the first place in.
Matt. 10:37; Luke 14:26.
False teachers seek to captivate.
Gal. 1:10; 4:17; 2 Tim. 3:6;
2 Pet. 2:3, 18; Rev. 2:14, 20.
Kindled by communion with Christ.
Luke 24:32.

Should be set
Upon the commandments of God.
Pss. 19:8–10; 119:20, 97, 103,
167.
Upon God supremely. Deut. 6:5;
12:30.
Upon heavenly things. Col. 3:1–2.
Upon the house and worship of
God. 1 Chron. 29:3; Pss. 26:8;
27:4; 84:1–2.
Upon the people of God.
Ps. 16:3; Rom. 12:10;
2 Cor. 7:13–15; 1 Thess. 2:8.
Should be zealously engaged for
God. Pss. 69:9; 119:139;
Gal. 4:18.
Should not grow cold.
Ps. 106:12–13; Matt. 24:12;
Gal. 4:15; Rev. 2:4.
Of the wicked, not sincerely set on
God. Isa. 58:1–2;
Ezek. 33:31–32; Luke 8:13.

Of the wicked, unnatural and
perverted. Rom. 1:31;
2 Tim. 3:3; 2 Pet. 2:10.
Worldly, crucified in believers.
Rom. 6:6; Gal. 5:24.
Worldly, should be put to death.
Rom. 8:13; 13:14; 1 Cor. 9:27;
Col. 3:5; 1 Thess. 4:5.

AFFLICTED BELIEVERS
See Believers, Afflicted

AFFLICTIONS
Always less than we deserve.
Ezra 9:13; Ps. 103:10.
Are consequences of the fall.
Gen. 3:16–19.
Believers appointed to. 1 Thess. 3:3.
Believers are to expect. John 16:33;
Acts 14:22.
Of believers, but temporary.
Pss. 30:5; 103:9; Isa. 54:7–8;
John 16:20; 1 Pet. 1:6; 5:10.
Of believers, comparatively light.
Acts 20:23–24; Rom. 8:18;
2 Cor. 4:17.
Of believers, end in joy and
blessedness. Ps. 126:5–6;
Isa. 61:2–3; Matt. 5:4;
1 Pet. 4:13–14.
Believers have joy under. Job 5:17;
James 5:11.
Exhibit the love and faithfulness of
God. Deut. 8:5; Ps. 119:75;
Prov. 3:12; 1 Cor. 11:32;
Heb. 12:6–7; Rev. 3:19.
Frequently result in good.
Gen. 50:20; Exod. 1:11–12;
Deut. 8:15–16; Jer. 24:5–6;
Ezek. 20:37.
God appoints. 2 Kings 6:33;
Job 5:6, 17; Ps. 66:11;
Amos 3:6; Mic. 6:9.

God determines the continuance of.
Gen. 15:13–14; Num. 14:33;
Isa. 10:25; Jer. 29:10.
God dispenses, as He will.
Job 11:10; Isa. 10:15; 45:7.
God does not willingly send.
Lam. 3:33.
God regulates the measure of.
Ps. 80:5; Isa. 9:1; Jer. 46:28.
Man is born to. Job 5:6–7; 14:1.
Often arise from being the followers
of Jesus. Christ. Matt. 24:9;
John 15:21; 2 Tim. 3:11–12.
Often severe. Job 16:7–16;
Pss. 42:7; 66:12; Jon. 2:3;
Rev. 7:14.
Sin produces. Job 4:8; 20:11;
Prov. 1:31.
Sin visited with. 2 Sam. 12:14;
Ps. 89:30–32; Isa. 57:17;
Acts 13:10–11.
Tempered with mercy.
Pss. 78:38–39;106:43–46;
Isa. 30:18–21; Lam. 3:32;
Mic. 7:7–9; Nah. 1:12.

**AFFLICTED, DUTY TOWARD
THE**
To bear them in mind. Heb. 13:3.
To comfort them. Job 16:5; 29:25;
2 Cor. 1:4; 1 Thess. 4:18.
To have compassion on them.
Job 6:14.
To pray for them. Acts 12:5; Phil.
1:16, 19; James 5:14–16.
To protect them. Ps. 82:3;
Prov. 22:22; 31:5.
To relieve them. Job 31:19–20;
Isa. 58:10; Phil. 4:14.
To sympathize with them.
Rom. 12:15; Gal. 6:2.
To visit them. James 1:27.

AFFLICTION, CONSOLATION UNDER

Believers should administer to each
    other. 1 Thess. 4:18; 5:11, 14.
Christ the Author and Giver of.
    Isa. 61:2; John 14:18;
    2 Cor. 1:5.
God the Author and Giver of.
    Ps. 23:4; Rom. 15:5.
Holy Spirit the Author and Giver of.
    John 14:16–17; 15:26; 16:7;
    Acts 9:31.

Is

Abundant. Ps. 71:21; Isa. 66:11.
A cause of praise. Isa. 12:1;
    49:13.
Everlasting. 2 Thess. 2:16.
Sought in vain from the world.
    Ps. 69:20; Eccles. 4:1;
    Lam. 1:2.
Strong. Heb. 6:18.
By ministers of the gospel.
    Isa. 40:1–2; 1 Cor. 14:3;
    2 Cor. 1:4, 6.
To the persecuted. Deut. 33:27.
To the poor. Pss. 10:14; 34:6,
    9–10.
Pray for. Ps. 119:82.
Promised. Isa. 51:3, 12; 66:13;
    Ezek. 14:22–23; Hos. 2:14;
    Zech. 1:17.
In prospect of death. Job 19:25–26;
    Ps. 23:4; John 14:2; 2 Cor. 5:1;
    1 Thess. 4:14; Heb. 4:9;
    Rev. 7:14–17; 14:13.
Through Scriptures. Ps. 119:50, 76;
    Rom. 15:4.
To the sick. Ps. 41:3.
Under the sufferings of old age.
    Ps. 71:9, 18.
To the tempted. Rom. 16:20;
    1 Cor. 10:13; 2 Cor. 12:9;

James 1:12; 4:7; 2 Pet. 2:9;
    Rev. 2:10.
To those deserted by friends.
    Pss. 27:10; 41:9–12;
    John 14:18; 15:18–19.
To those who mourn for sin.
    Ps. 51:17; Isa. 1:18; 40:1–2;
    61:1; Mic. 7:18–19; Luke 4:18.
To the troubled in mind. Pss. 42:5;
    94:19.

AFFLICTION, PRAYER UNDER

For deliverance. Pss. 25:17, 22;
    39:10; Isa. 64:9–12; Jer. 17:14.
For divine comfort. Pss. 4:6;
    119:76.
For divine teaching and direction.
    Job 34:32; Pss. 27:11; 143:10.
Encouragement to. James 5:13–16.
For increase of faith. Mark 9:24.
For mercy. Ps. 6:2; Hab. 3:2.
For mitigation of troubles.
    Ps. 39:12–13.
For pardon and deliverance from sin.
    Pss. 39:8, 51:1; 79:8.
For the presence and support of
    God. Pss. 10:1; 102:2.
For protection and preservation from
    enemies. 2 Kings 19:19;
    2 Chron. 20:12; Ps. 17:8–9.
For restoration to joy.
    Pss. 51:8, 12; 69:29; 90:14–15.
That God would consider our trouble.
    2 Kings 19:16; Neh. 9:32;
    Ps. 9:13; Lam. 5:1.
That the Holy Spirit may not be
    withdrawn. Ps. 51:11.
That we may be delivered.
    Ps. 143:11.
That we may be taught the
    uncertainty of life. Ps. 39:4.
That we may be turned to God.
    Pss. 80:7; 85:4–6; Jer. 31:18.

That we may know the causes of our trouble. Job 6:24; 10:2; 13:23–24.

AFFLICTIONS MADE BENEFICIAL

In convincing us of sin. Job 36:8–9; Ps. 119:67; Luke 15:16–18.

In exercising our patience. Ps. 40:1; Rom. 5:3; James 1:3; 1 Pet. 2:20.

In exhibiting the power and faithfulness of God. Ps. 34:19–20; 2 Cor. 4:8–11.

In furthering the gospel. Acts 8:3–4; 11:19–21; Phil. 1:12; 2 Tim. 2:9–10; 4:16–17.

In humbling us. Deut. 8:3, 16; 2 Chron. 7:13–14; Lam. 3:19–20; 2 Cor. 12:7.

In keeping us from again departing from God. Job 34:31–32; Isa. 10:20; Ezek. 14:10–11.

In leading us to confession of sin. Num. 21:7; Pss. 32:5; 51:3, 5.

In leading us to seek God in prayer. Judg. 4:3; Jer. 31:18; Lam. 2:17–19; Hos. 5:14–15; Jon. 2:1.

In promoting the glory of God. John 9:1–3; 11:3–4; 21:18–19

In purifying us. Eccles. 7:2–3; Isa. 1:25–26; 48:10; Jer. 9:6–7; Zech. 13:9; Mal. 3:2–3.

In rendering us fruitful in good works. John 15:2; Heb. 12:10–11.

In teaching us the will of God. Ps. 119:71; Isa. 26:9; Mic. 6:9.

In testing and exhibiting our sincerity. Job 23:10; Ps. 66:10; Prov. 17:3.

In trying our faith and obedience. Gen. 22:1–2, with Heb. 11:17; Exod. 15:23–25; Deut. 8:2, 16; 1 Pet. 1:7; Rev. 2:10.

In turning us to God. Deut. 4:30–31; Neh. 1:8–9; Ps. 78:34; Isa. 10:20–21; Hos. 2:6–7.

AFFLICTIONS OF THE WICKED

See Wicked, Afflictions of the

AGRICULTURE

Beasts used in
Donkey. Deut. 22:10.
Horse. Isa. 28:28.
Ox. Deut. 25:4.
Climate of Canaan favorable to. Gen. 13:10; Deut. 8:7–9.
Contributes to the support of all. Eccles. 5:9.
Cultivates the earth. Gen. 3:23.
Diligence in, rewarded. Prov. 12:11; 13:23; 28:19; Heb. 6:7.

Illustrative of
The culture of the church. 1 Cor. 3:9.
The culture of the heart. Jer. 4:3; Hos. 10:12.

Threshing with Sled and Oxen

Plow and Hoe

Implements of
Ax. 1 Sam. 13:20.
Cart. 1 Sam. 6:7; Isa. 28:27–28.
Fan. Isa. 30:24; Matt. 3:12.
Flail. Isa. 28:27.
Fork. 1 Sam. 13:21.
Harrow. 2 Sam. 12:31.
Mattock. 1 Sam. 13:20.
Plow. 1 Sam. 13:20.
Pruning hook. Isa. 18:5;
    Joel 3:10.
Shovel. Isa. 30:24.
Sickle. Deut. 16:9; 23:25.
Sieve. Amos 9:9.
Teethed threshing instrument.
    Isa. 41:15.
The Jews loved and followed.
    Judg. 6:11; 1 Kings 19:19;
    2 Chron. 26:10.

Labor of, supposedly lessened by
    Noah. Gen. 5:29, with 9:20.
Man doomed to labor in, after the
    fall. Gen. 3:23.
Man's occupation, before the fall.
    Gen. 2:15.
Not to be engaged in during the
    sabbatical year. Exod. 23:10–11.
Often performed by hired workers.
    1 Chron. 27:26; 2 Chron. 26:10;
    Matt. 20:8; Luke 17:7.

Laws to protect
Against injuring the produce of.
    Exod. 22:6.
Against the trespass of cattle.
    Exod. 22:5.
Grief occasioned by the failure of
    the fruits of. Joel 1:11;
    Amos 5:16–17.
Not to covet the fields of another.
    Deut. 5:21.
Not to cut down crops of another.
    Deut. 23:25.
Not to move landmarks.
    Deut. 19:14; Prov. 22:28.

Operations in
Binding. Gen. 37:7; Matt. 13:30.
Digging. Isa. 5:6; Luke 13:8;
    16:3.
Gathering out the stones. Isa. 5:2.
Gleaning. Lev. 19:9; Ruth 2:3.
Grafting. Rom. 11:17–19, 24.
Harrowing. Job 39:10;
    Isa. 28:24.

Plowing and Sowing

Hedging. Isa. 5:2, 5; Hos. 2:6.

Manuring. Isa. 25:10;
Luke 14:34–35.

Mowing. Ps. 129:7; Amos 7:1.

Planting. Prov. 31:16; Isa. 44:14;
Jer. 31:5.

Plowing. Job 1:14.

Pruning. Lev. 25:3; Isa. 5:6;
John 15:2.

Reaping. Isa. 17:5.

Sowing. Eccles. 11:4; Isa. 32:20;
Matt. 13:3.

Stacking. Exod. 22:6.

Storing in barns. Matt. 6:26;
13:30.

Threshing. Deut. 25:4;
Judg. 6:11.

Watering. Deut. 11:10;
1 Cor. 3:6–8.

Weeding. Matt. 13:28.

Winnowing. Ruth 3:2; Matt. 3:12.

Patriarchs engaged in. Gen. 4:2;
9:20.

Peace favorable to. Isa. 2:4;
Jer. 31:24.

Persons engaged in, called
Husbandmen. 2 Chron. 26:10.
Laborers. Matt. 9:37; 20:1.
Tillers of the ground. Gen. 4:2.

Produce of
Acknowledges providence of God.
Jer. 5:24; Hos. 2:8.
Exported. 1 Kings 5:11;
Ezek. 27:17.
Given as rent for land.
Matt. 21:33–34.
Often blasted because of sin.
Isa. 5:10; 7:23; Jer. 12:13;
Joel 1:10–11.

Promoted among the Jews by
Allotments to each family.
Num. 36:7–9.
Prohibition against interest.
Exod. 22:25.
Promises of God's blessing.
Lev. 26:4; Deut. 7:13;
11:14–15.
Right of redemption.
Lev. 25:23–28.
Separation from other nations.
Exod. 33:16.
Rendered laborious by the curse on
the earth. Gen. 3:17–19.

Requires
Diligence. Prov. 27:23–27;
Eccles. 11:6.
Patience. James 5:7.
Toil. 2 Tim. 2:6.

Threshing and Winnowing

Wisdom. Isa. 28:26.
Soil of Canaan suited to.
Gen. 13:10; Deut. 8:7–9.
War destructive to. Jer. 50:16;
51:23.

AIDS

Consequence of the Fall. Rom 1:27.

Injunctions regarding
Cultivate a pure lifestyle. Phil. 4:8;
Col. 3:1–7.
Have empathy for those who
suffer. Rom. 12:15.
Jesus' compassion on lepers and the
sick generally. Matt. 9:36; 14:14;
20:34; Mark 1:41.

Principles relevant to
All sufferers comforted by God.
2 Cor. 1:4.
Nothing can separate the Christian
from God. Rom. 8:31–39.
People responsible for their own
actions. Hos. 8:7; Gal. 6:7–8.

**ALLIANCE, WITH THE
ENEMIES OF GOD**

Believers
Are separate from. Exod. 33:16;
Ezra 6:21.
Are tempted by the wicked to.
Neh. 6:2–4.
Deprecate. Gen. 49:6; Pss. 6:8;
15:4; 101:4, 7; 119:115;
139:19.
Grieve to meet with. Pss. 57:4;
120:5–6; 2 Pet. 2:7–8.
Grieve to witness in their brethren.
Gen. 26:35; Ezra 9:3; 10:6.
Hate and avoid. Pss. 26:4–5;
31:6; 101:7; Rev. 2:2.

Should be cautious when
unintentionally thrown into.
Matt. 10:6; Col. 4:5;
1 Pet. 2:12.
Blessedness of avoiding. Ps. 1:1.
Blessedness of forsaking. Ezek. 9:12;
Prov. 9:6; 2 Cor. 6:17–18.
A call to come out from.
Num. 16:26; Ezra 10:11; Jer.
51:6, 45; 2 Cor. 6:17;
2 Thess. 3:6; Rev. 18:4.
Children who enter into, bring shame
upon their parents. Prov. 28:7.
Evil consequences of. Prov. 28:19;
Jer. 51:7.
Exhortations to avoid all inducements
to. Prov. 1:10–15; 4:14–15;
2 Pet. 3:17.
Exhortations to hate and avoid.
Prov. 14:7; Rom. 16:17;
1 Cor. 5:9–11; Eph. 5:6–7;
1 Tim. 6:5; 2 Tim. 3:5.
Forbidden. Exod. 23:32; 34:12;
Deut. 7:2–3; 13:6, 8;
Josh. 23:6–7; Judg. 2:2;
Ezra 9:12; Prov. 1:10, 15;
2 Cor. 6:14–17; Eph. 5:11.
Has led to murder and human
sacrifice. Ps. 106:37–38.

Is
Defiling. Ezra 9:1–2.
Degrading. Isa. 1:23.
Enslaving. 2 Pet. 2:18–19.
Ensnaring. Exod. 23:33;
Num. 25:18; Deut. 12:30;
13:6; Ps. 106:36.
Proof of folly. Prov. 12:11.
Ruinous to moral character.
1 Cor. 15:33.
Ruinous to spiritual interests.
Prov. 29:24; Heb. 12:14–15;
2 Pet. 3:17.

Leads to idolatry. Exod. 34:15–16;
   Num. 25:1–8; Deut. 7:4;
   Judg. 3:5–7; Rev. 2:20.
Means of preservation from.
   Prov. 2:10–20; 19:27.
Persons in authority should
   denounce. Ezra 10:9–11;
   Neh. 13:23–27.
Pious parents prohibit, to their
   children. Gen. 28:1.
Provokes God to leave men to reap
   the fruits of them.
   Josh. 23:12–13; Judg. 2:1–3.
Provokes the anger of God.
   Deut. 7:4; 31:16–17;
   2 Chron. 19:2; Ezra 9:13–14;
   Ps. 106:29, 40; Isa. 2:6.
Punishment of. Num. 33:56;
   Deut. 7:4; Josh. 23:13;
   Judg. 2:3; 3:5–8; Ezra 9:7, 14;
   Ps. 106:41–42;
   Rev. 2:16, 22–23.
Sin of, to be confessed, deeply
   regretted, and forsaken. Ezra 10.
Unbecoming in those called
   believers. 2 Chron. 19:2;
   2 Cor. 6:14–16; Phil. 2:15.

The wicked are prone to. Ps. 50:18;
   Jer. 2:25.

ALTAR OF BURNT OFFERING
See Burnt Offering, Altar of

ALTAR OF INCENSE
See Incense, Altar Of

ALTARS
See also additional topics: Burnt
   Offering, Altar of; Incense, Altar of

Afforded no protection to murderers.
   Exod. 21:14; 1 Kings 2:18–34.

Of brick, insulting to God. Isa. 65:3.

For burnt offering. Exod. 27:1–8.

Designed for sacrifice. Exod. 20:24.

Idolaters planted groves near.
   Judg. 6:30; 1 Kings 16:32–33;
   2 Kings 21:3.

For idolatrous worship, often erected
   on roofs of houses.
   2 Kings 23:12;
   Jer. 19:13; 32:29.

Altar of Burnt Offering

For idolatrous worship, to be destroyed. Exod. 34:13; Deut. 7:5.

For incense. Exod. 30:1–6.

The Jews not to plant groves near. Deut. 16:21.

Natural rocks sometimes used as. Judg. 6:19–21; 13:19–20.

Not to have steps up to them. Exod. 20:26.

Probable origin of inscriptions on. Deut. 27:8.

Protection afforded by. 1 Kings 1:50–51.

Should be made of earth, or uncut stone. Exod. 20:24–25; Deut. 27:5–6.

Those of, mentioned

Abraham. Gen. 12:7–8; 13:18; 22:9.

Ahaz. 2 Kings 16:10–12.

Athenians. Acts 17:23.

Balaam. Num. 23:1, 14, 29.

David. 2 Sam. 24:21, 25.

Gideon. Judg. 6:26–27.

Isaac. Gen. 26:25.

Jacob. Gen. 33:20; 35:1, 3, 7.

Jeroboam at Bethel. 1 Kings 12:33.

Joshua. Josh. 8:30–31.

Moses. Exod. 17:15; 24:4.

Noah. Gen. 8:20.

People of Israel. Judg. 21:4.

Reubenites, etc. Josh. 22:10.

Samuel. 1 Sam. 7:17.

Second temple. Ezra 3:2–3.

Temple of Solomon. 2 Chron. 4:1, 19.

AMBASSADOR

Sent to

Congratulate. 1 Kings 5:1; 2 Sam. 8:10.

Make alliance. Josh. 9:4.

Negotiate. 2 Kings 18:17–19:8.

Protest injustice. Judg. 11:12.

Seek favors. Num. 20:14.

Spiritual

For Christ. 2 Cor. 5:20.

In chains. Eph. 6:20.

Suffering imprisonment. Philem. 1:9.

AMBITION

Believers avoid. Ps. 131:1–2.

And covetousness. Hab. 2:8–9.

And cruelty. Hab. 2:12.

Condemned by Christ. Matt. 18:1, 3–4; 20:25–26; 23:11–12.

Condemned by God. Gen. 11:7; Isa. 5:8.

Leads to strife and contention. James 4:1–2.

And pride. Hab. 2:5.

Punishment of. Prov. 17:19; Isa. 14:12–15; Ezek. 31:10–11; Obad. 1:3–4.

Vanity of. Job 20:5–9; 24:24; Ps. 49:11–20.

AMEN

Affirms an oath. Num. 5:22; Deut. 27:15ff.

Christ as. Rev. 3:14.

Concludes a benediction or prayer. Matt. 6:13; Gal. 6:18.

Expresses agreement with a statement of praise or benediction. Pss. 41:13; 72:19; 1 Chron. 16:36; Rom. 16:24.

Uttered through Christ. 2 Cor. 1:20.

AMPUTATION
See Maiming

AMUSEMENTS AND PLEASURES, EVIL
Abstinence from, seems strange to
the wicked. 1 Pet. 4:4.
Are all vanity. Eccles. 2:11.
Are transitory. Job 21:12–13;
Heb. 11:25.
Avoided by the early Christians.
1 Pet. 4:3.
Belong to the works of the sinful
nature. Gal. 5:19, 21.
Choke the word of God in the heart.
Luke 8:14.
Denounced by God. Isa. 5:11–12.
Formed a part of idolatrous worship.
Exod. 32:4, 6, 19, with
1 Cor. 10:7; Judg. 16:23–25.

Indulgence in
An abuse of riches. James 5:1, 5.
A characteristic of the wicked.
Isa. 47:8; Eph. 4:17, 19;
2 Tim. 3:4; Titus 3:3;
1 Pet. 4:3.
A proof of folly. Eccles. 7:4.
A proof of spiritual death.
1 Tim. 5:6.

Lead to
Disregard of the judgments and
works of God. Isa. 5.12;
Amos 6:1–6.
Poverty. Prov. 21.17.
Rejection of God. Job 21:14–15.
May lead to greater evil. Job 1:5;
Matt. 14:6–8.
Punishment of. Eccles. 11:9;
2 Pet. 2:13.
Terminate in sorrow. Prov. 14:13.
Wisdom of abstaining from.
Eccles. 7:2–3.

ANARCHY
In man's final rebellion. 2 Tim. 4:3.
When violence reigns. Jer. 51:46.
Without law or government.
Judg. 2:19; 21:25.
Without self-discipline. Prov. 25:28.

ANGELS
Announced the
Ascension and second coming of
Christ. Acts 1:11.
Birth of Christ. Luke 2:10–12.
Conception of Christ.
Matt. 1:20–21; Luke 1:31.
Conception of John the Baptist.
Luke 1:13, 36.
Resurrection of Christ.
Matt. 28:5–7; Luke 24:23.

Are
Elect. 1 Tim. 5:21.
Examples of meekness.
2 Pet. 2:11; Jude 9.
Holy. Matt. 25:31.
Innumerable. Job 25:3;
Heb. 12:22.
Mighty. Ps. 103:20.
Ministering spirits. 1 Kings 19:5;
Pss. 68:17; 104:4; Luke 16:22;
Acts 12:7–11; 27:23;
Heb. 1:7, 14.
Not to be worshiped. Col. 2:18;
Rev. 19:10; 22:9.
Of different orders. Isa. 6:2;
1 Thess. 4:16; 1 Pet. 3:22;
Jude 9; Rev. 12:7.
Subject to Christ. Eph. 1:21;
Col. 1:16; 2:10; 1 Pet. 3:22.
Wise. 2 Sam. 14:20.
Celebrate the praises of God.
Job 38:7; Ps. 148:2; Isa. 6:3;
Luke 2:13–14; Rev. 5:11–12;
7:11–12.

Communicate the will of God and Christ. Dan. 8:16–17; 9:21–23; 10:11; 12:6–7; Matt. 2:13, 20; Luke 1:19, 28; Acts 5:20; 8:26; 10:5; 27:23; Rev. 1:1.

Execute the judgments of God. 2 Sam. 24:16; 2 Kings 19:35; Ps. 35:6–6; Acts 12:23; Rev. 16:1.

Execute the purposes of God. Num. 22:22; Ps. 103:21; Matt. 13:39–42; 28:2; John 5:4; Rev. 5:2.

Have charge over the children of God. Pss. 34:7; 91:11–12; Dan. 6:22; Matt. 18:10.

Know and delight in the gospel of Christ. Eph. 3:9–10; 1 Tim. 3:16; 1 Pet. 1:12.

The law given by. Ps. 68:17; Acts 7:53; Heb. 2:2.

Minister to Christ. Matt. 4:11; Luke 22:43; John 1:51.

Help of, obtained by prayer. Matt. 26:53; Acts 12:5, 7.

Obey the will of God. Ps. 103:20; Matt. 6:10.

Rejoice over every repentant sinner. Luke 15:7, 10.

Will attend Christ at His second coming. Matt. 16:27; 25:31; Mark 8:38; 2 Thess. 1:7.

Will execute the purposes of Christ. Matt. 13:41; 24:31.

Were created by God and Christ. Neh. 9:6; Col. 1:16.

Worship God and Christ. Neh. 9:6; Phil. 2:9–11; Heb. 1:6.

ANGER

Avoid those given to. Gen. 49:6; Prov. 22:24.

Be slow to. Prov. 15:18; 16:32; 19:11; Titus 1:7; James 1:19.

Brings its own punishment. Job 5:2; Prov. 19:19; 25:28.

A characteristic of fools. Prov. 12:16; 14:29; 27:3; Eccles. 7:9.

Children should not be provoked to. Eph. 6:4; Col. 3:21.

Connected with
Cruelty. Gen. 49:7; Prov. 27:3–4.
Harsh words and evil-speaking. Eph. 4:31.
Malice and blasphemy. Col. 3:8.
Pride. Prov. 21:24.
Strife and contention. Prov. 21:19; 29:22; 30:33.

Forbidden. Eccles. 7:9; Matt. 5:22; Rom. 12:19.

Harsh words stir up. Judg. 12:4; 2 Sam. 19:43; Prov. 15:1.

May be turned away by wisdom. Prov. 29:8.

Meekness pacifies. Prov. 15:1; Eccles. 10:4.

In prayer be free from. 1 Tim. 2:8.

Should not betray us into sin. Ps. 37:8; Eph. 4:26.

A work of the sinful nature. Gal. 5:20.

ANGER OF GOD
See God, Anger of

ANIMAL RIGHTS

All animals
Created by God as living beings. Gen. 1:20–25.
Given to people for food after the flood. Gen. 9:3.
God's possession. Ps. 50:10–11.

Named by Adam. Gen. 2:19.
Of lesser value than people.
Gen. 1:26–28.
To be under the dominion of
people. Gen. 1:26–28;
Ps. 8:5–8.

Domesticated animals
Cared for by people. Prov. 12:10.
To be fed adequately. Deut. 25:4;
1 Cor. 9:9; 1 Tim. 5:18.
To be helped with their loads.
Exod. 23:5.
To rest on the Sabbath.
Exod. 20:10; Deut. 5:14.

Wild animals
Can glean fields after poor people.
Exod. 23:11.
Can have eggs taken from nest but
should spare the mother bird.
Deut. 22:6–7.
Cared for by God. Job 38:39–41;
Ps. 104:21; 147:9; Matt. 6:26.

ANOINTING

Applied to
Eyes. Rev. 3:18.
Face. Ps. 104:15.
Feet. Luke 7:38–39; John 12:3.
Head. Ps. 23:5; Eccles. 9:8.
Deprivation of, threatened as a
punishment Deut. 28:40;
Mic. 6:15.
Neglect of, to guests, a mark of
disrespect. Luke 7:46.
Neglected in times of affliction.
2 Sam. 12:20; 14:2; Dan. 10:3.

Ointment for
An article of commerce.
Ezek. 27:17; Rev. 18:13.

Most expensive. 2 Kings 20:13;
Amos 6:6; John 12:3, 5.
Richly perfumed. Song of Sol.
4:10; John 12:3.
Recommended by Christ in times
of fasting. Matt. 6:17–18.

Used for
Curing the sick. Mark 6:13;
James 5:14.
Decorating the person. Ruth 3:3.
Healing wounds. Isa. 1:6;
Luke 10:34.
Preparing the dead for burial.
Matt. 26:12; Mark 16:1, with
Luke 23:56.
Preparing weapons for war.
Isa. 21:5.
Purifying the body. Esther 2:12;
Isa. 57:9.
Refreshing the body.
2 Chron. 28:15.
The wealthy very fond of.
Prov. 27:9; Amos 6:6.
With oil. Ps. 92:10.
With ointment. John 11:2.

ANOINTING OF THE HOLY SPIRIT
See Holy Spirit, Anointing of the

ANOINTING, SACRED
Antiquity of. Gen. 28:18; 35:14.
Consecrates to God's service.
Exod. 30:29.

Oil or ointment for
Compounded by priests.
1 Chron. 9:30.
Divinely prescribed.
Exod. 30:23–25.
Holy forever. Exod. 30:25, 31.
Not to be imitated. Exod. 30:32;
Ezek. 23:41.

Persons who received
   Kings. Judg. 9:8; 1 Sam. 9:16;
     1 Kings 1:34.
   Priests. Exod. 40:13–15.
   Prophets. 1 Kings 19:16;
     Isa. 61:1.

Things which received
   Bronze altar. Exod. 29:36; 40:10.
   Bronze basin. Exod. 40:11.
   Tabernacle, etc. Exod. 30:26–27;
     40:9.

Those who partook of
   Not to be injured or insulted.
     1 Sam. 24:6; 26:9;
     2 Sam. 1:14–15; 19:21.
   Protected by God.
     1 Chron. 16:22; Ps. 105:15.
   To be put on no stranger.
     Exod. 30:33.

ANTEDILUVIAN

Antediluvian, meaning "before the
flood," refers to those who lived
before the Flood. Gen. 6–8.

ANTICHRIST

Deceit characteristic of. 2 John 7.
Denies Father and Son.
   1 John 2:22.
Denies incarnation of Christ.
   1 John 4:3; 2 John 7.
Spirit prevalent in apostolic times.
   1 John 2:18.

ANXIETY

Articulated. Ps. 38:6.
Makes the Word of God unfruitful.
   Mark 4:19.
Overcome. Ps. 23:4.
Prevented. Ps. 121:4; 1 Pet. 5:7.
Prohibited. Matt. 6:34.

APOSTASY

At end of age. 2 Tim. 3:6–9; 4:3–4;
   2 Pet. 3:3.
At present. Rom. 1:18;
   Titus 1:10–14.

APOSTATES

Believers do not become.
   Ps. 41:18–19; Heb. 6:9; 10:39.
Cautions against becoming.
   Heb. 3:12; 2 Pet. 3:17.
Described. Deut. 13:13; Heb. 3:12.
Guilt and punishment of.
   Zeph. 1:4–6; Heb. 10:25–31, 39;
   2 Pet. 2:17, 20–22.
Impossible to restore. Heb. 6:4–6.
Made by persecution.
   Matt. 24:9–10; Luke 8:13.
Made by a worldly spirit.
   2 Tim. 4:10.
Never belonged to Christ.
   1 John 2:19.
Will abound in the latter days.
   Matt. 24:12; 2 Thess. 2:3;
   1 Tim. 4:1–3.

APOSTLES

Called by
   Christ. Matt. 10:1; Mark 3:13;
     Acts 20:24; Rom. 1:5.
   God. 1 Cor. 1:1; 12:28; Gal. 1:1,
     15–16.
   The Holy Spirit. Acts 13:2, 4.
Christ always present with.
   Matt. 28:20.
Christ as preeminent. Heb. 3:1.
Empowered to work miracles.
   Matt. 10:1, 8; Mark 16:20;
   Luke 9:1; Acts 2:43.
Equal authority given to each of.
   Matt. 16:19, with 18:18;
   2 Cor. 11:5.

Guided by the Spirit into all truth.
John 14:26; 15:26; 16:13.
The Holy Spirit given to.
John 20:22; Acts 2:1–4; 9:17.
Humility urged upon.
Matt. 20:26–27; Mark 9:33–37;
Luke 22:24–30.
Instructed by the Spirit to answer
adversaries. Matt. 10:19–20;
Luke 12:11–12.
Mutual love urged upon.
John 15:17.
Ordained by Christ. Mark 3:14;
John 15:16.
Persecutions and sufferings of.
Matt. 10:16, 18; Luke 21:16;
John 15:20; 16:2.
Received their title from Christ.
Luke 6:13.
Saw Christ in the flesh. Luke 1:2;
Acts 1:22; 1 Cor. 9:1;
1 John 1:1.
Selected from obscure positions.
Matt. 4:18.
Self-denial urged upon.
Matt. 10:37–39.
Sent first to the house of Israel.
Matt. 10:5–6; Luke 24:47;
Acts 13:46.
Sent to preach the gospel to all
nations. Matt. 28:19–20;
Mark 16:15; 2 Tim. 1:11.
Specially devoted to the office of the
ministry. Acts 6:4, 20:27.
Warned against a timid profession of
Christ. Matt. 10:27–33.
Were hated by the world.
Matt. 10:22; 24:9; John 15:18.
Were not of the world. John 15:19;
17:16.
Were unlearned men. Acts 4:13.
Witnesses of the resurrection and
ascension of Christ.

Luke 24:33–41, 51;
Acts 1:2–9; 10:40–41;
1 Cor. 15:8.

APPLIANCES
Mankind's ability to progress.
Gen. 11:6.

Principles relevant to.
Seek God first. Matt. 6:31–33.
Stewardship of creation.
Gen. 2:15.
Things not to be used for one's
own pleasure. James 4:3.

ARK, NOAH'S
Building commanded. Gen. 6:14.
Exhibited Noah's faith and
righteousness. 1 Pet. 3:20;
Heb. 11:7.
Set forth surrounding
unrighteousness. Luke 17:26–27.
Specifications. Gen. 6:15 ff
Successful test. Gen. 7–9.

ARK OF THE COVENANT
Anointed with sacred oil.
Exod. 30:26.
At Kiriath-jearim twenty years.
1 Sam. 7:1–2.
Brought by Solomon into the temple
with great seriousness. 1 Kings
8:1–6; 2 Chron. 5:2–9.
Brought into the city of David.
2 Sam. 6:12–15;
1 Chron. 15:25–28.

Called the
Ark of the Covenant of the Lord.
Num. 10:33.
Ark of God. 1 Sam. 3:3.
Ark of God's strength.
2 Chron. 6:41; Ps. 132:8.

Ark of the testimony. Exod. 30:6;
Num. 7:89.
Captured by the Philistines.
1 Sam. 4:11.

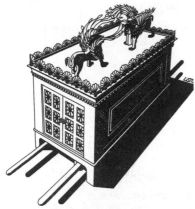

Ark of the Covenant

Carried
Before the Israelites in their
journeys. Num. 10:33;
Josh. 3:6.
By priests or Levites alone.
Deut. 10:8; Josh. 3:14;
2 Sam. 15:24; 1 Chron. 15:2.
Sometimes to the camp in war.
1 Sam. 4:4–5.
A copy of the law laid in the side of.
Deut. 31:26.
Covered with the veil by the priests
before removal. Num. 4:5–6.
David made a tent for. 2 Sam. 6:17;
1 Chron. 15:1.
Dimensions of. Exod. 25:10; 37:1.
Entirely covered with gold.
Exod. 25:11; 37:2.
Furnished with rings and staves.
Exod. 25:12–15; 37:3–5.
The Israelites inquired of the Lord
before. Josh. 7:6–9; Judg. 20:27;
1 Chron. 13:3.

Mercy seat laid upon. Exod. 25:21;
26:34.

Miracles connected with
Fall of Dagon. 1 Sam. 5:1–4.
Fall of the walls of Jericho.
Josh. 6:6–20.
Jordan divided. Josh. 4:7.
Manner of its restoration.
1 Sam. 6:1–18.
Philistines plagued.
1 Sam. 5:6–12.
Placed in the Holy of Holies.
Exod. 26:33; 40:21; Heb. 9:3–4.
Pot of manna and Aaron's rod laid up
before. Heb. 9:4, with
Exod. 16:33–34; Num. 17:10.
Profanation of, punished. Num. 4:5,
15; 1 Sam. 6:19;
1 Chron. 15:13.
Protecting of, rewarded.
1 Chron. 13:14.
Removed from Kiriath-jearim to the
house of Obed-edom.
2 Sam. 6:1–11.
Sanctified its resting place.
2 Chron. 8:11.
Surrounded with a crown of gold.
Exod. 25:11.
Symbol of the presence and glory of
God. Num. 14:43–44; Josh. 7:6;
1 Sam. 14:18–19; Ps. 132:8.
Tables of testimony alone placed in.
Exod. 25:16, 21.
A type of Christ. Ps. 40:8;
Rev. 11:19.
Valued the glory of Israel.
1 Sam. 4:21–22.
Was holy. 2 Chron. 35:3.

ARMIES
Accompanied by beasts of burden
and wagons for baggage.

Judg. 7:12; 2 Kings 7:7;
Ezek. 23:2.
Ancient, often numerous.
Josh. 11:4; 1 Sam. 13:5.
Antiquity of. Gen. 14:1–8.
Began their battles with a shout.
1 Sam. 17:20; 2 Chron. 13:15;
Jer. 51:14.
Began their campaigns in the spring.
2 Sam. 11:1.
Brought their idols with them.
1 Chron. 14:12.

Called the
Bands. 1 Chron. 7:4.
Hosts. Josh. 10:5; Judg. 8:10.
Power of kings. 2 Chron. 32:9.
Wings of a nation. Isa. 8:8;
Jer. 48:40.

Compared to
Caterpillars. Jer. 51:14, 27.
Clouds. Ezek. 38:9–16.
Flies. Isa. 7:18–19.
Grasshoppers. Judg. 6:3–5; 7:12.
Locusts. Isa. 33:4; Rev. 9:3, 7.
Overflowing torrents. Isa. 28:2;
Dan. 11:10, 26.
Waters of a river. Isa. 8:7.
Whirlwinds. Jer. 25:32.

Composed of
Bowmen and slingers.
1 Chron. 12:2, Jer. 4:29.
Cavalry. Exod. 14:9;
1 Kings 20:20.
Spearmen or heavy troops.
Ps. 68:30; Acts 23:23.
War chariots. Josh. 17:16;
Judg. 4:3.
Devastation occasioned by.
Isa. 37:18; Jer. 5:17.

Of different nations often
confederated. Josh. 9:2; 10:5;
Judg. 3:13; 1 Kings 20:1.
Divided the spoil. Exod. 15:9;
Zech. 14:1.

Employed in
Assaulting cities. Josh. 7:3–4.
Besieging cities. Deut. 20:12;
Isa. 29:3.
Fighting battles. 1 Sam. 17:2–3;
1 Chron. 19:17.

Encamped
Before cities. Josh. 10:5;
1 Sam. 11:1.
In the open fields. 2 Sam. 11:11;
1 Chron. 11:15.
Exercised savage cruelties on the
vanquished. Jer. 50:42;
Lam. 5:11–13; Amos 1:13.
Fear occasioned by. Num. 22:3;
Jer. 6:25.
Frequently the instrument of God's
vengeance. Isa. 10:5–6; 13:5.
Furnished with standards. Song of
Sol. 6:4; Isa. 10:18; Jer. 4:21.
Generally in three divisions.
Gen. 14:15; Job 1:17.

Illustrative of
The church. Dan. 8:10–13;
Song of Sol. 6:4, 10.
Multitudes of angels.
1 Kings 22:19; Ps. 148:2;
Dan. 4:35; Matt. 26:53.
Numerous and heavy afflictions.
Job 19:12.
In latter ages received pay.
Luke 3:14; 1 Cor. 9:7.

Led by
Experienced captains.
2 Kings 18:17, 24.

Kings in person. 2 Kings 18:13; 25:1.

Marched
Often in open line. Hab. 1:6, 8.
With noise and tumult.
Isa. 17:12–13; Joel 2:5.
With order and precision.
Isa. 5:27; Joel 2:7–8.
With rapidity. Jer. 48:40;
Hab. 1:8.
Often consisted of the whole effective strength of nations. Num. 21:23; 1 Sam. 29:1.

Often destroyed by
Supernatural means. Josh. 10:11; 2 Kings 19:35.
Their enemies. Exod. 17:13;
Josh. 10:10, 20; Judg. 11:33; 2 Sam. 18:7; 1 Kings 20:21.
Themselves through divine intervention. Judg. 7:22; 1 Sam. 14:15–16; 2 Chron. 20:23.
Often surprised their enemies.
Josh. 8:2; 2 Chron. 13:13; Jer. 51:12.
Often went on foreign service.
Jer. 5:15; 50:3.
Sent out foraging parties.
2 Kings 5:2.
Toil and fatigue often endured by.
Ezek. 29:18.
Troops often hired for.
1 Chron. 19:7; 2 Chron. 25:6.

ARMIES OF ISRAEL
See Israel, Armies of

ARMS, MILITARY
Armories built for. 2 Kings 20:13;
Song of Sol. 4:4.

Before using
Anointed. Isa. 21:5.
Burnished. Jer. 46:4;
Ezek. 21:9–11, 28.
Tried and proved. 1 Sam. 17:39.
Of conquered nations taken away to prevent rebellion. Judg. 5:8; 1 Sam. 13:19–22.

Of the Defeated
Sometimes burned.
Ezek. 39:9–10.
Sometimes kept as trophies.
1 Sam. 17:54.
Taken off them. 2 Sam. 2:21;
Luke 11:22.

Defensive
Belt, sash. 1 Sam. 18:4;
2 Sam. 18:11.
Buckler. 1 Chron. 5:18;
Ezek. 26:8.
Called armor. Luke 11:22.
Called harness. 1 Kings 22:34.
Coat of mail, breastplate, habergeon, or brigandine.
Exod. 28:32; 1 Sam. 17:5, 38;
Jer. 46:4; Rev. 9:9.
Greaves. 1 Sam. 17:6.
Helmet. 1 Sam. 17:5, 38;
2 Chron. 26:14.
Shield. 1 Kings 10:16–17;
14:26–27.
Target. 1 Sam. 17:6.

For sieges
Battering rams. 2 Sam. 20:15;
Ezek. 4:2.
Engines for casting stones, etc.
2 Chron. 26:15.
Great stores of, prepared.
2 Chron. 32:5.
Hung on the walls of cities.
Ezek. 27:10–11.

Illustrative of
Judgments of God. Isa. 13:5;
Jer. 50:25.
Spiritual armor. Rom. 13:12;
2 Cor. 6:7; Eph. 6:11–14;
1 Thess. 5:8.
Spiritual weapons. 2 Cor. 10:4;
Eph. 6:17.
Inferior to wisdom. Eccles. 9:18.
Made of iron, steel, or brass.
Job 20:24; 1 Sam. 17:5–6.
Not worn in ordinary. 1 Sam. 21:8.

Offensive
Battle-ax. Ezek. 26:9; Jer. 51:20.
Bow and arrows. Gen. 48:22;
1 Kings 22:34.
Called instruments of death.
Ps. 7:13.
Called instruments of war.
1 Chron. 12:33, 37.
Called weapons of war.
2 Sam. 1:27.
Dagger. Judg. 3:16, 21–22.
Dart or javelin. 1 Sam. 18:10–11;
2 Sam. 18:14.
Handstaff. Matt. 26:47.
Sling. 1 Sam. 17:50;
2 Kings 3:25
Spear or lance. 1 Sam. 26:7;
Jer. 50:42.
Sword. Judg. 20:15; Ezek. 32:27.
Two-edged sword. Ps. 149:6;
Prov. 5:4.
Often given as presents.
1 Kings 10:25.
Part of, borne by armor bearers.
Judg. 9:54; 1 Sam. 14:1; 16:21.
Put on at the first alarm. Isa. 8:9;
Jer. 46:3–4.

Were provided
By individuals themselves.
1 Chron. 12:33, 37.

From the public arsenals.
2 Chron. 11:12; 26:14.

ARROWS
Bright and polished. Isa. 49:2;
Jer. 51:11.
Called shafts. Isa. 49:2.
Carried in a quiver. Gen. 27:3;
Isa. 49:2; Jer. 5:16; Lam. 3:13.
Deadly and destructive weapons.
Prov. 26:18.

Discharged
Against enemies. 2 Kings 19:32;
Jer. 50:14.
At the beasts of the earth.
Gen. 27:3.
At a mark for amusement.
1 Sam. 20:20–22.
From a bow. Ps. 11:2; Isa. 7:24.
From engines. 2 Chron. 26:15.
With great force. Num. 24:8;
2 Kings 9:24.
Fleetness of, alluded to. Zech. 9:14.

Illustrative of
Bitter words. Ps. 64:3.
Christ. Isa. 49:2.
Destruction of power (when
broken) Ps 76:3.
Devices of the wicked. Ps. 11:2.
False witnesses. Prov. 25:18.
God's judgment. Deut. 32:23–42;
Pss. 7:13; 21:12; 64:7;
Ezek. 5:16.
Lightnings. Ps. 77:17–18;
Hab. 3:11.
Paralyzing power (when falling
from the hand). Ezek. 39:3.
Severe afflictions. Job 6:4;
Ps. 38:2.
Sharp. Ps. 120:4; Isa. 5:28.
Sometimes poisoned. Job 6:4.
Slanderous tongues. Jer. 9:8.

Word of Christ. Ps. 45:5.
Young children. Ps. 127:4.
The people in the ancient times
divined by. Ezek. 21:21.

ARTS

Apothecary or perfumer.
Exod. 30:25, 35.
Armorer. 1 Sam. 8:12.
Baker. Gen. 40:1; 1 Sam. 8:13.
Blacksmith. Gen. 4:22;
1 Sam. 13:19.
Brickmaker. Gen. 11:3;
Exod. 5:7–8, 18.
Calker. Ezek. 27:8, 27.
Carpenter. 2 Sam. 5:11; Mark 6:3.
Carver. Exod. 31:5; 1 Kings 6:18.
Confectioner. 1 Sam. 8:13.
Dyer. Exod. 25:5.
Embalmer. Gen. 50:2–3, 26.
Embroiderer. Exod. 35:35; 38:23.
Engraver. Exod. 28:11; Isa. 49:16;
2 Cor. 3:7.
Farmer. Gen. 4:2; 9:20.
Founder. Judg. 17:4; Jer. 10:9.
Fuller. 2 Kings 18:17; Mark 9:3.
Gardener. Jer. 29:5; John 20:15.
Goldsmith. Isa. 40:19.
Mariner. Ezek. 27:8–9.
Mason. 2 Sam. 5:11;
2 Chron. 24:12.
Metalworker. Gen. 4:22;
2 Tim. 4:14.
Musician. 1 Sam. 18:6;
1 Chron. 15:16.
Potter. Isa. 64:8; Jer. 18:3;
Lam. 4:2; Zech. 11:13.
Refiner of metals. 1 Chron. 28:18;
Mal. 3:2–3.
Ropemaker. Judg. 16:11.
Shipbuilder. 1 Kings 9:26.
Silversmith. Acts 19:24.
Smelter of metals. Job 28:2.

Spinner. Exod. 35:25; Prov. 31:19.
Stonecutter. Exod. 20:25;
1 Chron. 22:15.
Tailor. Exod. 28:3.
Tanner. Acts 9:43; 10:6.
Tentmaker. Gen. 4:20; Acts 18:3.
Weaver. Exod. 35:35; John 19:23.
Winemaker. Neh. 13:15; Isa. 63:3.
Writer. Judg. 5:14.

ASCENSION OF CHRIST

See Christ, Ascension of

ASP

Deprived of poison, illustrates
conversion. Isa. 11:8–9.
Describes injurious effects of wine.
Deut. 32:33; Prov. 23:32.
Poison of, illustrates speech of the
wicked. Ps. 140:3; Rom. 3:13.
A poisonous snake. Deut. 32:33;
Job 20:14, 16; Isa. 11:8;
Rom. 3:13.

ASSAULT AND BATTERY

Of parents, punishment of.
Exod. 21:15.
Of a pregnant woman. Exod. 21:22.
Response commanded by Jesus.
Matt. 5:38–39.
Of a servant. Exod. 21:26–27.

ASSISTED SUICIDE

See Suicide, Assisted

ASSURANCE

Abundant in the understanding of the
gospel. Col. 2:2; 1 Thess. 1:5.

Believers privileged to have, of
Answers to prayer. 1 John 3:22;
5:14–15.

Comfort in affliction. Ps. 73:26;
Luke 4:18–19; 2 Cor. 4:8–10,
16–18.
Continuance in grace. Phil. 1:6.
Crown. 2 Tim. 4:7–8.
Eternal life. 1 John 5:13.
Glorious resurrection. Job 19:26;
Ps. 17:15; Phil. 3:21;
1 John 3:2.
Kingdom. Heb. 12:28; Rev. 5:10.
Peace with God by Christ.
Rom. 5:1.
Preservation. Pss. 3:6, 8; 27:3–5;
46:1–3.
Support in death. Ps. 23:4.
Their adoption. Rom. 8:16;
1 John 3:2.
Their election. Ps. 4:3;
1 Thess. 1:4.
Their redemption. Job 19:25.
Their salvation. Isa. 12:2.
Unalienable love of God.
Rom. 8:38–39.
Union with God and Christ.
1 Cor. 6:15; 2 Cor. 13:5;
Eph. 5:30; 1 John 2:5; 4:13.
Confident hope in God restores.
Ps. 42:11.
Confirmed by love. 1 John 3:14, 19;
4:18.
Give diligence to attain.
2 Pet. 1:10–11.
Made full by hope. Heb. 6:11, 19.
Need to maintain. Heb. 3:14, 18.
Produced by faith. Eph. 3:12;
2 Tim. 1:12; Heb. 10:22.
Results from righteousness.
Isa. 32:17.

ASSYRIA
Antiquity and origin of.
Gen. 10:8–11.
Armies of, described. Isa. 5:26–29.

As a power, was
An instrument of God's
vengeance. Isa. 7:18–19;
10:5–6.
Cruel and destructive. Isa. 10:7.
Intolerant and oppressive.
Nah. 3:19.
Most formidable. Isa. 28:2.
Proud and haughty.
2 Kings 19:22–24; Isa. 10:8.
Selfish and reserved. Hos. 8:9.
Unfaithful, etc.
2 Chron. 28:20–21.

Called
Asshur. Hos. 14:3.
Land of Nimrod. Mic. 5:6.
Shinar. Gen. 11:2; 14:1.

Celebrated for
Extensive commerce.
Ezek. 27:23–24.
Extent of conquests.
2 Kings 18:33–35; 19:11–13.
Fertility. 2 Kings 18:32;
Isa. 36:17.
Chief men of, described.
Ezek. 23:6, 12, 23.
Condemned for oppressing God's
people. Isa. 52:4.
Governed by kings.
2 Kings 15:19, 29.
Greatness, extent, duration, and fall
of, illustrated. Ezek. 31:3–17
Idolatry, the religion of.
2 Kings 19:37.
Idolatry brought into Samaria.
2 Kings 17:29.
Israel condemned for trusting to.
Hos. 5:13; 7:11; 8:9.
The Jews condemned for following
the idolatries of. Ezek. 16:28;
23:5, 7, etc.

Judah condemned for trusting to.
Jer. 2:18, 36.
Manasseh taken captive to.
2 Chron. 33:11.
Nineveh, chief city of. Gen. 10:11;
2 Kings 19:36.

Predictions regarding
Conquest and captivity of Israel by.
Isa. 8:4; Hos. 9:3; 10:6; 11:5.
Conquest of the Kenites by.
Num. 24:22.
Conquest of Syria by. Isa. 8:4.
Destruction of. Isa. 10:19–19;
14:24–25; 30:31–33; 31:8–9;
Zech. 10:11.
Invasion of Judah by.
Isa. 5:26; 7:17–20; 8:8;
10:5–6, 12.
Participation in the blessings of the
gospel. Isa. 19:23–25;
Mic. 7:12.
Restoration of Israel from.
Isa. 27:12–13; Hos. 11:11;
Zech. 10:10.

Pul, king of
Bought off by Menahem.
2 Kings 15:19–20.
Invaded Israel. 2 Kings 15:19.
Populating of Samaria from,
completed by Asnapper.
Ezra 4:10.

Sennacherib, king of
Assassinated by his sons.
2 Kings 19:37.
Blasphemed the Lord.
2 Kings 18:33–35.
Bought off by Hezekiah.
2 Kings 18:14–16.
His army destroyed by God.
2 Kings 19:35.

Insulted and threatened Judah.
2 Kings 18:17–32; 19:10–13.
Invaded Judah. 2 Kings 18:13.
Prayed against by Hezekiah.
2 Kings 19:14–19.
Reproved for pride and
blasphemy. 2 Kings 12:20–34;
Isa. 37:21–29.

Shalmaneser, king of
Carried Israel captive.
2 Kings 17:5–6.
Imprisoned Hoshea.
2 Kings 17:4.
Reduced Israel to tribute.
2 Kings 17:3.
Repopulated Samaria from
Assyria. 2 Kings 17:24.
Was conspired against by Hoshea.
2 Kings 17:4.
Situated beyond the Euphrates.
Isa. 7:20.

Tiglath-pileser, king of
Asked to aid Ahaz against Syria.
2 Kings 16:7–8.
Conquered Syria. 2 Kings 16:9.
Ravaged Israel. 2 Kings 15:29.
Took money from Ahaz, but
strengthened him not.
2 Chron. 28:20–21.
Watered by the Tigris. Gen. 2:14.

ASTROLOGY
Futility of. Isa. 47:13.
Delusion of. Jeremiah 10:1–2.

ASTRONOMY
Constellations. Job 38:31.
Astral phenomena. Josh. 10:12–14;
Job 9:6–9.

ATHEISM
Arguments against. Job 12:7–25.

Espoused by a fool. Pss. 14:1: 53:1.
Without excuse. Rom. 1:19–20.

ATOMIC POWER

NOTE: 2 Pet. 3:10–12 has been interpreted as describing the effects of an atomic blast.

Some Christians have interpreted Col. 1:17, "In him (i.e., Christ) all things hold together," as a reference to the force that holds together the nucleus of an atom. Others contend that this verse, like Heb. 1:3, speaks more broadly of Christ as the sustainer of creation and unifying principle of life.

ATOMS

Elementary particles. Prov. 8:26.

ATONEMENT

Acceptable to God. Eph. 5:2.

Access to God by. Heb. 10:19–20.

Believers glorify God for.
1 Cor. 6:20; Gal. 2:20;
Phil. 1:20–21.

Believers praise God for.
Rev. 5:9–13.

Believers rejoice in God for.
Rom. 5:11.

Commemorated in the Lord's
Supper. Matt. 26:26–28;
1 Cor. 11:23–26.

Effected by Christ alone. John 1:29,
36; Acts 4:10, 12; 1 Thess. 1:10;
1 Tim. 2:5–6; Heb. 2:9;
1 Pet. 2:24.

Exhibits the
Grace and mercy of God.
Rom. 8:32; Eph. 2:4–5, 7;
1 Tim. 2:4; Heb. 2:9.

Love of Christ. John 15:13;
Gal. 2:20; Eph. 5:2, 25;
Rev. 1:5.

Love of God. Rom. 5:8;
1 John 4:9–10.

Explained. Rom. 5:8–11;
2 Cor. 5:18–19; Gal. 4:1–7;
1 John 2:2; 4:10.

Faith in, indispensable. Rom. 3:25;
Gal. 3:13–14.

Foreordained. 1 Pet. 1:11, 20;
Rev. 13:8.

Has delivered believers from the
Power of the devil. Col. 2:15;
Heb. 2:14–15.

Power of sin. Rom. 8:3;
1 Pet. 1:18–19.

Power of the world. Gal. 1:4;
6:14.

Justification by. Rom. 5:9;
2 Cor. 5:21.

Made but once.
Heb. 7:27; 9:24–28; 10:10, 12,
14; 1 Pet. 3:18.

Ministers should fully set forth.
Acts 5:29–31, 42; 1 Cor. 15:3;
2 Cor. 5:18–21.

Necessity for. Isa. 59:16;
Luke 19:10; Heb. 9:22.

Predicted. Isa. 53:4–6, 8–12;
Dan. 9:24–27; Zech. 13:1, 7;
John 11:50–51.

Reconciles the justice and mercy of
God. Isa. 45:21; Rom. 3:25–26.

Reconciliation to God effected by.
Rom. 5:10; 2 Cor. 5:18–20;
Eph. 2:13–16; Col. 1:20–22;
Heb. 2:17; 1 Pet. 3:18.

Redemption by. Matt. 20:28;
Acts 20:28; 1 Tim. 2:6;
Heb. 9:12; Rev. 5:9.

Remission of sins by. John 1:29;
Rom. 3:25; Eph. 1:7;
1 John 1:7; Rev. 1:5.

Sanctification by. 2 Cor. 5:15;
Eph. 5:26–27; Titus 2:14;
Heb. 10:10; 13:12.

Typified. Gen. 4:4, with Heb. 11:4;
Gen. 22:2, with Heb. 11:17, 19;
Exod. 12:5, 11, 14, with
1 Cor. 5:7; Exod. 24:8, with
Heb. 9:20; Lev. 16:30, 34, with
Heb. 9:7, 12, 28; Lev. 17:11,
with Heb. 9:22.

Was voluntary. Ps. 40:6–8, with
Heb. 10:5–9; John 10:11, 15,
17–18.

ATONEMENT, DAY OF

Atonement made on, for the
High priest. Lev. 16:11;
Heb. 9:7.

Holy place. Exod. 30:10;
Lev. 16:15–16.

Whole congregation.
Lev. 16:17, 24; 23:28;
Heb. 9:7.

For humiliation. Lev. 16:29–31;
23:27.

High priest entered into the holy
place on. Lev. 16:2–3; Heb. 9:7.

Observed as a Sabbath. Lev. 23:28,
32.

Offerings to be made on.
Lev. 16:3, 5–15.

Punishment for not observing.
Lev. 23:29–30.

Tenth day of seventh month.
Lev. 23:26–27.

Typical. Heb. 9:8, 24.

Year of Jubilee began on. Lev. 25:9.

ATONEMENT, UNDER THE LAW

Extraordinary cases of.
Exod. 32:30–34; Num. 16:47;
25:10–13.

Made by sacrifice. Lev. 1:4–5.

Necessary for
Propitiating God. Exod. 32:30;
Lev. 23:27–28; 2 Sam. 21:3.

Purifying. Exod. 29:36.

Ransoming. Exod. 30:15–16;
Job 33:24.

Offered for
Altar. Exod. 29:36–37;
Lev. 16:18–19.

Congregation. Num. 15:25;
2 Chron. 29:24.

Healed lepers. Lev. 14:18.

Holy place. Lev. 16:16–17.

Leprous house healed.
Lev. 14:53.

Persons sinning ignorantly.
Lev. 4:20, etc.

Persons sinning willfully. Lev. 6:7.

Persons swearing rashly.
Lev. 5:4, 6.

Persons unclean. Lev. 5:2–3, 6.

Persons withholding evidence.
Lev. 5:1, 6.

Priests. Exod. 29:31–33;
Lev. 8:34.

Women after childbirth.
Lev. 12:8.

By priests alone. 1 Chron. 6:49;
2 Chron. 29:24.

Typical of Christ's atonement.
Rom. 5:6–11.

ATTAINMENT

See also Accomplishment

Of divine knowledge, beyond man.
Ps. 139:6.

Of perfection, disclaimed by Paul.
Phil. 3:1, 2–14.

Of the resurrection, desired by Paul.
Phil. 3:11.

Of wisdom through understanding.
Prov. 1:5.

Of the world at the cost of loss of
one's soul. Matt. 16:26.

AUTHORITY
Of Christ's power over spirits.
Mark 1:27.

Of Christ's teaching. Matt. 7:29.

In the family. 1 Cor. 11:3;
Eph. 5:22; 6:1–4; 1 Tim. 2:12;
3:4, 12; 1 Pet. 3:1–6.

Given to the disciples. Luke 9:1.

Of God. Ps. 29:10; Dan. 4:34–35.

Of government. Prov. 29:2;
Rom. 13:1–7.

Promised to believers. Luke 19:17;
Rev. 2:26.

Of rulers, prayer for. 1 Tim. 2:1, 2.

Submission to. Rom. 13:7;
Heb. 13:17.

AVARICE
Guilty of, the descendants of Joseph.
Josh. 17:14–18.

Ministers must avoid. 1 Tim. 3:2–3.

Never satisfied. Eccles. 4:7–8;
5:10–11.

The root of all evil. 1 Tim. 6:10.

AWL
A tool. Exod. 21:6; Deut. 15:17.

AX
Battle–ax. Ezek. 26:9.

Elisha causes to swim.
2 Kings 6:5–6.

In figurative sense. Jer. 46:22;
51:20; Matt. 3:10.

An implement. Deut. 19:5;
1 Sam. 13:20, 21;
2 Sam. 12:31; Ps. 74:5–6.

Axes

B

BABIES

In a figurative sense, of weak
Christians. Rom. 2:20;
1 Cor. 3:1; Heb. 5:13;
1 Pet. 2:2.
A picture of the innocent. Ps. 8:2;
Matt. 11:25; Luke 10:21.
Praise perfected in the mouths of.
Matt. 21:16.

BABYLON

Ambassadors of, sent to Hezekiah.
2 Kings 20:12.
Armies of, described. Hab. 1:7–9.

As a power was
Arrogant. Isa. 14:13–14;
Jer. 50:29, 31–32.
Babylon the chief province of.
Dan. 3:1.
Covetous. Jer. 51:13.
Cruel and destructive. Isa. 14:17;
47:6; Jer. 51:25; Hab. 1:6–7.
Grand and stately. Isa. 47:1, 5.
An instrument of God's vengeance
on other nations. Isa. 47:6;
Jer. 51:7.
Oppressive. Isa. 14:4.
Secure and self-confident.
Isa. 47:7–8.

Capital of
Antiquity of. Gen. 11:4, 9.
Called Babylon the great.
Dan. 4:30.
Called beauty of Chaldees, etc. Isa.
13:19.
Called the city of merchants.
Ezek. 17:4.

Called the glory of kingdoms.
Isa. 13:19.
Called the golden city. Isa. 14:4.
Enlarged by Nebuchadnezzar.
Dan. 4:30.
Surrounded with a great wall and
fortified. Jer. 51:53, 58.
Composed of many nations.
Dan. 3:4, 29.
Destroyed by the Medes.
Dan. 5:30–31.
Formerly a part of Mesopotamia.
Acts 7:2.
Founded by the Assyrians, and part
of their empire. 2 Kings 17:24,
with Isa. 23:13.
Gospel preached in. 1 Pet. 5:13.
Grief of the Jews in. Ps. 137:1–6.

Inhabitants of
Addicted to magic. Isa. 47:9,
12–13; Dan. 2:1–2.
Idolatrous. Jer. 50:38; Dan. 3:18.
Profane and sacrilegious.
Dan. 5:1–3.
Wicked. Isa. 47:10.
The Jews exhorted to be subject to,
and settle in. Jer. 27:17; 29:1–7.
Languages spoken in. Dan. 1:4; 2:4

Nebuchadnezzar, king of
Besieged and took Jerusalem.
2 Kings 24:10–11; 25:1–4.
Burned Jerusalem, etc. 2 Kings
25:9–10.
Made Jehoiakim tributary. 2 Kings
24:1.
Made Zedekiah king. 2 Kings
24:17.

Rebelled against by Zedekiah.
2 Kings 24:20.

Spoiled and burned the temple.
2 Kings 24:13; 25:9, 13–17;
2 Chron. 36:18–19.

Took Jehoiachin captive to
Babylon. 2 Kings 24:12, 14–16;
2 Chron. 36:10.

Took Zedekiah, etc., captive to
Babylon. 2 Kings 25:7, 11,
18–21; 2 Chron. 36:20.

Origin of. Gen. 10:10.

Origin of name. Gen. 11:8–9.

Predictions respecting

Captivity of the Jews by.
Jer. 20:4–6; 22:20–26;
25:9–11; Mic. 4:10.

Conquests by.
Jer. 21:3–10; 27:2–6;
49:28–33; Ezek. 21:19–32;
29:18–20.

Destruction of.
Isa. 13; 14:4–22; 21:1–10; 47;
Jer. 25:12, 50, 51.

Perpetual desolation of.
Isa. 13:19–22; 14:22–23;
Jer. 50:13, 39; 51:37.

Preaching of the gospel in.
Ps. 87:4.

Presidents placed over.
Dan. 2:48; 6:1.

Remarkable for

Antiquity. Jer. 5:15.

Commerce. Ezek. 17:4.

Manufacture of garments.
Josh. 7:21.

Military power. Jer. 5:16; 50:23.

National greatness. Isa. 13:19;
Jer. 51:41.

Naval power. Isa. 43:14.

Wealth. Jer. 50:37; 51:13.

Represented by a

Great eagle. Ezek. 17:3.

Head of gold. Dan. 2:32, 37–38.

Lion with eagle's wings. Dan. 7:4.

Restoration of the Jews from.
2 Chron. 36:23; Ezra 1; 2:1–67;
Isa. 14:1–4; 44:28; 48:20;
Jer. 29:10; 50:4, 8, 19.

Revolt of the Jews from, and their
punishment illustrated. Ezek. 17.

Treatment of the Jews in. 2 Kings
25:27–30; Dan. 1:3–7.

A type of Antichrist. Rev. 16:19;
17:5.

Was called

Desert of the sea. Isa. 21:1, 9.

Lady of kingdoms. Isa. 47:5.

Land of the Chaldeans.
Ezek. 12:13.

Land of Merathaim. Jer. 50:21.

Land of Shinar. Dan. 1:2;
Zech. 5:11.

Sheshach. Jer. 25:12, 26.

Watered by the rivers Euphrates and
Tigris. Ps. 137:1; Jer. 51:13.

With Media and Persia, divided by
Darius into 120 provinces.
Dan. 6:1.

BACKBITING

See also Slander

Consequence of not acknowledging
God. Rom. 1:28.

Persons who practice will not dwell in
God's tabernacle. Ps. 15:1–3.

Potential problem in the church at
Corinth. 2 Cor. 12:20.

BACKSLIDING

Afflictions sent to heal. Hos. 5:15.

Blessedness of those who keep
from. Prov. 28:14; Isa. 26:3–4;
Col. 1:21–23.
Brings its own punishment.
Prov. 14:14; Jer. 2:19.
Endeavor to bring back those guilty
of. Gal. 6:1; James 5:10, 20.
Exhortations to return
from. 2 Chron. 30:6; Isa. 31:6;
Jer. 3:12, 14, 22; Hos. 6:1.
God is displeased at. Ps. 78:57, 59.
Guilt and consequences of.
Num. 14:43; Ps. 125:5;
Isa. 59:2, 9–11;
Jer. 5:6; 8:5, 13; 15:6;
Luke 9:62.
Hateful to believers. Ps. 101:3.
A haughty spirit leads to.
Prov. 16:18.
Healing of, promised. Jer. 3:22;
Hos. 14:4.

Is

Departing from the simplicity of
the gospel. 2 Cor. 11:3;
Gal. 3:1–3; 5:4, 7.
Leaving the first love. Rev. 2:4.
Turning from God. 1 Kings 11:9.
Likely to continue and increase.
Jer. 8:5; 14:7.
Not hopeless. Ps. 37:24;
Prov. 24:16
Pardon of, promised.
2 Chron 7:14; Jer. 3:12; 31:20;
36:3.
Pray to be restored from. Pss. 80:3;
85:4; Lam. 5:21.
Proneness to. Prov. 24:16;
Hos. 11:7.
Punishment of tempting others to the
sin of. Prov. 28:10; Matt. 18:6.
Sin of, to be confessed.
Isa. 59:12–14; Jer. 3:13–14;
14:7–9.

Warnings against. Ps. 85:8;
1 Cor. 10:12.

BAD COMPANY
Commandment to avoid. Jer. 51:6;
2 Cor. 6:14.
Consequences of involvement with.
1 Cor. 5:6; 15:33.

BALANCES
False balances, an abomination.
Prov. 11:1; 20:23.
False balances used. Hos. 12:7;
Amos 8:5; Mic. 6:11.
In figurative senses, used of
judgment. Dan. 5:27.
Money weighed with. Isa. 46:6;
Jer. 32:10.
Must be just. Lev. 19:36;
Prov. 16:11; Ezek. 45:10.
Used for weighing. Job 31:6;
Isa. 40:12, 15; Ezek. 5:1.

BALDNESS
Artificial, as an idolatrous practice,
forbidden. Lev. 21:5; Deut. 14:1.
Artificial, a sign of mourning.
Isa. 22:12; Jer. 16:6;
Ezek. 27:31; 29:18; Amos 8:10;
Mic. 1:16.
Elisha ridiculed for. 2 Kings 2:23.
A judgment. Isa. 3:24; Jer. 47:5;
48:37; Ezek. 7:18.
Levitical laws on. Lev. 13:40–43.

BALM
Anointing the king. Ps. 89:20.
Healing the Lord's people. Jer. 51:8.
Producing joy. Isa. 61:3.
Restoring sight. Rev. 3:18.
Sought. Jer. 8:22.

Balm

BANISHMENT
Of Adam and Eve, from Eden.
Gen. 3:22–24.
Of Cain to be a fugitive and
vagabond. Gen. 4:14.
Of Jews, from Rome. Acts 18:2.
Of John, to Patmos. Rev. 1:9.

BANKRUPTCY

Borrowing
Borrowed item repaid in full even if
at borrower's loss. Exod. 22:14.
Borrower becomes lender's slave.
Prov. 22:7.
Wicked do not repay what is owed.
Ps. 37:21.

Examples of financial destitution
Assets mortgaged for food.
Neh. 5:3.
Man unable to finish building
tower. Luke 14:28–29.

Prophet's wife. 2 Kings 4:1–7.
Widow. Luke 21:1–4.
Remission of debts every seven
years. Deut. 15:1–3.

Surety
Everything seized by creditor.
Ps. 109:11.
Hater of, is secure. Prov. 11:15.

BANNER
Raised to celebrate God's victory.
Ps. 20:5.

BAPTISM
See also Purification

Administered to
Households. Acts 16:15;
1 Cor. 1:16.
Individuals. Acts 8:38; 9:16.
Adopted by Christ. John 3:22;
4:1–2.
Appointed an ordinance of the
Christian church. Matt. 28:19–20;
Mark 16:15–16.
As administered by John.
Matt. 3:5–12; John 3:23;
Acts 13:24; 19:4.
Confession of sin necessary to.
Matt. 3:6.
Emblematic of the influences of the
Holy Spirit. Matt. 3:11; Titus 3:5.
Faith necessary to. Acts 8:37; 18:8.
Regeneration, the inward and
spiritual grace of. John 3:3, 5–6;
Rom. 6:3–4, 11.
Remission of sins, signified by.
Acts 2:38; 22:16.
Repentance necessary to. Acts 2:38.
Sanctioned, by Christ's submission to
it. Matt. 3:13–15; Luke 3:21.
There is but one. Eph. 4:5.

To be administered in the name of the Father, the Son, and the Holy Spirit. Matt. 28:19.

Typified. 1 Cor. 10:2; 1 Pet. 3:20, 21.

Unity of the church effected by. 1 Cor. 12:13; Gal. 3:27–28.

Water, the outward and visible sign in. Acts 8:36; 10:47.

BAPTISM WITH THE HOLY SPIRIT

See Holy Spirit, Baptism with the

BARBARIAN

A foreigner. Acts 28:2–4; Rom. 1:14; 1 Cor. 14:11; Col. 3:11.

BARBER

Uses razor. Ezek. 5:1.

BARLEY

Absalom burns Joab's field of. 2 Sam. 14:30.

Fed to horses. 1 Kings 4:28.

Jesus' miracle uses loaves of. John 6:9, 13.

Priests estimated value of. Lev. 27:16; 2 Kings 7:1; Rev. 6:6.

Product of Egypt. Exod. 9:31.

Product of Palestine. Deut. 8:8; 1 Chron. 11:13; Jer. 41:8.

Traffic in. 2 Chron. 2:10; Hos. 3:2.

Tribute in. 2 Chron. 27:5.

Used in offerings. Num. 5:15; Ezek. 45:15.

BARN, STOREHOUSE

Place where grain is stored. Matt. 3:12.

BARRENNESS

Miraculously removed

Elizabeth. Luke 1:5–25.

Hannah. 1 Sam. 1:6–20.

Manoah's wife. Judg. 13.

Rebekah. Gen. 25:21.

Sarai. Gen. 17:15–21.

Sent as a judgment. Gen. 20:17–18.

Sterility, a reproach. Gen. 30:22–23; 1 Sam. 1:6–7; Isa. 4:1; Luke 1:25.

BASIN

Altered by Ahaz. 2 Kings 16:17.

Brazen, made by Solomon for the temple. 1 Kings 7:23–26, 30, 38–39; 2 Chron. 4:2–14.

Broken and carried by Babylon by the Chaldeens. 2 Kings 25:13, 16; Jer. 52:17, 20.

Directions for making. Exod. 30:18–20.

Sanctified. Exod. 30:28–29; 40.11; Lev. 8:11.

Situation of, in a tabernacle, tent of the congregation, and the altar. Exod. 40:7.

Used for washing. Exod. 40:30–32.

Used in a figurative sense. Rev. 4:6; 15:2, in connection with Exod. 38:8 and 1 Kings 7:23.

BASKET

Paul let down from the wall in. Acts 9:25; 2 Cor. 11:33.

Received fragments after the miracle of the loaves. Matt. 14:20; 15:37; 16:9–10.

BASTARD

David's child by Bathsheba. 2 Sam. 11:2–5.

Excluded from the congregation.
Deut. 23:2.
Figurative sense. Zech. 9:6;
Heb. 12:8.
Ishmael. Gen. 16:3, 15; Gal. 4:22.
Jephthah. Judg. 11:1.
Moab and Ammon. Gen. 19:36–38.

BATHING

Ritual acts of purification.
Exod. 30:19–21.

BATTLE

Prayer before, by Asa.
2 Chron. 14:11.
Prayer before, by Jehoshaphat.
2 Chron. 20:3–12.
Priests in. 2 Chron. 13:12.
Shouting in. Judg. 7:20;
1 Sam. 17:20.

BEAR

Ferocity of. 2 Sam. 17:8;
Prov. 17:12; 28:15; Isa. 11:7;
59:11; Lam. 3:10; Hos. 13:8;
Amos 5:19.
Killed by David. 1 Sam. 17:34–37.
Symbolic use. Dan. 7:5; Rev. 13:2.
To destroy the children of Bethel,
who mocked Elisha. 2 Kings 2:24.

BEARD

Beards of David's ambassadors
half-shaven by the king of the
Amorites. 2 Sam. 10:4.
Cut. Isa. 7:20; 15:2; Jer. 41:5;
48:37.
David. 1 Sam. 21:13; Ezek. 5:1.
Idolatrous practice of marring
forbidden. Lev. 19:27; 21:5.
Lepers required to shave.
Lev. 13:29–33; 14:9.
Plucked. Ezra 9:3.

Samson. Judg. 16:17.
Shaven by Egyptians. Gen. 41:14.
Untrimmed in mourning.
2 Sam. 19:24.
Worn long by Aaron. Ps. 133:2.

Beards

BEASTS

Belong to God. Ps. 50:10.

Clean
Chamois. Deut. 14:5.
Fallow deer. Deut. 14:5.
Goat. Deut. 14:4.
Hart. Deut. 14:5, with
2 Sam. 2:18.
Ox. Exod. 21:28, with
Deut. 14:4.
Pygarg. Deut. 14:5.
Roebuck. Deut. 14:5, with
2 Sam. 2:18.
Sheep. Deut. 7:13, with 14:4.
Wild goat. Deut. 14:5.
Wild ox. Deut. 14:5.
Created by God. Gen. 1:24–25;
2:19.
Creation of, exhibits God's power.
Jer. 27:5.

Described as
Being four-footed. Acts 10:12.
By nature wild, etc. Ps. 50:11;
Mark 1:13.

Capable of being tamed.
James 3:7.

Differ in flesh from birds and
fishes. 1 Cor. 15:39.

Lacking immortality.
Ps. 49:12–15.

Lacking speech. 2 Pet. 2:16.

Lacking understanding.
Pss. 32:9; 73:22.

Possessed of instinct. Isa. 1:3.

Domestic

Not to be cruelly used.
Num. 22:27–32; Prov. 12:10.

To be taken care of. Lev. 25:7;
Deut. 25:4.

To enjoy the Sabbath.
Exod. 20:10; Deut. 5:14.

Early differentiated as clean or
unclean. Gen. 7:2.

Found in

Deserts. Isa. 13:21.

Fields. Deut. 7:22; Joel 2:22.

Forests. Isa. 56:9; Mic. 5:8.

Mountains. Song of Sol. 4:8.

Frequently suffered on account of the
sins of men. Joel 1:18, 20;
Hag. 1:11.

Given to man for food after the flood.
Gen. 9:3.

Herb of the field given to, for food.
Gen. 1:30.

History of, written by Solomon.
1 Kings 4:33.

Illustrative of

Antichrist. Rev. 13:2; 20:4.

Kingdoms. Dan. 7:11, 17; 8:4.

People of different nations.
Dan. 4:12, 21–22.

Persecutors. 1 Cor. 15:32;
2 Tim. 4:17.

Ungodly professors. 2 Pet. 2:12;
Jude 10.

Wicked men. Ps. 49:20;
Titus 1:12.

Instinctively fear humans. Gen. 9:2.

Lessons of wisdom to be learned
from. Job 12:7.

Liable to diseases. Exod. 9:3.

Made for the praise and glory of God.
Ps. 148:10.

Man by nature no better than.
Eccles. 3:18–19.

Many kinds of, domestic. Gen. 36:6;
45:17.

Many kinds of, dangerous and
destructive. Lev. 26:6;
Ezek. 5:17.

Named by Adam. Gen. 2:19–20.

No likeness of, to be worshiped.
Deut. 4:17.

Not to be eaten alive or with blood.
Gen. 9:4; Deut. 12:16, 23.

Often cut off for the sins of men.
Gen. 6:7, with 7:23; Exod. 11:5;
Hos. 4:3.

Often used as instruments of
punishment. Lev. 26:22;
Deut. 32:24; Jer. 15:3;
Ezek. 5:17.

Power over, given to man.
Gen. 1:26, 28; Ps. 87.

Representations of, worshiped by the
heathen. Rom. 1:23,

Settlements of

Dens and caves. Job 37:8, 38:40.

Deserted cities. Isa. 13:21–22;
Zeph. 2:15.

Under spreading trees. Dan. 4:12.

Subjects of God's care.
Pss. 36:6; 104:10–11.

Supply clothing to man. Gen. 3:21;
Job 31:20.

That died naturally or were torn, not
to be eaten. Exod. 22:31;
Lev. 17:15; 22:8.

Those clean
Firstborn of, not redeemed.
Num. 18:17.
How distinguished. Lev. 11:3;
Deut. 14:6.
Used for food. Lev. 11:2;
Deut. 12:15.
Used for sacrifice. Gen. 8:20.

Those unclean
Caused uncleanness when dead.
Lev. 5:2.
Firstborn of, redeemed.
Num. 18:15.
How distinguished. Lev. 11:26.
Not eaten. Lev. 11:4–8;
Deut. 1:7–8.
Not offered in sacrifice.
Lev. 27:11.

Unclean
Ape. 1 Kings 10:22.
Badger. Exod. 25:5; Ezek. 16:10.
Bear. 2 Sam. 17:8.
Behemoth. Job 40:15.
Camel. Gen. 24:64, with
Lev. 11:4.
Coney. Lev. 11:5; Ps. 104:18.
Dog. Exod. 22:31; Luke 16:2.
Donkey. Gen. 22:3; Matt. 21:2.
Ferret. Lev. 11:30.
Fox. Ps. 63:10; Song of Sol. 2:5.
Horse. Job 39:19–25.
Leopard. Song of Sol. 4:8.
Lion. Judg. 14:5, 6.
Mole. Lev. 11:30; Isa. 2:20.
Mouse. Lev. 11:29; Isa. 66:17.
Mule. 2 Sam. 13:29;
1 Kings 10:25.
Rabbit. Lev. 11:6; Deut. 14:7.

Swine. Lev. 11:7; Isa. 66:17.
Unicorn. Num. 23:22.
Weasel. Lev. 11:29.
Wild donkey. Job 6:5; 39:5–8.
Wolf. Gen. 49:27; John 10:12.

BEATING

Examples of
Of the evil tongue. Job 5:21.
Jesus. Matt. 20:19.
Paul. Acts 21:32; 2 Cor. 11:24,
25.
Paul and Silas. Acts 16:23.
Sosthenes. Acts 18:17.
Used in a figurative sense of the
oppressions of rulers.
1 Kings 12:11.
Fatal. Job 9:23.
Forty lashes the maximum limit.
Deut. 25:3.
Predicted by Jesus as a persecution
of Christians. Matt. 10:17.
Prescribed for other offenses.
Deut. 25:2.
Prescribed in the Mosiac law for
sexual immorality. Lev. 19:20;
Deut. 22:18.
As a punishment. Exod. 5:14; Deut.
25:3; Mark 13:9; Acts 5:40;
16:22, 37; 18:17; 21:32; 22:19.
Of servant avenged. Exod. 21:20.

BEAUTY
Abishag. 1 Kings 1:3–4.
Absalom. 2 Sam. 14:25.
Bathsheba. 2 Sam. 11:2.
Of the church. Eph. 5:27;
Rev. 21:2.
David. 1 Sam. 16:12, 18.
Emptiness of. Prov. 11:22; 31:30;
Ezek. 16:15.
Esther. Esther 2:7.
Fades away. Pss. 39:11; 49:14.

Of holiness. 1 Chron. 16:29;
2 Chron. 20:21; Pss. 29:2; 96:9.
Joseph. Gen. 39:6.
Of the Lord. Pss. 27:4; 90:17;
Isa. 33:17.
Moses. Exod. 2:2; Heb. 11:23.
Rachel. Gen. 29:17.
Rebekah. Gen. 24:16.
Sarah. Gen. 12:11.
Spiritual beauty. 1 Chron. 16:29;
Pss. 27:4; 29:2; 45:11; 90:17;
110:3; Isa. 52:7; Ezek. 16:14;
Zech. 9:17.
Tamar. 2 Sam. 13:1.
Of the temple. Ps. 96:6.
Vanity of. Ps. 39:11; Prov. 6:25;
31:30; Isa. 3:24; Ezek. 16:14.
Vashti. Esther 1:11.
Of Zion. Pss. 48:2; 50:2.

BED

Exempt from execution for debt.
Prov. 22:27.
Figurative sense. Ps. 139:8.
Of gold and silver. Esther 1:6.
Of iron. Deut. 3:11.
Of ivory. Amos 6:4.
Made of wood. Song of Sol. 3:7–9.
Perfumed. Prov. 7:17.
Used at meals. Amos 6:4.

BEE

Called by hissing. Isa. 7:18.
In Palestine. Deut. 1:44; Judg. 14:8;
Ps. 118:12; Isa. 7:18.

BEELZEBUB

The prince of devils. Matt. 10:25;
12:24, 27; Mark 3:22;
Luke 11:15, 18–19.
Messengers sent to inquire of, by
Ahaziah. 2 Kings 1:2.

BEETLE

Authorized as food. Lev. 11:22.

BEGGARS

Bartimeus. Mark 10:46.
The blind man. John 9:8.
Children of the wicked. Ps. 109:10;
Prov. 20:4; Luke 16:3.
The lame man at the temple.
Acts 3:2–5.
Lazarus. Luke 16:20–22.
Not the children of the righteous.
Ps. 37:25.
Set among princes. 1 Sam. 2:8.

BEGINNING

Christ as. Rev. 1:8.
Of creation. Gen. 1:1; Heb. 1:10.
Of eternity. John 1:1.
Of the gospel. Mark 1:1.
Of life on earth. Gen. 1:11.
Of light. Gen. 1:3.
Of man. Gen. 1:26.
Of the new creation. Col. 1:18.
Of wisdom. Ps. 111:10.

BEHEADING

Execution by
Of James. Acts 12:2.
Of John. Matt. 14:10; Mark 6:27.
Of the martyrs. Rev. 20:4.

BELIEF

In Christ. John 3:16; 14:1; 20:31;
Acts 8:37.
In God required. 2 Chron. 20:20.
Making all things possible.
Mark 9:23.
Of devils. James 2:19.
Producing healing. Matt. 9:22.

BELIEVERS

Are perfected through the church's ministry. Eph. 4:12.

Belong to Christ. Pss. 31:23; 34:9; Rom. 1:7.

Christ will appear with and be glorified in. 1 Thess. 3:13; 2 Thess. 1:10; Jude 1:14.

Compared to

Babes. Matt. 11:25; 1 Pet. 2:2.

Branches of a vine. John 15:2, 4–5.

Calves of the stall. Mal. 4:2.

Cedars in Lebanon. Ps. 92:12.

Corn. Hos. 14:7.

Dew and showers. Mic. 5:7.

Doves. Ps. 68:13; Isa. 60:8.

Eagles. Ps. 103:5; Isa. 40:31.

Fruitful trees. Ps. 1:3; Jer. 17:8.

Gold. Job 23:10; Lam. 4:2.

Good figs. Jer. 24:2–7.

Good fishes. Matt. 13:48.

Good servants. Matt. 25:21.

Green olive trees. Ps. 52:8; Hos. 14:6.

Jewels. Mal. 3:17.

Lambs. Isa. 40:11; John 21:15.

Lebanon. Hos. 14:5–7.

Lights. Matt. 5:14; Phil. 2:15.

Lilies. Song of Sol. 2:2; Hos. 14:5.

Lions. Prov. 28:1; Mic. 5:8.

Little children. Matt. 18:3; 1 Cor. 14:20.

Lively stones. 1 Pet. 2:5.

Members of the body. 1 Cor. 12:20, 27.

Mount Zion. Ps. 125:1–2.

Obedient children. 1 Pet. 1:14.

Palm trees. Ps. 92:12.

Pomegranates. Song of Sol. 4:13.

Runners in a race. 1 Cor. 9:24; Heb. 12:1.

Salt. Matt. 5:13.

Sheep. Ps. 78:52; Matt. 25:33; John 10:4.

Soldiers. 2 Tim. 2:3–4.

Stars. Dan. 12:3.

Stones of a crown. Zech. 9:16.

Strangers and pilgrims. 1 Pet. 2:11.

Sun. Judg. 5:31; Matt. 13:43.

Thirsting deer. Ps. 42:1.

Treasure. Exod. 19:5; Ps. 135:4.

Trees planted by rivers. Ps. 1:3.

Unfailing springs. Isa. 58:11.

Utensils of gold and silver. 2 Tim. 2:20.

Vines. Song of Sol. 6:11; Hos. 14:7.

Watered gardens. Isa. 58:11.

Wheat. Matt. 3:12; 13:29–30.

Willows by streams. Isa. 44:4.

Wrestlers. 2 Tim. 2:5.

Divine intercession for. Rom. 8:27.

God will not forsake. Ps. 37:28; 1 Sam. 2:9.

Paul considered himself the least. Eph. 3:8.

Paul ministered to. Rom. 15:25.

Will judge the world. 1 Cor. 6:2.

BELIEVERS, AFFLICTED

Christ

Comforts. Isa. 61:2; Matt. 11:28–30; Luke 7:13; John 14:1; 16:33.

Delivers. Rev. 3:10.

Is with. John 14:18.

Preserves. Isa. 63:9; Luke 21:18.

Supports. 2 Tim. 4:17; Heb. 2:18.

God

Comforts. Isa. 49:13; Jer. 31:13; Matt. 5:4; 2 Cor. 1:4–5; 7:6.

Delivers. Ps. 34:4, 19;
Prov. 12:13; Jer. 39:17–18.
Is a refuge and strength to.
Ps. 27:5–6; Isa. 25:4.
Is with. Ps. 46:5, 7; Isa. 43:2.
Preserves. Ps. 34:20.

Should
Acknowledge the justice of their
punishments. Neh. 9:33;
Job 2:10; Isa. 64:5–7;
Lam. 3:39; Mic. 7:9.
Avoid sin. Job 34:31–32;
John 5:14; 1 Pet. 2:12.
Be frequent in prayer.
Pss. 50:15; 55:16–17. (*See
also* Affliction, Prayer Under.)
Be patient. Luke 21:19;
Rom. 12:12; 2 Thess. 1:4;
James 1:4; 1 Pet. 2:20.
Be resigned. 1 Sam. 3:18;
2 Kings 20:19; Job 1:21;
Ps. 39:9.
Imitate Christ. Heb. 12:1–3;
1 Pet. 2:21–23.
Imitate the prophets. James 5:10.
Keep the resolutions made during
affliction. Ps. 66:13–15.
Not despise disciplining. Job 5:17;
Prov. 3:11; Heb. 12:5.
Praise God. Pss. 13:5–6;
56:8–10; 57:6–7; 71:20–23.
Take encouragement from former
mercies. Ps. 27:9; 2 Cor. 1:10.
Trust in the goodness of God. Job
13:15; Ps. 71:20; 1 Cor. 1:9.
Turn and devote themselves to
God. Josh. 6:1; Ps. 116:7–9;
Jer. 50:3–4.

BELIEVERS, CHARACTER OF
Attentive to Christ's voice.
John 10:3–4.
Blameless and harmless. Phil. 2:15.

Bold. Prov. 28:1; Rom. 13:3.
Contrite. Isa. 57:15; 66:2.
Desirous of good works. Titus 2:14;
3:8.
Devout. Acts 8:2; 22:12.
Faithful. Rev. 17:14.
Fearing God. Matt. 3:16; Acts 10:2.
Following Christ. John 10:4, 27.
Generous. Isa. 32:8; 2 Cor. 9:13.
Gentle. Prov. 16:19.
Godly. Ps. 4:3; 2 Pet. 2:9.
Holy. Deut. 7:6; 14:2; Col. 3:12.
Humble. Ps. 34:2; 1 Pet. 5:5.
Hungering after righteousness.
Matt. 5:6.
Just. Gen. 6:9; Hab. 2:4; Luke 2:25.
Led by the Spirit. Rom. 8:14.
Loving. Col. 1:4; 1 Thess. 4:9.
Meek. Isa. 29:19; Matt. 5:5.
Merciful. Ps. 37:26; Matt. 5:7.
New creatures. 2 Cor. 5:17;
Eph. 2:10.
Obedient. Rom. 16:19; 1 Pet. 1:14.
Poor in spirit. Ps. 51:17; Matt. 5:3.
Prudent. Prov. 16:21.
Pure in heart. Matt. 5:8; 1 John 3:3.
Righteous. Isa. 60:21; Luke 1:6.
Sincere. 2 Cor. 1:12; 2:17;
John 1:47.
Steadfast. Acts 2:42; Col. 2:5.
Taught of God. Isa. 54:13;
1 John 2:27.
True. 2 Cor. 6:8.
Undefiled. Ps. 119:1.
Upright. 1 Kings 3:6; Ps. 15:2.
Watchful. Luke 12:37.

BELIEVERS, COMMUNION OF
According to the prayer of Christ.
John 17:20–21.
Christ is present in. Matt. 18:20.
Delight of. Pss. 16:3; 42:4;
133:1–3; Rom. 15:32.

Exhortation to. Eph. 4:1–3.
In exhortation. Col. 3:16;
  Heb. 10:25.
God marks, with His approval.
  Mal. 3:16.
In holy conversation. Mal. 3:16.

Is with
  Believers in heaven.
    Heb. 12:22–24.
  Each other. Gal. 2:9;
    1 John 1:3, 7.
  God. 1 John 1:3.
In the Lord's Supper. 1 Cor. 10:17.
In mutual comfort and edification.
  1 Thess. 4:18; 5:11.
In mutual sympathy and kindness.
  Rom. 12:15; Eph. 4:32.
Opposed to communion with the
  wicked. 2 Cor. 6:14–17;
  Eph. 5:11.
In prayer for each other.
  2 Cor. 1:11; Eph. 6:18.
In public and social worship.
  Pss. 34:3; 55:14; Acts 1:14;
  Heb. 10:25.

BELIEVERS, DEATH OF
Asleep in Christ. 1 Cor. 15:18;
  1 Thess. 4:14.
Blessed. Rev. 14:13.
Disregarded by the wicked. Isa. 57:1.
God is with them in. Ps. 23:4.

Is full of
  Faith. Heb. 11:13.
  Hope. Prov. 14:32.
  Peace. Isa. 57:2.
Is gain. Phil. 1:21.

Leads to
  Christ's presence. 2 Cor. 5:8;
    Phil. 1:23.
  Comfort. Luke 16:25.

A crown of life. 2 Tim. 4:8;
  Rev. 2:10.
A joyful resurrection. Isa. 26:19;
  Dan. 12:2.
Rest. Job 3:17; 2 Thess. 1:7.
Met with resignation. Gen. 50:24;
  Josh. 23:14; 1 Kings 2:2.
Met without fear. 1 Cor. 15:55.
Precious in God's sight. Ps. 116:15.
Preserved by God in. Ps. 48:14.
Removes from coming evil.
  2 Kings 22:20; Isa. 57:1.
Sometimes desired. Luke 2:29.
Survivors consoled for.
  1 Thess. 4:13–18.
Waited for. Job 14:14.
The wicked wish theirs to resemble.
  Num. 23:10.

BELIEVERS, HAPPINESS OF
Abundant and satisfying. Pss. 36:8;
  63:5.

Derived from
  Divine chastening. Job 5:17;
    James 5:11.
  Fear of God. Ps. 128:1–2;
    Prov. 28:14.
  Finding wisdom. Prov. 3:13.
  God being their help. Ps. 146:5.
  God being their Lord. Ps. 144:15.
  Having mercy on the poor.
    Prov. 14:21.
  Hope in the Lord. Ps. 146:5.
  Hope of glory. Rom. 5:2.
  Obedience to God. Ps. 40:8;
    John 13:17.
  Praising God. Ps. 135:3.
  Salvation. Deut. 33:29;
    Isa. 12:2–3.
  Suffering for Christ. 2 Cor. 12:10;
    1 Pet. 3:14; 4:13–14.
  Their mutual love. Ps. 133:1.

Trust in God. Prov. 16:20;
Phil. 4:6–7.
Words of Christ. John 17:13.
Described by Christ in the Beatitudes.
Matt. 5:3–12.
Found only in the ways of wisdom.
Prov. 3:17–18.
Is in God. Ps. 73:25–26.

BELIEVERS, PRIVILEGES OF
Abiding in Christ. John 15:4–5.
Access to God by Christ. Eph. 3:12.
All things working together for their
good. Rom. 8:28;
2 Cor. 4:15–17.
Being of the household of God.
Eph. 2:19.
Calling upon God in trouble.
Ps. 50:15.
Committing themselves to God.
Ps. 31:5; Acts 7:59; 2 Tim. 1:12.

Having
Christ for their intercessor.
Rom. 8:34; Heb. 7:25;
1 John 2:1.
Christ for their Shepherd.
Isa. 40:11, with John 10:14,
16.
The promises of God. 2 Cor. 7:1;
2 Pet. 1:4.

Having God for their
Deliverer. 2 Sam. 22:2; Ps. 18:2.
Father. Deut. 32:6; Isa. 63:16;
64:8.
Friend. 2 Chron. 20:7, with
James 2:23.
Glory. Ps. 3:3; Isa. 60:19.
Guide. Ps. 48:14; Isa. 58:11.
Habitation. Pss. 90:1; 91:9.
Helper. Ps. 33:20; Heb. 13:6.
Keeper. Ps. 121:4–5.
King. Pss. 5:2; 41:4; Isa. 44:6.

Lawgiver. Neh. 9:13–14;
Isa. 33:22.
Light. Ps. 27:1; Isa. 60:19;
Mic. 7:8.
Portion. Ps. 73:26; Lam. 3:24.
Redeemer. Ps. 19:14; Isa. 43:14.
Refuge. Ps. 46:1, 11; Isa. 25:4.
Salvation. Pss. 18:2; 27:1;
Isa. 12:2.
Shield. Gen. 15:1; Ps. 84:11.
Strength. Pss. 18:2; 27:1; 46:1.
Tower. 2 Sam. 22:3; Ps. 61:3.
Interceding for others.
Gen. 18:23–33; James 5:16.
Membership with the church of the
firstborn. Heb. 12:23.
Partaking of the divine nature.
2 Pet. 1:4.
Possession of all things.
1 Cor. 3:21–22.
Profiting by punishment.
Ps. 119:67; Heb. 12:10–11.
Secure during public calamities.
Job 5:20, 23; Pss. 27:1–5;
91:5–10.
Suffering for Christ. Acts 5:41;
Phil. 1:29.
Their names written in the book of
life. Rev. 13:8; 20:15.
Union in God and Christ.
John 17:21.

BELIEVERS, REWARD OF
As servants of Christ. Col. 3:24.
Be careful not to lose. 2 John 1:8.
Believers may feel confident of.
Ps. 73:24; Isa. 25:8–9;
2 Cor. 5:1; 2 Tim. 4:8.

Described as
Being glorified with Christ.
Rom. 8:17–18; Col. 3:4;
Phil. 3:21; 1 John 3:2.

Being with Christ. John 12:26;
14:3; Phil. 1:23; 1 Thess. 4:17.
A city which had foundation.
Heb. 11:10.
A crown of glory. 1 Pet. 5:4.
A crown of life. James 1:12;
Rev. 2:10.
A crown of righteousness.
2 Tim. 4:8.
An enduring substance.
Heb. 10:34.
Entering into the joy of the Lord.
Matt. 25:21, with Heb. 12:2.
An eternal weight of glory. 2
Cor. 4:17.
Everlasting life. Luke 18:30;
John 6:40; 17:2–3; Rom. 2:7;
6:23; 1 John 5:11.
Everlasting light. Isa. 60:19.
Fullness of joy. Ps. 16:11.
A house, eternal in the heavens.
2 Cor. 5:1.
An incorruptible crown.
1 Cor. 9:25.
Inheritance eternal. Heb. 9:15.
Inheritance incorruptible, etc.
1 Pet. 1:4.
Inheritance of all things.
Rev. 21:7.
Inheritance with believers in light.
Acts 20:32; 26:18; Col. 1:12.
Joint heirship with Christ.
Rom. 8:17.
A kingdom. Matt. 25:34;
Luke 22:29.
A kingdom immovable.
Heb. 12:28.
The prize of the high calling of
God in Christ. Phil. 3:14.
Reigning forever and ever.
Rev. 22:5.
Reigning with Christ. 2 Tim. 2:12;
Rev. 3:21; 5:10; 20:4.

Rest. Heb. 4:9; Rev. 14:13.
Seeing the face of God. Ps. 17:15;
Matt. 5:8; Rev. 22:4.
Seeing the glory of Christ.
John 17:24.
Shining as the stars. Dan. 12:3.
Sitting in judgment with Christ.
Dan. 7:22; Matt. 19:28;
Luke 22:30, with 1 Cor. 6:2.
Treasure in heaven. Matt. 19:21;
Luke 12:33.
Hope of, a cause of rejoicing.
Rom. 5:2.

Is
From God. Rom. 2:7; Col. 3:24;
Heb. 11:6.
Full. 2 John 1:8.
Great. Matt. 5:12; Luke 6:35;
Heb. 10:35.
Incomparable. Isa. 64:4, with
1 Cor. 2:9.
Of God's good pleasure.
Matt. 20:14–15; Luke 12:32.
Of grace through faith alone.
Rom. 4:4–5, 16; 11:6.
Satisfying. Ps. 17:15.
Sure. Prov. 11:18.
Not because of their merits
Rom. 4:4–5.
Prepared by Christ. John 14:2.
Prepared by God. Heb. 11:16.
Present afflictions not to be
compared with. Rom. 8:18;
2 Cor. 5:17.

Prospect of, should lead to
Diligence. 2 John 8.
Enduring suffering for Christ.
2 Cor. 4:16–18; Heb. 11:26.
Faithfulness until death.
Rev. 2:10.
Pressing forward. Phil. 3:14.

Will be given at the second coming of
Christ. Matt. 16:17; Rev. 22:12.

BELIEVERS, TITLES AND NAMES OF

Believers. Acts 5:14; 1 Tim. 4:12.
Blessed of the Father. Matt. 25:34.
Blessed of the Lord. Gen. 24:31;
26:29.
Brothers. Matt. 23:8; Acts 12:17;
1 Thess. 5:27; Heb. 3:1.
Brothers of Christ. Luke 8:21; John
20:17.
Called of Jesus Christ. Rom. 1:6.
Children of Abraham. Gal. 3:7.
Children of the bride chamber.
Matt. 9:15.
Children of the day. 1 Thess. 5:5.
Children of the Father. Matt. 5:45.
Children of the free woman.
Gal. 4:31.
Children of God. John 11:52;
1 John 3:10.
Children of the highest. Luke 6:35.
Children of Jacob. Ps. 105:6.
Children of the kingdom.
Matt. 13:38.
Children of light. Luke 16:8;
Eph. 5:8; 1 Thess. 5:5.
Children of the Living God. Rom.
9:26.
Children of the Lord. Deut 14:1.
Children of promise. Rom. 9:8;
Gal. 4:28.
Children of the resurrection.
Luke 20:36.
Children of Zion. Ps. 149:2;
Joel 2:23.
Chosen generation. 1 Pet. 2:9.
Chosen ones. 1 Chron. 16:13.
Chosen vessels. Acts 9:15.
Christians. Acts 11:26; 26:28.

Dear brothers. 1 Cor. 15:58; James
2:5.
Dear children. Eph. 5:1.
Disciples of Christ. John 8:31; 15:8.
Elect of God. Col. 3:12; Titus 1:1.
Epistles of Christ. 2 Cor. 3:3.
Excellent. Ps. 16:3.
Faithful. Ps. 12:1.
Faithful brothers in Christ. Col. 1:2.
Faithful of the land. Ps. 101:6.
Fellow citizens with God's people.
Eph. 2:19.
Fellow heirs. Eph. 3:6.
Fellow servants. Rev. 6:11.
Friends of Christ. John 15:15.
Friends of God. 2 Chron. 20:7;
James 2:23.
Godly. Ps. 4:3; 2 Pet. 2:9.
Heirs of God. Rom. 8:17.
Heirs of the grace of life. 1 Pet. 3:7.
Heirs of the kingdom. James 2:5.
Heirs of promise. Heb. 6:17;
Gal. 3:29.
Heirs of salvation. Heb. 1:14.
Holy nation. Exod. 19:6; 1 Pet. 2:9.
Holy people. Deut. 26:19;
Isa. 62:12.
Holy priesthood. 1 Pet. 2:5.
Joint heirs with Christ. Rom. 8:17.
Just. Hab. 2:4.
Kingdom of priests. Exod. 19:6.
Kings and priests to God. Rev. 1:6.
Lambs. Isa. 40:11; John 21:15.
Lights of the world. Matt. 5:14.
Little children. John 13:33;
1 John 2:1.
Lively stones. 1 Pet. 2:5.
Lord's freemen. 1 Cor. 7:22.
Loved by God. Rom. 1:7.
Members of Christ. 1 Cor. 6:15;
Eph. 5:30.
Men of God. Deut. 33:1;
1 Tim. 6:11; 2 Tim. 3:17.

Obedient children. 1 Pet. 1:14.

Objects of mercy. Rom. 9:23.

Objects to honor. 2 Tim. 2:21.

Peculiar people. Deut. 14:2; Titus 2:14; 1 Pet. 2:9.

Peculiar treasure. Exod. 19:5; Ps. 135:4.

People near to God. Ps. 148:14.

People of God. Heb. 4:9; 1 Pet. 2:10.

People saved by the Lord. Deut. 33:29.

Pillars in the temple of God. Rev. 3:12.

Ransomed of the Lord. Isa. 35:10.

Redeemed of the Lord. Isa. 51:11.

Royal priesthood. 1 Pet. 2:9.

Salt of the earth. Matt. 5:13.

Servants of Christ. 1 Cor. 7:22; Eph. 6:6.

Servants of righteousness. Rom. 6:18.

Sheep of Christ. John 10:1–16; 21:16.

Sojourners with God. Lev. 25:23; Ps. 39:12.

Sons of God. John 1:12; Phil. 2:15; 1 John 3:1–2.

Trees of righteousness. Isa. 61:3.

Witnesses for God. Isa. 44:8.

BELIEVERS, WARFARE OF

Armor for

Breastplate of righteousness. Eph. 6:14.

Belt of truth. Eph. 6:14.

Called armor of God. Eph. 6:11.

Called armor of light. Rom. 13:12.

Called armor of righteousness. 2 Cor. 6:7.

Helmet of salvation. Eph. 6:17; 1 Thess. 5:8.

Mighty through God. 2 Cor. 10:4–5.

Must be put on. Rom. 13:12; Eph. 6:11.

Not worldly. 2 Cor. 10:4.

Preparation of the gospel. Eph. 6:15.

Shield of faith. Eph. 6:16.

Sword of the Spirit. Eph. 6:17.

To be on right hand and left. 2 Cor. 6:7.

The whole, is required. Eph. 6:13.

Believers

All engaged in. Phil. 1:30.

Comforted by God in. 2 Cor. 7:5–6.

Delivered by Christ in. 2 Tim. 4:18.

Encouraged in. Isa. 41:11–12; 51:12; Mic. 7:8; 1 John 4:4.

Exhorted to diligence in. 1 Tim. 6:12; Jude 1:3.

Helped by God in. Ps. 118:13; Isa. 41:13–14.

Must stand firm in. Eph. 6:13–14.

Protected by God in. Ps. 140:7.

Strengthened by Christ in. 2 Cor. 12:9; 2 Tim. 4:17.

Strengthened by God in. Pss. 20:2; 27:14; Isa. 41:70.

Thank God for victory in. Rom. 7:25; 1 Cor. 15:57.

Called the good fight of faith. 1 Tim. 6:12.

Illustrated. Isa. 9:5; Zech. 10:5.

Is

A good warfare. 1 Tim. 1:18–19.

Not after the sinful nature. 2 Cor. 10:3.

Is against
  Death. 1 Cor. 15:26, with Heb.
    2:14–15.
  The devil. Gen. 3:15; 2 Cor. 2:11;
    Eph. 6:12; James 4:7;
    1 Pet. 5:8; Rev. 12:17.
  Enemies. Pss. 38:19; 56:2; 59:3.
  The sinful nature. Rom. 7:23;
    1 Cor. 9:25–27; 2 Cor. 12:7;
    Gal. 5:17; 1 Pet. 2:11.
  The world. John 16:33;
    1 John 5:4–5.
Mere professors do not maintain.
  Jer. 9:3.
Often arises from the opposition of
  friends or relatives. Mic. 7:6, with
  Matt. 10:35–36.

Those who overcome in, will
  Be clothed in white. Rev. 3:5.
  Be confessed by Christ before God
    the Father. Rev. 3:5.
  Be pillars in the temple of God.
    Rev. 3:12.
  Be sons of God. Rev. 21:7.
  Eat of the hidden manna.
    Rev. 2:17.
  Eat of the tree of life. Rev. 2:7.
  Have God as their God. Rev. 21:7.
  Have the morning star. Rev. 2:28.
  Have the name of God written
    upon them by Christ. Rev. 3:12.
  Have power over the nations.
    Rev. 2:26.
  Have a white stone, and in it a new
    name written. Rev. 2:17.
  Inherit all things. Rev. 21:7.
  Not be hurt by the second death.
    Rev. 2:11.
  Not have their names blotted out
    of the book of life. Rev. 3:5.
  Sit with Christ on His throne.
    Rev. 3:21.

To be carried on
  Under Christ, as our captain.
    Heb. 2:10.
  Under the Lord's banner.
    Ps. 60:4.
  With a good conscience.
    1 Tim. 1:18–19.
  With confidence in God.
    Ps. 27:1–3.
  With earnestness. Jude 3.
  With endurance of hardship.
    2 Tim. 2:3, 10.
  With faith. 1 Tim. 1:18–19.
  With prayer. Ps. 35:1–3;
    Eph. 6:18.
  With self-denial. 1 Cor. 9:25–27.
  With sobriety. 1 Thess. 5:6;
    1 Pet. 5:8.
  With steadfastness in the faith.
    1 Cor. 16:13; 1 Pet. 5:9, with
    Heb. 10:23.
  With watchfulness. 1 Cor. 16:13;
    1 Pet. 5:8.

Victory in, is
  By faith. Heb. 11:33–37;
    1 John 5:4–5.
  From God. 1 Cor. 15:57;
    2 Cor. 2:14.
  Over all that exalts itself.
    2 Cor. 10:5.
  Over death and the grave.
    Isa. 25:8; 26:19; Hos. 13:14;
    1 Cor. 15:54–55.
  Over the devil. Rom. 16:20;
    1 John 2:14.
  Over the sinful nature.
    Rom. 7:24–25; Gal. 5:24.
  Over the world. 1 John 5:4–5.
  Through Christ. Rom. 7:25;
    1 Cor. 15:27; 2 Cor. 12:9;
    Rev. 12:11.
  Triumphant. Rom. 8:37;
    2 Cor. 10:5.

BELL
Attached to the hem of the priest's robe. Exod. 28:33–34; 39:25–26.
On horses. Zech. 14:20.

BELLOWS
Used with the furnace of the founder. Jer. 6:29.

BELLY
Used figuratively for the seat of the affections. Job 15:2, 35; 20:20; Ps. 44:25; Prov. 18:20; 20:27, 30; Hab. 3:16; John 7:38.

BELT
Embroidered. Exod. 28:8, 27–28; 29:5; Lev. 8:7.
Made of leather. 2 Kings 1:8; Matt. 3:4.
Made of linen. Prov. 31:24.
Traffic in. Prov. 31:24.
Used in a figurative sense. Isa. 11:5; 22:21; Eph. 6:14.
Used in symbolic sense.
Jer. 13:1–11; Acts 21:11; Rev. 15:6.
Used to bear arms. 1 Sam. 18:4; 2 Sam. 20:8; 2 Kings 3:21.
Worn by other priests. Exod. 28:40; 29:9; Lev. 8:13.
Worn by the high priest.
Exod. 28:4, 39; 39:29; Lev. 8:7; 16:4.
Worn by women. Isa. 3:24.

BEN-HUR
Solomon's district supervisor over Mt. Ephraim. 1 Kings 4:8.

BEREAVEMENT
Abram, of Sarah. Gen. 23:2.

David, of Absalom. 2 Sam. 18:33; 19:4.
David, of his child by Bathsheba. 2 Sam. 12:15–23.
The Egyptians of their firstborn. Exod. 12:29–33.
From God. Exod. 12:29; Hos. 9:12.
Jacob, of Joseph. Gen. 37:34–35.
Mourning forbidden to Ezekiel for his wife. Ezek. 24:16–18.
Mourning in, forbidden to Aaron on account of his son's wickedness. Lev. 10:6.
Naomi, of her husband. Ruth 1:3, 5, 20, 21.

Resignation in
David. 2 Sam. 12:22–23.
Job. Job 1:18–21.
Resignation in. Eccles. 7:2–4; 1 Thess. 4:13–18.

BETRAYAL
Of cities. Judg. 1:24–25.
Of David by Doeg. 1 Sam. 22:9, 10.
Of Jesus. Matt. 26:14–16.
Of others, predicted. Matt. 20:18; 24:10.

BETTING
By Samson. Judg. 14:12–19.

BIBLE, INSPIRATION OF THE
See also Scriptures, the; Word of God

Apostles appealed to. Acts 8:32; 28:23.
Continually affirmed. Deut. 6:6; 1 Kings 16:1; Jer. 13:1; 1 Cor. 2:13; 2 Pet. 1:21.
Inspired by God. 2 Tim. 3:16; Heb. 1:1.

Inspired by the Holy Spirit.
Acts 1:16; 2 Pet. 1:21.
Presents Christ. John 5:39;
Acts 18:28.
Will judge those not accepting it.
John 12:48; Heb. 10:28.

BIG BROTHER
Live quietly, minding one's own
affairs. 1 Thess. 4:11;
2 Thess. 3:12; 1 Tim. 2:2.
Look to interests of others. Phil 2:4.

BIGOTRY
Of the disciples in forbidding children
to be brought to Jesus. Matt. 9:13;
Mark 10:13; Luke 18:15.
Of the early Christians in opposing
the preaching of the gospel to the
Gentiles. Acts 10:45; 11:2, 3;
21:20–25.
Falsely accusing Jesus of being a
glutton and drunkard.
Matt. 11:18, 19.
Falsely accusing Jesus of blasphemy.
John 5:18.
God's view of. Isa. 65:5.
James and John in desiring to call
down fire on the Samaritans who
would not receive Jesus.
Luke 9:51–56.
Jesus' disciples as examples of.
Luke 9:49.
Jews with regard to the Samaritans.
John 4:9, 27.
Of John in forbidding the casting out
of devils by one who followed not
Jesus. Mark 9:38–40.
Joshua, through envy seeking to
suppress Eldad and Medad.
Num. 11:27–29.
Of keeping company with sinners.
Luke 7:39; 15:2; 19:5–7.

Of not conforming to traditions.
Luke 11:38–39.
Paul's argument against.
Rom. 3:1–23; 4:1–25.
In persecutions. 1 Thess. 2:15–16.
In regard to circumcision.
Acts 15:1–10, 24; Gal. 2:3–5.
With regard to Paul's preaching.
Acts 21:28–29; 22:22.
In rejecting the teachings of Jesus at
Nazareth. Luke 4:28.
Of the Samaritans in refusing to
receive Jesus. Luke 9:52–53.
Of Saul, in persecuting the
Christians. Acts 22:3–4;
9:1–5; 26:9;
Gal. 1:13–14; Phil. 3:6.
In the treatment of the young man
who was born blind whom Jesus
restored to sight.
John 9:28–29, 34.
Tribes and Pharisees as examples of.
Mark 2:16; Luke 15:2; 18:9–14.
In zeal. Rom. 10:2–3.

BIRDS
Are hostile to strange kinds.
Jer. 12:9.
Blood of, not to be eaten. Lev. 7:26.

Called
Birds of the air. Matt. 8:20.
Fowls of the air. Gen. 7:3.
Fowls of heaven. Job 35:11.
Winged fowl. Deut 4:17.
Can all be tamed. James 3:7.

Clean
Cock and hen. Matt. 23:37;
26:34, 74.
Crane. Isa. 38:14; Jer. 8:7.
Dove. Gen. 8:8.
Partridge. 1 Sam. 26:20;
Jer. 17:11.

Pigeon. Lev. 1:14; 12:6.

Quail. Exod. 16:12–13;
Num. 11:31–32.

Sparrow. Matt. 10:29–31.

Swallow. Ps. 84:3; Isa. 38:14.

Turtledove. Lev. 14:22; Song of
Sol. 2:12.

Confinement in cages of, alluded to.
Jer. 5:27.

Created by God. Gen. 1:20–21;
2:19.

Created for the glory of God.
Ps. 148:10.

Differ in flesh from beasts and fishes.
1 Cor. 15:39.

Domesticated. Job 41:5; James 3:7.

Early differentiated as clean or
unclean. Gen. 8:20.

Fly above the earth. Gen. 1:20.

Furnished with claws. Dan. 4:33.

Given as food to man. Gen. 9:2–3;
Deut. 14:11–20.

God provides for. Job 38:41;
Ps. 104:10–12; 147:9;
Matt. 6:26; 10:29;
Luke 12:6, 23–24.

Habits of. Job 39:13–18, 26–30.

Have each their peculiar note or
song. Ps. 104:12; Eccles. 12:4;
Song of Sol. 2:12.

Herb of the field given as food to.
Gen. 1:30.

Illustrative of
Cruel and ravenous kings.
Isa. 46:11.
Death (when snared).
Eccles. 9:12.
Plans of the wicked (when snared).
Ps. 124:7; Prov. 1:10–17;
7:23.
The devil and his spirits.
Matt. 13:4, 19.
Hostile nations. Jer. 12:9.

People of different countries.
Ezek. 31:6; Matt. 13:32.
Unsettled persons, etc.
Prov. 27:8; Isa. 16:2.

Inhabit
Deserted cities. Isa. 34:11,
14–15.
Deserts. Ps. 102:6.
Marshes. Isa. 14:23.
Mountains. Ps. 50:11.

Instinct of, inferior to man's reason.
Job 35:11.

Instinctively fear man. Gen. 9:2.

Lessons of wisdom to be learned
from. Job 12:7.

Make and dwell in nests. Matt. 8:20.

Make their nests
In clefts of rocks. Num. 24:21;
Jer. 48:28.
In trees. Ps. 104:17; Ezek. 31:6.
On the ground. Deut. 22:6.

Man's dominion over.
Gen. 1:26–28; 9:2–3; Ps. 8:5–8;
Jer. 27:6; Dan. 2:38; James 3:7.

Many kinds of
Carnivorous. Gen. 15:11; 40:19;
Deut. 28:26.
Granivorous. Matt. 13:4.
Migratory. Jer. 8:7.

Named by Adam. Gen. 2:19–20.

No likeness of, to be made for
worship. Deut. 4:17.

Not to be eaten, when unclean.
Lev. 11:13, 17; Deut. 14:12.

Often leave places suffering
calamities. Jer. 4:25; 9:10.

Often suffered for man's sins.
Gen. 6:7; Jer. 12:4; Ezek. 38:20;
Hos. 4:3.

Often worshiped by idolaters.
Rom. 1:23.

Power over, given to man.
Gen. 1:26; Ps. 8:6–8.
Propagated by eggs. Deut. 22:6;
Jer. 17:11.
Property of God. Ps. 50:11.
Rapid flight of, alluded to. Isa. 31:5;
Hos. 9:11; 11:11.
Rest in trees. Dan. 4:12;
Matt. 13:32.
Solomon wrote the history of.
1 Kings 4:33.
Songs of, at the break of day.
Ps. 104:12; Eccles. 12:4;
Song of Sol. 2:12.
Taken in snares or nets. Prov. 1:17.
To be eaten, when clean.
Deut. 14:11, 20.
To be offered in sacrifice, when
clean. Gen. 8:20; Lev. 1:14.

Unclean
Bat. Lev. 11:19; Isa. 2:20.
Bittern. Isa. 14:23; 34:11.
Cormorant. Lev. 11:17;
Isa. 34:11.
Cuckoo. Lev. 11:16.
Eagle. Lev. 11:13; Job 39:27.
Gier eagle. Lev. 11:18.
Glede. Deut. 14:13.
Great owl. Lev. 11:17.
Hawk. Lev. 11:16; Job 39:26.
Heron. Lev. 11:19.
Kite. Lev. 11:14.
Lapwing. Lev. 11:19.
Little owl. Lev. 11:17.
Night hawk. Lev. 11:16.
Osprey. Lev. 11:13.
Ossifrage. Lev. 11:13.
Ostrich. Job 39:13, 18.
Owl. Lev. 11:16; Job 30:29.
Peacock. 1 Kings 10:22;
Job 39:13.
Pelican. Lev. 11:18; Ps. 102:6.

Raven. Lev. 11:15; Job 38:41.
Stork. Lev. 11:19; Ps. 104:17.
Swan. Lev. 11:18.
Vulture. Lev. 11:14; Job 28:7;
Isa. 34:15.
Used for sacrifice. *See* Dove; Pigeon.

BIRTH
From above. John 1:13; 3:5;
1 Pet. 1:23.
Act of God. Acts 17:25.
Into trouble. Job 5:7.

Of Christ
Firstborn of many brethren.
Rom. 8:29.
Joy from. Luke 1:14.
Narrated. Matt. 1:18–2:23;
Luke 1:26–2:20.
Prophesied. Isa. 9:6.
Purpose. John 18:37.
Giving, ordained to be in sorrow.
Gen. 3:16.
Pangs in giving. Ps. 48:6; Isa. 13:8;
21:3; Jer. 4:31; 6:24; 30:6;
31:8.
Time for. Eccles. 3:2.

BIRTH CONTROL
Command to be fruitful and multiply.
Gen. 1:28; 9:1, 7.

Examples of
Castration. Matt. 19:12.
Treated lightly. Gen. 38:9.

Barren woman. Ps. 113:9.
Elizabeth. Luke 1:13, 18.
Hannah. 1 Sam. 1:2–10.
Rachel. Gen. 30:22.
Rebekkah. Gen. 25:21.
Sarah. Gen. 16:1–2; 17:15–16;
21:1–2; Heb. 11:11.
Wife of Manoah. Judg. 13:2–3.

BIRTHDAY

Celebrated by feasts. Gen. 40:20;
Matt. 14:6.
Cursed. Job 3:1–3; Jer. 20:14, 18.

BIRTH DEFECTS

Development of the unborn child.
Controlled by God. Job 10:11;
Ps. 119:73; 139:13–15;
Isa. 44:2; 46:3.
For a purpose. Isa. 49:5; Jer. 1:5;
Rom. 8:28.
Unknown by people. Eccles. 11:5.

Examples of
Blindness. John 9:1.
Lameness. Acts 3:2; 14:8.
Male sterility. Matt. 19:12.

BIRTHRIGHT

Adonijah. 1 Kings 2:15.
Belonged to the firstborn.
Deut. 21:15–16.
Coveted. Gen. 25:31.
Defined. Deut. 21:17.
Despised. Gen. 25:32, 34;
Heb. 12:16.
Entitled the firstborn to a double
portion of inheritance.
Deut. 21:15–17.
Forfeited by Reuben.
1 Chron. 5:1–2.
An honorable title. Exod. 4:22; Ps.
89:27; Jer. 31:9; Rom. 8:29;
Col. 1:15; Heb. 1:6; 12:23;
Rev. 1:5.
Hosah's son. 1 Chron. 26:10.
Loss mourned. Gen. 27:36.
Royal succession. 2 Chron. 21:3.
Set aside: that of Manasseh.
Gen. 48:15–20.

Sold by Esau. Gen. 25:29–34;
27:36; Rom. 9:12–13;
Heb. 12:16.

BISEXUALITY

Gender distinction at creation.
Gen. 1:27; 2:20–24.
Gender distinguished by hair length.
1 Cor. 11:14–15.
Men forbidden to wear women's
clothing and vice versa.
Deut. 22:5.

BISHOP

Appointed by the Holy Spirit.
Acts 20:28.
Among the recipients of Paul's letter
to Philippi. Phil. 1:1.
Requirements for serving as.
1 Tim. 3:2–11.
A title of Jesus. 1 Pet. 2:25.

BIT

Part of a bridle. Ps. 32:9; James 3:3.

BITTER HERBS

See Herbs, Bitter

BITTER WATER

See Water, Bitter

BITTERNESS

Christians must put away. Eph. 4:31;
Heb. 12:15.
Of the harlot. Prov. 5:4.
Known in the heart. Prov. 14:10.
Of the militaristic Chaldeans.
Hab. 1:6.
Of the prophet Jeremiah.
Lam. 3:15.
Of the wicked. Ps. 140:3;
Rom. 3:14.
Against wives proscribed. Col. 3:19.

BLASPHEMY

Backslidden Ephesians. Rev. 2:9.

Believers grieved to hear.
Pss. 44:15–16; 74:10, 18, 22.

Christ assailed with.
Matt. 10:25; Luke 22:64–65;
1 Pet. 4:14.

Christ charged with.
Matt. 9:2–3; 26:64–65;
John 10:33, 36.

Connected with folly and pride.
2 Kings 19:22; Ps. 74:18.

The depraved sons of Shelomith who
cursed God. Lev. 24:10–16.

Early Christians accused of.
Acts 6:11, 13.

The early Christians, persecuted by
Saul of Tarsus. Acts 26:11;
1 Tim. 1:13.

The enemies of Jesus when He was
crucified. Matt. 27:40–44, 63.

False indictments for
Of Jesus. Matt. 26:65;
Mark 14:58; Luke 22:70–71;
John 19:7.
Of Naboth. 1 Kings 21:13.
Of Stephen. Acts 6:11, 13.

Forbidden. Exod. 20:7; Col. 3:8.

Give no occasion for. 2 Sam. 12:14;
1 Tim. 6:1.

Against the Holy Spirit,
unpardonable. Matt. 12:31–32.

Hymenaeus and Alexander, who
were delivered to Satan that they
might learn not to blaspheme.
1 Tim. 1:20.

Hypocrisy counted as. Rev. 2:9.

Idolatry counted as. Isa. 65:7;
Ezek. 20:27–28.

Infidels who used the adultery of
David as an occasion to
blaspheme. 2 Sam. 12:14.

The Israelites murmuring against
God. Num. 21:5–6.

Job's wife when she exhorted Job to
curse God and die. Job 2:9.

The man of sin. 2 Thess. 2:3–4.

Peter, when accused of being a
disciple of Jesus. Matt. 26:74;
Mark 14:71.

Proceeds from the heart.
Matt. 15:19.

Punishment of. Lev. 24:16;
Isa. 65:7; Ezek. 20:27–33;
35:11–12.

Rabshakeh, in the siege of
Jerusalem. 2 Kings 18:22; 19;
Isa. 36:15–20; 37:10–33.

Shimei in his malice toward David.
2 Sam. 16:5.

The wicked addicted to. Ps. 74:18;
Isa. 52:5; 2 Tim. 3:2;
Rev. 16:11, 21.

BLEMISH

Prevented sons of Aaron from
exercise of priestly offices.
Lev. 21:17–23.

Animals with, forbidden to be used
for sacrifice. Lev. 22:19–25.

Figurative uses. Eph. 5:27;
1 Pet. 1:19.

BLESSED, THE

Believers at the judgment day.
Matt. 25:34.

The bountiful. Deut. 15:10;
Ps. 41.1, Prov. 22.9,
Luke 14:13–14.

The children of the just. Prov. 20:7.

The faithful. Prov. 28:20.

The generation of the upright.
Ps. 112:2.

Holy mourners. Matt. 5:4;
Luke 6:21.

The just. Ps. 106:3; Prov. 10:6.

The meek. Matt. 5:5.

The merciful. Matt. 5:7.

The peacemakers. Matt. 5:9.

The poor in spirit. Matt. 5:3.

The pure in heart. Matt. 5:8.

The righteous. Ps. 5:12.

To whom God imputes righteousness without works. Rom. 4:6–9.

The undefiled. Ps. 119:1.

Who are not offended at Christ. Matt. 11:6.

Who are on guard against sin. Rev. 16:15.

Who avoid the wicked. Ps. 1:1.

Who believe. Luke 1:45; Gal. 3:9.

Who delight in the commandments of God. Ps. 112:1.

Who die in the Lord. Rev. 14:13.

Who endure temptation. James 1:12.

Who favor believers. Gen. 12:3; Ruth 2:10.

Who fear God. Pss. 112:1; 128:1, 4.

Who frequent the house of God. Pss. 65:4; 84:4.

Who have the Lord for their God. Ps. 144:15.

Who have part in the first resurrection. Rev. 20:6.

Who hear and keep the word of God. Ps. 119:2; Matt. 13:16; Luke 11:28; James 1:25; Rev. 1:3; 22:7.

Who hunger and thirst after righteousness. Matt. 5:6.

Who keep the commandments of God. Rev. 22:14.

Who know Christ. Matt. 16:16–17.

Who know the gospel. Ps. 89:15.

Who reprimand sinners. Prov. 24:25.

Who suffer for Christ. Luke 6:22.

Who trust in God. Pss. 2:12; 34:8; 40:4; 84:12; Jer. 17:7.

Who wait for the Lord. Isa. 30:18.

Who will eat bread in the kingdom of God. Luke 14:15; Rev. 19:9.

Who watch for the Lord. Luke 12:37.

Whom God calls. Isa. 51:2; Rev. 19:9.

Whom God chastens. Job 5:17; Ps. 94:12.

Whom God chooses. Ps. 65:4; Eph. 1:3–4.

Whose sins are forgiven. Ps. 32:1–2; Rom. 4:7.

Whose strength is in the Lord. Ps. 84:5.

BLESSINGS

By Aaron. Lev. 9:22–23.

Apostolic forms of. Rom. 1:7; 1 Cor. 1:3; 2 Cor. 1:2; Gal. 1:3; Eph. 1:2; Phil. 1:2; Col. 1:2; 1 Thess. 1:1; 2 Thess. 1:2; 2 Tim. 1:2; Philem. 3.

By Araunah upon David. 2 Sam. 24:23.

By Bethuel's household upon Rebekah. Gen. 24:60.

By David upon Barzillai. 2 Sam. 19:39.

By David upon the people. 2 Sam. 6:18.

Divinely appointed. Num. 6:23–26; Deut. 10:8; 21:5.

By Eli upon Elkanah. 1 Sam. 2:20.

Upon Esau. Gen. 27:39–40.

By God, upon creatures He had made. Gen. 1:22.

Blessing

By half the tribes who stood on Mt. Gerizim. Deut. 11:29–30; 27:11–13; Josh. 8:33.

Upon his own sons. Gen. 40:9.

By Isaac upon Jacob. Gen. 27:23–29, 37; 28:1–4.

By Jacob upon Pharaoh. Gen. 47:7–10.

By Jesus upon His disciples. Luke 24:50.

Upon Joseph's sons. Gen. 48.

By Joshua upon Caleb. Josh. 14:13.

Levitical. Num. 6:23–26.

By Melchizedek upon Abraham. Gen. 14:19–20; Heb. 7:7.

Upon man. Gen. 1:28.

By Moses upon the tribes of Israel. Deut. 3:3.

By Naomi upon Ruth and Orpah. Ruth 1:8–9.

Upon Noah. Gen. 9:1–2.

By the people upon Ruth. Ruth 4:11–12.

Upon the Reubenites and Gadites and half the tribe of Manasseh. Josh. 22:6–7.

By Simeon upon Jesus. Luke 2:34.

By Solomon upon the people. 1 Kings 8:14, 55–58; 2 Chron. 6:3.

BLINDNESS, SPIRITUAL

Believers delivered from. John 8:12; Eph. 5:8; Col. 1:13; 1 Thess. 5:4–5; 1 Pet. 2:9.

Christ appointed to remove. Isa. 42:7; Luke 4:18; John 8:12.

Christ's ministers are lights to remove. Matt. 5:14; Acts 26:18.

The effect of sin. Isa. 29:10; Matt. 6:23; John 3:19–20.

Explained. John 1:5; 1 Cor. 2:14.

Is inconsistent with communion with God. 1 John 1:6–7.

Judicially inflicted. Ps. 69:23; Isa. 29:10; 44:18; Matt. 13:13–14; John 12:40.

Leads to all evil. Eph. 4:17–19.

Of ministers, fatal to themselves and to the people. Matt. 15:14.

Pray for the removal of. Pss. 13:3; 119:18.

Removal of, illustrated. John 9:7, 11, 25; Acts 9:18; Rev. 3:18.

The self-righteous are in. Matt. 23:19, 26; Rev. 3:17.

Unbelief the effect of. Rom. 11:8; 2 Cor. 4:3–4.

Uncharitableness, a proof of. 1 John 2:9, 11.

The wicked are in. Ps. 82:5; Jer. 5:21.

The wicked willfully guilty of. Isa. 26:11; Rom. 1:19–21.

A work of the devil. 2 Cor. 4:4.

BLOOD

Of animals slain for food to be
poured on the earth and covered.
Lev. 17:13; Deut. 12:16, 24.
Beasts of prey delight in.
Num. 23:24; Ps. 68:23.
Birds of prey delight in. Job 39:30.

Eating of, forbidden to
Early Christians. Acts 15:20, 29.
Israelites under the law.
Lev. 3:17; 17:10, 12.
Human after the flood. Gen. 9:4.
Fluid. Deut. 12:16.
Idolaters made drink offerings of.
Ps. 16:4.

Illustrative of
Guilt, when on one's head.
Lev. 20:9; 2 Sam. 1:16;
Ezek. 18:13.
Oppression and cruelty, when
building with. Hab. 2:12.
Ripening for destruction, when
preparing to. Ezek. 35:6.
Severe judgments, when given to
drink. Ezek. 16:38; Rev. 16:6.
Victories, when washing the feet
in. Pss. 58:10; 68:23.
The Jews often guilty of eating.
1 Sam. 14:32–33; Ezek. 33:25.

Of legal sacrifices
For atonement. Exod. 30:10;
Lev. 17:11.
How disposed of. Exod. 29:12;
Lev. 4:7.
Ineffective to remove sin.
Heb. 10:4.
Not offered with leaven.
Exod. 23:18; 34:25.
Price of, not to be consecrated.
Matt. 27:6.

For purification.
Heb. 9:13, 19–22.
Red. 2 Kings 3:22; Joel 2:31.
The life of animals. Gen. 9:4;
Lev. 17:11, 14.
Of all men the same. Acts 17:26.

Shedding of human
Always punished. Gen. 9:6.
Defiling to the land. Ps. 106:38.
Defiling to the person. Isa. 59:3.
Forbidden. Gen. 9:5.
Hateful to God. Prov. 6:16–17.
Jews often guilty of. Jer. 22:17;
Ezek. 22:4.
Mode of clearing those accused of.
Deut. 21:1–9.
Water turned into, as a sign.
Exod. 4:9, 30.
Waters of Egypt turned into, as a
judgment. Exod. 7:17–21.

BOASTING

About the Christians of Corinth.
2 Cor. 8:24; 9:3.
In the last days. 2 Tim. 3:2.
In the Lord. Pss. 34:2; 44:8;
Jer. 9:23–24; 2 Cor. 10:13;
10:17; Gal. 6:14.
Of the man of perdition.
2 Thess. 2:3–4.
Warned against. Deut. 8:17; 32:27;
Prov. 27:1.
Of the wicked.
Pss. 10:3; 12:3; 17:10; 52:1;
94:4.

BOLDNESS, HOLY

A characteristic of believers.
Prov. 28:1.
Christ set an example of. John 7:26.
Exhortations to. Josh. 1:17;
2 Chron. 19:11; Jer. 1:8;
Ezek. 3:9.

Express your trust in God with.
Heb. 13:6.
Through faith in Christ. Eph. 3:12;
Heb. 10:19.
Have, in prayer. Eph. 3:12;
Heb. 4:16.

Ministers should exhibit in
Condemning sin. Isa. 58:1;
Mic. 3:8.
The face of opposition.
Acts 13:46; 1 Thess. 2:2.
Faithfulness to their people.
2 Cor. 7:4; 10:1.
Preaching. Acts 4:31; Phil. 1:14.
Pray for. Acts 4:29; Eph. 6:19–20.

Produced by
Faithfulness to God. 1 Tim. 3:13.
Fear of God. Acts 4:19; 5:29.
Trust in God. Isa. 50:7.
Believers will have, in judgment.
1 John 4:17.

BONDAGE, SPIRITUAL
Believers are delivered
from. Rom. 6:18, 22.
Christ delivers from. Luke 4:18, 21;
John 8:36; Rom. 7:24–25;
Eph. 4:8.
Deliverance from, illustrated.
Deut. 4:20.
Deliverance from, promised.
Isa. 42:6–7.
To the devil. 1 Tim. 3:7;
2 Tim. 2:26.
To the fear of death. Heb. 2:14–15.
The gospel as instrument of
deliverance from. John 8:32;
Rom. 8:2.
To sin. John 8:34; Acts 8:23;
Rom. 6:16; 7:23; Gal. 4:3;
2 Pet. 2:19.

BOOKS
Divine communications recorded in.
Exod. 17:14; Isa. 30:8; Jer. 36:2;
Rev. 1:19.
Erasures in, alluded to. Exod. 32:33;
Num. 5:23.

Illustrative of
Memorials of conversation and
conduct of men. Dan. 7:10;
Mal. 3:16; Rev. 20:12.
Memorials of God's providence.
Pss. 56:8; 139:16.
Record of the church of Christ.
Dan. 12:1; Heb. 12:23;
Rev. 20:12, 15; 22:19.
Important events recorded in.
Ezra 4:15; 6:1–2; Esther 2:23.

Made of
Papyrus or paper reed. Isa. 19:7.
Parchment. 2 Tim. 4:13.

Not extant, but mentioned in
Scripture
Acts of Solomon. 1 Kings 11:41.
Ahijah the Shilonite.
2 Chron. 9:29.
Chronicles of David.
1 Chron. 27:24.
Gad the seer. 1 Chron. 29:29.
History of the kings.
1 Chron. 9:1.
Jasher. Josh. 10:13;
2 Sam. 1:18.
Jehu the son of Hanani.
2 Chron. 20:34.
Nathan. 1 Chron. 29:29;
2 Chron. 9:29.
Natural history by Solomon.
1 Kings 4:32–33.
Samuel concerning the kingdom.
1 Sam. 10:25.
Samuel the seer. 1 Chron. 29:29.

Sayings of the seers.
2 Chron. 33:19.
Shemaiah. 2 Chron. 12:15.
Visions of Iddo. 2 Chron. 9:29;
12:15.
Wars of the Lord. Num. 21:14.
Numerous and most expensive.
Acts 19:19.
Often dedicated to persons of
distinction. Luke 1:3; Acts 1:1.
Often sealed. Isa. 29:11; Dan. 12:4;
Rev. 5:1.
Often written on both sides.
Ezek. 2:10.
The people in ancient times fond of
making. Eccles. 12:12.
Probable origin of. Job 19:23–24.
In a roll. Isa. 34:4; Jer. 36:2;
Ezek. 2:9.
Written with pen and ink.
Jer. 36:18; 3 John 13.

BOTTLES

Bottles

First mention of, in Scripture.
Gen. 21:14.

Illustrative of
The afflicted, when dried up.
Ps. 119:83.
The clouds. Job 38:37.
God's remembrance. Ps. 56:8.

The impatient, when ready to
burst. Job 32:19.
Severe judgments, when broken.
Isa. 30:14; Jer. 19:10; 48:12.
Sinners ripe for judgment.
Jer. 13:12–14.

Made of skins
Marred by age and use.
Josh. 9:4, 13.
Shriveled and dried by smoke.
Ps. 119:83.
Sometimes probably of large
dimensions. 1 Sam. 25:18;
2 Sam. 16:1.
When old, unfit for holding new
wine. Matt. 9:17; Mark 2:22.
The people in ancient times often
drank from. Hab. 2:15.
Some made of earthenware.
Jer. 19:1.

Used for holding
Milk. Judg. 4:19.
Water. Gen. 21:14–15, 19.
Wine. 1 Sam. 1:24; 16:20.

Bottles

BOW
Called the battle bow. Zech. 9:10;
10:4.
Drawn with full force. 2 Kings 9:24.
Given as a sign of friendship.
1 Sam. 18:4.
Held in the left hand. Ezek. 39:3.

An instrument of war. Gen. 48:22;
Isa. 7:24.

Illustrative of
The hypocrite, when deceitful.
Ps. 78:57; Hos. 7:16.
The overthrow of power, when
broken. 1 Sam. 2:4; Jer. 49:35;
Hos. 1:5; 2:18.
Strength and power. Job 29:20.
The tongue of the wicked.
Ps. 11:2; Jer. 9:3.
The Jews taught to use.
2 Sam. 1:18.
Often furnished by the state.
2 Chron. 26:14.
For shooting arrows. 1 Chron. 12:2.
Sometimes used in hunting.
Gen. 27:3.

Those who use, called
Archers. 1 Sam. 31:3; Jer. 51:3.
Bowmen. Jer. 4:29.

Used expertly by
Benjamites. 1 Chron. 12:2;
2 Chron. 14:8.
Elamites. Jer. 49:35.
Lydians. Jer. 46:9.
Philistines. 1 Sam. 31:2–3.
Sons of Reuben, Gad, and
Manasseh. 1 Chron. 5:18.
Usually of steel. 2 Sam. 22:35;
Job 20:24.
Of the vanquished, broken and
burned. Ps. 37:15; Ezek. 39:9.

BOWELS

Emotions
Strong emotion. Job 30:27.
Love. Song of Sol. 5:4.
Compassion. Col. 3:12.
Sexual reproductive system. 2 Sam.
16:11; Ps. 71:6.

BRANCH
Figurative sense. Prov. 11:28;
Hos. 14:6; Isa. 60:21;
John 15:2–5.
Fruitless, cut off. John 15:2, 6.
Pruning of. Isa. 18:5; Dan. 4:14;
John 15:6; Rom. 11:17, 21.
A title of Christ. Isa. 11:1; Jer. 23:5;
33:15; Zech. 3:8; 6:12.
Symbolic name of Joshua.
Zech. 6:12.

BRASS (OR COPPER)
Antiquity of working in. Gen. 4:22.
Canaan abounded in. Deut. 8:9;
33:25.

Characterized by
Fusibility. Ezek. 22:18, 20.
Hardness. Lev. 26:19.
Sonorousness. 1 Cor. 13:1.
Strength. Job 40:18.
Yellow color. Ezra 8:27.
Coined for money. Matt. 10:9;
Mark 12:41.
Collected by David for the temple.
1 Chron. 22:3, 14, 16; 29:2.
Dug out of the mountains. Deut. 8:9.
Extensive commerce in.
Ezek. 27:13; Rev. 18:12.

Illustrative of
Decrees of God. Zech. 6:1.
Earth made barren. Lev. 26:19.
Extreme drought. Deut. 28:23.
Macedonian Empire. Dan. 2:39.
Obstinate sinners. Isa. 48:4;
Jer. 6:28.
Strength and firmness of Christ.
Dan. 10:6; Rev. 1:15.
Strength given to believers.
Jer. 15:20; Mic. 4:13.
Inferior in value to gold and silver.
Isa. 60:17; Dan. 2:32, 39.

Made into
Altars. Exod. 27:2; 39:39.
Bars for gates. 1 Kings 4:13.
Basins. Exod. 30:18;
1 Kings 7:38.
Chains. Judg. 16:21;
2 Kings 25:7.
Gates. Ps. 107:16; Isa. 45:2.
Greaves for the legs. 1 Sam. 17:6.
Helmets. 1 Sam. 17:5.
Household utensils. Mark 7:4.
Idols. Dan. 5:4; Rev. 9:20.
Instruments of music.
1 Chron. 15:19.
Mirrors. Exod. 38:8.
Pillars. 1 Kings 7:15–16.
Sacred articles. Exod. 27:3;
1 Kings 7:45.
Shields. 1 Kings 14:27;
2 Chron. 12:10.
Sockets for pillars.
Exod. 38:10–11, 17.
Moses made the serpent of.
Num. 21:9; 2 Kings 18:4.

Offerings of
Purified by smelting. Job 28:2.
For the tabernacle. Exod. 38:29.
For the temple. 1 Chron. 29:6–7.

Taken in war
Cleansed by fire. Num. 31:21–23.
Generally consecrated to God.
Josh. 6:19, 24;
2 Sam. 8:10–11.
Often in great quantities.
Josh. 22:8; 2 Sam. 8:8;
2 Kings 25:13–16.
Takes a high polish. 2 Chron. 4:16;
Ezek. 1:7.
Working in, a trade. Gen. 4:22;
1 Kings 7:14; 2 Chron. 24:12;
2 Tim. 4:14.

BRAZEN SERPENT
Made by Moses for the healing of the
Israelites. Num. 21:9.
A symbol of Christ. John 3:14–15.
Worshiped by Israelites.
2 Kings 18:4.

BREAD

Baked
In ovens. Lev. 26:26; Hos. 7:4–7.
On coals of fire. Isa. 44:19;
John 21:9.
On hearths. Gen. 18:6.
Broken for use. Lam. 4:4;
Matt. 14:19.
Corn ground for making. Isa. 28:28.
Crumb of, used to wipe the fingers,
thrown under the table.
Matt. 15:27; Luke 16:21.
Firstfruits of, offered to God.
Num. 15:19–20.

Formed into
Cakes. 2 Sam. 6:19;
1 Kings 17:13.
Given by God. Ruth 1:6;
Matt. 6:11.
Loaves. 1 Sam. 10:3–4;
Matt. 14:17.
Wafers. Exod. 16:31; 29:23.

Illustrative of
Abundance, when plentiful.
Deut. 8:9; Ezek. 16:49.
Affliction (of adversity). Isa. 30:20.
Christ. John 6:33–35.
Communion of believers, when
partaking of. Acts 2:46;
1 Cor. 10:17.
Death of Christ, when broken.
Matt. 26:26, with
1 Cor. 11:23–24.

Oppression (of wickedness).
Prov. 4:17.
Poverty, when in lack of.
1 Sam. 2:36; Ps. 37:25;
Prov. 12:9; Isa. 3:7; Lam. 1:11.
Sloth (of idleness). Prov. 31:27.
Sorrow (of tears). Ps. 80:5.
Unlawful gain (of deceit).
Prov. 20:17.
Kept in baskets. Gen. 40:16;
Exod. 29:32.

Made of
Barley. Judg. 7:13; John 6:9.
Beans, millet, etc. Ezek. 4:9.
Manna (in the wilderness).
Num. 11:8.
Wheat. Exod. 29:2; Ps. 81:16.
Making of, a trade. Gen. 40:2;
Jer. 37:21.
Multitudes miraculously fed by Christ
with. Matt. 14:19–21; 15:34–37.
Nutritious and strengthening.
Ps. 104:15.
Offered with sacrifices.
Exod. 29:2, 23; Num. 28:2.
Often given as a present.
1 Sam. 25:18; 2 Sam. 16:2;
1 Chron. 12:40.
Often put for the whole sustenance
of man. Gen. 3:19; 39:6;
Matt. 6:11.
Ordinary, called common.
1 Sam. 21:4
Placed on table of shipboard.
Exod. 25:30.
Plenty of, promised to the obedient.
Lev. 26:5.
Principal food of the people in
ancient times. Gen. 18:5; 21:14;
27:17; Judg. 19:5.
Publicly sold. Matt. 14:15; 15:33.
Sacred, called hallowed.
1 Sam. 21:4, 6.

Scarceness of, sent as a punishment.
Ps. 105:16; Isa. 3:1; Ezek. 4:16.
Served after funerals.
Ezek. 24:17–22.
Sometimes unleavened.
Exod. 12:18; 1 Cor. 5:8.
In times of scarcity, sold by weight.
Lev. 26:26; Ezek. 4:16.
Troughs used for kneading.
Exod. 12:34.
Usually leavened. Lev. 23:17;
Matt. 13:33.
Was kneaded. Gen. 18:6; Jer. 7:18;
Hos. 7:4.
When old dry and moldy. Isa.
9:5, 12.
With water, the food of prisons.
1 Kings 22:27.
Yielded by the earth. Job 28:5;
Isa. 55:10.

BREASTPLATE
Armor for soldiers. Rev. 9:9, 17.
Directions for the making of.
Exod. 28:15–30.
Figurative sense. Isa. 59:17;
Eph. 6:14; 1 Thess. 5:8.
Freewill offering of materials for.
Exod. 35:5–9, 27.
For the high priest. Exod. 25:7.
Made by Bezaleel. Exod. 39:8, 21.
Worn by Aaron. Exod. 29:5;
Lev. 8:8.

BREATH
Figurative sense. Ezek. 37:9.
Of God. 2 Sam. 22:16;
Job 4:9; 33:4; 37:10;
Pss. 18:15; 33:6; Isa. 30:33.
Of life. Gen. 2:7; 7:22; Acts 17:25.

BREECHES
See Undergarments

BRIBES
Characterize the wicked. Ps. 26:10;
Amos 5:12.
Create injustice. Deut. 16:19.
Forbidden by God. Exod. 23:8;
Lev. 19:13.
Punishment for. Job 15:34.

BRICK
Made by Israelites. Exod. 5:7–19;
2 Sam. 12:31; Jer. 43:9;
Nah. 3:14.

Used in building
Altars. Isa. 65:3.
Babel. Gen. 11:3.
Cities in Egypt. Exod. 1:11, 14.
Houses. Isa. 9:10.

BRIDE
Figurative sense. Ps. 45:10–17;
Rev. 19:7–8; 21:2, 9; 22:17.
Ornaments of. Isa. 49:18; 61:10;
Jer. 2:32; Rev. 21:2.
Presence to. Gen. 24:53.
Maids of. Gen. 24:59, 61; 29:24,
29.

BRIDEGROOM
Companions of. Judg. 14:7–11.
Exempt from military duty.
Deut. 24:5.
Figurative sense. Ezek. 16:8–14.
Joy with. Matt. 9:15; Mark 2:19–20;
Luke 5:34–35.
Ornaments of. Isa. 61:10.
Parable of. Matt. 25:1–13.
Song of. Song of Sol. 4:7–16.

BRIDLE
For animals. Ps. 32:9; Prov. 26:3;
Rev. 14:20.
Figurative sense. 2 Kings 19:28; Ps.
39:1; James 1:26.

BRIER
Symbolic. Isa. 5:6; 55:13; Ezek. 2:6;
28:24.

BRIMSTONE
Fire and, rained upon Sodom.
Gen. 19:24; Luke 17:29.
In Palestine. Deut. 29:23.
Symbolic sense. Job 18:15; Ps 11:6;
Isa. 30:33; Ezek. 38:22;
Rev. 9:17–18; 14:10; 19:20;
21:8.

BROTH
Literal. Judg. 6:19–20;
2 Kings 4:38; Isa. 65:4.
Symbolic sense. Ezek. 24:5.

BROTHER
Any Israelite. Jer. 34:9; Obad. 10.
Brother's widow, law concerning
Levirate marriage of.
Deut. 25:5–10; Matt. 22:24;
Mark 12:19; Luke 20:28.
Companion. 2 Sam. 1:26;
1 Kings 13:30; 20:33.
A fraternal epithet, especially among
Christians, instituted by Christ.
Matt. 12:50; 25:40;
Heb. 2:11–12.
Humankind. Gen. 9:5; Matt. 18:35;
1 John 3:15.
Joseph's love for his brothers.
Gen. 43:30–34; 45:1–5;
50:19–25.
Love of. Prov. 17:17; 18:24;
Song of Sol. 8:1.
Neighbor. Deut. 23:7; Judg. 21:6;
Neh. 5:7.
Peter. 1 Pet. 1:22.
Reuben's love for
Joseph. Gen. 37:21, 22.

Signifies a relative. Gen. 14:16;
29:12.
Unfaithful. Prov. 27:10.
Used among the Israelites.
Lev. 19:17; Deut. 22:1–4.
Used by disciples. Acts 9:17; 21:20;
Rom. 16:23; 2 Cor. 2:13.

BROTHERHOOD
Basis for peace in. Gen. 13:8.
Betrayal of. Gen. 4:1–16; 37:1–36;
James 2:1–5.
Blessings of. Ps. 133:1;
Prov. 17:17.
Danger of offending brethren.
Rom. 14:21; 1 Cor. 8:11.
Responsibility of. Gen. 4:9;
Deut. 15:11; Rom. 12:10.
Test of. 1 John 2:9; 3:14; 4:20.

BROTHERLY LOVE
See Love, Brotherly

BUILDER
Used of God. Ps. 118:22;
Matt. 21:42; Acts 4:11;
Heb. 11:10; 1 Pet. 2:7.

BUILDING
Symbolic of eternal dwelling.
2 Cor. 5:1.

BULL
Blood of, in sacrifice. Heb. 9:13;
10:4.
Wild, caught in net. Isa. 51:20.

BULRUSH
Boats made of. Isa. 18:2.
Moses, ark of. Exod. 2:3.
Symbolic sense. Isa. 58:5.

BULWARK
Literal sense. Deut. 20:20;
2 Chron. 26:15; Eccles. 9:14.
Symbolic sense. Ps. 48:13;
Isa. 26:1.

BURDENS
Relief of. Ps. 55:22;
Matt. 11:28–30.
Sharing of. Gal. 6:2.
Weight of. 1 Kings 12:9; Job 7:20;
Ps. 119:28.

BURIAL
Antiquity of coffins for. Gen. 50:26.
Antiquity of purchasing places for.
Gen. 23:7–16.

Attended by
Family of the dead.
Gen. 50:5–6, 8; Matt. 8:21.
Female friends. Mark 15:47;
Luke 7:13.
Great lamentation at.
Gen. 50:10–11;
2 Sam. 3:31–32.
Hired mourners. Jer. 9:17–18.
Number of friends, etc. Gen. 50:7,
9; 2 Sam. 3:31; Luke 7:13.

Body was
Anointed for. Matt. 26:12.
Carried on a bier to. 2 Sam. 3:31;
Luke 7:14.
Preserved with spices.
John 19:39–40.
Sometimes burned before.
1 Sam. 31:12.
Washed before. Acts 9:37.
Wound in linen for. John 11:44;
19:40.
Design of. Gen. 23:3–4.
Dishonorable, compared to the burial
of a donkey. Jer. 22:10.

Of enemies, sometimes performed by the conquerors. 1 Kings 11:15; Ezek. 39:11–14.

Followed by a feast. 2 Sam. 3:35; Jer. 16:7–8; Hos. 9:4.

Of the friendless, a kind act. 2 Sam. 2:5.

Illustrative of regeneration. Rom. 6:4; Col. 2:12.

Jews anxious to be interred in their family places of. Gen. 47:29–31; 49:29–30;   50:25; 2 Sam. 19:37.

Often took place immediately after death. John 11:17, 39, with Acts 5:6, 10.

Orations sometimes made at. 2 Sam. 3:33–34.

Perfumes burned at. 2 Chron. 16:14; Jer. 34:5.

Of persons embalmed, deferred for seventy days. Gen. 50:3–4.

Of persons hanged, always on the days of execution. Deut. 21:23; John 19:31.

Places of

For criminals, marked by heaps. Josh. 7:26.

Frequently prepared and pointed out during life. Gen. 50:5; 2 Chron. 16:14; Matt. 27:60.

Held in high veneration. Neh. 2:3, 5.

Members of a family interred in the same. Gen. 25:10; 49:31; 2 Sam. 2:32.

Often desecrated by idolatry. Isa. 65:3–4.

Pillars erected on. Gen. 35:20.

Provided for aliens and strangers. Matt. 27:7.

Provided for the common people. Jer. 26:23.

Sometimes had inscriptions. 2 Kings 23:17.

Sometimes not apparent. Luke 11:44.

Tombs erected over. Matt. 23:27–29.

Visited by sorrowing friends. John 11:31.

Were ceremonially unclean. Num. 19:16, 18.

Places used for

Caves hewn out of rocks. Isa. 22:16; Matt. 27:60.

City of David for the kings of Judah. 1 Kings 2:10; 2 Chron. 21:20; 24:16.

Gardens. 2 Kings 21:18, 26; John 19:41.

Houses of the deceased. 1 Sam. 25:1; 1 Kings 2:34.

Natural caves. Gen. 23:19; John 11:38.

Tops of the hills. Josh. 24:33; 2 Kings 23:16.

Under trees. Gen. 35:8; 1 Sam. 31:13.

Privation of

Considered a calamity. Eccles. 6:3.

Probable origin of. Gen. 4:9–10.

Right of all nations. Judg. 16:31; John 19:38.

Threatened as a punishment. 2 Kings 9:10; Jer. 8:2; 16:4.

BURNING BUSH
Moses at. Exod. 3:2–5; Acts 7:30.

BURNT OFFERING
See Offering, Burnt

BURNT OFFERING, ALTAR OF

Ahaz removed and profaned.
2 Kings 16:10–16.

All gifts to be presented at.
Matt. 5:23–24.

All its articles of brass.
Exod. 27:3; 38:3.

All sacrifices to be offered on.
Exod. 29:38–42; Isa. 56:7.

Anointed and sanctified with holy oil.
Exod. 40:10; Lev. 8:10–11.

The blood of sacrifices put on the
horns and poured at the foot of.
Exod. 29:12; Lev. 4:7, 18, 25;
8:15.

Called
Altar of God. Ps. 43:4.
Altar of the Lord. Mal. 2:13.
Bronze altar. Exod. 39:39;
1 Kings 8:64.
Cleansed and purified with blood.
Exod. 29:36–37.
Covered with brass. Exod. 27:2.
Dimensions, etc., of. Exod. 27:1;
38:1.
Furnished with rings and staves.
Exod. 27:6–7; 38:5–7.
Horns on the corners of.
Exod. 27:2; 38:2.

Its fire
Came from before the Lord.
Lev. 9:24.
Consumed the sacrifices.
Lev. 1:8–9.
Was continually burning.
Lev. 6:13.

The Jews condemned for swearing
lightly by. Matt. 23:18–19.

Made after a divine pattern.
Exod. 27:8.

Network grate of brass placed in.
Exod. 27:4–5; 38:4.

Nothing polluted or defective to be
offered on. Lev. 22:22;
Mal. 1:7–8.

Offering at the dedication of.
Num. 7.

Placed in the court before the door of
the tabernacle. Exod. 40:6, 29.

Priests
Alone to serve. Num. 18:3, 7.
Derived support from.
1 Cor. 9:13.
Sacrifices bound to the horns of.
Ps. 118:27.
Sanctified by God. Exod. 29:44.
Sanctified whatever touched it.
Exod. 29:37.
A type of Christ. Heb. 13:10.
Was most holy. Exod. 40:10.

BUSYBODY

Commandment against. Prov. 20:3;
2 Thess. 3:11; 1 Tim. 5:13;
1 Pet. 4:15.

BUTLER

Pharaoh's imprisoned and released.
Gen. 40.

BUTTER

Made by churning. Prov. 30:33.

CAGE
For birds, unclean. Jer. 5:27;
Rev. 18:2.

CALF
Altars of, destroyed. 2 Kings 23:4,
15–20.
Golden, made by Aaron. Exod. 32;
Deut. 9:16; Neh. 9:18;
Ps. 106:19; Acts 7:41.
Images of, set up in Bethel and Dan
by Jeroboam. 1 Kings 12:28–33;
2 Kings 10:29.
Offered in sacrifice. Mic. 6:6.
Prophecies against the golden calves
at Bethel. 1 Kings 13:1–5, 32;
Jer. 48:13; Hos. 8:5–6; 10:5–6,
15; 13:2; Amos 3:14; 4:4; 8:14.
Worshiped by Jehu. 2 Kings 10:29.

CALL OF GOD
See God, Call of

CAMEL
Docility of. Gen. 24:11.
Forbidden as food. Lev. 11:4.
Hair of, made into cloth. Matt. 3:4;
Mark 1:6.
Herds of. Gen. 12:16; 24:35;
30:43; 1 Sam. 30:17;
1 Chron. 27:30; Job 1:3, 17.
Ornaments of. Judg. 8:21, 26.
Stables for. Ezek. 25:5.

Uses of
For carrying burdens. Gen. 24:10;
37:25; 1 Kings 10:2;
2 Kings 8:9; 1 Chron. 12:40;
Isa. 30:6.
For cavalry. 1 Sam. 30:17.
Drawing chariots. Isa. 21:7.
For milk. Gen. 32:15.
Posts. Esther 8:10, 14; Jer. 2:23.
For riding. Gen. 24:10, 61, 64;
31:17.

CAMP
Of the Israelites about the tabernacle.
Num. 2; 3.

CANNIBALISM
Moses prophesied. Lev. 26:29;
Deut. 28:53–57.

CAPITAL LABOR
See Labor, Capital

CAPITAL PUNISHMENT
See **PUNISHMENT, CAPITAL**

CAPTAIN
Angel of the Lord, called.
Josh. 5:14; 2 Chron. 13:12.
Christ called. Heb. 2:10.
Commander-in-chief of an army.
Deut. 20:9; Judg. 4:2;
1 Sam. 14:50; 1 Kings 2:35;
16:16; 1 Chron. 27:34.
David's. 2 Sam. 23,
1 Chron. 11–12
Of fifties. 2 Kings 1:9; Isa. 3:3.
Of the guard. Gen. 37:36;
2 Kings 25:8.
Of hundreds. 2 Kings 11:15.
King appoints. 1 Sam. 18:13;
2 Sam. 17:25; 18:1.
Leader. 1 Chron. 11:21; 12:34;
2 Chron. 17:14–19; John 18:12.

Signifying any commander.
1 Sam. 9:16; 22:2; 2 Kings 20:5.
Of thousands. Num. 31:48;
1 Sam. 17:18; 1 Chron. 28:1.
Of the tribes. Num. 2.
Of the ward. Jer. 37:13.

CAPTIVE
Advance to positions in state.
Gen. 41:39–45; Esther 2:8–9;
Dan. 1.
Blinded. Judg. 16:21; Jer. 39:7.
Confined in pits. Isa. 51:14.
Cruelty to. Num. 31:9–20; 21:10;
Josh. 8:29; 10:15–40; 11:11;
Judg. 7:25; 8:21; 21:11;
1 Sam. 15:32–33; 2 Sam. 8:2;
2 Kings 8:12; Jer. 39:6;
Luke 20:13;.
Enslaved. Deut. 20:14; 2 Kings 5:2;
Ps. 44:12; Joel 3:6.
Kindness to. 2 Kings 25:27–30;
Ps. 106:46.
Maimed. Judg. 1:6–7.
Other indignities to. Isa. 20:4.
Prisoner of war. Gen. 14:12;
1 Sam. 30:1–2.
Ravished. Lam. 5:11–13;
Zech. 14:2.
Ripping women with child.
2 Kings 8:12; Amos 1:13.
Robbed. Ezek. 23:25–26.
Tortured under saws and harrows.
2 Sam. 12:31; 1 Chron. 20:3.
Twenty thousand by Amaziah.
2 Chron. 25:11–12.

CAPTIVITY
Hope in. Ezra 9:9; Zeph. 2:7.
Lessons of. Exod. 13:3; Isa. 5:13;
Lam. 1:3.
Redemption from. Deut. 30:3;
Job 42:10; Ps. 14:7; Jer. 29:14.

Of sin. Rom. 7:23.
Of thoughts. 2 Cor. 10:5.

CARE, GOD'S
Affirmed in faith. Ps. 23.
Assured through trust. Ps. 55:22.
Illustrated in the church.
1 Cor. 12:25.
Promised. 1 Pet. 5:7.

CAREER
Assigned by God. Exod. 31:1–11;
1 Cor. 7:17.
Dedication in. Ps. 119:32.
Diversity of. Rom. 12:68;
Eph. 4:11.
Faithfulness in. 1 Cor. 7:24.
Reward of. 2 Tim. 2:6.

CAREER DECISIONS
See Decisions, Career

CARELESSNESS
Admonition against. Heb. 2:1.
Danger of. Ezek. 39:6; Matt. 12:36.
Folly of. Prov. 14:16;
Matt. 7:26–27.
Warning against. Deut. 8:11;
Isa. 47:8; Luke 8:15.

CARNAL MINDEDNESS
See Worldly Mindedness

CARPENTRY
Building the ark. Gen. 6:14–16.
Carpenters. Jer. 24:1; Zech. 1:20.
David's palace. 2 Sam. 5:11.
Jesus. Mark 6:3.
Joseph. Matt. 13:55.
Making idols. Isa. 41:7; 44:13.
Tabernacle, and furniture of.
Exod. 31:2–9.
Temple. 2 Kings 12:11; 22:6.

CARVING
Beds decorated with. Prov. 7:16.
Idols manufactured by. Deut. 7:5;
  Isa. 44:9–17; 45:20;
  Hab. 2:18–19.

Persons skilled in
  Bezaleel. Exod. 31:5.
  Hiram. 1 Kings 7:13–51;
  2 Chron. 2:13–14.
Woodwork of the temple.
  1 Kings 6:18, 29, 32, 35;
  Ps. 74:6.

CASTLE
Bars of. Prov. 18:19.
"The house is my castle."
  Deut. 24:10–11.
A tower. Gen. 25:16; Num. 31:10;
  1 Chron. 11:5, 7;
  2 Chron. 17:12; 27:4;
  Acts 21:34, 37; 23:10, 16, 32.

CATERPILLAR
Sent as a judgment. 1 Kings 8:37;
  Pss. 78:46; 105:34; Jer. 51:27;
  Joel 1:4; 2:25.

CATTLE
Bashan. Ps. 22:12; Ezek. 39:18;
  Amos 4:1.
Gilead adapted to the raising of.
  Num. 32:1–4.
Sheltered. Gen. 33:17.
Stall-fed. Prov. 15:17.
Used for sacrifice. 1 Kings 8:63.

CAVALRY
On camels. 1 Sam. 30:17.
Mounted on horses. Exod. 14:23;
  1 Sam. 13:5; 2 Sam. 8:4;
  1 Kings 4:26; 2 Chron. 8:6;
  9:25; 12:3; Isa. 30:16; 31:1;

  Jer. 4:29; Zech. 10:5;
  Rev. 9:16–18.

CAVE
Of Adullam. 1 Sam. 22:1;
  2 Sam. 23:13; 1 Chron. 11:15.
Burial place.
  Gen. 23:9–20; 25:9; 49:29–32;
  50:13; John 11:38.
En-gedi. 1 Sam. 24:3–8.
Place of refuge. Josh. 10:16–27;
  Judg. 6:2; 1 Sam. 13:6;
  1 Kings 18:4, 13; 19:9, 13.

Used as a dwelling
  Believers. Heb. 11:38.
  Elijah. 1 Kings 19:9.
  Israelites. Ezek. 33:27.
  By Lot. Gen. 19:30.

CEDAR
David's ample provision of, in
  Jerusalem for the temple.
  2 Chron. 1.15; 2:3–4.
In David's palace. 2 Sam. 5:11;
  1 Chron. 17:1.
Furnished by Hiram, king of Tyre for
  Solomon's temple.
  1 Kings 5:6–10; 9:11;
  2 Chron. 2:16.
For masts of ships. Ezek. 27:5.
In purifications. Lev. 14:4, 6,
  49–52; Num. 19:6.
In Solomon's palace. 1 Kings 7:2.
Used in rebuilding the temple.
  Ezra 3:7.
Valuable for building purposes.
  Isa. 9:10.

CELIBACY
Jesus' teaching concerning.
  Matt. 19:10–12.
Paul's teaching concerning.
  1 Cor. 7:1–9, 25–26, 32–39.

Wrongly insisted on by some
teachers. 1 Tim. 4:1–3.

CENSER
For the temple, made of gold.
1 Kings 7:50; 2 Chron. 4:22;
Heb. 9:4.
Those that Korah used were
converted into plates.
Num. 16:37–39.
Used for offering incense.
Lev. 16:12; Num. 4:14; 16:6–7,
16–18, 46; Rev. 8:3.
Used in idolatrous rights. Ezek. 8:11.

CENSUS
By David. 2 Sam. 24:1–9;
1 Chron. 21:1–8; 27:24.
Numbering of Israel by Moses.
Exod. 38:26; Num. 1;
3:14–43; 26.
A poll tax to be levied at each.
Exod. 30:12–16; 38:26.
Of the Roman Empire. Luke 2:1–3.

CENTURION
Of Capernaum, comes to Jesus in
behalf of his servant.
Matt. 8:5–13; Luke 7:1–10.
In charge of soldiers who crucified
Jesus. Matt. 27:54; Mark 15:39;
Luke 23:47.
A commander of one hundred
soldiers in the Roman army.
Mark 15:44–45;
Acts 21:32; 22:25–26;
23:17, 23; 24:23.

CERTAINTY
Of faith. John 6:69; Heb. 10:22.
Of hope. Heb. 6:11.
Of judgment for sin. Num. 32:23;
Heb. 9:27.

Of reward for righteousness.
Prov. 11:18.
Of salvation. 2 Pet. 1:10.
Of truth. Prov. 22:21.

CHAFF
Literal sense. Jer. 23:28.
Symbolic sense. Job 21:18;
Pss. 1:4; 35:5; Isa. 5:24; 17:13;
Dan. 2:35; Hos. 13:3;
Matt. 3:12; Luke 3:17.

CHAINS
On the breastplate of the high priest.
Exod. 28:14; 39:15.
As ornaments on camels.
Judg. 8:26.
A partition of, in the temple.
1 Kings 6:21; 7:17.
Used as ornaments, worn by
princesses. Gen. 41:42; Dan. 5:7,
29.
Used in a symbolic sense. Ps. 73:6;
Prov. 1:9; Lam. 3:7;
Ezek. 7:23–27; 2 Pet. 2:4;
Jude 6; Rev. 20:1.
Used to confine prisoners. Pss. 68:6;
149:8; Jer. 40:4; Acts 12:6–7;
21:33; 28:20; 2 Tim. 1:16.
Worn on ankles. Num. 31:50;
Isa. 3:19.

CHAMPIONSHIP
How battles were decided
Goliath and David.
1 Sam. 17:8–53.
Young men of David's and Abner's
armies. 2 Sam. 2:14–17.
Representatives of the Philistines'
and David's armies.
2 Sam. 21:15–22.

CHANCELLOR
A state officer. Ezra 4:8–9, 17.

CHANGE OF VENUE
See Venue, Change of

CHARACTER

Of believers
Attentive to Christ's voice.
  John 10:3–4.
Blameless and harmless.
  Phil. 2:15.
Bold. Prov. 28:1.
Contrite. Isa. 57:15; 66:2.
Devoted. Acts 8:2; 22:12.
Eager to do good works.
  Titus 2:14.
Faithful. Rev. 17:14.
Fearing God. Mal. 3:16.
Following Christ. John 10:4, 27.
Generous. Isa. 32:8; 2 Cor. 9:13.
Gentle. Prov. 16:19.
Godly. Ps. 4:3; 2 Pet. 2:9.
Holy. Deut. 7:6; 14:2; Col. 3:12.
Humble. Ps. 34:2; 1 Pet. 5:5.
Hungering for righteousness.
  Matt. 5:6.
Just. Gen. 6:9; Hab. 2:4;
  Luke 2:25.
Led by the Spirit. Rom. 8:14.
Loathing themselves.
  Ezek. 20:43.
Meek. Isa. 29:19.
Merciful. Ps. 37:26; Matt. 5:7.
New creatures. 2 Cor. 5:17;
  Eph. 2:10.
Obedient. Rom. 16:19;
  1 Pet. 1:14.
Poor in spirit. Matt. 5:3.
Prudent. Prov. 16:21.
Pure in heart. Matt. 5:8;
  1 John 3:3.
Righteous. Isa. 60:21; Luke 1:6.

Sincere. John 1:47; 2 Cor. 1:12;
  2:17.
Steadfast. Acts 2:42; Col. 2:5.
Taught of God. Isa. 54:13;
  1 John 2:27.
True. 2 Cor. 6:8.
Undefiled. Ps. 119:1.
Upright. 1 Kings 3:6; Ps. 15:2.
Watchful. Luke 12:37.
Defamation of, punished.
  Deut. 22:13–19.
Firmness of. Ps. 57:7; Heb. 10:23.
Good. Prov. 22:1; Eccles. 7:1.
Instability of. Prov. 24:21.

Instance of instable character
King Saul in his treatment of
  David. 1 Sam. 18–19.

Instances of firm character
Joseph in resisting Potiphar's wife.
  Gen. 39:7–12.
Pilate. John 19:22.
Paul. Acts 20:22–24; 21:13–14.

Of the wicked
Abominable. Rev. 21:8.
Alienated from God. Eph. 4:18;
  Col. 1:21.
Antagonistic, disobedient.
  Prov. 21:8; Isa. 57:17.
Blasphemous. Luke 22:65;
  Rev. 16:9.
Blinded. 2 Cor. 4:4; Eph. 4:18.
Boastful. Ps. 10:3; 49:6.
Condemned. 2 Cor. 13:5;
  2 Tim. 3:8; Titus 1:16.
Conspiring against believers.
  Neh. 4:8; 6:2; Ps. 38:12.
Corrupt. Matt. 7:17; Eph. 4:22.
Covetous. Mic. 2:2; Rom. 1:29.
Deceitful. Ps. 5:6; Rom. 3:13.
Delighting in the sin of others.
  Prov. 2:14; Rom. 1:32.

Despising believers. Neh. 2:19; 4:2; 2 Tim. 3:3–4.

Destructive. Isa. 59:7.

Disobedient. Neh. 9:26; Titus 3:3; 1 Pet. 2:7.

Enticing to evil. Prov. 1:10–14; 2 Tim. 3:6.

Envious. Neh. 2:10; Titus 3:3.

Evildoers. Jer. 13:23; Mic. 7:3.

Fearful. Prov. 28:1; Rev. 21:8.

Fierce. Prov. 16:29; 2 Tim. 3:3.

Foolish. Deut. 32:6; Ps. 5:5.

Forgetting God. Job 8:13.

Fraudulent. Ps. 37:21; Mic. 6:11.

Glorying in their shame. Phil. 3:19.

Hard-hearted. Ezek. 3:7.

Hating the light. Job 24:13; John 3:20.

Heady and high-minded. 2 Tim. 3:4.

Hostile to God. Rom. 8:7; Col. 1:21.

Hypocritical. Isa. 29:13; 2 Tim. 3:5.

Ignorant of God. Hos. 4:1; 2 Thess. 1:8.

Impudent. Ezek. 2:4.

Incontinent. 2 Tim. 3:3.

Infidel. Pss. 10:4; 14:1.

Loathsome. Prov. 13:5.

Lovers of pleasure, not of God. 2 Tim. 3:4.

Lying. Pss. 58:3; 62:4; Isa. 59:4.

Mischievous. Prov. 28:8; Mic. 7:3.

Opposing. Pss. 10:8; 94:6.

Persecuting. Pss. 69:26; 109:16.

Perverse. Deut. 32:5.

Prayerless. Job 21:15; Ps. 53:4.

Proud. Ps. 59:12.

Rejoicing in the affliction of believers. Ps. 35:15.

Revealed in one's face. Isa. 3:9.

Selfish. 2 Tim. 3:2.

Sensual. Phil. 3:19; Jude 19.

Stiff-hearted. Ezek. 2:4.

Stiff-necked. Exod. 33:5; Acts 7:51.

Uncircumcised in heart. Jer. 9:26.

Unclean. Isa. 64:6; Eph. 4:19.

Unjust. Prov. 11:7; Isa. 26:18.

Ungodly. Prov. 16:27.

Unholy. 2 Tim. 3:2.

Unmerciful. Rom. 1:31.

Egyptian Chariot

Unprofitable. Matt. 25:30;
Rom. 3:12.
Unruly. Acts 2:40; Titus 1:10.
Unthankful. Luke 6:35;
2 Tim. 3:2.
Unwise. Deut. 32:6.

CHARACTER, STABILITY OF
Expression of. Ps. 57:7.
In one's calling. 1 Cor. 7:20.
Rewards of. Matt. 10:22.

CHARIOT
Chariots of God. 2 Kings 6:17;
Ps. 104:3; Isa. 66:15; Hab. 3:8;
Rev. 9:9.
Cherubim in Solomon's temple
mounted on. 1 Chron. 28:18.
Cities for. 1 Kings 9:19;
2 Chron. 1:14; 8:6; 9:25.
Commanded by captains.
Exod. 14:7; 1 Kings 9:22;
22:31–33; 2 Kings 8:21.
Drawn by camels. Isa. 21:7;
Mic. 1:13.
Imported from Egypt by Solomon.
1 Kings 10:26–29.

Introduced among Israelites by David.
2 Sam. 8:4.
Kings ride in. 2 Chron. 35:24;
Jer. 17:25; 22:4.
Made of iron. Josh. 17:18;
Judg. 1:19.
Royal. Gen. 41:43; 46:29;
2 Kings 5:9; 2 Chron. 35:24;
Jer. 17:25; Acts 8:29.
Symbolic sense. 2 Kings 2:11–12;
Zech. 6:1–8.
Traffic in. Rev. 18:13.
For war. Exod. 14:7, 9, 25;
Josh. 11:4; 1 Sam. 13:5;
1 Kings 20:1, 25; 2 Kings 6:14;
2 Chron. 12:2–3;
Pss. 20:7; 46:9; Jer. 46:9; 47:3;
51:21; Joel 2:5; Nah. 2:3, 4; 3:2.
Wheels of Pharaoh's, providentially
taken off. Exod. 14:25.

CHARISM
An inspired gift, bestowed on the
apostles and early Christians.
Matt. 10:1, 8; Mark 16:17–18;
Luke 10:1, 9, 17, 19; Acts 2:4;
10:44–46; 19:6; 1 Cor. 12.

Egyptian Chariot

CHARITY
See Love

CHASTISEMENT
See Punishment

CHASTITY
See Purity

CHEERFULNESS
And love. Rom. 12:8.
And praise. James 5:13.
And redemption. Isa. 52:9;
Zech. 8:19.
And sharing. Philem. 1:20.
And stewardship. 2 Cor. 9:7.
Value of. Prov. 15:15; 17:22.

CHEESE
Food. 1 Sam. 17:18; 2 Sam. 17:29;
Job 10:10.

CHERUBIM
Animated by the Spirit of God.
Ezek. 1:12, 20.
Called the cherubim of glory.
Heb. 9:5.
Engaged in accomplishing the
purposes of God. Ezek. 1:15, 21;
10:9–11, 16–17.
Form and appearance of.
Ezek. 1:5–11, 13–14.
Glory of God exhibited upon.
Ezek. 1:22, 26–28; 10:4, 18, 20.

Of Gold
Formed out of, and at each end of
the mercy seat.
Exod. 25:18–20.
God's presence manifested
between. 2 Sam. 6:2;
2 Kings 19:15; Pss. 80:1; 99:1.

Oracles or answers of God
delivered from between.
Exod. 25:22; Num. 7:89.
Placed over the ark of the
covenant. 1 Sam. 4:4;
1 Kings 8:6–7; 2 Chron. 5:7–8.
Placed at the entrance of Eden.
Gen. 3:24.

Representations of, made on the
Bases of bronze lavers.
1 Kings 7:28, 36.
Curtains of the tabernacle.
Exod. 26:1, 31.
Doors of the temple.
1 Kings 6:32, 35.
Veil of the tabernacle.
Exod. 26:31.
Veil of the temple. 2 Chron. 3:14.
Walls of the temple. 2 Chron. 3:7.
Riding on, illustrative of majesty and
power of God. 2 Sam. 22:11;
Ps. 18:10.
Sound of their wings was as the voice
of God. Ezek. 1:24; 10:5.

CHICKEN
Broods her young. Matt. 23:37;
Luke 13:34.

CHILD ABUSE

Examples of
Daughter
Of Jephthah. Judg. 11:30–40.
Of Lot. Gen. 19:8.
Infant
Fig. of Jerusalem. Ezek. 16:5.
Israelites in Egypt.
Exod. 1:16–17, 22.
Jews in Bethlehem. Matt. 2:16.
Son
Of Ahab. 2 Kings 16:3.
Of Israelites. 2 Kings 23:10.

Of Manasseh. 2 Chron. 33:6.
Of Mesha. 2 Kings 3:4, 27.
Generational influence. Exod. 34:7.
God better than human fathers.
Luke 11:11–13.
God like compassionate father.
Ps. 103:13.

Injunctions regarding
Expose deeds of darkness.
Eph. 5:11.
Parents not to exasperate children.
Eph. 6:4; Col. 3:21.
Jesus and little children.
Mark 10:13–16.

CHILDISHNESS

As instability and folly. Prov. 22:15;
Eph. 4:14.
Of thought rebuked. 1 Cor. 14:20.
Versus freedom. Gal. 4:3.
Versus spiritual maturity.
1 Cor. 13:11.

CHILDLESSNESS

A reproach. Gen. 16:2; 29:32;
30:1–3, 13; 1 Sam. 1:6; Isa. 4:1;
Luke 1:25.

CHILDLIKENESS

And growth. 1 Pet. 2:2;
1 Cor. 14:20.
And the kingdom. Matt. 10:14.
And obedience. 1 Pet. 1:14.
As saving faith. Matt. 18:3;
Mark 10:15.
As trust. Ps. 131:1–2.

CHILDREN

See also subtopics: Children,
Wicked; Children, Good; Child
Abuse

Amusements of. Zech. 8:5;
Matt. 11:16–17.
Anxiety of the Jews for. Gen. 30:1;
1 Sam. 1:5, 8.
Capable of glorifying God.
Gen. 33:5; Ps. 127:3.
Casting out of weak, etc., alluded to.
Ezek. 16:5.
Christ an example to. Luke 2:51;
John 19:26–27.
Circumcised on the eighth day.
Phil. 3:5.
Could demand their portion during
their father's life. Luke 15:12.
Destruction of, a punishment.
Lev. 26:22; Ezek. 9:6;
Luke 19:44.

Female
Inherited property in default of
sons. Num. 27:1–8;
Josh. 17:1–6.
Taken care of by nurses.
Gen. 35:8.
Usefully employed. Gen. 24:13;
Exod. 2:16.
Fondness and care of mothers for.
Exod. 2:2–10; 1 Sam. 2:19;
1 Kings 3:27; Isa. 49:15;
1 Thess. 2:7–8.
Frequently bore the curse of parents.
Exod. 20:5; Ps. 109:9–10.
Gifts from God. Gen. 33:5;
Ps. 127:3.
Of God's people, holy. Ezra 9:2;
1 Cor. 7:14.
Of God's people, interested in the
promises. Deut. 29:29;
Acts 2:39.
Grief occasioned by loss of.
Gen. 37:35; 44:27–29;
2 Sam. 13:37; Jer. 6:26; 31:15.
Heritage from the Lord. Pss. 113:9;
127:3.

Illegitimate
Despised by their brethren.
Judg. 11:2.
Excluded from the congregation.
Deut. 23:2.
Had no inheritance.
Gen. 21:10, 14; Gal. 4:30.
Not cared for by the father.
Heb. 12:8.
Sometimes sent away with gifts.
Gen. 25:6.
Inhuman practice of offering to idols.
2 Kings 17:31; 2 Chron. 28:3;
33:6.

Male
Birth of, announced to the father
by a messenger. Jer. 20:15.
Under the care of tutors, until they
came of age. 2 Kings 10:1;
Gal. 4:1–2.
If firstborn, belonged to God and
were redeemed.
Exod. 13:12–13, 15.
Inherited the possessions of their
father. Deut. 21:16–17;
Luke 12:13–14.
Received the blessing of their
father before his death.
Gen. 27:1–4; 48:15; 49.
Usefully employed. 1 Sam. 9:3;
17:15.
Mode of giving public instruction to.
Luke 2:46; Acts 22:3.
Mostly nursed by the mothers.
1 Sam. 1:22; 1 Kings 3:21;
Ps. 22:9; Song of Sol. 8:1.
Named at circumcision. Luke 1:59;
2:21.

Not to have
Considered an affliction.
Gen. 15:2–3; Jer. 22:30.

A reproach in Israel.
1 Sam. 1:6–7; Luke 1:25.
Numerous considered a special
blessing. Pss. 115:14; 127:4–5.
Often given in answer to prayer.
Gen. 25:21; 1 Sam. 1:27;
Luke 1:13.
Often numerous. 2 Kings 10:1;
1 Chron. 4:27.
Often prayed for. 1 Sam. 1:10–11;
Luke 1:13.
Often wicked and rebellious.
2 Kings 2:23.
Power of parents over, during
patriarchal age. Gen. 9:24–25;
21:14; 38:24.
Prosperity of, greatly depended on
obeying parents. Deut. 4:40;
12:25, 28; Ps. 128:1–3.
Rebellious, punished by the civil
power. Exod. 21:15–17;
Deut. 21:18–21.
Resignation manifested at loss of.
Lev. 10:19–20;
2 Sam. 12:18–23; Job 1:19–21.

Should
Attend to parental teaching.
Prov. 1:8–9.
Fear God. Prov. 24:21.
Fear parents. Lev. 19:3.
Honor parents. Exod. 20:12;
Heb. 19:9.
Honor the aged. Lev. 19:32;
1 Pet. 5:5.
Not imitate bad parents.
Ezek. 20:18.
Obey God. Deut. 30:2.
Obey parents. Prov. 6:20;
Eph. 6:1.
Remember God. Eccles. 12:1.
Take care of parents. 1 Tim. 5:4.

Should be

Brought early to the house of God.
1 Sam. 1:21.

Brought to Christ.
Mark 10:13–16.

Instructed in the ways of God.
Deut. 31:12–13; Prov. 22:6.

Judiciously trained. Prov. 22:15;
29:17; Eph. 6:4.

Sometimes born when parents were
old. Gen. 15:3, 6; 17:17;
Luke 1:18.

Sometimes devoted their property to
God to avoid supporting parents.
Matt. 15:5; Mark 7:11–12.

Treatment of, after birth, noticed.
Ezek. 16:4.

Weaning of, a time of joy and
feasting. Gen. 21:8; 1 Sam. 1:24.

Were named

From circumstances connected
with their birth. Gen. 25:25–26;
35:18; 1 Chron. 4:9.

Often by God. Isa. 8:3;
Hos. 1:4, 6, 9.

After relatives. Luke 1:59, 61.

From remarkable events.
Gen. 21:3, 6, with 18:13;
Exod. 2:10; 18:3–4.

Were required

To attend to instruction.
Deut. 4:9; 11:19.

To honor their parents.
Exod. 20:12.

To respect the aged. Lev. 19:32.

To submit to discipline.
Prov. 29:17; Heb. 12:9.

CHILDREN, GOOD

Adduced as a motive for submission
to God. Heb. 12:9.

Attend to parental teaching.
Prov. 13:1.

Honor the aged. Job 32:6–7.

Illustrative of a teachable spirit.
Matt. 18:4.

Know the Scriptures. 2 Tim. 3:15.

The Lord is with. 1 Sam. 3:19.

Make their parents' hearts glad.
Prov. 10:1; 29:17.

Obey parents. Gen. 28:7; 47:30.

Observe the law of God. Prov. 28:7.

Partake of the promises of God.
Acts 2:39.

Show love to parents. Gen. 46:29.

Spirit of, a requisite for the kingdom
of heaven. Matt. 18:3.

Take care of parents. Gen. 45:9, 11;
47:12.

Their obedience to parents is well
pleasing to God. Col. 3:20.

Will be blessed. Prov. 3:1–4;
Eph. 6:2–3.

CHILDREN, WICKED

Are proud. Isa. 3:5.

Are void of understanding. Prov. 7:7.

Despise their elders. Job 19:18.

Know not God. 1 Sam. 2:12.

Punished for

Cursing parents. Exod. 21:15,
with Mark 7:10.

Dishonoring parents.
Deut. 27:16.

Disobeying parents. Deut. 21:21.

Gluttony and drunkenness.
Deut. 21:20–21.

Mocking a prophet.
2 Kings 2:23–24.

Mocking parents. Prov. 30:17.

Striking parents. Exod. 21:15.

With regard to parents
Are a calamity to them.
Prov. 19:13.
Are a grief to them. Prov. 17:25.
Bring reproach on them.
Prov. 19:26.
Curse them. Prov. 30:11.
Despise them. Prov. 15:5, 20;
Ezek. 22:7.
Do not listen to them.
1 Sam. 2:25.
Rob them. Prov. 28:24.

CHOICE

By God. Ps. 65:4; Col. 3:12;
James 2:5.
Of life or death. Deut. 30:19.
Of a master. Josh. 24:15.
And wisdom. 1 Kings 3:9.

CHOSEN OF GOD

See God, Chosen of

CHRIST

See specific topics: Christ, Advent of;
Christ, Ascension of; Christ,
Character of; Christ, Death of;
Christ, Compassion and
Sympathy of; Christ, Deity of;
Christ, Denial of; Christ, Example
of; Christ, Glory of; Christ, Hatred
of; Christ, the Head of the Church;
Christ, the High Priest; Christ,
Humility of; Christ, the King;
Christ, the Lord; Christ, Love of;
Christ, the Mediator; Christ,
Miracles of; Christ, Power of;
Christ, Preciousness of; Christ,
Prophecies concerning; Christ, the
Prophet; Christ, Resurrection of;
Christ, Second Coming of; Christ,
the Shepherd; Christ, Titles and
Names of; Christ, Types of; Christ,
Union with.

CHRIST, ADVENT OF

Attested in the Lord's Supper.
1 Cor. 11:26.
Celebrated. Matt. 21:5–9.
Coming again. Luke 21:27;
Acts 1:11; Rev. 1:7.
Meaning for Christians.
2 Pet. 3:10–12; Rev. 22:12–14.
Prophesied. Isa. 52:13–53:12;
Mic. 4:1–8; 5:2; Mal. 4:2.

CHRIST, ASCENSION OF

Compared to His second coming.
Acts 1:10–11.
Described. Acts 1:9.
As the forerunner of His people.
Heb. 6:20.
Forty days after His resurrection.
Acts 1:3.
From Mount Olivet. Luke 24:50,
with Mark 11:1; Acts 1:12.
Predicted by Himself.
John 6:62; 7:33; 14:28; 16:5;
20:17.
Prophecies respecting. Pss. 24:7;
68:18, with Eph. 4:7, 8.
To intercede. Rom. 8:34;
Heb. 9:24.
To prepare a place for His people.
John 14:2.
To receive gifts for men. Ps. 68:18,
with Eph. 4:8, 11.
To send the Holy Spirit. John 16:7;
Acts 2:33.
Typified. Lev. 16:15, with
Heb. 6:20; Heb. 9:7, 9, 12.
Was to supreme power and dignity.
Luke 24:26; Eph. 1:20–21;
1 Pet. 3:22.
Was triumphant. Ps. 68:18.

When He had atoned for sin.
Heb. 9:12; 10:12.
While blessing His disciples.
Luke 24:50.

CHRIST, CHARACTER OF
See also Christ, Titles and Names of

Altogether lovely. Song of Sol. 5:16.
Believers are conformed to.
Rom. 8:29.
Benevolent. Matt. 4:23–24;
Acts 10:38.
Compassionate. Isa. 40:11;
Luke 19:41.
Faithful. Isa. 11:5; 1 Thess. 5:24.
Forgiving. Luke 23:34.
Good. Matt. 19:16.
Harmless. Heb. 7:26.
Holy. Luke 1:35; Acts 4:27;
Rev. 3:7.
Humble. Luke 22:27; Philem. 2:8.
Innocent. Isa. 53:9; Matt. 27:4;
1 Pet. 2:22.
Just. Zech. 9:9; John 5:30;
Acts 22:14.
Long-suffering. 1 Tim. 1:16.
Loving. John 13:1; 15:13.
Gentle in heart. Matt. 11:29.
Meek. Isa. 53:7; Zech. 9:9;
Matt. 11:29.
Merciful. Heb. 2:17.
Obedient to God the Father.
Ps. 40:8; John 4:34; 15:10.
Patient. Isa. 53:7; Matt. 27:14.
Resigned. Luke 22:42.
Resisting temptation. Matt. 4:1–10.
Righteous. Isa. 53:11; Heb. 1:9.
Self-denying. Matt. 8:20;
2 Cor. 8:9.
Sinless. John 8:46; 2 Cor. 5:21.
Spotless. 1 Pet. 1:19.
Subject to His parents. Luke 2:51.

True. John 1:14; 7:18;
1 John 5:20.
Zealous. Luke 2:49; John 2:17;
8:29.

CHRIST, COMPASSION AND SYMPATHY OF
An encouragement to prayer.
Heb. 4:15.

Manifested for the
Afflicted. Luke 7:13;
John 11:33, 35.
Diseased. Matt. 14:14;
Mark 1:41.
Perishing sinners. Matt. 9:36;
Luke 19:41; John 3:16.
Poor. Mark 8:2.
Tempted. Heb. 2:18.
Weak in faith. Isa. 40:11; 42:3,
with Matt. 12:20.
Weary and heavy-laden.
Matt. 11:28–30.
Necessary to His priestly office.
Heb. 5:2, 7.

CHRIST, DEATH OF
Acceptable, as a sacrifice to God.
Matt. 20:28; Eph. 5:2;
1 Thess. 5:10.
Accompanied by supernatural signs.
Matt. 27:45, 51–53.
Appointed by God. Isa. 53:6, 10;
Acts 2:23.
Commemorated in the sacrament of
the Lord's Supper.
Luke 22:19–20;
1 Cor. 11:26–29.
In the company of criminals.
Isa. 53:12, with Matt. 27:38.
Demanded by the Jews.
Matt. 27:22–23.
Inflicted by the
Gentiles. Matt. 27:26–35.

Mode of
Accursed. Gal. 3:13.
Exhibited His humility. Phil. 2:8.
Foolishness to
Gentiles. 1 Cor. 1:18, 23.
Predicted by Christ.
Matt. 20:18–19;
John 12:32–33.
Prefigured. Num. 21:8, with
John 3:14.
Shameful. Heb. 12:2.
A stumbling block to Jews.
1 Cor. 1:23.
Necessary for redemption.
Luke 24:46; Acts 17:3.
Predicted. Isa. 53:8; Dan. 9:26;
Zech. 13:7.
Symbolizes the death to sin.
Rom. 6:3–8; Gal. 2:20.
Undeserved. Isa. 53:9.
Voluntary. Isa. 53:12; Matt. 26:53;
John 10:17–18.

CHRIST, DEITY OF
Acknowledged by His apostles.
John 20:28.
Acknowledged by Old Testament
believers. Gen. 17:1, with
48:15–16; 32:24–30, with
Hos. 12:3–5; Judg. 6:22–24;
13:21–22; Job 19:25–27.
Believers live to Him as. Rom. 6:11;
Gal. 2:19, with 2 Cor. 5:15.
As Creator of all things. Isa. 40:28;
John 1:3; Col. 1:16; Heb. 1:2.
As discerning the thoughts of the
heart. 1 Kings 8:39, with
Luke 5:22; Ezek. 11:5, with
John 2:24–25; Rev. 2:23.
As Emmanuel. Isa. 7:14, with
Matt. 1:23.
As entitled to equal honor with the
Father. John 5:23.

As eternal. Isa. 9:6; Mic. 5:2;
John 1:1; Col. 1:17;
Heb. 1:8–10; Rev. 1:8.
As the eternal God and Creator.
Ps. 102:24–27, with Heb. 1:8,
10–12.
As giver of pastors to the church.
Jer. 3:15, with Eph. 4:11–13.
As God, He presents the church to
Himself. Eph. 5:27, with
Jude 24–25.
As God, He redeems and purifies the
church to Himself. Rev. 5:9, with
Titus 2:14.
As God over all. Ps. 45:6–7;
Rom. 9:5.
As God the Judge. Eccles. 12:14,
with 1 Cor. 4:5; 2 Cor. 5:10;
2 Tim. 4:1.
As God the Word. John 1:1.
As the great God and Savior.
Hos. 1:7, with Titus 2:13.
As having power to forgive sins.
Col. 3:13, with Mark 2:7, 10.
As the Holy One. 1 Sam. 2:2, with
Acts 3:14.
As husband of the church. Isa. 54:5,
with Eph. 5:25–32; Isa. 62:5,
with Rev. 21:2, 9.
As King of kings and Lord of lords.
Dan. 10:17, with Rev. 1:5;
Rev. 17:14.
As the Lord from heaven.
1 Cor. 15:47.
As Lord of all. Acts 10:36;
Rom. 10:11–13.
As Lord of the Sabbath. Gen. 2:3,
with Matt. 12:8.
As the mighty God. Isa. 9:6.
As the object of divine worship.
Acts 7:59; 2 Cor. 12:8–9;
Heb. 1:6; Rev. 5:12.

As the object of faith. Ps. 2:12, with
1 Pet. 2:6; Jer. 17:5, 7, with
John 14:1.

As omnipotent. Ps. 45:3; Phil. 3:21;
Rev. 1:8.

As omnipresent. Matt. 18:20;
28:30; John 3:13.

As omniscient. John 16:30; 21:17.

As one with the Father.
John 10:30, 38; 12:45;
14:7–10; 17:10.

As the only begotten Son of the
Father. John 1:14, 18; 3:16, 18;
1 John 4:9.

As owner of all things equally with
the Father. John 16:15.

As possessed of the fullness of the
Godhead. Col. 2:9; Heb. 1:3.

As raising the dead. John 5:21;
6:40, 54.

As raising Himself from the dead.
John 2:19, 21; 10:18.

As sending the Spirit equally with the
Father. John 14:16, with 15:26.

As Son of God. Matt. 26:63–67.

As the source of grace equally with
the Father. 1 Thess. 3:11;
2 Thess. 2:16–17.

As supporter and preserver of all
things. Neh. 9:6, with Col. 1:17;
Heb. 1:3.

As the true God. Jer. 10:10, with
1 John 5:20.

As unchangeable. Mal. 3:6, with
Heb. 1:12; Heb. 13:8.

As unrestricted by the law of the
Sabbath, equally with the Father.
John 5:17.

As unsearchable, equally with the
Father. 1 Thess. 3:11;
2 Thess. 2:16–17.

As Yahweh. Isa. 40:3, with
Matt. 3:3.

As Yahweh above all. Ps. 97:9, with
John 3:31.

As Yahweh the first and the last.
Isa. 44:6, with Rev. 1:17;
Isa. 48:12–16, with Rev. 22:13.

As Yahweh, for whose glory all
things were created. Prov. 16:4,
with Col. 1:16.

As Yahweh (invoked). Joel 2:32,
with Acts 2:21 and 1 Cor. 1:2.

As Yahweh the messenger of the
covenant. Mal. 3:1, with Mark 1:2
and Luke 2:27.

As Yahweh of glory. Ps. 24:7, 10,
with 1 Cor. 2:8; James 2:1.

As Yahweh of hosts. Isa. 6:1–3, with
John 12:41; Isa. 8:13–14, with
1 Pet. 2:8.

As Yahweh our righteousness.
Jer. 23:5–6, with 1 Cor. 1:30.

As Yahweh the Shepherd.
Isa. 40:11; Heb. 13:20.

As Yahweh's fellow and equal.
Zech. 13:7; Phil. 2:6.

CHRIST, DENIAL OF

A characteristic of false teachers.
2 Pet. 2:1; Jude 4.

Christ will deny those guilty of.
Matt. 10:33; 2 Tim. 2:12.

In doctrine. Mark 8:38; 2 Tim. 1:8.

Is the spirit of Antichrist
1 John 2:22–23, 4:3.

Leads to destruction. 2 Pet. 2:1;
Jude 4, 15.

In practice. Phil. 3:18–19;
Titus 1:16.

CHRIST, EXAMPLE OF

Conformity to, progressive.
2 Cor. 3:18.

Conformity to, required in
Being not of the world.
John 17:16.
Being sincere. 1 Pet. 2:21–22.
Believers predestined to follow.
Rom. 8:29.
Benevolence. Acts 20:35;
2 Cor. 8:7, 9.
Forgiving injuries. Col. 3:13.
Holiness. 1 Pet. 1:15–16, with
Rom. 1:6.
Humility. Luke 22:27;
Phil. 2:5, 7.
Is perfect. Heb. 7:26.
Love. John 13:34; Eph. 5:2;
1 John 3:16.
Meekness. Matt. 11:29.
Ministering to others.
Matt. 20:28; John 13:14–15.
Obedience. John 15:10.
Overcoming the world.
John 16:33, with 1 John 5:4.
Purity. 1 John 3:3.
Righteousness. 1 John 2:6.
Self-denial. Matt. 16:24;
Rom. 15:3.
Suffering for righteousness.
Heb. 12:3–4.
Suffering wrongly.
1 Pet. 2:21–22.

CHRIST, GLORY OF
Believers will behold, in heaven.
John 17:24.
Believers will rejoice at the revelation
of. 1 Pet. 4:13.
As the blessed of God. Ps. 45:2.
In the calling of the Gentiles.
Ps. 72:17; John 12:21, 23.
Celebrated by the redeemed.
Rev. 5:8–14; 7:9–12.
As Creator. John 1:3; Col. 1:17;
Heb. 1:2.

As the firstborn. Col. 1:15, 18;
Heb. 1:6.
Followed His resurrection.
1 Pet. 1:21.
Followed His sufferings.
1 Pet. 1:10–11.
As the foundation of the church.
Isa. 28:16.
In the fullness of His grace and truth.
Ps. 45:2, with John 1:14.
As God. John 1:1–5;
Phil. 2:6, 9–10.
As head of the church. Eph. 1:22.
In His exaltation. Acts 7:55–56;
Eph. 1:21.
In the restoration of the Jews.
Ps. 102:16.
In His sinless perfection.
Heb. 7:26–28.
In His transfiguration. Matt. 17:2,
with 2 Pet. 1:16–18.
In His triumph. Isa. 63:1–3, with
Rev. 19:11, 16.
In His words. Luke 4:22; John 7:46.
In His works. Matt. 13:54;
John 2:11.
As the image of God. Col. 1:15;
Heb. 1:3.
Is unchangeable. Heb. 1:10–12.
Imparted to believers. John 17:22;
2 Cor. 3:18.
As incarnate. John 1:14.
Is incomparable. Song of Sol. 5:10;
Phil. 2:9.
As Judge. Matt. 16:27; 25:31, 33.
As King. Isa. 6:1–5, with
John 12:41.
As the Life. John 11:25; Col. 3:4;
1 John 5:11.
As Lord of lords, etc. Rev. 17:14.
As Mediator. 1 Tim. 2:5; Heb. 8:6.
As one with the Father.
John 10:30, 38.

As Priest. Ps. 110:4; Heb. 4:15.

As Prophet. Deut. 18:15–16, with
Acts 3:22.

Revealed in the gospel. Isa. 40:5.

As Shepherd. Isa. 40:10–11;
John 10:11, 14.

As the Son of God. Matt. 3:17;
Heb. 1:6, 8.

As the true Light. Luke 1:78–79;
John 1:4, 9.

As the Truth. 1 John 5:20; Rev. 3:7.

As the Way. John 14:6;
Heb. 10:19–20.

CHRIST, HATRED TO

Illustrated. Luke 19:12–14, 17.

Involves

Hatred to His Father.
John 15:23–24.

Hatred to His people.
John 15:18.

Is because of His testimony against
the world. John 7:7.

Is without cause. Ps. 69:4, with
John 15:25.

No escape for those who persevere
in. 1 Cor. 15:25; Heb. 10:29–31.

Punishment of. Pss. 2:2, 9; 21:8.

CHRIST, THE HEAD OF THE CHURCH

Appointed by God. Eph. 1:22.

Believers are complete in. Col. 2:10.

Commissioned His apostles.
Matt. 10:1, 7; 28:19;
John 20:21.

Declared by Himself. Matt. 21:42.

Has the preeminence in all things.
1 Cor. 11:3; Eph. 1:22;
Col. 1:18.

As His mystical body. Eph. 4:12, 15;
5:23.

Imparts gifts. Ps. 68:18, with
Eph. 4:8.

Instituted the sacraments.
Matt. 28:19; Luke 22:19–20.

Perverters of the truth do not hold.
Col. 2:18–19.

Predicted. Ps. 118:22, with
Matt. 21:42.

CHRIST, THE HIGH PRIEST

Appointed and called by God.
Heb. 3:1–2; 5:4–5.

Appointment of, and encouragement
to steadfastness. Heb. 4:14.

Blesses. Num. 6:23–26, with
Acts 3:26.

Consecrated with an oath.
Heb. 7:20–21.

Entered into heaven. Heb. 4:14;
10:12.

Faithful. Heb. 3:2.

Has an unchangeable priesthood.
Heb. 7:23, 28.

His sacrifice superior to all others.
Heb. 9:13–14, 23.

On His throne. Zech. 6:13.

Intercedes. Heb. 7:25; 9:24.

Is of unblemished purity.
Heb. 7:26, 28.

Made reconciliation. Heb. 2:17.

Needed no sacrifice for Himself.
Heb. 7:27

Obtained redemption for us
Heb. 9:12.

Offered Himself as a sacrifice.
Heb. 9:14, 26.

Offered sacrifice but once.
Heb. 7:27; 9:25–26.

After the order of Melchizedek.
Ps. 110:4, with Heb. 5:6;
Heb. 6:20; 7:15, 17.

Superior to Aaron and the Levitical priests. Heb. 7:11, 16, 22; 8:1–2, 6.

Sympathizes with those who are tempted. Heb. 2:18; 4:15.

CHRIST, HUMAN NATURE OF

Acknowledged by men. Mark 6:3; John 7:27; 19:5; Acts 2:22.

Confession of, a test of belonging to God. John 4:2.

Denied by Antichrist. 1 John 4:3; 2 John 1:7.

Genealogy of. Matt. 1:1, etc.; Luke 3:23, etc.

Like our own in all things except sin. Acts 3:22; Phil. 2:7–8; Heb. 2:17.

Necessary to His mediatorial office. 1 Tim. 2:5.

Proved by His

Being a man of sorrows. Isa. 53:3–4; Luke 22:44; John 11:33; 12:27.

Being beaten. Matt. 26:67; Luke 22:64.

Being nailed to the cross. Ps. 22:16, with Luke 23:33.

Being flogged. Matt. 27:26; John 19:1.

Being subject to weariness. John 4:6.

Birth. Matt. 1:16, 25; 2:2; Luke 2:7, 11.

Burial. Matt. 27:59–60; Mark 15:46.

Circumcision. Luke 2:21.

Conception in the virgin's womb. Matt. 1:18; Luke 1:31.

Death. John 19:30.

Enduring indignities. Luke 23:11.

Having a human soul. Matt. 26:38; Luke 23:46; Acts 2:31.

Hungering. Matt. 4:2; 21:18.

Increase in wisdom and stature. Luke 2:52.

Partaking of flesh and blood. John 1:14; Heb. 2:14.

Resurrection. Acts 3:15; 2 Tim. 2:8.

Side being pierced. John 19:34.

Sleeping. Matt. 8:24; Mark 4:38.

Thirsting. John 4:7; 19:28.

Weeping. Luke 19:41; John 11:35.

Self-manifested. Matt. 8:20; 16:13.

Submitted to the evidence of the senses. Luke 24:39; John 20:27; 1 John 1:1–2.

Was of the offspring of

Abraham. Gen. 22:18, with Gal. 3:16; Heb. 2:16.

David. 2 Sam. 7:12, 16; Ps. 89:35–36; Jer. 23:5; Matt. 22:42; Mark 10:47; Acts 2:30; 13:23; Rom. 1:3.

The woman. Gen. 3:15; Isa. 7:4; Jer. 31:22; Luke 1:31; Gal. 4:4.

Without sin. John 8:46; 18:38; Heb. 4:15; 7:26, 28; 1 Pet. 2:22; 1 John 3:5.

CHRIST, HUMILITY OF

Believers should imitate. Phil. 2:5–8.

Declared by Himself. Matt. 11:29.

Exhibited in His

Associating with the despised. Matt. 9:10–11; Luke 15:1–2.

Becoming a servant. Matt. 20:28; Luke 22:27; Phil. 2:7.

Birth. Luke 2:4–7.

Death. John 10:15, 17–18;
Phil. 2:8; Heb. 12:2.

Entry into Jerusalem. Zech. 9:9,
with Matt. 21:5, 7.

Exposing Himself to reproach and
contempt. Pss. 22:6; 69:9, with
Rom. 15:3; Isa. 53:3.

Obedience. John 6:38;
Heb. 10:9.

Partaking of our sufferings.
Heb. 4:15; 5:7.

Position in life. Matt. 13:55;
John 9:29.

Poverty. Luke 9:58; 2 Cor. 8:9.

Refusing honors. John 5:41;
6:15.

Subjection to His parents.
Luke 2:51.

Submitting to sufferings. Isa. 50:6;
53:7, with Acts 8:32;
Matt. 26:37–39.

Submitting to ordinances.
Matt. 3:13–15.

Taking our nature. Phil. 2:7;
Heb. 2:16.

Washing His disciples' feet.
John 13:5.

His exaltation, the result of.
Phil. 2:9.

On account of, He was despised.
Mark 6:3; John 9:29.

CHRIST, THE KING

Acknowledged by
His followers. Luke 19:38;
John 12:13.

Nathanael. John 1:49.

The wise men from the East.
Matt. 2:2.

Believers receive a kingdom from.
Luke 22:29–30; Heb. 12:28.

Believers, the subjects of. Col. 1:13;
Rev. 15:3.

Believers will behold. Isa. 33:17;
Rev. 22:3–4.

Declared by Himself. Matt. 25:34;
John 18:37.

Glorious. Ps. 24:7–10; 1 Cor. 2:8;
James 2:1.

Has a righteous kingdom. Ps. 45:6,
with Heb. 1:8–9; Isa. 32:1;
Jer. 23:5.

Has a universal kingdom. Pss. 2:8;
72:8; Zech. 14:9; Rev. 11:15.

Has an everlasting kingdom.
Dan. 2:44; 7:14; Luke 1:33.

His kingdom not of this world.
John 18:36.

The Jews will strive to. Hos. 3:5.

King of Zion. Ps. 2:6; Isa. 52:7;
Zech. 9:9; Matt. 21:5;
John 12:12–15.

Kings will give respect, honor to.
Ps. 72:10; Isa. 49:7.

Predicted. Num. 24·17; Pss. 2:6;
45; Isa. 9:7; Jer. 23:5; Mic. 5:2.

Supreme. Ps. 89:27; Rev. 1:5;
19:16.

On the throne of David. Isa. 9:7;
Ezek. 27:24–25; Luke 1:32;
Acts 2:30.

In the throne of God. Rev. 3:21.

Will overcome all His enemies.
Ps. 110:1; Mark 12:36;
1 Cor. 15:25; Rev. 17:14.

Written on His cross. John 19:19.

CHRIST, THE LORD

Accepted. John 6:68.

Confessed. Phil. 2:11.

Named. Luke 2:11.

Seen. John 20:25.

Sovereign. Matt. 12:8; 1 Tim. 6:15.

CHRIST, LOVE OF
The banner over His believers.
Song of Sol. 2:4.

To believers is
Permanent. Rom. 8:35.
Restraining. 2 Cor. 5:14.
Unchangeable. John 13:1.
Unquenchable. Song of Sol. 8:7.
Believers obtain victory through.
Rom. 8:37.
To believers, will be acknowledged
even by enemies. Rev. 3:9.
To the Father. Ps. 91:14;
John 14:31.
The ground of His believers' love to
Him. Luke 7:47.
To His church. Song of Sol. 4:8–9;
5:1; John 15:9; Eph. 5:25.
Illustrated. Matt. 18:11–13.

Manifested in
His coming to seek the lost.
Luke 19:10.
Dying for us. John 15:13;
1 John 3:16.
Giving Himself for us. Gal. 2:20.
Interceding for us. Heb. 7:25;
9:24.
Praying for His enemies.
Luke 23:34.
Rebukes and chastisements.
Rev. 3:19.
Sending the Spirit. Ps. 68:18;
John 16:7.
Washing away our sins. Rev. 1:5.
Obedient believers abide in.
John 15:10.
Surpasses knowledge. Eph. 3:19.
To those who love Him. Prov. 8:17;
John 14:21.
To be imitated. John 13:34; 15:12;
Eph. 5:2; 1 John 3:16.

CHRIST, LOVE TO
Absence of, denounced.
1 Cor. 16:22.
A characteristic of believers.
Song of Sol. 1:4.
Decrease of, rebuked. Rev. 2:4.
An evidence of adoption. John 8:42.
Exhibited by believers. 1 Pet. 1:8.
Exhibited by God. Matt. 17:5;
John 5:20.
His love to us a motive to.
2 Cor. 5:14.
His personal excellence is deserving
of. Song of Sol. 5:9–16.
Increase of, to be prayed for.
Phil. 1:9.

Manifested in
Ministering to Him. Matt. 27:55,
with 25:40.
Obeying Him.
John 14:15, 21, 23.
Preferring Him to all others.
Matt. 10:37.
Seeking Him. Song of Sol. 3:2.
Taking up the cross for Him.
Matt. 10:38.
Pray for grace to those who have.
Eph. 6:24.
Promises to. 2 Tim. 4:8;
James 1:12.

Should be
Even to death. Acts 21:13;
Rev. 12:11.
Fervent. Song of Sol. 2:5; 8:6.
In proportion to our forgiveness.
Luke 7:47.
Sincere. Eph. 6:24.
With the soul. Song of Sol. 1:7.
Supreme. Matt. 10:37.
Unquenchable. Song of Sol. 8:7.

Those who have
    Are loved by Christ. Prov. 8:17;
        John 14: 21.
    Are loved by the Father.
        John 14:21, 23; 16:27.
    Enjoy communion with God and
        Christ. John 14:23.
The wicked, destitute of. Ps. 35:19,
    with John 15:18, 25.

CHRIST, THE MEDIATOR
Of the gospel covenant. Heb. 8:6;
    12:24.
The only one between God and man.
    1 Tim. 2:5.
In virtue of His atonement.
    Eph. 2:13–18; Heb. 9:15; 12:24.

CHRIST, MIRACLES OF
Blind restored to sight.
    Matt. 9:27–30; Mark 8:22–25;
    John 9:1–7.
Centurion's servant healed.
    Matt. 8:5–13.
Crippled woman healed.
    Luke 13:11–13.
Cures performed before the
    messengers of John.
    Luke 7:21–22.
Dead raised to life. Matt. 9:18–19,
    23–25; Luke 7:12–15;
    John 11:11–44.
Deaf and mute cured.
    Mark 7:32–35.
Devils cast out.
    Matt. 8:28–32; 9:32–33;
    15:22–28; 17:14–18;
    Mark 1:23–27.
Fig tree withered. Matt. 21:19.
Hemorrhage of blood stopped.
    Matt. 9:20–22.
His appearance to His disciples, the
    doors being shut. John 20:19.

His ascension. Acts 1:9.
His resurrection. Luke 24:6, with
    John 10:18.
His transfiguration. Matt. 17:1–8.
His walking on the sea.
    Matt. 14:25–27.
Invalid man healed. John 5:5–9.
Lepers cleansed. Matt. 8:3;
    Luke 17:14.
Malchus healed. Luke 22:50–51.
Many diseases healed.
    Matt. 4:23–24; 14:14; 15:30;
    Mark 1:34; Luke 6:17–19.
The multitude fed.
    Matt. 14:15–21; 15:32–38.
Nets full of fish. Luke 5:4–6;
    John 21:6.
Nobleman's son healed.
    John 4:46–53.
Paralytic healed. Mark 2:3–12.
Peter's mother-in-law healed.
    Matt. 8:14–15.
Peter walking on the sea.
    Matt. 14:29.
Severe swelling cured. Luke 14:2–4.
Shriveled hand restored.
    Matt. 12:10–13.
Sudden arrival of the ship.
    John 6:21.
Storm stilled. Matt. 8:23–26; 14:32.
Tribute money from fish.
    Matt. 17:27.
Water turned into wine.
    John 2:6–10.

CHRIST, POWER OF
Able to subdue all things. Phil. 3:21.

Believers
    Bodies of will be changed by.
        Phil. 3:21.
    Helped by. Heb. 2:18.
    Made willing by. Ps. 110:3.
    Preserved by. 2 Tim. 1:12; 4:18.

Strengthened by. Phil. 4:13;
2 Tim. 4:17.

Described as
Everlasting. 1 Tim. 6:16.
Glorious. 2 Thess. 1:9.
Over all flesh. John 17:2.
Over all things. John 3:35;
Eph. 1:22.
Supreme. Eph. 1:20–21;
1 Pet. 3:22.
Unlimited. Matt. 28:18.

Exhibited in
Creation. John 1:3, 10;
Col. 1:16.
Destroying the works of Satan.
1 John 3:8.
Enabling others to work miracles.
Matt. 10:1; Mark 16:17–18;
Luke 10:17.
Forgiving sins. Matt. 9:6;
Acts 5:31.
Giving eternal life. John 17:2.
Giving spiritual life.
John 5:21, 25–26.
His teaching. Matt. 7:28–29;
Luke 4:32.
Overcoming Satan. Col. 2:15;
Heb. 2:14.
Overcoming the world.
John 16:33.
Raising Himself from the dead.
John 2:19–21; 10:18.
Raising the dead. John 5:28–29.
Salvation. Isa. 63:1; Heb. 7:25.
Upholding all things. Col. 1:17;
Heb. 1:3.
Working miracles. Matt. 8:27;
Luke 5:17.
As man, from the Father.
Acts 10:38.
Ministers should make known.
2 Pet. 1:16.

Present in the assembly of believers.
1 Cor. 5:4.
Rests upon believers. 2 Cor. 12:9.
As Son of God, the power of God.
John 5:17–19; 10:28–30.
Will be specially shown at His second
coming. Mark 13:26; 2 Pet. 1:16.
Will subdue all power. 1 Cor. 15:24.
The wicked will be destroyed by.
Ps. 2:9; Isa. 11:4; 63:3;
2 Thess. 1:9.

CHRIST, PRECIOUSNESS OF

Because of His
Atonement. 1 Pet. 1:19, with
Heb. 12:24.
Care and tenderness. Isa. 40:11.
Excellence and grace. Ps. 45:2.
Goodness and beauty. Zech. 9:17.
Name. Song of Sol. 1:3;
Heb. 1:4.
Promises. 2 Pet. 1:4.
Words. John 6:68.
To believers. Song of Sol. 5:10;
Phil. 3:8; 1 Pet. 2:7.
As the cornerstone of the church.
Isa. 28:16, with 1 Pet. 2:6.
To God. Matt. 3:17; 1 Pet. 2:4.
Illustrated. Song of Sol. 2:3;
5:10–16; Matt. 13:44–46.
As the source of all grace.
John 1:14; Col. 1:19.
Unsearchable. Eph. 3:8.

CHRIST, PROPHECIES CONCERNING

Anointed with the Spirit. Ps. 45:7;
Isa. 11:2; 61:1. *Fulfilled:*
Matt. 3:16; John 3:34;
Acts 10:38.
Ascension. Ps. 68:18. *Fulfilled:*
Luke 24:51; Acts 1:9.

Bearing reproach. Pss. 22:6; 69:7, 9, 20. *Fulfilled:* John 1:11; 7:3.

Betrayed by a friend. Pss. 41:9; 55:12–14. *Fulfilled:* John 13:18, 21.

Born in Bethlehem of Judea. Mic. 5:2. *Fulfilled:* Matt. 2:1; Luke 2:4–6.

Born of a virgin. Isa. 7:14. *Fulfilled:* Matt. 1:18; Luke 2:7.

Buried with the rich. Isa. 53:9. *Fulfilled:* Matt. 27:57–60.

Called Immanuel. Isa. 7:14. *Fulfilled:* Matt. 1:22–23.

Called out of Egypt. Hos. 11:1. *Fulfilled:* Matt. 2:15.

Chief cornerstone of the church. Isa. 28:16. *Fulfilled:* 1 Pet. 2:6–7.

Coming at a set time. Gen. 49:10; Dan. 9:24–25. *Fulfilled:* Luke 2:1.

Coming into the temple. Hag. 2:7, 9; Mal. 3:1. *Fulfilled:* Matt. 21:12; Luke 2:27–32; John 2:13–16.

Conversion of the Gentiles to Him. Isa. 11:10; 42:1. *Fulfilled:* Matt. 1:17, 21; John 10:16; Acts 10:45, 47.

Death, Isa. 53:12. *Fulfilled:* Matt. 27:50.

Descendants of Abraham. Gen. 17:7; 22:18. *Fulfilled:* Gal. 3:16.

Descendants of David. Ps. 132:11; Jer. 23:5. *Fulfilled:* Acts 13:23; Rom. 1:3.

Descendants of Isaac. Gen. 21:12. *Fulfilled:* Heb. 11:17–19.

Descendants of the woman. Gen. 3:15. *Fulfilled:* Gal. 4:4.

Disciples forsaking Him. Zech. 13:7. *Fulfilled:* Matt. 26:31, 56.

Entering on His public ministry. Isa. 61:1–2. *Fulfilled:* Luke 4:16–21, 43.

Entering publicly into Jerusalem. Zech. 9:9. *Fulfilled:* Matt. 21:1–5.

Exercising the priestly office in heaven. Zech. 6:13. *Fulfilled:* Rom. 8:34.

Face marred. Isa. 52:14; 53:3. *Fulfilled:* John 19:5.

Flesh not seeing corruption. Ps. 16:10. *Fulfilled:* Acts 2:31.

Forsaken by God. Ps. 22:1. *Fulfilled:* Matt. 27:46.

Gall and vinegar given Him to drink. Ps. 69:21. *Fulfilled:* Matt. 27:34.

Lots cast for His garments. Ps. 22:18. *Fulfilled:* Matt. 27:35.

Great persons coming to adore Him. Ps. 72:10. *Fulfilled:* Matt. 2:1–11.

Hands and feet nailed to the cross. Ps. 22:16. *Fulfilled:* John 19:18; 20:25.

Hated by the Jews. Ps. 69:4; Isa. 49:7. *Fulfilled:* John 15:24–25.

Intensity of His sufferings. Ps. 22:14–15. *Fulfilled:* Luke 22:42, 44.

Intercession for His murderers. Isa. 53:12. *Fulfilled:* Luke 23:34.

Jews and Gentiles joining against Him. Ps. 2:1–2. *Fulfilled:* Luke 23:12; Acts 4:27.

King in Zion. Ps. 2:6. *Fulfilled:* Luke 1:32; John 18:33–37.

Meekness and humility. Isa. 42:2. *Fulfilled:* Matt. 12:15–16, 19.

Ministry beginning in Galilee.
Isa. 9:1–2. *Fulfilled:*
Matt. 4:12–16, 23.

Mocked. Ps. 22:7–8. *Fulfilled:*
Matt. 27:39–44.

Murder of the children of Bethlehem.
Jer. 31:15. *Fulfilled:*
Matt. 2:16–18.

Numbered with the transgressors.
Isa. 53:12. *Fulfilled:* Mark 15:28.

Patience and silence under
sufferings. Isa. 53:7. *Fulfilled:*
Matt. 26:63; 27:12–14.

Permanence of His kingdom.
Isa. 9:7; Dan. 7:14. *Fulfilled:*
Luke 1:32–33.

Pierced. Zech. 12:10. *Fulfilled:*
John 19:34, 37.

Preaching by parables. Ps. 78:2.
Fulfilled: Matt. 13:34–35.

Preceded by John the Baptist.
Isa. 40:3; Mal. 3:1. *Fulfilled:*
Matt. 3:1, 3; Luke 1:17.

Price given for the potter's field.
Zech. 11:13. *Fulfilled:*
Matt. 27:7.

A priest after the order of
Melchizedek. Ps. 110:4. *Fulfilled:*
Heb. 5:5–6.

A prophet like Moses.
Deut. 18:15–18. *Fulfilled:*
Acts 3:20–22.

Poverty. Isa. 53:2. *Fulfilled:*
Mark 6:3; Luke 9:58.

Rejected by His brethren. Ps. 69:8;
Isa. 63:3. *Fulfilled:* John 1:11;
7:3.

Rejected by the Jewish rulers.
Ps. 118:22. *Fulfilled:*
Matt. 21:42; John 7:48.

Resurrection. Ps. 16:10; Isa. 26:19.
Fulfilled: Luke 24:6, 31, 34.

Righteous government. Ps. 45:6–7.
Fulfilled: John 5:30; Rev. 19:11.

Sitting on the right hand of God.
Ps. 110:1. *Fulfilled:* Heb. 1:3.

Struck on the cheek. Mic. 5:1.
Fulfilled: Matt. 27:30.

Sold for thirty pieces of silver.
Zech. 11:12. *Fulfilled:*
Matt. 26:15.

Son of God. Ps. 2:7. *Fulfilled:*
Luke 1:32, 35.

Spit on and whipped. Isa. 50:6.
Fulfilled: Mark 14:65;
John 19:1.

A stone of stumbling to the Jews.
Isa. 8:4. *Fulfilled:* Rom. 9:32;
1 Pet. 2:8.

Suffering for others. Isa. 53:4–6, 12;
Dan. 9:26. *Fulfilled:*
Matt. 20:28.

Tenderness and compassion.
Isa. 40:11; 42:3. *Fulfilled:*
Matt. 12:15, 20; Heb. 4:15.

That none of His bones would be
broken. Exod. 12:46; Ps. 34:20.
Fulfilled: John 19:33, 36.

Universal dominion. Ps. 72:8;
Dan. 7:14. *Fulfilled:* Phil. 2:9,
11.

Without deceit. Isa. 53:9. *Fulfilled:*
1 Pet. 2:22.

Working miracles. Isa. 35:5–6.
Fulfilled: Matt. 11:4–6;
John 11:47.

Zeal. Ps. 69:9. *Fulfilled:* John 2:17.

CHRIST, THE PROPHET

Abounds in wisdom. Luke 2:40, 47,
52; Col. 2:3.

Alone knows and reveals God.
Matt. 11:27; John 3:2, 13, 34;
17:6, 14, 26; Heb. 1:1–2.

Anointed with the Holy Spirit.
Isa. 61:1, with Luke 4:18;
John 3:34.
Declared His doctrine to be that of
the Father. John 8:26, 28;
12:49–50; 14:10, 24; 15:15;
17:8, 16.
Faithful to His trust. Luke 4:32;
John 17:8; Heb. 3:2; Rev. 1:5;
3:14.
God commands us to hear.
Deut. 18:15; Matt. 17:25;
Acts 3:22; 7:37.
God will severely punish our neglect
of. Deut. 18:19; Acts 3:23;
Heb. 2:3.
Meek and unpretentious in His
teaching. Isa. 42:2;
Matt. 12:17–20.
Mighty in deed and word.
Matt. 13:54; Mark 1:27;
Luke 4:32; John 7:46.
Preached the gospel and worked
miracles. Matt. 4:23; 11:5;
Luke 4:43.
Predicted. Deut. 18:15, 18;
Isa. 52:7; Nah. 1:15.
Predicted things to come.
Matt. 24:3–35; Luke 19:41, 44.

CHRIST, RESURRECTION OF

The apostles
At first did not understand the
predictions about. Mark 9:10;
John 20:9.
Criticized for their unbelief of.
Mark 16:14.
Very slow to believe. Mark 16:13;
Luke 24:9, 11, 37–38.
Asserted and preached by the
apostles. Acts 25:19; 26:23.
An assurance of the judgment.
Acts 17:31.

Attested by
Angels. Matt. 28:5–7;
Luke 24:4–7, 23.
Apostles. Acts 1:22; 2:32; 3:15;
4:33.
His enemies. Matt. 28:11–15.

Believers
Desire to know the power of.
Phil. 3:10.
Given a living hope.
1 Pet. 1:3, 21.
Should keep, in remembrance.
2 Tim. 2:8.
Will rise in the likeness of.
Rom. 6:5; 1 Cor. 15:49, with
Phil. 3:21.

Effected by
His own power. John 2:19;
10:18.
The power of God. Acts 2:24;
3:15; Rom. 8:11; Eph. 1:20;
Col. 2:12.
The power of the Holy Spirit.
1 Pet. 3:18.
First fruits of our resurrection.
Acts 26:23; 1 Cor. 15:20, 23.
On the first day of the week.
Mark 16:9.
Followed by His exaltation.
Acts 4:10–11; Rom. 8:34;
Eph. 1:20; Phil. 2:9–10;
Rev. 1:18.
Fraud impossible in.
Matt. 27:63–66.

He appeared after, to
All the apostles. Luke 24:51;
Acts 1:9; 1 Cor. 15:7.
Apostles at the sea of Tiberias.
John 21:1.
Apostles, except Thomas.
John 20:19, 24.

Apostles in Galilee.
Matt. 28:16–17.
Apostles, Thomas being present.
John 20:26.
Above five hundred believers.
1 Cor. 15:6.
James. 1 Cor. 15:7.
Mary Magdalene. Mark 16:9;
John 20:18.
Paul. 1 Cor. 15:8.
Simon Peter. Luke 24:34.
Two disciples. Luke 24:13–31.
The women. Matt. 28:9.
He gave many infallible proofs of.
Luke 24:35, 39, 43;
John 20:20, 27; Acts 1:3.

Necessary to
Forgiveness of sins. 1 Cor. 15:17.
The fulfillment of Scripture.
Luke 24:45–46.
Hope. 1 Cor. 15:19.
Justification. Rom. 4:25; 8:34.
The validity of faith.
1 Cor. 15:14, 17.
The validity of preaching.
1 Cor. 15:14.
A picture of the new birth. Rom. 6:4;
Col. 2:12.
Predicted by Him. Matt. 20:9;
Mark 9:9; 14:28; John 2:19–22.
Predicted by the prophets.
Ps. 16:10, with Acts 13:34–35;
Isa. 26:19.
A proof of His being the Son of God.
Ps. 2:7, with Acts 13:33;
Rom. 1:4.
On the third day after His death.
Luke 24:26; Acts 10:40;
1 Cor. 15:4.
Truth of the gospel involved in.
1 Cor. 15:14–15.

CHRIST, THE SAVIOR

Announced at His birth. Matt. 1:21;
Luke 2:11.
Our Healer. Acts 9:34.
Our Liberator. Isa. 61:1; Rom. 8:2.
Our Redeemer. 1 Cor. 1:30;
2 Cor. 5:21.
Our Sin Bearer. John 1:29.
Preached by disciples. Acts 2:21;
3:6; 8:4.
Proclaimed by Himself. Matt. 20:28.

CHRIST, SECOND COMING OF

Believers
Assured of. Job 19:25–26.
Faith of, will be found to praise at.
1 Pet. 1:7.
Look for. Phil. 3:20; Titus 2:13.
Look forward to. 2 Pet. 3:12.
Love. 2 Tim. 4:8.
Pray for. Rev. 22:20.
Should be patient until.
2 Thess. 3:5; James 5:7–8.
Should be ready for. Matt. 24:44;
Luke 12:40.
Should watch for. Matt. 24:42;
Mark 13:35–37; Luke 21:36.
Wait for. 1 Cor. 1:7;
1 Thess. 1:10.
Will appear with Him in glory at.
Col. 3:4.
Will be blameless at. 1 Cor. 1:8;
1 Thess. 3:13; 5:23; Jude 24.
Will be like Him at. Phil. 3:21;
1 John 3:2.
Will be preserved until. Phil. 1:6.
Will not be ashamed at.
1 John 2:28; 4:17.
Will receive a crown of glory at.
2 Tim. 4:8; 1 Pet. 5:4.
Will reign with Him at. Dan. 7:27;
2 Tim. 2:12; Rev. 5:10; 20:6;
22:5.

Will see Him as He is, at.
1 John 3:2.
Believers alive at, will be caught up to
meet Him. 1 Thess. 4:17.
Blessedness of being prepared for.
Matt. 24:6; Luke 12:37–38.

Called the
Appearing of Jesus Christ.
1 Pet. 1:7.
Day of the Lord Jesus Christ.
1 Cor. 1:8.
Coming of the day of God.
2 Pet. 3:12.
Glorious appearing of the great
God and Savior. Titus 2:13.
Last time. 1 Pet. 1:5.
Revelation of Jesus Christ.
1 Pet. 1:13.
Times of refreshing from the
presence of the Lord. Acts 3:19.
Times of restitution of all things.
Acts 3:21, with Rom. 8:21.
Every eye will see Him at. Rev. 1:7.
Heavens and earth will be dissolved,
etc., at. 2 Pet. 3:10, 12.
Illustrated. Matt. 25:6;
Luke 12:36, 39; 19:12, 15.
The man of sin to be destroyed at.
2 Thess. 2:8.

Manner of
Accompanied by angels.
Matt. 16:27; 25:31;
Mark 8:38; 2 Thess. 1:7.
With believers. 1 Thess. 3:13;
Jude 14.
In clouds. Matt. 24:30; 26:64;
Rev. 1:7.
In flaming fire. 2 Thess. 1:8.
In the glory of His Father.
Mal. 16:27.
As He ascended. Acts 1:9, 11.
In His own glory. Matt. 25:31.

As the lightning. Matt. 24:27.
With power and great glory.
Matt. 24:30.
With a shout and the voice of the
Archangel, etc. 1 Thess. 4:16.
Suddenly. Mark 13:36.
As a thief in the night. 1 Thess.
5:2; 2 Pet. 3:10; Rev. 16:15.
Unexpectedly. Matt. 24:44;
Luke 12:40.
Not to make atonement. Heb. 9:28,
with Rom. 6:9–10 and
Heb. 10:14.

Predicted by
Angels. Acts 1:10–11.
Apostles. Acts 3:20; 1 Tim. 6:14.
Christ Himself. Matt. 25:31;
John 14:3.
Prophets. Dan. 7:13; Jude 14.

Purposes of, to
Be admired in those who believe.
2 Thess. 1:10.
Be glorified in believers.
2 Thess. 1:10.
Bring to light the hidden things of
darkness, etc. 1 Cor. 4:5.
Complete the salvation of
believers. Heb. 9:28; 1 Pet. 1:5.
Destroy death. 1 Cor. 15:25–26.
Judge. Ps. 50:3–4, with
John 5:22; 2 Tim. 4:1;
Jude 15; Rev. 20:11–13.
Reign. Isa. 24:23; Dan. 7:14;
Rev. 11:15.
Should be always considered as
imminent. Rom. 13:12; Phil. 4:5;
1 Pet. 4:7.
Signs preceding. Matt. 24:3, etc.
Those who have died in Christ will
rise first at. 1 Thess. 4:16.
Time of, unknown. Matt. 24:36;
Mark 13:32.

The wicked
Presume upon the delay of.
Matt. 24:28.
Scoff at. 2 Pet. 3:3–4.
Will be punished at. 2 Thess.
1:8–9.
Will be surprised by.
Matt. 24:37–39; 1 Thess. 5:3.

CHRIST, THE SHEPHERD
As Chief. 1 Pet. 5:4.
As good. John 10:11, 14.
As great. Mic. 5:4; Heb. 13:20.

His sheep
He calls. John 10:3.
He cherishes tenderly. Isa. 40:11.
He feeds. Ps. 23:1–2; John 10:9.
He gathers. Isa. 40:11;
John 10:16.
He gives eternal life to.
John 10:28.
He guides. Ps. 23:3;
John 10:3–4.
He knows. John 10:14, 27.
He laid down His life for. Zech.
13:7; Matt. 26:31;
John 10:11, 15; Acts 20:28.
He protects and preserves.
Jer. 31:10; Ezek. 34:10;
Zech. 9:16; John 10:28.
Predicted. Gen. 49:24; Isa. 40:11;
Ezek. 34:23; 37:24.

CHRIST, TITLES AND NAMES OF
Adam, second. 1 Cor. 15:45.
Advocate. 1 John 2:1.
Almighty. Rev. 1:8.
Alpha and Omega. Rev. 1:8; 22:13.
Amen. Rev. 3:14.
Angel. Gen. 48:16;
Exod. 23:20–21.
Angel of God's presence. Isa. 63:9.

Angel of the Lord. Exod. 3:2;
Judg. 13:15–18.
Apostle. Heb. 3:1.
Arm of the Lord. Isa. 51:9; 53:1.
Author and Finisher of our faith.
Heb. 12:2.
Beginning of the creation of God.
Rev. 3:14.
Blessed and only ruler. 1 Tim. 6:15.
Branch. Jer. 23:5; Zech. 3:8; 6:12.
Bread of life. John 6:35, 48.
Captain of the Lord's hosts.
Josh. 5:14–15.
Captain of salvation. Heb. 2:10.
Chief Cornerstone. Eph. 2:20;
1 Pet. 2:6.
Chief Shepherd. 1 Pet. 5:4.
Christ of God. Luke 9:20.
Commander. Isa. 55:4.
Consolation of Israel. Luke 2:25.
Counselor. Isa. 9:6.
David. Jer. 30:9; Ezek. 34:23.
Deliverer. Rom. 11:26.
Desire of all nations. Hag. 2:7.
Door. John 10:7.
Elect of God. Isa. 42:1.
Emmanuel. Isa. 7:14, with
Matt. 1:23.
Eternal life. 1 John 1:2; 5:20.
Everlasting Father. Isa. 9:6.
Faithful witness. Rev. 1:5; 3:14.
First and Last. Rev. 1:17; 2:8.
Firstborn of every creature.
Col. 1:15.
Firstborn of the dead. Rev. 1:5.
Forerunner. Heb. 6:20.
Glory of the Lord. Isa. 40:5.
God. Isa. 40:9; John 20:28.
God blessed forever. Rom. 9:5.
God's fellow. Zech. 13:7.
Good Shepherd. John 10:14.
Governor. Matt. 2:6.
Great High Priest. Heb. 4:14.

Head of the church. Eph. 5:23;
   Col. 1:18.
Heir of all things. Heb. 1:2.
Holy One. Ps. 16:10, with
   Acts 2:27, 31.
Holy One of God. Mark 1:24.
Holy One of Israel. Isa. 41:14.
I Am. Exod. 3:14, with John 8:58.
Jehovah. Isa. 26:4.
Jesus. Matt. 1:21; 1 Thess. 1:10.
Judge of Israel. Mic. 5:1.
Just One. Acts 7:52.
King. Zech. 9:9, with Matt. 21:5.
King of believers. Rev. 15:3.
King of Israel. John 1:49.
King of kings. 1 Tim. 6:15;
   Rev. 17:14.
King of the Jews. Matt. 2:2.
Lamb. Rev. 5:6, 12; 13:8; 21:22;
   22:3.
Lamb of God. John 1:29, 36.
Lawgiver. Isa. 33:22.
Leader. Isa. 55:4.
Life. John 14:6; Col. 3:4;
   1 John 1:2.
Light of the world. John 8:12.
Lion of the tribe of Judah. Rev. 5:5.
Lord God Almighty. Rev. 15:3.
Lord God of the holy prophets.
   Rev. 22:6.
Lord of all. Acts 10:36.
Lord of Glory. 1 Cor. 2:8.
Lord our righteousness. Jer. 23:6.
Mediator. 1 Tim. 2:5.
Messenger of the covenant.
   Mal. 3:1.
Messiah. Dan. 9:25; John 1:41.
Mighty God. Isa. 9:6.
Mighty One of Jacob. Isa. 60:16.
Morning star. Rev. 22:16.
Nazarene. Matt. 2:23.
Offspring of David. Rev. 22:16.
Only begotten. John 1:14.

Our Passover. 1 Cor. 5:7.
Plant of renown. Ezek. 34:29.
Prince of the kings of the earth.
   Rev. 1:5.
Prince of life. Acts 3:15.
Prince of peace. Isa. 9:6.
Prophet. Luke 24:19; John 7:40.
Ransom. 1 Tim. 2:6.
Redeemer. Job 19:25; Isa. 59:20;
   60:16.
Resurrection and life. John 11:25.
Rising sun. Luke 1:78.
Rock. 1 Cor. 10:4.
Root of David. Rev. 22:16.
Root of Jesse. Isa. 11:10.
Ruler of Israel. Mic. 5:2.
Savior. 2 Pet. 2:20; 3:18.
Servant. Isa. 42:1; 52:13.
Shepherd and overseer of souls.
   1 Pet. 2:25.
Shiloh. Gen. 49:10.
Son of David. Matt. 9:27.
Son of God. Luke 1:35; John 1:49.
Son of man. John 5:27; 6:37.
Son of the blessed. Mark 14:61.
Son of the highest. Luke 1:32.
Star. Num. 24:17.
Sun of righteousness. Mal. 4:2.
Surety. Heb. 7:22.
True God. 1 John 5:20.
True light. John 1:9.
True vine. John 15:1
Truth. John 14:6.
Way. John 14:6.
Wisdom. Prov. 8:12.
Witness. Isa. 55:4.
Wonderful. Isa. 9:6.
Word. John 1:1; 1 John 5:7.
Word of God. Rev. 19:13.
Word of life. 1 John 1:1.

CHRIST, TYPES OF

Aaron. Exod. 28:1, with
Heb. 5:4–5; Lev. 16:15, with
Heb. 9:7, 24.

Abel. Gen. 4:8, 10; Heb. 12:24.

Abraham. Gen. 17:5, with
Eph. 3:15.

Adam. Rom. 5:14; 1 Cor. 15:45.

Ark. Gen. 7:16, with
1 Pet. 3:20–21.

Ark of the Covenant. Exod. 25:16,
with Ps. 40:8; Isa. 42:6.

Atonement, sacrifices offered on the
Day of. Lev. 16:15–16, with
Heb. 9:12, 24.

Basin of brass. Exod. 30:18–20,
with Zech. 13:1; Eph. 5:26–27.

Bronze altar. Exod. 27:1–2, with
Heb. 13:10.

Bride, a type of the church.
Rev. 21:2, 9; 22:17.

Bronze serpent. Num. 21:9, with
John 3:14–15.

Burnt offering. Lev. 1:2, 4, with
Heb. 10:10.

Cities of refuge. Num. 35:6, with
Heb. 6:18.

David. 2 Sam. 8:15, with
Ezek. 37:24; Ps. 89:19–20, with
Phil. 2:9.

Eliakim. Isa. Isa. 22:20–22, with
Rev. 3:7.

First fruits. Exod. 22:29, with 1 Cor.
15:20.

Golden altar. Exod. 40:5, 26–27,
with Rev. 8:3; Heb. 13:15.

Golden candlestick. Exod. 25:31,
with John 8:12.

Isaac. Gen. 22:1–2, with
Heb. 11:17–19.

Jacob. Gen. 32:28, with
John 11:42; Heb. 7:25.

Jacob's ladder. Gen. 28:12, with
John 1:51.

Jonah. Jon. 1:17, with Matt. 12:40.

Joseph. Gen. 50:19–20, with
Heb. 7:52.

Joshua. Josh. 1:5–6, with
Heb. 4:8–9; Josh. 11:23, with
Acts 20:32.

Leper's offering. Lev. 14:4–7, with
Rom. 4:25.

Manna. Exod. 16:11–15, with
John 6:32–35.

Melchizedek. Gen. 14:18–20, with
Heb. 7:1–17.

Mercy seat. Exod. 25:17–22, with
Rom. 3:25; Heb. 4:16.

Morning and evening sacrifices.
Exod. 29:38–41, with
John 1:29, 36.

Moses. Num. 12:7, with Heb. 3:2;
Deut. 18:15, with Acts 3:20–22.

Noah. Gen. 5:29; 2 Cor. 1:5.

Paschal lamb. Exod. 12:3–6, 46,
with John 19:36; 1 Cor. 5:7.

Peace offering. Lev. 3:1, with
Eph. 2:14, 16.

Red heifer. Num. 19:2–6, with
Heb. 9:13–14.

Rock of Horeb. Exod. 17:6, with
1 Cor. 10:4.

Samson. Judg. 16:30, with
Col. 2:14–15.

The sanctuary, a type of the heavenly
sanctuary. Exod. 40:2, 24;
Heb. 8:2, 5; 9:1–12.

The saving of Noah and his family, a
type of the salvation through
Christ. 1 Pet. 3:20–21.

Scapegoat. Lev. 16:20–22, with
Isa. 53:6, 12.

Sin offering. Lev. 4:2–3, 12, with
Heb. 13:11–12.

Solomon. 2 Sam. 7:12–13, with
Luke 1:32–33; 1 Pet. 2:5.
Tabernacle. Exod. 40:2, 34, with
Heb. 9:11; Col. 2:9.
Table and shewbread.
Exod. 25:23–30, with John 1:16;
John 6:48.
Temple. 1 Kings 6:1, 38, with
John 2:19, 21.
Tree of life. Gen. 2:9, with John 1:4;
Rev. 22:2.
Trespass offering. Lev. 6:1–7, with
Isa. 53:10.
Veil of the tabernacle and temple.
Exod. 40:21; 2 Chron. 3:14,
with Heb. 10:20.
Zerubbabel. Zech. 4:7–9, with
Heb. 12:2–3.

CHRIST, UNION WITH

Believers
Are complete through. Col. 2:10.
Enjoy, in the Lord's Supper.
1 Cor. 10:16–17.
Exhorted to maintain. John 15:4;
Acts 11:23; Col. 2:7.
Have assurance of. John 14:20.
Have in His death. Rom. 6:3–8;
Gal. 2:20.
Have in love. Song of Sol. 2:16;
7:10.
Have in mind. 1 Cor. 2:16;
Phil. 2:5.
Have in spirit. 1 Cor. 6:17.
Have in sufferings. Phil. 3:10;
2 Tim. 2:12.
Identified with Christ by.
Matt. 25:40, 45; Acts 9:4, with
8:1.

Beneficial, results of
Abundant fruitfulness. John 15:5.
Answers to prayer. John 15:7.

Being created anew. 2 Cor. 5:17.
Confidence at His coming.
1 John 2:28.
Freedom from condemnation.
Rom. 8:1.
Freedom from life of sin.
1 John 3:6.
Righteousness attributed. 2 Cor.
5:21; Phil. 3:9.
The spirit alive to righteousness.
Rom. 8:10.
Christ prayed that all believers might
have. John 17:21, 23.

Described as
Christ being in us. Eph. 3:17;
Col. 1:27.
Our being in Christ. 2 Cor. 12:2;
1 John 5:20.
False teachers do not have.
Col. 2:18–19.
The gift of the Holy Spirit an
evidence of. 1 John 4:13.
As head of the church.
Eph. 1:22–23; 4:15–16;
Col. 1:18.
The Holy Spirit witnesses.
1 John 3:24.
Includes union with the Father.
John 17:21; 1 John 2:24.

Is
Of God. 1 Cor. 1:30.
Permanent. Rom. 8:35.

Maintained by
Abiding in Him. John 15:4, 7.
Faith. Gal. 2:20; Eph. 3:17.
Feeding on Him. John 6:56.
His Word abiding in us.
John 15:7; 1 John 2:24;
2 John 1:9.
Obeying Him. 1 John 3:24.

Necessary to fruitfulness.
John 15:4–5.
Necessary to growth in grace.
Eph. 4:15–16; Col. 2:19.
Punishment of those who have not.
John 15:6.
Those who have, should walk as He
walked. 1 John 2:6.

CHRISTIANS
Almost persuaded. Acts 26:28.
Daily life. Matt. 5:46–48; Eph. 4:17.
First named. Acts 11:26.
Under suffering. 1 Pet. 4:16.

CHRISTIANS, NATURE OF

New
Created by Christ. 2 Cor. 5:17.
Promised by the prophets.
Jer. 31:33; Ezek. 36:26.
Voluntarily put on. Eph. 4:24;
Col. 3:10.

Old
Corrupt. Eph. 4:22.
Crucified with Christ. Rom. 6:6.
Voluntarily put off. Eph. 4:22;
Col. 3:9.

CHRONOLOGY
Jewish year instituted. Exod. 12:2.

CHURCH, THE
Believers baptized into, by one Spirit.
1 Cor. 12:13.
Believers continually added by the
Lord. Acts 2:47; 5:14; 11:24.
Belongs to God. 1 Tim. 3:15.
As body of Christ. Eph. 1:23;
Col. 1:24.
Christ, the foundation stone of.
1 Cor. 3:11; Eph. 2:20;
1 Pet. 2:4, 6.

Christ, the head of. Eph. 1:22; 5:23.
Clothed in righteousness. Rev. 19:8.
Defiling of, will be punished.
1 Cor. 3:17.
Displays the wisdom of God.
Eph. 3:10.
Elect. 1 Pet. 5:13.
Extent of, predicted. Isa. 2:2;
Ezek. 17:22–24; Dan. 2:34–35;
Hab. 2:14.
Glorious. Ps. 45:13; Eph. 5:27.
Glory to be ascribed to God by.
Eph. 3:21.
God defends. Ps. 89:18; Isa. 4:5;
49:25; Matt. 16:18.
God provides ministers for.
Jer. 3:15; Eph. 4:11–12.
Is edified by the Word.
1 Cor. 14:4, 13; Eph. 4:15–16.
Loved by Christ. Song of Sol. 7:10;
Eph. 5:25.
Ministers commanded to feed.
Acts 20:28.
Not to be despised. 1 Cor. 11:22.
Object of the grace of God. Isa. 27:3;
2 Cor. 8:1.
Persecuted by the wicked.
Acts 8:1–3; 1 Thess. 2:14–15.
Purchased by the blood of Christ.
Acts 20:28; Eph. 5:25;
Heb. 9:12.
Sanctified and cleansed by Christ.
1 Cor. 6:11; Eph. 5:26–27.
Shows forth the praises of God.
Isa. 60:6.
Subject to Christ. Rom. 7:4;
Eph. 5:24.
Unity of. Rom. 12:5; 1 Cor. 10:17;
12:12; Gal. 3:28.

CHURCH, DISCIPLINE OF THE

Consists in
Maintaining sound doctrine.
1 Tim. 1:3; Titus 1:13.
Ordering its affairs. 1 Cor. 11:34;
Titus 1:5.
Rebuking offenders. 1 Tim. 5:20;
2 Tim. 4:2.
Removing obstinate offenders.
1 Cor. 5:3:5, 13; 1 Tim. 1:20.
Decency and order, the objects of.
1 Cor. 14:40.
Exercise, in a spirit of charity.
2 Cor. 2:6–8.
Ministers authorized to establish.
Matt. 16:19; 18:18.
Prohibits women preaching.
1 Cor. 14:34; 1 Tim. 2:12.
Should be submitted to. Heb. 13:17.

CHURCH, GLORY OF THE

Believers delight in. Isa. 66:11.

Consists in its
Being the body of Christ.
Eph. 1:22–23.
Being the bride of Christ.
Ps. 45:13–14; Rev. 19:7–8;
21:2.
Being established. Ps. 48:8;
Isa. 33:20.
Being the seat of God's worship.
Ps. 96:6.
Being the temple of God.
1 Cor. 3:16 17, Eph. 2:21–22.
Eminent position. Ps. 48:2;
Isa. 2:2.
Graces of character.
Song of Sol. 2:14.
Members being righteous.
Isa. 60:21; Rev. 19:8.
Perfection of beauty. Ps. 50:2.
Sanctification. Eph. 5:26–27.

Strength and defense.
Ps. 48:12–13.
Derived from Christ. Isa. 60:1;
Luke 2:34.
Derived from God. Isa. 28:5.
God delights in. Ps. 45:11;
Isa. 62:3–5.
Grew by increase of its members.
Isa. 49:18; 60:4–14.
Is abundant. Isa. 66:11.
Result from the favor of God.
Isa. 43:4.
Sin obscures. Lam. 2:14–15.

CHURCH, OF ISRAEL

Admission into, by circumcision.
Gen. 17:10–14.
All Israelites members of. Rom. 9:4.
Attachment of the Jews to.
Acts 6:11.

Called the
Congregation of Israel.
Exod. 12:47; Lev. 4:13.
Congregation of the Lord.
Num. 27:17; 31:16.
Converts admitted into.
Num. 9:14; 15:15, 29.
Depository of Holy Scripture.
Rom. 3:2.
Established by God. Deut. 4:5–14;
Deut. 26:18, with Acts 7:35, 38.

Had
Appointed feasts. Lev. 23:2;
Isa 1:14.
Appointed ordinances.
Exod. 18:20; Heb. 9:1, 10.
An appointed place of worship.
Deut. 12:5.
In covenant with God.
Deut. 4:13, 23; Acts 3:25.
The divine presence manifested in
it. Exod. 29:45–46;

Lev. 26:11–12;
1 Kings 8:10–11.

An ordained ministry. Exod. 29:9;
Deut. 10:8.

A spiritual church within it.
Rom. 9:6–8; 11:2–7.

Members of

Excommunicated for heavy
offenses. Num. 15:30–31;
19:20.

Required to attend its worship.
Exod. 23:17.

Required to keep its statutes.
Deut. 16:12.

Required to know its statutes.
Lev. 10:11.

Separated from, while unclean.
Lev. 13: 46; 15:31;
Num. 5:2–4.

Persons excluded
from. Exod. 12:48;
Deut. 23:1–4; Ezek. 44:7, 9.

Privileges of. Rom. 9:4.

Supported by the people.
Exod. 34:20; Deut. 16:17.

A type of the church of Christ.
Gal. 4:24–26; Heb. 12:23.

Was relatively holy. Exod. 31:13;
Num. 16:3.

Worship of, consisted in

Praise. 2 Chron. 5:13; 30:21.

Prayer. Exod. 24:1; Pss. 5:7;
95:6.

Preaching, Neh. 8:4, 7.

Reading God's Word. Exod. 24:7;
Deut. 31:11.

Sacrifice. Exod. 10:25; Lev. 1:2;
Heb. 10:1.

CHURCH/STATE SEPARATION

God

Bestows civil power. Job 12:18;
Jer. 22:1–5; 27:5–6; Dan 2:21;
John 19:11; Rom 13:1.

Controls history. Isa. 46:9–10.

Owns earth. Gen. 14:22;
Ps. 24:1.

Rules over all. Ps. 103:19.

Governmental authorities

Ministers of God. Rom 13:6.

Servants of God. Rom 13:4.

Examples of God's people holding
high positions in nontheocratic
government.

Daniel. Dan 2:48.

Esther. Esther 2:16–17.

Joseph. Gen. 41:39–44.

Nehemiah. Neh. 1:11.

Injunctions concerning

Be subject to governmental
authorities. Eccles. 8:2–5;
Rom. 13:1–5; Titus 3:1;
1 Pet 2:13–14.

Honor the governmental leaders.
1 Pet. 2:17.

Obey God rather than people.
Exod. 1:17; Dan 3;
Acts 4:19–20; 5:29.

Pay taxes due to state.
Matt. 17:24–27; 22:17–21;
Rom. 13:6–7.

Pray for governmental authorities.
1 Tim 2:1–2.

Jesus' kingdom not of this world.
John 18:36.

CHURCH, TITLES AND NAMES OF THE

Assembly of the saints. Ps. 89:7.

Assembly of the upright. Ps. 111:1.

Body of Christ. Eph. 1:22–23;
Col. 1:24.

Branch of God's planting.
Isa. 60:21.

Bride of Christ. Rev. 21:9.

Church of God. Acts 20:28.

Church of the firstborn. Heb. 12:23.

Church of the living God.
1 Tim. 3:15.

City of the living God. Heb. 12:22.

Congregation of believers.
Ps. 149:1.

Congregation of the Lord's poor.
Ps. 74:19.

Dove. Song of Sol. 2:14; 5:2.

Family in heaven and earth.
Eph. 3:15.

Flock of God. Ezek. 34:15;
1 Pet. 5:2.

Fold of Christ. John 10:16.

General assembly of the firstborn.
Heb. 12:23.

Golden candlestick. Rev. 1:20.

God's building. 1 Cor. 3:9.

God's field. 1 Cor. 3:9.

God's heritage. Joel 3:2; 1 Pet. 5:3.

Habitation of God. Eph. 2:22.

Heavenly Jerusalem. Gal. 4:26;
Heb. 12:22.

Holy city. Rev. 21:2.

Holy hill. Ps. 15:1.

Holy mountain. Zech. 8:3.

House of Christ. Heb. 3:6.

House of God. 1 Tim. 3:15;
Heb. 10:21.

House of the God of Jacob. Isa. 2:3.

Household of God. Eph. 2:19.

Inheritance. Ps. 28:9; Isa. 19:25.

Israel of God. Gal. 6:16.

King's daughter. Ps. 45:13.

Lamb's wife. Rev. 19:7; 21.

Lot of God's inheritance. Deut. 32:9.

Mount Zion. Ps. 2:6; Heb. 12:22.

Mountain of the Lord's house.
Isa. 2:2.

New Jerusalem. Rev. 21:2.

Pillar and ground of the truth. 1 Tim.
3:15.

Sanctuary of God. Ps. 114:2.

Sought out, a city not forsaken.
Isa. 62:12.

Spiritual house. 1 Pet. 2:5.

Spouse of Christ. Song of Sol. 4:12;
5:1.

Temple of God. 1 Cor. 3:16–17.

Temple of the living God.
2 Cor. 6:16.

Vineyard. Jer. 12:10; Matt. 21:41.

CINNAMON

An ingredient of the sacred oil.
Exod. 30:23.

A spice. Prov. 7:17;
Song of Sol. 4:14; Rev. 18:13.

CIRCUMCISION

Abolished by the gospel.
Eph. 2:11, 15; Col. 3:11.

Accompanied with naming the child.
Gen. 21:3–4; Luke 1:59; 2:21.

Believers the true spiritual. Phil. 3:3;
Col. 2:11.

Called the
Circumcision in the flesh.
Eph. 2:11.

Concision. Phil. 3:2.

Covenant of circumcision.
Acts 7:8.

Described. Gen. 17:11; Exod. 4:25.

Enforced by the law. Lev. 12:3, with
John 7:22.

First performed on Abraham and his
family. Gen. 17:24–27.

Illustrative of
Purity of heart. Deut. 10:16; 30:6.
Purity of speech. Exod. 6:12.
Readiness to hear and obey. Jer. 6:10.
Instituted by God. Gen. 17:9–10.
Introductory Jewish sacrament. Gal. 5:3.
Inward grace of. Rom. 2:29.

The Jews
Denominated by. Acts 10:45; Gal. 2:9.
Despised as unclean those not of the. 1 Sam.14:6; 17:26; Matt. 15:26–27; Eph. 2:11.
Did not associate with Gentiles. Acts 10:28; 11:3; Gal. 2:12.
Held it unlawful to intermarry with those not of the. Gen. 34:14; Judg. 14:3.
Necessary to enjoying the privileges of the Jewish church. Exod. 11:48; Ezek. 44:7.
Necessity of, asserted by false teachers. Acts 15:24; Gal. 6:12; Titus 1:10.
Necessity of, denied by Paul. Gal. 2:3–5.
Not performed in the wilderness. Josh. 5:5.
Outward sign of. Rom. 2:28.
A painful and bloody rite. Exod. 4:26; Josh. 5:8.
Paul denounced for opposing. Acts 21:21.
Performed by Joshua at Gilgal. Josh. 5:2, 7.
Performed on Timothy as a matter of expediency because of the Jews. Acts 16:3.
Promises to Abraham previous to. Rom. 4:9, 13.

Punishment for neglecting. Gen. 17:14; Exod. 4:24, 26.
A seal of the covenant. Gen. 17:11; Rom. 4:11.
Sometimes performed on slain enemies. 1 Sam. 18:25–27; 2 Sam. 3:14.
Trusting to, a denial of Christ. Gal. 3:3–4, with 5:3–4.

Was performed
By the heads of families. Gen. 17:23; Exod. 4:25.
On the eighth day. Gen. 17:12; Lev. 12:3.
With knives of flint. Exod. 4:25; Josh. 5:3.
On males home-born and bought. Gen. 17:12–13.
By persons in authority. Josh. 5:3.
In the presence of the family, etc. Luke 1:58–61.
Even on the Sabbath day. John 7:22–23.
Without faith, vain. Rom. 3:30; Gal. 5:6.
Without obedience, vain. Rom. 2:25; 1 Cor. 7:19.

CITIES
Afforded refuge in times of danger. Jer. 8:14–16.
Arranged in streets and lanes. Zech. 8:5; Luke 14:21.

Built
Beside rivers. Pss. 46:4, 137:1.
Of brick and mortar. Exod. 1:11, 14.
Of brick and tar. Gen. 11:3.
With compactness. Ps. 122:3.
In desert places. 2 Chron. 8:4; Ps. 107:35–36.

On hills. Matt. 5:14; Luke 4:29;
Rev. 17:9.
Often of a square form.
Rev. 21:16.
In plains. Gen. 11:2, 4; 13:12.
In pleasant situations.
2 Kings 2:19; Ps. 48:2.
On solid foundations. Ezra 6:3;
Rev. 21:14.
Of stone and wood. Ps. 102:14;
Ezek. 26:12.

Called after the
Country in which built.
Dan. 4:29–30.
Family of the founder. Gen. 4:17;
Judg. 18:29.
Proprietor of the land.
1 Kings 16:24.
Densely inhabited. Jon. 4:11;
Nah. 3:8.
Designed for settlements.
Ps. 107:7, 36.

Different kinds of
Chariot. 2 Chron. 1:14; 9:25.
Commercial. Isa. 23:11;
Ezek. 27:3.
Fenced. Josh. 10:20; Isa. 36:1.
Levitical. Lev. 25:32–33;
Num. 35:7–8.
Refuge. Num. 35:6.
Royal. Num. 21:26; Josh. 10:2;
2 Sam. 12:26.
Store. 2 Chron. 8:4, 6.
Treasure. Exod. 1:11.
Difficulty of taking, alluded to.
Prov. 18:19; Jer. 1:18–19.
Entered through gates. Gen. 34:24;
Neh. 13:19, 22.
First mentioned Gen. 4:17.
Furnished with troops.
2 Chron. 11:11–12.
Fortified in war. 2 Chron. 17:2, 19.

Under governors. 2 Chron. 33:14;
2 Cor. 11:32.
A great defense to a country.
2 Chron. 11:5.

Illustrative of
Apostasy. Rev. 16:10; 17:18.
Church triumphant. Rev. 21:2;
22:19.
Heavenly inheritance.
Heb. 11:16.
Riches. Prov. 10:15.
Believers. Matt. 5:14.
Visible church.
Song of Sol. 3:2–3; Rev. 11:2.
Infested by dogs. 1 Kings 14:11;
Ps. 59:6, 14.
Inhabitants of, called citizens.
Acts 21:13.
Numerous. Josh. 15:21;
1 Chron. 2:22; Jer. 2:28.
Often built to perpetuate a name.
Gen. 11:4.
Often deserted on the approach of
an enemy. 1 Sam. 31:7;
Jer. 4:29.
Often fortified by art.
2 Chron. 11:5–10, 23;
Ps. 48:12–13; Jer. 4:5;
Dan. 11:15.
Often fortified by nature. Ps. 125:2;
Isa. 33:16.
Often founded and enlarged by
bloodshed and plunder. Mic. 3:10;
Hab. 2:12.
Often great and goodly. Gen. 10:12;
Deut. 6:10; Dan. 4:30; Jon. 3:3.
Often had fortresses. Judg. 9:51.
Often insignificant. Gen. 19:20;
Eccles. 9:14.
Often of great antiquity.
Gen. 10:11–12.
Perishable nature of. Heb. 13:14.

Prosperity of, increased by
commerce. Gen. 49:13, with
Deut. 33:18–19; Ezek. 28:5.

Protected at night by watchmen.
Ps. 127:1; Song of Sol. 5:7;
Isa. 21:11.

Provided with judges. Deut. 16:18;
2 Chron. 19:5.

Sometimes had suburbs. Num. 35:2;
Josh. 21:3.

Surrounded by walls. Deut. 1:28;
3:5.

Water supplied artificially to.
2 Kings 18:17; 20:20.

Were frequently
Besieged. Deut. 28:52;
2 Kings 19:24–25.

Burned. Judg. 20:38, 40; Isa. 1:7.

Depopulated. Isa. 17:9;
Ezek. 26:19.

Destroyed and sown with salt.
Judg. 9:45.

Made heaps of ruins. Isa. 25:2.

Pillaged. Isa. 13:16; Jer. 20:5.

Stormed. Josh. 8:3–7;
Judg. 9:44.

Wasted by famine. Jer. 52:6;
Amos 4:6.

Wasted by plagues. 1 Sam. 5:11.

CITIES OF REFUGE
See Refuge, Cities of

CITIZENS

Duties of
Be subject to rulers. Rom. 13:1–7.

Pay taxes. Matt. 17:24–27.

Pray for rulers. 1 Tim. 2:1–2.

Strive after the peace of the city.
Jer. 29:7.

Will not curse their ruler.
Acts 23:5.

Will obey the law of the
governmental leaders.
Ezra 7:26.

Will pray for the life of the
governmental leaders.
Ezra 6:10.

*Examples of wicked and
treasonable*
Absalom. 2 Sam. 15:10–13.

Adonijah. 1 Kings 1:5–7.

Ahithophel. 2 Sam. 17:1–4.

Amaziah. 2 Kings 14:18–19.

Amon. 2 Kings 21:23.

Baasha. 1 Kings 15:27.

Barabbas. Mark 15:7.

Bigthan and Teresh. Esther 2:21.

An Egyptian. Acts 21:38.

Ephraimites. Judg. 12:1–4.

Hadad and Jeroboam.
1 Kings 11:14–26.

Hoshea. 2 Kings 15:30.

Ishmael. Jer. 40:14–16; 41.

Israelites. 1 Sam. 10:27;
1 Kings 12:16–19.

Jews. Ezek. 17:12–20.

Jozachar and Jozabad.
2 Kings 12:19–21; 14:5.

Korah, Dathan, and Abiram.
Num. 16; 26:9.

Menahem. 2 Kings 15:14.

Miriam and Aaron.
Num. 12:1–11.

Pekah. 2 Kings 15:25.

Shallum. 2 Kings 15:10.

Sheba. 2 Sam. 20:1–2.

Shechemites. Judg. 9:22–25.

Sons of Sennacherib.
2 Kings 19:36–37.

Theudas and four hundred
seditious persons.
Acts 5:36–37.

Zimri. 1 Kings 16:9.

Loyal, instances of
Barzillai. 2 Sam. 19:32.
David. 1 Sam. 24:6–10;
26:6–16; 2 Sam. 1:14.
David's soldiers.
2 Sam. 18:12–13; 23:15–16.
Hushai. 2 Sam. 17:15–16.
Israelites. Josh. 1:16–18;
2 Sam. 3:36, 37; 15:23, 30;
18:3; 21:17; 1 Chron. 12:38.
Jehoiada. 2 Kings 11:4–12.
Joab. 2 Sam. 19:5–6.
Mordecai. Esther 2:21–23.
Wicked and treasonable,
punishment to. Prov. 17:11;
19:10; 2 Pet. 2:10; Jude 8.
Of God's kingdom. Phil. 3:20;
Eph. 2:19.

Rights of
Roman citizens not to be beaten.
Acts 16:37; 22:25–29.

CIVIL DISOBEDIENCE
See Disobedience, Civil

CIVIL ENGINEERING
See Engineering, Civil

CIVIL LIBERTIES
See Liberties, Civil

CIVIL RIGHTS
See Rights, Civil

CIVIL SERVICE
See Service, Civil

CLAIRVOYANCE
The witch at Endor.
1 Sam. 28:13–14.

CLAY
Blind man's eyes anointed with.
John 9:6.
Humans formed from. Job 33:6.
Seals made of. Job 38:14.
Symbolic sense. Job 4:19; Ps. 40:2;
Isa. 45:9; 64:8; Jer. 18:6;
Rom. 9:21; Dan. 2:33–41.
Used by potter. Isa. 29:16; 41:25;
45:9.

CLEMENCY
Of David toward disloyal subjects.
2 Sam. 19:13, 16–23.

CLERK
Town. Acts 19:35.

CLOAK
Figurative sense. John 15:22;
1 Pet. 2:16.
Paul, left at Troas. 2 Tim. 4:13.

CLOSET
Used as a place for prayer. Matt. 6:6.

CLOTHING
Distinction between men's and
women's clothing. Deut. 22:5.

Headdress

Sandals

Of the Israelites, did not grow old. | Deut. 8:4; 29:5; Neh. 9:21.

Headdress   **Egyptian Headdress**   **Headdress**

CLOUD FORMATIONS

Are the garment of the sea.
Job 38:9.

Called the
Bottles of heaven. Job 38:37.
Chambers of God. Ps. 104:3, 13.
Clouds of heaven. Dan. 7:13;
Matt. 24:30.
Dust of God's feet. Nah. 1:3.
Waters above the heavens.
Gen. 1:7.
Windows of heaven. Gen. 7:11;
Isa. 24:18.

Different kinds of, mentioned
Black. 1 Kings 18:45.
Bright. Job 37:11; Zech. 10:1.
Great. Ezek. 1:4.
Small. 1 Kings 18:44.
Swift. Isa. 19:1.
Thick. Job 22:14; 37:11.
White. Rev. 14:14.
Formed from the sea.
1 Kings 18:44; Amos 9:6.

Frequently the instruments of God's
judgments. Gen. 7:11–12;
Job 37:13; Ps. 77:17.

God
Balanced in the air. Job 37:16.
Binds up. Job 26:8.
Brings over the earth. Gen. 9:14.
Disposed in order. Job 37:15.
Established. Prov. 8:28.
Scatters. Job 37:11.
Spreads out. Job 26:9.

Human
Cannot cause to rain. Job 38:34.
Cannot number. Job 38:37.
Cannot say. Job 38:37.
Ignorant of the balancing of.
Job 37:16.
Ignorant of the disposing of.
Job 37:15.
Ignorant of the spreading of.
Job 36:29.

Illustrative of
False teachers. 2 Pet. 2:17;
Jude 12.
The favor of good rulers.
Prov. 16:15.
The fraudulent. Prov. 25:14.
Goodness of prosperity of
hypocrites. Hos. 6:4; 13:3.
Hostile armies. Jer. 4:13;
Ezek. 38:9, 16.
Judgments of God. Lam. 2:1;
Ezek. 30:3; 34:12; Joel 2:2.
Multitudes of persons. Isa. 60:8;
Heb. 12:1.
The power and greatness of God.
Ps. 104:3; Isa. 19:1.
Human sin. Isa. 44:22.
Unsearchableness of God.
2 Sam. 22:12; Ps. 97:2;
Ezek. 1:4.
Wise rulers. 2 Sam. 23:3–4.
Often cover the heavens. Ps. 147:8.
Often dispersed by the wind.
Hos. 13:3.
Often obscure the sun, etc.
Job 36:32; Ezek. 32:7.
Power and wisdom of God exhibited
in condensing. Job 36:27–28;
37:10–11; Prov. 3:20.
Power and wisdom of God exhibited
in forming. Pss. 135:6–7; 147:5,
8; Jer. 10:13; 51:16.
The rainbow appears in.
Gen. 9:13–14.
Though small, often bring much rain
1 Kings 18:44–45.
Thunder and lightning come from.
Ps. 77:17–18.
Made for the glory of God.
Ps. 148:4.

Uses of
To give rain. Judg. 5:4;
Ps. 104:13–14.

To moderate heat. Isa. 25:5.
To supply dew. Prov. 3:20;
Isa. 18:4.
From the west, bring rain.
Luke 12:54.

CLOUD OF GLORY
See Glory, Cloud of

COAL
Symbolic sense. 2 Sam. 14:7;
Prov. 25:22; Isa. 6:6–7.

COERCION, RELIGIOUS
In Babylon. Dan. 3:2–6, 29;
6:26–27.

COFFER
A chest. 1 Sam. 6:8, 11, 15;
Ezek. 27:24.

COLLUSION
In sin. Lev. 20:4–5.

COLONIZATION
Of conquered countries and people.
2 Kings 17:6, 24; Ezra 4:9–10.

COLORS

Symbolic uses of
Of authorities. Judg. 8:26;
Dan. 5:7, 16, 29; Matt. 27:28.
Black, a symbol of affliction and
calamity. Job 3:5; 10:20–22;
30:26, Pss. 107:10; 143:3;
Isa. 5:30; 8:22; 9:19; 24:11;
50:3; Joel 2:6; 10; 3:14–15;
Amos 5:8; Nah. 2:10;
Zeph. 1:14–15;
Matt. 8:12; 22:13; 25:30;
2 Pet. 2:4; Jude 13;
Rev. 16:10.

Blue, symbol of deity.
Exod. 24:10; 25:3–4; 26:1;
28:28; 38:18; 39:1–5, 21, 24,
29, 31; Num. 4:5–12;
15:38–40; 2 Chron. 2:7;
Jer. 10:9.
Of conquest. Nah. 2:3; Rev. 12:3.

*Crimson, red, purple, and scarlet,
symbols of various ideas.*
Of iniquity. Isa. 1:18;
Rev. 17:3–4; 18:12, 16.
Of prosperity. 2 Sam. 1:24;
Prov. 31:21; Lam. 4:5.
Symbol of authorities.
Esther 8:15; Ezek. 23:6.
As types and shadows of the
atonement. Exod. 25:3–4;
Num. 4:7–8; Isa. 63:1–3;
Heb. 9:19–23.

White, symbol of holiness
Choir singers arrayed in white.
2 Chron. 5:12.
High priest holy garments of white
linen, Lev. 16:4, 32.
Of purity and holiness. Ps. 51:7;
Eccles. 9:8; Isa. 1:18;
Rev. 7:9, 13–14; 15:6;
19:8–11; 20:11.

COMFORT
According to the Word. Ps. 119:76.
Through Christ. 2 Cor. 1:5.
False. Job 16:2.
From God. Ps. 86:17; Isa. 40:1;
61:1–2.
Promised. Matt. 5:4.
True. Job 35:10; Ps. 23:4.

COMFORTER
See also Advocate

Abides forever. John 14:16.

Convicts the world. John 16:8.
Guides into truth. John 16:13.
Teaches all things. John 14:26.
Witnesses to Christ. John 15:26.

COMING OF CHRIST
See Christ, Second Coming of

COMMANDMENTS, TEN
See also Law of God

Enumerated. Exod. 20:3–17.
Law of, is spiritual. Matt. 5:28;
Rom. 7:14.
Spoken by God. Exod. 20:1;
Deut. 5:4, 22.
Summed up by Christ.
Matt. 22:35–40.
Written by God. Exod. 32:16;
34:1, 28; Deut. 4:13; 10:4.

COMMERCE
Of the Arabians. Isa. 60:6;
Jer. 6:20; Ezek. 27:21–24.

Articles of
Apes. 1 Kings 10:22.
Balm. Gen. 37:25.
Bodies and souls of men.
Rev. 18:13.
Blue cloth. Ezek. 27:24.
Brass. Ezek. 27:13.
Cattle. Ezek. 27:21.
Chest of rich apparel.
Ezek. 27:24.
Chariots. 1 Kings 10:29;
Rev. 18:13.
Cinnamon. Rev. 18:13.
Citron wood. Rev. 18:12.
Clothes for chariots. Ezek. 27:20.
Corn. 1 Kings 5:11; Ezek. 27:17.
Embroidery. Ezek. 27:16, 24.
Frankincense. Jer. 6:20;
Rev. 18:13.

Gold. 1 Kings 9:28; 10:22;
  2 Chron. 8:18; Isa. 60:6;
  Rev. 18:2.
Honey. Ezek. 27:17.
Horses. 1 Kings 10:29;
  Ezek. 27:14; Rev. 18:13.
Iron and steal. Ezek. 27:12, 19.
Ivory. 1 Kings 10:22;
  2 Chron. 9:21; Ezek. 27:15;
  Rev. 18:12.
Land. Gen. 23:13–16; Ruth 4:3.
Lead. Ezek. 27:12.
Linen. 1 Kings 10:28;
  Rev. 18:12.
Oil. 1 Kings 5:11; Ezek. 27:17.
Pearls. Rev. 18:12.
Peacocks. 1 Kings 10:22.
Perfumes. Song of Sol. 3:6.
Precious stones.
  Ezek. 27:16, 22; 28:13, 16;
  Rev. 18:12.
Purple. Ezek. 27:16; Rev. 18:12.
Sheep. Rev. 18:13.
Silk. Rev. 18:12.
Silver. 1 Kings 10:22;
  2 Chron. 9:21; Rev. 18:12.
Slaves. Gen. 37:28, 36;
  Deut. 24:7.
Sweet cane. Jer. 6:20.
Timber. 1 Kings 5:6–8.
Tin. Ezek. 27:12.
Wheat. Rev. 18:13.
White wool. Ezek. 27:18.
Wine. 2 Chron. 2:15;
  Ezek. 27:18; Rev. 18:13.
Babylonians. Rev. 18:3, 11–13.
Carried on by means of caravans.
  Gen. 37:25, 27; Isa. 60:6.
Conducted in fairs. Ezek. 27:12, 19;
  Matt. 11:16.
Egyptians. Gen. 42:2–34.
Ethiopians. Isa. 45:14.

Evil practices connected with.
  Prov. 29:14; Ezek. 22:13;
  Hos. 12:7.
Ishmaelites. Gen. 37:27–28.
Israelites. 1 Kings 9:26–28;
  Neh. 3:31–32; Ezek. 27:17.
Jews. Ezek. 27:17.
Laws concerning. Lev. 19:36–37;
  25:14, 17.
Ninevites. Nah. 3:16.
Ships. 1 Kings 9:27–28; 10:11;
  Ps. 107:23–30; Prov. 31:14;
  Rev. 18:19.
Syrians. Ezek. 27:16, 18.
Tarshish. Jer. 10:9; Ezek. 27:25.
Tyrians. 2 Sam. 5:11; 1 Kings 5:6;
  Isa. 23:8; Ezek. 27; 28:5.
Zidonians. Isa. 23:2; Ezek. 27:8.
Transportation of passengers.
  Jon. 1:3; Acts 21:2; 27:2, 6, 37.

COMMISSARY
For armies, cattle driven with.
  2 Kings 3:9.
For royal households.
  1 Kings 4:7–19, 27–28.

COMMON GOOD
Do not withhold good. Prov 3:27.

COMMUNICATION
Enhanced through interpretation.
  Neh. 8:8.

From God
  By means of Jesus. Heb 1:2.
  In various times and ways.
    Heb. 1:1.
  Spoken. Exod. 20:1; 33:11.
  Through creation. Ps. 19:1–4.
  Written. Jer. 36:1–2;
    2 Tim. 3:16.

Hindered
By foreign language.
Gen. 11:1, 7; Ezek. 3:6.
By human frailty. Mark 4:33;
8:14–21; Heb 5:11.
By sin. Gen. 3:8–10.

Intimate
With friend. Exod. 33:11;
Ps. 55:13–14; Gal. 6:2.
With God. Exod. 33:11;
Num. 12:8; Matt. 6:9;
Rom. 8:26–27.

Nonverbal
Actions. 1 Kings 21:4;
Matt. 5:16.
Eyes. 2 Kings 8:11; Luke 22:61.
Face. Gen. 4:6.
Hands. Exod. 17:11–12;
Gal. 2:9; 1 Tim. 2:8.
Kiss. 1 Cor. 16:20.
Touch. Mark 10:13; Luke 7:39.
Preaching. Rom. 10:17;
2 Tim. 4:2.
Propaganda. 2 Kings 18:26–27.
Songs. Eph. 5:19.

Speech
Bold. Acts 13:46.
Childish. 1 Cor. 13:11.
Clear. Num. 12:8; Col. 4:4.
Deliberate. James 1:19.
Dirty. Eph. 5:4.
Edifying. Eph. 4:15, 29.
Eloquent. Exod. 4:14; Prov. 17:7.
As example. 1 Tim. 4:12.
False. Prov. 17:7.
Gracious. Prov. 22:11; Col. 4:6.
Pure. Zeph. 3:9.
Timely. Eccles. 3:7; Eph. 4:29.
Truthful. Eph. 4:25.
Untrained. Exod. 4:10; Jer. 1:6.
Weak. 2 Cor. 10:10.

Without love. 1 Cor. 13:1.

Written
For instruction. Rom.. 15:4.
Prophetic. Jer. 36:2; Hab. 2:2.
As Scripture. 2 Tim. 3:16.
Strong. 2 Cor. 10:10.

COMMUNITY
Agreement in. Ps. 55:13–14;
Amos 3:3.
Corporate nature of. Exod. 20:5–6;
Num. 16:27–32; 1 Kings 22:52;
Ezek. 18:2; Acts 16:31;
Rom. 14:7–8; 1 Cor. 12:26.

Established by God.
From creation. Gen. 2:18.
In heaven. Rev. 5:9–10; 7:9;
21:2.
On earth. Exod. 6:2–8; Deut. 5:3;
32:8; Jer. 30:20;
1 Pet. 2:9–10.
Diversity in. Exod. 12:38;
1 Cor. 12:12; Rev. 5:9–10.
Lord's Supper as sign of.
1 Cor. 10:16.
Reconciliation. 2 Cor. 5:17–19.

Responsibilities in.
Bear one another's burdens.
Eccles. 4:9–12; Rom.. 12:15;
Gal. 6:2.
Edification. Luke 22:32;
Rom. 15:2; 1 Thess. 5:11.
Provide for others.
James 2:15–16;
1 John 3:17–18.
Worship. Pss. 22:22, 25; 107:32.
Unity in. John 15:5; 17:21;
Eph. 4:3.

COMMUNITY SERVICE
See Service, Community

COMMUNION OF BELIEVERS
See Believers, Communion of

COMMUNION
See Lord's Supper, The

COMMUNION WITH GOD
See God, Communion with

COMPANIONSHIP
With the disciples. Acts 2:44–47;
 Gal. 2:9; 1 John 1:7.
With God. Col. 13:14; 1 John 1:3.
With the righteous. Ps. 119:63.
With the unrighteous. Ps. 1:1.

COMPANY, EVIL
See also Peer Pressure

Command to avoid.
 Exod. 23:2, 32–33;
 1 Cor. 5:6–11; 2 Cor. 6:14–17.
Council to strive after good peers.
 Prov. 13:20.

COMPASSION AND SYMPATHY
Christ set an example of.
 Luke 19:41–42.

Exercise toward
 The afflicted. Job 6:14;
  Heb. 13:3.
 Believers. 1 Cor. 12:25–26.
 The disciplined. Isa. 22:4;
  Jer. 9:1.
 Enemies. Ps. 35:13.
 The poor. Prov. 19:17.
 The weak. 2 Cor. 11:29;
  Gal. 6:2.
Exhortation to. Rom. 12:15;
 1 Pet. 3:8.
Inseparable from love to God.
 1 John 3:17; 4:20.

Motives to
 The compassion of God.
  Matt. 13:27, 33.
 Promise to those who show.
  Prov. 19:17; Matt. 10:42.
 The sense of our sufferings.
  Heb. 5:2.
 The wicked made to feel, for
  believers. Ps. 106:46.

COMPASSION AND SYMPATHY OF CHRIST
See Christ, Compassion and
 Sympathy of

COMPLAINT

Examples of
 Asaph. Ps. 73:3.
 Cain. Gen. 4:13–14.
 David. 2 Sam. 6:8;
  Ps. 116:10–11.
 Elijah. 1 Kings 19:4, 10.
 Hezekiah. Isa. 38:9–20.
 Israelites. Exod. 5:21; 14:11–12;
  15:23–24; 16:2–3; 17:2–3;
  Num. 11:1–10, 33; 14; 16:41;
  20:2–5; 21:5–6;
  Deut. 1:27–28; Ps. 106:24–26.
 Jeremiah. Jer. 20:14–18.
 Jews, against Jesus.
  John 6:41–43, 52.
 Job. Job 3; 6; 7; 9; 10; 13; 19;
  23; 30.
 Jonah. Jon. 4.
 Korah. Num. 16:8–11.
 Moses. Exod. 5:22–23;
  Num. 11:11–15.
 Solomon. Eccles. 2:17–18.
Against God. Exod. 5:22–23;
 Job 15:11–13; 33:12–13; 34:37;
 Ps. 44:9–26.
Israelites against Moses.
 Exod. 5:21; 15:24; 16:2, 3;

Num. 16:2–3, 13–14, 41;
20:2–4.

COMPLICITY

Examples of
The daughter of Herodias in
asking for the head of John the
Baptist. Matt. 14:8; Mark 6:25.
Pilate in the death of Jesus.
Matt. 27:17–26;
Mark 15:1–15; Luke 23:13–25;
John 19:13–16.
Paul, in the stoning of Stephen.
Acts 7:58.
With a thief. Ps. 50:18; Prov. 29:24.

COMPROMISE

Encouraged, before litigation.
Prov. 25:8–10; Luke 12:58–59.

CONCEIT

Example of, the Pharisee.
Luke 18:11–12.
Of God's people, Israel.
Rom. 11:25.
Warning against. Prov. 3:5–7.

CONCEPTION

Miraculous
Elizabeth. Luke 1:24–25, 36–37,
58.
Hanna. 1 Sam. 1:19–20.
Manoah's wife. Judg. 13:3–24.
Mary. Matt. 1:18, 20;
Luke 1:26–35.
Rachel. Gen. 30:22.
Rebecca. Gen. 25:21.
Sarah. Gen. 21:1–2.

CONCUBINES

Called wives. Gen. 37:2.

Children of, not heirs. Gen. 15:4;
21:10.
Laws concerning. Exod. 21:7–11;
Lev. 19:20–22; Deut. 21:10–14.
Subject to be dismissed.
Gen. 21:10–14.

CONCUBINAGE

Practiced by
Abijah. 2 Chron. 13:21.
Abraham. Gen. 16:3; 25:6;
1 Chron. 1:32.
Belshazzar. Dan. 5:2.
Caleb. 1 Chron. 2:46–48.
David. 2 Sam. 5:13; 15:16.
Eliphaz. Gen. 36:12.
Jacob. Gen. 30:4.
Gideon. Judg. 8:31.
A Levite. Judg. 19:1.
Manasseh. 1 Chron. 7:14.
Nahor. Gen. 22:23–24.
Rehoboam. 2 Chron. 11:21.
Saul. 2 Sam. 3:7.
Solomon. 1 Kings 11:3.

CONDEMNATION

According to men's deserts.
Matt. 12:37; 2 Cor. 11:15.
Apostates ordained for. Jude 4.
Chastisements are designed to rescue
us from. Ps. 94:12–13;
1 Cor. 11:32.
Conscience testifies to the justice of.
Job 9:20; Rom. 2:1; Titus 3:11.

Increased by
Hypocrisy. Matt. 23:14.
Impenitence. Matt. 11:20–24.
Oppression. James 5:1–5.
Pride. 1 Tim. 3:6.
Unbelief. John 3:18–19.
Inseparable consequence of sin.
Prov. 12:2; Rom. 6:23.

The law is the ministration of.
2 Cor. 3:9.
The law testifies to the justice of.
Rom. 3:19.
Of the wicked, an example.
2 Pet. 2:6; Jude 7.
Saints are delivered from, by Christ.
John 3:18; 5:24; Rom. 8:1,
33–34.
The sentence of God against sin.
Matt. 25:41.
Unbelievers remain under.
John 3:18, 36.
Universal, caused by the sin of Adam.
Rom. 5:12, 10, 18.

CONDESCENSION OF GOD
See God, Condescension of

CONDOLENCE
Examples of
David to Hanun. 2 Sam. 10:2.
Jesus to Mary and Martha.
John 11:23–35.
King of Babylon to Hezekiah.
2 Kings 20:12–13.
The three friends to Job.
Job 2:11.

CONDUCT
According to men's deserts.
Matt. 12:37; 2 Cor. 11:15.
Believers are delivered from, by
Christ. John 3:18; 5:24;
Rom. 8:1, 33–34.
Conscience testifies to the justice of.
Job 9:20; Rom. 2:1; Titus 3:11.
The godless condemned to. Jude 4.

Increased by
Hypocrisy. Matt. 23:14.
Oppression. James 5:1–5.
Pride. 1 Tim. 3:6.

Refusal to repent.
Matt. 11:20–24.
Unbelief. John 3:18–19.
Inseparable consequence of sin.
Prov. 12:2; Rom. 6:23.
The law is the instrumentality.
2 Cor. 3:9.
The law testifies to the justice of.
Rom. 3:19.
Punishments are designed to rescue
us from. Ps. 94:12–13;
1 Cor. 11:32.
The sentence of God against sin.
Matt. 25:41.
Unbelievers remain under.
John 3:18, 36.
Universal, caused by the offense of
Adam. Rom. 5:12, 16, 18.
Of the wicked, an example.
2 Pet. 2:6; Jude 7.

CONDUCT, CHRISTIAN
Abounding in the work of the Lord.
1 Cor. 15:58; 2 Cor. 8:7;
1 Thess. 4:1.
Abstaining from all appearance of
evil. 1 Thess. 5:22.
Adorning the gospel. Matt. 5:16;
Titus 2:10.
Avoiding the wicked. Ps. 1:1;
2 Thess. 3:6.
Being contented. Phil. 4:11;
Heb. 13:5.
Being generous to others.
Acts 20:35; Rom. 12:13.
Believing God. Mark 11:22;
John 14:11–12.
Believing in Christ. John 6:29;
1 John 3:23.
Controlling the body. 1 Cor. 9:27;
Col. 3:5.
Doing as we would be done by.
Matt. 7:12; Luke 6:31.

Fearing God. Eccles. 12:13;
1 Pet. 2:17.
Following after that which is good.
Phil. 4:8; 1 Thess. 5:15;
1 Tim. 6:11.
Following God. Eph. 5:1;
1 Pet. 1:15–16.
Following the example of Christ.
John 13:15; 1 Pet. 2:21–24.
Forgiving injuries. Matt. 6:14;
Rom. 12:20.
Fulfilling domestic duties.
Eph. 6:1–8; 1 Pet. 3:1–7.
Hating defilement. Jude 23.
Honoring others. Ps. 15:4;
Rom. 12:10.

Living
Soberly, righteously, and godly.
Titus 2:12.
To Christ. Rom. 14:8;
2 Cor. 5:15.
For righteousness. Mic. 6:8;
Rom. 6:18; 1 Pet. 2:24.
Living peaceably with all.
Rom. 12:18; Heb. 12:14.
Loving Christ. John 21:15;
1 Pet. 1:7–8.
Loving God. Deut. 6:5; Matt. 22:37.
Loving one another. John 15:12;
Rom. 12:10; 1 Cor. 13;
Eph. 5:2; Heb. 13:1.
Obeying Christ. John 14:21; 15:14.
Obeying God. Luke 1:6; 1 John 5:3.
Overcoming the world.
1 John 5:4–5.
Perfecting holiness. Matt. 5:48;
2 Cor. 7:1; 2 Tim. 3:17.
Putting away all sin. 1 Cor. 5:7;
Heb. 12:1.
Rejoicing in Christ. Phil. 3:1; 4:4.
Rejoicing in God. Ps. 33:1;
Hab. 3:18.

Showing a good example.
1 Tim. 4:12; Titus 2:7;
1 Pet. 2:12.
Striving for the faith. Phil. 1:27;
Jude 3.
Subduing the temper. Eph. 4:26;
James 1:19.
Submitting to authorities.
Rom. 13:1–7.
Submitting to injuries.
Matt. 5:39–41; 1 Cor. 6:7.
Sympathizing with others. Gal. 6:2;
1 Thess. 5:14.
Visiting the afflicted. Matt. 25:36;
James 1:27.

Walking
As children of light. Eph. 5:8.
Honestly. 1 Thess. 4:12.
In newness of life. Rom. 6:4.
After the Spirit. Rom. 8:1.
In the Spirit. Gal. 5:25.
Worthy of God. 1 Thess. 2:12.
Worthy of our vocation. Eph. 4:1.
Worthy of the Lord. Col. 1:10.
Worth of maintaining.
Pss. 1:1–3; 19:9–11; 50:23;
Matt. 5:3–12; John 7:17; 15:10.

CONFESSING CHRIST
Consequences of not. Matt. 10:33.
Ensures His confessing us.
Matt. 10:32.
As evidence of union with God.
1 John 4:15.
Fear of others prevents.
John 7:13; 12:42–43.
Influences of the Holy Spirit
necessary to. 1 Cor. 12:3;
1 John 4:2.
Must be connected with faith.
Rom. 10:9.
Necessary to salvation.
Rom. 10:9–10.

Persecution should not prevent us from. Mark 8:35; 2 Tim. 2:12.
As test of being believers.
1 John 2:23; 4:2–3.

CONFESSION OF SIN
See Sin, Confession of

CONFIDENCE
See also subtopics: Confidence, Betrayed; Confidence, False

Foolish. Ps. 49:13; Phil. 3:3.
For the judgment. 1 John 4:17.
Before God. 1 John 3:21.
In the Lord. Ps. 118:8–9; Gal. 5:10; 2 Thess. 3:4.
In the Lord's people. Phil. 1:21.
Producing results. Matt. 17:20; Mark 9:23.
Sustaining. Heb. 3:14.
Wise (in the Lord). Ps. 118:8.

CONFIDENCE, BETRAYED
Examples of
Ahimelech by David.
1 Sam. 21:1–9.
Joshua by the Gideonites.
Josh. 9:3–15.
Eglon by Ehud. Judg. 3:15–23.
Abner by Joab. 2 Sam. 3:27.
Amasa by Joab. 2 Sam. 20:9–10.
The worshipers of Baal by Jehu.
2 Kings 10:18–28.

CONFIDENCE, FALSE
Examples of
Asa, in relying on Ben-hadad rather than on God.
2 Chron. 16:7–9.
Builders of Babel. Gen. 11:4.

Hezekiah, in the defenses of Jerusalem. Isa. 22:11.
Jonah. Jon. 1:3–5.
Paul. Phil. 1:25; 2:23–24.
Peter. Matt. 26:33–35.
Saul. 1 Sam. 13:8–14.
Sennacherib. 2 Kings 19:23.
Sennacherib, in the siege of Jerusalem. 2 Kings 19:23.
In outward resources. Ps. 20:7.
In people. Ps. 33:16; Isa. 2:22.
In self. Deut. 29:19; Rom. 12:16.

CONFISCATION
As a penalty. Ezra 10:8.

Of property
By Ahab of Naboth's vineyard.
1 Kings 21:7–16.
By Ahasuerus, of Haman's house.
Esther 8:1.
By David, that of Mephibosheth.
2 Sam. 16:4.

CONFLICT, INTERPERSONAL
See also Sibling Rivalry

Caused by
Jesus. Matt. 10:34–36.
Passions. James 4:1–3.

Examples of
Abram and Lot. Gen. 13:8–18
Corinthian believers.
1 Cor. 1:10–12; 3:2–4, 11.18.
Disciples of Jesus. Mark 9:33–37; Luke 22:24–27.
Isaac and Abimelech.
Gen. 26:26–30.
Jacob and Esau. Gen. 25:22–34; 27:1–45; 32:3–33:17.
Jacob and Laban. Gen. 29–31.
Joseph and brothers. Gen. 37–50.

Mary and Martha.
Luke 10:38–42.
Paul and Barnabas.
Acts 15:36–41.
Sarai and Hagar. Gen. 16:4–6.
Saul and David. 1 Sam. 18–31.
Saul and Jonathan.
1 Sam. 20:30–34.
Shepherds of Isaac and shepherds
of Abimelech. Gen. 26:19–22.
Hated by God. Prov. 6:16, 19.

Injunctions concerning
Be at peace with one another.
Mark 9:50; 1 Thess. 5:13.
Be united in mind and judgment.
1 Cor. 1:10.
Behave decently, as in the
daytime. Rom. 13:13.
Have the mind of Jesus.
Phil. 2:3–8.
Strive for peace. Ps. 34:14;
Rom. 14:19; Heb. 12:14;
1 Pet. 3:11.

Rather, live
In harmony. Rom. 15:5–6.
In peace. John 16:33;
1 Cor. 7:15.
In unity. Ps. 133:1.

Results in
Discord. Prov. 6:12–15.
Strife. Prov. 10:12; 16:28.

Stirred up by
Angry man. Prov. 15:18; 29:22.
Greedy man. Prov. 28:25.
Hating man. Prov. 10:12.
Perverse man. Prov. 16:28.
Tattler. Prov. 16:28.
Worthless man. Prov. 6:12–15.
As a work of the sinful nature.
Gal. 5:20.

CONFUSION
Of tongues. Gen. 11:1–9.

CONGESTION
Sent as judgment of God.
Deut. 28:22.

CONSCIENCE
Accuses of sin. Gen. 42:21;
2 Sam. 24:10; Matt. 27:3;
Acts 2:37.
Of believers, pure and good.
Heb. 13:18; 1 Pet. 3:16, 21.
Blood of Christ alone can purify.
Heb. 9:14; 10:2–10, 22.
Keep the faith in purity of.
1 Tim. 1:19; 3:9.
Ministers should commend
themselves to that of their people.
2 Cor. 4:2; 5:11.
Of others, not to be offended.
Rom. 14:21; 1 Cor. 10:28–32.
Submit to authority for. Rom. 13:5.
Suffer patiently for. 1 Pet. 2:19.
Testimony of, a source of joy.
2 Cor. 1:12; 1 John 3:21.
We should have the approval of.
Job 27:6; Acts 24:16; Rom. 9:1;
14:22.
Of the wicked, defiled. Titus 1:15.
Of the wicked, seared. 1 Tim. 4:2.
Without spiritual illumination, a false
guide. Acts 23:1, with 26:9.
Witnesses in man. Prov. 20:27;
Rom. 2:15.

CONSCIENTIOUS OBJECTORS

Injunctions concerning
Be subject to governing authorities
for sake of conscience.
Rom. 13:5.
Live peaceably as far as it depends
on you. Rom. 12:18.

Obey God rather than people.
Acts 5:29.

Principles relevant to
Accept consequences when
disobeying state. Dan 6:10–16;
Acts 5:40–42; 25:11.
Individual conscience before God.
Rom. 14:4.
Value of a good conscience.
1 Tim. 1:19.

CONSCRIPTION
Of soldiers. 1 Sam. 14:52.

CONSECRATION
Conditional. Gen. 28:20;
2 Sam. 15:7–8.

Examples of
Abraham of Isaac. Gen. 22:9–12.
David, of the water obtained by his
valiant warriors. 2 Sam. 23:16.
Hannah, of Samuel. 1 Sam. 1:11,
24–28.
Jephthah, of his daughter.
Judg. 11:30–31, 34–40.
Zichri, of himself.
2 Chron. 17:16.
Personal. Ps. 51:17;
Matt. 13:44–46; Rom. 6:13, 16,
19; 12:1–2; 2 Cor. 8:5.

CONSERVATISM

Hold fast to
Confession. Heb. 4:14; 10:23.
Faith. 1 Cor. 16:13.
Sure word as taught. Titus 1:9.
Teachings of elders. Prov. 1:8;
4:1–4; Mark 7:3–4.
Teachings of Paul. 1 Cor. 11:2;
2 Thess. 2:15; 2 Tim. 1:13.
What has been learned. 2 Tim. 3:14.

CONSISTENCY
Encouraged by Jesus. Matt. 6:24.
By Paul. 1 Cor. 10:21.

CONSPIRACY

Examples of
Abimelech against Gideon's sons.
Judg. 9:1–6.
Abner, against Ishbosheth.
2 Sam. 3:7–21.
Of Absalom. 2 Sam. 15:10–13.
Ahasuerus. Esther 2:21–23.
Amaziah. 2 Chron. 25:27.
Amon. 2 Kings 21:23.
Of Baasha. 1 Kings 15:27.
Daniel. Dan. 6:4–17.
Delilah, against Samson.
Judg. 16:4–21.
Gaal, against Abimelech.
Judg. 9:23–41.
Of Jehoiada. 2 Kings 11:4–16.
Of Jehu. 2 Kings 9:14–26.
Jeremiah. Jer. 18:18.
Of Jeroboam. 1 Kings 14:2.
Against Jesus. Jer. 11:9, 19;
Matt. 12:14; 21:38–41;
26:3–4; 27:1–2; Mark 3:6.
Of Jezebel, against Naboth.
1 Kings 21:8–13.
Joseph brethren against Joseph.
Gen. 37:18–20.
Miriam, Aaron, and Israelites
against Moses. Num. 12; 14:4;
16:1–35.
Against Paul. Acts 18:12;
23:12–15.
Pekah. 2 Kings 15:30.
Pekahiah. 2 Kings 15:23–25.
People in Jerusalem, against
Amaziah. 2 Kings 14:19.
Of servants, against Joash.
2 Kings 12:20.
Sennacherib. 2 Kings 19:36–37.

Shadrach, Meshach, Abednego.
Dan. 3:8–18.
Shalum against Zachariah.
2 Kings 15:10.
Of Zimri. 1 Kings 16:9.
Falsely accused of, Jonathan.
1 Sam. 22:8.
Law against. Exod. 23:1–2.

CONSTANCY
In doing good. Gal. 6:9.

Examples of
Ruth. Ruth 1:14.
Jonathan. 1 Sam. 18:1; 20:16.
Priscilla and Aquila. Rom. 16:3–4.
In friendship. Prov. 27:10.
In obedience. Ps. 119:31–33.
In prayer. Luke 18:1; Rom. 12:12;
Eph. 6:18; Col. 4:2;
1 Thess. 5:17.
In profession. Heb. 10:23.
Under suffering. Matt. 5:12;
Heb. 12:5; 1 Pet. 4:12–16.

CONSTELLATIONS
Orion. Job 9:9; Amos 5:8.
The serpent. Job 26:13.

CONSTITUTION
Agreement between a ruler and a
people. Deut. 17:18–20;
2 Sam. 5:3; 2 Chron. 23:2–3;
Jer. 34:8–11; Dan. 6:12–15.

CONSUMPTION
As judgment of God. Deut. 28:22.

CONTEMPT
Believers sometimes guilty of.
James 2:6.
Causes believers to cry to God.
Neh. 4:4; Ps. 123:3.

A characteristic of the wicked.
Prov. 18:3; Isa. 5:24; 2 Tim. 3:3.
Folly of. Prov. 11–12.

Forbidden toward
Believing masters. 1 Tim. 6:2.
Christ's little ones. Matt. 18:10.
Parents. Prov. 23:22.
The poor. James 2:1–3.
Weak brethren. Rom. 14:3.
Young ministers. 1 Cor. 16:11.
Ministers should give no occasion for.
1 Tim. 4:12.
Of ministers, is a despising of God.
Luke 10:16; 1 Thess. 4:8.
Pride and prosperity prompt to.
Ps. 123:4.
Self-righteousness prompts to.
Isa. 65:5; Luke 18:9, 11.
Sin of. Job 31:13–14; Prov. 14:21.

The wicked exhibit toward
The afflicted. Job 19:18.
Authorities. 2 Pet. 2:10; Jude 18.
Christ. Ps. 22:6; Isa. 53:3;
Matt. 27:29.
Parents. Prov. 15:5, 20.
The poor. Ps. 14:6; Eccles. 9:16.
Believers. Ps. 119:111.

Toward the church
Often punished. Ezek. 28:26.
Often turned into respect.
Isa. 60:14.

CONTENTMENT

Believers should exhibit
With appointed wages. Luke 3:14.
With food and clothing.
1 Tim. 6:8.
In their respective callings.
1 Cor. 7:20.
With what things they have.
Heb. 13:5.

Commandment. Heb. 13:5.

Examples of
Barzillai, in refusing to go with David to Jerusalem. 2 Sam. 19:33–37.
Esau, in refusing Jacob's present. Gen. 33:9.
The Shunammite, in refusing to make a request of Elisha. 2 Kings 4:13.
God's promises should lead to. Heb. 13:5.
From a good heritage. Ps. 16:6.
Paul's. Phil. 4:11.
Source of contentment. Prov. 16:8; 17:1; 30:8.
Value of. 1 Tim. 6:6.
The wicked want. Isa. 5:8; Eccles. 5:10.
With godliness is great gain. Ps. 37:16; 1 Tim. 6:6.

CONTINENCE
Job. Job 31:1.
Jesus' command. Matt. 5:27.
Paul's command. Rom. 13:13; 1 Cor. 7:1–9, 25–38; 9:27; Col. 3:5; 1 Tim. 4:12; 5:1.

Examples of
Boaz. Ruth 3:6–13.
Joseph. Gen. 39:7–12.
Joseph, husband of Mary. Matt. 1:24–25.
Paul. 1 Cor. 7:8.
Uriah. 2 Sam. 11:8–13.

CONTINENTS
Creation of. Gen. 1:9–10.

CONTINGENCIES
Cain. Gen. 4:7.

Eating the fruit from the tree of the knowledge of good and evil. Gen. 2:16–17.
The Lord's promise to Israel. Exod. 19:5; Deut. 11:26–28; 30:15–19; Josh. 24:15.
Promise to Solomon. 1 Kings 3:14.

CONTRACTS
Between Abraham and Abimelech concerning wells of water. Gen. 21:25–32.
The binding force of. Matt. 20:1–16.
By blotting out. Col. 2:14.
For cattle. Gen. 30:27–29, 31–34.
By consummating in the presence of the public at the gate of the city. Gen. 23:18; Ruth 4:1–2.
Dissolved, by mutual consent. Exod. 4:18.
By erecting a heap of stones. Gen. 31:44–54.
First contract between Laban and Jacob for Laban's daughter. Gen. 29:15–20, 27–30.
By joining hands. Prov. 6:1; 11:21; 17:18; 22:26; Ezek. 17:18.
Modes of ratifying, by giving presents. Gen. 21:25–30.
By oaths. Gen. 26:3, 31; Josh. 9:15, 20; 1 Chron. 16:16; Heb. 6:16–17.
With salt. Num. 18:19.
Second contract. Gen. 30:28–34.
Between Solomon and Hiram. 1 Kings 5:9–11; 9:11.
By taking of the shoe. Ruth 4:6–8.
Violated. Gen. 26:15; 29:23–27; 30:37–43; 31:7.
Written instruments. Jer. 32:10–15.

CONVERSATION
Jesus' command concerning.
Matt. 5:37.
Paul's commands concerning.
Gal. 3:8; 4:6; Eph. 4:29.

CONVERSION
By Christ. Acts 3:26; Rom. 15:18.
Commanded. Job 36:10.
Danger of neglecting. Ps. 7:12;
Jer. 44:5, 11; Ezek. 3:19.
Duty of leading sinners to. Ps. 51:13.
Encouragement for leading sinners
to. Dan. 12:3; James 5:19–20.
Exhortations to. Prov. 1:23;
Isa. 31:6; 55:7; Jer. 3:7;
Ezek. 33:11.
Follows repentance. Acts 3:19;
26:20.
Of Gentiles, predicted.
Isa. 2:2; 11:10; 60:5; 66:12.
By God. 1 Kings 18:37; John 6:44;
Acts 21:19.

Through the instrumentality of
Affliction. Ps. 78:34.
Ministers. Acts 26:18;
1 Thess. 1:9.
Scripture. Ps. 19:7.
Self-examination. Ps. 119:59;
Lam. 3:40.
Is accompanied by confession of sin,
and prayer. 1 Kings 8:35.
Is necessary. Matt. 18:3.
Is of grace. Acts 11:21, with v. 23.
Is the result of faith. Acts 11:21.
Of Israel, predicted.
Ezek. 36:25–27.
By the power of the Holy Spirit.
Prov. 1:23.
Pray for. Pss. 80:7; 85:4;
Jer. 31:18; Lam. 5:21.
Promises connected with. Neh. 1:9;
Isa. 1:27; Jer. 3:11; Ezek. 18:27.

Of sinners, a cause of joy
To believers. Acts 15:3;
Gal. 1:23–24.
To God. Ezek. 18:23;
Luke 15:32.

CONVERTS

Examples of
Andrew. John 1:40–41.
A blind man. John 9:8–38.
Cornelius. Acts 10.
The eunuch from Ethiopia.
Acts 8:35–38.
The Gadarenes. Luke 8:35–39.
Greeks. Acts 17:4, 12.
Jailer. Acts 16:27–34.
Jews and Greeks at Antioch.
Acts 13:43.
Lydia. Acts 16:14–15.
The Mariners with Jonah.
Jon. 1:5–6, 9, 14, 16.
Nebuchadnezzar. Dan. 4.
Ninevites. Jon. 3.
Philip. John 1:43–45.
Ruth. Ruth 1:16.
The Samaritans. John 4:28–42.
Saul of Tarsus. Acts 9:3–18.
Sergius Paulus. Acts 13:7–12;
26:12–23.
The thief on the cross.
Luke 23:39–43.
Three thousand at Pentecost.
Acts 2:41.
The woman of Samaria.
John 4:28–29.

CONVICTION, COURAGE OF
Abraham, in leaving his fatherland.
Gen. 12:1–9.
Abraham, in offering Isaac.
Gen. 22:1–14.

Agag, in the indifference with which he faced death.
1 Sam. 15:32–33.

The apostles, under persecution.
Acts 5:21, 29–32.

Daniel, in persisting in prayer, regardless of the edict against praying. Dan. 6:10.

David, in entering into the tent of Saul and carrying away Saul's spear. 1 Sam. 26:7–12.

David, in slaying Goliath.
1 Sam. 17:32–50.

David's captains. 2 Sam. 23.

Debra, in leading Israel's armies.
Judg. 4.

Esther, in going to the king to save her people. Esther 4:8, 16.

Ezra, in undertaking the perilous journey from Babylon to Palestine without a guard. Ezra 8:22–23.

Gideon, in attacking the confederate armies of the Midianites and Amalekites with 300 men.
Judg. 7:7–23.

Gideon, in destroying the altar of Baal. Judg. 6:25–31.

Jael, in slaying Sisera.
Judg. 4:18–22.

The Jews, in returning answer to Tatnai. Ezra 5:11.

Joab, in reproving King David.
2 Sam. 19:5–7.

Joseph of Arimathaea, in coming for the body of Jesus. Mark 15:43.

Joshua and Caleb, in advising that Israel go at once and possess the land. Num. 13:30; 14:6–12.

Nehemiah, in refusing to take refuge in the temple. Neh. 6:10–13.

Othniel, in smiting Kirjathsepher.
Josh. 15:16–17.

Paul, in going to Jerusalem, despite his impressions that bonds and imprisonment awaited him.
Acts 20:22–24; 24:14, 25.

Peter and John, in refusing to obey men, rather than God. Acts 4:19; 5:29.

Peter and the other disciples.
Acts 3:12–26; 4:9–13, 19–20, 31.

The three Hebrews who refused to bow down to the image of Nebuchadnezzar. Dan. 3:16–18.

Thomas, in being willing to die with Jesus. John 11:16.

CONVICTION OF SIN
See Sin, Conviction of

COOKING
Ephraim, a cake unturned. Hos. 7:8.

Prohibition against a kid being seethed in its mother's milk.
Deut. 14:21.

Spice used in. Ezek. 24:10.

In the temple. Ezek. 46:19–24.

CORD
Binding prisoners. Judg. 15:13.

In casting lots. Mic. 2:5.

Fastening tents. Exod. 35:18; 39:40.

Of friendship. Eccles. 4:12; Hos. 11:4.

Hitching to cart or plow. Job 39:10.

Leading or binding animals.
Ps. 118:27; Hos. 11:4.

Of life. Eccles. 12:6.

Measuring ground. 2 Sam. 8:2.

Sign in mourning.
1 Kings 20:31–33; Job 36:8.

Of sin. Prov. 5:22.

Symbolically used of spiritual
blessings. Ps. 16:6.
Worn on the head as a sign of
submission. 1 Kings 20:31.

CORN
Eaten by Israel. Josh. 5:11–12.
Ground. 2 Sam. 17:19.
Heads of, plucked by Christ's
disciples. Matt. 12:1.
Mosaic laws concerning. Exod. 22:6;
Deut. 23:25.
In Palestine. Deut. 33:28;
Ezek. 27:17.
Parched. Ruth 2:14; 1 Sam. 17:17;
2 Sam. 17:28.
A product of Egypt. Gen. 41:47–49.
Shocks of, burnt. Judg. 15:5.
Symbolic sense. Gen. 41:5.
In valleys. Ps. 65:13; Mark 4:28.

CORPORAL PUNISHMENT
See Punishment, Corporal

CORRECTION
Of children. Prov. 13:24; 19:15.
As discipline. Ps. 39:11.
From government. 1 Pet. 2:14.
In love. Heb. 12:5–7.
For righteousness of life.
Heb. 12:11.
From Scripture. 2 Tim. 3:16.

CORRUPTION
Figurative, of sin. Isa. 38:17.
Mount of. 2 Kings 23:13.
Physical, decomposition.
Lev. 22:25.

COSMETICS
Jezebel's use of. 2 Kings 9:30.

COST OF LIVING
See Living, Cost of

COUNSEL
Rejected. Prov. 1:24–33.

Examples of
By Rehoboam. 1 Kings 12:8–16.
By the rich young ruler.
Matt. 19:22.

COUNSELOR
Ahithophel was to Absalom.
2 Sam. 16:23.
Ahithophel was, to David.
2 Sam. 16:23.; 1 Chron. 27:33.
Joseph of Arimathea, was member
of the Sanhedrin at Jerusalem.
Mark 15:43; Luke 23:50–51.
A title of Christ. Isa. 9:6.
A wise man, versed in law and
diplomacy. 1 Chron. 27:32–33.

COUNSELS AND PURPOSES OF GOD
See God, Counsels and Purposes of

COUNTENANCE
Angry. Prov. 25:23.
Cheerful. Job 29:24; Ps. 4:6; 21:6;
44:3; Prov. 15:13; 27:17.
Fierce. Deut. 28:50; Dan. 8:23.
Guilty. Gen. 4:5; Isa. 3:9.
Health indicated in. Ps. 42:11; 43:5.
Pride in. 2 Kings 5:1; Ps. 10:4.
Reading of. Gen. 31:2, 5.
Sad. 1 Sam. 1:18; Neh. 2:2–3;
Eccles. 7:3; Ezek. 27:35;
Dan. 1:15; 5:6.
Transfigured. Exod. 34:29–35;
Luke 9:29; 2 Cor. 3:7, 13.

COUNTRY, LOVE OF
Expressed in captivity. Ps. 137:1–6.

COURAGE

Commanded. Deut. 31:6; Josh. 1:7;
Isa. 41:10.
Commanded upon the Israelites.
Lev. 26:6–8; 2 Chron. 32:7–8.
Commanded by Jehoshaphat upon
the judicial and executive officers
he appointed. 2 Chron. 19:11.
Commanded upon Joshua.
Deut. 31:7–8, 22–23;
Josh. 1:1–9.
Despite enemies. Phil. 1:28.
Imposed upon Asa.
2 Chron. 15:1–7.
Imposed upon Solomon.
1 Chron. 22:13; 28:20.
From the Lord. Heb. 13:6.

COURAGE OF CONVICTION

See Conviction, Courage of

COURTS OF JUSTICE

See Justice, Courts of

COVENANT

An agreement between two parties.
Gen. 26:28; Dan. 11:6.

Conditions of
Clearly specified. 1 Sam. 11:1–2.
Confirmed by oath.
Gen. 21:23, 31; 26:31.
Witnessed. Gen. 23:17–18;
Ruth 4:9–11.
Written and sealed. Neh. 9:38;
10:1.

Designed for
Establishing friendship.
1 Sam. 18:8.
Establishing peace.
Josh. 9:15–16.
Mutual protection.
Gen. 26:28–29; 31:50–52.

Procuring assistance in war.
1 Kings 15:18–19.
Promoting commerce.
1 Kings 5:6–11.
Selling land. Gen. 23:14–16.
Followed by a feast. Gen. 26:30;
31:54.
God often called to witness.
Gen. 31:50, 53.

Illustrative of
Worldly security (with death and
hell). Isa. 28:15, 18.
God's promises to humans.
Gen. 9:9–11; Eph. 2:12.
Good resolutions. Job 31:1.
Marriage contract. Mal. 2:14.
Peace and prosperity (with stones
and beasts of the earth).
Job 5:23; Hos. 2:18.
The united determination of a
people to serve God.
2 Kings 11:17;
2 Chron. 15:12; Neh. 10:29.

The Jews
Condemned for making with
idolatrous nations. Isa. 30:2–5;
Hos. 12:1.
Forbidden to make with the
nations of Canaan.
Exod. 23:32; Deut. 7:2.
Frequently made with other
nations. 1 Kings 5:12;
2 Kings 17:4.
Regarded as sacred.
Josh. 9:16–19; Ps. 15:4.
Made by passing between the pieces
of the divided sacrifices.
Gen. 15:9–17; Jer. 34:18–19.
Names given to places where made.
Gen. 21:31; 31:47–49.
Pillars raised in sign of.
Gen. 31:45–46.

Presents given as tokens of.
Gen. 21:27–30; 1 Sam. 18:3–4.
Ratified by joining hands.
Prov. 11:21; Ezek. 17:18.
Salt a sign of permanence in.
Num. 18:19; 2 Chron. 13:5.
Violated by the wicked. Rom. 1:31;
2 Tim. 3:3.
When confirmed, unalterable.
Gal. 3:15.

COVENANT, THE
All believers interested in.
Pss. 25:14; 89:29–37;
Heb. 8:10.
Be mindful of. 1 Chron. 16:15.
Blessings connected with.
Isa. 56:4–7; Heb. 8:10–12.
Caution against forgetting.
Deut. 4:23.
Christ the mediator of.
Heb. 8:6; 9:15; 12:24.
Christ the messenger of. Mal. 3:1.
Christ the substance of. Isa. 42:6;
49:8.
Confirmed in Christ. Gal. 3:17.
Everlasting. Ps. 111:9; Isa. 55:3;
61:8; Ezek. 16:60–63;
Heb. 13:20.
Fulfilled in Christ. Luke 1:68–79.
God is ever mindful of. Pss. 105:8;
111:5; Luke 1:72.
God is faithful to. Deut. 7:9;
1 Kings 8:23; Neh. 1:5;
Dan. 9:4.

Made with
Abraham. Gen. 15:7–18;
17:2–14; Luke 1:72–75;
Acts 3:25; Gal. 3:16.
David. 2 Sam. 23:5; Ps. 89:3–4.
Isaac. Gen. 17:19, 21; 26:3–4.
Israel. Exod. 6:4; Acts 3:25.

Jacob. Gen. 28:13–14, with
1 Chron. 16:16–17.
One of peace. Isa. 54:9–10;
Ezek. 34:25; 37:26.
Plead, in prayer. Ps. 74:20;
Jer. 14:21.
Punishment for despising.
Heb. 10:29–30.
Ratified by the blood of Christ.
Heb. 9:11–14, 16–23.
Renewed under the gospel.
Jer. 31:31–33; Rom. 11:27;
Heb. 8:8–10, 13.
Unalterable. Ps. 89:34; Isa. 54:10;
59:21; Gal. 3:17.
The wicked have no interest in.
Eph. 2:12.

COVETOUSNESS
Abhorred by God. Ps. 10:3.
Affliction, calamity denounced
against. Prov. 1:18–19; Isa. 5:8;
Hab. 2:9; Ezek. 22:12.
Avoid those guilty of. 1 Cor. 5:11.
Believers must rid themselves of.
Col. 3:5.
Beware of. Luke 12:15.
A characteristic of the lazy.
Prov. 21:25–26.
A characteristic of the wicked.
Rom. 1:29.
Comes from the heart.
Mark 7:22–23.
Commended by the wicked alone.
Ps. 10:3.
Engrosses the heart. Ezek. 33:31;
2 Pet. 2:14.
Excludes from heaven. 1 Cor. 6:10;
Eph. 5:5.
Forbidden. Exod. 20:17.
Hated by believers. Exod. 18:21;
Acts 20:33.

Is

Idolatry. Eph. 5:5; Col. 3:5.
Never satisfied. Eccles. 5:10;
Hab. 2:5.
The root of all evil. 1 Tim. 6:10.
Vanity. Ps. 39:6; Eccles. 4:8.

Is inconsistent

In believers. Eph. 5:3; Heb. 13:5.
In ministers. 1 Tim. 3:3.

Leads to

Departure from the faith.
1 Tim. 6:10.
Domestic affliction. Prov. 15:27.
Foolish and hurtful lusts.
1 Tim. 6:9.
Injustice and oppression.
Prov. 28:20; Mic. 2:2.
Lying. 2 Kings 5:22–25.
Misery. 1 Tim. 6:10.
Murder. Prov. 1:18–19;
Ezek. 22:12.
Poverty. Prov. 28:22.
Theft. Josh. 7:21.
Pray against. Ps. 119:36.
Punishment of. Job 20:15;
Isa. 57:17; Jer. 22:17–19;
Mic. 2:2–3.
Reward of those who hate.
Prov. 28:16.
Will abound in the last days.
2 Tim. 3:2; 2 Pet. 2:1–3.

COWARDICE

God creates, in the enemies of His
people. Lev. 26:36–37.
Contagious among God's people.
Deut. 20:8.
A characteristic of the wicked.
Prov. 28:1.
A trait of some of Paul's companions.
2 Tim. 4:16.

Examples of

Aaron, in yielding to the Israelites
when they demanded an idol.
Exod. 32:22–24.
Abraham, in calling his wife his
sister. Gen. 12:11–19;
20:2–12.
Adam, in attempting to shift
responsibility for his sin upon
Eve. Gen. 3:12.
In the battle with the people of Ai.
Josh. 7:5.
Canaanites. Josh. 2:11; 5:1.
David, in fleeing from Absalom.
2 Sam. 15:13–17.
Disciples, in the storm at sea.
Matt. 8:26; Mark 4:38;
Luke 8:25.
Disciples, when they saw Jesus
walking on the sea.
Matt. 14:25–26; Mark 6:50;
John 6:19.
Disciples, when Jesus was
apprehended. Matt. 26:56.
Early converts among the rulers.
John 12:42–43.
Ephramites. Ps. 78:9.
To fight with the Philistines.
1 Sam. 13:6–7.
Guards of the tomb of Jesus.
Matt. 28:4.
Isaac, in calling his wife his sister.
Gen. 26:7–9.
Israelites, in fearing to attempt the
conquest of Canaan.
Num. 14:1–5; Deut. 26–28.
Jacob, in fleeing from Laban.
Gen. 31:31.
Joseph of Arimathaea. Secretly a
disciple of Jesus. John 19:38.
Kings of the Amorites.
Josh. 10:16.
Manassehites. Josh. 17:14–18.

To meet Goliath. 1 Sam. 17:24.

Nicodemus, in coming to Jesus by night. John 3:1–2.

Parents of the blind man who was restored to sight. John 9:22.

Peter and other Christians at Antioch. Gal. 2:11–14.

Peter, in denying the Lord. Matt. 26:69–74; Mark 14:66–72; Luke 22:54–60; John 18:16–17, 25, 27.

The Philippian jailer. Acts 16:27.

Pilate, in condemning Jesus, through fear of the people. John 19:12–16.

Samuel, fearing to obey God's command to anoint a king in Saul's place. 1 Sam. 16:2.

The ten spies. Num. 13:28; 31–33.

Twenty-two thousand of Gideon's army. Judg. 7:3.

CRAFTINESS

Examples of

Gibeonites, in deceiving Joshua and the Israelites into a treaty. Josh. 9:3–15.

Jacob, in management of Laban's flocks and herds. Gen. 30:31–43.

Jacob, in purchase of Esau's birthright. Gen. 25:31–33.

Jacob, obtaining Isaac's blessing. Gen. 27:6–29.

Jewish leaders, in striving to enslave Jesus. Matt. 26:4; Mark 14:1.

Jewish leaders, in striving to entangle Jesus. Matt. 22:15–17, 24–28.

Sanballat, in trying to deceive Nehemiah into a conference. Neh. 6.

Satan, in the temptation of Eve. Gen. 3:1–5.

CREATION

Approved of by God. Gen. 1:31.

By faith we believe, to be God's work. Heb. 11:3.

Effected

According to God's purpose. Ps. 135:6.

In the beginning. Exod. 20:11; 31:17.

By Christ. John 1:3, 10; Col. 1:16.

For Christ. Col. 1:16.

By the command of God. Ps. 33:9; Heb. 11:3.

By God. Gen. 1:1; 2:4–5; Prov. 26:10.

For God's pleasure. Prov. 16:4; Rev. 4:11.

By the Holy Spirit. Job 26:13; Ps. 104:30.

In six days. Exod. 20:11; 31:17.

Exhibits

The deity of God. Rom. 1:20.

The glory and handiwork of God. Ps. 19:1.

God as the sole object of worship. Isa. 45:16–18; Acts 17:24–27.

The goodness of God. Ps. 33:5.

The power of God. Isa. 40:26–28; Rom. 1:20.

The wisdom of God. Pss. 104:24; 136:5.

Formation of things that had no previous existence. Rom. 4:17, with Heb. 11:3.

Glorifies God. Pss. 145:10; 148:5.

God rested from, on the seventh day.
Gen. 2:2–3.

God to be praised for. Neh. 9:6;
Ps. 136:3–9.

Groans because of sin. Rom. 8:22.

Illustrative of
Daily renewal of believers.
Ps. 51:40; Eph. 4:24.
New birth. 2 Cor. 5:17;
Eph. 2:10.
Renewal of the earth. Isa. 65:17;
2 Pet. 3:11, 13.
Insignificance of humans seen
from. Ps. 9:3–4; Isa. 40:12, 17.
Leads to confidence. Pss. 124:8;
146:5–6.

Order of
First day, making light and dividing
it from darkness. Gen. 1:3–5;
2 Cor. 4:6.
Second day, making the
firmament or atmosphere, and
separating the waters.
Gen. 1:6–8.
Third day, separating the land
from the water and making it
fruitful. Gen. 1:9–13.
Fourth day, placing the sun, moon,
and stars to give light, etc.
Gen. 1:14–19.
Fifth day, making birds, insects,
and fishes. Gen. 1:20–23.
Sixth day, making beasts of the
earth and man. Gen. 1:24, 28.
A subject of joy to angels. Job 38:7.

CREDIT CARDS

See also Creditors

Covetousness. Exod. 20:17;
Acts 20:33.
Daily bread. Prov. 30:8; Matt. 6:11.

Exorbitant interest. Ps. 15:5;
Prov. 28:8; Ezek. 18:8, 13.
Inability to repay debts. Hab. 2:6–7.
Indulgence enriches merchants.
Rev. 18:3.

Principles relevant to borrowing
Borrowed item repaid in full even if
at borrower's loss. Exod. 22:14.
Borrower is slave of lender.
Prov. 22:7.
Owe no one anything. Rom. 13:8.
Wicked do not repay what is owed.
Ps. 37:21.

CREDITORS
Defined. Philem. 1:18.

Illustrative of
The demands of the law. Gal. 5:3.
God's claim upon people.
Matt. 5:25–26, with 18:23, 35;
Luke 7:41, 47.

Might demand
Bills or promissory notes.
Luke 16:6–7.
Mortgages on property. Neh. 5:3.
Pledges. Deut. 24:10–11;
Prov. 22:27.
Security of others. Prov. 6:1;
22:26.
Might take interest from strangers.
Deut. 23:20.
Often cruel in exacting debts.
Neh. 5:7–9; Job 24:3–9;
Matt. 18:28–30.

Often exacted debts
By imprisonment. Matt. 5:25–26;
18:34.
By selling the debtor or taking him
for a servant. Matt. 18:25, with
Exod. 21:2.

By selling the debtor's family.
2 Kings 4:1; Job 24:9;
Matt. 18:25.
By selling the debtor's property.
Matt. 18:25.
From those who have become
legally liable for another person's
debt. Prov. 11:15; 22:26–27.

Prohibited from
Exacting debts from brethren
during sabbatical year.
Deut. 15:2–3.
Exacting interest from brethren.
Exod. 22:25; Lev. 25:36–37.
Taking millstones in pledge.
Deut. 24:6.
Violently selecting pledges.
Deut. 24:10.
Sometimes entirely remitted debts.
Neh. 5:10–12; Matt. 18:27;
Luke 7:42.
To return before sunset, garments
taken in pledge. Exod. 22:26–27;
Deut. 24:12–13; Ezek. 18:7, 12.
Were often defrauded. 1 Sam. 22:2;
Luke 16:5–7.

CREEPING THINGS
Clean. Lev. 11:21–22.
A general term for animals.
Gen. 1:26; Lev. 11:20–23,
29–31, 42; Ps. 104:20, 25;
Rom. 1:23.
Unclean. Lev. 5:2; 11:20, 29–44;
Deut. 14:19.
Uses of, in idolatrous worship.
Ezek. 8:10.

CREMATION

Examples of
Casualties of war. Amos 6:9–10.
King of Edom. Amos 2:1.

Men of Bethel. 1 Kings 13:2;
2 Kings 23:16.
People of Babylon (fig).
Ezek. 24:10.
Priests of Samaria. 2 Kings 23:20.

Principles relevant to
Individual integrity of body at final
judgment. Rev. 20:13.
Joshua and Israel carry out, on
their enemies. Josh. 7:25.
Carried out on Saul and his sons.
1 Sam. 31:12.

CRIB
Used for grain. Job 39:9;
Prov. 14:4; Isa. 1:3.

CRIME
Craftiness of criminals.
Prov. 1:11, 15, 18.
Rebuked. Isa. 1:16–17; Jon. 3:8.
Results of bloodshed. Gen. 9:6;
Matt. 26:52.
Significance of. John 3:19;
1 Cor. 6:10.
Source. Matt. 15:19–20.
Totality of disorder. Jer. 7:9;
Ezek. 7:23.

CRIMINALS
Confined in dungeons. Gen. 40:15;
41:14; Exod. 12:29; Isa. 24:22;
Jer. 37:16; 38:10;
Lam. 3:53, 55.
Confined in prisons.
Gen. 39:20–23; Ezra 7:26;
Acts 4:3; 12:4–5; 16:19–40.
Released at feasts. Matt. 27:15, 21.

CRITICISM
Abimelech criticizes Abraham for a
like offense. Gen. 20:9–10.

Abimelech criticizes Isaac for similar conduct. Gen. 26:9–10.

Cain criticizes God. Gen. 4:13–14.

David criticizes Joab for slaying Abner. 2 Sam. 3:28–21.

Deborah criticizes Israel in her epic. Judg. 5:16–23.

Isaac and Laban criticize each other. Gen. 31:26–42.

Israelites criticize Moses and tempt God. Exod. 17:7.

Jacob criticizes Simeon and Levi for slaying Hamor and Shechem. Gen. 34:30.

Jesus criticizes His disciples for forbidding children to come to Him. Matt. 19:14; Mark 10:14; Luke 18:16.

Jesus criticizes His disciples for showiness of heart. Matt. 15:16; 16:8–9, 11; Mark 7:18; Luke 24:25; John 14:9.

Jesus criticizes His disciples for sleeping in Gethsemane. Matt. 26:40; Mark 14:27.

Jesus criticizes His disciples for their unbelief. Matt. 8:26; 14:31; 16:8–11; 17:17; Mark 4:40; Luke 8:25.

Joab criticizes David for lamenting the death of Absalom. 2 Sam. 19:5–7.

Pharaoh criticizes Abraham for calling his wife his sister. Gen. 12.18 19.

Reuben criticizes his brethren for their treatment of Joseph. Gen. 42:22.

CROSS
To be carried by Jesus' followers. Matt. 10:38.

Borne by Jesus. John 19:17.

Borne by Simon. Matt. 27:32; Mark 15:21; Luke 23:26.

Enemies of. Phil. 3:18.

Jesus crucified on. Matt. 27:32; Luke 23:26; Acts 2:23, 36; 4:10; 1 Cor. 1:23; 2:2, 8; Eph. 2:16; Phil. 2:8; Col. 1:20; 2:14; Heb. 12:2.

Offensive. Gal. 5:11.

Paul's glory in. Gal. 6:14.

Preaching of, is foolishness. 1 Cor. 1:17.

CROSS-DRESSING
Forbidden. Deut. 22:5.

CROWN
Corruptible and incorruptible. 1 Cor. 9:25.

Eternal. Rev. 3:11.

Of glory. 1 Pet. 5:4.

Of life. James 1:12.

Made of gold. Ps. 21:3; Zech. 6:11.

An ornament. Ezek. 23:42.

Prescribed for priests. Exod. 29:6; 39:30; Lev. 8:9.

Of righteousness. 2 Tim. 4:8.

Set with gems. 2 Sam. 12:30; 1 Chron. 20:2; Isa. 62:3; Zech. 9:16.

Symbolic sense. Rev. 4:4, 10; 6:2; 9:7; 12:1, 3; 13:1; 14:14; 19:12.

Of thorns. Matt. 27:29; John 19:5.

Of victory. 2 Tim. 2:5.

Worn by kings. 2 Sam. 1:10; 12:30; 2 Kings 11:12; Esther 6:8; Song of Sol. 3:11; Rev. 6:2.

Worn by queens. Esther 1:11; 2:17.

CRUCIFIXION
With Christ. Gal. 2:20.

Of disciples, predicted. Matt. 23:34.

Of our old self. Rom. 6:6.
The reproach of. Gal. 3:13; 5:11.
Of two criminals. Matt. 27:38.

CRUELTY

Instances of
Egyptians to the Israelites.
Exod. 5:6–18.
Jewish leaders to Jesus.
Matt. 26:67; 27:28–31.
Peninnah to
Hannah. 1 Sam. 1:4–7; 2:3.
Roman soldiers to Jesus.
Luke 22:64; John 19:3.
Sarah to Hagar. Gen. 16:6;
21:9–14.
In war. Isa. 13:16, 18.

CUCUMBER

Eaten by Hebrews in Egypt.
Num. 11:5.
Field. Isa. 1:8.

CUD

Chewing of, was one of the facts by
which clean and unclean animals
were distinguished. Lev. 11:3–8;
Deut. 14:3–8.

CUP

Of consolation. Jer. 16:7.
Figurative, of sorrow. Pss. 11:6;
73:10; 75:8; Isa. 51:17, 22;
Jer. 25:15–28; Ezek. 23:31–34;
Matt. 20:22, 23; 26:39;
Mark 14:36; Luke 22:42;
John 18:11; Rev. 14:10.
Of joy. Ps. 23:5.
Made of gold. 1 Chron. 28:17;
Jer. 52:19.
Made of silver. Gen. 44:2.
Of salvation. Ps. 116:13.
Of the table of devils. 1 Cor. 10:21.

Used in the institution of the Lord's
Supper. Mark 14:23;
1 Cor. 10:21.

CURIOSITY

Examples of
Of Abraham to know whether God
would destroy the righteous in
Sodom. Gen. 18:23–32.
Of angels, to look into the
mysteries of salvation.
1 Pet. 1:12.
Of the Athenians, to hear some
new things. Acts 17:19–21.
Of the Babylonians, to see
Hezekiah's treasures.
2 Kings 20:13.
Of Daniel, to know a vision.
Dan. 12:8–9.
A disciple, to know if there by few
that will be saved. Luke 13:23.
Of the disciples, to know whether
Jesus would restore the kingdom
at the present time. Acts 1:6–7.
The first of Eve. Gen. 3:6.
Of the Greeks to see Jesus.
John 12:20–21.
Of Herod, to see Jesus. Luke 9:9;
23:8.
Of the Israelites, to see God.
Exod. 19:21–24.
Of Jacob, to know the name of the
angel. Gen. 32:29.
Of the Jewish leaders, to see
Lazarus, after he was raised from
the dead. John 12:9.
Of Manoah, to know the name of
an angel. Judg. 13:17–18.
Of the people of Bethshemesh, to
see inside the ark. 1 Sam. 6:19.
Of Peter, to know what was being
done with Jesus. Matt. 26:58.

Of Peter, to know what
John would be appointed to do.
John 21:21–22.

To witness the offering in the Holy
of Holies. Num. 4:19, 20.

A trait of human beings.
Prov. 27:20.

CURSE

Against Adam and Eve.
Gen. 3:15–19.

Barak commands Balaam to curse
Israel. Num. 22:6; 23:11.

Against Cain. Gen. 4:11–16.

Against Canaan. Gen. 9:24–27.

Denounced against the serpent.
Gen. 3:14–15.

Against Gehazi. 2 Kings 5:27.

Against the ground. Gen. 3:17–18.

Against Meroz. Judg. 5:23.

Of the Mosaic law. Deut. 27:1–26;
Josh. 8:30–34.

CURSING

The laws of Jesus concerning.
Matt. 5:44; Luke 6:28.

Of parents. Exod. 21:17;
Matt. 15:4; Mark 7:10.

Shimei curses David.
2 Sam. 16:5–8.

CYMBAL

Of brass. 1 Chron. 15:19, 28;
1 Cor. 13:1.

In the temple service. 1 Chron. 16:5,
42; 2 Chron. 5:12–13; 25:1, 6;
Ps. 150:5.

Used in the tabernacle service.
2 Sam. 6:5; 1 Chron. 13:8;
15:16, 19, 28.

Used on special occasions
Day of Atonement.
2 Chron. 29:25.
Dedication of the wall.
Neh. 12:27, 36.
Laying of the foundation of the
second temple. Ezra 3:10–11.

D

DAILY SACRIFICES
See Sacrifices, Daily

DAMAGES AND COMPENSATION
For accidentally causing an abortion. Exod. 21:22.
For damages resulting from lying. Lev. 6:1–5.
For injury by an animal. Exod. 21:28–32.
For injury to a neighbor's animal. Exod. 21:33–34.
For loss of time. Exod. 21:18–19.
For wrong to a young woman. Deut. 22:13–19.

DANCING
Children's game in Jesus' day. Luke 7:32.
In celebration of the prodigal's return. Luke 15:25.
The daughters of Shiloh. Judg. 21:19.
David. 2 Sam. 6:14.
Herodias, before Herod. Matt. 14:6; Mark 6:22.
Idolatrous. Exod. 32:19, 25.
Jephthah's daughter. Judg. 11:34.
Miriam. Exod. 15:20.
Praising God with. Ps. 150:4.
A time for. Eccles. 3:4.
Turned into mourning. Lam. 5:15.
Turning mourning into. Ps. 30:11.
Women of Israel in response to returning army. 1 Sam. 18:6.

DARKNESS
Called night. Gen. 1:5.
Called the swaddling band of the sea. Job 38:9.
Cannot hide us from God. Ps. 139:11–12.
Caused by setting of the sun. Gen. 15:17; John 6:17.
Created by God. Ps. 104:20; Isa. 45:7.

Degrees of, mentioned
Great. Gen. 15:12.
Gross. Jer. 13:16.
Outer or extreme. Matt. 8:12.
That may be felt. Exod. 10:21.
Thick. Deut. 5:22; Joel 2:2.

Effects of
Causes us to go astray. John 12:35; 1 John 2:11.
Causes us to stumble. Isa. 59:10.
Keeps us from seeing objects. Exod. 10:23.
Exhibits God's power and greatness. Job 38:8–9.

Illustrative of
Anything hateful. Job 3:4–9.
A course of sin. Prov. 2:13, Eph. 5:11.
The gravel. 1 Sam. 2:9; Job 10:21–22.
The greatness and unsearchableness of God. Exod. 20:21; 2 Sam. 22:10, 12; 1 Kings 8:12; Ps. 97:2.
Heavy afflictions. Job 23:17; Ps. 112:4; Eccles. 5:17; Isa. 5:30; 8:22; 59:9.

Ignorance and error. Job 37:19;
Isa. 60:2; John 1:5; 3:19;
12:35; Acts 26:18.

The power of Satan. Eph. 6:12;
Col. 1:13.

The punishment of devils and
wicked men. Matt. 22:13;
2 Pet. 2:4, 17; Jude 6, 13.

Secrecy. Isa. 45:19; Matt. 10:27.

Wisdom. Job 28:3.

Inexplicable nature of.
Job 38:19–20.

Miraculous

At the death of Christ.
Matt. 27:45.

Before the destruction of
Jerusalem. Matt. 24:29.

Over the land of Egypt.
Exod. 10:21–22.

On Mount Sinai. Exod. 19:16,
with Heb. 12:18.

Often put for night. Ps. 91:6.

Originally covered the earth.
Gen. 1:2.

Separated from the light. Gen. 1:4.

The wicked

Are children of. 1 Thess. 5:5.

Are full of. Matt. 6:23.

Live in. Ps. 107:10.

Perpetrate their plans in.
Job 24:16.

Walk in. Ps. 82:5.

DART

In a figurative sense, of the wicked.
Eph. 6:16.

A light javelin. Num. 25:7;
1 Sam. 18:10; 2 Sam. 18:14;
Job 41:29.

DAUGHTER

Forbidden to be the wife of her
mother's husband. Lev. 20:14.

Given in marriage by her parents.
Judg. 1:12–13; 1 Sam. 17:25;
18:20–21.

Property right of. Num. 27:1–11;
36; Josh. 17:3–6; Ruth 4:3.

Used also for granddaughter.
Gen. 36:2.

Sold as a concubine. Exod. 21:7–10.

DAUGHTER-IN-LAW

Filial, Ruth. Ruth 1:11–18; 4:15.

Unfilial, prophecy of. Mic. 7:6;
Matt. 10:35.

DAY

Artificial, divided into

Break of. Gen. 32:24, 26;
Song of Sol. 2:17.

Morning. Exod. 29:39;
2 Sam. 23:4.

Noon. Gen. 43:16; Ps. 55:17.

Decline of. Judg. 19:8–9;
Luke 9:12; 24:29.

Evening. Gen. 8:11; Ps. 104:23;
Jer. 6:4.

Artificial, the time of the sun's
continuance above the horizon.
Gen. 31:39–40; Neh. 4:21–22.

Divided into four parts. Neh. 9:3.

Illustrative of

The path of the just. Prov. 4:18.

Spiritual light. 1 Thess. 5:5, 8;
2 Pet. 1:19.

Time of judgment. 1 Cor. 3:13,
with 4:3.

Latterly subdivided into twelve hours.
Matt. 20:3, 5–6; John 11:9.

The light first called. Gen. 1:5.

Made for the glory of God.
  Ps. 74:16.
Natural, from evening to evening.
  Gen. 1:5; Lev. 23:32.
Proclaims the glory of God. Ps. 19:2.
Prophetical, a year. Ezek. 4:6;
  Dan. 12:12.
Succession, of, secured by covenant.
  Gen. 8:22.
Time ascertained by the dial.
  2 Kings 20:11.
Time for labor. Ps. 104:23;
  John 9:4.

A time of festivity called a
  Day of gladness. Num. 10:10.
  Day of good tidings. 2 Kings 7:9.
  Day which the Lord has made.
    Ps. 118:24.
  Good day. Esther 8:17; 9:19.
  Solemn day. Num. 10:10;
    Hos. 9:5.

A time of judgment called a day of
  Adversity. Prov. 24:10.
  Anger. Lam. 2:21.
  Calamity. Deut. 32:35;
    Jer. 18:17.
  Darkness. Joel 2:2, Zeph. 1:15.
  Destruction. Job 21:30.
  Evil. Jer. 17:17; Amos 6:3;
    Eph. 6:13.
  The Lord. Isa. 2:12; 13:6;
    Zeph. 1:14.
  Slaughter. Isa. 30:25; Jer. 12:3.
  Trouble. Ps. 102:2.
  Vengeance. Prov. 6:34; Isa. 61:2.
  Visitation. Mic. 7:4.
  Wrath. Job 20:28;
    Zeph. 1:15, 18; Rom. 2:5.

A time of mercy called a day of
  God's power. Ps. 110:3.
  Redemption. Eph. 4:30.

  Salvation. 2 Cor. 6:2.
  Visitation. Jer. 27:22;
    1 Pet. 2:12.
Under the control of God. Amos 5:8;
  8:9.
Wild beasts hide during. Ps. 104:22.

DAY OF ATONEMENT
See Atonement, Day of

DEACON
An ecclesiastic charged with the
  temporal affairs of the church.
  Ordained by the
  apostles. Acts 6:1–6.
Qualifications of. 1 Tim. 3:8–13.

DEACONESS
Phoebe. Rom. 16:1.

DEAD, THE
All offerings to, forbidden.
  Deut. 26:14.

Characterized by
  Absence of all human passions.
    Eccles. 9:6.
  Being incapable of motion.
    Matt. 28:4; Rev. 1:17.
  Being without the Spirit.
    James 2:26.
  Ignorance of all human affairs.
    Eccles. 9:5.
  Inability to glorify God.
    Ps. 115:17.
Even bones of, caused uncleanness.
  Num. 19:16; *See also*
  2 Chron. 34:5.
Eyes of, closed by nearest of kin.
  Gen. 46:4.
Heathenish expressions of grief for,
  forbidden. Lev. 19:28;
  Deut. 14:1–2.

High priest in no case to mourn for.
Lev. 21:10–11.

In a house, rendered it unclean.
Num. 19:14–15.

Idolaters
Consecrated part of their crops to.
Deut. 26:14.

Invoked and consulted.
1 Sam. 28:7–8.

Offered sacrifices for. Ps. 106:28.

Tore themselves for. Jer. 16:7.

Illustrative of
Fortune-tellers, etc. Isa. 8:19.

Faith without works. 1 Tim. 5:6;
James 2:17, 26.

Freedom from the law. Rom. 7:4.

Freedom from the power of sin.
Rom. 6:2, 8, 11; Col. 3:3.

Impotence. Gen. 20:3;
Rom. 4:19.

Human's state by nature.
2 Cor. 5:4; Eph. 2:1, 5.

A state of deep affliction, etc.
Pss. 88:5–6; 143:3; Isa. 59:10.

Instances of, restored by Christ, etc.
Matt. 9:25; Luke 7:15;
John 11:44; Acts 9:40; 20:12.

Instances of, restored to life before
Christ. 1 Kings 17:22;
2 Kings 4:34–36; 13:21.

The Jews looked for a resurrection
from. Isa. 26:19; Acts 24:15.

Mourning for, often
By hired mourners. Jer. 9:17–18;
Amos 5:16.

Lasted many days. Gen. 37:34;
50:3, 10.

Loud and clamorous. Jer. 16:6;
Mark 5:38.

Testified by change of apparel.
2 Sam. 14:2.

Testified by covering the head.
2 Sam. 19:4.

Testified by rending the garments.
Gen. 37:34; 2 Sam. 3:31.

Testified by tearing the hair.
Jer. 16:7.

Very great. Gen. 37:35;
Jer. 31:15; Matt. 2:18;
John 11:33.

With plaintive music. Jer. 48:36;
Matt. 9:23.

Nazarites not to touch or mourn for.
Num. 6:6–7.

Priests not to mourn for, except
when near of kin. Lev. 21:1–3;
Ezek. 44:25.

Regard often shown to the memory
of. Ruth 1:8.

Return not to this life.
Job 7:9–10; 14:10, 14.

Terms used to express
Carcasses. Num. 14:29, 32–33;
1 Kings 13:24.

Corpses. 2 Kings 19:35;
Nah. 3:3.

Deceased. Isa. 26:14;
Matt. 22:25.

They who have departed this life.
Gen. 23:2; 25:8; Job 1:19.

Those defiled by, removed from the
camp. Num. 5:2.

Those who are not. Matt. 2:18.

Too soon forgotten. Ps. 31:12;
Eccles. 9:5.

Touching of, caused uncleanness.
Num. 9:6–7; 19:11, 13, 16.

Uncleanness contracted from,
removed by the water of
separation. Num. 19:12, 18.

Were washed and laid out.
Acts 9:37.

Were wrapped in linen with spices.
John 19:40.

DEAFNESS

Figurative sense, of moral
insensibility. Isa. 6:10; 29:18;
35:5; Ezek. 12:2; Matt. 13:15;
John 12:40; Acts 28:26–27.
Inflicted by God. Exod. 4:11.
Law concerning. Lev. 19:14.
Miraculous cure of. Matt. 11:5;
Mark 7:32; 9:25.

DEATH

See specific topics: Death, Eternal;
Death, Natural; Death, Spiritual;
Christ, Death of; Believers, Death
of; Wicked, Death of the

DEATH, ETERNAL

Believers will escape. Rev. 2:11;
20:6.

Called
Damnation of hell. Matt. 23:33.
Destruction. Rom. 9:22;
2 Thess. 1:9.
Everlasting punishment.
Matt. 25:46.
Perishing. 2 Pet. 2:12.
A resurrection to damnation.
John 5:29.
A resurrection to shame, etc.
Dan. 12:2.
The second death. Rev. 2:11.
The wrath to come.
1 Thess. 1:10.
Christ the only way of escape from.
John 3:16; 8:51; Acts 4:12.

Described as
Banishment from God.
2 Thess. 1:9.
Indignation, wrath, etc.
Rom. 2:8–9.
A lake of fire. Rev. 19:20; 21:8.

A mist of darkness forever.
2 Pet. 2:17.
Outer darkness. Matt. 25:30.
Society with the devil, etc.
Matt. 25:41.
The worm that doesn't die.
Mark 9:44.
God alone can inflict. Matt. 10:28;
James 4:12.
The necessary consequence of sin.
Rom. 6:16, 21; 8:13;
James 1:15.
The portion of the wicked.
Matt. 25:41, 46; Rom. 1:32.
Self–righteousness leads to.
Prov. 14:12.
Will be inflicted by Christ.
Matt. 25:31, 41; 2 Thess. 1:7–8.
Strive to preserve others
from. James 5:20.
The wages of sin. Rom. 6:23.
The way to, described. Ps. 9:17;
Matt. 7:13.

DEATH, NATURAL

Abolished by Christ. 2 Tim. 1:10.
By Adam. Gen. 3:19;
1 Cor. 15:21–22.
All will be raised from. Acts 24:15.
Christ delivers from the fear of.
Heb. 2:15.
Conquered by Christ. Rom. 6:9;
Rev. 1:18.
Consequence of sin. Gen. 2:17;
Rom. 5:12.
Consideration of, a motive to
diligence. Eccles. 9:10; John 9:4.

Described as
Being cut down. Job 14:2.
Departing. Phil. 1:23.
The earthly house of this
tabernacle being dissolved.
2 Cor. 5:1.

Fleeing as a shadow. Job 14:2.

Gathering to our people.
Gen. 49:33.

God requiring the soul.
Luke 12:20.

Going down into silence.
Ps. 115:17.

Going the way of no return.
Job 16:22.

Putting off this tabernacle.
2 Pet. 1:14.

Returning to dust. Gen. 3:19;
Ps. 104:29.

A sleep. Deut. 31:16;
John 11:11.

Yielding up the Spirit. Acts 5:10.

Enoch and Elijah exempted from.
Gen. 5:24, with Heb. 11:5;
2 Kings 2:11.

Illustrates the change produced in
conversion. Rom. 6:2; Col. 2:20.

Levels all ranks. Job 3:17–19.

Lot of all. Eccles. 8:8; Heb. 9:27.

None subject to, in heaven.
Luke 20:36; Rev. 21:4.

Ordered by God. Deut. 32:39;
Job 14:5.

Pray to be prepared for.
Pss. 39:4, 13; 90:12.

Prepare for. 2 Kings 20:1.

Puts an end to earthly projects.
Eccles. 9:10.

Regard as at hand. Job 14:1–2;
Pss. 39:4–5; 90:9; 1 Pet. 1:24.

Will finally be destroyed by Christ.
Hos. 13:14; 1 Cor. 15:26.

Strips of earthly possessions.
Job 1:21; 1 Tim. 6:7.

When averted for a season, a motive
to increased devotedness.
Pss. 56:12–13; 118:17;
Isa. 38:18, 20.

DEATH, SPIRITUAL

Alienation from God. Eph. 4:18.

Believers are raised
from. Rom. 6:13.

A call to arise from. Eph. 5:14.

A consequence of the fall.
Rom. 5:15.

Deliverance from is through Christ.
John 5:24–25; Eph. 2:5;
1 John 5:12.

The fruits of, dead works. Heb. 6:1;
9:14.

Hypocrisy. Rev. 3:1–2.

Illustrated. Ezek. 37:2–3;
Luke 15:24.

Living in pleasure. 1 Tim. 5:6.

Love of the brethren, a proof of
being raised from. 1 John 3:14.

Spiritual ignorance. Isa. 9:2;
Matt. 4:16; Luke 1:79;
Eph. 4:18.

The state of all persons by nature.
Rom. 6:13; 8:6.

Unbelief. John 3:36; 1 John 5:12.

Walking in trespasses and sins.
Eph. 2:1; Col. 2:13.

Worldly-mindedness. Rom. 8:6.

DEATH OF BELIEVERS
See Believers, Death of

DEATH OF CHRIST
See Christ, Death of

DEATH OF THE WICKED
See Wicked, Death of the

DEBTS

Material
Excessive interest prohibited.
Exod. 22:25.

Necessity of paying promptly.
Deut. 24:14–15; Prov. 3:27;
Rom. 13:8.
Parables about. Luke 7:41–42;
Matt. 18:23–25.
Protection of borrowers.
Deut. 24:6, 17.

Spiritual
Condition of forgiveness.
Matt. 6:12, 14–15; 18:23–25.
Deliverance through Christ.
Rom. 6:20–23.
God's claim. Matt. 25–26;
Luke 7:41, 47; 16:5.
Our responsibility. Rom. 1:14–15;
13:8.

DECALOGUE
Called tables of testimony.
Exod. 31:18; 34:29; 40:20.
Called words of the covenant.
Exod. 34:28; Deut. 4:13.
Divine authority of. Exod. 20:1;
34:27–28; Deut. 5:4–22.
Written by God. Exod. 24:12;
31:18; 32:16; Deut. 5:22; 9:10;
Hos. 8:12.

DECEIT
Abhorred by God. Ps. 5:6.

Believers
Are delivered from those who use.
Ps. 72:14.
Are free from. Ps. 24:4;
Zeph. 3:13; Rev. 14:5.
Avoid. Job 31:5.
Avoid those addicted to.
Ps. 101:7.
Pray for deliverance from those
who use. Pss. 43:1; 120:2.
Purpose against. Job 27:4.

Should beware of those who
teach. Eph. 5:6; Col. 2:8.
Should lay aside, in seeking truth.
1 Pet. 2:1.
Blessedness of being free from.
Pss. 24:4–5; 32:2.
A characteristic of Antichrist.
2 John 1:7.
A characteristic of the apostasy.
2 Thess. 2:10.
Characteristic of the heart. Jer. 17:9.
Christ was perfectly free
from. Isa. 53:9, with 1 Pet. 2:22.
Comes from the heart. Mark 7:22.

Evil of
Keeps from knowledge of God.
Jer. 9:6.
Keeps from turning to God.
Jer. 8:5.
Leads to lying. Prov. 14:25.
Leads to pride and oppression.
Jer. 5:27–28.
Falsehood. Ps. 119:118.

False Teachers
Are workers of. 2 Cor. 11:13.
Impose on others by. Rom. 16:18;
Eph. 4:14.
Preach. Jer. 14:14; 23:26.
Openly revel in. 2 Pet. 2:13.
False witnesses use. Prov. 12:17;
14:5.
The folly of fools. Prov. 14:8.
Forbidden. Prov. 24:28;
1 Pet. 3:10.
Hatred often concealed by.
Prov. 26:24–28.
Hypocrites devise. Job 15:35.
Hypocrites practice. Hos. 11:12.
The kisses of an enemy. Prov. 27:6.
Ministers should lay aside.
2 Cor. 4:2; 1 Thess. 2:3.

Often accompanied by fraud and injustice. Pss. 10:7; 43:1.

Punishment of. Ps. 55:23; Jer. 9:7–9.

Tongue as the instrument of. Rom. 3:13.

The wicked
Are full of. Rom. 1:29.
Delight in. Prov. 20:17.
Devise. Pss. 35:20, 38:12; Prov. 12:5.
Increase in. 2 Tim. 3:13.
Use to each other. Jer. 9:5.
Use to themselves. Jer. 37:9 Obad. 1:3, 7.
Utter. Pss. 10:7; 36:3.
Work. Prov. 11:18.

DECEPTION

Abraham. Gen. 12:13; 20:2.
Absalom. 2 Sam. 13:24–28; 15:7.
Amnon. 2 Sam. 13:6–14.
Ananias and Sapphira. Acts 5:1.
Chief priests. Mark 14:1.
David. 1 Sam. 21:10–15.
Delilah. Judg. 16:4–20.
Doeg. Ps. 52:2.
Ehud. Judg. 3:15–30.
Gehazi. 2 Kings 5:20.
The Gibeonites. Josh. 9:3–15.
Herod. Matt. 2:8.
Isaac. Gen. 26:7.
Jacob and Rebecca. Gen. 27:6–23.
Jacob's sons. Gen. 34:13–31.
Job's friends. Job 6:15.
Joseph. Gen. 42–44.
Lawyer. Luke 10:25.
The old prophet. 1 Kings 13:18.
The Pharisees. Matt. 22:16.
Sanballat. Neh. 6.
By Satan. Gen. 3:4.

DECISION

Blessedness of. Josh. 1:7.

Exhibited in
Being on the Lord's side. Exod. 32:26.
Following God fully. Num. 14:24; 32:12; Josh. 14:8.
Keeping the commandments of God. Neh. 10:29.
Loving God perfectly. Deut. 6:5.
Seeking God with the heart. 2 Chron. 15:12.
Serving God. Isa. 56:6.
Exhortations to. Josh. 24:14–15.
Necessary to the service of God. Luke 9:62.

Opposed to
A divided service. Matt. 6:24.
Double-mindedness. James 1:8.
Halting between two opinions. 1 Kings 18:21.
Turning to the right or left. Deut. 5:32.
Unfaithfulness. Ps. 78:8, 37.

DECISIONS, CAREER

Career that contradicts gospel to be avoided. Acts 16:16, 19; 19:23–27.

Injunctions regarding
Be ready for any honest work. Titus 3:1.
Office of bishop is a noble task. 1 Tim. 3:1.

Whatever you do
Do it for the glory of God. 1 Cor. 10:31.
Do it in the name of Jesus. Col. 3:17.
Do it with might. Eccles. 9:10.

Work heartily as serving the Lord.
Col. 3:23.
Worthless pursuits bring poverty.
Prov. 28:19.

DECREES
Ecclesiastical, of the church at
Jerusalem. Acts 15:28–29; 16:4.
Of the Medes, irrevocable.
Dan. 6:14–15.

DEDICATION
Consecration of a place of worship.
2 Chron. 2:4.
Devoting anything to sacred uses.
1 Chron. 28:12.
Illustrative of devotedness to God.
Ps. 119:38.
Of idolaters in setting up idols.
Dan. 3:2–3.
Of property, often perverted.
Mark 7:9–13.
Solemn confirmation of a covenant.
Heb. 9:18.

Subjects of   .
Houses when built. Deut. 20:5;
Ps. 30.
Persons. Exod. 22:29;
1 Sam. 1:11.
Property. Lev. 27:28; Matt. 15:5.
Second temple. Ezra 6:16–17.
Spoils of war. 2 Sam. 8:11;
1 Chron. 18:11.
Tabernacle. Num. 7.
Temple of Solomon.
1 Kings 8:1–63; 2 Chron. 7:5.
Tribute from foreigners.
2 Sam. 8:10–11.
Walls of cities. Neh. 12:27.

Things dedicated to God
Applied to the repair and
maintenance of the temple.

2 Kings 12:4–5;
1 Chron. 26:27.
Given to appease enemies.
2 Kings 12:17–18.
Law respecting the release of.
Lev. 27.
Levites placed over.
1 Chron. 26:20, 26;
2 Chron. 31:12.
Placed with the treasures of the
Lord's house. 1 Kings 7:51;
2 Chron. 5:1.
Special chambers prepared for.
2 Chron. 31:11–12.
For support of priests.
Num. 18:14; Ezek. 44:29.
Valued holy. Lev. 27:28;
2 Kings 12:18.

DEDICATION, FEAST OF
To commemorate the cleansing of
the temple after its defilement by
Antiochus. Dan. 11:31.
Held in the winter month, Chislev.
John 10:22.

DEEDS
Of a child, significance of.
Prov. 20:11.
Of Christians. Matt. 5:16;
Luke 6:46; Col. 3:17.
Of evil men. John 3:19.
Of God, glory of. Exod. 15:11;
1 Sam. 12:7; Ps. 9:11.
Of Jesus, good. Matt. 11:5;
Luke 24:19.
Judgment according to. Rom. 2:5–6;
Rev. 20:12.
Of love, required. 1 John 3:18.
Of the old nature. Col. 3:9.

DEER
Coloring of. Jer. 14:5.

Designated among the clean animals, to be eaten. Deut. 12:15; 14:5.
Fleetness of. 2 Sam. 2:18; 1 Chron. 12:8; Prov. 6:5; Song of Sol. 8:14; Isa. 35:6.
Gentleness of. Prov. 5:19.
Provided for Solomon's household. 1 Kings 4:23.
Sure footedness of. 2 Sam. 22:34.

DEFENSE
Of Jeremiah. Jer. 26:12–16.
Of Paul.
Acts 22; 23:1–6; 24:10–21; 26:1–23.
Of Peter. Acts 4:8–13; 5:23–29.
Of Stephen. Acts 7.

DEFILEMENT
Causes of, improperly enlarged by tradition. Mark 7:2, with Matt. 15:20.
Ceremonial, abolished under the gospel. Acts 10:15; Rom. 14:14; Col. 2:20–22.

Ceremonial, caused by
Being alone with a dead body. Num. 19:14.
Burning the red heifer. Num. 19:8.
Childbearing. Lev. 12:2.
Eating things that died. Lev. 17:15.
Eating unclean things. Lev. 11:8; Acts 10:11, 14.
Gathering ashes of the red heifer. Num. 19:10.
Going into a leprous house. Lev. 14:46.
Having a discharge, etc. Lev. 15:2; Num. 5:2.
Having a leprosy. Lev. 13:3, 11; Num. 5:2–3.

Mourning for the dead. Lev. 21:1–3.
Sacrificing the red heifer. Num. 19:7.
Touching a dead beast. Lev. 5:2; 11:24–28.
Touching a dead body or a bone. Num. 9:6–7; 19:11, 16.
Touching a grave. Num. 19:16.
Touching an unclean person. Num. 19:22.
Touching anything defiled by a discharge, etc. Lev. 15:5–11.
Cleansed by ceremonial washings. Num. 19:18–19; Heb. 9:13.
Forbidden to the Jews. Lev. 11:44–45.

Illustrative of
Sin. Matt. 15:11, 18; Jude 8.
Unholy doctrines. 1 Cor. 3:16–17.

Moral, caused by
Following the sins of the heathen. Lev. 18:24.
Giving children to Molech. Lev. 20:3.
Making and serving idols. Ezek. 20:17–18; 22:3–4; 23:7.
Seeking after wizards. Lev. 19:31.
Shedding blood. Isa. 59:3.
Moral, punished. Lev. 18:24–25, 28–29.
Neglecting purification from, punished by cutting off. Num. 19:13, 20.

Priests
Not to eat holy things while under. Lev. 22:2, 4–6.
Punished for eating of the holy things while under. Lev. 22:3.

Specially required to avoid.
Lev. 21:1–6, 11–12.
To decide in all cases of.
Lev. 10:10; 13:3.

Things liable to ceremonial
Furniture, etc. Lev. 15:9–10;
Num. 19:14–15.
Garments. Lev. 13:59.
Houses. Lev. 14:44.
The land. Lev. 18:25;
Deut. 21:23.
The person. Lev. 5:3.
The sanctuary. Lev. 20:3;
Zeph. 3:4.
Those under, removed from the
camp. Num. 5:3–4; Deut. 23:14.

DELIGHTING IN GOD
See God, Delighting in

DEMAGOGISM
Absalom's. 2 Sam. 15:2 6.
Felix. Acts 24:27.
Herod. Acts 12:3.
Pilate. Matt. 27:17–26;
Mark 15:15; Luke 23:13–24;
John 18:38–40; 19:6–13.

DEMONS
Adversaries of human beings.
Matt. 12:45.
Believe and tremble. James 2.19.
Cast out by Jesus. Matt. 4:24; 8:16;
Mark 3:22; Luke 4.41.
Cast out by Paul. Acts 16:16–18;
19:12.
Cast out by Peter. Acts 5:16.
Cast out by Phillip. Acts 8:5–7.
Cast out by the disciples. Mark 9:38;
Luke 10:17.
Disciples could not expel.
Mark 9:18, 28–29.

Jesus falsely accused of being
possessed. Mark 3:22–30;
John 7:20; 10:20.
Messages given false prophets by.
1 Kings 22:21–23.
Parable of the man repossessed.
Matt. 12:43–45.

Possession by
The blind and dumb man.
Matt. 12:22; Luke 11:14.
The daughter of the
Syrophenician. Matt. 15:22–29;
Mark 7:25–30.
The dumb man. Matt. 9:32–33.
A herd of swine. Matt. 8:30–32.
The lunatic child. Matt. 17:14–18;
Mark 9:17–27; Luke 9:37–43.
The man in the synagogue.
Mark 1:23–26; Luke 4:33–35.
Mary Magdalene. Mark 16:9;
Luke 8:2–3.
Saul. 1 Sam. 16:14–23;
18:10–11; 19:9–10.
Two men of the Gergesenes.
Matt. 8:28–34; Mark 5:2–20.
Power over, given to the disciples.
Matt. 10:1; Mark 6:7; 16:7.
Punishment of. Matt. 8:29; 25:41;
Luke 8:28; 2 Pet. 2:4; Jude 6;
Rev. 12:7–9.
Sceva's son exorcise.
Acts 19:13–16.
Sent to incite trouble between
Abimelech and the
Shechemites. Judg. 9:23.
Testify to the divinity of Jesus.
Matt. 8:29; Mark 1:23–24; 3:11;
5:7; Luke 8:28; Acts 19:15.
To be judged at the general
judgment. Matt. 8:29; 2 Pet. 2:4;
Jude 6.
Worship of. Lev. 17:7; Deut. 32:17;
2 Chron. 11:15; Ps. 106:37;

Matt. 4:9; Luke 4:7;
1 Cor. 10:20–21; 1 Tim. 4:1;
Rev. 13:4.
Worship of, forbidden. Lev. 17:7;
Zech. 13:2; Rev. 9:20.

DENARIUS
Unit of Roman currency. Matt. 20:2.

DENIAL OF CHRIST
See Christ, Denial of

DENS
Used as places of refuge. Judg. 6:2;
Heb. 11:38; Rev. 6:15.

DEPRAVITY, HUMAN
See Human, Depravity of

DEPUTY
An officer who administers the
functions of a superior in his
absence. 1 Kings 22:47;
Acts 13:7–8; 18:12; 19:38.

DERISION
See Ridicule

DESERT
An arid region bearing only a sparse
vegetation. Lev. 16:22;
Deut. 8:15; Jer. 2:2, 6; 17:6.
Danger of traveling in. Exod. 14:3;
2 Cor. 11:26.

Described as
Desolate. Ezek. 6:14.
Dry and without water.
Exod. 17:1; Deut. 8:15.
Great and terrible. Deut. 1:19.
Trackless. Isa. 43:19.
Uncultivated. Num. 20:5;
Jer. 2:2.

Uninhabited and lonesome.
Jer. 2:6.
Waste and howling. Deut. 32:10.
The discontented fled to.
1 Sam. 22:2; Acts 21:38.
Guides required in. Num. 10:31;
Deut. 32:10.
Heath often found in. Jer. 17:6.

Illustrative of
Barrenness. Pss. 106:9;
107:33, 35.
Desolation by armies.
Jer. 12:10–13; 50:12.
The Gentiles. Isa. 35:1, 6; 41:19.
Those deprived of all blessings.
Hos. 2:3.
What affords no support.
Jer. 2:31.
The world. Song of Sol. 3:6; 8:5.

Infested with
Robbers. Jer. 3:2; Lam. 4:19.
Serpents. Deut. 8:15.
Wild beasts. Isa. 13:21;
Mark 1:13.
Inhabited by wandering tribes.
Gen. 21:20–21; Jer. 25:24.

Mentioned in Scripture
Arabian or great desert.
Exod. 23:31.
Beersheba. Gen. 21:14;
1 Kings 19:3–4.
Bethaven. Josh. 18:12.
Damascus. 1 Kings 19:15.
Edom. 2 Kings 3:8.
En-gedi. 1 Sam. 24:1.
Gibeon. 2 Sam. 2:24.
Jeruel. 2 Chron. 20:16.
Judea. Matt. 3:1.
Kadesh. Ps. 29:8.
Kedemoth. Deut. 2:26.
Maon. 1 Sam. 23:24–25.

Near Gaza. Acts 8:26.
Of the Red Sea. Exod. 13:18.
Paran. Gen. 21:21; Num. 10:12.
Shur. Gen. 16:7; Exod. 15:22.
Sin. Exod. 16:1.
Sinai. Exod. 19:1–2;
  Num. 33:16.
Zin. Num. 20:1; 27:14.
Ziph. 1 Sam. 23:14–15.
Parts of, afforded pasture.
  Gen. 36:24; Exod. 3:1.
The persecuted fled to.
  1 Sam. 23:14; Heb. 11:38.

Phenomena of, alluded to
  Clouds of sand and dust.
    Deut. 28:24; Jer. 4:12–13.
  Mirage or deceptive appearance of
    water. Jer. 15:18.
  Scorching or deadly wind.
    Jer. 4:11.
  Tornadoes or whirlwinds.
    Isa. 21:1.
Uninhabited places. Matt. 14:15;
  Mark 6:31.
Vast barren plains. Exod. 5:3.
Used in a figurative sense. Isa. 35:1.

**DESERT, JOURNEY OF ISRAEL
THROUGH THE**
Begun in haste. Exod. 12:39.
By a circuitous route.
  Exod. 13:17–18,
Caused universal terror and dismay.
  Exod. 15:14–16; Num. 22:3–4.
Circumcision omitted during.
  Josh. 5:5.
Conducted with regularity.
  Exod. 13:18.
Constant goodness and mercy of
  God to them during.
  Pss. 106:10, 43–46; 107:6, 13.

Continued forty years

As a punishment.
  Num. 14:33–34.
To test and humble them, etc.
  Deut. 8:2.
To teach them to live on God's
  word. Deut. 8:3.
Date of its commencement.
  Exod. 12:41–42.
Difficulty and danger of. Deut. 8:15.
Illustrative of the pilgrimage of the
  church. Song of Sol. 8:5;
  1 Pet. 1:17.
Justice administered during.
  Exod. 18:13, 26.
Marked by constant murmurings and
  rebellions. Pss. 78:40; 95:10;
  106:7–39.
A mixed multitude accompanied
  them in. Exod. 12:38;
  Num. 11:4.
Obstructed, etc., by the surrounding
  nations. Exod. 17:8; Num. 20:21.
Order of encamping during. Num. 2.
Order of marching during.
  Num. 10:14–28.
Territory acquired during.
  Deut. 29:7–8.
Their clothing preserved during.
  Deut. 8:4; 29:5; Neh. 9:21.
Their healthy state commencing.
  Ps. 105:37.
Their number commencing.
  Exod. 12:37.
Under God's guidance.
  Exod. 13:21–22; 15:13;
  Neh. 9:12; Ps. 78:52;
  Isa. 63:11–14.
Under God's protection.
  Exod. 14:19–20, with
  Ps. 105:39; Exod. 23:20, with
  Ps. 78:53.

Under Moses as leader.
Exod. 3:10–12,
with Acts 7:36, 38.
With miraculous provision.
Exod. 16:35; Deut. 8:3.
Worship of God celebrated during.
Exod. 24:5–8; 29:38–42;
40:24–29.

Began from Rameses in Egypt.
Exod. 12:37.
To Succoth. Exod. 12:37;
Num. 33:5.
To Etham. Exod. 13:20;
Num. 33:6.

Between Baalzephon and
Pihahiroth. Exod. 14:2;
Num. 33:7.
Overtaken by Pharaoh.
Exod. 14:9.
Exhorted to look to God.
Exod. 14:13–14.
The cloud removed to the rear.
Exod. 14:19–20.
The Red Sea divided.
Exod. 14:16, 21.

Through the Red Sea. Exod. 14:22,
29.
Faith exhibited in passing.
Heb. 11:29.
Pharaoh and his host destroyed.
Exod. 14:23–28; Ps. 106:11.
Israel's song of praise.
Exod. 15:1–21; Ps. 106:12.

Through the wilderness of Shur or
Etham. Exod. 15:22;
Num. 33:8.
To Marah. Exod. 15:23;
Num. 33:8.
Murmuring of the people on
account of bitterwater.
Exod. 15:24.

Water sweetened. Exod. 15:25.
To Elim. Exod. 15:27;
Num. 33:9.

By the Red Sea. Num. 33:10.

Through the wilderness of Sin.
Exod. 16:1; Num. 33:11.
Murmuring for bread.
Exod. 16:2–3.
Quails given for one night.
Exod. 16:8, 12–13.
Manna sent.
Exod. 16:14, 8, 16–31.

To Dophkah. Num. 33:12.

To Alush. Num. 33:13.

To Rephidim. Exod. 17:1;
Num. 33:14.
Murmuring for water.
Exod. 17:2–3.
Water brought from the rock.
Exod. 17:5–6.
Called Massah and Meribah.
Exod. 17:7.
Amalek opposes Israel.
Exod. 17:8.
Amalek overcome.
Exod. 17:9–13.

To Mount Sinai. Exod. 19:1–2;
Num. 33:15.
Jethro's visit. Exod. 18:1–6.
Judges appointed.
Exod. 18:14–26; Deut. 1:9–15.
Moral law given. Exod. 19:3; 20.
Covenant made. Exod. 24:3–8.
Moral law written on
tables. Exod. 31:18.
Order for making the tabernacle,
etc. Exod. 24–27.
Tribe of Levi taken instead of the
firstborn. Num. 3:11–13.

Aaron and his sons selected for priesthood. Exod. 28–29; Num. 3:1–3, 10.

Levites set apart. Num. 3:5–9.

Golden calf made. Exod. 32:1, 4.

Tables of testimony broken. Exod. 32:19.

People punished for idolatry. Exod. 32:25–29, 35.

God's glory shown to Moses. Exod. 33:18–23; 34:5–8.

The tables of testimony renewed. Exod. 34:1–4, 27–29; Deut. 10:1–5.

Tabernacle first set up. Exod. 40.

Nadab and Abibu destroyed for offering strange fire. Lev. 10:1–2; Num. 3:4.

Passover first commemorated. Num. 9:1–5.

Second numbering of the people. Num. 1:1–46, with Exod. 38:25–26.

To Kibroth-Hattaavah. Num. 33:16.

Complaining punished by fire. Num. 11:1–3.

Called Taberah. Num. 11:3.

Murmuring of the mixed multitude and of Israel, for flesh. Num. 11:4–9.

Meat promised. Num. 11:10–15, 18–23.

Seventy elders appointed to assist Moses. Num. 11:16–17, 24–30.

Quails sent for a month. Num. 11:19–20, 31–32.

Their murmuring punished. Num. 11:23; Ps. 78:30–31.

Why called Kibroth-hattaavah. Num. 11:34.

To Hazeroth. Num. 11:35; 33:17.

Aaron and Miriam envy Moses. Num. 12:1–2.

Miriam punished by leprosy. Num. 12:10.

Delayed seven days for Miriam. Num. 12:14–15.

To Kadesh-Barnea in wilderness of Rith Mahor Paran. Deut. 1:19, and Num. 32:8 with 12:16 and 33:18.

The people anxious to have the land of Canaan searched. Deut. 1:22.

Moses commanded to send spies. Num. 13:1–2.

Persons selected as spies. Num. 13:3–16.

Spies sent. Josh. 14:7, with Num. 13:17–20.

Spies bring back evil report. Num. 13:26–33.

The people terrified and rebel. Num. 14:1–4.

Punishment for rebellion. Num. 14:26, 35; 32:11–13; Deut. 1:35–36, 40.

Guilty spies slain by plague. Num. 14:36–37.

People stricken by Amalek for going up without the Lord. Num. 14:40–45; Deut. 1:41–44.

Returned by the way of the Red Sea. Num. 14:25; Deut. 1:40; 2:1.

Sabbath breaker stoned. Num. 15:32–36.

Rebellion of Korah. Num. 16:1–19.

Korah, etc., punished.
Num. 16:30–35.

Plague sent. Num. 16:41–46.

Plague stayed. Num. 16:47–50.

God's choice of Aaron confirmed.
Num. 17.

To Rimmon-Parez. Num. 33:19.

*To Libnah or Laban. Num. 33:20;
Deut. 1:1.*

To Rissah. Num. 33:21.

To Kehelathah. Num. 33:22.

To Mount Shapher. Num. 33:23.

To Haradah. Num. 33:24.

To Makheloth. Num. 33:25.

To Tahath. Num. 33:26.

To Tarah. Num. 33:27.

To Mithcah. Num. 33:28.

To Hashmonah. Num. 33:29.

*To Moseroth or Mosera.
Num. 33:30.*

To Bene-Jaakan. Num. 33:31.

*To Horhagidgad or Gudgodah.
Num. 33:32; Deut. 10:7.*

*To Jotbathah or Land of Rivers.
Num. 33:33; Deut. 10:7.*

*Several of these positions probably
revisited. Deut. 10:6–7, with
Num. 33:30–32.*

To Ebronah. Num. 33:34.

To Ezion-Gaber. Num. 33:35.

*To Kadesh in the wilderness of Zin.
Num. 20:1; 33:36; Judg. 11:16.*

Miriam dies and is buried.
Num. 20:1.

Second murmuring for water.
Num. 20:2–6.

Moses striking the rock instead of
speaking to it, disobeys God.
Num. 20:7–11.

Moses and Aaron punished.
Num. 20:12.

Called Meribah to commemorate
the murmuring. Num. 20:13;
27:14.

Orders given respecting Edom.
Deut. 2:3–6.

The king of Edom refuses a
passage. Num. 20:14–21;
Judg. 11:17.

*To Mount Hor. Num. 20:22;
33:37.*

Aaron dies. Num. 20:28–29;
33:38–39.

Arad conquered. Num. 21:1–3;
33:40.

Called Hormah. Num. 21:2–3.

To Zalmonah. Num. 33:41.

Murmuring of the people.
Num. 21:4–5.

Fiery serpents sent. Num. 21:6.

Bronze serpent raised up.
Num. 21:7–9.

To Punon. Num. 33:42.

To Oboth. Num. 21:10; 33:43.

*To Ije-Abarim Before Moab.
Num. 21:11; 33:44.*

Orders given respecting Moab.
Deut. 2:8–9.

*To Zared or Dibon-gad.
Num. 21:12; 33:45.*

*To Almon-Diblathaim.
Num. 33:46.*

*Across the Brook Zered. Deut.
2:13.*
Time occupied in going from
Kadesh–barnea to this position.
Deut. 2:14.
Order to pass through Ar.
Deut. 2:18.
Orders given respecting Ammon.
Deut. 2:19.

*Across the Arnon. Num. 21:13–15.
Deut. 2:24.*

To Beer or the Well. Num. 21:16.

To Mattanah. Num. 21:18.

To Nahaliel. Num. 21:19.

To Bamoth. Num. 21:19.

*To the mountains of Abarim.
Num. 21:20; 33:47.*
The Amorites refuse a passage to
Israel. Num. 21:21–23; Deut.
2:26–30.
Sihon conquered.
Num. 21:23–32;
Deut. 2:32–36.
Og conquered. Num. 21:33–35;
Deut. 3:1–11.
Reubenites, etc., obtained the land
taken from the
Amorites. Num. 32;
Deut. 3:12–17.

*Return to the plains of Moab.
Num. 22:1; 33:48–49.*
Balak sends for Balaam.
Num. 22:5–6, 15–17.
Balaam not permitted to curse
Israel. Num. 22:9–41; 23–24.

Israel seduced to idolatry, etc., by
advice of Balaam. Num. 25:1–3;
Rev. 2:14.
Israel punished. Num. 25:5, 9.
Third numbering. Num. 26:1–62.
All formerly numbered over twenty
years old, except Caleb and
Joshua, dead. Num. 26:63–65,
with 14:29.
The law of female inheritance
settled. Num. 27:1–11, with
36:1–9.
Appointment of Joshua.
Num. 27:15–23.
Midianites destroyed and Balaam
slain. Num. 31, with 25:17–18.
The law rehearsed. Deut. 1:3.
The law written by
Moses. Deut. 31:9.
Moses beholds Canaan.
Deut. 34:1–4.
Moses dies and is buried.
Deut. 34:5–6.
Joshua ordered to cross
Jordan. Josh. 1:2.
Two spies sent to Jericho.
Josh. 2:1.

Across the River Jordan. Josh. 2:1.

DESPAIR
Believers enabled to overcome.
2 Cor. 4:8–9.
Believers sometimes tempted to
Job 7:6; Lam. 3:18.

Leads to
Blasphemy. Isa. 8:21;
Rev. 16:10–11.
Continuing in sin. Jer. 2:25;
18:12.
Produced in the wicked by divine
judgments. Deut. 28:34, 67;
Rev. 9:6; 16:10.

Trust in God a preservative against.
Ps. 42:5, 11.

Will seize upon the wicked at the
appearing of Christ. Rev. 6:16.

DESIGN

In nature, evidence of. Job 12:7–11;
Prov. 16:4.

DESIRE

Spiritual. Ps. 42; Phil. 3:12–14;
Heb. 11:6.

DESPONDENCY

Cain, when God pronounced
judgment upon him for the murder
of Abel. Gen. 4:13–14.

Comfort in. Isa. 35:3–4;
Luke 18:1–8; Heb. 12:12–13.

Elijah, when he fled from Jezebel to
the wilderness. 1 Kings 19:4.

Hagar, when cast out of the
household of Abraham on account
of the jealousy of Sarah.
Gen. 21:15–16.

The Israelites on account of the cruel
oppression of the Egyptians.
Exod. 6:9.

Jonah, after he preached to the
Ninevites. Jon. 4:3, 8.

Moses, when sent on his mission to
the Israelites. Exod. 4:1, 10, 13;
6:12.

At the Red Sea. Exod. 14:15.

The sailors traveling to Rome with
Paul. Acts 27:20.

When the people lusted for flesh.
Num. 11:15.

DETECTIVES

Sent to spy on Jesus. Luke 20:20.

DEVIL, THE

The apostasy is of. 2 Thess. 2:9;
1 Tim. 4:1.

Assumes the form of an angel of
light. 2 Cor. 11:14.

Author of the fall.
Gen. 3:1, 6, 14, 24.

Believers

Are afflicted by, only as God
permits. Job 1:12; 2:4–7.

Are sifted by. Luke 22:31.

Are tempted by. 1 Chron. 21:1;
1 Thess. 3:5.

Overcome. 1 John 2:13;
Rev. 12:10–11.

Should be armed against.
Eph. 6:11–16.

Should be watchful against.
2 Cor. 2:11.

Should resist. James 4:7;
1 Pet. 5:9.

Sinned against God. 2 Pet. 2:4;
1 John 3:8.

Will be condemned at the
judgment. Jude 6; Rev. 20:10.

Will finally triumph over.
Rom. 16:20.

Cast down to hell. 2 Pet. 2:4;
Jude 6.

Cast out of heaven. Luke 10:18.

Character of

Cowardly. James 4:7.

Deceitful. 2 Cor. 11:14;
Eph. 6:11.

Fierce and cruel. Luke 8:29;
9:39, 42; 1 Pet. 5:8.

Malignant. Job 1:9; 2:4.

Powerful. Eph. 2:2; 6:12.

Presumptuous. Job 1:6;
Matt. 4:5–6.

Proud. 1 Tim. 3:6.

Subtle. Gen. 3:1, with
2 Cor. 11:3.
Wicked. 1 John 2:13.

Compared to
Fowls. Matt. 13:4.
A roaring lion. 1 Pet. 5:8.
A serpent. Rev. 12:9; 20:2.
A sower of weeds.
Matt. 13:25, 28.
A wolf. John 10:12.
A trapper. Ps. 91:3.
Everlasting fire is prepared for.
Matt. 25:41.
Hinders the gospel. Matt. 13:19;
2 Cor. 4:4.
Opposes God's work. Zech. 3:1;
1 Thess. 2:18.
Perverts the Scriptures. Matt. 4:6,
with Ps. 91:11–12.
Tempted Christ. Matt. 4:3–10.

Triumph over, by Christ
In casting out the spirits of.
Luke 11:20; 13:32.
Completed by His death. Col. 2:15;
Heb. 2:14.
In destroying the works of.
1 John 3:8.
In empowering His disciples to cast
out. Matt. 10:1; Mark 16:17.
Illustrated. Luke 11:21–22.
Predicted. Gen. 3:15.
In resisting his temptations.
Matt. 4:11.

The wicked
Are blinded by. 2 Cor. 4:4.
Are the children of. Matt. 13:38;
Acts 13:10; 1 John 3:10.
Are deceived by.
1 Kings 22:21–22;
Rev. 20:7–8.

Are ensnared by. 1 Tim. 3:7;
2 Tim. 2:26.
Are possessed by. Luke 22:3;
Acts 5:3; Eph. 2:2.
Are punished, together with.
Matt. 25:41.
Are troubled by. 1 Sam. 16:14.
Do the lusts of. John 8:44.
Turn aside after. 1 Tim. 5:15.
Works lying wonders. 2 Thess. 2:9;
Rev. 16:14.

**DEVIL, TITLES AND NAMES OF
THE**
Abbadon. Rev. 9:11.
Accuser of our brethren. Rev. 12:10.
Adversary. 1 Pet. 5:8.
Angel of the bottomless pit.
Rev. 9:11.
Apollyon. Rev. 9:11.
Beelzebub. Matt. 12:24.
Belial. 2 Cor. 6:15.
Crooked serpent. Isa. 27:1.
Dragon. Isa. 27:1; Rev. 20:2.
Enemy. Matt. 13:39.
Evil spirit. 1 Sam. 16:14.
Father of lies. John 8:44.
God of this world. 2 Cor. 4:4.
Great red dragon. Rev. 12:3.
Leviathan. Isa. 27:1.
Liar. John 8:44.
Lying spirit. 1 Kings 22:22.
Murderer. John 8:44.
Old serpent. Rev. 12:9; 20:2.
Piercing serpent. Isa. 27:1.
Power of darkness. Col. 1:13.
Prince of the devils. Matt. 12:24.
Prince of the power of the air. Eph.
2:2.
Prince of this world. John 14:30.
Ruler of the darkness of this world.
Eph. 6:12.
Satan. 1 Chron. 21:1; Job 1:6.

Serpent. Gen. 3:4, 14; 2 Cor. 11:3.
Spirit that works in the children of
disobedience. Eph. 2:2.
Tempter. Matt. 4:3; 1 Thess. 3:5.
Unclean spirit. Matt. 12:43.
Wicked one. Matt. 13:19, 38.

DEVOTEDNESS TO GOD
See God, Devotedness to

DEW
Absence of. 1 Kings 17:1.
Called the dew of heaven.
Dan. 4:15.
Forms imperceptibly. 2 Sam. 17:12.
Forms in the night. Job 29:19.
A merciful providence. Deut. 33:13.
Miraculous profusion and absence of.
Judg. 6:36–40.
Used in a figurative sense. Ps. 110:3;
Isa. 26:19; Hos. 6:4; 13:3; 14:5.

DIAL
A device for indicating time by the
sun's rays. 2 Kings 20:11;
Isa. 38:8.

DIAMOND
One of the jewels in the breastplate.
Exod. 28:18; 39:11; Jer. 17:1;
Ezek. 28:13.

DIET OF THE JEWS
See Jews, Diet of the

DIETING
Principles relevant to
Body a temple of the Holy Spirit.
1 Cor. 6:19.
Eat, drink, and be merry.
Eccles. 5:18; 9:7;
1 Cor. 15:32.

Eating for strength, not excess.
Eccles. 10:17.
Excessive eating. Prov. 23:20–21;
25:16; Phil. 3:19.
Honor God with body. 1 Cor.
6:20.
Restraint in eating. Prov. 23:2.
Rich foods refused. Dan. 1:5–16.
Subdue body. 1 Cor. 9:27.

DIFFICULTIES
God and. Gen. 18:14; Jer. 32:17.
Overcoming. Phil. 1:19.
Power over. Phil. 4:13.
Reality of. Ps. 137:15.
Of the true way. Matt. 7:14.

DILIGENCE
Believers should abound in.
2 Cor. 8:7.
Christ an example. Mark 1:35;
Luke 2:49.
God rewards. Deut. 11:14;
Heb. 11:6.
Illustrated. Prov. 6:6–8.

Required by God in
Cultivating Christian
graces. 2 Pet. 1:5.
Discharging official
duties. Deut. 19:18.
Following every good work.
1 Tim. 5:10.
Guarding against defilement.
Heb. 12:15.
Instructing children.
Deut. 6:7; 11:19.
Keeping the heart.
Deut. 4:9; Prov. 4:23.
Labors of love. Heb. 6:10–12.
Lawful business. Prov. 27:23;
Eccles. 9:10.
Listening to Him. Isa. 55:2.

Making our calling, etc., sure.
2 Pet. 1:10.
Obeying Him. Deut. 6:17; 11:13.
Seeking Him. 1 Chron. 22:19;
Heb. 11:6.
Seeking to be found spotless.
2 Pet. 3:14.
Self-examination. Ps. 77:6.
Striving after perfection.
Phil. 3:13–14.
Teaching religion. 2 Tim. 4:2;
Jude 3.

In the service of God
Is not in vain. 1 Cor. 15:58.
Leads to assured hope. Heb. 6:11.
Preserves from evil. Exod. 15:26.
Should be persevered in. Gal. 6:9.

In temporal matters, leads to
Favor. Prov. 11:27.
Honor. Prov. 12:24; 22:29.
Prosperity. Prov. 10:4; 13:4.

DIPLOMACY
Of Abigail. 1 Sam. 25:23–31.
Of Abimelech. Gen. 21:22–23;
26:26–31.
Absalom winning the people.
2 Sam. 15:2–6.
Ahaz purchases aid from the king of
Asyria. 2 Kings 16:7–9.
Ambassadors from Ben-hadad to
Aliab. 1 Kings 20:31–34.
Corrupt practices in, the officers of
Nebuchadnezzar's court to secure
the destruction of Daniel.
Dan. 6:4–15.
David, in sending Hushai to
Absalom's court.
2 Sam. 15:32–37.
Ecclesiastical, Paul, in circumcising
Timothy. Acts 16:3.
Of the Gibeonites. Josh. 9:3–16.

Of Hiram, to secure the good will of
David. 2 Sam. 5:11.
By intermarriage with other nations.
1 Kings 1:1–5.
Jehoash purchased peace from
Hazael. 2 Kings 12:18.
Of Jephthah, with the king of Moab,
unsuccessful. Judg. 11:12–28.
Paul, in arraying the Pharisees and
Sadducees against each other at
his trial. Acts 23:6–10.
Paul, in performing certain temple
services to placate the Jews.
Acts 21:20–25; Gal. 6:12.
In Paul's witness to all human beings.
1 Cor. 9:20–23.
The people of Tyre and Sidon, in
securing the favor of Herod.
Acts 12:20–22.
Rabshakeh, in trying to induce
Jerusalem to capitulate by
bombastic harangues.
2 Kings 18:17–37; 19:1–13;
Isa. 36:11–22.
Sanballat, in an attempt to prevent
the rebuilding of Jerusalem by
Nehemiah. Neh. 6.
Solomon, in his alliance with Hiram.
1 Kings 5:1–12; 9:10–14,
26–27; 10:11.
Of Toi, to promote the friendship of
David. 2 Sam. 8:10.
The wise woman of Abel
2 Sam. 20:16–22.

DIRECTION
Affirmations of. Ps. 23.
By an angel. Acts 10:22.
Through Christ. John 10:3.
Toward the highest. 2 Thess. 3:5.
Of the Lord. Deut. 32:12;
Exod. 13:21.
Prayer for. Pss. 31:3; 43:3.

Promise of. Ps. 32:8; Prov. 3:6.

DISAPPOINTMENT
Cannot be carried. Prov. 18:14.
Comfort for. Matt. 5:4.
Counselor for. Deut. 1:38;
    Job 4:3–4.
Encouragement in. Josh 1:6–7;
    Isa. 35:3–4; Luke 18:1–8; Col.
    2:2; Heb. 12:12–13.
Examples of. Lev. 26:16;
    1 Chron. 22:7; Acts 16:7.

Examples of
    Men on road to Emmaus.
        Luke 24:17–21.
    Paul. 1 Thess 2:17–20.
Has physical effects. Prov. 17:22;
    18:14.
From heartache. Prov. 15:13.
Hope in. Rom 5:3–5.
Judgment and. Heb. 6:10–12.
One reason for. Prov. 15:22.
Victory over. Hab. 3:17; Rom. 8:28.

DISCIPLES
First called Christians at Antioch.
    Acts 11:26.
Of Jesus. Matt. 10:1; 20:17;
    Acts 9:26; 14:2; 21:4.
Of John the Baptist. Matt. 9:14.
The seventy sent for. Luke 10:1.

DISCIPLESHIP
Tests of. Matt. 10:32–39;
    Luke 14:26–27, 33;
    John 21:15–19.

DISCIPLINE
Of armies, for disobedience of
    orders. Josh. 7:10–26;
    Judg. 21:5–12.

DISCIPLINE OF THE CHURCH
See Church, Discipline of the

DISCOURAGEMENT
Conquering. Hab. 3:17–19;
    Hag. 1:2–14; Acts 28:15;
    2 Cor. 12:9.
Danger of causing. Col. 3:21;
    1 Thess. 5:19.
Illustrated. 1 Kings 19:4; Neh. 4:10;
    Ps. 43:3; Isa. 49:14; Luke 5:5;
    24:24.
Reasons for. Prov. 13:12;
    2 Cor. 12:7.

DISCRIMINATION
See also Racial tension

No distinctions of race or gender.
    Gal. 3:28.

DISEASES
Alcohol abuse a cause of. Hos. 7:5.
In answer to prayer, Hezekiah
    healed. 2 Kings 20:1–11;
    Isa. 38:1–8.
Art of curing, defective. Job 13:4;
    Mark 5:26.
Children subject to. 2 Sam. 12:15;
    1 Kings 17:17.
Over excitement a cause of.
    Dan. 8:27.

Frequently
    Complicated. Deut. 28:60–61;
        Acts 28:8.
    Incurable. 2 Chron. 21:18;
        Jer. 14:19.
    Loathsome. Pss. 38:7; 41:8.
    Painful. 2 Chron. 21:15;
        Job 33:19.
    Tedious. Deut. 28:59; John 5:5;
        Luke 13:16.

God often entreated to cure.
2 Sam. 12:16; 2 Kings 20:1–3;
Ps. 6:2; James 5:14.

Healing of, from God. Exod. 15:26;
Ps. 103:3.

Illustrates sin. Isa. 1:5.

As judgment. Ps. 107:17; Isa. 3:17.

Medicine used for curing.
Prov. 17:22; Isa. 1:6.

Mentioned in Scripture
Abscess. 2 Kings 20:7.
Atrophy. Job 16:8.
Bleeding. Matt. 9:20.
Blindness. Job 29:15; Matt. 9:27.
Boils. Exod. 9:10.
Consumption. Lev. 26:16;
Deut. 28:22.
Deafness. Ps. 38:13; Mark 7:32.
Debility. Ps. 102:23; Ezek. 7:17.
Demon possession. Matt. 15:22;
Mark 5:15.
Dumbness. Prov. 31:8;
Matt. 9:32.
Dysentery. 2 Chron. 21:12–19;
Acts 28:8.
Fever. Lev. 26:16; Deut. 28:22;
Matt. 8:14.
Hemorrhoids. Deut. 28:27;
1 Sam. 5:6, 12.
Impediment speech. Mark 7:32.
Inflammation. Deut. 28:22.
Insanity. Matt. 4:24; 17:15.
Itch. Deut. 28:27.
Lameness. 2 Sam. 4:4;
2 Chron. 16:12.
Leprosy. Lev. 13:2; 2 Kings 5:1.
Loss of appetite. Job 33:20;
Ps. 107:18.
Melancholy. 1 Sam. 16:14.
Palsy. Matt. 8:6; 9:2.
Plague. Num. 11:33;
2 Sam. 24:15, 21, 25.
Scab. Deut. 28:27.

Sunstroke. 2 Kings 4:18–20;
Isa. 49:10.
Swelling, edema. Luke 14:2.
Ulcers. Isa. 1:6; Luke 16:20.
Worms. Acts 12:23.

Miraculous healing of, a sign to
accompany the preaching of the
word. Mark 16:18.

Not looking to God in, condemned.
2 Chron. 16:12.

Ointments used for. Isa. 1:6;
Jer. 8:22.

Physicians employed for.
2 Chron. 16:12; Jer. 8:22;
Matt. 9:12; Mark 5:26;
Luke 4:23.

Poultices used for. 2 Kings 20:7.

Regarded as visitations. Job 2:7–10;
Ps. 38:2, 7.

Remedies used. Prov. 17:22; 20:30;
Isa. 38:21; Jer. 30:13; 46:11.

Sent
From God. Lev. 14:34.
As punishment. Deut. 28:21;
John 5:14.
Through Satan.
1 Sam. 16:14–16; Job 2:7.

Sins of youth a cause of. Job 20:11.

Those afflicted with
Anointed. Mark 6:13;
James 5:14.
David's child. 2 Sam. 12:15.
Gehazi. 2 Kings 5:27.
Jeroboam. 2 Chron. 13:20.
Jehoram. 2 Chron. 21:12–19.
Laid in the streets to receive advice
from passers-by. Mark 6:56;
Acts 5:15.
Nabal. 1 Sam. 25:38.
Often divinely cured.
2 Kings 20:5; James 5:15.

Often divinely supported.
Ps. 41:3.
Uzziah. 2 Chron. 26:17–20.
Were many and various.
Matt. 4:24.

DISHONESTY
In business. Deut. 25:13–16.

Examples of
Abimlech's servants seize a well of
water. Gen. 21:25; 26:15–22.
Achan hides the wedge of gold and
the Babylonian garment.
Josh. 7:11–26.
Ahab seizes Nabob's vineyard.
1 Kings 21:2–16.
Jacob obtains his brother's
birthright by unjust advantage.
Gen. 25:29–33.
Jacob steals his father's blessing.
Gen. 27:6–29.
Jacob steals Laban's flocks.
Gen. 30:31–43.
Joab's deceit in securing
Absalom's return.
2 Sam. 14:2–20.
Judas' hypocritical sympathy for
the poor. John 12:6.
Laban's treatment of Jacob.
Gen. 29:21–30; 31:36–42.
Micah steals 1,100 pieces of silver.
Judg. 17:2.
Micah's priest steals his images.
Judg. 18:14–21.
Rachel steals the household gods.
Gen. 31:19.
Rebekah's deceit in Jacob's behalf.
Gen. 27:6–17.
Simeon and Levi deceive the
Shechemites. Gen. 34:15–31.
God's attitude toward. 1 Thess. 4:6;
James 5:4.
Penalty and restoration. Lev. 6:2–7.

DISOBEDIENCE, CIVIL

Practiced by
Apostles. Acts 4:1–3.
Daniel. Dan. 3, 6.
Moses' parents. Exod. 1:16–2:10.
Urged by Jeremiah. Jer. 38:1–6.

Warning against by
Paul. Rom. 13:1–7.
Peter. 1 Pet. 2:11–17.

DISOBEDIENCE TO GOD
See God, Disobedience to

DISPERSION
After building the tower of Babel.
Gen. 11:1–9; Deut. 32:8.
The descendants of Noah. Gen. 10.
Of the Jews, predicted. Jer. 16:15;
24:9; John 7:35.

DISSIPATION
Dangers of. Job 1:5.

DIVERSITY

Found in
Israel. Exod. 12:38.
Ministries. 1 Cor. 12:5–6, 14–31.
Population of earth. Acts 17:26–27.
Population of heaven. Rev. 5:9–10;
7:9.
Spiritual gifts. 1 Cor. 12:4, 7–31;
Eph. 4:11.

DIVINATION

Effected through
Cups. Gen. 44:2, 5.
Dreams. Jer. 29:8; Zech. 10:2.
Enchantments. Exod. 7:11;
Num. 24:1.
The flight of arrows.
Ezek. 21:21–22.

Inspecting the inside of beasts.
Ezek. 21:21.
Observing heavenly
bodies. Isa. 37:13.
Observing times. 2 Kings 21:6.
Raising the dead.
1 Sam. 28:11–12.
Rods. Hos. 4:12.
Sorcery. Isa. 47:12; Acts 8:11.
Frustrated by God. Isa. 44:25.
The Jews prone to. 2 Kings 17:17;
Isa. 2:6.

The Law
Forbade its practice for Israelites.
Lev. 19:26; Deut. 18:10–11.
Forbade seeking to. Lev. 19:31;
Deut. 18:14.
Punished those who sought to.
Lev. 20:6.
Punished with death those who
used. Exod. 22:18; Lev. 20:27.
A lucrative employment. Num. 22:7;
Acts 16:16.

Magic
An abominable practice.
1 Sam. 15:23.
All who practiced it, abominable.
Deut. 18:12.
Books of, numerous and expensive.
Acts 19:19.
Connected with idolatry.
2 Chron. 33:5–6.
Could not injure the Lord's people.
Num. 23:23.

Practiced by
Astrologers. Isa. 47:13; Dan. 4:7.
Psychics. Deut. 18:11.
Fortune-tellers. Deut. 18:14;
Isa. 2:6; Dan. 2:27.
False prophets. Jer. 14:14;
Ezek. 13:3, 6.

Magicians. Gen. 41:8; Dan. 4:7.
Mediums. Deut. 18:11.
Sorcerers. Deut. 18:10; Jer. 27:9;
Acts 13:6, 8.
Witches. Exod. 22:18;
Deut. 18:10.
Wizards. Deut. 18:11;
1 Sam. 28:3.
A system of fraud. Ezek. 13:6–7;
Jer. 29:8.

Those who practiced
Consulted in difficulties Dan. 2:2;
4:6–7.
Regarded as wise men.
Dan. 2:12, 27.
Regarded with awe. Acts 8:9, 11.
Used mysterious words and
gestures. Isa. 8:19.

DIVISIONS

Are contrary to the
Desire of Christ. John 17:21–23.
Purpose of Christ. John 10:16.
Spirit of the primitive church.
1 Cor. 11:16.
Unity of Christ. 1 Cor. 1:13;
12:12.
Are proof of a worldly spirit.
1 Cor. 3:3.
Avoid those who cause.
Rom. 16:17.
Condemned in the church.
1 Cor. 1:11–13; 11:18.
Evil of, illustrated. Matt. 12:25.
Forbidden in the church.
1 Cor. 1:10.
Unbecoming in the church.
1 Cor. 12:24–25.

DIVORCE
Of captives, regulated by law.
Deut. 21:13–14.

Forbidden by Christ except for
adultery. Matt. 5:32; 19:9.

Forced on those who had idolatrous
wives. Ezra 10:2–17.

Illustrative of God's casting off of the
Jewish church. Isa. 50:1; Jer. 3:8.

The Jews condemned for love of.
Mal. 2:14–16.

Law of marriage against. Gen. 2:24;
Matt. 19:6.

Not allowed to those who falsely
accused their
wives. Deut. 22:18–19.

Permitted
Because of hardness of heart.
Matt. 19:8.
By Mosaic law. Deut. 24:1.
Priests not to marry women after.
Lev. 21:14.
Prohibition of, offended the Jews.
Matt. 19:10.
Sought on slight grounds.
Matt. 5:31; 19:3.
Of servants, regulated by law.
Exod. 21:7, 11.
Often sought by the Jews. Mic. 2:9;
Mal. 2:14.

Women
Afflicted by. Isa. 54:4, 6.
Could obtain. Prov. 2:17, with
Mark 10:12.
Could remarry. Deut. 24:2.
Remarried, could not return to first
husband. Deut. 24:3–4;
Jer. 3:1.
Responsible for vows after.
Num. 30:9.

DOCTRINES, FALSE

Curse on those who teach.
Gal. 1:8–9.

Destructive to faith. 2 Tim. 2:18.

Hateful to God. Rev. 2:14–15.

Punishment of those who teach.
Mic. 3:6–7; 2 Pet. 2:1, 3.

Should be avoided by
All men. Jer. 23:16; 29:3.
Believers. Eph. 4:14; Col. 2:8.
Ministers. 1 Tim. 1:4; 6:20.

Teachers of
Attract many. 2 Pet. 2:2.
Bring reproach on religion.
2 Pet. 2:2.
Deceive many. Matt. 24:5.
Not to be tolerated. 2 John 10.
Pervert the gospel of Christ.
Col. 1:6–7.
Should be avoided.
Rom. 16:17–18.
Speak perverse things.
Acts 20:30.
Will abound in the latter days.
1 Tim. 4:1.
Will be exposed. 2 Tim. 3:9.

Teachers of, described as
Corrupt and depraved.
2 Tim. 3:8.
Covetous. Titus 1:11; 2 Pet. 2:3.
Cruel. Acts 20:29.
Deceitful. 2 Cor. 11:13.
Proud and ignorant.
1 Tim. 6:3–4.
Ungodly. Jude 4, 8.
Try, by Scripture. Isa. 8:20;
1 John 4:1.
Unprofitable and vain. Titus 3:9;
Heb. 13:9.
The wicked given up to believe.
2 Thess. 2:11.
The wicked love. 2 Tim. 4:3–4.

DOCTRINES, OF THE GOSPEL

Are from God. John 7:16;
Acts 13:12.
Are godly. 1 Tim. 6:3; Titus 1:1.
Are taught by Scripture.
2 Tim. 3:16.
Bring no reproach on. 1 Tim. 6:1;
Titus 2:5.
A faithful walk makes attractive.
Titus 2:10.
Immorality condemned by.
1 Tim. 1:9–11.
Lead to fellowship with the Father
and with the Son. 1 John 1:3;
2 John 9.
Lead to holiness. Rom. 6:17–22;
Titus 2:12.

Ministers should
Attend to. 1 Tim. 4:13, 16.
Believers abide in. Acts 2:42.
Believers obey, from the heart.
Rom. 6:17.
Be nourished up in. 1 Tim. 4:6.
Continue in. 1 Tim. 4:16.
Hold in sincerity. 2 Cor. 2:17;
Titus 2:7.
Hold steadfastly. 2 Tim. 1:13;
Titus 1:9.
Speak things which become.
Titus 2:1.
Not endured by the wicked.
2 Tim. 4:3.
Obedience of believers leads to
surer knowledge of. John 7:17.

Those who oppose are
Ignorant. 1 Tim. 6:4.
Not to be received. 2 John 10.
Proud. 1 Tim. 6:3–4.
Quarrelsome. 1 Tim. 6:4.
To be avoided. Rom. 16:17.

DOCTOR

A teacher or master. Matt. 8:19;
Luke 2:46; Acts 5:34;
1 Tim. 1:7.

DOG

Described as
Carnivorous. 1 Kings 14:11;
2 Kings 9:35–36.
Dangerous and destructive.
Ps. 22:16.
Fond of blood. 1 Kings 21:19;
22:38.
Impatient of injury. Prov. 26:17.
Unclean. Luke 16:21;
2 Pet. 2:22.
Despised by the Jews. 2 Sam. 3:8.
Epithet of contempt. 1 Sam. 17:43;
24:14; 2 Sam. 3:8; 9:8; 16:9;
2 Kings 8:13; Isa. 56:10–11;
Matt. 15:26.
Greyhound. Prov. 30:31.

Illustrative of
Apostates. 2 Pet. 2:22.
Covetous ministers. Isa. 56:11.
False teachers. Phil. 3:2.
Fools. Prov. 26:11.
Gentiles. Matt. 15:22, 26.
The mean (when dead).
1 Sam. 24:14; 2 Sam. 9:8.
Obstinate sinners. Matt. 7:6;
Rev. 22:15.
Persecutors. Ps. 22:16, 20.
Unfaithful ministers (when dumb).
Isa. 56:10.
Infested cities by night.
Ps. 59:14–15.
Manner of drinking alluded to.
Judg. 7:5.
Nothing holy to be given to.
Matt. 7:6; 15:26.

Sacrificing of, an abomination.
Isa. 66:3.
Things torn by beasts given to.
Exod. 22:31.

When domesticated
Employed in watching flocks.
Job 30:1.
Fed with the crumbs, etc.
Matt. 15:27.

DONKEY
Bridles for. Prov. 26:3.
Carrying burdens. Gen. 42:26;
2 Sam. 16:1; Isa. 30:6.
Drawing chariots. Isa. 21:7.
Firstlings of, redeemed.
Exod. 13:13, 34:20.
For food. 2 Kings 6:25.
Herds of. Gen. 12:16; 24:35; 32:5;
34:28; Num. 31:34, 45;
1 Chron. 5:21; Ezra 2:67;
Neh. 7:69.
Jawbone of, used by Samson to slay
Philistines. Judg. 15:15–17.
Not to be yoked with a ox.
Deut. 22:10.
Rest on Sabbath. Exod. 23:12.
Used for riding. Gen. 22:3;
Num. 22:21–33; Josh. 15:18;
Judg. 1:14; 5:10; 1 Sam. 25:23;
2 Chron. 28:15; Zech. 9:9.
Used for riding by Jesus. Zech. 9:9;
Matt. 21:2, 5; Luke 13:15;
John 12:14–15.

DOOR
Doors of the temple made of two
leaves, cherubim and flowers
carved upon, covered with gold.
1 Kings 6:31–35.
Hinges for. Prov. 26:14.
The law to be written on.
Deut. 11:20.

Made of gold. 1 Kings 7:50.
Post of, sprinkled with the blood of
the Paschal lamb. Exod. 12:22.

Used in a figurative sense
Closed. Matt. 25:10; Luke 13:25;
Rev. 3:7.
Door of hope. Hos. 2:15.
Of opportunity. 1 Cor. 16:9;
Rev. 3:8.

DOUBTING

Examples of
Abraham. Gen. 12:12–13.
Ananias. Acts 9:13–14.
The disciples. Matt. 8:23–27.
Elijah. 1 Kings 19:13–18.
Jeremiah. Jer. 1:6; 32:24–25.
John the Baptist. Matt. 11:2–3.
Lot. Gen. 19:30.
Moses. Exod. 3:11.
Philip. John 14:8–11.
Samuel. 1 Sam. 16:1–2.
Sarah. Gen. 18:12–14.
Some persons who witnessed
Jesus' ascension. Matt. 28:17.
God's help in. Ps. 73:13–17;
Isa. 40:27–28.

DOUGH
First of, offered to God.
Num. 15:19–21; Neh. 10:37.
Kneaded. Jer. 7:18; Hos. 7:4.
Part of, for Priest. Ezek. 44:30.

DOWNSIZING

Principle relevant to
All things work for good through
God. Rom 8:28.

Injunctions concerning
Be content in all situations.
Phil. 4:11–12.

Do not worry in times of hardship.
Matt. 6:25–33.

DOWRY
Law concerning. Exod. 22:16–17.
Ruth. Ruth 4:3.

DOVE

Characterized by
Attractiveness. Song of Sol. 2:14.
Clean and used as food.
Deut. 14:11.
Dwells in rocks. Song of Sol. 2:14;
Jer. 48:28.
Frequents streams and rivers.
Song of Sol. 5:12.
The harbinger of spring.
Song of Sol. 2:12.
Richness of plumage. Ps. 68:13.
Simplicity. Matt. 10:16.
Softness of eyes. Song of Sol.
1:15.
Sweetness of voice.
Song of Sol. 2:14.

Dove

Illustrative of
The church.
Song of Sol 2:14; 5:2.
Converts to the church. Isa. 60:8.

The Holy Spirit. Matt. 3:16;
John 1:32.
The meekness of Christ.
Song of Sol. 5:12.
Mourners. Isa. 38:14; 59:11.
The return of Israel from captivity
(in its flight). Hos. 11:11.
Impiously sold in the court of the
temple. Matt. 21:12; John 2:16.
Mournful cries of, alluded to.
Nah. 2:7.
Offered in sacrifice. Gen. 15:9;
Lev. 1:14.
Sent from the ark by Noah.
Gen. 8:8, 10, 12.
Why considered the emblem of
peace. Gen. 8:11.

DRAGON

Described as
Of a mournful voice. Mic. 1:8.
Often of a red color. Rev. 12:3.
Poisonous. Deut. 32:33.
Powerful. Rev. 12:4.
Snuffing up the air. Jer. 14:6.
Of solitary habits. Job 30:29.
Swallowing its prey. Jer. 51:34.
Wailing. Mic. 1:8.

Found in
Deserted cities. Isa. 13:22;
Jer. 9:11.
Dry places. Isa. 34:13; 43:20.
Rivers (a species). Ps. 74:13;
Isa. 27:1.
The wilderness. Mal. 1:3.

Illustrative of
Cruel and persecuting kings.
Isa. 27:1; 51:9; Ezek. 29:3.
The devil. Rev. 13:2; 20:2, 7.
Enemies of the church. Ps. 91:13.
Wicked people. Ps. 44:19.

Wine (poison of). Deut. 32:33.

DRAWING
Of pictures on tile. Ezek. 4:1.

DREAMS
Excess of business frequently leads to. Eccles. 5:3.

False prophets
Condemned for pretending to. Jer. 23:32.
Not to be regarded in. Deut. 13:1–3; Jer. 27:9.
Pretended to. Jer. 23:25–28; 29:8.
God the only interpreter of. Gen. 40:8; 41:16; Dan. 2:27–30; 7:16.
God's will often revealed in. Num. 12:6; Job 33:15.

Illustrative of
Enemies of the church. Isa. 29:7–8.
Impure imaginations. Jude 8.
Prosperity of sinners. Job 20:5–8; Ps. 73:19–20.

Mentioned in Scripture, of
Abimelech. Gen. 20:3–7.
Daniel. Dan. 7.
Jacob. Gen. 28:12; 31:10.
Joseph. Gen. 37:5–9; Matt. 1:20–21; 2:13, 19–20.
Laban. Gen. 31:24.
Midianite. Judg. 7:13–15.
Nebuchadnezzar. Dan. 2:1, 31; 4:5, 8.
Pharaoh. Gen. 41:1–7.
Pharaoh's butler and baker. Gen. 40:5–19.
Pilate's wife. Matt. 27:19.
Solomon. 1 Kings 3:5–15.

Wise men. Matt. 2:11–12.
Often but imaginary. Job 20:8; Isa. 29:8.

The people in ancient times
Anxious to have explained. Gen. 40:8; Dan. 2:3.
Consulted magicians on. Gen. 41:8; Dan. 2:2–4.
Often perplexed by. Gen. 40:6; 41:8; Job 7:14; Dan. 2:1; 4:5.
Put great faith in. Judg. 7:15.
Vanity of trusting to natural. Eccles. 5:7.
Visions in sleep. Job 33:15; Dan. 2:28.

DRESS
Ceremonial purification of. Lev. 11:32; 13:47–59; Num. 31:20.
Changes of clothing, the folly of excessive. Job 27:16.
Of fig leaves. Gen. 3:7.

Of the head
Bonnets prescribed by Moses, for the priests. Exod. 28:40; 29:9; 39:28.
Bonnets, worn by women. Isa. 3:20; Ezek. 24:17, 23.
Hats, worn by men. Dan. 3:21.
Handkerchiefs. Ezek. 13:18, 21.
Hoods. Isa. 3:23.
Men forbidden to wear women's, and women forbidden to wear men's. Deut. 22:5.
Mixed materials in, forbidden. Deut. 22:11.
Not to be held overnight as a pledge for debt. Exod. 22:26.
Presents made of changes of clothing. Gen. 45:22;

1 Sam. 18:4; 2 Kings 5:5;
Dan. 5:7.
Rules with respect to women's.
1 Tim. 2:9–10; 1 Pet. 3:3.
Of skins. Gen. 3:21.
Symbolic sense, filthy, of
unrighteousness. Isa. 64:6.
Uniform vestment kept in store for
worshipers of Baal.
2 Kings 10:22–23; Zeph. 1:8.

Various articles of
Mantle. Ezra 9:3; 1 Kings 19:13;
1 Chron. 15:27; Job 1:20.
Multicolored. 2 Sam. 13:18.
Purple. John 19:2, 5.
Robe. Exod. 28:4; 1 Sam. 18:4.
Shawls. Isa. 3:22.
Embroidered coat. Exod. 28:4,
40; 1 Sam. 2:19; Dan. 3:21.
Sleeveless shirt, called coat.
Matt. 5:40; Luke 6:29;
John 19:23; Acts 9:39.
Coat. 2 Tim. 4:13; John 19:2, 5.
Skirts. Ezek. 5:3.
Robes. Isa. 3:19.
Purses. Isa. 3:22.
Sashes. Isa. 3:20.
Trousers. Dan. 3:21.
For wedding feasts. Matt. 22:11.

DRINK OFFERING
See Offering, Drink

DRIVING
Rapid, by Jehu. 2 Kings 9:20.

DROSS
See Impurities

DROUGHT
Figurative sense. Ps. 32:4; Isa. 44:3.
Sent by God as judgment. Deut.
28:23–24.

DRUGS, FERTILITY
Mandrakes as an aphrodisiac.
Gen. 30:14–18.

DRUGS (ILLEGAL NARCOTICS)
Effects of bad company.
1 Cor. 15:33.
Hopeless cycle. Rom 7:18–20.

Injunctions concerning
Do not gratify desires of the sinful
nature. Gal. 5:16.
Honor God with body.
1 Cor. 6:20.
Prepare mind for acton.
1 Pet. 1:13.
Remain alert. 1 Thess. 5:6;
1 Pet. 5:8.

Principles relevant to
Body a living sacrifice. Rom 12:1.
Body as temple of the Holy Spirit.
1 Cor. 6:19.
Temptation. 1 Cor. 10:13.
Value of self-control. Prov 25:28;
Gal. 5:23.

DRUNKENNESS
Avoid those given to. Prov. 23:20;
1 Cor. 5:11.
Caution against. Luke 21:34.
Degrades. Isa. 28:8.

Denunciations against
Those given to. Isa. 5:11–12;
28:1–3.
Those who encourage. Hab. 2:15.
Excludes from heaven. 1 Cor. 6:10;
Gal. 5:21.
False teachers often addicted to.
Isa. 56:12.
Folly of yielding to. Prov. 20:1.
Forbidden. Eph. 5:18.
Inflames. Isa. 5:11.

Leads to

Affliction and sorrow.
Prov. 29–30.
Contempt of God's works.
Isa. 5:12.
Error. Isa. 28:7.
Poverty. Prov. 21:17; 23:21.
Scorning. Hos. 7:5.
Strife. Prov. 23:29–30.
Overcharges the heart. Luke 21:34.
Punishment of. Deut. 21:20–21;
Joel 1:5–6; Amos 6:6–7;
Matt. 24:49–51.
Takes away the heart. Hos. 4:11.
The wicked addicted to. Dan. 5:1–4.
A work of the sinful nature.
Gal. 5:21.

DUKE
Of the Midianites. Josh. 13:21.
Title of the princes of Edom.
Gen. 36:15–43.

DUMB
Miraculous healing of, by Jesus.
Matt. 9:32–33.
Stricken of God. Exod. 4:11;
Luke 1:20, 64.

DUNGEON
In prisons. Jer. 38:6; Lam. 3:53.

DUST
Casting of, in anger. 2 Sam. 16:13.
Man made from. Gen. 2:7; 3:19;
Eccles. 3:20.
Put on the head in mourning.
Josh. 7:6; Job 2:12; 42:6.
Shaking from feet. Matt. 10:14;
Acts 13:51.

DUTY
Before God. Deut. 6:18;
1 Chron. 16:29; Eccles. 12:13.
And stagnation. Deut. 1:6.
Summarized in love. Rom. 13:9.
Toward children. Eph. 6:4.
Toward fellow Christians.
Rom. 15:1; 1 Cor. 8:11.
Toward government. Luke 20:25;
1 Pet. 2:17.
Toward men. Prov. 3:27;
Rom. 13:7; 1 John 4:11.

DWARFS
Forbidden to be priests. Lev. 21:20.

DYSPEPSIA
Of Timothy. 1 Tim. 5:23.

EAGLE

A bird of prey. Job 9:26;
Matt. 24:28.
Called the eagle of the heavens.
Lam. 4:19.
Delights in the lofty cedars.
Ezek. 17:3–4.

Described as
Long-sighted. Job 39:29.
Soaring to heaven. Prov. 23:5.
Swift. 2 Sam. 1:23.
Different kinds of. Lev. 11:13, 18;
Ezek. 17:3.
Dwells in the high rocks.
Job 39:27–28.

Eagle

Feeds her young with blood.
Job 39:29–30.
Greatness of its wings alluded to.
Ezek. 17:3, 7.

Illustrative of
Calamities, in its increased
baldness in the molting season.
Mic. 1:16.
The fancied but fatal security of the
wicked in the height and security
of its dwelling. Jer. 49:16;
Obad. 1:4.
God's care of His church in its
mode of teaching the young to
fly. Exod. 19:4; Deut. 32:11.
Great and powerful kings.
Ezek. 17:3; Hos. 8:1.
The melting away of riches, in its
swiftness. Prov. 23:5.
Protection afforded to the church,
by its wings. Rev. 12:14.
Renewal of believers, in its
renewed strength and beauty.
Ps. 103:5.
The saint's rapid progress toward
heaven, in its upward flight.
Isa. 40:31.
The swiftness of hostile armies, in
its swiftness. Deut. 28:49;
Jer. 4:13; 48:40; Lam. 4:19.
The swiftness of human life in
swooping down on the prey.
Job 9:26.
Wisdom and zeal of God's
ministers. Ezek. 1:10; Rev. 4:7.
Peculiarity of its flight alluded to.
Prov. 30:19.

Strength of its feathers alluded to.
Dan. 4:33.
Unclean. Lev. 11:13; Deut. 14:12.
Was the standard of the Roman
armies. Matt. 24:15, with 28.

EAR

Blood put on the right ear of
The healed leper in cleansing him.
Lev. 14:14.
Priests at consecration.
Exod. 29:20; Lev. 8:23.
Capable of trying and distinguishing
words. Job 12:11.
Christ opens. Isa. 35:5; 43:8, 10.

God
Judicially closes. Isa. 6:10, with
Matt. 13:15.
Made. Prov. 20:12.
Opens. Job 33:16; 36:10.
Planted. Ps. 94:9.
Instruction received through.
Isa. 30:21.
Not satisfied with earthly things.
Eccles. 1:8.
Not to be stopped at cry of the poor.
Prov. 21:13.
Often adorned with rings.
Ezek. 16:12; Hos. 2:13.
Organ of hearing. Job 13:1; 29:11.
Of servants who refused to leave their
masters, pierced. Exod. 21:6;
Deut. 15:17.

Should
Be bowed down to instructions.
Prov. 5:1.
Be given to the law of God.
Isa. 1:10.
Be inclined to wisdom. Prov. 2:2.
Hear and obey correction.
Prov. 15:31; 25:12.

Receive the Word of God.
Jer. 9:20.
Seek knowledge. Prov. 18:15.
That hears and receives the Word of
God, blessed. Exod. 15:26;
Matt. 13:16.

Of the wicked
Itching. 2 Tim. 4:3.
Not inclined to hear God.
Jer. 7:24; 35:15.
Stopped against God's word.
Ps. 58:4; Zech. 7:11.
Turned away from God's law.
Prov. 28:9.
Uncircumcised. Jer. 6:10;
Acts 7:51.

EARNESTNESS
In all things. Col. 3:23.
In awaiting redemption. Rom. 8:19;
2 Cor. 5:2.
In obedience. Josh. 22:5; Eph. 6:6.
In prayer. 2 Chron. 6:12–42;
Acts 12:5.
In seeking God. Acts 16:30–34.
In spiritual perseverance. Heb. 2:1;
12:15.
In the work of the church.
2 Cor. 8:16–22.

EARRING
Of gold. Prov. 25:12.
Offering of, for the golden calf.
Exod. 32:2, 3.
For the tabernacle. Exod. 35:22.
Worn for idolatrous purposes.
Gen. 35:4; Isa. 3:20.

EARTH
Believers will inherit. Ps. 25:13;
Matt. 5:5.
Corrupted by sin. Gen. 6:11–12;
Isa. 24:5.

Created to be inhabited. Isa. 45:18.

Described as
Burning at God's presence.
Nah. 1:5.
Full of God's glory. Num. 14:21;
Isa. 6:3.
Full of God's goodness. Ps. 33:5.
Full of God's mercy. Ps. 119:64.
Full of God's riches. Ps. 104:24.
God's footstool. Isa. 66:1;
Matt. 5:35.
Melting at God's voice. Ps. 46:6.
Shining with God's glory.
Ezek. 43:2.
Trembling before God. Ps. 68:8;
Jer. 10:10.
Diversified by hills and mountains.
Hab. 3:6.
The dry land as divided from
waters. Gen. 1:10.
First division of. Gen. 10:25.
Full of minerals. Deut. 8:9;
Job 28:1–5, 15–19.

God
Created. Gen. 1:1; Neh. 9:6.
Enlightens. Gen. 1:14–16;
Job 33:25.
Establishes. Ps. 78:69; 119:90.
Formed. Ps. 90:2.
Governs supremely. Job 34:13;
Ps. 135:6.
Inspects. Zech. 4:10.
Laid the foundation of. Job 38:4;
Ps. 102:25.
Makes fruitful. Gen. 1:11; 27:28.
Reigns in. Exod. 8:22; Ps. 97:1.
Will be exalted in. Ps. 46:10.
Spread abroad. Isa. 42:5; 44:24.
Supports. Ps. 75:3.
Suspended in space. Job 26:7.
Waters. Pss. 65:9; 147:8.

Ideas of the people in ancient times
respecting the form of. Job 11:9;
38:18; Prov. 25:3.
Is the Lord's. Exod. 9:29;
1 Cor. 10:26.
Made barren by sin. Deut. 28:23;
Ps. 107:34.
Made to mourn and languish by sin.
Isa. 24:4; Jer. 4:28; 12:4;
Hos. 4:3.

Man
Brought a curse on. Gen. 3:17.
By nature is of. 1 Cor. 15:47–48.
By nature minds the things of.
Phil. 3:19.
Formed out of. Gen. 2:7;
Ps. 103:14.
Given dominion over. Gen. 1:26;
Ps. 115:16.
Will return to. Gen. 3:19;
Ps. 146:4.
Not to be again flooded. Gen. 9:11;
2 Pet. 3:6–7.
Once flooded. Gen. 7:17–24.
Satan goes to and fro in. Job 1:7;
1 Pet. 5:8.
Subject to God's judgments.
Ps. 46:8; Isa. 11:4.
To be dissolved by fire. 2 Pet. 3:7,
10, 12.
To be renewed. Isa. 65:17;
2 Pet. 3:13.
Will be filled with the knowledge of
God. Isa. 11:9; Hab. 2:14.
The world in general. Gen. 1:2.

EARTHQUAKES

Are visible tokens of
God's anger. Pss. 18:7; 60:2;
Isa. 13:13.
God's power. Job 9:6;
Heb. 12:26.

God's presence. Pss. 68:7–8;
114:7.

At Christ's second coming,
predicted. Zech. 14:4.

Before destruction of Jerusalem,
predicted. Matt. 24:7;
Luke 21:11.

Frequently accompanied by
Convulsion and receding of the
sea. 2 Sam. 22:8, 16;
Pss. 18:7, 15; 46:3.

Opening of the earth.
Num. 16:31–32.

Overturning of mountains.
Ps. 46:2; Zech. 14:4.

Rending of rocks. Matt. 27:51.

Volcanic eruptions. Ps. 104:32;
Nah. 1:5.

Illustrative of
The judgments of God.
Isa. 24:19–20; 29:6; Jer. 4:24;
Rev. 8:5.

The overthrow of kingdoms.
Hag. 2:6, 22; Rev. 6:12–13;
16:18–19.

Islands and mountainous districts
liable to. Ps. 114:4, 6; Rev. 6:14;
16:18, 20.

Mentioned in Scripture
At Christ's death. Matt. 27:51.

At Christ's resurrection.
Matt. 28:2.

At Mount Sinai. Exod. 19:15.

At Philippi. Acts 16:26.

In strongholds of Philistines.
1 Sam. 14:15.

In Uzziah's reign. Amos 1:1;
Zech. 14:5.

In the wilderness.
Num. 16:31–32.

When Elijah fled from Jezebel.
1 Kings 19:11.

People always terrified by.
Num. 16:34; Zech. 14:5;
Matt. 27:54; Rev. 11:13.

EATING

Favored guests served a double
portion. Gen. 43:34.

The host acting as waiter. Gen. 18:8.

Reclining on couches. Amos 6:4, 7;
Luke 7:37–38; John 13:25.

Sitting at table. Exod. 32:6.

Table used in. Judg. 1:7.

Washing before. Matt. 15:2.

ECLIPSE

Of the sun and moon. Isa. 13:10;
Ezek. 32:7–8; Joel 2:10, 31;
3:15; Amos 8:9; Mic. 3:6;
Matt. 24:29; Mark 13:24;
Acts 2:20; Rev. 6:12–13; 8:12.

ECONOMICS

Household. Prov. 24:27; 31:10–31;
Eccles. 11:4–6; John 6:12–13.

Political. Gen. 41:33–57.

EDIFICATION

All to be done to. 2 Cor. 12:19;
Eph. 4:29.

Described. Eph. 4:12–16.

Exhortation to. Jude 20–21.

Foolish questions opposed to.
1 Tim. 1:4.

Gospel as the instrument of.
Acts 20:32.

Is the object of
The church's union in Christ.
Eph. 4:16.

Ministerial authority. 2 Cor. 10:8;
13:10.

Ministerial gifts. 1 Cor. 14:3–5,
12.
The ministerial office.
Eph. 4:11–12.
Love leads to. 1 Cor. 8:1.
Mutual, commanded. Rom. 14:19;
1 Thess. 5:11.
Peace of the church favors.
Acts 9:31.
Use self-denial to promote, in others.
1 Cor. 10:23, 33.

EDUCATION
Of children in God's Word.
Deut. 6:7; Eph. 6:4;
2 Tim. 3:15–16.
From life. Isa. 28:10; Prov. 6:6.
In the pastoral ministry. 1 Tim. 4:11.
From personal experience.
Ps. 78:1–8.
In the prophetic ministry. Isa. 28:10.

EGYPT

Armies of
Assistance of, sought by Judah
against the Chaldees.
Ezek. 17:15, with Jer. 37:5, 7.
Besieged and plundered Jerusalem
in Rehoboam's time.
1 Kings 14:25–26.
Captured and burned Gazer.
1 Kings 9.16.
Deposed Jehoahaz and made
Judea a tributary.
2 Kings 23:31–35.
Described. Exod. 14:7–9.
Destroyed in the Red Sea.
Exod. 14:23–28.
Invaded Assyria and killed Josiah
who assisted it. 2 Kings 23:29.
Boundaries of. Ezek. 29:10.

Called
House of bondmen.
Exod. 13:3, 14; Deut. 7:8.
Land of Ham. Pss. 105:23;
106:22.
Rahab. Pss. 87:4; 89:10.
Sihor. Isa. 23:3.
The South. Jer. 13:19;
Dan. 11:14, 25.

Celebrated for
Commerce. Gen. 41:57;
Ezek. 27:7.
Fertility. Gen. 13:10; 45:18.
Fine horses. 1 Kings 10:28–29.
Fine linen, etc. Prov. 7:16;
Isa. 19:9.
Literature. 1 Kings 4:30;
Acts 7:22.
Wealth. Heb. 11:26.
Diet used in. Num. 11:5.
Dry climate of. Deut. 11:10–11.
Under a governor. Gen. 41:41–44.
Had princes and counselors.
Gen. 12:15; Isa. 19:11.

History of Israel in
Their sojourn there, predicted.
Gen. 15:13.
Joseph sold into. Gen. 37:28;
39:1.
Potiphar blessed for Joseph's
sake. Gen. 39:2–6.
Joseph unjustly cast into prison.
Gen. 39:7–20.
Joseph interprets the chief baker's
and the chief butler's dreams.
Gen. 40:5–19.
Joseph interprets Pharaoh's
dreams. Gen. 41:14–32.
Joseph counsels Pharaoh.
Gen. 41:33–36.
Joseph made governor.
Gen. 41:41–44.

Joseph successfully provides against the years of famine. Gen. 41:46–56.

Joseph's ten brothers arrive. Gen. 42:1–6.

Joseph recognizes his brothers. Gen. 42:7–8.

Benjamin brought. Gen. 43:15.

Joseph makes himself known to his brothers. Gen. 45:1–8.

Joseph sends for his father. Gen. 45:9–11.

Pharaoh invites Jacob into. Gen. 45:16–20.

Jacob's journey. Gen. 46:5–7.

Jacob, etc., presented to Pharaoh. Gen. 47:1–10.

Israel placed in the land of Goshen. Gen. 46:34; 47:11, 27.

Joseph enriches the king. Gen. 47:13–26.

Jacob's death and burial. Gen. 49:33; 50:1–13.

Israel's increase and oppression. Exod. 1:1–14.

Male children killed. Exod. 1:15–22.

Moses born and hid for three months. Exod. 2:2.

Moses exposed on the Nile. Exod. 2:3–4.

Moses adopted and brought up by Pharaoh's daughter. Exod. 2:5–10.

Moses kills an Egyptian. Exod. 2:11–12.

Moses flees to Midian. Exod. 2:15.

Moses sent to Pharaoh. Exod. 3:2–10.

Pharaoh increases their affliction. Exod. 5.

Moses proves his divine mission by miracles. Exod. 4:29–31; 7:10.

Egypt is plagued for Pharaoh's stubbornness. Exod. 7:14–10.

The passover instituted. Exod. 12:1–28.

Destruction of the firstborn. Exod. 12:29–30.

Israel plunders the Egyptians. Exod. 12:35–36.

Israel driven out of. Exod. 12:31–33.

Date of the Exodus. Exod. 12:41; Heb. 11:27.

Pharaoh pursues Israel and is miraculously destroyed. Exod. 14:5–25.

Idolatry of, followed by Israel. Exod. 32:4, with Ezek. 20:8, 19.

Inhabitants of

Abhorred shepherds. Gen. 46:34.

Abhorred the sacrifice of oxen, etc. Exod. 8:26.

Hospitable. Gen. 47:5–6; 1 Kings 11:18.

Might be received into the congregation in third generation. Deut. 23:8.

Not to be abhorred by Israel. Deut. 23:7.

Often intermarried with strangers. Gen. 21:21; 1 Kings 3:1; 11:19; 1 Chron. 2:34–35.

Superstitious. Isa. 19:3.

Magic practiced in. Exod. 7:11–12, 22; 8:7.

Mode of embalming in. Gen. 50:3.

Mode of entertaining in. Gen. 43:32–34.

Often a refuge to strangers. Gen. 12:10; 47:4.

Populated by Mizraim's posterity. Gen. 10:6, 13–14.

As a power was
Ambitious of conquests. Jer. 46:8.
Mighty. Isa. 30:2–3.
Pompous. Ezek. 32:12.
Proud and arrogant. Ezek. 29:3;
30:6.
Treacherous. Isa. 36:6;
Ezek. 29:6–7.

Prophecies regarding
Allies to share its misfortunes.
Ezek. 30:4, 6.
Armies destroyed by Babylon.
Jer. 46:2–12.
Captivity of its people. Isa. 20:4;
Jer. 46:19, 24, 26; Ezek. 30:4.
Christ to be called out of.
Hos. 11:1; Matt. 2:15.
Civil war and domestic strife.
Isa. 19:2.
Conversion of. Isa. 19:18–20.
Destruction of its cities.
Ezek. 30:14–18.
Destruction of its idols.
Jer. 43:12–13; 46:25;
Ezek. 30:13.
Destruction of its power.
Ezek. 30:24–25.
Dismay of its inhabitants.
Isa. 19:1, 16–17.
Ever to be a gentle kingdom.
Ezek. 29:15.
Failure of internal resources.
Isa 19:5–10
Flooding of, alluded to. Amos 8:8.
Infatuation of its princes.
Isa. 19:3, 11–14.
Invasion by Babylon.
Jer. 46:2–12.
The Jews who practiced its idolatry
to share its punishments.
Jer. 44:7–28.

Prophetic illustration of its
destruction. Jer. 43:9–10;
Ezek. 30:21–22; 32:4–6.
Spoil of, a reward to Babylon for
services against Tyre.
Ezek. 29:18–20.
Terror occasioned by its fall.
Ezek. 32:9–10.
To be numbered and blessed along
with Israel. Isa. 19:23–25.
Utter desolation of, for forty years.
Ezek. 29:8–12; 30:12; 32:15.
Religion of, idolatrous. Exod. 12:12;
Num. 33:4; Isa. 19:1; Ezek. 29:7.
Ruled by kings who assumed the
name of Pharaoh.
Gen. 12:14–15; 40:1–2;
Exod. 1:8, 22.
Sometimes visited by famine.
Gen. 41:30.
Subject to plague, etc. Deut. 7:15;
28:27, 60.
Watered by the Nile. Gen. 41:1–3;
Exod. 1:22.

ELECTION
Believers may have assurance of.
1 Thess. 1:4.

Of believers, is
According to the foreknowledge of
God. Rom. 8:29; 1 Pet. 1:2.
According to the purpose of God.
Rom. 9:11; Eph. 1:11.
To adoption. Eph. 1:5.
By Christ. John 13:18; 15:16.
In Christ. Eph. 1:4.
To conformity with Christ.
Rom. 8:29.
Eternal. Eph. 1:4.
To eternal glory. Rom. 9:23.
Through faith. 2 Thess. 2:13.
For the glory of God. Eph. 1:6.
Of God. 1 Thess. 1:4; Titus 1:1.

To good works. Eph. 2:10.
Of grace. Rom. 11:5.
Personal. Matt. 20:16, with
John 6:44; Acts 22:14;
2 John 1:13.
Recorded in heaven. Luke 10:20.
Regardless of merit. Rom. 9:11.
To salvation 2 Thess. 2:13.
Through sanctification of the
Spirit. 1 Pet. 1:2.
Sovereign. Rom. 9:15–16;
1 Cor. 1:27; Eph. 1:11.
To spiritual warfare. 2 Tim. 2:4.
Of Christ, as Messiah. Isa. 42:1; 1
Pet. 2:6.
Of churches. 1 Pet. 5:13.

Ensure to believers
Acceptance with God. Rom. 11:7.
Belief in Christ. Acts 13:48.
Blessedness. Pss. 33:12; 65:4.
Divine teaching. John 17:6.
Effectual calling. Rom. 8:30.
The inheritance. Isa. 65:9;
1 Pet. 1:4–5.
Protection. Mark 13:20.
Vindication of their wrongs.
Luke 18:7.
Working of all things for good.
Rom. 8:28.
Of good angels. 1 Tim. 5:21.
Of Israel. Deut. 7:6; Isa. 45:4.
Of ministers. Luke 6:13; Acts 9:15.
Should be evidenced by diligence.
2 Pet. 1:10.
Should lead to growth of graces.
Col. 3:12.

ELECTIONEERING
By Absalom. 2 Sam. 15:1–6.
By Adonijah. 1 Kings 1:7.

ELDER
In the Christian church, requirements
of. Titus 1:5–9.
In the Mosaic system. Deu 1:13, 15.

ELEGY
See Lament

EMANCIPATION
Of all Jewish servants at the Jubilee.
Lev. 25:8–17.
Proclamation of, by Cyrus.
2 Chron. 36:23; Ezra 1:1–4.
Proclamation of, by Zedekiah.
Jer. 34:8–11.

EMBALMING
Of Asa. 2 Chron. 16:14.
An attempt to defeat God's purpose.
Gen. 3:19.
How performed by the Jews.
2 Chron. 16:14; Luke 23:56,
with John 19:40.
Of Jacob. Gen. 50:2, 3.
Of Jesus. Mark 15:46; 16:1.
Of Joseph. Gen. 50:26.
Learned by the Jews in Egypt.
Gen. 50:2, 26.
Not always practiced by the Jews.
John 11:39.
Time required for. Gen. 50:3.
Unknown to early patriarchs.
Gen. 23:4.

EMBEZZLEMENT
Parable of. Luke 16:1–7.

EMBROIDERY
On the belt and coat of the high
priests. Exod. 28:4, 39.
Bezaleel and Aholiab divinely
inspired for, in the work of the

tabernacle.
Exod. 35:30–35; 38:22–23.
On the curtains of the tabernacle.
Exod. 26:1, 36; 27:16.
On the garments of princes.
Ezek. 26:16.
On the garments of Sisera.
Judg. 5:30.
On the garments of women.
Ps. 45:14.

EMERALD

Color of the rainbow. Rev. 4:3.
Merchandise of, in Tyre.
Ezek. 27:16; 28:13.
Set in a breastplate. Exod. 28:18.
Symbolic sense, in the foundation of
the Holy City. Rev. 21:19.

EMERODS

Disease(s). Deut. 28:27; 1 Sam. 5–6.

EMPLOYEE

How to treat. Deut. 24:14.
Just wages for. Lev. 19:13.
Rest for. Lev. 25:6.

EMPLOYER

Instructions for. Col. 4:1.

EMPLOYMENT

See also Career Decisions; Industry

Duties of employers. Lev. 19:13;
Luke 10:17; Col. 4:1.
Duties of workers. Exod. 20:9;
Eph. 6:5; 2 Thess. 3:12.
Payment of wages. Deut. 24:15;
Mal. 3:5; James 5:4.
People expected to work for a living.
Eph. 4:28; 1 Thess. 4:11;
2 Thess. 3:7–12.

Spiritual work. Mic. 3:11;
Matt. 9:37–38; John 10:12;
1 Cor. 3:10.
Value of. Gen. 2:15;
2 Thess. 3:7–12.
Vanity of overwork. Ps. 127:2.
Work all day. Ps. 104:23.
Worker worthy of fair wages.
Matt. 10:10; 1 Cor. 9:3–10;
1 Tim. 5:18.
Worker worthy of timely wages.
Lev. 19:13; Deut. 24:14–15;
Prov. 3:27–28.

ENCOURAGEMENT

Exhorted. Acts 27:22;
1 Thess. 5:14; Heb. 3:13.
Needed by all. Neh. 4:17–23;
Dan. 6:18–23.
Needed by prophets.
1 Kings 19:1–19.
Through Christ's presence.
Matt. 14:27.
Through fellow believers.
Acts 28:15.
Through God's care. Matt. 10:30.
Through God's help. Isa. 41:13.
Through salvation. Isa. 43:1.

ENDURANCE

Of Christians encouraged.
Matt. 10:22; 2 Tim. 2:3.
Of love. 1 Cor. 13:4–8.
Needed in spiritual life. Rom. 2:5–7;
Col. 1:23.
Rewards of. 2 Tim. 3:11;
James 1:12.
Of the things of God. Heb. 12:27;
Ps. 52:1.

ENEMIES

Be affectionately concerned for.
Ps. 35:13.

Of believers, God will destroy.
Ps. 60:12.

Christ prayed for His. Luke 23:34.

Curse them not. Job 31:30.

Desire not the death of.
1 Kings 3:11.

Friendship of, deceitful.
2 Sam. 20:9–10; Prov. 26:26;
27:6; Matt. 26:48–49.

God defends against. Pss. 59:9;
61:3.

God delivers from. 1 Sam. 12:11;
Ezra 8:31; Ps. 18:48.

Goods of, to be taken care of.
Exod. 23:4–5.

Lives of, to be spared.
1 Sam. 24:10; 2 Sam. 16:10–11.

Made to be at peace with believers.
Prov. 16:7.

Praise God for deliverance from.
Ps. 136:24.

Pray for deliverance from.
1 Sam. 12:10; Pss. 17:9; 59:1;
64:1.

Rejoice not at the failings of.
Prov. 24:17.

Rejoice not at the misfortunes of.
Job 31:29.

Should be
Assisted. Prov. 25:21, with
Rom. 12:20.
Loved. Matt. 5:44.
Overcome by kindness.
1 Sam. 26:21.
Prayed for. Acts 7:60.

EMPOWERMENT

Through anointing, given to
Absalom, to be king. 2
Sam. 19:10.
Cyrus, to subdue nations.
Isa. 45:1.

David, to be king. 1 Sam 16:13;
1 Chron. 11:3.

Elisha, to be prophet.
1 Kings 19:16; 2 Kings 2:9, 15.

Hazael, to be king. 1 Kings 19:15.

Jehu, to be king. 1 Kings 19:16;
2 Kings 9:3, 6, 12.

Jesus, to minister and heal.
Acts 10:38.

Joash, to be king. 2 Kings 11:12;
2 Chron. 23:11.

Jehoahaz, to be king.
2 Kings 23:30.

Saul, to be ruler. 1 Sam 10:1.

Servant of the Lord, to minister.
Isa. 61:1–3.

Solomon, to be king.
1 Kings 1:39; 1 Chron. 29:22.

Zadok, to be priest.
1 Chron. 29:22.

Azariah, to prophecy.
2 Chron. 15:1–7.

By the beast, given to the Dragon, to
deceive. Rev. 13:2, 4.

Beasts
To blaspheme. Rev. 13:5.
To cause life and death.
Rev. 13:13–15.
To control economy.
Rev. 13:16–17.
To make war. Rev. 13:7.

Believers
For life. Eph. 1:19.
To abound in hope. Rom. 15:13.
To become children of God.
John 1:12.

Bezalel and Oholiab
To make tabernacle and
furnishings. Exod. 31:1–11;
35:30–35.

To teach craftsmanship.
Exod. 35:34.

Claimed to be given by Satan to
Jesus. Luke 4:6.
Deacons, to serve. Acts 6:3–6.
Death, to kill. Rev. 6:8.

By divine authority, given to
apostles
To cast out demons, heal and
preach. Matt. 10:1;
Mark 3:14–15; 6:7;
Luke 9:1–2; 10:19;
Acts 4:7–10.
To be witnesses. Matt. 28:18–20;
Luke 24:49; Acts 1:8; 2:1–4.
Faint ones, to be renewed.
Isa. 40:29–31.
Gideon, to deliver Israel. Judg. 6:34.

By human authority, given to
The beast, to make war on the
Lamb. Rev. 17:12–14.
Jahaziel, to encourage
troops. 2 Chron. 20:14–17.
Jephthah, to deliver Israel.
Judg. 11:29.

Jesus
To empower disciples.
Matt. 28:18–20.
To forgive sins. Matt. 9:6;
Mark 2:10; Luke 5:24.
To give eternal life. John 17:2.
To heal. Luke 5:17.
To lay down own life. John 10:18.
To minister. Luke 4:18–21.
To raise up own life. John 10:18.
Locust (fig.), to harm those without
seal of God. Rev. 9:3–5.
Micah, to prophesy. Mic. 3:8.
Moses, to deliver Israel.
Exod. 3:1–4:17.
Nebuchadnezzar, to rule. Dan. 2:37.

Othniel, to deliver Israel. Judg. 3:10.

Paul
To bear own weaknesses.
2 Cor. 12:9.
To win gentiles. Acts 15:12;
Rom. 15:18–20; 2 Cor. 12:12.
People of God. Ps. 68:35.

People with ability and intelligence
To make holy garments.
Exod. 28:3.
To make tabernacle and
furnishings. Exod. 31:6–11;
36:1.
Pharaoh, so God's name would be
great. Rom. 9:17.
Pilate, to crucify or release Jesus.
John 19:10–11.
Samson, to deliver Israel.
Judg. 13:25; 14:6, 19; 15:14.
Servant of the Lord, to minister.
Isa. 41:8–16; 42:1–7; 49:5–6;
50:4–9; 52:13–53:12.
Stephen, to do signs and wonders.
Acts 6:8.
Those in Thyatira who conquer, over
the nations. Rev. 2:26.
Two witnesses, to prophesy. Rev.
11:3.
Through weakness. 2 Cor. 12:9.
Zechariah, to prophesy. 2
Chron. 24:20.

ENGINE
Of war. 2 Chron. 26:15;
Ezek. 26:9.

ENGINEERING, CIVIL
In the conquest of Canaan.
Josh. 18:9.
God involved in. Job 28:9–11.

ENGRAVING

In making idols. Exod. 32:4.
In the priest's crown. Exod. 39:30.
On the stones set in the priest's
    breastplate. Exod. 28:9–11, 21,
    36; 39:8–14.

ENJOYMENT

Abundant. 1 Tim. 6:17.
Of all things. 1 Tim. 6:17.
Blessings of. Ps. 112:1.
Despite temptations or tests.
    James 1:2.
Despite trouble. 2 Cor. 7:4.
Sacrifices of. Ps. 27:6.
Satisfying. Isa. 55:1–2.
Way to. 1 Pet. 3:10–11.

ENTERTAINMENT

Anxiety to have many guests at,
    alluded to. Luke 14:22–23.
Began with thanksgiving.
    1 Sam. 9:13; Mark 8:6.
A choice portion reserved in, for
    principal guests. Gen. 43:43;
    1 Sam. 1:5; 9:23–24.
Concluded with a hymn.
    Mark 14:26.
Custom of presenting dipped bread
    to one of the guests, alluded to.
    John 13:26.
Forwardness to take chief seats at,
    condemned. Matt. 23:6;
    Luke 14:7–8.
Given by the guests in return.
    Job 1:4; Luke 14:2.

Given on occasions of
    Birthdays. Mark 6:21.
    Coronations. 1 Kings 1:9, 18–19;
        1 Chron. 12:39–40; Hos. 7:5.
    Festivals. 1 Sam. 20:5, 24–26.
    Harvest home. Ruth 3:2–7;
        Isa. 9:3.

Leaving friends. 1 Kings 19:21.
Marriage. Matt. 22:2.
National deliverance.
    Esther 8:17; 9:17–19.
Offering voluntary sacrifice.
    Gen. 31:54; Deut. 12:6–7;
    1 Sam. 1:4–5, 9.
Ratifying covenants. Gen. 26:30;
    31:54.
Return of friends. 2 Sam. 12:4;
    Luke 15:23, etc.
Sheep shearing. 1 Sam. 25:2, 36;
    2 Sam. 13:23.
Vintage. Judg. 9:27.
Weaning children. Gen. 21:8.

Guests at
    Arranged according to rank.
        Gen. 43:33; 1 Sam. 9:22;
        Luke 14:10.
    Had their feet washed when they
        came a distance. Gen. 18:4;
        43:24; Luke 7:38, 44.
    Often ate from the same dish.
        Matt. 26:23.
    Often had separate dishes.
        Gen. 43:34; 1 Sam. 1:4.
    Saluted by the master. Luke 7:45.
    Usually anointed. Ps. 23:5;
        Luke 7:46.

Invitations to
    Often addressed to many.
        Luke 14:16.
    Often by the master in person.
        2 Sam. 13:24; Esther 5:4;
        Zeph. 1:7; Luke 7:36.
    Often only to relatives and friends.
        1 Kings 1:9; Luke 14:12.
    Repeated through servants when
        all things were ready.
        Prov. 9:1–5; Luke 14:17.
    Should be sent to the poor, etc.
        Deut. 14:29, with Luke 14:13.

Kinds of, mentioned in Scripture
Banquet of wine. Exod. 5:6.
Dinner. Gen. 43:16; Matt. 22:4;
Luke 14:12.
Supper. Luke 14:12; John 12:2.
Men and women did not usually meet
at. Esther 1:8–9; Mark 6:21, with
Matt. 14:11.
Music and dancing often introduced
at. Amos 6:5; Mark 6:22;
Luke 15:25.
None admitted to, after the master
had risen and shut the door.
Luke 13:24–25.
None asked to eat or drink more than
he liked at. Esther 1:8.
Offense given by refusing to go to.
Luke 14:18, 24.

Often given in
Outdoors, beside fountains.
1 Kings 1:9.
The court of the house. Esther
1:5–6; Luke 7:36–37.
The house. Luke 5:29.
The upper room or guest
chamber. Mark 14:14–15.
Often great. Gen. 21:8; Dan. 5:1;
Luke 5:29.
Often scenes of great drunkenness.
1 Sam. 25:36; Dan. 5:3–4;
Hos. 7:5.
Portions of, often sent to the absent.
2 Sam. 11:8; Neh. 8:10; Esther
9:19.
Preparations made for.
Gen. 18:6–7; Prov. 9:2;
Matt. 22:4; Luke 15:23.
Served often by hired servants.
Matt. 22:13; John 2:5.
Served often by members of the
family. Gen. 18:8; Luke 10:40;
John 12:2.

Under the direction of a master of the
feast. John 2:8–9.

ENTHUSIASM
Commanded. Rom. 12:8; Col. 3:23.
In everything. Col. 3:23.
Gideon. Judg. 6–7.
For God. Num. 25:13;
2 Kings 10:16; John 2:17.
Jehu. 2 Kings 9:1–14; 10:1–28.
Of spirit. Rom. 12:11.
Unfounded. Rom. 10:2; Phil. 3:6.
In work. Neh. 4:6; Eccles. 9:10.

ENVIRONMENT
Affected by the fall. Gen. 3:17–19;
Rom. 8:19–22.
Created to be good. Gen. 1–2;
Job 38; Ps. 104:1–30.

Responds to God
In devastation. Ps. 29:3–9;
Isa. 33:9; Joel 1:15–20;
Amos 1:3.
With joy. Pss. 65:13; 98:7–8;
148:3–10.
Responds to Jesus. Luke 8:22–25.
Restored. Isa. 35:1–7; 55:10–13;
Amos 9:13–15.

ENVIRONMENTAL
PROTECTION

Adam's role
To care for Eden. Gen. 2:15.
To have dominion over earth and
its resources. Gen. 1:26–28.
To name the animals.
Gen. 2:19–20.

Disobedience
Affects fertility of the land.
Gen. 3:17–19;
Deut. 11:16–17; 28:15–19.

Creates ecological imbalance.
Deut. 29:22–28; Jer. 4:23–28;
Hos. 4:2–3.
Defiles the land. Lev. 18:24–28.

Earth and its resources
Belong to God. Lev. 25:23;
Job 41:11; Pss. 24:1; 89:11.
Cared for by God. Deut. 11:12;
Ps. 104:10–22.
Given by God to people.
Gen. 1:29–30; 9:1–4;
Deut. 8:7–10.
Fruit picked from young trees only
after four years. Lev. 19:23–25.
Land to lay uncultivated every seven
years. Lev. 25:4.
Obedience affects fertility of the land.
Deut. 11:13–15; 28:1–4.
People have responsibility for what is
entrusted to them.
Luke 12:41–48.
Restoration of the land.
Isa. 35:1–7; 55:10–13;
Amos 9:13–15.

ENVY
Excited by good deeds of others.
Eccles. 4:4.
Forbidden. Prov. 3:31; Rom. 13:13.
Hinders growth in grace.
1 Pet. 2:1–2.
Hurtful to the envious. Job 5:2;
Prov. 14:30.
Inconsistent with the gospel.
James 3:14.
Leads to every evil work.
James 3:16.
None can stand before. Prov. 27:4.
Produced by foolish disputations.
1 Tim. 6:4.
A proof of worldly mindedness.
1 Cor. 3:1, 3.

Prosperity of the wicked should not
excite. Pss. 37:1, 35;
73:3, 17–20.
Punishment of. Isa. 26:11.

The wicked
Are full of. Rom. 1:29.
Live in. Titus 3:3.
A work of the sinful nature.
Gal. 5:21; James 4:5.

EPHOD
Emblem of the priestly office.
Hos. 3:4.

For the high priest
Breastplate of judgment
inseparably united to.
Exod. 28:25–28; 39:20–21.
Commanded to be made.
Exod. 28:4.
Fastened on with its own belt,
sash. Lev. 8:7.
Generally of linen. 1 Sam. 2:18;
2 Sam. 6:14.
Had a belt, sash of curious work.
Exod. 28:8.
Israel deprived of, for sin.
Hos. 3:4.
Made of gold, blue, purple, scarlet,
etc. Exod. 28:6.
Made of offerings of the people.
Exod. 25:4, 7.
Shoulders joined by onyx stones
engraved with names of the
twelve tribes of Israel.
Exod. 28:7; 9:12; 39:4, 6–7.
Used by idolatrous priests.
Judg. 8:27; 17:5; 18:14.
Worn or held by him when
consulted. 1 Sam. 23:6, 9–12;
30:7–8.
Worn over the robe. Exod. 28:31;
Lev. 8:7.

Worn by

The high priest. 1 Sam. 2:28; 14:3.

Ordinary priests. 1 Sam. 22:18.

Persons engaged in the service of God. 1 Sam. 2:18; 2 Sam. 6:14.

EPIC

Heroic poetry

David's war song. 2 Sam. 22.

Deborah's song. Judg. 5.

Miriam's song. Exod. 15:1–19, 21.

EPICUREANS

Dispute with Paul. Acts 17:18.

Doctrines taught by, familiar to Paul. 1 Cor. 15:32.

Doctrines taught by, familiar to Solomon. Eccles. 2:1–10.

Reject John the Baptist. Matt. 11:18; Luke 7:33.

EQUALITY

Among believers. Gen. 13:8; Matt. 23:8.

In Christ. Gal. 3:28.

Under God. Prov. 22:2.

In justice. Prov. 24:23.

In salvation. John 3:16; Rom. 5:18–21.

In sin and guilt. Rom. 3:10–19; 5:12–21.

ETERNITY

God inhabits. Isa. 57:15; Mic. 5:2.

God rules. Jer. 10:10.

ETHNIC CLEANSING

Examples of

Assyria, against Israel. 2 Kings 17:6, 24.

Failed, Ahasuerus against the Jews. Esther 3:8–15; 8:3–17.

Gaza, against an unnamed people. Amos 1:6.

Joshua, against the Canaanites. Josh. 6:21; 8:24–25; 10:40; 11:21–22.

Saul, against the Gibeonites. 2 Sam. 21:1–2.

Tyre, against unnamed people. Amos 1:9.

Punished by God. Amos 1:6, 9.

EUNUCH

Baptism of the Ethiopian. Acts 8:26–38.

Influential court officials. Jer. 38:7–13; 52:25; Dan. 1:3.

Prohibited from certain privileges of the congregation. Deut. 23:1; Isa. 56:3–5.

Those who voluntarily became, for the kingdom of heaven's sake. Matt. 19:12.

EUPHRATES RIVER

See River, Euphrates

EUTHANASIA

May lead to devaluing of life. Gen. 1:27.

Violates God's command. Exod. 20:13.

EVANGELISM

Beauty of. Isa. 52:7.

Commanded. Matt. 28:19–20; Mark 16:5; 2 Tim. 4:5.

Philip and the Enunch

Exemplified
  Paul. Rom. 1:16.
  Peter. Acts 2:14–42.
  Philip. Acts 8:5; 21:8.
  Timothy. 2 Tim. 4:5.
Glory of. Dan. 12:3.
Wisdom of. Prov. 11:30.
Work of God. Eph. 4:11.

EVE
Children of. Gen. 4:1–2, 25; 5:3–4.
Clothed with fig leaves. Gen. 3:7.
Clothed with skins. Gen. 3:21.
Creation of. Gen. 1:26–28;
  2:21–24.

Cursed, denounced against.
  Gen. 3:16.
Deceived by Satan. Gen. 3;
  2 Cor. 11:3; 1 Tim. 2:14.
Messiah promised to. Gen. 3:15.
Names by Adam. Gen. 2:23; 3:20.

EVENING
All defiled persons unclean until.
  Lev. 11:24–28; 15:5–7; 17:15;
  Num. 19:19.

Called
  Cool of the day. Gen. 3:8.
  Even. Gen. 19:1; Deut. 28:67.
  Evening. Josh. 8:29; Acts 4:3.

Custom of sitting at the gates in.
Gen. 19:1.

The day originally began with.
Gen. 1:5, etc.

Golden candlestick lighted in.
Exod. 27:21, with 30:8.

Humiliation often continued until.
Josh. 7:6; Judg. 20:23, 26; 21:2;
Ezra 9:4–5.

Man ceases from labor in. Ruth 2:17;
Ps. 104:23.

The outgoings of, praise God.
Ps. 65:8.

Part of the daily sacrifice offered in.
Exod. 29:41; Ps. 141:2;
Dan. 9:21.

Paschal lamb killed in.
Exod. 12:6, 18.

A season for
Exercise. 2 Sam. 11:2.

Meditation. Gen. 24:63.

Prayer. Ps. 55:17;
Matt. 14:15, 23.

Taking food. Mark 14:17–18;
Luke 24:29–30.

The sky red in, a sign of fair weather.
Matt. 16:2.

Stretches out its shadows. Jer. 6:4.

Wild beasts to come forth in.
Ps. 59:6, 14; Jer. 5:6.

EVICTION

Of tenants. Matt. 21:41; Mark 12:9.

EVIDENCE

Laws concerning. Num. 35:30;
Deut. 17:6.

Self-incriminating. Josh. 7:19–21.

EVIL, APPEARANCE OF, TO BE AVOIDED

Examples of
Paul, in refusing to eat that which
had been offered to idols.
1 Cor. 8:13.

Paul, in supporting himself.
1 Cor. 9:7–23.

EVIL FOR GOOD

David, to Joab. 1 Kings 2:4–6.

David, to Uriah. 2 Sam. 11.

Examples of
Israelites, to Moses.
Exod. 5:2; 14:11; 15:24;
16:2–3; 17:3–4.

Joseph accused his brothers of
rendering. Gen. 44:4.

Nabal returns, to David.
1 Sam. 25:21.

Saul returns, to David.
1 Sam. 19:1, 4–5, 10.

EVOLUTION

See also Creation

Contrary to the consistent teaching
of Scripture. Gen. 1–2;
Job 38–39; John 1:1–3;
Col. 1:16–17; Hab. 11:3.

EXAMINATION

Of the heart. Ps. 139:23–24.

Of one's faith and life. 1 Cor. 11:28.

Of the Scriptures. Acts 17:11.

Wrong standard of. 2 Cor. 10:12.

EXAMPLE OF CHRIST

See Christ, Example of

EXCELLENCE

Found in
Actions of God. Isa. 12:5.
Believers in the land. Ps. 16:3.
Building up the church. 1
   Cor. 14:12.
Dispensation of the Spirit.
   2 Cor. 3:7–11.
Doing what is good. Titus 3:8.
Fruit of the land. Isa. 4:2.
Greatness of God. Ps. 150:2.
Knowledge of Christ. Phil. 3:8.
Love. 1 Cor. 12:31–13:13.
Love of God. Ps. 36:7.
Ministry of Jesus. Heb. 8:6.
Name of God. Pss. 8:1, 9;
   148:13.
Name of Jesus. Heb. 1:4.
One's beloved. Song of Sol. 5:10.
Power of God. Job 37:23;
   2 Cor. 4:7.
Speech. Prov. 17:7; 1 Cor. 2:1.
Theophilus. Luke 1:3.
Things to have been approved by
   Jews. Rom 1:17–21.
Things to be approved by
   Christians. Phil. 1:10.
Things spoken of. Prov. 8:6.
Things thought. Phil. 4:8.
Virtuous woman. Prov. 31:29.
Wisdom of God. Isa. 28:29.
Wisdom of man. Eccles. 2:13.
Wisdom of Solomon.
   1 Kings 4:29–30.

EXCUSES

Adam and Eve to the Lord.
   Gen. 3:12–13.
A disciple to Jesus. Matt. 8:21.
Elisha to Elijah. 1 Kings 19:19–21.
Felix to Paul. Acts 24:25.
Humanity to God. Rom. 1:20.
Jeremiah to the Lord. Jer. 1:1–10.

Moses to the Lord. Exod. 4:1–14.
Naaman to Elijah. 2 Kings 5:10–14.

EXERCISE

Principles regarding
Body a living sacrifice. Rom 12:1.
Body a temple of the Holy Spirit.
   1 Cor. 6:19.

Injunctions concerning
Honor God with body.
   1 Cor. 6:20.
Subdue body. 1 Cor. 9:27.
Of some value. 1 Tim. 4:8.

EXILE

Absalom. 2 Sam. 14:13–14, 24.
Ittai. 2 Sam. 15:19.

EXPERIENCE, SPIRITUAL

Basis of confidence. John 4:42;
   2 Pet. 1:16; 1 John 1:1.
Basis of sharing. 2 Cor. 1:4.
Basis of witness. Mark 5:19.
Educational. Gen. 30:27.
Slow growth of. Mark 4:28.

EXPERIMENT

Concerning diet. Dan. 1.
Solomon's, in worldly pleasure.
   Eccles. 1:2.

EXPORTS

From Arabia
Of sheep and goats. Ezek. 27:21.

From Egypt
Of corn. Gen. 42; 43.
Of horses and chariots.
   1 Kings 10:28–29;
   2 Chron. 1:16–17.

From Gilead
　Of spices. Gen. 37:25.

From Ophir
　Of gold. 1 Kings 10:11; 22:48;
　　1 Chron. 29:4.

From Palestine

From Tarshish
　Of gold. 1 Kings 10:22.
　Honey. Ezek. 27:17.
　Of ivory, apes, and peacocks.
　　1 Kings 10:22.
　Of silver, iron, tin, lead, brass,
　　slaves. Ezek. 27:12–13.

EXTORTION

Examples of
　Jacob, in demanding Esau's
　　birthright for a bowl of stew.
　　Gen. 25:31–34.
　Pharaoh, in exacting of the
　　Egyptian lands and persons for
　　corn. Gen. 47:13–26.

EXTRADITION

Christians from Damascus by Saul of
　Tarsus. Acts:9:1–2.
Uriah from Egypt. Jer. 26:21–23.

EXTRAVAGANCE

Consequences of. Prov. 21:17–20;
　Luke 16:19.

EYE

Actions of, mentioned in Scripture
　Directing. Num. 10:31; Ps. 32:8.
　Seeing. Job 7:8; 28:10.
　Weeping. Job 16:20; Ps. 88:9;
　　Lam. 1:16.
　Winking. Prov. 10:10.
Consumed by grief. Ps. 6:7; 31:9.

Consumed by sickness. Lev. 26:16.

Eye of the Lord
　On those that fear Him. Ps.
　　33:18.
　On the righteous. Ps. 34:15.
　Promise to Isaiah. Isa. 1:15.

Figurative sense
　The offending. Matt. 5:29.
　Frequently fair. 1 Sam. 16:12.

God
　Enlightens. Ezra 9:8; Ps. 13:3.
　Formed. Ps. 94:9.
　Made. Prov. 20:12.
　Opens. 2 Kings 6:17; Ps. 146:8.
　Grows dim by age. Gen. 27:1;
　　1 Sam. 3:2.
　Grows dim by sorrow. Job 17:7.
　A guard to be set on. Job 31:1;
　　Prov. 23:31.

Illustrative of
　Healing by the Spirit (when
　　anointed with salve). Rev. 3:18.
　The mind. Matt. 6:22–23.
　Spiritual illumination (when open).
　　Ps. 119:18, 37.
　Jewish women often painted.
　　2 Kings 9:30; Jer. 4:30;
　　Ezek. 23:40.

The Jews
　Not to make baldness between.
　　Deut. 14:1.
　Raised up, in prayer. Ps. 122:1.
　Wore their phylacteries between.
　　Exod. 13:16, with Matt. 23:5.
　Light of, rejoices the heart.
　　Prov. 15:30.
　The light of the body. Matt. 6:22;
　　Luke 11:34.
　Made red by wine. Gen. 49:12;
　　Prov. 23:29.

No evil thing to be set before.
Ps. 101:3.
Not satisfied with riches. Eccles. 4:8.
Not satisfied with seeing.
Prov. 27:20; Eccles. 1:8; 1
John 2:16.
Often put out as a punishment. Judg.
16:21; 1 Sam. 11:2;
2 Kings 25:7.

Parts of, mentioned in Scripture
Apple or ball. Deut. 32:10.
Brow. Lev. 14:9.
Lid. Job 16:16.
Punishment for injuring.
Exod. 21:24, 26; Lev. 24:20;
Matt. 5:38.
Sometimes blemished. Lev. 21:20.
Sometimes tender. Gen. 29:17.

F

FABLE
Have nothing to do with. 1 Tim. 1:4; 4:7.

FACE
Character revealed in. Isa. 3:9.
Covering of. Isa. 6:2.
Disfiguring of, in fasting. Matt. 6:16.
Transfigured, of Jesus. Matt. 17:2; Luke 9:29.
Transfigured, of Moses. Exod. 34:29–35.

FAINTING
Daniel, in response to a vision from God. Dan. 8:27.
John, upon seeing the risen Christ. Rev. 1:17.

FAIRNESS
See also Justice

As criteria for judging people. Isa. 11:4; John 7:24.
Demanded by John. Luke 3:12–13.
Desired for living wisely. Prov. 1:3.

Examples of
Solomon. 1 Kings 3:16–27.
Jacob. Gen. 31:38–41.
Jesus and the woman that was caught in adultery. John 7:53–8:11.
Thief on the cross. Luke 23:40–41.
Exemplified in God. 2 Chron. 19:7; Ezek. 18:29; Rev. 15:3.
Expected of Christians. Luke 10:7; 1 Tim. 5:21; James 2:4.

Of God
Established on earth. Ps. 99:4.
In holding individuals responsible for actions. Ezek. 18:14–20.
In judging people. Ps. 98:9.
In punishing sin. Rom. 3:3–6.
Throne established on. Ps. 89:14.
Reciprocity. Exod. 21:24; Matt. 7:2; Mark 4:24; 2 Cor. 11:15.
Upheld when living wisely. Prov. 2:9–10.

Injunctions concerning
In business. Lev. 19:36; Deut. 25:15; 1 Tim 5:18.
In legal judgment. Exod. 23:3; Deut. 16:19; Prov 29:14.
In life generally. Isa. 56:1; Amos 5:24.
In speech. Exod. 23:1.
In treatment of slaves. Col. 4:1.
Lacking. Ps. 82:2–4; Prov. 18:17; Isa. 59:9–11; Mic. 3:9; Hab. 1:4.
Required by God. Deut. 1:17; Prov. 11:1.
Through faith. Heb. 10:38.
Through wisdom. Prov. 8:15.

FAITH
All difficulties overcome by. Matt. 17:20; 21:21; Mark 9:23.
All things should be done in. Rom. 14:22.
Believers die in. Heb. 11:13.

Believers should
Abound in. 2 Cor. 8:7.

Be grounded and settled in.
Col. 1:23.
Be sincere in. 1 Tim. 1:5;
2 Tim. 1:5.
Be strong in. Rom. 4:20–24.
Continue in. Acts 14:22;
Col. 1:23.
Have full assurance of.
2 Tim. 1:12; Heb. 10:22.
Hold, with a good conscience.
1 Tim. 1:19.
Pray for the increase of.
Luke 17:5.
Stand fast in. 1 Cor. 16:13.
Christ dwells in the heart by.
Eph. 3:17.

In Christ, is
Accompanied by repentance.
Mark 1:15; Luke 24:47.
Followed by conversion.
Acts 11:21.
Fruitful. 1 Thess. 1:3.
The gift of God. Rom. 12:3;
Eph. 2:8; 6:23; Phil. 1:29.
Most holy. Jude 20.
Precious. 2 Pet. 1:1.
The work of God. Acts 11:21;
1 Cor. 2:5.
Christ precious to those having. 1
Pet. 2:7.
Christ the author and finisher of.
Heb. 12:2.
Commanded. Mark 11:22;
1 John 3:23.
Essential to the profitable reception
of the gospel. Heb. 4:2.
Evidence of the new birth.
1 John 5:1.
Evidence of things not seen.
Heb. 11:1.
Examine whether you are in.
2 Cor. 13:5.
Excludes boasting. Rom. 3:27.

Excludes self-justification.
Rom. 10:3–4.
A gift of the Holy Spirit. 1 Cor. 12:9.
The gospel effectual in those who
have. 1 Thess. 2:13.
Impossible to please God without.
Heb. 11:6.

By it, believers
Are supported. Ps. 27:13;
1 Tim. 4:10.
Live. Gal. 2:20.
Obtain a good report. Heb. 11:2.
Overcome the devil. Eph. 6:16.
Overcome the world.
1 John 5:4–5.
Resist the devil. 1 Pet. 5:9.
Stand. Rom. 11:20; 2 Cor. 1:24.
Walk. Rom. 4:12; 2 Cor. 5:7.

Through it is
Access to God. Rom. 5:2;
Eph. 3:12.
Adoption. John 1:12; Gal. 3:26.
Edification. 1 Tim. 1:4; Jude 20.
Eternal life. John 3:15–16;
6:40, 47.
The gift of the Holy Spirit.
Acts 11:15–17; Gal. 3:14;
Eph. 1:13.
Inheritance of the promises.
Gal. 3:22; Heb. 6:12.
Justification. Acts 13:39;
Rom. 3:21–22, 28, 30; 5:1;
Gal. 2:16.
Preservation. 1 Pet. 1:5.
Remission of sins. Acts 10:43;
Rom. 3:25.
Rest in heaven. Heb. 4:3.
Salvation. Mark 16:16;
Acts 16:31.
Sanctification. Acts 15:9; 26:18.
Spiritual life. John 20:31;
Gal. 2:20.

Spiritual light. John 12:36, 46.

Its protection illustrative of a
Breastplate. 1 Thess. 5:8.
Shield. Eph. 6:16.
Justification is by, to be of grace.
Rom. 4:16.
Necessary in prayer. Matt. 21:22;
James 1:6.
Necessary in the Christian warfare.
1 Tim. 1:18–19; 6:12.

Objects of
Christ. John 6:29; Acts 20:21.
God. John 14:1.
The gospel. Mark 1:15.
Promises of God. Rom. 4:21;
Heb. 11:13.
Writings of Moses. John 5:46;
Acts 24:14.
Writings of the prophets.
2 Chron. 20:20; Acts 26:27.
Often tried by affliction.
1 Pet. 1:6–7.
Preaching designed to produce.
John 17:20; Acts 8:12;
Rom. 10:14–15, 17; 1 Cor. 3:5.

Produces
Boldness in preaching.
Ps. 116:10, with 2 Cor. 4:13.
Confidence. Isa. 28:16, with
1 Pet. 2:6.
Hope. Rom. 5:2.
Joy. Acts 16:34; 1 Pet. 2:6.
Peace. Rom. 15:13.
The Scriptures designed to produce.
John 20:31; 2 Tim. 3:15.
The substance of things hoped for.
Heb. 11:1.
Those who are not Christ's have not.
John 10:26–27.
Trial of, works patience. James 1:3.

True, evidenced by its fruits.
James 2:21–25.
Whatsoever is not of, is sin.
Rom. 14:23.
The wicked destitute of. John 10:25;
12:37; Acts 19:9; 2 Thess. 3:2.
The wicked often profess.
Acts 8:13, 21.

FAITHFULNESS
Associate with those who exhibit.
Ps. 101:6.
Blessedness of. 1 Sam. 26:23;
Prov. 28:20.
A characteristic of believers.
Eph. 1:1; Col. 1:2; 1 Tim. 6:2;
Rev. 17:14.
Difficulty of finding. Prov. 20:6.

Especially required in
Children of ministers. Titus 1:6.
Ministers. 1 Cor. 4:2; 2 Tim. 2:2.
Wives of ministers. 1 Tim. 3:11.

Examples of
Abijah. 2 Chron. 13:4–20.
Abraham. Gal. 3:9.
David. 2 Sam. 22:22–25.
Elijah. 1 Kings 19:10, 14.
Jehoshaphat. 2 Chron. 20:1–30.
Job. Job 1:21, 22; 2:9, 10.
Moses. Heb. 3:5.

Exhibited in
All things. 1 Tim. 3:11.
Bearing witness. Prov. 14:5.
Care of dedicated things.
2 Chron. 31:12.
Conveying messages.
Prov. 13:17; 25:13.
Declaring the word of God.
Jer. 23:28; 2 Cor. 2:17; 4:2.
Doing work. 2 Chron. 34:12.
Helping the believers. 3 John 1:5.

Keeping secrets. Prov. 11:13.
Service to God. Matt. 24:45.
Situations of trust. 2 Kings 12:15;
Neh. 13:13; Acts 6:1–3.
The smallest matters.
Luke 16:10–12.
Should be until death. Rev. 2:10.
The wicked lacking. Ps. 5:9.

FAITHFULNESS OF GOD
See God, Faithfulness of

FALLOW
Soil which has either never or not
recently been planted. Jer. 4:3;
Hos. 10:12.

FALL OF MAN
See Man, Fall of

FALSE CONFIDENCE
See Confidence, False

FALSEHOOD
Consequence of. Rev. 21:8, 27.

Examples of
Aaron, in attempting to shift
responsibility for making the
golden calf. Exod. 32:1–24.
Abraham, in denying Sarah was
his wife. Gen. 12:11–19; 20:2.
Adam and Eve, in attempting to
evade responsibility.
Gen. 3:12–13.
The Amalekite, who claimed to
have slain Saul.
2 Sam. 1:10–12.
Ananias and Sapphira falsely state
that they had sold their land for a
given sum. Acts 5:1–10.
Cain, in denying knowledge of his
brother's death. Gen. 4:9.

David, in feigning madness.
1 Sam. 21:13–15.
David, in the falsehood he put in
the mouth of Hushai.
2 Sam. 15:34–37.
David in lying to Ahimelech.
1 Sam. 21.
David, in other deceits with the
Philistines. 1 Sam. 27:8–12.
The disobedient son, who
promised to work in the vineyard
but did not. Matt. 21:30.
Ehud, in pretending to bear secret
messages to Eglon.
Judg. 3:16–23.
The Gibeonites, ambassadors, in
the deception they perpetrated
upon Joshua. Josh. 9.
Haman, in his conspiracy against
the Jews. Esther 3:8.
Herod, to the wise men in
professing to desire to worship
Jesus. Matt. 2:8.
Hushai, in false professions to
Absalom. 2 Sam. 16:16–19.
Hushai, in his deceitful counsel to
Absalom. 2 Sam. 17:7–14.
Isaac, denying that Rebekah was
his wife. Gen. 26:7–10.
Jacob's sons, in a scheme to
destroy the Shechemites.
Gen. 34.
Jeremiah's adversaries, in
accusing him of joining the
Chaldeans. Jer. 37:13–15.
Joseph, in the deception he
carried on with his brothers.
Gen. 42–44.
Joseph's brothers, in deceiving
their father. Gen. 37:29–35.
Michal, in the false statement that
David was sick.
1 Sam. 19:12–17.

Paul's enemies, falsely accusing him of treason to Caesar. Acts 16:20–21.

Peter, in denying Jesus. Matt. 26:69–75.

Pharaoh, in dealing deceitfully with the Israelites. Exod. 7–12.

Potiphar's wife, in falsely accusing Joseph. Gen. 39:14–17.

Rahab, in denying that the spies were in her house. Josh. 2:4–6.

Rebekah and Isaac, in conspiracy against Esau. Gen. 27:6–24, 46.

The Roman soldiers, who said the disciples stole the body of Jesus. Matt. 28:13, 15.

Sarah in denying to the king of Gerar that she was Abraham's wife. Gen. 20:2

Sarah to the angels, denying her scornful laugh life of unbelief. Gen. 18:15.

Satan, in deceiving Eve. Gen. 3:4–5.

Satan, in his false pretensions to Jesus. Luke 4:6–7.

Satan, in impugning Job's motive for being righteous. Job 1:9–10.

Saul, in accusing Ahimelech of conspiring with David. 1 Sam. 22.11 16.

Saul, in professing to Samuel to have obeyed the commandment to destroy all the spoils of the Amalekites. 1 Sam. 15:1–26.

Sisera, who instructed Jael to mislead his pursuers. Judg. 4:20.

Stephen's accusers, who falsely accused him of blaspheming Moses and God. Acts 6:11–14.

FAMILIES

Of believers blessed. Ps. 128:3–6.

Deceivers and liars should be removed from. Ps. 101:7.

Punishment of irreligious. Jer. 10:25.

Should

Be duly regulated. Prov. 31:27; 1 Tim. 3:4–5, 12.

Be taught the Scriptures. Deut. 4:9–10.

Live in mutual forbearance. Gen. 50:17–21; Matt. 18:21–22.

Live in unity. Gen. 45:24; Ps. 133:1.

Rejoice together before God. Deut. 14:26.

Worship God together. 1 Cor. 16:19.

Warning against departing from God. Deut. 29:18.

FAMINE

Caused

Blackness of the skin. Lam. 4:8; 5:10.

Burning and fever. Deut. 32:24.

Death. 2 Kings 7:4; Jer. 11:22.

Faintness. Gen. 47:13.

Grief and mourning. Joel 1:11–13.

Wasting of the body. Lam. 4:8; Ezek. 4:17.

Caused by

Blight and mildew. Amos 4:9; Hag. 2:17.

Devastation by enemies. Deut. 28:33, 51.

God's blessing withheld. Hos. 2:8–9; Hag. 1:6.

Rotting of the seed in the ground.
Joel 1:17.
Swarms of insects.
Deut. 28:38, 42; Joel 1:4.
Lack of seasonable rain.
1 Kings 17:1; Jer. 14:1–4;
Amos 4:7.

Expressed by
Arrows of famine. Ezek. 5:16.
Cleanness of teeth. Amos 4:6.
God provided for His people
during. 1 Kings 17:4, 9;
Job 5:20; Pss. 33:19; 37:19.
Taking away the supply of bread.
Isa. 3:1.

Illustrative of
An absence of the means of grace.
Amos 8:11–12.
Destruction of idols. Zeph. 2:11.

Instances of, in Scripture
After the captivity. Neh. 5:3.
In the days of Abraham.
Gen. 12:10.
In the days of Isaac. Gen. 26:1.
In the days of Joseph.
Gen. 41:53–56.
In the days of the judges. Ruth 1:1.
Before destruction of Jerusalem.
Matt. 24:7.
In the reign of
Ahab. 1 Kings 17:1; 18:5.
In the reign of Claudius Caesar.
Acts 11:28.
In the reign of David.
2 Sam. 21:1.
Of seven years predicted by Elisha.
2 Kings 8:1.
During the siege of Jerusalem.
2 Kings 25:3.
During the siege of Samaria.
2 Kings 6:25.

In the time of Elisha.
2 Kings 4:38.
In the time of Jeremiah. Jer. 14:1.
The Jews in their restored state not
to be afflicted by. Ezek. 36:29–30.
Often accompanied by war.
Jer. 14:15; 29:18.
Often followed by plagues.
Jer. 42:17; Ezek. 7:15;
Matt. 24:7.
Often long continued. Gen. 41:27;
2 Kings 8:1–2.
Often on account of sin.
Lev. 26:21, 26; Lam. 4:4–6.
Often severe. Gen. 12:10;
1 Kings 18:2; Jer. 52:6.
One of God's four dreadful
judgments. Ezek. 14:21.
Provisions sold by weight during.
Ezek. 4:16.
Sent by God. Ps. 105:16.
Suffering of brute creation from.
Jer. 14:5–6.

Things eaten during
Donkey's flesh. 2 Kings 6:25.
Excrement. 2 Kings 6:25;
Lam. 4:5.
Human flesh. Lev. 26:29;
2 Kings 6:28–29.
Wild herbs. 2 Kings 4:39–40.

FARMER
An agriculturist. Matt. 21:33–46;
Mark 12:1–9; John 15:1;
1 Cor. 3:9.

FASHION
Elegant. Ezek. 16:10–14.
Excessive clothing. Job 27:16–17.

Fine
For kings. Matt. 11:8.

For priests. Exod. 28:1–43;
39:1–31.
To show righteousness.
Rev 3:4–5; 7:9, 13.
To show status. Gen. 37:3;
Luke 15:22.

Garments
Coveted. Josh 7:21.
Course, for prophets. 2 Kings 1:8;
Zech. 13:4; Matt. 3:4;
Mark 1:6.
Filthy, fig. for unrighteousness.
Isa. 64:6; Zech. 3:3–4;
Rev. 3:4.
As gifts. Gen. 45:22; 2 Kings 5:5;
Esther 6:8.
Jewelry. Exod. 35:22;
Judg. 8:24–26; Isa. 3:18–21.
Judgment for showiness.
Isa. 3:16–26.
Modest. 1 Tim. 2:9; 1 Pet. 3:3–5.

FASTING

Accompanied by
Confession of sin. 1 Sam. 7:6;
Neh. 9:1–2.
Humiliation. Deut. 9:18;
Neh. 9:1.
Mourning. Joel 2:12.
Prayer. Ezra 8:23; Dan. 9:3.
For the chastening of the soul.
Ps. 69:10.
For the humbling of the soul
Ps. 35:13.
Not to be made a subject of display.
Matt. 6:16–18.

Observed on occasions of
Afflictions. Ps. 35:13; Dan. 6:18.
Afflictions of the church.
Luke 5:33–35.
Approaching danger. Esther 4:16.

Judgments of God. Joel 1:14;
2:12.
Ordination of ministers.
Acts 13:3; 14:23.
Private afflictions. 2 Sam. 12:16.
Public calamities. 2 Sam. 1:12.

Of hypocrites
Boasted of, before God.
Luke 18:12.
Described. Isa. 58:4–5.
Pretentious. Matt. 6:16.
Rejected. Isa. 58:3; Jer. 14:12.
Promises connected with.
Isa. 58:8–12; Matt. 6:18.
Should be to God. Zech. 7:5;
Matt. 6:18.
Spirit of, explained. Isa. 58:6–7.

FATHER

God as
Chose a son. 1 Chron. 28:6.
Everlasting. Isa. 9:6.
In heaven. Matt. 6:9; 23:9.
Of Jesus. Luke 2:49; John 8:49;
15:1.
Love of. 1 John 3:1.
Of Spirits. Heb. 7:3.

Natural
Duties. Eph. 6:4.
Happiness of. Prov. 10:1.
Messiah to humanize. Mal. 4:6.
Not to be dishonored.
Prov. 20:20.
To be honored. Exod. 20:12;
Eph. 6:2.

Spiritual
Of all that believe. Rom. 4:11.
Of Onesimus. Philem. 1:10.
Only one. 1 Cor. 4:15.
To the poor. Job 29:16.

FATHERLESS
See Orphans

FAVOR OF GOD
See God, Favor of

FEAR, GODLY
Advantages of. Prov. 15:16; 19:23;
Eccles. 8:12–13.
A characteristic of believers.
Mal. 3:16.
Commanded. Deut. 13:4;
Ps. 22:23; Eccles. 12:13;
1 Pet. 2:17.

Described as
Familial and reverential.
Heb. 12:9, 28.
A fountain of life. Prov. 14:27.
Hatred of evil. Prov. 8:13.
Sanctifying. Ps. 19:9.
A treasure to believers.
Prov. 15:16; Isa. 33:6.
Wisdom. Job 28:28; Ps. 111:10.
God the author of. Jer. 32:39–40.
God the object of. Isa. 8:13.

Motives to
Forgiveness of God. Ps. 130:4.
Goodness of God. 1 Sam. 12:24.
Greatness of God.
Deut. 10:12, 17.
Holiness of God. Rev. 15:4.
Judgments of God. Rev. 14:7.
Wondrous works of God.
Josh. 4:23–24.

Necessary to
Avoiding sin. Exod. 20:20.
Impartial administration of justice.
2 Chron. 19:6–9.
Perfecting holiness. 2 Cor. 7:1.
Righteous government.
2 Sam. 23:3.

The service of God. Ps. 2:11;
Heb. 12:28.
The worship of God. Pss. 5:7;
89:7.
Searching the Scriptures gives
understanding of. Prov. 2:3–5.
Should accompany the joy of
believers. Ps. 2:11.

Should be
Constantly maintained.
Deut. 14:23; Josh. 4:24;
Prov. 23:17.
Exhibited in giving a reason for our
hope. 1 Pet. 3:15.
Exhibited in our callings.
Col. 3:22.
Prayed for. Ps. 86:11.
Taught to others. Ps. 34:11.

Those who have
Afford pleasure to God.
Ps. 147:11.
Are accepted of God. Acts 10:35.
Are blessed. Pss. 112:1; 115:13.
Are pitied by God. Ps. 103:13.
Confide in God. Ps. 115:11;
Prov. 14:26.
Converse together of holy things.
Mal. 3:16.
Days of, prolonged. Prov. 10:27.
Depart from evil. Prov. 16:6.
Desires of, fulfilled by God.
Ps. 145:19.
Receive mercy from God.
Ps. 103:11, 17; Luke 1:50.
Should not fear people.
Isa. 8:12–13; Matt. 10:28.
The wicked destitute of. Ps. 36:1;
Prov. 1:29; Jer. 2:19;
Rom. 3:18.

FEAR, UNHOLY

Believers delivered from. Prov. 1:33;
  Isa. 14:3.

Believers sometimes tempted to.
  Ps. 55:5.

A characteristic of the wicked.
  Rev. 21:8.

Described as

  Consuming. Ps. 73:19.

  Fear of future punishment.
    Heb. 10:27.

  Fear of idols. 2 Kings 17:38.

  Fear of judgments. Isa. 2:19;
    Luke 21:26; Rev. 6:16–17.

  Fear of people. 1 Sam. 15:24;
    John 9:22.

  Overwhelming. Exod. 15:16;
    Job 15:21, 24.

Exhortations against. Isa. 8:12;
  John 14:27.

God mocks. Prov. 1:26.

A guilty conscience leads to.
  Gen. 3:8, 10; Ps. 53:5;
  Prov. 28:1.

Seizes the wicked. Job 15:24;
  18:11.

Surprises the hypocrite.
  Isa. 33:14, 18.

Trust in God, a preservative
  from. Ps. 27:1.

The wicked judicially filled with.
  Lev. 26:16–17; Deut. 28:65–67;
  Jer. 49:5.

Will be realized. Prov. 1:27; 10:24.

FEASTS, ANNIVERSARY

All males to attend. Exod. 23:17;
  34:23.

Children began attending, when
  twelve years old. Luke 2:42.

Christ attended. John 5:1; 7:10.

Dangers and difficulties encountered
  in going up to, alluded to.
  Ps. 84:6–7.

Enumerated. Exod. 23:15–16.

Females often attended.
  1 Sam. 1:3, 9; Luke 2:41.

Illustrative of general assembly of the
  church. Heb. 12:23.

Instituted by God. Exod. 23:14.

The Jews

  Attended gladly. Ps. 122:1–2.

  Dispersed in distant parts often
    attended. Acts 2:5–11; 8:27.

  Went up to, in large companies.
    Ps. 42:4; Luke 2:44.

Land divinely protected during.
  Exod. 34:24.

Offerings to be made at.
  Exod. 34:20; Deut. 16:16–17.

Rendered futile by the irreverence of
  the Jews. Isa. 1:13–14;
  Amos 5:21.

Ten tribes seduced by Jeroboam
  from attending. 1 Kings 12:27.

Were called

  Appointed feasts. Isa. 1:14.

  Feasts of the Lord. Lev. 23:4.

  Solemn feasts. 2 Chron. 8:13;
    Lam. 1:4.

  Solemn meetings. Isa. 1:13.

  Were eucharistic. Ps. 122:4.

Were seasons of

  Entertainments. 1 Sam. 1:4, 9.

  Joy and gladness. Ps. 42:4;
    Isa. 30:29.

  Sacrificing. 1 Sam. 1:3;
    1 Kings 9:25; 2 Chron. 8:13.

FEET

Of believers
Established by God. Pss. 66:9;
121:3.
Guided by Christ. Isa. 48:17;
Luke 1:79.
Kept by God. 1 Sam. 2:9;
Ps. 116:8.
At liberty. Pss. 18:36; 31:8.
Condemnation expressed by shaking
the dust from. Matt. 10:14;
Mark 6:11.

Of criminals
Bound with chains. Ps. 105:18.
Of enemies, often maimed and cut
off. Judg. 1:6–7; 2 Sam. 4:14.
Placed in stocks. Job 13:27;
Acts 16:24.
Early use of shoes for. Exod. 12:11.

Illustrative of
Abundance, when washed or
dipped in oil. Deut. 33:24;
Job 29:6.
Complete destruction, when
trampled under. Isa. 18:7;
Lam. 1:15.
Liberty, when set in a large place.
Ps. 31:8.
Stability, when set on a rock.
Ps. 40:2.
Victory, when dipped in blood.
Ps. 68:23.
Yielding to temptation, when
sliding. Job 12:5; Pss. 17:5;
38:16; 94:18.

Of the Jews
Bare in affliction. 2 Sam. 15:30.
Neglected in affliction.
2 Sam. 19:24; Ezek. 24:17.
Washed frequently. 2 Sam. 11:8;
Song of Sol. 5:3.

Necessary members of the body.
1 Cor. 15:15, 21.
Neglect of washing, disrespectful to
guest. Luke 7:44.
Often swift. 2 Sam. 2:18; 22:34.
Origin of uncovering in consecrated
places. Exod. 3:5; Josh. 5:15.

Parts of, mentioned
Heel. Pss. 41:9; 49:5; Hos. 12:3.
Sole. Deut. 11:24; 1 Kings 5:3.
Toes. Exod. 29:20;
2 Sam. 21:20; Dan. 2:41.
Path of, to be pondered. Prov. 4:26.
Respect exhibited by falling at.
1 Sam. 25:24; 2 Kings 12:9;
Esther 8:3; Mark 5:22;
Acts 10:25.
Reverence expressed by kissing.
Luke 7:38, 45.
Sleep expressed by covering.
1 Sam. 24:3.
Stamped on the ground in extreme
joy or grief. Ezek. 6:11; 25:6.
Of strangers and travelers washed.
Gen. 18:4; 19:2; 24:32;
1 Tim. 5:10.
Subjection expressed by licking the
dust of. Isa. 49:23.
Subjugation of enemies shown by
placing on neck. Josh 10:24;
Ps. 110:1.
To be directed by God's word.
Ps. 119:105.
To be guided by wisdom and
discretion. Prov. 3:21, 23, 26.
To be refrained from evil.
Prov. 1:15; Heb. 12:13.
To be turned to God's testimonies.
Ps. 119:59.
Washing for others, a menial office.
1 Sam. 25:41; John 13:5–14.

Were liable to
Disease. 1 Kings 15:23.
Injury from stones, etc. Ps. 91:12.
Swelling from walking. Deut. 8:4.

Of the wicked
Ensnared. Job 18:8; Ps. 9:15.
Swift to mischief. Prov. 6:18.
Swift to shed blood. Prov. 1:16;
Rom. 3:15.
Of women often adorned with
tinkling ornaments. Isa. 3:16, 18.

FELLOWSHIP

Blessings of. 1 John 1:7.
In Christ. Matt. 18:20; 1 Cor. 1:9;
Rev. 3:20.
In the Holy Spirit. 2 Cor. 13:14.
Kinds and results. Prov. 13:20.
Responsibilities of. Gal. 6:2.
With God's people. Pss. 55:14;
119:63; Gal. 3:28.

FERTILITY DRUGS

See Drugs, Fertility

FIG TREE

See Tree, Fig

FILE

Used for sharpening edges of tools.
1 Sam. 13:21.

FINANCIAL PLANNING

Examples of
Good. Gen. 41:34–36;
Eccles. 11:2; Luke 19:23; 1
Cor. 16:2; 2 Cor. 9:4–5.
Poor. Luke 12:16–21; 14:28–30;
19:20–21.

God
Causes plans to succeed. Ps. 20:4;
Prov. 16:1.
Knows all plans. Isa. 29:15.
Provides counsel. Ps. 32:8.
Provides direction. Prov. 3:6;
16:9.

Having plans
Avoids trouble. Prov. 6:6–8;
30:25.
Leads to success. Prov. 21:5;
Isa. 32:8; 2 Cor. 9:5.

Plans
To be formed with counsel.
Prov. 13:18; 20:18.
To be submitted to God.
Prov. 16:1–4.
Trust in God. Prov. 3:5–6.
Wait for God. Ps. 37:7, 34.

FINANCIAL RESPONSIBILITY

Ability to lend
By righteous persons.
Ps. 37:25–26; 112:5.
Evidence of God's blessing.
Deut. 15:6; 28:12.
Be godly and content. 1
Tim. 6:6–10.

Borrowing
Borrowed item repaid in full even if
at borrower's loss. Exod. 22:14.
Borrower is slave of lender.
Prov. 22:7.
Diversification. Eccles. 11:2.
Owe no one anything. Rom. 13:8.
Wicked do not repay what is owed.
Ps. 37:21.

Earth and its resources
Belong to God. Lev. 25:23;
Job 41:11; Ps. 24:1; 89:11.

Given by God to people.
Gen. 1:29–30; 9:1–4;
Deut. 8:7–10.

Fairness in requiring collateral or
exacting interest for loans
required.
Exod. 22:26–27;
Deut. 24:6, 10–13.

Generosity
Brings blessing. Prov. 22:9;
Mal. 3:10; 2 Cor. 9:7–10.
In eyes of God. Luke 21:1–4.
Reciprocal. Prov. 11:25;
Luke 6:38.
Sow and reap bountifully.
2 Cor. 9:6.

Giving
According to ability. Deut. 16:17;
1 Chron. 29:2; Ezra 2:69;
Acts 11:29; Rom 12:6–8;
1 Cor. 16:2–3.
Better than receiving. Acts 20:35.
First fruits. Exod. 34:26;
Num. 18:12–13; Prov. 3:9–10;
Ezek. 44:30.
Tithe. Gen. 14:20; Deut. 14:22;
Mal. 3:8–10.
Willing. Deut. 15:10–11, 14;
Matt. 5:42; 2 Cor. 8:3; 9:5, 7.
Without love, is nothing.
1 Cor. 13:3.
Without pretense. Matt. 6:3–4.
Without thought of return.
Rom. 11:35.

Hope
Placed in God, not money.
1 Tim. 6:17.
Placed in money, not God.
Ps. 49:5–9; Matt. 19:22.
Illicit gain. Prov. 13:11; 15:27;
Acts 5:1–10.

Inability to handle material wealth
indicative of inability to handle
spiritual wealth. Luke 16:11.

Inheritance, given to
Children. Num. 27:7–11;
Prov. 13:22.
Protected. Ruth 4:6.
Squandered. Eccles. 5:14;
Luke 15:12.
Stolen. Matt. 21:38–41.
Strangers. Num. 36:3–9;
Lam. 5:2.

Injunctions concerning
Be godly and content. 1
Tim. 6:6–10.
Be honest in business dealings.
Lev. 19:35–36;
Deut. 25:13–16; Prov. 11:1;
1 Tim. 3:8.
Give if asked. Matt. 5:42.
Pay debts when due.
Prov. 3:27–28.
Provide for the oppressed.
Job 20:18–19; Zech. 7:9–10;
Matt. 25:31–46; 1 Tim. 6:18.
Provide for own family. 1
Tim. 5:8.
Work. Prov. 20:4; Eph. 4:28;
2 Thess. 3:10.

Interest
Charged by wicked. Ezek. 18:13;
Luke 6:34.
Charged to foreigner.
Deut. 23:20.
Not charged by righteous.
Deut. 23:19; Neh 5:7–12;
Ps. 15:5; Luke 6:34.
Love of money. Prov. 23:4–5;
28:22; 1 Tim. 6:9–10.
Must provide for own family.
1 Tim. 5:8.

No interest charged on loans.
  Ezek. 18:7–9.
To brother/fellow believer.
  Deut. 23:19.
To the poor. Exod. 22:25.
Parable of the minas.
  Luke 19:11–27.
Parable of the talents.
  Matt. 25:14–30.
People are God's stewards.
  Luke 16:1–13.
Provide for times of need.
  Gen. 41:1–57; Prov. 6:6–8.
Rich must provide for others. 1
  Tim. 6:18.

Savings
  Plans for. Gen. 41:1–57;
    Prov. 6:6–8; 21:20;
    Eccles. 11:2; Matt. 6:19–21;
    Luke 12:16–21;
    1 Cor. 16:2.
Silver and gold belong to God.
  Hag. 2:8.
Spent. Job 20:20–22; Prov. 21:20.

Stewardship parables
  Minas. Luke 19:11–27.
  Shrewd manager. Luke 16:1–13.
  Talents. Matt. 25:14–30.

Work
  For adequate provision.
    Prov. 28:19
  Lack of work leads to poverty.
    Prov. 24:33–34.
  With might. Eccles. 9:10.
Workman worthy of fair wages.
  1 Cor. 9:3–10; 1 Tim. 5:18.

FINE
As penalty. Exod. 22:1–9.

FINGER
Six on one hand. 2 Sam. 21:20.

FIR TREE
See Tree, Fir

FIRE
Can be increased in intensity.
  Dan. 3:19, 22.

Characterized as
  Bright. Ezek. 1:13.
  Consuming. Judg. 15:4–5;
    Ps. 46:9; Isa. 10:16–17.
  Drying. Job 15:30; Joel 1:20.
  Enlightening. Pss. 78:14; 105:39.
  Heating. Mark 14:54.
  Insatiable. Prov. 30:16.
  Melting. Ps. 68:2; Isa. 64:2.
  Purifying. Num. 31:23;
    1 Pet. 1:7; Rev. 3:18.
  Spreading. James 3:5.
Christ will appear in. Dan. 7:10;
  2 Thess. 1:8.
Frequently employed as an
  instrument of divine vengeance.
  Ps. 97:3; Isa. 47:14; 66:16.
God appeared in. Exod. 3:2; 19:18.

In houses
  Lighted in the winter. Jer. 36:22.
  Lighted on spring mornings.
    John 18:18.
  Made of charcoal. John 18:18.
  Made of wood. Acts 28:3.
  Not to be lighted on the Sabbath.
    Exod. 35:3.

Illustrative of
  Affliction. Isa. 43:2.
  Christ as Judge. Isa. 10:17;
    Mal. 3:2.
  God's enemies. Isa. 10:17;
    Obad. 1:18.

God's protection. Num. 9:16;
Zech. 2:5.

God's vengeance. Deut. 4:24;
Heb. 12:29.

The Holy Spirit. Isa. 4:4; Acts 2:3.

The hope of hypocrites.
Isa. 50:11.

Judgments. Jer. 48:45;
Lam. 1:13; Ezek. 39:6.

Lust. Prov. 6:27–28.

Persecution. Luke 12:49–53.

The self-righteous. Isa. 65:5.

The tongue. Prov. 16:27;
James 3:6.

The Word of God. Jer. 5:14;
23:29.

Wickedness. Isa. 9:18.

Zeal of angels. Ps. 104:4;
Heb. 1:7.

Zeal of believers. Pss. 39:3;
119:139.

Injury from, to be made good by the
person who kindled it. Exod. 22:6.

Miraculous
Angel ascended in. Judg. 13:20.

In the burning bush. Exod. 3:2.

Consumed the company of Korah.
Num. 16:35.

Consumed the sacrifice of Elijah.
2 Kings 1:18, 38.

Consumed the sacrifice of Gideon.
Judg. 6:21.

Destroyed the enemies of Elijah.
2 Kings 1:10, 12.

Destroyed Nadab and Abihu.
Lev. 10:2.

Destroyed the people at Taberah.
Num. 11:1.

Elijah taken up in a chariot of.
2 Kings 2:11.

Led the people of Israel in the
desert. Exod. 13:22; 40:38.

On Mount Sinai at giving of law.
Deut. 4:11, 36.

Plagued the Egyptians.
Exod. 9:23–24.

Punishment of the wicked will be
in. Matt. 13:42; 25:41.

Sacred
All burnt offerings consumed by.
Lev. 6:9, 12.

Always burning on the altar.
Lev. 6:13.

Came from before the Lord.
Lev. 9:24.

Guilt of burning incense without.
Lev. 10:1.

Incense burned with. Lev. 16:12;
Num. 16:46.

Restored to the temple.
2 Chron. 7:1–3.

Things connected with
Ashes. 1 Kings 13:3; 2 Pet. 2:6.

Burning coals. Prov. 26:21.

Flame. Song of Sol. 8:6;
Isa. 66:15.

Smoke. Isa. 34:10; Joel 2:30.

Sparks. Job 18:5; Isa. 1:31.

Though small, kindles a great matter.
James 3:5.

FIRMAMENT

The expanse above the earth.
Gen. 1:6–8, 14–17, 20.

FIRST

In the beginning
Chosen. Eph. 1:4.

God. Gen. 1:1.

Jesus Christ. Col. 1:15;
Rev. 1:17; 3:14.

The Word. John 1:1.

Priorities
God's kingdom and righteousness.
Matt. 6:33.
Love. Matt. 22:35–40.
What has been received.
1 Cor. 15:3.

FIRSTBORN

The beginning of strength and
excellency of power. Gen. 49:3;
Deut. 21:17.

Of clean animals
Antiquity of offering. Gen. 4:4.
Could not be a freewill offering.
Lev. 27:26.
Flesh of, the priests' portion.
Num. 18:18.
Not sheared. Deut. 15:19.
Not taken from the dam for seven
days. Exod. 22:30; Lev. 22:27.
Not to labor. Deut. 15:19.
Offered in sacrifice. Num. 18:17.
Dedicated to commemorate the
sparing of the firstborn of Israel.
Exod. 13:15; Num. 8:17.
Of the donkey to be redeemed with a
lamb or its neck broken.
Exod. 13:13; 34:20.
Of Egyptians slain. Exod. 11:5;
12:12, 29.
Of idolaters, sacrificed. Ezek. 20:26.

Illustrative of
The dignity, etc., of Christ.
Ps. 89:27; Rom. 8:29;
Col. 1:18.
The dignity, etc., of the church.
Heb. 12:23.

Instances of being superseded
Aaron. Exod. 7:1–2, with
Num. 12:2, 8.
Adonijah. 1 Kings 2:15, 22.

Cain. Gen. 4:4–5.
David's brothers.
1 Sam. 16:6–12.
Esau. Gen. 25:23;
Rom. 9:12–13.
Hosah's son. 1 Chron. 26:10.
Ishmael. Gen. 17:19–21.
Japheth. Gen. 10:21.
Manasseh. Gen. 48:15–20.
Reuben, etc. 1 Chron. 5:1–2.

Of Israel
Price of, given to the priests.
Num. 3:48–51.
Price of redemption for.
Num. 3:46–47.
To be redeemed. Exod. 34:20;
Num. 18:15.
Tribe of Levi taken for.
Num. 3:12, 40–43; 8:18.

Laws respecting
Observed at Christ's birth.
Luke 2:22–23.
Restored after the captivity.
Neh. 10:36.
Of man and beast dedicated to God.
Exod. 13:2, 12; 22:29–30.
Objects of special love. Gen. 25:28;
Jer. 31:9, 20.
Precious and valuable. Mic. 6:7;
Zech. 12:10.

Privileges of
Authority over the younger
children. Gen. 4:7; 27:29;
1 Sam. 20:29.
In case of death the next brother to
raise up children to.
Deut. 25:5–6; Matt. 22:24–28.
Could be forfeited by misconduct.
Gen. 49:3–4, 8; 1 Chron. 5:1.
Could be sold. Gen. 25:31, 33;
Heb. 12:16–17.

A double portion of inheritance.
Deut. 21:17.

Honorable distinction of.
Ps. 89:27; Rom. 8:29;
Rev. 1:5.

The father's title and power.
2 Chron. 21:3.

Not to be alienated by parents
through whim. Deut. 21:15–16.

Precedence in the family.
Gen. 48:13–14.

Special blessing by the father.
Gen. 27:4, 39.

Of unclean animals
Law of redemption for.
Num. 18:16.

To be redeemed. Num. 18:15.

FIRST FRUITS
See Fruits, First

FISH
Cannot live without water. Isa. 50:2.

Catching of, a trade. Matt. 4:18;
Luke 5:2.

Created by God. Gen. 1:20–21;
Exod. 20:11.

Different in flesh from beasts, etc.
1 Cor. 15:39.

Distinction between clean and
unclean. Lev. 11:9–12;
Deut. 14:9–10.

Illustrative of
Believers (when good).
Matt. 13:48–49.

Men ignorant of future events.
Eccles. 9:12.

Mere professors (when bad).
Matt. 13:48–49.

Those ensnared by the wicked.
Hab. 1:14.

The visible church. Matt. 13:48.

The whole population of Egypt.
Ezek. 29:45.

Inhabit
Ponds. Song of Sol. 7:4;
Isa. 19:10.

Rivers. Exod. 7:18; Ezek. 29:5.

Seas. Num. 11:22; Ezek. 47:10.

Made for God's glory. Job 12:8–9;
Ps. 69:34.

Man given dominion over.
Gen. 1:26, 28; Ps. 8:8.

Man permitted to eat. Gen. 9:2–3.

Mentioned in Scripture
Leviathan. Job 41:1; Ps. 74:14.

Whale. Gen. 1:21; Matt. 12:40.

Miracles connected with
Dressed on the shore. John 21:9.

Immense numbers of. Luke 5:6, 9;
John 21:6, 11.

Multiplying a few.
Matt. 14:17–21; 15:34.

Procuring tribute money
from. Matt. 17:27.

Mode of cooking alluded to.
Luke 24:42; John 21:9.

No likeness of, to be made for
worship. Exod. 20:4; Deut. 4:18.

Number and variety of. Ps. 104:25.

Sold near the fish gate at Jerusalem.
2 Chron. 33:14; Zeph. 1:10.

Solomon wrote the history of.
1 Kings 4:33.

Suffered for men's sin. Exod. 7:21;
Ezek. 38:20.

Taken with
Hooks. Amos 4:2; Matt. 17:27.

Nets. Luke 5:4–6; John 21:6–8.

Spears. Job 41:7.

The Tyrians traded in. Neh. 13:16.

Used as food
By the Egyptians. Num. 11:5.
By the Jews Matt. 7:10.

FISHERMEN
Certain apostles. John 21:2–3.
In a figurative sense. Jer. 16:16;
Matt. 4:19.

FISHHOOK
Used as an instrument of God's
judgment. Amos 4:2.

FLATTERY
Avoid persons given to. Prov. 20:19.
Believers should not use.
Job 32:21–22.
Compared to honest reprimand.
Prov. 28:23.
Danger of. Prov. 7:21–23; 29:5.

Examples of
Absalom. 2 Sam. 15:2–6.
Adonijah. 1 Kings 1:42.
Agrippa. Acts 26:2–3.
Ahab. 1 Kings 20:4.
Citizens of Tyre. Acts 12:22.
Darius's court attendants.
Dan. 6:7.
Herodians. Luke 20:21.
False prophets. 1 Kings 22:13.
Gideon. Judg. 8:1–3.
Israel and Judah.
2 Sam. 19:41–43.
Jacob. Gen. 33:10.
Mephibosheth. 2 Sam. 9:8.
Paul. Acts 24:10.
A woman of Tekoah.
2 Sam. 14:17–20.
Tertullus. Acts 24:2–4.
False prophets and teachers use.
Ezek. 12:24, with Rom. 16:18.

Hypocrites use, to
God. Ps. 78:36.
Those in authority. Dan. 11:34.
Ministers should not use.
1 Thess. 2:5.
Paul avoided, in dealing with young
Christians. 1 Thess. 2:4–6.
A practice of the wicked. Ps. 5:8.
Punishment of. Job 17:5; Ps. 12:3.
Seldom gains respect. Prov. 28:23.

The wicked use, to
Others. Pss. 5:9; 12:2.
Themselves. Ps. 36:2.
Wisdom a preservative against.
Prov. 4:5.
Worldly advantage obtained by.
Dan. 11:21–22.

FLAX
In Egypt. Exod. 9:31.
Figurative sense. Smoking flax not
quenched. Isa. 42:3; Matt. 12:20.
Linen made from. Prov. 31:13.
In Palestine. Josh 2:6.

FLESH
Figurative sense, fruits of.
Gal. 5.19 21.
Symbolic sense, body of Christ
symbolized by bread.
John 6:51–63.

FLIES
Figurative sense. Isa. 7:18.
Plague of. Exod. 8:21–31.

FLINT
Rock from which God brought water
for the Israelites. Deut. 8:15;
32:13; Ps. 114:8.

FLOOD
Called the waters of Noah. Isa. 54:9.

Came suddenly and unexpectedly.
Matt. 24:38–39.
Causes of its abatement. Gen. 8:1–2.
Complete destruction effected by.
Gen. 7:23.
Date of its commencement.
Gen. 7:11.
Date of its complete removal.
Gen. 8:13.
Decrease of, gradual. Gen. 8:3, 5.
Extreme height of. Gen. 7:19–20.
Face of the earth changed by.
2 Pet. 3:5–6.

Illustrative of
Baptism. 1 Pet. 3:20–21.
The destruction of sinners.
Ps. 32:6; Isa. 28:2, 18.
Suddenness of Christ's coming (in
its unexpectedness).
Matt. 24:36–39;
Luke 17:26–30.
Increased gradually. Gen. 7:17–18.
Long-suffering of God exhibited in
deferring. Gen. 6:3, with
1 Pet. 3:20.
Noah prewarned of. Gen. 6:13;
Heb. 11:7.
Noah saved from. Gen. 6:18–22;
7:13–14.

Produced by
Forty days' incessant rain.
Gen. 7:4, 12, 17.
Opening up of the fountains of the
great deep. Gen. 7:11.
Sent as a punishment for the extreme
wickedness of humanity.
Gen. 6:5–7, 11–13, 17.

That it will never again occur
Confirmed by covenant.
Gen. 9:9–11.

A pledge of God's faithfulness.
Isa. 54:9–10.
Promised. Gen. 8:21–22.
The rainbow a sign.
Gen. 9:12–17.
Time of its increase and prevailing.
Gen. 7:24.
Traditional notice of. Job 22:15–17.
Wicked warned of. 1 Pet. 3:19–20;
2 Pet. 2:5.

FLOWERS
Appear in spring. Song of Sol. 2:12.
Cultivated in gardens.
Song of Sol. 6:2–3.

Described as
Beautiful. Matt. 6:29.
Sweet. Song of Sol. 5:13.
Temporary. Ps. 103:16;
Isa. 40:8.
Garlands of, used in worship of idols.
Acts 14:13.

Illustrative of
Glory of humanity. 1 Pet. 1:24.
Graces of Christ.
Song of Sol. 5:13.
Kingdom of Israel. Isa. 28:1.
Rich persons. James 1:10–11.
Shortness of life. Job 14:2;
Ps. 103:15.

Representations of, on the
Golden candlestick. Exod. 25:31,
33; 2 Chron. 4:21.
Sea of brass. 1 Kings 7:26;
2 Chron. 4:5.
Woodwork of the temple.
1 Kings 6:18, 29, 33, 35.

Those mentioned in Scripture
Flower of grass. 1 Pet. 1:24.
Lily. Hos. 14:5; Matt. 6:28.
Lily of the valley. Song of Sol. 2:1.

Rose. Isa. 35:1.
Rose of Sharon. Song of Sol. 2:1.
Wild in fields. Ps. 103:15.

FLUTE
Instrument used in Babylon.
Dan. 3:5–7, 10, 15.

FOOD

Articles of
Bread. Gen. 18:5.
Butter. Deut. 32:14.
Cheese. 1 Sam. 17:18.
Dried fruit. 1 Sam. 25:18.
Fish. Matt. 7:10.
Flesh. 2 Sam. 6:19.
Fruit. 2 Sam. 16:2.
Herbs. Prov. 15:17.
Honey. Song of Sol. 5:1.
Milk. Gen. 49:12.
Oil. Deut. 12:17.
Parched corn. Ruth 2:14.
Vinegar. Num. 6:3.
Wine. 2 Sam. 6:19.
From God. Gen. 1:29–30.
A hymn sung after. Matt. 26:30.
Men and women did not partake
together. Gen. 18:8–9.
Prepared by females. Gen. 27:9.
Thanks given before. Mark 8:6.
Things prohibited as. Exod. 22:31;
Lev. 1:1–47.

FOOLS
All persons are, without the
knowledge of God. Titus 3:3.

Are
Angry. Eccles. 7:9.
Contentious. Prov. 18:6.
Corrupt and abominable.
Ps. 14:1.
Full of words. Eccles. 10:14.

Given to meddling. Prov. 20:3.
A grief to parents. Prov. 17:25;
19:13.
Liars. Prov. 10:18.
Mere professors of religion.
Matt. 25:2–12.
Self-confident. Prov. 14:16.
Self-deceivers. Prov. 14:8.
Self-sufficient. Prov. 12:15;
Rom. 1:22.
Slanderers. Prov. 10:18.
Slothful. Eccles. 4:5.
To be avoided. Prov. 9:6; 14:7.
Blaspheme God. Ps. 74:18.
Cling to their folly. Prov. 26:11;
27:22.
Come to shame. Prov. 3:35.
Do not delight not in understanding.
Prov. 18:2.
Deny God. Pss. 14:1; 53:1.
Depend upon their wealth.
Luke 12:20.
Despise instruction. Prov. 1:7; 15:5.
Destroy themselves by their speech.
Prov. 10:8, 14; Eccles. 10:12.
Exhorted to seek wisdom. Prov. 8:5.
God has no pleasure in. Eccles. 5:4.
Hate knowledge. Prov. 1:22.
Hate to depart from evil.
Prov. 13:19.
Hear the gospel and do not obey it.
Matt. 7:26.
Honor is unbecoming for.
Prov. 26:1, 8.
Make a mock at sin. Prov. 14:9.
Punishment of. Ps. 107:17;
Prov. 19:29; 26:10.
Reproach God. Ps. 74:22.
Sport themselves in mischief.
Prov. 10:23.
Their company ruinous.
Prov. 13:20.

Their lips a snare to the soul.
Prov. 18:7.
Their mouths pour out foolishness.
Prov. 15:2.
Their worship hateful to God.
Eccles. 5:1.
Trust to their own hearts.
Prov. 28:26.
Walk in darkness. Eccles. 2:14.
Will not stand in the presence of
God. Ps. 5:5.
Worship idols. Jer. 10:8;
Rom. 1:22–23.

FOOT
Washing the feet of the disciples by
Jesus. John 13:4–16.
By disciples. 1 Tim. 5:10.

FOOTMAN
A runner before kings and
princesses. 1 Sam. 8:11;
2 Sam. 15:1; 1 Kings 1:5.

FOOTSTOOL
Figurative sense, the earth is God's.
Isa. 60:13; 66:1; Lam. 2:1;
Acts 7:49.

FORD
A shallow place in a stream or river.
Gen. 32:22; Josh. 2:7;
Judg. 3:28; 12:5, 6; Isa. 16:2;
Jer. 51:32.

FOREIGN AID

Examples of
Gift by church to other churches.
Acts 11:27–30; Rom 15:26;
2 Cor. 8:1–4.
Loan by Israel to nations.
Deut. 15:6; 28:12.

Sale of grain by Egypt to Jacob.
Gen. 41:57.

FORESTS
Abounded with wild honey.
1 Sam. 14:25–26.
Called on to rejoice at God's mercy.
Isa. 44:23.

Illustrative of
Destruction of the wicked (when
destroyed by fire). Isa. 9:18;
10:17–18; Jer. 21:14.
The Jews rejected by God (when
fruitful fields turned into).
Isa. 29:17; 32:15.
The unfruitful world. Isa. 32:19.
Infested by wild beasts. Pss. 50:10;
104:20; Isa. 56:9; Jer. 5:6;
Mic. 5:8.
Jotham built towers, etc., in.
2 Chron. 27:4.

Mentioned in Scripture
Arabian. Isa. 21:13.
Bashan. Isa. 2:13; Ezek. 27:6;
Zech. 11:2.
Carmel. 2 Kings 19:23;
Isa. 37:24.
Ephraim. 2 Sam. 18:6, 8.
Hareth. 1 Sam. 22:5.
The king's. Neh. 2:8.
Lebanon. 1 Kings 7:2; 10:17.
The south. Ezek. 20:46–47.
Often afforded pasture. Mic. 7:14.
Often destroyed by enemies.
2 Kings 19:23; Isa. 37:24.
Places of refuge. 1 Sam. 22:5;
23:16.
Power of God extends over.
Ps. 29:9.
Supplied timber for building.
1 Kings 5:6–8.

Tracts of land covered with trees.
Isa. 44:14.
Underbrush often in. Isa. 9:18.

FORGERY
By Jezebel. 1 Kings 21:8.

FORGETTING GOD
See God, Forgetting

FORGIVENESS OF INJURIES
A characteristic of believers. Ps. 7:4.
Christ set an example of.
Luke 23:34.
Commanded. Mark 11:25;
Rom. 12:19.
A glory to believers. Prov. 19:11.
Illustrated. Matt. 18:23–35.

Motives to
Christ's forgiveness of us.
Col. 3:13.
God's forgiveness of us.
Eph. 4:32.
The mercy of God. Luke 6:36.
Our need of forgiveness.
Mark 11:25.
No forgiveness without. Matt. 6:15;
James 2:13.
Promises to. Matt. 6:14; Luke 6:37.

Should be accompanied by
Blessing and prayer. Matt. 5:44.
Leniency. Col. 3:13.
Kindness. Gen. 45:5–11;
Rom. 12:20.
To be unlimited. Matt. 18:22;
Luke 17:4.

FORGIVENESS OF SIN
See Sin, Forgiveness of

FORK
An agricultural implement.
1 Sam. 13:21.

FORMALISM
Insufficient in the worship of God.
1 Sam. 15:22; Ps. 51:16–17;
Matt. 9:13.

FORSAKING GOD
See God, Forsaking

FORT
Caves used for. Judg. 6:2;
Isa. 33:16.
Defenses of cities. 2 Chron. 26:15;
Isa. 25:12.
Erected in vineyards and herding
grounds. 2 Chron. 26:10;
Isa. 5:2; Luke 20:9.
Figurative sense of, God's care.
2 Sam. 22:2–3, 47.
A military defense. Deut. 20:19–20.

FORTUNE
Changes of, in the lives of
Joseph, from slave to prime
minister. Gen. 40–41.
Pharaoh's butler and baker.
Gen. 40.

FORTY
*Remarkable coincidences in the
number*
Christ's stay after the resurrection.
Acts 1:3.
Days, of rain, at the time of the
flood. Gen. 7:7–12.
Egypt, to be desolated.
Ezek. 29:11.
Egypt, to be restored after.
Ezek. 29:13.

Elijah. 1 Kings 19:8.

For embalming. Gen. 50:3.

Of fasting by Moses. Exod. 24:18;
34:28; Deut. 9:9, 25.

Of flood, before sending the raven.
Gen. 8:6.

Jesus. Matt. 4:2.

Peace in Israel. Judg. 3:11; 5:31;
8:28.

Of probation, given to the
Ninevites. Jon. 3:4.

Spies in the land of promise.
Num. 13:25.

Symbolic sense. Ezek. 4:6.

Stripes, administered in punishing
criminals. Deut. 25:3;
2 Cor. 11:24.

Year's, wandering of the Israelites
in the wilderness. Exod. 16:35.

FOUNDATION

Described as
Deep laid. Luke 6:48.

Joined together by cornerstones.
Ezra 4:12, with 1 Pet. 2:6 and
Eph. 2:20.

Of stone. 1 Kings 5:17.

Strongly laid. Ezra 6:3.

Figuratively applied to
The earth. Job 38:4; Ps. 104:5.

The heavens. 2 Sam. 22:8.

Kingdoms. Exod. 9:18.

The mountains. Deut. 32:22.

The ocean. Ps. 104:8.

The world. Ps. 18:15;
Matt. 13:35.

Illustrative of
Christ. Isa. 28:16; 1 Cor. 3:11.

Decrees and purposes of God.
2 Tim. 2:19.

Doctrines of the apostles, etc.
Eph. 2:20.

First principles of the gospel.
Heb. 6:1–2.

Hope of believers. Ps. 87:1.

Magistrates. Ps. 82:5.

The righteous. Prov. 10:25.

Security of believers' inheritance.
Heb. 11:10.

Laid for
Cities. Josh 6:26; 1 Kings 16:34.

Houses. Luke 6:48.

Temples. 1 Kings 6:37;
Ezra 3:10.

Towers. Luke 14:28–29.

Walls. Ezra 4:12; Rev. 21:14.

The lowest part of a building, on
which it rests. Luke 14:29;
Acts 16:26.

Security afforded by. Matt. 7:25;
Luke 6:48.

FOUNTAINS AND SPRINGS

Abound in Canaan. Deut. 8:7;
1 Kings 18:5.

Afford
Drink to the beasts. Ps. 104:11.

Fruitfulness to the earth.
1 Kings 18:5; Joel 3:18.

Refreshment to the birds.
Ps. 104:12.

Came from the great deep.
Gen. 7:11; Job 38:16.

Constantly flowing
Could not be ceremonially defiled.
Lev. 11:36.

Especially valued. Isa. 58:11.

Created by God. Pss. 74:15;
104:10.

Drying up of, a severe punishment.
Ps. 107:33–34; Hos. 13:15.

Found in hills and valleys. Deut. 8:7;
Ps. 104:10.
Frequented by travelers. Gen. 16:7.
God to be praised for. Rev. 14:7.

Illustrative of
Christ. Zech. 13:1.
The church (when not failing).
Isa. 58:11.
The church (when sealed up).
Song of Sol. 4:12.
Constant supplies of grace.
Ps. 87:7.
Eternal life. John 4:14; Rev. 21:6.
God. Ps. 36:9; Jer. 2:13; 17:13.
Godly fear. Prov. 14:27.
A good wife. Prov. 5:18.
The Holy Spirit. John 7:38–39.
The law of the wise. Prov. 13:14.
The means of grace. Isa. 41:18;
Joel 3:18.
The natural heart (when corrupt).
James 3:11, with
Matt. 15:18–19.
Numerous posterity. Deut. 33:28.
Believers led astray (when
troubled). Prov. 25:26.
Spiritual wisdom. Prov. 16:22;
18:4.
Unceasing wickedness of the Jews
(when always flowing). Jer. 6:7.

Mentioned in Scripture
Of Jezreel. 1 Sam. 29:1.
Of Pisgah. Deut. 4:49.
Upper and lower springs.
Josh. 15:19; Judg. 1:15.
Of the waters of Nephtoah.
Josh. 15:9.
On the way to Shur. Gen. 16:7.
Send forth each but one kind of
water. James 3:11.
Sometimes dried up. Isa. 58:11.

Sometimes stopped or turned off to
distress enemies.
2 Chron. 32:3–4.

FOX
Dens of. Matt. 8:20.

Figurative sense of
Craftiness. Luke 13:32.
Heretics. Song of Sol. 2:15.
Unfaithful prophets. Ezek. 13:4.
Held in contempt. Neh. 4:3.
Ravages of. Ps. 63:10;
Song of Sol. 2:15.
Samson uses, to burn the field of the
Philistines. Judg. 15:4.

FRANKINCENSE
See also Incense

Burned in worship. Lev. 16:12–13.
A gift for the Christ child. Matt. 2:11.
No substitute for true worship.
Isa. 60:3.
Symbolized devotion. Ps. 141:2.
Used to anoint priests. Exod. 30:34.

FRANKNESS
Characterized Christ. John 16:29.
Characterized Paul the apostle.
1 Thess. 2:3.
Characterizes Christian love.
Eph. 6:24.
Sought by Job. Job 33:3.

FRATRICIDE
Examples of
Abimelech. Judg. 9:5.
Absalom. 2 Sam. 13:28–29.
Cain. Gen. 4:8.
Jehoram. 2 Chron. 21:4.
Solomon. 1 Kings 2:23–25.

FREEDOM

Characterizes the good news of the
gospel. Isa. 61:1; Luke 4:18.
The Christian's law. James 1:25;
2:12.
Granted believers. Ps. 119:45;
Rom. 8:21.
Our glorious heritage. John 8:36;
Gal. 5:1.
Proclaimed by God. Lev. 25:10.
Responsibility of. 1 Pet. 2:16.

FRIENDS

Jesus calls His disciples.
John 15:14–15.

False friends, examples of
Ahithophel to David.
2 Sam. 15:12.
David to Joab. 1 Kings 2:5–6.
David to Uriah. 2 Sam. 11.
David's friends to David.
Ps. 35:11–16; 41:9;
55:12–14, 20–21; 88:8, 18.
Delilah to Samson.
Judg. 16:1–20.
Disciples to Jesus.
Matt. 26:56, 58.
The Ephraimite's wife.
Judg. 19:1–2.
Judas to Jesus. Matt. 26:48–49.
Pharoah's butler to Joseph.
Gen. 40:23.

FRIENDSHIP

Characteristic of. Prov. 27:6–19.
Constancy of. Prov. 17:17.
Of Christ. Luke 7:34; John 15:14.
Of the disciples. Acts 28:15;
2 Cor. 2:13; 3 John 1:14.

Examples of
Abraham and Lot.
Gen. 14:14–16.

Daniel and his three companions.
Dan. 2:49.
David and Abiathar.
1 Sam. 22:23.
David and Hiram. 1 Kings 5:1.
David and Hushai.
2 Sam. 15:32–37.
David and Ittai. 2 Sam. 15:19–21.
David and Jonathan.
1 Sam. 18:1–4, 20; 23:16–18.
David and Nahash. 2 Sam. 10:2.
Job and his three friends.
Job 2:11–13.
Joram and Ahaziah.
2 Kings 8:28–29.
Luke and Theophilus. Acts 1:1.
Mary, Martha, Lazarus, and Jesus.
Luke 10:38–42.
The Marys and Joseph of
Arimathaea. Matt. 27:55–61.
Paul and his nephew. Acts 23:16.
Paul, Priscilla, and Aquilla.
Rom. 16:3–4.
Paul, Timothy, and Epaphroditus.
Phil. 2:19–20, 22, 25.
Ruth and Naomi. Ruth 1:16–17.
Samuel and Saul. 1 Sam. 15:35;
16:1.
Friend closer than brother. Prov.
18:24.
Helpfulness of. Eccles. 4:9–10.

FROGS

Plague of. Exod. 8:2–14; Ps. 78:45;
105:30.
Symbolic sense. Rev. 16:13.

FRONTLETS

A leather band worn on the forehead,
containing certain
commandments. Exod. 13:6, 16;
Deut. 6:1–8; 11:18.

FRUGALITY

Examples of
  The provisions made by the
    Egyptians against famine.
    Gen. 41:48–49, 53–54.
  The gathering of manna.
    Exod. 16:17–18, 22–24.
  A trait of the virtuous wife.
    Prov. 31:27.

FRUIT

Called the
  Fruit of the earth. Isa. 4:2.
  Fruit of the ground. Gen. 4:3;
    Jer. 7:20.
  Increase of the land. Ps. 85:12.

Divided into
  Evil or bad. Matt. 7:17.
  Goodly. Jer. 11:16.
  Hasty or early ripening of.
    Isa. 28:4.
  New and old. Song of Sol. 7:13.
  Pleasant. Song of Sol. 4:16.
  Precious. Deut. 33:14.

  Summer. 2 Sam. 16:1.
First of, devoted to God. Deut. 26:2.
Given by God. Acts 14:17.

Illustrative of
  Conduct and conversation of evil
    persons, when bad. Matt. 7:17;
    12:33.
  Converts to the church. Ps. 72:16;
    John 4:36.
  Doctrines of Christ.
    Song of Sol. 2:3.
  Effects of industry.
    Prov. 31:16, 31.
  Effects of repentance. Matt. 3:8.
  Example, etc., of the godly.
    Prov. 11:30.
  Good works. Matt. 7:17–18;
    Phil. 4:17.
  A holy conversation. Prov. 12:14;
    18:20.
  Praise. Heb. 13:15.
  The reward of believers. Isa. 3:10.
  The reward of the wicked.
    Jer. 17:9–10.

Carob Fruit

Date Palm

Works of the Spirit. Gal. 5:22–23;
Eph. 5:9.

Often destroyed
By blight. Joel 1:12.
By drought. Hag. 1:10.
By enemies. Ezek. 25:4.
By locusts, etc. Deut. 28:38–39;
Joel 1:4.
In God's anger. Jer. 7:20.
Often sent as presents. Gen. 43:11.
Preserved to us by God. Mal. 3:11.
The produce of corn, etc.
Deut. 22:9; Ps. 107:37.
The produce of trees. Gen. 1:29;
Eccles. 2:5.
Produced in their due seasons.
Matt. 21:41.

Require
A fruitful land. Ps. 107:34.
Influence of the sun and moon.
Deut. 33:14.
Rain from heaven. Ps. 104:13;
James 5:18.
To be waited for with patience.
James 5:7.

FRUITS, FIRST
Allotted to the priests.
Num. 18:12–13; Lev. 23:20;
Deut. 18:3–5.

Different kinds of
All agricultural produce.
Deut. 26:2.
Barley harvest. Lev. 23:10–14.
Fruit of new trees in fourth year.
Lev. 19:23–24.
Honey. 2 Chron. 31:5.
Wheat harvest. Exod. 23:16;
Lev. 23:16–17.
Wine and oil. Deut. 18:4.
Wood. Deut. 18:4.

God honored by the offering of.
Prov. 3:9.
Holy to the Lord. Ezek. 48:14.

Illustrative of
Church of Christ. James 1:18;
Rev. 14:4.
Early Jewish church. Jer. 2:3.
First converts in any place.
Rom. 16:5.
Resurrection of Christ.
1 Cor. 15:20, 23.
Law of, restored after the captivity.
Neh. 10:35, 37; 13:31.
Offering of, consecrated the whole.
Rom. 11:16.
To be best of their kind.
Num. 18:12.
To be brought to God's house.
Exod. 34:26.

To be offered
In a basket. Deut. 26:2.
With thanksgiving.
Deut. 26:3–10.
Without delay. Exod. 22:29.

FRUIT TREES
See Tree, Fruit

FRUSTRATION

Examples of
Ahab. 1 Kings 18:17.
Caravans, fig. for Job. Job 6:20.
Crafty people. Job 5:12.
Israel under Zerubbabel.
Ezra 4:4–5.
Liars. Isa. 44:25.
Pharaoh. Exod. 8:8, 25, 28;
9:27–28; 10:7, 10–11, 16–17,
24; 12:31–32.
Pilate. John 19:1–16.

Principles relevant to
Comfort. Isa. 40:1; 1 Cor. 1:3–7.
Contentment. 1 Tim. 6:6–10.
Everything works for good for
those who love God. Rom 8:28.

Spiritual maturity
Growth in. Phil. 1:6.
Through trials. James 1:2–4.
Trust. Ps. 22:5; Prov. 3:5–6.

FRYING PAN
Grain offering made in. Lev. 2:7.

FUEL
For temple, how provided.
Neh. 10:34; 13:30–31.

FUGITIVES
Absalom. 2 Sam. 13:34–38.
David, from the wrath of Saul.
1 Sam. 21:10.

Examples of
Onesimus. Philem. 1.
Shimei's servants. 1 Kings 2:39.
From justice, Moses. Exod. 2:15.
From servitude, not to be returned.
Deut. 23:15–16.
Jeroboam. 1 Kings 11:40.
Joseph, to Egypt. Matt. 2:13–15.

FURNACE

In figurative senses
Of affliction. Deut. 4:20.
Of lust. Hos. 7:4.
Of hell. Mal. 4:1; Matt. 13:42,
50; Rev. 9:2.
For refining gold. Prov. 17:3.
For refining silver. Ezek. 22:22;
Mal. 3:3.
For melting lead and tin.
Ezek. 22:20.
For punishment, Shadrach, Mesach,
and Abednego. Dan. 3:6–26.

G

GABRIEL

Heavenly messenger. Dan. 8:15–27;
9:20–27; Luke 1:8–20, 26–38.

GALILEE

Christ

Appeared in, to His disciples after
His resurrection. Matt. 26:32;
28:7.

Brought up in. Matt. 2:22;
Luke 2:39, 51.

Chose His apostles
from. Matt. 4:18, 21;
John 1:43–44; Acts 1:11.

Despised as of. Matt. 26:69, with
John 7:52.

Followed by the people of.
Matt. 4:25.

Kindly received in. John 4:45.

Ministered to by women of.
Matt. 27:55; Mark 15:41;
Luke 8:3.

Performed many miracles in.
Matt. 4:23–24; 15:29–31.

Preached throughout. Mark 1:39;
Luke 4:44.

Preaching in, predicted.
Isa. 9:1–2; Matt. 4:14–15.

Sought refuge in. John 4:1, 3.

Christian churches established in.
Acts 9:31.

Conquered by the Assyrians.
2 Kings 15:29.

Conquered by the Syrians.
1 Kings 15:20.

Inhabitants of

Called Galileans. Acts 2:7.

Cruelly treated by Pilate.
Luke 13:1.

Despised by the Jews.
John 7:41, 52.

Opposed the Roman taxation.
Acts 5:37.

Used a peculiar dialect.
Matt. 26:73; Mark 14:70.

Jurisdiction of, granted to Herod by
the Romans. Luke 3:1; 23:6–7.

Kadesh, the city of refuge for.
Josh 21:32.

Lake of Gennesaret called the sea of.
Matt. 15:29; Luke 5:1.

Separated from Judea by Samaria.
John 4:3–4.

Supplied Tyre, etc., with provisions.
Acts 12:20.

Towns of

Accho or Ptolemais. Judg. 1:31.

Bethsaida. Mark 6:45; John 1:44.

Cana. John 2:1; 21:2.

Capernaum. Matt. 4:13.

Cesarea. Acts 9:30; 10:24.

Cesarea Philippi. Matt. 16:13;
Mark 8:27.

Chorazin. Matt. 11:21.

Nain. Luke 7:11.

Nazareth. Matt. 2:22–23;
Luke 1:26.

Tiberias. John 6:23.

Twenty cities of, given to Hiram.
1 Kings 9:11.

Upper part called Galilee of the
Gentiles. Isa. 9:1; Matt. 4:15.

GALL

Any bitter or poisonous substance, as
the bile. Job 16:13.
A bitter herb. Deut. 29:18.
Given Jesus. Ps. 69:21; Matt. 27:34.
Symbolic sense of, gall of bitterness.
Acts 8:23.
Venom of serpents. Job 20:14.

GAMBLING

Attempts to avoid God-ordained
work. Gen. 3:19.
Can result in destructive lifestyle.
1 Tim. 6:9.
Harms the poor and families.
Prov. 14:3; 1 Tim. 5:8.
Poor example for those who may
become addicted. 1 Cor. 8:13.
Practiced by those who crucified
Jesus. Mark 12:30.
Stems from covetousness.
Luke 12:15; Phil. 2:3–4;
1 Tim. 6:10.

GAMES

Fighting wild beast, of spiritual
conflict. 1 Cor. 4:9; 9:26; 15:32;
2 Tim. 4:7.
Figurative sense, of the Christian life.
1 Cor. 9:24, 26; Gal. 5:7;
Phil. 2:16; 3:14; Heb. 12:1.
Foot races. 1 Cor. 9:24, 26;
Gal. 2:2; Phil. 2:16; Heb. 12:1.
Gladiatorial. 1 Cor. 4:9; 9:26;
15:32; 2 Tim. 4:7.
Of a successful ministry. Gal. 2:2;
Phil. 2:16.

GANGS

As followers of
Abimelech. Judg. 9:4.
David. 1 Sam. 22:2.
Jephthah. Judg. 11:3.

Jeroboam. 2 Chron. 13:6–7.
Against Job. Job 30:1–8.

Rape by
Attempted. Gen. 19:4–11.
Committed. Judg. 19:22–26.

GARDENS

Blasting of, a punishment.
Amos 4:9.

Of Eden
Called the garden of God.
Ezek. 28:13.
Called the garden of the Lord.
Gen. 13:10.
Fertility of Canaan like.
Gen. 13:10; Joel 2:3.
Future state of the Jews will be
like. Isa. 51:3; Ezek. 36:35.
Had every tree good for food.
Gen. 2:9.
Man placed in, to dress and keep.
Gen. 2:8.
Man sent from, after the fall.
Gen. 3:23–24.
Planted by the Lord. Gen. 2:8.
Watered by a river. Gen. 2:10–14.

Illustrative of
The church. Song of Sol. 5:1;
6:2, 11.
Pleasantness, fruitfulness, and
security of the church (when
enclosed). Song of Sol. 4:12.
Spiritual prosperity of the church
(when well watered). Isa. 58:11;
Jer. 31:12.
The wicked (when dried up).
Isa. 1:30.
Jews ordered to plant, in Babylon.
Jer. 29:5, 28.

Kinds of, mentioned
Cucumbers. Isa. 1:8.

Fruit trees. Eccles. 2:5–6.
Herbs. Deut. 11:10;
  1 Kings 21:2.
Spices, etc. Song of Sol. 4:16;
  6:2.
Lodges erected in. Isa. 1:8.
Often enclosed. Song of Sol. 4:12.
Often made by the banks of rivers.
  Num. 24:6.
Often refreshed by fountains.
  Song of Sol. 4:15.
Taken care of by gardeners.
  John 20:15.

Used also for
  Burial. 2 Kings 21:18, 26;
    John 19:41.
  Entertainments. Song of Sol. 5:1.
  Idolatrous worship. Isa. 1:29;
    65:3.
  Retirement. John 18:1.

GARLIC
Food Israelites ate in Egypt.
  Num. 11:5.

GARMENTS

Called
  Clothes. Gen. 28:20; Deut. 8:4;
    Prov. 6:27; Ezek. 16:39.
  Clothing. Job 22:6; 31:19.
  Robes. Gen. 41:42; Rev. 19:16.
Cleansed by water from ceremonial
  uncleanness. Lev. 11:32;
  Num. 31:20.

Colors of, mentioned
  Blue. Ezek. 23:6.
  Purple. Ezek. 7:27; Luke 16:19.
  Scarlet. 2 Sam. 1:24; Dan. 5:7.
  Variegated. Gen. 37:3;
    2 Sam. 13:18.
  White. Eccles. 9:8.

Given as a sign of covenants.
  1 Sam. 18:4.
Given as presents. Gen. 45:22;
  2 Kings 5:22.
Grew old and wore out. Josh 9:5;
  Ps. 102:26.

Illustrative of
  Abundance (washed in wine).
    Gen. 49:11.
  Righteousness (white). Matt. 28:3;
    Rev. 3:18.
  Victory (rolled in blood). Isa. 9:5.
Of Israel preserved for forty years.
  Deut. 8:4.
Liable to plague and leprosy.
  Lev. 13:47–59.

Made of
  Camel's hair. Matt. 3:4.
  Linen. Lev. 6:10; Esther 8:15.
  Sackcloth. 2 Sam. 3:31;
    2 Kings 19:1.
  Silk. Prov. 31:22.
  Skins. Heb. 11:37.
  Wool. Prov. 27:26; Ezek. 34:3.

Mentioned in Scripture
  Belt. 1 Sam. 18:4; Acts 21:11.
  Bonnet or hat. Lev. 8:13;
    Dan. 3:21.
  Cloak. Luke 6:29; 2 Tim. 4:13.
  Cloak or upper garment.
    Deut. 24:13; Matt. 21:8.
  Shoe or sandal. Exod. 3:5;
    Mark 6:9.
  Tunic or coat. John 19:23; 21:7.
  Veil. Gen. 24:65.
Not to be made of mixed materials.
  Deut. 22:11.
Often changed. Gen. 35:2; 41:14.
Often fringed and bordered.
  Num. 15:38; Deut. 22:12.

Often torn in affliction.
2 Sam. 15:32; Ezra 9:3, 5.

Of the poor
Not to be retained in pledge.
Deut. 24:12–13.
Provided specially by God.
Deut. 10:18.
Used as a covering by night.
Deut. 24:13.
Vile. James 2:2.

Of the rich
Embroidered. Ps. 45:14;
Ezek. 16:18.
Fine. James 2:2–3.
Of the finest materials. Matt. 11:8.
Gorgeous. Luke 7:25;
Acts 12:21.
Multiplied and heaped up.
Job 27:16; Isa. 3:22.
Often moth-eaten. Job 13:28;
James 5:2.
Perfumed. Ps. 45:8;
Song of Sol. 4:11.
Origin of. Gen. 3:7, 21.
Of the sexes, not to be interchanged.
Deut. 22:5.
Scribes and Pharisees condemned for
making broad the borders of.
Matt. 23:5.
Of those slain with a sword not used.
Isa. 14:19.
Worn long and flowing. Luke 20:46;
Rev. 1:13.

GARNER
See Barn, Storehouse

GARRISON
A military camp. 1 Sam. 13:3; 14:1;
2 Sam. 8:6, 14; 23:14.

GATES
Bodies of criminals exposed to view
at. 2 Kings 10:8.
Carcass of sin offering burned outside
of. Lev. 4:12; Heb. 13:11–13.

Of cities
Battering rams used against.
Ezek. 21:22.
Chief places of speeches.
Prov. 1:21.
Chief points of attack in war.
Judg. 5:8; Isa. 22:7;
Ezek. 21:15.
Conferences held at. Gen. 34:20;
2 Sam. 3:27.
Councils of state held at.
2 Chron. 18:9; Jer. 39:3.
Courts of justice held at.
2 Sam. 15:2; Prov. 22:22–23.
Criminals punished at. Deut. 17:5;
Jer. 20:2.
Custom of sitting at, in the
evening, alluded to. Gen. 19:1.
Experienced officers placed over.
2 Kings 7:17.
Idolatrous rites performed at.
Acts 14:13.
Land redeemed at. Ruth 4:1.
Land sold at. Gen. 23:10, 16.

Jaffa Gate, Jerusalem

Golden Gates, Jerusalem

Markets held at. 2 Kings 7:1, 18.

Often demolished and burned.
Neh. 1:3; Lam. 2:9.

Proclamations made at.
Prov. 1:21; Jer. 17:19.

Public censure passed at. Job 5:4;
Isa. 29:21.

Public commendation given at.
Prov. 31:23, 31.

Shut at nightfall. Josh 2:5;
Neh. 13:19.

Troops reviewed at. 2 Sam. 18:4.

Closed at night. Josh 2:5, 7.

Closed on the Sabbath. Neh. 13:19.

Criminals generally punished outside
of. Lev. 24:23; John 19:17, with
Heb. 13:12.

Of death. Job 38:17; Ps. 9:13.

Design of. Isa. 62:10.

Double doors. Isa. 45:1;
Ezek. 41:24.

Fastened with bars of iron.
Ps. 107:16; Isa. 45:2.

Figurative sense, of the people of a
city. Isa. 3:26.

Of the gospel. Isa. 60:11.

Of the grave. Isa. 38:10.

Guards stationed at. 2 Kings 7:17.

Illustrative of

Access to God (heaven).
Gen. 28:12–17.

Christ. John 10:9.

Death (the grave). Isa. 38:10.

The entrance to destruction, when
wide. Matt. 7:13

The entrance to life, when narrow.
Matt. 7:14.

Satan's power (hell). Matt. 16:18.

Jails made in the towers of.
Jer. 20:2.

Of Jerusalem

Benjamin Gate. Jer. 20:2; 37:13.

Corner Gate. 2 Chron. 26:9.
Dung Gate. Neh. 3:14; 12:31.
Fish Gate. 2 Chron. 33:14;
　Neh. 3:3.
Fountain Gate. Neh. 2:14; 3:15.
Gate of Ephraim. Neh. 12:39.
Gate of Miphkad. Neh. 3:31.
Horse Gate. 2 Chron. 23:15;
　Neh. 3:28.
Old Gate. Neh. 3:6; 12:39.
Sheep Gate. Neh. 3:1; John 5:2.
Valley Gate. 2 Chron. 26:29;
　Neh. 2:13.
Water Gate. Neh. 3:26; 8:3.
The law read at. Neh. 8.

Made of
　Brass. Ps. 107:16; Isa. 45:2.
　Iron. Acts 12:10.
　Wood. Neh. 1:3.

Made to
　Camps. Exod. 32:26.
　Cities. 1 Kings 17:10.

Houses. Luke 16:20; Acts 12:14.
Palaces. Esther 5:13.
Prisons. Acts 12:10.
Rivers. Nah. 2:6.
Temples. Acts 3:2.
Made of brass. Ps. 107:16;
　Isa. 45:2.
Made of iron. Acts 12:10.
Made of wood. Neh. 1:3.
Place for conferences on public
　affairs. Gen. 34:20.
Place for courts of justice.
　Deut. 16:18.
A place for idlers. Gen. 19:1.
Place for public business,
　announcements, and legal
　transactions. Gen. 23:10, 16.
Place for public speech. Gen. 23:10;
　Prov. 1:21.
Of the powers of hell. Matt. 16:18.
Punishment of criminals outside of.
　Deut. 17:5; Acts 7:58;
　Heb. 13:12.

Gate of Nicea, Bithynia

Religious services held at. Acts 14:3.
Of righteousness. Ps. 118:19.
Of salvation. Gen. 28:17;
    Ps. 24:7; 18:19, 20;
    Isa. 26:2; Matt. 7:13.
Symbolic sense.
    Rev. 21:12, 13, 21, 25.

Of the temple
    Called gates of righteousness.
        Ps. 118:19.
    Called gates of the Lord.
        Ps. 118:20.
    Called gates of Zion. Lam. 1:4.
    Charge of, given by lot.
        1 Chron. 26:13–19.
    Frequented by beggars. Acts 3:2.
    Levites the gatekeepers of.
        2 Chron. 8:14; 23:4.
    One specially beautiful. Acts 3:2.
    Overlaid with gold.
        2 Kings 18:16.
    Pious Israelites delighted to enter.
        Pss. 118:1–20; 100:4.
Thrones of kings at. 1 Kings 22:10.
Treasury placed at. 2 Chron. 24:8;
    Mark 12:41.

GEM CUTTER
One who cuts precious stones.
    Exod. 31:5 35:33.

**GENDERS, RELATIONSHIP
BETWEEN**
Be subject to one another.
    Eph. 5:21.
Mankind created male and female in
    image of God. Gen. 1:26–27;
    5:1–2.
Men and women equal as regards
    salvation. Gal. 3:28.
No partiality shown by God in
    salvation. Acts 10:34;
    Rom. 2:9–11.

One flesh in marriage. Gen. 2:24.
Partnership in childrearing.
    Prov. 1:8; Eph. 6:1–4; Col. 3:20.
Woman a coworker or enabler of
    man. Gen. 2:18.

Women in roles of responsibility
    Deborah. Judg. 4–5.
    Huldah. 2 Kings 22:12–20.
    Mary. Matt. 28:1–10.
    Miriam. Exod. 15:20; Mic. 6:4.
    Phoebe. Rom. 16:1.
    Priscilla. Rom. 16:3–4.
Virtuous woman. Prov. 31:10–31.

GENEALOGIES
Of Abraham, by his wife Keturah.
    Gen. 25:1–4; 1 Chron. 1:32–33.
To Abraham. Gen. 11:10–32;
    1 Chron. 1:4–27; Luke 3:34–38.
From Adam to Noah. Gen. 4:16–22;
    5; 1 Chron. 1:1–4;
    Luke 3:36–38.

Of Christ
    Given. Matt. 1:1–17;
        Luke 3:23–38.
    Test His descent from Judah.
        Heb. 7:14.
Of the descendants of Noah.
    Gen. 10.
Of Esau. Gen. 36;
    1 Chron. 1:35–54.
Illustrative of the record of believers
    in the book of life. Luke 10:20;
    Heb. 12:23; Rev. 3:5.
Of Ishmael. Gen. 25:12–16;
    1 Chron. 1:28–31.
Of Jacob. Gen. 35:23–26;
    Exod. 1:5; 6:14–27; Num. 26;
    1 Chron. 2–9.
The Jews reckoned by.
    1 Chron. 9:1; 2 Chron. 31:19.

Of the Jews who returned from the
captivity. Ezra 7:1–5; 8:1–15;
Neh. 7; 11:12.
Of Joseph. Matt. 1; Luke 3:23–38.
Of Nahor. Gen. 22:20–24.
Of no spiritual significance.
Matt. 3:9; 1 Tim. 1:4; Titus 3:9.
Of Pharez to David. Ruth 4:18–22.
Priests who could not prove their
own, excluded from the
priesthood. Ezra 2:62; Neh. 7:64.
Public registers kept of.
2 Chron. 12:15; Neh. 7:5.
Subject of, to be avoided.
1 Tim. 1:4; Titus 3:9.

GENEROSITY
Affirmed. 1 Chron. 29:14.
Blessings connected with. Ps. 41:1;
Prov. 22:9; Acts 20:35.
Characteristic of believers.
Ps. 112:9; Isa. 32:8.
Christ set an example of. 2 Cor. 8:9.
Commanded. Deut. 16:17;
2 Cor. 9:7.
Encouraged. Acts 20:35;
2 Cor. 8:7.
Exercise of, provokes others to.
2 Cor. 9:2.
Exhortations to. Luke 3:11; 11:41;
Acts 20:35; 1 Cor. 16:1;
1 Tim. 6:17–18.
Of God. Ps. 107:9; Rom. 8:32;
James 1:5.
God never forgets. Heb. 6:10.
Of Jesus. Acts 10:38; 2 Cor. 8:9.
Toward Jesus. Luke 8:3.
Labor to be enabled to exercise.
Acts 20:35; Eph. 4:28.

Lack of
Brings many a curse. Prov. 28:27.
A proof of not having faith.
James 2:14–16.

A proof of not loving God.
1 John 3:17.
Pleasing to God. 2 Cor. 9:7;
Heb. 13:16.
Promises to. Ps. 112:9;
Prov. 11:25; 28:27;
Eccles. 11:1–2; Isa. 58:10.

Should be exercised
Abundantly. 2 Cor. 8:7; 9:11–13.
According to ability. Deut. 16:10,
17; 1 Cor. 16:2.
Toward all men. Gal. 6:10.
Toward believers. Rom. 12:13;
Gal. 6:10.
Toward enemies. Prov. 25:21.
In forwarding missions.
Phil. 4:14–16.
In giving alms. Luke 12:33.
In lending to those in need.
Matt. 5:42.
Toward the poor. Deut. 15:11;
Isa. 58:7.
In relieving the destitute. Isa. 58:7.
In rendering personal services.
Phil. 2:30.
Toward servants.
Deut. 15:12–14.
In the service of God.
Exod. 35:21–29.
Without showiness. Matt. 6:1–3.
With simplicity. Rom. 12:8.
Toward strangers. Lev. 25:35.
Willingly. Exod. 25:2;
2 Cor. 8:12.
Rewarded. Prov. 19:17; 22:9;
28:27; Eccles. 11:1.
Unprofitable, without love.
1 Cor. 13:3.

GENIUS
Mechanical, a divine inspiration.
Exod. 28:3; 31:2–11; 35:30–35;
36:1.

GENOCIDE

See also War Crimes

Attempted in Persia. Esther 1–10.

GENTILES

All nations except the Jews.
Rom. 2:9; 3:9; 9:24.

Called
Greeks. Rom. 1:16; 10:12.
Heathen. Ps. 2:1; Gal. 3:8.
Nations. Pss. 9:20; 22:28;
Isa. 9:1.
Strangers. Isa. 14:1; 60:10.
Uncircumcised. 1 Sam. 14:6;
Isa. 52:1; Rom. 2:26.

Characterized as
Blasphemous and reproachful.
Neh. 5:9.
Constant to their false gods.
Jer. 2:11.
Depraved and wicked.
Rom. 1:28–32; Eph. 4:19.
Idolatrous. Rom. 1:23, 25;
1 Cor. 12:2.
Ignorant of God. Rom. 1:21;
1 Thess. 4:5.
Refusing to know God.
Rom. 1:28.
Superstitious. Deut. 18:14.
Without the law. Rom. 2:14
Christ given as a light to. Isa. 42:6;
Luke 2:32.
Conversion of, predicted. Isa. 2:2;
11:10.
Counsel of, ineffective. Ps. 33:10.
Excluded from Israel's privileges.
Eph. 2:11–12.
First general introduction of the
gospel to. Acts 13:48–49, 52;
15:12.

First special introduction of the
gospel to. Acts 10:34–45; 15:14.
Given to Christ as His inheritance.
Ps. 2:8.
The gospel not to be preached to,
until preached to the Jews.
Matt. 10:5; Luke 24:47;
Acts 13:46.
Hated and despised the Jews.
Esther 9:1, 5; Pss. 44:13–14;
123:3.
Israel rejected till the fullness of.
Rom. 11:25.
Jerusalem trodden down by, etc.
Luke 21:24.

The Jews
Despised, as if dogs. Matt. 15:26.
Dispersed among. John 7:35.
Never associated with.
Acts 10:28; 11:2–3.
Not to follow the ways of.
Lev. 18:3; Jer. 10:2.
Not to intermarry with. Deut. 7:3.
Often corrupted by.
2 Kings 17:7–8.
Permitted to have, as servants.
Lev. 25:44.
Not allowed to enter the temple.
Acts 21:28–29.
Often ravaged and defiled the holy
land and sanctuary. Ps. 79:1;
Lam. 1:10.
Outer court of temple for. Eph. 2:14;
Rev. 11:2.
Paul the apostle of. Acts 9:15;
Gal. 2:7–8.
Punished by God. Pss. 9:5; 94:10.
Ruled by God. 2 Chron. 20:6;
Ps. 47:8.
United with the Jews against Christ.
Acts 4:27.

GENTLENESS
Of Christ. Isa. 40:1; 42:3;
  2 Cor. 10:1; Matt. 18:2;
John 13:23.
Exhorted. Eph. 4:32; 1 Pet. 3:8;
  5:5.
Fruit of the Spirit. Gal. 5:22.
Mark of divine wisdom. James 3:17.

GEOLOGY
Foundations of the world.
  2 Sam. 22:16.
The Lord carved out rivers among
  the rocks. Job 28:9.
Pillars of the earth. 1 Sam. 2:8.

GIANTS
Inhabited the earth. Gen. 6:4.

GIDEON
Launched surprise attack against
  Midianites. Judg. 7:15–22.

GIFT OF THE HOLY SPIRIT
See Holy Spirit, Gift of the

GIFTS OF GOD
See God, Gifts of

GIRDLE
See Belt

GIVING
How. 2 Cor. 8:11; 9:6.
Rules for. Matt. 6:1.
When. 1 Cor. 16:2.

GLADIATOR
Contend with the wild beast.
  1 Cor. 15:32.

GLADNESS
Gift of God. Pss. 4:7; 30:11.

Should mark Christians. Matt. 5:12;
  Rev. 19:7.
Source of strength. Neh. 8:10.

GLASS
Symbolic sense. Rev. 21:18, 21.
Sea of. Rev. 15:2.

GLEANING

Example of
  Ruth in the field of Boaz.
    Ruth 2:2–3.
Laws concerning. Lev. 19:9–10;
  23:22; Deut. 24:19–20.
Used in a figurative sense. Judg. 8:2;
  Isa. 17:6; Jer. 49:9; Mic. 7:1.

GLORIFYING GOD
See God, Glorifying

GLORY
Believers desire to behold.
  Pss. 63:2; 90:16.
Believers will be, of their ministers.
  1 Thess. 2:19–20.
Bodies of believers will be raised in.
  1 Cor. 15:43; Phil. 3:21.
Christ is, to His people. Isa. 60:1;
  Luke 2:32.
Of the church will be rich and
  abundant. Isa. 60:11–13.

Eternal
  Accompanies salvation by Christ.
    2 Tim. 2:10.
  Believers called to. 2 Thess. 2:14;
    1 Pet. 5:10.
  Believers prepared for.
    Rom. 9:23.
  Enhanced by present afflictions.
    2 Cor. 4:17.

Inherited by believers. 1 Sam. 2:8;
Ps. 73:24; Prov. 3:35; Col. 3:4;
1 Pet. 5:10.

Present afflictions not worthy to be
compared with. Rom. 8:18.

Procured by the death of Christ.
Heb. 2:10.

God is to His people. Ps. 3:3;
Zech. 2:5.

Gospel ordained to be, to believers.
1 Cor. 2:7.

Of the gospel, exceeds that of the
law. 2 Cor. 3:9–10.

Of hypocrites turned to shame.
Hos. 4:7.

Joy of believers is full of. 1 Pet. 1:8.

Seek not, from persons. Matt. 6:2;
1 Thess. 2:6.

Spiritual

Is given by Christ. John 17:22.

Is given by God. Ps. 84:11.

Is the work of the Holy Spirit.
2 Cor. 3:18.

Temporal

The devil tries to seduce by.
Matt. 4:8.

Is given by God. Dan. 2:37.

Passes away. 1 Pet. 1:24.

Of the wicked

Ends in destruction. Isa. 5:14.

Is in their shame. Phil. 3:19.

GLORY, CLOUD OF

Called

The cloud. Exod. 34:5.

Cloud of the Lord. Num. 10:34.

Cloudy pillar. Exod. 33:9–10.

Pillar of cloud and pillar of fire.
Exod. 13:22.

The presence of God.
Exod. 33:14–15.

Christ will make His second
appearance in. Luke 21:27;
Acts 1:11.

Continued during the journeyings of
Israel. Exod. 13:22; 40:38.

First manifestation of.
Exod. 13:20–21.

God came down in. Exod. 34:5;
Num. 11:25.

God spoke from. Exod. 24:16;
Ps. 99:7.

God's glory manifested in.
Exod. 16:10; 40:35.

Illustrative of

The glory of Christ. Rev. 10:1.

The protection of the church.
Isa. 4:5.

Manifested in the temple of
Solomon. 1 Kings 8:10–11;
2 Chron. 5:13; Ezek. 10:4.

Special appearances of

At Christ's ascension. Acts 1:9.

At Christ's transfiguration.
Matt. 17:5.

At giving of the law.
Exod. 19:9, 16; 24:16–18.

At the murmuring for bread.
Exod. 16:10.

At the murmuring of Israel on
account of Korah's death.
Num. 16:42.

At the murmuring of Israel on
report of the spies. Num. 14:10.

At the rebellion of Korah, etc.
Num. 16:19.

At sedition of Aaron and Miriam.
Num. 12:5.

Was dark to the enemies of Israel.
Exod. 14:20.

Was designed to
  Cover the tabernacle.
    Exod. 40:34; Num. 9:15.
    Defend Israel. Exod. 14:19;
    Ps. 105:39.
    Guide Israel. Exod. 13:21;
    Neh. 9:19.
  Regulate the movements of Israel.
    Exod. 40:36–37;
    Num. 9:17–25.
  Show light to Israel. Pss. 78:14;
    105:39.
Was the Shekinah over the mercy
  seat. Lev. 16:2.

GLORY OF GOD
See God, Glory of

GLUTTONY
Caution against. Prov. 23:2–3;
  Luke 21:34; Rom. 13:13–14.
Christ falsely accused of.
  Matt. 11:19.
Commandment against.
  Rom. 13:13–14.
Consequences of. Prov. 23:21.
Danger of, illustrated.
  Luke 12:45–46.

Examples of
  Belshazzar. Dan. 5:1.
  Esau. Gen. 25:30–34;
    Heb. 12:16–17.
  Israel. Num. 11:4; Ps. 78:18.
  Sons of Eli. 1 Sam. 2:12–17.
Foolishness of. Luke 12:19–46.
Inconsistent in believers. 1 Pet. 4:3.

Leads to
  Poverty. Prov. 23:21.
  Worldly security. Isa. 22:13, with
    1 Cor. 15:32; Luke 12:19.
Pray against temptations to.
  Ps. 141:4.

Of princes, ruinous to their people.
  Eccles. 10:16–17.
Punishment of. Num. 11:33–34,
  with Ps. 78:31; Deut. 21:21;
  Amos 6:4, 7.
The wicked addicted to. Phil. 3:19;
  Jude 12.

GNASHING OF TEETH
See Teeth, Gnashing of

GOAD
See Prod

GOAT
Designated as one of the clean
  animals to be eaten. Deut. 14:4;
  Lev. 11:1–8.
Hair of, used for clothing.
  Num. 31:20.
Hair of ,used for curtains of the
  tabernacle. Exod. 26:7.
Hair of, used for pillows.
  1 Sam. 19:13.
Milk of, used for food. Prov. 27:27.
Should not be killed as an offering
  before it was eight days old.
  Lev. 22:27.
Used as a sacrifice by Abraham.
  Gen. 15:9.
Used by Gideon. Judg. 6:19.
Used by Manoah. Judg. 13:19.
Used for food. Gen. 27:9.
Used for the Paschal feast.
  Exod. 12:5; 2 Chron. 35:7.
Wild goats in Palestine. 1 Sam. 24:2;
  Ps. 104:18.
Young goat should not be cooked in
  its mother's milk. Exod. 23:19.

GOD
See also: God, Access to; God,
Anger of; God, Call of; God,

Goat of Aoudad

Goat

Chosen of; God, Communion with; God, Condescension of; God, Counsels and Purposes of; God, Delighting in; God, Devotion to; God, Disobedience to; God, Faithfulness of; God, Favor of; God, Forgetting; God, Forsaking; God, Gifts of; God, Glorifying; God, Glory of; God, Goodness of; God, Holiness of; God, House of; God, Ingratitude to; God, Joy of over His people; God, Justice of; God, Justification before; God, Kingdom of; God, Lamb of; God, Law of; God, Longsuffering of; God, Love of; God, Love to; God, Loving-kindness of; God, Mercy of; God, Messengers of; God, Obedience to; God, Power of; God, Promises of; God, Providence of; God, Rebellion against; God, Righteousness of; God, Sovereignty of; God, Submission to; God, Truth of; God, Unity of; God, Waiting upon; God, Walking with; God, Will of; God, Wisdom of; God, Voices of

Declared to be

Compassionate. 2 Kings 13:23.
A consuming fire. Heb. 12:29.
Eternal. Deut. 33:27; Ps. 90:2;
  Rev. 4:8–10.
Faithful. 1 Cor. 10:13;
  1 Pet. 4:19.
Glorious. Exod. 15:11; Ps. 145:5.
Good. Pss. 25:8; 119:68.
Gracious. Exod. 34:6; Ps. 116:5.
Great. 2 Chron. 2:5; Ps. 86:10.
Holy. Ps. 99:9; Isa. 5:16.
Immortal. 1 Tim. 1:17; 6:16.
Incorruptible. Rom. 1:23.
Invisible. Job 23:8, 9; John 1:18;
  5:37; Col. 1:15; 1 Tim. 1:17.
Jealous. Josh 24:19; Nah. 1:2.
Just. Deut. 32:4; Isa. 45:21.
Light. Isa. 60:19; James 1:17;
  1 John 1:5.
Long-suffering. Num. 14:18;
  Mic. 7:1.
Love. 1 John 4:8, 16.
Merciful. Exod. 34:6–7; Ps. 86:5.

Most High. Ps. 83:18; Acts 7:48.

Omnipotent (all-powerful).
Gen. 17:1; Exod. 6:3.

Omnipresent (ever-present).
Ps. 139:7; Jer. 23:23.

Omniscient (all-knowing).
Ps. 139:1–6; Prov. 5:21.

Only wise. Rom. 16:27;
1 Tim. 1:17.

Perfect. Matt. 5:48.

Righteous. Ezra 9:15;
Ps. 145:17.

True. Jer. 10:10; John 17:3.

Unsearchable. Job 11:7; 37:23;
Ps. 145:3; Isa. 40:28;
Rom. 11:33.

Upright. Pss. 25:8; 92:15.

Fills heaven and earth. 1 Kings 8:27;
Jer. 23:24.

None before Him. Isa. 43:10.

None beside Him. Deut. 4:35;
Isa. 44:6.

None good but He. Matt. 19:17.

None like Him. Exod. 9:14;
Deut. 33:26; 2 Sam. 7:22;
Isa. 46:5, 9; Jer. 10:6.

Should be worshiped in spirit and in truth. John 4:24.

A spirit. John 4:24; 2 Cor. 3:17.

Unchanging. Ps. 102:26–27;
James 1:17.

GOD, ACCESS TO

Believers earnestly seek.
Pss. 27:4; 42:1–2; 43:3; 84:1–2.

Believers have, with confidence.
Eph. 3:12; Heb. 4:16; 10:19, 22.

Blessedness of. Pss. 16:11; 65:4;
73:28.

Follows upon reconciliation to God.
Col. 1:21–22.

Granted to repenting sinners.
Hos. 14:2; Joel 2:12. (*See also* Repentance.)

In His temple.
Pss. 15:1; 27:4; 43:3; 65:4.

Is a privilege of believers. Deut. 4:7;
Pss. 15; 23:6; 24:3–4.

Is by Christ. John 10:7, 9; 14:6;
Rom. 5:2; Eph. 2:13; 3:12;
Heb. 7:19, 25; 10:19;
1 Pet. 3:18.

Is by the Holy Spirit. Eph. 2:18.

Is of God. Ps. 65:4.

To obtain mercy end grace.
Heb. 4:16.

Obtained through faith. Acts 14:27;
Rom. 5:2; Eph. 3:12; Heb. 11:6.

In prayer. Deut. 4:7; Matt. 6:6;
1 Pet. 1:17; (*See also* Prayer.)

Promises connected with.
Ps. 145:18; Isa. 55:3; Matt. 6:6;
James 4:8.

Typified. Lev. 16:12–15, with
Heb. 10:19–22.

Urge others to seek. Isa. 2:3;
Jer. 31:6.

Wicked commanded to seek.
Isa. 55:6; James 4:8.

GOD, ANGER OF

Against
Apostasy. Heb. 10:26–27.

Idolatry. Deut. 29:20, 27–28;
32:19–20, 22; Josh. 23:16;
2 Kings 22:17; Ps. 78:58–59;
Jer. 44:3.

Refusal to repent, unrepentant.
Ps. 7:12; Prov. 1:30–31;
Isa. 9:13–14; Rom. 2:5.

Sin, in believers.
Pss. 89:30–32; 90:7–9; 99:8;
102:9–10; Isa. 47:6.

Those who forsake Him.
Ezra 8:22; Isa. 1:4.
Those who oppose the gospel,
extreme. Ps. 2:2–3, 5;
1 Thess. 2:16.
Unbelief. Ps. 78:21–22;
John 3:36. Heb. 3:18–19.
The wicked. Pss. 7:11; 21:8–9;
Isa. 3:8; 13:9; Nah. 1:2–3;
Rom. 1:18; 2:8; Eph. 5:6;
Col. 3:6.
Aggravated by continual
provocation. Num. 32:14.
Cannot be resisted. Job 9:13; 14:13;
Ps. 76:7; Nah. 1:6.
Folly of provoking. Jer. 7:19;
1 Cor. 10:22.
Justice of, not to be questioned.
Rom. 9:18, 20, 22.
Manifested in judgments and
afflictions. Job 21:17;
Pss. 78:49–51; 90:7; Isa. 9:19;
Jer. 7:20; Ezek. 7:19; Heb. 3:17.
Manifested in terrors. Exod. 14:24;
Ps. 76:6–8; Jer. 10:10;
Lam. 2:20–22.
Removal of, should be prayed for.
Pss. 39:10; 79:5; 80:4;
Dan. 9:16; Hab. 3:2.
Righteous. Ps. 58:10–11;
Lam. 1:18; Rom. 2:6, 8; 3:5–6;
Rev. 16:6–7.
To seek to be avoided. Exod. 32:11;
Pss. 6:1; 38:1; 74:1–2; Isa. 64:9.
Should lead to repentance.
Isa. 42:24–25; Jer. 4:8.
Slow. Ps. 103:8; Isa. 48:9; Jon. 4:2;
Nah. 1:3.
Specially reserved for the day of
wrath. Zeph. 1:14–18;
Matt. 25:41; Rom. 2:5, 8;
2 Thess. 1:8; Rev. 6:17; 11:18;
19:15.

Tempered with mercy to believers.
Ps. 30:5; Isa. 26:20; 54:8;
57:15–16; Jer. 30:11; Mic. 7:11.
To be borne with submission.
2 Sam. 24:17; Lam. 3:39, 43;
Mic. 7:9.
To be dreaded. Pss. 2:12; 76:7;
90:11; Matt. 10:28.

Turned away
By Christ. Luke 2:11, 14;
Rom. 5:9; 2 Cor. 5:18–19;
Eph. 2:14, 17; Col. 1:20;
1 Thess. 1:10.
From them that believe.
John 3:14–18; Rom. 3:25; 5:1.
Upon confession of sin and
repentance. Job 33:27–28;
Ps. 106:43–45; Jer. 3:12–13;
18:7–8; 31:18–20;
Joel 2:12–14; Luke 15:18–20.

GOD, CALL OF

Addressed to all. Isa. 45:22;
Matt. 20:16.
Blessedness of receiving. Rev. 19:9.
By Christ. Isa. 55:5; Rom. 1:6.
Effectual to believers. Ps. 110:3;
Acts 2:47; 13:48; 1 Cor. 1:21.
By His gospel. 2 Thess. 2:14.
By His ministers. Jer. 35:15;
2 Cor. 5:20.
By His Spirit. Rev. 22:17.
By His works. Ps. 19:2–3;
Rom. 1:20.
Illustrated. Prov. 9:3–4;
Matt. 23:3–9.
Is from darkness. 1 Pet. 2:9.

To man is
According to the purpose of God.
Rom. 8:28; 9:11, 23–24.
To the eternal glory of Christ.
2 Thess. 2:14; 1 Pet. 5:10.

To eternal life. 1 Tim. 6:12.
To fellowship with Christ.
  1 Cor. 1:9.
To glory and virtue. 2 Pet. 1:3.
Heavenly. Heb. 3:1.
High. Phil. 3:14.
To holiness. 1 Thess. 4:7.
Holy. 1 Tim. 1:19.
Of grace. Gal. 1:15; 2 Tim. 1:9.
To liberty. Gal. 5:13.
To peace. 1 Cor. 7:15; Col. 3:15.
Walk worthy of. Eph. 4:1.
Most reject. Prov. 1:24;
  Matt. 20:16.

Its rejection leads to
  Condemnation. John 12:48;
    Heb. 2:1–3; 12:25.
  Delusion. Isa. 66:4;
    2 Thess. 2:10–11.
  Destruction. Prov. 29:1;
    Matt. 22:3–7.
  Judicial blindness. Isa. 6:9; with
    Acts 28:24–27; Rom. 11:8–10.
  Rejection by God. Prov. 1:24–32;
    Jer. 6:19, 30.
  Partakers of, justified. Rom. 8:30.
  Praise God for. 1 Pet. 2:9.
  Temporal judgments. Isa. 28:12;
    Jer. 6:16, 19; 35:17;
    Zech. 7:12–14.
  Withdrawal of the means of grace.
    Jer. 26:4–6; Acts 13:46; 18:6;
    Rev. 2:5.

GOD, CHOSEN OF

In Christ. John 15:16; Rom. 1:6;
  Gal. 1:1.
By grace. Deut. 7:7; Eph. 2:1–10.
For holiness. Num. 16:7; Eph. 1:4.
Separated for service. 1 Pet. 2:9.
Through the Spirit. 1 Pet. 1:2.

GOD, COMMUNION WITH

Believers
  Desire. Ps. 42:1; Phil. 1:23.
  Have, in the Lord's Supper.
    1 Cor. 10:16.
  Have, in meditation. Ps. 63:5–6.
  Have, in prayer. Phil. 4:6;
    Heb. 4:16.
  Should always enjoy. Ps. 16:8;
    John 14:16–18.
Holiness essential to.
  2 Cor. 6:14–16.
Is communion with the Father.
  1 John 1:3.
Is communion with the Holy Spirit.
  1 Cor. 12:13; 2 Cor. 13:14;
  Phil. 2:1.
Is communion with the Son.
  1 Cor. 1:9; 1 John 1:3;
  Rev. 3:20.
Promised to the obedient.
  John 14:23.
Reconciliation must precede.
  Amos 3:3.

GOD, CONDESCENSION OF

Enters into convenant with Abraham.
  Gen. 15:11–21; 18:1–22.
Indulges Abraham's intercession for
  Sodom. Gen. 18:23–33.
Indulges Gideon's test.
  Judg. 6:36–40.
Indulges Moses' prayer to behold His
  glory. Exod. 33:18–23.
Invites sinners. Isa. 1:18–20.
Reasons with backsliding Israel.
  Isa. 41:21–24; Jer. 3:1–15;
  Ezek. 18:25–32; Hos. 2;
  Mic. 6:1–9; Mal. 3:7–15.
Reasons with Job.
  Job 38; 39; 40; 41.
Reasons with Moses. Exod. 4:2–17.

Sends flesh to the Israelites in the desert. Exod. 16:12.

Sets forth His reasons for sending the flood. Gen. 6:11–13.

Warns Abimelech in a dream. Gen. 20:3–7.

GOD, COUNSELS AND PURPOSES OF

Are

Eternal. Eph. 3:11.

Faithfulness and truth. Isa. 25:1.

Great. Jer. 32:19.

Immutable. Ps. 33:11; Prov. 19:21; Jer. 4:28; Rom. 9:11; Heb. 6:17.

Sovereign. Isa. 40:13–14; Dan. 4:35.

Wonderful. Isa. 28:29.

Attend to. Jer. 49:20; 50:45.

Believers called and saved according to. Rom. 8:28; 2 Tim. 1:9.

None can annul, cancel. Isa. 14:27.

Secret not to be searched into. Deut. 29:29; Matt. 24:36; Acts 1:7.

Should be declared by ministers. Acts 20:27.

Sufferings and death of Christ were according to. Acts 2:23; 4:28.

Union of all believers in Christ is according to. Eph. 1:9–10.

The wicked

Despise. Isa. 5:19.

Do not understand. Mic. 4:12.

Reject. Luke 7:30.

Will be performed. Isa. 14:24; 46:11.

Works of God are according to. Eph. 1:11.

GOD, DELIGHTING IN

Believers, experience in

The comforts of God. Ps. 94:19.

Communion with God. Song of Sol. 2:3.

The goodness of God. Neh. 9:25.

The law of God. Pss. 1:2; 119:24, 35.

Commanded. Ps. 37:4.

Hypocrites

Blessedness of. Ps. 112:1.

In heart despise. Job 27:10; Jer. 6:10.

Pretend to. Isa. 58:2.

Promises to. Ps. 37:4.

Observing the Sabbath leads to. Isa. 58:13–14.

Reconciliation leads to. Job 22:21, 26.

GOD, DEVOTION TO

A characteristic of believers. Job 23:12.

Christ an example of. John 4:34; 17:4.

Grounded upon

The call of God. 1 Thess. 2:12.

The death of Christ. 2 Cor. 5:15.

The goodness of God. 1 Sam. 12:24.

The mercies of God. Rom. 12:1.

Our creation. Ps. 86:9.

Our preservation. Isa. 46:4.

Our redemption. 1 Cor. 6:19–20.

Lack of condemned. Rev. 3:16.

Should be

Abounding. 1 Thess. 4:1.

In life and death. Rom. 14:8; Phil. 1:20.

Persevering. Luke 1:74–75; 9:62.

Unreserved. Matt. 6:24;
Luke 14:33.

With our bodies. Rom. 6:12, 13;
12:1; 1 Cor. 6:20; 1 Pet. 4:2.

With our spirit. 1 Cor. 6:20;
1 Pet. 4:6.

With our substance. Exod. 22:29;
Prov. 3:9.

Should be exhibited

Bearing the cross. Mark 8:34.

Doing all to God's glory.
1 Cor. 10:31.

Giving up all for Christ.
Matt. 19:21, 28–29.

Living to Christ. 2 Cor. 5:15.

Loving God. Deut. 6:5;
Luke 10:27.

Self-denial. Mark 8:34.

Serving God. 1 Sam. 12:24;
Rom. 12:11.

Walking worthy of God.
1 Thess. 2:12.

GOD, DISOBEDIENCE TO

Acknowledge the punishment of, to
be just. Neh. 9:32–33;
Dan. 9:10–11, 14.

Bitter results of, illustrated. Jer. 9:13,
15.

Brings a curse. Deut. 11:28; 28:15,
etc.

A characteristic of the wicked.
Eph. 2:2; Titus 1:16; 3:3.

Examples of

Aaron, at the striking of the rock
by Moses. Num. 20:23–24.

Achan, in hiding the wedge of
gold. Josh. 7:15–26.

Adam and Eve, eating the
forbidden fruit. Gen. 3:6–11.

Ahab, in allowing the king of Syria
to escape out of his hands.
1 Kings 20:42.

Balaam, in accompanying the
messengers from Balak.
Num. 22:22.

The blind men Jesus healed and
commanded not to disclose their
healing. Matt. 9:30–31.

The children of Israel, in refusing
to enter the promised land.
Deut. 1:26.

The children of Israel, in gathering
excessive quantities of manna.
Exod. 16:19–20.

David, in his adultery, and in the
slaying of Uriah. 2 Sam. 12:9.

Jonah, in refusing to deliver the
message to the Ninevites.
Jon. 1.

The leper whom Jesus healed and
commanded not to let people
know about it. Mark 1:45.

Lot, in refusing to go to the
mountain as commanded by the
angels. Gen. 19:19–20.

Lot's wife, in looking back upon
Sodom. Gen. 19:26.

A man of Israel, who refused to
smite the prophet.
1 Kings 20:35–36.

Moses, in making excuses when
commissioned to deliver Israel.
Exod. 4:13–14.

Moses, when he struck the rock.
Num. 20:11, 23–24.

Nadab and Abihu, in offering
strange fire. Lev. 10:1–2.

Paul, in going to Jerusalem
contrary to repeated
admonition. Acts 21:4, 10–14.

The people of Judah, in going to dwell in Egypt contrary to divine commandment. Jer. 44:12–14.

Pharaoh, in refusing to let the children of Israel go. Exod. 5:2; 7:13, 22, 23; 8:15, 19, 32; 9:12, 34; 10:20, 27; 11:10; 14:8.

Priests, in not performing their functions after the due order. 1 Chron. 15:13.

The prophet of Judah, in not keeping the commandment to deliver his message to Jeroboam without delay. 1 Kings 13.

Saul, in offering a sacrifice. 1 Sam. 13:13.

Saul, in sparing Agag and the spoils of the Amalekites. 1 Sam. 15; 28:18.

Solomon, in building places for idolatrous worship. 1 Kings 11:7–10.

Forfeits his favor. 1 Sam. 13:14.

Forfeits his promised blessings. Josh. 5:6; 1 Sam. 2:30; Jer. 18:10.

Heinousness of, illustrated. Jer. 35:14, etc.

Humans prone to excuse. Gen. 3:12–13.

Provokes His anger. Ps. 78:10, 40; Isa. 3:8.

Will be punished. Isa. 42:24, 25; Heb. 2:2.

Warnings against. Deut. 28:15–68; 1 Sam. 12:15; Jer. 12:17.

The wicked persevere in. Jer. 22:21.

GOD, FAITHFULNESS OF

Believers encouraged to depend on. 1 Pet. 4:19.

Declared to be
Established. Ps. 89:2.
Everlasting. Pss. 119:90; 146:6.
Great. Lam. 3:23.
Incomparable. Ps. 89:8.
Infinite. Ps. 36:5.
Unfailing. Ps. 89:33; 2 Tim. 2:13.

Manifested
In afflicting believers. Ps. 119:75.
In executing His judgments. Jer. 23:20; 51:29.
In forgiving sins. 1 John 1:9.
In fulfilling His promises. 1 Kings 8:20; Ps. 132:11; Mic. 7:20; Heb. 10:23.
In His counsels. Isa. 25:1.
In His testimonies. Ps. 119:138.
In keeping His covenant. Deut. 7:9; Ps. 111:5.
To His believers. Ps. 89:24; 2 Thess. 3:3.
Part of His character. Isa. 49:7; 1 Cor. 1:9; 1 Thess. 5:24.

Should be
Magnified. Pss. 89:5; 92:2.
Pleaded in prayer. Ps. 143:1.
Proclaimed. Pss. 40:10; 89:1.

GOD, FAVOR OF

To be acknowledged. Ps. 85:1.

Believers
Encompassed by. Ps. 5:12.
Exalted in. Ps. 89:17.
Obtain. Prov. 12:2.
Preserved through. Job 10:12.
Sometimes tempted to doubt. Ps. 77:7.
Strengthened by. Ps. 30:7.
Victorious through. Ps. 44:3.

Christ the special object of.
Luke 2:52.
Disappointment of enemies an
assured evidence of. Ps. 41:11.
Domestic blessings traced to.
Prov. 18:22.
Given in answer to prayer.
Job 33:26.
Mercy and truth lead to.
Prov. 3:3–4.
Plead, in prayer. Exod. 33:13;
Num. 11:15.
Pray for. Pss. 106:4; 119:58.

The source of
Mercy. Isa. 60:10.
Spiritual life. Ps. 30:5.
Spiritual wisdom leads to.
Prov. 8:35.

The Wicked
Do not obtain. Isa. 27:11;
Jer. 16:13.
Uninfluenced by. Isa. 26:10.

GOD, FORGETTING

Backsliders are guilty of.
Jer. 3:21–22.
Cautions against. Deut. 6:12; 8:11.
A characteristic of the wicked.
Prov. 2:17; Isa. 65:11.
Encouraged by false teachers.
Jer. 23:27.
Exhortation to those guilty of.
Ps. 50:22.

Is forgetting His
Benefits. Pss. 103:2; 106:7.
Church. Ps. 137:5.
Covenant. Deut. 4:23;
2 Kings 17:38.
Law. Ps. 119:153, 176;
Hos. 4:6.

Past deliverance. Judg. 8:34;
Ps. 78:42.
Power to deliver. Isa. 51:13–15.
Word. Heb. 12:5; James 1:25.
Works. Pss. 78:7, 11; 106:13.
Prosperity often leads to.
Deut. 8:12–14; Hos. 13:6.
Punishment of. Job 8:12–13;
Ps. 9:17; Isa. 17:10–11;
Ezek. 23:35; Hos. 8:14.
Resolve against. Ps. 119:16, 93.
Trials should not lead to.
Ps. 44:17–20.

GOD, FORSAKING

Backsliders guilty of. Jer. 15:6.
Brings confusion. Jer. 17:13.
Brings down His wrath. Ezra 8:22.
Curse pronounced upon. Jer. 17:5.
Followed by remorse. Ezek. 6:9.
Idolaters guilty of. 1 Sam. 8:8;
1 Kings 11:33.

Is forsaking
His commandments. Ezra 9:10.
His covenant. Deut. 29:25;
1 Kings 19:10; Jer. 22:9;
Dan. 11:30.
His house. 2 Chron. 29:6.
The right way. 2 Pet. 2:15.
Leads people to follow their own
devices. Jer. 2:13.
Prosperity tempts to. Deut. 31:20;
32:15.
Provokes God to forsake humankind.
Judg. 10:13; 2 Chron. 15:2;
24:20, 24.
Punishment of. Deut. 28:20;
2 Kings 22:16–17; Isa. 1:28;
Jer. 1:16; 5:19.
Resolve against. Josh 24:16;
Neh. 10:29–30.
Sin of, to be confessed. Ezra 9:10.
Trusting in humankind is. Jer. 17:5.

Unreasonableness and ingratitude of.
Jer. 2:5–6.
Warnings against. Josh 24:20;
1 Chron. 28:9.
The wicked guilty of. Deut. 28:20.
Wickedness of. Jer. 2:13; 5:7.

GOD, GIFTS OF
All blessings. James 1:17;
2 Pet. 1:3.
Dispensed according to His will.
Eccles. 2:26; Dan. 2:21;
Rom. 12:6; 1 Cor. 7:7.
Free and abundant. Num. 14:8;
Rom. 8:32.
Illustrated. Matt. 25:15–30.

Spiritual
Acknowledge. Pss. 4:7; 21:2.
Are through Christ. Ps. 68:18,
with Eph. 4:7–8; John 6:27.
Christ the chief of. Isa. 42:6;
55:4; John 3:16; 4:10;
6:32–33.
Eternal life. Rom. 6:23.
Faith. Eph. 2:8; Phil. 1:29.
Glory. Ps. 84:11; John 17:22.
Grace. Ps. 84:11; James 4:6.
The Holy Spirit. Luke 11:3;
Acts 8:20.
A new heart. Ezek. 11:19.
Not regretted by Him.
Rom. 11:29.
Peace. Ps. 29:11.
Pray for. Matt. 7:7, 11;
John 16:23–24.
Repentance. Acts 11:18.
Rest. Matt. 11:28; 2 Thess. 1:7.
Righteousness. Rom. 5:16–17.
Strength and power. Ps. 68:35.
To be used for mutual profit.
1 Pet. 4:10.
Wisdom. Prov. 2:6; James 1:5.

Temporal
All creatures partake of.
Pss. 136:25; 145:15–16.
All good things. Ps. 34:10;
1 Tim. 6:17.
Food and clothing.
Matt. 6:25–33.
Life. Isa. 42:5.
Peace. Lev. 26:6; 1 Chron. 22:9.
Pray for. Zech. 10:1; Matt. 6:11.
Rain and fruitful seasons.
Gen. 27:28; Lev. 26:4–5;
Isa. 30:23.
Should cause us to remember God.
Deut. 8:18.
To be used and enjoyed.
Eccles. 3:13; 5:19–20;
1 Tim. 4:4–5.
Wisdom. 2 Cor. 1:12.

GOD, GLORIFYING
Acceptable through Christ.
Phil. 1:11; 1 Pet. 4:11.

Accomplished by
Bringing forth fruits of
righteousness. John 15:8;
Phil. 1:11.
Confessing Christ. Phil. 2:11.
Doing all to Him. 1 Cor. 10:31.
Dying for Him. John 21:19.
Faithfulness. 1 Pet. 4:11.
Glorifying Christ. Acts 19:17;
2 Thess. 1:12.
Patience in affliction. Isa. 24:15.
Praising Him. Ps. 50:23.
Relying on His promises.
Rom. 4:20.
Suffering for Christ.
1 Pet. 4:14, 16.
All by nature fail in. Rom. 3:23.

Believers should
Persevere in. Ps. 86:12.

Resolve on. Pss. 69:30; 118:28.
Unite in. Ps. 34:3; Rom. 15:6.
Blessings of God lead to. Isa. 60:21;
61:3.
Christ an example of. John 17:4.
Commanded. 1 Chron. 16:28;
Ps. 22:23; Isa. 42:12.
Due to Him. 1 Chron. 16:29.

For His
Deliverance. Ps. 50:15.
Faithfulness and truth. Isa. 25:1.
Grace to others. Acts 11:18;
2 Cor. 9:13; Gal. 1:24.
Holiness. Ps. 99:9; Rev. 15:4.
Judgments. Isa. 25:3;
Ezek. 28:22; Rev. 14:7.
Mercy and truth. Ps. 115:1;
Rom. 15:9.
Wondrous works. Matt. 15:31;
Acts 4:21.
Heavenly hosts engaged in.
Rev. 4:11.
Holy example of believers may lead
others to. Matt. 5:16; 1 Pet. 2:12.
Obligation of believers to.
1 Cor. 6:20.
Punishment for not. Dan. 5:23, 30;
Mal. 2:2; Acts 12:23; Rom. 1:21.
Required in body and spirit.
1 Cor. 6:20.
Will be universal. Ps. 86:9;
Rev. 5:13.
The wicked averse to. Dan. 5:23;
Rom. 1:21.

GOD, GLORY OF

Believers desire to behold. Pss. 63:2;
90:16.

Described as
Eternal. Ps. 104:31.
Great. Ps. 138:5.
Highly exalted. Pss. 8:1; 113:4.

Rich. Eph. 3:16.
Earth is full of. Isa. 6:3.
Enlightens the church. Isa. 60:1-2;
Rev. 21:11, 23.
Exhibited in Christ. John 1:14;
2 Cor. 4:6; Heb. 1:3.

Exhibited in His
Holiness. Exod. 15:11.
Majesty. Job 37:22;
Pss. 93:1; 104:1; 145:5, 12;
Isa. 2:10.
Name. Deut. 28:58; Neh. 9:5.
Power. Exod. 15:1, 6; Rom. 6:4.
Works. Pss. 19:1; 111:3.

Exhibited to
His church. Deut. 5:24;
Ps. 102:16.
Moses. Exod. 34:5-7, with
33:18-23.
Stephen. Acts 7:55.
God jealous of. Isa. 42:8.
Knowledge of will fill the earth.
Hab. 2:14.

People to
Declare. 1 Chron. 16:24;
Ps. 145:5, 11.
Magnify. Ps. 57:5.
Plead in prayer. Ps. 79:9.
Reverence. Isa. 59:19.

GOD, GOODNESS OF

Declared to be
Abundant. Exod. 34:6; Ps. 33:5.
Despise not. Rom. 2:4.
Enduring. Pss. 23:6; 52:1.
Great. Neh. 9:35; Zech. 9:17.
Leads to repentance. Rom. 2:4.
Magnify. Ps. 107:8; Jer. 33:11.
Rich. Ps. 104:24; Rom. 2:4.
Satisfying. Ps. 65:4;
Jer. 31:12, 14.

Universal. Ps. 145:9; Matt. 5:45.

Manifested
In doing good. Pss. 119:68;
145:9.
In forgiving sins. 2 Chron. 30:18;
Ps. 86:5.
To His church. Ps. 31:19;
Lam. 3:25.
In providing for the poor.
Ps. 68:10.
In supplying temporary needs.
Acts 14:17.
Part of His character. Ps. 25:8;
Nah. 1:7; Matt. 19:17.
Pray for the manifestation of.
2 Thess. 1:11.
Recognize, in His dealings.
Ezra 8:18; Neh. 2:18.
Reverence. Jer. 33:9; Hos. 3:5.
Urge others to confide in. Ps. 34:8.
The wicked disregard. Neh. 9:35.

GOD, HOLINESS OF
Believers are commanded to imitate.
Lev. 11:44, with 1 Pet. 1:15–16.
Believers should praise. Ps. 30:4.

Exhibited in
His character. Ps. 22:3;
John 17:11.
Kingdom. Ps. 47:8; Matt. 13:41;
1 Cor. 6:9–10; Rev. 21:27.
Name. Isa. 57:15, Luke 1:49.
Words. Ps. 60:6; Jer. 23:9
Works. Ps. 145:17.
Heavenly hosts adore. Isa. 6:3;
Rev. 4:8.
Incomparable. Exod. 15:11;
1 Sam. 2:2.

Pledged for the fulfillment of His
Judgments. Amos 4:2.
Promises. Ps. 89:35.

Requires holy service. Josh. 24:19;
Ps. 93:5.
Should be magnified.
1 Chron. 16:10;
Pss. 48:1; 99:3, 5; Rev. 15:4.
Should produce reverential fear.
Rev. 15:4.

GOD, HOUSE OF
A place of prayer. Matt. 21:13;
Mark 11:17; Luke 19:46.
Holy. Eccles. 5:1; Isa. 62:9;
Ezek. 43:12; 1 Cor. 3:17.

GOD, INGRATITUDE TO
A characteristic of the wicked.
Rom. 1:21.
Exceeding folly of. Deut. 32:6.
Guilt of. Ps. 106:7, 21;
Jer. 2:11–13.
Illustrated. Isa. 5:1–7;
Ezek. 16:1–15.
Inexcusable. Isa. 1:2–3; Rom. 1:21.
Prosperity likely to produce.
Deut. 31:20; 32:15; Jer. 5:7–11.
Punishment of. Neh. 9:20–27;
Hos. 2:8–9.
Unreasonable. Jer. 5:5–6, 31;
Mic. 6:2–3.
Warnings against. Deut. 8:11–14;
1 Sam. 12:24–25.

GOD, JOY OF, OVER HIS PEOPLE
On account of their
Faith. Heb. 11:5–6.
Fear of Him. Ps. 147:11.
Hope in His mercy. Ps. 147:11.
Meekness. Ps. 149:4.
Praying to Him. Prov. 15:8.
Repentance. Luke 15:7, 10.
Uprightness. 1 Chron. 29:17;
Prov. 11:20.

Greatness of, described. Zeph. 3:17.
Illustrated. Isa. 62:5;
Luke 15:23–24.

Leads Him to
Comfort them. Isa. 65:19.
Deliver them. 2 Sam. 22:20.
Do them good. Deut. 28:63;
Jer. 32:41.
Give them the inheritance.
Num. 14:8.
Prosper them. Deut. 30:9.

GOD, JUSTICE OF
Acknowledge. Ps. 51:4, with
Rom. 3:4.

Declared to be
The habitation of His throne.
Ps. 89:14.
Impartial. 2 Chron. 19:7;
Jer. 32:19.
Incomparable. Job 4:1.
Incorruptible. Deut. 10:17;
2 Chron. 19:7.
Plenteous. Job 37:23.
Undeviating. Job 8:3; 34:12.
Unfailing. Zeph. 3:5.
Without favoritism. Rom. 2:11;
Col. 3:25; 1 Pet. 1:17.
Denied by the ungodly. Ezek.
33:17, 20.

Exhibited in
All His ways. Ezek. 18:25, 29.
The final judgment. Acts 17:31.
Forgiving sins. 1 John 1:9.
His government. Ps. 9:4;
Jer. 9:24.
His judgments. Gen. 18:25;
Rev. 19:2.
Redemption. Rom. 3:26.
Magnify. Pss. 98:9; 99:3–4.
Not to be sinned against. Jer. 50:7.

A part of His character. Deut. 32:4;
Isa. 45:21.

GOD, JUSTIFICATION BEFORE
The act of God. Isa. 50:8;
Rom. 8:33.

By faith
Does not make void the law.
Rom. 3:30–31; 1 Cor. 9:21.
Excludes boasting. Rom. 3:27;
4:2; 1 Cor. 1:29–31.
Revealed in the Old Testament.
Hab. 2:4, with Rom. 1:17.

Under the gospel
Blessedness of. Ps. 32:1–2, with
Rom. 4:6–8.
By the blood of Christ. Rom. 5:9.
By imputation of Christ's
righteousness. Isa. 61:10;
Jer. 23:6; Rom. 3:22; 5:18;
1 Cor. 1:30; 2 Cor. 5:21.
Ensures glorification. Rom. 8:30.
Entitles to an inheritance.
Titus 3:7.
Frees from condemnation.
Isa. 50:8–9; 54:17, with
Rom. 8:33–34.
Is by faith alone. John 5:24;
Acts 13:39; Rom. 3:30; 5:1;
Gal. 2:16.
Is not of faith and works united.
Acts 15:1–29; Rom. 3:28;
11:6; Gal. 2:14–21; 5:4.
Is not of works. Acts 13:39;
Rom. 8:3; Gal. 2:16; 3:11.
Is of grace. Rom. 3:24; 4:16;
5:17–21.
In the name of Christ.
1 Cor. 6:11.
By the resurrection of Christ.
Rom. 4:25; 1 Cor. 15:17.

Under the law
  Persons cannot attain to.
    Job 9:2–3, 20; 25:4;
    Pss. 130:3; 143:2, with
    Rom. 3:20; Rom. 9:31–32.
  Requires perfect obedience.
    Lev. 18:5, with Rom. 10:5;
    2:13; James 2:10.
Promised to Christ. Isa. 45:25;
  53:11.
The wicked will not attain to.
  Exod. 23:7.

GOD, KINGDOM OF
Announced. Matt. 3:2; 4:23.
Compared to growing things.
  Mark 4:1–11, 26–32.
A future certainty. Matt. 6:10;
  Luke 22:16; 1 Cor. 6:9.
A present reality. Luke 17:21;
  Col. 1:13.
Promised. Dan. 2:44.

GOD, LAMB OF
A designation for of Jesus.
  John 1:29; Rev. 22:1, 3.

GOD, LAW OF
Absolute and perpetual. Matt. 5:18.
All men have transgressed.
  Rom. 3:9, 19.

Believers
  Delight in. Ps. 119:77;
    Rom. 7:22.
  Freed from the bondage of.
    Rom. 6:14; 7:4, 6; Gal. 3:13.
  Freed from the curse of.
    Gal. 3:13.
  Have written on their hearts.
    Jer. 31:33, with Heb. 8:10.
  Keep. Ps. 119:55.
  Love. Ps. 119:97, 113.

  Pledge themselves to walk in.
    Neh. 10:29.
  Pray for power to keep.
    Ps. 119:34.
  Pray to understand. Ps. 119:18.
  Prepare their hearts to seek.
    Ezra 7:10.
  Should make the subject of their
    conversation. Exod. 13:9.
  Should remember. Mal. 4:4.
  Sorrow over the violation of by
    others. Ps. 119:136.
Blessedness of keeping. Ps. 119:1;
  Matt. 5:19; 1 John 3:22, 24;
  Rev. 22:14.

Christ
  Came to fulfill. Matt. 5:17.
  Explained. Matt. 7:12; 22:37–40.
  Magnified. Isa. 42:21.
Conscience testifies to. Rom. 2:15.

Described as
  Exceedingly broad. Ps. 119:96.
  Holy, just, and good. Rom. 7:12.
  Not grievous. 1 John 5:3.
  Perfect. Ps. 19:7; Rom. 12:2.
  Pure. Ps. 19:8.
  Spiritual. Rom. 7:14.
  Truth. Ps. 119:142.
Designed to lead to Christ.
  Gal. 3:24.
Established by faith. Rom. 3:31.

Given
  To Adam. Gen. 2:16–17, with
    Rom. 5:12–14.
  To the Israelites. Exod. 20:2, etc.;
    Ps. 78:5.
  Through the ministry of angels.
    Acts 7:53; Gal. 3:19; Heb. 2:2.
  Through Moses. Exod. 31:18;
    John 7:19.
  To Noah. Gen. 9:6.

Gives the knowledge of sin.
Rom. 3:20; 7:7.
Humans by nature not in subjection
to. Rom. 7:5; 8:7.
Humans cannot be justified by.
Acts 13:39; Rom. 3:20, 28;
Gal. 2:16; 3:11.
Humans cannot render perfect
obedience to. 1 Kings 8:46;
Eccles. 7:20; Rom. 3:10.
Humans have duty to keep.
Eccles. 12:13.
Love of, produces peace.
Ps. 119:165.
Love the fulfilling of. Rom. 13:8, 10;
Gal. 5:14; James 2:8.

Obedience to
A characteristic of believers.
Rev. 12:17.
Of prime importance.
1 Cor. 7:19.
A test of love. 1 John 5:3.
Punishment for disobeying.
Neh. 9:26–27; Isa. 65:11–13;
Jer. 9:13–16.

Requires
Obedience of the heart. Ps. 51:6;
Matt. 5:28; 22:37.
Perfect obedience. Deut. 27:26;
Gal. 3:10 James 2:10.
The rule of life to believers.
1 Cor. 9:21; Gal. 5:13–14.
The rule of the judgment.
Rom. 2:12.
Sin is a transgression of. 1 John 3:4.
To be used lawfully. 1 Tim. 1:8.

The wicked
Brings punishment. Rom. 4:15.
Cast away. Isa. 5:24.
Despise. Amos 2:4.
Forget. Hos. 4:6.

Forsake. 2 Chron. 12:1;
Jer. 9:13.
Refuse to hear. Isa. 30:9;
Jer. 6:19.
Refuse to walk in. Ps. 78:10.

GOD, LONG-SUFFERING OF
Through Christ's intercession.
Luke 13:8.
An encouragement to repent.
Joel 2:13.

Exercised toward
His people. Isa. 30:18;
Ezek. 20:17.
The wicked. Rom. 9:22;
1 Pet. 3:20.
Exhibited in forgiving sins.
Rom. 3:25.
Illustrated. Luke 13:6, 9.
Limits set to. Gen. 6:3; Jer. 44:22.
Part of His character. Exod. 34:6;
Num. 14:18; Ps. 86:15.
Plead in prayer. Jer. 15:15.
Salvation the object of. 2 Pet. 3:15.
Should lead to repentance.
Rom. 2:4; 2 Pet. 3:9.

The wicked
Abuse. Eccles. 8:11;
Matt. 24:48-49.
Despise. Rom. 2:4.
Punished for despising.
Neh. 9:30; Matt. 24:48–51;
Rom. 2:5.

GOD, LOVE OF
Believers know and believe.
1 John 4:16.
Believers should abide in. Jude 21.
Christ abides in. John 15:10.
Christ the special object of.
John 15:9; 17:26.

Described as
Abiding. Zeph. 3:17.
Constraining. Hos. 11:4.
Everlasting. Jer. 31:3.
Great. Eph. 2:4.
Inseparable. Rom. 8:39.
Sovereign. Deut. 7:8; 10:15.
Unfailing. Isa. 49:15–16.

Exhibited in
Adoption. 1 John 3:1.
Corrections. Heb. 12:6.
Christ's dying for us while sinners.
Rom. 5:8; 1 John 4:10.
Defeating evil counsels.
Deut. 23:5.
Drawing us to Himself. Hos. 11:4.
Election. Mal. 1:2–3;
Rom. 9:11–13.
Forgiving sin. Isa. 38:17.
Free salvation. Titus 3:4–7.
The giving of Christ. John 3:16.
New life. Eph. 2.4–5.
Redemption. Isa. 43:3–4; 63:9.
The sending of Christ. 1 John 4:9.
Temporal blessings. Deut. 7:13.

Manifested toward
The cheerful giver. 2 Cor. 9:7.
The destitute. Deut. 10:18.
His disciples. John 16:27; 17:23;
2 Thess. 2:16; 1 John 4:16.
Perishing sinners. John 3:16;
Titus 3:4.
A part of His character.
2 Cor. 13:11; 1 John 4:8.

Perfected in believers
By brotherly love. 1 John 4:12.
By obedience. 1 John 2:5.
Poured out in the heart by the Holy
Spirit. Rom. 5:5.
Regardless of merit. Deut. 7:7;
Job 7:17.

The source of our love to Him.
1 John 4:19.
To be sought in prayer.
2 Cor. 13:14.

GOD, LOVE TO
Better than all sacrifices.
Mark 12:33.
A characteristic of believers.
Ps. 5:11.
Commanded. Deut. 11:1;
Josh 22:5.
Exhibited by Christ. John 14:31.
Encourage one another to.
Ps. 31:23.
The first great commandment.
Matt. 22:38.
God faithful to those who have.
Deut. 7:9.
God tries the sincerity of. Deut. 13:3.
Hypocrites, without. Luke 11:42;
John 5:42.
Love of the world a proof of not
having. 1 John 2:15.
Perfected, gives boldness.
1 John 4:17–18.
Perfected in obedience. 1 John 2:5.
Persevere in. Jude 21.
Pray for. 2 Thess. 3:5.

Produced by
Answers to prayer. Ps. 116:1.
The Holy Spirit. Gal. 5:22;
2 Thess. 3:5.
The love of God to us.
1 John 4:19.
Promises connected with.
Deut. 11:13–15; Ps. 69:36;
Isa. 56:6–7; James 1:12.

Should produce
Hatred of sin. Ps. 97:10.
Joy. Ps. 5:11.
Love to believers. 1 John 5:1.

Obedience to God. Deut. 30:20;
1 John 5:3.
Those who do not love others, lack.
1 John 3:17; 4:20.

Those who have
Are delivered by Him. Ps. 91:14.
Are known of Him. 1 Cor. 8:3.
Are preserved by Him.
Ps. 145:20.
Have all things working for their
good. Rom. 8:28.
Partake of His mercy. Exod. 20:6;
Deut. 7:9.
With all the heart. Deut. 6:5, with
Matt. 22:37.

GOD, LOVING-KINDNESS OF
See also Pity

Believers
Are ever mindful of. Pss. 26:3;
48:9.
Are heard according to.
Ps. 119:149.
Bound in a nuptial covenant.
Hos. 2:19.
Comforted by. Ps. 119:76.
Crowned with. Ps. 103:4.
Drawn by. Jer. 31:3.
Lifegiving. Ps. 119:88.
Look for mercy through. Ps. 51:1.
Preserved by. Ps. 40:11.
Receive mercy through. Isa. 54:8.
Should expect, in affliction.
Ps. 42:7–8.
Consideration of the dealings of God
gives a knowledge of. Ps. 107:43.
Constant. Ps. 89:33; Isa. 54:10.
Through Christ. Eph. 2:7;
Titus 3:4–6.

Described as
Better than life. Ps. 63:3.

Everlasting. Isa. 54:8.
Excellent. Ps. 36:7.
Good. Ps. 69:16.
Great. Neh. 9:17.
Innumerable. Isa. 63:7.
Marvelous. Pss. 17:7; 31:21.
Merciful. Ps. 117:2.
Former displays of, to be pleaded in
prayer. Pss. 25:6; 89:49.
Praise God for. Pss. 92:2; 138:2.

Pray for its
Continuance. Ps. 36:10.
Exhibition. Pss. 17:7; 143:8.
Extension. Gen. 24:12;
2 Sam. 2:6.
Proclaim to others. Ps. 40:10.

GOD, MERCY OF

Described as
Abundant. 1 Pet. 1:3.
Everlasting. 1 Chron. 16:34;
Pss. 89:28; 106:1; 107:1; 136.
Filling the earth. Ps. 119:64.
Great. Num. 14:18; Isa. 54:7.
High as heaven. Pss. 36:5,
103:11.
Manifold. Neh. 9:27; Lam. 3:32.
New every morning. Lam. 3:23.
Over all His works. Ps. 145:9.
Plenteous. Pss. 86:5, 15; 103:8.
Rich. Eph. 2:4.
Sure. Isa. 55:3; Mic. 7:20.
Tender. Pss. 25:6; 103:4;
Luke 1:78.
God's delight. Mic. 7:18.
A ground of hope. Pss. 130:7;
147:11.
A ground of trust. Ps. 52:8.

Manifested
To the afflicted. Isa. 49:13; 54:7.

With everlasting kindness.
Isa. 54:8.
To the fatherless. Hos. 14:3.
To His people. Deut. 32:43;
1 Kings 8:23.
In long-suffering. Lam. 3:22;
Dan. 9:9.
To repentant sinners. Ps. 32:5;
Prov. 28:13; Isa. 55:7;
Luke 15:18–20.
To returning backsliders.
Jer. 3:12; Hos. 14:4; Joel 2:13.
In salvation. Titus 3:5.
In the sending of Christ.
Luke 1:78.
To those who fear Him.
Ps. 103:17; Luke 1:50.
To whom He will. Hos. 2:23, with
Rom. 9:15, 18.
Part of His character. Exod. 34:6–7;
Neh. 9:17; Ps. 62:12; Jon. 4:2,
10–11; 2 Cor. 1:3.

Should be
Magnified. 1 Chron. 16:34;
Pss. 115:1; 118:1–4, 29;
Jer. 33:11.
Pleaded in prayer. Pss. 6:4; 25:6;
51:1.
Rejoiced in. Ps. 31:7.
Sought for others. Gal. 6:16;
1 Tim. 1:2; 2 Tim. 1:18.
Sought for ourselves. Ps. 6:2.
Typified by. Exod. 25:17.

GOD, MESSENGERS OF

Sent for the world's salvation.
John 3:17; Heb. 1:1–2.
Sent to assure of God's presence.
Hag. 1:13.
Sent to minister. Heb. 1:14.
Sent to prepare for the Messiah.
Mal. 3:1; Luke 1:76.
Sent to prepare the way. Gen. 24:7.

Sent to reveal God's word.
Matt. 23:34.

GOD, OBEDIENCE TO

Angels engaged in. Ps. 103:20.
Believers elected to. 1 Pet. 1:2.
Better than sacrifice. 1 Sam. 15:22.
Blessedness of. Deut. 11:27;
28:1–13; Luke 11:28;
James 1:25.
A characteristic of believers.
1 Pet. 1:14.
Christ an example of. Matt. 3:15;
John 15:10; Phil. 2:5–8;
Heb. 5:8.
Commanded. Deut. 13:4.
Confess your failure in. Dan. 9:10.
Exhortations to. Jer. 26:13; 38:20.
Impossible without faith. Heb. 11:6.

Includes
Keeping His commandments.
Eccles. 12:13.
Obeying Christ. Exod. 23:21;
2 Cor. 10:5.
Obeying His law. Deut. 11:27;
Isa. 42:24.
Obeying His voice. Exod. 19:5;
Jer. 7:23.
Obeying the gospel.
Rom. 1:5; 6:17; 10:16–17.
Submission to higher powers.
Rom. 13:1.
Justification obtained by that of
Christ. Rom. 5:19.
Obligations to. Acts 4:19–20; 5:29.
Pray to be taught. Pss. 119:35;
143:10.
Prepare the heart for. 1 Sam. 7:3;
Ezra 7:10.
Promises to. Exod. 23:22;
1 Sam. 12:14; Isa. 1:19;
Jer. 7:23.

Punishment of refusing.
Deut. 11:28.
Resolve upon. Exod. 24:7;
Josh 24:24.

Should be
Constant. Deut. 28:14;
Phil. 2:12.
From the heart. Deut. 11:13;
Rom. 6:17.
Unreserved. Josh. 22:2–3.
With willingness. Ps. 18:44;
Isa. 1:19.
To be universal in the last days.
Dan. 7:27.
The wicked refuse. Exod. 5:2;
Neh. 9:17.

GOD, POWER OF
All things possible to. Matt. 19:26.

Believers
Delivered by. Neh. 1:10;
Dan. 3:17.
Exalted by. Job 36:22.
Have confidence in. Jer. 20:11.
Long for exhibitions of.
Ps. 63:1–2.
Protected by until the coming of
salvation. 1 Pet. 1:5.
Receive increase of grace by.
2 Cor. 9:8.
Strengthened by. Eph. 6:10;
Col. 1:11.
Supported in affliction by.
2 Cor. 6:7; 2 Tim. 1:8.
Upheld by. Ps. 37:17; Isa. 41:10.
Can save by many or by few.
1 Sam. 14:6.

Described as
Effectual. Isa. 43:13; Eph. 3:7.
Everlasting. Isa. 26:4; Rom. 1:20.
Glorious. Exod. 15:6; Isa. 63:12.

Great. Ps. 79:11; Nah. 1:3.
Incomparable. Exod. 15:11–12;
Deut. 3:24; Job 40:9; Ps. 89:8.
Incomprehensible. Job 26:14;
Eccles. 3:11.
Irresistible. Deut. 32:39;
Dan. 4:35.
Mighty. Job 9:4; Ps. 89:13.
Sovereign. Rom. 9:21.
Strong. Pss. 89:13; 136:12.
Unsearchable. Job 5:9; 9:10.
Efficiency of ministers is through.
1 Cor. 3:6–8; Gal. 2:8; Eph. 3:7.
Exerted in behalf of believers.
2 Chron. 16:9.

Exhibited in
Creation. Ps. 102:25; Jer. 10:12.
Delivering His people. Ps. 106:8.
Destruction of the wicked.
Exod. 9:16; Rom. 9:22.
Establishing and governing all
things. Pss. 65:6; 66:7.
Making the gospel fruitful.
Rom. 1:16; 1 Cor. 1:18, 24.
Miracles of Christ. Luke 11:20.
Resurrection of Christ.
2 Cor. 13:4; Col. 2:12.
Resurrection of believers.
1 Cor. 6:14.

Expressed by the
Arm of God. Job 40:9;
Isa. 52:10.
Finger of God. Exod. 8:19;
Ps. 8:3.
Hand of God. Exod. 9:3, 15;
Isa. 48:13.
Thunder of His power, etc.
Job 26:14.
Voice of God. Pss. 29:3, 5;
68:33.
The faith of believers stands in.
1 Cor. 2:5.

A ground of trust. Isa. 26:4;
Rom. 4:21.
The heavenly host magnify.
Rev. 4:11; 5:13; 11:17.
Nothing too hard for. Gen. 18:14;
Jer. 32:27.
One of His attributes. Ps. 62:11.

Should be
Acknowledged. 1 Chron. 29:11;
Isa. 33:13.
Feared. Jer. 5:22; Matt. 10:28.
Magnified. Ps. 21:13; Jude 25.
Sought in prayer. Ps. 79:11;
Matt. 6:13.
The source of all strength.
1 Chron. 29:12; Ps. 68:35.

The wicked
Have against them. Ezra 8:22.
Do not know. Matt. 22:29.
Will be destroyed by. Luke 12:5.
Works in and for believers.
2 Cor. 13:4; Eph. 1:19; 3:20.

GOD, PROMISES OF

Are
Confirmed by an oath.
Ps. 89:3–4; Heb. 6:17.
Confirmed in Christ. Rom. 15:8.
Contained in the Scriptures.
Rom. 1:2.
Fulfilled in Christ. 2 Sam 7, 12,
with Acts 13:23; Luke 1:69–73.
Given to those who believe.
Gal. 3:22.
Good. 1 Kings 8:56.
Great and precious. 2 Pet. 1:4.
Holy. Ps. 105:42.
Inherited through faith and
patience. Heb. 6:12, 15; 10:36.
Made in Christ. Eph. 3:6;
2 Tim. 1:1.

Obtained through faith.
Heb. 11:33.
Performed in due season.
Jer. 33:14; Acts 7:17; Gal. 4:4.
Through the righteousness of
faith. Rom. 4:13, 16.
Yes and amen in Christ.
2 Cor. 1:20.

Believers
Children of. Rom. 9:8; Gal. 4:28.
Do not waver at. Rom. 4:20.
Expect the performance of.
Luke 1:38, 45; 2 Pet. 3:13.
Have implicit confidence in.
Heb. 11:11.
Heirs of. Gal. 3:29; Heb. 6:17;
11:9.
Plead, in prayer. Gen. 32:9, 12;
1 Chron. 17:23, 26; Isa. 43:26.
Sometimes, through suffering,
tempted to doubt. Ps. 77:8, 10.
The covenant established upon.
Heb. 8:6.
Be careful not to fall short of.
Heb. 4:1.
Gentiles will be partakers of.
Eph. 3:6.
God faithful to. Titus 1:2;
Heb. 10:23.
God remembers. Ps. 105:42;
Luke 1:54–55.
Inheritance of the believers is.
Rom. 4:13; Gal. 3:18.
The law could not do away with.
Gal. 3:17.
The law not against. Gal. 3:21.

Made to
Abraham. Gen. 12:3, 7, with
Gal. 3:16.
All who are called of God.
Acts 2:39.
Christ. Gal. 3:16, 19.

David. 2 Sam. 7:12;
Ps. 89:3–4, 35–36.
The fathers. Acts 13:32;
Acts 26:6–7.
Isaac. Gen. 26:3–4.
The Israelites. Rom. 9:4.
Jacob. Gen. 28:14.
Those who love Him. James 1:12;
2:5.
Not one will fail. Josh. 23:14;
1 Kings 8:56.
Persons, by nature, have no interest
in. Eph. 2:12.
Scoffers despise. 2 Pet. 3:3–4.
Should lead to perfecting holiness.
2 Cor. 7:1.
Should wait for the performance of.
Acts 1:4.

Subjects of
Adoption. 2 Cor. 6:18, with 7:1.
Blessing. Deut. 1:11.
Christ. 2 Sam. 7:12–13, with
Acts 13:22–23.
A crown of life. James 1:12.
Entering into rest. Josh. 22:4,
with Heb. 4:1.
Eternal life. Titus 1:2;
1 John 2:25.
Forgiveness of sins. Isa. 1:18;
Heb. 8:12.
The gospel. Rom. 1:1–2.
The Holy Spirit. Acts 2:33;
Eph. 1:13.
Life in Christ. 2 Tim. 1:1.
The life that now is. 1 Tim. 4:8.
New heavens and earth.
2 Pet. 3:13.
Preservation in affliction.
Isa. 43:2.
Putting the law into the heart.
Jer. 31:33, with Heb. 8:10.
Second coming of Christ.
2 Pet. 3:4.

GOD, PROVIDENCE OF

All things ordered by
For good to believers. Rom. 8:28.
For His glory. Isa. 63:14.

Believers should
Commit their works to.
Prov. 16:3.
Encourage themselves in.
1 Sam. 30:6.
Have full confidence in. Pss. 16:8;
139:10.
Pray in dependence upon.
Acts 12:5.
Pray to be guided by.
Gen. 24:12–14; 28:20–21;
Acts 1:24.
Trust in.
Matt. 6:33–34; 10:9, 29–31.
Cannot be defeated.
1 Kings 22:30, 34; Prov. 21:30.
Care over His works. Ps. 145:9.
Danger of denying. Isa. 10:13–17;
Ezek. 28:2–10; Dan. 4:29–31;
Hos. 2:8–9.
Ever watchful. Ps. 121:4; Isa. 27:3.

Exercised in
Bringing His words to pass.
Num. 26:65 Josh. 21:45;
Luke 21:32–33.
Defeating wicked plans.
Exod. 15:9–19;
2 Sam. 17:14–15; Ps. 33:10.
Delivering believers. Ps. 91:3;
Isa. 31:5.
Determining the period of human
life. Pss. 31:15; 39:5;
Acts 17:26.
Directing all events. Josh. 7:14;
1 Sam. 6:7–10, 12;
Prov. 16:33; Isa. 44:7;
Acts 1:26.

Leading believers. Deut. 8:2, 15;
Isa. 63:12.
Ordaining the conditions and
circumstances of persons.
1 Sam. 2:7–8; Ps. 75:6–7.
Ordering the minutest matters.
Matt. 10:29–30; Luke 21:18.
Ordering the ways of persons.
Prov. 16:9; 19:21; 20:24.
Overruling wicked plans for good.
Gen. 45:5–7; 50:20; Phil. 1:12.
Preserving His creation. Neh. 9:6;
Ps. 36:6; Matt. 10:29.
Preserving the course of nature.
Gen. 8:22; Job 26:10;
Ps. 104:5–9.
Prospering believers. Gen. 24:48,
56.
Protecting believers. Pss. 91:4;
140:7.
Providing for His creation.
Pss. 104:27–28; 136:25;
147:9; Matt. 6:26.
Ruling the elements.
Job 37:9–13; Isa. 50:2;
Nah. 1:4; John 1:4, 15.
Special preservation of believers.
Pss. 37:28; 91:11;
Matt. 10:30.
Person's efforts are useless without.
Ps. 127:1–2; Prov. 21:31.
Pervasive throughout the universe.
Ps. 139:1–5.
Righteous. Ps. 145:17; Dan. 4:37.
Seen in secondary causes.
1 Kings 21:19, with 22:37–38;
Mic. 5:2, with Luke 2:1–4;
Acts 27:22, 31–32.

Should be acknowledged
In adversity. Job 1:21;
Ps. 119:75.
In all things. Prov. 3:6.
For His daily care. Gen. 48:15.

In prosperity. Deut. 8:18;
1 Chron. 29:12.
In public disasters. Amos 3:6.
Sometimes dark and mysterious.
Pss. 36:6; 73:16; 77:19;
Rom. 11:33.
Those who depend on Him.
Luke 22:35.
The wicked made to promote the
plans of. Isa. 10:5–12;
Acts 3:17–18.

GOD, REBELLION AGAINST

Connected with
Contempt of God. Ps. 107:11.
Injustice and corruption. Isa 1:23.
Stubbornness. Deut. 31:27.

Exhibited in
Departing from Him. Isa. 59:13.
Departing from His instituted
worship. Exod. 32:8–9;
Josh. 22:16–19.
Departing from His laws.
Dan. 9:5.
Despising His counsels.
Ps. 107:11.
Despising His law. Neh. 9:26.
Distrusting His power.
Ezek. 17:15.
Murmuring against Him.
Num. 20:3, 10.
Rebelling against governors
appointed by Him. Josh. 1:18.
Refusing to listen to Him
Deut. 9:23; Ezek. 20:8;
Zech. 7:11.
Rejecting His government.
1 Sam. 8:7; 15:23.
Revolting from Him. Isa. 1:5;
31:6.
Sinning against light. Job 24:13;
John 15:22; Acts 13:41.

Unbelief. Deut. 9:23;
Ps. 106:24–25.
Walking after our own thoughts.
Isa. 65:2.
Forbidden. Num. 14:9; Josh. 22:19.
Forgiven upon repentance.
Neh. 9:26–27.
God alone can forgive. Dan. 9:9.
God ready to forgive. Neh. 9:17.
Grieves the Holy Spirit. Isa. 63:10.

Guilt of
To be confessed. Lam. 1:18, 20;
Dan. 9:5.
To be condemned. Josh. 22:29.
Worsened by God's fatherly care.
Isa. 1:2.
Worsened by God's unceasing
invitations to return to Him. Isa.
65:2.
The heart is the seat of. Jer. 5:23;
Matt. 15:18–19; Heb. 3:12.
Heinousness of. 1 Sam. 15:23.
Humans are prone to. Deut. 31:27;
Rom. 7:14–18.
Ingratitude of, illustrated. Isa. 1:2–3.

Ministers
Cautioned against. Ezek. 2:8.
Sent to those guilty of.
Ezek. 2:3–7; 3:4–9;
Mark 12:4–8.
Should remind their people of
past. Deut. 9:7; 31:27.
Should testify against. Isa. 30:8–9;
Ezek. 17:12; 44:6.
Should warn against. Num. 14:9.
Promises to those who avoid.
Deut. 28:1–13; 1 Sam. 12:14.
Provokes Christ. Exod. 23:20–21,
with 1 Cor. 10:9.
Provokes God. Num. 16:30;
Neh. 9:26.

Punished. Lev. 26:14–39;
1 Sam. 12:15; Isa. 1:20; Jer.
4:16–18; Ezek. 20:8, 38.
Punishment for teaching. Jer. 28:16.
Religious instruction designed to
prevent. Ps. 78:5, 8.

They who are guilty of
Banished from the church for.
Ezek. 20:38.
Banished in their sins for.
Ps. 5:10.
Delivered into the hands of
enemies because of.
Neh. 9:26–27.
Denounced. Isa. 30:1.
Have God as their enemy.
Isa. 63:10.
Have God's hand against them.
1 Sam. 12:15, with
Ps. 106:26–27.
Humbled. Ps. 107:11–12.
Impoverished for. Ps. 68:6.
Increase in, though punished.
Isa. 1:5.
Persevere in. Deut. 9:7, 24.
Practice hypocrisy to hide.
Hos. 7:14.
Restored through Christ alone.
Ps. 68:18.
Warned not to exalt themselves.
Ps. 66:7.
Worsen their sin by. Job 34:37.

GOD, RECONCILIATION WITH
Canceling record of charges
necessary to. Eph. 2:16;
Col. 2:14.

Effected for persons
By the blood of Christ. Eph. 2:13.
Col. 1:20.
By Christ as High Priest.
Heb. 2:17.

By the death of Christ.
Rom. 5:10; Eph. 2:16;
Col. 1:21–22.
By God in Christ. 2 Cor. 5:19.
While alienated from God.
Col. 1:21.
While enemies to God.
Rom. 5:10.
Without strength. Rom. 5:6.
Yet sinners. Rom. 5:8.

Effects of
Access to God. Rom. 5:2;
Eph. 2:18.
Peace of God. Rom. 5:1;
Eph. 2:16–17.
Union of Jews and Gentiles.
Eph. 2:14.
Union of things in heaven and
earth. Col. 1:20, with
Eph. 1:10.
Ministers, in Christ's place, should
encourage persons to seek.
2 Cor. 5:20.
The ministry of, committed to
believers. 2 Cor. 5:18–19.
Necessity for, illustrated.
Matt. 5:24–26.
A pledge of final salvation.
Rom. 5:10.
Predicted. Dan. 9:24, with Isa. 53:5.
Proclaimed by angels at the birth of
Christ. Luke 2:14.
Types. Lev. 8:15; 16:20.

GOD, RIGHTEOUSNESS OF
Angels acknowledge. Rev. 16:5.

Believers
Acknowledge in His dealings.
Ezra 9:15.
Acknowledge, though the wicked
prosper. Jer. 12:1, with
Ps. 73:12–17.

Ascribe to Him. Job 36:3;
Dan. 9:7.
Confident of seeing. Mic. 7:9.
Declare to others. Ps. 22:31.
Do not conceal. Ps. 40:10.
Magnify. Pss. 7:17; 51:14;
145:7.
Mention, only. Ps. 71:16.
Plead, in prayer. Ps. 143:11;
Dan. 9:16.
Recognize in the fulfillment of His
promises. Neh. 9:8.
Talk of. Pss. 35:28; 71:15, 24.
Upheld by. Isa. 41:10.
Christ acknowledged. John 17:25.
Christ committed His cause to.
1 Pet. 2:23.

Described as
Abundant. Ps. 48:10.
Beyond comprehension.
Ps. 71:15.
Enduring forever. Ps. 111:3.
Everlasting. Ps. 119:142.
The habitation of His throne.
Ps. 97:2.
Very high. Ps. 71:19.

Exhibited in
The final judgment. Acts 17:31.
The gospel. Ps. 85:10, with
Rom. 3:25–26.
His acts. Judg. 5:11;
1 Sam. 12:7.
His commandments. Deut. 4:8;
Ps. 119:172.
His government. Pss. 96:13;
98:9.
His judgments. Pss. 19:9;
119:7, 62.
His testimonies.
Ps. 119:138, 144.
His ways. Ps. 145:17.
His word. Ps. 119:123.

The punishment of the wicked.
Rom. 2:5; 2 Thess. 1:6;
Rev. 16:7; 19:2.
God delights in the exercise of.
Jer. 9:24.
Heavens will declare. Pss. 50:6;
97:6.
His care and defense of His people
designed to teach. Mic. 6:4–5.
Illustrated. Ps. 36:6.
Leads Him to love righteousness.
Ps. 11:7.
Part of His character.
Pss. 7:9; 11:6:5; 119:137.
Shown openly before the heathen.
Ps. 98:2.
Shown to the descendants of
believers. Ps. 103:17.

We should pray
For its continued manifestation.
Ps. 36:10.
To be answered in. Ps. 143:1.
To be delivered in. Pss. 31:1;
71:2.
To be judged according to.
Ps. 35:24.
To be led in. Ps. 5:8.
To be made alive in. Ps. 119:40.
The wicked have no interest in.
Ps. 69:27.

GOD, SOVEREIGNTY OF

Features of
Dominion. Rev. 1:6.
Glory. 1 Chron. 29:11; Rev. 1:6.
Greatness. 1 Chron. 29:11;
Ps. 135:5; Mal. 1:14.
Immortality. 1 Tim. 6:16.
Majesty. 1 Chron. 29:11.
Power. 1 Chron. 29:11;
Dan. 2:20; Matt. 6:13;
1 Tim. 6:16; Rev. 19:6.

Salvation. Rev. 19:1.
Victory. 1 Chron. 29:11.
Wisdom. Dan. 2:20.

God
Controls events. Lam. 3:37.
Gives and takes life. Job 1:21;
Rom. 14:7–8.
Is ruler over all kingdoms on earth.
2 Kings 19:15; 2 Chron. 29:11;
Ps. 10:16.
Is greater than all gods.
Exod. 18:11; Deut. 10:14.
Is the only God. Deut. 6:4;
Isa. 44:6.
Made heaven and earth. Gen. 1:1;
Neh. 9:6.
Owns the earth. Deut. 10:14;
Ps. 24:1.
Reduces rulers of the world to
nothing. Isa. 40:23.
Reigns forever. Exod. 15:18;
Ps. 93:1–2; 146:10; Rev 11:15.
Recognition of, by people.
Isa. 45:23; Rom. 14:11.

Titles and epithets showing
Father of all. Eph 4:6.
God Most High. Gen. 14:18–19.
God of heaven and earth. Gen.
24:3.
King of all the earth. Ps. 47:7.
King of kings. 1 Tim. 6:15.
LORD Most High. Ps. 47:2.
Lord of lords. 1 Tim. 6:15.
Maker of heaven and earth.
Gen. 14:19.

GOD, SUBMISSION TO

Christ set an example of.
Matt. 26:39–44. John 12:27;
18:11.
Commanded. Pss. 37:7; 46:10.
Exhortation to. Ps. 37:1–11.

Motives to
God's faithfulness. 1 Pet. 4:19.
God's greatness. Ps. 46:10.
God's justice. Neh. 9:33.
God's love. Heb. 12:6.
God's wisdom. Rom. 11:32–33.
Our own sinfulness. Lam. 3:39;
Mic. 7:9.

Should be exhibited in
Bodily suffering. Job 2:8–10.
Loss of children.
Job 1:18–19, 21.
Loss of goods. Job 1:15–16, 21.
The prospect of death.
Acts 21:13; 2 Cor. 4:16–51.
Punishment. Heb. 12:9.
Submission to the sovereignty of in
His purposes. Rom. 9:20–21.
Submission to His will.
2 Sam. 15:26; Ps. 42:5, 11;
Matt. 6:10.
The wicked lack. Prov. 19:3.

GOD, TRUTH OF
Always goes before His face.
Ps. 89:14.

Denied by
The devil. Gen. 3:4–5.
The self-righteous. 1 John 1:10.
Unbelievers. 1 John 5:10.

Described as
Abundant. Exod. 34:6.
Certain and fully trustworthy.
Num. 23:19; Titus 1:2.
Enduring to all generations.
Ps. 100:5.
Great. Ps. 57:10.
Plenteous. Ps. 86:15.
Reaching to the clouds. Ps. 57:10.

Exhibited in His
Administration of justice.
Ps. 96:13.
Counsels of old. Isa. 25:1.
Dealings with believers. Ps. 25:10.
Deliverance of believers. Ps. 57:3.
Fulfillment of His covenant.
Mic. 7:20.
Fulfillment of promises in Christ.
2 Cor. 1:20.
Judicial statutes. Ps. 19:9.
Punishment of the wicked.
Rev. 16:7.
Ways. Rev. 15:3.
Word. Ps. 119:160; John 17:17.
Works. Pss. 33:4; 111:7;
Dan. 4:37.
He keeps, forever. Ps. 146:6.
One of His attributes. Deut. 32:4;
Isa. 65:16.
Remembered toward believers.
Ps. 98:3.
A shield and refuge to believers.
Ps. 91:4.
United with mercy in redemption.
Ps. 85:10.

We should
Ask for, in prayer. Ps. 89:49.
Confide in. Ps. 31:5; Titus 1:2.
Magnify. Pss. 71:22; 138:2.
Make known to others. Isa. 38:19.
Pray that others might see in us.
2 Sam. 2:6.
Pray for revelation of.
2 Chron. 6:17.

GOD, UNITY OF
All believers acknowledge, in
worshiping Him. 2 Sam. 7:22;
2 Kings 19:15; 1 Chron. 17:20.
All should know and acknowledge.
Deut. 4:35; Ps. 83:18.

Asserted by

The apostles. 1 Cor. 8:4, 6;
Eph. 4:6; 1 Tim. 2:5.

Christ. Mark 12:29; John 17:3.

God Himself. Isa. 44:6, 8;
45:18 21.

Moses. Deut. 4:39; 6:4.

Consistent with the deity of Christ
and of the Holy Spirit.
John 10:30, with 1 John 5:7;
John 14:9–11.

Exhibited in His

Being only one who has all
knowledge. Isa. 46:9–11.

Being only one who is good.
Matt. 19:17.

Being the only Savior.
Isa. 45:21–22.

Being the only source of pardon.
Mic. 7:18, with Mark 2:7.

Being the sole object of worship in
heaven and earth. Neh. 9:6;
Matt. 4:10.

Exercise of uncontrolled
sovereignty. Deut. 32:39.

Greatness and wonderful works.
2 Sam. 7:22; Ps. 86:10.

Unparalleled election and care of
His people. Deut. 4:32–35.

Works of creation and providence.
Isa. 44:24; 45:5–8.

A ground for loving Him supremely.
Deut. 6:4–5, with Mark
12:29–30.

A ground for obeying Him
exclusively. Deut. 4:39–40.

Knowledge of, necessary to eternal
life. John 17:3.

May be acknowledged without saving
faith. James 2:19–20.

GOD, VOICE OF

As the Father's testimony to the Son.
John 12:28–29.

GOD, WAITING UPON

As the

Giver of all temporal blessings.
Pss. 104:27–28; 145:15–16.

God of providence. Jer. 14:22.

God of salvation. Ps. 25:5.

Believers

Have expectation from. Ps. 62:5.

Plead, in prayer. Ps. 25:21;
Isa. 33:2.

Resolve on. Pss. 52:9; 59:9.

Exhortations and encouragements
to. Pss. 27:14; 37:7; Hos. 12:6.

For

Coming of Christ. 1 Cor. 1:7;
1 Thess. 1:10.

The consolation of Israel.
Luke 2:25.

The fulfillment of His promises.
Acts 1:4.

The fulfillment of His Word.
Hab. 2:3.

Guidance and teaching. Ps. 25:5.

Hope of righteousness by faith.
Gal. 5:5.

Mercy. Ps. 123:2.

Pardon. Ps. 39:7–8.

Protection. Pss. 33:20; 59:9–10.

Salvation. Gen. 49:18;
Ps. 62:1–2.

God calls us to. Zeph. 3:8.

Illustrated. Ps. 123:2; Luke 12:36;
James 5:7.

Is good. Ps. 52:9.

The patience of believers often tried
in. Ps. 69:3.

Predicted of the Gentiles.
Isa. 42:4; 60:9.

Should be
All the day. Ps. 25:5.
Continually. Hos. 12:6.
Especially in adversity. Ps. 59:1–9;
Isa. 8:17.
With earnest desire. Ps. 130:6.
With full confidence. Mic. 7:7.
With hope in His Word. Ps.
130:5.
With patience. Pss. 37:7, 40:1.
With resignation. Lam. 3:26.
With the soul. Ps. 62:1, 5.
In the way of His judgments.
Isa. 26:8.

Those who engage in
Are blessed. Isa. 30:18;
Dan. 12:12.
Are heard. Ps. 40:1.
Experience His goodness.
Lam. 3:25.
Wait upon Him only. Ps. 62:5.
Will be saved. Prov. 20:22;
Isa. 25:9.
Will inherit the earth. Ps. 37:9.
Will not be ashamed. Ps. 25:3;
Isa. 49:23.
Will receive the glorious things
prepared by God for them.
Isa. 64:4.
Will rejoice in salvation. Isa. 25:9.
Will renew their strength, etc.
Isa. 40:31.

GOD, WALKING WITH

We are not to walk
According to the sinful nature.
Rom. 8:4.
Deceitfully. 2 Cor. 4:2.

In darkness. John 8:12;
1 John 1:6.
In disorder. 2 Thess. 3:6.
In our own ways. Acts 14:16.
By sight but by faith. 2 Cor. 5:7.
In the way of Cain. Jude 1:11.

We are to walk
As children of light. Eph. 5:8.
As Christ walked. 1 John 2:6.
Cautiously. Eph. 5:15.
By faith, not sight. 2 Cor. 5:7.
In the light. 1 John 1:7.
In love. Eph. 5:2.
In newness of life. Rom. 6:4.
In the Spirit. Gal. 5:16, 25.

GOD, WILL OF

Characteristics of
Giving. 2 Cor. 8:5; Gal. 1:4.
Good and perfect. Rom. 12:2.
To create people. Rev. 4:11.

Desire to do
By Jesus. Matt. 26:42; John 5:30;
Heb. 10:5–7.
By Paul, for Colossians. Col. 4:12.
By psalmist. Ps. 40:8.
Doers of, are family of Jesus.
Matt. 12:50.
Doers of, live forever. 1 John 2:17.

Doing
Confirms teachings of Jesus.
John 7:17.
Sustained Jesus. John 4:34.

Examples of
Joseph sold into Egypt.
Gen. 45:5, 7; 50:20.
Paul looking for. Rom 1:10.
Paul resigned to. Acts 21:14.
Suffering Servant. Isa. 53:10.

Jesus aimed to do God's.
  John 6:38–40.
Prayer of Jesus' followers.
  Luke 11:2.
Request to be done. Matt. 6:10.
To be followed. Col. 4:12; 1
  Pet. 3:17.
To be understood. Eph. 5:17.
To do good. 1 Pet. 2:15.
To save people. Matt. 18:14;
  Gal. 1:4.
To sanctify people. 1 Thess. 4:3.

GOD, WISDOM OF
All human wisdom derived from.
  Ezra 7:25.
Believers ascribe to Him. Dan. 2:20.

Described as
  Beyond human comprehension.
    Ps. 139:6.
  Incomparable. Isa. 44:7;
    Jer. 10:7.
  Infinite. Ps. 147:5; Rom. 11:33.
  Mighty. Job 36:5.
  Perfect. Job 36:4; 37:16.
  Underived. Job 21:22; Isa. 40:44.
  Universal. Job 28:24; Dan. 2:22;
    Acts 15:18.
  Unsearchable. Isa. 40:28;
    Rom. 11:33.
  Wonderful. Ps. 139:6.

Exhibited in
  His counsels. Isa. 28:29;
    Jer. 32:19.
  His foreshowing events.
    Isa. 42:9; 46:10.
  His works. Job 37:16;
    Pss. 104:24; 136:5; Prov. 3:19;
    Jer. 10:12.
  Redemption. 1 Cor. 1:24;
    Eph. 1:8; 3:10.

Searching the heart.
  1 Chron. 28:9; Rev. 2:23.
Understanding the thoughts.
  1 Chron. 28:9; Ps. 139:2.

Exhibited in knowing
  The actions. Job 34:21;
    Ps. 139:2–3.
  The afflictions of believers.
    Exod. 3:7; Ps. 142:3.
  The heart. Ps. 44:21; Prov.
    15:11; Luke 16:15.
  His believers. 2 Sam. 7:20;
    2 Tim. 2:19.
  The most secret things.
    Matt. 6:18.
  The sufferings of believers.
    Ps. 103:14.
  The smallest matters.
    Matt. 10:29–30.
  The time of judgment.
    Matt. 24:36.
  The wants of believers. Deut. 2:7;
    Matt. 6:8.
  The way of believers. Job 23:10;
    Ps. 1:6.
  The wicked. Neh. 9:10;
    Job 11:11.
  The words. Ps. 139:4.
  The works of the wicked.
    Isa. 66:18.
The gospel contains treasures of.
  1 Cor. 2:7.
Nothing concealed from.
  Ps. 139:12.
One of His attributes. 1 Sam. 2:3;
  Job 9:4.
Should be magnified. Rom. 16:27;
  Jude 25.
The wicked question. Ps. 73:11;
  Isa. 47:10.
Wisdom of believers derived from.
  Ezra 7:25.

GODLESSNESS
Of idolators. Ezek. 14:5.
Of those without hope. Eph. 2:12.
Of the unrighteous. Pss. 10:4; 53:1.

GODLINESS
Expected of Christians. 1 Tim. 6:11;
Titus 2:12; 2 Pet. 1:5.
Honored by God. Pss. 4:3; 97:11;
1 Tim. 4:7–8.
May be distorted. 1 Tim. 6:5.
Mystery of. 1 Tim. 3:16.
Rewarded. Matt. 5:6; 1 Tim. 6:6.
Value of. 1 Tim. 4:8; 2 Pet. 2:9.

GOLD
Abounded in
Havilah. Gen. 2:11.
Ophir. 1 Kings 9:28; 10:11;
1 Chron. 29:4;
2 Chron. 4:8–18; Job 22:24;
Ps. 45:9.
Parvaim. 2 Chron. 3:6.
Sheba. 1 Kings 10:10; Ps. 72:15;
Isa. 60:6.
Abundance of, in Solomon's reign.
2 Chron. 1:15.
An article of commerce.
Ezek. 27:22.
Belongs to God. Ezek. 16:17;
Joel 3:5; Hag. 2:8.

Described as
Malleable. Exod. 39:3;
1 Kings 10:16–17.
Melted down. Exod. 32:3–4;
Prov. 17:3.
Precious. Ezra 8:27; Isa. 13:12.
Valuable. Job 28:15–16.
Yellow. Ps. 68:13.
Estimated by weight.
1 Chron. 28:14.

Exacted as tribute. 1 Kings 20:3, 5;
2 Kings 23:33, 35.
Figurative sense. Eccles. 12:6,
Jer. 51:7; Lam. 4:1; 1 Cor. 3:12.
Found in the earth. Job 28:1, 6.
Given as presents. 1 Kings 15:19;
Matt. 2:11.

Illustrative of
Babylonian empire. Dan. 2:38.
Believers after affliction.
Job 23:10.
The doctrines of grace. Rev. 3:18.
Tried faith. 1 Pet. 1:7.
True converts. 1 Cor. 3:12.
Imported by Solomon.
1 Kings 9:11, 28; 10:11.
Jews condemned for multiplying.
Isa. 2:7.
Kings of Israel not to multiply.
Deut. 17:17.
Likely to grow dim. Lam. 4:1.
Most valuable when pure and fine.
Job 28:19; Pss. 19:10; 21:3;
Prov. 3:14.
Offerings of, for tabernacle.
Exod. 35:22.
Offerings of, for temple.
1 Chron. 22:14; 29:4, 7.
From Parvaim. 2 Chron. 3:6.
Patriarchs were rich in. Gen. 13:2.
Priestly and royal garments adorned
with. Exod. 28:4–6; Ps. 45:9, 13.
Refined and tried by fire. Job 28:19;
31:24; Prov. 8:19, 17:3; 27:21;
Zech. 13:9; Mal. 3:3; 1 Pet. 1:7.
Rusted. James 5:3.
Solomon rich in.
1 Kings 10:2, 14, 21.
Symbolic sense. Dan. 2:32–45;
Rev. 21:18, 21.
Taken in war, dedicated to God.
Josh. 6:19; 2 Sam. 8:11;
1 Kings 15:15.

From Tarshish. 1 Kings 22:48.
From Uphaz. Jer. 10:9.
Used as money. Matt. 10:9;
 Acts 3:6.

Used for
 Altar, lamps, and other articles
  made of. 1 Kings 7:48, 49–51;
  2 Kings 25:15; Ezra 8:27;
  Jer. 52:19; Dan. 5:3.
 Apparel. Ps. 45:9, 13.
 Beaten work. 2 Chron. 9:15.
 Candlesticks, for the tabernacle.
  Exod. 25:31–38; 37:17–24.
 Chains. Gen. 41:42; Dan. 5:29.
 Couches. Esther 1:6.
 Crowns. Exod. 25:25; 37:2–11;
  39:30; 2 Sam. 12:30;
  Esther 8:15; Ps. 21:3;
  Zech. 6:11.
 Earrings. Judg. 8:24, 26.
 Footstools. 2 Chron. 9:18.
 Forms of fruits. Prov. 25:11.
 Idols. Exod. 20:23; Ps. 115:4;
  Dan. 5:4.
 Instruments. 1 Kings 10:21;
  Esther 1:7.
 Mercy seat and cherubims.
  Exod. 25:17–18.
 Money. Gen. 44:8.
 Ornamenting the priest's
  garments. Exod. 39.
 Ornaments. Gen. 24:22;
  Exod. 3:22; 11:2; 28:11;
  Num. 31:50, 51;
  Song of Sol. 1:10; 5:14;
  Jer. 4:30; Ezek. 16:17.
 Overlaying cherubim in the
  temple. 2 Chron. 3:10.
 Overlaying the ark, etc.
  Exod. 25:11–13.
 Overlaying the floor of temple.
  1 Kings 6:30.

Overlaying the tabernacle.
 Exod. 36:34, 38.
Overlaying the temple.
 1 Kings 6:21–22.
Overlaying the throne of Solomon.
 1 Kings 10:18.
Rings. Song of Sol. 5:14;
 James 2:2.
Sacred candlesticks. Exod. 25:31;
 2 Chron. 4:7, 20.
Sacred utensils. Exod. 25:29, 38;
 2 Chron. 4:19–22.
Scepters. Esther 4:11.
Shields. 2 Sam. 8:7;
 1 Kings 10:16–17.
Wedge made of. Josh 7:21;
 Isa. 13:12.
Wire threads and woven into
 embroidered tapestry.
 Exod. 39:3.
Vanity of storing up. Eccles. 2:8, 11.
Working in, a trade. Neh. 3:8;
 Isa. 40:19.

GOLDEN RULE
Is the law and prophets. Matt. 7:12.
Stated by Christ. Luke 6:31.

GOOD AND EVIL
Choice between by Adam and Eve.
 Gen. 3.
Conflict between. Rev. 16:13–21.
Exhortation to choose between.
 Josh 24:15.
Subjective conflict between.
 Rom. 7:9–25.

GOOD FOR EVIL
Jesus' commandment.
 Matt. 5:42–48.

Examples of
 Abraham to Abimelech.
  Gen. 20:14–18.

David, to Saul. 1 Sam. 24:17; 26.
Elijah, to the Syrians.
  2 Kings 6:22–23.
David to his enemies.
  Ps. 35:12–14.
Jesus, to His crucifiers.
  Luke 23:34.
Stephen, to those who stoned him.
  Acts 7:60.

GOODNESS
And others. Matt. 7:12.
And prayer. Prov. 15:29.
Need of. Rom. 12:9; Gal. 6:10.
Power of. Rom. 12:21.

GOODNESS OF GOD
See God, Goodness of

GOOD NEWS
Contributes to health. Prov. 30:30.
Like cold water to a thirsty person.
  Prov. 25:25.

GOSHEN
General description of territory
  occupied by Joshua's forces.
  Josh. 10:41; 11:16.

GOSPEL, THE
Be careful not to hinder.
  1 Cor. 9:12.
Believers have fellowship in
  Phil. 1:5.
Brings peace. Luke 2:10, 14;
  Eph. 6:15.

Called the
  Dispensation of the grace of God.
    Eph. 3:2.
  Doctrine according to godliness.
    1 Tim. 6:3.
  Form of sound words.
    2 Tim. 1:13.

Glorious gospel of Christ.
  2 Cor. 4:4.
Gospel of Christ. Rom. 1:9, 16;
  2 Cor. 2:12; 1 Thess. 3:2.
Gospel of God. Rom. 1:1;
  1 Thess. 2:8; 1 Pet. 4:17.
Gospel of the grace of God.
  Acts 20:24.
Gospel of the kingdom.
  Matt. 24:14.
Gospel of peace. Eph. 6:15.
Gospel of salvation. Eph. 1:13.
Ministry of the Spirit. 2 Cor. 3:8.
Mystery of the gospel. Eph. 6:19.
Preaching of Jesus Christ.
  Rom. 16:25.
Word of Christ. Col. 3:16.
Word of faith. Rom. 10:8.
Word of God. 1 Thess. 2:13.
Word of grace. Acts 14:3; 20:32.
Word of life. Phil. 2:16.
Word of reconciliation.
  2 Cor. 5:19.
Word of salvation. Acts 13:26.
Word of truth. Eph. 1:13;
  James 1:18.
Everlasting. 1 Pet. 1:25; Rev. 14:6.
Exhibits the grace of God. Acts 14:3;
  20:32.
Glorious. 2 Cor. 4:4.
Good tidings of great joy for all
  people. Luke 2:10–11, 31–32.
Hid to the lost. 2 Cor. 4:3.
Knowledge of the glory of God by.
  2 Cor. 4:4, 6.
Let him who preaches another be
  cursed. Gal. 1:8.
Life and immortality brought to light
  by Jesus through. 2 Tim. 1:10.
Ministers have a command to
  preach. 1 Cor. 9:17.
Must be believed. Mark 1:15;
  Heb. 4:2.

The power of God for salvation.
Rom. 1:16; 1 Cor. 1:18;
1 Thess. 1:5.
Preached by Christ. Matt. 4:23;
Mark 1:14.

Preached to
Abraham. Gen. 22:18, with
Gal. 3:8.
Every creature. Mark 16:15;
Heb. 4:2.
The Gentiles. Mark 13:10;
Gal. 2:2, 9.
The Jews. Luke 24:47;
Acts 13:46.
The poor. Matt. 11:5; Luke 4:18.
Preached under the old testament.
Heb. 4:2.
Predicted. Isa. 41:27; 52:7; 61:1–3;
Mark 1:15.
Produces hope. Col. 1:23.
Profession of, accompanied by
afflictions. 2 Tim. 3:12.
Promises to sufferers for. Mark 8:35;
10:30.
Rejection of, by many, predicted.
Isa. 53:1, with Rom. 10:15–16.
Rejection of, by the Jews, a blessing
to the Gentiles. Rom. 11:28.
Terrible consequences of not
obeying. 2 Thess. 1:8–9.
Testifies to the final judgment.
Rom. 2:16.
There is fullness of blessing in.
Rom. 15:29.

Those who receive, should
Conduct themselves in a manner
worthy of. Phil. 1:27.
Hold to the truth of. Gal. 1:6–7,
2:14; 2 Tim. 1:13.
Earnestly contend for the faith of.
Phil. 1:17, 27; Jude 13.
Live in subjection to. 2 Cor. 9:13.

Not be ashamed of. Rom. 1:16;
2 Tim. 1:8.
Sacrifice friends and property for.
Matt. 10:37.
Sacrifice life itself for. Mark 8:35.

GOSSIP
Avoid people who do. Prov. 20:19.
Destructive. Ezek. 22:9.
Forbidden. Lev. 19:16.

GOSSIPER
A slanderer. Rom. 1:29;
2 Cor. 12:20.

GOURD
Jonah's. Jon. 4:6–10.
Wild gourd. 2 Kings 4:39.

GOVERNMENT
Church
Through apostles. Matt. 10:1–4;
Acts 6:1–2.
Through bishops. Phil. 1:1;
1 Tim. 3:2.
Christ the head. Eph. 5:23;
Col. 2:19.
Through church councils. Acts 15.
Through deacons. Acts 6:3–7.
Through elders. Acts 14:23;
1 Tim. 5:17.
Through lots. Acts 1:26.
Through the people. Acts 6:5.
Through prayer. Acts 1:24.
Through prophets and evangelists.
Eph. 4:11.
Through teachers. Acts 13:1.

Divine
Through Christ. Isa. 9:6;
Matt. 29:18; John 3:35;
1 Cor. 15:24–25; Eph. 1:22;
Rev. 11:15.

Through human government.
1 Sam. 16:1; Judg. 2:14–18.

Through the kingdom. Pss. 22:28;
99:1; 1 Cor. 4:20; Heb. 1:8;
Rev. 19:6.

Through providence.
Judg. 2:14–16; Hos. 4:5;
Mal. 1:14.

Through special spokesmen.
Hos. 12:13; Jer. 1:13–19.

Human

By divinely appointed leaders.
Exod. 12:35; Judg. 2:16.

By elders. Exod. 12:21.

By governors. Ezra 6:7.

By judges. Exod. 18:13–26;
Deut. 1:9–18.

By kings. 1 Sam. 10:24.

Of the people. Judg. 11:11.

To be obeyed when possible.
Rom. 13; Titus 3:1;
1 Pet. 2:13.

To be subordinate to God, and
therefore to be obeyed when
consistent with His will.
Jer. 32:1–5; Dan. 3; Acts 5:29;
Rom. 13:4.

GRACE

Believers

Abound in gifts of. Acts 4:33;
2 Cor. 8:1; 9:8, 14.

Are heirs of. 1 Pet. 3:7.

Are under. Rom. 6:14.

Are what they are by.
1 Cor. 15:10; 2 Cor. 1:12.

Receive, from Christ. John 1:16.

Should be established in.
Heb. 13:9.

Should be strong in. 2 Tim. 2:1.

Should grow in. 2 Pet. 3:18.

Should speak with. Eph. 4:29;
Col. 4:6.

Came by Christ. John 1:17;
Rom. 5:15.

Christ spoke with. Ps. 45:2, with
Luke 4:22.

Christ was full of. John 1:14.

Come short of God's. Heb. 12:15.

Described as

All-abundant. Rom. 5:15, 17, 20.

All-sufficient. 2 Cor. 12:9.

Exceeding. 2 Cor. 9:14.

Glorious. Eph. 1:6.

Great. Acts 4:33.

Manifold. 1 Pet. 4:10.

Rich. Eph. 1:7; 2:7.

Sovereign. Rom. 5:21.

Given by Christ. 1 Cor. 1:4.

Glory of, exhibited in our acceptance
in Christ. Eph. 1:6.

God the Giver of. Ps. 84:11;
James 1:17.

God the God of all. 1 Pet. 5:10.

God's throne, the throne of.
Heb. 4:16.

God's work completed in believers
by. 2 Thess. 1:11–12.

The gospel a declaration of.
Acts 20:24, 32.

Holy Spirit is the Spirit of.
Zech. 12:10; Heb. 10:29.

Inheritance of the promises by.
Rom. 4:16.

Justification by, opposed to that by
works. Rom. 4:4–5; 11:16;
Gal. 5:4.

Manifestation of, in others, a cause of
gladness. Acts 11:23; 3
John 1:3–4.

Necessary to the service of God.
Heb. 12:28.

Not to be abused. Rom. 3:8; 6:1, 15.

Not to be received in vain.
2 Cor. 6:1.

Pray for
For others. 2 Cor. 13:14;
Eph. 6:24.
For yourselves. Heb. 4:16.
Predicted by the prophets.
1 Pet. 1:10.
Riches of, exhibited in God's
kindness through Christ. Eph. 2:7.
Some used as license for immorality.
Jude 4.

Source of
The call of God. Col. 1:15.
Consolation. 2 Thess. 2:16.
Election. Rom. 11:5.
Faith. Acts 18:27.
Forgiveness of sins. Eph. 1:7.
Hope. 2 Thess. 2:16.
Justification. Rom. 3:24;
Titus 3:7.
Salvation. Acts 15:11;
Eph. 2:5, 8.

Specially given
To the humble. Prov. 3:24, with
James 4:6.
To ministers. Rom. 12:3, 6;
15:15; 1 Cor. 3:10; Gal. 2:9;
Eph. 3:7.
To those who walk uprightly.
Ps. 84:11.
Special manifestation of, at the
second coming of Christ. 1
Pet. 1:13.
Success and completion of the work
of God to be attributed to.
Zech. 4:7.
Was upon Christ. Luke 2:40;
John 3:34.

GRAFTING
Symbolic use. Rom. 11:17–24.

GRANDFATHER
Called father. Gen. 10:21.

GRAPE
Cultivated by the Amorites.
Num. 21:22.
Cultivated by the Canaanites.
Num. 13:24; Deut. 6:11;
Josh. 24:13.
Cultivated by the Edomites.
Num. 20:17.
Cultivated by the Philistines.
Judg. 15:5.
Cultivated in vineyards by Noah.
Gen. 9:20.
Culture of. Lev. 25:3, 11;
Deut. 28:39; 2 Chron. 26:10;
Song of Sol. 6:11; Isa. 5:1;
Jer. 31:5.
Fable of. Judg. 9:12–13.
Grown at Abel. Judg. 11:33.
Grown at Baalhamon.
Song of Sol. 8:11.
Grown at Carmel. 2 Chron. 26:10.
Grown at Engedi. Song of Sol. 1:14.
Grown at Jezreel. 1 Kings 21:1.
Grown at Lebanon. Hos. 14:7.
Grown at Samaria. Jer. 31:5.
Grown at Shechem. Judg. 9:27.
Grown at Shiloh. Judg. 21:20–21.
Grown at Timnath. Judg. 14:5.
Parables of the vine. Ps. 80:8–14;
Ezek. 17:6–10; 19:10–14;
John 15:1–5.
Proverb of. Ezek. 18:2.
Used in a figurative sense.
Deut. 32:32.
Wine of, forbidden to Nazirites.
Num. 6:4.

GRASS

Called
Of the earth. Rev. 9:4.
Of the field. Num. 22:4.
Cattle fed upon. Job 6:5; Jer. 50:11.
Created on the third day. Gen. 1:11.

Destroyed by
Drought. 1 Kings 17:1, with 18:5.
Hail and lightning. Rev. 8:7.
Locusts. Rev. 9:4.
Failure of, a great calamity.
Isa. 15:5–6.

God
Adorns and clothes. Matt. 6:30.
Causes to grow. Pss. 104:14;
147:8.
The giver of. Deut. 11:15.
Originally created. Gen. 1:11–12.
A green herb. Mark 6:39.

Illustrative of
Believers refreshed by grace (when
refreshed by dew and showers).
Ps. 72:6; Mic. 5:7.
Prosperity of the wicked. Ps. 92:7.
Shortness and uncertainty of life.
Pss. 90:5; 103:15; Isa. 40:6–7;
1 Pet. 1:24.
The wicked (when on housetops).
2 Kings 19:26; Isa. 37:27.
Often grew on the tops of houses.
Ps. 129:6.
Ovens often heated with. Matt. 6:30.
Mown. Ps. 72:6.
Refreshed by rain and dew.
Deut. 32:2; Prov. 19:12.
Soft and tender when young.
Prov. 27:25.
Springs out of the earth.
2 Sam. 23:4.
Sufferings of animals from failure of,
described. Jer. 14:54.

Used in a figurative sense.
Ps. 90:5–6; Isa. 40:6;
1 Pet. 1:24; James 1:10–11.

GRASSHOPPER
Israelites felt like, compared to the
Canaanites. Num. 13:33.

GRAVE
The Lord will ransom
from. Hos. 13:14.
The Lord robs, of its victory.
1 Cor. 15:55.

GRIEF
Of the Holy Spirit. Eph. 4:30.
Marked Christ. Isa. 53:3–10;
John 11:35.
May mark the righteous. Ps. 139:21;
1 Pet. 2:19.
Of men, lifted by God. Isa. 61:3;
2 Cor. 1:5.

GROUND
Animals from. Gen. 2:19.
Cursed. Gen. 3:17; 5:29.
Human beings made from.
Gen. 2:7; 3:19, 23; Job 4:19;
33:6.
Vegetables from. Gen. 2:9.

GROWTH
Of Christians. Eph. 4:14 15.
Of faith. 2 Thess. 1:3.
Through God's Word. 1 Pet. 2:2.
In grace. 2 Pet. 3:18.
Of the kingdom. Mark 4:30–32.
In the life of Jesus. Luke 12:40, 52.
Obstacles to. Acts 18:24–28;
1 Cor. 3:1–3.
In spiritual knowledge. 2 Pet. 3:18.
In spiritual things. Mark 4:28.

GUIDANCE

Of believers. Ps. 32:8; John 10:3.
Through divine light. Ps. 43:3.
Of Israel. Exod. 15:13; Deut. 32:12;
   Neh. 9:19.
To love and endurance.
   2 Thess. 3:5.
To repentance. Rom. 2:4.
To satisfaction. Rev. 7:17.
Through the Word of God.
   Isa. 30:21.

Through witnessing. Prov. 3:6.

GUILT

See Conscience; Forgiveness of
   Injuries; Forgiveness of Sin; Grace;
   Redemption; Sacrifices; Salvation;
   Sin.

GUN CONTROL

Philistines deny Israelites swords and
   spears. 1 Sam 13:19, 22.

❧H❧

HADES

The unseen world.
Matt. 10:28; 11:23; 16:18;
Rev. 1:18; 6:8; 20:13–14.

HAIL

Destroys army of the Amorites.
Josh. 10:11.
Plague of, in Egypt. Exod. 9:18–29.
Used in a figurative sense. Isa. 28:2;
Rev. 8:7; 11:19; 16:21.

HAIR

Black, particularly valued.
Song of Sol. 5:11.
Color of, changed by leprosy.
Lev. 13:3, 10, 20.
Cut off in affliction. Jer. 7:29.

God
Numbers. Matt. 10:30.
Takes care of. Dan. 3:27;
Luke 21:18.
Growth of. Judg. 16:22.
Of the healed leper, to be shaved.
Lev. 14:9.
Innumerable. Pss. 40:12; 69:4.

Judgments expressed by
Sending baldness. Isa. 3:24,
Jer. 47:5.
Shaving. Isa. 7:20.
Man cannot even change the color
of. Matt. 5:36.
Men condemned for wearing long.
1 Cor. 11:14.
Natural covering of the head.
Ps. 68:21.

Of Nazarites
Not to be cut or shaved during
their vow. Num. 6:5;
Judg. 16:7, 19–20.
Shaved after completion of vow.
Num. 6:18.
Often expensively anointed.
Eccles. 9:8.
Pulled out in extreme grief. Ezra 9:3.
Pulling out of, a reproach.
Neh. 13:25; Isa. 50:6.
Sometimes worn long by men.
2 Sam. 14:26.

White or gray
An emblem of wisdom. Dan. 7:9,
with Job 12:12.
A sign of age. 1 Sam. 12:2;
Ps. 71:18.
A sign of weakness and decay.
Hos. 7:9.
To be reverenced. Lev. 19:32.
With righteousness, a crown of
glory. Prov. 16:31.

Of women
Neglected in grief. Luke 7:38;
John 12:3.
Plaited and braided. 1 Tim. 2:9;
1 Pet. 3:3.
Well set and decorated. Isa. 3:24.
Worn long for a covering.
1 Cor. 11:15.

HALLELUJAH

Exclamation of praise. Ps. 146–150.

HANDBREADTH

A measure about four inches.
Exod. 25:25.

HANDKERCHIEF

Carried from Paul's body to a sick person. Acts 19:12.

HANDS

Application of, used in
Blessing. Gen. 48:14;
Mark 10:16.
Conferring civil power.
Num. 27:18; Deut. 34:9.
Imparting the gifts of the Holy
Spirit. Acts 8:17; 19:6.
Ordaining ministers. Acts 6:6;
1 Tim. 4:14.
Setting apart the Levites.
Num. 8:10.
Transferring guilt of sacrifices.
Lev. 1:4; 3:2; 16:21–22.
Believers blessed in the work of.
Deut. 2:7; 30:9; Job 1:10;
Ps. 90:17.
Clapped together in joy.
2 Kings 11:12; Ps. 47:1.

Criminals often
Bound by. Matt. 22:13.
Deprived of. Deut. 25:12;
2 Sam. 4:12.
Hung by. Lam. 5:12.
Mutilated in. Judg. 1:6–7.

Distinguished as
Left. Gen. 14:15; Acts 21:3.
Right. Acts 3:7.
God strengthens. Gen. 49:24.
Keeps from being effective.
Job 5:12.

Illustrative of
Generosity, when opened.
Deut. 15:8; Ps. 104:28.
Power. 1 Kings 18:46;
2 Kings 13:5.
Stinginess, when shut. Deut. 15:7.
Rebellion, when lifted up against
another. 2 Sam. 20:21.
Instruction of, a first principle of the
doctrine of Christ. Heb. 6:1–2.
The Jews carried a staff in.
Exod. 12:11; 2 Kings 4:29.
The Jews ate with. Matt. 26:23.
Kissed in idolatrous worship.
Job 31:27.
Many expert with both.
1 Chron. 12:2.
Many with more command of the
left. Judg. 3:15, 21; 20:16.
Necessary members of the body.
1 Cor. 12:21.
Often spread out in prayer.
Ps. 68:31; Isa. 1:15.

Of the wicked, described as
Bloody. Isa. 1:15; 59:3.
Ensnaring to themselves.
Ps. 9:16.
Lazy. Prov. 6:10; 21:25.
Mischievous. Ps. 26:10; Mic. 7:3.
Violent. Ps. 58:2; Isa. 59:6.

Parts of, mentioned
Fingers. 2 Sam. 21:20; Dan. 5:5.
Palm. Isa. 49:16; Matt. 26:67.
Thumb. Exod. 29:20;
Lev. 14:14, 17.
Placed under the thigh of a person to
whom an oath was made.
Gen. 24:2–3; 47:29–31.

Right hand
Accuser stood at, of the accused.
Ps. 109:6; Zech. 3:1.

Given as sign of friendship.
Gal. 2:9.

Of healed leper, touched with
blood of his sacrifice.
Lev. 14:14, 17, 25.

Of healed leper, touched with oil.
Lev. 14:28.

Place of honor. 1 Kings 2:19;
Ps. 45:9.

Place of power. Ps. 110:1;
Mark 14:62.

Of priests, touched with blood of
consecration ram. Exod. 29:20;
Lev. 8:23–24.

Ring worn on. Jer. 22:24.

Sworn by. Isa. 62:8.

Used in embracing. 2 Sam. 20:9;
Song of Sol. 2:6; 8:3.

Right hand, illustrative of
Corruption, when full of bribes.
Ps. 26:10.

Deceitfulness, when full of
falsehood. Ps. 144:8, 11;
Isa. 44:20.

Extreme self-denial, when cutting
off. Matt. 5:30.

Protection, when standing at.
Pss. 16:8; 109:31; 110:5.

Strength and power. Exod. 15:6;
Ps. 17:7.

Support, when holding by.
Ps. 73:23; Isa. 41:13.

Support withheld, when
withdrawn. Ps. 74:11.

Servants directed by movements of.
Ps. 123:2.

Servants pour water on, by custom.
2 Kings 3:11.

Should be employed in
Acts of goodness. Prov. 3:27;
31:20.

God's service. Neh. 2:18;
Zech. 8:9, 13.

Work. Eph. 2:28; 1 Thess. 4:11.

Struck together in extreme anger.
Num. 24:10; Ezek. 21:14, 17.

Stretched out to ridicule. Hos. 7:5;
Zeph. 2:15.

Security entered into by striking.
Job 17:3; Prov. 6:1; 17:18;
22:26.

Treaties made by joining.
2 Kings 10:15; Prov. 11:21.

Uses of, mentioned
Feeling. Ps. 115:7; 1 John 1:1.

Holding. Judg. 7:20; Rev. 10:2.

Making signs. Isa. 13:2;
Acts 12:17.

Striking. Mark 14:65; John 19:3.

Taking. Gen. 3:22; Exod. 4:4.

Writing. Isa. 44:5; Gal. 6:11.

Working. Prov. 31:19;
1 Thess. 4:11.

Were lifted up in
Blessing. Lev. 9:22.

Praise. Ps. 134:2.

Prayer. Ps. 141:2; Lam. 3:41.

Taking an oath. Gen. 14:22;
Rev. 10:5.

Were washed
Before eating. Matt. 15:2;
Mark 7:3.

As symbol of innocence.
Deut. 21:6–7; Matt. 27:24.

After touching an unclean person.
Lev. 15:11.

The wicked repaid for the work of.
Ps. 28:4; Prov. 12:14; Isa. 3:11.

HANGING
Capital punishment by.
  Gen. 40:19–22; Josh. 8:29;
  2 Sam. 4:12; Esther 7:10.
The curse of death by.
  Deut. 21:22–23; Gal. 3:13.

HAPPINESS OF BELIEVERS
See Believers, Happiness of

HAPPINESS OF THE WICKED
See Wicked, Happiness of

HARD-HEARTEDNESS
Warning against. Ps. 95:8–11;
  Prov. 21:9; Rev. 9:20–21.

Examples of
  Israelites. Num. 14:22.
  The people of Noah's generation.
    Gen. 6:3, 5, 7.
  Sodomites. Gen. 19:9, 14.
  Sons of Eli. 1 Sam. 2:22–25.

HARDSHIP
Of believers. Ps. 137:4.
Of Christian workers. 2 Tim. 2:3.
Of Christians. John 16:33;
  Acts 15:26.
Of Paul. 2 Cor. 11:23–27.
Of sinners. Prov. 13:15.
Overcome. John 16:33;
  2 Cor. 4:17; 12:10.

HARE
See Rabbit

HARLOT
To be avoided. Prov. 5:3–20;
  7:25–27.
Craftiness of. Prov. 7:10; 9:14–17;
  Isa. 23:15–16; Hos. 2:13.
Higher of, not to be received at the
  temple. Deut. 23:18.

Rahab. Josh. 2:3–6; 6:17, 23, 25;
  Heb. 11:31.
Shamelessness of.
  Prov. 2:16; 7:11–27; 9:13–18.

HARLOTRY
Forbidden. Lev. 19:29;
  Deut. 23:17.
Punishment of. Lev. 21:9.

HARMONY
Blessing of. Ps. 133:1.
Condition of. Amos 3:3.
Desirability of. Rom. 12:18;
  Eph. 4:3.

HARP
David skillful in manipulating.
  1 Sam. 16:16, 23.
Discordant. 1 Chron. 14:7.
Heard in heaven in John's
  apocalyptic vision. Rev. 5:8; 14:2;
  15:2.
Hung on the trees by the captive in
  Babylon. Ps. 137:2.
Made of Almug wood.
  1 Kings 10:12.
Originated with Jubal. Gen. 4:21.
A stringed instrument of music.
  Isa. 38:20; Ezek. 33:32;
  Hab. 3:19.
Ten strings. Ps. 33:2; 9:3; 144:9;
  150:4.
With three strings. 1 Sam. 18:6.
Used in festivities. Gen. 21:27;
  Rev. 18:22.
Used in mourning. Job 30:31.
Used in national celebrations after
  the triumph over Goliath.
  1 Sam. 18:6.
Used in national celebrations after
  the triumph over the armies of

Ammon and Moab.
2 Chron. 20:28.
Used in worship. 1 Sam. 10:5;
1 Chron. 16:5; Ps. 33:2; 150:3.
Used when the walls of Jerusalem
were dedicated. Neh. 12:27, 36.

HARROW
An agricultural implement used as an
instrument of torture.
2 Sam. 12:31; 1 Chron. 20:3.

HARVEST
Of barley at the passover. Lev. 23:6,
10; Ruth 1:22.

Called the
Appointed weeks of harvest.
Jer. 5:24.
Harvest time. 2 Sam. 23:13;
Jer. 50:16.

Failure of
A cause of great grief. Isa. 16:9;
Joel 1:11.
Occasioned by drought.
Amos 4:7.
Occasioned by locusts. Joel 1:4.
A punishment for sin.
Isa. 17:10–11.
Sometimes continued for years.
Gen. 45:6.
Fields appeared white before.
John 4:35.
Former and latter rain necessary to
abundance of. Jer. 5:24;
Amos 4:7.

Illustrative of
The end of the world.
Matt. 13:30, 39.
God's protection, etc. (dew in).
Isa. 18:4.

Honor given to fools (rain in).
Prov. 26:1.
A refreshing message (cold in).
Prov. 25:13.
Ripeness for wrath. Joel 3:13;
Rev. 14:15.
Seasons of grace. Jer. 8:20.
A time of judgment. Jer. 51:33;
Hos. 6:11.
A time when many are ready to
receive the gospel.
Matt. 9:37–38; John 4:35.
In gathering of fruits of the fields.
Mark 4:29.
Legal provision for the poor during.
Lev. 19:9–10; 23:22;
Deut. 24:19.
Men and women engaged in.
Ruth 2:8–9.
Miraculous thunder, etc., in.
1 Sam. 12:17–18.
Not to begin until the first fruits had
been offered to God.
Lev. 23:10, 14.
Omitted in the sabbatical year.
Lev. 25:5.
Omitted in year of jubilee.
Lev. 25:11–12.
Patience required in waiting for.
James 5:7.

Persons engaged in
Binders. Gen. 37:7; Ps. 129:7.
Called reapers. Isa. 17:5.
Called laborers. Matt. 9:37.
Fed by the farmer during. Ruth
2:14.
Often defrauded of their wages.
James 5:4.
Reapers. Ruth 2:4.
Received wages. John 4:36.
The Sabbath to be observed during.
Exod. 34:21.
Laziness during, ruinous. Prov. 10:5.

Time of great joy. Ps. 126:6;
Isa. 9:3.
To continue without intermission.
Gen. 8:22.
Of wheat at Pentecost. Exod. 34:22;
1 Sam. 12:17.

HASTE

In judgment by Moses and the
Israelites. Num. 32:1–19;
Josh. 22:10–34.

HATRED

Believers should
Expect. Matt. 10:22;
John 15:8–19.
Give no cause for. Prov. 25:17.
Not marvel at. 1 John 3:13.
Not rejoice in the calamities of
those who exhibit.
Job 31:29–30; Ps. 35:13–14.
Return good for. Exod. 23:5;
Matt. 5:44.
Christ experienced. Ps. 35:19, with
John 7:7; 15:18, 24–25.
Embitters life. Prov. 15:17.
Forbidden. Lev. 19:17; Col. 3:8.

Inconsistent with
The knowledge of God.
1 John 2:9, 11.
The love of God. 1 John 4:20.
Is murder. 1 John 3:15.
Leads to deceit. Prov. 26:24–25.
Liars prone to. Prov. 26:28.
Often cloaked by deceit.
Prov. 10:18; 26:26.
Punishment of. Pss. 34:21; 44:7;
89:23; Amos 1:11.
Stirs up strife. Prov. 10:12.

We should exhibit against
Backsliding. Ps. 101:3.

Evil. Ps. 97:10; Prov. 8:13.
False ways. Ps. 119:104, 128.
Hatred and opposition to God.
Ps. 139:21–22.
Lying. Ps. 119:163.

The wicked exhibit toward
Believers. Ps. 25:19;
Prov. 29:10.
Each other. Titus 3:3.
God. Rom. 1:30.

HATRED TO CHRIST

See Christ, Hatred to

HAWK

A carnivorous and unclean bird.
Lev. 11:16; Deut. 14:15;
Job 39:26.

Arabian Hawk

HEAD

All the other members necessary to.
1 Cor. 12:21.

Body supported and supplied by.
Eph. 4:16.

Bowed down
As a sign of respect. Gen. 43:28.
In worshiping God. Gen. 24:26;
Exod. 4:31.

Of criminals often cut off.
Matt. 14:10.

Of enemies slain in war, often cut off.
Judg. 5:26; 1 Sam. 17:51, 57;
31:9.

In grief
Covered up. 2 Sam. 15:30;
Esther 6:12.
One's hands placed on.
2 Sam. 13:19; Jer. 2:37.
Shaved. Job 1:20.
Sprinkled with dust. Josh 7:6;
Job 2:12.

Illustrative of
The chief city of a kingdom.
Isa. 7:8.
Chief men. Isa. 9:14–15.
Christ. 1 Cor. 11:3; Eph. 1:22;
Col. 2:19.
Defense and protection, when
covered. Ps. 140:7.
Exaltation, when lifted up.
Gen. 40:13; Ps. 27:6.
God. 1 Cor. 11:3.
Heavy judgments, when made
bald. Isa. 3:24; 15:2; 22:12;
Mic. 1:16.
Joy and confidence, when lifted
up. Ps. 3:3; Luke 21:28.
Joy and prosperity, when
anointed. Pss. 23:5; 92:10.

Pride, etc., when lifted up.
Ps. 83:2.
Rulers. 1 Sam. 15:17; Dan. 2:38.
Subjection, when covered.
1 Cor. 11:5, 10.
The Jews censured for swearing by.
Matt. 5:36.
Of the leper always uncovered.
Lev. 13:45.

Liable to
Baldness. Lev. 13:40–41;
Isa. 15:2.
Internal disease. 2 Kings 4:19;
Isa. 1:5.
Leprosy. Lev. 13:42–44.
Scab. Isa. 3:17.

Nazarites forbidden to shave.
Num. 6:5.

Often anointed. Eccles. 9:8;
Matt. 6:17.

Parts of, mentioned
Crown. Gen. 49:26; Isa. 3:17.
Face. Gen. 48:12; 2 Kings 9:30.
Forehead. 1 Sam. 17:49;
Ezek. 9:4.
Hair. Judg. 16:22; Ps. 40:12.
Scalp. Ps. 68:21.
Skull. 2 Kings 9:35; Matt. 27:33.
Temples. Judg. 4:21–22;
Song of Sol. 4:3.

Priests forbidden to shave, etc.
Lev. 21:5, 10.

Put for the life. Dan. 1:10;
1 Sam. 28:2.

Put for the whole person.
Gen. 49:26; Prov. 10:6.

Ridicule expressed by shaking, etc.
2 Kings 19:21; Pss. 22:7;
109:25; Matt. 27:39.

Uppermost and chief member of the
body. Isa. 1:6; 2 Kings 6:31.

When white with age to be respected. Lev. 19:32.

Of women generally covered in public. Gen. 24:65; 1 Cor. 11:5.

HEALTH

Communicated through gifts. 1 Cor. 12:9.

Connected with spiritual health. 1 Cor. 11:30; 3 John 1:2.

Promise of. Exod. 15:26; Deut. 7:15; Jer. 30:17.

Restoration of. Ps. 147:3.

Restored through faith. James 5:15.

Through Christ. Mark 3:15; Luke 7:21–22; Acts 9:34.

HEARERS

Contrasted with doers. Rom. 2:13; James 1:19–25.

HEART

Faith, the means of purifying. Acts 15:9.

God

Creates a new. Ps. 51:10; Ezek. 36:26.

Enlightens. 2 Cor. 4:6; Eph. 1:18.

Establishes. Ps. 112:8; 1 Thess. 3:13.

Influences. 1 Sam. 10:26; Ezra 6:22; 7:27; Prov. 21:1; Jer. 20:9.

Knows. Ps. 44:21; Jer. 20:12.

Opens. Acts 16:14.

Ponders. Prov. 21:2; 24:12.

Prepares. 1 Chron. 29:18; Prov. 16:1.

Searches. 1 Chron. 28:9; Jer. 17:10.

Strengthens. Ps. 27:14.

Tries. 1 Chron. 29:17; Jer. 12:3.

Understands the thoughts of. 1 Chron. 28:9; Ps. 139:2.

Harden not, against God. Ps. 95:8, with Heb. 4:7.

Harden not against the poor. Deut. 15:7.

He that trusts in, is a fool. Prov. 28:26.

Issues of life are out of. Prov. 4:23.

Know the plague of. 1 Kings 8:38.

No man can cleanse. Prov. 20:9.

Pray that it may be

Cleansed. Ps. 51:10.

Directed into the love of God. 2 Thess. 3:5.

Inclined to God's testimonies. Ps. 119:36.

United to fear God. Ps. 86:11.

The pure in, will see God. Matt. 5:8.

Regard not iniquity in. Ps. 66:18.

Renewal of, promised under the gospel. Ezek. 11:19; 36:26; Heb. 3:10.

Should be

Applied to wisdom. Ps. 90:12; Prov. 2:2.

Given to God. Prov. 23:26.

Guided in the right way. Prov. 23:19.

Kept with diligence. Prov. 4:23.

Perfect with God. 1 Kings 8:61.

Prepared to God. 1 Sam. 7:3.

Purified. James 4:8.

Single. Eph. 6:5; Col. 3:22.

Tender. Eph. 4:32.

Take heed lest it be deceived. Deut. 11:16.

We should

Believe with the. Acts 8:37; Rom. 10:10.

Do the will of God from the.
Eph. 6:6.
Keep God's statutes with all.
Deut. 26:16.
Love God with all. Matt. 22:37.
Love one another with a pure.
1 Pet. 1:22.
Return to God with all.
Deut. 30:2.
Sanctify God in the. 1 Pet. 3:15.
Serve God with all. Deut. 11:13.
Trust in God with all. Prov. 3:5.
Walk before God with all.
1 Kings 2:4.
When broken and contrite, not
despised by God. Ps. 51:17.

HEART, RENEWED

Awed by the Word of God.
Ps. 119:161.
Broken, contrite. Pss. 34:18; 51:17.
Circumcised. Deut. 30:6;
Rom. 2:29.
Clean. Ps. 73:1.
Confident in God. Ps. 112:7.
Desirous of God. Ps. 84:2.
Enlarged. Ps. 119:32; 2 Cor. 6:11.
Faithful to God. Neh. 9:8.
Filled with the fear of God.
Jer. 32:40.
Filled with the law of God.
Pss. 40:8; 119:11.
Fixed on God. Pss. 57:7; 112:7.
Honest and good. Luke 8:15.
Inclined to obedience. Ps. 119:112.
Joyful in God. 1 Sam. 2:1;
Zech. 10:7.
Meditative. Pss. 4:4; 77:6.
Obedient. Ps. 119:112; Rom. 6:17.
Perfect with God. 1 Kings 8:61;
Ps. 101:2.
Prayerful. 1 Sam. 1:13; Ps. 27:8.

Prepared to seek God.
2 Chron. 19:3; Ezra 7:10;
Ps. 10:17.
Pure. Ps. 24:4; Matt. 5:8.
Sincere. Acts 2:46; Heb. 10:22.
Sympathizing. Jer. 4:19; Lam. 3:51.
Tender. 1 Sam. 24:5;
2 Kings 22:19.
A treasury of good. Matt. 12:35.
Upright. Pss. 97:11, 125:4.
Void of fear. Ps. 27:3.
Wholly devoted to God.
Pss. 9:1; 199:10, 69, 145.
Wise. Prov. 10:8; 14:33; 23:15.
Zealous. 2 Chron. 17:6; Jer. 20:9.

HEART, UNRENEWED

Blind. Eph. 4:18.
Covetous. Jer. 22:17; 2 Pet. 2:14.
Darkened. Rom. 1:21.
Deceitful. Jer. 17:9.
Deceived. Isa. 44:20; James 1:26.
Desperately wicked. Jer. 17:9.
Despiteful. Ezek. 25:15.
Disobedient. Ps. 101:4; Prov. 6:14;
17:20.
Divided. Hos. 10:2.
Double. 1 Chron. 12:33; Ps. 12:2.
Elated by prosperity.
2 Chron. 26:16; Dan. 5:20.
Elated by sensual indulgence.
Hos. 13:6.
Ensnaring. Eccles. 7:26.
Far from God. Isa. 29:13, with
Matt. 15:8.
Foolish. Prov. 12:23, 22:15.
Full of evil. Eccles. 9:3.
Full of evil imaginations. Gen. 6:5;
8:21; Prov. 6:18.
Full of vain thoughts. Jer. 4:14.
Fully set to do evil. Eccles. 8:11.
Hard. Ezek. 3:7; Mark 10:5;
Rom. 2:5.

Hateful to God. Prov. 6:16, 18; 11:20.

Haughty. Prov. 18:12; Jer. 48:29.

Idolatrous. Ezek. 14:3–4.

Influenced by the devil. John 13:2.

Of little worth. Prov. 10:20.

Mad. Eccles. 9:3.

Mischievous. Pss. 28:3; 140:2.

Not perfect with God. 1 Kings 15:3; Acts 8:21; Prov. 6:18.

Not prepared to seek God. 2 Chron. 12:14.

Often judgment is impaired. Isa. 6:10; Acts 28:26–27.

Often judicially hardened. Exod. 4:21; Josh. 11:20.

Perverse. Prov. 12:8.

Prone to depart from God. Deut. 29:18; Jer. 17:5.

Prone to error. Ps. 95:10.

Proud. Ps. 101:5; Jer. 49:16.

Rages against the Lord. Prov. 19:3.

Rebellious. Jer. 5:23.

Stiff. Ezek. 2:4.

Stony. Ezek. 11:19; 36:26.

Stout. Isa. 10:12; 46:12.

Studies destruction. Prov. 24:2.

A treasury of evil. Matt. 12:35; Mark 7:21.

Unbelieving. Heb. 3:12.

Uncircumcised. Lev. 26:41; Acts 7:51.

Unrepentant. Rom. 2:5.

Worldly. Rom. 8:7.

HEARTH

A place for fire. Isa. 30:14.

HEAT

Jonah overcome with. Jon. 4:8.

HEATHEN

Aid missions to. 2 Cor. 11:9; 3 John 1:6–7.

Are without God and Christ. Eph. 2:12.

Baptism to be administered to. Matt. 28:19.

Cautions against imitating. Jer. 10:2; Matt. 6:7.

The church will be avenged of. Ps. 149:7; Jer. 10:25; Obad. 1:15.

Conversion of, acceptable to God. Acts 10:35; Rom. 15:16.

Danger of mingling with. Ps. 106:35.

Degradation of. Lev. 25:44.

Described as

Cruel. Ps. 74:20; Rom. 1:31.

Filthy. Ezra 6:21; Eph. 4:19; 5:12.

Having no hope. Eph. 2:12.

Idolatrous. Ps. 135:15; Rom. 1:23, 25.

Ignorant. 1 Cor. 1:21; Eph. 4:18.

Persecuting. Ps. 2:1–2; 2 Cor. 11:26.

Scoffing at believers. Ps. 79:10.

Strangers to the covenant of promise. Eph. 2:12.

Worshipers of the devil. 1 Cor. 10:20.

Employed to punish the church. Lev. 26:33; Jer. 39:14; Lam. 1:3; Ezek. 7:24; 25:7; Dan. 4:27; Hab. 1:5–9.

Evil of imitating. 2 Kings 16:3; Ezek. 11:12.

Given to Christ. Ps. 2:8; Dan. 7:14.

Glory of God to be declared among. 1 Chron. 16:24; Ps. 96:3.

God

Punishes. Ps. 44:2; Joel 3:11–13;
Mic. 5:15; Hab. 3:12;
Zech. 14:18.

Rules over. 2 Chron. 20:6;
Ps. 47:8.

Thwarts the counsels of.
Ps. 33:10.

Will be exalted among.
Pss. 46:10; 102:15.

Will finally judge. Rom. 2:12–16.

Gospel received by.
Acts 11:1–13:48; 15:3, 23.

Gospel to be preached to.
Matt. 24:14; 28:19; Rom. 16:26;
Gal. 1:16.

Have

Evidence of the goodness of God.
Acts 14:17.

Evidence of the power of God.
Rom. 1.19–20; Acts 17:27.

The testimony of conscience.
Rom. 2:14–15.

The Holy Spirit poured out on.
Acts 10:44–45; 15:8.

Necessity for preaching to.
Rom. 10:14.

Praise God for success of the gospel
among. Ps. 98:1–3; Acts 11:18.

Pray for. Ps. 67:2–5.

Salvation of, predicted. Gen. 12:3,
with Gal. 3:8; Isa. 2:2–4; 52:10;
60:1–8.

Salvation provided for. Acts 28:28;
Rom. 15:9–12.

HEAVEN

Angels are in. Matt. 18:10; 24:36.

Believers rewarded in. Matt. 5:12;
1 Pet. 1:4.

Christ

Is all-powerful in. Matt. 28:18;
1 Pet. 3:22.

As mediator, entered into.
Acts 3:21; Heb. 6:20; 9:12, 24.

Created by God. Gen. 1:1;
Rev. 10:6.

Enoch and Elijah translated into.
Gen. 5:24, with Heb. 11:5;
2 Kings 2:11.

Everlasting. Ps. 89:29; 2 Cor. 5:1.

Flesh and blood cannot inherit.
1 Cor. 15:50.

God

Answers His people from.
1 Chron. 21:26;
2 Chron. 7:14; Neh. 9:27;
Ps. 20:6.

Fills. 1 Kings 8:27; Jer. 23:24.

Is the Lord of. Dan. 5:23;
Matt. 11:25.

Reigns in. Pss. 11:4; 135:6;
Dan. 4:35.

Sends His judgments
from. Gen. 19:24;
1 Sam. 2:10; Dan. 4:13–14;
Rom. 1:18.

God's dwelling place. 1 Kings 8:30;
Matt. 6:9.

God's throne. Isa. 66:1, with
Acts 7:49.

Happiness of, described.
Rev. 7:16–17.

High. Ps. 103.11, Isa. 57:15.

Holy. Deut. 26:15; Ps. 20:6;
Isa. 57:15.

Immeasurable. Jer. 31:37.

Is called

The Father's house. John 14:2.

A barn. Matt. 3:12.

A heavenly country. Heb. 11:16.

The kingdom of Christ and of God.
Eph. 5:5.
Paradise. 2 Cor. 12:2, 4.
A rest. Heb. 4:9.
Lay up treasure in. Matt. 6:20;
Luke 12:33.
Names of believers are written in.
Luke 10:20; Heb. 12:23.
Repentance occasions joy in.
Luke 15:7.
The wicked excluded from: Gal.
5:21; Eph. 5:5; Rev. 22:15.

HEAVE OFFERING
See Offering, Heave

HEBREW
Applied to Abraham. Gen. 14:13.
Applied to Abraham's descendants.
Gen. 39:14; Exod. 2:6;
Deut. 15:12; 1 Sam. 4:9;
Jon. 1:9; Acts 6:1; 2 Cor. 11:22.
Used to denote the language of the
Jews. John 5:2; Acts 21:40;
Rev. 9:11.
A word supposed to be a corruption
of the name Eber who was an
ancestor of Abraham.
Gen. 10:24, 11:14–26.

HEDGE
A fence. Job 1:10; Isa. 5:5;
Mark 12:1.
People dwelled in. Luke 14:23.
Of thorns. Prov. 15:19.

HEEDFULNESS
Commanded. Exod. 23:13;
Prov. 4:25–27.

Necessary
In the care of the soul. Deut. 4:9.
In conduct. Eph. 5:15.

Against false Christs, and false
prophets. Matt. 24:4–5, 23–25.
Against false teachers. Phil. 3:2;
Col. 2:8; 2 Pet. 3:16–17.
In giving judgment.
1 Chron. 19:6–7.
In the house and worship of God.
Eccles. 5:1.
In how we hear. Luke 8:18.
Against idolatry. Deut. 4:15–16.
In keeping God's commandments.
Josh. 22:5.
Against presumption. 1 Cor.
10:12.
Promises to. 1 Kings 2:4;
1 Chron. 22:13.
Against sin. Heb. 12:15–16.
In speech. Prov. 13:3;
James 1:19.
In what we hear. Mark 4:24.
In worldly company. Ps. 39:1;
Col. 4:5.
Against unbelief. Heb. 3:12.

HEIFER
An atonement for murder.
Deut. 21:1–9.
The red heifer used for the water of
separation. Num. 19; Heb. 9:13.
Stubborn. Hos. 4:16.
Used as a sacrifice. Num. 19:2;
Deut. 21:3.
Used for plowing. Judg. 14:18.
Used for treading out wheat.
Hos. 10:11.
Used in a figurative sense, of
backsliders. Hos. 4:16.
Used of the obedient. Hos. 10:11.

HEIR
Ishmael not to be Abraham's.
Gen. 21:10.

Those in Christ are, according to the promise. Gal. 3:29.

Used in a figurative sense. Those born of God are, with Christ. Rom. 8:17.

HELL

The beast, false prophets, and the devil will be thrown into. Rev. 19:20; 20:10.

Body suffers in. Matt. 5:29; 10:28.

Described as
Devouring fire. Isa. 33:14.
Everlasting burnings. Isa. 33:14.
Everlasting fire. Matt. 25:41.
Everlasting punishment. Matt. 25:46.
Fire and brimstone. Rev. 14:10.
A furnace of fire. Matt. 13:42, 50.
A lake of fire. Rev. 20:15.
Unquenchable fire. Matt. 3:12.

Devils are confined in, until the judgment day. 2 Pet. 2:4; Jude 6.

Human power cannot preserve from. Ezek. 32:27.

Illustrated. Isa. 30:33.

The place of disembodied spirits
And a place of torment. Luke 16:23.
Contains, a place of rest, Abraham's bosom. Luke 16:23.
Paradise. Luke 23:43.
Which Christ visited. Luke 23:43; Acts 2:31; 1 Pet. 3:19.

The place of future punishment
Destruction from the presence of God. 2 Thess. 1:9.
Eternal. Isa. 33:14; Rev. 20:10.

Powers of, cannot prevail against the church. Matt. 16:18.

Prepared for the devil, etc. Matt. 25:41.

Society of the wicked leads to. Prov. 5:5; 9:18.

Soul suffers in. Matt. 10:28.

Strive to keep others from. Prov. 23:14; Jude 23.

The wicked will be turned into. Ps. 9:17.

The wise avoid. Prov. 15:24.

HELM

Of a ship. Acts 27:40.

Used in a figurative sense of the tongue. James 3:4.

HELMET

A defensive headgear worn by soldiers. 1 Sam. 17:5; 2 Chron. 26:14; Jer. 46:4; Ezek. 23:24.

Used in a figurative sense. Isa. 59:17; Eph. 6:17; 1 Thess. 5:8.

HELP

Exemplified by
Christians. Acts 16:9.
Gamaliel. Acts 5:17–42.
Good Samaritan. Luke 10:25–37.
Moses' helpers. Exod. 17:11–12.
Neighbors. Isa. 41:6.
Testimony of. Pss. 86:17; 118:13; Heb. 13:6.

HEMORRHAGE

Menstruation. Lev. 15:19; Matt. 9:20; Luke 8:43.

A woman suffers twelve years. Mark 5:25–29.

HEMORRHOIDS
A disease with the Philistines were
afflicted. Deut. 28:27;
1 Sam. 5:6, 12; 6:4, 11.

HEN
Used in a figurative sense.
Matt. 23:37; Luke 13:34.

HERALD
Signify by the word preacher.
1 Tim. 2:7; 2 Tim. 1:11;
2 Pet. 2:5.

HERBS
Given for food. Gen. 1:29, 30;
Prov. 15:17.

HERBS, BITTER
Eaten symbolically with the Passover.
Exod. 12:8; Num. 9:11.

HEREDITY
Death transmitted through.
1 Cor. 15:22.
Not sufficient for right standing with
God. Matt. 3:9; John 3:6–7.
Seen in Adam's son. Gen. 5:3.
Sin transmitted through. Eph. 2:3.

HERESY
Paul accused of. Acts 18:13.
Paul and Silas accused of.
Acts 16:20–21, 23.
Propagandism of, forbidden under
severe penalties. Deut. 12;
Titus 3:10–11; 2 John 10–11.
Repudiated by Paul. Acts 24:13–16.
Teachers of, among early Christians.
Acts 15:24; 2 Cor. 11:4;
Gal. 1:7; 2:4; 2 Pet. 2;
Jude 3–16; Rev. 2:2.

HIGH PLACES
Asa destroys. 2 Chron. 14:3.
Hezekiah destroys. 2 Kings 18:4.
The idolatrous, to be destroyed.
Lev. 26:30.
Jehoshaphat destroys.
2 Chron. 17:6.
Josiah destroys. 2 Kings 23:8.
Sexual immorality at.
Ezek. 16:24–43.
Signify a place of idolatrous worship.
Num. 22:41; 2 Kings 17:9, 29;
Jer. 7:31.
A term used to describe places of
worship. Gen. 12:8; 22:2, 14;
31:54; 1 Sam. 9:12;
2 Sam. 24:25; 1 Kings 3:2, 4;
18:30, 38; 1 Chron. 6:39.

HIGH PRIEST
Assisted by a deputy. 2 Sam. 15:24;
Luke 3:2.

Jewish High Priest

Called

God's high priest. Acts 23:4.

The priest. Exod. 29:30;
Neh. 7:65.

Ruler of the people. Exod. 22:28,
with Acts 23:5.

Consecrated to his office.
Exod. 40:13; Lev. 8:12.

Deputy of

Called the second priest.
2 Kings 25:18.

Had oversight of the Levites.
Num. 3:32.

Had oversight of the tabernacle.
Num. 4:16.

Duties of

Appointing priests to offices.
1 Sam. 2:36.

Bearing before the Lord the names
of Israel for a memorial.
Exod. 28:12, 29.

Blessing the people.
Lev. 9:22–23.

Consecrating the Levites.
Num. 8:11–21.

Inquiring of God by Urim and
Thummim. 1 Sam. 23:9–12;
30:7–8.

Lighting the sacred
lamps. Exod. 30:8; Num. 8:3.

Making atonement in the most
holy place once a year. Lev. 16;
Heb. 9:7.

Offering gifts and sacrifices.
Heb. 5:1.

Presiding in the superior court.
Matt. 26:3, 57–62;
Acts 5:21–28; 23:1–5.

Taking charge of money collected
in the sacred treasury.
2 Kings 12:10; 22:4.

Taking the census of the people.
Num. 1:3.

Family of Eli removed from office of,
for bad conduct. 1 Sam. 2:27–36.

Forbidden to mourn for any.
Lev. 21:10–12.

Inferior to Christ in

Being made without an oath.
Heb. 7:20–22.

Being of the order of Aaron.
Heb. 6:20; 7:11–17; 8:4–5,
with 1–2, 6.

Entering into Holy of Holies every
year. Heb. 9:7, 12, 25.

Needing to make atonement for
his own sins. Heb. 5:2–3;
7:26–28; 9:7.

Not being able to continue.
Heb. 7:23–24.

Offering the same sacrifices.
Heb. 9:25–26, 28; 10:11–12,
14.

Needed to sacrifice for himself.
Heb. 5:1–3.

Next in rank to the king. Lam. 2:6.

Office of

Hereditary. Exod. 29:29.

Made annual by the Romans.
John 11:49–51, with Acts 4:6.

Promised to the posterity of
Phinehas for his zeal.
Num. 25:12–13.

Often exercised chief civil power.
1 Sam. 4:18.

Sometimes deposed by the kings.
1 Kings 2:27.

Sometimes enabled to prophesy.
John 11:49–52.

Special garments of

Breastplate. Exod. 28:15–29.

Crown of gold, etc.
Exod. 28:36–38.
Embroidered coat. Exod. 28:4,
39.
Ephod. Exod. 28:6–7.
Linen turban. Exod. 28:4, 39.
Made by divine wisdom given to
Bezaleel, etc. Exod. 28:3; 36:1;
39:1.
Robe of the ephod.
Exod. 28:31–35.
Sash. Exod. 28:4, 39.
Went to his successors.
Exod. 29:29.
Were for beauty and ornament.
Exod. 28:2.
Worn at his consecration.
Lev. 8:7, 9.
Worn seven days after
consecration. Exod. 29:30.
Specially called of God.
Exod. 28:1–2; Heb. 5:4.
To be tender and compassionate.
Heb. 5:2.
To marry a virgin of Aaron's family.
Lev. 21:13–14.

Typified Christ in
Alone entering into most holy
place. Heb. 9:7, 12, 24, with
4:14.
Bearing the names of Israel upon
his heart. Exod. 28:29, with
Song of Sol. 8:6.
Being called of God. Heb. 5:4–5.
Being liable to temptation.
Heb. 2:18.
Blessing. Lev. 9:22–23;
Acts 3:26.
Compassion and sympathy for the
weak and ignorant. Heb. 4:15;
5:1–2.
His appointment. Isa. 61:1;
John 1:32–34.

His title. Heb. 3:1.
Holiness of office. Lev. 21:15,
with Heb. 7:26.
Interceding. Num. 16:43–48;
Heb. 7:25.
Making atonement. Lev. 16:33;
Heb. 2:17.
Marrying a virgin. Lev. 21:13–14;
2 Cor. 11:2.
Performing by himself all the
services on Day of Atonement.
Lev. 16, with Heb. 1:3.
Splendid dress. Exod. 28:2, with
John 1:14.
Wore the ordinary priest's garments
when making atonement in the
holy place. Lev. 16:4.

HIGHWAYS

All obstructions removed from,
before persons of distinction.
Isa. 40:3–4, with Matt. 3:3.
Beggars sat beside. Matt. 20:30;
Mark 10:46.
Bypaths more secure in times of
danger. Judg. 5:6.
Called the king's highway.
Num. 20:17.
Desolation of, threatened as a
punishment. Lev. 26:22;
Isa. 33:8.
Generally broad. Judg. 20:32, 45;
Matt. 7:13.
Generally straight. 1 Sam. 6:12;
Isa. 40:3.

Illustrative of
Christ. John 14:6.
Facilities for the restoration of the
Jews. Isa. 11:16; 62:10.
Facilities for the spread of the
gospel, when made in the
deserts. Isa. 40:3; 43:19.
The way of holiness. Isa. 3:5:8.

The way to destruction, when broad. Matt. 7:13.
The way to life, when narrow. Matt. 7:14.

Infested with
Robbers. Jer. 3:2; Luke 10:30–33.
Serpents. Gen. 49:17.
Wild beasts. 1 Kings 13:24, with Isa. 35:9.
Made to all cities of refuge. Deut. 19:2–3.
Marked out by heaps of stones. Jer. 31:21.
Often made in deserts. Isa. 40:3.
Often obstructed. Jer. 18:15.
Roads for public use. Num. 20:19; Deut. 2:27.

HIRE
Law concerning property. Exod. 22:14–15.

HOLIDAY
For rest. Lev. 25:2–7.

HOLINESS
Becoming in the church. Ps. 93:5.
Behavior of aged women should be as becomes. Titus 2:3.

Believers
Should lead to separation from the wicked. Num. 16:21, 26; 2 Cor. 6.17 18.
The wicked are without. 1 Tim. 1:9; 2 Tim. 3:2.
The Word of God the means of producing. John 17:17; 2 Tim. 3:16–17.
Called to. 1 Thess. 4:7; 2 Tim. 1:9.
Elected to. Rom. 8:29; Eph. 1:4.

New created in. Eph. 4:24.
Possess. 1 Cor. 3:17; Heb. 3:1.
Should continue in. Luke 1:75.
Should follow after. Heb. 12:14.
Should have their conversation in. 1 Pet. 1:15; 2 Pet. 3:11.
Should present their bodies to God in. Rom. 12:1.
Should seek perfection in. 2 Cor. 7:1.
Should serve God in. Luke 1:74–75.
Should yield their members as instruments of. Rom. 6:13, 19.
Will be presented to God in. Col. 1:22; 1 Thess. 3:13.
Will continue in, forever. Rev. 22:11.
Character of Christ, the standard of. Rom. 8:29; Phil. 2:5; 1 John 2:6.
Character of God, the standard of. Lev. 19:2, with 1 Pet. 1:15–16; Eph. 5:1.
Chastisements are intended to produce, in believers. Heb. 12:10; James 1:2–3.

Christ
An example of. Heb. 7:26; 1 Pet. 2:21–22.
Desires for His people. John 17:17.
Effects in His people. Eph. 5:25–27.
Church is the beauty of. 1 Chron. 16:29; Ps. 29:2.
Commanded. Lev. 11:45; 20:7; Eph. 5:8; Col. 3:12; Rom. 12:1.
Gospel the way of. Isa. 35:8.

Ministers should
Avoid everything inconsistent with. Lev. 21:6; Isa. 52:11.
Be examples of. 1 Tim. 4:12.

Exhort to. Heb. 12:14;
1 Pet. 1:14–16.
Possess. Titus 1:8.

Motives to
The destruction of all things.
2 Pet. 3:11.
The glory of God. John 15:8;
Phil. 1:11.
The love of Christ.
2 Cor. 5:14–15.
The mercies of God.
Rom. 12:1–2.
Necessary to God's worship.
Ps. 24:3–4.
None will see God without. Eph. 5:5;
12:14.
Promised to the church. Isa. 35:8;
Obad. 1:17; Zech. 14:20–21.
Promise to women to continue in.
1 Tim. 2:15.
Required in prayer. 1 Tim. 2:8.

Result of
God's keeping. John 17:15.
The manifestation of God's grace.
Titus 2:3, 11–12.
Subjection to God. Rom. 6:22.
Union with Christ. John 15:4–5;
17:9.

HOLINESS OF GOD
See God, Holiness of

HOLOCAUST
See Ethnic Cleansing; Genocide; and
War Crimes.

HOLY LAND
Abounded in minerals. Deut. 8:9;
33:25.
All inheritances in, inalienable.
Lev. 25:10, 23.
Allotment of, specified Josh. 14–19.

Burial place of the patriarchs.
Gen. 49:29–31; 50:13, 25;
Josh. 24:32.

Called
Glorious land. Dan. 11:16.
Good land. Num. 14:7;
Deut. 3:25.
The land. Lev. 26:42; Luke 4:25.
Land of Canaan. Gen. 11:31;
Lev. 14:34.
Land of Immanuel. Isa. 8:8.
Land of Israel. 1 Sam. 13:19;
Matt. 2:20–21.
Land of Judah. Isa. 26:1.
Land of promise. Heb. 11:9.
Land of the Hebrews. Gen. 40:15.
The Lord's land. Hos. 9:3.
Palestina. Exod. 15:14;
Isa. 14:29, 31.
Pleasant land. Ps. 106:24;
Dan. 8:9.
Conquered by Joshua. Josh. 6–12.
Divided by lot. Num. 34:16–29,
with 13:7–14.

Divided into
Four provinces by the Romans.
Luke 3:1.
Twelve provinces by Solomon.
1 Kings 47:7–19.
Two kingdoms in the time of
Rehoboam. 1 Kings 11:35–36;
12:19–20.
Extensive commerce of, in
Solomon's reign.
1 Kings 9:26–28; 10:22–29.

Extent of
As at first divided. Num. 34:1–12.
As promised. Gen. 15:18;
Deut. 1:7; Josh. 1:4.
Under Solomon. 1 Kings 4:21,
24; 2 Chron. 9:26.

Extremely fruitful. Exod. 3:8;
Num. 13:27; Deut. 8:7–9;
11:10–12.
Given by covenant to Israel.
Exod. 6:4.
Inhabitants of, expelled for
wickedness. Gen. 15:16;
Exod. 23:23; Lev. 18:25;
Deut. 18:12.
Numerous population of, in
Solomon's reign. 1 Kings 3:8;
2 Chron. 1:9.
Obedience the condition of
continuing in. Lev. 23:3, etc.;
Deut. 5:33; 11:16–17, 22–25.
Original inhabitants of.
Gen. 10:15–20; Deut. 7:1.

Promised to
Abraham. Gen. 12:7; 13:15;
17:8.
Isaac. Gen. 26:3.
Jacob. Gen. 28:13, 15; 35:12.
Prosperity of, in Solomon's reign.
1 Kings 4:20.
A sabbath of rest appointed for.
Lev. 25:2–5.
Twelve men sent to spy. Num. 13.
A type of the rest that remains for
believers. Heb. 4:1–2, 9;
1 Pet. 1:4.

HOLY OF HOLIES
Believers have boldness to enter the
true. Heb. 10:19.

Called the
Holiest of all. Heb. 9:3.
Holy place. Exod. 28:29;
Lev. 16:2–3.
Holy sanctuary. Lev. 16:33.
Most holy place. Exod. 26:31–33.
Oracle. 1 Kings 6:5, 16, 20.
Sanctuary. Lev. 4:6; Ps. 20:2.

Contained
Aaron's rod. Num. 17:10;
Heb. 9:4.
Ark of testimony. Exod. 26:33;
40:3, 21.
Cherubim. Exod. 25:18–22;
1 Kings 6:23–28.
Golden jar. Heb. 9:4.
Mercy seat. Exod. 26:34.
Pot of manna. Exod. 16:33;
Heb. 9:4.
A written copy of the divine law.
Deut. 31:26; 2 Kings 22:8.
Divided from the outward tabernacle
by a veil. Exod. 26:31–33.
God appeared in. Exod. 25:22;
Lev. 16:2.

High priest
Alone to enter, once a year.
Heb. 9:7.
Entered, in ordinary priest's dress.
Lev. 16:4.
Entered, not without blood of
atonement. Lev. 16:14–15;
Heb. 9:7.
Made atonement for.
Lev. 16:15–16, 20, 33.
Not to enter, at all times.
Lev. 16:2.
Offered incense in. Lev. 16:12.
Laid open to view at Christ's death.
Matt. 27:51.
Priests allowed to enter and prepare
the holy things for removal.
Num. 4:5.
A type of heaven. Ps. 102:19;
Heb. 9:12–13, 24.

**HOLY SPIRIT, ANOINTING OF
THE**
Abiding in believers. 1 John 2:27.
Believers receive. Isa. 61:3;
1 John 2:20.

From God. 2 Cor. 1:21.
God preserves those who receive.
Pss. 18:50; 20:6; 89:20–23.
Guides into all truth. 1 John 2:27.

That Christ should receive
Predicted. Ps. 45:7; Isa. 61:1;
Dan. 9:24.
Fulfilled. Luke 4:18, 21;
Acts 4:27; 10:38; Heb. 1:9.
Types. Exod. 40:13–15; Lev. 8:12;
1 Sam. 16:13; 1 Kings 19:16.

HOLY SPIRIT, BAPTISM WITH THE

All believers partake of.
1 Cor. 12:13.
Christ administered. Matt. 3:11;
John 1:33.
Is through Christ. Titus 3:6.
Necessity for. John 3:5;
Acts 19:2–6.
Predicted. Ezek. 36:25.
Promised to believers.
Acts 1:5; 2:38–39; 11:16.
Renews and cleanses the soul.
Titus 3:5; 1 Pet. 3:20–21.
Typified. Acts 2:1–4.
Word of God instrumental to.
Acts 10:44; Eph. 5:26.

HOLY SPIRIT, THE COMFORTER

As such He
Abides forever with believers.
John 14:16.
Communicates joy to believers.
Rom. 14:17; Gal. 5:22;
1 Thess. 1:6.
Dwells with and in believers.
John 14:17.
Edifies the church. Acts 9:31.

Imparts hope. Rom. 15:13;
Gal. 5:5.
Imparts the love of God.
Rom. 5:3–5.
Is known by believers.
John 14:17.
Proceeds from the Father.
John 15:26.
Teaches believers. John 14:26.
Testifies of Christ. John 15:26.

Given
By Christ. Isa. 61:3.
Through Christ's intercession.
John 14:16.
By the Father. John 14:16.
Sent in the name of Christ.
John 14:26.
The world cannot receive.
John 14:17.

HOLY SPIRIT, DEITY OF

As appointing and sending ministers.
Acts 13:2, 4, with Matt. 9:38;
Acts 20:28.
As author of the new birth.
John 3:5–6, with 1 John 5:4.
Being invoked as Jehovah.
Luke 2:26–29; Acts 4:23–25,
with 1:16, 20; 2 Thess. 3:5.
As called God. Acts 5:3–4.
As Comforter of the church.
Acts 9:31, with 2 Cor. 1:3.
As convincing of sin, righteousness,
and judgment. John 16:8–11.
As Creator. Gen. 1:26–27, with
Job 33:4.
As directing where the gospel should
be preached. Acts 16:6–7, 10.
As dwelling in believers. John 14:17,
with 1 Cor. 14:25; 1 Cor. 3:16,
with 6:19.
As equal to, and one with the Father.
Matt. 28:19; 2 Cor. 13:14.

As eternal. Heb. 9:14.
As inspiring Scripture. 2 Tim. 3:16,
　with 2 Pet. 1:21.
As Jehovah. Exod. 17:7, with
　Heb. 3:7–9; Num. 12:6, with
　2 Pet. 1:21.
As Jehovah Most High. Ps. 78:17,
　21, with Acts 7:51.
As Jehovah of hosts. Isa. 6:3, 8–10,
　with Acts 28:25.
As joined with the Father and the
　Son in the baptismal formula.
　Matt. 28:19.
As omnipotent (all-powerful).
　Luke 1:35; Rom. 15:19.
As omnipresent (all-present).
　Ps. 139:7–13.
As omniscient (all-knowing).
　1 Cor. 2:10.
As raising Christ from the dead.
　Acts 2:24, with 1 Pet. 3:18;
　Heb. 13:20, with Rom. 1:4.
As sanctifying the church.
　Ezek. 37:28, with Rom. 15:16.
As sovereign Disposer of all things.
　Dan. 4:35, with 1 Cor. 12:6, 11.
As the source of miraculous power.
　Matt. 12:28, with Luke 11:20;
　Acts 19:11, with Rom. 15:19.
As the source of wisdom. Isa. 11:2;
　John 16:13; 14:26; 1 Cor. 12:8.
As the Spirit of glory and of God. 1
　Pet. 4:14.
As the Witness. Heb. 10:15, with
　1 John 5:9.

HOLY SPIRIT, GIFT OF THE

Causes the wilderness to become
　fertile. Isa. 32:15.
Evidence of union with Christ.
　1 John 3:24; 4:13.
By the Father. Neh. 9:20;
　Luke 11:13.

Guarantee of the inheritance of the
　believers. 2 Cor. 1:22; 5:5;
　Eph. 1:14.

Given
　According to promise.
　　Acts 2:38–39.
　In answer to prayer. Luke 11:13;
　　Eph. 1:16–17.
　To Christ without measure.
　　John 3:34.
　For comfort of believers.
　　John 14:16.
　Upon the exaltation of Christ.
　　Ps. 68:18; John 7:39.
　To the Gentiles.
　　Acts 10:44–45; 11:17; 15:8.
　For instruction. Neh. 9:20.
　Through the intercession of Christ.
　　John 14:16.
　To those who obey God.
　　Acts 5:32.
　To those who repent and believe.
　　Acts 2:38.
Permanent. Isa. 59:21; Hag. 2:5;
　1 Pet. 4:14.
A pledge of the continued favor of
　God. Ezek. 39:29.
Received through faith. Gal. 3:14.
By the Son. John 20:22.

HOLY SPIRIT, INDWELLING OF THE

Believers enjoy. Isa. 63:11;
　2 Tim. 1:14.
Believers full of. Acts 6:5; Eph. 5:18
In the body of believers, as His
　temple. 1 Cor. 6:19; 2 Cor. 6:16.
In His church, as His temple.
　1 Cor. 3:16.
Is abiding. 1 John 2:27.

Is the means of
　Guiding. John 16:13; Gal. 5:18.

New Life. Rom. 8:11.

Producing fruit. Gal. 5:22.

Opposed by the worldly nature. Gal. 5:17.

Promised to believers. Ezek. 36:27.

A proof of adoption. Rom. 8:15; Gal. 4:5.

A proof of being Christ's. Rom. 8:9; 1 John 4:13.

Those who have not

Are sensual. Jude 19.

Are without Christ. Rom. 8:9.

HOLY SPIRIT, INSPIRATION OF THE

All Scripture given by. 2 Sam. 23:2; 2 Tim. 3:16.

Design of

To control ministers. Acts 16:6.

To direct ministers. Ezek. 3:24–27; Acts 11:12; 13:2.

To give power to ministers. Mic. 3:8; Acts 1:8.

To reveal future events. Acts 1:16; 28:25; 1 Pet. 1:11.

To reveal the mysteries of God. Amos 3:7; 1 Cor. 2:10.

To testify against sin. 2 Kings 17:13; Neh. 9:30; Mic. 3:8; John 16:8–9.

Despisers of, punished. 2 Chron. 36:15–16; Zech. 7:12.

Irresistible. Amos 3:8.

Modes of

By dreams. Num. 12:6; Dan. 7:1.

By secret impulse. Judg. 13:25; 2 Pet. 1:21.

Various. Heb. 1:1.

By visions. Num. 12:6; Ezek. 11:24.

By a voice. Isa. 6:8; Acts 8:29; Rev. 1:10.

Necessary to prophesying. Num. 11:25–27; 2 Chron. 20:14–17.

Predicted. Joel 2:28, with Acts 2:16–18.

HOLY SPIRIT, MIRACULOUS GIFTS OF THE

Christ endowed with. Matt. 12:28.

Communicated

For the confirmation of the gospel. Mark 16:20; Acts 14:3; Rom. 15:19; Heb. 2:4.

For the edification of the church. 1 Cor. 12:7; 14:12–13.

By the laying on of the apostles' hands. Acts 8:17–18; 19:6.

Upon the preaching of the gospel. Acts 10:44–46.

Counterfeited by Antichrist. Matt. 24:24; 2 Thess. 2:9; Rev. 13:13–14.

Of different kinds. 1 Cor. 12:4–6.

Dispensed, according to His sovereign will. 1 Cor. 12:11.

Listed. 1 Cor. 12:8–10, 28; 14:1.

Might be possessed without saving grace. Matt. 7:22–23; 1 Cor. 13:1–2.

Poured out on the day of Pentecost. Acts 2:1–4.

Predicted. Isa. 35:4–6; Joel 2:28–29.

Temporary nature of. 1 Cor. 13:8.

To be sought after. 1 Cor. 12:31; 14:1.

HOLY SPIRIT, OFFENSES AGAINST THE

Blasphemy against Him, unpardonable. Matt. 12:31–32; 1 John 5:16.

Exhibited in
Danger of being frivolous with the Holy Spirit. Heb. 6:4–6.
Disregarding His testimony. Neh. 9:30.
Grieving Him. Isa. 63:10; Eph. 4:30.
Insulting Him. Heb. 10:29.
Lying to Him. Acts 5:3–4.
Quenching Him. 1 Thess. 5:19.
Resisting Him. Acts 7:51.
Tempting Him. Acts 5:9.
Undervaluing His gifts. Acts 8:19–20.
Exhortations against. Eph. 4:30; 1 Thess. 5:19.

HOLY SPIRIT, PERSONALITY OF

He appoints and commissions ministers. Isa. 48:16; Acts 13:2; 20:28.
He can be grieved. Isa. 63:10; Eph. 4:30.
He can be resisted. Acts 7:51.
He can be tempted. Acts 5:9.
He comforts. Acts 9:31.
He convicts. John 16:8.
He creates and gives life. Job 33:4.
He directs ministers where not to preach. Acts 16:6–7.
He directs ministers where to preach. Acts 8:29; 10:19–20.
He dwells with believers. John 14:17.
He glorifies Christ. John 16:14.
He guides. John 16:13.

He has a power of His own. Rom. 15:13.
He helps our sufferings. Rom. 8:26.
He instructs ministers what to preach. 1 Cor. 2:13.
He sanctifies. Rom. 15:16; 1 Cor. 6:11.
He searches all things. Rom. 11:33–34, with 1 Cor. 2:10–11.
He spoke in, and by, the prophets. Acts 1:16; 1 Pet. 1:11–12; 2 Pet. 1:21.
He strives with sinners. Gen. 6:3.
He teaches. John 14:26; 1 Cor. 12:3.
He testifies of Christ. John 15:26.
He works according to His own will. 1 Cor. 12:11.

HOLY SPIRIT, POWER OF THE

Believers
Abound in hope by. Rom. 15:13.
Enabled to speak the truth boldly by. Mic. 3:8; Acts 6:5, 10; 2 Tim. 1:7–8.
Helped in prayer by. Rom. 8:26.
Strengthened by. Eph. 3:16.
Upheld by. Ps. 51:12.
Christ began His ministry in. Luke 4:14.
Christ performed His miracles by. Matt. 12:28.

Exhibited in
The conception of Christ. Luke 1:35.
Creation. Gen. 1:2; Job 26:13; Ps. 104:30.
Giving spiritual life. Ezek. 37:11–14, with Rom. 8:11.

Making the gospel effective.
1 Cor. 2:4; 1 Thess. 1:5.
Overcoming all difficulties.
Zech. 4:6–7.
Raising Christ from the dead.
1 Pet. 3:18.
Working miracles. Rom. 15:19.
God's Word the instrument of.
Eph. 6:17.
The power of God. Matt. 12:28,
with Luke 11:20.
Promised by Christ. Acts 1:8.
Promised by the Father. Luke 24:49.
Qualifies ministers. Luke 24:49;
Acts 1:8.

HOLY SPIRIT, SEALING OF THE

Believers receive. 2 Cor. 1:22;
Eph. 1:13.
Christ received. John 6:27.
Is until the day of redemption.
Eph. 4:30.
Judgment suspended until all
believers receive. Rev. 7:3.
Type. Rom. 4:11.
The wicked do not receive. Rev. 9:4.

HOLY SPIRIT, SYMBOLS OF

A dove
Descending. Matt. 3:16.
Gentle. Matt. 10:16, with
Gal. 5:22.

Fire
Baptizing. Matt. 3:11.
Illuminating. Exod. 13:21;
Ps. 78:14.
Purifying. Isa. 4:4; Mal. 3:2–3.
Searching. Zeph. 1:12, with
1 Cor. 2:10.

Oil
Comforting. Isa. 61:3; Heb. 1:9.
Consecrating. Exod. 29:7; 30:30;
Isa. 61:1.
Giving joy. Ps. 45:7.
Healing. Luke 10:34; Rev. 3:18.
Illuminating. Matt. 25:3–4;
1 John 2:20, 27.

Rain and dew
Abundant. Ps. 133:3.
Fertilizing. Ezek. 34:26–27;
Hos. 6:3; 10:12; 14:5.
Imperceptible. 2 Sam. 17:12,
with Mark 4:26–28.
Refreshing. Pss. 68:9; 72:6;
Isa. 18:4.

A seal
Authenticating. John 6:27;
2 Cor. 1:22.
For servants of God. Rev. 7:2.
Securing. Eph. 1:13–14; 4:30.

A voice
Guiding. Isa. 30:21, with
John 16:13.
Speaking. Matt. 10:20.
Warning. Heb. 3:7–11.

Tongues of fire
Of Galileans. Acts 2:3.
Understood by others.
Acts 2:6–11.

Water
Abundant. John 7:37–38.
Believing. John 7:38.
Born of. John 3:5.
Cleansing. Ezek. 16:9; 36:25;
Eph. 5:26; Heb. 10:22.
Fertilizing. Ps. 1:3;
Isa. 27:3, 6; 44:3–4; 58:11.
Freely given. Isa. 55:1;
John 4:14; Rev. 22:17.

Refreshing. Ps. 46:4;
Isa. 41:17–18.

Wind
Independent. John 3:8;
1 Cor. 12:11.
Powerful. 1 Kings 19:11, with
Acts 2:2.
Reviving. Ezek. 37:9–10, 14.
Sensible in its effects. John 3:8.

HOLY SPIRIT, THE TEACHER
Attend to the instruction of.
Rev. 2:7, 11, 29.

As such He
Brings the words of Christ to
remembrance. John 14:26.
Directs in the way of godliness.
Isa. 30:21; Ezek. 36:27.
Directs the decisions of the
Church. Acts 15:28.
Enables ministers to teach.
1 Cor. 12:8.
Guides into all truth. John 14:26;
16:13.
Reveals the future. Luke 2:26;
Acts 21:11.
Reveals the things of Christ.
John 16:14.
Reveals the things of God.
1 Cor. 2:10, 13.
Teaches believers to answer
persecutors. Mark 13:11;
Luke 12:12.

Given
In answer to prayer.
Eph. 1:16–17.
To believers. Neh. 9:20; 1 Cor.
2:12–13.
Natural man will not receive the
things of. 1 Cor. 2:14.
Necessity for. 1 Cor. 2:9–10.

Promised. Prov. 1:23.
Spirit of wisdom. Isa. 11:2;
40:13–14.

HOLY SPIRIT, TITLES AND NAMES
Breath of the Almighty. Job 33:4.
Comforter. John 14:16, 26; 15:26.
Eternal Spirit. Heb. 9:14.
Free Spirit. Ps. 51:12.
God. Acts 5:3–4.
Good Spirit. Neh. 9:20; Ps. 143:10.
Holy Spirit. Ps. 51:11; Luke 11:13;
Eph. 1:13; 4:30.
Lord. 2 Thess. 3:5.
Power of the highest. Luke 1:35.
Seven Spirits of God. Rev. 1:4.
Spirit. Matt. 4:1; John 3:6;
1 Tim. 4:1.
Spirit of adoption. Rev. 19:10.
Spirit of burning. Isa. 4:4.
Spirit of Christ. Rom. 8:9;
1 Pet. 1:11.
Spirit of counsel. Isa. 11:2.
Spirit of the Father. Matt. 10:20.
Spirit of the fear of the Lord.
Isa. 11:2.
Spirit of glory. 1 Pet. 4:14.
Spirit of God. Gen. 1:2; Job 33:4;
1 Cor. 2:11.
Spirit of grace. Zech. 12:10; Heb.
10:29.
Spirit of holiness. Rom. 1:4.
Spirit of judgment. Isa. 4:4; 28:6.
Spirit of knowledge. Isa. 11:2.
Spirit of life. Rom. 8:2; Rev. 11:11.
Spirit of the Lord. Isa. 11:2;
Acts 5:9.
Spirit of the Lord God. Isa. 61:1.
Spirit of might. Isa. 11:2.
Spirit of prophecy. Rev. 19:10.
Spirit of revelation. Eph. 1:17.
Spirit of the Son. Gal. 4:6.

Spirit of truth. John 14:17; 15:26.
Spirit of understanding. Isa. 11:2.
Spirit of wisdom. Isa. 11:2;
Eph. 1:17.

HOLY SPIRIT, WITNESS OF THE

Borne against all unbelievers.
Neh. 9:30; Acts 28:25–27.

Borne to Christ
As coming to redeem and sanctify.
1 John 5:6.
On earth. 1 John 5:8.
As exalted to be Prince and Savior
to give repentance.
Acts 5:31–32.
In heaven. 1 John 5:7, 11.
As Messiah. Luke 3:22, with
John 1:32–33.
As perfecting believers.
Heb. 10:14–15.
As predicted by Himself.
John 15:26.
Faithful preaching of the apostles
accompanied by. 1 Cor. 2:4;
1 Thess. 1:5.
First preaching of the gospel
confirmed by. Acts 14:3, with
Heb. 2:4.

Given to believers
On believing. Acts 15:8;
1 John 5:10.
As an evidence of adoption.
Rom. 8:16.
As an evidence of Christ in them.
1 John 3:24.
As an evidence of God in them.
1 John 4:13.
To testify to them of Christ.
John 15:26.
Is truth. 1 John 5:6.

To be implicitly received.
1 John 5:6, 9.

HOMELESSNESS

Examples of
Absalom. 2 Sam. 14:13–14.
Believers. Heb. 11:37–38.
Blind people in the streets.
Lam. 4:14–15.
Exiled people. Jer. 12:7; Lam 5:2;
Hos. 9:17; Amos 7:17.
Jesus. Matt. 8:20.
Paul. 1 Cor. 4:11.

Homeless persons
Given a home. Job 31:32.
Like a bird away from its nest.
Prov. 27:8.
Not separated from the love of
God. Rom 8:38–39.
Not to be oppressed. Zech 7:10.
To be given equal rights under the
law. Lev 24:22; Deut. 24:17.
To be provided for. Lev 19:10;
Deut. 10:18–19;
Matt. 25:31–46.
Watched over by the Lord.
Ps. 146:9.

HOMESTEAD

Mortgaged. Neh. 5:3.
When alienable, and when
inalienable. Lev. 25:25–34.

HOMICIDE

Accidental, laws concerning.
Exod. 21:13–32.

Examples of
Abimelech. Judg. 9:5, 18, 56.
Abner. 2 Sam. 2:18–24.
Absalom. 2 Sam. 13:22–29.

Adrammelech and Sharezer.
2 Kings 19:37.
Ahab and Jezebel.
1 Kings 21:10–24.
Amalekite. 2 Sam. 1:16.
Amaziah's soldiers.
2 Chron. 25:12.
Amonites. Amos 1:13–15.
Athaliah. 2 Kings 11:1.
Baasha. 1 Kings 15:27–29.
Barabbas. Mark 15:7.
Cain. Gen. 4:8.
David. 2 Sam. 11:14–17.
Ehud. Judg. 3:16–23.
Hazael. 2 Kings 8:15.
Herod. Acts 12:2, 19.
Herod the Great. Matt. 2:16.
Herod Antipas. Matt. 14:10.
Ishmael. Jer. 41:1–7.
Jael. Judg. 4:21.
Jehoram. 2 Chron. 21:4.
Jehu. 2 Kings 9:24–37.
Joab. 2 Sam. 3:24–27.
Joash's servants.
2 Kings 12:20–21.
Lamech. Gen. 4:23–24.
Manasseh. 2 Kings 21:16.
Menahem. 2 Kings 15:16.
Moses. Exod. 2:11–12.
Nebuchadnezzar. Jer. 39:6.
Pharaoh. Exod. 1:16, 22.
Rechab and
Baanah. 2 Sam. 4:5–8.
Sanhedrin. Acts 7:54–60.
Sanhedrin and Pilate.
Matt. 26, 27.
Servants of Amon. 2 Kings 21:23.
Simeon and Levi. Gen. 34:25–31.
Zimri. 1 Kings 16:9–11.

Examples of punishment for
Cain. Gen. 4:11–15.
David. 2 Sam. 12:9–10.
Joab. 1 Kings 2:31–34.

Haman. Esther 7:10.
The murderer of Saul.
2 Sam. 1:15–16.
The murderer of Ishbosheth.
2 Sam. 4:11–12.
The murderers of Joash.
2 Kings 14:5.
Felonious, punishment concerning.
Gen. 4:9–11; Exod. 20:13;
Deut. 15:17; Rom. 13:9.
By raping. Judg. 19:25–28.

HOMOSEXUALITY

Declared as wicked. Gen. 19:7;
Rom. 1:26–27, 32;
1 Tim. 1:8–10.
Forbidden. Lev. 18:22; 20:13.
Practiced at Sodom. Gen. 19:4–5.

Principles relevant to
People created male and female.
Gen. 1:27; 2:18–25;
Matt. 19:4–6.
Those who practice, will not
inherit the kingdom of God.
1 Cor. 6:9–11.

HONESTY

Delights the Lord. Prov. 12:22.
Demanded by God. Prov. 11:18;
Amos 8:4–7.
Imperative for Christians.
Rom. 12:17; 13:13; 2 Cor. 4:2;
8:21; Eph. 4:25; 1 Pet. 2:12.
Important for fellowship. Zech. 8:16.
Necessary in speaking.
Prov. 12:19; 17:20;
Matt. 5:33–37; 1 Kings 22:16;
Ps. 101:7; Rev. 22:15.
Required in business. Lev. 19:35;
Deut. 25:13; Prov. 11:1.

HONEY

Abounded in
Assyria. 2 Kings 18:32.
Canaan. Exod. 3:8; Lev. 20:24;
Deut. 8:8.
Egypt. Num. 16:13.
In the comb, sweetest and most
valuable. Prov. 16:24; 24:13.
Exported from Canaan.
Ezek. 27:17.
First fruits of, offered to God.
2 Chron. 31:5.

Found in
Carcasses of dead animals.
Judg. 14:8.
Rocks. Deut. 32:13; Ps. 81:16.
Woods. 1 Sam. 14:25–26;
Jer. 41:8.
Gathered and prepared by bees.
Judg. 14:18.
God the giver of. Ps. 81:16;
Ezek. 16:19.

Illustrative of
Holy speech of believers.
Song of Sol. 4:11.
Lips of a strange woman.
Prov. 5:3.
Pleasant words. Prov. 16:24.
Wisdom. Prov. 24:13–14.
The Word of God. Pss. 19:10;
119:103.
Loathed by those who are full.
Prov. 27:7.
Moderation needful in the use of.
Prov. 25:16, 27.
Not to be offered with any sacrifice.
Lev. 2:11.
Often sent as a present. Gen. 43:11;
1 Kings 14:3.
Sweetness of. Judg. 14:18.

Valued as a wholesome food.
Prov. 24:13.

Was eaten
With butter. Isa. 7:15, 22.
With the comb. Song of Sol. 5:1;
Luke 24:42.
With locusts. Matt. 3:4; Mark 1:6.
With milk. Song of Sol. 4:11.
Mixed with flour. Exod. 16:31;
Ezek. 16:13.
Plain. 1 Sam. 14:25–26, 29.

HONOR

Belongs to God. Ps. 145:5;
Rev. 4:11.
Due the old. Lev. 19:32; 1 Tim. 5:1.
Due to parents. Exod. 20:12;
Matt. 15:4.
Obtained by honoring God.
Prov. 15:33; 21:31.
Received from God. Esther 8:16;
Dan. 5:18; John 12:26.
Refused by Paul and Barnabas.
Acts 14:11–18.
Refused by Peter. Acts 10:26.
Refused by the angel seen by John in
his vision. Rev. 19:10; 22:8–9.
Rendered to kings.
1 Kings 1:16, 23, 31.
Rendered to princes. Esther 3:2, 5.

HOOF

Parting of, one of the physical marks
used for distinguishing clean and
unclean animals. Lev. 11:3–8;
Deut. 14:3–8.

HOOKS

For pruning. Isa. 2:4; 18:5;
Joel 3:10.
Silver. Exod. 27:10;
38:10–12, 17, 19.

For tabernacle, made of gold.
Exod. 26:32, 37; 36:36.
In the temple, seen in Ezekiel's
vision. Ezek. 40:43.
Used for catching fish. Ezek. 29:4.
Used in a figurative sense.
Ezek. 38:4.

HOPE
Be ready to give an answer
concerning. 1 Pet. 3:15.

Believers
Are called to. Eph. 4:4.
Have all, the same. Eph. 4:4.
Have, in death. Prov. 14:32.
Rejoice in. Rom. 5:2; 12:12.
Should abound in. Rom. 15:3.
Should continue in. Ps. 71:14;
1 Pet. 1:13.
Should hold fast. Heb. 3:6.
Should look for the object of.
Titus 2:13.
Should not be ashamed of.
Ps. 119:116.
Should not be moved
from. Col. 1:23.
A better, brought in by Christ.
Heb. 7:19.
In Christ. 1 Cor. 15:19; 1 Tim. 1:1.
Connected with faith and love.
1 Cor 13:13.

Described as
Blessed. Titus 2:13.
Good. 2 Thess. 2:16.
Happiness. Prov. 10:28.
Lively. 1 Pet. 1:3.
Sure and steadfast. Heb. 6:19.
Does not disappoint. Rom. 5:5.
Encouragement to. Hos. 2:15;
Zech. 9:12.
Encourage others to. Ps. 130:7.

Encourages boldness in preaching.
2 Cor. 3:12.
In God. Ps. 39:7; 1 Pet. 1:21.
In God's promises. Acts 26:6–7;
Titus 1:2.
Happiness of. Ps. 146:5.
Leads to patience. Rom. 8:25;
1 Thess. 1:3.
Leads to purity. 1 John 3:3.
Life is the season of. Eccles. 9:4;
Isa. 38:18.
In the mercy of God. Ps. 33:18.

Objects of
Christ's glorious appearing.
Titus 2:13.
Eternal life. Titus 1:2; 3:7.
Glory. Rom. 5:2; Col. 1:27.
A resurrection. Acts 23:6; 24:15.
Righteousness. Gal. 5:5.
Salvation. 1 Thess. 5:8.

Obtained through
Faith. Rom. 5:1–2; Gal. 5:5.
The gospel. Col. 1:5, 23.
Grace. 2 Thess. 2:16.
Patience and comfort of the
Scriptures. Rom. 15:4.

Of the wicked
Is in their worldly possessions.
Job 31:24.
Will be extinguished in death.
Job 27:8.
Will make them ashamed.
Isa. 20:5–6; Zech. 9:5.
Will perish. Job 8:13; 11:20;
Prov. 10:28.
Results from experience. Rom. 5:4.
Seek for full assurance of. Heb. 6:11.
Triumphs over difficulties.
Rom. 4:18.
The wicked have no ground for.
Eph. 2:12.

The work of the Holy Spirit.
Rom. 15:13; Gal. 5:5.

HORN
Figurative sense, of divine protection.
2 Sam. 22:3.
Of power. 1 Kings 22:11;
Ps. 89:24.
Used in a symbolic sense.
Dan. 7:7–24; Hab. 3:4;
Rev. 17:3–16.
Used to hold the anointing oil.
1 Sam. 16:1; 1 Kings 1:39.

HORSE
Adorned with bells on the neck.
Zech. 14:20.
In battle protected by armor.
Jer. 46:4.

Colors of, mentioned
Bay. Zech. 6:3, 7.
Black. Zech. 6:2, 6; Rev. 6:5.
Dappled. Zech. 6:3, 6.
Pale or ash color. Rev. 6:8.
Red. Zech. 1:8; 6:2; Rev. 6:4.
Speckled. Zech. 1:8.
White. Zech. 1:8; 6:3; Rev. 6:2.
Dedicated to the sun by idolaters.
2 Kings 23:11.

Described as
Fearless. Job 39:20, 22.
Fierce and impetuous.
Job 39:21, 24.
Strong. Pss. 33:17; 147:10.
Surefooted. Isa. 63:13.
Swift. Isa. 30:16; Jer. 4:13;
Hab. 1:8.
Warlike in disposition. Job 39:21;
Jer. 8:6.
Endowed with strength by God.
Job 39:19.

Fed on grain and herbs.
1 Kings 4:23; 18:5.
Governed by bit and bridle. Ps. 32:9;
James 3:3.
Hard hoofs of, alluded to. Isa. 5:28.

Illustrative of
Beauty of the church.
Song of Sol. 1:9; Zech. 10:3.
Dull headstrong disposition.
Ps. 32:9.
Glorious and triumphant
deliverance of the church.
Isa. 63:13.
Impulsiveness of the wicked in sin.
Jer. 8:6.

The Jews
Brought back from Babylon.
Ezra 2:66.
Condemned for multiplying.
Isa. 2:7.
Condemned for trusting to.
Isa. 30:16; 31:3.
Forbidden to multiply.
Deut. 17:16.
Imported from Egypt.
1 Kings 10:28–29.
Multiplied in Solomon's reign.
1 Kings 4:26.
Not to trust in. Hos. 14:3.
Kings and princes rode on.
Esther 6:8–11; Ezek. 23:23.
Loud snorting of, alluded to.
Jer. 8:16, with Job 39:20.
Notice of early traffic in. Gen. 47:17.
Numbers of, kept for war.
Jer. 51:27; Ezek. 26:10.

Often suffered
In battle. Jer. 51:21; Hag. 2:22.
From bites of serpents.
Gen. 49:17.
From blindness. Zech. 12:4.

In the hoof from prancing.
Judg. 5:22.
From pestilence. Exod. 9:3.
From plague. Zech. 14:15.
Prepared and trained for war.
Prov. 21:31.
Sold in fairs and markets.
Ezek. 27:14; Rev. 18:13.
Urged on by whips. Prov. 26:3.

Used for
Bearing burdens. Ezra 2:66;
Neh. 7:68.
Conveying posts, etc.
2 Kings 9:17–19; Esther 8:10.
Drawing chariots. Mic. 1:13;
Zech. 6:2.
Hunting. Job 39:18.
Mounting cavalry. Exod. 14:9;
1 Sam. 13:5.
Vanity of trusting to. Ps. 33:17;
Amos 2:15.
Lack of understanding in, alluded to.
Ps. 32:9.

HOSANNA
Words drawn from Ps. 118:25–26
that greeted Jesus on the occasion
of His triumphal entry. Mark 11:9.

HOSPITALITY
Commanded. Lev. 19:33–34;
Rom. 12:13; 1 Pet. 4:9.
Encouragement to. Luke 14:14;
Heb. 13:2.
Expected by travelers.
Gen. 19:1–11; Judg. 19:16–30.
Required in ministers. 1 Tim. 3:2;
Titus 1:8.

Specially to be shown to
Enemies. 2 Kings 6:22–23;
Rom. 12:20.
The poor. Isa. 58:7; Luke 14:13.

Strangers. Heb. 13:2.
A test of Christian character.
1 Tim. 5:10.

HOSTAGE
Jehoash took, and returned to
Samaria. 2 Kings 14:14.

HOT SPRINGS
The sons of Zibeon found, in the
wilderness. Gen. 36:24.

HOURS
In the night. Acts 23:23.
Used in a symbolic sense. Rev. 8:1;
9:15.
Twelve, in a day. John 11:9.

HOUSE
Altars on roof. 2 Kings 23:12.

Architecture of
Cornerstone. Job 38:6.
Figurative. Ps. 87:1; 118:22.
Foundations of stone.
1 Kings 5:17.
Porches. Judg. 3:23.
Battlements required in Mosaic law.
Deut. 22:8.
Booth on roof. Neh. 8:16.
Built into city walls. Josh. 2:15.
Built of brick. Gen. 11:3;
Exod. 1:11–14; Isa. 9:10.
Built of stone. Lev. 14:40–45,
Isa. 9:10; Amos 5:11.
Built of wood. Song of Sol. 1:17;
Isa. 9:10.
Ceiled and plastered. Dan. 5:5.
In a chamber. 1 Kings 22:25.
Chambers. Gen. 43:30.
Chimneys of. Hos. 13:3.
Courts. Esther 1:5.
With courts. Neh. 8:16.
Dedicated. Deut. 20:5; Ps. 30.

Housetops

Figurative sense. 2 Sam. 7:18; Heb. 3:2.

Flat roofs. Josh. 2:6.

Guest chamber. Mark 14:14.

Hinges. Prov. 26:14.

Lattice. Judg. 5:28.

Laws regarding sale of. Lev. 25:29–33.

"A man's castle." Deut. 24:10, 11.

Painted. Jer. 22:14.

Pillars. Prov. 9:1.

Prayer on roof. Acts 10:9.

Roof used as a dwelling place. Prov. 21:9.

Roof used as a place to sleep. Josh. 2:8.

Summer apartment. Judg. 3:20.

Text of Scripture on doorpost. Deut. 6:9.

Used for worship. Acts 1:13–14; 12:12; Rom. 16:5; 1 Cor. 16:19; Col. 4:15; Philem. 2.

Windows. Judg. 5:28.

HOUSE OF GOD
See God, House of

HUMAN, DEPRAVITY OF
Described by David. Ps. 51:5.

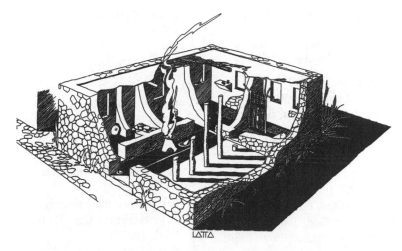

House

Described by Paul.
   Rom. 2:1; 3:9–23; 7:5–25.
Prior to the flood. Gen. 6:5–13;
   8:21.

HUMANITY

Care in construction. Deut. 22:8.
Concern for the needy. Deut. 24:19;
   Matt. 25:40.
Love for brethren. 1 Pet. 2:17;
   1 John 2:10.
Love for enemies. Matt. 5:44.
Love for neighbors. Lev. 19:18;
   Luke 10:27; Gal. 5:14
Regard for animals. Exod. 23.5,
   Deut. 22:6; Prov. 12:10; Job
   5:23; Matt. 18:12.

HUMAN NATURE OF CHRIST

See Christ, Human Nature of

HUMILITY

Accompanies the presence of God.
   Isa. 57:15; Matt. 5:3.

Afflictions intended to produce.
   Lev. 26:41; Deut. 8:3;
   Lam. 3:20.
Before honor. Prov. 15:33.

Believers should
   Be clothed with. 1 Pet. 5:5.
   Beware of false. Col. 2:18, 23.
   Put on. Col. 3:12.
   Walk with. Eph. 4:1–2.
Blessedness of. Matt. 5:3.
Brings wisdom. Prov. 11:2;
   Matt. 11:25.
A characteristic of believers.
   Ps. 34:2.
Christ an example of. Matt 11:29;
   John 13:14–15; Phil. 2:5–8.
Encouraged. Rom. 12:16; Phil. 2:3.
Excellency of. Prov. 16:19.
Lack of, condemned.
   2 Chron. 33:23; 36:12;
   Jer. 44:10; Dan. 5:22.
Leads to riches, honor, and life.
   Prov. 22:4.
Marks the person God
   helps. Matt. 8:8; Luke 18:9–14.

Necessary to the service of God.
Mic. 6:8.
Temporary judgments averted by.
2 Chron. 7:14; 12:6–7.

They who have
Delivered by God. Job 22:29.
Enjoy the presence of God.
Isa. 57:15.
Exalted by God. Luke 14:11;
18:14.
Greatest in Christ's kingdom.
Matt. 18:4; 20:26–28.
Heard by God. Pss. 9:12; 10:17.
Lifted up by God. James 4:10.
Receive more grace. Prov. 3:34;
James 4:6.
Regarded by God. Ps. 138:6;
Isa. 66:2.
Upheld by honor. Prov. 18:12;
29:23.

HUMILITY OF CHRIST
See Christ, Humility of

HUNGER
Absence of, in heaven.
Rev. 7:16–17.
Of Jesus. Matt. 4:2–4; 21:18;
Mark 11:12; Luke 4:2–4;
John 4:8.
Spiritual sense. Matt. 5:6.
A stimulus to work. Prov. 16:26.

HUNTING
Authorized in the Mosaic law.
Lev. 17:13.
By Esau. Gen. 27:3, 5, 30, 33.
Fowling. 1 Sam. 26:20.
By Ishmael. Gen. 21:20.
Of lion. Job 10:16.
By Nimrod. Gen. 10:9.
Used in a figurative sense.
Jer. 16:16.

HUSBANDMAN
See Farmer

HUSBANDS
Duty of, to wives
Be faithful to them. Prov. 5:19;
Mal. 2:14–15.
Comfort them. 1 Sam. 1:8.
Consult with them. Gen. 31:4–7.
Love them. Eph. 5:25, etc.;
Col. 3:19.
Not to leave them though
unbelieving. 1 Cor. 7:11–12,
14, 16.
Regard them as themselves.
Gen. 2:23, with Matt. 19:5.
Respect them. 1 Pet. 3:7.
Stay with them for life. Gen. 2:24;
Matt. 19:3–9.
Have authority over their wives.
Gen. 3:16; 1 Cor. 11:3;
Eph. 5:23.
Not to interfere with their duties to
Christ. Luke 14:26, with
Matt. 19:29.
Should have but one wife.
Gen. 2:24; Mark 10:6–8;
1 Cor. 7:2–4.

HYBRIDIZING
Forbidden. Lev. 19:19.

HYPOCRITES
Affliction to. Isa. 29:15;
Matt. 23:13.
The apostasy to abound with.
1 Tim. 4:2.
Beware of the principles of.
Luke 12:1.
Christ knew and detected.
Matt. 22:18.

Described as

Apparently zealous in the things of
God. Isa. 58:2.

Censorious. Matt. 7:3–5;
Luke 13:14–15.

Covetous. Ezek. 33:31;
2 Pet. 2:3.

Devouring widows' houses.
Matt. 23:14.

Exact in minor, but neglecting
important duties.
Matt. 23:23–14.

Glorying in appearance only.
2 Cor. 5:12.

Having but a form of godliness.
2 Tim. 3:5.

Loving preeminence.
Matt. 23:6–7.

Professing but not practicing.
Ezek. 33:31–32; Matt. 23:3;
Rom. 2:17–23.

Regarding tradition more than the
Word of God. Matt. 15:1–3.

Seeking only outward purity.
Luke 11:39.

Self-righteous. Isa. 65:5;
Luke 18:11.

Showy. Matt. 6:2, 5, 16; 23:5.

Trusting in privileges. Jer. 7:4;
Matt. 3:9.

Using but lip worship. Isa. 29:13,
with Matt. 15:8.

Vile. Isa. 32:6.

Willfully blind. Matt. 23:17, 19,
26.

Zealous in making converts.
Matt. 23:15.

Destroy others by slander.
Prov. 11:9.

Fearfulness will surprise. Isa. 33:14.

God has no pleasure in. Isa. 9:17.

God knows and detects.
Isa. 29:15–16.

Heap up wrath. Job 36:13.

Hope of, perishes. Job 8:13;
27:8–9.

Joy of, but for a moment. Job 20:5.

In power, are a snare. Job 34:30.

Punishment of. Job 15:34;
Isa. 10:6; Jer. 42:20, 22;
Matt. 24:51.

Spirit of, hinders growth in grace.
1 Pet. 2:1.

Will not come before God.
Job 13:16.

Worship of, not acceptable to God.
Isa. 1:11–15; 58:3–5; Matt. 15:9.

Hyssop

HYSSOP

An indigenous plant to Western Asia
and Northern Africa.
1 Kings 4:33.

Israelites used, in sprinkling the blood
of the Paschal lamb upon the
lintels of their doors. Exod. 12:22.

In sprinkling blood in purifications.
Lev. 14:4; Heb. 9:19.

Used in the sacrifices of separation.
Num. 19:6.

Used in giving Jesus vinegar on the
cross. John 19:29.

Used in a figurative sense, of spiritual
cleansing. Ps. 51:7.

IDLENESS AND LAZINESS

Accompanied by conceit.
Prov. 26:16.
Akin to extravagance. Prov. 18:9.
Effects of, afford instruction to
others. Prov. 24:30–32.
False excuses for. Prov. 20:4; 22:13.
Forbidden. Rom. 12:11; Heb. 6:12.
Grievance against. Prov. 6:6, 9.
Illustrated. Prov. 26:14;
Matt. 25:18, 26.

Lead to
Bondage. Prov. 12:24.
Disappointment. Prov. 13:4;
21:25.
Hunger. Prov. 19:15; 20:4;
24:34.
Poverty. Prov. 10:4; 20:13.
Ruin. Prov. 24:30–31;
Eccles. 10:18.
Tattling and meddling.
1 Tim. 5:13.
Produce apathy. Prov. 12:27;
26:15.

IDOLATRY

Accompanied by feasts.
2 Kings 10:20; 1 Cor. 10:27–28.
Adopted by Solomon.
1 Kings 11:5–8.
Adopted by the wicked kings.
1 Kings 21:26; 2 Kings 21:21;
2 Chron. 28:2–4; 33:3, 7.
All forms of, forbidden by the law of
Moses. Exod. 20:4–5.
All pagan nations given up to.
Ps. 96:5; Rom. 1:23, 25;
1 Cor. 12:2.

Altars raised for. 1 Kings 18:26;
Hos. 8:11.
Angels refuse to receive the worship
of. Rev. 22:8–9.
Believers preserved by God from.
1 Kings 19:18, with Rom. 11:4.
Believers refuse to receive the
worship of. Acts 10:25–26;
14:11–15.

Believers should
Flee from. 1 Cor. 10:14.
Keep from. Josh 23:7;
1 John 5:21.
Not covenant with those who
practice. Exod. 34:12, 15;
Deut. 7:2.
Not have anything connected with,
in their houses. Deut. 7:26.
Not have religious dealings with
those who practice. Josh 23:7;
1 Cor. 5:11.
Not intermarry with those who
practice. Exod. 34:16;
Deut. 7:3.
Not partake of anything connected
with. 1 Cor. 10:19–20.
Refuse to engage in, though
threatened with death.
Dan. 3:18.
Testify against. Acts 14:15;
19:26.
Calamity denounced against.
Hab. 2:19.
Captivity of Israel because of.
2 Kings 17:6–18.
Captivity of Judah because of.
2 Kings 17:19–23.

Changing the glory of God into an image. Rom. 1:23, with Acts 17:29.

Changing the truth of God into a lie. Rom. 1:25, with Isa. 44:20.

Consists in
Bowing down to images. Exod. 20:5; Deut. 5:9.
Covetousness. Eph. 5:5; Col. 3:5.
Fearing other gods. 2 Kings 17:35.
Looking to other gods. Hos. 3:1.
Sacrificing to images Ps. 106:38; Acts 7:41.
Sacrificing to other gods. Exod. 22:20.
Sensuality. Phil. 3:19.
Serving other gods. Deut. 7:4; Jer. 5:19.
Setting up idols in the heart. Ezek. 14:3–4.
Speaking in the name of other gods. Deut. 18:20.
Swearing by other gods. Exod. 23:13; Josh. 23:7.
Walking after other gods. Deut. 8:19.
Worshiping angels. Col. 2:18.
Worshiping dead men. Ps. 106:28.
Worshiping devils. Matt. 4:9–10; Rev. 9:20.
Worshiping images. Isa. 44:17; Dan. 3:5, 10, 15.
Worshiping other gods. Deut. 30:17; Ps. 81:9.
Worshiping the host of heaven. Deut. 4:19; 17:3.
Worshiping the true God by an image, etc. Exod. 32:4–6, with Ps. 106:19–20.
Curse denounced against. Deut. 27:15.

Described as
Abominable. 1 Pet. 4:3.
An abomination to God. Deut. 7:25.
Bloody. Ezek. 23:39.
Defiling. Ezek. 20:7; 36:18.
Hateful to God. Deut. 16:22; Jer. 44:4.
Irrational. Acts 17:29; Rom. 1:21–23.
Unprofitable. Judg. 10:14; Isa. 46:7.
Vain and foolish. Ps. 115:4–8; Isa. 44:19; Jer. 10:3.
Destruction of, promised. Ezek. 36:25; Zech. 13:2.
Divination connected with. 2 Chron. 33:6.
Early notice of, among God's professing people. Gen. 31:19, 30; 35:1–4; Josh 24:2.
Everything connected with, should be destroyed. Deut. 7:5; 2 Sam. 5:21; 2 Kings 23:14; Ezek. 34:13.
Example of the kings encouraged Israel in. 1 Kings 12:30; 2 Kings 21:11; 2 Chron. 33:9.
Exhortations to turn from. Ezek. 14:6; 20:7; Acts 14:15.
Forbidden. Exod. 20:2–3; Deut. 5:7.
Good kings of Judah endeavored to destroy. 2 Chron. 15:16; 34:7.
Great prevalence of, in Israel. Isa. 2:8; Jer. 2:28; Ezek. 8:10.

Idols, etc., mentioned in Scripture
Adrammelech. 2 Kings 17:31.
Anammelech. 2 Kings 17:31.
Ashima. 2 Kings 17:30.
Ashtoreth. Judg. 2:13; 1 Kings 11:33.
Baal. Judg. 2:11–13; 6:25.

Baal-berith. Judg. 8:33; 9:4, 46.
Baal-peor. Num. 25:1-3.
Baal-zebub. 2 Kings 1:2, 16.
Baal-zophon. Exod. 14:2.
Bel. Jer. 50:2; 51:44.
Chemosh. Num. 21:29;
 1 Kings 11:33.
Chinn. Amos 5:26.
Dagon. Judg. 16:23;
 1 Sam. 5:1-3.
Diana. Acts 19:24, 27.
Huzzab. Nah. 2:7.
Jupiter. Acts 14:12.
Mercury. Acts 14:12.
Merodach. Jer. 50:2.
Molech or Milcom. Lev. 18:21;
 1 Kings 11:5, 33.
Nebo. Isa. 46:1.
Nergal. 2 Kings 17:30.
Nibhaz and Tartak.
 2 Kings 17:31.
Nisroch. 2 Kings 19:37.
Queen of heaven. Jer. 44:17, 25.
Remphan. Acts 7:43.
Rimmon. 2 Kings 5:18.
Succoth-benoth. 2 Kings 17:30.
Tammuz. Ezek. 8:14.
Incompatible with the service of God.
 Gen. 35:2-3; Josh. 24:23.

The Jews
 Brought, out of Egypt with them.
  Ezek. 23:8, with Acts 7:39-41.
 Followed the Assyrians in.
  Ezek. 16:28-30; 23:5-7.
 Followed the Canaanites in.
  Judg. 2:11-13; 1 Chron. 5:25.
 Followed the Moabites in.
  Num. 25:1-3.
 Followed the Syrians in.
  Judg. 10:6.
 Forbidden to practice.
  Exod. 20:1-5; 23:24.

Often mixed up, with God's
 worship. Exod. 32:1-5;
 1 Kings 12:27-28.
 Practiced, in Egypt. Josh 24:14;
  Ezek. 23:3, 19.
Led the heathen to consider their
 gods to have but a local influence.
 1 Kings 20:23; 2 Kings 17:26.
Led the heathen to think their gods
 visited the earth in bodily shapes.
 Acts 14:11.
Led to abominable sins. Acts 15:20;
 Rom. 1:26-32;.
Making idols for the purpose of,
 described and ridiculed.
 Isa. 44:10-20.

Objects of
 Angels. Col. 2:18.
 Departed spirits.
  1 Sam. 28:14-15.
 Earthly creatures. Rom. 1:23.
 Heavenly bodies. 2 Kings 23:5;
  Acts 7:42.
 Images. Deut. 29:17; Ps. 115:4;
  Isa. 44:17.
Objects of, carried in procession.
 Isa. 46:7; Amos 5:26; Acts 7:43.

Objects of, described as
 Abominations. Isa. 44:19;
  Jer. 32:34.
 Dumb idols. Hab. 2:18;
  1 Cor. 12:2.
 Dumb stones. Hab. 2:19.
 Gods that cannot save. Isa. 45:20.
 Gods that have not made the
  heavens. Jer. 10:11.
 Graven images. Isa. 45:20;
  Hos. 11:2.
 Helpless. Jer. 10:5.
 Idols of abomination. Ezek. 16:36.
 Images of abomination.
  Ezek. 7:20.

Molten gods. Exod. 34:17;
Lev. 19:4.
Molten images. Deut. 27:15; Hab.
2:18.
New gods. Deut. 32:17;
Judg. 5:8.
No gods. Jer. 5:7; Gal. 4:8.
Nothing. Isa. 41:24; 1 Cor. 8:4.
Numerous. 1 Cor. 8:5.
Other gods. Judg. 2:12, 17;
1 Kings 14:9.
Senseless idols. Deut. 4:28;
Ps. 115:5, 7.
Stocks. Jer. 3:9; Hos. 4:12.
Strange gods. Gen. 35:2, 4;
Josh. 24:20.
Stumbling blocks. Ezek. 14:3.
Teachers of lies. Hab. 2:18.
Vanities of the Gentiles.
Jer. 14:22.
Vanity. Jer. 18:15.
Wind and confusion. Isa. 41:29.

Objects of, worshiped
By bowing to them.
1 Kings 19:18; 2 Kings 5:18.
By burning children. Deut. 12:31;
2 Chron. 33:6; Jer. 19:4, 5;
Ezek. 16:21.
By cutting the flesh.
1 Kings 18:28.
With drink offerings. Isa. 57:6;
Jer. 19:13.
In groves. Exod. 34:13.
On high places. Num. 22:41;
Jer. 2:20.
With incense. Jer. 48:35.
By kissing the hand to them.
Job 31:26–27.
By kissing them. 1 Kings 19:18;
Hos. 13:2.
With prayer. 1 Kings 18:26;
Isa. 44:17.
In private houses. Judg. 17:4–5.

In secret places. Isa. 57:8.
In temples. 2 Kings 5:18.
With sacrifices. Num. 22:40;
2 Kings 10:24.
With singing and dancing.
Exod. 32:18–19; 1 Cor. 10:7.
On the tops of houses.
2 Kings 23:12; Zeph. 1:5.
Under trees. Isa. 56:5; Jer. 2:20.
Obstinate sinners judicially given up
to. Deut. 4:28; 28:64; Hos. 4:17.

Punishment of
Banishment. Jer. 8:3;
Hos. 8:5–8; Amos 5:26–27.
Dreadful judgments ending in
death. Jer. 8:2; 16:1–11.
Eternal torments. Rev. 14:9–11;
21:8.
Exclusion from heaven.
1 Cor. 6:9–10; Eph. 5:5.
Judicial death Deut. 17:2–5.
Renounced on conversion.
1 Thess. 1:9.
Rites of, obscene and impure.
Exod. 32:25; Num. 25:1–3;
2 Kings 17:9;
Isa. 57:6, 8–9; 1 Pet. 4:3.
Temples built for. Hos. 8:14.

They who practice
Are estranged from God.
Ezek. 14:5.
Are ignorant and foolish.
Rom. 1:21–22.
Experience madness. Jer. 50:38.
Are vain in their imaginations.
Rom. 1:21.
Ask counsel of their idols.
Hos. 4:12.
Boast of it. Ps. 97:7.
Carried away by it. 1 Cor. 12:2.
Defile the sanctuary of God.
Ezek. 5:11.

Forget God. Deut. 8:19;
Jer. 18:15.
Forsake God. 2 Kings 22:17;
Jer. 16:11.
Go after it in heart. Ezek. 20:16.
Go astray from God. Ezek. 44:10.
Hate God. 2 Chron. 19:2–3.
Have fellowship with devils.
1 Cor. 10:20.
Hold fast their deceit. Jer. 8:5.
Inflame themselves. Isa. 56:5.
Look to idols for deliverance.
Isa. 44:17; 45:20.
Pollute the name of God.
Ezek. 20:39.
Provoke God. Deut. 31:20;
Isa. 65:3; Jer. 25:6.
Swear by their idols. Amos 8:14.
Victims sacrificed for, often adorned
with garlands. Acts 14:13.
A virtual forsaking of God.
Jer. 2:9–13.
Warnings against. Deut. 4:15–19.
A work of the sinful nature.
Gal. 5:19–20.

IGNORANCE

Associated with unrighteousness.
Prov. 12:2; Jer. 4:22;
Acts 17:30; Rom. 10:3.
Offerings for. Lev. 5:15–16;
Num. 15:22, 24, 28.
Results of. Isa. 5:13; Rom. 10:3;
2 Pet. 3:5.

IGNORANCE OF GOD

See Man's Ignorance of God

IMAGE

Used in a figurative sense
Christ, of God. Col. 1:15;
Heb. 1:3.
Of jealousy. Ezek. 8:3, 5.

Man created in, of God.
Gen. 1:26, 27; 5:1; 9:5;
James 3:9.
Regenerated into. Ps. 17:15;
Rom. 8:29.

IMAGINATION

Wickedness of. Gen. 6:5;
Matt. 5:28; Rom. 1:21;
2 Cor. 10:3.

IMITATION

Of Christ. 1 Pet. 2:23.
Of God. Eph. 5:1.
Of people of faith, value of.
Heb. 6:12.
Of prophets, need of. James 5:10.
Of the apostles. 1 Thess. 1:6.
Of the good, protection in.
1 Pet. 3:13; 3 John 1:11.
Of the wicked, evil of.
2 Kings 17:15.

IMMANUEL

Fulfilled. Matt. 1:22–23.
In prophecy. Isa. 7:14.

IMMORTALITY

David's hope. 2 Sam. 12:23.
Jesus' promise of. John 6:39–58.

IMPENITENT

See also Unrepentant

Examples of
Amaziah. 2 Chron. 25:16.
Amon. 2 Chron. 33:23.
Belshazzar. Dan. 5:22–23.
Eli's sons. 1 Sam. 2:22–25.
Israelites. Num. 14:22–23.
Jehoiakim and his servants.
Jer. 36:22–24.
Manasseh. 2 Chron. 33:10.
Pharaoh. Exod. 9:30, 34.

The rich young man. Matt. 19:22.
Zedekiah. 2 Chron. 36:12–13.
Warnings against. Lev. 26:21;
Rom. 2:4; Heb. 12:17.

IMPORTS

Of Egypt, spices. Gen. 37:25.
Gold, ivory, apes, peacocks.
2 Chron. 9:21.
Of Jerusalem, horses, chariots, and
linen. 1 Kings 10:28–29;
2 Chron. 1:16.
Of Tyre. Ezek. 27:12–25.

IMPOSSIBILITY

Does not apply to faith. Matt. 17:20.
Of escaping God. Ps. 139:7–12.
Of God to fail. Titus 1:2.
Of loving God without loving people.
1 John 4:20.
Means nothing to God. Matt. 19:26;
Luke 1:37; 18:27.
Of pleasing God without faith.
Heb. 11:6.

IMPRECATION (PROVOKE EVIL UPON)

Examples of
David. 2 Sam. 1:21; 3:28–29.
Ruth. Ruth 1:17.
Samuel. 1 Sam. 3:17.
Shimei. 2 Sam. 16:5, 13.

IMPRISONMENT

Apostles. Acts 5:18.
Of debtors. Matt 5:26; 18:30.
Jeremiah. Jer. 38:6.
John the Baptist. Matt. 11:2; 14:3.
Of Joseph. Gen. 39:20.
Paul and Silas. Acts 16:24.
Peter. Acts 12:4.

IMPURITIES

Figurative sense of. Ps. 119:119;
Prov. 25:4; 26:23; Isa. 1:22;
Ezek. 22:18–19.

INCENSE

By Amnon. 2 Sam 13:11–14.
An article of extensive commerce.
Rev. 18:13.
Brought from Sheba. Jer. 6:20.
Called frankincense.
Song of Sol. 4:6, 14.
Common, not to be offered to God.
Exod. 30:9.
Designed for atonement.
Num. 16:46–47.
For God's service mixed with sweet
spices. Exod. 25:6; 37:29.

Illustrative of
The merits of Christ. Rev. 8:3–4.
Prayer. Ps. 141:2; Mal. 1:11;
Rev. 5:8.

The Jews
Not accepted in offering, because
of sin. Isa. 1:13; 66:3.
Offered to idols on altars of brick.
Isa. 65:3.
Prayed when offering. Luke 1:10.
Punished for offering to idols.
2 Chron. 34:25.
Korah and his company punished for
offering. Num. 16:16–35.
Levites had charge of.
1 Chron. 9:29.
Nadab and Abihu destroyed for
offering, with strange fire.
Lev. 10:1–2.
None but priests to offer.
Num. 16:40; Deut. 33:10.

Offered
On the altar of gold.
Exod. 30:1, 6; 40:5.
In censers. Lev. 10:1;
Num. 16:17, 46.
Continually. Exod. 30:8.
With fire from off the altar of burnt offering. Lev. 16:12;
Num. 16:46.
By the high priest in the most holy place on the Day of Atonement.
Lev. 16:12–13.
Morning and evening.
Exod. 30:7–8.
Offering of, allotted to the priests.
Luke 1:9.
Presented to Christ by the wise men.
Matt. 2:11.
Put on meat offerings.
Lev. 2:1–2, 15–16; 6:15.
Recipe for mixing. Exod. 30:34–36.
Used in idolatrous worship.
Jer. 48:35.
Uzziah punished for offering.
2 Chron. 26:16–21.

INCENSE, ALTAR OF
Anointed with holy oil.
Exod. 30:26–27.
Atonement made for, by the high priest once every year.
Exod. 30:10; Lev. 16:18–19.
Blood of all sin offerings put on the horns of. Lev. 4:7, 18.
Called the golden altar. Exod. 39:38.
Covered by the priests before removal from the sanctuary.
Num. 4:11.
Covered with gold. Exod. 30:3;
37:26.
Dimensions, etc., of. Exod. 30:1–2;
37:25.

Had four rings of gold under crown for staves. Exod. 30:4; 37:27.
Incense burned on, every morning and evening. Exod. 30:7–8.
No strange incense nor any sacrifice to be offered on. Exod. 30:9.
Placed before the veil in the outer sanctuary Exod. 30:6; 40:5, 26.

Punishment for
Offering strange fire on.
Lev. 10:1–2.
Unauthorized offering on.
2 Chron. 26:16–19.
Said to be before the Lord. Lev. 4:7;
1 Kings 9:25.
Staves of, covered with gold.
Exod. 30:5.
Top of, surrounded with a crown of gold. Exod. 30:3; 37:26.
A type of Christ. Rev. 8:3; 9:3.

INCEST

Examples of
Abraham. Gen. 20:12–13.
Absalom. 2 Sam. 16:21–22.
Amnon. 2 Sam. 13:14.
Amram. Exod. 6:20.
Herod. Matt. 14:3–4.
Israel. Amos 2:7.
Judah. Gen. 38:16–18.
Lot. Gen. 19:31–36.
Nahor. Gen. 11:29.
Reuben. Gen. 35:22; 49:4.
Forbidden. Lev. 18:6–18;
1 Cor. 5:1.

Instances of marriage of near of kin
Isaac with Rebekah.
Gen. 24:15, 67.
Jacob with Leah and Rachel.
Gen. 29:23, 30.
Rehoboam. 2 Chron. 11:18.

INCLUSIVENES

See also Community; Racial Tension

In the family of God, shown by
Cornelius. Acts 10:9–48.
Every tribe, tongue, people and nation in heaven. Rev. 5:9–10; 7:9.

Israelites
Brothers of Edomites. Deut. 23:7.
Like Ethiopians. Amos 9:7.
Mixed multitude. Exod. 12:38.
Naaman. 2 Kings 5:1–19; Luke 4:27.

Principles relevant to
Abraham's family to be a channel of God's blessing to others. Gen. 12:1–3; Gal. 3:6–9.
Dividing wall of hostility broken. Eph. 2:11–14.
Foreigners to have equal rights. Lev. 24:22; Deut. 24:17.
No partiality shown by God in salvation. Acts 10:34; Rom. 2:9–11.
No racial distinction in Christ. Gal. 3:28–29.
Rahab. Josh. 6:25; Matt. 1:5.
Roman centurion. Matt. 8:5–13.
Ruth. Ruth 1:4; Matt. 1:5.
Samaritan woman. John 4:1–42.
Simon of Cyrene. Mark 15:21.
Syrophenician women.
1 Kings 17:8–24; Matt. 8:5–13; Luke 4:25–26.
Timothy. Acts 16:1.

INCONSISTENCY

Jesus criticizes. Matt. 7:3–5; 23:3–4.

Examples of
Jehu. 2 Kings 10:16–31.
The Jewish leaders in accusing Jesus of violating the Sabbath. John 7:22–23.
The Jews, in oppressing the poor. Neh. 5:9.
Paul criticizes. Rom. 2:1, 21–23.

INDECISION

Elijah criticizes. 1 Kings 18:21.

Examples of
Esther. Esther 5:8.
Felix. Acts 24:25.
Joshua at Ai. Josh. 7:10.
Moses at the Red Sea. Exod. 14:15.
Rulers who believed in Jesus. John 12:42.
Leads to instability. James 1:8.
Neutrality impossible. Matt. 6:24.

INDIA

Probably the eastern limit of the kingdom of Ahasuerus. Esther 1:1; 8:9.

INDICTMENTS

Examples of
Daniel indicted again. Dan. 6:13.
Jeremiah for treasonable prophesy. Jer. 26:1–24.
Jeremiah indicted again. Jer. 37:13–15.
Jesus charged with treason. Matt. 27:11, 37.
Jesus, on two charges. Matt. 26:61, 63–65; Mark 14:58, 61–64; Luke 22:67–71; John 19:7.
Naboth on charge of blasphemy. 1 Kings 21:13.

Paul. Acts 17:7; 18:13; 24:5;
  25:18, 19, 26, 27.
Paul and Silas. Acts 16:20, 21.
Stephen for blasphemy.
  Acts 6:11, 13.
Three Hebrew captives.
  Dan. 3:12.
Indictment quashed. Acts 18:14–16.

INDIVIDUAL, VALUE OF
God and one sparrow. Luke 12:6–7.
Joy over one recovered child.
  Luke 15:4, 7.
One-by-one love. Isa. 27:12.

INDUSTRY
Characteristic of godly women.
  Prov. 31:13, etc.
Commanded. Eph. 4:28;
  1 Thess. 4:11.
Early rising necessary to.
  Prov. 31:15.

Examples of
  Jeroboam. 1 Kings 11:28.
  Paul. Acts 18:3; 20:33, 34;
    2 Thess. 3:8.
  God's purpose for human beings.
    Gen. 2:15; Exod. 23:12.
  Illustrated. Prov. 6:6–8.

Leads to
  Affection of relatives.
    Prov. 31:28.
  General commendation.
    Prov. 31:31.
  Increase of substance.
    Prov. 13:11.
  Required of man after the fall.
    Gen. 3:23.
  Required of man in a state of
    innocence. Gen. 2:15.

Paul commands. Rom. 12:11;
  Eph. 4:28; 1 Thess. 4:11;
  2 Thess. 3:10–12; 1 Tim. 5:8.

Requisite to supply
  To be suspended on the Sabbath.
    Exod. 20:10.
  The lazy lacking. Prov. 24:30–31.
  Our own wants. Acts 20:34;
    1 Thess. 2:9.
  Wants of others. Acts 20:35;
    Eph. 4:28.

INDWELLING OF THE HOLY SPIRIT
See Holy Spirit, Indwelling of the

INERRANCY

Certainty of Word of God
  Law will not pass away.
    Matt. 5:18–19.
  Saying sure and worthy of full
    acceptance. 1 Tim. 1:15;
    2 Tim. 2:11; Titus 3:8.
  Scripture cannot be broken.
    John 10:35.
  Testimonies of God sure.
    Ps. 19:7.
  Word of God true. Prov. 30:5–6.

Divine nature of Scripture
  As Word of God. 1 Thess. 2:13.
  Inspired by God. 2 Tim. 3:16.
  Revealed through Jesus Christ.
    Gal. 1:12.
  Spoken by God. Exod. 20:1;
    Matt. 22:31; Acts 13:32–35;
    1 Cor. 14:37;
    2 Pet. 1:21.
  Spoken by Holy Spirit. Acts 1:16;
    1 Cor. 2:13; Heb 3:7.
  Written by men moved by Holy
    Spirit. 2 Pet. 1:21.

Human nature of Scripture
  Spoken by David, inspired by Holy
    Spirit. Mark 12:36; Acts 4:25.
  Spoken by Paul.
    1 Cor. 7:10, 12, 25, 40; 14:37;
    2 Pet. 3:15.
  Written by men moved by Holy
    Spirit. 2 Pet. 1:21.

INFERTILITY
See also Barrenness

Barren womb not satisfied.
  Prov. 30:16.

INFANTICIDE
Of the Hebrew babies.
  Exod. 1:15–16.
Of the young children in Bethlehem.
  Matt. 2:16–18.

INFIDELITY
Israel at Massah and Meribah.
  Exod. 17:7.
In the last days. 2 Pet. 3:3–4.

INFIDELS
Compared to nonproviding father.
  1 Tim. 5:8.
Described. Titus 1:15–16.
Destined for lake of fire. Rev. 21:8.
Have nothing in common with
  believers. 2 Cor. 6:15.
Not to be married to believers.
  2 Cor. 6:14.

INFIRMITY
Exempt from
  Moses. Deut. 34:7.
  Caleb. Josh. 14:11.

INFLUENCE
Evil, examples of
  Satan over Adam and Eve.
    Gen. 3:1–5.
  Eve over Adam. Gen. 3:6.

Good, examples of
  Ezra. Ezra 10:1.
  Hezekiah. 2 Chron. 29:31.
  Josiah. 2 Kings 22–23.
  Manasseh. 2 Chron. 33:12–19.
  Nehemiah. Neh. 4; 5.
Political. 1 Kings 2:13–18.

INGRATITUDE
Believers avoid the guilt of.
  Ps. 7:4–5.
A characteristic of the wicked.
  Ps. 38:20; 2 Tim. 3:2.

Often exhibited
  To benefactors. Ps. 109:5;
    Eccles. 9:15.
  To friends in distress. Ps. 38:11.
  By relations. Job 19:14.
  By servants. Job 19:15–16.
Punishment of. Prov. 17:13;
  Jer. 18:20–21.

Should be met with
  Faithfulness. Gen. 31:38–42.
  Persevering love. 2 Cor. 12:15.
  Prayer. Pss. 35:12–13; 109:4.

INGRATITUDE TO GOD
See God, Ingratitude to

INHERITANCE
Figurative sense. Ps. 37:29;
  Rom. 8:16–17; Eph. 1:11–14;
  Titus 3:7; Heb. 1:14.
Provisions for inheritance under
  levirate marriages. Gen. 38:7–11;

Num. 36:6–9; Deut. 25:5–10;
Ruth 3:1–8; 4:7–17.
Standing firm on. 1 Kings 21:3.

INHOSPITABLENESS

Examples of
Toward the Israelites. Edom.
Num. 20:18–20.
Toward the Israelites. Sihon.
Num. 21:22–23.
Toward the Israelites, Ammonites
and Moabites. Deut. 23:3–6.
Men of Gibeah toward a Levite.
Judg. 19:15.
Nabal toward David.
1 Sam. 25:10–17.
Samaritans toward Jesus.
Luke 9:53.

INJUSTICE
A bad example leads to. Exod. 23:2.

Believers should
Bear patiently. 1 Cor. 6:7.
Hate. Prov. 29:27.
Take no vengeance for.
Matt. 5:39.
Testify against. Ps. 58:1–2;
Mic. 3:8–9.
Brings a curse. Deut. 27:17, 19.
Covetousness leads to. Jer. 6:13;
Ezek. 22:12; Mic. 2:2.
Drunkenness leads to. Prov. 31:5.
Forbidden. Lev. 19:15, 35;
Deut. 16:19.

God
Despises. Prov. 17:15; 20:10.
Disapproves of. Lam. 3:35–36.

Hears the cry of those who suffer
Provoked to avenge. Ps. 12:5.
Regards. Eccles. 5:8; James 5:4.

Of the least kind, condemned.
Luke 16:10.
Punishment of. Prov. 11:7; 28:8;
Amos 5:11–12; 8:5, 8;
1 Thess. 4:6.

Specially to be avoided toward
The poor. Exod. 23:6;
Prov. 22:16, 22–23.
Servants. Deut. 24:14;
Job 31:13–14; Jer. 22:13.
The stranger and fatherless.
Exod. 22:21–22; Deut. 24:17;
Jer. 22:3.

The wicked
Deal with. Isa. 26:10.
Judge with. Ps. 82:2;
Eccles. 3:16; Hab. 1:4.
Practice without shame.
Jer. 6:13, 15; Zeph. 3:5.

INK
Baruch uses, to record the words of
Jeremiah. Jer. 36:18.
The Corinthians, a letter of Christ
written not in. 2 Cor. 3:3.

INN
Place where Jesus was born.
Luke 2:7.
Place where Joseph's brothers stayed
in Egypt. Gen. 42:27.

INNOCENCE
Contrasted with guilt. Gen. 2:25;
3:7–11.
Found in Daniel. Dan. 6:22.
Found in Jeremiah. Jer. 2:35.
Professed by Pilate. Matt. 27:24.
Signified by washing the hands.
Deut. 21:6; Ps. 26:6;
Matt. 27:24.

Ink Bottle

INNUENDO
Communicated by body language.
Prov. 6:13.

INSANITY
Cured by Jesus. Matt. 4:24; 17:15.
Demonic, Saul. 1 Sam. 16:14;
18:10.
Jesus accused of. Mark 3:21;
John 10:20.
Nebuchadnezzar's. Dan. 4:32–34.
Pretended by David.
1 Sam. 21:13–15.
Paul accused of. Acts 26:24, 25.
Person who deceives his neighbor is
likened to a person with.
Prov. 26:18.
Sent as a judgment from God.
Deut. 28:28; Zech. 12:4.

INSCRIPTIONS
On gravestones. 2 Kings 23:17.
Over Jesus at the crucifixion.
John 19:19.

INSECTS
Created by God. Gen. 1:24–25.

Divided into
Clean and fit for food.
Lev. 11:21–22.
Clean and unclean. Deut. 14:19;
Lam. 11:21–25.
Unclean and abominable.
Lev. 11:23–24.
Fed by God. Pss. 104:25, 27;
145:9, 15.

Mentioned in Scripture
Ant. Prov. 6:6; 30:25.
Bald locust. Lev. 11:22.
Bee. Judg. 14:8; Ps. 118:12;
Isa. 7:18.
Beetle. Lev. 11:22.
Caterpillar. Ps. 78:46; Isa. 33:4.
Earthworm. Job 25:6; Mic. 7:17.
Flea. 1 Sam. 24:14.
Fly. Exod. 8:22; Eccles. 10:1;
Isa. 7:18.
Gnat. Matt. 23:24.
Grasshopper. Lev. 11:22;
Judg. 6:5; Job 39:20.
Hornet. Deut. 7:20.
Locust. Exod. 10:12–13;
Joel 1:4; Amos 4:9;
Nah. 3:15–16.
Lice. Exod. 8:16; Ps. 105:31.
Maggot. Exod. 16:20.
Moth. Job 4:19; 27:18; Isa. 50:9.
Spider. Job 8:14; Prov. 30:28.

Locust

INSOMNIA

Instances of
Ahasuerus. Esther 6:1.
Nebuchadnezzar. Dan. 6:18.

INSPIRATION OF THE BIBLE
See Bible

INSPIRATION OF THE HOLY SPIRIT
See Holy Spirit, Inspiration of the

INSTABILITY
Avoid persons given to. Prov. 24:21.
Caused by competing loyalties.
Matt. 6:24; 12:25.
Doubt produces. James 1:6–8.

Examples of
David, in yielding to lust.
2 Sam. 11:2–9.
Ephaim and Judah. Hos. 6:4.
Jesus' disciples. John 6:66;
Acts 15:38.
Lot's wife. Luke 17:32.
Reuben. Gen. 49:4.
Saul, in his feelings toward David.
1 Sam. 18:19.
Solomon, in yielding to his
idolatrous wives. 1 Kings 1–8.
Grace and antidote to. Heb. 13:9.

INSTINCT
Of animals. Prov. 1:17; Isa. 1:3.
Of birds. Jer. 8:7.

INSTRUCTION
From nature. Prov. 24:30–34;
Eccles. 1:13–18; 3; 4:1;
Matt. 6:25–30.

By object lessons
Basket of figs. Jer. 24.

The boiling pot. Ezek. 24:1–14.
Bonds and yokes.
Jer. 27:2–11; 28.
Of children. Deut. 4:9;
Prov. 22:6; 2 Tim. 3:15.
Eating and drinking sparingly.
Ezek. 12:18–20.
Eating bread mixed with dung.
Ezek. 4:9–17.
Fringes on the borders of
garments. Num. 15:38–39.
Illustrations on a tile. Ezek. 4:1–3.
Linen belt. Jer. 13:1–11.
Lying on one side in public view
for a long period. Ezek. 4:4–8.
Moving household goods.
Ezek. 12:3–16.
The pillow of twelve stones at the
fords of the Jordan.
Josh 4:19–24.
A pot of manna. Exod. 16:32.
Potter's vessel. Jer. 19:1–12.
In religion. Exod. 13:11–16;
Matt. 5:1–2.
Shaving the head. Ezek. 5.
Sighing. Ezek. 21:6–7.
Symbolically wearing sack cloth
and going barefoot. Isa. 20:2–3.
Two sticks joined together.
Ezek. 37:16–22.
Widowhood. Ezek. 24:16–27.
From the study of human nature.
Eccles. 3–12.

INSURGENTS
Army of, David's. 1 Sam. 22:1–2.

INSURRECTION
Described by David in Ps. 64:2; 55.
Lead by Sheba. 2 Sam. 20.
Lead by Barabbas. Mark 15:7.

INTEGRATION
See Racial tension

INTEGRITY
And bribes. Acts 8:18–23.
And honesty. 2 Cor. 7:2.
Characterizes righteous men.
Num. 16:15; Job 27:5;
Ps. 26:11; Prov. 11:3.
Protects the righteous. Ps. 25:21;
Prov. 11:3.
Required of humankind. Deut. 6:5.

INTELLIGENCE

Found in
Daniel. Dan. 5:12 (NIV).
Jesus. Luke 2:47.
A person's spirit. Job 32:8.

Gained by
One who seeks wisdom.
Pro 2:5, 9.
Solomon. 1 Kings 4:29.

Lacking in
Idol makers. Isa. 44:18–19.
Job. Job 37:5; 38:4; 42:3.
Psalmist. Ps. 139:6.
Of value in understanding
Scripture. 2 Pet. 3:16–17.
Requested. Ps. 119:27, 34, 125;
Prov 2:3.

Surpassed by
Love of God. Eph. 3:19.
Peace of God. Phil. 4:7.
Will vanish. Isa. 29:14;
1 Cor. 1:19–20.

INTERCESSION
Brings special blessings.
1 Sam. 7:5–9; Num. 6:23–26;
James 5:14–16.

Divine examples
Christ. John 17:1–26;
Rom. 8:34; Heb. 7:25;
1 John 2:1.
Holy Spirit. Rom. 8:26.

Human examples
Job. Job 42:8–10.
Moses. Num. 14:19.
Stephen. Acts 7:60.
Should be made for everyone.
Eph. 6:18; 1 Tim. 2:1.
Should be made for specific
individuals. Rom. 15:30;
Heb. 13:18.

INTEREST
See also Usury

Curse attending the giving or
receiving of unlawful, alluded to.
Jer. 15:10.
Illustrative of the improvement of
talents received from God.
Matt. 25:27; Luke 19:23.

The Jews
Allowed to take, from strangers.
Deut. 23:20.
Forbidden to take, from brethren.
Deut. 23:19.
Forbidden to take, from brethren
especially when poor.
Exod. 22:25; Lev. 25:35–37.
Often guilty of taking. Neh. 5:6–7;
Ezek. 22:12.
Required to restore. Neh. 5:9–13.
Judgments denounced against those
who exacted unlawful.
Isa. 24:1–2;
Ezek. 18:13.
Lending of money or other property
for in crease. Lev. 25:37.

Those enriched by unlawful, not
allowed to enjoy their gain.
Ps. 28:8.
True and faithful Israelites never
took, from their brethren.
Ps. 15:5; Ezek. 18:8–9.

INTERPRETATION
Of foreign tongues. 1 Cor. 14:9–19.

INTERPRETER
In Christian churches.
1 Cor. 12:10, 30;
14:5, 13, 26–28.
Of dreams. Gen. 40:8; 41:16;
Dan. 2:18–30.
Of languages. Gen. 42:23;
2 Chron. 32:31; Neh. 8:8;
Job 33:23.
Used in a figurative sense.
Job 33:23.

INTOLERANCE, RELIGIOUS

Examples of
Cain. Gen. 4:8.
Elijah. 1 Kings 18:40.
James and John. Mark 9:38–39.
Jehu. 2 Kings 10:18–31.
Joshua. Num. 11:24–28.
Of idolatrous religions, taught by
Moses. Exod. 22:20; Deut. 13;
17:1–7.
The Jewish leaders, in persecuting
the disciples. Acts 4:1–3.
By the Jews at the time of the
religious revival under the
leadership of Asa.
2 Chron. 15:12–13.
In persecuting Stephen.
Acts 6:9–15; 7:57–59; 8:1–3.
In persecuting Paul. Acts 13:50;
17:5; 18:13; 21:28–31; 22:22;
23:2.

INTOXICATION
Brings affliction. Prov. 23:29–30.
Causes shame. Joel 1:5; Ps. 69:12.
Inconsistent with Christianity.
Rom. 13:13; Eph. 5:18.

INVENTION
Engines of war. 2 Chron. 26:15.

Of musical instruments
By David. 1 Chron. 23:5;
2 Chron. 7:6; 29:26.
By Jubal. Gen. 4:21.
The use of metals. Gen. 4:22.

INVESTIGATION
Of the whole of life.
Eccles. 1:13–18; 2:1–12;
12:9–14.

INVESTING
Assets devoured by foolish person.
Prov. 21:20.

Business ventures
Joint. Eccles. 4:9.
Poor. Eccles. 5:14.
Successful, over time.
Eccles. 11:1.
Uncertain. Eccles. 11:6;
Luke 12:16–21;
James 4:13–14.
Fig., for eternity. 1 Cor. 3:12–15.
Illicit gain. Prov. 13:11; 15:27.

Injunctions concerning
Charge no interest. Exod. 22:25;
Ps. 15:5.
Diversify assets. Eccles. 11:2.
Do not toil to acquire wealth.
Prov. 23:4.
Plan for return on investment.
Prov. 21:5.

Kingdom of heaven compared to.
Matt. 13:44–46.

Purchase of property
By Boaz, in Bethlehem.
Ruth 4:3–4.
By David, in Jerusalem.
1 Chron. 21:24–25.
By Jeremiah, in Anathoth.
Jer. 32:7–14.

By sons of Jacob
In Goshen. Gen. 47:27.
In Shechem. Gen. 34:10.
Stewardship. Luke 16:1–13;
19:11–27; 1 Cor 4:2.
Trade. Gen. 34:10;
Ezek. 27:12–36.

IRAN
See Persia

IRON
An article of commerce.
Ezek. 27:12, 19; Rev. 18:12.
Canaan abounded with. Deut. 8:9;
33:25.

Described as
Fusible. Ezek. 22:20.
Malleable. Isa. 2:4.
Strong and durable. Job 40:18;
Dan. 2:40.
Dug out of the earth. Job 28:2.
Great quantity of, provided for the
temple. 1 Chron. 22:3, 14, 16;
29:2.
Of greater gravity than water.
2 Kings 6:5.
Hardened into steel. 2 Sam. 22:35;
Job 20:24.

Illustrative of
A hard barren soil. Deut. 28:23.

Insensibility of conscience, when
seared with. 1 Tim. 4:2.
Severe affliction. Deut. 4:20;
Ps. 107:10.
Severe exercise of power. Ps. 2:9;
Rev. 2:27.
Strength. Dan. 2:33, 40.
Stubbornness. Isa. 48:4.

Made into
Armor. 2 Sam. 23:7; Rev. 9:9.
Bars. Ps. 107:16; Isa. 45:2.
Bed. Deut. 3:11.
Chains. Pss. 105:18; 149:8.
Chariots. Judg. 4:3.
Engraving tools. Job 19:24;
Jer. 17:1.
Farm implements for husbandry.
1 Sam. 13:20–21;
2 Sam. 12:31.
Gates. Acts 12:10.
Idols. Dan. 5:4, 23.
Nails and hinges. 1 Chron. 22:3.
Pillars. Jer. 1:18.
Rods. Ps. 2:9; Rev. 2:27.
Tools for stonemasons.
Josh 8:31; 1 Kings 6:7.
Weapons of war. 1 Sam. 13:19;
17:7.
Yokes. Deut. 28:48;
Jer. 28:33–14
Miraculously made to swim.
2 Kings 6:6.
Mode of purifying, taken in war.
Num. 31:21–23.
From the north hardest and best.
Jer. 15:12.
Sharpens things made of it.
Prov. 27:17.
Of small comparative value.
Isa. 60:17.
Taken in war often dedicated to God.
Josh 6:19, 24.

Used from the earliest age.
Gen. 4:22.
Working in, a trade. 1 Sam. 13:19;
2 Chron. 2:7, 14.
Wrought iron. Ezek. 27:19.

IRONY

Examples of
Agrippa to Paul. Acts 26:28.
Amos to the Samaritans.
Amos 4:4.
Elijah to the priest of Baal.
1 Kings 18:27.
Ezekiel to the prince of Tyre.
Ezek. 28:3–5.
Jesus to Pharisees. Mark 2:17.
Job to his accusers. Job 12:2.
Michaiah. 1 Kings 22:15.
Michal to David. 2 Sam. 6:20.
Pharisees and Herodians to Jesus.
Matt. 22:16.
Pilate, calling Jesus king.
Mark 15:19; John 19:15.
Roman soldiers to Jesus.
Matt. 27:29; Mark 15:17–19;
Luke 23:11; John 19:2–3.
Superscription of Pilate over
Jesus. Matt. 27:37;
Mark 15:26; Luke 23:38;
John 19:19.

IRRIGATION

Practiced by the Hebrews in Egypt.
Deut. 11:10.
Solomon employed. Eccles. 2:6.
Used in a figurative sense.
Isa. 58:11.

I.R.S.

See also Tax

In connection with census
By religious authority.
Exod. 30:11–16.
By state. Luke 2:1.
Taxes paid by Jesus.
Matt. 17:24–27.
Excessive taxation.
1 Kings 12:4–15;
Neh 5:4.

Injunctions concerning taxes
To be collected fairly. Luke 3:13;
19:8.
To be paid. Matt. 22:17–21;
Rom 13.1, 5 7.

*Purpose for taxation by religious
authority*
For tabernacle service.
Exod. 30:16; 38:24, 26.
To repair temple. 2 Kings 12:4–5.

Purpose for taxation by state
To build temple.
1 Kings 5:13–18; 9:15.
To establish royal power.
1 Sam. 8:13–17; 1 Kings 9:15.
To pay foreign king.
2 Kings 23:35.
Tax collectors. Matt. 5:46; 9:11;
21:31; Mark 2:14;
Luke 3:12–13; 18:11; 19:1–10.
Tax exemption for religious
personnel. Gen. 47:26;
Ezra 7:24.

Taxes imposed
As conscripted labor.
1 Sam. 8:13, 16; 1 Kings 5:13,
15; 9:15.
On land. 2 Kings 23:35.

Taxes imposed on product
Best of produce. 1 Sam. 8:14.

One-fifth of produce. Gen. 41:34;
47:26.
One-tenth of livestock.
1 Sam. 8:17.
One-tenth of produce.
1 Sam. 8:15.

ISLAND

Prophesies concerning. Ps. 97:1;
Isa. 11:11; 41:1, 5; 49:1;
Zeph. 2:11; Rev. 16:20.

ISRAEL

See also Holy Land, Jews, Judea

Name given to Jacob.
Gen. 32:24–82.
A name of Christ in prophecy.
Isa. 49:3.
A name given to Jacob's
descendents. Exod. 1:1–5.

ISRAEL, ARMIES OF

With the aid of God, all powerful.
Lev. 26:3, 7–8; Deut. 7:24;
32:30; Josh. 1:5.
Ark of God frequently brought with.
Josh. 6:6–7; 1 Sam. 4:4–5;
2 Sam. 11:11; 15:24.
Attended by priests with trumpets.
Num. 10:9; 31:6;
2 Chron. 13:13–14.

Before going to war
Consulted the Lord. Judg. 1:1;
20:27–28.
Were encouraged by their
commanders. 2 Chron. 20:20.
Were numbered and reviewed.
2 Sam. 18:1–2, 4;
1 Kings 10:15, 27.
Were required to keep from
iniquity. Deut. 23:9.

Bravery and fidelity in, rewarded.
Josh. 15:16; 1 Sam. 17:25;
18:17; 2 Sam. 18:11;
1 Chron. 11:6.

Called
The armies of the living God.
1 Sam. 17:26.
The host. Deut. 23:9;
1 Sam. 28:19.

Collected by
Extraordinary means.
Judg. 19:29, with 20:1;
1 Sam. 11:7.
Sound of trumpets. Judg. 3:27;
6:34.
Special messengers. Judg. 6:35;
2 Sam. 20:14.
Commanded by the captain of the
host. 2 Sam. 2:8; 17:25; 20:23.
Composed of infantry. Num. 11:21;
Judg. 5:15.
Congratulated on returning
victorious. 1 Sam. 18:6–7, with
Exod. 15:1–21.
Directed in their movements by God.
Josh. 8:1–2; Judg. 1:2;
2 Sam. 5:25; 1 Chron. 14:16.
Disbanded after war. 1 Sam. 13:2;
1 Kings 22:36.

Divided into
Companies of thousands, etc.
Num. 31:14; 2 Kings 1:9, 11;
1 Chron. 13:1; 27:1.
Three divisions. Judg. 7:16;
1 Sam. 11:11.
Van and rear. Josh. 6:9.
Educated in the art of war. Isa. 2:4;
Mic. 4:3.
Enrolled by the chief scribe.
2 Kings 25:19.

Fearful ones allowed to leave.
Deut. 20:8; Judg. 7:3.
First mention of. Exod. 7:4.
Without God, easily overcome.
Lev. 26:17; Num. 14:22.45.
Horsemen and chariots introduced
into, after David's reign.
1 Kings 1:5; 4:26.

Inferior officers of, appointed by
The captain of the host.
2 Sam. 18:11; 2 Kings 4:13.
The chief officers. Deut. 20:9.
The king. 2 Sam. 18:1;
2 Chron. 25:5.
Men selected from, for difficult
enterprises. Exod. 17:9;
Num. 31:5–6; Josh. 7:4; 8:3;
Judg. 7:5–6; 2 Sam. 17:1.

Mode of provisioning
Food brought by themselves.
Josh. 1:11.
Food sent by their families.
1 Sam. 17:17.
Levies. Judg. 8:5;
1 Sam. 25:4–8.
Presents. 2 Sam. 17:27–29.
Often led by the king in person.
1 Sam. 8:20; 15:4–5;
2 Sam. 12:29; 1 Kings 22.
Often supplied with arms from public
armories. 2 Chron. 11:12; 26:14.
Part of, retained in times of peace by
the kings. 1 Sam. 13:1–2;
1 Chron. 27:1–15.

Persons exempted from serving in
Who had built a house.
Deut. 20:5.
Who had planted a vineyard.
Deut. 20:6.
Who were lately betrothed.
Deut. 20:7.

Who were newly married.
Deut. 24:5.
Persons liable to serve in.
Num. 1:2–3.
Praises of God often sung before.
2 Chron. 20:21–22.
Purified on returning from war.
Num. 31:19–25.
Refusal to join, often punished.
Judg. 21:5, 8–11; 1 Sam. 11:7.
Refusal to join, stigmatized.
Judg. 5:15–17.
Sometimes consisted of the whole
nation. Judg. 20:11;
1 Sam. 11:7.
Strict discipline observed in.
Josh. 7:16–21;
1 Sam. 14:24–44.

ISRAEL, TRIBES OF

All inheritance to remain in the tribe
and family to which allotted.
Num. 36:3–9.
Canaan divided among nine and a
half of, by lot. Josh. 14:1–5.
Canaan to be divided among
according to their numbers.
Num. 33:54.
Descended from Jacob's sons.
Gen. 35:22–26.
Divided into four divisions while in
the wilderness. Num. 10:14–28.
Divided on mounts Ebal and Gerizim
to hear the law. Deut. 27:12–13.
Each family of, had a chief or head.
Num. 36:1; 1 Chron. 4:38.

Each of them
Divided into families. Num. 1:2;
26:5–50; Josh. 7:14.
Under a president or chief.
Num. 1:4–16.
Usually furnished an equal number
of men for war. Num. 31:4.

Encamped in their divisions and by
their standards around the
tabernacle. Num. 2:2–31.

Manasseh and Ephraim numbered
among, instead of Joseph and
Levi. Gen. 48:5; Josh. 14:3–4.

Names of, engraver on the
breastplate of the high priest.
Exod. 28:21; 39:14.

Predictions regarding each of.
Gen. 49:3–27; Deut. 33:6–35.

Remained as one people until the
reign of Rehoboam.
1 Kings 12:16–20.

Reuben, Gad, and half Manasseh
Settled on east side of Jordan.
Deut. 3:12–17;
Josh. 13:23–32.
Were required to assist in subduing
Canaan. Num. 32:6–32;
Deut. 3:18–20.

Situation of and bounds of the
inheritance of each. Josh. 15–17.

Total strength of, on entering the
land of Canaan. Num. 26:51.

Total strength of, on leaving Egypt.
Exod. 12:37; Num. 1:44–46;
2:32.

Twelve in number. Gen. 49:28;
Acts 26:12; James 1:1.

ITCH
Part of God's judgment.
Deut. 28:27.

IVORY
Ahab's palace made of.
1 Kings 22:39.

Articles made of. Rev. 18:12.

Beds made of. Amos 6:4.

Benches made of. Ezek. 27:6.

Exported from Chittim. Ezek. 27:6.

Exported from Tarshih.
1 Kings 10:22; 2 Chron. 9:21.

Other houses made of. Ps. 45:8;
Amos 3:15.

Stringed instruments made of.
Ps. 45:8.

Thrones made of. 1 Kings 10:18;
2 Chron. 9:17.

J

JAILER
Of Philippi, converted.
Acts 16:27–34.

JAVELIN
A heavy lance. Ezek. 39:9.
Used by Goliath. 1 Sam. 17:6.
Used by Saul. 1 Sam. 18:11;
19:9–10.

JEALOUSY
Attributed to God. Exod. 20:5;
1 Kings 14:22; Ps. 78:58;
Isa. 30:1–2; 1 Cor. 10:22.

Examples of
The brother of the prodigal son.
Luke 15:25–32.
Cain, of Abel. Gen. 4:5–8.
Ephraimites, of Gideon.
Judg. 8:1.
Ephraimites, of Jephthah.
Judg. 12:1.
Joab, of Abner. 2 Sam. 3:24–27.
Joseph's brothers, of Joseph.
Gen. 37:4–8, 18, 28.
Nathan, of Adonijah.
1 Kings 1:24–26.
Sarah of Hagar. Gen. 16:5.
Saul, of David.
1 Sam. 18:8–30; 19:8–24;
20:24–34.
Sectional, between Israel and the
tribe of Judah.
2 Sam. 19:41–43.
Image of. Ezek. 8:3–4.
Law concerning, when husband is
jealous of his wife. Num. 5:12–31.

A spirit of emulation. Rom. 10:19;
11:11.

JEHOSHAPHAT
Sent Levites throughout the territory
of Judah to instruct the people in
the Book of the Law.
2 Chron. 17:1–9.
The place to which the Lord
summoned the nations for
judgment. Joel 3:2.

JERUSALEM
Allotted to the tribe of Benjamin.
Josh. 18:28.
Ancient Jebusi or Jebus. Josh. 15:8;
18:28; Judg. 19:10.
Ancient Salem. Gen. 14:18;
Ps. 76:2.

Calamities of, mentioned
Besieged but not taken by Rezin
and Pekah. Isa. 7:1;
2 Kings 16:5.
Besieged but not taken by
Sennacherib.
2 Kings 18:17; 19.
Besieged by Nebuchadnezzar.
2 Kings 24:10–11.
Taken and burned by
Nebuchadnezzar. 2 Kings 25;
Jer. 39:1–8.
Taken and made tributary by
Pharaoh Necho.
2 Kings 23:33–35.
Taken and plundered by Jehoash
king of Israel.
2 Kings 14:13–14.

Jerusalem, Dome of the Rock

Taken and plundered by Shishak.
1 Kings 14:25–26;
2 Chron. 12:1–4.
Threatened by Sanballat.
Neh. 4:7–8.

Called
A city not forsaken. Isa. 62:12.
City of God. Pss. 46:4; 48:1.
City of Judah. 2 Chron. 25:28.
City of righteousness. Isa. 1:26.
City of solemnities. Isa. 33:20.
City of the great king. Ps. 48:2;
Matt. 5:5.
City of the Lord. Isa. 60:14.
City of truth. Zech. 8:3.
Faithful city. Isa. 1:21, 26.
Holy city. Neh. 11:1; Isa. 48:2;
Matt. 4:5.
Throne of the Lord. Jer. 3:17.
Zion. Ps. 48:12; Isa. 33:20.

Zion of the holy one of Israel.
Isa. 60:14.

Christ
Did many miracles in. John 4:45.
Lamented over. Matt. 23:37;
Luke 19:41.
Preached in. Luke 21:37–38;
John 18:20.
Publicly entered, as king.
Matt. 21:9–10.
Was put to death at. Luke 9:31;
Acts 13:27, 29.

Described as
Beautiful. Song of Sol. 6:4.
Beautiful for situation. Ps. 48:2.
Compact. Ps. 122:3.
Full of business and tumult.
Isa. 22:3.
Great. Jer. 22:8.
Joy of the whole earth. Ps. 48:2;
Lam. 2:15.

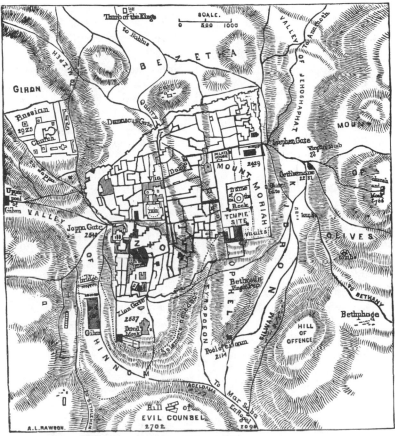

Plan of Jerusalem

The perfection of beauty.
Lam. 2:15.
Populous, Lam. 1:1.
Princess among the provinces.
Lam. 1:1.
Wealth, etc., in the time of
Solomon. 1 Kings 10:26–27.
Enlarged by David. 2 Sam. 5:9.
Entered by gates. Ps. 122:2; Jer.
17:19–21.
First Christian council held at.
Acts 15:4, 6.

Gospel first preached at.
Luke 24:47; Acts 2:14.
Hezekiah made an aqueduct for.
2 Kings 20:20.
Idolatry of. 2 Chron. 28.24,
Ezek. 8:7–10.

Illustrative of
Believers under God's protection
(by its strong position).
Ps. 125:2.
The church. Gal. 4:25–26;
Heb. 12:22.

The church glorified. Rev. 3:12; 21:2, 10.

Instances of God's care and protection of. 2 Sam. 24:16; 2 Kings 19:32–34; 2 Chron. 12:7.

The Jebusites

Finally dispossessed of, by David. 2 Sam. 5:6–8.

Formerly lived in. Judg. 19:10–11.

Held possession of, with Judah and Benjamin. Josh. 15:63; Judg. 1:21.

The Jews

Lamented the affliction of. Neh. 1:2–4.

Loved. Ps. 137:5–6.

Prayed for prosperity of. Pss. 51:18; 122:6.

Prayed toward. Dan. 6:10, with 1 Kings 8:44.

Went up to, at the feasts. Luke 2:42, with Ps. 122:4.

The king of, defeated and slain by Joshua. Josh. 10:5–23.

Made the royal city. 2 Sam. 5:9; 20:3.

Miraculous gift of the Holy Spirit first given at. Acts 1:4; 2:1–5.

Partly taken and burned by Judah. Judg. 1:8.

Persecution of the Christian church began at. Acts 4:1; 8:1.

Prophecies regarding

Christ to enter, as king. Zech. 9:9.

The gospel to go forth from. Isa. 2:3; 40:9.

Its capture accompanied by severe calamities. Matt. 24:21, 29; Luke 21:23–24.

Signs preceding its destruction Matt. 24:6–15; Luke 21:7–11, 25, 28.

To be a quiet habitation. Isa. 33:20.

To be a terror to their enemies. Zech. 12:2–3.

To be a wilderness. Isa. 64:10.

View of Jerusalem

To be destroyed by the Romans.
Luke 19:42–44.

To be made a heap of ruins.
Jer. 9:11; 26:18.

To be rebuilt by Cyrus.
Isa. 44:26–28.

To be taken by king of Babylon.
Jer. 20:5.

Protected by forts and bulwarks.
Ps. 48:12–13.

Protected by God. Isa. 31:5.

Rebuilt after the captivity by order of
Cyrus. Isa. 44:26–28.

Roman government transferred
from, to Caesarea.
Acts 23:23–24; 25:1–13.

Seat of government under the
Romans. Matt. 27:2, 19.

Specially chosen by God.
2 Chron. 6:6; Ps. 135:21.

Spoils of war placed in.
1 Sam. 17:54; 2 Sam. 8:7.

Surrounded by a wall. 1 Kings 3:1.

Surrounded by mountains.
Ps. 125:2.

The temple built in. 2 Chron. 3:1;
Ps. 68:29.

Was the tomb of the prophets.
Luke 13:33–34.

Wickedness of. Isa. 1:1–4;
Jer. 5:1 5, Mic. 3:10.

Wickedness of, the cause of its
calamities. 2 Kings 21:12–15;
2 Chron. 24:18;
Lam. 1:8; Ezek. 5:5–8.

JESTING
Foolish, forbidden. Eph. 5:4.

JESUS CHRIST
See specific topics under Christ

JEWELS AND PRECIOUS STONES

Forms

Agate, possibly used in windows.
Exod. 28:9; Isa. 54:12.

Alabaster, used in bottles to hold
perfume or myrrh. Mark 16:3;
Luke 7:37.

Amethyst, a purple quartz stone.
Exod. 39:12; Rev. 21:20.

Beryl, a green or red stone.
Exod. 28:20; Rev. 21:20.

Carbunele, a green or red stone.
Exod. 28:17; Isa. 54:12.

Carnelian, a red quartz.
Exod. 28:17; Ezek. 28:13;
Rev. 4:3; 21:20.

Chalcedony, a green stone.
Rev. 21:19.

Chrysolite, yellow topaz or quartz.
Rev. 21:20.

Chrysoprasus, a light green
chalcedony. Rev. 21:20.

Co °l, a red or black marine
growth. Job 28:18;
Ezek. 27:16.

Crystal, a form of quartz, glass, or
ice. Job 28:17; Rev. 4:6;
21:11.

Diamond, a hard opaque stone
probably quite different from the
modern diamond. Exod. 28:18;
Ezek. 28:13.

Emerald, a green or red stone.
Exod. 28:18; Rev. 4:3.

Hyacinth, *See* Jacinth.

Jacinth, a blue or blue-green stone.
Rev. 9:17; 21:20.

Jasper, green jade or green or
translucent quartz. Exod. 29:20;
Ezek. 28:13; Rev. 4:3,
21:11, 18–19.

Lapis lazuli, *See* Sapphire.

Ligure, a yellow stone.
Exod. 39:12.
Onyx, a green or black and white
stone. Gen. 2:12; Exod. 25:7;
Job 28:16.
Pearl, a stone produced by an
oyster. Matt. 13:45–46;
Rev. 17:4.
Ruby, a bright red stone.
Job 28:18; Prov. 8:11.
Sapphire, a deep blue stone.
Exod. 24:10; Isa. 54:11.
Sardius, a brown or red form of
quartz. Exod. 28:17; Ezek.
28:13; Rev. 21:20.
Sardonyx, a multicolored stone.
Rev. 21:20.
Topaz, a yellow stone.
Exod. 28:17; Job 28:19;
Rev. 21:20.

Illustrative of
Love and affection. Gen. 24:22;
Mal. 3:17.
Selfish ornamentation.
1 Tim. 2:9; Rev. 17:4.

Used as
Adornment. Isa. 3:18ff.
Investment and merchandise.
Prov. 3:15; James 2:2;
Rev. 18:12.
Offerings. Exod. 32:1; 35:22.

JEWS
An agricultural people. Gen. 46:32.

All other nations
Envied. Neh. 4:1; Isa. 26:11;
Ezek. 35:11.
Hated. Ps. 44:10; Ezek. 35:5.
Oppressed. Exod. 3:9;
Judg. 2:18; 4:3.
Persecuted. Lam. 1:3; 5:5.

Rejoiced at calamities of.
Pss. 44:13–14; 80:5–6;
Ezek. 36:4.
Believers remember. Ps. 102:14;
137:5; Jer. 51:50.
Beloved for their fathers' sake.
Deut. 4:37; 10:15, with
Rom. 11:28.

Blessedness of
Blessing. Gen. 27:29.
Favoring. Gen. 12:3; Ps. 122:6.

Called
Children of Israel. Gen. 50:25;
Isa. 27:12.
Children of Jacob.
1 Chron. 16:13.
Hebrews. Gen. 14:13; 40:15;
2 Cor. 11:22.
Israelites. Exod. 9:7; Josh. 3:17.
Jeshurun. Deut. 32:15.
Offspring of Abraham. Ps. 105:6;
Isa. 41:8.
Offspring of Israel.
1 Chron. 16:13.
Offspring of Jacob. Jer. 33:36.
Cast off for unbelief.
Rom. 11:17, 20.
Chosen and loved by God.
Deut. 7:6–7.

Christ
Descended from. John 4:22;
Rom. 9:5.
Expected by. Ps. 14:7;
Matt. 11:3; Luke 2:25, 38;
John 8:56.
Murdered by. Acts 7:52;
1 Thess. 2:15.
Promised to. Gen. 49:10;
Dan. 9:25.

Regarded as the restorer of national greatness. Matt. 20:21; Luke 24:21; Acts 1:6.

Rejected by. Isa. 53:3; Mark 6:3; John 1:11.

Sent to. Matt. 15:24; 21:37; Acts 3:20, 22, 26.

Sprang from. Rom. 9:5; Heb. 7:14.

Circumcised in sign of their covenant relation. Gen. 17:10–11; Acts 7:8.

A commercial people. Ezek. 27:17.

Compassion of Christ for. Matt. 23:37; Luke 19:41.

Condemned for associating with other nations. Judg. 2:1–3; Jer. 2:18.

Covenant established with. Exod. 6:4; 24:6–8; 34:27.

Degenerated as they increased in national greatness. Amos 6:4.

Denunciations against those who
Aggravated the afflictions of. Zech. 1:14–15.

Contended with. Isa. 41:11; 49:25.

Cursed. Gen. 27:29; Num. 24:9.

Hated. Ps. 129:5; Ezek. 35:5–6.

Oppressed. Isa. 49:26; 51:21–23.

Slaughtered. Ps. 79:1–7; Ezek. 35:5 6.

Deprived of civil and religious privileges. Hos. 3·4

Descended from Abraham. Ps. 105:6; Isa. 51:2; John 8:33, 39; Rom. 9:7.

Described as
A holy nation. Exod. 19:6.
A holy people. Deut. 7:6; 14:21.
A kingdom of priests. Exod. 19:6.
The Lord's portion. Deut. 32:9.

A peculiar people. Deut. 14:2.
A peculiar treasure. Exod. 19:5; Ps. 135:4.
A special people. Deut. 7:6.

In the desert forty years. Num. 14:33; Josh. 5:6.

Desired and obtained kings. 1 Sam. 8:5, 22.

Despised all strangers. 1 Sam. 17:36; Matt. 16:26–27; Eph. 2:11.

Despised by the nations. Ezek. 36:3.

Distinction of castes among, noticed. Isa. 65:5; Luke 7:39; 15:2; Acts 26:5.

Divided into twelve tribes. Gen. 35:22; 49:28.

Divided into two kingdoms after Solomon. 1 Kings 11:31–32; 12:19–20.

Enemies of, obliged to acknowledge them as divinely protected. Josh. 2:9–11; Esther 6:13.

Gentiles made one with, under the gospel. Acts 10:15, 28; 15:8–9; Gal. 3:28; Eph. 2:14–16.

God mindful of. Ps. 98:3; Isa. 49:15–16.

Under God's special protection. Deut. 32:10–11; 33:27–29; Pss. 105:13–15; 121:3–5.

Gospel preached first to. Matt. 10:6; Luke 24:47; Acts 1:8.

Had an ecclesiastical establishment. Exod. 28:1, Num. 18:6; Mal. 2:4–7.

Had courts of justice. Deut. 16:18.

Had a series of prophets to promote national reformation. Jer. 7:25; 26:4–5; 35:15; 44:4; Ezek. 38:17.

Held no dealings with strangers. John 4:9; Acts 11:2–3.

Invoked the blood of Christ upon themselves and their children. Matt. 27:25.

Many of, believed the gospel. Acts 21:20.

Modern, divided into
Hebrews or pure Jews. Acts 6:1; Phil. 3:5.
Hellenists or Grecians. Acts 6:1; 9:29.
Many sects and parties. Matt. 16:6; Mark 8:15.

National character of
Attached to customs of the law. Acts 6:14; 21:21; 22:3.
Attached to Moses. John 9:28–29; Acts 6:11.
Backsliding. Jer. 2:11–13; 8:5.
Covetous. Jer. 6:13; Ezek. 33:31; Mic. 2:2.
Cowardly. Exod. 14:10; Num. 14:3; Isa. 51:12.
Distrustful of God. Num. 14:11; Ps. 78:22.
Fond of their brethren. Exod. 2:11–12; Rom. 9:1–3.
Fond of traditionary customs. Jer. 44:17; Ezek. 20:18, 30, with 21; Mark 7:3–4.
Formal in religion. Isa. 29:13; Ezek. 33:31; Matt. 15:7–9.
Idolatrous. Isa. 2:8; 57:5.
Ignorant of the true sense of Scripture. Acts 13:27; 2 Cor. 3:13–15.
Love their country. Ps. 137:6.
Proud of descent, etc. Jer. 13:9; John 8:33, 41.
Rebellious. Deut. 9:7, 24; Isa. 1:2.
Self-righteous. Isa. 65:5; Rom. 10:3.

Stubborn and stiff-necked. Exod. 32:9; Acts 7:51.
Unfaithful to covenant engagements. Jer. 3:6–8; 31:32; Ezek. 16:59.
Ungrateful to God. Deut. 32:15; Isa. 1:2.
None hated or oppressed, with impunity. Ps. 137:8–9; Ezek. 25:15–16; 35:6; Obad. 1:10–16.

Objects of God's
Choice. Deut. 7:6.
Love. Deut. 7:8; 23:5; Jer. 31:3.
Protection. Ps. 105:15; Zech. 2:8.
Obliged to unite against enemies. Num. 32:20–22; Judg. 19:29, 20; 1 Sam. 11:7–8.
Often displeased God by their sins. Num. 25:3; Deut. 32:16; 1 Kings 16:2; Isa. 1:4; 5:24–25.
Often distinguished in war. Judg. 7:19–23; 1 Sam. 14:6–13; 17:32–33; Neh. 4:16–22.
Often subdued and made tributary. Judg. 2:13–14; 4:2; 6:2, 6; 2 Kings 23:33.
The only people who had knowledge of God. Ps. 76:1, with 1 Thess. 4:5; Ps. 48:3, with Rom. 1:28.
The only people who worshiped God. Exod. 5:17, with Ps. 96:5; Ps. 115:3–4; John 4:22.
People of God. Deut. 32:9; 2 Sam. 7:24; Isa. 51:16.
Pray persistently for. Ps. 122:6; Isa. 62:1, 6–7; Jer. 31:7; Rom. 10:1.
Privileges of. Ps. 76:1–2; Rom. 3:1–2; 9:4–5.

Prohibited from
Associating with others.
Acts 10:28.
Covenanting with others.
Exod. 23:32; Deut. 7:2.
Following practices of others.
Deut. 12:29–31; 18:9–14.
Marrying others. Deut. 7:3;
Josh. 23:12.

Promises regarding
Blessing to the Gentiles by
conversion. Isa. 2:1–5; 60:5;
66:19; Rom. 11:12, 15.
Future glory. Isa. 60:19; 62:3–4;
Zeph. 3:19–20; Zech. 2:5.
Future prosperity. Isa. 60:6–7, 9,
17; 61:4–6; Hos. 14:5–6.
Gentiles assisting in their
restoration. Isa. 49:22–23;
60:10, 14; 61:4–6.
Joy occasioned by conversion of.
Isa. 44:23; 49:13; 52:8–9;
66:10.
Pardon of sin. Isa. 44:22;
Rom. 11:27.
The pouring out of the Spirit upon
them. Ezek. 39:29;
Zech. 12:10.
The removal of their blindness.
Rom. 11:25; 2 Cor. 3:14–16.
Restoration to their own land.
Isa. 11:15–16; 14:1–3;
27:12–13; Jer. 16:14–15;
Ezek. 36:24; 37:21, 25; 39:25,
28; Luke 21:24.
Reunion of. Jer. 3:18;
Ezek. 37:16–17, 20–22;
Hos. 1:11; Mic. 2:12.
Salvation. Isa. 59:20, with
Rom. 11:26.
Sanctification. Jer. 33:8;
Ezek. 36:25; Zech. 12:1, 9.

Subjection of Gentiles to.
Isa. 60:11–12, 14.
That Christ will dwell among.
Ezek. 43:7, 9; Zech. 14:4.
Their humiliation for the rejection
of Christ. Zech. 12:10.
Their return and seeking to God.
Hos. 3:5.

Promises regarding, made to
Abraham.
Gen. 12:1–3; 13:14–17; 15:1;
17:7–8.
Isaac. Gen. 26:2–5, 24.
Jacob. Gen. 28:12–15; 35:9–12.
Themselves. Exod. 6:7–8;
19:5–6; Deut. 26:18–19.

Punished for
Breaking the covenant. Isa. 23:5;
Jer. 11:10.
Changing the ordinances.
Isa. 24:5.
Idolatry. Ps. 78:58–64;
Isa. 65:3–7.
Killing the prophets.
Matt. 23:37–38.
Transgressing the law. Isa. 1:4, 7;
24:5–6.
Unbelief. Rom. 11:20.
Punishment for rejecting and killing
Christ illustrated. Matt. 21:37–43.
Received converts from other
nations. Acts 2:10, with
Exod. 12:44, 48.

Religion of
According to rites prescribed by
God. Lev. 18:4; Deut. 12:8–11;
Heb. 9:1.
Typical. Heb. 9:8–11; 10:1.
Restored to their own land by Cyrus.
Ezra 1:1–4.

Scattered among the nations.
Deut. 28:64; Ezek. 6:8; 36:19.

Scattered and peeled. Isa. 18:2, 7;
James 1:1.

Separated from all other nations.
Exod. 33:16; Lev. 20:24;
1 Kings 8:53.

Separated to God. Exod. 33:16;
Num. 23:9; Deut. 4:34.

Settled in Canaan. Num. 32:32;
Josh. 14:1–5.

Sojourned in Egypt.
Exod. 12:40–41.

Spiritual offspring of true believers
always among. 1 Kings 19:18;
Isa. 6:13; Rom. 9:6–7; 11:1, 5.

Strengthened by God in war.
Lev. 26:7–8; Josh. 5:13–14;
8:1–2.

Taken captive to Assyria and
Babylon. 2 Kings 17:23; 18:11;
24:16; 25:11.

Taken out of Egypt by God.
Exod. 12:42; Deut. 5:15; 6:12.

Their country trodden under foot by
the Gentiles. Deut. 28:49–52;
Luke 21:24.

Their house desolate. Matt. 24:38.

Their national greatness. Gen. 12:2;
Deut. 33:29.

Their national privileges. Rom. 3:2;
9:4–5.

Their vast numbers. Gen. 22:17;
Num. 10:36.

Under the theocracy until the time of
Samuel. Exod. 19:4–6, with
1 Sam. 8–7.

Trusted to their privileges for
salvation. Jer. 7:4; Matt. 3:9.

Unbelieving, persecuted the
Christians. Acts 17:5, 13;
1 Thess. 2:14–16.

Will finally be saved.
Rom. 11:26–27.

JEWS, DIET OF THE

Articles used for
Bread. Gen. 18:5; 1 Sam. 17:17.
Butter. Deut. 32:14;
2 Sam. 17:29.
Cheese. 1 Sam. 17:18;
Job 10:10.
Dried fruit. 1 Sam. 25:18; 30:12.
Fish. Matt. 7:10; Luke 24:42.
Flesh. 2 Sam. 6:19; Prov. 9:2.
Fruit. 2 Sam. 16:2.
Herbs. Prov. 15:17; Rom. 14:2;
Heb. 6:7.
Honey. Song of Sol. 5:1;
Isa. 7:15.
Milk. Gen. 49:12; Prov. 27:27.
Oil. Deut. 12:17; Prov. 21:17;
Ezek. 16:13.
Parched corn. Ruth 2:14;
1 Sam. 17:17.
Vinegar. Num. 6:3; Ruth 2:14.
Water. Gen. 21:14; Matt. 10:42.
Wine. 2 Sam. 6:19; John 2:3, 10.

In Egypt. Exod. 16:3; Num. 11:5.

Expressed by bread and water.
1 Kings 13:9, 16.

Generally prepared by
females. Gen. 27:9; 1 Sam. 8:13;
Prov. 31:15.

A hymn sung after. Matt. 26:30.

In the wilderness. Exod. 16:4–12.

Items of, often sent as presents.
1 Sam. 17:18; 25:18, 27;
2 Sam. 16:1–2.

Men and women did not partake of,
together. Gen. 18:8–9;
Esther 1:3, 9.

In patriarchal age. Gen. 18:7–8;
27:4.

Of the poor, frugal. Ruth 2:14;
Prov. 15:17.

Purification before. 2 Kings 3:11;
Matt. 15:2.

Of the rich, luxurious. Prov. 23:1–3;
Lam. 4:5; Amos 6:4–5;
Luke 16:19.

Thanks given before. Mark 8:6;
Acts 27:35.

Was taken
In the evening. Gen. 24:11, 33;
Luke 24:29–30.

In the morning, sparingly. Judg.
19:5, with Eccles. 10:16–17.

At noon. Gen. 43:16;
John 4:6, 8.

Often reclining. Amos 6:4;
John 13:23.

Often sitting. Gen. 27:19; 43:33.

With the hand. Matt. 26:23, with
Luke 22:21.

JEZEBEL
Wife of King Ahab. 1 Kings 16:31;
18:4, 19.

JOB SECURITY
See also Downsizing; Employment

For Levites, until retirement.
Num. 8:24–25.

Principles relevant to
Diligence. Prov. 12:24.

Faithfulness leads to.
Luke 12:42–44.

Servant hired year by year.
Lev. 25:53.

JORDAN RIVER
See River, Jordan

JOT
Vowel point in Hebrew. Matt. 5:18.

JOY
Afflictions of believers succeeded by.
Pss. 30:5; 126:5; Isa. 35:10;
John 16:20.

Of believers is
In Christ. Luke 1:47; Phil. 3:3.

For deliverance from bondage.
Ps. 105:43; Jer. 31:10–13.

For divine protection. Pss. 5:11;
16:8–9.

For divine support. Pss. 28:7;
63:7.

For election. Luke 10:20.

In God. Pss. 89:16; 149:2;
Hab. 3:18; Rom. 5:11.

In the Holy Spirit. Rom. 14:17.

For manifestation of goodness.
2 Chron. 7:10.

For salvation. Ps. 21:1;
Isa. 61:10.

For supplies of grace. Isa. 12:3.

For temporal blessings.
Joel 2:23–24.

For the hope of glory. Rom. 5:2.

For the success of the gospel.
Acts 15:3.

For the victory of Christ.
John 16:33.

Of believers made full by
Abiding in Christ.
John 15:10–11.

Answers to prayer. John 16:24.

Communion. 2 Tim. 1:4;
1 John 1:3–4; 2 John 1:12.

Faith in Christ. Rom. 15:13.

The favor of God. Acts 2:28.

The word of Christ. John 17:13.

Believers will be presented to God
with exceeding. 1 Pet. 4:13, with
Jude 24.

Believers should afford, to their
ministers. Phil. 2:2; Philem. 1:20.

Of believers should be
Abundant. 2 Cor. 8:2.
Animated. Ps. 32:11; Luke 6:23.
With awe. Ps. 2:11.
Constant. 2 Cor. 6:10; Phil. 4:4.
Under calamities. Hab. 3:17–18.
Exceeding. Pss. 21:6; 68:3.
Expressed in hymns. Eph. 5:19;
James 5:13.
Forevermore. 1 Thess. 5:16.
Full of glory. 1 Pet. 1:8.
Great. Zech. 9:9; Acts 8:8.
In hope. Rom. 12:12.
Under persecutions.
Matt. 5:11–12; Luke 6:22–23;
Heb. 10:34.
In sorrow. 2 Cor. 6:10.
Under trials. James 1:2;
1 Pet. 1:6.
Unspeakable. 1 Pet. 1:8.
Will be taken away. Isa. 16:10.

Believers should have, in all their
undertakings. Deut. 12:18.

Christ appointed to give. Isa. 61:3.

The coming of Christ will bring
exceeding, to believers.
1 Pet. 4:14.

Commanded to Believers. Ps. 32:11;
Phil. 3:1.

Experienced by
Believers. Luke 24:52;
Acts 16:34.
The just. Prov. 21:15.
Parents of good children.
Prov. 23:24.
Peacemakers. Prov. 12:20.

The wise and discreet.
Prov. 15:23.

A fruit of the Spirit. Gal. 5:22.

Fullness of, in God's presence.
Ps. 16:11.

Generosity in God's service should
cause. 1 Chron. 29:9, 17.

God gives. Eccles 2:26; Ps. 4:7.

God's Word affords. Neh. 8:12;
Jer. 15:6.

Gospel good tidings of.
Luke 2:10–11.

Gospel to be received with.
1 Thess. 1:6.

Holy, illustrated. Isa. 9:3;
Matt. 13:44.

Increased to the meek. Isa. 29:19.

Ministers should
Come to their people with.
Rom. 15:32.
Desire to render an account with.
Phil. 2:16; Heb. 13:17.
Esteem their people as their.
Phil. 4:1; 1 Thess. 2:20.
Finish their course with.
Acts 20:24.
Have, in the faith and holiness of
their people. 2 Cor. 7:4;
1 Thess. 3:9; 3 John 1:4.
Pray for, for their people.
Rom. 15:13.
Promote, in their people.
2 Cor. 1:24; Phil. 1:25.

Pray for restoration of. Pss. 51:8,
12; 85:6.

Prepared for believers. Ps. 97:11.

Promised to believers. Ps. 132:16;
Isa. 35:10; 55:12; 56:7.

Promote, in the afflicted. Job 29:13.

The reward of believers at the
judgment day. Matt. 25:21.

Serve God with. Ps. 100:2.

Strengthening to believers.
  Neh. 8:10.
Vanity of seeking, from earthly
  things. Eccles. 2:10–11; 11:8.

Of the wicked
  Is delusive. Prov. 14:13.
  Is derived from earthly pleasures.
    Eccles 2:10; 11:9.
  Is derived from folly. Prov. 15:21.
  Is short-lived. Job 20:5;
    Eccles. 7:6.
  Should be turned into mourning.
    James 4:9.

**JOY OF GOD OVER HIS
PEOPLE**
See God, Joy of, over His People

JUBILEE, FEAST OF
Began on the Day of Atonement.
  Lev. 25:9.

Called the
  Acceptable year. Isa. 61:2.
  Year of liberty. Ezek. 46:17.
  Year of the redeemed. Isa. 63:4.

Enactments regarding
  Cessation of all field labor.
    Lev. 25:11.
  Fruits of the earth to be common
    property. Lev. 25:12.
  Redemption of sold property.
    Lev. 25:23–27.
  Release of Hebrew servants.
    Lev. 25:40–41, 54.
  Restoration of all inheritances.
    Lev. 25:10, 13, 28; 27:24.
Held every fiftieth year. Lev. 25:8,
  10.
Houses in walled cities not redeemed
  within a year, exempted from the
  benefit of. Lev. 25:30.

Illustrative of the gospel. Isa. 61:1–2;
  Luke 4:18–19.
Proclaimed by trumpets. Lev. 25:9;
  Ps. 89:15.
Sale of property calculated from.
  Lev. 25:15–16.
Value of devoted property calculated
  from. Lev. 27:14–23.
Was specially holy. Lev. 25:12.

JUDAH, TRIBE OF
With Benjamin, alone adhered to the
  house of David. 1 Kings 12:21.
Bounds of inheritance.
  Josh. 15:1–12.
Censured for tardiness in bringing
  back David after Absalom's
  rebellion. 2 Sam. 19:11–15.
Christ in lineage of. Matt. 1:3–16;
  Luke 3:23–33; Heb. 7:14.
Descended from Jacob's fourth son.
  Gen. 29:35.
Encamped with its standard east of
  the tabernacle. Num. 2:3.
Families of. Num. 26:19–21.
First and most vigorous in driving out
  the Canaanites. Judg. 1:3–20.
First to submit to David.
  2 Sam. 2:10.
First went against Gibeah.
  Judg. 20:18.
Furnished kings to Israel.
  1 Sam. 13:14; 15:28; 16:6, 13;
  2 Sam. 2:4; 7:16–17.
Furnished to Israel the first judge.
  Judg. 3:9.
On Gerizim said amen to the
  blessings. Deut. 27:12.
Helped Saul in his wars.
  1 Sam. 11:8; 15:4.
Last tribe carried into captivity.
  2 Kings 17:18, 20; 25:21.

Led the first division of Israel in their journeys. Num. 10:14.

Offering of, at dedication. Num. 7:12–17.

Officer placed over by David. 1 Chron. 27:18.

Other tribes jealous of, because of David. 2 Sam. 19:41–43; 20:1–2.

Persons selected from to
Divide the land. Num. 34:19.
Number the people. Num. 1:7.
Spy out the land. Num. 13:6.

Predictions regarding. Gen. 49:8–12; Deut. 33:7.

Reigned over alone by David seven years and a half. 2 Sam. 2:11; 5:5.

Remarkable persons of
Absalom. 2 Sam. 15:1.
Achan. Josh. 7:18.
Adonijah. 1 Kings 1:5–6.
Bezaleel. Exod. 31:2.
Boaz. Ruth 2:1.
Caleb. Num. 14:24.
David. 1 Sam. 16:1, 13.
Elhanan. 2 Sam. 21:19.
Elihu. 1 Chron. 27:18.
Elimelech. Ruth 1:1–2.
Jesse. Ruth 4:22.
Jonathan. 2 Sam. 21:21.
Kings of Judah. 1 and 2 Kings.
Nashon. Num. 7:12.
Obed. Ruth 4:21.
Pethahiah. Neh. 11:2:4.
Solomon. 1 Kings 1:32–39.

Strength of, on leaving Egypt. Num. 1:26–27; 2:4.

JUDEA

Called
Judah. Dan. 5:13, with John 7:1.
The land of Judah. Matt. 2:6.

Christ
Born in. Matt. 2:1, 5–6.
Frequently visited. John 11:7.
Often left, to escape persecution. John 4:1–3.
Tempted in the wilderness of. Matt. 4:1.

Comprised the whole of the ancient kingdom of Judah. 1 Kings 12:21–24.

Jerusalem the capital of. Matt. 4:23.

John the Baptist preached in. Matt. 3:1.

A mountainous district. Luke 1:39, 65.

One of the divisions of the Holy Land under the Romans. Luke 3:1.

Parts of, desert. Matt. 3:1; Acts 8:26.

Several Christian churches in. Acts 9:31; 1 Thess. 2:14.

Towns of
Arimathea. Matt. 27:57; John 19:38.
Azotus or Ashdod. Acts 8:40.
Bethany. John 11:1, 18.
Bethlehem. Matt. 2:1, 6, 16.
Bethphage. Matt. 21:1.
Emmaus. Luke 24:13.
Ephraim. John 11:54.
Gaza. Acts 8:26.
Jericho. Luke 10:30; 19:1.
Joppa. Acts 9:36; 10:5, 8.
Lydda. Acts 9:32, 35, 38.

JUDGE
Appointed by Persian. Ezra 7:25.

Corrupt, examples of
Eli's sons.
1 Sam. 2:12–17, 22, 25.
Felix. Acts 24:26–27.
The judges of Jezreel.
1 Kings 21:8–13.
Pilate. Matt. 27:24.
Samuel's sons. 1 Sam. 8:1–5.
Held circuit courts. 1 Sam. 7:16.
Kings and other rules as.
2 Sam. 8:15; 15:2; 1 Kings
3:16–28.
Priests and Levites as. Deut. 17:9;
2 Chron. 9:8; Ezek. 44:23–24;
Matt. 26:57–62.
Women as, Deborah. Judg. 4:4.

JUDGES, EXTRAORDINARY

During four hundred and fifty years.
Acts 13:20.
Israel not permanently or spiritually
benefited by. Judg. 2:17–19.

Names of
Abdon. Judg. 12:13.
Abimelech. Judg. 9:6.
Deborah. Judg. 4:4.
Ehud. Judg. 3:15.
Eli. 1 Sam. 4:18.
Elon. Judg. 12:11.
Gideon. Judg. 6:11.
Ibzan. Judg. 12:8.
Jair. Judg. 10:3.
Jephthah. Judg. 11:1.
Othniel. Judg. 3:9–10.
Samson. Judg. 13:24–25; 16:31.
Samuel. 1 Sam. 7:6, 15–17.
Shamgar. Judg. 3:31.
Tola. Judg. 10:1.
Not without intermission.
Judg. 17:6; 18:1; 19:1; 21:25.
The office of, not always for life or
hereditary. Judg. 8:23, 29.

Raised up to deliver Israel.
Judg. 2:16.
Remarkable for their faith.
Heb. 11:32.
Upheld and strengthened by God.
Judg. 2:18.

JUDGMENT

Believers will be enabled to stand in.
Rom. 8:33–34.
Believers will be rewarded at.
2 Tim. 4:8; Rev. 11:18.
Believers will sit with Christ in.
1 Cor. 6:2; Rev. 20:4.
The books will be opened at.
Dan. 7:10.

Called the
Day of destruction. Job 21:30.
Day of judgment and perdition of
ungodly men. 2 Pet. 3:7.
Day of wrath. Rom. 2:5;
Rev. 6:17.
Judgment of the great day. Jude 6.
Revelation of the righteous
judgment of God. Rom. 2:5.

Certainty of, a motive to
Faith. Isa. 28:16–17.
Holiness. 2 Cor. 5:9–10;
2 Pet. 3:11, 14.
Prayer and watchfulness.
Mark 13:33.
Repentance. Acts 17:30–31.
Christ will acknowledge believers at.
Matt. 25:34–40; Rev. 3:5.
Of Christians, by the gospel. James
2:12.
A day appointed for. Acts 17:31;
Rom. 2:16.
Devils will be condemned at.
2 Pet. 2:4; Jude 6.
Final punishment of the wicked will
succeed. Matt. 13:40–42; 25:46.

A first principle of the gospel.
Heb. 6:2.

Of heathens, by the law of
conscience. Rom. 2:12, 14–15.

Of Jews by the law of Moses.
Rom. 2:12.

Neglected advantages increase
condemnation at.
Matt. 11:20–24; Luke 11:31–32.

None, by nature, can stand in.
Pss. 130:3; 143:2; Rom. 3:19.

Perfect love will give boldness in.
1 John 4:17.

Predicted in the Old Testament.
1 Chron. 16:33; Pss. 9:7; 96:13;
Eccles. 3:17.

The wicked dread. Acts 24:25;
Heb. 10:27.

The wicked will be condemned in.
Matt. 7:22–23; 25:41.

The word of Christ will be a witness
against the wicked in. John 12:48.

Time of, unknown to us.
Mark 13:32.

Warn the wicked of. Acts 24:25;
2 Cor. 5:11.

Will be administered by Christ.
John 5:22, 27; Acts 10:42;
Rom. 14:10; 2 Cor. 5:10.

Will be held upon
All men. Heb. 9:27; 12:23.
All nations. Matt. 25:32.
Living and dead. 2 Tim. 4:1;
1 Pet. 4:5.
The righteous and wicked.
Eccles. 3:17.
Small and great. Rev. 20:12.
Will be in righteousness. Ps. 98:9;
Acts 17:31.

Will be of all
Actions. Eccles. 11:9; 12:14;
Rev. 20:13.

Thoughts. Eccles 12:14; 1 Cor.
4:5.

Words. Matt. 12:36–37; Jude 15.

Will take place at the coming of
Christ. Matt. 25:31; 2 Tim. 4:1.

JUDGMENTS

Are frequently tempered with mercy.
Jer. 4:27; 5:10, 15–18;
Amos 9:8.

Are from God. Deut. 32:39;
Job 12:23; Amos 3:6; Mic. 6:9.

Are in all the earth. 1 Chron. 16:14.

Are sent as punishment for
Despising the warnings of God.
2 Chron. 36:16;
Prov. 1:24–31; Jer. 44:4–6.
Disobedience to God.
Lev. 26:14–16;
2 Cor. 7:19–20.
Idolatry. 2 Kings 22:17;
Jer. 16:18.
Iniquity. Isa. 26:21;
Ezek. 24:13–14.
Murmuring against God.
Num. 14:29.
Persecuting Believers.
Deut. 32:43.
Sins of rulers. 1 Chron. 21:2, 12.

Believers
Acknowledge the justice of.
2 Sam. 24:17; Ezra 9:13;
Neh. 9:33; Jer. 14:7.
Pray for those under.
Exod. 32:11–13; Num. 11:2;
Dan. 9:3.
Preserved during. Job 5:19–20;
Ps. 91:7; Isa. 26:20; Ezek. 9:6;
Rev. 7:3.
Provided for, during. Gen. 47:12;
Pss. 35:19; 37:19.

Sympathize with those under.
Jer. 9:1; 13:17; Lam. 3:48.

Different kinds of
Abandonment by God. Hos. 4:17.
Blotting out the name.
Deut. 29:20.
Captivity. Deut. 28:41;
Ezek. 39:23.
Continued sorrows. Pss. 32:10;
78:32–33; Ezek. 24:23.
Cursing men's blessings. Mal. 2:2.
Desolation. Ezek. 33:29;
Joel 3:19.
Destruction. Job 31:3; Ps. 34:16;
Prov. 2:22.
Enemies. 2 Sam. 24:13.
Famine. Deut. 28:38–40;
Amos 4:7–9.
Famine of hearing the word.
Amos 8:11.
Plagues. Deut. 28:21–22;
Amos 4:10.
The sword. Exod. 22:24;
Jer. 19:7.

Inflicted upon
All enemies of believers.
Jer. 30:16.
False gods. Exod. 12:12;
Num. 33:4.
Individuals. Deut. 29:20;
Jer. 23:34
Nations. Gen. 15:14;
Jer. 51:20–21.
Posterity of sinners. Exod. 20:5;
Ps. 37:28; Lam. 5:7.
Manifest the righteous character of
God. Exod. 9:14–16;
Ezek. 39:21; Dan. 9:14.

May be averted by
Forsaking iniquity. Jer. 18:7–8.

Humiliation. Exod. 33:3–4, 14;
2 Chron. 7:14.
Prayer. Judg. 3:9–11;
2 Chron. 7:13–14.
Turning to God. Deut. 30:1–3.
Sent for correction. Job 37:13;
Jer. 30:11.
Sent for the deliverance of believers.
Exod. 6:6.
Should be a warning to others.
Luke 13:3, 5.

Should lead to
Humiliation. Josh. 7:6;
2 Chron. 12:6; Lam. 3:1–20;
Joel 1:13; Jon. 3:5–6.
Learning righteousness. Isa. 26:9.
Prayer. 2 Chron. 20:9.
Remorse. Neh. 1:4; Esther 4:3;
Isa. 22:12.

JUDGMENT SEAT
Of Christ. Rom. 14:10.
Pilate. Matt. 27:19.

JURY
Of seventy men. Number 11:16; 17;
24–25.
Of ten men. Ruth 4:2.

JUSTICE
Believers should
Always do. Ps. 119:121;
Ezek. 18:8 9.
Pray for wisdom to execute.
1 Kings 3:9.
Receive instruction in. Prov. 1:3.
Study the principles of. Phil. 4:8.
Take pleasure in doing.
Prov. 21:15.
Teach others to do. Gen. 18:19.
Brings its own reward. Jer. 22:15.

Christ an example of. Ps. 98:9;
Isa. 11:4; Jer. 23:5.
Commanded. Deut. 16:20;
Isa. 56:1.
Gifts impede. Exod. 23:8.

God
Delights in. Prov. 11:1.
Displeased with the lack of.
Eccles 5:8.
Gives wisdom to execute.
1 Kings 3:11–12; Prov. 2:6, 9.
Requires. Mic. 6:8.
Sets the highest value on.
Prov. 21:3.
Promises to. Isa. 33:15–16;
Jer. 7:5, 7.
Specially required in rulers.
2 Sam. 23:3; Ezek. 45:9.

To be done
In buying and selling. Lev. 19:36;
Deut. 25:15.
In executing judgment.
Deut. 16:18; Jer. 21:12.
To the fatherless and widows.
Isa. 1:17.
To the poor. Prov. 29:14; 31:9.
To servants. Col. 4:1.

The wicked
Abhor. Mic. 3:9.
Afflict those who act with.
Job 12:4; Amos 5:12.
Banish. Isa. 59:14.
Do not call for. Isa. 59:4.
Pass over. Luke 11:42.
Scorn. Prov. 19:28.

JUSTICE, COURTS OF

The accused
Evidence of two or more witnesses
required in. Deut. 17:6; 19:15;
John 8:17; 2 Cor. 13:1.

Examined on oath. Lev. 5:1;
Matt. 26:63.
Exhorted to confess. Josh. 7:19.
Might have advocates.
Prov. 31:8–9; Isa. 1:17.
Permitted to plead their own
cause. 1 Kings 3:22;
Acts 24:10; 26:1.
Sometimes examined by torture.
Acts 22:24, 29.
Sometimes treated with insult.
Matt. 26:67; John 18:22–23;
Acts 23:2–3.
Stood before the judge.
Num. 35:12; Matt. 27:11.
Witnesses sometimes laid their
hands on the criminal's head
before punishment. Lev. 24:14.
Both the accusers and accused
required to appear before.
Deut. 25:1; Acts 25:16.

Causes in, were opened by
Advocate. Acts 24:1.
Complainant. 1 Kings 3:17–21;
Acts 16:19–21.
Corruption and bribery often
practiced in. Isa. 10:1;
Amos 5:12; 8:6.
False witnesses in to receive the
punishment of the accused.
Deut. 19:19.
Generally held in the morning.
Jer. 21:12; Matt. 27:1;
Luke 22:66; Acts 5:21.
Have authority from God.
Rom. 13:1–5.

Inferior
All minor cases decided by.
Exod. 18:26; 2 Sam. 15:4.
All transfers of property made
before. Gen. 23:17–20;
Ruth 4:1–2.

Held at the gates. Gen. 34:20;
Deut. 16:18; 21:19; Job 5:4.
In all cities. Deut. 16:18;
2 Chron. 19:5–7.
Judges of, appointed by the
governor. Exod. 18:21, 25;
Deut. 1:9–15; 2 Sam. 15:3.

Judges of
Called elders. Deut. 25:7;
1 Sam. 16:4.
Called magistrates. Luke 12:58.
Conferred together before giving
judgment.
Acts 5:34–40; 25:12;
26:30–31.
To decide according to law.
Ezek. 44:24.
Examined the parties. Acts 24:8.
To investigate every case.
Deut. 19:18.
To judge as for God.
2 Chron. 19:6–7, 9.
To judge righteously. Lev. 19:15;
Deut. 1:16.
To judge without favoritism.
Exod. 23:3, 6; Lev. 19:15;
Deut. 1:17; Prov. 22:22.
Not to take bribes. Exod. 23:8;
Deut. 16:19.
Pronounced the judgment of the
court. Matt. 26:65–66;
Luke 23:24; Acts 5:40.
Rode often on white donkeys.
Judg. 5:10.
Sat on the judgment seat while
hearing causes. Exod. 18:13;
Judg. 5:10; Isa. 28:6;
Matt. 27:19.
To promote peace. Zech. 8:16.

Judgment of
Alluded to. Job 5:4; Ps. 127:5;
Matt. 5:22.

Illustrative of the last judgment.
Matt. 19:28; Rom. 14:10;
1 Cor. 6:2.
Immediately executed. Deut. 25:2;
Josh. 7:25; Mark 15:15–20.
Not given until accused was heard.
John 7:51.
Recorded in writing. Isa. 10:1.
Witnesses first to execute.
Deut. 17:7; Acts 7:58.

Provided with
Judges. Deut. 16:18.
Officers. Deut. 16:18; Matt. 5:25.
Reestablished by Ezra. Ezra 7:25.
Reestablished by Jehoshaphat.
2 Chron. 19:5–10.
Tormentors or executioners.
Matt. 18:34.

Of the Romans in Judea
Appeals from, made to the
emperor. Acts 25:11; 26:32;
28:19.
Could alone award death.
John 18:31.
Never examined their own citizens
by torture. Acts 22:25–29.
Never interfered in any dispute
about minor masters or about
religion. Acts 18:14–15.
Place of, called the hall of
judgment. John 18:28, 33;
19:9.
Presided over by the governor or
deputy. Matt. 27:2, 11;
Acts 18:12.

Sanhedrin or Court of the Seventy
Consisted of chief priests, etc.
Matt. 26:57, 59.
Mentioned in the latter part of
sacred history. Luke 22:66;
John 11:47; Acts 5:27.

Presided over by high priest.
Matt. 26:62–66.

Probably derived from the seventy
elders appointed by Moses.
Exod. 24:9; Num. 11:16–17,
24–30.

Sat in high priest's palace.
Matt. 26:57–58.

Sometimes held in synagogues.
Matt. 10:17; Acts 22:19; 26:11.

Superior

Consisted of priests and Levites.
Deut. 17:9, with Mal. 2:7.

Decided on all appeals and difficult
cases. Exod. 18:26; Deut. 1:17;
17:8–9.

Decisions of, conclusive.
Deut. 17:10–11.

Held at the seat of government.
Deut. 17:8.

Held first by Moses alone in the
wilderness. Exod. 18:13–20.

Presided over by the governor or
the high priest. Deut. 17:12;
Judg. 4:4–5.

JUSTICE OF GOD
See God, Justice of

JUSTIFICATION BEFORE GOD
See God, Justification before

JUVENILE DELINQUENCY

Delinquent son
Correction of. Prov 19:18.
Refusing correction.
Deut. 21:18–21; Jer. 2:30.
Responsible for own actions.
Ezek 18:10–13.

Examples of
Boys jeering Elisha.
2 Kings 2:23–25.
Prodigal son. Luke 15:12–13.
Sons of Eli. 1 Sam 2:22–25.

Treatment of parents as
Cursing. Exod. 21:17.
Dishonoring. Deut. 27:16.
Striking. Exod. 21:15.
With contempt. Ezek 22:7.
With insolence. Isa. 3:5.

❧K❧

KEY
A symbol of authority. Isa. 22:22;
Matt. 16:19; Rev. 1:18; 3:7; 9:1;
20:1.
Used in a figurative sense.
Luke 11:52.

KIDNAPPING
Example of. Judg. 21:20–23.
Forbidden. Exod. 21:16;
Deut. 24:7.

KIDNEY
Burnt offering of. Exod. 29:13, 22.

KINDNESS
An attribute of God. Isa. 54:8;
Eph. 2:7; Titus 3:4–7.
A characteristic of decent people.
Job 29:15; Prov. 31:26;
1 Cor. 13:4.
A Christian necessity. Col. 3:12;
2 Pet. 1:7.
A fundamental requirement.
Mic. 6:8; Matt. 25:40.

KING
Acts as judge. 2 Sam. 8:15.

Ceremonial recognition of
Bowing. 1 Kings 1:16.
Kneeling before. Matt. 27:29.
Prostration. 1 Sam. 25:41.
Salutation to. Dan. 2:4; 6:6, 21.
Chronicles of, kept. 1 Kings 11:41.
Constitutional restrictions of.
Deut. 17:18–20.
Decrees of, irrevocable. Esther 8:8;
Dan. 6:8–9, 12–15.

Deification of. Ezek. 28:2, 9.
Divinely authorized. Deut. 17:15;
1 Sam. 9:16–17; Dan. 2:21, 37;
4:17.
Drunkenness of, forbidden.
Prov. 31:4–5.
Exercise executive clemency.
1 Sam. 11:13.

How chosen
By divine appointment, Saul.
1 Sam. 10:1.
David and the Davidic dynasty.
1 Sam. 16:1–13.
Hereditary succession.
2 Sam. 7:12–16;
1 Kings 1:28–30;
2 Chron. 21:3–4;
Ps. 89:35–37.
Not hereditary.
1 Chron. 1:43–51.
By lot. 1 Sam. 10:20, 21.

Influenced by popular opinion
David. 2 Chron. 20:21.
Herod. Matt. 14:5; Acts 12:2–3.
Hezekiah. 2 Chron. 30:2.
Pilate. John 19:6–13.
Saul. 1 Sam. 14:45.
Zedekiah. Jer. 38:19, 24–27.

Influence of queens over
Bathsheba. 1 Kings 1:28–34.
Esther. Esther 5:1–8.
Jezebel. 1 Kings 18:4–13.
Laws concerning. Deut. 17:14–19.
Loyalty to, commanded.
Prov. 16:14–15.

Modes of induction into office

By anointing Judg. 9:8;
1 Sam. 9:16; 1 Kings 1:34.

By an oath. 2 Kings 11:4.

By proclamation. 2 Sam. 15:10.

Obedience to, commanded.
Eccles 8:2–5.

Prayer for. Ezra 6:10.

Prayer for, commanded.
1 Tim. 2:1–2.

Religious duties of. Ezek. 45:9–25.

Respect due to. Job 34:18;
Matt. 22:21.

Rights and duties of.
Prov. 25:2, 5, 6, 15; 29:4,
12, 14; Jer. 21:12.

KINGDOM OF GOD

See God, Kingdom of

KISS

Of affection. Gen. 27:26–27;
31:55; Exod. 18:7; Ruth 1:14;
2 Sam. 14:33; Luke 15:20;
Acts 20:37.

Deceitful. Prov. 27:6.

Deceitful, of Joab, when he killed
Amasa. 2 Sam. 20:9–10.

The feet of Jesus kissed by the
penitent woman. Luke 7:38.

Holy. Rom. 16:16.

Of Judas when he betrayed Jesus.
Matt. 26:48.

KNIFE

An edged tool used by Abraham in
offering Isaac. Gen. 22:6.

Of the temple, return from Babylon.
Ezra 1:9.

Used for sharpening pens.
Jer. 36:23.

Self-mutilation with, idolatrous.
1 Kings 18:28.

KNOWLEDGE

Of Christ. Phil. 3:8.

Desire for. 1 Kings 3:9; Ps. 119:66;
Prov. 2; 3; 12:1; 15:14; 18:15.

A divine gift. 1 Cor. 12:8.

The earth will be full of. Isa. 11:9.

Fear of the Lord is the beginning of.
Prov. 1:7.

Fools hate. Prov. 1:22, 29.

Of God more than burnt offerings.
Hos. 6:6.

Of good and evil. Gen. 2:9, 17;
3:22.

His power. Prov. 3:20; 24:5.

Is pleasant. Prov. 2:10.

Key of. Luke 11:52.

Of more value than gold. Prov. 8:10.

Now we know in part.
1 Cor. 13:9–12.

The priest's lips should keep.
Mal. 2:7.

Rejected. Hos. 4:6.

Of salvation. Luke 1:77.

Those who reject are destroyed.
Hos. 4:6.

Will be increased. Dan. 12:4.

LABOR

Divinely ordained. Gen. 2:5, 15;
3:19; 2 Thess. 3:10, 12.
Required in the Christian life.
Heb. 4:11; 1 Cor. 3:9; Col. 4:12.
To be done well. Eccles. 9:10.
Worthwhile in the Lord.
1 Cor. 15:58.

LABOR, CAPITAL

Strife between. Matt. 21:33–41;
Mark 12:1–9; Luke 20:9–16.

LADDER

In Jacob's vision. Gen. 28:12.

LAKE OF FIRE

See also Hell

Description of hell.
Rev. 19:20; 20:10, 14, 15; 21:8.

LAMA SABACHTHANI

The dying cry of Jesus. Matt. 27:46
with Ps. 22:1.

LAMB

Considered a great delicacy.
Amos 6:4.
Covenants confirmed by gift of.
Gen. 21:28–30.

Described as
Patient. Isa. 53:7.
Playful. Ps. 114:4, 6.
Exposed to danger from wild beasts.
1 Sam. 17:34.
An extensive commerce in.
Ezra 7:17; Ezek. 27:21.

The firstborn of an ass to be
redeemed with. Exod. 13:13;
34:20.

Illustrative of
Anything dear or cherished.
2 Sam. 12:3, 9.
Christ as a sacrifice. John 1:29;
Rev. 5:6.
Complete destruction of the
wicked (when consumed in
sacrifice). Ps. 37:20.
Israel deprived of God's protection
(when deserted and exposed).
Hos. 4:16.
The Lord's people. Isa. 5:17;
11:6.
Ministers among the ungodly
(when among wolves).
Luke 10:3.
Patience of Christ. Isa. 53:7;
Acts 8:32.
Purity of Christ. 1 Pet. 1:19.
Weak believers. Isa. 40:11;
John 21:15.
The wicked under judgments
(when brought to slaughter).
Jer. 51:40.
Not to be cooked in its mother's milk.
Exod. 23:19.
Numbers of, given by Josiah to the
people for sacrifice.
2 Chron. 35:7.

Offered in sacrifice
During the earliest times.
Gen. 4:4; 22:7–8.
Every morning and evening.
Exod. 29:38–39; Num. 28:3–4.

Females. Num. 6:14.

Males. Exod. 12:5.

At the Passover. Exod. 12:3, 6–7.

While sucking. 1 Sam. 7:9.

At a year old. Exod. 12:5;
Num. 6:14.

By the wicked not accepted.
Isa. 1:11; 66:3.

Offering of. Exod. 29:38–41.

Shepherds care for. Isa. 40:11.

Tribute often paid in. 2 Kings 3:4;
Isa. 16:1.

Used for

Clothing. Prov. 27:26.

Food. Deut. 32:14; 2 Sam. 12:4.

Sacrifice. 1 Chron. 29:21;
2 Chron. 29:32.

The young of the flock. Exod. 12:5;
Ezek. 45:15.

LAMB OF GOD

See God, Lamb of

LAMENESS

Disqualified animals for sacrificial
uses. Deut. 15:21.

Disqualified priests from exercising
the priestly office. Lev. 21:18.

Hated by David. 2 Sam. 5:8.

Healed by Jesus. Matt. 11:5;
Luke 7:22.

Healed by Peter. Acts 3:2–11.

Used in a figurative sense.
Heb. 12:13.

LAMENT

David's on Abner. 2 Sam. 3:33–34.

David's, on Saul and Jonathan.
2 Sam. 1:17–27.

LAMPS

Earthen Lamp

Described as

Burning. Gen. 15:17.

Shining. John 5:35.

Design of. 2 Pet. 1:19.

Illumination of the tents of Arab
chiefs by, alluded to. Job 29:3–4.

Illustrative of

Complete destruction of those
who curse parents (when totally
quenched). Prov. 20:20.

Destruction of the wicked (when
put out). Job 18:5–6; 21:17;
Prov. 13:9.

Glory of the cherubim. Ezek. 1:13.

God's guidance. 2 Sam. 22:29;
Ps. 18:28.

Graces of the Holy Spirit.
Rev. 4:5.

Human spirit. Prov. 20:27.

Ministers. John 5:35.

Omniscience of Christ. Dan. 10:6;
Rev. 1:14.

Salvation of God. Gen. 15:17;
Isa. 62:1.

Earthen Lamp

Severe judgments. Rev. 8:10.
A succession of heirs.
  1 Kings 11:36; 15:4.
Wise rulers. 2 Sam. 21:17.
The Word of God. Ps. 119:105;
  Prov. 6:23.
Lighted with oil. Matt. 25:3, 8.
Often kept lighting all night.
  Prov. 31:18.
Oil for, carried in vessels. Matt. 25:4.
Placed on a stand to give light to all in
  the house. Matt. 5:15.
Probable origin of dark lantern.
  Judg. 7:16.
Required to be constantly trimmed.
  Matt. 25:7.
Sometimes supplied with oil from a
  bowl through pipes. Zech. 4:2.

Used for lighting
  Chariots of war by night.
    Nah. 2:3-4.
  Marriage processions. Matt. 25:1.
  Persons going out at night.
    John 18:3.
  Private apartments. Acts 20:8.
  The tabernacle. Exod. 25:37.

LAND

Appeared on the third day. Gen. 1:9.
Bought and sold. Gen. 23:3-18;
  Acts 4:34; 5:1-8.
Conveyance of, by written deeds and
  other forms. Gen. 23:3-20.
Conveyance of, witness.
  Gen. 23:10, 11; Ruth 4:9, 11;
  Jer. 32:9-14.
Kings' part in. Ezek. 48:21.
Monopoly of. Gen. 47:20-26;
  Isa. 5:8; Mic. 2:1-2.
Original title to, from God.
  Gen. 13:14-17.
Priests' part in. Gen. 47:22;
  Ezek. 48:10.

Products of, for all. Eccles. 5:9.
To rest every seventh year for the
  benefit of the poor. Exod. 23:11.
Rights in, alienated. 2 Kings 8:1-6.
Rights in, leased. Luke 20:9-16.
Sale and redemption of, laws
  concerning. Lev. 25:15;
  Num. 36:4; Jer. 32:7-16;
  Ezek. 46:18.
Sold for debt. Neh. 5:3-5.
Widow's dower in. Ruth 4:3-9.
Unmarried woman's rights in.
  Num. 27:1-11; 36:1-11.

LANDMARKS

Protected from fraudulent removal.
  Deut. 19:14; Job 24:2;
  Prov. 22:28; Hos. 5:10.

LANGUAGE

Of all people one at first.
  Gen. 11:1, 6.
Ancient kingdoms often
  comprehended nations of
  different. Esther 1:22; Dan. 3:4;
  6:25.

Called
  Speech. Mark 14:70; Acts 14:11.
  Tongue. Acts 1:19; Rev. 5:9.

Confusion of
  Divided people into separate
    nations. Gen. 10:5, 20, 31.
  Originated the varieties in.
    Gen. 11:7.
  A punishment for presumption,
    etc. Gen. 11:2-6.
  Scattered people over the earth.
    Gen. 11:8-9.
Great variety of, spoken by men.
  1 Cor. 14:10.

Interpretation of
Antiquity of engaging persons for.
Gen. 42:23.
A gift of the Holy Spirit.
1 Cor. 12:10.
The Jews punished by being given
up to people of a strange.
Deut. 28:49; Isa. 28:11;
Jer. 5:15.
Most important in the early
church. 1 Cor. 14:5, 13,
27–28.

Kinds of, mentioned
Arabic, etc. Acts 2:11.
Chaldee. Dan. 1:4.
Egyptian. Pss. 81:5; 114:1;
Acts 2:10.
Greek. Acts 21:37.
Hebrew. 2 Kings 18:28;
Acts 26:14.
Latin. Luke 23:38.
Lycaonian. Acts 14:11.
Syriac. 2 Kings 18:26; Ezra 4:7.

Power of speaking different
Conferred by laying on of the
apostles' hands. Acts 8:17–18;
19:6.
Followed receiving the gospel.
Acts 10:44–46.
A gift of the Holy Spirit.
1 Cor. 12:10.
Given on the day of Pentecost.
Acts 2:3–4.
Necessary to spread of the gospel.
Acts 2:7–11.
Promised. Mark 16:17.
A sign to unbelievers.
1 Cor. 14:22.
Sometimes abused.
1 Cor. 14:2–12, 23.
Of some nations difficult.
Ezek. 3:5–6.

Term *barbarian* applied to those
who spoke a strange.
1 Cor. 14:11.

LANTERN
Used at night by Roman soldiers.
John 18:3.

LASCIVIOUSNESS

Examples of
Amnon. 2 Sam. 13:1–14.
David. 2 Sam. 5:13; 11:2–27.
Eli's sons. 1 Sam. 2:22.
Gibeahites. Judg. 19:22–25.
Judah. Gen. 38:15–16.
Lot's daughters. Gen. 19:30–38.
Persian kings.
Esther 2:3, 13, 14, 19.
Rehoboam. 2 Chron. 11:21–23.
Sodomites. Gen. 19:5.
Solomon. 1 Kings 11:1–3.
Those who practice, will not inherit
God's kingdom. Gal. 5:19.
Used in a figurative sense.
Ezek. 16:15–59.
Warning against. Prov. 5:3–27.

LAST

Christ
Alpha and Omega. Rev. 21:6.
Beginning and end. Rev. 2:3.

God
At the end. 1 Cor. 15:24.
The first and the. Isa. 44:6.
With the. Isa. 41:4.

Times
Of the apostles'. 1 Cor. 4:9.
Day. John 6:39.
Days. Acts 2:17; 2 Tim. 3:1.
These days. Heb. 1:1.
Time. Matt. 21:37; 1 John 2:18.

Times. 1 Pet. 1:20.

LAUGHTER
Attributed to God. Pss. 37:13; 59:8;
  Prov. 1:26.
A time for. Eccles. 3:4.

LAVER
See Basin

LAW OF GOD
See God, Law of

LAW OF MOSES
See Moses, Law of

LAWSUITS
To be avoided. Prov. 25:8–10;
  Matt. 5:25–26; 1 Cor. 6:1–8.

LAWYER
Jesus' satire against.
  Luke 11:45–52.
Test Jesus with questions.
  Matt. 22:35; Luke 10:25–37.
Zenas. Titus 3:13.

LAZINESS
Consequences of. Prov. 15:19.
Contrasted with diligence.
  Prov. 13:4.

LEAD
Lead founder. Jer. 6:29;
  Ezek. 22:18, 20.
A mineral. Exod. 15:10.
Purified by fire. Num. 31:22;
  Jer. 6:29; Ezek. 22:18, 20.
Trade in. Ezek. 27:12.
Used for weighing. Zech. 5:7–8.
Used in making inscriptions on
  stone. Job 19:24.

LEASE
Of real estate. Matt. 21:33–41.

LEATHER
Belts. 2 Kings 1:8; Matt. 3:4.
Called skin. Gen. 3:21; Mark 1:6.
Hide. Lev. 8:17.
Tanning of. Acts 9:43; 10:5–6.

LEAVEN
Expansive properties of. 1 Cor. 5:6.
Feast of. Exod. 14–20.
First fruits of wheat offered with.
  Lev. 23:17.

Forbidden
  During the feast of Passover.
    Exod. 12:15–20.
  To be offered, etc., with meat
    offerings which were burned.
    Lev. 2:11; 10:12.
  To be offered with blood.
    Exod. 34:25.

Illustrative of
  Doctrines of Pharisees, etc.
    Matt. 16:6, 12.
  False teachers. Gal. 5:8–9.
  Malice and wickedness.
    1 Cor. 5:8.
  The rapid spread of the gospel.
    Matt. 13:33; Luke 13:21.
  Ungodly professors. 1 Cor. 5:6–7.
Prepared in times of haste.
  1 Sam. 28:24.
Used in making bread. Hos. 7:4.
Used with thank offerings.
  Lev. 7:13; Amos 4:5.

LEFT-HANDED
Ehud. Judg. 3:15.
Seven hundred choice men.
  Judg. 20:16.

LEGENDS

On bells of horses, on pots and bowls. Zech. 14:20.

"Holiness to the Lord," engraved on the high priest's turban. Exod. 28:36; 39:30.

Laws written on doorposts and gates, and worn on the hand and forehead. Deut. 6:6–9; 11:18–20; Isa. 57:8.

"This is Jesus, the king of the Jews." Matt. 27:37.

LEGION

Of angels. Matt. 26:53.

Devils. Mark 5:9, 15.

LEGISLATION

Class, forbidden. Exod. 12:49; Lev. 24:22; Num. 9:14; 15:15, 29; Gal. 3:28.

Inheritance. Num. 27:1–11.

Supplemental, concerning Sabbath breaking. Num. 15:32–35.

LEGS

Of the crucified broken. John 19:31–32.

LEISURE TIME

Honeymoon. Deut. 24:5.

Jesus not able to have. Mark 6:31.

Misused. Isa. 5:11–12; Amos 6:4–6.

LENDING

Jesus' teaching concerning. Matt. 5:42; Luke 6:34–35.

Mosaic teaching concerning. Exod. 22:25–27; Lev. 25:35–37; Deut. 15:1–11.

LENTILS

Bread made with. Ezek. 4:9.

Lentils

LEOPARD

A carnivorous animal. Song of Sol. 4:8.

Fierceness of. Jer. 5:6.

Use in a figurative sense, taming of, the triumph of the gospel. Isa. 11:6.

LEPROSY

Ceremonies at cleansing of. Lev. 14:3–32.

Christ gave power to heal. Matt. 10:8.

A common disease among the Jews. Luke 4:27.

Garments

Incurably infected with, burned. Lev. 13:51–52.

Infected with, to have the piece first torn out. Lev. 13:56.

Suspected of but not infected, washed and pronounced clean. Lev. 13:53–54, 58–59.

Suspected of, shown to priest. Lev. 13:49.

Suspected of, shut up seven days. Lev. 13:50.

Houses

Ceremonies at cleansing of. Lev. 14:49–53.

To have the part infected with, first removed, and the rest scraped, etc. Lev. 14:39, 42.

Incurably infected with, pulled down and removed. Lev. 14:43–45.

Infected with, communicated uncleanness to everyone who entered them. Lev. 14:46–47.

Suspected of, but not infected, pronounced clean. Lev. 14:48.

Suspected of, emptied. Lev. 14:36.

Suspected of, inspected by priest. Lev. 14:37.

Suspected of, reported to priest. Lev. 14:35.

Suspected of, shut up seven days. Lev. 14:38.

An incurable disease. 2 Kings 5:7.

Infected

Garments. Lev. 13:47.

Houses. Lev. 14:34.

Men. Luke 17:12.

Women. Num. 12:10.

Often began with a bright red spot. Lev. 13:2, 24.

Often hereditary. 2 Sam. 3:29; 2 Kings 5:27.

Often sent as a punishment for sin. Num. 12:9–10; 2 Chron. 26:19.

Parts affected by

The beard. Lev. 13:20.

The forehead. 2 Chron. 26:19.

The hand. Exod. 4:6.

The head. Lev. 13:44.

The whole body. Luke 5:12.

Person pronounced clean when it covered the whole body. Lev. 13:13.

Power of Christ manifested in curing. Matt. 8:3; Luke 5:13; 17:13–14.

Power of God manifested in curing. Num. 12:13–14; 2 Kings 5:8–14.

The priests

Examined all persons healed of. Lev. 14:2; Matt. 8:4; Luke 17:14.

Examined persons suspected of. Lev. 13:2, 9.

Had rules for distinguishing. Lev. 13:5–44.

Judged and directed in cases of. Deut. 24:8.

Shut up for seven days persons, suspected of. Lev. 13:4.

Those afflicted with

Associated together. 2 Kings 7:3; Luke 17:12.

Ceremonially unclean. Lev. 13:8, 11, 22, 44.

To cry unclean when approached. Lev. 13:45.

Cut off from God's house. 2 Chron. 26:21.

Excluded from priest's office. Lev. 22:2–4.

Had their heads bare, clothes rent, and lip covered. Lev. 13:45.

Lived in a separate house. 2 Kings 15:5.

Separated from contact with others. Num. 5:2; 12:14–15.

Turned the hair white or yellow.
Lev. 13:3, 10, 30.
Turned the skin white. Exod. 4:6;
2 Kings 5:27.

LETTERS
Artaxerxes to Nehemiah.
Neh. 2:7–9.
Claudius Lysias to Felix.
Acts 23:35–30.
David to Joab. 2 Sam. 11:14.
King of Babylon to Hezekiah.
Isa. 39:1.
King of Syria to King of Israel.
2 Kings 5:5–6.
Letters of intercession by Paul to
Philemon on behalf of Onesimus.
Philem. 1.
Letters of recommendation.
2 Cor. 3:1.
Luke to Theophilus, the Books of
Luke and Acts. Acts 1:1.
Open letter from Sanballat to
Nehemiah. Neh. 6:5.
Rabshakeh to Hezekiah.
Isa. 37:9–14.
Sennacherib to Hezekiah.
2 Kings 19:14.

LEVIATHAN
Possibly a crocodile. Job 41:1;
Ps. 104:26.
Used in a figurative sense. Ps. 74:14.

LEVIRATE MARRIAGE
Israelite custom. Deut. 25:5–10.

LEVITES
Ceremonies at consecration of
Cleansing and purifying.
Num. 8:7.
Elders of Israel laying their hands
on them. Num. 8:9–10.

Making a sin offering for.
Num. 8:8, 12.
Presenting them to God as an
offering for the people.
Num. 8:11, 15.
Setting before the priests and
presenting them as their offering
to God. Num. 8:13.
Chosen by God for service of the
sanctuary. 1 Chron. 15:2, with
Num. 3:6.

David
Divided them into four classes.
1 Chron. 23:4–6.
By his last words had them
numbered from twenty years old.
1 Chron. 23:24, 27.
Made them attend in divisions.
2 Chron. 8:14; 31:17.
Made them serve from twenty on
account of the lightness of their
duties. 1 Chron. 23:26, 28–32.
Numbered them first from thirty
years old. 1 Chron. 23:2–3.
Subdivided them into twenty-four
divisions. 1 Chron. 23:6, with
25:8–31.
Descended from Jacob's third son.
Gen. 29:34; Heb. 7:9–10.
Encamped around the tabernacle.
Num. 1:50, 52–53; 3:23, 29, 35.
Entered on their service at age
twenty-five. Num. 8:24.

Families, as numbered
Of Gershon. Num. 3:18, 21–22.
Of Kohath. Num. 3:19, 27–28.
Of Merari. Num. 3:20, 33–34.
Forty-eight cities appointed for.
Num. 35:2–8.
Given to Aaron and sons. Num. 3:9;
8:19.

Had a part of the offerings.
Deut. 18:1–2.
Had chiefs or officers over them.
Num. 3:24, 30, 35;
1 Chron. 15:4–10;
2 Chron. 35:9; Ezra 8:29.
Had no inheritance in Israel.
Deut. 10:9; Josh. 13:33; 14:3.
The Jews to be kind and benevolent
to. Deut. 12:12, 18–19; 14:29;
16:11, 14.
Marched in the center of Israel.
Num. 2:17.
Not numbered with Israel.
Num. 1:47–49.
Numbered as ministers at age thirty.
Num. 4:3, 23, etc.
Numbered separately after the
people from a month old.
Num. 3:14–16, 39.
Originally consisted of three families
or divisions. Num. 3:17;
1 Chron. 6:16–48.
Priests to get a tenth of their tithes.
Num. 18:26–32.
Prophecies regarding. Gen. 49:5, 7;
Deut. 33:8–11.
Punished with death for encroaching
on the priestly office. Num. 18:3.
Punishment of Korah and others, for
offering incense. Num. 16:1–35.
Served in divisions after captivity.
Ezra 6:18.

Services of
  Blessing the people. Deut. 10:8
  Conducting the sacred music.
  1 Chron. 23:5–30;
  2 Chron. 5:12–13;
  Neh. 12:24, 27–43.
  Doing the service of tabernacle.
  Num. 8:19, 22.
  Guarding king's person and house
  in time of danger.

2 Kings 11:5–9;
2 Chron. 23:5, 7.
Judging and deciding in
controversies. Deut. 17:9;
1 Chron. 23:4; 2 Chron. 19:8.
Keeping sacred instruments and
vessels. Num. 3:8;
1 Chron. 9:28–29.
Keeping sacred oil, flour, etc.
1 Chron. 9:29–30.
Keeping sacred treasures.
1 Chron. 26:20.
Keeping the charge of the
sanctuary. Num. 18:3;
1 Chron. 23:32.
Keeping the gates of the temple.
1 Chron. 9:17–26.
Ministering to priests.
Num. 3:6–7; 18:2.
Ministering to the Lord.
Deut. 10:8.
Ministering to the people.
2 Chron. 35:3.
Preparing the sacrifices for the
priests. 1 Chron. 23:31;
2 Chron. 35:11.
Preparing the shewbread.
1 Chron. 9:31–32; 23:29.
Purifying the holy things.
1 Chron. 23:28.
Regulating weights and measures.
1 Chron. 23:29.
Singing praises before the army.
2 Chron. 20:21–22.
Taking charge of the tithes,
offerings, etc.
2 Chron. 31:11–19;
Neh. 12:44.
Taking down, putting up, and
carrying the tabernacle, etc.
Num. 1:50–51; 4:5–33.

Teaching the people.
2 Chron. 17:8–9; 30:22; 35:3;
Neh. 8:7.
Retired at age fifty. Num. 8:25.
Taken instead of the firstborn of
Israel. Num. 3:12–13,
40–45; 8:16–18.
Tithes given to, for their support.
Num. 18:21, 24;
2 Chron. 31:4–5;
Neh. 12:44–45; *(See also*
Heb. 7:5.)
Were all under control of the high
priest's deputy. Num. 3:32;
1 Chron. 9:20.
Were consecrated. Num. 8:6, 14.
When retired, required to perform
less arduous duties. Num. 8:26.
While in attendance, lodged around
the temple. 1 Chron. 9:27.
Zeal against idolatry a cause of their
appointment. Exod. 32:26–28,
with Deut. 33:9–10.

LIARS

All people liars. Ps. 116:11.
Satan, a liar. John 8:44, 55.
Prohibited in the kingdom of heaven.
Rev. 21:8.

LIBERALISM

Personal freedom
Given to believers. Rom. 14:22;
1 Cor. 6:12; 10:23; 2
Cor. 3:17;
Gal. 2:4; 5:1; James 1:25.
Not determined by others'
opinions. Rom. 14:14;
1 Cor. 10:29.
Not to be used as license for
irresponsible behavior.
Rom. 14:15;
1 Cor. 6:12; 8:9–13;

Gal. 5:13; James 2:12; 1
Pet. 2:16.
Willingly set aside. 1 Cor. 9:12,
15.
Tolerance. 2 Kings 5:18–19;
Matt. 7:1; John 7:24; 8:15;
Rom. 14:3–12; 1 Cor. 9:19–22;
James 2:8–9.

LIBERALITY
See Generosity

LIBERTIES, CIVIL

Injunctions concerning
Be subject to governmental
authorities. Eccles. 8:2–5;
Rom. 13:1–5; Titus 3:1;
1 Pet. 2:13–14.
Do not become enslaved to
people. 1 Cor. 7:23.
Everything to be done in name of
Jesus. Col. 3:17.
Everything to be done to glory of
God. 1 Cor. 10:31.
Give freely to others.
1 John 3:17–18.
Live quietly. 1 Thess. 4:11;
2 Thess. 3:12.
Live responsibly. Gal. 5:13–15;
1 Pet. 2:16.
Obey God rather than people.
Exod. 1:17; Dan. 3;
Acts 4:19–20; 5:29.
Pay taxes due to state.
Matt. 17:24–27; 22:17–21;
Rom. 13:6–7.
Pray for governmental leaders, to
allow. 1 Tim. 2:2.
Liberty where Spirit of the Lord is.
2 Cor. 3:17.
Set free by Christ. Gal. 5:1.
Voluntary subordination of
personal liberty. Luke 22:26;

1 Cor. 8:9–13; 9:12, 15;
Eph. 5:21; Phil. 2:4.

LIBERTINES
Freedmen. Acts 6:9.

LIBERTY, CHRISTIAN
Believers are called to. Gal. 5:13.

Believers should
Assert. 1 Cor. 10:29.
Not abuse. Gal. 5:13; 1 Pet. 2:16.
Not offend others by.
1 Cor. 8:9; 10:29, 32.
Praise God for. Ps. 116:16–17.
Stand fast in. Gal. 2:5; 5:1.
Walk in. Ps. 119:45.
Called the glorious liberty of the
children of God. Rom. 8:21.

Conferred
By Christ. Gal. 4:3–5; 5:1.
By God. Col. 1:13.
Through the gospel. John 8:32.
By the Holy Spirit. Rom. 8:15;
2 Cor. 3:17.
Confirmed by Christ. John 8:36.

False teachers
Abuse. Jude 4.
Promise to others. 2 Pet. 2:19.
Try to destroy. Gal. 2:4.
The gospel is the law of. James 1:25;
2:12.

Is freedom from
Corruption. Rom. 8:21.
Curse of the law. Gal. 3:13.
Fear of death. Heb. 2:15.
Human bondage. 1 Cor. 9:19.
Jewish ordinances. Gal. 4:3;
Col. 2:20.
Law. Rom. 7:6; 8:2.
Sin. Rom. 6:7, 18.
Predicted. Isa. 42:7; 61:1.

Proclaimed by Christ. Isa. 61:1;
Luke 4:18.
The service of Christ is. 1 Cor. 7:22.
Types. Lev. 25:10–17;
Gal. 4:22–26, 31.
The wicked, lacking. John 8:34, with
Rom. 6:20.

LICE
Plague of. Exod. 8:16–19;
Ps. 105:31.

LIFE, ETERNAL

Believers
Are preserved for.
John 10:28–29.
Have hope of. Titus 1:2; 3:7.
Have promises of. 1 Tim. 4:8;
2 Tim. 1:1; Titus 1:2;
1 John 2:25.
Look to the mercy of God for.
Jude 21.
May have assurance of.
2 Cor. 5:1; 1 John 5:13.
Should lay hold of.
1 Tim. 6:12, 19.
Will go into. Matt. 25:46.
Will inherit. Matt. 19:29.
Will reap, through the Spirit
Gal. 6:8.
Will reign in. Dan. 7:18;
Rom. 5:17.
Will arise to. Dan. 12:2;
John 5:29.
Cannot be inherited by works.
Rom. 2:7, with 3:10–19.
Christ is. 1 John 1:2; 5:20.
Exhortation to seek. John 6:27.

Given
To all given to Christ. John 17:2.
In answer to prayer. Ps. 21:4.
By Christ. John 6:27; 10:28.

In Christ. 1 John 5:11.
Through Christ. Rom. 5:21; 6:23.
By God. Ps. 113:3; Rom. 6:23.
To those who believe in Christ.
John 3:15–16; 6:40, 47.
To those who believe in God.
John 5:24.
To those who hate life for Christ.
John 12:25.

Results from
Drinking the water of life.
John 4:14.
Eating of the tree of life. Rev. 2:7.
Eating the bread of life.
John 6:50–58.
Revealed by Christ. John 6:68;
2 Tim. 1:10.
Revealed in the Scriptures.
John 5:39.
The self-righteous think to inherit, by
works. Mark 10:17.
Those who are ordained to, believe
the gospel. Acts 13:48.
To know God and Christ is.
John 17:3.

The wicked
Do not have. 1 John 3:15.
Judge themselves unworthy of.
Acts 13:46.

LIFE, NATURAL

Be thankful for
Its preservation. Ps. 103:4;
John 2:6.
The supply of its wants.
Gen. 48:15.
Believers have true enjoyment of.
Ps. 128:2; 1 Tim. 4:8.
Of believers, specially protected by
God. Job 2:6; Acts 18:10;
1 Pet. 3:13.

Cares and pleasures of, dangerous.
Luke 8:14; 21:34; 2 Tim. 2:4.

Compared to
A dream. Ps. 73:20.
An eagle swooping to the prey.
Job 9:26.
A flower. Job 14:2.
Grass. 1 Pet. 1:24.
A pilgrimage. Gen. 47:9.
A shadow. Eccles. 6:12.
A shepherd's tent removed.
Isa. 38:18.
A sleep. Ps. 90:5.
A swift post. Job 9:25.
A swift ship. Job 9:26.
A tale told. Ps. 90:9.
A thread cut by the weaver.
Isa. 38:12.
A vapor. James 4:14.
Water spilled on the ground.
2 Sam. 14:14.
A weaver's tool. Job 7:6.
Width of the hand. Ps. 39:5.
Wind. Job 7:7.

Described as
Full of trouble. Job 14:1.
Limited. Job 7:1; 14:5.
Short. Job 14:1; Ps. 89:47.
Uncertain. James 4:13–15.
Vain. Eccles. 6:12.
The dissatisfied despise.
Eccles. 2:17.
Do not be overanxious to provide for
the needs of. Matt. 6:25.
Enjoyment does not consist in
abundance of possessions.
Luke 12:15.
Forfeited by sin. Gen. 2:17;
3:17–19.
God as the author of. Gen. 2:7;
Acts 17:28.
God preserves. Pss. 36:6; 66:9.

God's loving-kindness better than.
Ps. 63:3.
In the hand of God. Job 12:10;
Dan. 5:23.
Miraculously restored by Christ.
Matt. 9:18, 25; Luke 7:15, 22;
John 11:43.
Obedience to God tends to prolong.
Deut. 30:20.
Obedience to parents tends to
prolong. Exod. 20:12;
Prov. 4:10.
Of others, not to be taken away.
Exod. 20:13.
Preserved by discretion. Prov. 13:3.
Shortness of, should lead to spiritual
improvement. Deut. 32:29;
Ps. 90:12.
Should be laid down, if necessary, for
Christ. Matt. 10:39; Luke 14:26;
Acts 20:24.
Should be laid down, if necessary, for
the fellow believers. Rom. 16:4;
1 John 3:16.

Should be spent in
Doing good. Eccles. 3:12.
Fear of God. 1 Pet. 1:17.
Living for God. Rom. 14:8;
Phil. 1:21.
Peace. Rom. 12:18; 1 Tim. 2:2.
Service of God. Luke 1:75.
Should be taken all due care of.
Matt. 10:23; Acts 27:34.
Sometimes judicially shortened.
1 Sam. 2:32-33; Job 36:14.
Sometimes prolonged, in answer to
prayer. Isa. 38:2-5; James 5:15.
Value of. Job 2:4; Matt. 6:25.
We do not know what is good for us
in. Eccles. 6:12.
The wicked have their portion of
good during. Ps. 17:14;
Luke 6:24; 16:25.

Of the wicked, not specially
protected by God. Job 36:6;
Ps. 78:50.

LIFE, ORIGIN OF
God acted before time. John 17:24;
Eph 1:4.

God created
By decisive acts.
Gen. 1:3, 6, 9, 14, 20, 24, 26;
Ps. 148:5; Rev. 4:11.
Everything that exists. John 1:3.
Heaven and earth. Gen. 1:1;
Isa. 45:18.
With intricate design.
Ps. 139:13-15.
With purpose. Isa. 43:7; 45:18;
Col. 1:16.
In self-reproducing "kinds."
Gen. 1:11-12, 21, 24.
Special creation of people.
Gen. 1:26-28; 2:7; Matt. 19:4;
1 Cor. 15:22.
Out of things not visible.
Heb. 11:3.

LIFE SPAN
Cut off prematurely. Gen. 4:8;
Job 21:21; Ps. 39:5, 11.
Lengthened before the flood.
Gen. 5:1-32.
Natural, of seventy to eighty years.
Ps. 90:10.
Reduced after the flood.
Gen. 11:10-32.

LIFE, SPIRITUAL
All believers have. Eph. 2:1, 5;
Col. 2:13.
Believers praise God for.
Ps. 119:175.

Christ the author of.
John 5:21, 25; 6:33, 51–53;
14:6; 1 John 4:9.

Described as a
Life for God. Rom. 6:11;
Gal. 2:19.
Living in the Spirit. Gal. 5:25.
Newness of life. Rom. 6:4.
Evidenced by love for fellow
believers. 1 John 3:14.
Fear of God is. Prov. 14:27; 19:23.
God the author of. Ps. 36:9;
Col. 2:13.
Has its infancy. Luke 10:21;
1 Cor. 3:1–2; 1 John 2:12.
Has its maturity. Eph. 4:13;
1 John 2:13–14.
Has its origin in the new birth.
John 3:3–8.
Has its youth. 1 John 2:13–14.
Hidden with Christ. Col. 3:3.
The Holy Spirit the author of.
Ezek. 37:14, with Rom. 8:9–13.
Hypocrites destitute of. Jude 12;
Rev. 3:1.
Illustrated. Ezek. 37:9–10;
Luke 15:24.
Lovers of pleasure destitute of.
1 Tim. 5:6.

Maintained by
Christ. John 6:57;
1 Cor. 10:3–4.
Faith. Gal. 2:20.
Prayer. Ps. 69:32.
The Word of God. Deut. 8:3, with
Matt. 4:4.
Pray for the increase of.
Pss. 119:25; 143:11.
Revived by God. Ps. 85:6; Hos. 6:2.
Seek to grow in. Eph. 4:15;
1 Pet. 2:2.

Should enliven the services of
believers. Rom. 12:1;
1 Cor. 14:15.
Spiritual-mindedness is. Rom. 8:6.
The wicked alienated
from. Eph. 4:18.
The Word of God is the instrument
of. Isa. 55:3; 2 Cor. 3:6;
1 Pet. 4:6.

LIFE SUPPORT (ARTIFICIAL)
Preference for death. 2 Cor. 5:8.
Preference for life. Deut. 30:19.

Principles relevant to
Fear of death removed. 1
Cor. 15:54–55; Heb. 2:14–15.
God gives and takes life. Job 1:21;
Rom. 14:7–8.
Sanctity of life. Gen. 1:26–27;
Ps. 8:5.

LIGHT
Communicated to the body through
the eye. Prov. 15:30; Matt. 6:22.
Created by God. Gen. 1:3; Isa. 45:7.

Described as
Agreeable. Eccles. 11:7.
Bright. Job 37:21.
Diffusive. Job 25:3, with 36:30.
Manifesting objects.
John 3:20–21; Eph. 5:13.
Shining. 2 Sam. 23:4; Job 41:18.
Useful and precious. Eccles. 2:13.

Divided into
Artificial. Jer. 25:10; Acts 16:29.
Extraordinary or miraculous.
Exod. 14:20; Ps. 78:14;
Acts 9:3; 12:7.
Natural. Job 24:14; Isa. 5:30.
God the only source of. James 1:17.

Illustrative of
Believers. Luke 16:8; Eph. 5:8;
  Phil. 2:15.
Christ the source of all wisdom.
  Luke 2:32; John 1:4, 9; 8:12;
  12:46.
Favor of God. Ps. 4:6; Isa. 2:5.
Future glory of believers.
  Ps. 97:11; Col. 1:12.
Glory of Christ. Acts 9:3, 5;
  26:13.
Glory of God. Ps. 104:2, with
  1 Tim. 6:16.
Glory of the church. Isa. 60:1–3.
Gospel. 2 Cor. 4:4; 1 Pet. 2:9.
Guidance of God. Pss. 27:1; 36:9.
Ministers. Matt. 5:14; John 5:35.
Path of the just. Prov. 4:18.
Purity of Christ. Matt. 17:2.
Purity of God. 1 John 1:5.
The soul of persons. Job 18:5–6.
Whatever makes things easy to
  see. John 3:21; Eph. 5:13.
Wisdom of God. Dan. 2:22.
Wise rulers. 2 Sam. 21:17; 23:4.
Word of God. Ps. 119:105, 130;
  2 Pet. 1:19.
Separated from darkness. Gen. 1:4.
Sun, moon, and stars appointed to
  communicate to the earth.
  Gen. 1:14–17; Jer. 31:35.
Theory of, beyond human
  comprehension.
  Job 38:19–20, 24.

LIGHTNING
God controls. Job 37:3.
Jesus saw Satan fall like.
  Luke 10:18.

LILY
Lessons to trust gathered from.
  Matt. 6:28–30.

Molded in the rim of the molten laver
  in the temple. 1 Kings 7:26;
  2 Chron. 4:5.
The principle capitals of the temple
  ornamented with carvings of.
  1 Kings 7:19, 22, 26.
Used in a figurative sense, of the lips
  of the beloved. Song of Sol. 5:13.

LIME
Bodies burned to. Isa. 33:12;
  Amos 2:1.
Used as a plaster. Deut. 27:2, 4.

LINEN
Bedding made of. Prov. 7:16.
The body of Jesus wrapped in.
  Mark 15:46; John 20:5.
Clothing of royal households made
  of. Gen. 41:42; Esther 8:15.
Curtains of the tabernacle made of.
  Exod. 26:1; 27:9.
Exported from Egypt.
  1 Kings 10:28; Ezek. 27:7.
Exported from Syria. Ezek. 27:16.
Garments for men made of.
  Gen. 41:42; Ezek. 9:2;
  Luke 16:19.
Garments for women made of.
  Isa. 3:23; Ezek. 16:10–13.
Mosaic law forbade its being mingled
  with wool. Lev. 19:19,
  Deut. 22:11.
Used in a figurative sense, pure and
  white, of righteousness.
  Rev. 15:6; 19:8, 14.
Vestments of priests made of.
  Exod. 28:5–8, 15, 39–42.

LINTEL
Every household which had blood on
  the lintel would be spared the

death of the firstborn.
Exod. 12:22–23.

LION

Attacks and destroys men.
1 Kings 13:24; 20:36.
Attacks the sheepfolds.
1 Sam. 17:34; Amos 3:12;
Mic. 5:8.
Canaan infested by.
2 Kings 17:25–26.
Conceals itself by day. Ps. 104:22.
Criminals often thrown to.
Dan. 6:7, 16, 24.

Described as
Active. Deut. 33:22.
Courageous. 2 Sam. 17:10.
Fearless even of man. Isa. 31:4;
Nah. 2:11.
Fierce. Job 10:16; 28:8.
Majestic in movement.
Prov. 30:29–30.
Ravenous. Ps. 17:12.
Superior in strength. Judg. 14:18;
Prov. 30:30.

Disobedient prophet slain by.
1 Kings 13:24, 26.
God provides for. Job 38:39;
Ps. 104:21, 28.
God's power exhibited in restraining.
1 Kings 13:28; Dan. 6:22, 27.
Greatness of its teeth alluded to.
Ps. 58:6; Joel 1:6.
Hunting of, alluded to. Job 10:16.

Illustrative of
Boldness of believers. Prov. 28:1.
Brave men. 2 Sam. 1:23; 23:20.
Christ. Rev. 5:5.
Cruel and powerful enemies.
Isa. 5:29; Jer. 49:19; 51:38.
The devil. 1 Pet. 5:8.
God in executing judgments.
Isa. 38:13; Lam. 3:10;
Hos. 5:14; 13:8.
God in protecting His church.
Isa. 31:4.
Imaginary fears of the lazy.
Prov. 22:13; 26:13.
Israel. Num. 24:9.
A king's wrath (when roaring).
Prov. 19:12; 20:2.

Lions

Natural man subdued by grace
(when tamed). Isa. 11:7; 65:25.
Persecutors. Ps. 22:13;
2 Tim. 4:17.
Tribe of Gad. Deut. 33:20.
Tribe of Judah Gen. 49:9.

Inhabits
Deserts. Isa. 30:6.
Forests. Jer. 5:6.
Mountains. Song of Sol. 4:8.
Thickets. Jer. 4:7.
Lurks for its prey. Ps. 10:9.
Often carries its prey to its den.
Nah. 2:12.
Often perishes for lack of food.
Job 4:11.
Roars when seeking prey.
Ps. 104:21; Isa. 31:4.

Slain by
Benaiah. 2 Sam. 23:20.
David. 1 Sam. 17:35–36.
Samson. Judg. 14:5–6.
Swarm of bees found in the carcass
of, by Samson. Judg. 14:8.
Tears its prey. Deut. 33:20; Ps. 7:2.

LIPS
Blessings and. 1 Sam. 1:13;
Pss. 45:2; 66:13–14;
Job 33:3; Heb. 13:15.
Evil and. Pss. 22:7; 140:9;
Prov. 24:2, 28; Isa. 59:3.
May glorify God. Ps. 51:15;
Rom. 10:9.
Require Christian control.
Pss. 19:14; 141:3; Matt. 5:37;
Col. 4:6.
Reveal the heart. Matt. 12:34.
Source of good or evil. Prov. 18:21;
James 3:9–10.

LISTENING
Emphasized in the way of faith.
Isa. 55:3; Matt. 11:15; Rev. 2:7.
Neglected by the unrighteous.
Neh. 9:16.
Required by God. Ps. 34:11.

LITIGATION
To be avoided. Matt. 5:25;
Luke 12:58; 1 Cor. 6:1–8.

LITURGY

In ancient Israel
In levitical service. 2 Chron. 8:14.
Music in.
1 Chron. 6:31–32; 15:16–22;
25:6–8; Neh. 12:46.
For Passover. 2 Chron. 35:1–6.
For sacrifice. Lev. 1–7.
In first century Judaism.
Acts 13:13–15.

In the church
Breaking bread. Acts 20:7;
1 Cor. 10:16; 11:23–26.
Prayer with lifted hands.
1 Tim. 2:8.
Public reading of Scripture.
1 Tim. 4:13.
Things to be done in an orderly
manner.
1 Cor. 14:26–33.

LIVER
Burnt in sacrifice. Lev. 3:5.
Superstitious rites with. Ezek. 21:21.

LIVING, COST OF
Godliness with contentment.
1 Tim. 6:6–8.
Increase in, due to war and famine.
2 Kings 6:24–25; 7:1.

Increase in riches
  As vanity. Eccles. 2:8–11.
  Not to be trusted. Ps. 62:10.
Middle-class resources.
  Prov. 30:8–9.
Prosperity and adversity from God.
  Job 2:10; Phil. 4:11–14.

LOAVES

Miracle of the five. Matt. 14:15–21;
  Luke 9:12–17.
Miracle of the seven.
  Matt. 15:24–38; 16:10.

LOBBYING

Against the people of Judah during
  the time of Zerubbabel.
  Ezra 4:4–5.

LOCK

Used on chamber door.
  Judg. 3:23–25.

LOCUST

Carried every way by the wind.
  Exod. 10:13, 19.
Clean and fit for food.
  Lev. 11:21–22.

Described as
  Like horses prepared for battle.
    Joel 2:4, with Rev. 9:7.
  Rapid in movement. Isa. 33:4.
  Voracious. Exod. 10:15.
  Wise. Prov. 30:24, 27.
Flies in swarms and with order.
  Prov. 30:27.

Illustrative of
  Destruction of God's enemies (by
    its destruction). Nah. 3:15.
  Destructive enemies. Joel 1:6–7;
    2:2–9.
  False teachers of the apostasy.
    Rev. 9:3.
  Ungodly rulers. Neh. 3:17.
Immensely numerous. Ps. 105:34;
  Nah. 3:15.

The Jews
  Often plagued by. Joel 1:4; 2:25.
  One of the plagues of Egypt.
    Exod. 10:4–15.
  Prayed in response to the plague
    of. 1 Kings 8:37–38.
  Promised deliverance from the
    plague of, on humiliation, etc.
    2 Chron. 7:13–14.
  A small insect. Prov. 30:24, 27.

Locust

Threatened with, as a punishment
for sin. Deut. 28:38, 42.
Used, as food. Matt. 3:4.

LOINS
Body's midsection. Exod. 28:42;
2 Kings 1:8; Isa. 11:5; Jer. 13:1;
Matt. 3:4.
Tying up garments around.
Exod. 12:11; 1 Kings 18:46;
2 Kings 9:1.
Girding up one's loins figuratively.
Luke 12:35; Eph. 6:14;
1 Pet. 1:13.

LONELINESS

May be an occasion for
Communion. Exod. 24:2.
Meditation. John 6:15.
Not good for man. Gen. 2:18;
Ps. 68:6.
Prayer. Luke 9:18.
Sometimes necessary. Ps. 38:11;
2 Tim. 4:16.
Thanksgiving. Dan. 6:10.

LONGEVITY
Promise of. Exod. 20:12.

Examples of
Adam, 930 years. Gen. 5:5.
Seth, 912 years. Gen. 5:8.
Enosh, 905 years. Gen. 5:11.
Kenan, 910 years. Gen. 5:14.
Mahalalel, 895 years. Gen. 5:17.
Jared, 962 years. Gen. 5:20.
Enoch, 365 years. Gen. 5:23.
Methuselah, 969 years.
Gen. 5:27.
Lamech, 777 years. Gen. 5:31.
Noah, 950 years. Gen. 9:29.
Shem. Gen. 11:11.
Arphaxad. Gen. 11:13.

Salah. Gen. 11:15.
Eber. Gen. 11:17.
Peleg. Gen. 11:19.
Reu. Gen. 11:21.
Serug. Gen. 11:23.
Nahor. Gen. 11:25.
Terah, 205 years. Gen. 11:32.
Sarah, 127 years. Gen. 23:1.
Abraham, 175 years. Gen. 25:7.
Isaac, 180 years. Gen. 35:28.
Jacob, 147 years. Gen. 47:28.
Joseph, 110 years. Gen. 50:26.
Amram, 137 years. Exod. 6:20.
Aaron, 123 years. Num. 33:39.
Moses, 120 years. Deut. 31:2;
34:7.
Joshua, 110 years. Josh 24:29.
Eli, 98 years. 1 Sam. 4:15.
Barzillai, 80 years. 2 Sam. 19:32.
Job. Job 42:16.
Jehoiada, 130 years.
2 Chron. 24:15.
Anna. Luke 2:36, 37.
Paul. Philem. 1:9.

LONG-SUFFERING OF GOD
See God, Long-Suffering of

LORD'S SUPPER, THE
Both bread and wine are necessary to
be received in. Matt. 26:27;
1 Cor. 11:26.
Continually partaken of, by the
primitive church. Acts 2:42; 20:7.
Instituted. Matt. 26:26;
1 Cor. 11:23.
Is taken to remember the body and
blood of Christ. 1 Cor. 10:16.
Newness of heart and life necessary
to the worthy partaking of. 1 Cor.
5:7–8.
Object of. Luke 22:19;
1 Cor. 11:24, 26.

Partakers of, should be wholly
separate to God. 1 Cor. 10:21.
Prefigured. Exod. 12:21–28;
1 Cor. 5:7–8.
Self–examination commanded
before partaking of.
1 Cor. 11:28, 31.

Unworthy partakers of
Are guilty of the body and blood of
Christ. 1 Cor. 11:27.
Are visited with judgments.
1 Cor. 11:30.
Do not recognize the Lord's body.
1 Cor. 11:29.

LOSS

Of a child, due to
Accident. 1 Kings 3:19.
For Jesus' sake. Matt. 19:29.
Murder. Gen. 4:25.
Rebelliousness of child.
2 Sam. 13:37; 18:33;
Luke 15:11–32.
Sibling rivalry. Gen. 37:33–35.
Sickness. 2 Sam 12:19;
1 Kings 14:1, 17; 17:17;
2 Kings 4:19–20; Luke 8:42.
Will of God. Job 1:12, 19.

Of a child, suffered by
Adam and Eve. Gen. 4:25.
David. 2 Sam. 12:19; 18:33.
Father of prodigal.
Luke 15:24, 32.
Harlot before Solomon.
1 Kings 3:19.
Jacob. Gen. 37:33–35.
Jairus. Luke 8:49.
Jeroboam. 1 Kings 14:17.
Job. Job 1:18–19.
Naomi. Ruth 1:5, 20–21.
Self-sufficient people. Isa. 47:9.

Shunamite. 2 Kings 4:20.
Widow from Nain. Luke 7:12.
Widow from Zarephath.
1 Kings 17:17

Of health, due to
Figurative for sins of people.
Jer. 8:22; Hos. 5:13.
Grief. Ps. 31:9–10.
Sin. 2 Chron. 21:15, 19;
Ps. 38:3–8.
Will of God. Job 2:7–8.

Of health, suffered by
Asa. 1 Kings 15:23
Centurion's servant. Luke 7:2.
Elisha. 2 Kings 13:14.
Epaphroditus. Phil. 2:27.
Hezekiah. 2 Kings 20:1.
Jehoram. 2 Chron. 21:15, 19.
Job. Job 2:7–8.
Lazarus. Luke 16:20.
Man at pool of Bethesda.
John 5:5.
Psalmist. Ps. 41:3.
Uzziah. 2 Chron. 26:21.
Woman with hemorrhage.
Luke 8:43.

Of home, due to
Famine. Neh 5:3.
Against homeowner. Mic. 2:2, 9.
Of homeowner. Jer. 6:12.
For Jesus' sake. Matt. 19:29.
War. 2 Kings 25:9.

Of home, suffered by
Absalom. 2 Sam 14:13.
Exiled people. 2 Kings 25:9;
Lam. :2.
Prodigal son. Luke 15:13–19.

Of hope suffered by
Exiled people. Lam 3:18;
Ezek. 37:11.

Godless people. Job 8:13;
Prov. 11:7.
Job. Job 7:6; 17:15; 19:10.
Lioness, fig. of leaders of Israel.
Ezek. 19:5.
Naomi. Ruth 1:1–13.

Of one's own life, figurative
For Christ. Gal. 2:20.
Is gain. Phil. 1:21.
For Israel. Rom. 9:3.
For Jesus' sake. 2 Cor. 4:11.

Of parents
For Jesus' sake. Matt. 19:29.
Suffered by exiled people.
Lam. 5:3.

Of sibling
For Jesus' sake. Matt. 19:29.
Lazarus. John 11:2, 13, 21, 32.

Of spouse, suffered by
Abraham. Gen. 23:2.
Ezekiel. Ezek 24:16–18.
Jacob. Gen. 48:7.
Judah. Gen. 38:12
Naomi. Ruth 1:3, 20–21.
Self-sufficient people. Isa. 47:9.

Of time
To be compensated. Exod. 21:19.

Of wealth
Commanded by Jesus.
Matt. 19.21.
For Jesus' sake. Matt. 19:29;
Phil. 3:7–8.

Of wealth, suffered by.
A father. Eccles. 5:14.
Job. Job 1:13–17.
Naboth. 1 Kings 21:1, 16.
Prodigal son. Luke 15:13.
Sailors. Acts 27:21–22.

LOVE
See also Love, Brotherly

Covers sin. Prov. 10:12.
Encouraged. Col. 3:14. (*See* Love to
Man.)
Explained. 1 Cor. 13:4–7.
Fulfills the law. Rom. 13:8.
God is. 1 John 4:8, 16.
The greatest thing in the world.
1 Cor. 13.
The highest principle.
Matt. 22:37–38.
Is of God. 1 John 4:7.
Marks the child of God. John 13:35;
1 John 4:7.

LOVE, BROTHERLY
Demonstrates Christian faith.
1 John 2:9–11.
Is to continue. Heb. 13:1.
Ordered, commanded of Christians.
Rom. 12:10; John 13:34.
Should increase. 1 Thess. 4:9–10.
Should supplement godliness and
love. 2 Pet. 1:7.

LOVE OF CHRIST
See Christ, Love of

LOVE OF GOD
See God, Love of

LOVE TO CHRIST
See Christ, Love to

LOVE TO GOD
See God, Love to

LOVE TO MAN
See Man, Love to

LOVING-KINDNESS OF GOD
See God, Loving-kindness of; Pity

LOWLINESS
See Humility

LOYALTY
Extolled. Ps. 31:23.
Must be wholehearted. Matt. 6:24;
James 1: 8.
To friends. Ruth 1:14; Prov. 27:6;
17:17.
To God. Matt. 6:24; Luke 9:62;
1 Cor. 10:21.

LUKEWARMNESS
Indicates spiritual instability.
Hos. 7:8; James 1:6, 8.
Offensive to God. 1 Kings 18:21;
Luke 16:13 Rev. 3:16.

LUST
See also Voyeurism

Injunctions concerning
Abstain from every form of evil.
1 Thess. 5:22.
Be satisfied with spouse.
Prov. 5:15–20.
Flee youthful lusts. 2 Tim. 2:22.
Pure thoughts. Phil. 4:8.
Marks false spiritual leaders.
Jude 16, 18.
May bring spiritual death.
James 1:15.
Must be controlled by God.
Rom. 13:14; Gal. 5:17.
Same as committing adultery.
Matt. 5:28.
With lustful actions. Ezek. 23:8

LYING
An abomination to God.
Prov. 12:22.
A characteristic of the apostasy.
2 Thess. 2:9; 1 Tim. 4:2.

Believers
Avoid. Isa. 63:8; Zeph. 3:13.
Hate. Ps. 119:163; Prov. 13:5.
Pray to be preserved
from. Ps. 119:29; Prov. 30:8.
Reject those who practice.
Ps. 101:7.
Respect not those who practice.
Ps. 40:4.
Those who are guilty of, will be
thrown into hell. Rev. 21:8.
Will be detected. Prov. 12:19.
The devil excites men to.
1 Kings 22:22; Acts 5:3.
The devil the father of. John 8:44.
The evil of rulers listening to.
Prov. 29:12.
Excludes from heaven. Rev. 21:27;
22:15.
False prophets addicted to.
Jer. 23:14; Ezek. 22:28.
False witnesses addicted to.
Prov. 14:5, 25.
Foolishness of concealing hatred by.
Prov. 10:18.
Forbidden. Lev. 19:11; Col. 3:9.
Hateful to God. Prov. 6:16–19.
A hindrance to prayer. Isa. 59:2–3.
Hypocrites addicted to. Hos. 11:12.
Hypocrites an offspring of. Isa. 57:4.
Lawless persons guilty of.
1 John 2:4.

Leads to
Hatred. Prov. 26:28.
Love of impure conversation.
Prov. 17:4.
Often accompanied by gross crimes.
Hos. 4:1–2.
Poverty preferable to. Prov. 19:22.
Punishment for. Pss. 5:6; 120:3–4;
Prov. 19:5; Jer. 50:36.
Unbecoming in rulers. Prov. 17:7.

Vanity of getting riches by.
Prov. 21:6.

The wicked
Are addicted to, from their
infancy. Ps. 58:3.
Bring forth. Ps. 7:14.

Delight in. Ps. 62:4.
Love. Ps. 52:3.
Pay attention to. Prov. 17:4.
Prepare their tongues for.
Jer. 9:3, 5.
Seek after. Ps. 4:2.

MAGI
Interpreted dreams and "magic arts."
Dan. 2:2; 4:7; 5:7.

MAGIC
Of the Egyptian sorcerers.
Exod. 7:1–12.
Forbidden. Deut. 13:1–18;
18:9–14.
Of Sceva and his sons.
Acts 19:11–20.
Of Simon of Samaria. Acts 8:9–24.

MAGISTRATES
Appointed by God. Rom. 13:1.
Ministers of God. Rom. 13:4, 6.
Not a terror to the good, but to the
evil. Rom. 13:3.
Purpose of their appointment.
Rom. 13:4; 1 Pet. 2:14.

Should
Be diligent in ruling. Rom. 12:8.
Be faithful to the governmental
leaders. Dan. 6:4.
Be impartial. Exod. 23:6;
Deut. 1:17.
Defend the poor, etc. Job 29:12,
16.
Enforce the laws. Ezra 7:26.
Hate covetousness. Exod. 18:21.
Judge for God, not for man.
2 Chron. 19:6.
Judge righteously.
Deut. 1:16; 16:18; 25:1.
Judge wisely. 1 Kings 3:16–28.
Know the law of God. Ezra 7:25.
Not take bribes. Exod. 23:8;
Deut. 16:19.
Rule in the fear of God.
2 Sam. 23:3; 2 Chron. 19:7.
Seek wisdom from God.
1 Kings 3:9.
Submission to their authority
commanded. Matt. 23:2–3;
Rom. 13:1; 1 Pet. 2:13–14.
Their office to be respected.
Acts 23:5.
To be prayed for. 1 Tim. 2:1–2.
To be wisely selected and appointed.
Exod. 18:21; Ezra 7:25.
Wicked, illustrated. Prov. 28:15.

MAIMING
Arm, as fig. for strength. 1
Sam. 2:31.
Castration. Matt. 19:12.
Ear. John 18:10.
Eye, fig., to prevent sin. Matt. 5:29;
Mark 9:47.
Hand, as penalty for wrongdoing.
Deut. 25:11–12.

Hands and feet
Fig., to prevent sin. Matt. 5:30;
18:8; Mark 9:43–45.
In death, as penalty for
wrongdoing. 2 Sam. 4:12.
Male procreative organ. Deut. 23:1.
Thumbs and great toes. Judg. 1:6–7.

MALICE
Believers avoid. Job 31:29–30;
Ps. 35:12–14.
Brings its own punishment.
Ps. 7:15–16.
Christian liberty not to be made a
cover for. 1 Pet. 2:16.

Forbidden. 1 Cor. 14:20; Col. 3:8;
Eph. 4:26–27.

God repays. Ps. 10:14; Ezek. 36:5.

A hindrance to growth in grace.
1 Pet. 2:1–2.

Incompatible with the worship of
God. 1 Cor. 5:7–8.

Pray for those who injure you
through. Matt. 5:44.

Punishment of. Amos 1:11–12;
Obad. 1:10–15.

Springs from an evil heart.
Matt. 15:19–20; Gal. 5:19.

The wicked
Are filled with. Rom. 1:29.
Conceive. Ps. 7:14.
Live in. Titus 3:3.
Speak with. 2 John 1:10.
Visit believers with. Ps. 83:3;
Matt. 22:6.

MAMMON
Money. Matt. 6:24;
Luke 16:9, 11, 13.

MAN
Able to sustain bodily affliction.
Prov. 18:14.

All the ways of, clean in his own eyes.
Prov. 16:2.

Allowed to eat flesh after the flood.
Gen. 9:3.

Approved of by God. Gen. 1:31.

Banished from paradise.
Gen. 3:23–24.

Blessed by God. Gen. 1:28; 5:2.

Born in sin. Ps. 51:5.

Born to trouble. Job 5:7.

Called
The clay of the earth. Isa. 45:9.
Flesh. Gen. 6:12; Joel 2:28.

Vain man. Job 11:12;
James 2:20.

A worm. Job 25:6.

Cannot be just with God. Job 9:2;
25:4; Ps. 143:2; Rom. 3:20.

Cannot cleanse himself. Job 15:14;
Jer. 2:22.

Cannot direct his ways. Jer. 10:23;
Prov. 20:24.

Cannot profit God. Job 22:2;
Ps. 16:2.

Cannot retain his spirit from death.
Eccles. 8:8.

Christ
Approved of God as. Acts 2:22.
As such, the cause of the
resurrection. 1 Cor. 15:21–22.
Called the second, as covenant
head of the church.
1 Cor. 15:47.
Head of every. 1 Cor. 11:3.
Knew what was in. John 2:25.
Made in the likeness of. Phil. 2:7.
A refuge, to sinners. Isa. 32:2.
Took on Him nature of.
John 1:14; Heb. 2:14, 16.
Was found in fashion as. Phil. 2:8.
Clothed by God with skins.
Gen. 3:21.

Compared to
Clay in the potter's hands.
Isa. 64:8; Jer. 18:2, 6.
A dream. Ps. 90:5.
Grass. Isa. 40:6–8; 1 Pet. 1:24.
Vanity. Ps. 144:4.
A wild donkey's colt. Job 11:12.
Covered himself with fig leaves.
Gen. 3:7.

Created
By Christ. John 1:3; Col. 1:16.

After consultation, by the Trinity.
Gen. 1:26.

From the dust. Gen. 2:7;
Job 33:6.

Upon the earth. Deut. 4:32;
Job 20:4.

By God. Gen. 1:27; Isa. 45:12.

By the Holy Spirit. Job 33:4.

In the image of God. Gen. 1:26;
James 3:9.

In knowledge (inferred). Col. 3:10.

A living soul. Gen. 2:7;
1 Cor. 15:45.

Male and female. Gen. 1:27; 5:2.

Under obligation to obedience.
Gen. 2:16–17.

On the sixth day. Gen. 1:31.

A type of Christ. Rom. 5:14.

In uprightness. Eccles. 7:29.

Days of, as the days of a laborer.
Job 7:1.

Days of, compared to a shadow.
1 Chron. 29:15.

Disobeyed God by eating part of the
forbidden fruit. Gen. 3:1–12.

Every herb and tree given to, for
food. Gen. 1:29.

Fearfully and wonderfully made.
Ps. 139:14.

Filled with shame after the fall.
Gen. 3:10.

Gave names to other creatures.
Gen. 2:19–20.

Does not profit from work and worry.
Eccles. 2:22; 6:12.

Given life by the breath of God.
Gen. 2:7; 7:22; Job 33:4.

God

Destroys the hopes of. Job 14:19.

Enables to speak. Prov. 16:1.

Instructs. Ps. 94:10.

Makes his beauty consume away.
Ps. 39:11.

Makes the wrath of, to praise Him.
Ps. 76:10.

Orders the goings of. Prov. 5:21;
20:24.

Prepares the heart of. Prov. 16:1.

Preserves. Job 7:20; Ps. 36:6.

Provides for. Ps. 145:15–16.

Turns, to destruction. Ps. 90:3.

God's purpose in creation completed
by making. Gen. 2:5, 7.

Has an appointed time on the earth.
Job 7:1.

Has but few days. Job 14:1.

Has sought out many inventions.
Eccles. 7:29.

Help of, vain. Ps. 60:11.

Ignorant of what is good for him.
Eccles. 6:12.

Ignorant of what is to come after him.
Eccles. 10:14.

Inferior to angels. Ps. 8:5, with
Heb. 2:7.

Intellect of, matured by age.
1 Cor. 13:11.

Involved posterity in his ruin.
Rom. 5:12–19.

Made by God in his successive
generations. Job 10:8–11; 31:15.

Made for God. Prov. 16:4, with
Rev. 4:11.

Made wise by the inspiration of the
Almighty. Job 32:8–9.

More valuable than other creatures.
Job 35:11.

Nature and constitution different
from other creatures.
1 Cor. 15:39.

Not good for, to be alone.
Gen. 2:18.

No trust to be placed in. Ps. 118:8;
Isa. 2:22.

Of every nation, made of one blood.
Acts 17:26.

Of the earth, earthy. 1 Cor. 15:47.
Ordinary limit of his life. Ps. 90:10.
Originally naked and not ashamed.
Gen. 2:25.
Placed in the garden of Eden.
Gen. 2:15.

Possessed of
Affections. 1 Chron. 29:3;
Col. 3:2.
Body. Matt. 6:25.
Conscience. Rom. 2:15;
1 Tim. 4:2.
Memory. Gen. 41:9; 1 Cor. 15:2.
Soul. Luke 12:20; Acts 14:22;
1 Pet. 4:19.
Spirit. Prov. 18:14; 20:27;
1 Cor. 2:11.
Understanding. Eph. 1:18; 4:18.
Will. 1 Cor. 9:17; 2 Pet. 1:21.
Punished for disobedience.
Gen. 3:16–19.
Received dominion over other
creatures. Gen. 1:28; Ps. 8:6–8.
Sinks under trouble of mind.
Prov. 18:14.
Unworthy of God's favor. Job 7:17;
Ps. 8:4.
Walks in a vain show. Ps. 39:6.
Whole duty of. Eccles. 12:13.
Will be rewarded according to his
deeds. Ps. 62:12; Rom. 2:6.
Wiser than other creatures.
Job 35:11.
Woman formed to be a help for.
Gen. 21:2–25.
Would give all his possessions for the
preservation of life. Job 2:4.

MAN, FALL OF
Adam and Eve. Gen. 3:1–19.
All persons partake of the effects of.
1 Kings 8:46; Gal. 3:22;
1 John 1:8; 5:19.

Cannot be remedied by man.
Prov. 20:9; Jer. 2:22; 13:23.
Dead in sin. Eph. 2:1; Col. 2:13.
By the disobedience of Adam.
Gen. 3:6, 11–12, with
Rom. 5:12, 15, 19.
Implications of. 2 Cor. 11:3;
1 Tim. 2:14.

Man, in consequence
Abominable. Job 15:16; Ps. 14:3.
Blinded in heart. Eph. 4:18.
In bondage to the devil.
2 Tim. 2:26; Heb. 2:14–15.
In bondage to sin. Rom. 6:19;
7:5, 23; Gal. 5:17; Titus 3:3.
Born in sin. Job 15:14; 25:4;
Ps. 51:5; Isa. 48:8; John 3:6.
A child of wrath. Eph. 2:3.
Conscious of guilt.
Gen. 3:7–8, 10.
Constant in evil. Ps. 10:5;
2 Pet. 2:14.
Corrupt and perverse. Gen. 6:12;
Ps. 10:5; Rom. 3:12–16.
Defiled in conscience. Titus 1:15;
Heb. 10:22.
Depraved in mind. Rom. 8:5–7;
Eph. 4:17; Col. 1:21; Titus
1:15.
Does not receive the things of
God. 1 Cor. 2:14.
Lacking the fear of God.
Rom. 3:18.
Estranged from God. Gen. 3:8;
Ps. 58:3; Eph. 4:18; Col. 1:21.
Evil in heart. Gen. 6:5; 8:21;
Jer. 16:12; Matt. 15:19.
Loves darkness. John 3:19.
Made in the image of Adam.
Gen. 5:3, with
1 Cor. 15:48–49.
Short of God's glory. Rom. 3:23.
Stubborn. Job 11:12.

Totally depraved. Gen. 6:5;
Rom. 7:18.
Turned to his own way. Isa. 53:6.
Without understanding.
Ps. 14:2–3, with
Rom. 1:31; 3:11.
Unrighteous. Eccles. 7:20;
Rom. 3:10.

Punishment consequent upon
Banishment from paradise.
Gen. 3:24.
Condemnation to labor and
sorrow. Gen. 3:16, 19;
Job 5:6–7.
Eternal death. Job 21:30;
Rom. 5:18, 21; 6:23.
Temporal death. Gen. 3:19;
Rom. 5:12; 1 Cor. 15:22.
Relationship to Christ. 1 Cor. 15:21.
Remedy for, provided by God.
Gen. 3:15; John 3:16.
Through temptation of the devil.
Gen. 3:1–5; 2 Cor. 11:3;
1 Tim. 2:14.

MAN, LOVE TO
An abiding principle.
1 Cor. 13:8, 13.
An active principle. 1 Thess. 1:3;
Heb. 6:10.
After the example of Christ.
John 13:34; 15:12; Eph. 5:2.
All things should be done with.
1 Cor. 16:14.

Believers should
Be fervent in. 1 Pet. 1:22; 4:8.
Be sincere in. Rom. 12:9;
2 Cor. 6:6; 8:8; 1 John 3:18.
Continue in. 1 Tim. 2:15;
Heb. 13:1.
Encourage each other to.
2 Cor. 8:7; 9:2; Heb. 10:24.

Follow after. 1 Cor. 14:1.
Have in abundance. Phil. 1:9;
1 Thess. 3:12.
Put aside self-interest.
1 Cor. 10:24; 13:5; Phil. 2:4.
Put on. Col. 3:14.
Binds all together in perfect unity.
Col. 3:14.
Brings unity. Col. 2:2.
Commanded by Christ. John 13:34;
15:12; 1 John 3:23.
Commanded by God. 1 John 4:21.
The end of the commandment.
1 Tim. 1:5.
Especially expected of upon
ministers. 1 Tim. 4:12;
2 Tim. 2:22.

An evidence of
Being in the light. 1 John 2:10.
Discipleship with Christ.
John 13:35.
Spiritual life. 1 John 3:14.
Explained. 1 Cor. 13:4–7.
Faith works by. Gal. 5:6.
A fruit of the Spirit. Gal. 5:22;
Col. 1:8.
The fulfilling of the law.
Rom. 13:8–10; Gal. 5:14;
James 2:8.
Of God. 1 John 4:7.
Good and pleasant. Ps. 133:1–2.
Greatest sacrifices are nothing
without. 1 Cor. 13:3
Hypocrites devoid of. 1 John 3:10.
Love of God is a motive to.
John 13:34; 1 John 4:11.
Love to self is the measure of.
Mark 12:33.
Necessary to true happiness.
Prov. 15:17.
Purity of heart leads to. 1 Pet. 1:22.
The second great commandment.
Matt. 22:37–39.

Should be connected with Christian kindness. Rom. 12:10; 2 Pet. 1:7.

Should be exhibited in
Clothing the naked. Isa. 58:7; Matt. 25:36.
Covering the faults of others. Prov. 10:12, with 1 Pet. 4:8.
Forbearing. Eph. 4:2.
Forgiving injuries. Eph. 4:32; Col. 3:13.
Loving each other. Gal. 5:13.
Ministering to the needs of others. Matt. 25:35; Heb. 6:10.
Rebuking. Lev. 19:17; Matt. 18:15.
Relieving strangers. Lev. 25:35; Matt. 25:35.
Supporting the weak. Gal. 6:2; 1 Thess. 5:14.
Sympathizing. Rom. 12:15; 1 Cor. 12:26.
Visiting the sick, etc. Job 31:16–22; James 1:27.

Should be exhibited toward
All men. Gal. 6:10.
Believers. 1 Pet. 2:17; 1 John 5:1.
Enemies. Exod. 23:4–5; 2 Kings 6:22; Matt. 5:44; Rom. 12:14, 20; 1 Pet. 3:9.
Families. Eph. 5:25; Titus 2:4.
Fellow citizens. Exod. 32:32; Rom. 9:2–3; 10:1.
Ministers. 1 Thess. 5:13.
Strangers. Lev. 19:34; Deut. 10:19.
Supernatural gifts are nothing without. 1 Cor. 13:1–2.
Taught by God. 1 Thess. 4:9.

MAN'S IGNORANCE OF GOD

Evidenced by
Absence of love. 1 John 4:8.
Living in sin. Titus 1:16; 1 John 3:6.
Not keeping His commandments. 1 John 2:4.
Ignorance of Christ is. John 8:19.
Is no excuse for sin. Lev. 4:2; Luke 12:48.

Leads to
Alienation from God. Eph. 4:18.
Error. Matt. 22:29.
Idolatry. Isa. 44:19; Acts 17:29–30.
Persecuting believers. John 15:21; 16:3.
Sinful lusts. 1 Thess. 4:5; 1 Pet. 1:14.

Ministers should
Aid those in. 2 Tim. 2:24–25; Heb. 5:2.
Labor to remove. Acts 17:23.
Punishment of. Ps. 79:6; 2 Thess. 1:8.
The wicked choose. Job 21:14; Rom. 1:28.
The wicked in a state of. Jer. 9:3; John 15:21; 17:25; Acts 17:30.

MANIFESTATION
Of the being and love of God. Rom. 1:19; Titus 3:4; 1 John 4:9.
Of Christ and His glory. Matt. 17; John 1:14; 2:11; 1 Tim. 3:16; 1 John 3:5.
Of everyone's work. 1 Cor. 3:13.
Of iniquity and evil. John 3:21; 2 Tim. 3:9.
Of the Holy Spirit. 1 Cor. 12:7.
Of the judgments of God. Rev. 15:4.

Of the righteousness of God.
Rom. 3:21.
Of the sons of God. Rom. 8:19;
1 John 3:10.

MANNA

Called
Angel's food. Ps. 78:25.
Bread from heaven. Exod. 16:4;
John 6:31.
Bread of heaven. Ps. 105:40.
Corn of heaven. Ps. 78:24.
God's manna. Neh. 9:20.
Spiritual meat. 1 Cor. 10:3.
Ceased when Israel entered Canaan.
Exod. 16:35; Josh. 5:12.

Described as
Like coriander seed. Exod. 16:31;
Num. 11:7.
Like in color to bedellium.
Num. 11:7.
Like frost. Exod. 16:14.
Like in taste to oil. Num. 11:8.
Like in taste to wafers made with
honey. Exod. 16:31.
White. Exod. 16:31.
Fell after the evening dew.
Num. 11:9.
Fell not on the Sabbath.
Exod. 16:26–27.
Gathered every morning.
Exod. 16:21.

Given
As a sign of Moses' divine mission.
John 6:30–31.
As a test of obedience.
Exod. 16:4.
For forty years. Neh. 9:21.
In answer to prayer. Ps. 105:40.
Through Moses. John 6:31–32.

To exhibit God's glory.
Exod. 16:7.
To humble and test Israel.
Deut. 8:16.
To teach that man does not live
only by bread. Deut. 8:3, with
Matt. 4:4.
When Israel grumbled for bread.
Exod. 16:2–3.
A golden pot of, reserved for a
memorial. Exod. 16:32–34;
Heb. 9:4.
He that gathered much or little had
sufficient and nothing over.
Exod. 16:18.

Illustrative of
Blessings given to believers.
Rev. 2:17.
Christ. John 6:32–35.

The Israelites
At first covetous of. Exod. 16:17.
Complaining. Num. 21:5.
Considered inferior to food of
Egypt. Num. 11:4–6.
Ground, made into cakes and
baked in pans. Num. 11:8.
Punished for despising.
Num. 11:10–20.
Punished for complaining.
Num. 21:6.
Kept longer than a day (except on the
Sabbath) became corrupt.
Exod. 16:19 20.
Melted away by the sun.
Exod. 16:21.
Miraculously given to Israel for food
in the wilderness. Exod. 16:4, 15;
Neh. 9:15.
Previously unknown. Deut. 8:3, 16.
Two portions of, gathered the sixth
day because of the Sabbath.
Exod. 16:5, 22–26.

Two quarts of, gathered for each person. Exod. 16:16.

MARRIAGE

See also Marriage, Christian; Marriage, Interracial

The bride
Adorned with jewels for. Isa. 49:18; 61:10.
Attended by bridesmaids. Ps. 15:9.
Called to forget her father's house. Ps. 45:10.
Given a handmaid at. Gen. 24:59; 29:24, 29.
Gorgeously appareled. Ps. 45:13–14.
Received presents before. Gen. 24:53.
Stood on the right of bridegroom. Ps. 45:9.

The bridegroom
Adorned with ornaments. Isa. 61:10.
Attended by many friends. Judg. 14:11; John 3:29.
Crowned with garlands. Song of Sol. 3:11.
Presented with gifts. Ps. 45:12.
Rejoiced over the bride. Isa. 62:5.
Returned with the bride to his house at night. Matt. 25:1–6.

Celebrated
For seven days. Judg. 14:12.
With feasting. Gen. 29:22; Judg. 14:10; Matt. 22:2–3; John 2:1–10.
With great rejoicing. Jer. 33:11; John 3:29.
Contracted at the gate and before witnesses. Ruth 4:1, 10–11.

Contracted in patriarchal age with near relations. Gen. 20:12; 24:24; 28:2.
Consent of the parties necessary to. Gen. 24:57–58; 1 Sam. 18:20; 25:41.
A covenant relationship. Mal. 2:4.

Designed for
Happiness of man. Gen. 2:18.
Increasing the species. Gen. 1:28; 9:1.
Preventing fornication. 1 Cor. 7:2.
Raising up godly offspring. Mal. 2:15.
Divinely instituted. Gen. 2:24.
Dowry given to the woman's parents before. Gen. 29:18; 34:12; 1 Sam. 18:27–28; Hos. 3:2.
Early introduction of polygamy. Gen. 4:19.

Expressed by
Giving daughters to sons and sons to daughters. Deut. 7:3; Ezra 9:12.
Joining together. Matt. 19:6.
Making affinity. 1 Kings 3:1.
Taking a wife. Exod. 2:1.
Followed by a benediction. Gen. 24:60; Ruth 4:11–12.
Garments provided for guests at. Matt. 22:12.
High priest not to contract with a widow or a divorced or profane person. Lev. 21:14.
Honorable for all. Heb. 13:4.

Illustrative of
Christ's union with His church. Eph. 5:23–24, 32.

God's union with the Jewish
nation. Isa. 54:5; Jer. 3:14;
Hos. 2:19–20.
Infidelity of those contracted in,
punished as if married.
Deut. 22:23–24; Matt. 1:19.
Permanent during the joint lives of
the parties. Matt. 19:6;
Rom. 7:2–3; 1 Cor. 7:39.

The Jews
Betrothed themselves some time
before. Deut. 20:7; Judg. 14:5,
7–8; Matt. 1:18.
Careful in contracting for their
children. Gen. 24:2–3; 28:1–2.
Considered avoidance of a
reproach. Isa. 4:1.
Contracted when young.
Prov. 2:17; Joel 1:8.
Exempted from going to war
immediately after. Deut. 20:7.
Forbidden to contract, with
idolaters. Deut. 7:3–4;
Josh. 23:12; Ezra 9:11–12.
Forbidden to contract with their
near relatives. Lev. 18:6.
Obliged to contract with a
brother's wife who died without
children. Deut. 25:5;
Matt. 22:24.
Often contracted in their own
tribe. Exod. 2:1;
Num. 36:6–13; Luke 1:5, 27.
Often contracted with foreigners.
1 Kings 11:1; Neh. 13:23.
Often punished by being
prevented from. Jer. 7:34;
16:9; 25:10.
Sometimes guilty of polygamy.
1 Kings 11:1, 3.
Were allowed divorce from,
because of hardness of their

hearts. Deut. 24:1, with
Matt. 19:7–8.
Lawful in all. 1 Cor. 7:2, 28;
1 Tim. 5:14.
Modes of demanding women in.
Gen. 24:3–4; 34:6, 8;
1 Sam. 25:39–40.
Often contracted by parents for
children. Gen. 24:49–51; 34:6, 8.
Older daughters usually given in,
before the younger. Gen. 29:26.
Parents might refuse to give their
children in. Exod. 22:17;
Deut. 7:3.
Priest not to contract with divorced
or improper persons. Lev. 21:7.
Should be only in the Lord.
1 Cor. 7:39.
Should be with the consent of
parents. Gen. 28:8;
Judg. 14:2–3.

MARRIAGE, CHRISTIAN

Christians not under Jewish
ceremonial laws. Acts 15:1–29;
Rom. 7:4–6; Gal. 3:1–5:6;.

Purposes of
Fellowship and well-being.
Gen. 2:18.
Glory of God. 1 Cor. 6:15, 20.
Godly seed. Mal. 2:14–15;
1 Cor. 7:14.
Prevention of sin. 1 Cor. 7:2, 9.

Restrictions of
In the Lord. 1 Cor. 6:16–20;
7:39; 2 Cor. 6:4.
Permanent. Matt. 19:6;
Rom. 7:2–3; 1 Cor. 7:39.

MARRIAGE, INTERRACIAL

Background
All nations of one blood.
Acts 17:26.
All races descended from Adam.
Gen. 1:27; 2:20; 5;
Rom. 5:12–21.
All races descended from Noah.
Gen. 7:23; 9:18–19.
David and Jesus descended from
interracial marriage. Ruth 4:22;
Matt. 1:1, 5–6.
God's interest in marriage not racial
but spiritual. Mal. 2:14–15;
Matt. 19:4–6.
Jews often married outside race.
1 Kings 11:1.
Punishment of Aaron and Miriam for
speaking against Moses' Ethiopian
wife. Num. 12:1–10.

*Restrictions on Jewish marriage
not racial but spiritual*
Daughters of Zelophehad not to
marry outside own tribe.
Num. 27:1–11.
High priest not to marry a widow.
Lev. 21:14.
Jews not to marry heathen.
Exod. 34:12–16.

MARTYRDOM
The apostasy guilty of inflicting.
Rev. 17:6; 18:24.

Believers
Forewarned of. Matt. 10:21;
24:9; John 16:2.
Should be prepared for.
Matt. 16:24–25; Acts 21:13.
Should not fear. Matt. 10:28;
Rev. 2:10.
Should resist sin to. Heb. 12:4.

Of believers, will be avenged.
Luke 11:50–51; Rev. 18:20–24.
Death suffered for the word of God
and testimony of Christ. Rev. 6:9;
20:4.
Inflicted at the instigation of the devil.
Rev. 2:10, 13.
Reward of. Rev. 2:10; 6:11.

MASSACRE

Attempted unsuccessfully against
Abimelech's rivals. Judg. 9:1–6.
Athaliah's rivals. 2 Kings 11:2.
Innocent and faith-filled
individuals. Acts 9:1;
Rev. 12:11; 20:4.
Jesus. Matt. 2:16.
The Jews. Exod. 1:16–18.
The work of the devil and his
servants. Gen. 9:6; Exod. 20:13;
Matt. 15:19; 19:18; 26:52;
John 8:44; 1 Pet. 4:15.

MASTERS
Authority of, established. Col. 3:22;
1 Pet. 2:18.
Benevolent, blessed. Deut. 15:18.

Duty of, toward servants
Not to defraud them. Gen. 31:7.
Not to keep back their wages.
Lev. 19:13; Deut. 24:15.
Not to rule over them with
ruthlessly. Lev. 25:43;
Deut. 24:14.
To act justly. Job 31:13, 15;
Col. 4:1.
To avoid threatening them.
Eph. 6:9.
To deal with them in the fear of
God. Eph. 6:9; Col. 4:1.
To esteem them highly, if
believers. Philem. 1:16.

To take care of them in sickness. Luke 7:3.

Should receive faithful advice from servants. 2 Kings 5:13–14.

Should select faithful servants. Gen. 24:2; Ps. 101:6–7.

Should with their households
Fear God. Acts 10:2.
Observe the Sabbath.
Exod. 20:10; Deut. 5:12–14.
Put away idols. Gen. 35:2.
Serve God. Josh 24:15.
Worship God. Gen. 35:3.

Unjust, denounced. Jer. 22:13; James 5:4.

MASTERY

Over the body. 1 Cor. 9:27.

Of Christ. 1 Cor. 15:28; Phil. 3:21; Heb. 2:8; 1 Pet. 3:22.

Of God. Ps. 98:1; 1 Chron. 29:12; Dan. 4:17; Rev. 19:6.

Over one's own spirit. Prov. 16:32; 25:28.

Over the realm of evil. Luke 10:19.

MATURATION

From adulthood to old age
Carried by God. Isa. 46:4.

Avoid youthful passions. 2 Tim. 2:22.

From childhood to adulthood
Be subject to elders. 1 Pet. 5:5.

Description of old age.
2 Sam. 19:35; 1 Kings 1:1; Eccles. 12:2–7.

Elderly to be honored. Lev. 19:32; Prov. 23:22; Lam. 5:12; 1 Tim. 5:1.

Example of from adulthood to old age
Solomon. 1 Kings 4:29; 11:4.

Examples of from childhood to adulthood
Jacob and Esau. Gen. 25:27.
Jesus. Isa. 53:2; Luke 2:40, 52.
John the Baptist. Luke 1:80.
Paul. 1 Cor. 13:11.
Samson. Judg. 13:24–25.
Samuel. 1 Sam. 2:26.
Shelah. Gen. 38:11, 14.

Glory found in. Prov. 20:29.

God proclaimed by. Ps. 71:17–18.

Let no one despise your youth. 1 Tim. 4:12.

Mature children. Ps. 144:12.

Pampered. Prov. 29:21.

Righteous not seen to be forsaken during. Ps. 37:25.

Spiritual maturity
Brought to completion. Phil. 1:6.
In Christ. Eph. 4:15.
In grace and knowledge of Jesus. 2 Pet. 3:18.
Growth in faith and love. 2 Thess. 1:3.
Likened to cedar of Lebanon. Ps. 92:12.
Prayed for. 2 Cor. 13:9.
Through Scripture. 2 Tim. 3:16–17.
To salvation. 1 Pet. 2:2.
Seek. Heb. 6:1.
With solid food. 1 Cor. 3:1–2; Heb. 5:12–14.
Through trials. James 1:2–4.

Trained correctly. Prov. 22:6.

MEAT OFFERINGS

Always seasoned with salt. Lev. 2:13.

Consisted of
Barley meal. Num. 5:15.
Fine flour. Lev. 2:1.
Fine flour baked in a frying pan.
Lev. 2:7.
Fine flour baked in a pan.
Lev. 2:5.
Green ears of corn parched.
Lev. 2:14.
Unleavened cakes baked in the
oven. Lev. 2:4.
High priest's deputy had care of.
Num. 4:16.
Of jealousy, without oil or incense.
Num. 5:15.

The Jews
Condemned for offering to idols.
Isa. 57:6.
Often not accepted in.
Amos 5:22.
Often prevented from offering, by
judgments. Joel 11:9, 13.
Laid up in a chamber of the temple.
Neh. 10:39; 13:5; Ezek. 42:13.
Materials for public, often provided
by the princes. Num. 7:13, 19,
25; Ezek. 5:17.
No leaven used with. Lev. 2:11;
6:17.
Not to be offered on altar of incense.
Exod. 30:9.

Offered
With all burnt sacrifices.
Num. 15:3–12.
On the altar of burnt offering.
Exod. 40:29.
With the daily sacrifices.
Exod. 29:40–42.
By the high priest every day, half
in the morning and half in the
evening. Lev. 6:20–22.

By the poor for a trespass offering.
Lev. 5:11.
Oil and incense used with.
Lev. 2:1, 4, 15.
The priest's portion. Lev. 2:3; 6:17.
A small part consumed on the altar
for a memorial. Lev. 2:2, 9, 16;
6:15.
To be eaten in the holy place.
Lev. 6:16.
To be eaten solely by the male
descendents of Aaron. Lev. 6:18.
Were most holy. Lev. 6:17.
When offered for a priest, entirely
consumed by fire. Lev. 6:23.

MEDIA

Injunctions concerning
Have pure thoughts. Phil. 4:8.
Test everything. 1 Thess.
5:21–22.
Use time wisely. Eph. 5:16.

Principle relevant to
Things used for own pleasure.
James 4:3.

MEDITATION

Brings vision and help. Ps. 63:1–8.
Characterizes the godly person.
Ps. 1:1–2.
A Christian duty. 1 Tim. 4:15.

Should be centered on
The good and true. Phil. 4:8.
The Lord. Ps. 63:6.
The message of God. Ps. 119:67.
The promises of God.
Ps. 119:148.
The works of God. Ps. 143:5.

MEEKNESS

Believers should
Answer for their hope with.
1 Pet. 3:15.
Exhibit. James 3:13.
Put on. Col. 3:12–13.
Receive the Word of God with.
James 1:21.
Restore the person who sins.
Gal. 6:1.
Seek. Zeph. 2:3.
Show, to all men. Titus 3:2.
Blessedness of. Matt. 5:5.
A characteristic of wisdom.
James 3:17.

Christ
Set an example of. Ps. 45:4;
Isa. 53:7; Matt. 11:29; 21:5;
2 Cor. 10:1; 1 Pet. 2:21–23.
Taught. Matt. 5:38–45.
A fruit of the Spirit. Gal. 5:22–23.
The gospel to be preached to those
who possess. Isa. 61:1.

Ministers should
Follow after. 1 Tim. 6:11.
Instruct opposers with.
2 Tim. 2:24–25.
Urge, on their people.
Titus 3:1–2.
Necessary to a Christian walk.
Eph. 4:1–2; 1 Cor. 6:7.
Precious in the sight of God.
1 Pet. 3:4.

Those who are gifted with
Are beautified with salvation.
Ps. 149:4.
Are exalted. Ps. 147:6;
Matt. 23:12.
Are guided and taught. Ps. 25:9.
Are preserved. Ps. 76:9.
Are richly provided for. Ps. 22:26.

Increase their joy. Isa. 29:19.
Will inherit the earth. Ps. 37:11.

MEMORY, MEMORIALS
Blessed, of the just. Prov. 10:7.

Divine
God's name and revelation.
Exod. 3:15; Ps. 135:13.
The Lord's Supper. Luke 22:19.
Passover. Exod. 12:14.

Things to remember
The apostolic testimony. Jude 17.
The heritage of the past.
Deut. 32:7.
The Lord's day. Exod. 20:8.
The Lord's deliverance.
Deut. 16:3.
The Lord's leadings. Deut. 8:2.
The Lord's resurrection.
2 Tim. 2:8.
The words of Jesus. Acts 20:35.
Value of. Ezra 9:5–15;
2 Pet. 1:15–21;.

MERCY
Beneficial to those who exercise.
Prov. 11:17.
Blessedness of showing.
Prov. 14:21; Matt. 5:7.
A characteristic of believers.
Ps. 37:26; Isa. 57:1.
Denunciations against those lacking.
Hos. 4:1, 3; Matt. 18:23–35;
James 2:13.
Encouraged. 2 Kings 6:21–23;
Hos. 12:6; Rom. 12:20–21;
Col. 3:12.
After the example of God.
Luke 6:36.
Hypocrites lacking. Matt. 23:23.

Should be shown
  To animals. Prov. 12:10.
  To backsliders. Luke 15:18–20;
    2 Cor. 2:6–8.
  To our brethren. Zech. 7:9.
  With cheerfulness. Rom. 12:8.
  To the poor. Prov. 14:31;
    Dan. 4:27.
  To those who are in distress.
    Luke 10:37.
To be engraved on the heart.
  Prov. 3:3.
Upholds the throne of kings.
  Prov. 20:28.

MERCY OF GOD
See God, Mercy of

MERCY SEAT
Bezaleel given wisdom to make.
  Exod. 31:2–3, 7.
Blood of sacrifices on the day of
  atonement
Sprinkled upon and before.
  Lev. 16:14–15.
Cherubim formed out of, and at each
  end of it. Exod. 25:18–20;
  Heb. 9:5.
Covered with a cloud of incense on
  the Day of Atonement.
  Lev. 16:13.

God
  Appeared over in the cloud.
    Lev. 16:2.
  Lived over. Ps. 80:1.
  Spoke from above. Exod. 25:22;
    Num. 7:89.

Illustrative of
  Christ. Rom. 3:25, with Heb. 9:3.
  The throne of grace. Heb. 4:16.
Made of pure gold. Exod. 25:17;
  37:6.

Moses commanded to make.
  Exod. 25:17.
Placed upon the ark of testimony.
  Exod. 25:21; 26:34; 40:20.

MESSENGERS OF GOD
See God, Messengers of

MESSIAH

Brings about
  An end to divisions and hostilities.
    Eph. 2:1–22.
  Everlasting righteousness.
    Dan. 9:24; 2 Cor. 5:21.
  A new covenant. Jer. 31:31–34;
    Matt. 26:26–30.
  Redemption from sin.
    1 Pet. 1:18–20.

Promised
  To Abraham. Gen. 12:1–3.
  Through Balaam.
    Num. 22–24:17.
  For Bethlehem. Mic. 5:2, 5.
  Through David's lineage.
    Isa. 11:1–10.
  At the Fall. Gen. 3:15.

Revealed
  Through the apostles. Acts 17:3;
    18:28.
  At His birth. Matt. 1:16, 23.
  To His followers.
    John 1:41; 6:41, 69.

METHUSELAH
Oldest human. Gen. 5:27.
Son of Enoch and grandfather of
  Noah. Gen. 5:21, 26–29).

MILK
Canaan abounded with. Exod. 3:8,
  17; Josh. 5:6.

Different kinds mentioned
Of camels. Gen. 32:15.
Of cows. Deut. 32:14;
1 Sam. 6:7.
Of goats. Prov. 27:27.
Of jackals. Lam. 4:3.
Of sheep. Deut. 32:14.
Flocks and herds fed for supply of.
Prov. 27:23, 27; Isa. 7:21–22;
1 Cor. 9:7.

Illustrative of
Blessings of the gospel. Isa. 55:1;
Joel 3:18.
Doctrines of the gospel.
Song of Sol. 5:1.
First principles of God's Word.
1 Cor. 3:2; Heb. 5:12;
1 Pet. 2:2.
Godly and edifying discourses.
Song of Sol. 4:11.
Temporary blessings. Gen. 49:12.
Wealth of the Gentiles. Isa. 60:16.
Kept by the Jews in bottles.
Judg. 4:19.

Made into
Butter. Prov. 30:33.
Cheese. Job 10:10.
Used as food by the Jews.
Gen. 18:8; Judg. 5:25.
Young animals not to be boiled in
that of the mother. Exod. 23:19.

MILLENNIUM
Description of. Rev. 20:1–6.

MILLS
Antiquity of. Exod. 11:5.
Female servants usually employed at.
Exod. 11:5; Matt. 24:41.

Illustrative of
Degradation, etc., when grinding.
Isa. 47:1–2.
Desolation, when ceasing.
Jer. 25:10; Rev. 18:22.
Male captives often employed at.
Judg. 16:21; Lam. 5:13.

Stones used in
Hard. Job 41:24.
Heavy. Matt. 18:6.
Large. Rev. 18:21.
Not to be taken in pledge.
Deut. 24:6.
Often thrown down on enemies
during sieges. Judg. 9:53;
2 Sam. 11:21.

Used for grinding
Corn. Isa. 47:2.
Manna in the wilderness.
Num. 11:8.

MILLSTONE
Abimelech killed by one being hurled
at him. Judg. 9:53.
Not to be taken in pledge.
Deut. 24:6.
Probably used in executions by
drowning. Matt. 18:6; Mark 9:42;
Luke 17:2.
Used in a figurative sense describing
the hard heart. Job 41:24.

MIND
Blinded. Luke 24:16; 2 Cor. 3:14.
Discouraged. Heb. 12:3.
Hardened. Isa. 5:13; Dan. 5:20.
Opened. Luke 24:31; Eph. 1:18.
Power of. Prov. 23:7; 4:23;
Rom. 8:6; 1 Pet. 1:13.
Protection of. Phil. 4:7.
Renewed. Rom. 12:1–2; Eph. 4:23.

MINISTERS

Are bound to
Build up the church.
2 Cor. 12:19; Eph. 4:12.
Comfort. 2 Cor. 1:4–6.
Convince gainsayers. Titus 1:9.
Endure hardness. 2 Tim. 2:3.
Exhort. Titus 1:9; 2:15.
Feed the church. Jer. 3:15;
John 21:15–17; Acts 20:28;
1 Pet. 5:2.
Pray for their people. Joel 2:17;
Col. 1:9.
Preach the gospel to all.
Mark 16:15; 1 Cor. 1:17.
Reprimand. Titus 1:13; 2:15.
Strengthen the faith of their
people. Luke 22:32;
Acts 14:22.
Teach. 2 Tim. 2:2.
Wage a good warfare.
1 Tim. 1:18; 2 Tim. 4:7.
Warn affectionately. Acts 20:31.
Watch for souls. Heb. 13:17.
Authority of, is for edification.
2 Cor. 10:8; 13:10.
Calamity to those who are called to
preach the gospel, who fail to do
so. 1 Cor. 9:16.
Called by God. Exod. 28:1, with
Heb. 5:4.
Commissioned by Christ.
Matt. 28:19.
Compared to earthly vessels.
2 Cor. 4:7.

Described as
Ambassadors for Christ.
2 Cor. 5:20.
Defenders of the faith. Phil. 1:7.
Ministers of Christ. 1 Cor. 4:1.
Servants of Christ's people.
2 Cor. 4:5.

Stewards of the mysteries of God.
1 Cor. 4:1.
Entrusted with the gospel.
1 Thess. 2:4.
Excellency of. Rom. 10:15.
Have authority from God.
2 Cor. 10:8; 13:10.
Labors of, vain, without God's
blessing. 1 Cor. 3:7; 15:10.
Necessity for. Matt. 9:37–38;
Rom. 10:14.
Pray for the increase of. Matt. 9:38.
Qualified by God. Isa. 6:5–7;
2 Cor. 3:5–6.
Sent by the Holy Spirit. Acts 13:2, 4.
Should avoid giving unnecessary
offense. 1 Cor. 10:32–33;
2 Cor. 6:3.

Should be
Affectionate to their people.
Phil. 1:7; 1 Thess. 2:8, 11.
Able to teach. 1 Tim. 3:2;
2 Tim. 2:24.
Blameless. 1 Tim. 3:2; Titus 1:7.
Devoted. Acts 20:24;
Phil. 1:20–21.
Disinterested. 2 Cor. 12:14;
1 Thess. 2:6.
Examples to the flock. Phil. 3:17;
2 Thess. 3:9; 1 Tim. 4:12;
1 Pet. 5:3.
Gentle. 1 Thess. 2:7;
2 Tim. 2:24.
Holy. Exod. 28:36; Lev. 21:6;
Titus 1:8.
Hospitable. 1 Tim. 3:2; Titus 1:8.
Humble. Acts 20:19.
Impartial. 1 Tim. 5:21.
Patient. 2 Cor. 6:4; 2 Tim. 2:24.
Prayerful. Eph. 3:14; Phil. 1:4.
Pure. Isa. 52:11; 1 Tim. 3:9.
Self-denying. 1 Cor. 9:27.

Sober, just, and temperate.
  Lev. 10:9; Titus 1:8.
Strict in ruling their own families.
  1 Tim. 3:4, 12.
Strong in grace. 2 Tim. 2:1.
Studious and meditative.
  1 Tim. 4:13, 15.
Watchful. 2 Tim. 4:5.
Willing. Isa. 6:8; 1 Pet. 5:2.
Should make full proof of their
  ministry. 2 Tim. 4:5.

Should not be
  Contentious. 1 Tim. 3:3;
    Titus 1:7.
  Crafty. 2 Cor. 4:2.
  Easily dispirited. 2 Cor. 4:8–9;
    6:10.
  Entangled by cares. Luke 9:60;
    2 Tim. 2:4.
  Given to wine. 1 Tim. 3:3;
    Titus 1:7.
  Greedy. Acts 20:33;
    1 Tim. 3:3, 8; 1 Pet. 5:2.
  Lords over God's heritage.
    1 Pet. 5:3.
  Men-pleasers. Gal. 1:10;
    1 Thess. 2:4.

Should preach
  According to the oracles of God.
    1 Pet. 4:11.
  With attentiveness. 1 Tim. 4:16.
  With boldness. Isa. 58:1;
    Ezek. 2:6; Matt. 10:27–28.
  Without charge, if possible. 1 Cor.
    9:18; 1 Thess. 2:9.
  Christ crucified. Acts 8:5, 35;
    1 Cor. 2:2.
  With consistency.
    2 Cor. 1:18–19.
  With constancy. Acts 6:4;
    2 Tim. 4:2.

Without deceitfulness.
  2 Cor. 2:17; 4:2; 1 Thess. 2:3,
  5.
Everywhere. Mark 16:20;
  Acts 8:4.
With faithfulness. Ezek. 3:17–18.
Fully, and without reserve.
  Acts 5:20; 20:20, 27;
  Rom. 15:19.
With good will and love.
  Phil. 1:15–17.
With plainness of speech.
  2 Cor. 3:12.
Not setting forth themselves.
  2 Cor. 4:5.
Not with enticing words of man's
  wisdom. 1 Cor. 1:17; 2:1, 4.
Repentance and faith. Acts 20:21.
With zeal. 1 Thess. 2:8.
Should seek the salvation of their
  flock. 1 Cor. 10:33.
Specially protected by God.
  2 Cor. 1:10.

Their people are bound to
  Attend to their instructions.
    Mal. 2:7; Matt. 23:3.
  Follow their holy example.
    1 Cor. 11:1; Phil. 3:17.
  Give them joy. 2 Cor. 1:14; 2:3.
  Help them. Rom. 16:9; Phil. 4:3.
  Hold them in reputation.
    Phil. 2:29; 1 Thess. 5:13;
    1 Tim. 5:17.
  Imitate their faith. Heb. 13:7.
  Love them. 2 Cor. 8:7;
    1 Thess. 3:6.
  Not to despise them. Luke 10:16;
    1 Tim. 4:12.
  Obey them. 1 Cor. 16:16;
    Heb. 13:17.
  Pray for them. Rom. 15:30;
    2 Cor. 1:11; Eph. 6:19;
    Heb. 13:18.

Regard them as God's messengers. 1 Cor. 4:1; Gal. 4:14.

Support them. 2 Chron. 31:4; 1 Cor. 9:7–11; Gal. 6:6.

When faithful

Approve themselves as the ministers of God. 2 Cor. 6:4.

Are rewarded. Matt. 24:47; 1 Cor. 3:14; 9:17, 18; 1 Pet. 5:4.

Commend themselves to the consciences of men. 2 Cor. 4:2.

Glory in their people. 2 Cor. 7:4.

Rejoice in the faith and holiness of their people. 1 Thess. 2:19–20; 3:6–9.

Thank God for His gifts to their people. 1 Cor. 1:4; Phil. 1:3; 1 Thess. 3:9.

When unfaithful

Deal treacherously with their people. John 10:12.

Described. Isa. 56:10–12; Titus 1:10–11.

Mislead men. Jer. 6:14; Matt. 15:14.

Seek gain. Mic. 3:11; 2 Pet. 2:3.

Will be punished. Ezek. 33:6–8; Matt. 24:48–51.

MINISTERS, TITLES AND NAMES OF

Ambassadors for Christ. 2 Cor. 5:20.

Angels of the church. Rev. 1:20; 2:1.

Apostles. Luke 6:13; Eph. 4:11; Rev. 18:20.

Apostles of Jesus Christ. Titus 1:1.

Bishops. Phil. 1:1; 1 Tim. 3:1; Titus 1:7.

Deacons. Acts 6:1; Phil. 1:1; 1 Tim. 3:8.

Elders. 1 Tim. 5:17; 1 Pet. 5:1.

Evangelists. Eph. 4:11; 2 Tim. 4:5.

Fishers of men. Matt. 4:19; Mark 1:17.

Laborers. Matt. 9:38, with Philem. 1:1; 1 Thess. 2:2.

Messengers of the church. 2 Cor. 8:23.

Messengers of the Lord of hosts. Mal. 2:7.

Ministers of Christ. Rom. 15:16; 1 Cor. 4:1.

Ministers of the church. Col. 1:24–25.

Ministers of God. 2 Cor. 6:4.

Ministers of the gospel. Eph. 3:7; Col. 1:23.

Ministers of the Lord. Joel 2:17.

Ministers of the New Testament. 2 Cor. 3:6.

Ministers of righteousness. 2 Cor. 11:15.

Ministers of the sanctuary. Ezek. 45:4.

Ministers of the word. Luke 1:2.

Overseers. Acts 20:28.

Pastors. Jer. 3:15; Eph. 4:11.

Preachers. Rom. 10:14; 1 Tim. 2:7.

Servants of the church. 2 Cor. 4:5.

Servants of God. Titus 1:1; James 1:1.

Servants of Jesus Christ. Phil. 1:1; Jude 1.

Servants of the Lord. 2 Tim. 2:24.

Shepherds. Jer. 23:4.

Soldiers of Christ. Phil. 2:25; 2 Tim. 2:3.

Stars. Rev. 1:20; 2:1.

Stewards of God. Titus 1:7.

Stewards of the grace of God. 1 Pet. 4:10.

Stewards of the mysteries of God.
1 Cor. 4:1.

Teachers. Isa. 30:20; Eph. 4:11.

Watchmen. Isa. 62:6; Ezek. 33:7.

Witnesses. Acts 1:8; 5:32; 26:16.

Workers together with God.
2 Cor. 6:1.

MINORS

Legal status of. Gal. 4:1, 2.

MIRACLES

See also Christ, Miracles of; Miracles
through Evil Agents; Miracles
Performed through Servants of
God; Holy Spirit, Miraculous Gifts
of the

Described as

Marvelous things. Ps. 78:12.

Marvelous works. Isa. 29:14;
Ps. 105.5.

Signs and wonders. Jer. 32:21;
John 4:48; 2 Cor. 12:12.

Evidences of a divine commission.
Exod. 4:1–5; Mark 16:20.

Faith required in

Those for whom they were
performed. Matt. 9:28; 13:58;
Mark 9:22–24; Acts 14:9.

Those who performed.
Matt. 17:20; 21:21;
John 14:12; Acts 3:16; 6-8

First preaching of the gospel
confirmed by. Mark 16:20;
Heb. 2:4.

A gift of the Holy Spirit.
1 Cor. 12:10.

Guilt of rejecting the evidence
afforded by. Matt. 11:20–24;
John 15:24.

Instrumental to the early spread of
the gospel. Acts 8:6;
Rom. 15:18–19.

Insufficient of themselves to produce
conversion. Luke 16:31.

Jesus followed because of.
Matt. 4:23–25; 14:35–36;
John 6:2, 26; 12:18.

Jesus proved to be the Messiah by.
Matt. 11:4–6; Luke 7:20–22;
John 5:36; Acts 2:22.

Manifest

The glory of Christ. John 2:11;
11:4.

The glory of God. John 11:4.

The works of God. John 9:3.

Messiah expected to perform.
Matt. 11:2–3; John 7:31.

Power of God necessary to.
John 3:2.

Should be remembered.
1 Chron. 16:12; Ps. 105:5.

Should be told to future generations.
Exod. 10:2; Judg. 6:13.

Should produce faith. John 2:23;
20:30–31.

Should produce obedience.
Deut. 11:1–3; 29:2–3, 9.

Those who perform, disclaimed all
power of their own. Acts 3:12.

Were performed

In the name of Christ.
Mark 16:17; Acts 3:16; 4:30.

By the power of Christ.
Matt. 10:1.

By the power of God. Exod. 8:19;
Acts 14:3; 15:12; 19:11.

By the power of the Holy Spirit.
Matt. 12:28; Rom. 15:19.

The wicked
Desire to see. Matt. 27:42;
Luke 11:29; 23:8.
Do not consider. Mark 6:52.
Do not understand. Ps. 106:7.
Forget. Neh. 9:17; Ps. 78:1, 11.
Often acknowledge. John 11:47;
Acts 4:16.
Proof against. Num. 14:22;
John 12:37.

MIRACLES OF CHRIST
See Christ, Miracles of

MIRACLES PERFORMED THROUGH SERVANTS OF GOD

The apostles
Signs and wonders and done.
Acts 2:43; 5:12.

Elijah
Child restored to life.
1 Kings 17:22–23.
Drought caused. 1 Kings 17:1;
James 5:17.
Meal and oil multiplied.
1 Kings 17:14–16.
Men destroyed by fire.
2 Kings 1:10–12.
Rain brought. 1 Kings 18:41–45;
James 5:18.
Sacrifice consumed by fire.
1 Kings 18:36, 38.
Taken to heaven. 2 Kings 2:11.
Waters of Jordan divided.
2 Kings 2:8.

Elisha
Child restored to life.
2 Kings 4:32–35.
Children torn by bears.
2 Kings 2:24.

Gehazi struck with leprosy.
2 Kings 5:27.
Iron ax head caused to float.
2 Kings 6:6.
Man restored to life.
2 Kings 13:21.
Naaman healed.
2 Kings 5:10, 14.
Oil multiplied. 2 Kings 4:1–7.
Syrians restored to sight.
2 Kings 6:20.
Syrians stricken with blindness.
2 Kings 6:18.
Waters healed. 2 Kings 2:21–22.
Waters of Jordan divided.
2 Kings 2:14.

Isaiah
Hezekiah healed. 2 Kings 20:7.
Shadow put back on the dial.
2 Kings 20:11.

Joshua
Jericho taken. Josh 6:6–20.
Jordan restored to its course.
Josh. 4:18.
Midianites destroyed.
Judg. 7:16–22.
Sun and moon signs stayed.
Josh. 10:12–14.
Waters of Jordan divided.
Josh. 3:10–17.

Moses and Aaron
Amalek vanquished.
Exod. 17:11–13.
Boils brought. Exod. 9:10–11.
Darkness covers Egypt.
Exod. 10:22.
Egyptians overwhelmed.
Exod. 14:26–28.
Firstborn destroyed. Exod. 12:29.
Flies cover Egypt. Exod. 8:21–24.
Flies removed. Exod. 8:31.

Frogs cover Egypt. Exod. 8:6.
Frogs removed. Exod. 8:13.
Hail sent on Egypt. Exod. 9:23.
Hail removed. Exod. 9:33.
Hand healed. Exod. 4:7.
Hand made leprous. Exod. 4:6.
Healing by bronze serpent.
  Num. 21:8–9.
Korah destroyed.
  Num. 16:28–32.
Lice brought. Exod. 8:17.
Locusts brought. Exod. 10:13.
Locusts removed. Exod. 10:19.
Pestilence of beasts. Exod. 9:3–6.
Red Sea divided. Exod. 14:21–22.
River turned into blood.
  Exod. 7:20.
Staff changed into a serpent.
  Exod. 4:3; 7:10.
Staff restored. Exod. 4:4.
Water brought from rock in
  Horeb. Exod. 17:6.
Water brought from rock in
  Kadesh. Num. 20:11.
Water sweetened. Exod. 15:25.
Water turned into blood.
  Exod. 4:9, 30.

Paul
  Elymas stricken with blindness.
    Acts 13:11.
  Eutychus restored to life.
    Acts 20:10, 12.
  Father of Publius healed.
    Acts 28:8.
  Lame man cured. Acts 14:10.
  Snake's bite made harmless.
    Acts 28:5.
  Special miracles. Acts 19:11–12.
  Unclean spirit cast out.
    Acts 16:18.

Paul and Barnabas
  Empowered to work signs and
    wonders. Acts 14:3.

Peter
  Aeneas made whole. Acts 9:34.
  Death of Ananias. Acts 5:5.
  Death of Sapphira. Acts 5:10.
  Dorcas restored to life. Acts 9:40.
  Lame man cured. Acts 3:7.
  The sick healed. Acts 5:15–16.

Philip
  Miracles and signs. Acts 8:13.
  Unclean spirits cast out, paralytics
    and crippled healed. Acts 8:6–7.

The prophet of Judah
  Altar split apart. 1 Kings 13:5.
  Jeroboam's hand withered.
    1 Kings 13:4.
  Withered hand restored.
    1 Kings 13:6.

Samson
  Dagon's house pulled down.
    Judg. 16:30.
  The gates of Gaza carried away.
    Judg. 16:3.
  A lion killed. Judg. 14:6.
  Philistines killed. Judg. 14:19;
    15:15.

Samuel
  Thunder and rain in harvest.
    1 Sam. 12:18.
  The seventy disciples
  Sent to heal sick. Luke 10:9.
  Empowered to overcome devils.
    Luke 10:17.

The seventy disciples
  Empowered to overcome devils.
    Luke 10:17.
  Sent to heal sick. Luke 10:9.

Stephen
  Wonders and miracles done.
    Acts 6:8.

MIRACLES THROUGH EVIL AGENTS

Deceive the ungodly.
  2 Thess. 2:10–12; Rev. 13:14;
  19:20.
A mark of the apostasy.
  2 Thess. 2:3, 9; Rev. 13:13.
Not to be regarded. Deut. 13:3.
Performed through the power of the
  devil. 2 Thess. 2:9; Rev. 16:14.

Performed
  By false christs. Matt. 24:24.
  By false prophets. Matt. 24:24;
    Rev. 19:20.
  In support of false religions.
    Deut. 13:1–2.

MIRACULOUS GIFTS OF THE HOLY SPIRIT

See Holy Spirit, Miraculous Gifts of
  the

MIRROR

Of brass. Job 37:18.
Given by the Israelite women to be
  melted for the basin. Exod. 38:8.
Used in a figurative sense.
  1 Cor. 13:12; 2 Cor. 3:18;
  James 1:23–24.

MISCARRIAGE/STILLBORN INFANT

Better than futile life. Eccles. 6:3.
Compared to one punished by God.
  Num. 12:12.

Desired by
  Hosea, for enemies. Hos. 9:14.

Job, for own mother. Job 3:11,
  16.
Psalmist, for enemies. Ps. 58:8.

MISCEGENATION

See also Marriage, Interracial

Examples of
  Esau. Gen. 26:34, 35.
  Israel. Num. 25:1, 6–8;
    Judg. 3:5–8.
  Moses. Num. 12:1.
Forbidden by Abraham. Gen. 24:3.
Forbidden by Jacob. Gen. 28:1.
Forbidden by Joshua. Josh. 23:12.
Forbidden by Moses.
  Exod. 34:12–16; Deut. 7:3–4.
Reasons for prohibition.
  Exod. 34:16.
Results of. Judg. 3:6, 7.

MISJUDGMENT

Examples of
  Hannah. 1 Sam. 1:14–17.
  The Reubenites and Gadites.
    Num. 32:1–33;
    Josh. 22:11–31.

MISSIONARIES

All Christians should be as
  In admonishing others.
    1 Thess. 5:14; 2 Thess. 3:15.
  In aiding ministers in their work.
    Rom. 16:3, 9; 2 Cor. 11:9;
    Phil. 4:14–16; 3 John 1:6.
  In declaring what God has done for
    them. Pss. 66:16; 116:16–19.
  In dedicating themselves to the
    service of God. Josh. 24:15;
    Ps. 27:4.
  In devoting all property to God.
    1 Chron. 29:2–3, 14, 16;

Eccles. 11:1; Matt. 6:19–20;
Mark 12:44; Luke 12:33;
18:22, 28; Acts 2:45; 4:32–34.

In encouraging the weak.
Isa. 35:3–4; Rom. 14:1; 15:1;
1 Thess. 5:14.

In the family. Deut. 6:7;
Ps. 78:5–8; Isa. 38:19; 1 Cor.
7:16.

In first giving themselves to the
Lord. 2 Cor. 8:5.

In following Christ. Luke 14:27;
18:22.

In forsaking all for Christ.
Luke 5:11.

In giving a reason for their faith.
Exod. 12:26–27.

In hating life for Christ.
Luke 14:26.

In holy boldness. Ps. 119:46.

In holy conduct. 1 Pet. 2:12.

In holy conversation. Ps. 37:30,
with Prov. 10:31; Prov. 15:7;
Eph. 4:29; Col. 4:6.

In holy example. Matt. 5:16;
Phil. 2:15; 1 Thess. 1:7.

In interceding for others. Col. 4:3;
Heb. 13:18; James 5:16.

In inviting others to embrace the
gospel. Ps. 34:8; Isa. 2:3;
John 1:46; 4:29.

In joyfully suffering for Christ.
Heb. 10:34.

In old age. Deut. 32:7; Ps. 71:18.

In openly confessing Christ.
Matt. 10:32.

In preferring Christ above all
relations. Luke 14:26; 1 Cor.
2:2.

In proclaiming God's praises.
Isa. 43:21.

In rebuking others. Lev. 19:17;
Eph. 5:11.

In seeking the edification of others.
Rom. 14:19; 15:2;
1 Thess. 5:11.

With a superabundant generosity.
Exod. 36:5–7; 2 Cor. 8:3.

In talking of God and His works.
Pss. 71:24; 77:12; 119:27;
145:11–12.

In teaching and exhorting.
Pss. 34:11; 51:13; Col. 3:16;
Heb. 3:13; 10:25.

In their interaction with the world.
Matt. 5:16; Phil. 2:15–16;
1 Pet. 2:12.

In visiting and helping the poor
and the sick. Lev. 25:35;
Ps. 112:9, with 2 Cor. 9:9;
Matt. 25:36; Acts 20:35;
James 1:27.

In youth. Pss. 71:17; 148:12–13.

With a willing heart. Exod. 35:29;
1 Chron. 29:9, 14.

Blessedness of. Dan. 12:3.

Encouragement to. Prov. 11:25, 30;
1 Cor. 1:27; James 5:19–20.

Faithful stewards. 1 Pet. 4:10–11.

Follow the example of Christ.
Acts 10:38.

However weak. 1 Cor. 1:27.

Illustrated. Matt. 25:14; Luke 19:13,
etc.

An imperative duty. John 5:23;
Luke 19:40.

Principle of. 2 Cor. 5:14–15.

Their calling as believers.
Exod. 19:6; 1 Pet. 2:9.

Women and children as well as men.
Ps. 8:2; Prov. 31:26;
Matt. 21:15–16; Phil. 4:3;
1 Tim. 5:10; Titus 2:3–5;
1 Pet. 3:1.

Zeal of idolaters should provoke.
Jer. 7:18.

MISSIONARY WORK BY MINISTERS

According to the purpose of God.
Luke 24:46–47; Gal. 1:15–16;
Col. 1:25–27.

Aid those engaged in. Rom. 16:1–2;
2 Cor. 11:9; 3 John 1:5–8.

Be ready to engage in. Isa. 6:8.

Christ engaged in. Matt. 4:17, 23;
11:1; Mark 1:38–39; Luke 8:1.

Christ sent His disciples to labor in.
Mark 3:14; 6:7; Luke 10:1–11.

Commanded. Matt. 28:19;
Mark 16:15.

Directed by the Holy Spirit.
Acts 13:2.

Excellency of. Isa. 52:7, with
Rom. 10:15.

God qualifies for.
Exod. 3:11, 18; 4:11–12, 15;
Isa. 6:5–9.

God strengthens for. Jer. 1:7–9.

Guilt and danger of shrinking
from. Jon. 1:3–4.

Harmony should characterize those
engaged in. Gal. 2:9.

Holy Spirit calls to. Acts 13:2.

No limits to the sphere of. Isa. 11:9;
Mark 16:15; Rev. 14:6.

Obligations to engage in.
Acts 4:19–20; Rom. 1:13–15;
1 Cor. 9:16.

Opportunities for, not to be
neglected. 1 Cor. 16:9.

Required. Luke 10:2;
Rom. 10:14–15.

Requires wisdom and meekness.
Matt. 10:16.

Success of
A cause of joy. Acts 15:3.
A cause of praise. Acts 11:18;
21:19–20.

To be prayed for. Eph. 6:18–19;
Col. 4:3.

Warranted by predictions concerning
the pagan, etc. Isa. 42:10–12;
66:19.

Worldly concerns should not delay.
Luke 9:59–62.

MITE

About one-fifth of a cent.
Mark 12:42.

Widow's. Luke 21:2.

MOB

At Ephesus. Acts 19:29–40.

At Jerusalem. Acts 21:28, 30.

At Thessalonica. Acts 17:5.

MOCKING

The Ammonites mock God.
Ezek. 25:3.

Believers endure, because of their
Being children of God. Gen. 21:9,
with Gal. 4:29.
Enthusiasm for God's house.
Neh. 2:19.
Faith. Heb. 11:36.
Faithfulness in declaring the Word
of God. Jer. 20:7–8.
Uprightness. Job 12:4.

Calamity denounced against.
Isa. 5:18–19.

Characteristic of the latter days.
2 Pet. 3:3; Jude 18.

Children mock Elisha. 2 Kings 2:23.

Christ endured. Matt. 9:24; 27:29.

Drunkards addicted to. Ps. 69:12;
Hos. 7:5.

Elijah mocks the priests of Baal.
1 Kings 18:27.

Idolaters addicted to. Isa. 57:3–6.

The persecutors of Jesus mock Him.
Matt. 26:67–68;
27:28–31, 39–44.
Punishment for. Prov. 19:29;
Isa. 29:20; Lam. 3:64–66.
Sufferings of Christ by, predicted.
Ps. 22:6–8; Isa. 53:3;
Luke 18:32.

Those who are addicted to
Are avoided by believers. Ps. 1:1;
Jer. 15:17.
Are belligerent. Prov. 22:10.
Are hated by men. Prov. 24:9.
Are proud and arrogant.
Prov. 21:24.
Are ridiculed by God. Prov. 3:34.
Bring others into danger.
Prov. 29:8.
Delight in. Prov. 1:22.
Do not go to the wise.
Prov. 15:12.
Do not hear reprimand.
Prov. 13:1.
Do not love those who reprimand.
Prov. 15:12.
Follow their own desires.
2 Pet. 3:3.
Hate those who reprimand.
Prov. 9:8.
Will themselves endure.
Ezek. 23:32.
The tormentors of Job mock.
Job 16:12; 30:1.
Tyre mocks Jerusalem. Ezek. 26:2.
Used in a figurative sense.
Prov. 1:26.

The wicked indulge in, against
All solemn warnings.
2 Chron. 30:6–10.
Believers. Ps. 123:4; Lam. 3:14,
63.
The gifts of the Spirit. Acts 2:13.

God's ministers. 2 Chron. 36:16.
God's ordinances. Lam. 1:7.
God's threatenings. Isa. 5:19; Jer.
17:15.
The resurrection of the dead. Acts
17:32.
The second coming of Christ.
2 Pet. 3:3–4.
The wicked mock. Isa. 28:15, 22;
2 Pet. 3:3.
Zedekiah mocks Micaiah.
1 Kings 22:24.

MODESTY

Examples of
Elihu. Job 32:4–7.
Saul. 1 Sam. 9:21.
Vashti. Esther 1:11–12.
Of women. 1 Tim. 2:9.

MOLDING

Of images. Exod. 32:4, 8.

MOMENT

Afflictions last but a. 2 Cor. 4:17.
Divine anger endures but a. Ps. 30:5.
We are kept every. Isa. 27:3.
We will be changed in a.
1 Cor. 15:52.

MONEY

Brass introduced as, by the Romans.
Matt. 10:9.
Changing of, a trade. Matt. 21:12;
John 2:15.
Custom of presenting a piece of.
Job 42:11.
Gold and silver used as. Gen. 13:2;
Num. 22:18.
Jews forbidden to take interest for.
Lev. 25:37.

Of the Jews regulated by the standard
of the sanctuary. Lev. 5:15;
Num. 3:47.
Love of, the root of all evil.
1 Tim. 6:10.

Pieces of, mentioned
Fourth of a shekel. 1 Sam. 9:8.
Gerah, the twentieth of a shekel.
Num. 3:47.
Half shekel or bekah.
Exod. 30:15.
Mite. Mark 12:42; Luke 21:2.
Penny. Matt. 5:26; 20:2;
Mark 6:37; Luke 12:6.
Pound. Luke 19:13.
Shekel of silver. Judg. 17:10;
2 Kings 15:20.
Talent of gold. 1 Kings 9:14;
2 Kings 23:33.
Talent of silver. 1 Kings 16:24;
2 Kings 5:22–23.
Third of a shekel. Neh. 10:32.
Power and usefulness of.
Eccles. 7:12; 10:19.
Of the Romans, stamped with the
image of Caesar. Matt. 22:20–21.
Usually taken by weight.
Gen. 23:16; Jer. 32:10.
Was current with the merchants.
Gen. 23:16.

Was given
As alms. 1 Sam. 2:36;
Acts 3:3, 6.
As offerings. 2 Kings 12:7–9;
Neh. 10:32.
As wages. Ezra 3:7; Matt. 20:2;
James 5:4.
For lands. Gen. 23:9; Acts 4:37.
For merchandise. Gen. 43:12;
Deut. 2:6.
For slaves. Gen. 37:28;
Exod. 21:21.

For tribute. 2 Kings 23:33;
Matt. 22:19.

MONEY CHANGERS
Jesus drives out of the temple.
Matt. 21:12.

MONOPOLY
Of food. Prov. 11:26.
Of lands. Isa. 5:8; Mic. 2:2.
By Pharaoh. Gen. 47:19–26.

MONOTHEISM
Christ and His Father are one.
John 10:30.
The Holy Spirit is sent by Father and
Son. John 14:16; 15:26.
The Holy Spirit is the Spirit of God
and of Christ. Rom. 8:9, 14;
1 Cor. 3:16.
There is only one God. Deut. 4:39;
6:4; 1 Cor. 8:4, 6; Eph. 4:5–6.

MONTHS
Commenced with first appearance of
new moon. Num. 10:10, with
Ps. 81:3.
Idolaters make predictions by.
Isa. 47:13.
The Jews computed time by.
Judg. 11:37; 1 Sam. 6:1;
1 Kings 4:7.

Names of the twelve
First, Nisan or Abib. Exod. 13:4;
Neh. 2:1.
Second, Zif. 1 Kings 6:1, 37.
Third, Sivan. Esther 8:9.
Fourth, Thammuz. Zech. 8:19.
Fifth, Ab. Zech. 7:3.
Sixth, Ehul. Neh. 6:15.
Seventh, Ethanim. 1 Kings 8:2.
Eighth, Bul. 1 Kings 6:38.
Ninth, Chisleu. Zech. 7:1.

Tenth, Tebeth. Esther 2:16.
Eleventh, Sebat. Zech. 1:7.
Twelfth, Adar. Ezra 6:15; Esther
3:7.
Observance of, condemned.
Gal. 4:10.
Originally had no names. Gen. 7:11;
8:4.
Patriarchs computed time by.
Gen. 29:14.
Sun and moon designed to mark out.
Gen. 1:14.
Year composed of twelve.
1 Chron. 27:2–15; Esther 2:12;
Rev. 22:2.

MOON, THE

Appointed
For the benefit of all. Deut. 4:19.
To divide day from night.
Gen. 1:14.
For a light in the heavens.
Gen. 1:15.
To light the earth by night.
Jer. 31:35.
By an ordinance forever.
Pss. 72:5, 7; 89:37;
Jer. 31:36.
To rule the night. Gen. 1:16;
Ps. 136:9.
For signs and seasons. Gen. 1:14;
Ps. 104:19.
Called the lesser light. Gen. 1:16.
Created by God. Gen. 1:14; Ps. 8:3.

Described as
Bright. Job 31:26.
Fair. Song of Sol. 6:10.
First appearance of, a time of
festivity. 1 Sam. 20:5–6;
Ps. 81:3.
Has a glory of its own. 1 Cor. 15:41.

Illustrative of
Changeableness of the world.
Rev. 12:1.
Deep calamities (when
withdrawing its light). Isa. 13:10;
Joel 2:10; 3:15; Matt. 24:29.
Fairness of the church. Song of
Sol. 6:10.
Glory of Christ in the church.
Isa. 60:20.
Judgments (when becoming as
blood). Rev. 6:12.
Influences vegetation. Deut. 33:14.
Insanity attributed to the influence of.
Ps. 121:6, with Matt. 4:24.
Made to glorify God. Ps. 148:3.

Miracles connected with
Signs in, before the destruction of
Jerusalem. Luke 21:25.
Standing still in Ajalon.
Josh. 10:12–13.
Worshiped as the queen of heaven.
Jer. 7:18; 41:17–19, 25.

Worshiping of
Condemned as atheism.
Job 31:26, 28.
Forbidden to the Jews.
Deut. 4:19.
Jews often guilty of. 2 Kings 23:5;
Jer. 8:2.
Jews punished for. Jer. 8:1–3.
To be punished with death.
Deut. 17:3–6.

MORAL DECLINE

At end of age. Matt. 24:12, 37;
2 Tim. 3:1–5.
Lack of morals. Gal. 5:19–21;
Eph. 5:3–5; Col. 3:5–6;
1 Tim. 1:9–10.

MORALITY
Characterizes the kingdom of God, and the new heavens and new earth. Rom. 14:17; 2 Pet. 3:13.

Conscience.
Accuses or excuses.
Rom. 2:14–15.
Clear. Acts 24:16;
1 Pet. 3:16, 21.
Defiled. Titus 1:15.
Good. Acts 23:1; 1 Tim. 1:19.
Renewed. Rom. 12:2.
Seared. 1 Tim. 4:2.
Weak. 1 Cor. 8:7–13.

Described
Fruit of the Spirit. Gal. 5:22–23.
Qualifications of Christian leaders.
1 Tim. 3:1–13;
2 Tim. 2:24–25;
Titus 1:5–9.
Things pertaining to life.
2 Pet. 1:3, 5–7.
Things to be thought. Phil. 4:8.
Enlightens the darkness. Isa. 58:10.
Exalts a nation. Prov. 14:34;
Isa. 26:2.

Examples of
Sermon on the Mount. Matt. 5–7.
Ten Commandments.
Exod. 20:1–17; Deut. 5:6–21.
The heart of religion. Mic. 6:6–8.
Indispensable for Christians.
Matt. 5:47; 1 John 2:29.

Nature of God
Good. Ps. 119:68.
Holy. Lev. 19:2; 1 Pet. 1:15–16.
Loving. 1 John 3:16; 4:7–8.
Righteous. Ps. 89:14–16;
Jer. 23:6; Rom. 10:3.
Wise. Eph. 3:10.

Prescribed by God. Prov. 3:1, 2;
Titus 2:7; Heb. 13:20–21.
Profitability of Scripture.
2 Tim. 3:16–17.
Religious ceremony useless without.
Amos 5:21, 24.
Word of God for instruction.
Ps. 119:9–16, 105.

Value of
Find favor and good repute with God and man. Prov. 3:1–4.
Gain life. Prov. 1:32–33.
Influence others. Phil. 2:15.

MORNING
Began with first dawn. Josh. 6:15;
Ps. 119:147.
Continued until noon.
1 Kings 18:26; Neh. 8:3.
First dawning of, called the eyelids of.
Job 3:9; 41:18.
First part of the natural day.
Mark 16:2.

Illustrative of
Glory of Christ (star of).
Rev. 22:16.
Glory of the church (when breaking forth).
Song of Sol. 6:10; Isa. 58:8.
Heavy calamities (spread upon the mountains). Joel 2:2.
Rapid movements (wings of).
Ps. 139:9.
Resurrection day. Ps. 49:14.
Reward of believers (star of).
Rev. 2:28.
Short–lived profession of hypocrites (clouds in). Hos. 6:4.

The Jews
Ate little in. Eccles. 10:16.

Began their journeys in.
Gen. 22:3.

Contracted covenants in.
Gen. 26:31.

Devoted a part of, to prayer and
praise. Pss. 5:3; 59:16; 88:13.

Gathered the manna in.
Exod. 16:21.

Generally rose early in.
Gen. 28:18; Judg. 6:28.

Held courts of justice in.
Jer. 21:12; Matt. 27:1.

Offered a part of the daily sacrifice
in. Exod. 29:38–39;
Num. 28:4–7.

Transacted business in.
Eccles. 11:6; Matt. 20:1.

Went to the temple in.
Luke 21:38; John 8:2.

Ordained by God. Job 38:12.

Outgoings of, made to rejoice.
Ps. 65:8.

A red sky in, a sign of bad weather.
Matt. 16:3.

Second part of the day at the
creation.
Gen. 1:5, 8, 13, 19, 23, 31.

Ushered in by the morning star.
Job 38:7.

Was frequently cloudless.
2 Sam. 23:4.

MORTAR

A cement. Exod. 1:14.

An instrument for pulverizing grains.
Num. 11:8; Prov. 27:22.

Makeshift, temporary.
Ezek. 13:10–15; 22:28.

Tar used as, in building the Tower of
Babel. Gen. 11:3.

To be trodden to make firm.
Nah. 3:14.

Used in a figurative sense.
Isa. 41:25.

Used to plaster houses.
Lev. 14:42, 45.

MORTGAGE

On land. Neh. 5:3.

MORTIFICATION

Examples of
David's ambassadors, sent to
Hanun. 2 Sam. 10:1–5.
Judas. Matt. 27:3–5.

MOSES, LAW OF

Additions made to, in the plains of
Moab by Jordan. Num. 36:13.

All Israelites required
To know. Exod. 18:16.
To lay up in their hearts.
Deut. 6:6; 11:18.
To observe. Deut. 4:6; 6:2.
To remember. Mal. 4:4.
To teach their children. Deut. 6:7;
11:19.

Book of, laid up in the Sanctuary.
Deut. 31:26.

A burdensome yoke. Acts 15:10.

Called
Book of Moses. 2 Chron. 25:4;
35:12.
Book of the law. Deut. 30:10;
Josh. 1:8.
A fiery law. Deut. 33:2.
Lively oracles. Acts 7:38.
Ministry of condemnation.
2 Cor. 3:9.
Ministry of death. 2 Cor. 3:7.
Royal law. James 2:8.
Word spoken by angels. Heb. 2:2.

Christ

Abrogated, as a covenant of
works. Rom. 7:4.

Attended all feasts of.
John 2:23; 7:2, 10, 37.

Bore the curse of. Deut. 21:23,
with Gal. 3:13.

Came not to destroy but to fulfill.
Matt. 5:17–18.

Circumcised according to.
Luke 2:21; Rom. 15:8.

Fulfilled all laws of. Ps. 40:7–8.

Fulfilled all types and shadows of.
Heb. 9:8, 11–14; 10:1, 11–14.

Made under. Gal. 4:4.

Magnified and made honorable.
Isa. 42:41.

Contrasted with the grace of God.
John 1:17; *(See also*
Rom. 8:3–4.)

Could not annul the covenant of
grace made in Christ. Gal. 3:17.

Could not give righteousness and life.
Gal. 3:21, with Rom. 8:3–4;
Heb. 10:1.

A covenant of works to the Jews as a
nation. Deut. 28:1, 15, with
Jer. 31:32.

Darkness, etc., at giving of,
illustrative of obscurity of Mosaic
covenant. Heb. 12:18–24.

Divided into

Ceremonial, relating to manner of
worshiping God. Lev. 7:37–38;
Heb. 9:1–7.

Civil, relating to administration of
justice. Deut. 17:9–11;
Acts 23:3; 24:6.

Moral, embodied in the Ten
Commandments. Deut. 5:22;
10:4.

Entire, written in a book. Deut. 31:9.

Given

After the Exodus. Deut. 4:45;
Ps. 81:4–5.

At Horeb. Deut. 4:10, 15; 5:2.

By ministry of angels. Acts 7:53.

From Mount Sinai.
Exod. 19:11, 20.

In the desert. Ezek. 20:10–11.

Through Moses as mediator.
Deut. 5:5, 27–28; John 1:17;
Gal. 3:19.

To no other nation. Deut. 4:8;
Ps. 147:20.

To the Jews. Lev. 26:46;
Ps. 78:5.

Good kings enforced.
2 Kings 23:24–25;
2 Chron. 31:21.

The Jews

Accused Christians of speaking.
Acts 6:11–14; 21:28.

Accused Christ of breaking.
John 19:7.

Broke it themselves. John 7:19.

Dishonored God by breaking.
Rom. 2:23.

From regard to, rejected Christ.
Rom. 9:31–33.

Held those ignorant of, accursed.
John 7:49.

Will be judged by. John 5:45;
Rom. 2:12.

Zealous for. John 9:28–29;
Acts 21:20.

Kings to write out and study.
Deut. 17:18–19.

The law of God. Lev. 26:46.

A means of national reformation.
2 Chron. 34:19–21;
Neh. 8:13–18.

None to approach the mount while
God gave. Exod. 19:13, 21–24;
Heb. 12:20.

Priests and Levites to teach.
Deut. 33:8–10; Neh. 8:7;
Mal. 2:7.
Primitive Jewish converts would have
all Christians observe. Acts 15:1.
Public instruction given to youth in.
Luke 2:46; Acts 22:3.

Publicly read
By Ezra. Neh. 8:2–3.
At the feast of tabernacles in the
sabbatical year.
Deut. 31:10–13.
By Joshua. Josh. 8:34–35.
In the synagogues every Sabbath.
Acts 13:15; 15:21.
Rehearsed by Moses. Deut. 1:1–3.
Remarkable phenomena connected
with, at giving. Exod. 19:16–19.
A tutor to lead to Christ. Gal. 3:24.
Scribes were learned in, and
expounded. Ezra 7:6; Matt. 23:2.
A shadow of good things to come.
Heb. 10:1.
Tables of, laid up in the ark.
Deut. 10:5.

Taught the Jews
All punishments awarded
according to. John 8:5; 19:7;
Heb. 10:28.
To love and fear God.
Deut. 6:5; 10:12–13;
Matt. 22:36, 38.
To love their neighbor.
Lev. 19:18; Matt. 22:39.
Strict justice and impartiality.
Lev. 19:35–36.
Terror of Israel at receiving.
Exod. 19:16; 20:18–20;
Deut. 5:5, 23–25.

MOTE
A small particle. Matt. 7:3–5.

MOTH
An insect. Job 4:19; 27:18;
Ps. 39:11.
Destructive of garments. Job 13:28;
Isa. 50:9; 51:8; Hos. 5:12.
Used in a figurative sense.
Matt. 6:19–20; James 5:2.

MOTHER
Blessings of. Ps. 113:9; Isa. 40:11.
Comfort of. Isa. 66:12–13.
Duties of. Prov. 31:26–27, 30;
Titus 2:4
Gift of God. Ps. 113:9.
Praised by her family. Prov. 31:28.
To be honored and cared for.
Gen. 32:11; Prov. 23:22;
John 19:27; Eph. 6:2.
Tribute to. Prov. 31:1–31.

MOTHER-IN-LAW
Not to be defiled. Lev. 18:17.
Loved by Ruth. Ruth 1:14–17.
Peter's, healed by Jesus.
Mark 1:30–31.

MOTIVE
Ascribe to God. Ps. 106:8;
Ezek. 36:21–22, 32.

Misunderstood
David's, by King Hanun.
2 Sam. 10:2–3;
1 Chron. 19:3–4.
Job's, in his righteousness.
Job 1:9–11; 2:4–5.
The king of Syria, in sending
presents to the king of Israel by
Naaman. 2 Kings 5:5–7.
The tribes of Reuben and Gad, in
asking inheritance east of the
Jordan. Num. 32:1–33.
When they built the memorial.
Josh 22:9–34.

Right, required. Matt. 6:1–18.
Sinful, illustrated by Cain. Gen. 4:7;
1 John 3:12.

MOUNTAINS

Abounded with
Deer. 1 Chron. 12:8;
Song of Sol. 2:8.
Forests. 2 Kings 19:23;
2 Chron. 2:2, 8–10.
Game. 1 Sam. 26:20.
Herbs. Prov. 27:25.
Minerals. Deut. 8:9.
Precious things. Deut. 33:15.
Spices. Song of Sol. 4:6; 8:14.
Stone for building.
1 Kings 5:14, 17; Dan. 2:45.
Vineyards. 2 Chron. 26:10;
Jer. 31:5.
Wild beasts. Song of Sol. 4:8;
Hab. 2:17.

Afforded
Pasture land. Exod. 3:1;
1 Sam. 25:7; 1 Kings 22:17;
Ps. 147:8; Amos 4:1.
Refuge in time of danger.
Gen. 14:10; Judg. 6:2;
Matt. 24:16; Heb. 11:38.
Beacons or banners often raised
upon. Isa. 13:2; 30:17.

Called
Ancient mountains. Deut. 33:15.
Everlasting hills. Gen. 49:26.
Everlasting mountains. Hab. 3:6.
God's mountains. Isa. 49:11.
Perpetual hills. Hab. 3:6.
Pillars of heaven. Job 26:11.
Canaan abounded in. Deut. 11:11.
Collect the vapors which ascend from
the earth. Ps. 104:6, 8.
Defenses. Ps. 125:2.

Elevated parts of the earth.
Gen. 7:19–20.

God
Causes to melt. Judg. 5:5;
Ps. 97:5; Isa. 64:1, 3.
Causes to skip. Ps. 114:4, 6.
Causes to smoke. Pss. 104:32;
144:5.
Causes to tremble. Nah. 1:5;
Hab. 3:10.
Formed. Amos 4:13.
Gives strength to. Ps. 95:4.
Makes waste. Isa. 42:15.
Overturns. Job 9:5; 28:9.
Parches with drought. Hag. 1:11.
Removes. Job 9:5.
Scatters. Hab. 3:6.
Set fast. Ps. 65:6.
Sets the foundations of, on fire.
Deut. 32:22.
Waters, from his chambers.
Ps. 104:13.
Weighs, in a balance. Isa. 40:12.

Illustrative of
Abundance (when dripping wine).
Amos 9:13.
The church of God. Isa. 2:2;
Dan. 2:35, 44–45.
Desolation (when made waste).
Isa. 42:15; Mal. 1:3.
Destructive enemies (when
burning). Jer. 51:25; Rev. 8:8.
Difficulties. Isa. 40:4; Zech. 4:7;
Matt. 17:20.
Exceeding joy (when breaking
forth into song). Isa. 44:23;
55:12.
God's righteousness. Ps. 36:6.
Heavy judgments (threshing of).
Isa. 41:15.
Persons in authority. Ps. 72:3;
Isa. 44:23.

Proud and haughty persons.
Isa. 2:14.
Made to glorify God. Ps. 148:9.
Many very high. Ps. 104:18;
Isa. 2:14.

Mentioned in Scripture
Abarim. Num. 33:47–48.
Amalek. Judg. 12:15.
Ararat. Gen. 8:4.
Bashan. Ps. 68:15.
Bethel. 1 Sam. 13:2.
Carmel. Josh. 15:55; 19:26;
2 Kings 19:23.
Ebal. Deut. 11:29; 27:13.
Ephraim. Josh. 17:15; Judg. 2:9.
Gerizim. Deut. 11:29; Judg. 9:7.
Gilboa. 1 Sam. 31:1; 2 Sam. 1:6,
21.
Gilead. Gen. 31:21, 25;
Song of Sol. 4:1.
Hachilah. 1 Sam. 23:19.
Hermon. Josh. 13:11.
Hor. Num. 20:22; 34:7–8.
Horeb. Exod. 3:1.
Lebanon. Deut. 3:25.
Mizar. Ps. 42:6.
Moroh. Judg. 7:1.
Moriah. Gen. 22:2; 2 Chron. 3:1.
Nebo (part of Abarim).
Num. 32:3; Deut. 34:1.
Olives, or mount of corruption.
1 Kings 11:7, with
2 Kings 23:13; Luke 21:37.
Pisgah (part of Abarim).
Num. 21:20; Deut. 34:1.
Seir. Gen. 14:6; 36:8.
Sinai. Exod. 19:2, 18, 20, 23;
31:18.
Sion. 2 Sam. 5:7.
Tabor. Judg. 4:6, 12, 14.
Often inhabited. Gen. 36:8;
Josh. 11:21.

Often selected as places for
idolatrous worship. Deut. 12:2;
2 Chron. 21:11.
Proclamations often made
from. Isa. 40:9.
Sometimes selected as places for
divine worship. Gen. 22:2, 5;
Exod. 3:12; Isa. 2:2.
Sources of springs and rivers.
Deut. 8:7; Ps. 104:8–10.
Volcanic fires of, alluded to.
Isa. 64:1–2; Jer. 51:25;
Nah. 1:5–6.

MOURNING
Abraham mourned for Sarah.
Gen. 23:2.

For calamities and other sorrows
Ashes put on the head.
Ezek. 27:30.
Covering the head and face.
2 Sam. 15:30.
Covering the upper lip.
Ezek. 24:17, 22.
Cutting or pulling out the hair and
beard. Ezra 9:3.
Dressing in black. Jer. 14:2.
Dust on the head. Josh. 7:6.
Laying aside ornaments.
Exod. 33:4, 6.
Laying the hand on the head.
2 Sam. 13:19; Jer. 2:37.
Sitting on the ground. Isa. 3:26.
Tearing the garments.
Gen. 37:29; Matt. 26:65;
Acts 14:14.
Walking barefoot. 2 Sam. 15:30;
Isa. 20:2.
Wearing mourning dress.
Gen. 38:14.
Caused ceremonial defilement.
Lev. 21:1; Num. 19:11–16;
31:19.

Cutting the flesh. Lev. 19:28;
   21:1–5; Deut. 14:1; Jer. 16:6–7;
   41:5.

David's lamentations
   Over the death of Saul and his
      sons. 2 Sam. 1:17–27.
   Over the death of Abner.
      2 Sam. 3:33–34.
   Over the death of Absalom.
      2 Sam. 18:33.
Egyptians for Jacob seventy days.
   Gen. 50:1–3.
Fasting. 1 Sam. 31:13;
   2 Sam. 1:12; 3:35.
Head uncovered. Lev. 10:6; 21:10.
Hired mourners. 2 Chron. 35:25;
   Matt. 9:23.
Israelites, for Aaron thirty days.
   Num. 20:29.
Jeremiah and the singing men and
   the singing women lament for
   Josiah. 2 Chron. 35:25.
Lamentations. Gen. 50:10;
   Exod. 12:30; 1 Sam. 30:4;
   Jer. 22:18; Matt. 2:17–18.
Lying on the ground. 2 Sam. 12:16.
Personal appearance neglected.
   2 Sam. 14:2.
Priests prohibited, except for nearest
   of kin. Lev. 21:1–11.
Prevented offerings from being
   accepted. Deut. 26:14; Hos. 9:4.
For Nadab and Abihu forbidden.
   Lev. 10:6.
Sexes separated in. Zech. 12:12, 14.

MOUTH
See Lips

MOWING
Grass. Ps. 72:6.

MULE
Tribute paid in. 1 Kings 10:25.
Used in barter. Ezek. 27:14.
Used by the captives in returning
   from Babylon. Ezra 2:66;
   Neh. 7:68.
Used in war. Zech. 14:15.

Uses of
   By believers in Isaiah's prophetic
      vision of the kingdom of Christ.
      Isa. 66:20.
   As pack animals. 2 Kings 5:17;
      1 Chron. 12:40.
   Ridden by messengers.
      Esther 8:10, 14.
   Royal riders. 2 Sam. 13:29; 18:9;
      1 Kings 1:33, 38.

MUNITIONS
Fortifications. Nah. 2:1.

MURDER
Believers
   Seek to avoid the guilt of.
      Ps. 51:14.
   Should warn others against.
      Gen. 37:22; Jer. 26:15.
   Specially warned against. 1 Pet.
      4:15.
Of believers, specially avenged.
   Deut. 32:43; Matt. 23:35;
   Rev. 18:20, 24.
A characteristic of the devil.
   John 8:44.
Comes from the heart. Matt. 15:19.
Connected with idolatry.
   Ezek. 22:3–4; 2 Kings 3:27.
Cries for vengeance. Gen. 4:10.

Defiles the
   Hands. Isa. 59:3.
   Land. Num. 35:33; Ps. 106:38.

Person and garments.
Lam. 4:13–14.

Described as killing
By the blow of a stone.
Num. 35:17.
By a hand weapon of wood.
Num. 35:18.
By an instrument of iron.
Num. 35:16.
By lying in wait. Num. 35:20;
Deut. 19:11.
From hatred. Num. 35:20–21;
Deut. 19:11.
With premeditation. Exod. 21:14.
Early introduction of. Gen. 4:8.
Excludes from heaven. Gal. 5:21;
Rev. 22:15.
Explained by Christ. Matt. 5:21–22.
Forbidden. Gen. 9:6; Exod. 20:13;
Deut. 5:17, with Rom. 13:9.
Forbidden by Mosaic law.
Exod. 20:13; Deut. 5:17.

God
Curses those guilty of. Gen. 4:11.
Hates. Prov. 6:16–17.
Rejects the prayers of those guilty
of. Isa. 1:15; 59:2–3.
Requires blood for. Gen. 9:5;
Num. 35:33; 1 Kings 2:32.
Will avenge. Deut. 32:43;
1 Kings 21:19; Ps. 9:12;
Hos. 1:4.
Hatred is. 1 John 3:15.
Imputed to the nearest city if
murderer unknown.
Deut. 21:1–3.
The Jews often guilty of. Isa. 1:21.
Killing a thief in the day, counted as.
Exod. 22:3.
The law made to restrain.
1 Tim. 1:9.

Mode of clearing those suspected of.
Deut. 21:3–9. (See Matt. 27:24.)
Not concealed from God. Isa. 26:21;
Jer. 2:34.
Often committed at night.
Neh. 6:10; Job 24:14.

Persons guilty of
Fearful and cowardly. Gen. 4:14.
Flee from God's presence.
Gen. 4:16.
Had no protection from altars.
Exod. 21:14.
Not protected in refuge cities.
Deut. 19:11–12.
Not to be pitied or spared.
Deut. 19:13.
Wanderers and vagabonds.
Gen. 4:14.

Punishment for
Curse of God. Gen. 4:11.
Death. Gen. 9:5–6; Exod. 21:12;
Num. 35:16, 30.
Inflicted by the nearest relative of
victim. Num. 35:19, 21.
Not to be commuted.
Num. 35:32.
Punishment of, not commuted under
the law. Num. 35:31.
Represented as a sin crying to
heaven. Gen. 4:10, with
Heb. 12:24; Rev. 6:10.
To be proved by at least two
witnesses. Num. 35:30;
Deut. 19:11, 15.
Why forbidden by God. Gen. 9:6.

The wicked
Devise. Gen. 27:41; 37:18.
Encourage others to commit.
1 Kings 21:8–10; Prov. 1:11.
Filled with. Rom. 1:29.
Have hands full of. Isa. 1:15.

Intent on. Jer. 22:17.
Lie in wait to commit.
Ps. 10:8–10.
Perpetrate. Job 24:14;
Ezek. 22:3.
Swift to commit. Prov. 1:16;
Rom. 3:15.
A work of the sinful nature.
Gal. 5:21.

MURMURING

Against
Christ. Luke 5:30; 15:2; 19:7;
John 6:41–43, 52.
Disciples of Christ. Mark 7:2;
Luke 5:30; 6:2.
God. Prov. 19:3.
Ministers of God. Exod. 17:3;
Num. 16:41.
The service of God. Mal. 3:14.
The sovereignty of God.
Rom. 9:19–20.
Believers cease from. Isa. 29:23–24.
A characteristic of the wicked.
Jude 10.
Forbidden. 1 Cor. 10:10; Phil. 2:14.
Guilt of encouraging others in.
Num. 13:31–33, with 14:36–37.
Illustrated. Matt. 20:11;
Luke 15:29–30.
Provokes God. Num. 14:2, 11;
Deut. 9:8, 22.
Punishment of.
Num. 11:1; 14:27–29;
16:45–46; Ps. 106:25–26.
Tempts God. Exod. 17:2.
Unreasonableness of. Lam. 3:39.

MUSIC

Appointed to be used in the temple.
1 Chron. 16:4–6; 23:5–6; 25:1;
2 Chron. 29:25.

Considered effective in dealing with
mental disorders.
1 Sam. 16:14–17, 23.
Custom of sending away friends with.
Gen. 3:27.
Designed to promote joy.
Eccles. 2:8, 10.

Divided into
Instrumental. Dan. 6:18.
Vocal. 2 Sam. 19:35; Acts 16:25.
Early invention of. Gen. 4:21.
Effects produced on the prophets of
old by. 1 Sam. 10:5–6.
Generally put aside in times of
affliction. Ps. 137:2–4;
Dan. 6:18.

Illustrative of
Calamities (when ceasing).
Isa. 24:8–9; Rev. 18:22.
Heavenly happiness. Rev. 5:8–9.
Joy and gladness. Zeph. 3:17;
Eph. 5:19.

Instruments
Great diversity of. Eccles. 2:8.
Invented by David. 1 Chron. 23:5;
2 Chron. 7:6.
The Jews celebrated for inventing.
Amos 6:5.
Made of brass. 1 Cor. 13:1.
Made of fir wood. 2 Sam. 6:5.
Made of horns of animals.
Josh 6:8.
Made of juniper wood.
1 Kings 10:12.
Made of silver. Num. 10:2.
Many with strings. Pss. 33:2;
150:4.
Often expensively ornamented.
Ezek. 28:13.

Instruments named

Cymbals. 1 Chron. 16:5; Ps. 150:5.

Cornet. Ps. 98:6; Hos. 5:8.

Dulcimer. Dan. 3:5.

Flute. Dan. 3:5.

Harp. Ps. 137:2; Isa. 14:11; Ezek. 26:13 Amos 5:23.

Lyre. Dan. 3:5.

Organ. Gen. 4:21; Job 21:12; Ps. 150:4.

Pipe. 1 Kings 1:40; Isa. 5:12; Jer. 48:36.

Psaltery. Pss. 33:2; 71:22.

Tambourine. 1 Sam. 10:5; Isa. 24:8.

Timbrel. Exod. 15:20; Ps. 68:25.

Trumpet. 2 Kings 11:14; 2 Chron. 29:27.

Movements of armies regulated by. Josh 6:8; 1 Cor. 14:8.

Used by the Jews

At consecration of temple. 2 Chron. 5:11–13.

At coronation of kings. 2 Chron. 23:11, 13.

At dedication of city walls. Neh. 12:27–28.

At laying foundation of temple. Ezra 3:9–10.

In commemorating great men. 1 Chron. 35:25.

In dances. Matt. 11:17; Luke 15:25.

In funeral ceremonies. Matt. 9:23.

In private entertainments. Isa. 5:12; Amos 6:5.

In religious feasts. 2 Chron. 30:21.

In sacred processions. 2 Sam. 6:4–5, 15; 1 Chron. 13:6–8; 15:27–28.

To celebrate victories. Exod. 15:20; 1 Sam. 18:6–7.

Used in idol worship. Dan. 3:5.

Vanity of all unsanctified. Eccles. 2:8, 11.

MUTABILITY

God has not. Pss. 89:34; 102:25; Mal. 3:6; James 1:17.

Heavens have. Isa. 34:4; Ps. 102:25–26; Heb. 1:12.

Times and seasons have. Dan. 2:20–21.

Universe has. 2 Pet. 3:10; Rev. 21:1.

Visible things have. 2 Cor. 4:18.

World has. 1 Cor. 7:31.

MUTINY

Israelites against Moses. Num. 14:4.

MYRRH

Given at Christ's birth. Matt. 2:11.

Offered at Christ's death. Mark 15:23.

Used in Christ's tomb. John 19:39–40.

MYSTERY

Of the faith. 1 Tim. 3:9.

Of God. Deut. 21:29; Rom. 11:33.

Of godliness. 1 Tim. 3:16.

Of heaven. 1 Cor. 2:9.

Of iniquity. 2 Thess. 2:7.

Of our coming transformation. 1 Cor. 15:51.

NAIL

Jael kills Sisera with. Judg. 4:21.
Made of iron. 1 Chron. 22:3.
Made of gold. 2 Chron. 3:9.
Used in a figurative sense. Ezra 9:8;
Isa. 22:23, 25; Zech. 10:4.

NAME

Of believers
In the book of life. Phil. 4:3.
Everlasting. Isa. 56:5.
Written in heaven. Luke 10:20.

Of God
Blessed. Ps. 72:19.
Eternal. Ps. 135:13.
Excellent. Ps. 148:13.
Glorious. Isa. 63:14; Deut. 28:58.
Great. Mal. 1:11.
Holy. Ps. 99:3.
Not to be taken in vain.
Exod. 20:7.
Importance of good. Prov. 22:1;
Eccles. 7:1.

Of Jesus Christ
Above every name. Eph. 3:15;
Phil. 2:9–10; Heb. 1:4.
We are baptized in. Acts 2.38,
8:16.
We are saved by. Acts 4.12.
We have life in. John 20:31.
We may pray in. John 14:13.
We should gather in. Matt. 18:20.
Wonderful. Isa. 9:6.

NATIONS

All one blood, Acts 17:26.
All will serve God. Ps. 72:11.

Divided after building the Tower of
Babel. Gen. 11:8.
Glory to be brought into the New
Jerusalem. Rev. 21:24.
Insignificant compared to God.
Isa. 40:15.
Israel separated from other.
Lev. 20:24.
Redeemed are from every nation.
Rev. 5:9.

NATURALIZATION

Used in a spiritual sense.
Eph. 2:12, 19.

NATURE, HUMAN

Assumed by Christ. John 1:14;
Phil. 2:7.
Born to trouble. Job 5:7.
Created by God. Gen. 1:26.
Crowned with honor. Pss. 8:5; 21:5.
Lower than angels. Ps. 8:5.

NATURE OF CHRISTIANS

See Christians, Nature of

NAVIGATION

Sounding in. Acts 27:28.

NAVEL

Treatment of, at birth. Ezek. 16:4.

NAVY

Of Chittim. Dan. 11:30, 40.
Hiram's. 1 Kings 10:11.
Solomon's. 1 Kings 9:26.

NAZARITES

On completion of vow, to
Be brought to tabernacle door.
Num. 6:13.
Have the left shoulder of the ram
of the peace offering waved
upon their hands by the priest.
Num. 6:19–20, with Lev. 7:32.
Offer sacrifices. Num. 6:14–17.
Shave their heads. Num. 6:18;
Acts 18:18; 21:24.

Different kinds of
By a particular vow. Num. 6:2.
From the womb. Judg. 13:5;
Luke 1:15.

If defiled during vow, to
Bring two turtledoves for a burnt
offering. Num. 6:10–11.
Repay their vow with a trespass
offering. Num. 6:12.
Shave the head the seventh day.
Num. 6:9.

Illustrative of
Christ. Heb. 7:26.
Believers. 2 Cor. 6:17; James
1:27.
Persons separated to the service of
God. Num. 6:2.

Prohibited from
Cutting or shaving the head.
Num. 6:5; Judg. 13:5; 16:17.
Defiling themselves by the dead.
Num. 6:6–7.
Grapes or anything made from the
vine. Num. 6:3–4; Judg. 13:14.
Wine or strong drink. Num. 6:3;
Luke 1:15.
Raised up for the good of the
nation. Amos 2:11.
Required to be holy. Num. 6:8.

Ungodly Jews tried to corrupt.
Amos 2:12.
Valued pure. Lam. 4:7.

NECROMANCY

Warnings against. Deut. 18:11;
26:14; Isa. 8:19; 29:4.
The witch of Endor.
1 Sam. 28:7–19.

NEEDLE

Eye of. Matt. 19:24.

NEEDY, THE

The early church cared for.
Acts 4:35; Rom. 12:13.
Jesus helped. Matt. 9:12.
The Lord regards.
Pss. 40:17; 102:17.
We are to aid. Deut. 15:11; 24:14;
Matt. 25:34–40.
The wicked trample. Job 24:4;
Isa. 10:2; Amos 8:6.

NEIGHBOR

Care for. Prov. 3:28–29;
Matt. 25:34–46; Luke 10:25–37.

NEPOTISM

Of David. 2 Sam. 8:16; 19:13.
Of Joseph. Gen. 47:11–12.
Of Nehemiah. Neh. 7:2.
Of Saul. 1 Sam. 14:50.

NEST

Bird's in a rock. Num. 24:21.
Birds rouse. Deut. 32:11.

NET

Fish caught in. Matt. 4:18–21;
13:47; Luke 5:4; John 21:6–11.
Hidden in a pit. Psalm 35:7–8.
Of lattice work. 1 Kings 7:17.

Set for birds. Prov. 1:17.
Set for wild animals. Isa. 51:20.

NEW BIRTH
All believers partake of.
  Rom. 8:16–17; 1 Pet. 2:2;
  1 John 5:1.
Connected with adoption.
  Isa. 43:6–7; John 1:12–13.
Corruption of human nature
  requires. John 3:6; Rom. 8:7–8.

Described as
  Circumcision of the heart,
    Deut. 30:6, with Rom. 2:29;
    Col. 2:11.
  The inward man. Rom. 7:22;
    2 Cor. 4:16.
  A new creation. 2 Cor. 5:17;
    Gal. 6:15; Eph. 2:10.
  A new heart. Ezek. 36:26.
  A new spirit. Ezek. 11:19;
    Rom. 6:6.
  Newness of life. Rom. 6:4.
  Partaking of the divine nature.
    2 Pet. 1:4.
  Putting on the new man.
    Eph. 4:24.
  A spiritual resurrection.
    Rom. 6:4–6; Eph. 2:1, 5;
    Col. 2:12; 3:1.
  The washing of regeneration.
    Titus 3:5.

Effected by
  Christ. 1 John 2:29.
  God. John 1:13; 1 Pet. 1:3.
  The Holy Spirit. John 3:6;
    Titus 3:5.

Evidenced by
  Brotherly love. 1 John 4:7.
  Faith in Christ. 1 John 5:1.
  Righteousness. 1 John 2:29.

For the glory of God. Isa. 43:7.
The ignorant question. John 3:4.
Manner of bringing about illustrated.
  John 3:8.
Of the mercy of God. Titus 3:5.
None can enter heaven without.
  John 3:3.
Preserves from Satan's devices.
  1 John 5:18.

Produces
  Delight in God's law. Rom. 7:22.
  Hatred of sin. 1 John 3:9; 5:18.
  Knowledge of God. Jer. 24:7;
    Col. 3:10.
  Likeness to Christ. Rom. 8:29;
    2 Cor. 3:18; 1 John 3:2.
  Likeness to God. Eph. 4:24;
    Col. 3:10.
  Victory over the world.
    1 John 5:4.

Through the instrumentality of
  The ministry of the gospel.
    1 Cor. 4:15.
  The resurrection of Christ.
    1 Pet. 1:3.
  The Word of God. James 1:18;
    1 Pet. 1:23.
Of the will of God. James 1:18.

NEW MOON, FEAST OF
Celebrated with blowing of trumpets.
  Num. 10:10; Ps. 8:3–4.
Disliked by the ungodly. Amos 8·5
Held first day of the month.
  Num. 10:10.
The Jews deprived of, for sin.
  Hos. 2:11.
Mere outward observance of, hateful
  to God. Isa. 1:13–14.
Observance of, by Christians,
  condemned. Col. 2:16, with
  Gal. 4:10.

Observed with great seriousness.
1 Chron. 23:31; 2 Chron. 2:4;
8:13; 31:3.

Restored after captivity. Ezra 3:5;
Neh. 10:33.

Sacrifices at. Num. 28:11–15.

A season for
Entertainments. 1 Sam. 20:5, 18.
Inquiring of God's messengers.
2 Kings 4:23.
Worship in God's house.
Isa. 66:23; Ezek. 46:1.

NEW NATURE
See Christians, Nature (New) of

NEWS (MEDIA-REPORTING)

Examples of
Bad news. Num. 13:32;
2 Sam. 1:19–20; Jer. 4:15–16.
Good news. Prov. 25:25;
Isa. 52:7; Jer. 50:2; Mark 7:36;
Luke 8:1, 39.

Heralds
Angelic. Luke 2:10–14.
Human. 1 Sam 31:9;
2 Chron. 30:6, 10; Esther 3:15;
8:14; Jer. 51:31; Hab 2:2.
With standard. Jer. 50:2.

Influence of
To disseminate information.
Neh. 8:15; Jer. 51:31.
To incite. 2 Sam. 1:20.
To prompt action. Num. 13:26;
Judg. 19:29–30;
2 Chron. 30:6–9; 36:22–23;
Esther 1:20, 22; 3:14–15;
8:13; Jer. 4:5; Luke 2:1.
To uplift. Prov 15:30; 25:25.

Injunctions regarding
Speak the truth. Prov 8:7; 12:17;
Eph 4:25.

NIGHT
Began at sunset. Gen. 28:11.
Belongs to God. Ps. 74:16.
Caused by God. Ps. 104:20.
Continued until sunrise. Ps. 104:22;
Matt. 28:1, with Mark 16:2.
The darkness first called. Gen. 1:5.
Designed for rest. Ps. 104:23.
Divided into four watches by the
Romans. Luke 12:38, with
Matt. 14:25; Mark 13:35.
Eastern fishermen continued their
employment during. Luke 5:5;
John 21:3.
Eastern shepherds watched over
their flocks during. Gen. 31:40;
Luke 2:8.
Favorable to the purposes of the
wicked. Gen. 31:39;
Job 24:14–15; Obad. 1:5;
1 Thess. 5:2.

Frequently
Accompanied by heavy dews.
Num. 11:9; Judg. 6:38, 40;
Job 29:19; Song of Sol. 5:2.
Cold and frosty. Gen. 31:40;
Jer. 36:30.
Very dark. Prov. 7:9.

God frequently
Executed His judgments in.
Exod. 12:12; 2 Kings 19:35;
Job 27:20; Dan. 5:30.
Revealed His will in. Gen. 31:24;
46:2; Num. 22:20; Dan. 7:2.
Visited His people in. 1 Kings 3:5;
Ps. 17:3.
Heavenly bodies designed to
separate day from. Gen. 1:14.

Illustrative of

Death. John 9:4.

Seasons of severe calamities.
Isa. 21:12; Amos 5:8.

Seasons of spiritual desertion.
Song of Sol. 3:1.

Spiritual darkness. Rom. 13:12.

The Jews

In affliction, spent in prayer.
Ps. 22:2.

In affliction, spent in sorrow and
humiliation. Pss. 6:6; 30:5;
Joel 1:13.

Forbidden to allow criminals to
hang during. Deut. 21:23.

Forbidden to keep the wages of
servants during. Lev. 19:13.

Often kept lamps burning during.
Prov. 31:18.

Moon and stars designed to rule and
give light by. Gen. 1:16–18;
Jer. 31:35.

Originally divided into three watches.
Lam. 2:19, with Judg. 7:19;
Exod. 14:24.

Regular succession of

Established by covenant.
Gen. 8:22; Jer. 33:20.

Ordained for the glory of God.
Ps. 19:2.

Unsuitable for labor. John 9:4.

Unsuitable for traveling.
John 11:10.

Tiresome to the sick. Job 7:3–4.

Wild beasts search for prey during.
2 Sam. 21:10; Ps. 104:21–22.

NILE RIVER

See River, Nile

NINEVEH

Ancient capital of Assyria.
2 Kings 19:36; Isa. 37:37.

Called the city of blood. Nah. 3:1.

Described as

Commercial. Nah. 3:16.

Extensive. Jon. 3:3.

Full of joy and carelessness.
Zeph. 2:15.

Full of lies and robbery. Nah. 3:1.

Full of witchcraft, etc. Nah. 3:4.

Great. Jon. 1:2; 3:2.

Idolatrous. Nah. 1:14.

Populous. Jon. 4:11.

Rich. Nah. 2:9.

Strong. Nah. 3:12.

Vile. Nah. 1:14.

Wicked. Jon. 1:2.

Destruction of, averted. Jon. 3:10;
4:11.

Inhabitants of, repented at Jonah's
preaching. Jon. 3:5–9;
Matt. 12:41; Luke 11:32.

Jonah sent to proclaim the
destruction of. Jon. 1:2; 3:1–2, 4.

Origin and antiquity of. Gen. 10:11.

Predictions respecting

Being taken while the people were
drunk. Nah. 1:10; 3:11.

Captivity of its people. Nah. 3:10.

Coming up of the Babylonian
armies against. Nah. 2:1–4; 3:2.

Complete desolation.
Zeph. 2:13–15.

Degradation and contempt put on.
Nah. 3:5–7; Zeph. 2:15.

Destruction of its idols.
Nah. 1:14; 2:7.

Destruction of its people.
Nah. 1:12; 3:3.

Plunder of its treasures. Nah. 2:9.

Utter destruction. Nah. 1:8–9.

Weakness of its people.
Nah. 3:13.
Situated on the river Tigris.
Nah. 2:6, 8.

NOLLE PROSEQUI
Of the complaint against Paul.
Acts 18:12–17.

NON-CHRISTIAN RELIGIONS
See Religions, Non-Christian

NOSE
Jewels for. Prov. 11:22; Isa. 3:21;
Ezek. 16:12.

Mutilated. Ezek. 23:25.

NUCLEAR WEAPONS
See Atomic Power

NURSE
Careless. 2 Sam. 4:4.
For Moses. Exod. 2:7.

NUT
A product Jacob sent with his sons to
Egypt. Gen. 43:11.

OAK TREE
See Tree, Oak

OAR
Used with boats. Isa. 33:21.

OATHS
Antiquity of. Gen. 14:22; 24:3, 8.
Custom of swearing by the life of the
king. Gen. 42:15–16.

Expressions used
  "By the fear of Isaac."
    Gen. 31:53.
  "God is witness." 1 Thess. 2:5.
  "Before God do not lie."
    Gal. 1:20.
  "I call God for a record."
    2 Cor. 1:23.
  "I charge you by the Lord."
    1 Thess. 5:27.
  "By the Lord." 2 Sam. 19:7;
    1 Kings 2:42.
  "As the Lord lives." Judg. 8:19;
    Ruth 3:13.
  "May God deal with you."
    1 Sam. 3:17.
  "May the Lord deal with me." Ruth
    1:17.
  "As my soul lives." 1 Sam. 1:26;
    25:26.
God used, to show the
  unchangeableness of His counsel.
  Gen. 22:16; Num. 14:28;
  Heb. 6:17.

Instances of rash, etc.
  Herod. Matt. 14:7–9.
  Jephthah. Judg. 11:30–36.

The Jews who sought to kill Paul.
  Acts 23:21.
Joshua. Josh. 9:15–16.
Saul. 1 Sam. 14:27, 44.

The Jews
  Condemned for false. Zech. 5:4;
    Mal. 3:5.
  Condemned for profane.
    Jer. 23:10; Hos. 4:2.
  Fell into many errors regarding.
    Matt. 23:16–22.
  Forbidden to take false. Lev. 6:3;
    Zech. 8:17.
  Forbidden to take in the name of
    any created thing.
    Matt. 5:34–36; James 5:12.
  Forbidden to take in the name of
    idols. Josh. 23:7.
  Forbidden to take rash, or unholy.
    Lev. 5:4.
  Generally respected the obligation
    of. Josh. 9:19–20;
    2 Sam. 21:7; Ps. 15:4;
    Matt. 14:9.
  Often guilty of falsely taking.
    Lev. 6:3; Jer. 5:2; 7:9.
  Often guilty of rashly taking.
    Judg. 21:7; Matt. 14:7; 26:72.
  To take in truth, judgment, etc.
    Jer. 4:2.
  To use God's name alone in.
    Deut. 6:13; 10:20; Isa. 65:16.
Judicial form of administering.
  1 Kings 22:16; Matt. 26:63.
Lawful purpose of, explained.
  Heb. 6:16.

Often accompanied by placing the hand under the thigh of the person sworn to. Gen. 24:2, 9; 47:29.

Often accompanied by raising up the hand. Gen. 14:22; Dan. 12:7; Rev. 10:5–6.

To be taken in fear and reverence. Eccles. 9:2.

Used for
Binding to performance of any particular act. Gen. 24:3–4; 50:25; Josh. 2:12.
Binding to performance of sacred duties. Num. 30:2; 2 Chron. 15:14–15; Neh. 10:29; Ps. 132:2.
Confirming covenants. Gen. 26:28; 31:44, 53; 1 Sam. 20:16–17.

OBEDIENCE TO GOD
See God, Obedience to

OBESITY

Examples of
Eglon. Judg 3:17, 22.
Eli. 1 Sam 2:29; 4:18.
Excessive eating. Prov. 23:20–21; 25:16; Phil. 3:19.
Restraint in eating. Prov. 23:2; 25:16.

OBLATION
Gift not involving blood. Lev. 7:38; 2 Chron. 31:14; Isa. 1:13; Ezek. 20:40; 44:30.

OBLIGATION
Acknowledgment of. Ps. 116:12–14, 17.
A motive of obedience. Deut. 4:32–40; 6–11; 26:16;

32:6; 1 Sam. 12:24; 1 Chron. 16:12; Rom. 2:4; 2 Cor. 5:15.

OBSTACLES
Christ can overcome. Rom. 8:35–37.
Faith can take away. Matt. 21:21.
God may set up. Jer. 6:21; Hos. 2:6.
God removes. Isa. 40:4; 45:2; Mark 16:4.
Religious leaders sometimes cause. Isa. 57:14.
Riches can be. Mark 10:24.
We must avoid creating. Rom. 14:13; 1 Cor. 8:9.

OBSTETRICS
Process described. Ezek. 16:4.

OCCULT
Belongs to the works of the flesh. Gal. 5:20.
Books of occult science destroyed. Acts 19:19.

Divination by an alleged assistance of evil spirits
Denounced. Isa. 8:19; Mal. 3:5.
Forbidden. Lev. 19:26–28, 31; 20:6; Deut. 18:9–14.
Divining by familiar spirits. Lev. 20:27; 1 Chron. 10:13; 2 Chron. 33:6; Isa. 8:19; 19:3; 29:4.
Divining by images. 2 Kings 23:24; Ezek. 21:21.
Divining by livers. Ezek. 21:21.
Divining by rods. Hos. 4:12.
Fortune-tellers will be put to shame. Mic. 3:7.
Messages of, false. Ezek. 21:29; Zech. 10:2; 2 Thess. 2:9.

Practiced by
Astrologers. Jer. 10:2;
Mic. 3:6–7.
Babylonians. Isa. 47:9–13.
Balaam. Num. 22:6; 23:23.
Belshazzar. Dan. 5:7, 15.
Egyptians. Isa. 19:3, 11, 12.
Elymas. Acts 13:8.
False prophets. Jer. 14:14; 27:9;
29:8– 9; Ezek. 13:6–9; 22:28;
Matt. 24:24.
Jezebel. 2 Kings 9:22.
Magicians. Exod. 7:11, 22;
8:7, 18.
Ninevites. Nah. 3:4–5.
Roving Jews. Acts 19:13.
Simon Magus. Acts 8:9, 11.
The slave girl at Philippi.
Acts 16:16.
Sons of Sceva. Acts 19:14–15.
Punishment for. Exod. 22:18;
Lev. 20:27; Deut. 13:5.
Saul consulted the witch of Endor.
1 Sam. 28:7–25.
Wickedness of. 1 Sam. 15:23.
Vainness of. Isa. 44:25.

OFFENSES

All things that cause, will be gathered
out of Christ's kingdom.
Matt. 13:41.
Blessedness of not taking, at Christ.
Matt. 11:6.

Believers should
Avoid those who cause.
Rom. 16:17.
Be cautious of giving. Ps. 73:15;
Rom. 14:13; 1 Cor. 8:9.
Be without. Phil. 1:10.
Cut off what causes, to themselves.
Matt. 5:29–30; Mark 9:43–47.
Have a conscience void of.
Acts 24:16.

Not let their liberty cause, to
others. 1 Cor. 8:9.
Not take. John 16:1.
Reprimand those who cause.
Exod. 32:21; 1 Sam. 2:24.
Use self-denial rather than cause.
Rom. 14:21; 1 Cor. 8:13.
Denunciation against those who
cause. Matt. 18:7; Mark 9:42.

Ministers should
Be cautious of giving. 2 Cor. 6:3.
Remove that which causes.
Isa. 57:14.
Occasions of, forbidden.
1 Cor. 10:32; 2 Cor. 6:3.
Occasions of, must arrive.
Matt. 18:7.
Persecution, a cause of, to mere
professors. Matt. 13:21; 24:10;
26:31.
Punishment for causing.
Ezek. 44:12; Mal. 2:8–9;
Matt. 18:6–7.

The wicked take, at
Christ as the Bread of life.
John 6:58–61.
Christ as the cornerstone.
Isa. 8:14, with Rom. 9.33;
1 Pet. 2:8.
Christ crucified. 1 Cor. 1:23;
Gal. 5:11.
The low position of Christ.
Isa. 53:1–3; Matt. 13:54–57.
The necessity of inward purity.
Matt. 15:11–12.
The righteousness of faith.
Rom. 9:32.

OFFENSES AGAINST THE HOLY SPIRIT

See Holy Spirit, Offenses against the

OFFERINGS

See also Offering, Burnt; Offering, Drink

Antiquity of. Gen. 4:3–4.
Could not make the giver perfect. Heb. 9:9.
Declared to be most holy. Num. 18:9.

Different kinds of
Burnt. Lev. 13–17; Ps. 66:15.
Drink. Gen. 35:14; Exod. 29:40; Num. 15:5.
First fruits. Exod. 22:29; Deut. 18:4.
Free-will. Lev. 23:38; Deut. 16:10; 23:23.
Gifts. Exod. 35:22; Num. 7:2–88.
Incense. Exod. 30:8; Mal. 1:11; Luke 1:9.
Jealousy. Num. 5:15.
Meat. Lev. 3; Num. 15:4.
Peace. Lev. 3:1–17; 7:11.
Personal, for redemption. Exod. 30:13, 15.
Set aside. Exod. 29:27–28; Lev. 7:14; Num. 15:19.
Sin. Lev. 4:3–35; 6:25; 10:17.
Thanksgiving. Lev. 7:12; 22:29; Ps. 50:14.
Tithe. Lev. 27:30; Num. 18:21; Deut. 14:22.
Trespass. Lev. 5:6–19; 6:6; 7:1.
Wave. Exod. 29:26; Lev. 7:30.
Hezekiah prepared chambers for. 2 Chron. 31:11.

Illustrative of
Christ's offering of Himself. Eph. 5:2.
The conversion of the Gentiles. Rom. 15:16.
The conversion of the Jews. Isa. 66:20.

The Jews often
Abhorred, on account of the sins of the priests. 1 Sam. 2:17.
Defrauded God of. Mal. 3:8.
Gave the worst they had as. Mal. 1:8, 13.
Presented to idols. Ezek. 20:28.
Rejected in, because of sin. Isa. 1:13; Mal. 1:10.
Slow in presenting. Neh. 13:10–12.
Laid up in the temple. 2 Chron. 31:12; Neh. 10:37.
Made by strangers, to be the same as by the Jews. Num. 15:14–16.
Many offenses under the law, beyond the efficiency of. 1 Sam. 3:14; Ps. 51:16.

Required to be
Best of their kind. Mal. 1:14.
Brought in a clean vessel. Isa. 66:20.
Brought to the place appointed of God. Deut. 12:6; Ps. 27:6; Heb. 9:9.
Brought without delay. Exod. 22:29–30.
Laid before the altar. Matt. 5:23–24.
Offered in love and charity. Matt. 5:23–24.
Offered in righteousness. Mal. 3:3.
Offered willingly. Lev. 22:19.
Perfect. Lev. 22:21.
Presented by the priest. Heb. 5:1.

Things forbidden as
The price of a dog. Deut. 23:18.

The price of fornication.
Deut. 23:18.
Whatever was blemished.
Lev. 22:20.
Whatever was imperfect.
Lev. 22:24.
Whatever was unclean.
Lev. 27:11, 27.
To be made to God alone.
Exod. 22:20; Judg. 13:16.
Unacceptable without gratitude.
Ps. 50:8, 14.

OFFERING, BURNT

Abraham tried by the command to
offer Isaac as. Gen. 22.
Ashes of, collected at foot of altar and
carried outside the camp.
Lev. 6:11.
An atonement for sin. Lev. 9:7.
Blood of, sprinkled round about upon
the altar. Lev. 1:5, 11.
Fat, etc., of all peace offerings laid on
and consumed with the daily.
Lev. 3:5; 6:12.
Guilt of offering, except in the place
appointed. Lev. 17:8–9.
Guilt of unauthorized persons
offering. 1 Sam. 13:12–13.
Guilt transferred to, by imposition of
hands. Lev. 1:4; Num. 8:12.
If a bird, blood wrung out at side of
altar. Lev. 1:15.
Of human victims denounced.
Deut. 12.31, 2 Kings 3.27;
Jer. 7:31; 19:5.
Incapable of removing sin and
reconciling to God. Pss. 40:6;
50:8; Heb. 10:6.
Knowledge of God better than.
Hos. 6:6.
Love of God better than.
Mark 12:33.

Most ancient of all sacrifices
Gen. 4:4,
with 8:20; 22:2, 13; Job 1:5.
Most costly, no adequate tribute to
God. Isa. 40:16, with
Ps. 50:9–13.
Obedience better than.
1 Sam. 15:22; Jer. 7:21–23.

Offered
On Atonement Day. Lev. 16:3, 5;
Num. 29:8.
At consecration of kings.
1 Chron. 29:21–23.
At consecration of Levites.
Num. 8:12.
At consecration of priests.
Lev. 9:2, 12–14.
At dedication of sacred places.
Num. 7:15, etc.; 1 Kings 8:64.
Every morning and evening.
Exod. 29:38–42.
Every Sabbath day.
Num. 28:9–10.
On the first day of every month.
Num. 28:11.
Before going to war. 1 Sam. 7:9.
After great mercies. 1 Sam. 6:14;
2 Sam. 24:22, 25.
For the healed leper. Lev. 14:13,
19–20.
By the Jews before the law.
Exod. 10:25; 24:5.
For Nazarites after defilement, or
at expiration of their vow.
Num. 6:11, 14.
At purification of women.
Lev. 12:6.
Seven days of unleavened bread.
Num. 28:19, 24.
With sound of trumpets at feasts.
Num. 10:10.

Required to be
Entirely burned. Lev. 1:8–9,
12–13; 6:9.
Killed, if a beast, by the person
who brought it. Lev. 1:5, 11.
Killed, if a bird, by the priest.
Lev. 1:15.
A male without blemish. Lev. 1:3;
22:19.
Offered by priests only. Lev. 1:9;
Ezek. 44:15.
Offered in righteousness.
Ps. 51:19.
For the people at large, killed and
prepared by the Levites.
Ezek. 44:11.
Presented at the door of the
tabernacle. Lev. 13;
Deut. 12:6, 11, 14.
Voluntary. Lev. 1:3; 22:18–19.
Skin of, given to the priests for
clothing. Lev. 7:8. (*See*
Gen. 3:21.)
Specially acceptable. Gen. 8:21;
Lev. 1:9, 13, 17.
To be offered only to the Lord.
Judg. 13:16.

To be taken from
The flock or herd. Lev. 1:2.
The fowls. Lev. 1:14.
Of the wicked, not accepted by God.
Isa. 1:10–11; Jer. 6:19–20;
Amos 5:22.

OFFERING, DRINK
Antiquity of. Gen. 35:14.
Idolaters often used blood for.
Ps. 16:4.

Idolatrous Jews
Offered to the queen of heaven.
Jer. 7:18; 44:17–19.

Rebuked for offering to idols.
Isa. 57:5–6; 65:11; Jer. 19:13;
Ezek. 20:28.

Illustrative of
Devotedness of ministers.
Phil. 2:17.
Offering of Christ. Isa. 53:12.
Pouring out of the Spirit.
Joel 2:28.
Not poured on the altar of incense.
Exod. 30:9.
Omission of, caused by bad vintage.
Joel 1:9, 13.
For public sacrifices, provided by the
state. Ezra 7:17; Ezek. 45:17.
Quantity appointed to be used for
each kind of sacrifice.
Num. 15:3–10.
Sacrifices accompanied by.
Exod. 29:40; Lev. 23:13.
Vanity of offering, to idols.
Deut. 32:37–38.

OFFERING, HEAVE

Consisted of
First fruits of bread.
Num. 15:19–21.
Part of all gifts. Num. 18:29.
Part of spoil taken in war.
Num. 31:26–47.
Part of the meat offering of all
peace offerings. Lev. 7:14.
Right shoulder of peace offerings.
Lev. 7:32.
Shoulder of the priest's
consecration ram. Exod. 29:27.
Given to the priests. Exod. 29:28;
Lev. 7:34.
Sanctified the whole offering.
Num. 18:27, 30.

To be

 Best of their kind. Num. 18:29.

 Brought to God's house.
 Deut. 12:6.

 Eaten in a clean place.
 Lev. 10:12–15.

 Set aside by the priest.
 Exod. 29:27.

OFFERING, SIN

Aaron, etc., rebuked for burning and
 not eating that of the
 congregation, its blood not having
 been brought into the tabernacle.
 Lev. 10:16–18, with 9:9, 15.

Blood of

 In every case, poured at the foot of
 the altar of burnt offering.
 Lev. 4:7, 18, 25, 30; 9:9.

 For a priest or for the
 congregation, brought by the
 priest into the tabernacle.
 Lev. 4:5, 16.

 For a priest or for the
 congregation, put upon the
 horns of the altar of incense.
 Lev. 4:7, 18.

 For a priest or for the
 congregation, sprinkled seven
 times before the Lord, outside
 the veil, by the priest with his
 finger. Lev. 4:6, 17.

 For a priest or the congregation,
 the skin, carcass, etc., burned
 outside the camp.
 Lev. 4:11–12, 21; 6:30; 9:11.

 For a ruler or for a private person,
 put upon the horns of the altar of
 burnt offering by the priest with
 his finger. Lev. 4:25, 30.

Consisted of

 A female goat or female lamb for a
 private person. Lev. 4:28, 32.

 A male goat for a ruler. Lev. 4:23.

 A young bull for priests.
 Lev. 4:3; 9:2, 8; 16:3, 6.

 A young bull or goat for the
 congregation. Lev. 4:14; 16:9;
 2 Chron. 29:23.

Eaten by the priests in a holy place,
 when its blood had not been
 brought into the tabernacle.
 Lev. 6:26, 29–30.

Fat of the inside, kidneys, etc.,
 burned on the altar of burnt
 offering. Lev. 4:8–10, 19, 26,
 31; 9:10.

Killed in the same place as the burnt
 offering. Lev. 4:24; 6:25.

Laws regarding the utensils used for
 boiling the flesh of. Lev. 6:28.

Offered

 At the consecration of Levites.
 Num. 8:8.

 At the consecration of priests.
 Exod. 29:10, 14; Lev. 8:14.

 On the Day of Atonement.
 Lev. 16:3, 9.

 At the expiration of a Nazarite's
 vow. Num. 6:14.

 For sins of ignorance.
 Lev. 4:2, 13, 22, 27.

Probable origin of. Gen. 4:4, 7.

Sins of the offerer transferred to, by
 imposition of hands. Lev. 4:4, 15,
 24, 29; 2 Chron. 29:23.

A type of Christ's sacrifice.
 2 Cor. 5:21; Heb. 13:11–13.

Whatever touched the flesh of, was
 rendered holy. Lev. 6:27.

OFFERING, TRESPASS

Accompanied by confession.
Lev. 5:5.

Atonement made by.
Lev. 5:6, 10, 13, 16, 18; 6:7;
19:22.

Belongs to the priest. Lev. 14:13;
Ezek. 44:29.

For minor offenses, was lessened for
the poor. Lev. 5, with 4.

Consisted of
A meat offering by the very poor.
Lev. 5:11–13.

A ram without blemish. Lev. 5:15;
6:6.

A female lamb or kid. Lev. 5:6.

Two turtle doves by those unable
to bring a lamb. Lev. 5:7–10.

Generally accompanied by
restitution. Lev. 5:16; 6:5.

Illustrative of Christ. Isa. 53:10;
Ezek. 46:20.

A most holy offering. Lev. 14:13.

Offered
For any sin of ignorance.
Lev. 5:17.

For breach of trust, or fraud.
Lev. 6:2–5.

For concealing knowledge of a
crime. Lev. 5:1.

For involuntarily touching unclean
things. Lev. 5:2–3.

For rash swearing. Lev. 5:4.

For sins of ignorance in holy
things. Lev. 5:15.

Sometimes waved alive before the
Lord. Lev. 14:12–13.

Special occasions of offering
Cleansing of a leper.
Lev. 14:2, 12–14, 21–22.

In connection with a sexual sin
involving a female slave engaged
to another man. Lev. 19:20–22.

Purification of Nazarites who had
broken their vow. Num. 6:12.

Purification of those with
hemorrhage. Lev. 15:14–15.

Purification of women.
Lev. 12:6–8.

To be slain where the sin offering and
burnt offering were slain.
Lev. 14:13; Ezek. 40:39.

Valued as a sin offering, and
frequently so called. Lev. 5:6, 9.

OFFERING, WAVE

Consisted of
Breast of all peace offerings.
Lev. 7:30; 9:18, 21;
Num. 6:17, 20.

Breast of the priest's consecration
ram. Exod. 29:26; Lev. 8:29.

Fat, right shoulder, etc., of the
priest's consecration ram.
Exod. 29:22–23; Lev. 8:25–26.

Firstfruits of barley harvest.
Lev. 23:10–11.

Firstfruits of wheat bread.
Lev. 23:20.

Jealousy offering. Num. 5:25.

Left shoulder of Nazarite's peace
offering. Num. 6:17, 19.

Leper's trespass offering.
Lev. 14:12, 24.

Fat, etc., of the consecration ram
burnt on the altar. Exod. 29:25;
Lev. 8:28.

Given to the priest as his due.
Exod. 29:26–28;
Lev. 7:31, 34; 8:29; 10:15;
23:20; Num. 18:11.

Placed in the hand of the priest and waved before the Lord. Exod. 29:24; Lev. 8:27.

To be eaten in a holy place by the priest's family. Lev. 10:14.

OIL

Ascribed by the law for a tithe. Deut. 12:17.

Canaan abounded in. Deut. 8:8.

Comes from the earth. Ps. 104:14–15; Hos. 2:22.

Dealing in, a trade. 2 Kings 4:7.

Described as
Healing. Isa. 1:6, with Luke 10:34.
Penetrating. Ps. 109:18.
Smooth. Prov. 5:3.
Soft. Ps. 55:21.

Exported. 1 Kings 5:11; Ezek. 27:17; Hos. 12:1.

Extracted by presses. Hag. 2:16, with Mic. 6:15.

Failure of, a severe calamity. Hag. 1:11.

First fruits of, given to God. Deut. 18:4; 2 Chron. 31:5; Neh. 10:37.

Given by God. Ps. 104:14–15; Jer. 31:12; Joel 2:19, 24.

Illustrative of
The anointing of the Holy Spirit. Pss. 45:7; 89:20; Zech. 4:12.
The consolation of the gospel. Isa. 61:3.
Kind reprimand. Ps. 141:5.

Jews often extravagant in the use of. Prov. 21:17.

Kept in
Boxes. 2 Kings 9:1.
Cellars. 1 Chron. 27:28.

Horns. 1 Kings 1:39.
Jars. 1 Kings 17:12.
Pots. 2 Kings 4:2.
Storehouses. 2 Chron. 32:28.

Kinds of, mentioned
Myrrh. Esther 2:12.
Olive. Exod. 30:24; Lev. 24:2.

Miraculous increase of. 2 Kings 4:2–6.

Ointments of the Jews made of perfumes mixed with. Exod. 30:23–25; John 12:3.

The poor employed in extracting. Job 24:11.

Sold by measure. 1 Kings 5:11; Luke 16:6.

Stores of, laid up in fortified cities. 2 Chron. 11:11.

Used
For anointing the person. Pss. 23:5; 104:15; Luke 7:46.
For anointing the sick. Mark 6:13; James 5:14.
For anointing to offices of trust. Exod. 29:7; 1 Sam. 10:1; 1 Kings 19:16.
For food. 1 Kings 17:12; Ezek. 16:13.
For lamps. Exod. 25:6; 27:20; Matt. 25:3.
In God's worship. Lev. 7:10; Num. 15:4–10.
In idolatrous worship. Lev. 7:10; Num. 15:4–10.

When fresh, especially valued. Ps. 92:10.

OINTMENT

The alabaster box of. Matt. 26:7.

Compounded by Bezaleel. Exod. 37:1, 29.

Not sacred. 2 Kings 20:13;
    Esther 2:12; Eccles. 7:1;
    Song of Sol. 1:3; Mark 14:3–5.
Sacred, formula for.
    Exod. 30:23–25.
Uses of. Exod. 30:26–33.

OMEN
Israelites prohibited from
    interpreting. Deut. 18:10.

OLD
Christ's new covenant replaces the
    old. Heb. 8:6–13.
Has given way to new. 2 Cor. 5:17.
Landmarks not to be removed.
    Prov. 22:28.
Men and women counseled.
    Titus 2:2–4.
Men will dream dreams. Acts 2:17.
And new both to be treasured.
    Matt. 13:52.
The new is implicit in the old
    commandment. 1 John 2:7.
Things may not go with new.
    Matt. 9:16–17; Luke 5:36–39.
Wine is better than new. Luke 5:39.

OLD AGE
See Senior Citizen

OLD NATURE
See Christians, Nature (Old) of

OLIVE TREE
See Tree, Olive

ONE
In Christ. Gal. 3:28.
God is one. Deut. 6:4.
Lord, one faith, one baptism.
    Eph. 4:5.
Thing have I desired. Ps. 27:4.

Thing I do. Phil. 3:13.
Thing I know. John 9:25.
Thing lacking. Luke 18:22.
Thing needful. Luke 10:42.

ONENESS
Of all nations. Acts 17:24–26.
Of the church. 1 Cor. 1:13;
    12:4–31.
Of the first believers. Acts 2:44–47;
    4:32.
Of husband and wife. Gen. 2:24;
    1 Cor. 6:16.
Of Jesus and His Father.
    John 10:30.

OPINION, PUBLIC
Concessions to, by Paul, in
    circumcising Timothy. Acts 16:3.

*Corrupt yielding to, by Herod, in
    the case*
    By Felix and Festus, concerning
      Paul. Acts 24:27; 25:9.

Olives

Of John the Baptist. Mark 6:26.
Of Peter. Acts 12:3.
By Peter, concerning Jesus.
  Matt. 26:69–75.
By Pilate. Matt. 27:23–27.
Disciples, who urged circumcision.
  Gal. 6:12.
Feared by chief priests who
  continued to further persecute the
  disciples. Acts 4:21; 5:26.
Feared by chief priests who feared to
  answer the questions of Jesus.
  Matt. 21:26.
Feared by Joseph of Arimathaea.
  John 19:38.
Feared by Nicodemus. John 3:2.
Feared by rulers, who believed in
  Jesus, but feared the Pharisees.
  John 12:42–43.
Feared by the parents of the man
  who was born blind.
  John 9:21–22.
James and the Christian elders, who
  required Paul to observe certain
  rites. Acts 21:18, 26.
Jesus inquires about. Matt. 16:13.
Peter and Barnabas with others.
  Gal. 2:11–14.

OPPORTUNITY
Easily lost. 1 Kings 20:40; Jer. 8:20;
  John 9:4.
For good deeds. Gal. 6:10.
Present and immediate. Esther 4:14;
  John 4:35; Rom. 13:11.
For salvation. 2 Cor. 6:2.
For satisfaction. Rev. 22:17.

OPPOSITION
To Christ. Matt. 26:3–4; Heb. 12:3.
Depth of spiritual. Eph. 6:12.
To the doer of righteousness.
  John 15:20.

To God. 2 Thess. 2:3–4;
  2 Tim. 6:20.
To the Holy Spirit. Acts 7:51.
Power over. Luke 10:19.
To the speaker of truth. Isa. 30:10;
  Jer. 11:21.
Technique for meeting.
  Eph. 6:11–19.

OPPRESSION
Divinely prohibited. Lev. 25:14;
  James 5:4.

Examples of
  Hagar, by Sarah. Gen. 16:6.
  Israelites by Egyptians.
    Exod. 1:10–22; 5.
  Jeroboam resolves to oppress the
    Israelites. 1 Kings 12:4.
God is a refuge from. Ps. 9:9.
God's aid promised against.
  Ps. 12:5; 72:4, 14; Jer. 50:34.
God will judge. Ps. 103:6;
  Eccles. 5:8; Isa. 10; Jer. 22:17;
  Ezek. 22:7; Mal. 3:5; James 5:4.
National, God judges. Acts 7:7.
National, relieved. Exod. 3:9;
  Deut. 26:7; Judg. 2:4; 6; 7; 8; 10;
  2 Kings 13; Ps. 9:9; Isa. 52:4.
To be opposed by the godly.
  Isa. 1:17; Acts 7:24;
  James 2:5–8; Gal. 6:2.
Prayers against.
  Pss. 17:9; 44.24; 119:121, 134;
  Isa. 38:14.
Warnings against. Exod. 22:21–24;
  James 2:6.

ORACLE
The holy place. 1 Kings 6:5;
  Ps. 28:2.
The Scriptures called oracles.
  Acts 7:38; Rom. 3:2; Heb. 5:12;
  1 Pet. 4:11.

ORGAN

Pipe or shrill flute. Gen. 4:21;
Job 21:12; 30:31; Ps. 150:4.

ORATOR

Examples of
The apostles. Acts 2:1–41.
Appollos. Acts 18:24–28.
Jonah. Jon. 3:4–10.
Tertullus. Acts 24:1.

ORIGIN OF LIFE

See Life, Origin of

ORPHANS

Afflict not. Exod. 22:23.
Blessedness of taking care of.
Deut. 14:29; Job 29:12–13;
Jer. 7:6–7.
A curse on those who oppress.
Deut. 27:19.
Commandments concerning.
Exod. 22:22–24; James 1:27.
Defend. Ps. 82:3; Isa. 1:17.
Do not defraud. Prov. 23:10.
Do not do violence to. Jer. 22:3.
Do not oppress. Zech. 7:10.
Do not take advantage of.
Deut. 24:17.

Examples of
Daughters of Zelophehad.
Num. 27:1–5.
Esther. Esther 2:7.
Joash. 2 Kings 11:1–12.
Jotham. Judg. 9:16–21.
Lot. Gen. 11:27–28.
Mephibosheth. 2 Sam. 9:3.
A picture of Zion in affliction.
Lam. 5:3.
Find mercy in God. Hos. 14:3.

God will
Be a father of. Ps. 68:5.
Be a helper of. Ps. 10:14.
Execute the judgment of.
Deut. 10:18; Ps. 10:18.
Hear the cry of. Exod. 22:23–24.
Punish those who mistreat.
Jer. 5:28–29.
Punish those who oppress.
Exod. 22:24; Isa. 10:1–3;
Mal. 3:5.
Let them share in our blessings.
Deut. 14:29.
Promises with respect to. Jer. 49:11.
Visit in their distress. James 1:27.

The wicked
Grieve. Ezek. 22:7.
Judge not for. Jer. 5:28.
Murder. Ps. 94:6.
Oppress. Job 24:3.
Overwhelm. Job 6:27.
Rob. Isa. 10:2.

OUTER SPACE

Astrology. Isa. 47:13; Jer. 10:2.
Created by God. Gen. 1:1, 14–19;
Job 9:7–10; 26:7; Ps. 8:3;
136:5–9.
Comets. Jude 13.
Darkened. Isa. 13:10; Joel 2:31;
Matt. 24:29; Rev. 6:12–13; 8:12.
Emptiness of. Job 26:7.
God's presence in. Ps. 139:8.

Lights of
Increased. Isa. 30:26.
Surpassed by God. Isa. 60:19–20;
Rev. 21:23.

Moon
Light of. Gen. 1:16; Job 25:5;
31:26; Song of Sol. 6:10.

Planets
Earth. Job 26:7.
Morning star. Job 38:7.

Stars
Of Bethlehem. Matt. 2:2, 7, 9–10.
In constellations. 2 Kings 23:5;
Job 9:9; 38:31–33; Isa. 13:10;
Amos 5:8.
Of differing magnitudes.
1 Cor. 15:41.
Evening. Neh. 4:21.
Morning. Job 38:7.
Moving. Matt. 2:9.
Numberless. Jer. 33:22.

Sun
Brightness of. Gen. 1:16;
2 Sam. 23:4; Song of Sol. 6:10.
Movement of, when viewed from
earth. Ps. 19:4–6; 104:19;
Eccles. 1:5.

Worship elements of
Forbidden. Deut. 4:19; 17:3.
Practiced. 2 Kings 23:5; Jer. 8:2.

OVEN
For baking. Exod. 8:3;
Lev. 2:4; 7:9; 11:35; 26:26.
Used in a figurative sense. Ps. 21:9;
Hos. 7:4, 6, 7; Mal. 4:1;
Matt. 6:30; Luke 12:28.

OVERCOMING
Faith overcomes the world.
1 John 5:4.

Overcomers will
Be clothed in the white of purity
and hear Christ confess their
names. Rev. 3:5.
Become a pillar in the temple of
God and be given three great
names. Rev. 3:12.

Be granted power over the
nations. Rev. 2:26.
Enjoy the tree of life. Rev. 2:7.
Not be subject to spiritual death.
Rev. 2:11.
Sit with Christ on His throne.
Rev. 3:21.
In practice we are to overcome evil
with good. Rom. 12:21.
In principle we have overcome evil.
1 John 2:13–14.

OX
Clean and fit for food. Deut. 14:4.
Custom of sending the pieces of, to
collect the people to war.
1 Sam. 11:7.

Described as
Beautiful. Jer. 46:20;
Hos. 10:11.
Not without discernment. Isa. 1:3.
Strong. Ps. 144:14; Prov. 14:4.

Fed
With corn. Isa. 30:24.
With grass. Job 40:15;
Ps. 106:20; Dan. 4:25.
On the hills. Isa. 7:25.
In stalls. Hab. 3:17.
In the valleys. 1 Chron. 27:29;
Isa. 65:10.

Formed a part of the
Patriarchal wealth. Gen. 13:2, 5;
26:14; Job 1:3.
Wealth of Israel in Egypt.
Gen. 50:8; Exod. 10:9; 12:32.
Wealth of the Jews. Num. 32:4;
Ps. 144:14.
Goes to the slaughter unconscious.
Prov. 7:22.
Herdmen appointed over.
Gen. 13:7; 1 Sam. 21:7.

Horns and hoofs of, alluded to.
Ps. 69:31.

Illustrative of
Backsliding Israel (a heifer sliding
back). Hos. 4:16.
Beauty and wealth of Egypt (a fair
heifer). Jer. 46:20.
Believers under persecution (when
led to slaughter). Jer. 11:19.
A beloved wife (a heifer).
Judg. 14:18.
Fierce enemies (bulls). Pss. 22:12;
68:30.
The glory of Joseph (a firstborn
bull). Deut. 33:17.
Greedy mercenaries (fattened
calves). Jer. 46:21.
The impatient under judgment (in
a net). Isa. 51:20.
Israel's fondness for ease, not
obedience (a heifer taught).
Hos. 10:11.
Luxurious Chaldees (a heifer at
grass). Jer. 50:11.
Ministers (when engaged in
farming). Isa. 30:24; 32:20.
Ministers' right to support (when
not muzzled in treading corn).
1 Cor. 9:9–10.
Moab in affliction (a heifer three
years old). Isa. 15:5; Jer. 48:34.
Proud and wealthy rulers (cattle).
Amos 4:1.
The provision of the gospel (when
prepared for a feast). Prov. 9:2;
Matt. 22:4.
A rash youth (when led to
slaughter). Prov. 7:22.
Stubborn sinners (when
unaccustomed to the yoke).
Jer. 31:18.
Years of plenty (when well
favored). Gen. 41:2, 26, 29.

Years of scarcity (when lean).
Gen. 41:3, 27, 30.

Includes the
Bull. Gen. 32:15; Job 21:10;
Ps. 50:9; Jer. 46:21.
Cow. Num. 18:17; Job 21:10.
Heifer. Gen. 15:9; Num. 19:2.
Increase of, promised. Deut. 7:13;
28:4.

Laws respecting
Fallen under its burden, to be
raised up again. Deut. 22:4.
Fat of, not to be eaten. Lev. 7:23.
If stolen to be restored double.
Exod. 22:4.
Killing a man, to be stoned.
Exod. 21:28–32.
Mode of reparation for one, killing
another. Exod. 21:35–36.
Not to be muzzled when treading
out the corn. Deut. 25:4;
1 Cor. 9:9.
Not to be yoked with a donkey in
the same plow. Deut. 22:10.
Of others, if lost or hurt through
neglect, to be made good.
Exod. 22:9–13.
Of others, not to be coveted.
Exod. 20:17; Deut. 5:21.
Straying to be brought back to its
owner. Exod. 23:4;
Deut. 22:1–2.
To rest on the Sabbath.
Exod. 23:12; Deut. 5:14.
Lowing of, alluded to. 1 Sam. 15:14;
Job 6:5.
Male firstborn of, belonged to God.
Exod. 34:19.
Often found wild. Deut. 14:5.
Often given as a present.
Gen. 12:16; 20:14.

Often stall-fed for slaughter.
Prov. 15:17.

Publicly sold. 2 Sam. 24:24;
Luke 14:19.

Rapid manner of collecting its food
alluded to. Num. 22:4.

Required great care and attention.
Prov. 27:23.

Sea of brass rested on figures of.
1 Kings 7:25.

Tithe of, given to the priests.
2 Chron. 31:6.

Urged on by the prod. Judg. 3:31.

Used for
Carrying burdens.
1 Chron. 12:40.

Drawing wagons, etc. Num. 7:3;
1 Sam. 6:7.

Food. 1 Kings 1:9; 19:21;
2 Chron. 18:2.

Plowing. 1 Kings 19:19;
Job 1:14; Amos 6:12.

Plowing the corn. Hos. 10:11.

Sacrifice. Exod. 20:24;
2 Sam. 24:22.

Tilling the ground. Isa. 30:24;
32:20.

The wicked often took, in pledge
from the poor. Job 24:3.

Young of, considered a great
delicacy. Gen. 18:7; Amos 6:4.

PAIN
Absence of, in heaven. Rev. 21:4.
Job's experience of. Job 33:19.
Present in hell. Rev. 16:10.

PAINTING
Around the eyes, to enlarge their
    appearance. 2 Kings 9:30;
    Jer. 4:30; Ezek. 23:40.
Of portraits. Ezek. 23:14.
Of rooms. Jer. 22:14.

PALACES
Archives kept in. Ezra 6:2.
At Babylon. Dan. 4:29; 5:5; 6:18.
Of David. 2 Sam. 7:2.

Described as
High. Ps. 78:69.
Pleasant. Isa. 13:22.
Polished. Ps. 144:12.
In a figurative sense, of a
    government. Amos 1:12; 2:2;
    Nah. 2:6.

Illustrative of
The godly children of believers.
    Ps. 144:12.
The place of Satan's dominion.
    Luke 11:21.
The splendor of the church.
    Song of Sol. 8:9.
Jerusalem celebrated for.
    Ps. 48:3, 13.

Of kings
Afforded support to all the king's
    servants. Ezra 4:14; Dan. 1:5.
Called the house of the kingdom.
    2 Chron. 2:1, 12.

Called the king's house. 2 Kings
    25:9; 2 Chron. 7:11.
Called the king's palace.
    Esther 1:5.
Called the royal house. Esther 1:9.
Contained treasures of the king.
    1 Kings 15:18; 2 Chron. 12:9.
Gorgeous apparel suited to, alone.
    Luke 7:25.
Under governors. 1 Kings 4:6;
    Neh. 7:2.
Often attended by eunuchs as
    servants. 2 Kings 20:18;
    Dan. 1:3–4.
Royal decrees issued from.
    Esther 3:15; 8:14.
Royal decrees laid up in. Ezra 6:2.
Splendidly furnished. Esther 1:6.
Surrounded with gardens.
    Esther 1:5.
Surrounded with terraces.
    2 Chron. 9:11.
Were strictly guarded.
    2 Kings 11:5–6.
For kings. 1 Kings 21:1.
Of Solomon. 1 Kings 7:1–12.

Often as a punishment
Burned with fire. 2 Chron. 36:19;
    Jer. 17:27.
Desolate. Ezek. 19:7.
Forsaken. Isa. 32:14.
The habitation of dragons, etc. Isa.
    13:22.
Overgrown with thorns, etc. Isa.
    34:13.
Scenes of bloodshed. Jer. 9:21.
Spoiled. Amos 3:11.

Often the storehouses of plunder.
Amos 3:10.
The spider makes its way even
into. Prov. 30:28.

Term applied to
House of the high priest.
Matt. 26:58.
Houses of great men. Amos 3:9;
Mic. 5:5.
Residences of kings. Dan. 4:4;
6:18.
Temple of God.
1 Chron. 29:1, 19.
Proclamations issued
from. Amos 3:9.
At Shushan. Neh. 1:1; Esther 1:2;
7:7; Dan. 8:2.
Were entered by gates. Neh. 2:8.

PALM TREE
See Tree, Palm

PALSY
Paralysis. Matt. 4:24; 9:2;
Luke 5:18; Acts 8:7.

PANIC
In armies. Lev. 26;17; Deut. 32:30;
Josh. 23:10; Ps. 35:5.
From God. Gen. 35:5;
Exod. 15:14–16; Judg. 7:22;
1 Sam. 14:15–20;
2 Kings 7:6, 7;
2 Chron. 20:22, 23.

PANTOMIME
By Agabus. Acts 21:11.
By Ezekiel. Ezek. 4:1–8; 12:18.
By Isaiah. Isa. 20:2–3.

PAPYRUS
The reeds of which grew in Egypt.
Exod. 2:3.

PARABLES

Of Christ
Barren fig tree. Luke 13:6–9.
Blind leading the blind. Luke 6:39.
Builder of a tower.
Luke 14:28–30, 33.
Children of the bride chamber.
Matt. 9:15.
Clean and unclean invited.
Matt. 15:10–15.
Cloud and wind. Luke 12:54–57.
Creditor and debtors.
Luke 7:41–47.
Faithful and evil servants.
Matt. 24:45–51.
Fig tree leafing. Matt. 24:32–34.
Good Samaritan. Luke 10:30–37.
Good shepherd. John 10:1–6.
House divided against itself.
Mark 3:25.

Papyrus

King going to war.
Luke 14:31–33.
Kingdom divided against itself.
Mark 3:24.
Laborers hired. Matt. 20:1–16.
Leaven. Matt. 13:33.
Lighted candle. Mark 4:21;
Luke 11:33–36.
Lost piece of silver.
Luke 15:8–10.
Lost sheep. Luke 15:3–7.
Man of the house watching.
Matt. 24:43.
Man taking a far journey.
Mark 13:34–37.
Marriage feast. Matt. 22:2–14.
Men invited to a feast.
Luke 14:7–11.
Mustard seed. Matt. 13:31–32;
Luke 13:19.
Net cast into the sea.
Matt. 13:47–50.
New cloth on an old garment.
Matt. 9:16.
New wine and old bottles.
Matt. 9:17.
Pearl of great price.
Matt. 13:45–46.
Persistent friend. Luke 11:5–9.
Persistent widow. Luke 18:1–8.
Pharisee and tax collector.
Luke 18:9–14.
Pounds. Luke 19:12–27.
Prodigal son. Luke 15:11–32.
Rich fool. Luke 12:16–21.
Rich man and Lazarus.
Luke 16:19–31.
Savor of salt. Luke 14:34–35.
Seed growing secretly.
Mark 4:26–29.
Shrewd manager. Luke 16:1–8.
Sower. Matt. 13:3, 18;
Luke 8:5, 11.

Speck and log. Luke 6:41–42.
Strong man armed. Mark 3:27;
Luke 11:21.
Talents. Matt. 25:14–30.
Ten virgins. Matt. 25:1–13.
Treasure hid in a field.
Matt. 13:44.
Tree and its fruit. Luke 6:43–45.
Two sons. Matt. 21:28–32.
Unclean spirit. Matt. 12:43.
Unmerciful servant.
Matt. 18:23–35.
Vine and branches. John 15:1–5.
Weeds. Matt. 13:24–30, 36–43.
Wicked farmers. Matt. 21:33–45.
Wise and foolish builders.
Matt. 7:24–27.
Of the Old Testament. Judg. 9:8–15;
2 Sam. 12:1–4; 14:5–7.

PARADISE
The place of the glorified spirits.
Luke 23:43; 2 Cor. 12:4;
Rev. 2:7.

Used to speak of
Garden of Eden. Gen. 2–3.
King Artaxerxes' forest. Neh. 2:8
Orchards of Solomon. Eccles. 2:5;
Song of Sol. 4:13.

PARADOX
Becoming wise and being foolish.
1 Cor. 3:18.
Chief of the apostles, yet nothing.
2 Cor. 12:1–11.
Concerning riches and poverty.
Prov. 13:7.
Having all things and possessing
nothing. 2 Cor. 6:4–10.

PARALYSIS
Cured by Jesus. Matt. 4:24.
Cured by Peter. Acts 9:33, 34.

Cured by Phillip. Acts 8:7.

PARCHMENT
Paul asks that they be brought.
2 Tim. 4:13.

PARDON
All believers enjoy. Col. 2:13;
1 John 2:12.
Blessedness of. Ps. 32:1, with
Rom. 4:7.
Blood of Christ alone is effective for.
Zech. 13:1, with 1 John 1:7.
Encouragement to pray for.
2 Chron. 7:14.

Exhibits God's
Compassion. Mic. 7:18–19.
Faithfulness. 1 John 1:9.
Goodness. 2 Chron. 30:18;
Ps. 86:5.
Grace. Rom. 5:15–16.
Justice. 1 John 1:9.
Loving-kindness. Ps. 51:1.
Mercy. Exod. 34:7; Ps. 51:1.
Patience. Rom. 3:25.

Expressed by
Casting sins into the sea.
Mic. 7:19.
Covering sin. Ps. 32:1.
Forgiving sin. Ps. 32:1.
Not mentioning transgression.
Ezek. 18:22.
Not remembering sins.
Heb. 10:17.
Not taking sin into account.
Rom. 4:8.
Removing sin. Ps. 103:12.
Wiping out sin. Acts 3:19.
Wiping out sin. Isa. 44:22.

Granted
Abundantly. Isa. 55:7; Rom. 5:20.

According to the riches of grace.
Eph. 1:7.
Through the blood of Christ.
Matt. 26:28; Rom. 3:25;
Col. 1:14.
By Christ. Mark 2:5; Luke 7:48.
Through Christ. Luke 1:69, 77;
Acts 5:31; 13:38.
By God alone. Dan. 9:9;
Mark 2:7.
Freely. Isa. 43:25.
In Christ's name. 1 John 2:12.
On the exaltation of Christ.
Acts 5:31.
Readily. Neh. 9:17; Ps. 86:5.
To those who believe. Acts 10:43.
To those who confess their sins.
2 Sam. 12:13; Ps. 32:5;
1 John 1:9.
To those who repent. Acts 2:38.
Legal sacrifices not effective for.
Heb. 10:4.
Ministers are appointed to proclaim.
Isa. 40:1–2; 2 Cor. 5:19.
None without shedding of blood.
Lev. 17:11, with Heb. 9:22.
Outward purifications not effective
for. Job 9:30–31; Jer. 2:22.

Pray for
Others. James 5:15;
1 John 5:16.
Yourselves. Pss. 25:11, 18; 51:1;
Matt. 6:12; Luke 11:4.
Promised. Isa. 1:18; Jer. 31:34, with
Heb. 8:12; Jer. 50:20.
Should be preached in the name of
Christ. Luke 24:47.

Should lead to
Fearing God. Ps. 130:4.
Loving God. Luke 7:47.
Praising God. Ps. 103:2–3.
Returning to God. Isa. 44:22.

Withheld from
Apostates. Heb. 10:26–27;
1 John 5:16.
Blasphemers against the Holy
Spirit. Matt. 12:32;
Mark 3:28–29.
The unrepentant. Luke 13:2–5.
The unbelieving. John 8:21, 24.
The unforgiving. Mark 11:26;
Luke 6:37.

PARENTING

Children
Characteristics revealed by
actions. Prov. 20:11.
Foolish. Prov. 17:21.
Forsaken by parents. Ps. 27:10.
A heritage of the Lord. Gen. 33:5;
Ps. 127:3–5; 128:3.
Mature. Ps. 144:12.
To obey parents. Eph. 6:1;
Col. 3:20.
Wise. Prov 13:1.
Children received from God.
Gen. 33:5; 1 Sam. 1:27;
Ps. 127:3.

Examples of
Eli. 1 Sam. 3:13.
Eunice. 2 Tim. 1:5; 3:14–15.
Hannah. 1 Sam. 1:21–28;
2:19–21.
Isaac and Rebekkah. Gen. 25:28.
Prodigal son. Luke 15:11–32.
Negligence of, sorely punished.
1 Sam. 3:13.

Parents are to
Bless them. Gen. 48:15;
Heb. 11:20.
Bring them to Christ.
Matt. 19:13–14.

Command them to obey God.
Deut. 32:46; 1 Chron. 28:9.
Correct them.
Prov. 13:24; 19:18; 23:13;
29:17; 1 Tim. 3:4; Heb. 12:7.
Have compassion for them.
Ps. 103:13.
Instruct them. Gen. 18:19;
Deut. 4:9; 6:7; 11:19;
Ps. 78:1–8; Prov. 4:3–4; 22:6;
Isa. 38:19; Eph. 6:4;
2 Tim. 3:14–15.
Love them. John 13:35; 15:12;
Titus 2:4.
Make the most of the time.
Prov. 4:3–4; Eph. 5:15–16.
Manage them. 1 Tim. 3:4, 12.
Nourish. Prov. 15:4; 19:18.
Not make unholy connections for
them. Gen. 24:1–4; 28:1–2.
Not provoke them. Eph. 6:4;
Col. 3:21.
Pray for. 1 Thess. 5:17.
Provide for them. Job 42:15;
2 Cor. 12:14; 1 Tim. 5:8.
Teach them God's Word.
Deut. 4:9; 11:19; Isa. 38:19.
Tell them of God's judgments.
Joel 1:3.
Tell them of the miraculous works
of God. Exod. 10:2; Ps. 78:4.
Train them up for God.
Prov. 22:6; Eph. 6:4.
Treat children fairly.
Deut. 21:15–17.

Should pray for their children
For their spiritual welfare.
Gen. 17:18; 1 Chron. 29:19.
When in sickness. 2 Sam. 12:16;
Mark 5:23; John 4:46, 49.
When in temptation. Job 1:5.
Sins of, visited on their children.
Exod. 20:5; Isa. 14:20; Lam. 5:7.

When faithful
Are blessed by their children.
Prov. 31:28.
Leave a blessing to their children.
Ps. 112:2; Isa. 65:23.

When wicked
Instruct their children in evil.
Jer. 9:14; 1 Pet. 1:18.
Set a bad example to their
children. Ezek. 20:18;
Amos 2:4.
Wicked children, a cause of grief to.
Prov. 10:1; 17:25.

PARRICIDE
Sennacherib. 2 Kings 19:36.

PARTAKERS

Should not take part in
Adultery. Ps. 50:18.
Other men's sins. 1 Tim. 5:22.
The table of devils. 1 Cor. 10:21.

Should take part in
The bread of communion.
1 Cor. 10:17.
Grace. Phil. 1:7.
The heavenly calling. Heb. 3:1.
The holiness of God. Heb. 12:10.
The Holy Spirit. Heb. 6:4.
The inheritance of believers.
Col. 1:12.
The nature of God. 2 Pet. 1:4.
The promise of salvation.
Eph. 3:6.
Spiritual blessings. Rom. 11:17.
The sufferings of Christ.
1 Pet. 4:13.

PARTIALITY
Its effect on other children.
Gen. 37:4.

There is none with God. Acts 10:34;
Rom. 10:12; Matt. 5:45.
There must be none with us.
Deut. 1:17; Job 13:10;
1 Tim. 5:21; James 2:4.
There should be none in the realm of
justice. Lev. 19:15; Col. 4:1.

PARTIES

Examples of
Nabal. 1 Sam 25:36.
Wild. Isa. 5:11-12.

PARTNERSHIP
With God. 1 Cor. 3:7, 9; 2 Cor. 6:1;
Phil. 2:13.

PASCHAL LAMB, TYPICAL NATURE OF
Blood of, not sprinkled on threshold.
Exod. 12:7; Heb. 10:29.
Blood of, sprinkled on lintel and door
posts. Exod. 12:22;
Heb. 9:13-14; 10:22; 1 Pet. 1:2.
Blood of, to be shed. Exod. 12:7;
Luke 22:20.
Chosen beforehand. Exod. 12:3;
1 Pet. 2:4.
Eaten in haste. Exod. 12:11;
Heb. 6:18.
Eaten with bitter herbs. Exod. 12:8;
Zech. 12:10.
Eaten fully dressed. Exod. 12:11;
Luke 12:35; Eph. 6:14;
1 Pet. 1:13.
Eaten with shoes on. Exod. 12:11;
Eph. 6:15.
Eaten with staff in hand.
Exod. 12:11; Ps. 23:4.
Eaten with unleavened bread.
Exod. 12:39; 1 Cor. 5:7-8. (*See
also* 2 Cor. 1:12.)

Killed at the place where the Lord put
his name. Deut. 16:2, 5–7;
2 Chron. 35:1; Luke 13:33.
Killed by the people. Exod. 12:6;
Acts 2:23.
Killed in the evening. Exod. 12:6;
Mark 15:34, 37.
A male of the first year. Exod. 12:5;
Isa. 9:6.
Not a bone of, broken. Exod. 12:46;
John 19:36.
Not eaten raw. Exod. 12:9;
1 Cor. 11:28–29.
Not taken out of the house.
Exod. 12:46; Eph. 3:17.
Roasted with fire. Exod. 12:8;
Ps. 22:14 15.
Shut up four days that it might be
closely examined. Exod. 12:6;
John 8:46; 18:38.
Taken out of the flock. Exod. 12:5;
Heb. 2:14, 17.
A type of Christ. Exod. 12:3;
1 Cor. 5:7.
What remained of it until morning to
be burned. Exod. 12:10;
Matt. 7:6; Luke 11:3.
Without blemish. Exod. 12:5;
1 Pet. 1:19.

PASSOVER, FEAST OF

All males to appear at. Exod. 23:17;
Deut. 16:16.
Began the fourteenth of the first
month at evening.
Exod. 12:2, 6, 18; Lev. 23:5;
Num. 9:3.

Called the
Days of unleavened bread.
Acts 12:3; 20:6.
Feast of unleavened bread.
Mark 14:1; Luke 22:1.

Jew's Passover. John 2:13;
11:55.
Lord's Passover. Exod. 12:11, 27.
Passover. Num. 9:5; John 2:23.
Children to be taught the nature and
design of. Exod. 12:26–27; 13:8.
Christ always observed.
Matt. 26:17–20; Luke 22:15;
John 2:13, 23.

Commemorates the
Deliverance of Israel from bondage
of Egypt. Exod. 12:17, 42;
13:9; Deut. 16:3.
Passing over the firstborn.
Exod. 12:12–13.
Custom of releasing a prisoner at.
Matt. 27:15; Luke 23:10–17.
Day before the Sabbath in, called the
preparation. John 19:14, 31.
First and last days of, holy
convocations. Exod. 12:16;
Num. 28:18, 25.
First sheaf of barley harvest offered
the day after the Sabbath in.
Lev. 23:10–14.
Illustrative of redemption through
Christ. 1 Cor. 5:7–8.
Improper keeping of, punished.
2 Chron. 30:18, 20.
Lasted seven days. Exod. 12:15;
Lev. 23:6.

Leaven
Nothing with, to be eaten.
Exod. 12:20.
Not to be in any of their quarters.
Exod. 13:7; Deut. 16:4.
Not to be in their houses during.
Exod. 12:19.
Punishment for eating.
Exod. 12:15, 19.
The Lord's Supper instituted at.
Matt. 26:26–28.

Might be kept in second month by those who were unclean at the appointed time. Num. 9:6–11; 2 Chron. 30:2–3, 15.

Moses kept through faith. Heb. 11:28.

Neglect of, punished with death. Num. 9:13.

No uncircumcised person to keep. Exod. 12:43, 45.

Ordained by God. Exod. 12:1–2.

Paschal lamb eaten first day of. Exod. 12:6, 8.

People of Jerusalem offered their rooms to strangers for. Luke 22:11–12.

Purification necessary to the due observance of. 2 Chron. 30:15–19; John 11:55.

Remarkable celebrations of

After the captivity. Ezra 6:19–20.

Before the death of Christ. Luke 22:15.

On entering the land of promise. Josh. 5:10–11.

In Hezekiah's reign. 2 Chron. 30:1.

In Josiah's reign. 2 Kings 23:22–23; 2 Chron. 35:1, 18.

On leaving Egypt. Exod. 12:28, 50.

In the wilderness of Sinai. Num. 9:3–5.

The Sabbath in, a high day. John 19:31.

Sacrifices during. Lev. 23:8; Num. 28:19–24.

Strangers and servants when circumcised might keep. Exod. 12:44, 48.

To be perpetually observed during the Mosaic period. Exod. 12:14; 13:10.

Unleavened bread eaten at. Exod. 12:15; Deut. 16:3.

PASSPORTS
Given to Nehemiah. Neh. 2:7–9.

PASTORS
See also Ministers; Shepherds

Good

Are examples to the flock. 1 Pet. 5:3.

Are faithful. 1 Sam. 2:35.

Are ministers for good. Rom. 13:4.

Do not quarrel. 2 Tim. 2:24.

Do not try to rule over the flock. 1 Pet. 5:3.

Do the work of evangelists. 2 Tim. 4:5.

Exhibit purity, knowledge, patience, kindness, the Holy Spirit, and unfeigned love. 2 Cor. 6:6.

Feed the sheep. Jer. 23:4; 1 Pet. 5:2.

Give themselves to prayer and the ministry of the Word. Acts 6:4.

Keep watch over themselves and their flock. Acts 20:28.

Serve God. Rev. 22:3.

Work willingly, not just for money. 1 Pet. 5:2.

Work eagerly. 1 Pet. 5:2.

Poor

Are senseless. Jer. 10:21.

Cannot understand. Isa. 56:11.

Do not care for the sheep. John 10:13.

Lead the sheep astray. Jer. 50:6.

Scatter the sheep. Jer. 23:1.

PATIENCE
Believers receive from God.
Col. 1:11.
Christ an example of. Isa. 53:7, with
Acts 8:32; Matt. 27:14.
Commanded. Titus 2:2; 2 Pet. 1:6.
Commended. Eccles. 7:8;
Rev. 2:2–3.
Exercise, toward all. 1 Thess. 5:14.
God the God of. Rom. 15:5.
Illustrated. James 5:7.
Ministers approved by. 2 Cor. 6:4.
Ministers should follow after.
1 Tim. 6:11.
Necessary to the inheritance of the
promises. Heb. 6:12; 10:36.

Produces
Experience. Rom. 5:4.
Hope. Rom. 15:4.

Should be accompanied by
Faith. 2 Thess. 1:4; Heb. 6:12;
Rev. 13:10.
Godliness. 2 Pet. 1:6.
Joyfulness. Col. 1:11.
Long-suffering. Col. 1:11.
Self-control. 2 Pet. 1:6.

Should be exercised in
Bearing the yoke. Lam. 3:27.
Bringing forth fruits. Luke 8:15.
Running the race set before us.
Heb. 12:1.
Troubles. Luke 21:19;
Rom. 12:12.
Waiting for Christ. 1 Cor. 1:7;
2 Thess. 3:5.
Waiting for God. Pss. 37:7; 40:1.
Waiting for God's salvation.
Lam. 3:26.

Waiting for the hope of the gospel.
Rom. 8:25; Gal. 5:5.
Well-doing. Rom. 2:7; Gal. 6:9.
Should have its perfect work.
James 1:4.
Suffering with, for well-doing, is
acceptable with God. 1 Pet. 2:20.
Those who are in authority should
exercise. Matt. 18:26; Acts 26:3.
Trials of believers lead to. Rom. 5:3;
James 1:3.

PATRIARCH
Abraham. Heb. 7:4.
Head of a family. Acts 7:9.
Jacob's twelve sons. Acts. 7:8–9.
David. Acts 2:29.

PATRICIDE
Of Sennacherib. 2 Kings 19:37;
Isa. 37:38.

PATRIOTISM

Examples of
Deborah. Judg. 4:5.
Eli. 1 Sam. 4:17–18.
Hadad. 1 Kings 11:21–22.
Joab. 2 Sam. 10:12.
The lepers of Samaria.
2 Kings 7:9.
Moses. Heb. 11:24–26.
Nehemiah. Neh. 1:2, 4–11; 2:3.
The tribes of Zebulun and
Naphtali. Judg. 5:18–20.
Uriah. 2 Sam. 11:11.
The wife of Phinehas.
1 Sam. 4:19–22.

Lacking in
Inhabitants of Meroz. Judg. 5:23.
Of Succoth and Penuel.
Judg. 8:4–17.

The tribes of Reuben, Asher, and Dan. Judg. 5:15–17.

PATTERN
Of the tabernacle. Hebrew 8:5; 9:23.

PAVILION
Image of God's protection. Pss. 27:5; 31:20.
Tents used in military compaigns. 1 Kings 20:12, 16; Jer. 43:10.
Thick canopy of clouds surrounding God. 2 Sam. 22:12; Ps. 18:11.

PAYMENT
To God
Should be made regularly. 1 Cor. 16:2.
Should be proportionate to what we have. Lev. 27:32.
Should honor Him. Prov. 3:9.

To men
Should be made when due. Prov. 12:14.
Should not be made in kind but in grace. Luke 6:35; 1 Pet. 3:9.

For our deeds
Bountiful sowing brings bountiful harvest. 2 Cor. 9:6.
Wage of sin is death. Rom. 6:23.
Will be made in kind. Luke 6:38.
Worker is worthy of wages. 1 Tim. 5:18.

PEACE
Advantages of. Prov. 17:1; Eccles. 4:6.

Believers should
Cultivate. Ps. 120:7.

Endeavor to have with all people. Rom. 12:18; Heb. 12:14.
Follow. 2 Tim. 2:22.
Follow the things which make for. Rom. 14:19.
Have with each other. Mark 9:50; 1 Thess. 5:13.
Live in. 2 Cor. 13:11.
Love. Zech. 8:19.
Seek. Ps. 34:14, with 1 Pet. 3:11.
Speak. Esther 10:3.
Blessedness of. Ps. 133:1.
Blessedness of promoting. Matt. 5:9.
A bond of union. Eph. 4:3.
The church will enjoy. Pss. 125:5; 128:6; Isa. 2:4; Hos. 2:18.
Exhort others to. Gen. 45:24.
Fruit of righteousness should be sown in. James 3:18.
God the author of. Ps. 147:14; Isa. 45:7; 1 Cor. 14:33.

God bestows upon those who
Endure His discipline. Job 5:17, 23–24.
Obey Him. Lev. 26:6.
Please Him. Prov. 16:7.
Ministers should exhort to. 2 Thess. 3:12.
Necessary to the enjoyment of life. Ps. 34:12, 14, with 1 Pet. 3:10–11.
Pray for that of the church. Ps. 122:6–8.

Results from
Government of Christ. Isa. 2:4.
Heavenly wisdom. James 3:17.
Praying for rulers. 1 Tim. 2:2.
Seeking the peace of those with whom we dwell. Jer. 29:7.
Will abound in the latter days. Isa. 2:4; 11:13; 32:18.

The wicked
Do not enjoy. Isa. 48:22;
Ezek. 7:25.
Do not speak. Ps. 35:20.
Hate. Ps. 120:6.
Hypocritically speak. Ps. 28:3.
Opposed to. Ps. 120:7.

PEACE, SPIRITUAL

Accompanies
Acquaintance with God.
Job 22:21.
Faith. Rom. 15:13.
Love of God's law. Ps. 119:165.
Righteousness. Isa. 32:17.
Spiritual-mindedness. Rom. 8:6.
Announced by angels. Luke 2:14.

Believers
Blessed with. Ps. 29:11.
Die in. Ps. 37:37; Luke 2:29.
Enjoy. Ps. 119:165.
Have in Christ. John 16:33.
Have with God. Isa. 27:5;
Rom. 5:1.
Kept by. Phil. 4:7.
Kept in perfect. Isa. 26:3.
Rest in. Ps. 4:8.
Ruled by. Col. 3:15.
Wish, to each other. Gal. 6:16;
Phil. 1:2; Col. 1:2;
1 Thess. 1:1.

Of believers
Abundant. Ps. 72:7, Jer. 33:6.
Consummated after death.
Isa. 57:2.
Great. Ps. 119:165; Isa. 54:13.
Passes all understanding.
Phil. 4:7.
Secure. Job 34:29.
Benediction of ministers should be.
Num. 6:26; Luke 10:5.

Christ gives. 2 Thess. 3:16.
Christ guides into the way of.
Luke 1:79.
Christ our. Eph. 2:14.
Christ the Lord of. 2 Thess. 3:16.
Christ the prince of. Isa. 9:6.
Divine wisdom is the way of.
Prov. 3:17.
Established by covenant. Isa. 54:10;
Ezek. 34:25; Mal. 2:5.
Follows upon justification. Rom. 5:1.
A fruit of the Spirit. Rom. 14:17;
Gal. 5:22.
Given by Christ. John 14:27.
God ordains. Isa. 26:12.
God speaks, to His believers.
Ps. 85:8.
God the God of. Rom. 15:33;
2 Cor. 13:11; 1 Thess. 5:23;
Heb. 13:20.
The gospel is good tidings of.
Rom. 10:15.

Preached
By Christ. Eph. 2:17.
Through Christ. Acts 10:36.
By ministers. Isa. 52:7, with
Rom. 10:15.

Promised to
Believers. Ps. 72:3, 7; Isa. 55:12.
The church. Isa. 66:12.
The Gentiles. Zech. 9:10.
The meek. Ps. 37:11.
Returning backsliders.
Isa. 57:18–19.
Those who confide in God.
Isa. 26:3.
Supports under trials. John 14:27;
16:33.
Through the atonement of Christ.
Isa. 53:5; Eph. 2:14–15;
Col. 1:20.
We should love. Zech. 8:19.

The wicked
Are promised, by false teachers.
Jer. 6:14.
Know not the things of.
Luke 19:42.
Know not the way of. Isa. 59:8;
Rom. 3:17.
Promise, to themselves.
Deut. 29:19.
There is none for. Isa. 48:22;
57:21.

PEARLS
Are not to be thrown before swine.
Matt. 7:6.
Are the gates of the heavenly city.
Rev. 21:21.
And excessive adorning are not
appropriate for children of God.
1 Tim. 2:9; Rev. 17:4.
The kingdom is like a merchant
seeking. Matt. 13:45.
Wisdom is worth more than.
Job 28:18.

PEER PRESSURE
Accepted by Rehoboam.
1 Kings 12:8; 2 Chron. 13:7.

Injunctions concerning
Do not conform. Rom 12:2.
Exhort one another for good.
Heb. 3:13.
Follow advice of elders.
Lev. 19:32; Prov. 23:22.

Principles relevant to
False friendship. Prov. 18:24.
Many companions bring ruin.
Prov. 18:24.
Set above peers. Ps. 45:7.

PEN
Made of iron. Job 19:24; Jer. 17:1.

PENITENCE
See Repentance

PENKNIFE
Used to cut up a scroll. Jer. 36:23.

PENNY
A day's wages. Matt. 20:2–14.
Roman, bore Caesar's image.
Matt. 22:19–21.
About seventeen cents. Matt. 18:28.

PENSION
Of Levites. 2 Chron. 31:16–18.

PENTECOST, FEAST OF
All males to attend. Exod. 23:16–17;
Deut. 16:16.

Called the
Day of Pentecost. Acts 2:1.
Day of the first fruits. Num. 28:26.
Feast of harvest. Exod. 23:16.
Feast of weeks. Exod. 34:22;
Deut. 16:10.
First fruits of bread presented at.
Lev. 23:17; Deut. 16:10.
Held fiftieth day after offering first
sheaf of barley harvest.
Lev. 23:15–16; Deut. 16:9.
A holy assembly. Lev. 23:21;
Num. 28:26.
Holy Spirit given to apostles at.
Acts 2:1–3.
Law given from Mount Sinai on.
Exod. 19:1, 11, with 12:6, 12.
Observed by the early church.
Acts 20:16; 1 Cor. 16:8.
Sacrifices at. Lev. 23:18–19;
Num. 28:27–31.
A time of holy rejoicing.
Deut. 16:11–12.
To be continually observed.
Lev. 23:21.

PEOPLE
Common, heard Jesus gladly.
Mark 6:2.

PERFECTION
All believers have, in Christ.
1 Cor. 2:6; Phil. 3:15; Col. 2:10.
Believers do not claim. Job 9:20;
Phil. 3:12.
Believers commanded to aim at.
Gen. 17:1; Deut. 18:13.
Believers follow after. Prov. 4:18;
Phil. 3:12.
Blessedness of. Ps. 37:37;
Prov. 2:21.
The church will attain to.
John 17:23; Eph. 4:13.
Exhortation to. 2 Cor. 7:1; 13:11.
Of God. Pss. 18:32; 138:8.
God's perfection the standard of.
Matt. 5:48.
Implies willingness to give up one's
most cherished possessions.
Matt. 19:21.
Love the bond of. Col. 3:14.
Impossibility of attaining to.
2 Chron. 6:36; Ps. 119:96.
Ministers appointed to lead believers
to. Eph. 4:12; Col. 1:28.
Patience leads to. James 1:4.
Pray for. Heb. 13:20–21; 1
Pet. 5:10.
Purity and holiness in speech.
James 3:2.

The Word of God
Designed to lead us to.
2 Tim. 3:16–17.
The rule of. James 1:25.

PERFUME
Beds perfumed with myrrh.
Prov. 7:17.
Used in the tabernacle. Exod. 30:7.

PERJURY
Commandment against. Lev. 6:2–7;
Matt. 5:33.

Examples of
David. Ps. 35:11.
Jesus. Matt. 26:59.
Peter, when he denied Jesus with
an oath. Mark 14:71.
Stephen. Acts 6:11, 13–14.
Witnesses against Naboth.
1 Kings 21:18–13.
Zedekiah. 2 Chron. 36:13.
Judgment against. Mal. 3:5;
1 Tim. 1:9.

PERSECUTION
All that live godly in Christ will suffer.
2 Tim. 3:12.
Of believers, a persecution of Christ.
Zech. 2:8, with Acts 9:4–5.
Believers may expect. Mark 10:30;
Luke 21:12; John 15:20.
Believers suffer, for the sake of God.
John 15:15.
Believers suffering, should
Commit themselves to God. 1
Pet. 4:19.
Exhibit patience. 1 Cor. 4:12.
Glorify God. 1 Pet. 4:16.
Pray for deliverance. Pss. 7:1;
119:86.
Pray for those who inflict.
Matt. 5:44.
Rejoice. Matt. 5:12; 1 Pet. 4:13.
Return blessing for. Rom. 12:14.
Blessedness of enduring, for Christ's
sake. Matt. 5:10; Luke 6:22.
Cannot separate from Christ.
Rom. 8:35.
Christ patient under. Isa. 53:7.
Christ suffered. Ps. 69:26;
John 5:16.

Christ voluntarily submitted to.
Isa. 50:6.

False teachers shrink
from. Gal. 6:12.

God delivers out of. Dan. 3:25, 28;
2 Cor. 1:10; 2 Tim. 3:11.

God doesn't forsake believers under.
2 Cor. 4:9.

Hope of future blessedness supports
under. 1 Cor. 15:19, 32;
Heb. 10:34–35.

Hypocrites cannot endure.
Mark 4:17.

Illustrated. Matt. 21:33–39.

Inconsistent with the spirit of the
gospel. Matt. 26:52.

Lawful means may be used to escape.
Matt. 2:13; 10:23; 12:14–15.

Persons born according to the flesh
are given to. Gal. 4:29.

Originates in
Hatred to God and Christ.
John 15:20, 24.
Hatred to the gospel. Matt. 13:21.
Ignorance of God and Christ.
John 16:3.
Mistaken zeal. Acts 13:50;
26:9–11.
Pride. Ps. 10:2.

Pray for those suffering.
2 Thess. 3:2.

Preachers of the gospel subject to.
Gal. 5:11.

Punishment for. Ps. 7:13;
2 Thess. 1:6.

Sometimes to death. Acts 22:4;
Jer. 15:15.

The wicked
Active in. Ps. 143:3; Lam. 4:19.
Addicted to. Pss. 10:2; 69:26.
Encourage each other in.
Ps. 71:11.

Rejoice in its success. Ps. 13:4;
Rev. 11:10.

PERSIA (MODERN DAY IRAN)

Captivity predicted. Hos. 13:16.

An empire when extended from
Indian to Ethiopia, comprising
127 provinces. Esther 1:1;
Dan. 6:1.

Government of, restricted by
constitutional limitations.
Esther 8:8; Dan. 6:8–12.

Israel captive in. 2 Chron. 26:20.

Men of, in the Tyrian army.
Ezek. 27:10.

Municipal governments in, provided
with dual governors. Neh. 3:9, 12,
16–18.

The princes advisory in matters of
administration. Dan. 6:1–7.

Prophecies concerning. Isa. 3:17;
21:1–10; Jer. 49:34–39;
51:11–64;
Ezek. 32:24–25; 38:5;
Dan. 2:31–45; 5:28; 7; 8;
11:1–4.

Rulers of
Ahasuerus. Esther 1:3.
Artaxerxes I. Ezra 4:7–24.
Artaxerxes II. Ezra 7;
Neh. 2; 5:14.
Cyrus. 2 Chron. 36:22–23;
Isa. 41:2; 3; 4:28; 45:1–4, 13.
Darius. Dan. 5:31; 6; 9:1.
Princes of. Esther 1:14.

Status of women in, queen sat on the
throne with the king. Neh. 2:6.

System of justice. Ezra 7:25.

Vashti divorced for refusing to
appear before the kings court
attendants. Esther 1:10–22; 2:4.

PERSEVERANCE

Blessedness of. James 1:25.

A characteristic of believers.
Prov. 4:18.

Encouragement to. Heb. 12:2–3.

An evidence of belonging to Christ.
John 8:31; Heb. 3:6, 14.

An evidence of reconciliation with
God. Col. 1:21–23.

Lack of
Excludes from the benefits of the
gospel. Heb. 6:4–6.

Illustrated. Mark 4:5, 17.

Punished. John 15:6;
Rom. 11:22.

Leads to increase of knowledge.
John 8:31–32.

Maintained through
Faith. 1 Pet. 1:5.

The fear of God. Jer. 32:40.

The intercession of Christ.
Luke 22:31–32; John 17:11.

The power of Christ. John 10:28.

The power of God. Ps. 37:24;
Phil. 1:6.

Ministers should exhort to.
Acts 13:43; 14:22.

Promised to believers. Job 17:9.

Promises to. Matt. 10:22; 24:13;
Rev. 2:26–28.

To be manifested in
Continuing in the faith.
Acts 14:22; Col. 1:23;
2 Tim. 4:7.

Holding fast hope. Heb. 3:6.

Prayer. Rom. 12:12; Eph. 6:18.

Seeking God. 1 Chron. 16:11.

Waiting on God. Hos. 12:6.

Well-doing. Rom. 2:7;
2 Thess. 3:13.

In well-doing
Is not in vain. 1 Cor. 15:58;
Gal. 6:9.

Leads to assurance of hope.
Heb. 6:10–11.

PERSISTENCE

Of God
Christ persisted with Peter.
Matt. 26:32–33; Luke 22:61;
John 21:1–17.

God loves and calls with
everlasting love. Jer. 31:3.

The Lord called Samuel three
times. 1 Sam. 3:8.

The Lord revealed Himself
repeatedly in spite of human
indifference. Luke 20:9–15;
Heb. 1:1; 2 Pet. 3:9.

Where sin abounds, grace abounds
all the more. Rom. 5:20.

In prayer
The early Christians' example.
Acts 2:42.

Paul's example. 2 Cor. 12:7–8;
Acts 20:18–35.

The psalmist's example.
Ps. 55:17.

Of the righteous
In good things. Gal. 6:9;
1 Thess. 5:21; 2 Thess. 3:13.

The just person's resilience.
Prov. 24:16.

Peter's continued knocking.
Acts 12:16.

PERSONIFICATION

Of wisdom. Prov. 1; 2:1–9; 8; 9.

PERSUASION
Our assurance. Rom. 8:38–39;
2 Tim. 1:12; Heb. 11:13.
Our duty. Acts 26:28; 2 Cor. 5:11;
1 Pet. 3:15.
Our security. Rom. 15:14.

PESTILENCE
Sent as an encouragment for
repentance. Amos 4:10.
Sent as failure to fulfill coveant
obligations. Lev. 26:25;
Deut. 28:21.
Sent as punishment for persistent
unbelief. Num. 14:12.
Sent by God. Exod. 9:15; Jer. 15:2;
Hab. 3:5; Amos 4:10.
Sent by means of a destroying angel.
2 Sam. 24:16; 1 Chron. 21:15.

PETITION

Right of, recognized
By David. 1 Kings 1:15–21.
By Israel. Num. 27:1–5; 32:1–5;
36:1–5; Josh. 17:4, 14, 16;
21:1–2.
By Jehoram. 2 Kings 8:3, 6.
By Jeroboam. 1 Kings 12:1–17;
2 Chron. 10.
By Pharaoh. Exod. 5:15–18.

PETROLEUM
Rock pours out streams of oil.
Job 29:6.

PETS
Lamb as. 2 Sam 12:3.

PHARISEES
Ascribed Christ's miracles to Satan's
power. Matt. 9:34; 12:24.
As a body, rejected John's baptism.
Luke 7:30.

Believed in the resurrection, etc.
Acts 23:8.

Character of
Active in proselytizing.
Matt. 23:15.
Cruel in persecuting. Acts 9:1–2.
Desired special treatment.
Matt. 23:6.
Fond of distinguished titles.
Matt. 23:7–10.
Fond of public greetings.
Matt. 23:7.
Greedy. Matt. 23:14;
Luke 16:14.
Outwardly moral. Luke 18:11;
Phil. 3:5–6.
Oppressive. Matt. 23:4.
Particular in paying all dues.
Matt. 23:23.
Rigid in fasting. Luke 5:33;
18:12.
Self-righteous. Luke 16:15; 18:9.
Zealous of the law. Acts 15:5;
Phil. 3:5.
Zealous of tradition. Mark 7:3,
5–8; Gal. 1:14.

Christ
Announced warnings against.
Matt. 23:13, etc.
Asked for signs by. Matt. 12:38;
16:1.
Called an evil and adulterous
generation. Matt. 12:39.
Called fools and blind guides.
Matt. 23:17, 24.
Called serpents and generation of
vipers. Matt. 23:33.
Compared to unmarked graves.
Luke 11:44.
Compared to whitewashed tombs.
Matt. 23:27.

Condemned by, for associating with sinners. Matt. 9:11; Luke 7:39; 15:1–2.

Declared their doctrines hypocritical. Matt. 16:6, 11–12; Luke 12:1.

Declared their righteousness not sufficient for. Matt. 5:20.

Left Judea for a time because of. John 4:1–3.

Offended by His doctrine. Matt. 15:12; 21:45; Luke 16:14.

Often invited by. Luke 7:36; 11:37.

Tempted by, with questions about the law. Matt. 19:3; 22:15–16, 35.

Watched by, for evidence of evil.

By descent especially esteemed. Acts 23:6.Luke 6:7.

Had disciples. Luke 5:33; Acts 22:3.

Made broad their phylacteries, etc. Matt. 23:5.

Many priests and Levites. John 1:19, 24.

Many rulers, lawyers, and scribes. John 3:1; Acts 5:34; 23:9.

Often sought to destroy Christ. Matt. 12:14; 21:46; John 11:47, 53, 57.

A sect of the Jews. Acts 15:5.

Sent officers to apprehend Christ. John 7:32, 45.

Some came to John for baptism. Matt. 3:7.

Strictest observers of the Mosaic ritual. Acts 26:5.

Their opinions a standard to others. John 7:48.

PHILISTINES
Always joined with the enemies of Israel. Ps. 83:7; Isa. 9:11–12.

Called
Caphtorites. Deut. 2:23.
Kerethites. 1 Sam. 30:14; Zeph. 2:5.

Character of
Idolatrous. Judg. 16:23; 1 Sam. 5:2.
Proud. Zech. 9:6.
Superstitious. Isa. 2:6.
Warlike. 1 Sam. 17:1; 28:1.
Conquered the Avites and the west coast of Canaan. Deut. 2:23.

Country of
Called Philistia. Pss. 87:4; 108:9.
Divided into five states or lordships. Josh. 13:3; Judg. 3:3; 1 Sam. 6:16.
Given by God to the Israelites. Josh. 13:2–3; 15:45, 47.
Had many flourishing cities. 1 Sam. 6:17.

David
Distrusted by. 1 Sam. 29:2–7.
Fled to, for safety. 1 Sam. 27:1–7.
Gained the confidence of Achish, king of. 1 Sam. 28:2; 29:9.
Had a guard composed of. 2 Sam. 8:18, with Ezek. 25.16, Zeph. 2:5
Often defeated during Saul's reign. 1 Sam. 19:8; 23:1–5.
Often defeated in the course of his reign. 2 Sam. 5:17–23; 8:1; 21:15–22; 23:8–12.
Received Saul's daughter in exchange for a hundred foreskins of. 1 Sam. 18:25–27.

Slew Goliath the champion of.
1 Sam. 17:40–50.

Defeated by Hezekiah. 2 Kings 18:8.

Defeated by Israel at Ephes-dammin
and pursued to Ekron.
1 Sam. 17:1, 52.

Defeated by Uzziah.
2 Chron. 26:6–7.

Defeated Israel and killed Saul.
1 Sam. 31:1–10.

Defeated Israel at Ebenezer.
1 Sam. 4:1–2.

Descended from Casluhimites.
Gen. 10:13–14.

Distressed Judah under Ahaz.
2 Chron. 28:18–19.

First lived in the land of Caphtor.
Jer. 47:4; Amos 9:7.

Gathered all their armies to Aphek
against Israel. 1 Sam. 28:1; 29:1.

Governed by kings in the patriarchal
age. Gen. 21:22, 34; 26:8.

Invaded the land of Israel with a great
army. 1 Sam. 13:5, 17–23.

Israel condemned for imitating.
Judg. 10:6; Amos 6:2; 9:7.

Jonathan and his armor bearer killed
a garrison of, at the passages.
1 Sam. 14:1–14.

Jonathan killed a garrison of, at
Geba. 1 Sam. 13:3–4.

Men of great strength and stature
among 1 Sam. 17:4–7;
2 Sam. 21:16, 18–20.

Miraculously panicked.
1 Sam. 14:15–23.

Miraculously routed at Mizpah.
1 Sam. 7:7–14.

Mocked Israel by their champion.
1 Sam. 17:4–10.

Nadab besieged in Gibbethon.
1 Kings 15:27.

Oppressed Israel after the death of
Jair for eighteen years.
Judg. 10:7–8.

Oppressed Israel for forty years after
the death of Abdon. Judg. 13:1.

Plagued for retaining the ark.
1 Sam. 5:6–12.

Prophecies concerning

Destruction and desolation of their
cities. Jer. 47:5; Zeph. 2:4.

Dismay at ruin of Tyre.
Zech. 9:3, 5.

Hatred and revenge against Israel
to be fully paid back.
Ezek. 25:15–17; Amos 1:6–8.

To help in Israel's restoration.
Isa. 11:14.

A mongrel people to be their
rulers. Zech. 9:6.

Punishment with other nations.
Jer. 25:20.

Put the ark into Dagon's house.
1 Sam. 5:1–4.

Their country to be a future
possession of Israel. Obad. 1:19;
Zeph. 2:7.

Union with Syria against Israel.
Isa. 9:11–12.

Utter destruction by Pharaoh king
of Egypt. Jer. 47:1–4;
Zeph. 2:5–6.

Samson

Blinded and imprisoned by.
Judg. 16:21.

Burned vineyards, etc., of.
Judg. 15:3–5.

Intermarried with. Judg. 14:1, 10.

Killed a thousand with the jawbone
of an donkey. Judg. 15:15–16.

Killed many for burning his wife.
Judg. 15:7–8.

Killed thirty near Ashkelon.
Judg. 14:19.
Promised as a deliverer
from. Judg. 13:5.
Pulled down the house of Dagon
and destroyed immense numbers
of. Judg. 16:29–30.
Saul constantly at war with.
1 Sam. 14:52.
Sent back the ark and were healed.
1 Sam. 6:1–18.
Sent by God against Jehoram.
2 Chron. 21:16–17.
Shamgar killed six hundred and
delivered Israel. Judg. 3:31.
Some left to test Israel. Judg. 3:1–3.
Took the ark. 1 Sam. 4:3–11.
Ziklag, a town of, taken and
plundered by the Amalekites.
1 Sam. 30:1–2, 16.

PHILOSOPHY
Employment of, was not Paul's
method of preaching the gospel.
1 Cor. 1:17, 19, 21; 2:1–5, 13.
Greek schools of. Acts 17:18.
Is not sufficient for an adequate
knowledge of God.
1 Cor. 1:21–22.
The nature of things. Eccles. 1–7.
Not sufficient for a knowledge of
salvation through the atonement
of Jesus Christ. 1 Cor. 2:6–10.
A philosophical discourse on
wisdom. Job 28.
Philosophical inductions and
deductions relating to God and His
providence. Job 5:8–20; 9;
10:2–21; 12:6–24; 33:12–30;
37.
Rabbinical. Gal. 2:8, 16–19;
1 Tim. 6:20.

Revealed the mysteries of
providence. Prov. 25:2;
Rom. 1:19–20.

PHILIPPI
Paul did missionary work there.
Acts 16:12
Paul wrote a letter to the church
there. Phil. 1:1.

PHYLACTERY
A small box containing slips of
parchment on which were written
portions of the law. Exod. 13:16;
Deut. 6:4–9; 11:18.
Worn showily by some Jewish
leaders on the head and left arm.
Matt. 23:5.

PHYSICIAN
Asa sought, for disease of the feet.
2 Chron. 16:12.
Jeremiah asked if there is any, in
Gilead? Jer. 8:22.
Job calls his friends worthless.
Job 13:4.
Luke. Col. 4:14.
Proverb about. Mark 2:17.

PHYSIOGNOMY
Character revealed in. Isa. 3:9.

PHYSIOLOGY
Description of. Job 10:11;
Ps. 139:14–16.
Used in a figurative sense.
Eph. 4:16; Col. 2:19.

PICTURE
Use of in worship, prohibited.
Lev. 26:1.

PILGRIMS

All believers are. Ps. 39:12;
1 Pet. 1:1.

Believers are called to be. Gen. 12:1,
with Luke 14:26–27, 33;
Acts 7:3.

Believers confess themselves.
1 Chron. 29:15; Pss. 39:12;
119:19; Heb. 11:13.

As believers they
Are moved by faith. Heb. 11:9.

Are exposed to persecution
Ps. 120:5–7; John 17:14.

Are not at home in this world.
Heb. 11:9.

Are not mindful of this world.
Heb. 11:15.

Are strengthened by God.
Deut. 33:25; Ps. 81:6–7.

Die in faith. Heb. 11:13.

Forsake all for Christ.
Matt. 19:27.

Hate worldly fellowship.
Ps. 120:5–6.

Have a heavenly citizenship.
Phil. 3:20.

Have the example of Christ.
Luke 9:58.

Have their faces toward Zion.
Jer. 50:5.

Invite others to go with them.
Num. 10:29.

Keep the promises in view.
Heb. 11:13.

Long for their pilgrimage to end.
Ps. 55:6; 2 Cor. 5:1–8.

Look for a heavenly city.
Heb. 11:10.

Shine as lights in the world.
Phil. 2:15.

Should abstain from fleshly
desires. 1 Pet. 2:11.

Should have their treasure in
heaven. Matt. 6:19;
Luke 12:33; Col. 3:1–2.

Should not be overanxious about
worldly things. Matt. 6:25.

Described. John 17:16.

God is not ashamed to be called their
God. Heb. 11:16.

Look for a heavenly country.
Heb. 11:16.

Pass their sojourning in fear.
1 Pet. 1:17.

Pray for direction. Ps. 43:3;
Jer. 50:5.

Rejoice in the statutes of God.
Ps. 119:54.

The world is not worthy of.
Heb. 11:38.

PILLARS

Divine glory appeared to Israel in the
form of. Exod. 13:21–22;
Num. 12:5.

Illustrative of
Believers who overcome in Christ.
Rev. 3:12.

The church. 1 Tim. 3:15.

Ministers. Jer. 1:18; Gal. 2:9.

Stability of Christ.
Song of Sol. 5:15; Rev. 10:1.

Stability of the earth. 1 Sam. 2:8;
Ps. 75:3.

Stability of the heavens.
Job 26:11.

Lot's wife became, of salt.
Gen. 19:26.

Made of
Brass. 1 Kings 7:15.

Iron. Jer. 1:18.

Marble. Esther 1:6.

Silver. Song of Sol. 3:10.

Wood. 1 Kings 10:12.

Of memorial
To commemorate remarkable
events. Exod. 24:4;
Josh. 4:20, 24.
In honor of idols. Lev. 26:1;
Deut. 7:5.
Often anointed. Gen. 28:18;
31:13.
Often had inscriptions. Job 19:24.
To mark the graves of the dead.
Gen. 35:20.
To perpetuate names.
2 Sam. 18:18.
To witness covenants.
Gen. 31:52.
To witness vows. Gen. 28:18;
31:13.
Sometimes of a heap of stones.
Josh. 4:8–9, 20.
Sometimes of a single stone.
Gen. 28:18.
The supports of a building.
Judg. 16:29.
Two placed in the temple porch.
1 Kings 7:15–21.
Veil and hangings of the tabernacle
supported by. Exod. 26:32, 37;
36:36, 38.

PILLOW
A cushion. Gen. 28:11, 18;
1 Sam. 26:7, 11–16.

A support for the head
Called bolster.
1 Sam. 26:7, 11–12, 16.
Jesus sleeps on. Mark 4:38.
Made of goats hair.
1 Sam. 19:13, 16.
Stones used for. Gen. 28:11, 18.
Used in a figurative sense, of false
teachers. Ezek. 13:18, 20.

PILOT
Used in a figurative sense.
Ezek. 27:8, 27–29.

PINNACLE
Of temple. Matt. 4:5.

PIPE
A wind instrument of music, used in
religious services. 1 Sam. 10:5;
Isa. 30:29.

PIT
Benaiah slays a lion in.
2 Sam. 23:20.
The bottomless pit.
Rev. 9:1–2, 11; 11:7; 17:8;
20:1, 3.
Used in a figurative sense.
Ps. 7:15–16; Prov. 23:27.

PITCHER
Earthen. Lam. 4:2.
Used by Gideon in his battle with the
Midianites. Judg. 7:10–20.

PITY
See also Compassion; God,
Loving-kindness of

God's is
Toward all. Ps. 145:9; Matt. 5:45;
John 3:16.
Toward His people. Joel 2:18.
Toward little ones. Matt. 10:42.
Toward the poor. Prov. 19:17.
Toward the weak and needy.
Ps. 72:13.
Toward those who trust Him.
Ps. 103:13.

Ours should be
At the heart of our life. Col. 3:12.
Characteristic. Matt. 5:7, 46–48.

Continual. 1 Pet. 3:8.
Fundamental to our faith.
Hos. 6:6.

PLAGUES

Attributed to a destroying angel.
Exod. 12:23, with 2 Sam. 24:16.
Desolating effects of. Ps. 91:7;
Jer. 16:6–7; Amos 6:9–10.
Described as deadly. Ps. 91:3.
Egypt often afflicted with.
Jer. 42:17, with Amos 4:10.
Equally fatal day and night.
Ps. 91:5–6.

Illustrative of
The diseased state of human
hearts. 1 Kings 8:38.
God's judgments upon the
apostasy. Rev. 18:4, 8.
Inflicted by God. Ps. 78:50;
Jer. 21:6; Ezek. 14:19; Hab. 3:5.
Israel threatened with, as a
punishment for disobedience.
Lev. 26:24–25; Deut. 28:21.
The Jews sought deliverance from,
by prayer. 1 Kings 8:37–38;
2 Chron. 20:9.
Often broke out suddenly.
Ps. 106:29.
Often followed war and famine.
Jer. 27:13; 28:8; 29:17–18.
One of God's four dreadful
judgments. Ezek. 14:21.
Predicted to happen before
destruction of Jerusalem.
Matt. 24:7; Luke 21:11.
Sent as a just punishment.
Lev. 26:16, 25.

Sent upon
David's subjects for his numbering
the people. 2 Sam. 24:15.
The Egyptians. Exod. 12:29–30.

Israel for despising manna.
Num. 11:33.
Israel for making a golden calf.
Exod. 32:35.
Israel for murmuring at destruction
of Korah. Num. 16:46–50.
Israel for worshiping Baal–peor.
Num. 25:18.
Specially fatal in cities. Lev. 26:25;
Jer. 21:6, 9.

PLANE

A tool. Isa. 44:13.

PLANS

Foolishness of forgetting God in.
Ps. 52:7.
Importance of. Luke 14:28, 31.
Urgency of including God in.
Prov. 3:6.

PLASTER

Used in the building of houses.
Lev. 14:42–43, 48; Deut. 27:2;
Dan. 5:5.

PLEADING

Of the guilty. Josh. 7:19–21.
Jesus declined to. Matt. 26:62.
Prisoners required to. Acts 7:1.

PLEASURE

Dangers in. Titus 3:3; Heb. 11:25.
Emptiness of worldly. Eccles. 2.
From God. Ps. 16:6, 11; Prov. 3:17;
Acts 2:26.
Of God. Ps. 149:4; Phil. 2:13.
Influence of. Luke 8:14; 2 Pet. 2:13.

PLEDGE

Creditor must not enter house of a
debtor to take. Deut. 24:10–13.

PLOWS AND PLOWING

Breaking up or tilling the earth.
Jer. 4:3; Hos. 10:12.
Difficulty of, on rocky ground.
Amos 6:12.
Followed by harrowing and sowing.
Isa. 28:24–25.

Illustrative of
Continued devotedness (by the
attention and constancy required
in). Luke 9:62.
A course of sin. Job 4:8;
Hos. 10:13.
The labor of ministers.
1 Cor. 9:10.
Peace and prosperity. Isa. 2:4;
Mic. 4:3.
Repentance and reformation.
Jer. 4:3.
A severe course of affliction.
Hos. 10:11.
By Job's servants. Job 1:14.
Noah the supposed inventor of.
Gen. 5:29.

Performed
During the cold winter season.
Prov. 20:4.
Generally by servants. Isa. 61:5;
Luke 17:7.
In long and straight furrows.
Ps. 129:3.
By a plow. Luke 9:62.
Sometimes by the owner of the
land himself. 1 Kings 19:19.
With oxen. 1 Sam. 14:14;
Job 1:14.
Shares of, sharpened by smiths of the
Philistines. 1 Sam. 13:20.
Used by Elisha with twelve yoke of
oxen. 1 Kings 19:19.
Used in a figurative senses, of
afflictions. Ps. 129:3.

With an ox and a donkey yoked
together, forbidden to the Jews.
Deut. 22:10.

PLOWSHARE

Swords hammered into. Isa. 2:4;
Mic. 4:3.
Plowshares hammered into spears.
Joel 3:10.

PLUMB LINE

Used in a figurative sense.
Amos 7:7–8.

POET

Greek. Acts 17:28; Titus 1:12.

POETRY

Acrostic. Ps. 25; 34; 37; 111; 112;
119; 145; Prov. 31:10–31;
Lam. 1–5.

Didactic
Book of Job.
Book of Proverbs.
Moses' song. Deut. 32.
Song of Solomon.

Epic
Moses' song. Exod. 15:1–19.
Miriam's song. Exod. 15:21.
Song of Deborah. Judg. 5.

Lament
On the death of Abner.
2 Sam. 3:33–34.
On the death of Saul.
2 Sam. 1:19–27.

Lyrics, sacred
Elizabeth's song. Luke 1:42–45.
Hannah's song. 1 Sam. 2:1–10.
Mary's song. Luke 1:46–55.
Moses' and Miriam's song.
Exod. 15.

Zacharias' song. Luke 1:68–79.

POLICE

Instruments of state to maintain order. Rom. 13:4.

Personal bodyguards. 1 Sam 14:13; 17:7; 2 Sam 15:1; 18:15.

Royal attendants as. 1 Kings 9:22.

POLITICS

Corruption in. Ps. 12:8.

Corruption in the court of Ahasuerus. Esther 3.

Corruption in the court of Darius. Dan. 6:4–15.

Examples of

Absalom, electioneering for the throne. 2 Sam. 15:2–6.

Pilate, condemning Jesus to gratify popular demand. Matt. 27:23–27.

Ministers in

Nathan, the prophet influences the selection of David's successor. 1 Kings 1:11–40.

Zadok the priest, a partisan of David. 2 Sam. 15:24–29.

Women in

Bathsheba, in securing the crown for Solomon. 1 Kings 1:15–21.

Herodias, in influencing the administration of Herod. Mark 6:17–28.

Mother of Zebedee's children, in seeking favor for her sons. Matt. 20:20–23.

The wise woman of Abel, who saved the city through diplomacy. 2 Sam. 20:16–22.

POLITICIANS

Principles relevant to leaders

To be diligent. Rom 12:8.

As worthless shepherds. Ezek. 34:2–10; Zech. 11:15–17.

Office seekers as examples of

Absalom. 2 Sam. 15:1–6.

Gaal. Judg 19:28–29.

POLLUTION

See also Environmental protection

Of the altar of God. Exod. 20:25; Dan. 8:11.

Of clear water. Ezek. 34:18–19.

Of the Lord's Day. Isa. 56:2.

Of rivers. Exod. 7:20–24; Ezek. 32:2; Rev. 8:9–10; 16:4.

Of the sea. Rev. 8:8–9; 16:3.

Of sin removed. 1 John 1:7.

Of the sinful nature. Eph. 4:22.

Of the ungodly. Lev. 19:31; Acts 15:20.

POLYGAMY

Authorized. 2 Sam. 12:8.

Domestic unhappiness, in Abraham's family. Gen. 16; 21:9–16.

The evil effects of

Elkanah's favoritism in. 1 Sam. 1:5.

Husband's favoritism in. Deut. 21:15–17.

Jacob's favoritism in. Gen. 29:30; 30:15.

Rehoboam's favoritism in. 2 Chron. 11:21.

Forbidden. Deut. 17:17; Lev. 18:18; Mal. 2:14–15; Matt. 19:4–5; 1 Tim. 3:2, 12; Titus 1:6.

Mosaic law respecting the firstborn in. Deut. 21:15–17.

Practiced by
Abijah. 2 Chron. 13:21.
Abraham. Gen. 16.
Ahab. 2 Kings 10:1.
Ashur. 1 Chron. 4:5.
Belshazzer. Dan. 5:2.
David. 1 Sam. 25:39–44.
Elkanah. 1 Sam. 1:2.
Esau. Gen. 26:34.
Gideon. Judg. 8:30.
Hosea. Hos. 3:1–2.
Jacob. Gen. 29:30.
Jehoiachin. 2 Kings 24:15.
Jehoram. 2 Chron. 21:14.
Joash. 2 Chron. 24:2–3.
Lamech. Gen. 4:19.
Rehoboam. 2 Chron. 11:18–23.
Solomon. 1 Kings 11:1–8.
Sought by women. Isa. 4:1.

Tolerated. Exod. 21:10; 1 Sam. 1:2; 2 Chron. 24:3.
Unhappiness in Elkanah's marriages. 1 Sam. 1:4–7.
Unhappiness in Jacob's family. Gen. 29:30–34; 30:1–23.
Upon Solomon. 1 Kings 11:4–8.

POMEGRANATE TREE
See Tree, Pomegranate

PONTIUS PILATE
Roman procurator in Judea during the time of Christ.
Luke 23:4, 14, 22, 24.

POOL
Of Heshbon. Song of Sol. 7:4.
Of Jerusalem, upper pool.
2 Kings 18:17; Isa. 36:2.
Lower pool. Isa. 22:9.
Of Samaria. 1 Kings 22:38.

Pool of Siloam

Siloah. Neh. 3:15; John 9:7, 11.

POOLS AND PONDS

Artificial, designed for
Preserving fish. Isa. 19:10.
Supplying cities with water.
2 Kings 20:20.
Supplying gardens, etc., with
water. Eccles. 2:6.
Egypt abundant in. Exod. 7:19.
Filled by the rain. Ps. 84:6.

Illustrative of
The gifts of the Spirit (in the
wilderness). Isa. 35:7; 41:18.
Great desolation (turning cities
into). Isa. 14:23.
Nineveh. Nah. 2:8.
Made by God. Isa. 35:7.
Made by man. Isa. 19:10.

Mentioned in Scripture
Bethesda. John 5:2.
Gibeon. 2 Sam. 2:13.
Hebron. 2 Sam. 4:12.
The king's pool. Neh. 2:14.
The lower pool. Isa. 22:9.
The old pool. Isa. 22:11.
Samaria. 1 Kings 22:38.
Siloam. John 9:7.
The upper pool. 2 Kings 18:17;
Isa. 7:3.
Water of, brought into the city by a
ditch or conduit. Isa. 22:11, with
2 Kings 20:20.

POLYTHEISM
Laban's household gods.
Gen. 31:19.
Jacob puts away household gods.
Gen. 35:2, 4.
Meat offered to idols. 1 Cor. 8.

Pool of Hebron

POOR, THE

Care for
A characteristic of believers.
Ps. 112:9, with 2 Cor. 9:9;
Prov. 29:7.
Christ delivers. Ps. 72:12.
Christ lived as one of. Matt. 8:20.
Christ preached to. Luke 4:18.
A fruit of repentance. Luke 3:11.
Illustrated. Luke 10:33–35.
Should be urged. 2 Cor. 8:7–8;
Gal. 2:10.

Condition of, often results from
Bad company. Prov. 28:19.
Drunkenness and gluttony.
Prov. 23:21.
Laziness. Prov. 20:18.
Defend. Ps. 82:3–4.
Do justice to. Ps. 82:3;
Jer. 22:3, 16.
Do not despise. Prov. 14:21;
James 2:2–4.
Do not rob. Prov. 22:22.
Do not rule over ruthlessly.
Lev. 25:39, 43.
Do not be stingy with. Deut. 15:7.
Do not deny justice to. Exod. 23:6.
Does not harden the heart against.
Deut. 15:7.

Give to
Cheerfully. 2 Cor. 8:12; 9:7.
Generously. Deut. 14:29;
15:8, 11.
Not grudgingly. Deut. 15:10;
2 Cor. 9:7.
Specially if believers. Rom. 12:13;
Gal. 6:10.
Without showiness. Matt. 6:1.

God
Delivers. Job 36:15; Ps. 35:10.

Does not despise the prayer of.
Ps. 102:17.
Does not forget. Ps. 9:18.
Exalts. 1 Sam. 2:8; Ps. 107:41.
Hears. Ps. 69:33; Isa. 41:17.
Is reproached by mocking.
Prov. 17:5.
Is reproached by oppressing.
Prov. 14:31.
Is the refuge of. Ps. 14:6.
Maintains the right of. Ps. 140:12.
Protects. Pss. 12:5; 109:31.
Provides for. Pss. 68:10; 146:7.
Regards equally with the rich.
Job 34:19.
Guilt of defrauding. James 5:4.
Made by God. Job 34:19;
Prov. 22:2.

May be
Generous. Mark 12:42;
2 Cor. 8:2.
Rich in faith. James 2:5.
Upright. Prov. 19:1.
Wise. Prov. 28:11.

Neglect toward, is
Inconsistent with love to God.
1 John 3:17.
A neglect of Christ.
Matt. 25:42–45.
A proof of unbelief.
James 2:15–17.
Offerings of, acceptable to God.
Mark 12:42–44; 2 Cor. 8:2, 12.
Oppression of, illustrated.
2 Sam. 12:1–6.
Oppress not. Deut. 24:14;
Zech. 7:10.
Pray for. Ps. 74:19, 21.
Provided for under the law.
Exod. 23:11; Lev. 19:9–10.

Punishment for
Acting unjustly toward.
Job 20:19, 29; 22:6, 10;
Isa. 10:1–3; Amos 5:11–12.
Oppressing. Prov. 22:16;
Ezek. 22:29, 31.
Refusing to assist. Job 22:7, 10;
Prov. 21:13.
Ruining. Isa. 3:13–15;
Ezek. 18:13.
Relieve. Lev. 25:35; Matt. 19:21.
Will always be present. Deut. 15:11;
Zeph. 3:12; Matt. 26:11.

Should
Commit themselves to God.
Ps. 10:14.
Hope in God. Job 5:16.
Rejoice in God. Isa. 29:19.
When converted, rejoice in their
exaltation. James 1:9.
Such by God's appointment.
1 Sam. 2:7; Job 1:21.
Take no interest from. Lev. 25:36.

Those who in faith believe
Are blessed. Deut. 15:10;
Ps. 41:1; Prov. 22:9;
Acts 20:35.
Are happy. Prov. 14:21.
Have promises. Prov. 28:27;
Luke 14:13–14.
Have the favor of God.
Heb. 13:16.

The wicked
Crush. Amos 4:1.
Do not care about. John 12:6.
Defraud. Amos 8:5–6.
Despise the counsel of. Ps. 14:6.
Devour. Hab. 3:14.
Grind the poor into the dirt.
Isa. 3:15.

Oppress. Job 24:4–10;
Ezek. 18:12.
Persecute. Ps. 10:2.
Regard not the cause of.
Prov. 29:7.
Sell. Amos 2:6.
Trample. Amos 5:11.
Grieve. Ezek. 22:20.

POOR, RESPONSIBILITY TOWARD
See Welfare Programs

POPULARITY

Examples of
Absalom. 2 Sam. 15:2–6, 13.
David. 2 Sam. 3:36.
Job. Job 29.

PORPOISE
Skins of, used in building the
tabernacle. Ex. 25:5.

PORTERS
Guards at the city gates, doors of the
king's palace, and doors of the
temple. 1 Chron. 9:17–32;
2 Chron. 34:13; 35:15.
One-third were porters of the gate of
the foundation. 2 Chron. 23:5.
One-third were porters of the king's
house. 2 Chron. 23:5.
One-third were porters of the temple.
2 Chron. 23:4.
Posts were determined by lot.
1 Chron. 24:31; 26:13–19.
Served also as porters of the gates of
the walls. Neh. 12:25.
Served in twenty-four divisions.
1 Chron. 26:13–19.
Stationed around the temple in order
to be present for opening the
doors. 1 Chron. 9:27.

POSSIBILITY

In anything. Rom. 8:37–38;
Eph. 3:20.

Through Christ. Rom. 8:37;
Phil. 4:13.

By faith. Matt. 17:20; 19:26;
Mark 9:23.

With God. Judg. 6:12; Mark 14:36.

Of strength. 2 Chron. 32:7;
Ps. 27:1; 55:22.

In weakness. 2 Cor. 12:10;
Heb. 11:34.

POST

Of Ahasuerus. Esther 3:13, 15;
8:10, 14.

A bearer of messages. Job 9:25;
Jer. 51:31.

Of Hezekiah. 2 Chron. 30:6, 10.

POTTERY

Clay prepared for, by treading.
Isa. 41:25.

Place for manufacture of, outside the
wall of Jerusalem. Matt. 27:7–10.

Pots made of. Jer. 18:3–4.

Used in a figurative sense, of
weakness, in the idol in
Nebuchadnezzar's vision.
Dan. 2:41.

POVERTY

See Poor, the

POWER OF CHRIST

See Christ, Power of

POWER OF GOD

See God, Power of

POWER OF THE HOLY SPIRIT

See Holy Spirit, Power of

PRAETORIAN GUARD

Assigned to a Roman provincial
governor. Phil. 1:13.

PRAISE

Acceptable through Christ.
Heb. 13:15.

Accompanied with musical
instruments. 1 Chron. 16:41–42;
Ps. 150:3, 5.

Believers should
Be endowed with the spirit of.
Isa. 61:3.
Declare. Isa. 42:12.
Exhibit. Isa. 43:21; 1 Pet. 2:9.
Express their joy by. James 5:13.
Glory in. 1 Chron. 16:35.
Invite others to. Pss. 34:3, 95:1.
Pray for ability to offer.
Pss. 51:15; 119:175.
Render, under affliction.
Acts 16:25.
Triumph in. Ps. 106:47.

Called the
Fruit of the lips. Hos. 14:2;
Heb. 13:15.
Garment of praise. Isa. 61:3.
Sacrifice of praise. Heb. 13:15.
Sacrifices of joy. Ps. 27:6.
Voice of a psalm. Ps. 98:5.
Voice of melody. Isa. 51:3.
Voice of praise. Ps. 66:8.
Voice of triumph. Ps. 47:1.
Christ worthy of. Rev. 5:12.

Due to God on account of
All spiritual blessings. Ps. 103:2;
Eph. 1:3.
All temporary blessings.
Pss. 104:1, 14; 136:25.
Answering prayer. Pss. 28:6;
118:21.

Constant preservation.
Ps. 71:6–8.
The continuance of blessings.
Ps. 68:19.
Deliverance. Pss. 40:1–3; 124:6.
Fulfilling of His promises.
1 Kings 8:56.
His comfort. Ps. 42:5; Isa. 12:1.
His counsel. Ps. 16:7; Jer. 32:19.
His excellency. Exod. 15:7;
Ps. 148:13.
His faithfulness and truth.
Isa. 25:1.
His glory. Ps. 138:5; Ezek. 3:12.
His goodness. Pss. 107:8, 118:1;
136:1; Jer. 33:11.
His greatness. 1 Chron. 16:25;
Ps. 145:3.
His holiness. Exod. 15:11;
Isa. 6:3.
His judgment. Ps. 101:1.
His loving-kindness and truth.
Ps. 138:2.
His majesty. Ps. 96:1, 6;
Isa. 24:14.
His mercy. 2 Chron. 20:21;
Pss. 89:1; 118:1–4; 136.
His power. Ps. 21:13.
His salvation. Ps. 18:46;
Isa. 35:10; 61:10;
Luke 1:68–69.
His wisdom. Dan. 2:20; Jude 25.
His wonderful works. Pss. 89:5;
150:2; Isa. 25:1.
The hope of glory. 1 Pet. 1:3–4.
Pardon of sin. Ps. 103:1–3;
Hos. 14:2.
Protection. Pss. 28:7; 59:17.
Spiritual health. Ps. 103:3.
God glorified by. Pss. 22:23; 50:23.
God worthy of. 2 Sam. 22:4.
Good and pleasant. Pss. 33:1;
147:1.

The heavenly host engage in.
Isa. 6:3; Luke 2:13; Rev. 4:9–11;
5:12.

Obligatory upon
All creation. Pss. 148:1–10;
150:6.
All people. Pss. 107:8; 145:21.
Angels. Pss. 103:20; 148:2.
Believers. Pss. 30:4; 149:5.
Children. Ps. 8:2, with
Matt. 21:16.
Gentiles. Ps. 117:1, with
Rom. 15:11.
High and low. Ps. 148:1, 11.
Small and great. Rev. 19:5.
Young and old. Ps. 148:1, 12.
Offered to Christ. John 12:13.
A part of public worship.
Pss. 9:14; 100:4; 118:19–20;
Heb. 2:12.
Offered in a standing position.
1 Chron. 23:30; Neh. 9:5.

Should be offered
Continually. Pss. 35:28, 71:6.
Day and night. Rev. 4:8.
Day by day. 2 Chron. 30:21.
During life. Ps. 104:33.
Forever and ever. Ps. 145:1–2.
In psalms and hymns, etc.
Ps. 105:2; Eph. 5:19;
Col. 3:16.
More and more Ps. 71:14.
Throughout the world. Ps. 113:3.
With gladness. 2 Chron. 29:30;
Jer. 33:11.
With joy. Pss. 63:5; 98:4.
With the lips. Pss. 63:3; 119:171.
With the mouth. Pss. 51:15; 63:5.
With the soul. Ps. 103:1;
104:1, 35.
With thankfulness. 1 Chron. 16:4;
Neh. 12:24; Ps. 147:7.

With the understanding. Ps. 47:7, with 1 Cor. 14:15.

With the whole heart. Pss. 9:1; 111:1; 138:1.

With uprightness of heart. Ps. 119:7.

PRAYER

See also subtopics: Prayer, Answers to; Prayer, Intercessory; Prayer, Private; Prayer, Public; Prayer, Social and Family; Prayerfulness; Prayerlessness.

Acceptable through Christ. John 14:13–14; 15:16; 16:23–24.

Accompanied with
Confession. Neh. 1:4, 7; Dan. 9:4–11.
Fasting. Neh. 1:4; Dan. 9:3; Acts 13:3.
Humility. Gen. 18:27.
Praise. Ps. 66:17.
Repentance. 1 Kings 8:33; Jer. 36:7.
Thanksgiving. Phil. 4:6; Col. 4:2.
Watchfulness. Luke 21:36; 1 Pet. 4:7.
Weeping. Jer. 31:9; Hos. 12:4.
Avoid hindrances in. 1 Pet. 3:7.
Commanded. Isa. 55:6; Matt. 7:7; Phil. 4:6.

Described as
Bowing the knees. Eph. 3:14.
Calling upon the name of the Lord. Gen. 12:8; Ps. 116:4; Acts 22:16.
Crying to heaven. 2 Chron. 32:20.
Crying to God. Pss. 27:7; 34:6.

Drawing near to God. Ps. 73:28; Heb. 10:22.
Lifting up the heart. Lam. 3:41.
Lifting up the soul. Ps. 25:1.
Looking up. Ps. 5:3.
Looking to God. Job 8:5.
Pleading. Job 8:5; Jer. 36:7.
Pouring out the heart. Ps. 62:8.
Pouring out the soul. 1 Sam. 1:15.
Seeking the face of the Lord. Ps. 27:8.
Seeking the favor of the Lord. Exod. 32:11.
An evidence of conversion. Acts 9:11.
Experience of past mercies an incentive to. Pss. 4:1; 116:2.
For mercy and grace to help in time of need. Heb. 4:16.
For spiritual blessings. Matt. 6:33.
For temporary blessings. Gen. 28:20; Prov. 30:8; Matt. 6:11.
God hears. Pss. 10:17; 65:2.
God responds. Ps. 99:6; Isa. 58:9.

The Holy Spirit
As the spirit of adoption, leads to. Rom. 8:15; Gal. 4:6.
Helps our sufferings in. Rom. 8:26.
Promised as a spirit of. Zech. 12:10.
Model for. Matt. 6:9–13.
Of the righteous, is powerful. James 5:16.
Of the upright, a delight to God. Prov. 15:8.
Pretentious in, forbidden. Matt. 6:5.
Persist in. Luke 18:1.

Plead in the
Covenant of God. Jer. 14:21.

Faithfulness of God. Ps. 143:1.
Mercy of God. Ps. 51:1;
Dan. 9:18.
Promises of God. Gen. 32:9–12;
Exod. 32:13; 1 Kings 8:26;
Ps. 119:49.
Righteousness of God. Dan. 9:16.

Postures in
Bowing down. Ps. 95:6.
Falling on the face. Num. 16:22;
Josh. 5:14; 1 Chron. 21:16;
Matt. 26:39.
Kneeling. 2 Chron. 6:13;
Ps. 95:6; Luke 22:41;
Acts 20:36.
Lifting up the hands. Ps. 28:2;
Lam. 2:19; 1 Tim. 2:8.
Spreading out the hands.
Isa. 1:15.
Standing. 1 Kings 8:22;
Mark 11:25.
Promises of Christ encourage to.
Luke 11:9–10; John 14:13–14.
Promises of God encourage to.
Isa. 65:24; Amos 5:4;
Zech. 13:9.
Repeating meaningless phrases,
forbidden. Matt. 6:5.
Reaches heaven. 2 Chron. 30:27;
Rev. 5:8.
Reviving grace necessary to.
Ps. 80:18.
Rise early for. Pss. 5:3; 119:147.
Seek divine teaching for. Luke 11:1.
Shortness of time a motive to.
1 Pet. 4:7.

Should be offered up
With boldness. Heb. 4:16.
Without ceasing. 1 Thess. 5:17.
With confidence in God.
Pss. 56:9; 86:7; 1 John 5:14.
With deliberation. Eccles. 5:2.

With desire to be answered.
Pss. 27:7; 102:2; 108:6;
143:1.
With desire to be heard. Neh. 1:6;
Pss. 17:1; 55:1–2; 61:1.
With earnestness. 1 Thess. 3:10;
James 5:17.
Everywhere. 1 Tim. 2:8.
In everything. Phil. 4:6.
In faith. Matt. 21:22; James 1:6.
In a forgiving spirit. Matt. 6:12.
In full assurance of faith.
Heb. 10:22.
With the heart. Jer. 29:13;
Lam. 3:41.
With holiness. 1 Tim. 2:8.
In the Holy Spirit. Eph. 6:18;
Jude 20.
With humility. 2 Chron. 7:14;
33:12.
Night and day. 1 Tim. 5:5.
With persistence. Gen. 32:26;
Luke 11:8–9; 18:1–7.
With preparation of heart.
Job 11:13.
With the soul. Ps. 42:4.
With the spirit and understanding.
John 4:22–24; 1 Cor. 14:15.
With submission to God.
Luke 22:42.
With a true heart. Heb. 10:22.
With truth. Ps. 145:18;
John 4:24.
With sincere lips. Ps. 17:1.
With the whole heart. Ps. 119:58,
145.

To be offered
Through Christ. Eph. 2:18;
Heb. 10:19.
To Christ. Luke 23:42; Acts 7:59.
To God. Ps. 5:2; Matt. 4:10.
To the Holy Spirit. 2 Thess. 3:5.

PRAYER, ANSWERS TO

Believers
Are assured of. 1 John 5:15.
Bless God for. Ps. 66:20.
Love God for. Ps. 116:1.
Praise God for. Pss. 116:17;
118:21.
Christ gives. John 4:10, 14; 14:14.
Christ received. John 11:42;
Heb. 5:7.

Denied those who
Are blood-shedders. Isa. 1:15;
59:3.
Are deaf to the cry of the poor.
Prov. 21:13.
Are hypocrites. Job 27:8–9.
Are idolaters. Jer. 11:11–14;
Ezek. 8:15–18.
Are proud. Job 35:12–13.
Are self-righteous.
Luke 18:11–12, 14.
Are the enemies of believers.
Ps. 18:40–41.
Are wavering. James 1:6–7.
Ask with wrong motives.
James 4:3.
Cruelly oppress believers.
Mic. 3:2–4.
Forsake God. Jer. 14:10, 12.
Do not hear the law. Prov. 28:9;
Zech. 7:11–13.
Harbor sin in the heart. Ps. 66:18.
Live in sin. Isa. 59:2; John 9:31.
Offer unworthy service to God.
Mal. 1:7–9.
Reject the call of God.
Prov. 1:24–25, 28.
God gives. Pss. 99:6; 118:5; 138:3.

Granted
Beyond expectation. Jer. 33:3;
Eph. 3:20.

Sometimes after delay. Luke 18:7.
Sometimes differently from our
desire. 2 Cor. 12:8–9.
Sometimes immediately.
Isa. 65:24; Dan. 9:21, 23;
10:12.
Through the grace of God.
Isa. 30:19.
A motive for continued prayer.
Ps. 116:2.
Promised. Isa. 58:9; Jer. 29:12;
Matt. 7:7.
Promised especially in times of
trouble. Pss. 50:15; 91:15.

Received by those who
Abide in Christ. John 15:7.
Are poor and needy. Isa. 41:17.
Are righteous. Ps. 34:15;
James 5:16.
Ask according to God's will.
1 John 5:14.
Ask in faith. Matt. 21:22;
James 5:15.
Ask in the name of Christ.
John 14:13.
Call on God in truth. Ps. 145:18.
Call on God under affliction.
Pss. 18:6; 106:44;
Isa. 30:19–20.
Call on God under oppression.
Isa. 19:20.
Fear God. Ps. 145:19.
Humble themselves.
2 Chron. 7:14; Ps. 9:12.
Keep God's commandments.
1 John 3:22.
Love God. Ps. 91:14–15.
Return to God. 2 Chron. 7:14;
Job 22:23–27.
Seek God. Ps. 34:4.
Seek God with all the heart.
Jer. 29:12–13.
Wait upon God. Ps. 40:1.

PRAYER, INTERCESSORY

Beneficial to the offerer. Job 42:10.

Christ set an example of.
Luke 22:32; 23:34;
John 17:9–24.

Commanded. 1 Tim. 2:1;
James 5:14, 16.

Encouragement to. James 5:16;
1 John 5:16.

Futile for the stubbornly unrepentant.
Jer. 7:13–16; 14:10–11.

By ministers for their people.
Eph. 1:16; 3:14–19; Phil. 1:4.

Seek an interest in. 1 Sam. 12:19;
Heb. 13:18.

Should be offered up for
All in authority. 1 Tim. 2:2.

All people. 1 Tim. 2:1.

All believers. Eph. 6:18.

Children. Gen. 17:18;
Matt. 15:22.

The church. Ps. 122:6;
Isa. 62:6–7.

Enemies among whom we dwell.
Jer. 29:7.

Fellow countrymen. Rom. 10:1.

Friends. Job 42:8.

Kings. 1 Tim. 2:2.

Masters. Gen. 24:12–14.

Ministers. 2 Cor. 1:11; Phil. 1:19.

Persecutors. Matt. 5:44.

Servants. Luke 7:2–3.

The sick. James 5:14.

Those who envy us. Num. 12:13.

Those who forsake us.
2 Tim. 4:16.

Those who grumble against God.
Num. 11:1–2; 14:13, 19.

Sin of neglecting. 1 Sam. 12:23.

PRAYER, PRIVATE

Christ was constant in.
Matt. 14:23; 26:36, 39;
Mark 1:35; Luke 9:18, 29.

Commanded. Matt. 6:6.

An evidence of conversion.
Acts 9:11.

Nothing should hinder. Dan. 6:10.

Rewarded openly. Matt. 6:6.

Should be offered
Day and night. Ps. 88:1.

Evening, morning, and noon.
Ps. 55:17.

Without ceasing. 1 Thess. 5:17.

Will be heard. Job 22:27.

PRAYER, PUBLIC

Acceptable to God. Isa. 56:7.

Believers delight in. Pss. 42:4;
122:1.

Christ
Attended. Matt. 12:9; Luke 4:16.

Exhortation to. Heb. 10:25.

God promises to bless in.
Exod. 20:24.

God promises to hear.
2 Chron. 7:14, 16.

Instituted form of. Luke 11:2.

Promises answers to. Matt. 18:19.

Sanctifies by His presence.
Matt. 18:20.

Should not be made in an unknown
language. 1 Cor. 14:14–16.

Urge others to join in. Ps. 95:6;
Zech. 8:21.

PRAYER, SOCIAL AND FAMILY

Christ promises to be present at.
Matt. 18:20.

Promise of answers to. Matt. 18:19.

Punishment for neglecting.
Jer. 10:25.

PRAYERFULNESS
Encouragement to. 1 Thess. 5:17.

PRAYERLESSNESS
Pastors in Jeremiah's time guilty of. Jer. 10:21.
Psalmist urges judgment on those guilty of. Ps. 79:6.

PREACHING

Purpose of
Convince, reprimand, exhort, teach. 2 Tim. 4:2.
Encourage, comfort, do people good. 1 Cor. 14:3.

Results of
Believers are built up through. 1 Cor. 14:3; Eph. 4:12.
Some consider foolishness. 1 Cor. 1:18–21.
Some find life through. Luke 11:32; 8:15; 1 Cor. 3:6–23.
Some postpone a decision. Acts 17:32; 26:28.
Some reject outright. 2 Pet. 2:4–5.

Subject of
Christ's cross. 1 Cor. 1:18, 23.
Christ's resurrection. Acts 17:18.
Forgiveness. Acts 13:38.
God's kingdom. Luke 9:2, 60.
Good news or gospel. Luke 4:18, 43; Rom. 1:15; 1 Cor. 1:17; Eph. 1:3.
Jesus Christ. 1 Cor. 1:23; 2 Cor. 4:5.
Peace. Acts 10:36.
Repentance. Mark 1:15.
Righteousness of life. Acts 24:25; 1 Tim. 4:11–65; 2 Pet. 2:5.

The unsearchable riches of Christ. Eph. 3:8.
The word of faith. Rom. 10:8.
The Word of God. 2 Tim. 4:2; Heb. 4:2.

PRECIOUSNESS OF CHRIST
See Christ, Preciousness of

PREDESTINATION
Of Abraham and his descendants. Gen. 21:12–13.

Examples of
Ahaziah. 2 Chron. 22:7.
Amaziah and the idolatrous Jews. 2 Chron. 25:20.
In the apostles. John 13:18; 15:19.
In the covenant with Abraham to have an heir. Gen. 21:12; Neh. 9:7–8.
In the destruction of Eli's sons. 1 Sam. 2:25.
The Hivites. Josh. 11:20.
Paul. Gal. 1:15.
Philistines. Judg. 14:4.
Rufus. Rom. 16:13.
In Zerubbabel. Hag. 2:23.
Paul's teaching concerning. Rom. 8:28–33; 9:11–29; 11:5–8.

Reason for God's
Of children. Matt. 11:25.
Of God's elect. Luke 18:7.
Of Israel. Deut. 7:7.
Of Jacob. Mal. 1:2.
Of Jeremiah. Jer. 1:4.
Of Judas. Luke 22:22.
Seen in the Lord's judgment on Egypt. Exod. 33:19.

PREJUDICE
Christ condemned for not having.
Matt. 9:11.
Christ rejected through. Luke 4:24;
John 1:46; 7:52.
Condemned. Prov. 28:21;
James 2:3–4, 9.
God's lack of. Job 13:10;
Acts 10:34; Eph. 6:9.

PREMARITAL SEX
See also Affairs; Sex Outside of
Marriage

Forbidden. Exod. 22:16–17;
Song of Sol. 2:7; 3:5; 4:12; 8:4;
1 Cor. 6:15–20.

Injunctions concerning
Better to marry than burn with
passion.
1 Cor. 7:2, 8–9, 36–37.
Control sexual desires. 1
Cor. 7:9, 37.
Flee youthful passions.
2 Tim. 2:22.
Premarital pregnancy without.
Matt. 1:18–20, 25.

Principles relevant to
With prostitute. 1 Cor. 6:15–20.
Temptation. 1 Cor. 10:12–13.
Unclean talk. Eph. 5:3–4.

PREPARATION
In God's plan
For deliverance of the Israelites
from Egypt. Gen. 2:1–4:31.
For the ministry of Christ.
Luke 4:1–15.
For our future. John 14:2;
1 Cor. 2:9–10.
For the work of Christ. Mal. 3:1;
Luke 1:76; 3:1–17.

In our lives
For the Lord's coming.
Luke 12:35–36.
To do good works. Titus 3:1.
To seek the Lord. Hos. 10:12.

PRESENCE
Of Christ
With His disciples. Matt. 28:20.
In all things. Rom. 8:35–38.
In our hearts. Eph. 3:17.
In our suffering. 2 Cor. 1:5;
Phil. 3:10.
When two or three worship.
Matt. 18:20.

Of God
Demands thanksgiving. Ps. 95:2.
Forever. Heb. 13:5.
In Eden. Gen. 3:8.
With His people. Exod. 33:14;
Josh. 3:10.
In our trials. Isa. 43:2.
Source of help. Ps. 46:5.
Source of joy. Ps. 16:11.

PRESENTS
Antiquity of. Gen. 32:13; 43:15.
Considered essential on all visits of
business. 1 Sam. 9:7.
Generally presented in person.
Gen. 43:15, 26; Judg. 3:17;
1 Sam. 25:27.
Generally gets a favorable reception.
Prov. 18:16; 19:6.

Given
On all occasions of public
rejoicing. Neh. 8:12;
Esther 9:19.
To appease the angry feelings of
others. Gen. 32:20;
1 Sam. 25:27–28, 35.

To confirm covenants.
Gen. 21:28–30.

To judges to secure a favorable
hearing. Prov. 17:23;
Amos 2:6.

By kings to each other in token of
inferiority. 1 Kings 10:25;
2 Chron. 9:23–24; Ps. 72:10.

To kings to engage their aid.
1 Kings 15:18.

At marriages. Gen. 24:53;
Ps. 45:12.

On occasions of visits. 2 Kings
8:8.

On recovering from sickness.
2 Kings 20:12.

On restoration to prosperity.
Job 42:10–11.

To reward service. 2 Sam. 18:12;
Dan. 2:6, 48.

On sending away friends.
Gen. 45:22; Jer. 40:5.

To show respect. Judg. 6:18.

In token of friendship.
1 Sam. 18:3–4.

As tribute. Judg. 3:15;
2 Sam. 8:2; 2 Chron. 17:5.

Laid out and presented with great
ceremony. Gen. 43:25;
Judg. 3:18; Matt. 2:11.

Not bringing, considered a mark of
disrespect and dislike. 1 Sam.
10:27; 2 Kings 17:4.

Of persons of rank, of great value
and variety. 2 Kings 5:5;
2 Chron. 9:1.

Often carried by servants.
Judg. 3:18.

Often carried on camels, etc.
1 Sam. 25:18; 2 Kings 8:9;
2 Chron. 9:1.

Receiving of, a sign of good will.
Gen. 33:10–11.

Sometimes sent before the giver.
Gen. 32:21.

Things given as
Cattle. Gen. 32:14–15, 18.

Food. Gen. 43:11; 1 Sam. 25:18;
1 Kings 14:3.

Garments. Gen. 45:22;
1 Sam. 18:4.

Gold and silver vessels.
1 Kings 10:25.

Horses and mules. 1 Kings 10:25.

Money. Gen. 45:22; 1 Sam. 9:8;
Job 42:11.

Ornaments. Gen. 24:22, 47;
Job 42:11.

Precious stones. 1 Kings 10:2.

Servants. Gen. 20:14; 29:24, 29.

Weapons of war. 1 Sam. 18:4.

When small or defective, refused.
Mal. 1:8.

PRESUMPTION

Believers avoid. Ps. 131:1.

A characteristic of Antichrist.
2 Thess. 2:4.

A characteristic of the wicked.
2 Pet. 2:10.

Exhibited in
Considering our own ways right.
Prov. 12:15.

Opposing God. Job 15:25–26.

Planning for future. Luke 12:18;
James 4:13.

Pray to be kept from sins of.
Ps. 19:13.

Pretending to prophecy.
Deut. 18:22.

Punishment for. Num. 15:30;
Rev. 18:7–8.

Seeking precedence.
Luke 14:7–11.

Self-righteousness. Hos. 12:8;
Rev. 3:17.
Spiritual pride. Isa. 65:5;
Luke 18:11.
Willful commission of sin.
Rom. 1:32.

PRIDE
Affliction to. Isa. 23:1, 3.

Believers
Do not give way to. Ps. 131:1.
Hate, in others. Ps. 101:5.
Mourn over in others. Jer. 13:17.
Do not respect in others. Ps. 40:4.

A characteristic of
The devil. 1 Tim. 3:6.
False teachers. 1 Tim. 6:3–4.
The wicked. Hab. 2:4–5;
Rom. 1:30.
The world. 1 John 2:16.
Comes from the heart.
Mark 7:21–23.
Defiles a person. Mark 7:20, 22.
Exhortation against. Jer. 13:15.

Followed by
Degradation. Prov. 29:23;
Isa. 28:3.
Destruction. Prov. 16:18; 18:12.
Shame. Prov. 11:2.
Forbidden. 1 Sam. 2:3; Rom. 12:3,
16.
Hardens the mind. Dan. 5:20.
Hateful to Christ. Prov. 8:12–13.
Hateful to God. Prov. 6:16–17;
15:5.
A hindrance to improvement.
Prov. 26:12.
A hindrance to seeking God.
Ps. 104; Hos. 7:10.

Leads people to
Anger. Prov. 21:24.

Contempt and rejection of God's
Word and ministers. Jer. 43:2.
Contention. Prov. 13:10; 28:25.
A persecuting spirit. Ps. 10:2.
Self-deception. Jer. 49:16;
Obad. 1:3.

Often originates in
Inexperience. 1 Tim. 3:6.
Possession of power. Lev. 26:19;
Ezek. 30:6.
Possession of wealth.
2 Kings 20:13.
Religious privileges. Zeph. 3:11.
Self-righteousness.
Luke 18:11–12.
Unsanctified knowledge.
1 Cor. 8:1.
A sin. Prov. 21:4.

Those who are guilty of, will be
Brought into contempt. Isa. 23:9.
Brought low. Ps. 18:27; Isa. 2:12.
Humbled. Dan. 4:37, with
Matt. 23:12.
Ruined. Jer. 13:9.
Punished. Zeph. 2:10–11;
Mal. 4:1.
Repaid. Ps. 31:23.
Resisted. James 4:6.
Scattered. Luke 1:51.
Subdued. Exod. 18:11;
Isa. 13:11.
The wicked clothed with. Ps. 73:6.
Will abound in the last days.
2 Tim. 3:2.

PRIESTS
After the Exodus, young men
(firstborn) assigned to act as.
Exod. 24:5, with 19:22.
All except offspring of Aaron
excluded from being. Num. 3:10;
16:40; 18:7.

Ceremonies at consecration of
Anointing with oil. Exod. 30:30;
40:13.
Clothing with the holy garments.
Exod. 29:8–9; 40:14;
Lev. 8:13.
Lasted seven days.
Exod. 29:35–37; Lev. 8:33.
Offering sacrifices.
Exod. 29:10–19; Lev. 8:14–23.
Partaking of the sacrifices of
consecration. Exod. 29:31–33;
Lev. 8:31–32.
Placing in their hands the wave
offering. Exod. 29:22–24; Lev.
8:25–26.
Purification by blood of the
consecration ram.
Exod. 29:20–21; Lev. 8:23–24.
Separated by David into
twenty-four divisions.
1 Chron. 24:1–19;
2 Chron. 8:14; 35:4–5.
Washing in water. Exod. 29:4;
Lev. 8:6.
During patriarchal age heads of
families acted as. Gen. 8:20;
12:8; 35:7.
Each division of, had its president or
chief. 1 Chron. 24:6, 31;
2 Chron. 36:14.
First notice of persons acting as.
Gen. 4:3–4
The four division that returned from
Babylon subdivided into
twenty-four. Ezra 2:36–39, with
Luke 1:5.

Garments of
Cap. Exod. 28:40; 39:28.
Coat or tunic. Exod. 28:40;
39:27.
Laid up in holy chambers.
Ezek. 44:19.

Linen undergarments.
Exod. 28:42; 39:28.
Often provided by the people.
Ezra 2:68–69; Neh. 7:70–72.
Purified by sprinkling of blood.
Exod. 29:21.
Sashes. Exod. 28:40.
Worn always while engaged in the
service of the tabernacle
Exod. 28:43; 39:41.
Worn at consecration.
Exod. 29:9; 40:15.
Worn by the high priest on the day
of atonement. Lev. 16:4.
Generally participated in punishment
of the people. Jer. 14:18;
Lam. 2:20.

Illustrative of
Believers. Exod. 19:6; 1 Pet. 2:9.
Christ. Heb. 10:11–12.
Made of the lowest of the people by
Jeroboam and others.
1 Kings 12:31; 2 Kings 17:32.
Might purchase and hold other lands
in possession. 1 Kings 2:26;
Jer. 32:8–9.
No blemished or defective persons
could be consecrated.
Lev. 21:17–23.
On special occasions, persons not of
Aaron's family acted as.
Judg. 6:24–27; 1 Sam. 7:9;
1 Kings 18:33.
Publicly consecrated. Exod. 28:3;
Num. 3:3.
Punishment for invading the office
of. Num. 16:1–35; 18:7;
2 Chron. 36:14.

Required to
Remain in the tabernacle seven
days after consecration.
Lev. 8:33–36.

Test their genealogy before they exercised the office. Ezra 2:62; Neh. 7:64.

Wash in the bronze basin before they performed their services. Exod. 30:18–21.

Revenues of

All devoted things. Num. 18:14.

All restitutions when the owner could not be found. Num. 5:8.

Firstborn of animals or their substitutes. Num. 18:17–18, with Exod. 13:12–13.

Firstfruits Num. 18:8, 12–13; Deut. 18:4.

First of the wool of sheep. Deut. 18:4.

A fixed portion of the spoil taken in war. Num. 31:29, 41.

Part of all sacrifices. Lev. 6:6–10, 31–34; Num. 6:19–20; 18:8–11; Deut. 18:3.

Redemption money of the firstborn. Num. 3:48, 51; 18:15–16.

Shewbread after its removal. Lev. 24:9; 1 Sam. 21:4–6; Matt. 12:4.

Tenth of the tithes paid to the Levites. Num. 18:26, 28; Neh. 10:37–38; Heb. 7:5.

Sanctified by God for the office. Exod. 29:44.

Services of

Blessing the people. Num. 6:23–27.

Blowing the trumpets on various occasions. Num. 10:1–10; Josh. 6:3–4.

Burning incense. Exod. 30:7–8; Luke 1:9.

Carrying the ark. Josh. 3:6, 17; 6:12.

Covering the sacred things of the sanctuary before removal. Num. 4:5–15.

Deciding in cases of jealousy. Num. 5:14–15.

Deciding in cases of leprosy. Lev. 13:2–59; 14:34–45.

Divided by lot. Luke 1:9.

Encouraging the people when they went to war. Deut. 20:1–4.

Ineffective for removing sin. Heb. 7:11; 10:11.

Judging in cases of controversy. Deut. 17:8–13; 21:5.

Keeping the charge of the tabernacle, etc. Num. 18:1, 5, 7.

Keeping the sacred fire always burning on the altar. Lev. 6:12–13.

Lighting and trimming the lamps of the sanctuary. Exod. 27:20–21; Lev. 24:3–4.

Offering first fruits. Lev. 23:10–11; Deut. 26:3–4.

Offering sacrifices. Lev. 1–6; 2 Chron. 29:34; 35:11.

Placing and removing shewbread. Lev. 24:5–9.

Purifying the unclean. Lev. 15:30–31.

Teaching the law. Deut. 33:8, 10; Mal. 2:7.

Valuing things devoted. Lev. 27:8.

Sons of Aaron appointed as, by perpetual statute. Exod. 29:9; 40:15.

Special laws respecting
  All bought and home-born
    servants to eat of their portion.
    Lev. 22:11.
  Children of, married to strangers,
    not to eat of their portion.
    Lev. 22:12.
  No foreigners or hired servant to
    eat of their portion. Lev. 22:10.
  Not to defile themselves by eating
    what died or was torn.
    Lev. 22:8.
  Not to defile themselves for the
    dead except for nearest relative.
    Lev. 21:1–6.
  Not to drink wine, etc., while
    attending in the tabernacle.
    Lev. 10:9; Ezek. 44:21.
  Not to marry divorced or
    prostitutes. Lev. 21:7.
  Restitution to be made to, by
    persons ignorantly eating of their
    holy things. Lev. 22:14–16.
  While unclean could not eat of the
    holy things. Lev. 22:3–7.
  While unclean could not perform
    any service. Lev. 22:1, 2, with
    Num. 19:6–7.
Thirteen of the Levitical cities given
  to, for residence.
  1 Chron. 6:57–60, with
  Num. 35:1–8.

Were sometimes
  Corrupters of the law. Isa. 28:7,
    with Mal. 2:8.
  Drunken. Isa. 28:7.
  Greedy. 1 Sam. 2:13–17.
  Profane and wicked.
    1 Sam. 2:22–24.
  Slow to sanctify themselves for
    God's service. 2 Chron. 29:34.
  Unjust. Jer. 6:13.

Were to live by the altar, because
  they had no inheritance.
  Deut. 18:1–2; 1 Cor. 9:13.

PRISONERS
Apostles. Acts 5:17–42.
Bound to soldiers. Acts 12:6,–7.
Confined in court of the palace.
  Jer. 32:2.
Confined in house of captain of the
  guard. Gen. 40:3.
Confined in house of the scribe.
  Jer. 37:15.
Cruelty to. Jer. 38:6.
Flogged. Matt. 27:26;
  Acts 16:23, 33; 2 Cor. 6:5;
  11:23–24.
Joseph. Gen. 39:20–23; 40;
  41:1–44.
Jeremiah. Jer. 38:6–28; 39:14.
John the Baptist. Matt. 11:2;
  14:3–12.
Keepers responsible for.
  Acts 12:18–19.
Kept in chains. Acts 12:6.
Kept in stocks. Prov. 7:22;
  Jer. 29:26; Acts 16:24.
Kept on bread and water of affliction.
  1 Kings 22:27.

Kindness to
  By Felix. Acts 24:23.
  By Julius, the centurion.
    Acts 27:1, 3; 28:16, 30–31.
  By the Philippian jailer to Paul and
    Silas. Acts 16:33.
  By the prison keeper to Jeremiah.
    Jer. 38:7–28.
Paul. Acts 16:19–40; 21; 27–40.
Permitted to make defense.
  Acts 24:10; 2 Tim. 4:16.
Peter. Acts 12:3–19.
Released at feasts. John 18:39.
Required to labor. Judg. 16:21.

Severe hardships of, mitigated.
Jer. 37:20–21.

Silas. Acts 16:19–40.

Visited by friends. Matt. 11:2;
Acts 24:23.

Tortured to extort self-incriminating
testimony. Acts 22:24.

Used in a figurative sense. Isa. 61:1;
Luke 4:18.

To be visited and ministered to.
Matt. 25:35–46.

Of war

Blinded. 2 Kings 25:7.

Put to death. Josh. 10:16–27.

Thumbs and toes cut off.
Judg. 1:6–7.

PRISONS

Antiquity of. Gen. 39:20.

Cisterns attached to. Jer. 38:6;
Zech. 9:11.

Confinement in, often awarded as a
punishment. Ezra 7:26.

Confinement in, considered a severe
punishment. Luke 22:33.

Illustrative of

Bondage to sin and Satan.
Isa. 42:7; 49:9; 61:1.

Deep afflictions. Ps. 142:7.

Hell. Rev. 20:7.

Keepers of

Often used severity.
Jer. 37:16, 20; Acts 16:24.

Put to death if prisoners escaped.
Acts 12:19.

Responsible for the prisoners.
Acts 16:23, 27.

Sometimes acted kindly.
Gen. 39:21; Acts 16:33–34.

Sometimes entrusted the care of
the prison to well-conducted
prisoners. Gen. 39:22–23.

Strictly guarded the doors.
Acts 12:6.

Kinds of, mentioned

Common. Acts 5:18.

State. Jer. 37:21, with
Gen. 39:20.

The king had power to commit to.
1 Kings 22:27.

The king had power to release
from. Gen. 40:21.

Magistrates had power to commit to.
Matt. 5:25.

Magistrates had power to release
from. Acts 16:35–36.

Persons confined in

Clothed in prison dress.
2 Kings 25:29.

Fed on bread and water.
1 Kings 22:27.

Might have their condition
improved by the king.
Jer. 37:20–21.

Often bound with chains.
Gen. 42:19; Ezek. 19:9;
Mark 6:17.

Often chained to two soldiers.
Acts 12:6.

Often executed in. Gen. 40:22;
Matt. 14:10.

Often fastened in stocks.
Jer. 29:26; Acts 16:24.

Often kept to hard labor.
Judg. 16:21.

Often placed in dungeons.
Jer. 38:6; Acts 16:24.

Often subjected to extreme
suffering. Pss. 79:11; 102:20;
105:18.

Said to be in jail. Acts 4:3.

Said to be in custody. Lev. 24:12.
Sometimes allowed to be visited by
their friends. Matt. 11:2; 25:36;
Acts 24:23.

Places used as
Court of the king's house.
Jer. 32:2.
House of the captain of the guard.
Gen. 40:3.
House of the king's scribe.
Jer. 37:15.
Prisoner's own house, where he
was kept bound to a soldier.
Acts 28:16, 30, with
2 Tim. 1:16–18.
Under the care of a keeper.
Gen. 39:21.

Used for confining
Condemned criminals until
executed. Lev. 24:12;
Acts 12:4–5.
Debtors until they paid.
Matt. 5:26; 18:30.
Enemies taken captive.
Judg. 16:21; 2 Kings 17:4;
Jer. 52:11.
Persons accused of crimes.
Luke 23:19.
Persons accused of heresy.
Acts 4:3; 5:18; 8:3.
Persons under the king's
displeasure. 1 Kings 22:27;
2 Chron. 16:10; Mark 6:17.
Suspected persons. Gen. 42:19.

PRIVACY
Communal responsibility.
Rom. 14:7–8.

Examples of
Heber the Kenite. Judg. 4:11.

Israel under Solomon.
1 Kings 4:25.
Residents of Laish.
Judg. 18:7, 27–28.
Tribe of Simeon. 1 Chron. 4:40.
Pray for king to allow. 1 Tim. 2:1–2.

Quiet living
As future hope. Mic. 4:4.
Commanded. 1 Thess. 4:10–11;
2 Thess. 3:12.

Retreat into
Before a fight. Gen. 32:23–24;
Josh. 8:13.
For prayer. Matt. 6:6; 14:23;
26:36.
For rest. Matt. 14:13; Mark 6:31.
For sacrifice. Gen. 22:5–6.
For transfiguration of Jesus.
Matt. 17:1.

PRIVILEGES OF BELIEVERS
See Believers, Privileges of

PRIZE
A reward of merit. 1 Cor. 9:24.
Used in a figurative sense. Phil. 3:14.

PROBATION
Adam on. Gen. 2:15–17; 3:3.
Amorites. Gen. 15:16.
None after death.
Matt. 12:32; 25:10–13; 26:24
Solomon. 1 Kings 3:14; 9:4–9.
Taught in the parable of the
embezzling manager.
Luke 16:1–12.
Taught in the parable of the fig tree.
Luke 13:6–9.
Taught in parables of the talents and
pounds. Matt. 25:14–30.

PROCLAMATION
Emancipation. 2 Chron. 36:23;
Ezra 1:1–4.
Imperial. 2 Chron. 30:1–10;
Esther 1:22; 6:9; 8:10–14;
Isa. 40:3, 9; Dan. 3:4–7; 4:1;
5:29.

PROCRASTINATION
Believers avoid. Pss. 27:8; 119:60.
Condemned by Christ.
Luke 9:59–62.
Danger of, illustrated. Matt. 5:25;
Luke 13:25.

Motives for avoiding
The present the accepted time.
2 Cor. 6:2.
The present the best time.
Eccles. 12:1.
The uncertainty of life. Prov. 27:1.

To be avoided in
Glorifying God. Jer. 13:16.
Keeping God's commandments.
Ps. 119:60.
Listening to God. Ps. 95:7–8, with
Heb. 3:7–8.
Making offerings to God.
Exod. 22:29.
Performance of vows.
Deut. 23:21; Eccles. 5:4.
Seeking God. Isa. 55:6.
Warning against. Prov. 27:1;
Matt. 25:2–12; 1 Thess. 5:2–3.

PROD
Figurative sense, of mental incentive.
Eccles. 12:11.
An instrument of torture.
1 Sam. 13:21.
Saul of Tarsus kicking against.
Acts 26:14.

Six hundred men slain with, by
Shamgar, a judge of Israel.
Judg. 3:31.

PROFITABLE THINGS
Doing God's will. Titus 3:8.
God's discipline. Heb. 12:10.
Godliness. 1 Tim. 4:8; 6:6.
Labor. Prov. 14:23.
Scripture. 2 Tim. 3:16.
Wisdom. Job 22:2.

PROGNOSTICATION
By astrologers. Isa. 47:13.

PROHIBITION
Of the use of intoxicating liquors
To Nazarites. Num. 6:3–4.
To priests on duty. Lev. 10:9.

PROMISES OF GOD
See God, Promises of

PROMOTION
As a reward of merit. 1 Chron. 11:6.

Examples of
Aaron, from slave to high priest.
Abraham. Gen. 12:2.
Baasha, "out of the dust" to
throne. 1 Kings 16:1–2.
Daniel, from captive to premier.
Dan. 2:48.
David, from shepherd to king.
Jeroboam, from slave to king.
1 Kings 11:26–35.
Joseph, from imprisoned slave to
prince. Gen. 41:1–45.
Moses, from exile to law giver.
Saul, from obscurity to king.
Shadrach, Meshach, Abednego.
Dan. 3:30.

PRODUCT SAFETY

Chariot wheels, coming off (NIV).
Exod. 14:25.

Lattice, Ahaziah falling through.
2 Kings 1:2.

Law concerning death due to lack of.
Deut. 19:5.

Loose axe head, instance of.
2 Kings 6:5.

Railing, law concerning, to prevent
falling off roof. Deut. 22:8.

Staff, broken and piercing hand, fig.
Isa. 36:6.

PROPAGATION

Of species, commanded.
Gen. 1:11, 12, 21–25, 28;
9:1, 7.

PROPHECIES CONCERNING CHRIST

See Christ, Prophecies Concerning

PROPHECY

See also Christ, Prophecies
Concerning

Blessedness of reading, hearing, and
keeping. Rev. 1:3; 22:7.

Christ the great subject of.
Acts 3:22–24; 10:43;
1 Pet. 1:10–11.

Did not come by the human will.
2 Pet. 1:21.

Do not despise. 1 Thess. 5:20.

Fulfilled respecting Christ.
Luke 24:44.

For the benefit of after ages. 1 Pet.
1:12.

A gift of Christ. Eph. 4:11;
Rev. 11:3.

A gift of the Holy Spirit.
1 Cor. 12:10.

Gift of, promised. Joel 2:28, with
Acts 2:16–17.

Gift of, sometimes possessed by
unconverted men. Num. 24:2–9;
1 Sam. 19:20, 23; Matt. 7:22;
John 11:49–51; 1 Cor. 13:2.

Given from the beginning.
Luke 1:70.

God accomplishes. Isa. 44:26;
Acts 3:18.

God gives, through Christ. Rev. 1:1.

God the author of. Isa. 44:7; 45:21.

Guilt of pretending to have the gift of.
Jer. 14:14; 23:13–14;
Ezek. 13:2–3.

How tested. Deut. 13:1–3; 18:22.

A light in a dark place. 2 Pet. 1:19.

Not of private interpretation.
2 Pet. 1:20.

Pay attention to. 2 Pet. 1:19.

Predicting future events. Gen. 49:1;
Num. 24:14.

Punishment for
Adding to, or taking from.
Rev. 22:18–19.
Not giving heed to. Neh. 9:30.
Pretending to the gift of.
Deut. 18:20; Jer. 14:15;
23:15.
Receive in faith. 2 Chron. 20:20;
Luke 24:25.
A sure word. 2 Pet. 1:19.

They who uttered
Filled with the Holy Spirit.
Luke 1:67.
Moved by the Holy Spirit.
2 Pet. 1:21.
Ordained by God. 1 Sam. 3:20;
Jer. 1:5.
Raised up by God. Amos 2:11.
Sent by Christ. Matt. 23:34.

Sent by God. 2 Chron. 36:15;
Jer. 7:25.
Spoke by the Holy Spirit.
Acts 1:16; 11:28; 28:25.
Spoke in the name of the Lord.
2 Chron. 33:18; James 5:10.
Spoke with authority.
1 Kings 17:1.

PROPHETS

See also Prophets, False

Assisted the Jews in their great
national undertakings. Ezra 5:2.
Christ exercised the office of.
Matt. 24; Mark 10:32–34.
Christ predicted to exercise the office
of. Deut. 18:15, with Acts 3:22.
Consulted in all difficulties.
1 Sam. 9:6; 28:15;
1 Kings 14:2–4; 22:7.

Extraordinary
Often endowed with miraculous
power. Exod. 4:1–4;
1 Kings 17:23; 2 Kings 5:3–8.
Specially raised up on occasions of
emergency. 1 Sam. 3:19–21;
Isa. 6:8–9; Jer. 1:5.
Felt deeply because of disasters they
predicted. Isa. 16:9–11;
Jer. 9:1–7.
God avenged all injuries done to.
2 Kings 9:7;
1 Chron. 16:21–22;
Matt. 23:35–38; Luke 11:50.

God communicated to
By angels. Dan. 8:15–26;
Rev. 22:8–9.
By an audible voice. Num. 12:8;
1 Sam. 3:4–14.
By dreams and visions.
Num. 12:6; Joel 2:28.

His secret things. Amos 3:7.
At many times and in various
ways. Heb. 1:1.
God spoke of old by. Hos. 12:10;
Heb. 1:1.
Great patience of, under suffering.
James 5:10.
Historiographers of the Jewish
nation. 1 Chron. 29:29;
2 Chron. 9:29.
Interpreters of dreams, etc.
Dan. 1:17.

The Jews
Often imprisoned them.
1 Kings 22:27; Jer. 32:2;
37:15–16.
Often left without, because of sin.
1 Sam. 3:1; Ps. 74:9;
Amos 8:11–12.
Often put them to death.
1 Kings 18:13; 19:10;
Matt. 23:34–37.
Often tried to make them speak
favorably. 1 Kings 22:13;
Isa. 30:10; Amos 2:12.
Persecuted them.
2 Chron. 36:16; Matt. 5:12.
Required to hear and believe.
Deut. 18:15, with
2 Chron. 20:20.

Mentioned in Scripture
Aaron. Exod. 7:1.
Agabus. Acts 11:28; 21:10.
Ahijah. 1 Kings 11:29; 12:15;
2 Chron. 9:29.
Amos. Amos 1:1; 7:14–15.
Anna. Luke 2:36.
Azariah the son of Oded.
2 Chron. 15:2, 8.
Daniel. Dan. 12:11, with
Matt. 24:15.
Daughters of Philip. Acts 21:9.

David. Ps. 16:8–11, with
  Acts 2:25, 30.
Deborah. Judg. 4:4.
Elijah. 1 Kings 17:1.
Elisha. 1 Kings 19:16.
Enoch. Gen. 5:21–24, with
  Jude 14.
Ezekiel. Ezek. 1:3.
Gad. 2 Sam. 24:11;
  1 Chron. 29:29.
Habakkuk. Hab. 1:1.
Haggai. Ezra 5:1; 6:14; Hag. 1:1.
Hanani. 2 Chron. 16:7.
Hosea. Hos. 1:1.
Huldah. 2 Kings 22:14.
Iddo. 2 Chron. 9:29; 12:15.
Isaiah. 2 Kings 19:2;
  2 Chron. 26:22; Isa. 1:1.
Jacob. Gen. 49:1.
Jeduthun. 2 Chron. 35:15.
Jehu the son of Hanani.
  1 Kings 16:1, 7, 12.
Jeremiah. 2 Chron. 36:12, 21;
  Jer. 1:1–2.
Joel. Joel 1:1; Acts 2:16.
John. Rev. 1:1.
Jonah. 2 Kings 14:25; Jon. 1:1;
  Matt. 12:39.
Malachi. Mal. 1:1.
Micah. Mic. 1:1.
Micaiah the son of Imlah.
  1 Kings 22:7–8.
Miriam. Exod. 15:20.
Moses. Deut. 18:18.
Nahum. Nah. 1:1.
Nathan. 2 Sam. 7:2; 12:1;
  1 Kings 1:10.
Noah. Gen. 9:25–27.
Obadiah. Obad. 1:1.
Oded. 2 Chron. 28:9.
Paul. 1 Tim. 4:1.
Peter. 2 Pet. 2:1–2.
Prophet of Judah. 1 Kings 13:1.

Prophet sent to Eli. 1 Sam. 2:27.
Prophet sent to Israel. Judg. 6:8.
Samuel. 1 Sam. 3:20.
Shemaiah. 1 Kings 12:22;
  2 Chron. 12:7, 15.
Zacharias the father of John.
  Luke 1:67.
Zadok. 2 Sam. 15:27.
Zechariah son of Iddo. Ezra 5:1;
  Zech. 1:1.
Zephaniah. Zeph. 1:1.
Messengers of God.
  2 Chron. 36:15; Isa. 44:26.
Often accompanied by music while
  predicting. 1 Sam. 10:5;
  2 Kings 3:15.
Often committed their predictions to
  writing. 2 Chron. 21:12;
  Jer. 36:2.
Often in their actions, etc., signs
  were made to the people.
  Isa. 20:2–4;
  Jer. 19:1, 10–11; 27:2–3; 43:9;
  51:63; Ezek. 4:1–13; 5:1–4;
  7:23; 12:3–7; 21:6–7; 24:1–24;
  Hos. 1:2–9.
Often led a wandering and unsettled
  life. 1 Kings 18:10–12;
  19:3, 8, 15; 2 Kings 4:10.
Often left without divine
  communications on account of
  sins of the people. 1 Sam. 28:6;
  Lam. 2:9; Ezek. 7:26.
Often spoke in parables and riddles.
  2 Sam. 12:1–6; Isa. 5:1–7;
  Ezek. 17:2–10.
One generally attached to the king's
  household. 2 Sam. 24:11;
  2 Chron. 29:25; 35:15.

Ordinary
  Numerous in Israel. 1 Sam. 10:5,
  1 Kings 18:4.

Trained up and instructed in schools, 2 Kings 2:3, 5, with 1 Sam. 19–20.

Predictions of
Frequently proclaimed at the gate of the Lord's house. Jer. 7:2.

Proclaimed in the cities and streets. Jer. 11:6.

Were all fulfilled, 2 Kings 10:10; Isa. 44:26; Acts 3:18; Rev. 10:7.

Written on scrolls and read to the people. Isa. 8:1; Jer. 36:2.

Written on tables and displayed in some public place. Hab. 2:2.

Presented with gifts by those who consulted them. 1 Sam. 9:7–8; 1 Kings 14:3.

Servants of God. Jer. 35:15.

Simple in their manner of life. Matt. 3:4.

Sometimes announced their predictions in verse. Deut. 32:44; Isa. 5:1.

Sometimes received divine communications and pronounced predictions under great bodily and mental excitement. Jer. 23:9; Ezek. 3:14–15; Dan. 7:28; 10:8; Hab. 3:2, 16.

Sometimes thought it right to reject presents. 2 Kings 5:15–16.

Spoke in the name of the Lord. 2 Chron. 33:18; Ezek. 3:11; James 5:10.

Watchmen of Israel. Ezek. 3:17.

Were called
Holy men of God. 2 Pet. 1:21.

Holy prophets. Luke 1:70; Rev. 18:20; 22:6.

Men of God. 1 Sam. 9:6.

Prophets of God. Ezra 5:2.

Seers. 1 Sam. 9:9.

Were mighty through faith. Heb. 11:32–40.

Were often married men. 2 Kings 4:1; Ezek. 24:18.

Were required
Not to speak anything but what they received from God. Deut. 18:20.

To be bold and fearless. Ezek. 2:6; 3:8–9.

To be vigilant and faithful. Ezek. 3:17–21.

To declare everything that the Lord commanded. Jer. 26:2.

To receive with attention all God's communications. Ezek. 3:10.

Were respected as holy men. 2 Kings 4:9.

Were sent to
Denounce the wickedness of kings. 1 Sam. 15:10, 16–19; 2 Sam. 12:7–12; 1 Kings 18:18; 21:17–22.

Exhort to faithfulness and constancy in God's service. 2 Chron. 15:1–2, 7.

Predict the coming, etc., of Christ. Luke 24:44; John 1:45; Acts 3:24; 10:43.

Predict the downfall of nations. Isa. 15:1; 17:1, etc.; Jer. 47–51.

Reprove the wicked and exhort to repentance. 2 Kings 17:13; 2 Chron. 24:19; Jer. 25:4–5.

Were under the influence of the Holy Spirit while prophesying. Luke 1:67; 2 Pet. 1:21.

Women sometimes endowed as. Joel 2:28.

Wore a garment of hair. 2 Kings 1:8;
Zech. 13:4; Matt. 3:4; Rev. 11:3.

Writings of, read in the synagogues
every Sabbath. Luke 4:17;
Acts 13:15.

PROPHETS, FALSE

Called foolish prophets. Ezek. 13:3.

Compared to foxes in the desert.
Ezek. 13:4.

Compared to wind. Jer. 5:13.

Described as

Arrogant and treacherous.
Zeph. 3:4.

Covetous. Mic. 3:11.

Crafty. Matt. 7:15.

Drunken. Isa. 28:7.

Immoral and profane.
Jer. 23:11, 14.

Influenced by evil spirits.
1 Kings 22:21–22.

Involved the people in their own ruin.
Isa. 9:15–16; Jer. 20:6;
Ezek. 14:10.

Judgments denounced against.
Jer. 8:1–2; 14:15; 28:16–17;
29:32.

Made use of by God to test Israel.
Deut. 13:3.

Mode of trying and detecting.
Deut. 13:1 2; 18:21–22;
1 John 4:1–3.

Not sent or commissioned by God.
Jer. 14:14; 23:21; 29:31.

Often deceived by God as a
judgment. Ezek. 14:9.

Often practiced divination and
witchcraft. Jer. 14:14;
Ezek. 22:28; Acts 13:6.

Often presented to dreams, etc.
Jer. 23:28, 32.

The people

Deprived of God's word by.
Jer. 23:30.

Encouraged and praised.
Jer. 5:31; Luke 6:26.

Led into error by. Jer. 23:13;
Mic. 3:5.

Made to forget God's name by.
Jer. 23:27.

Oppressed and defrauded by.
Ezek. 22:25.

Taught wickedness and sin by.
Jer. 23:14–15.

Warned not to listen to.
Deut. 13:3; Jer. 23:16;
27:9, 15–16.

Predicted to arise

Before destruction of Jerusalem.
Matt. 24:11, 24.

In the latter times. 2 Pet. 2:1.

Pretended to be sent by God.
Jer. 23:17–18, 31.

Prophesied

Falsely. Jer. 5:31.

Lies in the name of the Lord.
Jer. 14:14.

In the name of false gods. Jer. 2:8.

Peace, when there was no peace.
Jer. 6:14; 23:17; Ezek. 13:10;
Mic. 3:5.

Out of their own heart.
Jer. 23:16, 26; Ezek. 13:2.

Women sometimes acted as.
Neh. 6:14; Rev. 2:20.

PROPERTY

Dwellings

By absence. 2 Kings 8:1–6.

Alienated for debt.
Lev. 25:29–30.

Confiscation of.
  1 Kings 21:15–16.
Dedicated. Lev. 27:14–15.
Inherited. Eccles. 2:21.
Landmarks of, not to be removed.
  Deut. 19:14; 27:17.
Limiting inheritance of.
  Num. 27:1–11; 36:1–9.
Priests exempt from taxes.
  Gen. 47:22.
In villages, inalienable.
  Lev. 25:31–33.

Personal
Dedicated to God, redemption of.
  Lev. 27:9–13, 26, 33.
Hired. Exod. 22:14–15.
Laws concerning trespassing of
  and violence to.
  Exod. 21:28–36; 22:9;
  Deut. 23:25.
Loaned. Exod. 22:10–15.

In real estate
Dedicated. Lev. 27:16–25.
Rights in, violated.
  Gen. 21:25–30; 26:18–22.
Rights in, sacred. Exod. 20:17;
  Deut. 5:21.
Rights of redemption of.
  Jer. 32:7.
Sold for debt. Prov. 22:26–27.
Strayed, to be returned to owner.
  Lev. 6:3, 4; Deut. 22:1–3.

PROPITIATION
Christ, our. 1 John 2:2; 4:10.

PROSELYTES
From the Ammonites and Moabites,
  restricted forever from holding
  office in the congregation.
  Deut. 23:3.
Described. Esther 8:17; Isa. 56:3.

From the Egyptians and Edomites,
  restricted to the third generation
  from holding office in the
  congregation. Deut. 23:7–8.
Entitled to all privileges.
  Exod. 12:48; Isa. 56:3–7.
Later called devout Greeks.
  John 12:20, with Acts 17:4.
Many embraced the gospel.
  Acts 6:5; 13:43.
Pharisees, etc., zealous in making.
  Matt. 23:15.

Required
To be circumcised. Gen. 17:13,
  with Exod. 12:48.
To enter into covenant to serve the
  Lord. Deut. 29:10–13, with
  Neh. 10:28–29.
To give up all heathen associates.
  Ruth 1:16; 2:11; Ps. 45:10;
  Luke 14:26.
To give up all pagan practices.
  Ezra 6:21.
To observe the law of Moses as
  Jews. Exod. 12:49.
Unfaithfulness in, punished.
  Ezek. 14:7.
Went up to the feasts. Acts 2:10;
  8:27.

PROSPERITY

Material
Dangers of. Ps. 73:12;
  Prov. 28:20; Mark 10:24;
  Luke 18:25.
From the Lord. 1 Sam. 2:7;
  2 Kings 18:7.
Limitations of. Ps. 49:10;
  1 Tim. 6:7; James 1:11.

Spiritual
Of the Christian. 3 John 1:2.

Of generous souls. Prov. 11:25.
Of those who love God.
Ps. 122:6.
Of those who trust God. Ps. 23:1.

PROSTITUTION
Forbidden. Lev. 19:29;
Deut. 23:17.

PROTECTION

Afforded to
The church. Ps. 48:3;
Zech. 2:4–5.
The perfect in heart.
2 Chron. 16:9.
The oppressed. Ps. 9:9.
The poor. Pss. 14:6; 72:12–14.
Returning sinners. Job 22:23, 25.
Those who hearken to God.
Prov. 1:33.

Believers
Acknowledge God as their.
Pss. 18:2; 62:2; 89:18.
Praise God for. Ps. 5:11.
Pray for. Ps. 17:5, 8; Isa. 51:9.
God able to provide. 1 Pet. 1:5;
Jude 24.
God faithful to provide.
1 Thess. 5:23–24; 2 Thess. 3:3.

Of God is
Encouraging. Isa. 41:10, 50:7.
Indispensable. Ps. 127:1.
Often afforded through means
inadequate in themselves.
Judg. 7:7; 1 Sam. 17:45, 50;
2 Chron. 14:11.
Perpetual. Ps. 121:8.
Seasonable. Ps. 46:1.
Sufficient. John 10:28–30;
2 Cor. 12:9.
Unfailing. Deut. 31:6; Josh. 1:5.

Uninterrupted. Ps. 121:3.

Granted to believers, in
All dangers. Ps. 91:3–7.
All places. Gen. 28:15;
2 Chron. 16:9.
Calamities. Pss. 57:1; 59:16.
Death. Ps. 23:4.
Defeating the plans of enemies.
Isa. 8:10.
Defending them against their
enemies. Deut. 20:1–4; 33:27;
Isa. 59:19.
Keeping their feet. 1 Sam. 2:9;
Prov. 3:26.
Keeping them from evil.
2 Thess. 3:3.
Keeping them from falling.
Jude 24.
Keeping them from temptation.
Rev. 3:10.
Preparing the way. Exod. 23:20.
Persecution. Luke 21:18.
Preserving them. Ps. 145:20.
Providing a refuge for them.
Prov. 14:26; Isa. 4:6; 32:2.
Sleep. Pss. 3:5; 4:8; Prov. 3:24.
Strengthening them. 2 Tim. 4:17.
Temptation. 1 Cor. 10:13;
2 Pet. 2:9.
Upholding them. Pss. 37:17, 24;
63:8.
Illustrated. Deut. 32:11;
Ps. 125:1–2; Prov. 18:10;
Isa. 25:4; 31:5; Luke 13:34.

Not to be found in
Horses. Ps. 33:17; Prov. 21:31.
Hosts. Josh. 11:4–8, with
Ps. 33:16.
Idols. Deut. 32:37–39; Isa. 46:7.
Persons. Ps. 146:3; Isa. 30:7.
Riches. Prov. 11:4, 28;
Zeph. 1:18.

Withdrawn from the
Backsliding. Josh. 23:12–13;
Judg. 10:13.
Disobedient. Lev. 26:14–17.
Obstinately unrepentant.
Matt. 23:38.
Presumptuous. Num. 14:40–45.
Unbelieving. Isa. 7:9.

PROTRACTED MEETINGS
During Solomon's reign.
1 Kings 8:65.

PROVERBS
Design of. Prov. 1:1–4.
Quoted by Jesus. Matt. 12:33;
Luke 4:23; 14:34.
Quoted by Nathanael. John 1:46.
Quoted by Paul. 1 Cor. 15:33;
Gal. 6:7.
Written by Solomon. Prov. 1:1;
25:1.

PROVIDENCE OF GOD
See God, Providence of

PROXY
In priest's service. 2 Chron. 30:17.

PRUNING
Pruninghook. Isa. 2:4; 18:5;
Joel 3:10; Mic. 4:3.

PRUDENCE
Believers act with. Ps. 112:5.
Believers should specially exercise, in
their dealings with unbelievers.
Matt. 10:16; Eph. 5:15; Col. 4:5.
Exemplified by Christ. Isa. 52:13;
Matt. 21:24–27; 22:15–21.
Exhibited in the expressions of God's
grace. Eph. 1:8.

Intimately connected with wisdom.
Prov. 8:12.
Necessity for, illustrated. Matt. 25:3,
9; Luke 14:28–32.

Those who have
Are preserved by it. Prov. 2:11.
Crowned with knowledge.
Prov. 14:18.
Deal with knowledge.
Prov. 13:16.
Foresee and avoid evil.
Prov. 22:3.
Get knowledge. Prov. 18:15.
Keep silence in the evil time.
Amos 5:12.
Learn from correction.
Prov. 15:5.
Not pretentious of knowledge.
Prov. 12:23.
Suppress angry feelings, etc.
Prov. 12:16; 19:11.
Understand the ways of God.
Hos. 14:9.
Understand their own ways.
Prov. 14:8.
Virtuous wives act with.
Prov. 31:16, 26.
Watch their steps. Prov. 14:15.
The wise celebrated for.
Prov. 16:21.
The young should cultivate.
Prov. 3:21.

Of the wicked
Defeated by God. Isa. 29:14;
1 Cor. 1:19.
Denounced by God. Isa. 5:21;
29:15.
Fails in the times of bewilderment.
Jer. 49:7.
Keeps them from the knowledge
of the gospel. Matt. 11:25.

475

PUBLIC RELATIONS

PSALMS

Psalms in the Bible include:
Hymns. Ps. 105.
Community complaints. Ps. 74.
Individual complaints. Ps. 13.
Individual songs of thanksgiving.
Ps. 18.
Royal psalms. Ps. 2.
Torah psalms. Pss. 1; 127.
Oracle psalms. Ps. 82.
Blessings psalms. Ps. 128.
Taunt songs. Ps. 52.
Songs of trust. Ps. 11.

PSALTERY

A harp, used in religious services.
2 Sam. 6:5; Ps. 33:2; Rev. 5:8.
Used at the dedication of a new wall
when the captives return.
Neh. 12:27.
Used in idolatrous worship.
Dan. 3:5, 7, 10, 15.

PSYCHIATRY

Inner peace. Ps. 4:8; Isa. 26:3;
Phil. 4:7.

Mind
Anxious. Deut. 28:65–67;
Prov. 3:25; Luke 10:41.
Corrupted. Titus 1:15.
Love God with. Luke 10:27.
Renewal of. Rom 12:2;
Eph. 4:23; Col. 3:9–10;
1 John 1:9.
Sound, given by God. 2 Tim. 1:7
(KJV).
New person in Christ. 2 Cor. 5:17.

Troubled
Examples of. 1 Sam. 16:14–23;
18:10–11; Dan. 4:33–34;
Mark 5:2–25.

Pretended. 1 Sam. 21:13–15.

PUBLICANS

Chiefs of, very rich. Luke 19:2.
Collectors of the public taxes.
Luke 5:27.

The Jews
Classed with the most infamous
characters. Matt. 11:19; 21:32.
Despised. Luke 18:11.
Despised Christ for associating
with. Matt. 9:11; 11:19.

Many of
Attended the preaching of Christ.
Mark 2:15; Luke 15:1.
Believed the preaching of John.
Matt. 21:32.
Embraced the gospel.
Matt. 21:31.
Matthew the apostle was of.
Matt. 10:3.
Often guilty of extortion.
Luke 19:8.
Often hospitable. Luke 5:29;
19:6.
Often kind to their friends.
Matt. 5:46–47.
Received John's baptism.
Luke 3:12; 7:29.
Suspected of extortion.
Luke 3:13.

PUBLIC RELATIONS

Examples of
Good. 1 Sam. 25:23–35;
2 Sam. 15:2–6.
Poor. 1 Kings 12:1–15.

Principles relevant to
Good reputation. Prov. 22:1;
31:23, 31; Eccles. 7:1.

Uplifting behavior.
1 Cor. 4:10–13.

PULPIT
Solomon used, in addressing the
people. 2 Chron. 6:13.
Used by Ezra as he addressed the
people of Jerusalem. Neh. 8:4.

PUNISHMENT
Antiquity of. Gen. 4:13–14.

Capital, kinds of
Beheading. Gen. 40:19;
Mark 6:16, 27.
Burning. Gen. 38:24; Lev. 20:14;
Dan. 3:6.
Crucifying. Matt. 20:19, 27:35.
Cutting in pieces. Dan. 2:5;
Matt. 24:51.
Exposing to wild beasts.
Dan. 6:16, 24. *(See also*
1 Cor. 15:32.)
Grinding like grain. Prov. 27:22.
Hanging. Num. 25:4;
Deut. 21:22–23; Josh. 8:29;
2 Sam. 21:12;
Esther 7:9–10.
Not permitted to the Jews by the
Romans. John 18:31.
Sawing in two. Heb. 11:37.
Slaying with the sword.
1 Sam. 15:33; Acts 12:2.
Stoning. Lev. 24:14;
Deut. 13:10; Acts 7:59.
Throwing head first from a rock.
2 Chron. 25:12.
Throwing into the sea. Matt. 18:6.

Secondary, kinds of
Banishment. Ezra 7:26; Rev. 1:9.
Binding with chains. Ps. 105:18.
Confinement in a dungeon.
Jer. 38:6; Zech. 9:11.

Confinement in stocks. Jer. 20:2;
Acts 16:24.
Confiscating the property.
Ezra 7:26.
Cutting off hands and feet.
2 Sam. 4:12.
Cutting off nose and ears.
Ezek. 23:25.
Fine, or giving of money.
Exod. 21:22; Deut. 22:19.
Imprisonment. Ezra 7:26;
Matt. 5:25.
Mutilating the hands and feet.
Judg. 1:5–7.
Pulling out the hair. Neh. 13:25;
Isa. 50:6.
Putting out the eyes. Judg. 16:21;
1 Sam. 11:2.
Restitution. Exod. 21:36; 22:1–4;
Lev. 6:4–5; 24:18.
Retaliation or injuring according to
the injury done. Exod. 21:24;
Deut. 19:21.
Selling the criminal, etc.
Matt. 18:25.
Torturing. Matt. 18:34;
Heb. 11:37.
Whipping. Deut. 25:2–3;
Matt. 27:26; Acts 22:25;
2 Cor. 11:24.
Sometimes deferred for a
considerable time. 1 Kings 2:5–6,
8–9.
Sometimes deferred until God was
consulted. Num. 15:34.
Strangers not exempted
from. Lev. 20:2.
A warning to others.
Deut. 13:11; 17:13; 19:20.

Were inflicted
Without compassion.
Deut. 19:13, 21.

On the guilty. Deut. 24:16;
Prov. 17:26.
Immediately after sentence was
passed. Deut. 25:2; Josh. 7:25.
On murderers without
commutation. Num. 35:31–32.
By order of kings.
2 Sam. 1:13–16;
1 Kings 2:23–46.
By order of magistrates.
Job 31:11; Acts 16:22;
Rom. 13:4.
Without partiality. Deut. 13:6–8.
By the people. Num. 15:35–36;
Deut. 13:9.
By soldiers. 2 Sam. 1:15;
Matt. 27:27–35.
By the witnesses. Deut. 13:9, with
17:7; John 8:7; Acts 7:58–59.
Were sometimes commuted.
Exod. 21:29–30.

PUNISHMENT, CAPITAL

For adultery. John 8:3–11.
For murder. Gen. 9:5–6;
Exod. 21:12.
Required to atone for murder.
Num. 35:33.
For violating Sabbath. Exod. 31:14.
Warning against putting innocent to
death. Exod. 23:7.

PUNISHMENT, CORPORAL

Effective. Prov 20:30.

Enacted by.
Gideon. Judg 8:16.
God (fig). 2 Sam 7:14.
Judge. Deut. 25:1–3.
Parents. Prov. 13:24; 22:15;
23:13–14.
Ineffective. Prov. 17:10.

PUNISHMENT OF THE WICKED
See Wicked, Punishment of the

PURIFICATION
Consequence of neglecting those
prescribed by law. Lev. 17:16;
Num. 19:13, 20.
Of the healed leper. Lev. 14:8–9.
Of high priest on Day of Atonement.
Lev. 16:4, 24.

Illustrative of
Purification by the blood of Christ.
Heb. 9:9–12.
Regeneration. Eph. 5:26;
1 John 1:7.
Of individuals who were ceremonially
unclean. Lev. 15:2–13; 17:15;
22:4–7; Num. 19:7–12, 21.
Insufficient for spiritual purification.
Job 9:30–31; Jer. 2:22.
Of Israel at the Exodus. Exod. 14:32;
1 Cor. 10:2.
Of Israel before receiving the law.
Exod. 19:10.
The Jews laid great stress on.
John 3:25.
Of Levites before consecration.
Num. 8:6–7.

Means used for
Running water. Lev. 15:13.
Water mixed with blood.
Exod. 24:5–8, with Heb. 9:19.
Water of separation. Num. 19:9.
Multiplied by traditions. Matt. 15:2,
Mark 7:3–4.
Of Nazarites after vow expired.
Acts 21:24, 26.
Of priests before consecration.
Exod. 29:4.
Of priests performed in the bronze
basin. Exod. 30:18; 2 Chron. 4:6.
Sanctified the flesh. Heb. 9:13.

Of things for burnt offerings.
2 Chron. 4:6.
Used by the devout before entering
God's house. Ps. 26:6;
Heb. 10:22.
Vessels in the houses of the Jews for.
John 2:6.

Was by
Sprinkling. Num. 19:13, 18;
Heb. 9:19.
Washing parts of the body.
Exod. 30:19.
Washing the whole body.
Lev. 8:6; 14:9.

PURIM, FEAST OF
Began fourteenth of twelfth month.
Esther 9:17.
Confirmed by royal authority.
Esther 9:29–32.
Instituted by Mordecai. Esther 9:20.
The Jews bound themselves to keep.
Esther 9:27–28.
Lasted two days. Esther 9:21.
To commemorate the defeat of
Haman's wicked design.
Esther 3:7–15, with 9:24–26.
Way of celebrating.
Esther 9:17–19, 22.

PURITY
Advantages of. 1 Pet. 3:1–2.
Avoid those lacking. 1 Cor. 5:11;
1 Pet. 4:3.
Believers are kept in. Eccles. 7:26.
Breach of, punished.
1 Cor. 3:16–17; Eph. 5:5–6;
Heb. 13:4; Rev. 22:15.
Commanded. Exod. 20:14;
Prov. 31:3; Acts 15:20;
Rom. 13:13; Col. 3:5;
1 Thess. 4:3.

Consequences of associating with
those lacking. Prov. 5:3–11;
7:25–27; 22:14.
Drunkenness destructive to.
Prov. 23:31–33.

Of heart
Blessing of. Matt. 5:8.
David's cry for. Ps. 51:7.
Command to have. James 4:8.
A condition for seeing God.
Matt. 5:8.
God's gift of, through Christ.
Heb. 9:13–14; 10:2.
Required to come to the hill of the
Lord. Ps. 24:3–5.
Keep the body in.
1 Cor. 6:13, 15–18.
Lack of, excludes from heaven.
Col. 5:19–21.
Of life, necessity of. Isa. 52:11;
1 Pet. 1:22.
Of mind, value of. Titus 1:15.
Motives for. 1 Cor. 6:19;
1 Thess. 4:7.
Preserved by wisdom.
Prov. 2:10–11, 16; 7:1–5.
Of religion, essence of. James 1:27.
Required in heart. Prov. 6:25.
Required in look. Job 31:1;
Matt. 5:28.
Required in speech. Eph. 5:3.
Of spirit, witness of. Phil. 2:15.
Temptation to deviate from,
dangerous. 2 Sam. 11:2–4.
Of thought, desirability of. Phil. 4:8.
The wicked are lacking. Rom. 1:29;
Eph. 4:19; 2 Pet. 2:14; Jude 8.

PURPOSE

Of Christ
To bring good news and
deliverance. Luke 4:18.

To bring life. John 10:10.
To witness to the truth.
  John 18:37.

Of Christians
  To achieve the heavenly goal.
    Phil. 3:13–14.
  To have the best gifts.
    1 Cor. 9:25.

To remain true to the Lord.
  Acts 11:22–23.
To seek the things above.
  Col. 3:1–2.

Of God
  Our purity. 1 Thess. 3:13.
  Our salvation. Eph. 3:11;
    2 Tim. 1:9.

QUATERNION
A squad composed of four soldiers.
John 19:23; Acts 12:4.

QUAIL
Miracle of, at Kibroth-Hattaavah.
Num. 11:31–32; Ps. 105:40.
Miracle of, in the wilderness of Sin.
Exod. 16:13.

QUEEN
Candace of Ethiopia. Acts 8:27.
Counsels the king. Dan. 5:10–12.
Crowned. Esther 1:11; 2:17.
Divorced. Esther 1:10–22.
Makes feasts for the women of the
royal household. Esther 1:9.

The moon called queen of heaven.
Jer. 7:18; 44:7–19, 25
Of Sheba, visits Solomon.
1 Kings 10:1–13.
Sits on the throne with the king.
Neh. 2:6.
The wife of a king. 1 Kings 11:19.

QUICKEN
See Regeneration

QUIET
Achievement of. Isa. 32:17.
Power of. Isa. 30:15.
Value of. Eccles. 4:6.

QUIVER
For arrows. Gen. 27:3; Isa. 22:6.

❖R❖

RABBI
Forbidden by Jesus as a title to His disciples. Matt. 23:8.
Jesus called Rabboni. Mark 10:51.
The title of a teacher. Matt. 23:7–8; John 3:2.
Used by the Pharisees in a showy way. Matt. 23:7.
Used in addressing Jesus.
John 1:38, 49; 3:2; 6:25.
Used in addressing John. John 3:26.

RABBIT
Forbidden as food. Lev. 11:6; Deut. 14:7.

RACE

Choice of Jewish
To bless all races. Gen. 12:1–3.
To special responsibility.
Amos 3:2.

Church and
Paul's proclamation of racial equality in Christ. Gal. 3:23–29; Eph. 2:11–22; Col. 3:1–17.
Peter's overcoming of racial prejudice. Acts 10:1–48; 11:1–18.
Philip's Ethiopian convert.
Acts 8:26–40.
Reconciling early racial divisions.
Acts 6:1–7.

God and
Loves the world. John 3:16.
Will gather all nations together.
Isa. 66:18.
Will heal all nations. Rev. 22:2.

Jesus and
Denounced as a Samaritan.
John 8:48.
Healing a Gentile. Matt. 8:5–13.
Healing a Syrophenician girl.
Mark 7:24–30.
Praising hated Samaritans.
Luke 10:25–37; 17:16.
Talking with a Samaritan woman.
John 4.
Transcending racial differences.
John 4:19–24; Col. 3:11.
Uniting races. Eph. 2:11–22.
Worldwide unity of.
Gen. 1:27; 7:23; 9:18–19;
Acts 17:26.

RACIAL TENSION
See also Genocide; Inclusiveness

Examples of
Egyptians against shepherds.
Gen. 46:34.
Greeks against Cretans.
Titus 1:12.
Haman against Jews.
Esther 3:1–6.
Israelites against Amalekites.
Deut. 25:17–19.
Israelites against Edomites.
Obad. 18.
Israelites against Gibeonites.
Josh. 9:22–27.
Israelites against Ninevites.
Jon. 4:2.
Jews against foreigners.
Luke 4:25–28.
Jews against Samaritans.
Luke 9:52–56; John 4:9.

Philistines against Israelites.
2 Sam. 21:21.

Injunctions concerning

Abraham's family to be a channel
of God's blessing to others.
Gen. 12:1–3; Gal. 3:6–9.

Dividing wall of hostility between
Jews and Gentiles broken.
Eph. 2:11–14.

Foreigners to have equal rights.
Lev. 24:22; Deut. 24:17.

No racial distinction in Christ.
Gal. 3:28–29; Eph. 2:19.

*Inclusiveness in the family of God
shown by*

Cornelius. Acts 10:9–48.

Every tribe, tongue, people, and
nation in heaven. Rev. 5:9–10;
7:9.

Foreigners to have equal rights.
Lev. 24:22; Deut. 24:17.

Mixed multitude. Exod. 12:38.

Naaman. 2 Kings 5:1–19;
Luke 4:27.

No partiality shown by God in
salvation. Acts 10:34;
Rom. 2:9–11.

No racial distinction in Christ.
Gal. 3:28–29.

Rahab. Josh 6:25; Matt. 1:5.

Roman centurion. Matt. 8:5–13.

Ruth. Ruth 1:4; Matt. 1:5.

Samaritan woman. John 4:1–42.

Simon of Cyrene. Matt. 27:32;
Mark 15:21; Luke 23:26.

Syrophenician women.
1 Kings 17:8–24;
Luke 4:25–26.

Timothy. Acts 16:1.

RAILING

Forbidden. 1 Cor. 5:11; 1 Tim. 6:4;
1 Pet. 3:9; 2 Pet. 2:11; Jude 9.

RAIN

Appearance of a cloud from the west
in indicated. 1 Kings 18:44;
Luke 12:54.

Canaan abundantly supplied with.
Deut. 11:11.

Caused by condensing of the clouds.
Job 36:27–28; Ps. 77:17;
Eccles. 11:3.

Designed for

Making the earth fruitful.
Heb. 6:7.

Refreshing the earth. Pss. 68:9;
72:6.

Replenishing the springs and
fountains of the earth.
Ps. 104:8.

Divided into

Great. Ezra 10:9.

Overflowing. Ezek. 38:22.

Plentiful. Ps. 68:9.

Small. Job 37:6.

Sweeping. Prov. 28:3.

The former, after harvest, to prepare
for sowing. Deut. 11:14;
Jer. 5:24.

Frequently withheld because of
iniquity. Deut. 11:17; Jer. 3:3;
5:25; Amos 4:7.

God

Causes to come down. Joel 2:23.

Exhibits goodness in giving.
Acts 14:17.

Exhibits greatness in giving.
Job 36:26–27.

Gives. Job 5:10.

Made a decree for. Job 28:26.

Prepares. Ps. 147:8.

Sends upon the evil and good. Matt. 5:45.

Should be feared because of. Jer. 5:24.

Should be praised for. Ps. 147:7–8.

Illustrative of

Christ in the communication of His graces. Ps. 72:6; Hos. 6:3.

The doctrine of faithful ministers. Deut. 32:2.

God's judgments (when destructive). Job 20:23; Ps. 11:6; Ezek. 38:22.

A poor man oppressing the poor (when destructive). Prov. 28:3.

Righteousness. Hos. 10:12.

Spiritual blessings. Pss. 68:9; 84:6; Ezek. 34:26.

Uselessness of idols exhibited in not being able to give. Jer. 14:22.

The Word of God. Isa. 55:10–11.

Instances of extraordinary

After long drought in Ahab's reign. 1 Kings 18:45.

After the captivity. Ezra 10:9, 13.

During wheat harvest in the days of Samuel. 1 Sam. 12:17–18.

Plague of, upon Egypt. Exod. 9:18, with 23.

Time of the flood. Gen. 7:4, 12.

Lack of

Causes the earth to open. Job 29:23; Jer. 14:4.

Dries up springs and fountains. 1 Kings 17:7.

Leads to famine. 1 Kings 18:1–2.

Removed by prayer. 1 Kings 8:35–36; James 5:18.

The latter, before harvest. Joel 2:23; Zech. 10:1.

The north wind drives away. Prov. 25:23.

Not sent upon the earth immediately after creation. Gen. 2:5.

Often destroyed houses, etc. Ezek. 13:13–15; Matt. 7:27.

Often impeded traveling in the east. 1 Kings 18:44, with Isa. 4:6.

Often succeeded by heat and sunshine. 2 Sam. 23:4; Isa. 18:4.

Promised in due season to the obedient. Lev. 26:4; Deut. 11:14; Ezek. 34:26–27.

Rainbows often appear during. Gen. 9:14, with Ezek. 1:28.

Rarely falls in Egypt. Deut. 11:10; Zech. 14:18.

Storms often accompanied. Matt. 7:25, 27.

Thunder and lightning often accompanied. Ps. 135:7.

Unusual in harvest time. Prov. 26:1.

Withheld for three years and six months in the days of Elijah. 1 Kings 17:1; James 5:17.

RAINBOW

A sign that the earth will not again be destroyed by water. Gen. 9:8–16; Ezek. 1:28.

Symbolic sense. Rev. 4:3; 10:1.

RAISIN

Given by Ziba to David. 2 Sam. 16:1.

Given to David at Ziklag. 1 Chron. 12:40.

Given to the famishing Egyptian to revive him. 1 Sam. 30:12.

Preserved grape, given by Abigail to David. 1 Sam. 25:18.

RAM

Seen in Daniel's vision.
Dan. 8:3, 20.
Skins of, used for the roof of the
tabernacle. Exod. 26:14.

RANSOM

Of a man's life. Exod. 21:30;
Ps. 49:7–8; Prov. 6:35.
Used in a figurative sense.
Job 33:24; Isa. 35:10; 51:10;
Matt. 20:28; 1 Tim. 2:6.

RAP MUSIC

Principles relevant to
Have pure thoughts. Phil. 4:8.
Test everything.
1 Thess. 5:21–22.

RAPE

See also Affairs; Self-esteem

Captives afflicted with. Isa. 13:16;
Lam. 5:11; Zech. 14:2.

Examples of
Dinah and Shechem. Gen. 34:2.
The servant of a Levite, by
Benjamites. Judg. 19:22–30;
20:35.
Of Tamar by Amnon.
2 Sam. 13:1–29, 32–33.
Forbidden. Deut. 22:25–28.

Gang rape
Attempted. Gen. 19:4–11.
Committed. Judg. 19:22–26.
Law imposes death penalty for.
Deut. 22:25–27.

RAPTURE

"Catching up" of believers.
1 Thess. 4:17.

RASHNESS

Consequences of.
Prov. 14:29; 19:2; 21:5; 25:8.

Examples of
The centurion, in rejecting Paul's
counsel. Acts 27:11.
David, in his generosity to Ziba.
2 Sam. 16:4.
Israel's vow to destroy the
Benjamites. Judg. 21:1–23.
James and John, in desiring to call
down fire on the Samaritans.
Luke 9:54.
Jephthah's vow. Judg. 11:31–39.
Josiah, in fighting against Necho.
2 Chron. 35:20–24.
Moses, in killing the Egyptian.
Exod. 2:11–12.
Moses, when he struck the rock.
Num. 20:10–12.
Naaman, in refusing to wash in the
Jordan. 2 Kings 5:11–12.
Paul, in persisting in going to
Jerusalem, against the repeated
warnings of the Holy Spirit.
Acts 21:4, 10–15.
Rehoboam, in forsaking the
counsel of the old men.
1 Kings 12:8–15.
Uzza, in steadying the ark.
2 Sam. 6:6–7.
Seen in quick generalizations.
Ps. 116:11.

RAVEN

Called the raven of the valley.
Prov. 30:17.

Described as
Black. Song of Sol. 5:11.
Carnivorous. Prov. 30:17.
Do not provide for the future.
Luke 12:24.

Live in desolate places. Isa. 34:11.
Elijah fed by. 1 Kings 17:4–6.
God provides food for. Job 38:41;
Ps. 147:9; Luke 12:24.
Plumage of, illustrative of the glory of
Christ. Song of Sol. 5:11.
Sent by Noah from the ark.
Gen. 8:7.
Unclean and not to be eaten.
Lev. 11:15; Deut. 14:14.

RAZOR
Nazarite forbidden to use. Num. 6:5.

REAPING
The ark of the Lord returned by the
Philistines at the time of.
1 Sam. 6:13.
Both men and women engaged in.
Ruth 2:8–9.
Corn after, tied in bundles.
Gen. 37:7; Ps. 129:7.
Cutting of the corn in harvest.
Job 24:6, with Lev. 23:10.

Illustrative of
The final judgment.
Matt. 13:30, 39–43.
Gathering in souls to God.
John 4:38.
The judgments of God on the
anti-Christian world.
Rev. 14:14–16.
Ministers receiving temporary
provision for spiritual labors.
1 Cor. 9:11.
Receiving the reward of
righteousness. Hos. 10:12;
Gal. 6:8–9.
Receiving the reward of
wickedness. Job 4:8;
Prov. 22:8; Hos. 8:7; Gal. 6:8.

The Jews not to reap
The corners of their fields.
Lev. 19:9, with 23:22.
During the sabbatical year.
Lev. 25:5.
During the year of jubilee.
Lev. 25:11.
The fields of others. Deut. 23:25.
The Jews often hindered from,
because of their sins. Mic. 6:15.
Mode of gathering the corn for,
alluded to. Ps. 129:7; Isa. 17:5.
Often unprofitable because of sin.
Jer. 12:13.

Persons engaged in
Fed by the master who himself
presided at their meals. Ruth
2:14.
Under the guidance of a steward.
Ruth 2:5–6.
Received wages. John 4:36;
James 5:4.
Visited by the master. Ruth 2:4;
2 Kings 4:18.
Sickle used for. Deut. 16:9;
Mark 4:29.
A time of great rejoicing.
Ps. 126:5–6.
Used in a figurative sense. Ps. 126:6;
Hos. 10:12–13.

REASONING
With God. Job 13:3, 17–28.
God reasoning with persons.
Exod. 4:11; 20:5, 11;
Isa. 1:18; 5:3–4; 43:26;
Hos. 4:1; Mic. 6:2.
The gospel cannot be explained by.
1 Cor. 1:18–28; 2:1–14.
Natural understanding. Dan. 4:36.
Not a sufficient guide in human
affairs. Deut. 12:8; Prov. 3:5.

Of Paul from the Scriptures.
  Acts 17:2; 18:4; 19; 24:25.
Of the Pharisees. Luke 5:21–22;
  20:5.
To be applied to religion.
  1 Cor. 10:15; 1 Pet. 3:15.

REBELLION

Examples of
  Absalom. 2 Sam. 15; 18.
  Revolt of the ten tribes.
    1 Kings 12:16–20;
    2 Chron. 10; 13:5–12.
  Sheba. 2 Sam. 20.
Treasonable. Prov. 17:11.

REBELLION AGAINST GOD
See God, Rebellion Against

RECIPROCITY
Among believers. Rom. 15:27.

RECONCILIATION WITH BRETHREN
Messiah to unite the generations.
  Mal. 4:6.
Prodigal son welcomed by his father
  but not by his self-righteous
  brother.
  Luke 15:25–32.
Racially divided Christians reconciled
  by appointment of deacons.
  Acts 6:1–7.
Worshiper first reconciled with an
  offended brother. Matt. 5:23–24.

RECONCILIATION WITH GOD
See God, Reconciliation with

RECONNAISSANCE
Of Bethel. Judg. 1:23.
Of Jericho. Josh 2:1–24.
Of Laish. Judg. 18:2–10.

RECREATION
Jesus takes, from the fatigues of His
  ministry. Mark 6:31–32; 7:24.

RECYCLING

Examples of jewelry
  For furnishings in tabernacle.
    Exod. 35:22.
  For golden calf. Exod. 32:2–4.
  For idols. Ezek. 7:20.
Of plunder, as clothing for the naked.
  2 Chron. 28:15.

Principles relevant to
  Care for Eden. Gen. 2:15.
  Dominion over earth and its
    resources. Gen. 1:26–28.
  Earth belongs to God. Lev. 25:23;
    Ps. 24:1.
  Earth given by God to people.
    Deut. 8:7–10.
  Environment created to be good.
    Gen. 1–2; Ps. 104:1–30.
  Responsibility for what is
    entrusted. Luke 12:41–48.

RED HEIFER
Ashes of, collected and mixed with
  water for purification.
  Num. 19:9, 11–22.
Blood of, sprinkled seven times
  before the tabernacle. Num. 19:4.
Cedar, hyssop, etc., burned with.
  Num. 19:6.

Communicated uncleanness to
  The one who burned her.
    Num. 19:8.
  The one who gathered the ashes.
    Num. 19:10.
  The priest who offered her.
    Num. 19:7.

Could only purify the flesh.
Heb. 9:13.
Entirety, to be burned. Num. 19:5.
To be given to Eleazar the priest to
offer. Num. 19:3.
To be slain outside the camp.
Num. 19:3.
To be without spot or blemish.
Num. 19:2.
A type of Christ. Heb. 9:12–14.

RED SEA

Exod. 2:3, 5; 2 Chron. 20:16;
Eccles. 3:11; Isa. 19:6; Joel 2:20.

REDEMPTION

Christ is made, for us. 1 Cor. 1:30.
Christ sent to effect. Col. 4:4–5.
Corruptible things cannot purchase.
1 Pet. 1:18.
Defined. 1 Cor. 6:20; 7:23.

Described as
Eternal. Heb. 9:12.
Full. Ps. 130:7.
Precious. Ps. 49:8.
Humans cannot effect. Ps. 49:7.
Is by the blood of Christ. Acts 20:28;
Heb. 9:12; 1 Pet. 1:19; Rev. 5:9.
Is by Christ. Matt. 20:28; Gal. 3:13.

Is from
All evil. Gen. 48:16.
All sin. Ps. 130:8; Titus 2:14.
All troubles. Ps. 25:22.
The bondage of the law. Gal. 4:5.
The curse of the law. Gal. 3:13.
Death. Hos. 13:14.
Destruction. Ps. 103:4.
Enemies. Ps. 106:110–11;
Jer. 15:21.
The power of sin. Rom. 6:18, 22.
The power of the grave.
Ps. 49:15.

This present evil world. Gal. 1:14.
Vain conversation. 1 Pet. 1:18.
Is of God. Isa. 43:1, with Luke 1:68;
Isa. 44:21–23.

Manifests the
Grace of God. Isa. 52:3.
Love and compassion of God.
Isa. 63:9; John 3:16; Rom. 6:8;
1 John 4:10.
Power of God. Isa. 50:2.
Old Testament believers share in
opportunity. Heb. 9:15.
Pray for the completion of.
Pss. 26:11; 44:26.
Present life the only season for.
Job 36:18–19.

Procures for us
Adoption. Gal. 4:4–5.
Forgiveness of sin. Eph. 1:7;
Col. 1:14.
Justification. Rom. 3:24.
Purification. Titus 2:14.
A subject for praise. Isa. 44:22–23;
51:11.
Should be without fear. Isa. 43:1.
Should glorify God for. 1 Cor. 6:20.

Subjects of
The body. Rom. 8:23.
The inheritance. Eph. 1:14.
The life. Ps. 103:4; Lam. 3:58.
The soul. Ps. 49:15.

Those who experience
Alone can learn the songs of
heaven. Rev. 14:3–4.
Are a peculiar people.
2 Sam. 7:23; Titus 2:14, with
1 Pet. 2:9.
Are assured of. Job 19:25;
Ps. 31:5.
Are first fruits to God. Rev. 14:4.

Are sealed until the day of.
Eph. 4:30.
Are the property of God.
Isa. 43:1; 1 Cor. 6:20.
Are zealous of good works.
Eph. 2:10; Titus 2:14;
1 Pet. 2:9.
Commit themselves to God.
Ps. 31:5.
Have a guarantee of the
completion of. Eph. 1:14, with
2 Cor. 1:22.
Praise God for. Pss. 71:23;
103:4; Rev. 5:9.
Wait for the completion of.
Rom. 8:23; Phil. 3:20–21;
Titus 2:11–13.
Walk safely in holiness. Isa. 35:8–9.
Will return to Zion with joy.
Isa. 35:10.

REED

Jesus struck with. Matt. 27:30;
Mark 15:19.
Mockingly given to Jesus as a symbol
of royalty. Matt. 27:29.
Used as a measuring device as six
cubits. Ezek. 40:3–8; Rev. 11:1;
21:15–16.
Used in a figurative sense, of
weakness. 1 Kings 14:15;
Matt. 11:7; 12:20.
A water plant. Isa. 19:6–7; 35:7;
Jer. 51:32.

REFINING

*The process of eliminating by fire
the impurities of metals*
Of gold. 1 Chron. 28:18.
Of silver. 1 Chron. 29:4.
Of the purity of the Word of God.
Pss. 18:30; 119:140.

Used in a figurative sense, of the
corrective judgments of God.
Isa. 1:25; 48:10; Jer. 9:7;
Zech. 13:9; Matt. 3:2–3.
Of wine. Isa. 25:6.

REFUGE, CITIES OF

Afforded no asylum to murderers.
Exod. 21:14; Num. 35:16–21.
Design of. Exod. 21:13;
Num. 35:11; Josh. 20:3.
From the avenger of blood.
Exod. 21:13–14.

Illustrative of
Christ. Ps. 91:2; Isa. 25:4.
The hope of the gospel.
Heb. 6:18.
The way to Christ. Isa. 35:8;
John 14:16.
List of. Josh. 20:7–9.
Names, etc., of. Deut. 4:41–43;
Josh. 20:7–8.

Required to be
Easy of access. Deut. 19:3;
Isa. 62:10.
Open to all murderers. Josh. 20:4.
Roads made to. Deut. 19:3.
Strangers might take advantage of.
Num. 35:15.

Those admitted to
Not protected outside of.
Num. 35:26–27.
Obliged to remain in, until the high
priest's death. Num. 35:25, 28.
Put on their trial. Num. 35:12, 24.
Used in a figurative sense, of Christ.
Heb. 6:18.

REGENERATION

See also New Birth; Redemption;
Salvation; Sin, Remission of

Of the church, by the Father.
Ps. 71:20; Rom. 4:17; Eph. 2:1.

Examples of
Jacob. Gen. 32:29.
Saul. 1 Sam. 10:9.
Saul of Tarsus. Acts 9:3–18.
By the Holy Spirit. John 6:63;
Rom. 8:11; 2 Cor. 3:6;
1 Pet. 3:18.

Pictures of
Being born again. John 3:3–16.
Being raised to new life.
Rom. 6:3 23.
Circumcision of the heart.
Deut. 30:6.
Leading captives. Ps. 68:18.
The Lord's giving His people the
desire to do His will.
1 Kings 8:58.
Opening blind eyes. Isa. 35:5.
Providing water for the thirsty.
Isa. 44:3.
Purging. Ps. 65:3.
Replace stony heart with a heart of
flesh. Ezek. 11:19.
Releasing prisoners. Isa. 49:9.
Washing. Ps. 51:2.
By the Son. John 5:21;
1 Cor. 15:45.

REGICIDE

Of Ahaziah. 2 Kings 9.27.
Of Amaziah. 2 Kings 14:19–20.
Of Ehud. Judg. 3:16–23.
Of Elah. 1 Kings 16:9–11.
Of Ishbosheth. 2 Sam. 4:5–8.
Of Joash. 2 Kings 12:20–21.
Of Joram. 2 Kings 9:24.
Of Nadab. 1 Kings 15:27–29.
Of Pekahiah. 2 Kings 15:25.
Of Saul. 2 Sam. 1:16.

Of Sennacherib. 2 Kings 19:36–37;
Isa. 37:37–38.
Of Shallum. 2 Kings 15:14.
Of Zechariah. 2 Kings 15:10.

RELATIONSHIP BETWEEN GENDERS

See Genders, Relationship Between

RELIGION

Of the Athenians. Acts 17:22.
Of the Christian. Heb. 10:23.
Of the heart. 1 Cor. 13.
At its best. Mic. 6:8; Mark 12:33;
Rom. 13:10; James 1:27
At its worst. Isa. 1:10–14; Hos. 6:6;
Mic. 6:6–7; James 1:26.
Of Paul before his conversion.
Acts 26:5.
Of the scribes and Pharisees.
Matt. 23.

RELIGIONS, NON-CHRISTIAN

Israelite religion
With Canaanite influences.
Judg. 2:11–19; 1 Sam 7:3;
1 Kings 12:28–33; 14:23–24;
18:20–29; 2 Kings 18:4;
Jer. 32:35; 44:17–18;
Zeph. 1:4–5.
Heart-felt. Deut. 6:4–9; 10:12;
30.6; Ps. 51:16–17; Mic 6.8

Judaism, holidays and festivals.
Civil New Year (Rosh Hashanah).
Lev. 23:23–25.
Day of Atonement (Yom Kippur).
Lev. 23:26–32.
Dedication (Hanukkah).
John 10:22.
Firstfruits (Yom haBikkurim)
Lev. 23:9–14.

New Moon (Hodesh).
  Num. 28:11–15.
Passover (Pesach). Lev. 23:4–8.
Purim. Esther 9:18–32.
Sabbath (Shabbat). Lev. 23:3.
Sabbatical Year. Exod. 23:10–11;
  Lev. 25:1–7.
Tabernacles (Sukkot).
  Lev. 23:33–36.
Weeks (Shavuot). Lev. 23:15–22.
Year of Jubilee (Shanat haYovel).
  Lev. 25:8–55.

Judaism, religious personnel
Chief priests. Matt. 2:4; 16:21.
High priest. Luke 3:2.
Pharisees. Matt. 3:7–10;
  23:2–36; Mark 7:3–4;
  John 3:1; Acts 23:6–8;
  Phil. 3:5–6.
Priests. Luke 1:8–9; 17:14;
  Acts 6:7.
Sadducees. Matt. 3:7–10;
  Acts 5:17; 23:6–8.
Scribes. Matt. 2:4; 23:2–36;
  Mark 1:22.

Judaism, sacrificial system
Burnt offering.
  Lev. 1:3–17; 6:8–13; 7:16;
  22:17–21.
Drink offering. Num. 15:5–10.
Freewill offering. Lev. 7:17;
  22:18–23.
Grain offering. Lev. 2:1–16;
  6:14–23.
Guilt offering. Lev. 5:14–6:7.
Peace offering. Lev. 3:1–17;
  7:11–21.
Sin offering. Lev. 4:1–35;
  6:24–30.
Wave offering. Exod. 29:22–28;
  Lev. 23:9–21.

Judaism, Scripture
Oral. Neh 8:8; Matt. 23:4;
  Mark 7:3–4; Acts 15:10.
Written. Exod. 20:1–17;
  Josh. 1:8; Luke 24:44.

Of nations
Ammon. Lev 18:21; 20:1–5;
  Judg. 11:24;
  1 Kings 11:5, 7, 33.
Assyria. 2 Kings 19:37.
Babylon. 2 Kings 17:30;
  Isa. 46:1–2; Jer. 50:2;
  Ezek. 8:14; Dan 1:20; 3:1–13;
  4:7.
Egypt. Gen. 41:8; Exod. 7:11.
Greece.
  Acts 14:12–13; 17:16–23;
  19:24–35.
Idols, in general. Isa. 40:18–20;
  44:9–17.
Moab. 1 Kings 11:7, 33;
  Jer. 48:7, 13.
Philistia. Judg. 16:23–27;
  1 Sam. 5:2–7; 1 Chron. 10:10.
Sidon. 1 Kings 11:5.
Syria. 2 Kings 5:18–19.

REMEMBRANCE

God's people are in His. Isa. 49:16;
  Mal. 3:16.
Lord's Supper is His. 1 Cor. 11:24.
Prayer should include. 2 Tim. 1:3.
Righteous to be in everlasting.
  Ps. 112:6.
We need a reminder. 2 Pet. 1:12.
Woman's generosity to be a.
  Matt. 26:13.

REMISSION OF SIN
See Sin, Remission of

REMORSE

Examples of
David. Ps. 51.
Judas. Matt. 27:3–5.
Peter. Matt. 26:75.

RENDING

Of garments, a sign of affliction.
Gen. 37:29, 34; Matt. 26:65;
Acts 14:14.
Used in a figurative sense as symbol
of tearing apart a kingdom.
1 Sam. 15:27–28.

RENEWAL

Of days. Lam. 5:21.
Of earth. Ps. 104:30.
Of inward nature. Ps. 51:10;
2 Cor. 4:16; Eph. 4:23; Col.
3:10; Titus 3:5.
Of the inner nature, daily.
2 Cor. 4:16.
Of the Lord's work, prayed for.
Hab. 3:2.
Of mind. Rom. 12:2.
Of mind, a means of transformation
of life. Rom. 12:1–2.
Of mind, our duty. Eph. 4:23.
Of people, in general. Ps. 85:6.
Of spirit, from God.
Pss. 23:3; 51:10; Isa. 57:15.
Of strength. Ps. 103:5;
Isa. 40:31–41:1.
Of strength, from waiting on the
Lord. Isa. 40:31.
Of those who have fallen away
impossible. Heb. 6:6.
Of works of God. Hab. 3:2.

RENTING

Houses. Acts 28:30.
Land. Matt. 21:33–41.

REPARATIONS

See Restitution

REPENTANCE

By the work of the Holy Spirit.
Zech. 12:10.
Called repentance to life.
Acts 11:18.
Called repentance to salvation.
2 Cor. 7:10.
Christ came to call sinners to.
Matt. 9:13.
Christ exalted to give. Acts 5:31.
Commanded by Christ. Rev. 2:5, 16;
3:3.
Commanded to all by God.
Ezek. 18:30–32; Acts 17:30.
Conviction of sin necessary to.
1 Kings 8:38; Prov. 28:13;
Acts 2:37–38; 19:18.
Danger of neglecting.
Matt. 11:20–24; Luke 13:3, 5;
Rev. 2:22.
Denied to those who fall away.
Heb. 6:4–6.
Exhortations to. Ezek. 14:6; 18:30;
Acts 2:38; 3:19.
Given by God. Acts 11:18;
2 Tim. 2:25.
Godly sorrow works. 2 Cor. 7:10.
Joy in heaven over one sinner
brought to. Luke 15:7, 10.
Ministers should rejoice over their
people on their. 2 Cor. 7:9.
Necessary to the pardon of sin.
Acts 2:38; 3:19; 8:22.
Neglect of, followed by swift
judgment. Rev. 2:5, 16.
Not to be regretted of. 2 Cor. 7:10.

Preached
By the apostles. Mark 6:12;
Acts 20:21.
By Christ. Matt. 4:17; Mark 1:15.

By John the Baptist. Matt. 3:2.
In the name of Christ.
Luke 24:47.
Present time the season for.
Ps. 95:7–8, with Heb. 3:7–8;
Prov. 27:1; Isa. 55:6; 2 Cor. 6:2;
Heb. 4:7.

Should be accompanied by
Confession. Lev. 26:40;
Job 33:27.
Conversion. Acts 3:19; 26:20.
Faith. Matt. 21:32; Mark 1:15;
Acts 20:21.
Greater seriousness in the path of
duty. 2 Cor. 7:11.
Humility. 2 Chron. 7:14;
James 4:9–10.
Prayer. 1 Kings 8:33; Acts 8:22.
Sorrow for sin. Job 42:6.
Shame and confusion.
Ezra 9:6–15; Jer. 31:19;
Ezek. 16:61, 63; Dan. 9:7–8.
Turning from idolatry. Ezek. 14:6;
1 Thess. 1:9.
Turning from sin. 2 Chron. 6:26.
Should be evidenced by fruits.
Isa. 1:16–17; Dan. 4:27;
Matt. 3:8; Acts 26:20.

We should be led to, by
The goodness of God. Rom. 2:4.
The long-suffering of God.
Gen. 6:3, with 1 Pet. 3:20;
2 Pet. 3:9.
The punishments of God.
1 Kings 8:47; Rev. 3:19.
What it is. Isa. 45:22;
Matt. 6:19–21; Acts 14:15;
2 Cor. 5:17; Col. 3:2;
1 Thess. 1:9; Heb. 12:1–2.

The wicked
Averse to. Jer. 8:6.

Condemned for neglecting.
Matt. 11:20.
Neglect the time given for.
Rev. 2:21.
Not led to, by the judgments of
God. Rev. 9:20–21; 16:9.
Not led to, by miraculous
interference. Luke 16:30–31.

REPROBACY

Examples of
Eli's house. 1 Sam. 3:14.
Israel. Num. 14:26–45;
Deut. 1:42–43.
Saul. 1 Sam. 15:23; 16:14;
18:12; 28:15.

REPROOF

Attention to, a proof of wisdom.
Prov. 15:5.

Because of
Fearfulness. Mark 4:40;
Luke 24:37–38.
Hardness of heart. Mark 8:17;
16:14.
Hypocrisy. Matt. 15:7; 23:13,
etc.
Not understanding.
Matt. 16:9, 11; Mark 7:18;
Luke 24:25;
John 8:43; 13:7–8.
Oppressing fellow believers.
Neh. 5:7.
Reviling Christ. Luke 23:40.
Sinful practices. Matt. 21:13;
Luke 3:19; John 2:16.
Unbelief. Matt. 17:17, 20;
Mark 16:14.
Unrepentance. Matt. 11:20–24.
Unruly conduct. 1 Thess. 5:14.
Vain boasting. Luke 22:34.

Believers should
Delight in those who give.
Prov. 24:25.
Give. Lev. 19:17; Eph. 5:11.
Give no occasion for. Phil. 2:15.
Love those who give. Prov. 9:8.
Receive kindly. Ps. 141:5.
Christ gives, in love. Rev. 3:19.
Christ sent to give. Isa. 2:4; 11:3.
Contempt of, leads to remorse.
Prov. 5:12.

Declared to be
Better than secret love.
Prov. 27:5.
Better than the praise of fools.
Eccles. 7:5.
An excellent oil. Ps. 141:5.
More profitable to believers than
stripes to a fool. Prov. 17:10.
Eventually brings more respect than
flattery. Prov. 28:23.
God gives, to His own children.
2 Sam. 7:14; Job 5:17;
Pss. 94:12; 119:67, 71, 75;
Heb. 12:6-7.
God gives, to the wicked. Ps. 50:21;
Isa. 51:20.
Hatred of, a proof of stupidity.
Prov. 12:1.
Hatred of, leads to destruction.
Prov. 15:10; 29:1.
The Holy Spirit gives. John 16:7-8.
Hypocrites not qualified to give.
Matt. 7:5.

Leads to
Happiness. Prov. 6:23.
Honor. Prov. 13:18.
Knowledge Prov. 19:25.
Understanding. Prov. 15:32.
Wisdom. Prov. 15:31; 29:15.
Ministers empowered to give.
Mic. 3:8.

Ministers sent to give. Jer. 44:4;
Ezek. 3:17.

Ministers should give
With all authority. Titus 2:15.
With Christian love.
2 Thess. 3:15.
Fearlessly. Ezek. 2:3-7.
With long-suffering, etc.
2 Tim. 4:2.
Openly. 1 Tim. 5:20.
Sharply, if necessary. Titus 1:13.
Unreservedly. Isa. 58:1.
A proof of faithful friendship.
Prov. 27:6.
Rejection of, leads to error.
Prov. 10:17.
The Scriptures are profitable for.
Ps. 19:7-11; 2 Tim. 3:16.
Should be accompanied by
exhortation to repent.
1 Sam. 12:20-25.
Those who give, disliked by those
who make fun of wisdom.
Prov. 9:8; 15:12.
Of those who offend, a warning to
others. Lev. 19:17; Acts 5:3-4,
9; 1 Tim. 5:20; Titus 1:10-13.

When from God
Is despised by the wicked.
Prov. 1:30.
Is for correction. Ps. 39:11.
Pray that it not be in anger.
Ps. 6:1.
Should not discourage believers.
Heb. 12:5.

REPTILES
Created by God. Gen. 1:24-25.
Jews condemned for worshiping.
Ezek. 8:10.
Made for praise and glory of God.
Ps. 148:10.

Mentioned in Scripture
    Adder or asp. Pss. 58:4; 91:13;
        Prov. 23:32.
    Chameleon. Lev. 11:30.
    Cobra. Isa. 11:8; 59:5.
    Dragon. Deut. 32:33; Job 30:29;
        Jer. 9:11.
    Flying fiery serpent. Deut. 8:15;
        Isa. 30:6.
    Frog. Exod. 8:2; Rev. 16:13.
    Horse leech. Prov. 30:15.
    Lizard. Lev. 11:30.
    Scorpion. Deut. 8:15.
    Serpent. Job 26:13; Matt. 7:10.
    Snail. Lev. 11:30; Ps. 58:8.
    Tortoise. Lev. 11:29.
    Viper. Acts 28:3.
No idol or image of, to be made for
    worshiping. Deut. 4:16, 18.
Placed under the dominion of man.
    Gen. 1:26.
Solomon wrote a history of.
    1 Kings 4:33.
Unclean and not eaten.
    Lev. 11:31, 40–43;
    Acts 10:11–14.
Worshiped by the Gentiles.
    Rom. 1:23.

REPUTATION, GOOD

Highly desirable. Prov. 22:1.

REQUIREMENTS

Of the entrance into the kingdom:
    conversion. Matt. 18:3.
Of the law: love. Rom. 13:10.
Of the Lord: justice, mercy, and
    humble fellowship with God.
    Mic. 6:8.
Of salvation: belief in Christ.
    John 8:24.
Of worship: sincerity and true
    devotion of spirit. John 4:24.

RESIGNATION

See God, Submission to

RESPECT

To the aged. Lev. 19:32.
To a host. Luke 14:10.
To one another. Rom. 12:10;
    Phil. 2:3; 1 Pet. 2:17.
To rulers. Prov. 25:6.

RESPONSIBILITY

Corporate. Josh. 22:16;
    1 Cor. 5:1–2.
For the earth. Gen. 1:28;
    Ps. 115:16.
Individual. Deut. 24:16; Jer. 31:30;
    Rom. 14:12.
Marital. 1 Cor. 7:3–5.
National. Prov. 14:34;
    Amos 1:3–3:2.
For one another. Rom. 14:13; 15:1;
    1 Cor. 8:11; 1 John 4:11.
Parental. 1 Sam. 3:13; Eph. 6:4.
For sexual partnerships.
    1 Cor. 6:12–20.
For what we hear. Mark 4:24.
For what we see. Mark 9:47.
For whatever we do. 1 Cor. 10:31.

REST

Christ's call to. Matt. 11:28.
Eternal. Ps. 104:23; Rev. 14:13.
God's day for. Exod. 23:12.
The Lord's provision for. Pss. 23:2;
    37:7; Heb. 4:9.

RESTITUTION

Divine provisions for, in the case of
    Accidentally destroying property.
        Exod. 22:5–6.
    Disappearing, injured, or
        destroyed property.
        Exod. 22:7–15.

Ill-gotten gains. Num. 5:6–10.
Seduction of a virgin.
   Exod. 22:16–17.
Stealing an animal. Exod. 22:1, 4.
Example approved by Christ.
   Luke 19:8–9.

RESTORATION
Of all things. Acts 3:21;
   Rev. 21:1–5.

RESURRECTION
Assumed and proved by Christ.
   Matt. 22:29–32; Luke 14:14;
   John 5:28–29.

Believers in, will
  Be as the angels. Matt. 22:30.
  Be glorified with Christ. Col. 3:4.
  Be repaid. Luke 14:14.
  Have bodies like Christ's.
    Phil. 3:21; 1 John 3:2.
  Have glorious bodies.
    1 Cor. 15:43.
  Have incorruptible bodies.
    1 Cor. 15:42.
  Have powerful bodies.
    1 Cor. 15:43.
  Have spiritual bodies.
    1 Cor. 15:44.
  Rise first. 1 Cor. 15:23;
    1 Thess. 4:16.
  Rise through Christ. John 11:25;
    Acts 4:2; 1 Cor. 15:21–22.
  Rise to eternal life. Deut. 12:2;
    John 5:29.
Believers should look forward to.
   Dan. 12:13; 2 Cor. 5:1;
   Phil. 3:11
Of believers, will be followed by the
   change of those then alive.
   1 Cor. 15:51, with 1 Thess. 4:17.
Blessedness of those who have part
   in the first. Rev. 20:6.

Called in question by some in the
   primitive church. 1 Cor. 15:12.
Certainty of, proved by the
   resurrection of Christ.
   1 Cor. 15:12–20.
Credibility of, shown by the
   resurrection of individuals.
   Matt. 9:25; 27:53; Luke 7:14;
   John 11:44; Heb. 11:35.
Denied by the Sadducees.
   Matt. 22:23; Luke 20:27;
   Acts 23:8.
Doctrine of the Old Testament.
   Job 19:26; Pss. 16:10; 49:15;
   Isa. 26:19; Dan. 12:2;
   Hos. 13:14.

Effected by the power of
  Christ. John 5:28–29;
    6:39–40, 44.
  God. Matt. 22:29.
  The Holy Spirit. Rom. 8:11.
Expected by the Jews. John 11:24;
   Heb. 11:35.
Explained away by false teachers.
   2 Tim. 2:18.
First principle of the gospel.
   1 Cor. 15:13–14; Heb. 6:1–2.
Illustrated. Ezek. 37:1–10;
   1 Cor. 15:36–37.
Illustrative of the new birth.
   John 5:25.
Not contrary to reason. John 12:24;
   1 Cor. 15:35–49.
Not incredible. Mark 12:24;
   Acts 26:8.
Preached by the apostles.
   Acts 4:2; 17:18; 24:15.

Preaching of, caused
  Mocking. Acts 17:32.
  Persecution. Acts 23:6;
    24:11–15.

Of the wicked, will be to
Judgment. John 5:29.
Shame and everlasting contempt.
Dan. 12:2.
Will be of all the dead. John 5:28;
Acts 24:15; Rev. 20:13.

RESURRECTION OF CHRIST
See Christ, Resurrection of

RETALIATION OR REVENGE
Be thankful for being kept from
taking. 1 Sam. 25:32–33.
Christ an example of abstaining
from. Isa. 53:7; 1 Pet. 2:23.

Examples of
Absalom. 2 Sam. 13:23–29.
Ahab. 1 Kings 22:27.
Chief priests. Acts 5:33.
David on Joab. 1 Kings 2:5–6.
David on Michal.
2 Sam. 6:21–23.
David on Shimei. 1 Kings 2:8–9.
The Edomites. Ezek. 25:12.
Gideon on Penuel. Judg. 8:9, 17.
Gideon on the kings of Midian.
Judg. 8:18–21.
Gideon on the princess of
Succoth. Judg. 8:7, 13–16.
Haman. Esther 3:8–15.
Herodias. Mark 6:19–24.
Israelites on the Amalekites.
Deut. 25:17–19;
1 Sam. 15:1–9.
James and John. Luke 9:54.
Jewish leaders. Acts 7:54–59;
23:12.
Jews on the Chaldeans. Esther 9.
Jezebel. 1 Kings 19:2.
Joab on Abner. 2 Sam. 3:27, 30.
Philistines. Ezek. 25:15.
Samson. Judg. 15:7–8;
16:28–30.

Simeon and Levi. Gen. 34:25.
Forbidden by Jesus. Matt. 5:39–41;
Rom. 12:17, 19; 1 Thess. 5:15;
1 Pet. 3:9.
Inconsistent with Christian spirit.
Luke 9:55.

Instead of taking, we should
Abstain from. Matt. 5:38–41.
Bless. Rom. 12:14.
Exhibit love. Lev. 19:18;
Luke 6:35.
Leave justice to God. Rom. 12:19.
Overcome others by kindness.
Prov. 25:21–22, with
Rom. 12:20.
Trust in God. Prov. 20:22.
Jesus' example. Luke 9:52–56.
Jesus' teaching. Matt. 5:38–44;
7:1–2.
Keep others from taking.
1 Sam. 24:10; 25:24–31; 26:9.
Law of. Exod. 21:23–25.
Paul's teaching. Rom. 12:17–19.
Proceeds from a spiteful heart.
Ezek. 25:15.
Punishment for. Ezek. 25:15–17;
Amos 1:11–12.
Rebuked by Christ. Luke 9:54–55.
The wicked are intent upon.
Jer. 20:10.

REVELATION
God reveals Himself to Moses.
Exod. 3:1–6, 14; 6:1–3.
God reveals His law. Exod. 20–35;
Lev. 1–7.
God reveals the pattern of the
temple. 1 Chron. 28:11–19.
God reveals the sonship of Jesus.
Matt. 3:17; 17:5.

REVENUE
Solomon's. 2 Chron. 9:13–14.

REVERENCE

For Christ. Matt. 8:2; 14:33;
28:16–17; Phil. 2:10; Heb. 1:6.
For God. 1 Chron. 16:25;
Hab. 2:20.
For the Lord's day. Esther 20:8;
Rev. 1:10.
For the Lord's house. Lev. 19:30;
John 2:16.
For the Lord's name. Exod. 20:7.
For parents. Exod. 20:12;
Eph. 6:1–3.
For spiritual leaders. Heb. 13:7, 17.

REVILING AND REPROACHING

Believers
Endure. 1 Tim. 4:10; Heb. 10:33.
Endure for Christ's sake.
Luke 6:22.
Endure for God's sake.
Prov. 69:7.
May take pleasure in.
2 Cor. 12:10.
Pray under. 2 Kings 19:4, 16;
Ps. 89:50.
Return blessings for. 1 Cor. 4:12;
1 Pet. 3:9.
Should expect. Matt. 10:25.
Should not fear. Isa. 51:7.
Sometimes depressed by.
Pss. 42:10–11; 44:16; 69:20.
Supported under. 2 Cor. 12:10.
Trust in God under. Pss. 57:3;
119:42.
Blessedness of enduring, for Christ's
sake. Matt. 5:11; Luke 6:22.
Of Christ, predicted. Ps. 69:9, with
Rom. 15:3; Ps. 89:51.
Conduct of Christ under.
1 Pet. 2:23.
Excludes from heaven. 1 Cor. 6:10.
Forbidden. 1 Pet. 3:9.

Happiness of enduring, for Christ's
sake. 1 Pet. 4:14.
Ministers should not fear. Ezek. 2:6.
Punishment for. Zeph. 2:8–9;
Matt. 5:22.
Of rulers specially forbidden.
Exod. 22:28, with Acts 23:4–5.

The wicked utter, against
Believers. Ps. 102:8; Zeph. 2:8.
Christ. Matt. 27:39; Luke 7:34.
God. Pss. 74:22; 79:12.
God, by oppressing the poor.
Prov. 14:31.
Rulers. 2 Pet. 2:10–11; Jude 8–9.

REVIVALS

Examples of
Under Asa. 2 Chron. 14:2–5;
15:1–14.
Under Elijah. 1 Kings 18:17–40.
Under Hezekiah. 2 Kings 18:1–7;
2 Chron. 29–31.
Under Jehoash and Jehoiada.
2 Kings 11–12;
2 Chron. 23–24.
Under Joshua. Josh. 5:2–9.
Under Josiah. 2 Kings 22–23;
2 Chron. 34–35.
Under Manasseh.
2 Chron. 33:12–19.
In Nineveh. Jon. 3:4–10.
At Pentecost. Acts 2:1–42, 46,
47.
Under Samuel. 1 Sam. 7:1–6.
Prayer for. Hab. 3:2.
Prophecies concerning. Isa. 32:15;
Joel 2:28; Mic. 4:1–8; Hab. 3:2.

REVISIONISM

Of commandment of God
Pharisees. Mark 7:2, 8, 13.

Of prophetic word
Micaiah. 1 Kings 22:5–23.
Rebellious people. Isa. 30:8–11.
Unbelievers 2 Pet 3:3–5.
Zedekiah. Jer. 32:3–5.

Rather, hold fast to
Faith. 1 Cor. 16:13.
Our confession. Heb 4:14; 10:23.
Sure word as taught. Titus 1:9.
Teachings of elders. Prov. 1:8;
4:1–4.
Teachings of Paul. 1 Cor. 11:2;
2 Thess. 2:15; 2 Tim. 1:13.
What has been learned. 2 Tim.
3:14.

Of sound doctrine
Persons who suppress truth.
Rom. 1:18.
Persons who teach different
doctrine. 1 Tim. 1:3–4.
Persons who teach whatever
wants to be heard. 2 Tim.
4:3–4.
Those who call good evil and evil
good. Isa. 5:20.

REVOLT
Of the ten tribes. 1 Kings 12:1–24.

REWARD OF BELIEVERS
See Believers, Reward of

RICH PERSONS
Abraham. Gen. 13:2; 24:35.
Hezekiah. 2 Kings 20:12–18.
Job. Job 1:3.
Joseph of Arimathea. Matt. 27:57.
Solomon. 1 Kings 10:23.
Zaccheus. Luke 19:2.

RICHES
Be not overanxious for. Prov. 30:8.

The blessing of the Lord brings.
Prov. 10:22.

Cannot
Deliver in the day of God's wrath.
Zeph. 1:18; Rev. 6:15–17.
Redeem the soul. Ps. 49:6–9.
Secure prosperity. James 1:11.
Danger of misusing, illustrated.
Luke 16:19–25.
Deceitfulness of, chokes the Word.
Matt. 13:22.

Denunciations against those who
Abuse. James 5:1, 5.
Get by vanity. Prov. 13:11; 21:6.
Get unlawfully. Jer. 17:11.
Hoard. Eccles. 5:13–14;
James 5:3.
Increase by oppression.
Prov. 22:16; Mic. 2:2–3;
Hab. 2:6–8.
Receive their reward from.
Luke 6:24.
Spend everything on their own
selfish appetites. Job 20:15–17.
Trust in. Prov. 11:28.

Described as
Corruptible. James 5:2;
1 Pet. 1:18.
Deceitful. Matt. 13:22.
Fleeting. Prov. 23:5;
Rev. 18:16–27.
Liable to be stolen. Matt. 6:19.
Perishable. Jer. 48:36.
Temporary. Prov. 27:24.
Thick clay. Hab. 2:6.
Uncertain. 1 Tim. 6:17.
Unsatisfying. Eccles. 4:8; 5:10.
Do not labor for. Prov. 23:4.
Do not profit in the day of wrath.
Prov. 11:4.

Folly and danger of trusting to, illustrated. Luke 12:16–21.

Give worldly power. Prov. 22:7.

God gives. 1 Sam. 2:7; Eccles. 5:19.

God gives power to obtain. Deut. 8:18.

Guilt of rejoicing in. Job 31:25, 28.

Guilt of trusting in. Job 31:24, 28; Ezek. 28:4–5, 8.

Heavenly treasure superior to. Matt. 6:19–20.

Life consists not in abundance of. Luke 12:15.

Love of, the root of all evil. 1 Tim. 6:10.

Often an obstruction to the reception of the gospel. Mark 10:23–25.

Often lead to
Anxiety. Eccles. 5:12.

Denying God. Prov. 30:8–9.

Forgetting God. Deut. 8:13–14.

Forsaking God. Deut. 32:15.

Fraud. James 5:4.

Oppression. James 2:6.

An overbearing spirit. Prov. 18:23.

Pride. Ezek. 28:5; Hos. 12:8.

Rebelling against God. Neh. 9:25–26.

Rejecting Christ. Matt. 19:22; Mark 10:22.

Self sufficiency. Prov. 28:11.

Sensual indulgence. Luke 16:19; James 5:5.

Violence. Mic. 6:12.

Those who covet
Bring trouble on their families. Prov. 15:27.

Bring trouble on themselves. 1 Tim. 6:10.

Fall into harmful desires. 1 Tim. 6:9.

Fall into temptation and a trap. 1 Tim. 6:9.

Use unlawful means to acquire. Prov. 28:20.

Wander from the faith. 1 Tim. 6:10.

Those who possess, should
Ascribe them to God. 1 Chron. 29:12.

Be generous in all things. 1 Tim. 6:18.

Devote them to God's service. 1 Chron. 29:3; Mark 12:42–44.

Consider it a privilege to be allowed to give. 1 Chron. 29:14.

Give of them to the poor. Matt. 19:21; 1 John 3:17.

Not be arrogant. 1 Tim. 6:17.

Not boast of obtaining them. Deut. 8:17.

Not glory in them. Jer. 9:23.

Not hoard them. Matt. 6:19.

Not set the heart on them. Ps. 62:10.

Not trust in them. Job 31:24; 1 Tim. 6:17.

Use them in promoting the salvation of others. Luke 16:9.

When converted, rejoice in being humbled. James 1:9–10.

This world's, belong to God. Hag. 2:8.

True, described. Eph. 3:8; 1 Cor. 1:30; Col. 2:3; 1 Pet. 2:7.

Vanity of accumulating. Ps. 39:6; Eccles. 5:10–11.

The wicked
Accumulate. Job 27:16; Ps. 39:6; Eccles. 2:26.

Boast themselves in. Pss. 49:6;
52:7.
Do not profit by. Prov. 11:4;
13:7; Eccles. 5:11.
Have trouble with. Prov. 15:6;
1 Tim. 6:9–10.
Keep, to their hurt. Eccles. 5:13.
Must leave, to others. Ps. 49:10.
Often increase in. Ps. 73:12.
Often spend their days in.
Job 21:13.
Swallow. Job 20:15.
Trust in the abundance of.
Ps. 52:7.
Of the wicked, laid up for the just.
Prov. 13:22.

RIDDLE

Used as a test of wit
By Agur. Prov. 30:15–16, 18–31.
At Samson's feast.
Judg. 14:12–18.

RIDICULE

The evil children of Bethel deride
Elisha. 2 Kings 2:23.
The people of Israel scoff at
Hezekiah. 2 Chron. 30:1–10.
Sarah, when the angels gave her the
promise of a child. Gen. 18:12.
The wicked held in, by God. Ps. 2:4;
Prov. 1:26.

RIGHTEOUSNESS

Believers
Are covered with the robe of.
Isa. 61:10.
Are led in the paths of. Ps. 23:3.
Are renewed in. Eph. 4:24.
Are servants of. Rom. 6:16, 18.
Characterized by. Gen. 18:25;
Ps. 1:5–6.

Count their own, as filthy rags.
Isa. 64:6.
Do. 1 John 2:29; 3:7.
Follow after. Isa. 51:1.
Have, credited. Rom. 4:11, 22.
Have, in Christ. Isa. 45:24;
54:17; 2 Cor. 5:21.
Hunger and thirst after. Matt. 5:6.
Know. Isa. 51:7.
Offer the sacrifice of. Ps. 4:5;
51:19.
Pray for the spirit of. Ps. 51:10.
Put no trust in their own.
Phil. 3:6–8.
Put on. Job 29:14.
Receive, from God. Ps. 24:5.
Should have on the breastplate of.
Eph. 6:14.
Should live in. Titus 2:12;
1 Pet. 2:24.
Should seek. Zeph. 2:3.
Should serve God in. Luke 1:75.
Should yield their bodies as
instruments of. Rom. 6:13.
Should yield their bodies servants
to. Rom. 6:19.
Wait for the hope of. Gal. 5:5.
Walk before God in. 1 Kings 3:6.
Will receive a crown of.
2 Tim. 4:8.
Will see God's face in. Ps. 17:15.
Work, by faith. Heb. 11:33.
Of believers endures forever.
Ps. 112:3, 9, with 2 Cor. 9:9.

Blessedness of
Being made right with God without
works. Rom. 4:6.
Being persecuted for. Matt. 5:10.
Doing. Ps. 106:3.
Hungering and thirsting after.
Matt. 5:6.
Suffering for. 1 Pet. 3:14.
Turning others to. Dan. 12:3.

Blessing of God not attributed to our works of. Deut. 9:5.

Brings its own reward. Prov. 11:18; Isa. 3:10.

Cannot come by the law. Gal. 2:21; 3:21.

Christ
Fulfilled all. Matt. 3:15.
Has brought in everlasting. Dan. 9:24.
Is the end of the law for. Rom. 10:4.
Is the Son of. Mal. 4:2.
Loves. Ps. 45:7, with Heb. 1:9.
Makes us right with God. 1 Cor. 1:30.
Preached. Ps. 40:9.
Put on, as a breastplate. Isa. 59:17.
Will execute. Ps. 99:4; Jer. 23:6.
Will judge with. Ps. 72:2; Isa. 11:4; Acts 17:31; Rev. 19:11.
Will reign in. Ps. 45:6; Isa. 32:1; Heb. 1:8.
Was surrounded with like a belt. Isa. 11:5.
Was sustained by. Isa. 59:16.

A crown of glory to the aged. Prov. 16:31.

Effect of, quietness and assurance forever. Isa. 32:17.

An evidence of the new birth. 1 John 2:29.

The fruit of the Spirit is in all. Eph. 5:9.

God looks for. Isa. 5:7.

God loves. Ps. 11:7.

Has no fellowship with unrighteousness. 2 Cor. 6:14.

Judgment should be executed in. Lev. 19:15.

Judgments designed to lead to. Isa. 26:9.

Keeps believers in the right way. Prov. 11:5; 13:6.

The kingdom of God is. Rom. 14:17.

Ministers should
Be armed with. 2 Cor. 6:7.
Be clothed with. Ps. 132:9.
Be preachers of. 2 Pet. 2:5.
Follow after. 1 Tim. 6:11; 2 Tim. 2:22.
Pray for fruit of, in their people. 2 Cor. 9:10; Phil. 1:11.
Reason of. Acts 24:25.

Nations exalted by. Prov. 14:34.

No justification by works of. Rom. 3:20; 9:31–32; Gal. 2:16.

None by nature have. Job 15:14; Ps. 14:3, with Rom. 3:10.

Obedience to God's law. Deut. 6:25, with Rom. 10:5; Luke 1:6, with Ps. 1:2.

Promised to the church. Isa. 32:16; 45:8; 61:11; 62:1.

Punishments yield the fruit of. Heb. 12:11.

Promised to believers. Isa. 60:21; 61:3.

The Scriptures instruct in. 2 Tim. 3:16.

Tends to life. Prov. 11:19; 12:28.

Those who walk in and follow
Are abundantly provided for. Prov. 13:25; Matt. 6:25–33.
Are accepted with God. Acts 10:35.
Are blessed by God. Ps. 5:12.
Are bold as a lion. Prov. 28:1.
Are delivered out of all troubles. Ps. 34:19; Prov. 11:8.
Are enriched. Ps. 112:3; Prov. 15:6.

Are exalted by God. Job 36:7.
Are heard by God. Luke 18:7;
   James 5:16.
Are loved by God. Ps. 146:8;
   Prov. 15:9.
Are never forsaken by God.
   Ps. 37:25.
Are objects of God's watchful care.
   Job 36:7; Ps. 34:15;
   Prov. 10:3; 1 Pet. 3:12.
Are righteous. 1 John 3:7.
Are the excellent of the earth.
   Ps. 16:3, with Prov. 12:26.
Are tried by God. Ps. 11:5.
Dwell in security. Isa. 33:15–16.
Find it with life and honor.
   Prov. 21:21.
Have their desires granted.
   Prov. 10:24.
Have their prayers heard.
   Ps. 34:17; Prov. 15:29;
   1 Pet. 3:12.
Know the secret of the Lord.
   Ps. 25:14; Prov. 3:32.
Will be ever remembered.
   Ps. 112:6.
Will flourish as a branch.
   Prov. 11:28.
Will hold on their way. Job 17:9.
Will never be moved. Pss. 15:2, 5;
   55:22; Prov. 10:30; 12:3.
Think and desire good.
   Prov. 11:23; 12:5.
The throne of kings established by.
   Prov. 16:12; 25:5.
Unregenerate persons seek
   justification by works of.
   Luke 18:9; Rom. 10:3.

The wicked
   Are enemies of. Acts 13:10.
   Are far from. Ps. 119:150;
      Isa. 46:12.
   Are free from. Rom. 6:20.

Do not. 1 John 3:10.
Do not follow after. Rom. 9:30.
Do not obey. Rom. 2:8, with
   2 Thess. 2:12.
Hate those who follow. Ps. 34:21.
Leave off. Amos 5:7, with
   Ps. 36:3.
Love lying rather than. Ps. 52:3.
Make mention of God, not in.
   Isa. 48:1.
Should awake to. 1 Cor. 15:34.
Should break off their sins by.
   Dan. 4:27.
Slay those who follow. Ps. 37:32;
   1 John 3:12, with Matt. 23:35.
Speak will contempt against those
   who follow. Ps. 31:18;
   Matt. 27:39–44.
Though favored, will not learn.
   Isa. 26:10, with Ps. 106:43.
Vainly wish to die as those who
   follow. Num. 23:10.
Will be glad in the Lord. Ps. 64:10.
Work of, will be peace. Isa. 32:17.

RIGHTEOUSNESS CREDITED

Believers
   Clothed with the robe of
      righteousness. Isa. 61:10.
   Desire to be found in. Phil. 3:9.
   Exalted in righteousness.
      Ps. 89:16.
   Glory in having. Isa. 45:24–25.
   Have, on believing.
      Rom. 4:5, 11, 24.
Blessedness of those who have.
   Rom. 4:6.
Christ brings in an everlasting
   righteousness. Dan. 9:24.
Christ called the Lord our
   righteousness. Jer. 23:6.
Christ the end of the law for.
   Rom. 10:4.

Described as
  Christ became righteousness for
    us. 1 Cor. 1:30.
  Our being made the righteousness
    of God, in Christ. 2 Cor. 5:21.
  The righteousness of faith.
    Rom. 4:13; 9:30; 10:6.
  The righteousness of God by faith
    in Christ. Rom. 3:22.
  The righteousness of God, without
    the law. Rom. 3:21.
Exhortation to seek righteousness.
  Matt. 6:33.
A free gift. Rom. 5:17.
The Gentiles attained to. Rom. 9:30.
God's righteousness never to be
  abolished. Isa. 51:6.

Israel
  Do not submit to. Rom. 10:3.
  Ignorant of. Rom. 10:3.
  Stumble at righteousness by faith.
    Rom. 9:32.
Of the Lord. Isa. 54:17.
Predicted. Isa. 56:1; Ezek. 16:14.
Promises made through. Rom. 4:13.
Revealed in the gospel. Rom. 1:17.

RIGHTEOUSNESS OF GOD
See God, Righteousness of

RIGHTS, CIVIL

All persons
  Equal in Christ. Gal. 3:28.
  Made in image of God.
    Gen. 1:27–28.

Impartiality
  As characteristic of God.
    Deut. 10:17–18; Acts 10:34.
  As characteristic of Jesus.
    Luke 20:21.

In judgment, shown to
  All people. Deut. 16:18–20.
  Authorities. 2 Sam. 12:7; 14:13;
    1 Kings 20:42.
  Citizens and noncitizens.
    Exod. 12:49; Lev. 24:22;
    Num. 15:15–16.
  Great and small. Deut. 1:17.
  Rich and poor. Lev. 19:15;
    Amos 5:12.
In matters of instruction. Mal. 2:9;
  1 Tim 5:21.
Right to asylum. Exod. 21:13.
Right to fair trial. Exod. 22:9.
Right to life. Exod. 20:13;
  21:22–25; Ps. 139:13–15;
  Matt. 5:21–22.

Right to work
  Fair wages. Matt. 10:10;
    1 Cor. 9:3–12; 1 Tim 5:18;
    James 5:4.
  Timely wages. Lev. 19:13;
    Deut. 24:14–15;
    Prov. 3:27–28.

To be upheld
  By God. Ps. 146:7–9.
  By people. Prov. 31:4–5, 8–9;
    Isa. 1:17; 1 Tim 6:17–18.
  Voluntary subordination of rights.
    Luke 22:26; 1 Cor. 8:9–13;
    Eph. 5:21; Phil 2:4.
  Witnesses. Deut. 19:15; Isa. 43:9.

RINGS
Antiquity of. Gen. 24:22; 38:18.

Illustrative of
  Favor (when put on the hands).
    Luke 15:22.
  The glory of Christ.
    Song of Sol. 5:14.

Of kings
Given to favorites as a mark of
honor. Gen. 41:42;
Esther 3:10; 8:2.
Used for sealing decrees.
Esther 3:12; 8:8, 10.
Made of gold and set with precious
stones. Num. 31:50–51;
Song of Sol. 5:14.
Numbers of, taken from Midianites.
Num. 31:50.
Offerings of, to the tabernacle.
Exod. 35:22; Num. 31:50.
Rich men distinguished by.
James 2:2.
Women of rank adorned with.
Isa. 3:16, 21.

Worn
On the arms. 2 Sam. 1:10.
In the ears. Job 42:11;
Ezek. 16:12; Hos. 2:11.
On the hands. Gen. 41:42.
In the nose. Prov. 11:22;
Isa. 3:21.

RISING EARLY
For devotions. Pss. 5:3; 59:16;
61:1; 88:13; Song of Sol. 7:12;
Isa. 26:9.

Examples of
Abimelech. Gen. 20:8.
Abraham. Gen. 19:27; 21:14;
22:3.
Apostles. Acts 5:21.
David. 1 Sam. 17:20.
Elkanah. 1 Sam. 1:19.
Gideon. Judg. 6:38.
Isaac. Gen. 26:31.
Jacob. Gen. 28:18; 32:31.
Joshua. Josh. 3:1; 6:12, 15;
7:16.
Laban. Gen. 31:55.

Lot. Gen. 19:23.
Mary. Mark 16:2.
Moses. Exod. 8:20; 9:13.
Samuel. 1 Sam. 15:12.
Illustrates spiritual diligence.
Rom. 13:11–12.
Practiced by drunkards. Isa. 5:11.
Practiced by the wicked.
Prov. 27:14; Mic. 2:1; Zeph. 3:7.

RISING LATE
Consequences of. Prov. 6:9–11;
24:33–34.

RIVER, EUPHRATES
Assyria bounded by. 2 Kings 23:29;
Isa. 7:20.
Babylon situated on. Jer. 51:13, 36.
A branch of the river of Eden.
Gen. 2:14.

Called
The flood. Josh. 24:2.
The great river. Gen. 15:18;
Deut. 1:7.
The river. Exod. 23:31; Neh. 2:7;
Ps. 72:8.
Captivity of Judah represented by the
marring of Jeremiah's belt in.
Jer. 13:3–9.
Egyptian army destroyed at.
Jer. 46:2, 6, 10.
Extreme eastern boundary of the
promised land. Gen. 15:18;
Deut. 1:7; 11:24.
Frequented by the captive Jews.
Ps. 137:1.
Often overflowed its banks.
Isa. 8:7–8.
Prophecies respecting Babylon
thrown into, as a sign. Jer. 51:63.
Will be the scene of future judgments.
Rev. 16:12.

Waters of, considered wholesome.
Jer. 2:18.

RIVER, JORDAN

Despised by foreigners.
2 Kings 5:12.

Eastern boundary of Canaan.
Num. 34:12.

Empties into the Dead Sea.
Num. 34:12.

Ferry boats often used on.
2 Sam. 19:18.

Fordable in some places. Josh. 2:7;
Judg. 12:5–6.

The Jews had great pride in.
Zech. 11:3.

Moses not allowed to cross.
Deut. 3:27; 31:2.

Often overflowed. Josh. 3:15;
1 Chron. 12:15.

Overflowing of, called the swelling of
Jordan. Jer. 12:5; 49:19.

Passage of Israel over
Accomplished.
Josh. 3:17; 4:1, 10–11.
Alluded to. Pss. 74:15; 114:3, 5.
In an appointed order.
Josh. 3:1–8.
Commemorated by a pillar of
stones in Gilgal.
Josh. 4:2–8, 20–24.
Commemorated by a pillar of
stones raised in it. Josh. 4:9.
A pledge that God would drive the
Canaanites, etc., out of their
land. Josh. 3:10.
Preceded by priests with the ark.
Josh. 3:6, 11, 14.
Promised. Deut. 4:22; 9:1;
11:31.

Plains of
Afforded clay for molding brass,
etc. 1 Kings 7:46;
2 Chron. 4:17.
Chosen by Lot for a residence.
Gen. 13:11.
Exceeding fertile. Gen. 13:10.
Infested with lions. Jer. 49:19;
50:44.
Thickly wooded. 2 Kings 6:2.

Remarkable events connected with
Baptism of multitudes by John the
Baptist. Matt. 3:6; Mark 1:5;
John 1:28.
Christ's baptism. Matt. 3:13, 15;
Mark 1:9.
Division of its waters by Elijah.
2 Kings 2:8.
Division of its waters by Elisha.
2 Kings 2:14.
Division of its waters to let Israel
pass over. Josh. 3:12–16; 5:1.
Healing of Naaman the leper.
2 Kings 5:10, 14.
Return of its waters to their place.
Josh. 4:18.
Slaughter of Moabites.
Judg. 3:28–29.
Slaughter of the Ephraimites.
Judg. 12:4–6.

RIVER, NILE

Abounded in
Crocodiles. Ezek. 29:3.
Fish. Exod. 7:21; Ezek. 29:4.
Reeds and rushes. Isa. 19:6–7.
Annual overflow of its banks alluded
to. Jer. 46:8; Amos 8:8; 9:5.

Called
The Egyptian sea. Isa. 11:15.
The river. Gen. 41:1, 3.

Sihor. Josh 13:3; Jer. 2:18.

The stream of Egypt. Isa. 27:12.

Empties itself into the Mediterranean Sea by seven streams. Isa. 11:15.

The Egyptians

Bathed in. Exod. 2:5.

Carried on extensive commerce by. Isa. 23:3.

Drank of. Exod. 7:21, 24.

Took great pride in. Ezek. 29:9.

Were punished by destruction of its fish. Isa. 19:8.

Were punished by failure of its waters. Isa. 19:5–6.

Remarkable events connected with

Its waters turned into blood. Exod. 7:15, 20.

Male children drowned in. Exod. 1:22.

Miraculous generation of frogs. Exod. 8:3.

Moses set afloat on its banks. Exod. 2:3.

RIVERS

See also: River, Euphrates; River, Jordan; River, Nile

Banks of

Covered with reeds. Exod. 2:3, 5.

Frequented by doves. Song of Sol. 5:12.

Frequented by wild beasts. Jer. 49:19.

Frequently overflowed. Josh. 3:15; 1 Chron. 12:15.

Peculiarly fruitful. Ps. 1:3; Isa. 32:20.

Places of common resort. Ps. 137:1.

Planted with trees. Ezek. 47:7.

Baptism often performed in. Matt. 3:6.

Of Canaan, abounded with fish. Lev. 11:9–10.

Cities often built beside. Pss. 46:6; 137:1.

Enclosed within banks. Dan. 12:5.

Flow through valleys. Ps. 104:8, 10.

Gardens often made beside. Num. 24:6.

God's power over, unlimited. Isa. 50:2; Nah. 1:4.

Illustrative of

Abundance. Job 20:17; 29:6.

The abundance of grace in Christ. Isa. 32:2, with John 1:16.

The gifts and graces of the Holy Spirit. Ps. 46:4; Isa. 41:18; 43:19–20; John 7:38–39.

God's judgments (when drying up). Isa. 19:1–8; Jer. 51:36; Nah. 1:4; Zech. 10:11.

God's judgments (when overflowing). Isa. 8:7–8; 28:3, 18; Jer. 47:2.

Heavy afflictions. Ps. 69:2; Isa. 43:2.

Peace of believers (in their steady course). Isa. 66:12.

People flying from judgments. Isa. 23:10.

The permanent prosperity of believers (fruitfulness of trees planted by). Ps. 1:3; Jer. 17:8.

Many, fordable in some places. Gen. 32:22; Josh. 2:7; Isa. 16:2.

Mentioned in Scripture

Abana. 2 Kings 5:12.

Of Ahava. Ezra 8:15.

Arnon. Deut. 2:36; Josh. 12:1.

Of Babylon. Ps. 137:1.

Chebar. Ezek. 1:1, 3; 10:15, 20.

Of Damascus. 2 Kings 5:12.
Of Eden. Gen. 2:10.
Of Egypt. Gen. 15:18.
Of Ethiopia. Isa. 18:1.
Euphrates. Gen. 2:14.
Gihon. Gen. 2:13.
Gozan. 2 Kings 17:6;
1 Chron. 5:26.
Hiddekel. Gen. 2:14.
Jabbok. Deut. 2:37; Josh. 12:2.
Jordan. Josh 3:8; 2 Kings 5:10.
Of Jotbath. Deut. 10:7.
Of Judah. Joel 3:18.
Kanah. Josh 16:8.
Kishon. Judg. 5:21.
Pharpar. 2 Kings 5:12.
Of Philippi. Acts 16:13.
Pison. Gen. 2:11.
Ulai. Dan. 8:16.
Often the boundaries of kingdoms,
etc. Josh 22:25; 1 Kings 4:24.
Run into the sea. Eccles. 1:7;
Ezek. 47:8.

Some are
Broad. Isa. 33:21.
Deep. Ezek. 47:5; Zech. 10:11.
Great and mighty. Gen. 15:18;
Ps. 74:15.
Parted into many streams.
Gen. 2:10; Ps. 11:15.
Rapid. Judg. 5:21.
Source of. Job 28:10;
Ps. 104:8, 10.

Useful for
Bathing. Exod. 2:5.
Commerce. Isa. 23:3.
Promoting vegetation. Gen. 2:10.
Supplying drink to the people.
Jer. 2:18.

ROADS
From Bethel to Shechem.
Judg. 21:19.
Built by rulers. Num. 20:17; 21:22.
To cities of refuge. Deut. 19:3.
From Gibeon to Beth-horon.
Josh 10:10.
To the house of God. Judg. 20:31.
From Judea to Galilee by way of
Samaria. John 4:3–5, 43.
Public highways. Deut. 2:27.

ROBBERS
Activities described. Prov. 1:11–16.
Bands of. Hos. 6:9; 7:1.
Dens of. Jer. 7:11.

ROBBERY
Examples of. Judg. 9:25;
Luke 10:30.
Forbidden. Lev. 19:13; Isa. 61:8.
Forgiven. Ezek. 33:15.
Punished with death.
Ezek. 18:10–13.

ROBE
Of righteousness. 2 Chron. 6:41;
Isa. 61:10; Rev. 6:11; 7:9, 13.
Parable of the man who was not
dressed in a wedding garment.
Matt. 22:11.

ROCKS
Bees often made their honey among.
Deut. 32:13; Ps. 1:16.
Casting down from, a punishment.
2 Chron. 25:12.
A defense to a country. Isa. 33:16.

Described as
Barren. Ezek. 26:4, 14;
Amos 6:12; Luke 8:6.
Durable. Job 19:24.
Hard. Jer. 5:3.

Via Dolorosa

Dreaded by mariners. Acts 27:29.

God's power exhibited in removing, etc. Job 14:18; Nah. 1:6.

Hammers used for breaking. Jer. 23:29.

Houses often built on. Matt. 7:24–25.

Illustrative of
  The ancestor of a nation. Isa. 51:1.

Christ as a stumbling stone to the wicked. Isa. 8:14; Rom. 9:33; 1 Pet. 2:8.

Christ as foundation of His church. Matt. 16:18, with 1 Pet. 2:6.

Christ as refuge for His people. Isa. 32:2.

Christ as source of spiritual gifts. 1 Cor. 10:4.

God as creator of His people. Deut. 32:18.

God as defense of His people.
Ps. 31:2–3.
God as refuge for His people.
Ps. 94:22.
God as salvation of His people.
Deut. 32:15; Pss. 89:26; 95:1.
God as the strength of His people.
Pss. 18:1–2; 62:7; Isa. 17:10.
A place of safety. Pss. 27:5; 40:2.
Whatever we trust in.
Deut. 32:31, 37.
Important events often engraved
upon. Job 19:24.

Inhabited by
Badgers. Ps. 104:18.
Doves. Song of Sol. 2:14;
Jer. 48:28.
Eagles. Job 39:28; Jer. 49:16.
Wild goats. Job 39:1.
Man's industry in cutting through.
Job 28:9–10.

Mentioned in Scripture
Adullam. 1 Chron. 11:15.
Bozez. 1 Sam. 14:4.
En-gedi. 1 Sam. 24:1–2.
Etam. Judg. 15:8.
Horeb in Rephidim. Exod. 17:1.
Meribah in Kadesh. Num. 20:11.
Oreb. Judg. 7:25; Isa. 10:26.
Rimmon. Judg. 20:45.
Sela-hammahlekoth in the
wilderness of Maon.
1 Sam. 23:25, 28.
Selah in the Valley of Salt.
2 Kings 14:7;
2 Chron. 25:11–12.
Seneh. 1 Sam. 14:4.

Miracles connected with
Broken in pieces by the wind.
1 Kings 19:11.

Broken at the death of Christ.
Matt. 27:51.
Fire ascended out of. Judg. 6:21.
Water brought from. Exod. 17:6;
Num. 20:11.
Often composed of flint. Deut. 8:15;
32:13.
Often had large cracks and clefts.
Exod. 33:22.
Often sharp pointed and craggy.
1 Sam. 14:4.
The olive tree flourished among.
Deut. 32:13; Job 29:6.
Shadow of, welcome to travelers
during the heat of the day.
Isa. 32:2.
Tombs often carved from.
Isa. 22:16; Matt. 27:60.

Used as
Altars. Judg. 6:20–21, 26; 13:19.
Places for idolatrous worship.
Isa. 57:5.
Places for shelter by the poor in
their distress. Job 24:8; 30:3, 6.
Places of observation.
Exod. 33:21; Num. 23:9.
Places of safety in danger.
1 Sam. 13:6; Isa. 2:19;
Jer. 16:16; Rev. 6:15.

ROMAN EMPIRE
Called the world (from its extent).
Luke 2:1.

Citizenship of
Exempted from the degradation of
beating. Acts 16:37–38; 22:25.
Obtained by birth. Acts 22:28.
Obtained by purchase.
Acts 22:28.

Emperors of, mentioned
Augustus. Luke 2:1.

Claudius. Acts 11:28.
Nero. Phil. 4:22; 2 Tim. 4:17.
Tiberius. Luke 3:1.

Grecian games adopted by
Crowning of conquerors.
1 Cor. 9:25; Phil. 3:14;
2 Tim. 4:8.
Foot races. 1 Cor. 9:24;
Phil. 2:16; 3:11–14;
Heb. 12:1–2.
Gladiatorial fights. 1 Cor. 4:9;
15:32.
Rules observed in conducting.
2 Tim. 2:5.
Training of combatants.
1 Cor. 9:25, 27.
Wrestling. Eph. 6:12.
Judea a province of, under a
procurator or a governor.
Luke 3:2; Acts 23:24, 26; 25:1.

Judicial affairs of
Accusation in writing placed over
the head of those executed.
John 19:19.

Accused persons protected from
popular violence.
Acts 23:20, 24–27.
Accusers and accused confronted
together. Acts 23:35;
25:16–19.
All appeals made to the emperor.
Acts 25:11–12.
Criminals delivered over to the
soldiers for execution.
Matt. 27:26–27.
Garments of those executed given
to the soldiers. Matt. 27:35;
John 19:23.
Persons accused, examined by
beating. Acts 22:24, 29.
Power of life and death given its
authorities.
John 18:31, 39–40; 19:10.
Prisoners chained to soldiers for
safety. Acts 21:33, with 12:6;
2 Tim. 1:16, with Acts 28:16.
Those who appealed to Caesar, to
be brought before him.
Acts 26:32.

Rome, the Forum

Military affairs of

Crowning of soldiers who distinguished themselves. 2 Tim. 4:7–8.

Danger of sentinels' sleeping. Matt. 28:13–14.

Different military officers, etc. Acts 21:31; 23:23–24.

Hardship endured by soldiers. 2 Tim. 2:3.

Italian and imperial regiments. Acts 10:1; 27:1.

Removing from the roster names of soldiers guilty of crimes. Rev. 3:5.

Soldiers not allowed to entangle themselves with earthly cares. 2 Tim. 2:4.

The soldier's special comrade who shared his toils and dangers. Phil. 2:25.

Strict obedience to superiors. Matt. 8:8–9.

Triumph of victorious generals. 2 Cor. 2:14–16; Col. 2:15.

Use of spiritual or defensive armor. Rom. 13:12; 2 Cor. 6:7; Eph. 6:11–17.

Predictions respecting

Its division into ten parts. Dan. 2:41–43; 7:20, 24.

Its universal dominion. Dan. 7:23.

Origin of papal power in. Dan. 7:8, 20–25.

Represented by

Legs of iron in Nebuchadnezzar's vision. Dan. 2:33, 40.

Terrible beast in Daniel's vision. Dan. 7:7, 19.

Rome the capital of. Acts 18:2; 19:21.

ROPE

Figurative sense

Of affliction. Job 36:8.

Of love. Hos. 11:4.

Of temptations. Ps. 140:5; Prov. 5:22.

Threefold. Eccles. 4:12.

Used in casting lots. Mic. 2:5.

Worn on the head as an emblem of servitude. 1 Kings 20:30, 32.

ROSE

Of Sharon. Song of Sol. 2:1.

RULERS

Examples of patriarchal

Abraham. Gen. 14:13–24; 17:6; 21:21–32.

Esau and the dukes of Edom. Gen. 36.

Heads of families. Exod. 6:14.

Isaac. Gen. 26:26–31.

Ishmael. Gen. 17:20.

Judah. Gen. 38:24.

Melchizedek. Gen. 14:18.

Nimrod. Gen. 10:8–10.

Character and qualifications of

A person who is mature. Eccles. 10:16–17.

A person who punishes the wicked. Prov. 20:8; 26–28.

A person who tells the truth. Prov. 17:7.

Persons not given to wine and strong drink. Prov. 31:4–5.

Persons of ability. Exod. 18:21.

Persons who are fair. Deut. 16:18–20.

Persons who fear the Lord. Ps. 2:10.

Persons who know the laws of God. Ezra 7:25.

Persons who will not take a bride. Exod. 23:8.

Wisdom and discretion. Gen. 41:33.

Examples of righteous rulers
Abimelech. Gen. 20.
Artaxerxes. Ezra 7; Neh. 2; 5:14.
Asa. 1 Kings 15:11–15;
2 Chron. 14:2–5.
Cyrus. Ezra 1.
Daniel. Dan. 1–6.
Darius. Ezra 6:1–12.
Hezekiah. 2 Kings 18:3;
20:1–11; 2 Chron. 30; 31.
Isaac. Gen. 26:6–11.
Jehoshaphat. 1 Kings 22:41–46;
2 Chron. 17:3–10; 19;
20:3–30.
Joseph. Gen. 41:37–57.
Josiah. 2 Kings 22; 23;
2 Chron. 34; 35.
King of Nineveh. Jon. 3:6–9.
Moses. Num. 16:15.
Nehemiah. Neh. 4–5.
Pharaoh.
Gen. 12:15–20; 47:5–10;
50:1–6.
Samuel. 1 Sam. 12:3–4.
Saul. 1 Sam. 11:12–13.
Solomon. 1 Kings 3:16–28.

Example of wicked rulers
Abijam. 1 Kings 15:3.
Abimelech. Judg. 9:1–5.
Adoni-bezek. Judg. 1:7.
Ahab.
1 Kings 16:30–33; 21:21–26;
22:38; 2 Kings 9:26.
Ahasuerus. Esther 3.
Ahaz. 2 Kings 16:3.
Ahaziah. 2 Chron. 22:1–9.

Amaziah. 2 Chron. 25:14.
Amon. 2 Kings 21:19–22.
Ananias. Acts 23:2.
Asa. 2 Chron. 16:10.
Baasha. 1 Kings 15:33–34.
Belshazzar. Dan. 5:22–23.
Chief priest, elders, and all the
council. Matt. 26:59.
Darius. Dan. 6:7, 9.
David. 2 Sam. 24:1–9;
1 Chron. 21:1–7; 27:23–24.
Eli's sons. 1 Sam. 2:12–17; 2:22.
Hanun. 2 Sam. 10:4;
1 Chron. 19:2–5.
Hazael. 2 Kings 8:12.
Herod Agrippa. Acts 12:1–19.
Herod Antipas. Matt. 14:1–11.
Herod the Great. Matt. 2:16–18.
Hoshea. 2 Kings 15:30.
Jehoahaz. 2 Kings 13:1–2.
Jehoash. 2 Kings 13:10.
Jehoiachin. 2 Kings 24:9.
Jehoiakim. 2 Kings 23:37.
Jehoram. 2 Kings 3:2–3; 8:18.
Jehu. 2 Kings 10:29.
Jeroboam.
1 Kings 12:26–33; 13:1–5;
13:33; 14:6; 2 Kings 14:23,
24; 2 Chron. 11:14–15;
Ezek. 44:7.
Joash. 2 Chron. 24:2, 17–25.
Manasseh. 2 Kings 21:1–17.
Nadab. 1 Kings 15:26.
Nebuchadnezzar. Dan. 2:13;
3:1–23.
Omri. 1 Kings 16:25–29.
Pharaoh. Exod. 1–11.
Pilate. Matt. 27:11–26.
Potiphar. Gen. 39:20.
Rehoboam. 1 Kings 12:8–11;
2 Chron. 10:1–15.
Samuel's sons. 1 Sam. 8:1–5.

Saul. 1 Sam. 15:8–35; 18:8, 29; 19; 22:7–19.

Solomon. 1 Kings 4:7–23; 11:1–13; 12:4.

Uzziah. 2 Chron. 26:16.

Zedekiah. 2 Kings 24:19.

Zimri. 1 Kings 16:19.

Punished. Dan. 4.

SABACHTHANI
Word Jesus quoted from the cross.
Ps. 22:1.

SABBATH, THE

Believers
Honor God in observing.
Isa. 58:13.
Observe. Neh. 13:22.
Rejoice in. Ps. 118:24; Isa. 58:13.
Testify against those who
desecrate. Neh. 13:15, 20–21.
Blessedness of honoring.
Isa. 58:13–14.
Blessedness of keeping. Isa. 56:2, 6.

Called
God's holy day. Isa. 58:13.
The Lord's day. Rev. 1:10.
The rest of the holy Sabbath.
Exod. 16:23.
The Sabbath of rest. Exod. 31:15.
The Sabbath of the Lord.
Exod. 20:10; Lev. 23:3;
Deut. 5:14.

Christ
Is Lord of. Mark 2:27.
Taught on. Luke 4:31; 6:6.
Was accustomed to observe.
Luke 4:16.
Denunciations against those who
profane. Exod. 31:14–15;
Num. 15:32–36.
Divine worship to be celebrated on.
Ezek. 46:3; Acts 16:13.
First day of the week kept as, by
primitive church. John 20:26;
Acts 20:7; 1 Cor. 16:2.

God
Blessed. Gen. 2:3; Exod. 20:11.
Commanded to be kept.
Lev. 19:3, 30.
Commanded to be sanctified.
Exod. 20:8.
Hallowed. Exod. 20:11.
Sanctified. Gen. 2:3; Exod. 31:15.
Shows considerate kindness in
appointing. Exod. 23:12.
Shows favor in appointing.
Neh. 9:14.
Will have His goodness
commemorated in the
observance of. Deut. 5:15.
Grounds of its institution.
Gen. 2:2–3; Exod. 20:11.
Instituted by God. Gen. 2:3.
Made for man. Mark 2:27.
Necessary needs may be supplied on.
Matt. 12:1; Luke 13:15; 14:1.
No burdens to be carried on.
Neh. 13:19; Jer. 17:21.
No manner of work to be done on.
Exod. 20:10; Lev. 23:3.
No purchases to be made on.
Neh. 10:31; 13:15–17.
Observance of, to be perpetual.
Exod. 31:16–17, with
Matt. 5:17–18.
Punishment of those who profane.
Exod. 31:14–15;
Num. 15:32–36.
The Scriptures to be read on.
Acts 13:27; 15:21.
Servants and cattle should be allowed
to rest on. Exod. 20:10;
Deut. 5:14.

Seventh day observed as.
Exod. 20:9, 11.
A sign of the covenant. Exod. 31:13,
17.
A type of the heavenly rest.
Heb. 4:4, 9.

The wicked
Bear burdens on. Neh. 13:15.
Buy and sell on. Neh. 10:31;
13:15–16.
Do their own pleasure on.
Isa. 58:13.
Hide their eyes from. Ezek. 22:26.
Laugh at. Lam. 1:7.
May be judicially deprived of.
Lam. 2:6; Hos. 2:11.
Pollute. Isa. 56:2;
Ezek. 20:13, 16.
Profane. Neh. 13:17; Ezek. 22:8.
Sometimes pretend to be zealous
for. Luke 13:14; John 9:16.
Wearied by. Amos 8:5.
Work on. Neh. 13:15.
The Word of God to be preached on.
Acts 13:14–15, 44; 17:2; 18:4.
Works connected with religious
service lawful on. Num. 28:9;
Matt. 12:5; John 7:23.
Works of mercy lawful on.
Matt. 12:12; Luke 13:16;
John 9:14.

SABBATICAL YEAR, FEAST OF

Enactments respecting
Cessation of all field labor.
Lev. 25:4–5.
The fruits of the earth to be
common property. Exod. 23:11;
Lev. 25:6–7.
No release to strangers during.
Deut. 15:3.

Public reading of the law at Feast
of Tabernacles. Deut.
31:10–13.
Release of all Hebrew servants.
Exod. 21:2; Deut. 15:12.
Remission of debts. Deut. 15:1–3;
Neh. 10:31.
Jews threatened for neglecting.
Lev. 26:34–35, 43;
Jer. 34:13–18.
Kept every seventh year.
Exod. 23:11; Lev. 25:4.
Release of, not to hinder the exercise
of benevolence. Deut. 15:9–11.
Restored after the captivity.
Neh. 10:31.
A sabbath for the land. Lev. 25:2.
The seventy years' captivity a
punishment for neglecting.
2 Chron. 36:20–21.
Surplus of sixth year to provide for.
Lev. 25:20–22.

SACKBUT
Musical instrument. Dan. 3:5.

SACKCLOTH
Of a black color. Rev. 6:12.

Illustrative of
Heavy afflictions. Isa. 3:24;
22:12; 32:11.
Joy and gladness (when taking off).
Ps. 30:11.
Severe judgments (when covering
the heavens with). Isa. 50:3.
Severe judgments (when heavens
became black as). Rev. 6:12.
The Jews lay in, when in deep
affliction. 2 Sam. 21:10;
1 Kings 21:27; Joel 1:13.
Made of coarse hair. Matt. 3:4, with
Rev. 6:12.

No one clothed in, allowed into the palaces of kings. Esther 4:2.

Rough and unsightly. Zech. 13:4.

Worn

With ashes on the head. Esther 4:1.

Frequently next to the skin in deep affliction. 1 Kings 21:27; 2 Kings 6:30; Job 16:15.

At funerals. 2 Sam. 3:31.

By God's prophets. 2 Kings 1:8; Isa. 20:2; Matt. 3:4; Rev. 11:3.

Often over the whole person. 2 Kings 19:1–2.

Often with ropes on the head. 1 Kings 20:31.

By persons in affliction. Neh. 9:1; Ps. 69:11; Jon. 3:5.

In the streets. Isa. 15:3.

Around the waist. Gen. 37:34; 1 Kings 20:31.

SACRIFICES

Always offered upon altars. Exod. 20:24.

Consisted of

Clean animals or bloody sacrifices. Gen. 8:20.

Fruits of the earth or unbloody sacrifices. Gen. 4:4; Lev. 2:1.

Could not take away sin. Ps. 40:6; Heb. 9:9; 10:1–11.

Covenants of God confirmed by. Gen. 15:9–17; Exod. 24:5–8, with Heb. 9:19–20; Ps. 50:5.

Different kinds of

Burnt offering totally consumed by fire. Lev. 1; 1 Kings 18:38.

Peace offering. Lev. 3.

Sin offering for sins of ignorance. Lev. 4.

Trespass offering for intentional sins. Lev. 6:1–7; 7:1–7.

Divine institution of. Gen. 3:21, with 1:29 and 9:3; 4:4–5, with Heb. 11:4.

Fat of, not to remain until morning. Exod. 23:8.

Generally the best of their kind. Gen. 4:4; 1 Sam. 15:22; Ps. 66:15; Isa. 1:11.

On great occasions, very numerous. 2 Chron. 5:6; 7:5.

Illustrative of

Benevolence. Phil. 4:18; Heb. 13:16.

A broken spirit. Ps. 51:17.

Devotedness. Rom. 12:1; Phil. 2:17.

Martyrdom. Phil. 2:7; 2 Tim. 4:6.

Prayer. Ps. 141:2.

Righteousness. Pss. 4:5; 51:19.

Thanksgiving. Pss. 27.6; 107:22; 116:17; Heb. 13:15.

Imparted a legal purification. Heb. 9:13, 22.

The Jews

Condemned for bringing defective and blemished. Mal. 1:13–14.

Condemned for not offering. Isa. 43:23–24.

Condemned for not treating with respect. 1 Sam. 2:29; Mal. 1:12.

Condemned for offering, to idols. 2 Chron. 34:25; Isa. 65:3, 7; Ezek. 20:28, 31.

Unaccepted in, on account of sin. Isa. 1:11, 15; 66:3; Hos. 8:13.

No leaven offered with, except for thanksgiving. Exod. 23:18, with Lev. 7:13.

Without obedience, worthless.
1 Sam. 15:22; Prov. 21:3;
Mark 12:33.

Offered
At all the feasts. Num. 10:10.
Daily. Exod. 29:38–39;
Num. 28:3–4.
After the departure of Israel from
Egypt. Exod. 5:3, 17; 18:12;
24:5.
From the earliest age. Gen. 4:3–4.
In faith of a coming Savior.
Heb. 11:4, 17, 28.
For individuals. Lev. 1:2; 17:8.
Monthly. Num. 28:11.
Under the Mosaic covenant.
Lev. 1–7; Heb. 10:1–3.
By the patriarchs.
Gen. 22:2, 13; 31:54; 46:1;
Job 1:5.
Weekly. Num. 28:9–10.
For the whole nation.
Lev. 16:15–30;
1 Chron. 29:21.
Yearly. Lev. 16:3;
1 Sam. 1:3, 21; 20:6.
Offered to false gods, are offered to
devils. Lev. 17:7; Deut. 32:17;
Ps. 106:37; 1 Cor. 10:20.
Offering of, an acknowledgment of
sin. Heb. 10:3.
Often consumed by fire from heaven.
Lev. 9:24; 1 Kings 18:38;
2 Chron. 7:1.

.Priests
Appointed to offer. 1 Sam. 2:28;
Ezek. 44:11, 15; Heb. 5:1; 8:3.
Had a portion of and lived by.
Exod. 29:27–28; Deut. 18:3;
Josh. 13:11; 1 Cor. 9:13.
For public use, often provided by the
state. 2 Chron. 31:3.

Required to be perfect and without
blemish. Lev. 22:19; Deut. 15:21;
17:1; Mal. 1:8, 14.
To be brought to the place appointed
by God. Deut. 12:6;
2 Chron. 7:12.
To be offered to God alone. Exod.
22:20; Judg. 13:16;
2 Kings 17:36.
Were accepted when offered in
sincerity and faith. Gen. 4:4, with
Heb. 11:4; Gen. 8:21.
Were bound to the horns of the altar.
Ps. 118:27.
Were seasoned with salt. Lev. 2:13;
Mark 9:49.
Were typical of Christ's sacrifice.
1 Cor. 5:7; Eph. 5:2; Heb. 10:1,
11–12.
When bloody, accompanied with
meat and drink offering.
Num. 15:3–12.
When offered to God, an
acknowledgment of His being the
supreme God. 2 Kings 5:17;
Jon. 1:16.

SACRIFICES, DAILY
Abolition of, predicted.
Dan. 9:26–27; 11:31.
Doubled on the Sabbath.
Num. 28:9–10.

Illustrative of
Acceptable prayer. Ps. 141:2.
Christ. John 1:29, 36;
1 Pet. 1:19.
A lamb as a burnt offering morning
and evening. Exod. 29:38–39;
Num. 28:3–4.
Ordained in Mount Sinai.
Num. 28:6.
Peculiarly acceptable. Num. 28:8;
Ps. 141:2.

Required to be
  With a meat and drink offering.
    Exod. 29:40–41; Num. 28:5–8.
  Perpetually observed.
    Exod. 29:42; Num. 28:3, 6.
  Slowly and entirely consumed.
    Lev. 6:9–12.
Restored after the captivity. Ezra 3:3.
Secured God's presence and favor.
    Exod. 29:43–44.
Times of offering were seasons of
    prayer. Ezra 9:5; Dan. 9:20–21,
    with Acts 3:1.

SACRILEGE

Examples of
  Ahaz. 2 Chron. 28:24.
  Esau sells his birthright.
    Gen. 25:33.
  Korah. Num. 16:40.
  Money changers in the temple.
    Matt. 21:12–13.
  Nadab and Abihu offer strange
    fire. Lev. 10:1–7; Num. 3:4.
  The people of Beth-Shemesh.
    1 Sam. 6:19.
  Those who profaned the Lord's
    Supper. 1 Cor. 11:29.
  Uzza. 2 Sam. 6:6–7.
  Uzziah. 2 Chron. 26:16–21.
Profaning holy things, forbidden.
    Lev. 19:8; 1 Cor. 3:17;
    Titus 1:11; 1 Pet. 5:2.

SADDUCEES

Christ
  Cautioned His disciples against
    their principles.
    Matt. 16:6, 11–12.
  Silenced. Matt. 22:34.
  Tempted by. Matt. 16:1.

Vindicated the resurrection
    against. Matt. 22:24–32;
    Mark 12:19–27.
Denied the resurrection and a future
    state. Matt. 22:23; Luke 20:27.
Persecuted the early Christians.
    Acts 4:1; 5:17–18, 40.
Refused baptism by John. Matt. 3:7.
The resurrection a cause of dispute
    between them and the Pharisees.
    Acts 23:6–9.
A sect of the Jews. Acts 5:17.

SAINTS (THOSE WHO BELONG TO GOD)
See Believers

SALT
Characterized as good and useful.
    Mark 9:50.

Illustrative of
  Believers. Matt. 5:13.
  Desolation (pits of). Zeph. 2:9.
  Grace in the heart. Mark 9:50.
  Graceless religious persons
    (without taste). Matt. 5:13;
    Mark 9:50.
  Preparation of the wicked for
    destruction (salted with fire).
    Mark 9:49.
  Wisdom in speech. Col. 4:6.
Generously given to the Jews after
    the captivity. Ezra 6:9; 7:22.
Lost its taste when exposed to the air.
    Matt. 5:13; Mark 9:50.

Miracles connected with
  Elisha healed the bad water with.
    1 Kings 2:21.
  Lot's wife turned into a pillar of.
    Gen. 19:26.

Often found
 Near the Dead Sea. Num. 34:12;
  Deut. 3:17.
 In pits. Zeph. 2:9.
 In springs. James 3:12.
Partaking of another's, a bond of
 friendship. Ezra 4:14.
Scattered over, to denote destroyed
 cities. Judg. 9:45.
Places where it abounded barren and
 unfruitful. Jer. 17:6; Ezek. 47:11.

Used for
 Ratifying covenants. Num. 18:19;
  2 Chron. 13:5.
 Seasoning food. Job 6:6.
 Seasoning sacrifices. Lev. 2:13;
  Ezek. 43:24.
 Strengthening newborn infants.
  Ezek. 16:4.
Valley of, celebrated for victories.
 2 Sam. 8:13; 2 Kings 14:7;
 1 Chron. 18:12.

SALUTATIONS
Antiquity of. Gen. 18:2; 19:1.
Denied to persons of bad character.
 2 John 1:10.

Expressions used as
 "The blessing of the Lord be upon
  you, we bless you in the name of
  the Lord." Ps. 129:8.
 "God be gracious to you."
  Gen. 43:29.
 "Good health to you and your
  household! And good health to
  all that is yours!" 1 Sam. 25:6.
 "Greetings." Matt. 26:49; 28:9;
  Luke 1:28.
 "How are you?" 2 Sam. 20:9.
 "The Lord be with you." Ruth 2:4.
 "The Lord bless you."
  1 Sam. 15:13; Ruth 2:4.

"Peace be with you." Judg. 19:20.
"Peace be to this house."
 Luke 10:5.

Given
 By all passersby. 1 Sam. 10:3–4;
  Ps. 129:8.
 By brothers to each other.
  1 Sam. 17:22.
 On entering a house. Judg. 18:15;
  Matt. 10:12;
  Luke 1:40–41, 44.
 By inferiors to their superiors.
  Gen. 47:7.
 By superiors to inferiors.
  1 Sam. 30:21.
Given to Christ in ridicule.
 Matt. 27:39, with Mark 15:18.
Jews condemned for giving only to
 their own countrymen. Matt. 5:47.

Often accompanied by
 Bowing frequently to the ground.
  Gen. 33:3.
 Embracing and kissing the feet.
  Matt. 28:9; Luke 7:38, 45.
 Falling on the neck and kissing.
  Gen. 33:4; 45:14–15;
  Luke 15:20.
 Falling on the ground. Esther 8:3;
  Matt. 2:11; Luke 8:41.
 Grabbing the beard with the right
  hand. 2 Sam. 20:9.
 Kissing the dust. Ps. 72:9;
  Isa. 49:23.
Often insincere. 2 Sam. 20:9;
 Matt. 26:49.
Often sent by letter. Rom.
 16:21–23; 1 Cor. 16:21;
 Col. 4:18; 2 Thess. 3:17.
Often sent through messengers.
 1 Sam. 25:5, 14; 2 Sam. 8:10.

Persons in a hurry excused from giving or receiving. 2 Kings 4:29; Luke 10:24.

Pharisees condemned for seeking in public. Matt. 23:7; Mark 12:38.

SALVATION

All the earth will see. Isa. 52:10; Luke 3:6.

Announced after the fall. Gen. 3:15.

Believers

Appointed to obtain. 1 Thess. 5:9.

Are heirs of. Heb. 1:14.

Ascribe, to God. Ps. 25:5; Isa. 12:2.

Beautified with. Ps. 149:4.

Chosen to. 2 Thess. 2:13; 2 Tim. 1:9.

Clothed with. Isa. 61:10.

Commemorate, with thanks. Ps. 116:13.

Daily approach nearer to. Rom. 13:11.

Declare. Pss. 40:10; 71:15.

Earnestly look for. Ps. 119:123.

Evidence, by works. Heb. 6:9–10.

Glory in. 1 Cor. 1:31; Gal. 6:14.

Have a sign of, in their patient suffering for Christ. Phil. 1:28–29.

Have, through grace. Acts 15:11.

Hope for. Lam. 3:26; Rom. 8:24.

Kept by the power of God to. 1 Pet. 1:5.

Long for. Ps. 119.81, 174.

Love. Ps. 40:16.

Praise God for. 1 Chron. 16:23; Ps. 96:2.

Pray for assurance of. Ps. 35:3.

Pray for a joyful sense of. Ps. 51:12.

Pray to be visited with. Pss. 85:7; 106:4; 119:41.

Rejoice in. Pss. 9:14; 21:1; Isa. 25:9.

Receive, as the end of their faith. 1 Pet. 1:9.

Satisfied by. Luke 2:30.

Wait for. Gen. 49:18; Lam. 3:26.

Welcome the tidings of. Isa. 52:7, with Rom. 10:15.

Came to the Gentiles through the fall of the Jews. Rom. 11:11.

Christ

Appointed for. Isa. 49:6.

The Author of. Heb. 5:9.

Brings, with Him. Isa. 62:11; Luke 19:9.

Came to effect. Matt. 18:11; 1 Tim. 1:15.

The Captain of. Heb. 2:10.

Died to effect. John 3:14–15; Gal. 1:4.

Exalted to give. Acts 5:31.

Has. Zech. 9:9.

Powerful effect. Isa. 63:1; Heb. 7:25.

Raised up for. Luke 1:69.

Confession of Christ necessary to. Rom. 10:10.

Deliverance from

The devil. Col. 2:15; Heb. 2:14–15.

Enemies. Luke 1:71, 74.

Eternal death. John 3:16–17.

Sin. Matt. 1:21, with 1 John 3:5.

This present evil world. Gal. 1:4.

Uncleanness. Ezek. 36:29.

Wrath. Rom. 5:9; 1 Thess. 1:10.

Described as

Common. Jude 1:3.

Complete. Heb. 7:25.

Eternal. Isa. 45:17; 51:6; Heb. 5:9.

From generation to generation.
Isa. 51:8.
Glorious. 2 Tim. 2:10.
Great. Heb. 2:3.
Final perseverance necessary to.
Matt. 10:22.
God is willing to give. Tim. 2:4.
Godly sorrow produces repentance
to. 2 Cor. 7:10.
The gospel is the power of God to.
Rom. 1:16; Col. 1:18.
The heavenly host ascribe to God.
Rev. 7:10; 19:1.

Illustrated by
Chariots. Hab. 3:8.
Clothing. 2 Chron. 6:41;
Pss. 132:16; 149:4; Isa. 61:10.
A cup. Ps. 116:13.
A helmet. Isa. 59:17.
A horn. Ps. 18:2; Luke 1:69.
A lamp. Isa. 62:1.
A rock. Deut. 32:15;
2 Sam. 22:47; Ps. 95:1.
A shield. 2 Sam. 22:36.
A tower. 2 Sam. 22:51.
A victory. 1 Cor. 15:57.
Walls and defenses. Isa. 26:1;
60:18.
Wells. Isa. 12:3.

Is
Of the appointment of God.
1 Thess. 5:9.
By Christ. Isa. 63:9; Eph. 5:23.
By Christ alone. Isa. 45:21–22;
59:16; Acts 4:12.
Through faith in Christ. Mark
16:16; Acts 16:31; Rom. 10:9;
Eph. 2:8; 1 Pet. 1:5.
Far from the wicked. Ps. 119:155;
Isa. 59:11.
Of God. Pss. 3:8; 37:39; Jer.
3:23.

Of grace. Eph. 2:5, 8; 2 Tim. 1:9;
Titus 2:11.
Of the long-suffering of God.
2 Pet. 3:15.
Of love. Rom. 5:8;
1 John 4:9–10.
Of mercy. Ps. 6:4; Titus 3:5.
Not by works. Rom. 11:6;
Eph. 2:9; 2 Tim. 1:9; Titus 3:5.
Of the purpose of God.
2 Tim. 1:9.

Ministers
Are aroma of Christ among those
being saved. 2 Cor. 2:15.
Give the knowledge of. Luke 1:77.
Should be clothed with.
2 Chron. 6:41; Ps. 132:16.
Should endure suffering that the
elect may obtain. 2 Tim. 2:10.
Should exhort to. Ezek. 3:18–19;
Acts 2:40.
Should labor to lead others to.
Rom. 11:14.
Should use self-denial to lead
others to. 1 Cor. 9:22.
Show the way of. Acts 16:17.
No escape for those who neglect.
Heb. 2:3.
Now is the day of. Isa. 49:8;
2 Cor. 6:2.
Of the Gentiles, predicted.
Isa. 45:22; 49:6; 52:10.
Of Israel, predicted. Isa. 35:4;
45:17; Zech. 9:16; Rom. 11:26.
Preaching the Word is the appointed
means of. 1 Cor. 1:21.
Reconciliation to God, a pledge of.
Rom. 5:10.
Regeneration necessary to.
John 3:3.
Revealed in the gospel. Eph. 1:13;
2 Tim. 1:10.

The Scriptures are able to make wise to. 2 Tim. 3:15; James 1:21.
Searched into and exhibited by the prophets. 1 Pet. 1:10.
From sin, to be worked out with fear and trembling. Phil. 2:12.

Sought in vain from
Earthly power. Jer. 3:23.
Idols. Isa. 45:20; Jer. 2:28.
Types. Num. 21:4–9, with John 3:14–15.

SAMARIA, ANCIENT
Had many cities. 1 Kings 13:32.
Inhabitants of, carried captive to Assyria. 2 Kings 17:6, 23; 18:11.
A mountainous country. Jer. 31:5; Amos 3:9.

People of, characterized as
Corrupt and wicked.
Ezek. 16:46–47; Hos. 7:1; Amos 3:9–10.
Idolatrous. Ezek. 23:5; Amos 8:14; Mic. 1:7.
Proud and arrogant. Isa. 9:9.
Predictions about its destruction.
Isa. 8:4; 9:11–12; Hos. 13:16; Amos 3:11–12; Mic. 1:6.
Repopulated from Assyria.
2 Kings 17:24–25.

Samaria the capital of
Besieged and taken by Shalmaneser. 2 Kings 17:5–6; 18:9–10.
Besieged by Ben-Hadad. 1 Kings 20:1–12.
Besieged second time by Ben-Hadad. 2 Kings 6:24.
Built by Omri king of Israel. 1 Kings 16:23–24.

Burial place of the kings of Israel. 1 Kings 16:28; 22:37; 2 Kings 13:13.
Called after Shemer, the owner of the hill on which it was built. 1 Kings 16:24.
Called the head of Ephraim. Isa. 7:9.
Called the mountain of Samaria. Amos 4:1; 6:1.
Deliverance of, effected. 1 Kings 20:15–21.
Deliverance of, predicted. 1 Kings 20:13–14.
Delivered by miraculous means. 2 Kings 7:6–7.
Elisha predicted plentifulness in. 2 Kings 7:1–2.
A fenced city, well provided with arms. 2 Kings 10:2.
Kings of Israel sometimes took their titles from. 1 Kings 21:1; 2 Kings 1:3.
Pool of Samaria near to. 1 Kings 22:38.
Prophet Elisha lived in. 2 Kings 2:25; 5:3; 6:32.
Remarkable plentifulness in, as predicted by Elisha. 2 Kings 7:16–20.
The residence of the kings of Israel. 1 Kings 16:29; 2 Kings 1:2; 3:1, 6.
Suffered severely from famine. 2 Kings 6:25–29.
Territory of Ephraim and Manasseh properly so-called. Josh. 17:17–18; Isa. 28:1.
Whole kingdom of Israel sometimes called. Ezek. 16:46, 51; Hos. 8:5–6.

SAMARIA, IN THE FIRST CENTURY

Christ after His resurrection commanded the gospel to be preached in. Acts 1:8.

Christ at first forbade His disciples to visit. Matt. 10:5.

Christ preached in. John 4:39–42.

Cities of, mentioned

Antipatris. Acts 23:31.

Samaria. Acts 8:5.

Sychar. John 4:5.

The gospel first preached in, by Philip. Acts 8:5.

Had many cities, etc. Matt. 10:5; Luke 9:52.

Inhabitants of

Boasted descent from Jacob. John 4:12.

Despised by the Jews. John 8:48.

Expected the Messiah. John 4:25, 29.

Had no dealings with the Jews. Luke 9:52–53; John 4:9.

More humane and grateful than the Jews. Luke 10:33–36; 17:16–18.

Opposed the Jews after their return from captivity. Neh. 4:1–18.

Professed to worship God. Ezra 4:2.

Ready to hear and embrace the gospel. John 4:39–42; Acts 8:6–8.

Their religion mixed with idolatry. 2 Kings 17:41, with John 4:22.

Their true descent. 2 Kings 17:24; Ezra 4:9–10.

Were superstitious. Acts 8:9–11.

Worshiped on Mount Gerizim. John 4:20.

Many Christian churches in. Acts 9:31.

Persecuted Christians fled to. Acts 8:1.

Situated between Judea and Galilee. Luke 17:11; John 4:3–4.

SANCTIFICATION

All believers are in a state of. Acts 20:32; 26:18; 1 Cor. 6:11.

Through the atonement of Christ. Heb. 10:10; 13:12.

Believers elected to salvation through. 2 Thess. 2:13; 1 Pet. 1:2.

Believers fitted for the service of God by. 2 Tim. 2:21.

Brought about by

Christ. Heb. 2:11; 13:12.

God. Ezek. 37:28; 1 Thess. 5:23; Jude 1:1.

The Holy Spirit. Rom. 15:16; 1 Cor. 6:11.

In Christ. 1 Cor. 1:2.

Christ became, of God, for us. 1 Cor. 1:30.

The church made glorious by. Eph. 5:26–27.

Described as separation to the service of God. Ps. 4:3; 2 Cor. 6:17.

God wills all believers to have. 1 Thess. 4:3.

Ministers

Set apart to God's service by. Jer. 1:5.

Should exhort their people to walk in. 1 Thess. 4:1, 3.

Should pray that their people may enjoy complete. 1 Thess. 5:23.

None can inherit the kingdom of God without. 1 Cor. 6:9–11.

Offering up of believers acceptable through. Rom. 15:16.

Should lead to
Holiness. Rom. 6:22; Eph. 5:7–9.
Putting to death of sin.
1 Thess. 4:3–4.
Through the Word of God.
John 17:17, 19; Eph. 5:26.
Types.
Gen. 2:3; Exod. 13:2; 19:14;
40:9–15; Lev. 27:14–16.

SANCTUARY
Brings understanding. Ps. 73:17.
A house of prayer for all peoples.
Isa. 56:7; Matt. 21:13.
Isaiah saw the Lord in. Isa. 6.
The Lord is in. Ps. 11:4.
Not to be desecrated. John 2:16.
The righteous love. Ps. 26:8.
Strength and beauty are in. Ps. 96:6.
To be reverenced. Lev. 19:30.

SANITATION
Carcasses. Lev. 11:24–40.
Childbirth. Ezek. 16:4.
Disinfection. Lev. 2:13.
Quarantine. Lev. 13:2–46.
Venereal diseases. Lev. 15:2–33;
22:4–6.
Women in childbirth. Lev. 12:2–5.

SARCASM
Examples of
Agrippa to Paul. Acts. 26:28.
Ahab's reply to Ben-Hadad.
1 Kings 20:11.
Balak blaming Balaam.
Num. 24:11.
Cain's self-justifying argument when God asked him where Abel was. Gen. 4:9.

David's reply to Michal's irony.
2 Sam. 6:21.
Eliab to David. 1 Sam. 17:28.
Elijah to the priests of Baal.
1 Kings 18:27.
God blaming Israel. Num. 11:20;
Judg. 10:14.
Israelites blaming Moses.
Exod. 14:11.
Jehoash to Amaziah.
2 Kings 14:9, 10; 2 Chron.
25:18–19.
Job to Zophar. Job 12:2–3.
Joshua to the descendants of
Joseph. Josh. 17:15.
Jotham. Judg. 9:7–19.
The man of Jabesh to Nahash.
1 Sam. 11:10.
The persecutors of Jesus.
Matt. 27:28–29.
Paul. 1 Tim. 4:7.
Rabshakeh to Hezekiah.
2 Kings 18:23–24.
Samson. Judg. 14:18.
Sanballat's address to the army of
Samaria. Neh. 4:2–3.
Solomon. Prov. 26:16.
Zophar to Job. Job 11:12.

SATAN
See Devil, the

SATIRE
Hannah's song of exaltation over
Peninnah. 1 Sam. 2:1–10.
Jesus against hypocrites.
Matt. 23:2–33.

SATISFACTION
From drinking divine waters.
Isa. 55:1; John 4:14.
From good news. Prov. 25:25.
With good things. Ps. 103:2, 5.

Of the humble, the mourning, the
meek. Matt. 5:3–12.
For the hungry. Luke 6:21.
With long life. Ps. 91:16.
From the Lord's likeness. Ps. 17:15.
Of the redeemed in heaven.
Rev. 7:16.

SATYR

A mythological creature, represented
as half-man and half-goat.
Lev. 17:7; 2 Chron. 11:15;
Isa. 13:21; 34:14.

SAVINGS (MONEY)

See also Financial Responsibility

Examples of
Joseph, for Pharaoh.
Gen. 41:1–57.
Man who built bigger barns.
Luke 12:16–21.
Fool devours treasure. Prov. 21:20.

Injunctions concerning
Be like industrious ant.
Prov. 6:6–8; 30:25.
Diversify assets. Eccles. 11:2.
Lay up treasures in heaven.
Matt. 6:19–21.
Save for offerings. 1 Cor. 16:2.

SAVIOR

See Christ, the Savior; Redemption;
Salvation

SAW

Used as an instrument of torture.
2 Sam. 12:31; Heb. 11:37.
Used for cutting stone. 1 Kings 7:9.
Used in a figurative sense. Isa. 10:15.

SCAB

Disease of the skin. Lev. 13:2, 6–8;
Isa. 3:17.

SCALES

Fell from Paul's eyes. Acts 9:18.

SCAPEGOAT

Chosen by lot. Lev. 16:8.

Communicated uncleanness to
The high priest. Lev. 16:24.
The man who led him away.
Lev. 16:26.
High priest transferred the sins of
Israel to, by confessing them with
both hands upon its head.
Lev. 16:21.
Part of the sin offering on the Day of
Atonement. Lev. 16:5, 7.
Sent into the wilderness by the hands
of a fit person. Lev. 16:21–22.
A type of Christ. Isa. 53:6, 11–12.

SCEPTER

Made of gold. Esther 4:11.
Made of iron. Ps. 2:9; Rev. 2:27;
12:5.
A symbol of authority. Num. 24:17;
Isa. 14:5.
A wand used by kings to signify favor
or disfavor to those who desired
audience. Esther 5:2; 8:4.
Used in a figurative sense.
Gen. 49:10; Num. 24:17;
Isa. 9:4.

SCHOOL

At Bethel. 2 Kings 2:3.
Bible school. Deut. 31:10–13.
Crowded attendance at. 2 Kings 6:1.
Of Gamaliel. Acts 5:34; 22:3.
At Gilgal. 2 Kings 4:38.

In the home. Deut. 4:9–10; 6:7, 9;
11:19–20; Ps. 78:5–8.

At Jericho. 2 Kings 2:5–15.

At Jerusalem. 2 Kings 22:14;
2 Chron. 34:22.

Of the prophets, at Naioth.
1 Sam. 19:20.

Schoolmaster. Gal. 3:24–25.

State school. 2 Chron. 17:7–9;
Dan. 1:3–21.

Of Tyrannus. Acts 19:9.

SCIENCES

Architecture. Deut. 8:12;
1 Chron. 29:19.

Arithmetic. Gen. 15:5; Lev. 26:8;
Job 29:18.

Astrology. Isa. 47:13.

Astronomy. Job 38:31–32;
Isa. 13:10.

Botany. 1 Kings 4:33.

Geography. Gen. 10:1–30;
Isa. 11:11.

History and chronology.
1 Kings 22:39; 2 Kings 1:18;
1 Chron. 9:1; 29:29.

Mechanics. Gen. 6:14–16; 11:4;
Exod. 14:6–7.

Medicine. Jer. 8:22; Mark 5:26.

Music. 1 Chron. 16:4–7; 25:6.

Navigation. 1 Kings 9:27;
Ps. 107:23.

Surveying. Josh. 18:4–9;
Neh. 2:12–16; Ezek. 40:5–6;
Zech. 2:2.

Zoology. 1 Kings 4:33.

SCOURGING

See Beating

SCORNING

See Mocking

SCRIBES

Acted as

Notaries in courts of justice.
Jer. 32:11–12.

Religious teachers. Neh. 8:2–6.

Royal secretaries. 2 Kings 25:19;
2 Chron. 26:11; Jer. 52:25.

Secretaries to kings. 2 Sam. 8:17;
20:25; 2 Kings 12:10;
Esther 3:12.

Secretaries to prophets.
Jer. 36:4, 26.

Writers of public documents.
1 Chron. 24:6.

Antiquity of. Judg. 5:14.

Families celebrated for furnishing

Kenites. 1 Chron. 2:55.

Levi. 1 Chron. 24:6;
2 Chron. 34:13.

Zebulun. Judg. 5:14.

Generally men of great wisdom.
1 Chron. 27:32.

Illustrative of well-instructed ministers
of the gospel. Matt. 13:52.

Modern

Active in bringing about Christ's
death. Matt. 26:3; Luke 23:10.

Condemned by Christ for
hypocrisy. Matt. 23:15.

Often offended at Christ's conduct
and teaching. Matt. 21:15;
Mark 2:6–7, 16; 3:22.

Persecuted the early Christians.
Acts 4:5, 18, 21; 6:12.

Regarded as interpreters of
Scripture. Matt. 2:4; 17:10;
Mark 12:35.

Sat in Moses' seat. Matt. 23:2.

Tempted Jesus. John 8:3.

Their manner of teaching contrasted with that of Christ. Matt. 7:29; Mark 1:22.
Valued wise and learned. 1 Cor. 1:20.
Were doctors of the law. Mark 12:28, with Matt. 22:35.

Were frequently Pharisees. Acts 23:9.
Wore long robes and loved preeminence. Mark 12:38–39.
Often learned in the law. Ezra 7:6.
Were ready writers. Ps. 45:1.
Wore an inkhorn at their belts. Ezek. 9:2–3.

Jewish Scribes

SCRIPTURES, THE

See also: Bible; Inspiration of; Word of God

Advantage of possessing. Rom. 3:2.
All should desire to hear. Neh. 8:1.

Are

Able to make one wise to salvation through faith in Christ. 2 Tim. 3:15.
Full and sufficient. Luke 16:29, 31.
Profitable both for doctrine and practice. 2 Tim. 3:16–17.
An unerring guide. Prov. 6:23; 2 Pet. 1:19.

Believers

Delight in. Ps. 1:2.

Grieve when people disobey. Ps. 119:158.
Hide in their hearts. Ps. 119:11.
Hope in. Ps. 119:74, 81, 147.
Keep in remembrance. Ps. 119:16.
Long for. Ps. 119:82.
Love exceedingly. Ps. 119:86, 113, 159, 167.
Meditate in. Pss. 1:2; 119:99, 148.
Obey. Ps. 119:67; Luke 8:21; John 17:6.
Plead the promises of, in prayer. Ps. 119:25, 28, 41, 76, 169.
Pray to be conformed to. Ps. 119:133.
Pray to be taught. Ps. 119:12–13, 33, 66.
Regard as sweet. Ps. 119:103.

Rejoice in. Ps. 119:162;
Jer. 15:16.
Speak of. Ps. 119:172.
Stand in awe of. Ps. 119:161;
Isa. 66:2.
Trust in. Ps. 119:42.
Value above all things. Job 23:12.
Value as a light. Ps. 119:105.
Blessedness of hearing and obeying.
Luke 11:28; James 1:25.

Called the
Book. Ps. 40:7; Rev. 22:19.
Book of the Law. Neh. 8:3;
Gal. 3:10.
Book of the Lord. Isa. 34:16.
Holy Scriptures. Rom. 1:2;
2 Tim 3:15.
Law of the Lord. Ps. 1:2;
Isa. 30:9.
Oracles of God. Rom. 3:2;
1 Pet. 4:11.
Scripture of truth. Dan. 10:21.
Sword of the Spirit. Eph. 6:17.
Word. James 1:21–23; 1 Pet. 2:2.
Word of Christ. Col. 3:16.
Word of God. Luke 11:28;
Heb. 4:12.
Word of truth. James 1:18.
Christ enables us to understand.
Luke 24:45.
Christ sanctioned, by appealing to
them. Matt. 4:4; Mark 12:10,
John 7:42.
Christ taught out of. Luke 24:27.
Contain the promises of the gospel.
Rom. 1:2.

Described as
Perfect. Ps. 19:7.
Precious. Ps. 19:10.
Pure. Pss. 12:6; 119:140;
Prov. 30:5.
Quick and powerful. Heb. 4:12.

True. Ps. 119:160; John 17:17.

Designed for
Admonishing. Ps. 19:11;
1 Cor. 10:11.
Building up in the faith.
Acts 20:32.
Cleansing the heart. John 15:3;
Eph. 5:26.
Cleansing the ways. Ps. 119:9.
Comforting. Ps. 119:82;
Rom. 15:4.
Converting the soul. Ps. 19:7.
Illuminating. Ps. 119:130.
Keeping from destructive paths.
Ps. 17:4.
Making wise the simple. Ps. 19:7.
Producing faith. John 20:31.
Producing hope. Ps. 119:49;
Rom. 15:4.
Producing obedience.
Deut. 17:19–20.
Promoting growth in grace.
1 Pet. 2:2.
Regenerating. James 1:18;
1 Pet. 1:23.
Rejoicing the heart. Pss. 19:8;
119:111.
Reviving. Ps. 119:50, 93.
Sanctifying. John 17:17;
Eph. 5:26.
Supporting life. Deut. 8:3, with
Matt. 4:4.
Destruction of, punished.
Jer. 36:29–31.
Everything should be tried by.
Isa. 9:20; Acts 17:11.
Given by inspiration of God.
2 Tim. 3:16.
Given by inspiration of the Holy
Spirit. Acts 1:16; Heb. 3:7;
2 Pet. 1:21.

The Holy Spirit enables us to understand. John 16:13; 1 Cor. 2:10–14.

Ignorance of, a source of error. Matt. 22:29; Acts 13:27.

Intended for the use of all persons. Rom. 16:26.

Let them dwell richly in you. Col. 3:16.

The letter of, without the spirit, kills. John 6:63, with 2 Cor. 3:6.

Mere hearers of, deceive themselves. James 1:22.

No prophecy of, is of any private interpretation. 2 Pet. 1:20.

Nothing to be taken from or added to. Deut. 4:2; 12:32.

One portion of, to be compared with another. 1 Cor. 2:13.

Record divine prophecies. 2 Pet. 1:19–21.

Reveal the laws, statutes, and judgments of God. Deut. 4:5, 14, with Exod. 24:3–4.

Should be
Appealed to. 1 Cor. 1:31; 1 Pet. 1:16.
Believed. John 2:22.
Kept in the heart. Deut. 6:6; 11:18.
Known. 2 Tim. 3:15.
Not handled deceitfully. 2 Cor. 4:2.
Not only heard, but obeyed. Matt. 7:24, with Luke 11:28; James 1:22.
Read. Deut. 17:19; Isa. 34:16.
Read publicly to all. Deut. 31:11–13; Neh. 8:3; Jer. 36:6; Acts 13:15.
Received, not as the word of men, but as the Word of God. 1 Thess. 2:13.

Received with meekness. James 1:21.
Searched. John 5:39; 7:52.
Searched daily. Acts 17:11.
The standard of teaching. 1 Pet. 4:11.
Talked of continually. Deut. 6:7.
Taught to all. 2 Chron. 17:7–9; Neh. 8:7–8.
Taught to children. Deut. 6:7; 11:19; 2 Tim. 3:15.
Used against our spiritual enemies. Matt. 4:4, 7, 10, with Eph. 6:11, 17.

Testify of Christ. John 5:39; Acts 10:43; 18:28; 1 Cor. 15:3.

Those who search, are truly noble. Acts 17:11.

Warnings against those who add to or take from. Rev. 22:18–19.

The wicked
Corrupt. 2 Cor. 2:17.
Do not obey. Ps. 119:158.
Frequently distort, to their own destruction. 2 Pet. 3:16.
Reject. Jer. 8:9.
Set aside to observe their traditions. Mark 7:9–13.
Stumble at. 1 Pet. 2:8.

Work effectually in those who believe. 1 Thess. 2:13.

Written for our instruction. Rom. 15:4.

SEA, THE

Called the
Deep. Job 41:31; Ps. 107:24; 2 Cor. 11:25.
Great and wide sea. Ps. 104:25.
Great waters. Ps. 77:19.

Caused to churn by crocodile. Job 41:31–32.

Clouds the clothes of. Job 38:9.

Commercial nations
Derived great wealth from.
Deut. 33:19.
Often built cities on the borders of.
Gen. 49:13; Ezek. 27:3;
Nah. 3:8.

Darkness the clothes of. Job 38:9.

Gathering together of waters
originally called. Gen. 1:10.

God
Created. Exod. 20:11; Ps. 95:5;
Acts 14:15.
Does what He pleases in.
Ps. 135:6.
Dries up, by His reprimand.
Isa. 50:2; Nah. 1:4.
Founded the earth upon. Ps. 24:2.
Made the birds and fishes out of.
Gen. 1:20–22.
Measures the waters of.
Isa. 40:12.
Set bounds to, by a perpetual
decree. Job 26:10; 38:8,
10–11; Prov. 8:27, 29.
Shakes, by His word. Hag. 2:6.
Stills, by His power.
Pss. 65:7; 89:9; 107:29.

Great rivers often called. Isa. 11:15;
Jer. 51:36.

Illustrative of
Devastating armies (its waves).
Ezek. 26:3–4.
Diffusion of spiritual knowledge
over the earth in the latter days
(covered with waters). Isa. 11:9;
Hab. 2:14.
Heavy afflictions. Isa. 43:2;
Lam. 2:13.
Hostile armies (when roaring).
Isa. 5:30; Jer. 6:23.

The peace of heaven (when
smooth as glass). Rev. 4:6; 15:2.
Righteousness (its waves).
Isa. 48:18.
The unsteady (its waves).
James 1:6.
The wicked (when troubled).
Isa. 57:20.

Inhabited by numerous large and
small creatures. Ps. 104:25–26.

Lakes often called. Deut. 3:17;
Matt. 8:24, 27, 32.

Made to glorify God. Pss. 69:34;
148:7.

Names mentioned
Adriatic or Sea of Adria.
Acts 27:27.
Of great depth. Ps. 69:22.
Of immense extent. Job 11:9;
Ps. 104:25.
Mediterranean or Great Sea.
Num. 34:6; Deut. 11:24; 34:2;
Zech. 14:8.
Numerous islands in. Ezek. 26:18.
Passed over in ships. Pss. 104:26;
107:23.
Raised by the wind.
Ps. 107:25–26; Jon. 1:4.
Red Sea. Exod. 10:19; 13:18;
23:31.
The renewed earth will be without.
Rev. 21:1.
Replenished by rivers. Eccles. 1:7;
Ezek. 47:8.
Rivers flowed into. Eccles. 1:7.
Sailing on, dangerous.
Acts 27:9, 20; 2 Cor. 11:26.
Salt or Dead Sea. Gen. 14:3;
Num. 34:12.
Sea of Galilee. Matt. 4:8; 8:32;
John 6:1.
Sea of Jazer. Jer. 48:32.

Sea of Joppa or Sea of the Philistines. Ezra 3:7, with Exod. 23:31.

Sand the barrier of. Jer. 5:22.

Shore of covered with sand. Gen. 22:17; 1 Kings 4:29; Job 6:3; Ps. 78:27.

Waves of
Mighty. Ps. 93:4; Acts 27:41.
Raised upon high. Pss. 93:3; 107:25.
Rise over land. Jer. 51:42.
Tossed about. Jer. 5:22.
Tumultuous. Luke 21:25; Jude 13.
Will give up its dead at the last day. Rev. 20:13.
Wonders of God seen in. Ps. 107:24.

SEALING OF THE HOLY SPIRIT
See Holy Spirit, Sealing of the

SEALS
Called pledges. Gen. 38:18, 25.
Generally worn as rings or bracelets. Jer. 22:24.

Illustrative of
Appropriation of believers to God by the Spirit. 2 Cor. 1:22; Eph. 1:13; 4:30.
Circumcision. Rom. 4:11.
Converts. 1 Cor. 9:2.
Full approval. John 3:33.
Restraint. Job 9:7; 37:7; Rev. 20:3.
Secrecy. Dan. 12:4; Rev. 5:1; 10:4.
Security. Song of Sol. 4:12; 2 Tim. 2:19; Rev. 7:2–8; 20:3.
What is dear or valued. Song of Sol. 8:6; Jer. 22:24; Hag. 2:23.

Impressions of
Attached to all royal decrees. 1 Kings 21:8; Esther 3:12; 8:8.
Attached to covenants. Neh. 9:38; 10:1.
Attached to leases and transfers of property. Jer. 32:9–12, 44.
Attached to the victims approved for sacrifice, alluded to. John 6:27.
Frequently taken in clay. Job 38:14.
Set upon treasures. Deut. 32:34.
Used for security. Dan. 6:17; Matt. 27:66.
Were given by kings as a badge of authority. Gen. 41:41–42.

Inscriptions upon, alluded to. 2 Tim 2:19.

Precious stones set in gold used as. Exod. 28:11.

SECOND COMING OF CHRIST
See Christ, Second Coming of

SECOND DEATH
Final punishment of the wicked. Rev. 20:14.

SECRET
Alms to be given in. Matt. 6:4.
Of others not to be divulged. Prov. 25:9; Matt. 18:15.
Prayer to be offered in. Matt. 6:6.

SECRETARY
Military. 2 Kings 25:19; 2 Chron. 26:11.
Recorder. 2 Sam. 20:24.

SECURITY

Of believers
Chosen before the foundation of
the world. Eph. 1:4.
None can take them from Christ's
hand, nor from God's.
John 10:28–29.
Predestined, called, justified,
glorified. Rom. 8:30.
Will never perish. John 10:28.

In God
Our caretaker. 1 Pet. 5:7.
Our champion. 2 Sam. 5:24;
2 Chron. 32:8.
Our defense. Ps. 62:2.
Our dwelling place. Ps. 90:1.
Our guardian. Ps. 125:2;
Isa. 31:5; 52:12.
Our help. Ps. 94:17.
Our keeper. Ps. 121:5.
Our rock. Deut. 32:31.
Our safety. Prov. 21:31.
Our stronghold in trouble.
Nah. 1:7.
Our sustainer. Ps. 55:22.

SEDITION

Charged against Paul. Acts 24:5.
How punished. Acts 5:36–37.

SEDUCTION

Examples of
Dinah. Gen. 34:2.
Tamar. 2 Sam. 13:1–14.
Laws concerning. Exod. 22:16–17;
Deut. 22:23–29.

SEED

Difference between, and the plant
that grows from it, noticed. 1 Cor.
15:37–38.

Each kind of, has its own body.
1 Cor. 15:38.
In Egypt required to be artificially
watered. Deut. 11:19.
Every herb, tree ,and grass yields its
own. Gen. 1:11–12, 29.
Ground carefully plowed and
prepared for. Isa. 28:24–25.

Illustrative of
Spiritual life. 1 John 3:9.
The Word of God. Luke 8:11;
1 Pet. 1:23.

The Jews punished by
Its being choked by thorns.
Jer. 12:13, with Matt. 13:7.
Its increase being consumed by
enemies. Lev. 26:16;
Deut. 28:33, 51.
Its increase being consumed by
locusts, etc. Deut. 28:38;
Joel 1:4.
Its rotting in the ground. Joel 1:17;
Mal. 2:3.
Its yielding but little increase.
Isa. 5:10; Hag. 1:6.

Mosaic laws regarding
Different kinds of, not to be sown
in the same field. Lev. 19:19;
Deut. 22:9.
If dry, exempted from uncleanness
though touched by an unclean
thing. Lev. 11:37.
If wet, rendered unclean by contact
with an unclean thing.
Lev. 11:38.
Not to be sown during the
sabbatical year. Lev. 25:4, 20.
Not to be sown in year of jubilee.
Lev. 25:11.
The tithe of, to be given to God.
Lev. 27:30.

Often sown beside rivers.
Eccles. 11:1; Isa. 32:20.
Often trodden into the ground, by the feet of oxen, etc. Isa. 32:20.
Required to be watered by the rain. Isa. 55:10.

Sowing
Necessary to its productiveness.
John 12:24; 1 Cor. 15:36.
Often attended with danger.
Ps. 126:5–6.
Often attended with great waste.
Matt. 13:4–5, 7.
Required constant diligence.
Eccles. 11:4, 6.
Time for, called seed time.
Gen. 8:22.

Sowing, illustrative of
The burial of the body.
1 Cor. 15:26–38.
Christian generosity. Eccles. 11:6; 2 Cor. 9:6.
The death of Christ and its effects.
John 12:24.
Human works producing a corresponding reward. Job 4:8; Hos. 10:12; Gal. 6:7–8.
Preaching the gospel.
Matt. 13:3, 32; 1 Cor. 9:11.
Scattering or dispersing a people.
Zech. 10:9.
Yearly return of time of sowing, secured by covenant.
Gen. 8:21–22.
Yielded an abundant increase in Canaan. Gen. 26:12. (*See also* Matt. 13:23.)

SEEKERS

Examples of
Asa. 2 Chron. 14:7.

Daniel. Dan. 9:3–4.
David. Ps. 34:4.
Ezra. Ezra 7:10.
Hezekiah. 2 Chron. 31:21.
Jehoshaphat. 2 Chron. 17:3–4.
Josiah. 2 Chron. 34:3.
The Magi. Matt. 2:1–2.
Uzziah. 2 Chron. 26:5.

SEEKING GOD

Afflictions designed to lead to.
Ps. 78:33–34; Hos. 5:15.

Believers
Characterized by. Ps. 24:6.
Desirous of. Job 5:8.
Engage in, with the whole heart.
2 Chron. 15:2; Ps. 119:10.
Make top priority. Job 8:5; Ps. 63:1; Song of Sol. 3:2, 4; Isa. 26:9.
Prepare their hearts for.
2 Chron. 30:19.
Purpose, in heart. Ps. 27:8.
Set their hearts to.
2 Chron. 11:16.
Specially exhorted to. Zeph. 2:3.
Blessedness of. Ps. 119:2.
Commanded. Isa. 55:6; Matt. 7:7.
Ends in praise. Ps. 22:26.

Ensures
Being heard of Him. Ps. 34:4.
Gifts of righteousness.
Hos. 10:12.
His being found. Deut. 4:29; 1 Chron. 28:9; Prov. 8:17; Jer. 29:13.
His favor. Lam. 3:25.
His not forsaking us. Ps. 9:10.
His protection. Ezra 8:22.
Life. Ps. 69:32; Amos 5:4, 6.
Prosperity. Job 8:5–6; Ps. 34:10.

Understanding all things.
  Prov. 28:5.
In His house. Deut. 12:5; Ps. 27:4.
Imperative upon all. Isa. 8:19.

Includes seeking
  Christ. Mal. 3:1; Luke 2:15–16.
  The city God has prepared.
    Heb. 11:10, 16; 13–14.
  His commandments.
    1 Chron. 28:8; Mal. 2:7.
  His face. Pss. 27:8; 105:4.
  His kingdom. Matt. 6:33;
    Luke 12:31.
  His laws. Ps. 119:45, 94.
  His name. Ps. 83:16.
  His righteousness. Matt. 6:33.
  His strength. 1 Chron. 16:11;
    Ps. 105:4.
  His word. Isa. 34:16.
  Honor that comes from Him.
    John 5:44.
  Justification by Christ.
    Gal. 2:16–17.
Is never in vain. Isa. 45:19.
Leads to joy. Pss. 70:4; 105:3.
None, by nature, are found to be
  engaged in. Ps. 14:2, with
  Rom. 3:11; Luke 12:23, 30.
Promise connected with. Ps. 69:32.
By prayer. Job 8:5; Dan. 9:3.
Punishment of those who neglect.
  Zeph. 1:4–6.

Should be
  In the day of trouble. Ps. 77:2.
  With diligence. Heb. 11:6.
  Evermore. Ps. 105:4.
  With the heart. Deut. 4:29;
    1 Chron. 22:19.
  Immediate. Hos. 10:12.
  While He may be found. Isa. 55:6.
They who neglect denounced.
  Isa. 31:1.

The wicked
  Are gone out of the way of. Ps.
    14:2–3, with Rom. 3:11–12.
  Not led to, by affliction. Isa. 9:13.
  Do not prepare their hearts for.
    2 Chron. 12:14.
  Refuse, through pride. Ps. 10:4.
  Rejected, when too late in.
    Prov. 1:28.
  Sometimes pretend to. Ezra 4:2;
    Isa. 58:2.
Will be rewarded. Heb. 11:6.

SEGREGATION
See also Racial Tension

Examples of
  Believers, from nonbelievers.
    Luke 6:22.

Israelites
  From foreigners. 1 Kings 8:53;
    Neh. 9:2.
  From inhabitants of the land.
    Ezra 10:11.
  Levites, from other Israelites.
    Num. 8:14.

Principles relevant to
  Abraham's family to be a channel
    of God's blessing to others.
    Gen. 12:1–3; Gal. 3:6–9.
  Dividing wall of hostility broken.
    Eph. 2:11–14.
  No racial distinction in Christ.
    Gal. 3:28–29.
  Foreigners to have equal rights.
    Deut. 24:17.

SELF-CONDEMNATION
Examples of
  Achan. Josh. 7:19–25.
  Ahab. 1 Kings 20:39–42.
  David. 2 Sam. 12:5–7.

SELF-CONTROL
For a clear conscience. Acts 24:16.
Through divine help. Jer. 10:23.
The fruit of the Holy Spirit.
Gal. 5:22–23.
Over our bodies. Rom. 6:12.
Over our lips. Ps. 141:3;
James 1:26.
Over our spirits. Prov. 16:32; 25:28.
Reward of. Rev. 21:7.
Value of. Prov. 16:32; 25:28.

SELF-DECEPTION
Hearing without doing results in.
James 1:26.

SELF-DEFENSE
Accused heard in. Matt. 27:11–14;
Acts 2:37–40; 22; 23; 24:10–21;
26.

SELF-DELUSION
A characteristic of the wicked.
Ps. 49:18.

Exhibited in thinking that
Christ will not come to judge.
2 Pet. 3:4.
Gifts entitle us to heaven.
Matt. 7:21–22.
God will not punish our sins.
Ps. 10:11; Jer. 5:12.
Our lives will be prolonged.
Isa. 56:12; Luke 12:19;
James 4:13.
Our own ways are right.
Prov. 14:12.
Privileges entitle us to heaven.
Matt. 3:9; Luke 13:25–26.
We are above adversity. Ps. 10:6.
We are better than others.
Luke 18:11.
We are pure. Prov. 30:12.

We are rich in spiritual things.
Rev. 3:17.
We may have peace while in sin.
Deut. 29:19.
We should adhere to established
wicked practices. Jer. 44:17.
Fatal consequences of.
Matt. 7:23, 24:48–51;
Luke 12:20; 1 Thess. 5:3.
Frequently persevered in, to the last.
Matt. 7:22; 25:11–12;
Luke 13:24–25.
Prosperity frequently leads to.
Ps. 30:6; Hos. 12:8; Luke
12:17–19.
Unrepentant sinners often given up
to. Ps. 81:11–12; Hos. 4:17;
2 Thess. 2:10–11.

SELF-DENIAL
Becomes strangers and pilgrims.
Heb. 11:13–15; 1 Pet. 2:11.
Christ set an example of.
Matt. 4:8–10; 8:20; John 6:38;
Rom. 15:3; Phil. 2:6–8.
Danger of neglecting.
Matt. 16:25–26; 1 Cor. 9:27.
Happy result of. 2 Pet. 1:4.
Ministers especially called to
exercise. 2 Cor. 6:4–5.

Necessary
In following Christ.
Luke 14:27–33.
To the triumph of believers.
1 Cor. 9:25–27.
In the warfare of believers.
2 Tim. 2:4.
Reward of. Matt. 19:28–29;
Rom. 8:13.

Should be exercised in
Abstaining from fleshly desires.
1 Pet. 2:11.

Assisting others. Luke 3:11.
Being crucified to the world.
Gal. 6:14.
Being crucified with Christ.
Rom. 6:6.
Controlling the appetite.
Prov. 23:2.
Crucifying the sinful nature.
Gal. 5:24.
Denying ungodliness and worldly
lusts. Rom. 6:12; Titus 2:12.
Even lawful things. 1 Cor. 10:23.
Forsaking all. Luke 14:33.
Mortifying deeds of the body.
Rom. 8:13.
Mortifying sinful desires.
Mark 9:43; Col. 3:5.
No longer living to the lusts of
men. 1 Pet. 4:2.
Not pleasing ourselves.
Rom. 15:1–3.
Not seeking our own profit.
1 Cor. 10:24, 33; 13:5;
Phil. 2:4.
Preferring Christ to all earthly
relations. Matt. 8:21–22;
Luke 14:26.
Preferring the profit of others.
Rom. 14:20–21;
1 Cor. 10:24, 33.
Putting off the old nature which is
corrupt. Eph. 4:22; Col. 3:9.
Taking up the cross and following
Christ. Matt. 10:38; 16:24.
A test of devotedness to Christ.
Matt. 10:37–38; Luke 9:23–24.

SELF-ESTEEM

Examples of arrogance
Edom. Obad. 3.
Laodiceans. Rev. 3:17.
Moab. Isa. 16:6.

Nebuchadnezzar. Dan. 4:30–33;
5:20–21.
People in last days. 2 Tim. 3:1–4.
Sodomites. Ezek. 16:49–50.
Uzziah. 2 Chron. 26:16.

Humble
Abraham. Gen. 18:27.
David. 1 Sam 13:14; 18:18;
Ps. 51:1–17.
Isaiah. Isa. 6:5.
Moses. Exod. 3:11; Num 12:3.
Paul. 1 Cor. 15:9–10;
Eph. 3:7–8.

In relation to others
Count others better than oneself.
Phil. 2:3.
Do not boast of oneself beyond
limit. 2 Cor. 10:7–13.
Do not think more highly of
oneself than is proper.
Rom. 12:3; Gal. 6:1–3.

Principles relevant to
Better to be humble than proud.
Prov. 16:19.

God
Lifts up humble but puts down
pride. Ps. 138:6; 1 Pet 5:5.
Loves everyone. John 15:12;
1 John 4:10.
No condemnation in Christ.
Rom. 8:1.
Nothing separates from love of God.
Rom. 8:35–39.

People
Are sinners. Rom. 3:23.
Are valuable. 1 Cor. 6:20.
Created in image of God.
Gen. 1:26–27.
Created with exalted status.
Ps. 8:4–8.

With new nature. 2 Cor. 5:16–17;
Eph. 4:24; Phil. 1:6; Col. 3:10.
With renewed spirit. Eph. 4:23.
Self-abasement to be avoided.
Col. 2:18, 23.
Self-confidence in Christ.
1 Cor. 9:24; 2 Cor. 3:5;
Phil. 3:4–7; 4:13.
Self-elation prevented by thorn in
flesh. 2 Cor. 12:7.

SELF-EXAMINATION

Advantages of. 1 Cor. 11:31;
Gal 6:4; 1 John 3:20–22.
Cause of difficulty in. Jer. 17:9.
Commanded. 2 Cor. 13:5.
Necessary before the Lord's Supper.
1 Cor. 11:28.

Should be engaged in
With diligent search. Ps. 77:6;
Lam. 3:40.
With holy reverence. Ps. 4:4.
With prayer for divine searching.
Pss. 26:2; 139:23–24.
With purpose of amendment.
Ps. 119:59; Lam. 3:40.

SELF-EXULTATION

Examples of
Belshazzar. Dan. 5:23.
Herod. Acts 12:20–23.
Korah, Dathan, and Abiram.
Num. 16:1–3.
Nebuchadnezzar. Dan. 4:30;
5:20.
Pharaoh. Exod. 9:17.
Prince of Tyre. Ezek. 28:2, 9.
Sennacherib. 2 Chron. 32:9–19.
Simon the Sorcerer. Acts 8:9.

SELF-IMAGE

Better to be humble than proud.
Prov. 16:19.
Competency comes from God.
2 Cor. 3:5.

Humble
Abraham. Gen. 18:27.
David. 1 Sam. 13:14; 18:18;
Ps. 51:1–17.
Isaiah. Isa. 6:5.
Moses. Exod. 3:11; Num. 12:3.
Paul. 1 Cor. 15:9–10;
Eph. 3:7–8.

SELF-INDULGENCE

Examples of
The rich fool. Luke 12:16–20.
The rich man. Luke 16:19.
Solomon. Eccles. 2:10.

SELFISHNESS

All humans addicted to. Eph. 2:3;
Phil. 2:21.
Believers falsely accused of.
Job 1:9–11.
Characteristic of the last days.
2 Tim. 3:1–2.
Contrary to the law of God.
Lev. 19:18; Matt. 22:39;
James 2:8.
Especially forbidden to believers.
1 Cor. 10:24; Phil. 2:4.
Example of (Christ condemns).
John 4:34; Rom. 15:3; 2 Cor.
8:9.

Exhibited in
Being lovers of ourselves.
2 Tim. 3:2.
Living to ourselves. 2 Cor. 5:15.
Neglect of the poor. 1 John 3:17.

Performing duty for reward.
  Mic. 3:11.
Pleasing ourselves. Rom. 15:1.
Seeking after gain. Isa. 56:11.
Seeking our own. 1 Cor. 10:33;
  Phil. 2:21.
Seeking undue precedence.
  Matt. 20:21.
Serving God for reward.
  Mal. 1:10.
God hates. Mal. 1:10.
Inconsistent with Christian love.
  1 Cor. 13:5.
Inconsistent with the communion of
  believers. Rom. 12:4–5, with
  1 Cor. 12:12–27.
Love of Christ should constrain us to
  avoid. 2 Cor. 5:14–15.
Ministers should be lacking.
  1 Cor. 9:19–23; 10:33.

SELF-RIGHTEOUSNESS

Believers renounce. Phil. 3:7–10.
Denunciation against.
  Matt. 23:27–28.
Folly of. Job 9:20.
Hateful to God. Luke 16:15.
Humans are prone to. Prov. 20:6;
  30:12.
Illustrated. Luke 18:10–12.
Is boastful. Matt. 23:30.

Is vain because our righteousness is
  Cannot bring salvation.
    Job 9:30–31; Matt. 5:20, with
    Rom. 3:20.
  No better than filthy rags.
    Isa. 64:6.
  Only external. Matt. 23:25–28;
    Luke 11:39–40.
  Only partial. Matt. 23:25;
    Luke 11:42.
  Unprofitable. Isa. 57:12.

They who are given to
  Are abominable before God.
    Isa. 65:5.
  Are pure in their own eyes.
    Prov. 30:12.
  Condemn others. Matt. 9:11–13;
    Luke 7:39.
  Consider their own way right.
    Prov. 21:2.
  Despise others. Isa. 65:5;
    Luke 18:9.
  Proclaim their own goodness.
    Prov. 20:6.
  Rashly approach God.
    Luke 18:11.
  Reject the righteousness of God.
    Rom. 10:3.
  Seek to justify themselves.
    Luke 10:29.
  Seek to justify themselves before
    others. Luke 16:15.
Warning against. Deut. 9:4.

SELF-WILL AND STUBBORNNESS

Characteristic of the wicked.
  Prov. 7:11; 2 Pet. 2:10.

Exhibited in
  Going backward and not forward.
    Jer. 7:24.
  Hardening the heart.
    2 Chron. 36:13.
  Hardening the neck. Neh. 9:16.
  Rebelling against God.
    Deut. 31:27; Ps. 78:8.
  Refusing to listen to God.
    Prov. 1:24.
  Refusing to listen to the
    messengers of God.
    1 Sam. 8:19; Jer. 44:16;
    Zech. 7:11.
  Refusing to listen to parents.
    Deut. 21:18–19.

Refusing to receive correction.
Deut. 21:18; Jer. 5:3; 7:28.

Refusing to walk in the ways of
God. Neh. 9:17; Ps. 78:10;
Isa. 42:24; Jer. 6:16.

Resisting the Holy Spirit.
Acts 7:51.

Walking in the counsels of an evil
heart. Jer. 7:24, with 23:17.

Forbidden. 2 Chron. 30:8;
Pss. 75:5; 95:8.

God knows. Isa. 48:4.

Heinousness of. 1 Sam. 15:23.

Illustrated. Ps. 32:9; Jer. 31:18.

Ministers should
Be without. Titus 1:7.

Pray that their people may be
forgiven for. Exod. 34:9;
Deut. 9:27.

Warn their people against.
Heb. 3:7–12.

Proceed from
An evil heart. Jer. 7:24.
Pride. Neh. 9:16, 29.
Unbelief. 2 Kings 17:14.

Punishment for. Deut. 21:21;
Prov. 29:1.

The wicked continue in. Judg. 2:19.

SENATE
The Sanhedrin. Acts 5:21.
Senator, an elder. Ps. 105:22.

The Sanhedrin

SENIOR CITIZEN

May be a time of danger or decline.
1 Kings 11:4; Ps. 71:9.

Should be a time of special blessing.
Prov. 22:6; Isa. 65:20; Acts 2:17.

A time of ripeness and fruition.
Ps. 92:14.

To be honored. Lev. 19:32;
Prov. 16:31.

SENSUALITY

Example of
The rich man. Luke 16:25.
Warning against. Jude 18.

SERGEANT

In Philippi. Acts 16:35, 38.

SERMON

Jesus' sermon on the mount.
Matt. 5;6; 7.

Jesus' sermon by the sea. Matt.
13:1–52.

SERPENTS

All kinds of, can be tamed.
James 3:7.

Called crooked. Job 26:13;
Isa. 27:1.

Characterized as subtle. Gen. 3:1;
Matt. 10:16.

Created by God. Job 26:13.

Cursed above all creatures.
Gen. 3:14.

Dangerous to travelers. Gen. 49:17.

Doomed to creep on their bellies.
Gen. 3:14.

Doomed to eat their food mingled
with dust. Gen. 3:14; Isa. 65:25;
Mic. 7:17.

Illustrative of
The devil. Gen. 3:1, with 2 Cor.
11:3; Rev. 12:9; 20:2.
Enemies who harass and destroy.
Isa. 14:29; Jer. 8:17.
Harmful effects of wine (by their
poisonous bite).
Prov. 23:31–32.
Hypocrites. Matt. 23:33.
Malice of the wicked (by their
sharp tongues). Ps. 140:3.
The tribe of Dan. Gen. 49:17.

Infest
Deserts. Deut. 8:15.
Hedges. Eccles. 10:8.
Holes in walls. Amos 5:19.
Human aversion and hatred to.
Gen. 3:15.
Many kinds of, poisonous.
Deut. 32:24; Ps. 58:4.

Miracles connected with
Israelites cured by looking at one
of brass. Num. 21:8–9;
John 3:14–15.
Moses' rod turned into.
Exod. 4:3; 7:9, 15.
Power over, given to the disciples.
Mark 16:18; Luke 10:19.
Often sent as a punishment.
Num. 21:6; Deut. 32:24;
1 Cor. 10:9.
Produced from eggs. Isa. 59:5.
Unclean and unfit for food.
Matt. 7:10.
Were often enchanted or fascinated.
Eccles. 10:11.

SERVANTS

Are inferior to their masters.
Luke 22:27.

To be honored. Gen. 24:31;
Prov. 27:18.

Characteristics of good
Adorn the doctrine of God their
Savior in all things. Titus 2:10.
Blessed by God. Matt. 24:46.
Bring God's blessing upon their
masters. Gen. 30:27, 30; 39:3.
Deserve the confidence of their
masters. Gen. 24:2, 4, 10;
39:4.
Fellow believers beloved in the
Lord. Philem. 1:16.
Guided by God. Gen. 24:7, 27.
Have God with them. Gen. 31:42;
39:21; Acts 7:9–10.
The Lord's freemen. 1 Cor. 7:22.
Often advanced by masters.
Gen. 39:4–5.
Often exalted. Gen. 41:40;
Prov. 17:2.
Partakers of gospel privileges.
1 Cor. 12:13; Gal. 3:28;
Eph. 6:8; Col. 3:11.
Prospered by God. Gen. 39:3.
Protected by God. Gen. 31:7.
Servants of Christ. Col. 3:24.
Will be rewarded. Eph. 6:8;
Col. 3:24.

Characteristics of wicked
Covetousness. 2 Kings 5:20.
Deceit. 2 Sam. 19:26;
Ps. 101:6–7.
Eye service. Eph. 6:6; Col. 3:22.
Gluttony. Matt. 24:49.
Lying. 2 Kings 5:22, 25.
Quarrelsomeness. Gen. 13:7;
26:20.
Stealing. Titus 2:10.
Unmerciful to their fellows.
Matt. 18:30.
Will be punished. Matt. 24:50.
Will not submit to correction.
Prov. 29:19.

Christ condescended to the office of.
Matt. 20:28; Luke 22:27;
John 13:5; Phil. 2:7.

Divided into
Female. Gen. 16:6; 32:5.
Hired. Mark 1:20; Luke 15:17.
Male. Gen. 24:34; 32:5.
Slave or bond. Gen. 43:18;
Lev. 25:46.

Duties of, to masters
Not to answer them rudely.
Titus 2:9.
Not to defraud them. Titus 2:10.
Not to serve them just to win favor
while they're watching.
Eph. 6:6; Col. 1:22.
To attend to their call. Ps. 123:2.
To be anxious for their welfare.
1 Sam. 25:14–17;
2 Kings 5:2–3.
To be earnest in transacting their
business. Gen. 24:54–56.
To be faithful to them.
Luke 16:10–12; 1 Cor. 4:2;
Titus 2:10.
To be industrious in laboring for
them. Neh. 4:16, 23.
To be kind and attentive to their
guests. Gen. 43:23–24.
To be profitable to them.
Luke 19:15–16, 18;
Philem. 1:11.
To be prudent in the management
of their affairs. Gen. 24:31–49.
To be subject to them.
1 Pet. 2:18.
To be submissive. Gen. 16:6, 9;
1 Pet. 2:18.
To bless God for mercies shown to
them. Gen. 24:27, 48.
To honor them. Mal. 1:6;
1 Tim. 6:1.

To obey them. Eph. 6:5;
Titus 2:9.

To please them well in all things.
Titus 2:9.

To pray for them. Gen. 24:12.

To prefer their business to their
own necessary food.
Gen. 24:33.

To revere them the more, when
they are believers. 1 Tim. 6:2.

To sympathize with them.
2 Sam. 12:18.

Early mention of. Gen. 9:25–26.

Hired

Anxiety of, for the end of their
day's work, alluded to. Job 7:2.

Called hirelings. Job 7:1;
John 10:12–13.

Engaged by the day. Matt. 20:2.

Engaged by the year. Lev. 25:53;
Isa. 16:14.

Hebrew slaves serving strangers to
be treated as. Lev. 25:39–40.

Hebrew slaves serving their
brethren to be treated as.
Lev. 25:39–40.

If foreigners not allowed to partake
of the Passover or holy things.
Exod. 12:45; Lev. 22:10.

Not to be oppressed. Deut. 24:14.

Often oppressed and their wages
kept back. Mal. 3:5; James 5:4.

Often stood in the marketplace
waiting for employment.
Matt. 20:1–3.

Often well fed and taken care of.
Luke 15:17.

To be considered worthy of their
pay. Luke 10:7.

To be paid without delay at the
expiration of their service.
Lev. 19:13; Deut. 24:15.

To partake of the produce of the
land in the sabbatical year.
Lev. 25:6.

Illustrations of bond

Believers. 1 Cor. 6:20; 7:23.

Christ. Ps. 40:6, with Heb. 10:5;
Phil. 2:7–8.

The wicked. 2 Pet. 2:19, with
Rom. 6:16, 19.

Persons devoted to God so called.
Ps. 119:49; Isa. 56:6; Rom. 1:1.

Persons devoted to the service of
another so called. Exod. 24:13;
1 Kings 19:21.

Persons of low condition so called.
Eccles. 10:7.

The property of masters increased by
faithful. Gen. 30:29–30.

Should be compassionate to their
fellows. Matt. 18:33.

Should be contented in their
situation. 1 Cor. 7:20–21.

Should follow Christ's example.
1 Pet. 2:21.

Should serve

For conscience toward God.
1 Pet. 2:19.

As doing the will of God from the
heart. Eph. 6:6.

In the fear of God. Eph. 6:5;
Col. 3:22.

With good will. Eph. 6:7.

As the servants of Christ.
Eph. 6:5–6.

In singleness of heart. Eph. 6:5;
Col. 3:22.

Wholeheartedly, as to the Lord,
and not to men. Eph. 6:7;
Col. 3:23.

Slave or bond

All Israelites sold as, to be free at the jubilee.
Lev. 25:10, 40–41, 54.

By birth. Gen. 14:14; Ps. 116:16; Jer. 2:14.

Called bondmen. Gen. 43:18; 44:9.

Captives taken in war often kept as. Deut. 20:14; 2 Kings 5:2.

Could not, when set free, demand wives or children procured during servitude. Exod. 21:3–4.

Crippled or injured by masters, to have their freedom.
Exod. 21:26–27.

Custom of branding alluded to. Gal. 6:17.

Engaged in the most menial offices. 1 Sam. 25:41; John 13:4–5.

Israelites sold as, refusing their liberty, to have their ears bored to the door. Exod. 21:5–6; Deut. 15:16–17.

Israelites sold to strangers as, might be redeemed by their nearest relative. Lev. 25:47–55.

Laws respecting marriage with female. Exod. 21:7–11.

Laws respecting, often violated. Jer. 34:8–16.

Laws respecting the killing of. Exod. 21:20–21.

Masters to be repaid for injury done to. Exod. 21:32.

More valuable than hired servants. Deut. 15:18.

Of others, not to be coveted or enticed away. Exod. 20:17; Deut. 5:21.

Persons belonging to other nations might be purchased as.
Lev. 25:44.

Persons of distinction had many. Gen. 14:14; Eccles. 2:7.

Persons unable to pay their debts liable to be sold as. 2 Kings 4:1; Neh. 5:4–5; Matt. 18:25.

By purchase. Gen. 17:27; 37:36.

Seeking protection, not to be delivered up to masters.
Deut. 23:15.

Seizing and stealing of men for, condemned and punished by the law. Exod. 21:16; Deut. 24:7; 1 Tim. 1:10.

Sometimes intermarried with their master's family.
1 Chron. 2:34–35.

Sometimes rose to rank. Eccles. 10:7.

Temporary residents in Israel might be purchased as.
Lev. 25:45.

Thieves unable to make restitution sold as. Exod. 22:3.

To be allowed to rest on the sabbath. Exod. 20:10.

To be furnished liberally, when their servitude expired.
Deut. 15:13–14.

To participate in all national rejoicings. Deut. 12:18; 16:11, 14.

When foreigners, to be circumcised. Gen. 17:13, 27; Exod. 12:44.

When Israelites, not to be treated ruthlessly. Lev. 25:39–40, 46.

When Israelites, to have their liberty after six years' service. Exod. 21:2; Deut. 15:12.

Subjects of a prince or king so called.
Exod. 9:20; 11:8.
The term often used to express
humility. Gen. 18:3; 33:5;
1 Sam. 20:7; 1 Kings 20:32.
When patient under injury,
acceptable to God.
1 Pet. 2:19–20.

SERVICE

Aiding Christ's followers.
Matt. 25:40.
Caring for one another. Gal. 5:13.
Dedication for. Isa. 6:8;
Rom. 12:1–2.
Doing good. Isa. 6:8.
Feeding the hungry. James 2:15–16.
Of God. Luke 1:74; Rom. 12:11.
Helping the weak. Rom. 15:1;
Acts 20:35.
Of the Lord. Eph. 6:7.
Through prayer. Heb. 12:12.

SERVICE, CIVIL

*Appointment in, on account of
merit*
Daniel, Hananiah, Mishael,
Azariah. Dan. 1:17–21.
Joseph. Gen. 39–41.
Jeroboam. 1 Kings 11:28.
Mordecai. Esther 6.1–11.
Corruption in. Neh. 5:15;
Dan. 6.4–17.
Disciples likened to.
Matt. 25:14–30.
Example of corruption, Pilate.
Mark 15:15.
Influence in. 1 Kings 1:11–31;
2 Kings 4:13.
Reform in. Neh. 5:14.
School for. Dan. 1:3–21.

SERVICE, COMMUNITY

Care for others
The homeless. Job 31:32;
Isa. 58:7.
The hungry. Isa. 58:7;
Matt. 25:25; Acts 6:1;
James 2:15–16.
Levites. Deut. 14:27, 29.
Orphans. Deut. 14:29.
The poor. Deut. 15:7–8.
Prisoners. Matt. 25:36.
The sick. Matt. 25:36.
Strangers. Lev. 19:10; Heb. 13:2.

Repair of infrastructure
Of city wall. Neh. 2:11–18;
Isa. 22:9.
Of roads. Isa. 40:3; 62:10.
Water supply. 2 Kings 20:20;
2 Chron. 26:10; Isa. 22:9.
Strive after the good of others.
Luke 10:29–37; Rom. 14:7–8;
1 Cor. 10:24; Phil 2:4.

SEVEN

Interesting facts concerning days
Consecration of priests and altars
lasted. Exod. 29:30–35.
Dedication of the temple lasted
double. 1 Kings 8:65.
Defilement lasted. Lev. 12:2.
The elders of Jabesh-gilead asked
for a truce of. 1 Sam. 11:3.
Ezekiel sits by the river Chebar in
astonishment. Ezek. 3:15.
Fasts of. 1 Sam. 31:13.
The feast of Ahasuerus continued.
Esther 1:5.
The feast of tabernacles lasted.
Lev. 23:34, 42.

The firstborn of flocks and sheep to remain with mother before being offered. Exod. 22:30.

The Israelites surrounded Jericho. Josh. 6:4.

Mourning for Jacob lasted. Gen. 50:10.

Mourning of Job. Job 2:13.

Noah and the ark before the flood. Gen. 7:4, 10.

Noah remains in the ark after sending out the dove. Ge 8:10, 12.

The Passover lasted. Exod. 12:15.

Paul tarries at Puteoli. Acts 28:14.

Paul tarries at Tyre. Acts 21:4.

The plague of bloody waters in Egypt lasted. Exod. 7:25.

Saul directed by Samuel to stay at Gilgal. 1 Sam. 10:8; 13:8.

Week consists of. Gen. 2:3; Exod. 20:11; Deut. 5:13–14.

Months

Holy convocations in the seventh month. Lev. 23:24–44; Num. 29; Ezek. 45:25.

Other instances of sevens

Abraham gives Abimelech seven lambs. Gen. 21:28.

Blood sprinkling seven times. Lev. 4:6.

Of clean beasts taken into the ark. Gen. 7:2.

Elijah's servant looks seven times for the appearance of rain. 1 Kings 18:43.

The heat of Nebuchadnezzar's furnace intensified sevenfold. Dan. 3:19.

The Israelites surrounded Jericho seven times, on the seventh day

sounding seven trumpets. Josh. 6:4.

The light of the sun intensified sevenfold. Isa. 30:26.

Naaman required to wash in Jordan seven times. 2 Kings 5:10.

Rams and bulls to the number of, required in sacrifices. Lev. 23:18.

Seven angels with seven plagues. Rev. 15:6.

Seven angels with seven trumpets. Rev. 8:2.

Seven churches in Asia Minor. Rev. 1:4, 20.

Scarlet-colored beast having seven heads. Rev. 17:3, 7.

Seven counselors at the court of Artaxerxes. Ezra 7:14.

Seven cows and seven ears of corn in Pharaoh's vision. Gen. 41:2–7.

Seven deacons in the early church. Acts 6:3.

Seven eunuchs at the court of Ahasuerus. Esther 1:10.

Seven eyes of the Lord. Zech. 3:9; 4:10; Rev. 5:6.

Seven golden bowls. Rev. 15:7.

Seven golden candlesticks. Rev. 1:12.

Seven heads and seven crowns. Rev. 12:3; 13:1; 17:9.

Seven horns and seven eyes. Rev. 5:6.

Seven kings. Rev. 17:9–10.

Seven lamps and pipes. Zech. 4:2.

Seven maidens given to Esther. Esther 2:9.

Seven magi. Prov. 26:16.

Seven plagues. Rev. 15:1.

Seven princes. Esther 1:14.

Seven seals. Rev. 5:1.

Seven shepherds to be sent forth
against Assyria. Mic. 5:5–6.

Seven spirits. Rev. 1:4; 3:1; 4:5;
5:6.

Seven stars. Rev. 1:16, 20.

Seven steps in the temple seen in
Ezekiel's vision.
Ezek. 40:22, 26.

Seven thunders. Rev. 10:3.

Seven women will seek
polygamous marriage. Isa. 4:1.

Silver purified seven times.
Ps. 12:6.

Symbolic of liberality.
Eccles. 11:1–2.

Symbolic of many sons.
Ruth 4:15.

The threatened sevenfold
punishment of Israel.
Lev. 26:18–21.

Worshiping seven times a day.
Ps. 119:164.

Years
Jacob serves for each of his wives.
Gen. 29:15–30.
Of plenty. Gen. 41:1–32, 53.
Famine lasted in Egypt.
Gen. 41:1–32, 54–56.
Famine lasted in Canaan.
2 Sam. 24:13.
Insanity of Nebuchadnezzar.
Dan. 4:32.
Seven times, the period between
jubilees. Lev. 25:8.

Weeks
In Daniel's vision concerning the
coming of the Messiah.
Dan. 9:25.
The period between the Passover
and Pentecost. Lev. 23:15.
Ten times. Dan. 9:24.

SEVENTY

The Jews in captivity in Babylon
seventy years. Jer. 25:11–12;
29:10; Dan. 9:2; Zech. 1:12; 7:5.

The senate of the Israelites
composed of seventy elders.
Exod. 24:1, 9;
Num. 11:16, 24–25.

Seventy disciples sent forth by Jesus.
Luke 10:1–17.

Seventy weeks in the vision of
Daniel. Dan. 9:24.

SEX
See Lust; Marriage

SEX OUTSIDE OF MARRIAGE
See also Premarital sex; Rape

Brings trouble. Prov. 6:24–32;
9:13–18.

Examples of
Amnon and Tamar.
2 Sam. 13:1–14.
David and Bathsheba.
2 Sam. 11:2–5.
Forbidden. Exod. 20:14;
Prov. 5:15–20; Matt. 5:27.
Judah and Tamar.
Gen. 38:12–26.
With prostitute. Prov. 7:6–23;
1 Cor. 6:13–20.
Lust equated with. Matt. 5:28.
Marriage partners one flesh.
Gen. 2:24; 1 Cor. 6:16–17.
Refused by Joseph. Gen. 39:7–18.

SHAME
Of Adam and Eve. Gen. 3:10.
Of the cross. Heb. 12:2.
Destitute of, the Israelites when they
worshipped the golden calf.
Exod. 32:25.

Jesus ashamed of those who deny Him. Luke 9:26.

The unjust. Zeph. 3:5.

SHAVING

Custom less common among Hebrews where beard was only trimmed. 2 Sam. 19:24; Ezek. 44:20.

SHEEP

Bleating of, alluded to. Judg. 5:16; 1 Sam. 15:14.

Clean and used as food. Deut. 14:4.

Constituted a great part of patriarchal wealth. Gen. 13:5; 25:35; 26:14.

Described as

Agile. Ps. 114:4, 6.

Covered with a fleece. Job 31:20.

Discerning. John 10:4–5.

Innocent. 2 Sam. 24:17.

Remarkably prolific. Pss. 107:41; 144:13; Song of Sol. 4:2; Ezek. 36:37.

False prophets assume the simple appearance of. Matt. 7:15.

Females of, called ewes. Ps. 78:71.

Firstborn of

Not to be dedicated as a freewill offering. Lev. 27:26.

Not to be redeemed. Num. 18:17.

Not to be shaved. Deut. 15:19.

First wool of, given to the priests. Deut. 18:4.

Flesh of, used extensively as food. 1 Sam. 25:18; 1 Kings 1:19; 4:23; Neh. 5:18; Isa. 22:13.

Flocks of

Attended by members of the family. Gen. 29:6; Exod. 2:16; 1 Sam. 16:11.

Attended by servants. 1 Sam. 17:20; Isa. 61:5.

Fed in the valleys. Isa. 65:10.

Fed on the mountains. Exod. 3:1; Ezek. 34:6, 13.

Fled from strangers. John 10:5.

Followed the shepherd. John 10:4, 27.

Frequently covered the pastures. Ps. 65:13.

Guarded by dogs. Job 30:1.

Kept in folds or pens. 1 Sam. 24:3; 2 Sam. 7:8; John 10:1.

Led to the richest pastures. Ps. 23:2.

Made to rest at noon. Ps. 23:2, with Song of Sol. 1:7.

Watered every day. Gen. 29:8–10; Exod. 2:16–17.

Frequently

Cut off by disease. Exod. 9:3.

Destroyed by wild beasts. Jer. 50:17; Mic. 5:8; John 10:12.

Given as presents. 2 Sam. 17:29; 1 Chron. 12:40.

Given as tribute. 2 Kings 3:4; 2 Chron. 17:11.

Taken in great numbers in war. Judg. 6:4; 1 Sam. 14:32; 1 Chron. 5:21; 2 Chron. 14:15.

Illustrative of

The Jews. Pss. 74:1; 78:52; 79:13.

The patience, etc., of Christ (in
their patience and simplicity).
Isa. 53:7.

The people of Christ.
John 10:7–26; 21:16–17;
Heb. 13:20; 1 Pet. 5:2.

Restored sinners (when found).
Luke 15:5, 7.

Separation of believers from the
wicked (when separated from
goats). Matt. 25:32–33.

Those under God's judgment.
Ps. 44:11.

Those who depart from God (in
their proneness to wander). Ps.
119:176; Isa. 53:6;
Ezek. 34:16.

The unregenerate (when lost).
Matt. 10:6.

The wicked (in their death).
Ps. 49:14.

Males of, called rams. 1 Sam. 15:23;
Jer. 51:40.

Under man's care from the earliest
age. Gen. 4:4.

Milk of, used as food. Deut. 32:14;
Isa. 7:21–22; 1 Cor. 9:7.

Offered in sacrifice from the earliest
age. Gen. 4:4; 8:20; 15:9–10.

Offered in sacrifice under the law.
Exod. 20:24; Lev. 1:10;
1 Kings 8:5, 63

Places celebrated for
Bashan. Deut. 32:14.
Bozrah. Mic. 2:12.
Kedar. Ezek. 27:21.
Nebaioth. Isa. 60:7.

Skins of, made into a covering for the
tabernacle. Exod. 25:5; 36:19;
39:34.

Skins of, worn as clothing by the
poor. Heb. 11:37.

Time of shearing, a time of rejoicing.
1 Sam. 25:2, 11, 36;
2 Sam. 13:23.

Tithe of, given to the Levites.
2 Chron. 31:4–6.

Washed and shorn every year.
Song of Sol. 4:2.

Wool of, made into clothing.
Job 31:20; Prov. 31:13;
Ezek. 34:3.

Young of, called lambs. Exod. 12:3;
Isa. 11:6.

SHEEPGATE
An ancient gate of Jerusalem.
Neh. 3:1, 32; 12:39; John 5:2.

SHEEP MARKET
Of Jerusalem. John 5:2.

SHEET
Of Peter's vision. Acts 10:11.

SHEKEL
Corrupted. Amos 8:5.

Of different standards: of the
sanctuary. Exod. 30:13.

Fees paid in. 1 Sam. 9:8.

Fines paid in. Deut. 22:19–29.

Fractions of, used in currency.
Neh. 10:32.

Sanctuary revenues paid in.
Exod. 30:13.

Used to weigh cinnamon.
Exod. 30:23.

Used to weigh gold. Gen. 24:22.

Used to weigh hair. 2 Sam. 14:26.

Used to weigh iron. 1 Sam. 17:7.

Used to weigh myrrh. Exod. 30:23.

Used to weigh rations. Ezek. 4:10.

Used to weigh silver. Josh. 7:21.

A weight, equal to 20 gerahs.
Exod. 30:13.

SHEKINAH

The visible sign of God's presence on
the ark of testimony in the Holy of
Holies. Exod. 25:22; Ps. 80:1;
Isa. 37:16; Heb. 9:5.

SHEPHERDS

An abomination to the Egyptians.
Gen. 46:34.

Assigned to younger sons, hirelings,
and slaves. 1 Sam. 16:11–13.

Care of sheep by, exhibited in
Attending them when sick.
Ezek. 34:16.

Defending them when attacked by
wild beasts. 1 Sam. 17:34–36;
Amos 3:12.

Going before and leading them.
Pss. 77:20; 78:52; 80:1.

Knowing them. John 10:14.

Numbering them when they return
from pasture. Jer. 33:13.

Searching them out when lost and
straying. Ezek. 34:12;
Luke 15:4–5.

Seeking out good pasture for
them. 1 Chron. 4:39–41;
Ps. 23:2.

Tenderness to the ewes in lamb,
and to the young.
Gen. 33:13–14; Ps. 78:71.

Watching over them by night.
Luke 2:8.

Carried a staff or rod. Lev. 27:32;
Ps. 23:4.

Early mention of. Gen. 4:2.

Had hired keepers under them.
1 Sam. 17:20.

Illustrative of
Bad ministers (when ignorant and
foolish). Isa. 56:11; Jer. 50:6;

Ezek. 34:2, 10; Zech. 11:7–8,
15–17.

Christ as the good shepherd. Ezek.
34:23; Zech. 13:7; John 10:14;
Heb. 13:20.

Christ seeking the lost (when
searching out straying sheep).
Ezek. 34:12; Luke 15:2–7.

God as leader of Israel. Pss. 77:20;
80:1.

Kings as the leaders of the people.
Isa. 44:28; Jer. 6:3; 49:19.

Ministers of the gospel. Jer. 23:4.

Tenderness of Christ (by their care
and tenderness). Isa. 40:11;
Ezek. 34:13–16.

Lived in tents while tending their
flocks. Song of Sol. 1:8;
Isa. 38:12.

Members of the family, both male
and female, acted as. Gen. 29:6;
1 Sam. 16:11; 17:15.

Unfaithfulness of hired hand, alluded
to. John 10:12.

Usually carried a staff or bag.
1 Sam. 17:40.

SHIELDS

A disgrace to lose or throw away.
2 Sam. 1:21.

Frequently made of or covered with
Brass. 1 Kings 14:27.
Gold. 2 Sam. 8:7; 1 Kings 10:17.

Illustrative of
Faith. Eph. 6:16.
Favor of God. Ps. 5:12.
Protection of God. Gen. 15:1;
Ps. 33:20.
Salvation of God. 2 Sam. 22:36;
Ps. 18:35.
Truth of God. Ps. 91:4.

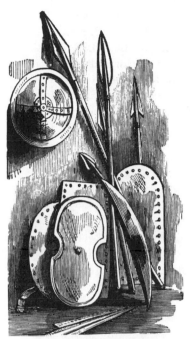

Ancient Shields and Spears

Kinds of

Large. 2 Chron. 9:15, with
1 Chron. 5:18; Ezek. 26:8.

Small shield. 2 Chron. 9:16.

Many of the Israelites used, with
expertness. 1 Chron. 12:8, 24,
34; 2 Chron. 14:8; 25:5.

Often carried by an armor bearer.
1 Sam. 17:7.

Part of defensive armor.
Ps. 115:9, with 140:7.

Provided by the kings of Israel in
great abundance. 2 Chron. 11:12;
26:14; 32:5.

Said to belong to God. Ps. 47:9.

Scarce in Israel in the days of
Deborah and Barak. Judg. 5:8.

In times of peace, hung up in towers
of armories. Ezek. 27:10, with
Song of Sol. 4:4.

Of the vanquished, often burned.
Ezek. 39:9.

Before war

Anointed. 2 Sam. 1:21, with Isa.
21:5.

Gathered together. Jer. 51:11.

Often made red. Nah. 2:3.

Repaired. Jer. 46:3.

Uncovered. Isa. 22:6.

SHIPS

Antiquity of, among the Jews.
Gen. 49:13; Judg. 5:17.

Commanded by a master. Jon. 1:6;
Acts 27:11.

Course of, frequently directed by the
heavenly bodies. Acts 27:20.

Course of, through the midst of the
sea, wonderful. Prov. 30:18–19.

Described as

Gallant. Isa. 33:21.

Large. James 3:4.

Strong. Isa. 23:14.

Swift. Job 9:26.

Employed in

Carrying passengers. Jon. 1:3;
Acts 27:2, 6; 28:11.

Fishing. Matt. 4:21; Luke 5:4–9;
John 21:3–8.

Trading. 1 Kings 22:48;
2 Chron. 8:18; 9:21.

War. Num. 24:24;
Dan. 11:30, 40.

Endangered by

Quicksands. Acts 27:17.

Rocks. Acts 27:29.

Storms. Jon. 1:4; Mark 4:37–38.

Generally propelled by sails.
Acts 27:2-7.

Generally made of the fir tree.
Ezek. 27:5.

Governed and directed by the helm.
James 3:4.

Guided in their course by pilots.
Ezek. 27:8, 27-29.

Illustrative of
Departure from the faith (when
wrecked). 1 Tim. 1:19.
Industrious women. Prov. 31:14.

Mentioned in Scripture
Adramyttium. Acts 27:2.
Alexandria. Acts 27:6.
Chaldea. Isa. 43:14.
Chittim. Num. 24:24;
Dan. 11:30.
Tarshish. Isa. 23:1; 60:9.
Tyre. 2 Chron. 8:18.

Navigated
Lakes. Luke 5:1-2.
The ocean. Pss. 104:26; 106:23.
Rivers. Isa. 33:21.

Often propelled by oars. Jon. 1:13;
John 6:19.

Often the property of individuals.
Acts 27:11.

Often wrecked. 1 Kings 22:48;
Ps. 48:7; Acts 27:41-44;
2 Cor. 11:25.

Parts of, mentioned
Anchors. Acts 27:29, 40.
Boats. Acts 27:30, 32.
Bow. Acts 27:30, 41.
Hind part or stern.
Acts 27:29, 41.
Hold or between the sides.
Jon. 1:5.
Mast. Isa. 33:23; Ezek. 27:5.
Oars. Isa. 33:21; Ezek. 27:6.

Rudder bands. Acts 27:40.
Rudder or helm. James 3:4.
Sails. Isa. 33:23; Ezek. 27:7.
Tackling. Isa. 33:23; Acts 27:19.

Probably originated from the ark
made by Noah. Gen. 7:17-18.

Seams of, calked. Ezek. 27:9, 27.

Solomon built a navy of.
1 Kings 9:26.

Sometimes made of papyrus.
Isa. 18:2.

Soundings usually taken for, in
dangerous places. Acts 27:28.

Stern of, occupied by passengers.
Mark 4:38.

Usually distinguished by signs or
figure heads. Acts 28:11.

When damaged, sometimes
undergirded with cables.
Acts 27:17.

Worked by mariners or sailors.
Ezek. 27:9, 27; Jon. 1:5;
Acts 27:30.

SHOES

The apostles prohibited from taking
for their journey more than the
pair they had on. Matt. 10:10;
Mark 6:9; Luke 10:4.

Bound around the feet with ratchets
or strings. John 1:27; Acts 12:8.

Called sandals. Mark 6:9; Acts 12:8.

Carrying for another, a degrading
office, only performed by slaves.
Matt. 3:11.

Customs connected with
A man who refused to marry a
deceased brother's wife
disgraced by her pulling off his
shoes. Deut. 25:9-10.
The right of redemption resigned
by a man's giving one of his

shoes to the nearest relative.
Ruth 4:7–8.
Early use of. Gen. 14:23.

Illustrative of
The beauty conferred on believers.
Song of Sol. 7:1, with
Luke 15:22.
Being engaged in war and
slaughter (when bloody).
1 Kings 2:5.
An degrading and menial
condition (when taken off). Isa.
47:2; Jer. 2:25.
The preparation of the gospel.
Eph. 6:15.
Subjection (when thrown over a
place). Pss. 60:8; 108:9.

The Jews
Never wore in mourning.
2 Sam. 15:30; Isa. 20:2–3;
Ezek. 24:17, 23.
Put off when they entered sacred
places. Exod. 3:5; Josh. 5:15.
Put on before beginning a journey.
Exod. 12:11.
Of Israel, preserved for forty years,
while journeying in the wilderness.
Deut. 29:5.

Of ladies of distinction
Often highly ornamental.
Song of Sol. 7:1.
Often made of badgers' skins.
Ezek. 16:10.
Probably often adorned with
chains. Isa. 3:18.
Often given as bribes. Amos 2:6;
8:6.
Soles of, sometimes plated with brass
or iron. Deut. 33:25.
Untying of, for another, a degrading
office. Mark 1:7; John 1:27.

Worn out by a long journey.
Josh. 9:5, 13.

SHEWBREAD
Cakes of fine flour (twelve).
Lev. 24:5.
Called hallowed bread. 1 Sam. 21:4.
Changed every Sabbath day.
Lev. 24:8.
Frankincense placed on. Lev. 24:7.
Had poles of acacia wood covered
with gold. Exod. 25:28.

Illustrative of
Christ as the Bread of life.
John 6:48.
The church. 1 Cor. 5:7; 10:17.
Materials for, provided by the people.
Lev. 24:8; Neh. 10:32–33.
Not lawful for any but priests to eat,
except in extreme cases.
1 Sam. 21:4–6, with Matt. 12:4.
Once removed from the table, given
to the priests. Lev. 24:9.
Placed in the north side of the
tabernacle. Exod. 40:22;
Heb. 9:2.
Placed in two rows on the table by
the priests. Exod. 25:30, 40:23;
Lev. 24:6.
Prepared by Levites. 1 Chron. 9:32;
23:29.

Table of
Covered with gold. Exod. 25:24.
Dimensions, etc., of. Exod. 25:23.
Directions for removing.
Num. 4:7.
Had an ornamental border.
Exod. 25:25.
Had dishes, spoons, covers, and
bowls of gold. Exod. 25:29.
Had rings of gold in the corners for
the poles. Exod. 25:26–27.

SHIBBOLETH
Used as a test in wartime.
Judg. 12:6.

SHOVEL
A utensil in the tabernacle.
Exod. 27:3; 1 Kings 7:40; Jer.
52:18.

SIBLING RIVALRY
Brothers in unity. Ps. 133:1.

Characteristics of
Brother betrays brother.
Matt. 10:21; Mark 13:12.
Brother born for adversity.
Prov. 17:17.

Examples of
Abimelech, Jotham, and brothers.
Judg. 9:1–57.
Absalom, Amnon, and Tamar.
2 Sam. 13:1–39.
✓Cain and Abel. Gen. 4:1–11.
David and Eliab.
1 Sam. 17:28–30.
Er and Onan. Gen. 38:1–10.
Jacob and Esau.
Gen. 25:22–28:9; 32:1–33:17;
Mal 1:2–3.
Joseph and brothers. Gen. 37,
39–50.
Leah and Rachel.
Gen. 29:16–30:24.
Moses, Aaron, and Miriam.
Num 12:1–15.
Prodigal son and older brother.
Luke 15:25–30.
Shem, Ham, and Japheth.
Gen. 9:20–27.
Solomon and Adonijah.
1 Kings 1:5–53.

SICKLE
An agricultural implement used for
cutting grain. Deut. 23:25;
Jer. 50:16; Mark 4:29.
Used in a figurative sense of the
judgment of God. Joel 3:13;
Rev. 14:14–19.

SICKNESS
The apostles endowed with power to
heal. Matt. 10:1.

Believers
Acknowledge that it comes from
God. Ps. 31:1–8;
Isa. 38:12, 15.
Are resigned under. Job 2:10.
Attribute recovery from to God.
Isa. 38:20.
Feel for others in. Ps. 35:13.
Mourn under, with prayer.
Isa. 38:14.
Praise God for recovery from.
Ps. 103:1–3; Isa. 38:19;
Luke 17:15.
Pray for recovery from.
Isa. 38:2–3.
Thank God publicly for recovery
from. Isa. 38:20; Acts 3:8.
Visit those in. Matt. 25:36.
Christ compassionate to those in.
Isa. 53:4, with Matt. 8:16–17.

Christ healed, by
Being present. Matt. 4:23; Mark
1:31.
Laying on of hands. Mark 6:5;
Luke 13:13.
Not being present. Matt. 8:13.
A touch. Matt. 8:3.
The touch of His garment.
Matt. 14:35–36; Mark 5:27–34.
A word. Matt. 8:8, 13.

Faith required in those healed of, by Christ. Matt. 9:28–29; Mark 5:34; 10:52.

God

Abandons the wicked to. Jer. 34:17.

Comforts believers in. Ps. 41:3.

Exhibits His love in healing. Isa. 38:17.

Exhibits His mercy in healing. Phil. 2:27.

Exhibits His power in healing. Luke 5:17.

Heals. Deut. 32:39; Ps. 103:3; Isa. 38:5, 9.

Hears the prayers of those in. Pss. 30:2; 107:18–20.

Often manifests saving grace to sinners during. Job 33:19–24; Ps. 107:17–21.

Permits believers to be tried by. Job 2:5–6.

Persecutes the wicked by. Jer. 29:18.

Preserves believers in time of. Ps. 91:3–7.

Promises to heal. Exod. 23:25; 2 Kings 20:5.

Strengthens believers in. Ps. 41:3.

God's aid should be sought in. 2 Chron. 16:12.

Healing of, lawful on the Sabbath. Luke 13:14–16.

Illustrates sin. Lev. 13:45–46; Isa. 1:5; Jer. 8:22; Matt. 9:12.

Not visiting those in, an evidence of not belonging to Christ. Matt. 25:43, 45.

Often brought on by drunkenness. Hos. 7:5.

Often incurable by human means. Deut. 28:27; 2 Chron. 21:18.

Often sent as a punishment of sin. Lev. 26:14–16; 2 Chron. 21:12–15; 1 Cor. 11:30.

One of God's four dreadful judgments on a guilty land. Ezek. 14:19–21.

The power of healing, one of the miraculous gifts given to the early church. 1 Cor. 12:9, 30; James 5:14–15.

Pray for those afflicted with. Acts 28:8; James 5:14–15.

Sent by

The devil. Job 2:6–7; Luke 9:39; 13:16.

God. Deut. 28:59–61; 32:39; 2 Sam. 12:15; Acts 12:23.

Visiting those in, an evidence of belonging to Christ. Matt. 25:34, 36, 40.

The wicked

Do not visit those in. Matt. 25:43.

Forsake those in. 1 Sam. 30:13.

Have much sorrow, etc., with. Eccles. 5:17.

SIEGE

Battering rams used in. 2 Sam. 20:15; Ezek. 4:2; 21:22.

Cannibalism in. 2 Kings 6:28–29.

Conducted by erecting embankments parallel to the walls of besieged city. Deut. 20:19–20; Isa. 29:3; 37:33.

Examples of

Abel. 2 Sam. 20:15.

Gibbethon. 1 Kings 15:27.

Jericho. Josh. 6.

Jerusalem, by David. 2 Sam. 5:6, 9.

Jerusalem, by Nebuchadnezzar.
2 Kings 24:10–11; Dan. 1:1;
2 Kings 25:1–3; Jer. 52.
Jerusalem, by Rezin, king of Syria,
and Pekah, son of Remaliah,
king of Israel. 2 Kings 16:5.
Jerusalem, by the children of
Judah. Judg. 1:8.
Jerusalem, by Sennacherib.
2 Chron. 32:1–23.
Rabbah. 2 Sam. 11:1.
Samaria. 1 Kings 20:1;
2 Kings 6:24; 17:5; 18:9–11.
Tirzah. 1 Kings 16:17.
Offer of peace must be made to the
city before beginning.
Deut. 20:10–12.
The stress of the inhabitants during.
2 Kings 6:24–29; 25:3; Isa. 9:20;
36:12; Jer. 9:19.

SIEVE

Used in a figurative sense. Isa. 30:28;
Amos 9:9; Luke 22:31.

SIGN

Asked for by, and given to, Abraham.
Gen. 15:8–17.
Given to Gideon.
Judg. 6:17, 36–40.
Given to Hezekiah. 2 Kings 20:8.
Given to Jeroboam. 1 Kings 13:3–5.
Given to Moses. Exod. 4:1–9.
Given to Zacharias. Luke 1:18.
A miracle to confirm faith.
John 2:11; 3:2; 4:48.
A sign of coming events.
Matt. 16:3–4; 24:3.

SIGNAL

Used in war. Isa. 18:3.

SILVER

Abundant during the reign of
Solomon. 1 Kings 10:21–22, 27;
2 Chron. 9:20–21, 27.

Called, when purified
Choice silver. Prov. 8:19.
Refined silver. 1 Chron. 29:4.
Comparative value of. Isa. 60:17.

Described as
Fusible. Ezek. 22:20, 22.
Malleable. Jer. 10:9.
White and shining. Ps. 68:13–14.
Found in the earth in veins. Job 28:1.
Generally found in an impure state.
Prov. 25:4.
Given by David and his subjects for
making the temple.
1 Chron. 28:14; 29:2, 6–9.
Given by the Israelites for making the
tabernacle. Exod. 25:3; 35:24.

Illustrative of
Believers purified by affliction.
Ps. 66:10; Zech. 13:9.
Diligence required for attaining
knowledge (in the labor of
seeking it). Prov. 2:4.
Good rulers. Isa. 1:22–23.
Medo-Persian kingdom.
Dan. 2:32, 39.
The tongue of the righteous.
Prov. 10:20.
The wicked (by its impurities).
Isa. 1:22; Ezek. 22:18.
The wicked (when depraved).
Jer. 6:30.
The words of the Lord. Ps. 12:6.

Made into
Beds or couches. Esther 1:6.
Bowls. Num. 7:13, 84.
Candlesticks. 1 Chron. 28:15.
Chains. Isa. 40:19.

Cups. Gen. 44:2.

Dishes. Num. 7:13, 84, 85.

Idols. Ps. 115:4; Isa. 2:20; 30:22.

Instruments. 2 Sam. 8:10;
Ezra 6:5.

Ornaments and hooks for the
pillars of the tabernacle.
Exod. 27:17; 38:19.

Ornaments for the person.
Exod. 3:22.

Sockets for the boards of the
tabernacle. Exod. 26:19, 25,
32; 36:24, 26, 30, 36.

Tables. 1 Chron. 28:16.

Thin plates. Jer. 10:9.

Wires (alluded to). Eccles. 12:6.

Often given as presents.
1 Kings 10:25; 2 Kings 5:5, 23.

Patriarchs rich in. Gen. 13:2; 24:35.

Purified by fire. Prov. 17:3;
Zech. 13:9.

Taken in war, often consecrated to
God. Josh. 6:19; 2 Sam. 8:11;
1 Kings 15:15.

Taken in war, purified by fire.
Num. 31:22–23.

Tarshish carried on extensive
commerce in. Jer. 10:9;
Ezek. 27:12.

Tribute often paid in.
2 Chron. 17:11; Neh. 5:15.

Used as money from the earliest age.
Gen. 23:15–16; 37:28;
1 Kings 16:24.

Wisdom to be valued more than. Job
28:15; Prov. 3:14; 8:10, 19;
16:16.

Working in, a trade. Acts 19:24.

SIMONY

Ecclesiastical corruption.
Acts 8:18–19.

SIMPLICITY

Beware of being corrupted from that
which is in Christ. 2 Cor. 11:3.

Exhortation to. Rom. 16:19;
1 Pet. 2:2.

Illustrated. Matt. 6:22.

Necessity for. Matt. 18:2–3.

Opposed to fleshly wisdom.
2 Cor. 1:12.

Should be exhibited
In acts of benevolence.
Rom. 12:8.

In all our conduct. 2 Cor. 1:12.

Concerning evil. Rom. 16:19.

Concerning malice. 1 Cor. 14:20.

Concerning our own wisdom.
1 Cor. 3:18.

In preaching the gospel.
1 Thess. 2:3–7.

Those who have the grace of
Are made wise by God.
Matt. 11:25.

Are made wise by the Word of
God. Pss. 19:7; 119:130.

Are preserved by God. Ps. 116:6.

Made cautious by instruction.
Prov. 1:4.

Profit by the correction of others.
Prov. 19:25; 21:11.

SIN

See also Sin, Confession of; Sin,
Conviction of; Sin, Forgiveness of;
Sin, Remission of; Sins, National;
Sin, Unpardonable

All men conceived and born in.
Gen. 5:3; Job 15:14; 25:4; Ps.
51:5.

All the imaginations of the
unregenerated heart are.
Gen. 6:5; 8:21.

All unrighteousness is. 1 John 5:17.

Believers
Ashamed of having committed.
Rom. 6:21.
Cannot live in. 1 John 3:9; 5:18.
Dead to. Rom. 6:2, 11; 1
Pet. 2:24.
Despise themselves because of.
Job 42:6; Ezek. 20:43.
Have still the remains of, in them.
Rom. 7:17, 23, with Gal. 5:17.
Made free from. Rom. 6:18.
Profess to have ceased from.
1 Pet. 4:1.
Resolve against. Job 34:32.
Blessings withheld because of.
Jer. 5:25.
Christ alone was without.
2 Cor. 5:21; Heb. 4:15; 7:26;
1 John 3:5.
Christ's blood cleanses from.
1 John 1:7.
Christ's blood redeems from.
Eph. 1:7.
Christ came to take away.
John 1:29; 1 John 3:5.
Death the punishment of. Gen. 2:17;
Ezek. 18:4.
Death the wages of. Rom. 6:23.

Described as
The abominable thing that God
hates. Prov. 15:9; Jer. 44:4, 11.
Blaming the Lord. Num. 15:30;
Ps. 74:18.
Coming from the heart.
Matt. 15:19.
Dead works. Heb. 6:1; 9:14.
Deceitful. Heb. 3:13.
Defiling. Prov. 30:12; Isa. 59:3.
Disgraceful. Prov. 14:34.
The fruit of lust. James 1:15.
A hindrance. Heb. 12:1.

Like scarlet and crimson.
Isa. 1:18.
Often numerous. Amos 5:12.
Often mighty. Amos 5:12.
Often presumptuous. Ps. 19:13.
Often very great. Exod. 32:30;
1 Sam. 2:17.
Reaching to heaven. Rev. 18:5.
Rebellion against God. Deut. 9:7;
Josh. 1:18.
Sometimes open and obvious.
1 Tim. 5:24.
Sometimes secret. Ps. 90:8;
1 Tim. 5:24.
The sting of death. 1 Cor. 15:56.
Works of darkness. Eph. 5:11.
Of the devil. 1 John 3:8, with John
8:44.
Entered into the world by Adam.
Gen. 3:6–7, with Rom. 5:12.
Excludes from heaven.
1 Cor. 6:9–10; Gal. 5:19–21;
Eph. 5:5; Rev. 21:27.
Fear of God restrains. Exod. 20:20;
Ps. 4:4; Prov. 16:6.

God
Alone can forgive. Exod. 34:7;
Dan. 9:9; Mic. 7:18; Mark 2:7.
Has opened a fountain for.
Zech. 13:1.
Hates. Deut. 25:16;
Prov. 6:16–19.
Is provoked to anger by.
1 Kings 16:2.
Is provoked to jealousy by.
1 Kings 14:22.
Punishes. Isa. 13:11; Amos 3:2.
Repays. Jer. 16:18; Rev. 18:6.
Remembers. Rev. 18:5.
Watches. Job 10:14.
God's Word keeps us from.
Pss. 17:4; 119:11.

Ground cursed because of.
  Gen. 3:17–18.
Guilt of concealing. Job 31:33;
  Prov. 28:13.
The Holy Spirit convinces of.
  John 16:8–9.
If we say that we have no, we deceive
  ourselves, and the truth is not in
  us. 1 John 1:8.
If we say that we have no, we make
  God a liar. 1 John 1:10.
Knowingly doing wrong.
  Luke 12:47; John 15:22.

The Law
  Curses those guilty of. Gal. 3:10.
  Gives knowledge of. Rom. 3:20;
    7:7.
  Is the strength of. 1 Cor. 15:56.
  Is transgressed by every.
    James 2:10–11, with
    1 John 3:4.
  By its strictness stirs up.
    Rom. 7:5, 8, 11.
  Made to restrain. 1 Tim. 1:9–10.
  Shows exceeding sinfulness of.
    Rom. 7:13.

Leads to
  Alarm. Ps. 38:3.
  Disease. Job 20:11.
  Shame. Rom. 6:21.
Ministers should warn the wicked to
  forsake. Ezek. 33:9; Dan. 4:27.
No one can atone for. Mic. 6:7.
No one is without. 1 Kings 8:46;
  Eccles. 7:20.
Omission of what we know to be
  good is. James 4:17.
People cannot cleanse themselves
  from. Job 9:30–31; Prov. 20:9;
  Jer. 2:22.
Prayer hindered by. Ps. 66:18;
  Isa. 59:2.

Scripture concludes all under.
  Gal. 3:22.
Shame belongs to those guilty of.
  Dan. 9:7–8.

Should be
  Avoided even in appearance.
    1 Thess. 5:22.
  Confessed. Job 33:27;
    Prov. 28:13.
  Departed from. Ps. 34:14;
    2 Tim. 2:19.
  Despised. Rom. 12:9.
  Fought. Heb. 12:4.
  Guarded against. Pss. 4:4; 39:1.
  Hated. Ps. 97:10; Prov. 8:13;
    Amos 5:15.
  Mortified. Rom. 8:13; Col. 3:5.
  Mourned over. Ps. 38:18;
    Jer. 3:21.
  Put away. Job 11:14.
  Totally destroyed. Rom. 6:6.
Throw off. Heb. 12:1.
The thought of foolishness is.
  Prov. 24:9.
Toil and sorrow originated in.
  Gen. 3:16–17, 19, with Job 14:1.
Transgression of the Law.
  1 John 3:4.

We should pray to God
  To cleanse us from. Ps. 51:2.
  To deliver us from. Matt. 6:13.
  To forgive our. Exod. 34:9;
    Luke 11:4.
  To keep us from. Ps. 19:13.
  To make us know our. Job 13:23.
  To search for, in our hearts.
    Ps. 139:23–24.
Whatever is not of faith is.
  Rom. 14:23.
When finished brings about death.
  James 1:15.

The wicked
Boast of. Isa. 3:9.
Cannot cease from. 2 Pet. 2:14.
Dead in. Eph. 2:1.
Defy God in committing.
Isa. 5:18–19.
Delight in those who commit.
Ps. 10:3; Hos. 7:3; Rom. 1:32.
Encourage themselves in. Ps 64:5.
Encouraged in by prosperity.
Job 21:7–15; Prov. 10:16.
Excuse. Gen. 3:12–13;
1 Sam. 15:13–15.
Expect impunity in.
Pss. 10:11; 50:21; 94:7.
Guilty of, in everything they do.
Prov. 21:4; Ezek. 21:24.
Heap up. Ps. 78:17; Isa. 30:1.
Led by despair to continue in.
Jer. 2:25; 18:12.
Mock at. Prov. 14:9.
Make excuses for.
1 Sam. 13:11–12.
Servants to. John 8:34;
Rom. 6:16.
Tempt others to. Gen. 3:6;
1 Kings 16:2; 21:25;
Prov. 1:10–14.
Throw the blame of, on God.
Gen. 3:12; Jer. 7:10.
Throw the blame of, on others.
Gen. 3:12–13;
Exod. 32:22–24.
Try to conceal, from God. Gen.
3:8, 10, with Job 31:33.
Will bear the shame of. Ezek.
16:52.
Will find out the wicked.
Num. 32:23.

SINCERITY
Blessedness of. Ps. 32:2.

A characteristic of the doctrines of
the gospel. 1 Pet. 2:2.
Christ an example of. 1 Pet. 2:22.
Exhortations to. Ps. 34:13;
1 Cor. 5:8; 1 Pet. 2:1.
The gospel sometimes preached
without. Phil. 1:16.
Ministers should exemplify.
Titus 2:7.
Opposed to human wisdom.
2 Cor. 1:12.
Pray for, on behalf of others.
Phil. 1:10.

Should characterize
Our faith. Tim. 1:5.
Our love to Christ. Eph. 6:24.
Our love to God. 2 Cor. 8:8, 24.
Our love for one another.
Rom. 12:9; 1 Pet. 1:22; 1 John
3:18.
Our service to God. Josh. 24:14;
John 4:23–24.
Our whole conduct. 2 Cor. 1:12.
The preaching of the gospel.
2 Cor. 2:17; 1 Thess. 2:3–5.
The wicked lack. Pss. 5:9; 55:21.

SIN, CONFESSION OF
Exhortation to. Josh. 7:19;
Jer. 3:13; James 5:16.
Followed by forgiveness. Ps. 32:5;
1 John 1:9.
God regards. Job 33:27, 28;
Dan. 9:20, etc.
God requires. Lev. 5:5; Hos. 5:15.
Illustrated. Luke 15:21; 18:13.
Promises to. Lev. 26:40–42;
Prov. 28:13.

Should be accompanied with
Forsaking sin. Prov. 28:13.
Godly sorrow. Ps. 38:18;
Lam. 1:20.

Prayer for forgiveness.
2 Sam. 24:10; Pss. 25:11;
51:1; Jer. 14:7–9, 20.
Restitution. Num. 5:6–7.
Self–abasement. Isa. 64:5–6;
Jer. 3:25.
Submission to punishment.
Lev. 26:41; Ezra 9:13;
Neh. 9:33.
Should be full and unreserved.
Pss. 32:5; 51:3; 106:6.

SIN, CONVICTION OF
Adam and Eve, after their
disobedience. Gen. 3:8–10.
Belshazzar, when Nebuchadnezzar
saw part of the hand that wrote on
the wall. Dan. 5:6.
Darius, when Daniel was in the lions'
den. Dan. 6:18.
David, after the plagues sent on
account of his numbering the
people. 1 Chron. 21:30.
The death of the ten spies and their
being sentenced to wander forty
years. Num. 14:39–40.
Felix, under the preaching of Paul.
Acts 24:25.
Herod, when he heard of the fame of
Jesus. Matt. 14:2; Mark 6:14;
Luke 9:7.
Israelites, after being bitten by fiery
serpents. Num. 21:7.
The Israelites, after worshiping the
golden calf. Exod. 33:4.
Jews, when Jesus commanded the
guiltless man to cast the first stone
at the woman taken in adultery.
John 8:9.
Jonah, in the whale's belly. Jon. 2.
Joseph's brothers on account of their
cruelty to him. Gen. 42:21–22;
44:16; 45:3; 50:15–21.

Judas, after his betrayal of Jesus.
Matt. 27:3–5.
Ninevites at the preaching of Jonah.
Jon. 3; Matt. 12:41; Luke 11:32.
Pharaoh, after the death of his
firstborn. Exod. 12:31.
Pharaoh, after the plague of hail.
Exod. 9:27–28.
Pharaoh, after the plague of locust.
Exod. 10:16–17.
Philippian jailor, after the
earthquake. Acts 16:30.
Sailors, after casting Jonah into the
sea. Jon. 1:16.
Saul, after sparing Agag and the best
of the spoils. 1 Sam. 15:24.
Saul of Tarsus, when he saw Jesus on
the way to Damascus. Acts 9:1–6.
The widow of Zarephath, when her
son died. 1 Kings 17:18.

SIN, FORGIVENESS OF
Accomplished by the cross.
Col. 1:14; Heb. 9:22.
Based on God's grace. Luke 7:42.
Conditioned by attitude toward
others. Matt. 6:12; Mark 11:25.
Connected with repentance.
Acts 2:38.
Found in God. Ps. 130:4; Dan. 9:9.
Granted by Christ. Luke 7:47;
Matt. 2:5.
Received through Christ.
1 John 2:12.

SIN OFFERING
See Offering, Sin

SIN, REMISSION OF
Baptism to accompany. Acts 2:38.
Blessing accompanies. Ps. 32:1.
Christian fellowship may grant.
John 20:22–23.

Confession necessary for.
1 John 1:9.

Faith receives. Acts 10:43.

Lack of a forgiving spirit negates.
Matt. 6:15.

Repentance is required for.
Mark 1:4; Acts 2:38.

Secured through Christ's blood.
Matt. 26:28; 1 Cor. 15:3.

SINS, NATIONAL

Aggravated by privileges. Isa. 5:4–7;
Ezek. 20:11–13; Amos 2:4;
3:1–2; Matt. 11:21–24.

Believers especially mourn over.
Ps. 119:136; Ezek. 9:4.

Bring down national judgments.
Matt. 23:35–36; 27:25.

Cause the withdrawal of privileges.
Lam. 2:9; Amos 8:11;
Matt. 23:37–39.

Defile
The land. Lev. 18:25;
Num. 35:33–34; Ps. 106:38;
Isa. 24:5; Mic. 2:10.
National worship. Isa. 1:10–15;
Amos 5:21–22; Hag. 2:14.
The people. Lev. 18:21;
Ezek. 14:11.

Denunciations against. Isa. 1:24;
30:1; Jer. 5:9; 6:27–30.

Lead the heathen to blaspheme.
Ezek. 36:20, 23; Rom. 2:24.

Ministers should
Mourn over. Ezra 10:6;
Jer. 13:17; Ezek. 6:11;
Joel 2:17.
Pray for forgiveness of.
Exod. 32:31–32; Joel 2:17.
Testify against. Isa. 30:8–9; 58:1;
Ezek. 2:3–5; 22:2; Jon. 1:2.

Try to turn the people from. Jer.
23:22.

National prayer rejected on account
of. Isa. 1:15; 59:2.

National worship rejected on account
of. Isa. 1:10–14; Jer. 6:19–20;
7:9–14.

Often caused and encouraged by
rulers. 1 Kings 12:26–33; 14:16;
2 Chron. 21:11–13; Prov. 29:12.

Often caused by prosperity.
Deut. 32:15; Neh. 9:28;
Jer. 48:11; Ezek. 16:49; 28:5.

Pervade all ranks. Isa. 1:5; Jer.
5:1–5; 6:13.

Punishment for. Isa. 3:8; Jer. 12:17;
25:12; Ezek. 28:7–10.

Punishment for, avoided on
repentance. Judg. 10:15–16;
2 Chron. 12:6–7;
Ps. 106:43–46; Jon. 3:10.

A reproach to a people. Prov. 14:34.

Should be
Confessed. Lev. 26:40;
Deut. 30:2; Judg. 10:10;
1 Kings 8:47–48.
Mourned over. Joel 2:12.
Regretted. Jer. 18:8; Jon. 3:5.
Turned from. Isa. 1:16;
Hos. 14:1–2; Jon. 3:10.

SIN, UNPARDONABLE

Of Manasseh. 2 Kings 24:4.

Israel. Numbers 14:26–45.

Eli's house. 1 Sam. 3:14.

Jesus' teaching concerning.
Matt. 12:31–32; Luke 12:10.

Warning against. Heb. 6:4–6.

SKEPTICISM

Job. Job 21:15; 22:17.

Pharaoh. Exod. 5:2.

Thomas. John 20:25–28.

SKIN

Clothes of. Gen. 3:21.
For covering the tabernacle.
    Exod. 25:5.
Diseases of. Lev. 13:38–39; Job 7:5.

SLANDER

An abomination to God.
    Prov. 6:16, 19.
A characteristic of the devil.
    Rev. 12:10.

Believers
    Blessed in enduring. Matt. 5:11.
    Characterized as avoiding.
        Ps. 15:1, 3.
    Exposed to. Pss. 38:12; 109:2;
        1 Pet. 4:4.
    Should be warned against.
        Titus 3:1–2.
    Should give no occasion for.
        1 Pet. 2:12; 3:16.
    Should keep their tongue from.
        Ps. 34:13, with 1 Pet. 3:10.
    Should lay aside. Eph. 4:31;
        1 Pet. 2:1.
    Should return good for.
        1 Cor. 4:13.
Christ exposed to. Ps. 35:11;
    Matt. 26:60.
Comes from the evil heart.
    Matt. 15:19; Luke 6:45.
A deceitful work. Ps. 52:2.
Destructive. Prov. 11:9.

Effects of
    Deadly wounds. Prov. 18:8;
        26:22.
    Discord among believers.
        Prov. 6:19.
    Murder. Ps. 31:13; Ezek. 22:9.
    Separating friends.
        Prov. 16:28; 17:9.
    Strife. Prov. 26:20.

End of, is mischievous madness.
    Eccles. 10:13.
Evokes anger. Prov. 25:23.
Forbidden. Exod. 23:1; Eph. 4:31;
    James 4:11.
Hypocrites addicted to. Prov. 11:9.
Idleness leads to. 1 Tim. 5:13.
Illustrated. Prov. 12:18; 25:18.

Includes
    Babbling. Eccles. 10:11.
    Backbiting. Rom. 1:30;
        2 Cor. 12:20.
    Bearing false witness.
        Exod. 20:16; Deut. 5:20;
        Luke 3:14.
    Conceit. 1 Tim. 6:4.
    Defaming. Jer. 20:10;
        1 Cor. 4:13.
    Evil speaking. Pss. 41:5; 109:20.
    Gossiping. 1 Tim. 5:13.
    Raising false reports. Exod. 23:1.
    Repeating matters. Prov. 17:9.
    Slandering. James 4:11–12.
    Tale-bearing. Lev. 19:16.
    Whispering. Rom. 1:29;
        2 Cor. 12:20.
Ministers exposed to. Rom. 3:8;
    1 Cor. 6:8.
Ministers' wives should avoid.
    1 Tim. 3:11.
Nearest relations exposed to.
    Ps. 50:20.
Often arises from hatred. Pss. 41:7;
    109:3.
People will give account for.
    Matt. 12:36; James 1:26.
Punishment for. Deut. 19:16–21;
    Ps. 101:5.
Rulers exposed to. 2 Pet. 2:10;
    Jude 1:8.
Should not be listened to.
    1 Sam. 24:9.

Those who indulge in are fools.
Prov. 10:18.
Those who indulge in, not to be
trusted. Jer. 9:4.
Tongue of, lashes. Job 5:21.
Venomous. Ps. 140:3;
Eccles. 10:11.
The wicked addicted to. Ps. 50:20;
Jer. 6:28; 9:4.
The wicked love. Ps. 52:4.
Women warned against. Titus 2:3.

SLEEP
From God. Ps. 127:2.
Of Jesus. Matt. 8:24.
Of the sluggard. Prov. 6:9–10.
A symbol of death. Job 14:12;
Mark 5:39; 1 Thess. 4:14.

SLIME
See Tar

SLING
David kills Goliath with.
1 Sam. 17:40–50.
Skilled use of. Judg. 20:16.
Used for throwing stones.
Prov. 26:8.
Used in war. 2 Chron. 26:14.

SLOTHFULNESS
See Laziness

SLUGGARD
Can learn from the ant.
Prov. 6:6–11.

SNOW
On Mount Lebanon. Jer. 18:14.
In Palestine. 2 Sam. 23:20.
In Uz. Job 6:16.
Used in a figurative sense, of purity.
Ps. 51:7; Isa. 1:18; Lam. 4:7.

SOAP
A washing compound. Jer. 2:22;
Mal. 3:2.

SOBRIETY
Commanded. 1 Pet. 1:13; 5:8.
The gospel designed to teach.
Titus 2:11–12.
Motives to. 1 Pet. 4:7; 5:8.

Required in
All believers. 1 Thess. 5:6, 8.
Ministers. 1 Tim. 3:2–3; Titus 1:8.
Older men. Titus 2:2.
Wives of ministers. 1 Tim. 3:11.
Young men. Titus 2:6.
Young women. Titus 2:4.
We should estimate our character
and talents with. Rom. 12:3.
We should live in. Titus 2:12.
With prayer. 1 Pet. 4:7.
With watchfulness. 1 Thess. 5:6.
Women should exhibit, in dress.
1 Tim. 2:9.

SOCIALISM

Principles relevant to
Common ownership. Acts 4:32.
Distribution of goods according to
need. Acts 2:45; 4:35.
Division of land according to need.
Num. 26:52–56.
Return of land to original owner.
Lev. 25.

SOLDIERS
Of the Christian. Eph. 6:11–17;
2 Tim. 2:3.
Come to John the Baptist.
Luke 3:14.
Cowards excused from duty as.
Deut. 20:8; Judg. 7:3.
Crucified Jesus. Mark 15:16–24.

Dressed in scarlet. Nah. 2:3.
Guard prisoners. Acts 12:4–6;
28:16.
Guard the tomb.
Matt. 27:65; 28:11–15.
Jesus called Captain of our salvation.
Heb. 2:10.
Maintain the peace. Acts 21:31–35.
Military enrollment of Israel in the
wilderness of Sinai. Num. 1; 2.
Mock Jesus. Matt. 27:27–31.
Officers concerned in the betrayal of
Jesus. Luke 22:4.
Others exempt from service.
Deut. 20:5–9; 24:5.
Perform escort duty. Acts 21:31–33,
35; 22:24–28; 23:23, 31–33;
27:1, 31, 42, 43; 28:16.
In the plains of Moab. Num. 26.
Supports the entire army with food.
Judg. 20:10.
Their duty as guards. Acts 12:19.
Used in figurative sense, of divine
protection. Isa. 59:16–17.

SON
Figurative, of man's relationship to
God. Exod. 4:22.

SON-IN-LAW
Faithful, Peter. Mark 1:29–30.
Unjust, Jacob. Gen. 30:37–42.

SONG
Didactic. Deut. 32.
Gift of a new. Pss. 33:3; 40:3;
Isa. 42:10.
In glad worship. Ps. 100:2.
God gives. Ps. 77:6.
Impersonation of the church.
Song of Sol. 1–8.
The Lord is our. Exod. 15:2;
Job 30:9.

Of Moses and the Lamb.
Rev. 15:3–4.
Of the redeemed. Rev. 14:2, 3–5.
Of redemption. Rev. 5:9–10.
Of salvation. Ps. 32:7; Isa. 35:6.
Solomon wrote 1,005.
1 Kings 4:32.
Spiritual, singing of, commanded.
Eph. 5:19; Col. 3:16.
Sung at Passover. Matt. 26:30.
War. Exod. 15:1–21.

SORCERY
Belongs to works of the sinful nature.
Gal. 5:20.
Denounced. Isa. 8:19; Mal. 3:5.
Divining by familiar spirits.
Lev. 20:27.
Forbidden. Lev. 19:26–28, 31;
20:6; Deut. 18:9–14.
Futility of. Isa. 44:25.
By images. 2 Kings 23:24.
By livers. Ezek. 21:21.

Practiced by
Astrologers. Jer. 10:2.
Babylonians. Isa. 47:9–13;
Ezek. 21:21–22.
Balaam. Num. 22:6; 23:23.
Belshazzar. Dan. 5:7, 15.
To cease. Ezek. 12:23–24.
By the Egyptian magicians.
Exod. 7:11, 22; 8:7, 18.
Elymas. Acts 13:8.
False prophets. Jer. 14:14.
Jezebel. 2 Kings 9:22.
Messages of, false. Ezek. 21:29.
Ninevites. Nahum 3:4–5.
Simon Magus. Acts 8:9.
The slave girl in Philippi.
Acts 16:16.
Sons of Sceva. Acts 19:14–15.
Those who practice will be
confounded. Mic. 3:7.

Wickedness of. 1 Sam. 15:23.
Punishment for. Exod. 22:18.
By rods. Hos. 4:12.

SORROW

From bereavement
　Of the lost. Matt. 8:12.
　Of Jacob for Joseph.
　　Gen. 37:34–35.
　Of Jacob for Benjamin.
　　Gen. 43:14.
Comforted. Isa. 40; 61:1–3;
　James 4:9.
Of David for Absalom.
　2 Sam. 18:33.
God takes notice of Hagar's.
　Gen. 21:17–20.
God takes notice of the Israelites.
　Exod. 3:7–10.
Of Hannah. 1 Sam. 1:15.
Of Jeremiah. Lam. 1:12.
Of Jesus. Luke 22:42–44.

Kinds of
　Godly. 2 Cor. 7:10.
　Natural. Luke 22:45; Rom. 9:2.
　Resulting from sin. Ps. 51.
Of Mary and Martha. John
　11:19–40.
For sin. 2 Cor. 7:10–11.
No sorrow in heaven. Rev. 21:4.

SOVEREIGNTY OF GOD
See God, Sovereignty of

SOWER
Parable of the. Mark 4:3–20.
Sowing. Eccles. 11:4; Isa. 28:25.
Used in a figurative sense. Ps. 126:5;
　Prov. 11:18; Isa. 32:20; Hos. 8:7;
　10:12; Gal. 6:7–8.

SPARROW
Nests of. Ps. 84:3.
Two sold for a penny. Matt. 10:29;
　Luke 12:6.

Sparrow

SPEAKING

Evil
  Command against cursing.
    Exod. 22:28.
  Flattery. Ps. 12:3.
  Gossip. Prov. 18:8.
  Power of speech. James 3:5–10.
  Provocative words. Prov. 15:1.
  Unclean speech. Isa. 6:5.
Thoughtful. James 1:19, 26.

Wise speech
  Benefits of. Prov. 10:11–13.

SPEAR
Called the glittering spear.
    Job 39:23; Hab. 3:11.

Different kinds of
  Darts. 2 Sam. 18:14;
    Job 41:26, 29.
  Javelins. Num. 25:7;
    1 Sam. 18:10.
  Lances. Jer. 50:42.
First mention of, in Scripture.
    Josh. 8:18.
Frequently thrown from the hand.
    1 Sam. 18:11; 19:10.
Frequently used by horse soldiers.
    Nah. 3:3.
Illustrative of the bitterness of the
    wicked. Ps. 57:4.

The Israelites
  Acquainted with the making of.
    1 Sam. 13:19.
  Frequently used. Neh. 4:13, 16.
  Ill provided with, in the times of
    Deborah and Saul. Judg. 5:8;
    1 Sam. 13:22.
Made into pruning hooks in peace.
    Isa. 2:4; Mic. 4:3.
An offensive weapon.
    2 Sam. 23:8, 18.

Often retained in the hand of the
    person using. Num. 25:7;
    2 Sam. 2:23.

Parts of, mentioned
  Head of iron or brass.
    1 Sam. 17:7, with
    2 Sam. 21:16.
  Staff of wood. 1 Sam. 17:7.
Polished before war. Jer. 46:4.
Probably pointed at both ends.
    2 Sam. 2:23.
Provided by the kings of Israel in
    great abundance. 2 Chron. 11:12;
    32:5.
Pruning hooks made into, before
    war. Joel 3:10.
Stuck in the ground beside the head
    during sleep. 1 Sam. 26:7–11.
Those who used, called spearmen.
    Ps. 68:30; Acts 23:23.

SPICES
Exported from Gilead. Gen. 37:25.
In the formula for sacred oil.
    Exod. 25:6.
Prepared for embalming the body of
    Jesus. Luke 23:56; 24:1.
Presented by the queen Sheba to
    Solomon. 1 Kings 10:2, 10.
Sent as a present by Jacob to Joseph.
    Gen. 43:11.
Sold in the markets of Tyre.
    Ezek. 27:22.
Stores of. 2 Kings 20:13.
Used in the embalming of Asa.
    2 Chron. 16:14.
Used in the temple. 1 Chron. 9:29.

SPIDER
Mentioned in one of Agur's riddles.
    Prov. 30:28.
Web of, figurative of the hope of the
    hypocrite. Job 8:14; Isa. 59:5.

SPIES
In the church of Galatia. Gal. 2:4.
Pharisees acted as. Luke 20:20.

Sent to investigate
    Canaan. Num. 13.
    Jaazer. Num. 21:32.
    Jericho. Josh. 2:1.
Used by David. 1 Sam. 26:4.
Used by David at the court of
    Absalom. 2 Sam. 15:10;
    17:1–17.

SPIKENARD
An aromatic plant.
    Song of Sol. 4:13–14.
A fragrant oil from, used in
    anointing. Mark 14:3.
Perfume prepared from.
    Song of Song 1:12.

Spikenard

SPINDLE
Used in spinning. Prov. 31:19.

SPINNING
By hand. Exod. 35:25.

SPIRIT
Called inner person. Rom. 7:22;
    Eph. 3:16.

SPIRITUALITY
Brings peace. Isa. 26:3; Rom. 8:6;
    14:17.
Described as the great and enduring
    good. Luke 10:42.
Indifference to worldly good.
    1 Cor. 7:29–31.
As love and devotion to God.
    Deut. 6:5.
Is produced by the indwelling of the
    Holy Spirit. John 14:16–17;
    Rom. 8:4.
Thirst for heavenly blessings.
    Matt. 5:6; John 6:27.

SPITTING
In the face, as an indignity. Num.
    12:14; Job 30:10; Matt. 26:67;
    27:30.
Jesus used saliva in healing.
    Mark 7:33; 8:23.

SPOILS
Dedicated to the Lord.
    1 Chron. 26:27; 2 Chron. 15:11.
Divided between the combatants and
    noncombatants of the Israelites,
    including priests and Levites. Num.
    31:25–54.
Of war. Gen. 14:11–12.

SPONGE
Filled with vinegar. Matt. 27:48;
    Mark 15:36; John 19:29.

SPOONS
Of the tabernacle. Exod. 25:29.
Of the temple. 1 Kings 7:50.

SPORTS

Described
Boxing. 1 Cor. 9:26.
Foot races. 1 Cor. 9:24–25.

*As figurative of living the
Christian life*
Boxing. 1 Cor. 9:27.
Foot races. 1 Cor. 9:24–25;
Gal. 2:2; 5:7; Phil. 2:16;
3:13–14; 2 Tim. 4:7;
Heb. 12:1.
Gladiatorial. 1 Cor. 4:9; 15:32.

SPOUSAL ABUSE

Examples of
Abraham and Sarah.
Gen. 12:10–20; 20:2–14.
Concubine. Judg. 19:22–30.
Isaac and Rebekah.
Gen. 26:6–11.

Principles relevant to
Generational influence.
Exod. 34:7.
Jealousy and revenge. Prov. 6:34.
Smooth speech masks violence.
Ps. 55:20–21.

Responsibilities of husband
Be considerate and show honor to
wife. 1 Pet. 3:7.
Be head of wife. 1 Cor. 11:3.
Be nonviolent and self-controlled.
1 Tim. 3:2–3; Titus 1:7–8.
Love wife as himself.
Eph. 5:25–33.
Marry with honor and holiness.
1 Thess. 4:4.
Not be harsh with wife. Col. 3:19.
Provide for family. 1 Tim. 5:8.

SPRING

Described. Prov. 27:25;
Song of Sol. 2:11–13.
Season of, promise annual return of.
Gen. 8:22.
Used in figurative sense to connote
corruption. Prov. 25:26;
James 3:11.
Of water. Hot. Gen. 36:24.

STAMMERING
Of Moses. Exod. 4:10.

STANDARD
Banners used as. Ps. 20:5;
Song of Sol. 6:4, 10.
Believers praise God for. Ps. 116:8.
Believers pray for. Ps. 17:5.
A flag used by each of the tribes of
Israel in camp and on marches.
Num. 1:52.
To call attention to news. Jer. 50:2;
51:12.
Used in war. Jer. 4:21.
Used in a figurative sense. Isa. 49:22;
62:10; Jer. 4:6.
Used to direct the route to defensive
cities. Jer. 4:6.

STARS
Appear after sunset. Neh. 4:21, with
Job 3:9.
Appear of different magnitudes.
1 Cor. 15.41.
Astrology and stargazing practiced by
the Babylonians, etc. Isa. 47:13.

Called
The host of heaven. Deut. 17:3;
Jer. 33:22.
Stars of heaven. Isa. 13:10.
Stars of light. Ps. 148:3.
Exhibit the greatness of God's power.
Ps. 8:3, with Isa. 40:26.

False gods frequently worshiped under the representation of. Amos 5:26; Acts 7:43.

God

Appointed to give light by night. Gen. 1:16, with v. 14; Ps. 136:9; Jer. 31:35.

Created. Gen. 1:16; Pss. 8:3; 148:5.

Established forever. Ps. 148:3, 6; Jer. 31:36.

Numbers and names. Ps. 147:4.

Obscures. Job 9:7.

Set, in the heavens. Gen. 1:17.

Idolaters worshiped. Jer. 8:2; 19:13.

Illustrative of

Angels. Job 38:7.

Christ. Num. 24:17.

Christ (bright and morning star). Rev. 22:16.

False teachers (wandering). Jude 1:13.

Glory to be given to faithful believers (morning star). Rev. 2:28.

Ministers. Rev. 1:16, 20; 2:10.

Pride and worldly security (setting the host among). Obad. 1:4.

Princes and subordinate governors. Dan. 8:10; Rev. 8:12.

The reward of faithful ministers (by shining). Dan. 12:3.

Severe judgments (when withdrawing their light). Isa. 13:10; Ezek. 32:7; Joel 2:10; 3:15.

Impure in the sight of God. Job 25:5.

Infinite in number. Gen. 15:5; Jer. 33:22.

The Israelites forbidden to worship. Deut. 4:19; 17:2–4.

Made to praise God. Ps. 148:3.

Mentioned in Scripture

Arcturus. Job 9:9; 38:32.

Mazzaroth. Job 38:32.

Morning star. Rev. 2:28.

Orion. Job 9:9; 38:31; Amos 5:8.

Pleiades. Job 9:9; 38:31; Amos 5:8.

One of extraordinary brightness appeared at Christ's birth. Matt. 2:2, 9.

Punishment for worshiping. Deut. 17:5–7.

Revolve in fixed orbits. Judg. 5:20.

Shine in the arch of heaven. Dan. 12:3.

Use of, in navigation alluded to. Acts 27:20.

When grouped together, called constellations. 2 Kings 23:5; Isa. 13:10.

STATECRAFT

School in. Dan. 1:3–5.

Skilled in

Jeroboam. 1 Kings 12:26–33.

Joseph. Gen. 47:15–26.

Nathan. 1 Kings 1:11–14.

Samuel. 1 Sam. 11:12–15.

Wisdom in. Prov. 28:2.

STEADFASTNESS

A characteristic of believers. Job 17:9; John 8:31.

Commanded. Phil. 4:1; 2 Thess. 2:15; James 1:6–8.

Exhibited by God in all His purposes and ways. Num. 23:19; Dan. 6:26; James 1:17.

Godliness necessary to. Job 11:13–15.

Lack of, illustrated. Luke 8:6, 13; John 15:6; 2 Pet. 2:17; Jude 12.

Ministers

Encouraged by, in their people. 1 Thess. 3:8.

Exhorted to. 2 Tim. 1:13–14; Titus 1:9.

Rejoiced by, in their people. Col. 2:5.

Should exhort to. Acts 13:43; 14:22.

Should pray for, in their people. 1 Thess. 3:13; 2 Thess. 2:17.

Principle of, illustrated. Matt. 7:24–25; John 15:4; Col. 2:7.

Secured by

The intercession of Christ. Luke 22:31–32.

The power of God. Pss. 55:22; 62:2; 1 Pet. 1:5; Jude 24.

The presence of God. Ps. 16:8.

Trust in God. Ps. 26:1.

Should be manifested

In clinging to God. Deut. 10:20; Acts 11:23.

In contending for the faith of the gospel. Phil. 1:27, with Jude 3.

In continuing in the apostles' doctrine and fellowship. Acts 2:42.

Even under affliction. Ps. 44:17–19; Rom. 8:35–37; 1 Thess. 3:3.

In holding firmly our profession. Heb. 4:14; 10:23.

In holding firmly the confidence and rejoicing of the hope. Heb. 3:6, 14.

In holding firmly what is good. 1 Thess. 5:21.

In keeping the faith. Col. 2:5; 1 Pet. 5:9.

In maintaining Christian liberty. Gal. 5:1.

In standing firm in the faith. 1 Cor. 16:13.

In the work of the Lord. 1 Cor. 15:58.

The wicked lack. Ps. 78:8, 37.

STEEL

(In some translations this term is rendered as *brass*.)

Bows of. 2 Sam. 22:35; Job 20:24; Ps. 18:34.

Strength of. Jer. 15:12.

STEWARD

Description of faithful. Luke 12:35–38, 42.

Description of unfaithful. Luke 16:1–8.

Must be faithful. 1 Cor. 4:1–2; Titus 1:7; 1 Pet. 4:10.

Seen in the parable of the talents. Matt. 25:14–30; Luke 19:12–27.

STINGINESS

Of the disciples, when the perfume was poured on Jesus. Matt. 26:8–9.

Of God's people toward God. Mal. 3:8–9.

Of the Jews toward the temple. Hag. 1:2, 4, 6, 9.

Punishment of. Hag. 1:9–11.

STOCKS

Feet fastened in, as punishment. Job 13:27; 33:11; Prov. 7:22.

In prisons. Jer. 20:2; Acts 16:24.

STOICISM
School of, at Athens. Acts 17:18.

STONES, PRECIOUS
Art of engraving upon, early known
to the Jews. Exod. 28:9, 11, 21.
Art of setting, known to the Jews.
Exod. 28:20.
Brilliant and glittering.
1 Chron. 29:2; Rev. 21:11.
Brought from Ophir. 1 Kings 10:11;
2 Chron. 9:10.
Brought from Sheba.
1 Kings 10:1–2; Ezek. 27:22.

Called
Jewels. Isa. 61:10; Ezek. 16:12.
Precious jewels. 2 Chron. 20:25;
Prov. 20:15.
Stones of fire. Ezek. 28:14, 16.
Stones to be set. 1 Chron. 29:2.
Dug out of the earth. Job 28:5–6.
Extensive commerce in.
Ezek. 27:22; Rev. 18:12.
Given by leaders for the temple.
1 Chron. 29:8.
Given by the Jews for the tabernacle.
Exod. 25:7.
Highly prized by the people in
ancient times. Prov. 17:8.

Illustrative of
Beauty and stability of the church.
Isa. 54:11–12.
Believers. Mal. 3:17; 1 Cor. 3:12.
Glory of heavenly Jerusalem.
Rev. 21:11.
Preciousness of Christ. Isa. 28:16;
1 Pet. 2:6.
Seductive splendor and false glory
of the apostasy.
Rev. 17:4; 18:16.
Stability of heavenly Jerusalem.
Rev. 21:19.

Worldly glory of nations.
Ezek. 28:13–16.

Mentioned in Scripture
Agate. Exod. 28:19; Isa. 54:12.
Amethyst. Exod. 28:19;
Rev. 21:20.
Beryl. Dan. 10:6; Rev. 21:20.
Carbuncle. Exod. 28:17;
Isa. 54:12.
Chalcedony. Rev. 21:19.
Chrysolyte. Rev. 21:20.
Chrysoprasus. Rev. 21:20.
Coral. Job 28:18.
Diamond. Exod. 28:18; Jer. 17:1;
Ezek. 28:13.
Emerald. Ezek. 27:16; Rev. 4:3.
Jacinth. Rev. 9:17; 21:20.
Jasper. Rev. 4:3; 21:11, 19.
Onyx. Exod. 28:20; Job 28:16.
Pearl. Job 28:18; Matt.
13:45–46; Rev. 21:21.
Ruby. Job 28:18; Lam. 4:7.
Sapphire. Exod. 24:10;
Ezek. 1:26.
Sardine or sardius. Exod. 28:17;
Rev. 4:3.
Sardonyx. Rev. 21:20.
Topaz. Job 28:19; Rev. 21:20.
Often given as presents.
1 Kings 10:2, 10.
A part of the treasure of kings.
2 Chron. 32:27.
Prepared by David for the temple.
1 Chron. 29:2.

Used for
Adorning the breastplate of
judgment. Exod. 28:17–20;
39:10–14.
Adorning the high priest's ephod.
Exod. 28:12.
Adorning the temple.
2 Chron. 3:6.

Decorating the person.
Ezek. 28:13.
Honoring idols. Dan. 11:38.
Ornamenting royal crowns.
2 Sam. 12:30.
Setting in seals and rings.
Song of Sol. 5:12.
Of various colors and variety.
1 Chron. 29:2.

STONING

Punishment by. Exod. 19:13;
Heb. 11:37.

Examples of
Achan. Josh. 7:25.
Naboth. 1 Kings 21:13.
Paul. Acts 14:19; 2 Cor. 11:25.
Sabbath-breaker. Num. 15:36.
Stephen. Acts 7:59.

STRANGERS IN ISRAEL

All foreigners residing in Israel
counted as. Exod. 12:49.
Under the care and protection of
God. Deut. 10:18; Ps. 146:9.

Chiefly consisted of
Captives taken in war.
Deut. 21:10.
Foreign servants. Lev. 25:44–45.
Persons who came into Israel for
the sake of religious privileges.
1 Kings 8:41.
Persons who sought employment
among the Jews. 1 Kings 7:13;
9:27.
The remnant of the mixed
multitude who came out of
Egypt. Exod. 12:38.
The remnant of the nations of the
land. 1 Kings 9:20;
2 Chron. 8:7.

Could worship in the outer court of
the temple. 1 Kings 8:41–43, with
Rev. 11:2. (*See also* Eph. 2:14.)
The Jews condemned for
oppressing. Ps. 94:6;
Ezek. 22:7, 29.

Laws regarding
Allowed to eat what died of itself.
Deut. 14:21.
The Jews might purchase and
have them as slaves.
Lev. 25:44–45.
The Jews might take interest from.
Deut. 23:20.
Might offer their burnt offerings on
the altar of God. Lev. 17:8;
22:18; Num. 15:14.
Might purchase Hebrew servants
subject to release. Lev.
25:47–48.
Not to be chosen as kings in Israel.
Deut. 17:15.
Not to be grieved or oppressed.
Exod. 22:21; 23:9; Lev. 19:33.
Not to blaspheme God.
Lev. 24:16.
Not to eat blood. Lev. 17:10–12.
Not to eat of the Passover while
uncircumcised.
Exod. 12:43–44.
Not to practice idolatrous rites.
Lev. 20:2.
Not to work on the Sabbath.
Exod. 20:10; 23:12;
Deut. 5:14.
Subject to the civil law.
Lev. 24:22.
To be loved. Lev. 19:34;
Deut. 10:19.
To be relieved in distress.
Lev. 25:35.
To enjoy the benefit of the cities of
refuge. Num. 35:15.

To have justice done to them in all disputes. Deut. 1:16; 24:17.

To have the gleaning of the harvest. Lev. 19:10; 23:22; Deut. 24:19–22.

To have the Law read to them. Deut. 31:12; Josh. 8:32–35.

To participate in the rejoicing of the people. Deut. 14:29; 16:11, 14; 26:11.

The Jews prohibited from oppressing. Exod. 22:21; 23:9.

Very numerous in Solomon's reign. 2 Chron. 2:17.

Were frequently employed in public works. 1 Chron. 22:2; 2 Chron. 2:18.

STRENGTH

Through Christ. Phil. 4:13.

God is our. Pss. 27:1; 73:26; Isa. 40:29.

Love with. Mark 12:30.

Must be demonstrated. 1 Cor. 16:13.

Quietness is. Isa. 30:7.

Through the Spirit. Eph. 3:16; Col. 1:11.

In weakness. 2 Cor. 12:10; Heb. 11:34.

STRANGLED

Things dying by strangulation, forbidden as food. Acts 15:20, 29; 21:25.

STRATEGY

In war. Gen. 14:14; Josh. 8:3–25; Judg. 7:16–23; 2 Sam. 15:31–34; Neh. 6; Jer. 6:5.

STRAW

For brick. Exod. 5:7.

Used food for animals. Gen. 24:32.

STRAY

Animals straying to be returned. Exod. 23:4.

Instance of animals straying, Kish's. 1 Sam. 9.

STRIFE

Appeased by patience. Prov. 15:18.

Believers kept from tongues of. Ps. 31:20.

Believers should
Avoid. Gen. 13:8; Eph. 4:3.
Avoid questions that lead to. 2 Tim. 2:14.
Do all things without. Phil. 2:14.
Not act from. Phil. 2:3.
Not walk in. Rom. 13:13.
Praise God for protection from. 2 Sam. 22:44; Ps. 18:43.
Seek God's protection from. Ps. 35:1; Jer. 18:19.
Submit to wrong rather than engage in. Prov. 20:22; Matt. 5:39–40; 1 Cor. 6:7.

Christ an example of avoiding. Isa. 42:2, with Matt. 12:15–19; Luke 9:52–56; 1 Pet. 2:23.

Danger of joining in, illustrated. Prov. 26:17.

Difficulty of stopping, a reason for avoiding it. Prov. 17:14.

Evidence of a worldly spirit. 1 Cor. 3:3.

Evidences a love of sin. Prov. 17:19.

Excited by
Antagonists. Prov. 16:28.
A belligerent disposition. Prov. 26:21.

Curious questions. 1 Tim. 6:4;
  2 Tim. 2:23.
Drunkenness. Prov. 23:29–30.
Gossiping. Prov. 26:20.
Hatred. Prov. 10:12.
Lusts. James 4:1.
Mocking. Prov. 22:10.
Pride. Prov. 13:10; 28:25.
Wrath. Prov. 15:18; 30:33.
Excludes from heaven.
  Gal. 5:20–21.
Existed in primitive church.
  1 Cor. 1:11.
Fools engage in. Prov. 18:6.
Forbidden. Prov. 3:30; 25:8.
Honorable to cease from.
  Prov. 20:3.
Hypocrites make religion a pretense
  for. Isa. 58:4.

Leads to
  Blasphemy. Lev. 24:10–11.
  Confusion and every evil work.
    James 3:16.
  Injustice. Hab. 1:3–4.
  Mutual destruction. Gal. 5:15.
  Violence. Exod. 21:18, 22.

Ministers should
  Avoid. 1 Tim. 3:3; 2 Tim. 2:24.
  Avoid questions that lead to.
    2 Tim. 2:23; Titus 3:9.
  Not preach through.
    Phil. 1:15–16.
  Reprove. 1 Cor. 1:11–12; 3:3;
    11:17–18.
  Warn against. 1 Cor. 1:10;
    2 Tim. 2:14.
Promoters of, should be expelled.
  Prov. 22:10.
Punishment for. Ps. 55:9.
Shameful in believers. 2 Cor. 12:20;
  James 3:14.

Strength and violence of, illustrated.
  Prov. 17:14; 18:19.
Temporary blessings embittered by.
  Prov. 17:1.
A work of the sinful nature.
  Gal. 5:20.

STUDENTS
Poverty of. 2 Kings 4:1.
In schools of the prophets.
  1 Sam. 19:20.
In state school. Dan. 1.

SUBMISSION
To authority, Jesus an example of.
  Matt. 26:39, 42; Heb. 5:8.

SUBSERVIENCE
Examples of
  Abigail. 1 Sam. 25:23–31, 41.
  Mephibosheth. 2 Sam. 9:8.
  The woman of Tekoah.
    2 Sam. 14:4–20.

SUBSTITUTION
The Levites for the firstborn of the
  Israelites. Num. 3:12.
The life of Ahab for that of
  Ben-hadad. 1 Kings 20:42.
The offering for the offerer. Lev. 1:4.

SUBURBS
Described. Num. 35:3–5;
  Josh. 14:4.

SUFFERING
For Christ. 2 Cor. 4:11–18.
Of Christ. Luke 24:46–47;
  Heb. 2:9–18; 5:8–9; 9:15–16.
Vicarious. John 15:13; Rom. 9:3;
  1 Pet. 2:21; 1 John 3:16.

SUICIDE

Temptation to, of the Philippian jailer. Acts 16:27.

Examples of
Ahithophel. 2 Sam. 17:23.
Judas. Matt. 27:5; Acts 1:18.
Samson. Judg. 16:29–30.
Saul and his armor bearer. 1 Sam. 31:4–5.
Zimri. 1 Kings 16:18.

SUICIDE, ASSISTED

Communal nature of life and death. Rom. 14:7–8.
Performed. Judg. 9:54.
Recovery of one near death. Phil. 2:27.
Refused. 1 Sam. 31:4; 1 Chron. 10:4.

Value of life
God gives and takes life. Job 1:21.
Preference for life. Deut. 30:15, 19; 1 Cor. 15:25–26.
Sanctity of life. Gen. 1:26–27; 2:7; Ps. 8:5.
Steadfastness in trial. 2 Cor. 12:7–10; Phil. 4:11–13; James 1:2–4.

SUMMER

Ants provide their winter food during. Prov. 6:8; 30:25.
Approach of, indicated by shooting out of leaves on trees. Matt. 24:32.

Characterized by
Excessive drought. Ps. 32:4.
Excessive heat. Jer. 17:8.
Illustrative of seasons of grace. Jer. 8:20.
Made by God. Ps. 74:17.

Many kinds of fruit ripened and used during. 2 Sam. 16:1; Jer. 40:10; 48:32.
The people in ancient times had houses or apartments suited to. Judg. 3:20, 24; Amos 3:15.
The wise are diligent during. Prov. 10:5.
Yearly return of, secured by covenant. Gen. 8:22.

SUN, THE

Called the greater light. Gen. 1:16.
Clearness of its light alluded to. Song of Sol. 6:10.

Compared to
A bridegroom coming forth from his chamber. Ps. 19:5.
A strong man rejoicing to run a race. Ps. 19:5.

God
Appointed to divide seasons, etc. Gen. 1:14.
Appointed to rule the day. Gen. 1:16; Ps. 136:8; Jer. 31:35.
Causes to know its time of setting. Ps. 104:19.
Causes to rise both on evil and good. Matt. 5:45.
Created. Gen. 1:14, 16; Ps. 74:16.
Exercises sovereign power over. Job 9:7.
Placed in the sky. Gen. 1:17.

Illustrative of
Christ's coming. Mal. 4:2.
The future glory of believers (in its brightness). Dan. 12:3, with Matt. 13:43.

The glory of Christ. Matt. 17:2;
Rev. 1:16; 10:1.

God's favor. Ps. 84:11.

Public disgrace (when before or in
sight of). 2 Sam. 12:11–12;
Jer. 8:3.

The purity of the church (in its
clearness). Song of Sol. 6:10.

Perpetual blessedness (no more
going down). Isa. 60:20.

Premature destruction (going
down at noon). Jer. 15:9;
Amos 8:9.

Severe calamities (darkened).
Ezek. 32:7; Joel 2:10, 31, with
Matt. 24:29; Rev. 9:2.

Supreme rulers. Gen. 37:9;
Isa. 13:10.

The triumph of believers (in its
power). Judg. 5:31.

Indicates the hours of the day by the
shadow on the dial. 2 Kings 20:9.

The Jews

Began their day with the rising of.
Gen. 19:23–24, with 27–28;
Judg. 9:33.

Began their evening with the
setting of. Gen. 28:11;
Deut. 24:13; Mark 1:32.

Consecrated chariots and horses,
as symbols of. 2 Kings 23:11.

Expressed the east by rising of.
Num. 21.11, Deut. 4:11, 47;
Josh. 12:1.

Expressed the west by setting of.
James 1:4.

Expressed the whole earth by,
from rising of, to setting of.
Pss. 50:1; 113:3; Isa. 45:6.

Forbidden to worship.
Deut. 4:19; 17:3.

Worshiped. 2 Kings 23:5;
Jer. 8:2.

Made to praise and glorify God.
Ps. 148:3.

Miracles connected with

Darkened at the crucifixion.
Luke 23:44–45.

Shadow put back on the dial.
2 Kings 20:11.

Standing still for a whole day in the
valley of Ajalon.
Josh. 10:12–13.

The power and brilliancy of its rising
alluded to. Judg. 5:31;
2 Sam. 23:4.

Rays of

Change the color of the skin.
Song of Sol. 1:6.

Frequently destructive to human
life. 2 Kings 4:18–20;
Ps. 121:6; Isa. 49:10.

Pleasant to humans. Job 30:28,
with Eccles. 11:7.

Produce and ripen fruit.
Deut. 33:14.

Soften and melt some substances.
Exod. 16:21.

Wither and burn up the herbs of
the field. Mark 4:6; James 1:11.

Worshipers of, turned their faces
toward the east. Ezek. 8:16.

SUNSTROKE

Cause of a child's death.
2 Kings 4:19.

SUPEREROGATION

The doctrine of excessive and
meritorious righteousness denied.
Ezek. 33:12, 13; Luke 17:10.

SUPERSTITION

Examples of

The belief of the Syrians concerning the help of the gods. 1 Kings 20:23.

The disciples, supposing they saw a spirit when Jesus came walking on the sea. Matt. 14:26.

The disciples, who were frightened at the appearance of Peter. Acts 12:14–15.

The Ephesians, in their sorceries. Acts 19:13–19.

The Gadarenes, on account of Jesus casting devils out of the demon-possessed man. Matt. 8:34.

Herod, imagining that John the Baptist had risen from the dead. Mark 6:14, 16.

Israelites, supposing that their defeat in the battle with the Philistines was due to their not having brought with them the Ark of the Covenant. 1 Sam. 4:3.

Jews, attributing their calamities to having ceased offering sacrifices to the queen of heaven. Jer. 44:17–19.

Nebuchadnezzar, supposing that the spirit of the gods was upon Daniel. Dan. 4:8–9.

The people of the island of Melita, in imagining Paul to be a god. Acts 28:6.

Philistines, refusing to tread the threshold of the temple of Dagon after the image of Dagon had repeatedly fallen. 1 Sam. 5:5.

The sailors who threw Jonah into the sea. Jon. 1:4–16.

SWEARING FALSELY

Believers keep from. Josh. 9:20; Ps. 15:4.

Blessedness of abstaining from. Ps. 24:4–5.

False witnesses guilty of. Deut. 19:16, 18.

Forbidden. Lev. 19:12; Num. 30:2; Matt. 5:33.

Fraud often leads to. Lev. 6:2–3.

Hateful to God. Zech. 8:17.

We should not love. Zech. 8:17.

The wicked

Addicted to. Jer. 5:2; Hos. 10:4.

Plead excuses for. Jer. 7:9–10.

Will be cut off for. Zech. 5:3.

Will be judged because of. Mal. 3:5.

Will have a curse upon their houses for. Zech. 5:4.

SWEARING, PROFANE

All kinds forbidden as desecration of God's name. Exod. 20:7; Matt. 5:34–36; 23:21–22; James 5:12.

Calamity denounced against. Matt. 23:16.

Guilt of. Exod. 20:7; Deut. 5:11.

Nations visited for. Jer. 23:10; Hos. 4:1–3.

Punishment for. Lev. 24:16, 23; Pss. 59:12; 109:17–18.

The wicked

Addicted to. Ps. 10:7; Rom. 3:14.

Clothe themselves with. Ps. 109:18.

Love. Ps. 109:17.

SWEAT

An offense in the sanctuary. Ezek. 44:18.

Of blood. Luke 22:44.

SWINE

Described as
Destructive to agriculture.
Ps. 80:13.
Fierce and ungenerous. Matt. 7:6.
Filthy in its habits. 2 Pet. 2:22.
Fed upon husks. Luke 15:16.
Feeding of. Luke 15:15–16.
The Gergesenes punished for having.
Matt. 8:31–32; Mark 5:11, 14.
Herding of considered as the greatest
degradation to a Jew. Luke 15:15.

Illustrative of
Hypocrites. 2 Pet. 2:22.
The wicked. Matt. 7:6.
Jesus sends devils into.
Matt. 8:28–32.
Jewels in the nose of. Prov. 11:22.
Kept in large herds. Matt. 8:30.
Sacrificing of, an abomination.
Isa. 66:3.
Unclean and not to be eaten.
Lev. 11:7–8.
Ungodly Jews condemned for eating.
Isa. 65:4; 66:17.
When wild, inhabited the woods.
Ps. 80:13.

SWORD

Brandished over the head.
Ezek. 32:10.
Carried in a sheath or scabbard.
1 Chron. 21:27; Jer. 47:6;
Ezek. 21:3–5.
David's army equipped with.
1 Chron. 21:5.

Described as
Bright. Nah. 3:3.

Glittering. Deut. 32:41;
Job 20:25.
Hurtful. Ps. 144:10.
Oppressive. Jer. 46:16.
Sharp. Ps. 57:4.
Frequently had two edges. Ps. 149:6.
Hebrews early acquainted with
making of. 1 Sam. 13:19.

Illustrative of
Deep mental affliction. Luke 2:35.
The end of the wicked. Prov. 5:4.
False witnesses. Prov. 25:18.
Judicial authority. Rom. 13:4.
The justice of God. Deut. 32:41;
Zech. 13:7.
Peace and friendship (when
sheathed). Jer. 47:6.
Perpetual calamity (not departing
from one's house).
2 Sam. 12:10.
Persecuting spirit of the wicked.
Ps. 37:14.
Plunder (when living by).
Gen. 27:40.
The protection of God.
Deut. 33:29.
Severe and heavy calamities.
Ezek. 5:2, 17; 14:17; 21:9.
The tongue of the wicked.
Pss. 57:4; 64:3; Prov. 12:18.
War and contention. Matt. 10:34.
War and destruction (when drawn).
Lev. 26:33; Ezek. 21:3–5.
The wicked. Ps. 17:13.
The word of Christ. Isa. 49:2, with
Rev. 1:16.
The Word of God. Eph. 6:17, with
Heb. 4:12.
Of judgments. Deut. 32:41.
Of the malicious tongue.
Prov. 25:18.
Often sent as a punishment.
Ezra 9:7; Ps. 78:62.

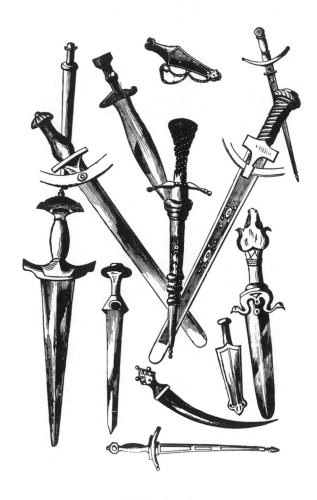

Ancient Swords

Often threatened as a punishment.
Lev. 26:25, 33; Deut. 32:25.

One of God's four dreadful
judgments. Ezek. 14:21.

Pointed. Ezek. 21:15.

Probable origin of. Gen. 3:24.

Sharpened and polished before going
to war. Ps. 7:12; Ezek. 21:9.

Suspended from the belt.
1 Sam. 17:39; 2 Sam. 20:8;
Neh. 4:18; Ps. 45:3.

Those slain by, communicated
ceremonial uncleanness.
Num. 19:16.

Thrust through enemies.
Ezek. 16:40.

In time of peace made into
plowshares. Isa. 2:4; Mic. 4:3.
In time of war plowshares made into.
Joel 3:10.
To be beaten into plowshares.
Isa. 2:4.
Two-edged. Heb. 4:12;
Rev. 1:16; 2:12.

Used
For destruction of enemies.
Num. 21:24; Josh. 6:21.
In a figurative sense, of war.
Gen. 27:40.
By Gideon. Judg. 7:20.
By Goliath. 1 Sam. 21:9.
By heathen nations. Judg. 7:22;
1 Sam. 15:33.
By the Jews. Judg. 20:2;
2 Sam. 24:9.
By the patriarchs.
Gen. 34:25; 48:22.
By Peter. Matt. 26:51.
For punishing criminals.
1 Sam. 15:33; Acts 12:2.
For self-defense. Luke 22:36.
Sometimes for self-destruction.
1 Sam. 31:4–5; Acts 16:27.
In a symbolic sense. Gen. 3:24;
Josh. 5:13; Rev. 1:16.

SYMBOLS
Almond rod. Jer. 1:11.
Basket. Zech. 5:6–11.
Basket of fruit. Amos 8:1–2.
Bow shot by Joash.
2 Kings 13:15–19.
Bow shot by Jonathan.
1 Sam. 20:21–37.
Book cast into Euphrates.
Jer. 51:63.
Bottles. Jer. 13:12.
Bread. Matt. 26:26.
Breaking of potter's vessel. Jer. 19.

Bring to life by water. Ps. 1:3.
The bronze serpent, of Christ.
Num. 21:8–9; John 3:14.
Canaan, of the spiritual rest.
Heb. 3:11–12; 4:5.
Cooking. Jer. 1:13.
Change of residence. Ezek. 12:3–11.
Childhood. Mark 10:14–15.
Circumcision, of the covenant of
Abraham. Gen. 17:11;
Rom. 4:11.
Cleansing by water.
Ezek. 16:9; 36:25.
Darkness, of God's mysteriousness.
Exod. 20:21; 1 Kings 8:12;
Ps. 18:11; 97:2; Heb. 12:18–19.
Of the divine presence, the pillar of
cloud. Exod. 13:21–22.
Dove. Matt. 3:16.
Dumbness. Luke 1:20–22, 62–64.
Eating bread with care.
Ezek. 12:17–20.
Eating and drinking in fear.
Ezek. 12:18.
Ezekiel's beard. Ezek. 5:1–4.
Fire, purifying by. Mal. 3:2–3.
Fire, illuminating. Exod. 13:21.
Fire, searching. Zeph. 1:12.
Food. Isa. 37:30.
Good and bad figs. Jer. 24.
Handwriting on the wall.
Dan. 5:5–6, 16–28.
Harvest. 2 Kings 19:29.
Invitation to approach.
1 Sam. 14:8–12.
Isaiah's children. Isa. 8:18.
Jeremiah's deeds of land.
Jer. 32:1–16.
Jonah. Matt. 16:4.
Lapping water. Judg. 7:4–8.
Manna. John 6:31–58.
Marrying a prostitute.
Hos 1:2–9; 3:1–4.

Men meeting Saul. 1 Sam. 10:2–7.
Mourning forbidden.
  Ezek. 24:15–18.
Nakedness. Isa. 20:2–4.
Passover, of the sparing of the
  firstborn, and of the atonement
  made by Christ. Exod. 12:3–28;
  1 Cor. 5:7.
Plumb line. Amos 7:7–8.
Posture. Ezek. 4:4–8.
Praying toward the temple.
  1 Kings 8:29; Dan. 6:10.
Offering water to drink.
  Gen. 24:13–15, 42–44.
Oil expressing healing. Isa. 1:6.
Oil, expressing comfort. Isa. 61:3.
Oil, illuminating.
  Zech. 4:2–3, 11–13.
Oil, consecrating. Isa. 61:1.
Rain and dew, abundant. Ps. 133:3.
Rain and dew, fertilizing. Hos. 6:3.
Rain and dew, imperceptible.
  2 Sam. 17:12.
Rain and dew, refreshing. Ps. 68:9.
Rain and thunder.
  1 Sam. 12:16–18.
Rainbow. Gen. 9:12–13.
Rock at Horeb. Exod. 17:6;
  1 Cor. 10:4.
Scroll. Zech. 5:2–4.
Sacrificial animals. Gen. 15:8–11;
  John 1:29, 36.
Salt. Num. 18:19; Col. 4:6.
Sanctuary. Ps. 20:2.
Seal, guarantee. Eph. 1:13–14.
Seal, impressing. Job 38:14.
Shadow on Ahaz's dial. Isa. 38:7–8.
Siege. Ezek. 4:1–3.
Split altar. 1 Kings 13:3, 5.
The sprinkled blood, of the covenant.
  Exod. 24:8.
Star in the East. Matt. 2:2.
Sticks. Ezek. 37:16–17.

Tabernacle. Ps. 15:1; Exod. 27:20;
  Heb. 8:2, 5; 9:1–12, 23–24.
Tearing of the veil. Mark 15:38.
Thunder on Mt. Sinai.
  Exod. 19:9, 16.
Tongues of fire. Acts 2:3, 6, 11.
Trees of life and knowledge.
  Gen. 2:9, 17; 3:3, 24; Rev. 22:2.
Two sticks. Ezek. 37:15–28.
Unclean food. Ezek. 4:9–17.
Vine. Ezek. 15:2.
Voice, speaking. Matt. 10:20.
Voice, guiding. Isa. 30:21.
Voice, warning. Heb. 3:7–11.
Water. John 3:5; 7:38–39.
Waving the wave offering.
  Exod. 29:24–28;
  Lev. 8:27–29; 9:21.
The whole system of Mosaic rights.
  Heb. 9:9–10, 18–23.
Wind, incomprehensible. John 3:8.
Wind, powerful. 1 Kings 19:11.
Wind, reviving. Ezek. 37:9–10, 14.
Wind, sensible in its effect. John 3:8.
Wine. Luke 22:17.
Wine, of the atoning blood. Matt.
  26:27–29; Luke 22:17–18, 20.
Wounding. 1 Kings 20:35–40.
Yokes. Jer. 27:2–3; 28:10.

SYMPATHY
Of Job's friends. Job 2:11.

SYNAGOGUES
The apostles frequently taught and
  preached in. Acts 9:20;
  13:5; 17:1, 17.
The building of, considered a noble
  and meritorious work. Luke 7:5.
Chief seats in, reserved for elders.
  Matt. 23:6.

Christ often
  Attended. Luke 4:16.

Performed miracles in.
Matt. 12:9–10; Mark 1:23;
Luke 13:11.

Preached and taught in. Matt.
4:23; Mark 1:39; Luke 13:10.

Each sect had its own. Acts 6:9.

Early notice of their existence.
Ps. 74:8.

Governed by

Ordinary rulers. Mark 5:22;
Acts 13:15.

A president or chief ruler.
Acts 18:8, 17.

Had seats for the congregation.
Acts 13:14.

Offenders were often

Expelled from.
John 9:22, 34; 12:42; 16:2.

Given up to, for trial. Luke 12:11;
21:12.

Punished in. Matt. 10:17; 23:34;
Acts 22:19.

Often used as courts of justice.
Acts 9:2.

Places in which the Jews assembled
for worship. Acts 13:5, 14.

Portion of Scripture for the day
sometimes read by one of the
congregation. Luke 4:16.

Probably originated in the schools of
the prophets. 1 Sam. 19:18–24;
2 Kings 4:23.

Provided with an attendant, who had
charge of the sacred books.
Luke 4:17, 20.

Revival of, after the captivity.
Neh. 8:1–8.

Service in, on the Sabbath day.
Luke 4:16; Acts 13:14.

Service of, consisted of

Expounding the Word of God.
Neh. 8:8; Luke 4:21.

Praise and thanksgiving. Neh. 9:5.

Prayer. Matt. 6:5.

Reading the Word of God.
Neh. 8:18; 9:3; 13:1;
Acts 15:21.

Sometimes several, in the same city.
Acts 6:9; 9:2.

Strangers invited to address the
congregation in. Acts 13:15.

SYRIA

Abana and Pharpar rivers of.
2 Kings 5:12.

Army of, miraculously scattered.
2 Kings 7:5–6.

Asa sought aid of, against Israel.
1 Kings 15:18–20.

Ben-hadad king of, besieged
Samaria. 1 Kings 20:1–12.

Besieged Samaria again.
2 Kings 6:24–29.

Damascus the capital of. Isa. 7:8.

David

Dedicated the spoils of.
2 Sam. 8:11–12.

Destroyed an army of, which
assisted Hadadezer. 2 Sam. 8:5.

Destroyed a second army of.
2 Sam. 10:15–19.

Fortified and made tributary.
2 Sam. 8:6.

Obtained fame by his victory over.
2 Sam. 8:13.

Sent Joab against the armies of,
hired by the Ammonites.
2 Sam. 10:6–14.

Death of the king of, and the cruelty
of his successor, predicted by
Elisha. 2 Kings 8:7, 15.

Elijah anointed Hazael king over, by divine direction. 1 Kings 19:15.

Elisha predicted to Joash his three victories over. 2 Kings 13:14–19.

God struck with blindness those sent against Elisha by the king of. 2 Kings 6:14, 18–20.

The gospel preached and many churches founded in. Acts 15:23, 41.

Governed by kings. 1 Kings 22:31; 2 Kings 5:1.

Inhabitants of

Called Syrians. 2 Sam. 10:11; 2 Kings 5:20.

Called Syrians of Damascus. 2 Sam. 8:5.

A commercial people. Ezek. 27:18.

An idolatrous people. Judg. 10:6; 2 Kings 5:18.

Spoke the Syriac language. 2 Kings 18:26; Ezra 4:7; Dan. 2:4.

A warlike people. 1 Kings 20:23, 25.

Israel delivered into the hands of, for the sins of Jehoahaz. 2 Kings 13:3, 7, 22.

Israel followed the idolatry of. Judg. 10:6.

The Israelites

At peace with, for three years. 1 Kings 22:1.

Craftily drawn into a league with. 1 Kings 20:31–43.

Defeated by, and Ahab slain. 1 Kings 22:30–36.

Encouraged and assisted by God, overcame a second time. 1 Kings 20:28–30.

Forewarned of invasion by, at the return of the year. 1 Kings 20:22–25.

Harassed by frequent incursions of. 2 Kings 5:2; 6:23.

Heard the secrets of, from Elisha. 2 Kings 6:8–12.

Insignificant before. 1 Kings 20:26–27.

Under Ahab, encouraged and assisted by God, overcame. 1 Kings 20:13–20.

Under Ahab, sought to recover Ramoth-gilead from. 1 Kings 22:3–29.

Joined with Israel against Ahaz and besieged Jerusalem. 2 Kings 16:5; Isa. 7:12.

Joram king of Israel, in seeking to recover Ramoth-gilead from, severely wounded. 2 Kings 8:28–29; 9:15.

More properly, the country around Damascus. 2 Sam. 8:6.

Originally included Mesopotamia. Gen. 25:20; 28:5; Deut. 26:5, with Acts 7:2.

Prophecies regarding

Burning of Damascus. Jer. 49:27; Amos 1:4.

Ceasing to be a kingdom. Isa. 17:1–3.

Destruction of its inhabitants. Jer. 49:26.

Destruction of Rezin, king of. Isa. 7:8, 16.

Invasion of Damascus. Isa. 8:4.

Its calamities, the punishments of its sins. Amos 1:3.

Its history in connection with the Macedonian empire. Dan. 11:6, etc.

Its inhabitants to be captives.
Amos 1:5.

Terror and dismay in, caused by its invasion. Jer. 49:23–24.

Retook Elath and drove out the Jews. 2 Kings 16:6.

A savior raised up for Israel against. 2 Kings 13:5, 23–25.

Subdued and governed by the Romans. Luke 2:2.

Subdued and its inhabitants taken captive by Assyria. 2 Kings 16:9.

T

TABERNACLE, THE

All offerings to be made at.
Lev. 17:4; Deut. 12:5–6, 11,
13–14.

Anointed and consecrated with oil.
Exod. 40:9; Lev. 8:10; Num. 7:1.

Ark and mercy seat put in the most
holy place. Exod. 26:33–34;
40:20–21; Heb. 9:4.

Boards of

Had each two tenons fitted into
sockets of silver.
Exod. 26:17, 19; 36:22–24.

Made of acacia wood.
Exod. 26:15; 36:20.

Six, and two corner boards for
west side. Exod. 26:22–25;
36:27–30.

Supported by bars of acacia wood
resting in rings of gold.
Exod. 26:26–29; 36:31–33.

Ten cubits high by one and a half
wide. Exod. 26:16; 36:21.

Twenty on north side.
Exod. 26:20; 36:25.

Twenty on south side.
Exod. 26:18; 36:23.

With the bars, covered with gold.
Exod. 26:29; 36:34.

Called the

House of the Lord. Josh. 6:24;
1 Sam. 1:7, 24.

Tabernacle of Joseph. Ps. 78:67.

Tabernacle of Shiloh. Ps. 78:60.

Tabernacle of testimony or
witness. Exod. 38:21;

Num. 1:50; 17:7–8; 2 Chron.
24:6; Acts 7:44.

Tabernacle of the congregation.
Exod. 27:21; 33:7; 40:26.

Tabernacle of the Lord.
Josh. 22:19; 1 Kings 2:28;
1 Chron. 16:39.

Temple of the Lord.
1 Sam. 1:9; 3:3.

The cloud of glory rested on, by night
and day, during its time in the
wilderness. Exod. 40:38;
Num. 9:15–16.

Court of

All the utensils of, made of brass.
Exod. 27:19.

All the pillars of, provided with
silver bases.
Exod. 27:17; 38:17.

Contained the bronze altar and
basin of brass. Exod. 40:29–30.

The gate of, a hanging of blue,
purple, etc., twenty cubits wide,
suspended from four pillars, etc.
Exod. 27:16; 38:18.

One hundred cubits long and fifty
cubits wide. Exod. 27:18.

Surrounded by curtains of fine
linen suspended from pillars in
sockets of brass. Exod. 27:9–15;
38:9–16.

Coverings of

First or inner, ten curtains of blue,
purple, etc., joined with loops
and golden clasps.
Exod. 26:1–6; 36:8–13.

Fourth or outward, badgers' skins.
Exod. 26:14; 36:19.

Second, eleven curtains of goats'
hair, etc. Exod. 26:7–13;
36:14–18.

Third, rams' skins dyed red.
Exod. 26:14; 36:19.

Designed for manifestation of God's
presence and for His worship.
Exod. 25:8, 29:42–43.

Divided by a veil of blue, purple, etc.,
suspended from four pillars of
acacia wood by gold hooks.
Exod. 26:31–33; 36:35–36;
40:21.

Divided into

The holy place. Exod. 26:33;
Heb. 9:2–6.

The most holy place. Exod. 26:34;
Heb. 9:3, 7.

Divine wisdom given to Bezaleel,
etc., to make. Exod. 31:2–7;
35:30–35; 36:1.

Door of, a curtain of blue and purple
suspended by gold rings from five
pillars of acacia wood, etc.
Exod. 26:36–37; 36:37–38.

First set up on the first day of the
second year after the Exodus.
Exod. 40:2, 17.

Freewill offerings made at the
dedication of the altar of. Num.
7:10–87.

Freewill offerings made when first set
up. Num. 7:1–9.

Had a court around it. Exod. 40:8.

Illustrative of

The body. 2 Cor. 5:1;
2 Pet. 1:13.

Christ. Isa. 4:6; John 1:14;
(Greek) Heb. 9:8–9, 11.

Christ's body (the veil).
Heb. 10:20.

The church. Ps. 15:1; Isa. 16:5;
54:2; Heb. 8:2; Rev. 21:2–3.

Heaven (the holy of holies).
Heb. 6:19–20; 9:12, 24; 10:19.

The mystery of the Old Testament
provision (the veil). Heb. 9:8,
10, with Rom. 16:25–26;
Rev. 11:19.

Journeys of Israel regulated by the
cloud on. Exod. 40:36–37.

The Levites

Appointed over and had charge of.
Num. 1:50; 8:24; 18:2–4.

Carried. Num. 4:15, 25, 31.

Did the inferior service of.
Num. 3:6–8.

Pitched their tents around.
Num. 1:53; 3:23, 29, 35.

Took down and put up.
Num. 1:51.

The Lord appeared in, over the
mercy seat. Exod. 25:22;
Lev. 16:2; Num. 7:89.

Made of the freewill offerings of the
people. Exod. 25:1–8;
35:4–5, 21–29.

Moses commanded to make, after a
divine pattern. Exod. 25:9; 26:30;
Heb. 8:5.

A movable tent suited to the unsettled
condition of Israel. 2 Sam. 7:6–7.

A permanent house substituted for,
when the kingdom was
established. 2 Sam. 7:5–13.

The priests

Alone could enter. Num. 18:3, 5.

Performed all services in.
Num. 3:10; 18:1–2; Heb. 9:6.

Were the ministers of. Heb. 8:2.

Punishment for defiling. Lev. 15:31;
Num. 19:13.
Sanctified by the glory of the Lord.
Exod. 29:43; 40:34; Num. 9:15.

Set up
At Gilgal. Josh. 5:10–11.
By Moses at Mount Sinai.
Exod. 40:18–19, with
Num. 10:11–12.
In Nob. 1 Sam. 21:1–6.
In Shiloh. Josh. 18:1; 19:51.
Lastly at Gibeon. 1 Chron. 16:39;
21:29.
Sprinkled and purified with blood.
Heb. 9:21.
The table of shewbread, the golden
candle stick, and the altar of
incense placed in the holy place.
Exod. 36:35; 40:22, 24, 26;
Heb. 9:2.

TABERNACLES, FEAST OF
All males obliged to appear at.
Exod. 23:6–17.
Began fifteenth of seventh month.
Lev. 23:34, 39.
Called the feast of ingathering.
Exod. 34:22.
Commemorated the sojourn of Israel
in the desert. Lev. 23:43.

Customs observed at
Bearing branches of palms.
Lev. 23:40; Rev. 7:9.
Drawing water from the pool of
Siloam. Isa. 12:3; John 7:2,
37–39.
Singing hosannas.
Ps. 118:24–29; Matt. 21:8–9.
First and last days of, holy
convocations. Lev. 23:35, 39;
Num. 29:12, 35.

Held after harvest and vintage.
Deut. 16:13.
Lasted seven days. Lev. 23:34, 41;
Deut. 16:13, 15.
The law publicly read every seventh
year at. Deut. 31:10–12;
Neh. 8:18.

Observed
Perpetually. Lev. 23:41.
With rejoicing. Deut. 16:14–15.
The people lived in booths during.
Lev. 23:42; Neh. 8:15–16.

Remarkable celebrations of
After the captivity. Ezra 3:4;
Neh. 8:17.
At the dedication of Solomon's
temple. 1 Kings 8:2, 65.
Sacrifices during. Lev. 23:36–37;
Num. 29:13–39.

TABLE
An article of furniture. Judg. 1:7;
John 2:15.
Of charities. Acts 6:2.
Of idolatrous feasts. 1 Cor. 10:21.
Of the Lord's Supper. 1 Cor. 10:21.
Made of silver. 1 Chron. 28:16.
Used in figurative sense, of the altar.
Mal. 1:7, 12.

TACT
The church council at Jerusalem.
Acts 21:20–25.
In David's popular methods, in
mourning for Abner.
2 Sam. 3:28–37.
Esther, in placating the king.
Esther 5–7.
Of Gideon. Judg. 8:1–3.
Joab's trick in obtaining David's
consent to the return of Absalom.
2 Sam. 14:1–22.

Table

Mordecai, in concealing Esther's nationality. Esther 2:10.

Nabal's wife. 1 Sam. 25:18–37.

In organizing the temple music. 1 Chron. 15:16–24.

Paul, in arraying the two religious factions of the Jews against each other when he was in trouble. Acts 23:6–10.

Paul, in circumcising Timothy. Acts 16:3.

Paul in stimulating the benevolent giving of the churches. 2 Cor. 8:1–8; 9:1–5.

Paul in turning the preaching of adversaries to good. Phil. 1:10–22.

In preaching. 1 Cor. 9:19–22; 2 Cor. 12:6.

Of Saul, in managing troublemakers. 1 Sam. 10:27.

In securing popular consent to bring the Ark to Jerusalem. 1 Chron. 13:1–4.

Solomon, in arbitrating between the harlots. 1 Kings 3:24–28.

The townclerk of Ephesus. Acts 19:35–41.

TAILORING
A God-given gift in building the tabernacle. Exod. 31:2–3, 6, 10; 39:1.

TALEBEARER
Commandment against. Lev. 19:16.

Examples of
Israelites. 2 Sam. 3:23.
Joseph. Gen. 37:2.
Tobiah. Neh. 6.

TALENT (ABILITY)
Differs in different individuals. Matt. 25:15.

Given by God. 1 Cor. 12:4.

To be used. 1 Tim. 4:14; Rom. 12:6.

TALENT (CURRENCY)
Parable of the. Matt. 18:24; 25:15, 28.

A weight equal to 3,000 shekels, about 125 pounds. Exod. 38:25–26.

TAPESTRY
Gold thread sewn in. Exod. 39:3.
In groves. 2 Kings 23:7.
In palaces. Esther 1:6;
Song of Sol. 1:5.
Of the tabernacle. Exod. 26:1–14, 31–37.

TAR
Found in the valley of Siddim. Gen. 14:10.
Inflammable. Isa. 34:9.
Used at Babel. Gen. 11:3.
Used in Noah's ark. Gen. 6:14.
Used in the ark of Moses. Exod. 2:3.

TARGET
A defensive article of armor, used by a spearman. 2 Chron. 14:8.
Made of brass. 1 Sam. 17:6.
Made of gold. 1 Kings 10:16;
2 Chron. 9:15.

TATTLING
See also Gossip; Gossiper

Destroys friendships. Prov. 16:28.

Examples of
In bedroom. Eccles. 10:20.
To save lives. 1 Sam. 19:11;
Esther 2:21–23.
Forbidden. Prov. 25:7–10.

TATTOOING
Forbidden. Lev. 19:28.

TAX
Collectors of. 2 Sam. 20:24;
Dan. 11:20; Mark 2:14.

Jesus pays. Matt. 17:24–27.
Land. Gen. 41:34.
Land mortgaged for. Neh. 5:3–4.
Paid in grain. Amos 5:11.
Paid in provisions. 1 Kings 4:7–28.
Personal. 1 Kings 9:15.
Poll. Exod. 30:11–16.
Priests exempted from. Gen. 47:26;
Ezra 7:24.
Resisted by Israelites. 1 Kings 12:18;
2 Chron. 10:18.
Stoned. 2 Chron. 10:18.
Unpopular. Matt. 5:46.
Worldwide, levied by Caesar.
Luke 2:1–3.

TEACHING
In the church. Acts 5:42; Rom. 12:7;
Col. 1:28; 1 Tim. 4:11;
Titus 1:11; Heb. 5:12.
Commanded. Prov. 19:20;
Col. 1:28.

False
Described. Isa. 56:11.
Motive in. Titus 1:10–11.
Warned against. Jer. 12:6;
Heb. 13:9.
From God, promised. 1 Sam. 12:23;
Exod. 4:15; Luke 12:12.
From God, requested. Ps. 25:4;
86:11.
From nature. Job 12:7–8;
1 Cor. 11:14.
Parents' duty. Deut. 4:10; 11:19.
Teachers worthy of honor.
1 Cor. 9:9; 1 Tim. 5:17.

TEARS
None in heaven. Rev. 21:4.
Observed by God. Ps. 56:8.
Used in a figurative sense. Ps. 80:5.
Wiped away. Rev. 7:17.

TEETH, GNASHING OF
In hell. Luke 13:28.
Job speaking of God. Job 16:9.

TEMPLE, THE FIRST
All dedicated things placed in.
2 Chron. 5:1.
Appointed as a house of prayer.
Isa. 56:7, with Matt. 21:13.
Appointed as a house of sacrifice.
2 Chron. 7:12.
Ark of God brought into, with great
seriousness. 1 Kings 8:1–9;
2 Chron. 5:2–10.
Built on Mt. Moriah on the threshing
floor of Ornan or Araunah.
1 Chron. 21:28–30, with 22:1;
2 Chron. 3:1.

Called
House of the God of Jacob.
Isa. 2:3.
The house of the Lord.
2 Chron. 23:5, 12.
The mountain of the Lord's house.
Isa. 2:2.
Mount Zion. Ps. 74:2.
Zion. Ps. 84:1–7.
Cedar of, carved with flowers, etc.
1 Kings 6:18.
Complete destruction of, predicted.
Jer. 26:18, with Mic. 3:12.

David
Anxious to build. 2 Sam. 7:2;
1 Chron. 22:7; 29:3;
Ps. 132:2–5.
Being a man of war, not permitted
to build. 2 Sam. 7:5–9, with
1 Kings 5:3; 1 Chron. 22:8.
Charged his princes to assist in
building. 1 Chron. 22:17–19.
Charged Solomon to build.
1 Chron. 22:6–7, 11.

Freewill offerings of the people for
building. 1 Chron. 29:6–9.
Made preparations for building.
1 Chron. 22:2–5, 14–16;
29:2–5.
Prayed that Solomon might have
wisdom to build.
1 Chron. 29:19.
Told by the prophet that Solomon
should build. 2 Sam. 17:12–13;
1 Chron. 17:12.
Dedicated to God by Solomon.
1 Kings 8:12–66; 2 Chron. 6.

Divided into
Oracle or most holy place.
1 Kings 6:19.
Porch. 2 Chron. 3:4.
Sanctuary or greater house.
2 Chron. 3:5.
Filled with the cloud of glory.
1 Kings 8:10–11;
2 Chron. 5:13; 7:2.
Floor and walls of, covered with
cedar and firwood. 1 Kings 6:15.
Garnished with precious stones.
2 Chron. 3:6.
God promised to dwell in. 1 Kings
6:12–13.

Historical notices of
Defiled and its treasures given by
Ahaz to the king of Assyria.
2 Kings 16:14, 18; 2 Chron.
28:20–21.
Its treasures, etc., given by
Hezekiah to the Assyrians, to
obtain a treaty.
2 Kings 18:13–16.
Pillaged and burned by the
Babylonians. 2 Kings 25:8,
13–17; 2 Chron. 36:18–19.

Pillaged by Shishak king of Egypt.
1 Kings 14:25–26;
2 Chron. 12:9.

Polluted by the idolatrous worship
of Manasseh. 2 Kings 21:4–7;
2 Chron. 33:4–5, 7.

Purified and divine worship
restored under Hezekiah.
2 Chron. 29:3–35.

Purified by Josiah.
2 Kings 23:4–7, 11–12.

Repaired by Jehoash at the
instigation of Jehoiada. 2 Kings
12:4–14; 2 Chron. 24:4–13.

Repaired by Josiah in the
eighteenth year of his reign.
2 Kings 22:3–7;
2 Chron. 34:8–13.

Treasures of given by Jehoash to
propitiate the Syrians.
2 Kings 12:17–18.

Illustrative of
The bodies of believers.
1 Cor. 6:19.

Christ. John 2:19, 21.

The spiritual church. 1 Cor. 3:16;
2 Cor. 6:16; Eph. 2:20–22.

Inside and out covered with gold.
1 Kings 6:21–22; 2 Chron. 3:7.

Its magnificence. 2 Chron. 2:5, 9.

Oracle or most holy place
Doors and posts of, olivewood
carved and covered with gold.
1 Kings 6:31–32.

A partition of chains of gold
between it and outer house.
1 Kings 6:21.

Separated from the outer house by
a veil. 2 Chron. 3:14.

Twenty cubits every way.
1 Kings 6:16, 20.

Two cherubim made of olivewood
within, covered with gold.
1 Kings 6:23–28;
2 Chron. 1:11–13.

Paneled with fir wood and gold
covered. 2 Chron. 3:5.

Porch
One hundred and twenty cubits
high. 2 Chron. 3:4.

Pillars with their tops described.
1 Kings 7:15–22;
2 Chron. 3:15–17.

Sacred fire sent down from heaven
at its dedication. 2 Chron. 7:3.

Twenty cubits long and ten wide.
1 Kings 6:3.

Sanctuary or greater house
Door posts of olivewood, carved
and gold covered. 1 Kings 6:33;
2 Chron. 3:7.

Folding doors of fir, carved and
gold covered. 1 Kings 6:34–35.

Forty cubits long. 2 Kings 6:17.

Solomon
Applied to Hiram for a skillful
workman to supervises, etc., the
building of. 2 Chron. 2:7,
13–14.

Begun second day of second
month of fourth year of
Solomon. 1 Kings 6:1, 37;
2 Chron. 3:2.

Built without the noise of
hammers, ax, or any tool.
1 Kings 6:7.

Contracted with Hiram for wood,
stone, and labor. 1 Kings
5:6–12; 2 Chron. 2:8–10.

Determined to build.
2 Chron. 2:1.

Employed all the strangers in preparing for. 2 Chron. 2:2, 17–18, with 1 Kings 5:15.

Employed thirty thousand Israelites in the work. 1 Kings 5:13–14.

Specially instructed for. 2 Chron. 3:3.

Surrounded with three stories of chambers communicating with the interior on the right side. 1 Kings 6:5–6, 8, 10.

Was but a temple built with hands. Acts 7:47–48.

Was finished in the eighth month of the eleventh year of Solomon. 1 Kings 6:38.

Was lighted by narrow windows. 1 Kings 6:4.

Was roofed with cedar. 1 Kings 6:9.

Was seven years in building. 1 Kings 6:38.

Was threescore cubits long, twenty wide, and thirty high. 1 Kings 6:2; 2 Chron. 3:3.

Temple

TEMPLE, SECOND

Beautiful gate of, mentioned. Acts 3:2.

Built on the site of the first temple. Ezra 2:6, etc.

Ceremony connected with laying the foundation of. Ezra 3:9–11.

Christ
To appear in. Hag. 2:7, with Mal. 3:1.
Frequently taught in. Mark 14:49.

Miraculously transported to a pinnacle of. Matt. 4:5; Luke 4:9.

Predicted its destruction. Matt. 24:2; Mark 13:2; Luke 21:6.

Presented in. Luke 2:22, 27.

Purified, at the close of His ministry. Matt. 21:12–13.

Purified, at the commencement of His ministry. John 2:15–17.

Completed the third of the twelfth month in the sixth year of Darius. Ezra 6:15.

Cyrus

Decree for building, predicted. Isa. 44:28.

Furnished means for building. Ezra 6:4.

Gave a decree for building, in the first year of his reign. Ezra 1:1–2; 6:3.

Gave permission to the Jews to go to Jerusalem to build. Ezra 1:3.

Gave the articles of the first temple for. Ezra 1:7–11, 6:5.

Ordered those who remained in Babylon to contribute to the building of. Ezra 1:4.

Decree of Cyrus found and confirmed by Darius. Ezra 6:1–2, 6–12.

Desecrated by the Romans. Dan. 9:27, with Matt. 24:15.

Dedication of, celebrated with joy and thankfulness. Ezra 6:16–18.

Desecration of, predicted. Dan. 9:27; 11:31.

Dimensions. Ezra 6:3–4.

Divine worship begun before foundation was laid. Ezra 3:1–6

Foundation of, laid the second month of the second year after the captivity. Ezra 3:8.

Future glory of, predicted. Hag. 2:7–9.

Grief of those who had seen the first temple. Ezra 3:12; Hag. 2:3.

Its completion by Zerubbabel predicted, to encourage the Jews. Zech. 4:4–10.

The Jews

Considered it blasphemy to speak against. Matt. 26:61; Acts 6:13; 21:28.

Desecrated by the selling of oxen, etc. John 2:14.

Encouraged to proceed in building. Hag. 1:8; 2:19; Zech. 8:9.

Prayed outside while the priest offered incense within. Luke 1:10. (*See also* Luke 18:10.)

Punished for not persevering in building. Heb. 1:6, 9–11; 2:15, 17; Zech. 8:10.

Reproved for not building. Hag. 1:1–5.

Joy of those who had not seen the first temple. Ezra 3:13.

Magnificence of its building and ornaments. John 2:20; Mark 13:1; Luke 21:5.

Materials for building, obtained from Tyre and Sidon. Ezra 3:7.

No Gentile allowed to enter the inner courts of. Acts 21:27–30.

Rededicated and cleansed by Judas Maccabaeus after its desecration by Antiochus. John 10:22.

Repaired and beautified by Herod, which occupied forty-six years. John 2:20.

Resumed by Zerubbabel and Jeshua. Ezra 5:2.

The Samaritans, etc.

Obtained its interruption for fifteen years. Ezra 4:24.

Proposed to assist in building. Ezra 4:1–2.

Their help refused by the Jews. Ezra 4:3.

Weakened the hands of the Jews in building. Ezra 4:4–5.

Wrote to Artaxerxes to interrupt the building. Ezra 4:6–16.

Separation between the outer or Gentile court and that of the Jews alluded to. Eph. 2:13–14.

Solomon's porch connected with. John 10:23; Acts 3:11.

Tatnai the governor wrote to Darius to know if the building had his sanction. Ezra 5:3–17.

Veil of, torn apart at the death of Christ. Matt. 27:51.

TEMPTATION

Believers may be suffer. 1 Pet. 1:6.

Believers should

Avoid the way of. Prov. 4:14–15.

Not occasion to others. Rom. 14:13.

Pray to be kept from. Matt. 6:13; 26:41.

Resist in faith. Eph. 6:16; 1 Pet. 5:9.

Restore those overcome by. Gal. 6:1.

Watch for. Matt. 26:41; 1 Pet. 5:8.

Blessedness of those who meet and overcome. James 1:2–4, 12.

Christ

Endured from the devil. Mark 1:13.

Endured from the wicked. Matt. 16:1; 22:18; Luke 10:25.

Intercedes for His people under. Luke 22:31–32; John 17:15.

Is able to help those under. Heb. 2:18.

Keeps faithful believers from the hour of. Rev. 3:10.

Overcame. Matt. 4:11.

Resisted by the Word of God. Matt. 4:4, 7, 10.

Sympathizes with those under. Heb. 4:15.

Comes from

Covetousness. Prov. 28:20; 1 Tim. 6:9–10.

Lust. James 1:14.

The devil is the author of. 1 Chron. 21:1; Matt. 4:1; John 13:2; 1 Thess. 3:5.

The devil will renew. Luke 4:13.

To distrust of God's providence. Matt. 4:3.

Does not come from God. James 1:13.

Evil associates, the instruments of. Prov. 1:10; 7:6; 16:29.

God

Cannot be the subject of. James 1:13.

Enables the believers to bear. 1 Cor. 10:13.

Knows how to deliver believers out of. 2 Pet. 2:9.

Will make a way for believers to escape out of. 1 Cor. 10:13.

Will not allow believers to be exposed to, beyond their powers to bear. 1 Cor. 10:13.

Has strength through human weakness. Matt. 26:41.

Mere professors fall away in time of. Luke 8:13.

Often arises through

Poverty. Prov. 30:9; Matt. 4:2–3.

Prosperity. Prov. 30:9; Matt. 4:8.

Worldly glory. Num. 22:17; Dan. 4:30; 5:2; Matt. 4:8.

Often ends in sin and perdition. 1 Tim. 6:9; James 1:15.

Often strengthened by not applying God's Word correctly. Matt. 4:6.

A part of every person's life. 1 Cor. 10:13.

Permitted as a trial of

Disinterestedness. Job 1:9–12.

Faith. 1 Pet. 1:7; James 1:2–3.

To presumption. Matt. 4:6.

To worshiping the god of this world. Matt. 4:9.

Tents

TENTS

Antiquity of. Gen. 4:20.

Called

Curtains. Isa. 54:2; Heb. 3:7.

Tabernacles. Num. 24:5; Job 12:6; Heb. 11:9.

Custom of sitting and standing at the door of. Gen. 18:1; Judg. 4:20.

Ease and rapidity of their removal alluded to. Isa. 38:12.

Fastened by cords to stakes or nails. Isa. 54:2; Jer. 10:20, with Judg. 4:21.

Illustrative of

The great extension of the church (when enlarging). Isa. 54:2.

The heavens (when spread out). Isa. 40:22.

Pitched

In the neighborhood of wells, etc. Gen. 13:10, 12; 26:17–18; 1 Sam. 29:1.

With order and regularity. Num. 1:52.

On the tops of houses. 2 Sam. 16:22.

Under trees. Gen. 18:1, 4; Judg. 4:5.

Sending persons to seek a
convenient place for, alluded to.
Deut. 1:33.
Separate, for females of the family.
Gen. 24:67.
Separate, for servants. Gen. 31:33.
Spread out. Isa. 40:22.
Those of the Jews contrasted with
those of the Arabs. Num. 24:5,
with Song of Sol. 1:5.

Used by
All eastern nations. Judg. 6:5;
1 Sam. 17:4; 2 Kings 7:7;
1 Chron. 5:10.
The Arabs. Isa. 13:20.
Israel in the desert. Exod. 33:8;
Num. 24:2.
Patriarchs. Gen. 13:5; 25:27;
Heb. 11:9.
The people of Israel in all their
wars. 1 Sam. 4:3, 10; 29:1;
1 Kings 16:16.
The Rechabites. Jer. 35:7, 10.
Shepherds while tending their flocks.
Song of Sol. 1:8; Isa. 38:12.

THANKSGIVING

Believers
Abound in the faith with. Col. 2:7.
Come before God with. Ps. 95:2.
Exhorted to. Ps. 105:1; Col. 3:15.
Habitually offer. Dan. 6:10.
Magnify God by. Ps. 69:30.
Offer sacrifices of. Ps. 116:17.
Resolved to offer. Pss. 18:49;
30:12.
Should enter God's gate with.
Ps. 100:4.
Christ set an example of.
Matt. 11:25; 26:27; John 6:11;
11:41.
Commanded. Ps. 50:14; Phil. 4:6.

Expressed in Psalms. 1 Chron. 16:7.
A good thing. Ps. 92:1.
The heavenly host engaged in.
Rev. 4:9; 7:11–12; 11:16–17.
Of hypocrites, full of boasting.
Luke 18:11.
Ministers appointed to offer in public.
1 Chron. 16:4, 7; 23:30;
2 Chron. 31:2.
Should always accompany praise.
Ps. 92:1; Heb. 13:15.
Should always accompany prayer.
Neh. 11:17; Phil. 4:6; Col. 4:2.
Should be accompanied by
intercession for others.
1 Tim. 2:1; 2 Tim. 1:3;
Philem. 1:4.

Should be offered
Always. Eph. 1:16; 5:20;
1 Thess. 1:2.
For all people. 1 Tim. 2:1.
For all things. 2 Cor. 9:11;
Eph. 5:20.
For appointment to the ministry.
1 Tim. 1:12.
In behalf of ministers. 2 Cor. 1:11.
Through Christ. Rom. 1:8;
Col. 3:17; Heb. 13:15.
To Christ. 1 Tim. 1:12.
For Christ's power and reign.
Rev. 11:17.
Upon the completion of great
undertakings. Neh. 12:31, 40.
For deliverance through Christ
from indwelling sin.
Rom. 7:23–25.
In everything. 1 Thess. 5:18.
For the conversion of others.
Rom. 6:17.
For faith exhibited by others.
Rom. 1:8; 2 Thess. 1:3.
To God. Ps. 50:14.
For the gift of Christ. 2 Cor. 9:15.

For the goodness and mercy of God. Pss. 106:1; 107:1; 136:1–3.

For the grace bestowed on others. 1 Cor. 1:4; Phil. 1:3–5; Col. 1:3–6.

For love exhibited by others. 2 Thess. 1:3.

Before meals. John 6:11; Acts 27:35.

In the name of Christ. Eph. 5:20.

For nearness of God's presence. Ps. 75:1.

In private worship. Dan. 6:10.

In public worship. Ps. 35:18.

For the reception and effective working of the word of God in others. 1 Thess. 2:13.

At the remembrance of God's holiness. Pss. 30:4; 97:12.

For the supply of our bodily needs. Rom. 14:6–7; 1 Tim. 4:3–4.

For the triumph of the gospel. 2 Cor. 2:14.

For victory over death and the grave. 1 Cor. 15:57.

For willingness to offer our property for God's service. 1 Chron. 29:6–14.

For wisdom and might. Dan. 2:23.

For the zeal exhibited by others. 2 Cor. 8:16.

The wicked are characterized by an absence of. Rom. 1:21.

THEFT

An abomination. Jer. 7:9–10.

All earthly treasure exposed to. Matt. 6:19.

Believers warned against. Eph. 4:28; 1 Pet. 4:15.

Brings a curse on those who commit it. Hos. 4:2–3; Zech. 5:3–4; Mal. 3:5.

Brings the wrath of God upon those who commit it. Ezek. 22:29, 31.

Calamity pronounced against. Isa. 10:2; Nah. 3:1.

Connected with murder. Jer. 7:9; Hos. 4:2.

Defiles a person. Matt. 15:20.

Excludes from heaven. 1 Cor. 6:10.

Forbidden. Exod. 20:15, with Mark 10:19; Rom. 13:9.

Heavenly treasure secure from. Matt. 6:20; Luke 12:33.

Illustrates the guilt of false teachers. Jer. 23:30; John 10:1, 8, 10.

Includes fraud concerning wages. Lev. 19:13; Mal. 3:5; James 5:4.

Includes fraud in general. Lev. 19:13.

Mosaic law regarding. Exod. 22:1–8.

From the poor, specially forbidden. Prov. 22:22.

Proceeds from the heart. Matt. 15:19.

Shame follows the detection of. Jer. 2:26.

Those who connive at
Hate their own souls. Prov. 29:24.
Will be reproved of God. Ps. 50:18, 21.

The wicked
Addicted to. Ps. 119:61.
Associate with those who commit. Isa. 1:23.
Commit, under shelter of the night. Job 24:14; Obad. 1:5.
Consent to those who commit. Ps. 50:18.
Destroy themselves by. Prov. 21:7.
Do not repent of. Rev. 9:21.

Lie in wait to commit. Hos. 6:9.
May, for a season, prosper in.
Job 12:6.
Plead excuses for. Jer. 7:9–10.
Store up the fruits of. Amos 3:10.

THRESHING
Cattle employed in, not to be
muzzled. Deut. 25:4; 1 Cor. 9:9;
1 Tim. 5:18.
Continued until the grape harvest in
years of abundance. Lev. 26:5.
Followed by a winnowing with a
shovel or fan. Isa. 30:24; 41:16;
Matt. 3:12.

Illustrative of
The church in her conquests.
Isa. 41:15–16; Mic. 4:13.
The church overcoming
opposition (an instrument for,
with teeth). Isa. 41:15.
Complete destruction (dust made
by). 2 Kings 13:7.
The judgments of God. Isa. 21:10;
Jer. 51:33; Hab. 3:12.
The labors of ministers.
1 Cor. 9:9–10.
Preparing the enemies of the
church for judgments (gathering
the sheaves). Mic. 4:12.

Performed
By cart wheels. Isa. 27:27–28.
By instruments with teeth.
Isa. 41:15; Amos 1:3.
By rod or staff. Isa. 28:27.
By the feet of horses and oxen.
Isa. 28:28; Hos. 10:11. *(See
also* 2 Sam. 24:22.)

Place for
Called the barn floor. 2 King 6:27.
Called the corn floor. Hos. 9:1.
Called the floor. Judg. 6:37;
Isa. 21:10.
Called the threshing floor.
Num. 18:27; 2 Sam. 24:18.
Fullness of, promised as a blessing.
Joel 2:24.
Generally on high ground.
1 Chron. 21:18, with
2 Chron. 3:1.
The Jews slept on, during the time
of. Ruth 3:7.
Often robbed. 1 Sam. 23:1.
Scarcity in, a punishment.
Hos. 9:2.
Sometimes beside the winepress
for concealment. Judg. 6:11.
Used also for winnowing the corn.
Ruth 3:2.
Was large and roomy.
Gen. 50:10.
Removing or separating corn, etc.,
from the straw. 1 Chron. 21:20.

TIME
All events of, predetermined by God.
Acts 17:26.
All God's purposes fulfilled in due
time. Mark 1:15; Gal. 4:4.
An appointed season. Neh. 2:6;
Eccles. 3:1, 17.

Computed by
Days. Gen. 8:3; Job 1:4;
Luke 11:3.
Hours, after the captivity.
Dan. 5:5; John 11:9.
Moments. Exod. 33:5; Luke 4:5;
1 Cor. 15:52.
Months. Num. 10:10;
1 Chron. 27:1; Job 3:6.
Weeks. Dan. 10:2; Luke 18:12.
Years. Gen. 15:13; 2 Sam. 21:1;
Dan. 9:2.

Duration of the world. Job 22:16;
Rev. 10:6.

Eras from which computed
Accession of kings. 1 Kings 6:1;
15:1; Isa. 36:1; Jer. 1:2;
Luke 3:1.
Building of the temple.
1 Kings 9:10; 2 Chron. 8:1.
The captivity. Ezek. 1:1; 33:21;
40:1.
The Exodus from Egypt.
Exod. 19:1; 40:17; Num. 9:1;
33:38; 1 Kings 6:1.
The jubilee. Lev. 25:15.
Nativity of the patriarchs during
the patriarchal age. Gen. 7:11;
8:13; 17:1.
Heavenly bodies appointed as a
means for computing. Gen. 1:14.
Measure of the continuance of
anything. Judg. 18:31.
Part of a period of, usually counted as
the whole. 1 Sam. 13:1;
Esther 4:16, with 5:1.

Particular periods of, mentioned
Accepted time. Isa. 49:8;
2 Cor. 6:2.
Ancient time. Isa. 45:21.
Evil time.Exod. 9:12; Ps. 37:19.
Time of healing. Jer. 14:19.
Time of need. Neh. 4:16.
Time of reformation. Heb. 9:10.
Time of refreshing. Acts 3:19.
Time of restitution of all things.
Acts 3:21.
Time of temptation. Luke 8:13.
Time of trouble. Ps. 27:5;
Jer. 14:8.
Time of visitation.
Jer. 46:21; 50:27.

In prophetic language, a prophetic
year, or 365 natural years.
Dan. 12:7; Rev. 12:14.
Shortness of main's portion of.
Ps 89:47.
Should be redeemed. Eph. 5:16;
Col. 4:5.
Should be spent in the fear of God.
1 Pet. 1:17.
Sundial early invented for pointing
out. 2 Kings 20:9–11.

TITHE
Antiquity of the custom of giving to
God's ministers. Gen. 14:20;
Heb. 7:6.
Considered a just return to God for
His blessings. Gen. 28:22.

Consisted of a tenth
Of all cattle. Lev. 27:32.
Of all the produce of the land.
Lev. 27:30.
Of holy things dedicated.
2 Chron. 31:6.
Given by God to the Levites for their
services. Num. 18:21, 24;
Neh. 10:37.
The Jews reprimanded for
withholding. Mal. 3:8.
The Jews slow in giving. Neh. 13:10.
The Pharisees scrupulous in paying.
Luke 11:42; 18:12.
Pious governors of Israel caused the
payment of. 2 Chron. 31:5;
Neh. 13:11–12.
Punishment for changing.
Lev. 27:33.
Reasonableness of appointing, for
the Levites. Num. 18:20, 23–24;
Josh. 13:33.
Rulers appointed over, for
distributing. 2 Chron. 31:12;
Neh. 13:13.

A second
  Or its value yearly brought to the
    tabernacle and eaten before the
    Lord. Deut. 12:6–7, 17–19;
    14:22–27.
  To be consumed at home every
    third year to promote hospitality
    and charity. Deut. 14:28–29;
    26:12–15.
The tenth of anything.
  1 Sam. 8:15, 17.
The tenth of, given by the Levites to
  the priests as their portion.
  Num. 18:26, 28; Neh. 10:38.
The tenth of, offered by the Levites
  as a set-aside offering to God.
  Num. 18:26–27.
Under the law, belonged to God.
  Lev. 27:30.
When redeemed, to have a fifth part
  of the value added. Lev. 27:31.

TITLES AND NAMES OF BELIEVERS
See Believers, Titles and Names of

TITLES AND NAMES OF CHRIST
See Christ, Titles and Names of

TITLES AND NAMES OF THE CHURCH
See Church, Titles and Names of the

TITLES AND NAMES OF THE DEVIL
See Devil, Titles and Names of the

TITLES AND NAMES OF THE HOLY SPIRIT
See Holy Spirit, Titles and Names of
the

TITLES AND NAMES OF MINISTERS
See Ministers, Titles and Names of

TITLES AND NAMES OF THE WICKED
See Wicked, Titles and names of

TOWERS
Antiquity of. Gen. 11:4.

Built
  In cities. Judg. 9:51.
  In the deserts. 2 Chron. 26:10.
  In the forests. 2 Chron. 27:4.
  In vineyards. Isa. 5:2; Matt. 21:33.
  On the walls of cities.
    2 Chron. 14:7; 26:9.
Frequently left desolate. Isa. 32:14;
  Zeph. 3:6.
Frequently strong and well fortified.
  Judg. 9:51, with 2 Chron. 26:9.
Frequently thrown down in war.
  Judg. 8:17; 9:49; Ezek. 26:4.
Frequently very high. Isa. 2:15.
Guards posted on, in times of danger.
  2 Kings 9:17; Hab. 2:1.

Illustrative of
  God as the protector of His
    people. 2 Sam. 22:3, 51;
    Pss. 18:2; 61:3.
  The grace and dignity of the
    church. Song of Sol. 4:4; 7:4;
    8:10.
  Ministers. Jer. 6:27.
  Mount Zion. Mic. 4:8.
  The name of the Lord.
    Prov. 18:10.
  The proud and haughty. Isa. 2:15;
    30:25.
Of Jerusalem, remarkable for
  number, strength, and beauty.
  Ps. 48:12.

Mentioned in Scripture
Babel. Gen. 11:9.
David. Song of Sol. 4:4.
Edar. Gen. 35:21.
Hananeel. Jer. 31:38;
 Zech. 14:10.
Jezreel. 2 Kings 9:17.
Lebanon. Song of Sol. 7:4.
Meah. Neh. 12:39.
Of the furnaces. Neh. 3:11.
Penuel. Judg. 8:17.
Shechem. Judg. 9:46.
Siloam. Luke 13:4.
Syene. Ezek. 29:10; 30:6.
Thebez. Judg. 9:50–51.
Used as armories. Song of Sol. 4:4.
Used as hiding places in times of war.
 Judg. 9:51; Ezek. 27:11.

TRAVELERS

After a long journey, described.
 Josh. 9:4–5, 13.
Called travelers. Judg. 19:17;
 Isa. 35:8.

Carried with them
Feed for their animals.
 Gen. 42:27; Judg. 19:19.
Presents for those who gave them
 a place to stay. Gen. 43:15;
 1 Kings 10:2; 2 Kings 5:5;
 Matt. 2:11.
Provisions for the journey. Josh.
 9:11–12; Judg. 19:19.
Skins filled with water, wine, etc.
 Gen. 21:14–15; Josh. 9:13.
Ceasing of, threatened as a calamity.
 Isa. 33:8.

Of distinction
Before setting out gave
 employment, etc., to their
 servants. Matt. 25:14.

Frequently extorted provisions by
 the way. Judg. 8:5, 8;
 1 Sam. 25:4–13.
Generally attended by running
 footmen. 1 Sam. 25:27;
 1 Kings 18:46; 2 Kings 4:24;
 Eccles. 10:7.
Generally performed their journey
 in great state. 1 Kings 10:2;
 2 Kings 5:5, 9, etc.
Often preceded by heralds, etc., to
 have the roads prepared. Isa.
 40:3–4, with Mark 1:2–3.
Rode in chariots. 2 Kings 5:9;
 Acts 8:27–28.
Rode on donkeys, camels, etc.
 Gen. 22:3; 24:64; Num. 22:21.

On errands requiring haste
Saluted no man by the way.
 2 Kings 4:29; Luke 10:4.
Went with great speed. Esther
 8:10; Job 9:25.
Estimated the length of their journey
 by the number of days it took.
 Gen. 31:23; Deut. 1:2;
 2 Kings 3:9.
On foot, how attired. Exod. 12:11.

Friends of
Frequently commended them to
 protection of God. Gen.
 43:13–14; Acts 21:5.
Frequently said good-bye to them
 with sorrow. Acts 20:37; 21:16.
Often sent them away with music.
 Gen. 31:27.
Often supplied them with
 provision. Gen. 21:14; 44:1;
 Jer. 40:5.
Sometimes accompanied them a
 short way. 2 Sam. 19:31;
 Acts 20:38; 21:5.

Frequently asked from where they came and where they went. Judg. 19:17.

Generally began their journey early in the morning. Judg. 19:5.

Generally stopped at wells or streams. Gen. 24:11; 32:21, 23; Exod. 15:27; 1 Sam. 30:21; John 4:6.

Generally rested at noon. Gen. 18:1, 3; John 4:6.

Generally stopped at night. Gen. 24:11.

Generally treated with great hospitality. Gen. 18:3–8; 19:2; 24:25, 32–33; Exod. 2:20; Judg. 19:20–21; Job 31:32. (See also Heb. 13:2.)

The Jews prohibited from taking long journeys on the Sabbath. Exod. 20:10, with Acts 1:12.

Often got together and formed caravans. Gen. 37:25; Isa. 21:13; Luke 2:44.

Often engaged persons acquainted with the country as guides. Num. 10:31–32; Job 29:15.

Often left the highways for security. Judg. 5:6.

Often traveled on foot. Gen. 28:10, with 32:10; Exod. 12:37; Acts 20:13.

Pledges of hospitality alluded to. Rev. 2:17.

Preparations made by, alluded to. Ezek. 12:3–4.

Protected by those who entertained them Gen. 19:6–8; Judg. 19:23.

Public inn for, noticed. Gen. 42:27; Exod. 4:24; Luke 2:7; 10:34.

Strangers civil to. Gen. 18:2; 24:18–19.

TREASURE CITIES

Built for the storage of the king's substance. Exod. 1:11; 1 Kings 9:19; 2 Chron. 8:4, 6.

TREASURE HOUSES

Chambers provided in the temple for various kinds of offerings. Neh. 10:38–39; 13:5, 9, 12; Mal. 3:10.

Under the charge of the Levites. 1 Chron. 26:20.

Heathen temples used for. Dan. 1:2.

Of kings. 2 Kings 20:13; 1 Chron. 27:25; 2 Chron. 32:27–28; Ezra 1:7–8; Esther 3:9.

Priests and Levites in charge of. 1 Chron. 9:26; 26:20–28; Neh. 12:44; 13:13.

Records preserved in. Ezra 5:17; 6:1.

Solomon's temple used for. 1 Kings 7:51; 2 Kings 12:4–14, 18; 22:4–5; 1 Chron. 28:11–12; Matt. 27:6; Mark 12:41, 43; Luke 21:1; John 8:20.

Treasures in charge of. Ezra 7:20–21.

Tabernacle used for. Num. 31:54; Josh. 6:19, 24.

TREATY

Acquiring of territory by. 1 Kings 9:10–14; 20:34.

Between nations
    Israel and the Gibeonites. Josh. 9:3–15.
    Judah and Syria. 1 Kings 15:19.

With idolatrous nations forbidden. Exod. 34:12–15.

Reciprocity. 1 Kings 5:1–12.

Sacredness of. Josh. 9:16–21.

TREES

See also Tree, Fig; Tree, Fir; Tree, Fruit; Tree, Oak; Tree, Olive; Tree, Palm; Tree, Pomegranate

Afford shade in eastern countries during the heat of the day. Gen. 18:4; Job 40:21.

Cut down
  With axes. Deut. 19:5; Ps. 74:5; Matt. 3:10.
  By besieging armies for erecting forts. Deut. 20:20; Jer. 6:6.
  For building. 2 Kings 6:2; 2 Chron. 2:8, 10.
  For fuel. Isa. 44:14–16; Matt. 3:10.
  For making idols. Isa. 40:20; 44:14, 17.
Designed to beautify the earth. Gen. 2:9.

Different kinds of, mentioned
  Bearing fruit. Neh. 9:25; Eccles. 2:5; Ezek. 47:12.
  Deciduous. Isa. 6:13.
  Evergreen. Ps. 37:35; Jer. 17:2.
  Of the forest. Isa. 10:19.
  Of the wood. Song of Sol. 2:3.
Each kind has its own seed for propagating its species. Gen. 1:11–12.
Each kind known by its fruit. Matt. 12:33.
Early custom of planting in consecrated grounds. Gen. 21:33.
Given as food to the animals. Gen. 1:29–30; Deut. 20:19.
God increases and multiplies the fruit of, for His people. Lev. 26:4; Ezek. 34:27; Joel 2:22.
God often renders barren as a punishment. Lev. 26:20.

Illustrative of
  Believers (when evergreen). Ps. 1:1–3.
  Believers (when good and fruitful). Num. 24:6; Ps. 1:3; Isa. 61:3; Jer. 17:8; Matt. 7:17–18.
  Christ. Rom. 11:24; Rev. 2:7; 22:2, 14.
  Continued prosperity of believers (in their duration). Isa. 65:22.
  The elect remnant in the church (casting their leaves yet retaining their substance). Isa. 6:13.
  The innocence of Christ (when green). Luke 23:31.
  Kings, etc. Isa. 10:34; Ezek. 17:24; 31:7–10; Dan. 4:10–14.
  The life and conversation of the righteous. Prov. 11:30; 15:4.
  The terror of the wicked (shaking of their leaves). Isa. 7:2.
  Useless persons (when dry). Isa. 56:3.
  The wicked (when producing evil fruit). Matt. 7:17–19.
  The wicked ripe for judgment (when dry). Luke 23:31.
  Wisdom. Prov. 3:18.

The Jews
  Considered trees on which criminals were executed abominable. Isa. 14:19.
  Made for the glory of God. Ps. 148:7–9.
  Often buried under. Gen. 35:8; 1 Sam. 31:13.
  Often executed criminals on. Deut. 21:22–23; Josh. 10:26; Gal. 3:13. (*See also* Gen. 40:19.)

Often pitched their tents under.
Gen. 18:1, 4; Judg. 4:5; 1 Sam.
22:6.
Prohibited from cutting down fruit-
bearing, for sieges. Deut. 20:19.
Prohibited from planting in
consecrated places.
Deut. 16:21.
Of knowledge.
Gen. 2:9, 17; 3:3–6, 11–12, 17.
Of life. Gen. 2:9; 3:22, 24;
Rev. 22:14.

Mentioned in Scripture
Acacia wood. Exod. 36:20;
Isa. 41:19.
Almond. Gen. 43:11;
Eccles. 12:5; Jer. 1:11.
Almug or algum. 1 Kings
10:11–12; 2 Chron. 9:10–11.
Aloe. Num. 24:6.
Apple. Song of Sol. 2:3; 8:5;
Joel 1:12.
Ash. Isa. 44:14.
Bay. Ps. 37:35.
Box. Isa. 41:19.
Cedar. 1 Kings 10:27; Isa. 41:19.
Chestnut. Ezek. 31:8.
Cyprus. Isa. 44:14.
Fig. Deut. 8:8.
Fir. 1 Kings 5:10; 2 Kings 19:23;
Ps. 104:17.
Juniper. 1 Kings 19:4–5.
Mulberry. 2 Sam. 5:23–24.
Mustard. Matt. 13:31–32.
Myrtle. Isa. 41:19; 55:13;
Zech. 1:8.
Oak. Isa. 1:30.
Oil tree. Isa. 41:19.
Olive. Deut. 6:11.
Palm. Exod. 15:27.
Pine. Isa. 41:19.
Pomegranate. Deut. 8:8;
Joel 1:12.

Sycamore. 1 Kings 10:27; Ps.
78:47; Amos 7:14; Luke 19:4.
Teil. Isa. 6:13.
Vine. Num. 6:4; Ezek. 15:2.
Willow. Isa. 44:4; Ezek. 17:5.

Nourished
By the earth. Gen. 1:12; 2:9.
By the rain from heaven.
Isa. 44:14.
Through their own sap.
Ps. 104:16.
Often propagated by birds who carry
the seeds along with them. Ezek.
17:3, 5.

Often suffered from
Fire. Joel 1:19.
Hail and frost. Exod. 9:25;
Ps. 78:47.
Locusts. Exod. 10:5, 15;
Deut. 28:42.
Originally created by God.
Gen. 1:11–12; 2:9.

Parts of, mentioned
Branches. Lev. 23:40; Dan. 4:14.
Fruit or seeds. Lev. 27:30;
Ezek. 36:30.
Leaves. Isa. 6:13; Dan. 4:12;
Matt. 21:19.
Roots. Jer. 17:8.
Stem or trunk. Isa. 11:1; 44:19.
Planted by man. Lev. 19:23.
Sold with the land on which they
grew. Gen. 23:17.
Specially flourished beside rivers and
streams of water. Ezek. 47:12.
Used in a figurative sense. Ps. 1:3;
Jer. 17:8.
Of various sizes. Ezek. 17:24.
When cut down, often sprouted from
the roots again. Job 14:7.

TREE, FIG

Abounded in
Canaan. Num. 13:23; Deut. 8:8.
Egypt. Ps. 105:33.
Afforded a thick shade.
John 1:48, 50.
In an allegory. Judg. 9:11.
Barren, parable of. Luke 13:6–9;
21:29–31.
Failure of, a great calamity.
Hab. 3:17.
Figurative sense. Matt. 24:32;
Rev. 6:13.

Fruit of
Eaten dried in cakes.
1 Sam. 30:12.
Eaten fresh from the tree.
Matt. 21:18–19.

First ripe valued. Jer. 24:2;
Hos. 9:10.
Formed after winter.
Song of Sol. 2 :11, 13.
Gathered and kept in baskets.
Jer. 24:1.
Sent as presents. 1 Sam. 25:18;
1 Chron. 12:40.
Sold in the markets. Neh. 13:15.
Used in the miraculous healing of
Hezekiah. 2 Kings 20:7;
Isa. 38:21.

Illustrative of
Mere professors of religion (when
barren). Matt. 21:19;
Luke 13·6–7.
Prosperity and peace (sitting under
one's own). 1 Kings 4:25;
Mic. 4:4.

Sycamore Fig

Fig

Its fruit illustrative of
Believers Jer. 24:2–3.
Fathers of the Jewish church
(when first ripe). Hos. 9:10.
Good works. Matt. 7:16.
Wicked men (when bad).
Jer. 24:2–8.
The wicked ripe for judgment
(when untimely and dropping).
Isa. 34:4; Nah. 3:12;
Rev. 6:13.
Jeremiah's parable of. Jer. 24:2–3.

The Jews punished by
Enemies devouring fruit of.
Jer. 5:17.
Failure of fruit on. Jer. 8:13;
Hag. 2:19.
God's breaking down. Hos. 2:12.
Stripping of bark and eating of, by
locusts, etc. Joel 1:4, 7, 12;
Amos 4:9.
Leaves of, a sign of the approach of
summer. Matt. 24:32.
Leaves of, used by Adam for
covering. Gen. 3:7.
Not found in desert places.
Num. 20:5.
Often unfruitful. Luke 13:7.
Produces a rich sweet fruit.
Judg. 9:11.
Reasonableness of expecting fruit
upon, when full of leaves.
Mark 11:13.
Required cultivation. Luke 13:8.
Sometimes planted in vineyards.
Luke 13:6.
A species of, produced vile and
worthless fruit. Jer. 29:17.
Taught by the Jews. Amos 4:9.

TREE, FIR
Instruments of music made of.
2 Sam. 6:5.

Ships made of. Ezek. 27:5.
Wood of, used for building.
1 Kings 6:15, 34;
Song of Sol. 1:17.

TREES, FRUIT
Care for. Deut. 20:19–20.

TREE, OAK
Absalom in his flight, intercepted by
and suspended
from. 2 Sam. 18:9–10, 14.
Bashan celebrated for. Isa. 2:13.

Described as
Strong. Amos 2:9.
A stump. Isa. 6:13.
Thick-spreading. 2 Sam. 18:9;
Ezek. 6:13.
Idolaters often made idols of.
Isa. 44:14.

Illustrative of
The church. Isa. 6:13.
Strong and powerful men.
Amos 2:9.
Wicked rulers. Isa. 2:13;
Zech. 11:2.
The wicked under judgments
(when fading). Isa. 1:30.
Jacob buried his family idols under.
Gen. 35:4.

The people in ancient times often
Buried their dead under.
Gen. 35:8; 1 Chron. 10:12.
Erected monuments under.
Josh. 24:26.
Performed idolatrous rites under.
Isa. 1:29; 57:5; Ezek. 6:13;
Hos. 4:13.
Rested under. Judg. 6:11, 19;
1 Kings 13:14.

The Tyrians made oars of.
Ezek. 27:6.

TREE, OLIVE

Assyria abounded in. 2 Kings 18:32.

Beaten to remove the fruit.
Deut. 24:20.

Canaan abounded in.
Deut. 6:11; 8:8.

Cultivated
Among rocks. Deut. 32:13.
In olive yards. 1 Sam. 8:14;
Neh. 5:11.
On the sides of mountains.
Matt. 21:1.

Described as
Bearing good fruit. Jer. 11:16,
with James 3:12.
Fair and beautiful. Jer. 11:16, with
Hos. 14:6.
Fatty and oily. Judg. 9:9;
Rom. 11:17.
Green. Jer. 11:16.

Failure of, a great calamity.
Hab. 3:17–18.

Fruit of, during sabbatical year left for
the poor, etc. Exod. 23:11.

Fruit of, trodden in presses to extract
the oil. Mic. 6:15, with Hag. 2:16.

Gleaning of, left for the poor.
Deut. 24:20.

Good for the service of God and
man. Judg. 9:9.

Grafting of, alluded to. Rom. 11:24.

Illustrative of
Children of pious parents.
Ps. 128:3.
Christ. Rom. 11:17, 24;
Zech. 4:3, 12.
Gentiles (when wild).
Rom. 11:17, 24.

The Jewish church. Jer. 11:16.

The remnant of grace (gleaning
of). Isa. 17:6; 24:13.

The righteous. Ps. 52:8;
Hos. 14:6.

The two witnesses. Rev. 11:3–4.

Kings of Israel largely cultivated.
1 Chron. 27:28.

Often grew wild. Rom. 11:17.

Often sheds its flowers. Job 15:33.

Often sheds its fruit. Deut. 28:40.

Often suffered from caterpillars.
Amos 4:9.

Oil procured from. Exod. 27:20;
Deut. 8:8.

Probable origin of its being the
emblem of peace. Gen. 8:11.

Pruning of, alluded to.
Rom. 11:18–19.

Shaken when fully ripe. Isa. 17:6.

Used for making
Booths at feast of tabernacles.
Neh. 8:15.
Cherubim in the temple.
1 Kings 6:23.
Doors and posts of the temple.
1 Kings 6:31–33.

TREE, PALM

Blasted as a punishment. Joel 1:12.

Branches were
Carried at feast of tabernacles.
Lev. 23:40.
The emblem of victory. Rev. 7:9.
Spread before Christ. John 12:13.
Used for constructing booths.
Neh. 8:15.

Deborah judged Israel under.
Judg. 4:5.

Described as
First mention of, in Scripture.
Exod. 15:27.
Fruitful to a great age. Ps. 92:14.
Tall. Song of Sol. 7:7.
Upright. Jer. 10:5.

Illustrative of
The church. Song of Sol. 7:7–8.
Jericho celebrated for. Deut. 34:3;
Judg. 1:16.
Represented in carved work on the
walls and doors of the temple of
Solomon. 1 Kings 6:29, 32, 35;
2 Chron. 3:5.
The righteous. Ps. 92:12.
The upright appearance of idols.
Jer. 10:5.

Jericho was called the "City of Palm
Trees." Deut. 34:3.

Requires a moist and fertile soil.
Exod. 15:27.

In the temple seen in the vision of
Ezekiel. Ezek. 40:16; 41:18.

Tents often pitched under the shade
of. Judg. 4:5.

Used as a symbol of victory.
Rev. 7:9.

Used in a figurative sense of the
prosperity of the righteous.
Ps. 92:12.

TREE, POMEGRANATE

Believers. Song of Sol. 6:11; 7:12.

Blasting of, a great calamity.
Joel 1:12.

Canaan abundant with. Num. 13:23;
Deut. 8:8.

Egypt abundant with. Num. 20:5.

God's favor exhibited, in making
fruitful. Hag. 2:19.

Pomegranate

Illustrative of
The church (as an orchard).
Song of Sol. 4:13.
The graces of the church (in its
fruit). Song of Sol. 4:3; 6:7.

The Jews
Cultivated, in orchards.
Son of Sol. 4:13.
Drank the juice of.
Song of Sol 8:2.
Often lived under shade of.
1 Sam. 14:2.

Representations of its fruit
On the high priest's robe.
Exod. 39:24–26.
On the pillars of the temple.
1 Kings 7:18.

TRESPASS OFFERING
See Offering, Trespass

TRIAL
Before court. Lev. 24:10–14.
Of faith. Heb. 11:17; 1 Pet. 4:12.

Of the heart. Ps. 66:10;
1 Thess. 2:4.
Of Jesus. Matt. 4:1.
Promised, with victory. John 16:33.
Rewarded. James 1:12; 1 Pet. 1:7.
Right of. John 7:51;
Acts 16:37–39; 22:25–30.
Of the righteous. Job 23:10.

TRIBES OF ISRAEL

See Israel, Tribes of

TRIBUTE

All believers exhorted to pay.
Rom. 13:6–7.
Arabians to Solomon.
2 Chron. 9:14.
Arabians to Jehoshaphat.
2 Chron. 17:11.
Christ, to avoid offense, performed a
miracle to pay for Himself and
Peter.
Matt. 17:24–27.
Exacted from all conquered nations.
Josh. 16:10; Judg. 1:30, 33, 35;
2 Kings 23:33, 35;
Matt. 17:24–27; 22:15–22;
Luke 2:1–5.
The Jews required to pay half a
shekel to God as.
Exod. 30:12–16.

Kings of Israel
Forbidden to levy unnecessary or
oppressive. Deut. 17:17.
Often oppressed the people with.
1 Kings 12:4, 11.
Set officers over. 2 Sam. 20:24;
1 Kings 1:6–7.

Often exacted in
Gold and silver.
2 Kings 23:33, 35.

Labor. 1 Kings 5:13–14;
9:15, 21.
Produce of land, etc. 1 Sam. 8:15;
1 Kings 4:7.
Priests and Levites exempted from.
Ezra 7:24.

Roman
Christ falsely accused of forbidding
to pay. Luke 23:2.
Christ showed to the Pharisees
and Herodians the propriety of
paying. Matt. 22:15–22;
Mark 12:13–17.
Collected by the publicans.
Luke 3:12–13; 5:27.
Decree of Augustus for. Luke 2:1.
First levied in Judea when
Cyrenius was governor.
Luke 2:2.
Paid in Roman coin.
Matt. 22:19–20.
Persons enrolled for, in the native
place of their tribe and family.
Luke 2:3–5.
Resisted by the Galileans under
Judas of Galilee. Acts 5:37, with
Luke 13:1.
Sometimes exacted by kings from
their own subjects.
1 Sam. 8:10–17.
When oppressive, frequently led to
rebellion. 1 Kings 12:14–20.

TRINITY, THE

Baptism administered in name of.
Matt. 28:19.
Benediction given in name of.
2 Cor. 13:14.
Divine titles applied to the three
Persons in. Exod. 20:2, with John
20:28, and Acts 5:3–4.
Doctrine of, proved from Scripture.
Matt. 3:16–17; 28:19; Rom. 8:9;

1 Cor. 12:3–6; 2 Cor. 13:14;
Eph. 4:4–6; 1 Pet. 1:2;
Jude 20–21; Rev. 1:4–5.

Each person in, described as
Author of all spiritual operations.
Heb. 13:21, with Col. 1:29, and
1 Cor. 12:11.
Creator. Gen. 1:1, with Col. 1:16,
and Job 33:4; Ps. 148:5, with
John 1:3, and Job 26:13.
Eternal. Rom. 16:26, with
Rev. 22:13, and Heb. 9:14.
Holy. Rev. 4:8; 15:4, with
Acts 3:14, and 1 John 2:20.
Inspiring the prophets, etc.
Heb. 1:1, with 2 Cor. 13:3, and
Mark 13:11.
Omnipotent (all-powerful).
Gen. 17:1, with Rev. 1:8, and
Rom. 15:19; Jer. 32:17, with
Heb. 1:3, and Luke 1:35.
Omnipresent (ever-present).
Jer. 23:24, with Eph. 1:23, and
Ps. 139:7.
Omniscient (all-knowing).
Acts 15:18, with John 21:17,
and 1 Cor. 2:10–11.
Raising Christ from the dead.
1 Cor. 6:14, with John 2:19,
and 1 Pet. 3:18.
Sanctifier. Jude 1:1, with
Heb. 2:11, and 1 Pet. 1:2.
Source of eternal life. Rom. 6:23,
with John 10:28, and Gal. 6:8.
Supplying ministers to the church,
Jer. 3:15, with Eph. 4:11, and
Acts 20:28; Jer. 26:5, with
Matt. 10:5, and Acts 13:2.
Teacher. Isa. 54:13, with
Luke 21:15, and John 14:26;
Isa. 48:17, with Gal. 1:12, and
1 John 2:20.
True. John 7:28, with Rev. 3:7.

Salvation the work of.
2 Thess. 2:13–14; Titus 3:4–6;
1 Pet. 1:2.

TRIUMPH
In Christ. Rom. 8:37; 2 Cor. 2:14.
Over death. Isa. 25:8; 1 Cor. 15:55.
Over evil. Rev. 2:17; 6:2.
In the Lord's praise. Ps. 106:47.
Over troubles. Isa. 43:2.
Over the world. 1 John 5:4.

TROPHIES
Goliath's head and armor.
1 Sam. 17:54; 21:9.
Saul's. 1 Sam. 31:8–10.

TROUBLE
See also Trial

Attitude toward. Matt. 6:25–34;
Phil. 4:6; 1 Pet. 5:7.

Examples of
The disciples as they faced a large
crowd of hungry people.
Mark 6:37.
The disciples in a storm on the Sea
of Galilee. Luke 8:22–24.
The disciples when Jesus was
resurrected. Luke 24:4–9,
24–31, 36–40.
Elijah under the juniper tree.
1 Kings 19:4–15.
Israelites about food.
Exod. 16:2–3; Num. 11:4–33.
Israelites about water.
Exod. 15:23–25; 17:2–3;
Num. 20:1–13.
Israelites at the Red Sea.
Exod. 14:10–12.
Mary at the tomb.
John 20:11–17.

The people in the shipwreck.
Acts 27:22–25, 30–36.

When Moses tarried on the mount.
Exod. 32:1.

When the spies brought their
unfavorable report. Num.
13:28–29, 31–33; 14:1–4.

TRUCE

Embattled. 2 Sam. 2:26–31.

TRUMPET

Called the trump. 2 Cor. 15:52.

Feast of trumpets celebrated by
blowing of. Lev. 23:24;
Num. 29:1.

An instrument of music.
1 Chron. 13:8.

Jubilee introduced by blowing of.
Lev. 25:9.

Made of
Rams' horns. Josh. 6:4.
Silver. Num. 10:2.

Miracles connected with
Confusion produced in the camp
of the Midianites by sound of.
Judg. 7:16, 22.

Falling of the walls of Jericho.
Josh. 6:20.

Heard at Mount Sinai at giving of
the law. Exod. 19:16; 20:18.

Moses commanded to make two, for
the tabernacle. Num. 10:2.

Priests to blow the sacred. Num.
10:8; 2 Chron. 5:12; 7:6.

Required to give an intelligible and
understood sound. 1 Cor. 14:8.

Solomon made a great many, for the
service of the temple.
2 Chron. 5:12.

Sounding of, illustrated
The bold and faithful preaching of
ministers. Isa. 58:1; Hos. 8:1;
Joel 2:1.

God's power to raise the dead.
1 Cor. 15:52; 1 Thess. 4:16.

The latter-day judgments.
Rev. 8:2, 13.

The proclamation of the gospel.
Ps. 89:15.

Used for
Assembling the people to war.
Judg. 3:27.

Blowing at all religious processions
and ceremonies. 1 Chron. 13:8;
15:24, 28; 2 Chron. 5:13;
15:14.

Blowing over the sacrifices on
feast day. Num. 10:10;
Ps. 81:3.

Calling assemblies.
Num. 10:2–3, 7.

Giving alarm in cases of danger.
Ezek. 33:2–6.

Proclaiming kings. 2 Kings 9:13;
11:14.

Regulating the journeys of the
children of Israel.
Num. 10:2, 5–6.

Sounding for a memorial when the
people went into battle.
Num. 10:9; 31:6–7.

War horse acquainted with the sound
of. Job 39:24–25.

TRUMPETS, FEAST OF

Held the first day of seventh month.
Lev. 23:24; Num. 29:1.

A holy convocation and rest.
Lev. 23:24–25.

A memorial of blowing of trumpets.
Lev. 23:24.

Sacrifices at. Num. 29:2–6.

TRUST

To be accompanied by doing good.
Ps. 37:3.
Believers plead, in prayer.
Pss. 25:21; 31:1; 141:8.
Of believers, illustrated. Ps. 91:12;
Prov. 18:10.

Of believers is
In Christ. Eph. 3:12.
Through Christ. 2 Cor. 3:4.
Despised by the wicked. Isa. 36:4,
7.
Fixed. 2 Sam. 22:3; Ps. 112:7.
Forever. Pss. 52:8; 62:5;
Isa. 26:4.
In God. Pss. 11:1; 31:14;
2 Cor 1:9.
Grounded on the covenant.
2 Sam. 23:5.
In the mercy of God. Pss. 13:5;
52:8.
Not in the sinful nature.
Phil. 3:3–4.
Not in themselves. 2 Cor. 1:9.
Strong in the face of death.
Ps. 23:4.
Not in worldly weapons.
1 Sam. 17:38–39, 45;
Ps. 44:6; 2 Cor. 10:4.
Unalterable. Job 13:15.
In the Word of God. Ps. 119:42.
Blessedness of placing in God.
Pss. 2:12; 34:8; 40:4; Jer. 17:7.
Calamity and curse of false.
Isa. 30:1–2; 31:1–3; Jer. 17:5.

Encouragements to
The care of God for us. 1 Pet. 5:7.
The everlasting strength of God.
Isa. 26:4.
Former deliverances. Ps. 9:10;
2 Cor. 1:10.
The goodness of God. Nah. 1:7.

The loving-kindness of God.
Ps. 36:7.
The rich bounty of God.
1 Tim. 6:17.
Exhortations to. Pss. 4:5; 115:9–11.
Fear of God leads to. Prov. 14:26.
God the true object of. Ps. 65:5.

Keeps from
Desolation. Ps. 34:22.
Fear. Ps. 56:11; Isa. 12:2;
Heb. 13:6.
Unwavering. Ps. 26:1.

Leads to
Being surrounded with mercy.
Ps. 32:10.
Deliverance from enemies.
Ps. 37:40.
Enjoyment of all temporal and
spiritual blessings. Isa. 57:13.
Enjoyment of happiness.
Prov. 16:20.
Enjoyment of perfect peace.
Isa. 26:3.
Fulfillment of all holy desires.
Ps. 37:5.
Prosperity. Prov. 28:25.
Rejoicing in God. Pss. 5:11;
33:21.
Safety in times of danger. Prov.
29:25.
Stability. Ps. 125:1.
The Lord knows those who have.
Nah. 1:7.
Should be from youth up. Ps. 71:5.
Should be with the whole heart.
Prov. 3:5.

Of the wicked
Is in earthly alliances. Isa. 30:2;
Ezek. 17:15.
Is in falsehood. Isa. 28:15;
Jer. 13:25.

Is in idols. Isa. 42:17; Hab. 2:18.
Is in man. Judg. 9:26;
 Ps 118:8–9.
Is in their own heart. Prov. 28:26.
Is in their own righteousness.
 Luke 18:9, 12.
Is in vanity. Job 15:31; Isa. 59:4.
Is in wealth. Pss. 49:6; 52:7; Prov.
 11:28; Jer. 48:7; Mark 10:24.
Is not in God. Ps. 78:22;
 Zeph. 3:2.
Is vain and delusive. Isa. 30:7;
 Jer. 2:37.
Will be destroyed. Job 18:14;
 Isa. 28:18.
Will make them ashamed.
 Isa. 20:5; 30:3, 5; Jer. 48:13.
Of the wicked, illustrated. 2 Kings
 18:21; Job 8:14.

TRUSTEE
Mosaic law concerning.
 Exod. 22:7–13; Lev. 6:2–7.
The parable of the pounds.
 Matt. 25:14–28; Luke 19:12–27.

TRUTH
Abides continually with believers.
 2 John 1:2.

Believers should
 Buy the truth and do not sell it.
  Prov. 23:23.
 Keep religious feasts with.
  1 Cor. 5:8.
 Meditate upon. Phil. 4:8.
 Rejoice in. 1 Cor. 13:6.
 Serve God in. Josh. 24:14;
  1 Sam. 12:24.
 Speak, to one another.
  Zech. 8:16; Eph. 4:25.
 Walk before God in. 1 Kings 2:4;
  2 Kings 20:3.

Worship God in. John 4:24, with
 Ps. 145:18.
Write upon the tables of the heart.
 Prov. 3:3.

Christ
 Bears witness to. John 18:37.
 Is. John 14:6, with 7:18.
 Spoke. John 5:45.
 Was full of. John 1:14.
The church the pillar and ground of.
 1 Tim. 3:15.
The devil lacking. John 8:44.
The fruit of the Spirit is in. Eph. 5:9.

God
 Desires in the heart. Ps. 51:6.
 Is a God of. Deut. 32:4; Ps. 31:5.
 Regards with favor. Jer. 5:3.
The gospel as, came by Christ.
 John 1:17.

The Holy Spirit
 Guides believers into all.
  John 16:13.
 Is the Spirit of. John 14:17.

Is
 According to godliness. Titus 1:1.
 In Christ. Rom. 9:1; 1 Tim. 2:7.
 Part of the Christian armor.
  Eph. 6:14.
 Purifying. 1 Pet. 1:22.
 Sanctifying. John 17:17, 19.
John bears witness to. John 5:33.
Judgments of God are according to.
 Ps. 96:13; Rom. 2:2.
Kings are preserved by. Prov. 20:28.
Magistrates should be men of.
 Exod. 18:21.

Ministers should
 Approve themselves by.
  2 Cor. 4:2; 6:7–8; 7:14.
 Speak. 2 Cor. 12:6; Gal. 4:16.

Teach in. 1 Tim. 2:7.
Revealed abundantly to believers.
Jer. 33:6.

Should be
Acknowledged. 2 Tim. 2:25.
Believed. 2 Thess. 2:12–13;
1 Tim. 4:3.
Loved. 2 Thess. 2:10.
Manifested. 2 Cor. 4:2.
Obeyed. Rom. 2:8; Gal. 3:1.
Rightly divided. 2 Tim. 2:15.

Those who speak
Are the delight of God.
Prov. 12:22.
Exhibit righteousness.
Prov. 12:17.
Will be established. Prov. 12:19.

The wicked
Are destitute of. Hos. 4:1;
1 Tim. 6:5.
Do not ask for. Isa. 59:4.
Do not defend. Jer. 9:3.
Do not speak. Jer. 9:5.
Do not uphold. Isa. 59:14–15.
Punished for lack of. Jer. 9:5, 9;
Hos. 4:1.
Resist. 2 Tim. 3:8.
Turn away from. 2 Tim. 4:4.

The Word of God is. Dan. 10:21;
John 17:17.

TRUTH OF GOD
See God, Truth of

TUMORS
God sends as judgment on the
Philistines.1 Sam. 5:6, 9, 12.
Philistines use golden likenesses of as
a guilt offering to the Lord.
1 Sam. 6:4, 5, 11, 17.

TWINS
Jacob and Esau. Gen. 25:24–26.
Pharez and Zarah. Gen. 38:27–30.

TYPES
Bride, a type of the church.
Rev. 21:2, 9; 22:17.
The sanctuary, a type of the heavenly
sanctuary. Exod. 40:2, 24;
Heb. 8:2, 5; 9:1–12.
The saving of Noah and his family, a
type of the salvation through
Christ. 1 Pet. 3:20–21.

TYPES OF CHRIST
See Christ, Types of

UNBELIEF

All, by nature, concluded in.
Rom. 11:32.
Believers should hold no communion
with those in. 2 Cor. 6:14.
Defilement inseparable from.
Titus 1:15.

Exhibited in
Departing from God. Heb. 3:12.
Not believing the works of God.
Ps. 78:32.
Questioning the power of God.
2 Kings 7:2; Ps. 78:19–20.
Rejecting Christ. John 16:9.
Rejecting evidence of miracles.
John 12:37.
Rejecting the gospel. Isa. 53:1;
John 12:38.
Rejecting the Word of God.
Ps 106:24.
Wavering at the promise of God.
Rom. 4:20.
A hindrance to the performance of
miracles. Matt. 17:20; Mark 6:5.
Is sin. John 16:9.
The Jews rejected for. Rom. 11:20.
Miracles designed to convince those
in. John 10:37–38; 1 Cor. 14:22.
The portion of, awarded to all
unfaithful servants. Luke 12:46.
Pray for help against. Mark 9:24.

Proceeds from
The devil blinding the mind.
2 Cor. 4:4.
The devil taking away the Word
out of the heart. Luke 8:12.
An evil heart. Heb. 3:12.

Hardness of heart. Mark 16:14;
Acts 19:9; John 12:39–40.
Not being Christ's sheep.
John 10:26.
Seeking honor from men.
John 5:44.
Slowness of heart. Luke 24:25.
Unwillingness to accept the truth.
John 8:45–46.
Questions the truthfulness of God.
1 John 5:10.
Rebuked by Christ. Matt. 17:17;
John 20:27.

Those who are guilty of
Are condemned already.
John 3:18.
Become belligerent.
2 Kings ç17:14.
Cannot please God. Heb. 11:6.
Do not have the Word of God in
them. John 5:38.
Excite others against believers.
Acts 14:2.
Have the wrath of God abiding
upon. John 3:36.
Malign the gospel. Acts 19:9.
Persecute the ministers of God.
Rom. 15:31.
Persevere in it. John 12:37.
Will be thrown into the lake of fire.
Rev. 21:8.
Will be condemned. Mark 16:16;
2 Thess. 2:12.
Will be destroyed. Jude 1:5.
Will die in their sins. John 8:24.
Will not be established. Isa. 7:9.
Will not enter the rest.
Heb. 3:19; 4:11.

Warnings against. Heb. 3:12; 4:11.

UNCHARITABLENESS

Examples of
Bildad toward Job. Job 8.
Eli toward Hannah.
1 Sam. 1:14–17.
Eliab toward David.
1 Sam. 17:28.
Eliphaz toward Job. Job 4:1–6;
20.
The Israelites toward Moses.
Exod. 5:21; 14:11–12.
The Jewish leaders regarding Paul.
Acts 21:28.
Nathaniel toward Jesus.
John 1:46.
Princes of Ammon toward David.
2 Sam. 10:3.
The tribes west of the Jordan
toward the two and one-half
tribes. Num. 32:1–33;
Josh. 22:11–31.
Jesus' warning against. Matt. 7:1–5.
Paul's teaching concerning. Rom.
14:1–15; 1 Cor. 4:3–7; 13:1–6;
James 4:11–12.

UNCTION
See also Anointing

From the Holy Spirit.
1 John 2:20, 27.

UNDERGARMENTS
For the priests. Exod. 28:42; 39:28;
Lev. 6:10; 16:4; Ezek. 44:18.

UNDERSTANDING
Belongs to God
His is infinite. Ps. 147:5.
His is unsearchable. Isa. 40:28.

Needed by
Believers. Luke 24:45;
Mark 12:33.
Pastors. Jer. 3:15.
Those who pray. 1 Cor. 14:15.
Those who sing. Ps. 47:4.
Those who would find good.
Prov. 19:8.

Sought by
The psalmist. Ps. 119:34, 125.
Solomon. 1 Kings 3:9–11; 4:29.

Value of having
A wellspring of life. Prov. 16:22.
Will keep the righteous.
Prov. 2:11.

UNFAITHFULNESS
Israel charged with. Hos. 10:1–2.
Judgment for. Matt. 3:10.
Parable regarding. Matt. 21:33–43.

UNFRUITFULNESS
Consequences of. Isa. 5:2;
John 15:2–6.

UNICORN
Great strength of. Num. 24:8;
Job 39:10–11.
Horned. Deut. 33:17; Pss. 22:21;
92:10.
Stubborn. Job 39:9–12.
Used in a figurative sense, of the
judgments of God. Isa. 34:7.

UNION
Advantages of. Prov. 15:22;
Eccles. 4:9–12.

UNION WITH CHRIST
See Christ, Union with

UNITY
See also Oneness

The early church a picture of.
Acts 4:32.
The goodness of brothers dwelling in.
Ps. 133:1.
Paul's urging believers toward.
Rom. 12:16; 14:19; 15:5;
Phil. 2:2; 3:16–17.

UNITY OF GOD
See God, Unity of

UNPARDONABLE SIN
See Sin, Unpardonable

UNSELFISHNESS
Commanded. Lev. 19:18;
Deut.10:19; Matt. 19:21;
John 15:12; Phil. 2:4.
Covers sin. 1 Pet. 4:8.
Described. 1 Cor. 13.
Encouraged. Rom. 15:1; 2 Cor. 9:7.

Examples of
Abraham. Gen. 13:9; 14:23–24.
Araunah. 2 Sam. 24:22–24.
Children of Heth. Gen. 23:6–11.
Daniel. Dan. 5:17.
David. 1 Sam. 24:17;
2 Sam. 15:19–20; 23:16–17;
1 Chron. 21:17; Ps. 69:6.
The disciples. Acts 4:34–35.
Gideon. Judg. 8:22–23.
The Jews. Esther 9:15.
Jonah. Jon. 1:12–13.
Jonathan. 1 Sam. 23:17–18.
Joseph. Matt. 1:19.
Judah. Gen. 44:33–34.
King of Sodom. Gen. 14:21.
Moses. Num. 11:29; 14:12–19.
Saul. 1 Sam. 11:12–13.
Nehemiah. Neh. 5:14–18.

Paul. 1 Cor. 10:33; Phil. 1:18;
4:17; 2 Thess. 3:8.
Philemon. Philem. 13–14.
Priscilla and Aquila. Rom. 16:3–4.
Measure of. Luke 6:31.
Paul's urging. Phil. 2:3–4.
Purpose of God's commandment.
1 Tim. 1:5.
Reward for. Matt. 7:2; 10:42;
Prov. 11:25, 22:9; Isa. 58:10;
2 Cor. 9:6.

UPRIGHTNESS
Admonish those who deviate from.
Gal. 2:14.
Being kept from willful sins necessary
to. Ps. 19:13.
Believers should resolve to walk in.
Ps. 26:11.
A characteristic of believers.
Ps. 111:1; Isa. 26:7.

God
Created human in. Eccles. 7:29.
Has pleasure in. 1 Chron. 29:17.
Is perfect in. Isa. 26:7.
With poverty, better than foolishness.
Prov. 19:1.
With poverty, better than sin with
riches. Prov. 28:6.
Pray for those who walk in.
Ps. 125:4.

Should be in
Heart. 2 Chron. 29:34;
Ps. 125:4.
Judging. Pss. 58:1; 75:2.
Ruling. Ps. 78:72.
Speech. Isa. 33:15.
Walk. Prov. 14:2.

Those who walk in
A blessing to others. Prov. 11:11.
Defended by God. Prov. 2:7.

Delighted in by God. Prov. 11:20.
Direct their way. Prov. 21:29.
Fear God. Prov. 14:2.
Find strength in God's way.
Prov. 10:29.
Guided by integrity. Prov. 11:3.
Hated by the wicked. Prov. 29:10,
21; Amos 5:10.
Kept by righteousness. Prov. 13:6.
Love Christ. Song of Sol. 1:4.
Obtain good from God's Word.
Mic. 2:7.
Obtain light in darkness.
Ps. 112:4.
Persecuted by the wicked.
Ps. 37:14.
Praise is fitting for. Ps. 33:1.
Prospered by God. Job 8:6;
Prov. 14:11.
Repaid by God. Ps. 18:23–24.
Ridiculed by the wicked. Job 12:4.
Their prayer delighted in by God.
Prov. 15:8.
Upheld in it by God. Ps. 41:12.
Walk securely. Prov. 10:9.
Will see God's face. Ps. 11:7.

Those who walk in will
Be blessed. Ps. 112:2.
Be delivered by righteousness.
Prov. 11:6.
Be delivered by their wisdom.
Prov. 12:6.
Be saved. Prov. 28:18.
Dwell in the land. Prov. 2:21.
Dwell on high and be provided for.
Isa. 33:16.
Dwell with God. Pss. 15:2;
140:13.
Enter into peace. Ps. 37:37;
Isa. 57:2.
Have dominion over the wicked.
Ps. 49:14.

Have an inheritance forever.
Ps. 37:18.
Have nothing good withheld.
Ps. 84:11.
Possess good things. Prov. 28:10.
The truly wise walk in. Prov. 15:21.
The way of, to depart from evil.
Prov. 16:17.

The wicked
Do not act with. Mic. 7:2, 4.
Do not have in heart. Hab. 2:4.
Leave the path of. Prov. 2:13.

URIM AND THUMMIM

Absent in the second temple.
Ezra 2:63; Neh. 7:65.
In the breastplate. Exod. 28:30;
Lev. 8:8.
Eleazar to ask counsel for Joshua
after the judgment of.
Num. 27:21.
God to be consulted by. Num. 27:21.
Illustrative of the light and perfection
of Christ, the true high priest.
Deut. 33:8. (*See also* John 1:4, 9,
17; Col. 2:3.)
Instances of consulting God by.
Judg. 1:1; 20 18, 28;
1 Sam. 23:9–11; 30:7–8.
Israelites consult. Judg. 1:1;
20:18, 23.
Only priests might interpret. Deut.
33:8; Ezra 2:63; Neh. 7:65.
Placed in the breastplate of the high
priest. Exod. 28:30; Lev. 8:8.
Sometimes no answer by, in
consequence of the sin of those
consulting. 1 Sam. 28:6.
Withheld answer from King Saul.
1 Sam. 28:6.

USURPATION

In ecclesiastical affairs
Ahaz. 2 Kings 16:12–13.
Saul, in assuming priestly
functions. 1 Sam. 13:8–14.
Solomon, in thrusting Abiathar out
of the priesthood.
1 Kings 2:26–27.
Uzziah, in assuming priestly
offices. 2 Chron. 26:16–21.

Of executive power
Ahaz, in ordering Naboth in
confiscation of his vineyard.
1 Kings 21:7–19.
Moses accused of. Numbers 16:3.
Pharaoh, making bond servants of
the Israelites. Exod. 1:9–22.
The scheme of Joseph to
dispossess the Egyptians of their
real and personal property.
Gen. 47:13–26.

Of political functions
Absalom. 2 Sam. 15:1–12.
Adonijah. 1 Kings 1:5–9.
Athaliah. 2 Kings 11:1–16.
Baasha. 1 Kings 15:27–28.
Jehu. 2 Kings 9:11–37.
Shallum. 2 Kings 15:10.
Zimri. 1 Kings 16:9–10.

USURY
See also Interest

Authorized, of strangers.
Deut. 23:20.
Exacted by Jews. Ezek. 22:12.
Exaction of, rebuked. Neh. 5:1–13.
Forbidden. Exod. 22:25;
Lev. 25:35–37; Deut. 23:19;
Ps 15:5; Prov. 28:8; Jer. 15:10;
Ezek. 18:8, 13, 17; 22:12.
Righteous men do not require.
Ezek. 18:8.

V

VALLEYS

Abounded with
Doves. Ezek. 7:16.
Fountains and springs. Deut. 8:7;
Isa. 41:18.
Lily of the valley. Song of Sol. 2:1.
Ravens. Prov. 30:17.
Rocks and caves. Job 30:6;
Isa. 57:5.
Trees. 1 Kings 10:27.

Called
Dales. Gen. 14:17; 2 Sam. 18:18.
Fertile, when fruitful. Isa. 28:1, 4.
Foothills. Deut. 1:7; Josh. 10:40.
Rough, when uncultivated and
barren. Deut. 21:4.
Canaan abounded in. Deut. 11:11.
The Canaanites held possession of,
against Judah. Judg. 1:19.
Described as tracts of land between
mountains. 1 Sam. 17:3.
The heathen believed that certain
deities presided over.
1 Kings 20:23, 28.

Illustrative of
Affliction and death (when dark).
Ps. 23:4.
The church of Christ.
Song of Sol. 6:11.
Removing all obstructions to the
gospel (when being filled up). Isa.
40:4; Luke 3:5.
The tents of Israel (when fruitful
and well watered). Num. 24:6.
Of Israel, well-tilled and fruitful.
1 Sam. 6:13; Ps. 65:13.

Mentioned in Scripture
Achor. Josh. 7:24; Isa. 65:10;
Hos. 2:15.
Ajalon. Josh. 10:12.
Baca. Ps. 84:6.
Berachah. 2 Chron. 20:26.
Bochim. Judg. 2:5.
Charashim. 1 Chron. 4:14.
Elah. 1 Sam. 17:2; 21:9.
Eshcol. Num. 32:9; Deut. 1:24.
Gad. 2 Sam. 24:5.
Gerar. Gen. 26:17.
Gibeon. Isa. 28:21.
Hamon-gog. Ezek. 39:11.
Hebron. Gen. 37:14.
Hinnom. Josh. 15:8, 18:16;
2 Kings 23:10; 2 Chron. 28:3;
Jer. 7:32.
Jehoshaphat or decision.
Joel 3:2, 14.
Jericho. Deut. 34:3.
Jezreel. Hos. 1:5.
Jiphthah-el. Josh. 19:14, 27.
Keziz. Josh. 18:21.
Lebanon. Josh. 11:17.
Megiddo. 2 Chron. 35:22;
Zech. 12:11.
Moab where Moses was buried.
Deut. 34:6.
Rephaim. Josh. 15:8; 18:16;
2 Sam. 5:18; Isa. 17:5.
Salt. 2 Sam. 8:13; 2 Kings 14:17.
Shaveh. Gen. 14:17;
2 Sam. 18:18.
Shittim. Joel 3:18.
Siddim. Gen. 14:3, 8.
Sorek. Judg. 16:4.
Succoth. Ps. 60:6.
Zared. Num. 21:12.

Zeboim. 1 Sam. 13:18.
Zephathah. 2 Chron. 14:10.

Miracles connected with
Ditches in, filled with water.
2 Kings 3:16–17.
The moon made to stand still over
Ajalon. Josh. 10:12.
Water in, made to appear to the
Moabites like blood.
2 Kings 3:22–23.
Often the scenes of great contests.
Judg. 5:15; 7:8, 22;
1 Sam. 17:19.
Often the scenes of idolatrous rites.
Isa. 57:5.
To be filled with hostile chariots,
threatened as a punishment.
Isa. 22:7.

VANITY

All earthly things are. Eccles. 1:2.
All should know and acknowledge.
Deut. 4:35.
Beauty of man is. Ps. 39:11;
Prov. 31:30.

Believers
Avoid. Ps. 24:4.
Avoid those given to. Ps. 26:4.
Hate the thoughts of.
Ps. 119:113.
Pray to be kept from. Ps. 119:37;
Prov. 30:8.
Childhood and youth are.
Eccles. 11:10.
Conduct of the ungodly is.
1 Pet. 1:18.
A consequence of the fall.
Rom. 8:20.
Days of man are. Job 7:16;
Eccles. 6:12.
Every man is. Ps. 39:11.
Every state of man is. Ps. 62:9.

Faith without works is. James 2:14.
False teaching is. Jer. 23:32.
Following those given to, leads to
poverty. Prov. 28:19.
Foolish questions, etc., are.
1 Tim. 1:6–7; 6:20; 2 Tim. 2:14,
16; Titus 3:9.
Fools follow those given to.
Prov. 12:11.
Giving without love is. 1 Cor. 13:3.
Heaping up riches is.
Eccles. 2:26; 4:8.
Help of man is. Ps. 60:11;
Lam. 4:17.
Idolatry is. 2 Kings 17:15; Ps. 31:6;
Isa. 44:9–10; Jer. 10:8; 18:15.
Love of riches is. Eccles. 5:10.
Lying words are. Jer. 7:8.
Man at his best estate is. Ps. 39:5.
Man like to. Ps. 144:4.
Man's own righteousness is.
Isa. 57:12.
Mere external religion is. 1 Tim. 4:8;
Heb. 13:9.
Riches gotten by falsehood are.
Prov. 21:6.
Religion of hypocrites is.
James 1:26.
Those who trust in, rewarded with.
Job 15:31.
Thoughts of man are. Ps. 94:11.
Treasures of wickedness are.
Prov. 10:2.
Unblessed riches are. Eccles. 6:2.
Wealth gotten by, diminishes.
Prov. 13:11.

The wicked
Allure others by words of.
2 Pet. 2:18.
Count God's service as.
Job 21:15; Mal. 3:14.
Especially characterized by.
Job 11:11.

Though full of, affect to be wise.
Job 11:12.
Imagine. Ps. 2:1; Acts 4:25;
Rom. 1:21.
Inherit. Jer. 16:19.
Judicially given up to. Ps. 78:33;
Isa. 57:13.
Love. Ps. 4:2.
Reap. Prov. 22:8; Jer. 12:13.
Speak. Pss. 10:7; 12:2; 41:6.
Walk after. Jer. 2:5.
Walk in. Ps. 39:6; Eph. 4:17.
Worldly anxiety is. Pss. 39:6; 127:2.
Worldly enjoyment is. Eccles. 2:3,
10–11.
Worldly labor is. Eccles. 2:11; 4:4.
Worldly pleasure is. Eccles. 2:1.
Worldly possessions are.
Eccles. 2:4–11.
Worldly wisdom is. Eccles. 2:15, 21;
1 Cor. 3:20.
Worship of the wicked is. Isa. 1:13;
Matt. 6:7.

VEGETARIANS

Persons who eat no meat.
Rom. 14:2.

VEIL

A covering for the head usually worn
by women. Gen. 38:14.

Illustrative of
The spiritual blindness of the
Gentile nations. Isa. 25:7.
The spiritual blindness of the
Jewish nation. 2 Cor. 3:14–16.
Moses put one on to conceal the
glory of his face. Exod. 34:33,
with 2 Cor. 3:13.
Removing of, considered rude and
insolent. Song of Sol. 5:7.

Removing of, threatened as a
punishment to ungodly women.
Isa. 3:23.

Worn
For concealment. Gen. 38:14.
As a symbol of modesty.
Gen. 24:65.
As a symbol of subjection.
1 Cor. 11:3, 6–7, 10.

VEIL, SACRED

At Christ's death torn. Matt. 27:51;
Mark 15:38; Luke 23:45.
Designed to conceal the ark, mercy
seat, and the symbol of the divine
presence. Exod. 40:3.

The high priest
Alone allowed to enter within.
Heb. 9:6–7.
Allowed to enter only once a year.
Lev. 16:2; Heb. 9:7.
Could not enter without blood.
Lev. 16:3, with Heb. 9:7.
Hung between the holy and most
holy place. Exod. 26:33;
Heb. 9:3.

Illustrative of
The death of Christ which opened
heaven to believers (when torn).
Heb. 10:19–20, with 9:24.
Flesh of Christ which concealed
His divinity. Heb. 10:20.
(See also Isa. 53:2.)
Obscurity of the Mosaic period.
Heb. 9:8.
Made by Bezaleel for the tabernacle.
Exod. 36:35.
Made by Solomon for the temple.
2 Chron. 3:14.
Moses commanded to make.
Exod. 26:31.

Suspended from four pillars of acacia
wood overlaid with gold.
Exod. 26:32.

VENGEANCE
Belongs to God. Ps. 94:1;
Rom. 12:19.
Instance of, sons of Jacob on Hamor
and Shechem. Gen. 34:20–31.

VENUE, CHANGE OF
Declined by Paul. Acts 25:9, 11.
Granted Paul. Acts 23:17–35.

VENTRILOQUISM
Divination by. Acts 16:16.

VERDICT
Against Jesus. Luke 23:24.

VICTORIES
In battle, from God. Ps. 55:18;
76:5–6.
Celebrated in song. Judg. 5;
2 Sam. 22.
By women. 1 Sam. 18:6–7;
2 Sam. 1:20.

VICTORY
See Overcoming; Triumph

VINE
Canaan abounded in. Deut.
6:11; 8:8.

Cultivated
On the sides of hills. Jer. 31:5.
In the valleys. Song of Sol. 6:11.
In vineyards from the time of
Noah. Gen. 9:20.
By the walls of houses. Ps. 128:3.
Degeneracy of. Jer. 2:21.
Dwarf and spreading particularly
valuable. Ezek. 17:6.

Fable of. Judg. 9:12–13.
Foxes destructive to.
Song of Sol. 2:15.
Frequently injured by hail and frost.
Pss. 78:47; 105:32–33.
Frequently made unfruitful as a
punishment. Jer. 8:13; Hos. 2:12;
Joel 1:7, 12; Hag. 2:19.

Fruit of
Called grapes. Gen. 40:10.
Eaten dried.
1 Sam. 25:18; 30:12.
Eaten fresh from the tree.
Deut. 23:24.
Made into wine. Deut. 32:14;
Matt. 26:29.
Peculiarly sour when unripe.
Jer. 31:30.
Sold in the markets. Neh. 13:15.
God made fruitful for His people
when obedient. Joel 2:22;
Zech. 8:12.

Illustrative of
Believers (by its fruitful branches).
John 15:5.
Christ. John 15:1–2.
God's purifying His people by
afflictions (when pruned).
John 15:2.
The graces of the church (by its
rich clusters). Song of Sol. 7:8.
The growth of believers in grace
(by its quick growth). Hos. 14:7.
Israel. Ps. 80:8; Isa. 5:2, 7.
Mere professors (by its unfruitful
branches). John 15:2, 6.
Peace and prosperity (when sitting
under one's own). 1 Kings 4:25;
Mic. 4:4; Zech. 3:10.
The wicked (when unfruitful).
Hos. 10:1.

By the worthlessness of its wood,
the unprofitableness of the
wicked. Ezek. 15:6–7.
Its flowers perfumed the air.
Song of Sol. 2:13; Hos. 14:7.
Nazarites prohibited from eating.
Num. 6:3–4.
Of Sodom, bad, and unfit for use.
Deut. 32:32.
Often degenerated. Isa. 5:2;
Jer. 2:21.
Often found wild. 2 Kings 4:39;
Hos. 9:10.
Parables of. Ps. 80:8–14;
Ezek. 17:6–10; 19:10–14.

Places celebrated for
Egypt. Pss. 78:47; 80:8.
Eshcol. Num. 13:23–24.
Lebanon. Hos. 14:7.
Sibmah. Isa. 16:8–9.
Probably produced two crops a year.
Num. 13:20.
Proverbial allusion to fathers eating
the unripe fruit of. Jer. 31:29–30;
Ezek. 18:2.
Pruned. Isa. 5:6; John 15:1–5.
Required to be dressed and pruned to
increase its fruitfulness. Lev. 25:3;
2 Chron. 26:10; Isa. 18:5.
Sometimes shed its fruit before ripe.
Job 15:33; Mal. 3:11.
Symbolic sense. John 15:1–5.
Wild boar destructive to. Ps. 80:13.
Wood of, fit only for burning.
Ezek. 15:2–5.
Young cattle fed on its leaves and
tender shoots. Gen. 49:11.

VINEGAR
Forbidden to Nazarites. Num. 6:3.
Offered to Christ on the cross.
John 19:29.
Used with food. Ruth 2:14.

VINEYARDS
Antiquity of. Gen. 9:20.
Cottages built in, for the keepers.
Isa. 1:8.
Design of planting. Ps. 107:37;
1 Cor. 9:7.
Estimated profit arising from, to the
cultivators. Song of Sol. 8:12.
Estimated rent of. Song of Sol. 8:11;
Isa. 7:23.
Frequently leased to the farmer.
Song of Sol. 8:11; Matt. 21:33.
Frequently walled or fenced with
hedges. Num. 22:24;
Prov. 24:31; Isa. 5:2, 5.

Illustrative of
The elect (when cleaning grapes
of). Isa. 24:13.
The Jewish church. Isa. 5:7; 27:2;
Jer. 12:10.
Severe calamities (when failing).
Isa. 32:10.

Laws regarding
Compensation in kind to be made
for injury done to. Exod. 22:5.
Fruit of new, not to be eaten for
three years. Lev. 19:23.
Fruit of new, to be eaten by the
owners from the fifth year.
Lev. 19:25.
Fruit of new, to be holy to the Lord
in the fourth year. Lev. 19:24.
Gleaning of, to be left for the poor.
Lev. 19:10; Deut. 24:21.
Not to be cultivated during the
sabbatical year. Exod. 23:11;
Lev. 25:4.
Not to be planted with different
kinds of seed. Deut. 22:9.
Planters of, not liable to military
service until they had eaten of
the fruit. Deut. 20:6.

Spontaneous fruit of, not to be gathered during the sabbatical or jubilee year. Lev. 25:5, 11.

Strangers entering, allowed to eat fruit but not to take any away. Deut. 23:24.

Of the lazy man, neglected and laid waste. Prov. 24:30–31.

Leased. Song of Sol. 8:11, 12; Matt. 21:33–39.

Members of the family often worked in. Song of Sol. 1:6; Matt. 21:28–30.

Mode of hiring and paying laborers for working in. Matt. 20:1–2.

Neglected. Prov. 24:30, 31.

Of kings. 1 Chron. 27:26–28.

Of the kings of Israel, supervised by officers of state. 1 Chron. 27:27.

Often mortgaged. Neh. 5:3–4.

The poor engaged in culture of. 2 Kings 25:12; Isa. 61:5.

Parables of. Isa. 5:1–7; Luke 13:6–9.

Plain of the. Judg. 11:33.

Pools in. Eccles. 2:4, 6.

Produce of, frequently destroyed by enemies. Jer. 48:32.

Produce of, often destroyed by insects, etc. Deut. 28:39; Amos 4:9.

Provided with the apparatus for making wine. Isa. 5:2; Matt. 21:33.

The Rechabites forbidden to plant. Jer. 35:7–9.

Of red grapes, particularly valuable. Isa. 27:2.

Rent of, frequently paid by part of the fruit. Matt. 21:34.

Stones carefully gathered out of. Isa. 5:2.

Vintage or ingathering of

Failure in, occasioned great grief. Isa. 16:9–10.

Sometimes continued to the time of sowing seed. Lev. 26:5.

A time of great rejoicing. Isa. 16:10.

The wicked judicially deprived of the enjoyment of. Amos 5:11; Zeph. 1:13.

Towers in. Isa. 5:2; Matt. 21:33.

In unfavorable seasons, produced but little wine. Isa. 5:10; Hag. 1:9, 11.

Winepress in. Isa. 5:2.

VIRGIN

Advised by Paul not to marry. 1 Cor. 7.

Character of, to be protected. Deut. 22:17–21, 23, 24.

Distinguishing apparel of. 2 Sam. 13:18.

Dowry of. Exod. 22:17.

Engagement of. Deut. 22:23–24.

Fruits of. Deut. 22:13–21.

Mary, mother of Jesus. Isa. 7:14; Matt. 1:23.

Mourn in the temple. Lam. 1:4; 2:10.

Priests might marry none but. Lev. 21:14.

Parable of the wise and foolish. Matt. 25:1–13.

Used in a figurative sense, of the church. Isa. 62:5; 2 Cor. 11:2.

Used in a figurative sense, of personal purity. 1 Cor. 7:25, 37; Rev. 14:4.

VIRTUE

Excellence. Phil. 4:8; 2 Pet. 1:5.

Power. Luke 6:19; 8:46.

VISIONS
Of Abraham, concerning his descendants. Gen. 15:1–17.

Of Amos, of fire. Amos 7:4.

Of Amos, of grasshoppers. Amos 7:1–2.

Of Amos, of a plumb line. Amos 7:7–8.

Of Amos, of summer fruit. Amos 8:1–2.

Of Amos, of the temple. Amos 9:1.

Of Ananias. Acts 9:12.

Of Ananias, of Christ. Acts 9:10–12.

Angel and the sun. Rev. 19:17–21.

Angel coming out of the temple. Rev. 14:7–19.

Angel having a book. Rev. 10:1–10.

An angel having power over fire. Rev. 14:18.

The angel having the everlasting gospel. Rev. 14:6–7.

The angel proclaiming the fall of Babylon. Rev. 14:8–13.

Angel reaping the harvest. Rev. 14:14–20.

Angels with the seven last plagues. Rev. 15.

Army of horsemen. Rev. 9:16–19.

The beast coming out of the sea. Rev. 13:1–10.

The beast coming out of the earth. Rev. 13:11–18.

The beast out of the bottomless pit. Rev. 11:7.

Book with seven seals. Rev. 5:1–5.

Bottomless pit. Rev. 9:2.

Of Christ and the golden candlesticks. Rev. 1:10–20.

Of Cornelius, the centurion, of an angel. Acts 10:3.

Court of the Gentiles. Rev. 11:2.

Of Daniel, of the Ancient of Days. Dan. 7:9–27.

Of Daniel, of the angel. Dan. 10.

Of Daniel, of the four beasts. Dan. 7.

Of Daniel, of the ram and the goat. Dan. 8.

Of David, of the angel of the Lord by the threshing floor of Ornan. 1 Chron. 21:15–18.

Death and hell. Rev. 20:14.

Destruction of Babylon. Rev. 18.

Earthquake and celestial phenomena. Rev. 6:12–14.

Of Elisha's servant, of the chariots of the Lord. 2 Kings 16:17.

Of Elisha, when Elijah was taken into heaven. 2 Kings 2:11.

Of Eliphaz's vision at night. Job 4:13–16.

Of Ezekiel, of the glory of God. Ezek. 1:3; 12:14; 23.

Of Ezekiel, of the coals of fire. Ezek. 10:1–7.

Of Ezekiel, of the city and the temple. Ezek. 40–48.

Of Ezekiel, of the dry bones. Ezek. 37:1–14.

Of Ezekiel, of the roll. Ezek. 2:9.

Of Ezekiel, of the man of fire. Ezek.. 8; 9.

Of Ezekiel, of the waters. Ezek. 47:1–12.

Fall of the city. Rev. 11:13.

Falling star. Rev. 8:10–11; 9:1.

False prophets pretended to have seen. Jer. 14:14; 23:16.

Four angels. Rev. 7:1.

Four angels loosed from the Euphrates. Rev. 9:14.

Of four horses. Rev. 6:2–8.

Four living creatures. Rev. 4:6–8.

Frequently difficult and perplexing to those who received them. Dan. 7:15; 8:15; Acts 10:17.

God often made known His will by.
Ps. 89:19.

Golden bowls. Rev. 5:8.

Great white throne. Rev. 20:11.

Hail and fire. Rev. 8:7.

Of Him who is faithful and true,
riding a white horse.
Rev. 19:11–16.

Of Isaiah, of the Lord and His glory
in the temple. Isa. 6.

Of Isaiah, of the valley of vision.
Isa. 22.

Of the Israelites, of the manifestation
of the glory of God. Exod. 24:10,
17; Heb. 12:18–21.

Of Jacob, at Beersheba. Gen. 46:2.

Of Jacob, of the ladder with
ascending and descending angels.
Gen. 28:12.

Of the jar. Rev. 8:5.

Of Jeremiah, of an almond branch.
Jer. 1:11.

Of Jeremiah, of the boiling pot. Jer.
1:13.

Of Job, of his spirit. Job 4:12–16.

Of John the Baptist, at the baptism of
Jesus. Matt. 3:16.

Of John on the island of Patmos. The
Book of Rev.

Of Joshua, of the captain of the
Lord's host. Josh. 5:13–15.

The lamb on Mt. Zion. Rev. 14:1–5.

Locusts. Rev. 9:3–11.

Of the man of Macedonia saying,
"Come over into Macedonia and
help us." Acts 16:9.

Measurement of the temple.
Rev. 11:1–2.

Of Micaiah, of the defeat of the
Israelites. 1 Kings 22:17–23;
2 Chron. 18:16–22.

A mode of revelation. Num. 12:6;
1 Sam. 3:1; 2 Chron. 26:5;

Ps. 89:19; Prov. 29:18;
Jer. 14:14; 23:16; Dan. 1:17;
Hos. 12:10; Joel 2:28; Obad. 1;
Hab. 2:2; Acts 2:17.

Of Moses, of the burning bush.
Exod. 3:2.

Of Moses, of the glory of God.
Exod. 24:9–11; 33:18–23.

Mountain thrown into the sea.
Rev. 8:8–9.

Multiplied for the benefit of the
people. Hos. 12:10.

Of the multitude praising.
Rev. 19:1–9.

Of Nebuchadnezzar's dream of the
stone image. Dan. 2:28; 4:5.

New Jerusalem. Rev. 21.

Often accompanied by
An appearance of angels.
Luke 1:22, with 1:11; 24:23;
Acts 10:3.
An appearance of human beings.
Acts 9:12; 16:9.
An audible voice from heaven.
Gen. 15:1; 1 Sam. 3:4–5.
A representative of the divine
person and glory. Isa. 6:1.

Often communicated
At night. Gen. 46:2; Dan. 2:19.
In a trance. Num. 24:16;
Acts 11:5.

Of the open door. Rev. 4:1.

Opening of the Book of Life.
Rev. 20:12.

Of Paul, in Corinth. Acts 18:9–10.

Of Paul, in a trance. Acts 22:17–21.

Of Paul, of Christ, on the way to
Damascus. Acts 9:3–6.

Of Paul, of Paradise. 2 Cor. 12:1–4.

Of Samuel. 1 Sam. 3:2–15.

Of Peter, James, and John, of the
transfiguration of Jesus and the

appearance of Moses and Elijah.
Matt. 17:1–9.

Of Peter, of the sheet let down from
heaven. Acts 10:9–18.

Of the people, of the tongues of fire
at Pentecost. Acts 2:2–3.

The plague upon the men who has
the mark of the beast. Rev. 16:2.

Prophets of God skilled in
interpreting. Dan. 1:17.

A rainbow and a throne. Rev. 4:2–3.

Recorded for the benefit of the
people. Hab. 2:2.

The red dragon. Rev. 12:3–17.

River of life. Rev. 22:1.

Satan bound a thousand years.
Rev. 20:1–3.

Sea of glass. Rev. 4:6; 15:2.

The sea turned into blood. Rev. 16:3.

Sealing of the 144,000. Rev. 7:2–8.

Second and third calamities.
Rev. 11:14.

The seven angels with the seven
bowls of the wrath of God.
Rev. 16; 17.

Seven lamps. Rev. 4:5.

Seven thunders. Rev. 10:3–4.

Of the seventh seal and seven angels.
Rev. 8–11.

Of the six seals. Rev. 6.

Sometimes withheld for a long time.
1 Sam. 3:1.

The Son of Man with a sickle
Rev. 14:14–16.

Of Stephen, of Christ. Acts 7:55–56.

The temple opened. Rev. 15:5.

Tree of life. Rev. 22:2.

The third part of the sun and moon
and stars darkened. Rev. 8:12.

Thrones of judgment, and the
resurrection, and the loosing of
Satan. Rev. 20:1–10.

Twenty-four elders. Rev. 4:4.

Two olive trees and two candlesticks.
Rev. 11:4.

Two witnesses. Rev. 11:3–12.

The vine and the winepress.
Rev. 14:18–20.

War in heaven. Rev. 12:7–9.

Withholding of, a great calamity.
Prov. 29:18; Lam. 2:9.

A woman clothed with the sun and
the birth of a male child. Rev. 12.

Of Zechariah, of horns and
carpenters. Zech. 1:18–21.

Of Zechariah, of horses.
Zech. 1:8–11.

Of Zechariah, of the flying roll.
Zech. 5:1–4.

Of Zechariah, of the golden
candlestick. Zech. 4.

Of Zechariah, of the high priest.
Zech. 3:1–5.

Of Zechariah, of the mountains and
chariots. Zech. 6:1–8.

Of Zacharias, and the temple.
Luke 1:13–22.

VOICE OF GOD
See God, Voice of

VOLCANO
At Horeb. Deut. 4:11; 5:23.

VOLUNTEERS

In financial giving
By leaders. 1 Chron. 29:6–9;
2 Chron. 35:8; Ezra 7:15.
By people. Exod. 25:2;
Judg. 8:25; Ezra 1:6; 2
Cor. 8:1–4; 9:7.
To live in Jerusalem. Neh. 11:1–2.

In military service
Commanders. Judg. 5:9.
Fighters. Judg. 5:2.

In temple service. 2 Chron. 17:16;
Ezra 1:5–6.

VOWS

Of children, void without consent of
parents. Num. 30:3–5.

Clean beasts the subjects of, not to be
redeemed. Lev. 27:9–10.

Danger of inconsiderately making.
Prov. 20:25.

Hire of a prostitute or price of a dog
could not be the subject of.
Deut. 23:18.

Made in reference to

Afflicting the soul. Num. 30:13.

Dedicating children to God.
1 Sam. 1:11.

Devoting property to God.
Gen. 28:22.

Devoting the person to God.
Num. 6:2.

Offering sacrifices. Lev. 7:16;
22:18, 22; Num. 15:3.

Of married women, void without
consent of husbands.
Num. 30:6–8, 10–13.

Recorded in Scripture of

Certain Jews with Paul.
Acts 21:23–24, 26.

David. Ps. 132:2–5.

Elkanah. 1 Sam. 1:21.

Hannah. 1 Sam. 1:11.

Israelites. Num. 21:2.

Jacob. Gen. 28:20–22; 31:13.

Jephthah. Judg. 11:30–31.

Jonah. Jon. 2:9.

Lemuel's mother. Prov. 31:1–2.

Mariners who cast out Jonah.
Jon. 1:16.

Paul. Acts 18:18.

Redeemed by paying a suitable
compensation. Lev. 27:1–8,
11–23.

Should be

Performed faithfully. Num. 30:2.

Performed without delay.
Deut. 23:21, 23.

Voluntary. Deut. 23:21–22.

Things dedicated by, to be brought
to the tabernacle. Deut. 12:6,
11, 17–18, 26.

As solemn promises to God.
Ps. 76:11.

Of things corrupt or blemished an
insult to God. Lev. 22:23;
Mal. 1:14.

Of widows and women divorced from
their husbands, binding.
Num. 30:9.

Of wives, could only be objected to at
the time of making.
Num. 30:14–15.

VOYEURISM

Abstained from. Job 31:1.

David and Bathsheba. 2 Sam. 11:2.

Injunctions concerning

Abstain from every form of evil.
1 Thess. 5:22.

Flee youthful lusts. 2 Tim. 2:22.

Potential for. Gen. 12:11; 39:6–7;
Esther 2:2–4.

Pure thoughts. Phil. 4:8.

Same as committing adultery.
Matt. 5:28.

With lustful actions. Ezek. 23:8.

WAGES

God's commandment concerning.
Lev. 19:13; Deut. 24:14–15;
Luke 3:14; Col. 4:1; James 5:4.
Of Jacob. Gen. 29:15–30.
Parable concerning. Matt. 20:1–15.

WAITING UPON GOD

See God, Waiting upon

WALKING WITH GOD

See God, Walking with

WALLS

Of cities

Battered by besieging armies.
2 Sam. 20:15; Ezek. 4:2–3.

Bodies of enemies sometimes
fastened on, as a disgrace.
1 Sam. 31:10.

Broad and places of public resort.
2 Kings 6:26, 30; Ps. 55:10.

Custom of dedicating.
Neh. 12:27.

Danger of approaching too near
to, in time of war.
2 Sam. 11:20–21.

Destruction of, a punishment and
cause of grief. Deut. 28:52;
Neh. 1:3; 2:12–17.

Falling of, sometimes occasioned
great destruction.
1 Kings 20:30.

Frequently laid in ruins.
2 Chron. 25:23; 36:19;
Jer. 50:15.

Had towers built on them.
2 Chron. 26:9; 32:5;
Ps. 48:12; Song of Sol. 8:10.

Houses often built on. Josh. 2:15.

Houses sometimes broken down
to repair and fortify. Isa. 22:10.

Idolatrous rites performed on.
2 Kings 3:27.

Instances of persons let down
from. Josh. 2:15; Acts 9:24–25;
2 Cor. 11:33.

Kept by watchmen night and day.
Song of Sol. 5:7; Isa. 62:6.

Often very high. Deut. 1:28; 3:5.

Skill of soldiers in scaling, alluded
to. Joel 2:7–9.

Sometimes burned. Jer. 49:27;
Amos 1:7.

Strongly fortified. Isa. 2:15;
25:12.

Strongly manned in war.
2 Kings 18:26.

Designed for defense. 1 Sam. 25:16.

Designed for separation. Ezek. 43:8;
Eph. 2:14.

Frequently made of stone and wood
together. Ezra 5:8; Hab. 2:11.

Of houses

Easily dug through. Gen. 49:6,
Ezek. 8:7–8; 12:5.

Had nails or pegs fastened into
them when built. Eccles. 12:11;
Isa. 22:23.

Often infested with serpents.
Amos 5:19.

Susceptible to mildew. Lev. 14:37.

The seat next, the place of
distinction. 1 Sam. 20:25.

Usually plastered. Ezek. 13:10,
with Dan. 5:5.
Probably often strengthened with
plates of iron or brass.
Jer. 15:20; Ezek. 4:3.
Hyssop frequently grew on.
1 Kings 4:33.

Illustrative of
The church as a protection to the
nation. Song of Sol. 8:9–10.
Hypocrites (whitewashed).
Acts 23:3.
Ordinances as a protection to the
church. Song of Sol. 2:9;
Isa. 5:5.
Prophets in their testimony against
the wicked (brazen). Jer. 22:20.
Protection of God. Zech. 2:5.
Salvation. Isa. 26:1; 60:18.
Separation of Jews and Gentiles.
Eph. 2:14.
The teaching of false prophets like
flimsy walls covered with
whitewash. Ezek. 13:10–15.
Those who provide protection.
1 Sam. 25:16; Isa. 2:15.
The wealth of the rich in their own
conceit. Prov. 18:11.
The wicked under judgments
(bowing or tottering). Ps. 62:3;
Isa. 30:12.

Mentioned in Scripture
Of cities. Num. 13:28.
Of houses. 1 Sam. 18:11.
Of temples. 1 Chron. 29:4;
Isa. 56:5.
Of vineyards. Num. 22:24;
Prov. 24:31.

Miracles connected with
Falling of the walls of Jericho.
Josh. 6:20.

Handwriting on Belshazzar's
palace. Dan. 5:5, 25–28.
Small towns and villages were not
surrounded by. Lev. 25:31;
Deut. 3:5.

WAR
Antiquity of. Gen. 14:2.
Frequently long. 2 Sam. 3:1.
Frequently dreadful and bloody.
1 Sam. 14:22; 1 Chron. 5:22;
2 Chron. 14:13; 28:6.

Illustrative of
The contest between Antichrist
and the church. Rev. 11:7;
13:4, 7.
The contest of believers with the
enemies of their salvation. Rom.
7:23; 2 Cor. 10:3; Eph. 6:12;
1 Tim. 1:18.
The malice of the wicked.
Ps 55:21.
Our contest with death.
Eccles. 8:8.

The Jews
Expert in. 1 Chron. 12:33,
35–36; Song of Sol. 3:8.
Frequently engaged in. Josh.
6–11; 1 Kings 14:30; 15:7–16.
Large armies frequently engaged in.
2 Chron. 13:3; 14:9.

Often attended by
Cruelty. Jer. 18:21;
Lam. 5:11–14.
Devastation. Isa. 1:7.
Famine. Isa. 51:19; Jer. 14:15;
Lam. 5:10.
Plagues. Jer. 27:13; 28:8.
Often sent as a punishment for sin.
Judg. 5:8.

Originates in the lusts of persons.
James 4:1.

Preceded By
Consultation. Luke 14:31, with
Prov. 24:6.
Great preparation. Joel 3:9.
Rumors. Jer. 4:19; Matt. 24:6.
Records often kept of.
Num. 21:14.
Weapons used in. Josh. 1:14;
Judg. 18:11.

WAR CRIMES
See also Ethnic Cleansing; Genocide

Examples of
Ambush of helpless.
Deut. 25:17–18.
Deportation of people as slaves.
Amos 1:6, 9.
Mistreatment of women.
Amos 1:13.
Unburied bodies. Ps. 79:2–3.

Principles relevant to
Rules of warfare. Deut. 20:1–20.
Treatment of captive women.
Deut. 21:10–14.

WARFARE OF BELIEVERS
See Believers, Warfare of

WATCHFULNESS
Believers pray to be kept in a state of.
Ps. 141:3.
Blessedness of. Luke 12:37;
Rev. 16:15.
Christ an example of. Matt. 26:38,
40; Luke 6:12.
Commanded. Mark 13:37; Rev. 3:2.
Danger of failing in.
Matt. 24:48–51; 25:5, 8, 12;
Rev. 3:3.

Exhortations to. 1 Thess. 5:6;
1 Pet. 4:7.
Faithful ministers approved by.
Matt. 24:45–46; Luke 12:41–44.
Faithful ministers exercise.
Heb. 13:17.
God especially requires in ministers.
Ezek. 3:17, with Isa. 62:6;
Mark 13:34.
Ministers exhorted to. Acts 20:31;
2 Tim. 4:5.

Motives to
Expected direction from God.
Hab. 2:1.
Liability to temptation.
Matt. 26:41.
Relentless assaults of the devil.
1 Pet. 5:8.
Uncertain time of the coming of
Christ. Matt. 24:42; 25:13;
Mark 13:35–36.

Should be
At all times. Prov. 8:34.
In all things. 2 Tim. 4:5.
With alertness. Mark 13:33.
With prayer. Luke 21:36;
Eph. 6:18.
With sobriety. 1 Thess. 5:6;
1 Pet. 4:7.
With steadfastness in the faith.
1 Cor. 16:13.
With thanksgiving. Col. 4:2.
Unfaithful ministers lacking.
Isa. 56:10.
The wicked averse to. 1 Thess. 5:7.

WATCHMEN
Citizens sometimes acted as.
Neh. 7:3.
Danger of sleeping on their posts
referred to. Matt. 28:13–14.

Illustrative of
Anxiously waiting for God (when looking for the morning). Ps. 130:5–6.
Careless ministers (when blind). Isa. 56:10.
Ministers. Isa. 52:8; 62:6; Ezek. 3:17; Heb. 13:17.

In time of danger
Increased in number. Jer. 51:12.
Reported the approach of all strangers. 2 Sam. 18:24–27; 2 Kings 9:18–20; Isa. 21:6–7, 9.
Sounded an alarm at the approach of enemies. Ezek. 33:2–3.
Vigilant night and day. Neh. 4:9; Isa. 21:8.
Neglecting to give warning punished with death. Ezek. 33:6.
Often interrogated by passengers. Isa. 21:11.
Paraded the streets at night to preserve order. Song of Sol. 3:3; 5:7.
Relieved by turns. Neh. 7:3.
Soldiers generally acted as. Matt. 27:65–66.

Stationed
In the streets of cities. Ps. 127:1.
Around the temple in Jerusalem on special occasions. 2 Kings 11:6.
On the walls of cities. Isa. 62:6.
On watchtowers. 2 Kings 9:17; Isa. 21:5.
Vigilance of, vain without God's protection. Ps. 127:1.

WATER
Artificial mode of conveying into large cities. 2 Kings 20:20.

Becomes ice. Job 38:29; Ps. 147:16–17.
Carried in vessels. Gen. 21:14; 1 Sam. 26:11; Mark 14:13.

Collected in
Brooks. 2 Sam. 17:20; 1 Kings 18:5.
Clouds. Gen. 1:7; Job 26:8–9.
Fountains. 1 Kings 18:5; 2 Chron. 32:3.
Ponds. Exod. 7:19; Isa. 19:10.
Pools. 1 Kings 22:38; Neh. 2:14.
Rivers. Isa. 8:7; Jer. 2:18.
The sea. Gen. 1:9–10; Isa. 11:9.
Springs. Josh. 15:19.
Streams. Ps. 78:16; Isa. 35:6.
Wells. Gen. 21:19.

Described as
Cleansing. Ezek. 36:25; Eph. 5:26.
Fluid. Ps. 78:16; Prov. 30:4.
Penetrating. Ps. 109:18.
Refreshing. Job 22:7; Prov. 25:25.
Unstable. Gen. 49:4.
Wearing the hardest substances. Job 14:19.
Drops from the clouds in rain. Deut. 11:11; 2 Sam. 21:10.
An element of the world. Gen. 1:2.
Frequently contaminated and unfit for use. Exod. 15:23; 2 Kings 2:19.

God originally
Collected into one place. Gen. 1:9.
Created the firmament to divide. Gen. 1:6–7.
Created birds and fishes from. Gen. 1:20–21.

Illustrative of

The career of the wicked (when
rapidly flowing away).
Job 24:18; Ps. 58:7.

Counsel in the heart (when deep).
Prov. 20:5.

Death (when spilled on the
ground). 2 Sam. 14:14.

Different nations and people
(when many). Jer. 51:13;
Rev. 17:1, 15.

Faintness and cowardliness (in its
weakness). Josh. 7:5;
Ezek. 7:17.

Faintness by terror (when poured
out). Ps. 22:14.

Gifts and graces of the Holy Spirit.
Isa. 41:17-18; 44:3;
Ezek. 36:25; John 7:38-39.

Hostile armies. Isa. 8:7; 17:13.

Numerous offspring (when poured
out of buckets). Num. 24:7.

The ordinances of the gospel
(when still). Ps. 23:2.

Persecutions. Ps. 88:17.

Persecutors. Ps. 124:4-5.

Severe affliction (when deep).
Pss. 66:12; 69:1; Isa. 30:20;
43:2.

Strife and contention (when
difficult to stop). Prov. 17:14.

Support of God. Isa. 8:6.

A variety of afflictions (when
many). 2 Sam. 22:17.

A wavering disposition (in its
instability). Gen. 49:4.

Widespread distribution of the
knowledge of God (when
covering the sea). Isa. 11:9;
Hab. 2:14.

The word of Christ (when many
and noisy). Rev. 1:15.

The words of the wise (when
deep). Prov. 18:4.

The wrath of God (when poured
out). Hos. 5:10.

Kept for purification in large pots.
John 2:6.

Lack of, a great calamity.
Exod. 17:1-3; Num. 20:2;
2 Kings 3:9-10; Isa. 3:1.

Miracles connected with

Brought from the jawbone of a
donkey. Judg. 15:19.

Brought from the rock.
Exod. 17:6; Num. 20:11.

Christ walked on. Matt. 14:26-29.

Consumed by fire from heaven.
1 Kings 18:38.

Divided and made to stand on
heap. Exod. 14:21-22.

Healing powers communicated to.
2 Kings 5:14; John 5:4; 9:7.

Iron made to swim in.
2 Kings 6:5-6.

Trenches filled with.
2 Kings 3:17-22.

Turned into blood.
Exod. 7:17, 20.

Turned into wine. John 2:7 9.

Necessary to the comfort and
happiness of person. Isa. 41:17,
with Zech. 9:11.

Necessary to vegetation. Gen. 2:5-6;
Job 14:9; Isa. 1:30.

Rises in vapor to the clouds.
Eccles. 1:7, with Ps. 104:8.

Some plants particularly require.
Job 8:11.

Used by the Jews

For cooking. Exod. 12:9.

For legal purification. Exod. 29:4;
Heb. 9:10, 19.

As their principal beverage.
Gen. 24:43; 1 Kings 13:19, 22;
18:4; Hos. 2:5.
For washing the person.
Gen. 18:4; 24:32.
When scarce, sold at an enormous
price. Lam. 5:4.
The world and its inhabitants once
destroyed by. Gen. 7:20–23, with
2 Pet. 3:6.
The world not to be again destroyed
by. Gen. 9:8–15; 2 Pet. 3:7.

WATER, BITTER
A ceremonial water used by the
priests. Num. 5:18–27.
At Marah. Exod. 15:23.

WAVE OFFERING
See Offering, Wave

WAY
Doctrines taught by Christ.
Acts 9:2; 19:23; 22:4;
24:14, 22.
Jesus the. John 14:6; Heb. 9:8.
Of righteousness. Matt. 7:14.
Of sin, broad. Matt. 7:13.
Used in a figurative sense, of
holiness. Ps. 16:11; Isa. 35:8–9;
Jer. 6:16; Hos. 14:9.

WEALTH
See Prosperity; Riches

WEEKS
The Feast of Pentecost called the
Feast of. Exod. 34:22, with Acts
2:1.
Origin of computing time by.
Gen. 2:2.
A period of time consisting of seven
days. Lev. 23:15–16; Luke 18:12.

A space of seven years sometimes so
called. Gen. 29:27–28;
Dan. 9:24–25, 27.

WEATHER
Sayings concerning. Job 37:9,
17, 22.
Signs of. Matt. 16:2–3.

WEAVING
Bezaleel skilled in. Exod. 35:35.
Of coats. Exod. 39:27.
Done by women. 2 Kings 23:7.
Of the Ephod. Exod. 28:32.
Weaver's shuttle. Job 7:6.
Weaver's loom. Judg. 16:14.

WEDDINGS
Anticipation of.
Song of Sol. 4:7–15.
Best man. John 3:29.
Bridesmaids. Ps. 45:14.

Dress for
Bride. Ps. 45:13; Isa. 49:18;
61:10; Jer. 2:32; Rev. 19:7–8;
21:2.
Groom. Isa. 61:10.
Guest. Matt. 22:12.
Excuses groom from military service.
Deut. 20:7; 24:5.

Feast for
Anticipated by guests.
Matt. 25:1–7, 10;
Luke 12:35–36.
Despised by guests.
Matt. 22:1–10.
Ignored by guests. Matt. 25:8–13.
Seating at. Luke 14:7–11.
Wine at. John 2:1–10.
Of the Lamb. Rev. 19:7–9.
Night. Gen. 29:23–25;
Song of Sol. 4:16.

Preparation for
By bride. Ps. 45:13–15;
Joel 2:16.
By groom. Ps. 19:5; Joel 2:16.
By guests. Matt. 25:1–13.

Rejoicing at
By groom. Isa. 62:5.
By guests. Matt. 9:15.

Requests for
Samson's. Judg. 14:2.
Michal's. 1 Sam. 18:20.

WEEPING
In hell. Matt. 8:12.

Instances of repentant weeping
Of Abraham for Sarah. Gen. 23:2.
Because of tribulation. Jer. 22:10;
Amos 5:16–17.
Of David.
2 Sam. 1:17; 3:32; 13:36;
15:23, 30; 18:33.
Of Esau. Gen. 27:38.
Of Hannah. 1 Sam. 1:7.
Of Hezekiah. 2 Kings 20:3;
Isa. 38:3.
The Israelites. Judg. 2:4–5.
Of Jacob. Gen. 37:35.
Of Jacob and Esau. Gen. 33:4.
Of Jesus at the grave of Lazarus.
John 11:35.
Of Jesus, over Jerusalem.
Luke 19:41.
Of Jonathan and David.
1 Sam. 20:41.
Of Joseph. Gen. 42:24; 43:30;
45:2, 14; 46:29; 50:1, 17.
Of Mary Magdalene. John 20:11.
Of Mary, when she washed the
feet of Jesus. Luke 7:38;
John 11:2, 33.
For others. Jer. 9:1.

Peter. Matt. 26:75.
Of Paul. Acts 20:19; Phil. 3:18.
While doing good. Ps. 126:5–6.
None in heaven. Rev. 7:17.
Repentant. Jer. 50:4; Joel 2:12.

WEIGHTS
All metals given by. Exod. 37:24;
1 Chron. 28:14.
Frequently used in scales or balances.
Job 31:6; Isa. 40:12.
Generally regulated by the standard
of the sanctuary. Exod. 30:24.

Illustrated
The exceeding glory reserved for
believers (when heavy).
2 Cor. 4:17.
Restraints put on the elements.
Job 28:25.
Sins. Heb. 12:1.

The Jews
Forbidden to have different.
Deut. 25:13–14.
Forbidden to have unjust.
Lev. 19:35–36.
Frequently used unjust. Mic. 6:11.

Mentioned in Scripture
Dram. Neh. 7:70–71.
Gerah. Exod. 30:13; Ezek. 45:12.
Maneh or pound. Neh. 7:71;
Ezek. 45:12.
Shekel. Exod. 30:13;
Ezek. 45:12.
Shekel or half shekel. Gen. 24:22.
Talent. 2 Sam. 12:30;
Rev. 16:21.
Provisions sold by, in times of
scarcity. Lev. 26:26;
Ezek. 4:10, 16.
Sometimes regulated by the king's
standard. 2 Sam. 14:26.

Value of money estimated according to. Gen. 23:16; 43:21; Jer. 32:9.

WELFARE PROGRAMS

Amount given mandated. Deut. 14:27–29.

Amount given to be willing, free and generous. Deut. 15:10, 11, 14; Acts 11:29; 1 Cor. 16:2–3; 2 Cor. 8:1–4; 9:5–7.

Equated with God's blessing. Job 31:16–22; Prov. 25:21–22; 28:27.

Meet needs of neighbors. Rom. 15:2; 1 Cor. 10:24; Phil. 2:4.

Meet needs of own family. 1 Tim. 5:8.

Mosaic Law

Poor to glean in fields, orchards and vineyards. Exod. 23:10–11; Lev. 19:9–10; 25:3–7; Deut. 24:19–22; Ruth 2:2–3, 15–17.

Provide for Levites. Deut. 14:27.

Tithe for Levite, foreigner, fatherless, widow. Deut. 14:28–29.

Year of release. Deut. 15:1–18.

People expected to work for a living. Prov. 20:4; Eph. 4:28; 1 Thess. 4:11; 2 Thess. 3:7–12.

Practiced by the church. Acts 2:45; 4:32, 34; 6:1–4; 10:1–2; 11:27–30; Rom. 15:25–27; 2 Cor. 8:1–4; Phil. 4:15–18.

Prophets. Isa. 58:6–7; Ezek. 18:7.

Share with those in need commanded by

Apostles. 1 Cor. 13:3; 16:1–3; Gal. 2:10; Eph. 4:28;

1 Tim. 5:8; 6:18; James 2:15–16; 1 John 3:17–18.

Jesus. Matt. 5:42; 19:21; 25:31–46; Mark 9:41; Luke 10:32–36.

John the Baptist. Luke 3:11.

Must be just. Lev. 19:35; Prov. 11:1.

WELLS

Canaan abounded with. Deut. 6:11.

First mention of. Gen. 16:14.

A frequent cause of strife. Gen. 21:25; 26:21–22; Exod. 2:16–17.

Frequented by

Travelers. Gen. 24:11, 13, 42; John 4:6.

Women who came to draw water. Gen. 24:13–14; John 4:7.

Frequently dug

In the courts of houses. 2 Sam. 17:18.

In the desert. 2 Chron. 26:10.

Near encampments. Gen. 21:30; 26:18.

Outside cities. Gen. 24:11; John 4:6, 8.

Had troughs placed near for watering cattle. Gen. 24:19–20; Exod. 2:16.

Illustrative of

Enjoyment of domestic happiness (when drinking from one's own). Prov. 5:15.

The Holy Spirit in believers. Song of Sol. 4:15, with John 4:14.

Human understanding and wisdom. Prov. 16:22; 18:4.

Hypocrites (when without water).
2 Pet. 2:17.
The mouth of the righteous.
Prov. 10:11.
The ordinances of the church.
Isa. 12:3.
Many supplied from Lebanon.
Song of Sol. 4:15.

Mentioned in Scripture
Beer (east of Jordan).
Num. 21:16–18.
Beer-lahai-roi. Gen. 16:14.
Beer-sheba. Gen. 21:30–31.
Bethlehem. 2 Sam. 23:15;
1 Chron. 11:17–18.
Elim. Exod. 15:27.
Esek. Gen. 26:20.
Hagar. Gen. 21:19.
Haran. Gen. 29:3–4.
Jacob. John 4:6.
Rehoboth. Gen. 26:22.
Sitnah. Gen. 26:21.
Names often given to. Gen. 16:14;
21:31.

The occasion of feuds
Between Abraham and
Abimelech. Gen. 21:25–30.
At Haran. Gen. 24:16.
Between Isaac and Abimelech.
Gen. 26:15–22, 32–33.
Of Jacob. John 4:6.
Of Solomon. Eccles. 2:6.
Of Uzziah. 2 Chron. 26:10.
Used in a figurative sense, of
salvation. Isa. 12:3; John 4:14.
Without water. Jer. 15:18;
2 Pet. 2:17.
Often afforded no water. Jer. 14:3;
Zech. 9:11.
Often covered to prevent their being
filled with sand. Gen. 29:2–3.

Often deep and difficult to draw
from. John 4:11.
Often stopped up by enemies.
Gen. 26:15, 18;
2 Kings 3:19, 25.
Strangers not to draw from, without
permission. Num. 20:17.
Supplied by springs. Prov. 16:22.
Supplied by the rain. Ps. 84:6.
Surrounded by trees. Gen. 49:22;
Exod. 15:27.
Water of, frequently sold.
Num. 20:19.

WHALE
Created. Gen. 1:21.

WHEAT
Chaff of. Jer. 23:28; Matt. 3:12.
Ground in a mortar. Prov. 27:22.
Grown in Palestine. 1 Kings 5:11;
Ps. 81:16; 147:14.
Growth of, figurative of vicarious
death. John 12:24.
Offerings of. Num. 18:12.
Parables of. Matt. 13:25.
Prophesy of the sale of the measure
of, for a penny. Rev. 6:6.
Used in a figurative sense, of God's
mercy. Ps. 81:16; 147:14.
Used in a figurative sense, of
self-righteousness. Jer. 12:13.
Winnowing of. Luke 3:17

WHEEL
Figurative sense. Prov. 20:26;
Eccles. 12:6.
Potter's. Jer. 18:3.
Used in a symbolic sense.
Ezek. 1:15–21; 3:13;
10:9–19; 11:22.

WHIP
For horses. Prov. 26:3.

WHIRLWIND
Arose from the earth. Jer. 25:32.
Called the whirlwind of the Lord.
Jer. 23:19; 30:23.
Destructive nature of. Prov. 1:27.
Frequently continued for a long time.
Jer. 30:23.
Generally came from the south. Job
37:9; Isa. 21:1; Zech. 9:14.

Illustrative of the
Fury of God's judgments.
Jer. 25:32; 30:23.
Speed with which God executes
His purposes. Nah. 1:3.
Sudden destruction of the wicked.
Ps. 58:9; Prov. 1:27;
Isa. 17:13; 40:24; 41:16;
Jer. 30:23.
Unavoidable fruit of a life of sin
and vanity. Hos. 8:7.
Velocity of the chariots in hostile
armies. Isa. 5:28; Jer. 4:13.
Velocity of Christ's second
coming. Isa. 66:15.

Miracles connected with
Elijah taken to heaven in.
2 Kings 2:1, 11.
God spoke to Job from. Job 38:1;
40:6.
Sometimes came from the north.
Ezek. 1:4.

WICKED

Character of
Abominable. Rev. 21:8.
Alienated from God. Eph. 4:18;
Col. 1:21.
Blasphemous. Luke 22:65;
Rev. 16:9.
Blinded. 2 Cor. 4:4; Eph. 4:18.
Boastful. Pss. 10:3; 49:6.
Conspiring against God's people.
Neh. 4:8; 6:2; Ps. 38:12.
Corrupt. Acts 2:40.
Covetous. Mic. 2:2; Rom. 1:29.
Deceitful. Ps. 5:6; Rom. 3:13.
Delighting in the iniquity of others.
Prov. 2:14; Rom. 1:32.
Despising the works of the faithful.
Neh. 2:19; 4:2; 2 Tim. 3:3–4.
Destructive. Isa. 59:7.
Disobedient. Neh. 9:26;
Prov. 21:8; Isa. 57:17;
Titus 3:3; 1 Pet. 2:7.
Enticing to evil. Prov. 1:10–14;
2 Tim. 3:6.
Envious. Neh. 2:10; Titus 3:3.
Fearful. Prov. 28:1; Rev. 21:8.
Fierce. Prov. 16:29; 2 Tim. 3:3.
Foolish. Deut. 32:6; Ps. 5:5.
Forgetting God. Job 8:13.
Fraudulent. Ps. 37:21; Mic. 6:11.
Glorying in their shame.
Phil. 3:19.
Hardhearted. Ezek. 3:7.
Hating the light. Job 24:13;
John 3:20.
Heady and high-minded.
2 Tim. 3:4.
Hostile to God. Rom. 8:7;
Col. 1:21.
Hypocritical. Isa. 29:13;
2 Tim. 3:5.
Ignorant of God. Hos. 4:1;
2 Thess. 1:8.
Infidel. Pss. 10:4; 14:1.
Loathsome. Prov. 13:5.
Lovers of pleasure more than of
God. 2 Tim. 3:4.
Lying. Pss. 58:3; 64:4; Isa. 59:4.

Mischievous. Prov. 24:8; Mic. 7:3.
Murderous. Pss. 10:8; 94:6;
  Rom. 1:29.
Prayerless. Job 21:15; Ps. 53:4.
Persecuting. Pss. 69:26; 109:16.
Perverse. Deut. 32:5.
Proud. Ps. 59:12; Obad. 1:3;
  2 Tim. 3:2.
Rejoicing in the affliction of
  believers. Ps. 35:15.
Rejected. 2 Cor. 13:5;
  2 Tim. 3:8; Titus 1:16.
Selfish. 2 Tim. 3:2.
Sensual. Phil. 3:19, Jude 1:19.
Sold under sin. 1 Kings 21:20;
  2 Kings 17:17.
Stiff-hearted. Ezek. 2:4.
Stiff-necked. Exod. 33:5;
  Acts 7:51.
Stubborn. Ezek. 2:4.
Uncircumcised in heart. Jer. 9:26;
  Acts 7:51.
Undisciplined. 2 Tim. 3:3.
Ungodly. Prov. 16:27.
Unholy. 2 Tim. 3:2.
Unjust. Prov. 11:7; Isa. 26:10.
Unmerciful. Rom. 1:31.
Unprofitable. Matt. 25:30;
  Rom. 3:12.
Unruly. Titus 1:10.
Unthankful. Luke 6:35;
  2 Tim. 3:2.
Unwise. Deut. 32:6.

Compared to
Abominable branches. Isa. 14:19.
Ashes under the feet. Mal. 4:3.
Bad fish. Matt. 13:48.
Beasts. Ps. 49:12; 2 Pet. 2:12.
Blind men. Zeph. 1:17;
  Matt. 15:14.
Brass and iron, etc. Jer. 6:28;
  Ezek. 22:18.

Briars and thorns. Isa. 55:13;
  Ezek. 2:6.
Bush in the desert. Jer. 17:6.
Bulls of Bashan. Ps. 22:12.
Carcasses trampled under foot.
  Isa. 14:19.
Chaff. Job 21:18; Ps. 1:4;
  Matt. 3:12.
Clouds without water. Jude 12.
Corn blasted. 2 Kings 19:26.
Corrupt trees. Luke 6:43.
Deaf snakes. Ps. 58:4.
Dogs. Prov. 26:11; Matt. 7:6;
  2 Pet. 2:22.
Early dew. Hos. 13:3.
Earthenware. Prov. 26:23.
Evil figs. Jer. 24:8.
Fading oaks. Isa. 1:30.
Fiery oven. Ps. 21:9; Hos. 7:4.
Fire of thorns. Ps. 118:12.
Fools building upon sand.
  Matt. 7:26.
Fuel of fire. Isa. 9:19.
Garden without water. Isa. 1:30.
Goats. Matt. 25:32.
Grass. Pss. 37:2; 92:7.
Grass on the housetop.
  2 Kings 19:26.
Green bay trees. Ps. 37:35.
Green herbs. Ps. 37:2.
Horses rushing into the battle.
  Jer. 8:6.
Idols. Ps. 115:8.
Impurities. Ps. 119:119;
  Ezek. 22:18–19.
Lions greedy of prey. Ps. 17:12.
Melting wax. Ps. 68:2.
Morning clouds. Hos. 13:3.
Moth-eaten garments. Isa. 50:9;
  51:8.
Passing whirlwinds. Prov. 10:25.
Raging waves of the sea.
  Jude 1:13.

Rejected silver. Jer. 6:30.
Scorpions. Ezek. 2:6.
Serpents. Ps. 58:4; Matt. 23:33.
Smoke. Hos. 13:3.
Stony ground. Matt. 13:5.
Stubble. Job 21:18; Mal. 4:1.
Swine. Matt. 7:6; 2 Pet. 2:22.
Troubled sea. Isa. 57:20.
Visions of the night. Job 20:8.
Wandering˘ stars. Jude 1:13.
Wayward children. Matt. 11:16.
Weeds. Matt. 13:38.
Wells without water. 2 Pet. 2:17.
Wheels. Ps. 83:13.
White-washed tombs.
    Matt. 23:27.
Wild donkey's colts. Job 11:12.

WICKED, AFFLICTIONS OF THE

Are continual. Job 15:20;
    Eccles. 2:23; Isa. 32:10.
Are for examples to others.
    Ps. 64:7–9; Zeph. 3:6–7;
    1 Cor. 10:5–11; 2 Pet. 2:6.
Are ineffective of themselves, for
    their conversion. Exod. 9:30;
    Isa. 9:13; Jer. 2:30; Hag. 2:17.
Are multiplied. Deut. 31:17;
    Job 20:12–18; Ps. 32:10.
Are often sent as judgment.
    Job 21:17; Ps. 107:17;
    Jer. 30:15.
Are often sudden. Ps. 73:19;
    Prov. 6:15; Isa. 30:13;
    Rev. 18:10.
Believers should not be alarmed at.
    Prov. 3:25–26.
Frequently make worse.
    Neh. 9:28–29; Jer. 5:3.
God glorified in. Exod. 14:4;
    Ezek. 38:22–23.

God holds in ridicule. Ps. 37:12;
    Prov. 1:26–27.
Produce slavish fear. Job 15:24;
    Ps. 73:19; Jer. 49:3, 5.
Rejecting God's correction a cause
    of. Prov. 1:30–31; Ezek. 24:13;
    Amos 4:6–12; Zech. 7:11–12;
    Rev. 2:21–22.
Sometimes humble them.
    1 Kings 21:27.
Their persecution of believers, a
    cause of. Deut. 30:7; Ps. 55:19;
    Zech. 2:9; 2 Thess. 1:6.

WICKED, DEATH OF THE

Frequently marked by terror.
    Job 18:11–15; 27:19–21;
    Ps. 73:19.
Frequently sudden and unexpected.
    Job 21:13, 23; 27:21;
    Prov. 29:1.
God has no pleasure in.
    Ezek. 18:23, 32.
Illustrated. Luke 12:20; 16:22–23.
Like the death of beasts. Ps. 49:14.
Punishment follows. Isa. 14:9;
    Acts 1:25.
The remembrance of them perishes
    in. Job 18:17; Ps. 34:16;
    Prov. 10:7.
Sometimes without fear. Jer. 34:5,
    with 2 Chron. 36:11–13.
In their sins. Ezek. 3:19; John 8:21.
Without hope. Prov. 11:7.

WICKED, HAPPINESS OF THE

Believers often permitted to see the
    end of. Ps. 73:17–20.

Derived from
    Drunkenness. Isa. 5:11; 56:12.
    Gluttony. Isa. 22:13; Hab. 1:16.
    Popular applause. Acts 12:22.

Successful oppression. Hab. 1:15;
James 5:6.

Their power. Job 21:7;
Ps. 37:35.

Their wealth. Job 21:13;
Ps. 52:7.

Their worldly prosperity.
Pss. 17:14; 73:3–4, 7.

Vain pleasure. Job 21:12;
Isa. 5:12.

Do not worry. Ps. 37:1.

Illustrated. Ps. 37:35–36;
Luke 12:16–20; 16:19–25.

Leads to recklessness. Isa. 22:13.

Leads to sorrow. Prov. 14:13.

Limited to this life. Ps. 17:14;
Luke 16:25.

Marred by jealousy. Esther 5:13.

Often interrupted by judgments.
Num. 11:33; Job 15:21;
Ps. 73:18–20; Jer. 25:10–11.

Short. Job 20:5.

Sometimes a stumbling block to
believers. Ps. 73:3, 16; Jer. 12:1;
Hab. 1:13.

Uncertain. Luke 12:20;
James 4:13–14.

Vain. Eccles. 2:1; 7:6.

Warning against. Amos 6:1;
Luke 6:25.

WICKED, PUNISHMENT OF THE

Because of
Covetousness. Isa. 57:17;
Jer. 51:13.

Disobeying God. Neh. 9:26–27;
Eph. 5:6.

Disobeying the gospel.
2 Thess. 1:8.

Evil ways and doings. Jer. 21:14;
Hos. 4:9; 12:2.

Idolatry. Lev. 26:30;
Isa. 10:10–11.

Ignorance of God. 2 Thess. 1:8.

Iniquity. Jer. 36:31;
Ezek. 3:17–18; 18:4, 13, 20;
Amos 3:2.

Oppressing. Isa. 49:26;
Jer. 30:16, 20.

Persecuting. Jer. 11:21–22;
Matt. 23:34–36.

Pride. Isa. 10:12; 24:21;
Luke 14:11.

Rejection of the law of God.
1 Sam. 15:23; Hos. 4:6–9.

Sin. Lam. 3:39.

Unbelief. Mark 16:16;
Rom. 11:20; Heb. 3:18–19;
4:2.

Comes from God. Lev. 26:18;
Isa. 13:11.

Commences frequently in this life.
Prov. 11:31.

Consummated at the day of
judgment. Matt. 25:31, 46;
Rom. 2:5, 16; 2 Pet. 2:9.

Deferred, encourages them in sin.
Eccles. 8:11.

The fruit of sin. Job 4:8; Prov. 22:8;
Rom. 6:21; Gal. 6:8.

Future, awarded by Christ.
Matt. 16:27; 25:31, 41.

Future, described as
Blackness of darkness.
2 Pet. 2:17; Jude 13.

Damnation of hell. Matt. 23:33.

Darkness. Matt. 8:12;
2 Pet. 2:17.

Death. Rom. 5:12–17; 6:23.

Eternal damnation. Mark 3:29.

Everlasting burnings. Isa. 33:14.

Everlasting destruction. Pss. 52:5;
92:7; 2 Thess. 1:9.

Everlasting fire. Matt. 25:41;
Jude 7.

Hell. Ps. 9:17; Matt. 5:29;
Luke 12:5; 16:23.

Often sudden and unexpected.
Pss. 35:8; 64:7; Prov. 29:1;
Luke 12:20; 1 Thess. 5:3.

Punished forever and ever.
Rev. 14:11.

Punished with fire. Rev. 14:10.

Resurrection of damnation.
John 5:29.

The righteousness of God requires.
2 Thess. 1:6.

Rising to shame and everlasting
contempt. Dan. 12:2.

Second death. Rev. 2:11; 21:8.

Wine of the wrath of God.
Rev. 14:10.

The wrath of God. John 3:36.

In this life by
Bringing down their pride.
Isa. 13:11.

Cutting off. Ps. 94:23.

Depraved mind. Rom. 1:28.

Deliverance to enemies.
Neh. 9:27.

Famine. Lev. 26:19–20, 26, 29;
Ps. 107:34.

Fear. Lev. 26:36–37; Job 18:11.

Put in slippery places.
Ps. 73:3–19.

Sickness. Lev. 26:16; Ps. 78:50.

Trouble and distress. Isa. 8:22;
Zeph. 1:15.

War. Lev. 26:25, 32–33;
Jer. 6:4.

Wild animals. Lev. 26:22.

No combination is effective against.
Prov. 11:21.

Often brought about by evil plans.
Esther 7:10; Pss. 37:1, 5; 57:6.

The reward of sin. Job 4:8;
Prov. 22:8; Rom. 6:21; Gal. 6:8.

Will be
Accompanied by remorse.
Isa. 66:24, with Mark 9:44.

According to their deeds.
Matt. 16:27; Rom. 2:6, 9;
2 Cor. 5:10.

According to the knowledge
possessed by them.
Luke 12:47–48.

Increased by neglect of privileges.
Matt. 11:21–24;
Luke 10:13–15.

Without mitigation.
Luke 16:23–26.

Should be a warning to others.
Num. 26:10; 1 Cor. 10:6–11;
Jude 7.

WICKED, TITLES AND NAMES OF

Adversaries of the Lord.
1 Sam. 2:10.

Children of gentle men. Job 30:8.

Children of Belial. Deut. 13:13;
2 Chron. 13:7.

Children of corruption. Isa. 1:4.

Children of the devil. Acts 13:10;
1 John 3:10.

Children of disobedience. Eph. 2:2;
Col. 3:6.

Children of fools. Job 30:8.

Children of hell. Matt. 23:15.

Children of iniquity. Hos. 10:9.

Children of pride. Job. 41:34.

Children of the sinful nature.
Rom. 9:8.

Children of strangers. Isa. 2:6.

Children of the wicked one.
Matt. 13:38.

Children of this world. Luke 16:8.

Children of transgression. Isa. 57:4.

Children of wickedness.
2 Sam. 7:10.
Children that will not hear the law of
the Lord. Isa. 30:9.
Corrupt generation. Acts 2:40.
Cursed children. 2 Pet. 2:14.
Enemies of all righteousness.
Acts 13:10.
Enemies of the cross of Christ.
Phil. 3:18.
Enemies of God. Ps. 37:20;
James 4:4.
Evil and adulterous generation.
Matt. 12:39.
Evildoers. Ps. 37:1; 1 Pet. 2:14.
Evil generation. Deut. 1:35.
Evil men. Prov. 4:14; 2 Tim. 3:13.
Faithless children. Deut. 32:20.
Fools. Prov. 1:7; Rom. 1:22.
Generation of serpents. Matt. 3:7;
12:34.
Hardened rebels. Jer. 6:28.
Haters of God. Ps. 81:15;
Rom. 1:30.
Impudent children. Ezek. 2:4.
Instruments of wrath. Rom. 9:22.
Inventors of evil things. Rom. 1:30.
Lying children. Isa. 30:9.
Men of the world. Ps. 17:14.
Objects of wrath. Eph. 2:3.
People laden with iniquity. Isa. 1:4.
Perverse and crooked generation.
Deut. 32:5; Matt. 17:17;
Phil. 2:15.
Perverse generation. Deut. 32:20.
Rebellious children. Isa. 30:1.
Rebellious house. Ezek. 2:5, 8; 12:2.
Rebellious people. Isa. 30:9; 65:2.
Reprobates. 2 Cor. 13:5–7.
Scornful. Ps. 1:1.
Seed of evil doers. Isa. 1:4; 14:20.
Seed of falsehood. Isa. 57:4.
Seed of the wicked. Ps. 37:28.

Serpents. Matt. 23:33.
Servants of corruption. 2 Pet. 2:19.
Servants of sin. John 8:34;
Rom. 6:20.
Sinful generation. Mark 8:28.
Sinners. Ps. 26:9; Prov. 1:10.
Sons of Belial. 1 Sam. 2:12;
1 Kings 21:10.
Senseless children. Jer. 4:22.
Strange children. Ps. 144:7.
Stubborn and rebellious generation.
Ps. 78:8.
Transgressors. Pss. 37:38; 51:13.
Ungodly. Ps. 1:1.
Ungodly men. Jude 1:4.
Unprofitable servants. Matt. 25:30.
Wicked doers. Ps. 101:8;
Prov. 17:4.
Wicked generation.
Matt. 12:45; 16:4.
Wicked of the earth. Ps. 75:8.
Wicked ones. Jer. 2:33.
Wicked servants. Matt. 25:26.
Wicked sinners. Ps. 59:5.
Workers of iniquity. Ps. 28:3; 36:12;
Matt. 12:39.

WIDOWS

Allowed to marry again. Rom. 7:3;
1 Cor. 7:39.

Believers
Cause joy to. Job 29:13.
Do not disappoint. Job 31:16.
Relieve. Acts 9:39.
Blessings on those who relieve.
Deut. 14:29.
Calamity to those who oppress.
Isa. 10:1–2.
Character of true. Luke 2:37;
1 Tim. 5:5, 10.
Clothed in mourning after the death
of husbands. Gen. 38:14, 19;
2 Sam. 14:2, 5.

Commandment regarding.
Exod. 22:22–24.

Curse for perverting judgment of.
Deut. 27:19.

Examples of
Anna. Luke 2:36–37.

Of Nain whose only son Jesus
raised from the dead.
Luke 7:11–15.

Naomi. Ruth 1:3.

Ruth. Ruth 1–4.

The widow of Zarephath, who
sustained Elijah during the
famine. 1 Kings 17.

The woman who gave two small
coins in the temple.
Mark 12:41–44; Luke 21:2.

The women whose sons Elisha
saved from being sold into
slavery. 2 Kings 4:1–7.

Exhorted to trust in God. Jer. 49:11.

Frequently oppressed and
persecuted. Job 24:3; Ezek. 22:7.

God
Establishes the border of.
Prov. 15:25.

Judges for. Deut. 10:18; Ps. 68:5.

Relieves. Ps. 146:9.

Surely hears the cry of.
Exod. 22:23.

Illustrative of
A desolate condition. Isa. 47:8–9.

Zion in captivity. Lam. 1:1.

Increase of, threatened as a
punishment. Exod. 22:24;
Jer. 15:8; 18:21.

Instances of great generosity in.
1 Kings 17:9–15;
Mark 12:42–43.

Intermarrying with by kings,
considered treason.
1 Kings 2:21–24.

Laws regarding
Allowed to glean in fields and
vineyards. Deut. 24:19.

Bound to perform their vows.
Num. 30:9.

Clothing not to be taken as
collateral by creditors.
Deut. 24:17.

Not to be oppressed. Exod. 22:22;
Deut. 27:19.

Priests forbidden to marry.
Lev. 21:14.

Share in public rejoicings.
Deut. 16:11, 14.

Share the tithe every three years.
Deut. 14:28–29; 26:12–13.

When daughters of priests, to be
supported by their fathers.
Lev. 22:13.

When left without children, to be
married by their husband's
nearest relative. Deut. 25:5–6;
Ruth 3:10–13, with 4:4–5;
Matt. 22:24–28.

Often devoted themselves entirely to
God's service. Luke 2:37;
1 Tim. 5:9–11.

Paul's commandments concerning.
1 Cor. 7:8–9; 1 Tim. 5:3–16.

Though poor, may be generous.
Mark 12:42–43.

Released from all obligation to
former husbands. Rom. 7:3.

Reproach connected with. Isa. 54:4.

Should be
Allowed to share in our blessings.
Deut. 14:29; 16:11, 14;
24:19–21.

Honored, if widows indeed.
1 Tim. 5:3.
Pleaded for. Isa. 1:17.
Relieved by the church. Acts 6:1;
1 Tim. 5:9.
Relieved by their friends.
1 Tim. 5:4, 16.
Visited in distresses. James 1:27.

Should not be
Afflicted. Exod. 22:22.
Deprived of clothing in pledge.
Deut. 24:17.
Oppressed. Zech. 7:10.
Treated with violence. Jer. 22:3.
Specially taken care of by the
primitive church. Acts 6:1;
1 Tim. 5:9.
A type of Zion in affliction. Lam. 5:3.
Under the special protection of God.
Deut. 10:18; Ps. 68:5.
When young, exposed to many
temptations. 1 Tim. 5:11–14.

The wicked
Do no good to. Job 24:21.
Grieve. Ezek. 22:7.
Kill. Ps. 94:6.
Make a prey of. Isa. 10:2;
Matt. 23:14.
Reject the cause of. Isa. 1:23.
Send away empty. Job 22:9.
Take pledges from. Job 24:3.

WIFE
Bathsheba. 2 Sam. 11:2–5.
Bought. Gen. 29; Exod. 21:7–11;
Ruth 4:10.
Called desire of the eyes.
Ezek. 24:16.
Called helper. Gen. 2:18, 20.
Called fruitful vine. Ps. 128:3.
Contentious, Zipporah. Exod. 4:25.

Domestic duties of. Gen. 18:6;
Prov. 31:13–27.
Gotten by violence. Judg. 21.
Hated. Gen. 29:31–33.
Idolatrous, Solomon's wives.
1 Kings 11:4–8; Neh. 13:26.
Incorruptible, Vashti.
Esther 1:10–22.
Jezebel. 1 Kings 21;
2 Kings 9:30–37.
The judgment denounced against
Eve. Gen. 3:16.
Loved, by Isaac. Gen. 24:67.
Loved, by Jacob. Gen. 29:30.
Loyal. Gen. 31:14–16.
Paul's instruction to. Eph. 5:22–33.
Potiphar's. Gen. 39:7.
Procured. Gen. 24; 34:4–10; 38:6.
Relation of, to husband. Gen. 2:18,
23–24; 1 Cor. 11:3–12.
Tactful, Abigail. 1 Sam. 25:3,
14–42.
Unfaithful. Num. 5:14–31.
Virtuous. Prov. 31:10–31.
Vows of. Num. 30:6–16.

WILDERNESS
Jesus' temptation in. Matt. 4:1.
Wandering of the Israelites in a
picture of the sinners' state.
Deut. 32:10.

WILL (THE MENTAL FACULTY)
Freedom of choice, recognized by
God. Gen. 4:6–10.

WILL (A TESTAMENT)
Of Abraham. Gen. 25:5–6.
David. 1 Kings 2:1–9.
Enforced after death only.
Heb. 9:16–17.
Jacob. Gen. 48; 49.
Jehoshaphat. 2 Chron. 21:3.

Made not be annulled. Gal. 3:15.

WILL OF GOD
See God, Will of

WIND
Accomplishes the purposes of God.
Ps. 148:8.
Drying nature of. Gen. 8:1;
Isa. 11:15.
Frequently brings rain.
1 Kings 18:44–45.
(*See also* 2 Kings 3:17.)
From the north, drives away rain.
Prov. 25:23.

God
Brings forth, out of His treasuries.
Ps. 135:7; Jer. 10:13.
Changes. Ps. 78:26.
Created. Amos 4:14.
Gathers in His hand. Prov. 30:4.
Quiets. Matt. 8:26; 14:32.
Raises. Ps. 107:25; Jon. 4:8.
Restrains. Job 28:25; Ps. 107:29.

Illustrative of
Disappointed expectations
(bringing forth). Isa. 26:18.
False doctrines Eph. 4:14.
Human life. Job 7:7.
Iniquity that leads to destruction.
Isa. 64:6.
The judgments of God (when
destructive). Isa. 27:8; 29:6;
41:16.
Molten images. Isa. 41:29.
One who boasts of a false gift
(when without rain).
Prov. 25:14.
The operations of the Holy Spirit.
Ezek. 37:9; John 3:8; Acts 2:2.
Sin (sowing). Hos. 8:7.

The speeches of the desperate.
Job 6:26.
Terrors that pursue the soul.
Job 30:15.
Vain hopes (feeding upon).
Hos. 12:1.
The wicked (as chaff or stubble
before). Job 21:18; Ps. 1:4.
Its movement of the leaves noticed.
Isa. 7:2; Matt. 11:7; Rev. 6:13.

Mentioned in Scripture
East. Job 27:21; Ezek. 17:10;
Hos. 13:15.
Northeastern. Acts 27:14.
North. Prov. 25:23;
Song of Sol. 4:16.
Simoon or scorching wind.
Jer. 4:11.
South. Job 37:17; Luke 12:55.
West. Exod. 10:19.
Whirlwind. Job 37:9.

Miracles connected with
Calmed by casting overboard
Jonah. Jon. 1:15.
Calmed by Christ. Matt. 8:26;
14:32.
Locusts brought by. Exod. 10:13.
Locusts removed by. Exod. 10:19.
Quails brought by. Num. 11:31.
Raised because of Jonah.
Jon. 1:4.
Red Sea divided by. Exod. 14:21.
Rocks and mountains torn by.
1 Kings 19:11.
Often destruction. Ps. 103:16;
Isa. 40:7.
Purifying nature of. Job 37:21;
Jer. 4:11.

Stormy
Destroys houses. Job 1:19;
Matt. 7:27.

Drives about the largest ships.
Matt. 14:24; Acts 27:18;
James 3:4.
Raises the sea in waves.
Ps. 107:25; John 6:18.
Theory of, above human
comprehension. John 3:8.
Variable nature of. Eccles. 1:6.

When violent, called
Fierce. James 3:4.
Great and strong. 1 Kings 19:11.
Mighty. Acts 2:2; Rev. 6:13.
Rough. Isa. 27:8.
Storm. Job 21:18; Ps. 83:15.
Stormy. Pss. 55:8; 148:8;
Ezek. 13:11, 13.
Storm. Job 9:17; 27:20; Jon. 1:4.

WINDOW
In Rahab's house. Josh. 2:15.

WINE
An article of extensive commerce.
Ezek. 27:18.

Characterized as
Cheering God and man.
Judg. 9:13; Zech. 9:17.
Making happy the heart.
Ps. 104:15.
Making happy. Esther 1:10;
Eccles. 10:19.
Strengthening. 2 Sam. 16:2;
Song of Sol. 2:5.
Consequence of putting (when new)
into old bottles. Mark 2:22.
Custom of giving to persons in pain
or suffering, mixed with drugs.
Prov. 31:6; Mark 15:23.
Custom of presenting to travelers.
Gen. 14:18; 1 Sam. 25:18.
Firstfruits of, to be offered to God.
Deut. 18:4; 2 Chron. 31:5.

First mention of. Gen. 9:20–21.
First mode of making, noticed.
Gen. 40:11.
Forbidden to Nazarites during their
separation. Num. 6:3.
Forbidden to the priests while
engaged in the tabernacle.
Lev. 10:9.
Generally made by treading the
grapes in a press. Neh. 13:15;
Isa. 63:2–3.
Given in abundance to the Jews
when obedient. Hos. 2:22;
Joel 2:19, 24; Zech. 9:17.

Illustrative of
The abominations of the apostasy.
Rev. 17:2; 18:3.
The blessings of the gospel.
Prov. 9:2, 5; Isa. 25:6; 55:1.
The blood of Christ.
Matt. 26:27–29.
Violence and plunder. Prov. 4:17.
The wrath and judgments of God.
Pss. 60:3; 75:8;
Jer. 13:12–14; 25:15–18.
Improved by age. Luke 5:39.

In excess
Forbidden. Eph. 5:18.
Impairs the health. 1 Sam. 25:37;
Hos. 4:11.
Impairs the judgment and
memory. Prov. 31:4–5;
Isa. 28:7.
Inflames the passions. Isa. 5:11.
Infuriates the temper. Prov. 20:1.
Leads to remorse. Prov. 29:32.
Leads to sorrow and contention.
Prov. 23:29–30.
In times of scarcity, mixed with
water. Isa. 1:22.
The Jews frequently deprived of, as a
punishment. Isa. 24:7, 11;

Hos. 2:9; Joel 1:10; Hag. 1:11; 2:16.

The Jews frequently drank to excess. Isa. 5:11; 113:3; Amos 6:6.

Kept in bottles. 1 Sam. 25:18; Hab. 2:15.

Love of Christ to be preferred to. Song of Sol. 1:2, 4.

Made of

Juice of the grape. Gen. 49:11.

Juice of the pomegranate. Song of Sol. 8:2.

Many kinds of. Neh. 5:18.

Never drunk by Rechabites. Jer. 35:5–6.

Often spiced to increase its strength, etc. Prov. 9:2, 5; 23:30.

Places celebrated for

Assyria. 2 Kings 18:32; Isa. 36:17.

Canaan in general. Deut. 33:28.

Helbon. Ezek. 27:18.

Lebanon. Hos. 14:17.

Moab. Isa. 16:8–10; Jer. 48:32–33.

Possessions of Judah. Gen. 49:8, 11–12.

Red, most valued. Prov. 23:31; Isa. 27:2.

Refining of, alluded to. Isa. 25:6.

Sometimes mixed with milk as a beverage. Song of Sol. 5:1.

Stored in cellars. 1 Chron. 27:27.

Sweet, valued for flavor and strength. Isa. 49:26; Amos 9:13; Mic. 6:15.

Used

At all feasts and entertainments. Esther 1:7; 5:6; Isa. 5:12; Dan. 5:1–4; John 2:3.

As a beverage from the earliest age. Gen. 9:21; 27:25.

For drink offerings in idolatrous worship. Deut. 32:37–38.

For drink offerings in the worship of God. Exod. 29:40; Num. 15:4–10.

As a medicine. Luke 10:34; 1 Tim. 5:23.

Water miraculously turned into. John 2:9.

With corn and oil, symbolized all temporal blessings. Gen. 27:28, 37; Ps. 4:7; Hos. 2:8; Joel 2:19.

WINNOWING

Fodder eaten by ox and donkey. Isa. 30:24.

Analogy of God's judgment. Matt. 3:12.

WINTER

God makes. Ps. 74:17.

Illustrative of seasons of spiritual adversity. Song of Sol. 2:11.

The Jews frequently had special houses for. Jer. 36:22; Amos 3:15.

Ships laid up in port during. Acts 27:9, 12; 28:11.

Unsuited for traveling. Matt. 24:20; 2 Tim. 4:21.

Yearly return of, secured by covenant. Gen. 8:22.

WISDOM

Natural

Foolishness with God. 1 Cor. 3:19.

Not to be trusted. 1 Cor. 2:5.

Spiritual
Begins with the fear of the Lord.
Ps. 111:10.
Granted those who ask.
James 1:5.
Priceless. Prov. 8:11.
Unknown by worldly leaders.
1 Cor. 2:7–8.

That of Christ
Amazed men during His ministry.
Luke 4:36.
Astonished men during His youth.
Luke 2:47.
Increased with His years.
Luke 2:52.
Should guide Christians.
1 Cor. 2:16; Phil. 2:5.

WISDOM OF GOD

See God, Wisdom of

WISE MEN

Of Babylon. Dan. 4:18; 5:8.
Of the East. Matt. 2:1–12.
Of Egypt. Gen. 41:8, 24;
Exod. 7:11.
Solomon. 1 Kings 4:29–34.

WITCHCRAFT

Law concerning. Exod. 22:18;
Lev. 19:31; 20:6, 27.
Witch of Endor. 1 Sam. 28:7–25.
Witches destroyed. 1 Sam. 28:3, 9.

WITNESS

Corrupted by money.
Matt. 28:11–15; Acts 6:11, 13.
Incorruptible. Ps. 15:4.
By laying hands on the accused.
Lev. 24:14.
To marriage to. Ruth 4:10–11;
Isa. 8:2–3.

Qualified by oath. Exod. 22:11;
Num. 5:19, 21; 1 Kings 8:31–32.
Required to cast the first stone in
executing sentence. Deut. 13:9;
17:5–7; Acts 7:58.
To the transfer of land.
Gen. 21:25–30; 23:11, 16–18;
Ruth 4:1–9; Jer. 32:9–12,,
25, 44.
Two necessary to establish a fact.
Num. 35:30; Deut. 17:6; 19:15;
Matt. 18:16; John 8:17;
2 Cor. 13:1; 1 Tim. 5:19;
Heb. 10:28.
Used in a figurative sense, of
instruction in righteousness.
Rev. 11:3.

WITNESS OF THE HOLY SPIRIT

See Holy Spirit, Witness of the

WITNESSING

For Christ. Acts 1:8.
For God. Isa. 43:10.
In our worship. 1 Cor. 14:25.
We must always be ready for.
1 Pet. 5:12.

WIVES

Duties of, to their husbands
To be faithful to them.
1 Cor. 7:3–5, 10.
To be subject to them. Gen. 3:16;
Eph. 5:22, 24; 1 Pet. 3:1.
To love them. Titus 2:4.
To obey them. 1 Cor. 14:34;
Titus 2:5.
To remain with them for life.
Rom. 7:2–3.
To reverence them. Eph. 5:33.

Good

Are benevolent to the poor.
Prov. 31:20.

Are a blessing to husbands.
Prov. 12:4; 31:10, 12.

Are diligent and prudent.
Prov. 31:13–27.

Are from the Lord. Prov. 19:14.

Are praised by husbands.
Prov. 31:28.

Are a sign of the favor of God.
Prov. 18:22.

Bring honor on husbands.
Prov. 31:23.

Duty of, to unbelieving husbands.
1 Cor. 7:13–14, 16;
1 Pet. 3:1–2.

Secure confidence of husbands.
Prov. 31:11.

Should be silent in the churches.
1 Cor. 14:34.

Not to be selected from among the
ungodly. Gen. 24:3; 26:34–35;
28:1.

Of ministers, should be exemplary.
1 Tim. 3:11.

Should be adorned

Not with ornaments. 1 Tim. 2:9;
1 Pet. 3:3.

With good works. 1 Tim. 2:10;
5:10.

With a meek and quiet spirit.
1 Pet. 3:4–5.

With modesty and sobriety.
1 Tim 2:9.

Should seek religious instruction from
their husbands. 1 Cor. 14:35.

WOLF

Destructive to flocks of sheep.
John 10:12.

Illustrative of

The change effected by conversion
(taming of). Isa. 11:6, 65:25.

The devil. John 10:12.

False teachers. Matt. 7:15;
Acts 20:29.

Fierce enemies. Jer. 5:6;
Hab. 1:8.

The tribe of Benjamin.
Gen. 49:27.

The wicked. Matt. 10:16;
Luke 10:3.

Wicked rulers. Ezek. 22:27;
Zeph. 3:3.

Particularly fierce in the evening
when it seeks its prey. Jer. 5:6;
Hab. 1:8.

Ravenous nature of. Gen. 49:27.

WOMAN

Allowed to join in the temple music
from the time of David. 1 Chron.
25:5–6; Ezra 2:65; Neh. 7:67.

Characterized as

Loving and affectionate.
2 Sam. 1:26.

Tender and constant to her
offspring. Isa. 49:15;
Lam. 4:10.

Timid. Isa. 19:16; Jer. 50:37;
51:30; Nah. 3:13.

Weaker than man. 1 Pet. 3:7.

Considered a valuable acquisition in
war. Deut. 20:14; 1 Sam. 30:2.

Curse pronounced on. Gen. 3:16.

Deceived by Satan. Gen. 3:1–6;
2 Cor. 11:3; 1 Tim. 2:14.

Of distinction

Arrogant in their behavior.
Isa. 3:16.

Fair and graceful. Gen. 12:11;
24:16; Song of Sol. 1:8;
Amos 8:13.

Fond of dress and ornaments.
Isa. 3:17–23.

Wore their hair braided and
adorned with gold and pearls.
Isa. 3:24, with 1 Tim. 2:9.

Generally wore a veil in the presence
of the opposite sex. Gen. 24:65.

Good and virtuous, described.
Prov. 31:10–28.

Had a court of the tabernacle
assigned to her. Exod. 38:8;
1 Sam. 2:22.

Illustrative of
Apostasy (when lewd).
Rev. 17:4, 18.

Backsliding Israel (when delicate).
Jer. 6:2.

Believers (when pure and holy).
Song of Sol. 1:3; 2 Cor. 11:2;
Rev. 14:4.

Believers (when wise).
Matt. 25:1–2, 4.

The church of Christ (when
gloriously arrayed). Ps. 45:13;
Gal. 4:26, with Rev. 12:1.

Israel in its captivity (when
forsaken). Isa. 54:6.

Mere professors (when foolish).
Matt. 25:1–3.

A state of worldly security (when at
ease and careless). Isa. 32:9, 11.

Led man to disobey God.
Gen. 3:6, 11–12.

Often engaged in
Agriculture. Ruth 2:8;
Song of Sol. 1:6.

Attending funerals as mourners.
Jer. 9:17, 20.

Celebrating the victories of the
nation. Exod. 15:20–21;
Judg. 11:34; 1 Sam. 18:6–7.

Domestic employments.
Gen. 18:6; Prov. 31:15.

Drawing and carrying water.
Gen. 24:11, 13, 15–16;
1 Sam. 9:11; John 4:7.

Embroidery. Prov. 31:22.

Grinding corn. Matt. 24:41;
Luke 17:35.

Spinning. Prov. 31:13–14.

Tending sheep. Gen. 29:9;
Exod. 2:16.

Origin of name. Gen. 2:23.

Originally made
By God in His own image.
Gen. 1:27.

For man. 1 Cor. 11:9.

From one of Adam's ribs.
Gen. 2:21–22.

Subordinate to man. 1 Cor. 11:3.

To be the glory of man.
1 Cor. 11:7.

To be a helper for man.
Gen. 2:18, 20.

Of the poorer classes, dark from
exposure to the sun.
Song of Sol. 1:5–6.

Punishment for injuring, when with
child. Exod. 21:22–25.

Required to hear and obey the law.
Josh. 8:35.

Safety in childbirth promised to the
faithful and holy. 1 Tim. 2:15.

Sometimes
Active in instigating to iniquity.
Num. 31:15–16;
1 Kings 21:25; Neh. 13:26.

Fond of self-indulgence.
Isa. 32:9–11.

Lived in a separate apartment or tent. Gen. 18:9; 24:67; Esther 2:9, 11.

Silly and easily led into error. 2 Tim. 3:6.

Subtle and deceitful. Prov. 7:10; Eccles. 7:26.

Zealous in promoting superstition and idolatry. Jer. 7:18; Ezek. 13:17, 23.

Submissive and respectful to husband. 1 Pet. 3:6, with Gen. 18:12.

To be governed by, considered a calamity by the Jews. Isa. 3:12.

To be slain by, considered a great disgrace. Judg. 9:54.

To wear her hair long as a covering. 1 Cor. 11:15.

Unfaithfulness of, when married, found out by the waters of jealousy. Num. 5:14–28.

Virtuous, held in high estimation. Ruth 3:11.

Vows of, when married, not binding upon the husband. Num. 30:6–8.

Young

Called girls. Gen. 24:55; Mark 5:39.

Called maids. Exod. 2:8; Luke 8:51–52.

Called virgins. Gen. 24:16; Lam. 1:4.

Could not marry without consent of parents. Gen. 24:3–4; 34:6; Exod. 22:17.

Of distinction, dressed in robes of various colors. 2 Sam. 13:18; Ps. 45:14.

Fond of ornaments. Jer. 2:32.

Happy and merry. Judg. 11:34; 21:21; Jer. 31:13; Zech. 9:17.

Inherited parents' property when there was no male heir. Num. 27:8.

Kind and courteous to strangers. Gen. 24:17.

Not to be given in marriage, considered a calamity. Judg. 11:37; Ps. 78:63; Isa. 4:1.

Often taken captive. Lam. 1:18; Ezek. 30:17–18.

Often treated with great cruelty in war. Deut. 32:25; Lam. 2:21; 5:11.

Punishment for seducing when engaged. Deut. 22:23–27.

Punishment for seducing when not engaged. Exod. 22:16–17; Deut. 22:28–29.

Required to learn from and imitate their elders. Titus 2:4.

WOOL

First fleece of, belonged to the priest. Deut. 18:4.

Fleece of. Judg. 6:37.

Mixing of, with other fabrics forbidden. Lev. 19:19; Deut. 22:11.

Prohibited in the priest's temple dress. Ezek. 44:17.

Used for clothing. Lev. 13:47–52, 59; Prov. 31:13; Ezek. 34:3; 44:17.

WORD OF GOD

See also Bible; Scriptures, the

Called book. Ps. 40:7, Rev. 22:19.

Called Book of the Lord. Isa. 34:16.

Called Book of the law. Neh. 8:3; Gal. 3:10.

Called good Word of God. Heb. 6:5.

Called Holy Scriptures. Rom. 1:2; 2 Tim. 3:15.

Called law of the Lord. Ps. 1:2;
Isa. 30:9.
Called oracles of God. Rom. 3:2;
1 Pet. 4:11.
Called Scriptures. 1 Cor. 15:3.
Called Scriptures of truth.
Dan. 10:21.
Called sword of the spirit. Eph. 6:17.
Called the word. James 1:21–23;
1 Pet. 2:2.
Called the Word of God. Luke 11:28;
Heb. 4:12.
Called word of Christ. Col. 3:16.
Called word of life. Phil. 2:16.
Called word of truth. 2 Tim. 2:15;
James 1:18.
Conviction of sin from reading.
2 Kings 22:9–13;
2 Chron. 17:7–10; 34.
Expounded. Neh. 8:8.
Expounded by Jesus.
Luke 4:16–27; 24:27, 45.
Fulfilled by Jesus. Matt. 5:17.
Likened to a two-edged sword.
Heb. 4:12.
Likened to seed. Matt. 13:3–8,
18–23, 37–38.
Not to be added to or taken from.
Deut. 4:2; 12:32; Rev.
22:18–19.
Not to be handled deceitfully.
2 Cor. 4:2.
The people stood and responded by
saying "amen." Neh. 8:5–6;
Exod. 24:7; Deut. 27:12–26.
Searched. Acts 17:11.
Searching of, encouraged.
John 5:39; 7:52.
The standard of judgment.
John 12:48; Rom. 2:16.
Taught by apostles. Acts 2; 3;
8:32, 35.
Testify of Jesus. John 5:39.

Texts of, to be written on the
doorpost. Deut. 6:9; 11:20.
To be read publicly. Deut. 31:11–13;
Josh. 8:33–35; 2 Kings 23:2;
2 Chron. 17:7–9; Neh. 8:1–8,
13, 18; Jer. 36:6; Acts 13:15,
27; Col. 4:16; 1 Thess. 5:27.

WORDS

Deceitful, or a snare to those who
speak them. Prov. 6:2.
Fool known by the multitude of.
Eccles. 5:3.
Fool will swallow himself.
Eccles. 10:12–14.
Of the gossiper, wounds to the soul.
Prov. 18:8.
Hasty, foolishness of. Prov. 29:20.
Idle, account must be given for in the
day of judgment. Matt. 12:36–37.

Of Jesus
Eternal life. John 6:68.
Gracious. Luke 4:22.
Spirit and life. John 6:63.
Will judge. John 12:47, 48.
Like a storm. Job 8:2.
In a multitude of, is sin. Prov. 10:19.

Of the perfect man
Gentle. James 3:2.
Seditious, deceive the simple.
Rom. 16:18.
Should be acceptable to God.
Ps. 19:14.
Of a teacher, should be plain.
1 Cor. 14:9, 19.
Unprofitable, to be avoided.
2 Tim. 2:14.
Unspeakable, heard by Paul in
Paradise. 2 Cor. 12:4.
Vain, not to be regarded. Exod. 5:9;
Eph. 5:6.

Without knowledge, darken counsel.
Job 38:2.

Of the wise
Appropriately spoken, like apples
of gold in pictures of silver.
Prov. 25:11.
As prods, and as nails well
fastened. Eccles. 12:11.
Gracious. Eccles. 10:12.
Spoken in season. Prov. 15:23;
Eccles. 10:12.

WORKS, GOOD

A blessing attends. James 1:25.

Believers
Are full of. Acts 9:36.
Are zealous of. Titus 2:14.
Bring to the light their. John 3:21.
Created in Christ for. Eph. 2:10.
Exhorted to put on. Col. 3:12–14.
Followed into rest by their.
Rev. 14:13.
Should abound to all. 2 Cor. 9:8.
Should avoid being pretentious in.
Matt. 6:1–18.
Should be careful to maintain.
Titus 3:8, 14.
Should be done, with meekness.
James 3:13.
Should encourage each other to.
Heb. 10:24.
Should be established in.
2 Thess. 2:17.
Should be fruitful in. Col. 1:10.
Should be furnished to all.
2 Tim. 3:17.
Should be perfect in. Heb. 13:21.
Should be prepared for all.
2 Tim. 2:21.
Should be ready to all. Titus 3:1.
Should be rich in. 1 Tim. 6:18.

Called
Fruits in keeping with repentance.
Matt. 3:8.
Fruits of righteousness. Phil. 1:11.
Good fruits. James 3:17.
Works and labors of love.
Heb. 6:10.
Christ as an example of. John 10:32;
Acts 10:38.
Designed to lead others to glorify
God. Matt. 5:16.1 Pet. 2:12.
God glorified by. John 15:8.
God remembers. Neh. 13:14,
with Heb. 6:9–10.
Heavenly wisdom full of.
James 3:17.
Holy women should manifest.
1 Tim. 2:10; 5:10.
Illustrated. John 15:5.
By Jesus Christ to the glory and
praise of God. Phil. 1:11.
In the judgment, will be an evidence
of faith. Matt. 25:34–40;
James 2:14–20.
Justification unattainable by.
Rom. 3:20; Gal. 2:16.

Ministers should
Be patterns of. Titus 2:7.
Exhort to. 1 Tim. 6:17–18;
Titus 3:1, 8, 14.
Only those who abide in Christ can
perform. John 15:4–5.
Performed by God in us. Isa. 26:12;
Phil. 2:13.
Salvation unattainable by. Eph.
2:8–9; 2 Tim. 1:9; Titus 3:5.
The Scripture designed to lead us to.
2 Tim. 3:16–17; James 1:25.
To be performed in Christ's name.
Col. 3:17.
The wicked unfit for. Titus 1:16.
Will be brought into the judgment.
Eccles. 12:14, with 2 Cor. 5:10.

WORLDLINESS

Examples of
Balaam. 2 Pet. 2:15; Jude 11.
Cretans. Titus 1:12.
Eli's sons. 1 Sam. 2:12–17.
Esau. Gen. 25:30–34.
Gehazi. 2 Kings 5:21–27.
Herod. Matt. 14:6–7.
Israelites. Num. 11:33–34;
   Ps. 78:18, 29–31.
Jacob. Gen. 25:31–34.
Judah. Gen. 37:26–27.
Jesus' warning against.
   Matt. 6:25–34; 10:39; 16:26;
   18:1–4; 24:38; Luke 18:14;
   16:1–25.
Paul's warning against. Rom. 12:2;
   1 Cor. 7:29–31; 2 Tim. 3:2–7;
   2 Pet. 2:12–18; 1 John 2:15–17;
   Jude 11–19.

WORLDLY MINDEDNESS
Consequences of. Rom. 8:6–8;
   Gal. 6:8.

WORMWOOD
Pictured as the opposite of justice
   and righteousness. Amos 5:7;
   Jer. 23:15.
One of the blzaing stars which brings
   destruction. Rev. 8:10–11.

WORRY
Be without. 1 Cor. 7:32; Phil. 4:6.
About earthly things, forbidden.
   Matt. 6:25; Luke 12:22, 29;
   John 6:27.
Futility of. Matt. 6:27;
   Luke 12:25–26.
God's promises should keep us from.
   Heb. 13:5.

God's providential goodness should
   keep us from. Matt. 6:26, 28, 30;
   Luke 22:35.
Obstructs the gospel. Matt. 13:22;
   Luke 8:14; 14:18–20.
Sent as a punishment to the wicked.
   Ezek. 4:16; 12:19.
Should be cast on God. Pss. 37:5;
   55:22; Prov. 16:3; 1 Pet. 5:7.
Trust in God should free us from.
   Jer. 17:7–8; Dan. 3:16.
Unbecoming in believers.
   2 Tim. 2:4.
Vanity of. Ps. 39:6; Eccles. 4:8.
Warning against. Luke 21:34.

WORSHIP
Commanded. Exod. 34:14;
   Pss. 95:6; 147:7–11.

Examples of
All people. Ps. 148:11–13.
All things. Ps. 148:1–10.
Angels. Isa. 6:1–6; Luke 2:13;
   Rev. 7:11–12.
Athenians. Acts 17:15–34.
Cain and Abel. Gen. 4:1–16.
Heavenly beings. Rev. 4:1–11.
Moses. Exod. 3:5.
Multitudes. Rev. 19:1–18.
The redeemed. Rev. 15:3–4.
Solomon. 2 Chron. 6:1–42.
Young and old. Ps. 148:12–13.
Prophesied. Isa. 66:23.

True
More than sacrifice desired.
   Hos. 6:6.
In spirit and in truth. John 4:24.
What God wants. Mic. 6:6–8.

Value of
Convinces unbelievers.
   1 Cor. 14:22–25.

Glorifies God. Ps. 50:23.
Strengthens fellowship.
  Acts 2:42–47.

WORSHIP STYLES

With dance
  David. 2 Sam. 6:14–16.
  Miriam. Exod. 15:20–21.

Examples of
  Bowing down. Exod. 12:27;
    1 Chron. 29:20; Ps. 95:6;
    Matt. 2:11.
  In private. Gen. 22:5; Dan. 6:10;
    Job 1:20.
  Kneeling. Ps. 95:6.
With fasting and prayer. Luke 2:37.
With fear and reverence.
  Pss. 5:7; 96:9; Isa. 6:1–7.

With music
  Believers. Eph. 5:19; Col. 3:16.
  Miriam. Exod. 15:20–21.
  Psalmist. Ps. 57:7–8; 150.

Place of worship
  Afar off. Gen. 22:5;
    Exod. 24:1–2.
  No longer required to be in
    Samaria or Jerusalem.
    John 4:20–21.
In spirit and truth. John 4:23.
With thanksgiving. Eph. 5:20.

WOUNDS
Treatment of. Prov. 20:30; Isa. 1:6;
  Luke 10:34.

WRESTLING
Jacob with God. Gen. 32:24, 25.
In a spiritual sense. Eph. 6:12.

YEARS

Commencement of, changed after the Exodus. Exod. 12:2.

Divided into
Days. Gen. 25:7; Esther 9:27.
Months. Gen. 7:11;
1 Chron. 27:1.
Seasons. Gen. 8:22.
Weeks. Dan. 7:27; Luke 18:12.
Early computation of time by.
Gen. 5:3.

Illustrative of
Judgments (of recompenses).
Isa. 34:8.
Manhood (coming to).
Heb. 11:24.
Old age (being full of). Gen. 25:8.
Old age (well stricken in).
Luke 1:7.
Prosperity (of the right hand of the Most High). Ps. 77:10.
Redemption by Christ (of the redeemed). Isa. 63:4.
Severe judgments (of visitation).
Jer. 11:23; 23:12.
Length of, during the patriarchal age.
Gen. 7:11; 8:13, with
Gen. 7:24; 8:3.
In prophetic computation, days reckoned as. Dan. 12:11–12.

Remarkable
Jubilee. Lev. 2:11.
Sabbatical. Lev. 25:4.
Sun and moon appointed to mark out. Gen. 1:14.

YOKE

Used in a figurative sense.
Matt. 11:29–30; Phil. 4:3.
Used to speak of slavery, bondage, and hardship. 1 Kings 12:4,
Jer. 27:8.

YOUTH

Cleansing of. Ps. 119:9.
Glory of. Prov. 20:29.
Must be serious. Titus 2:6.
No one should despise. 1 Tim. 4:12.
Power of. 1 John 2:13.
Rejoice in. Eccles. 11:9.
Renewed. Ps. 103:5.
A time to remember the Creator.
Eccles. 12:1.
Will see visions. Acts 2:17.

ZEAL

Of believers. Ps. 119:139.
Christ an example of. Ps. 69:9;
John 2:17.
Exhortation to. Rom. 12:11;
Rev. 3:19.
Godly sorrow leads to.
2 Cor. 7:10–11.

Should be exhibited
In contending for the faith. Jude 3.
In desiring the salvation of others.
Acts 26:29; Rom. 10:1.
For the glory of God.
Num. 25:11, 13.
Against idolatry. 2 Kings 23:4–14.
In missionary labors.
Rom. 15:19, 23.
In spirit. Rom. 12:11.

For the welfare of believers.
Col. 4:13.
In well-doing. Gal. 4:18;
Titus 2:14.
Sometimes not according to
knowledge.Acts 21:20;
Rom. 10:2; Gal. 1:14.
Sometimes wrongly directed.
2 Sam. 21:2; Acts 22:3–4;
Phil. 3:6.
Stimulates others to do good.
2 Cor. 9:2.

Ungodly men sometimes pretend to.
2 Kings 10:16; Matt. 23:15.

ZEALOT
Simon, one of the twelve disciples.
Luke 6:15.

ZIGGURAT
Tower of Babel. Gen. 11:3–9.

ZODIAC
Signs of. Job 38:32.

INDEX OF TOPICS